February 7–9, 2012
San Antonio, TX, USA

Association for
Computing Machinery

Advancing Computing as a Science & Profession

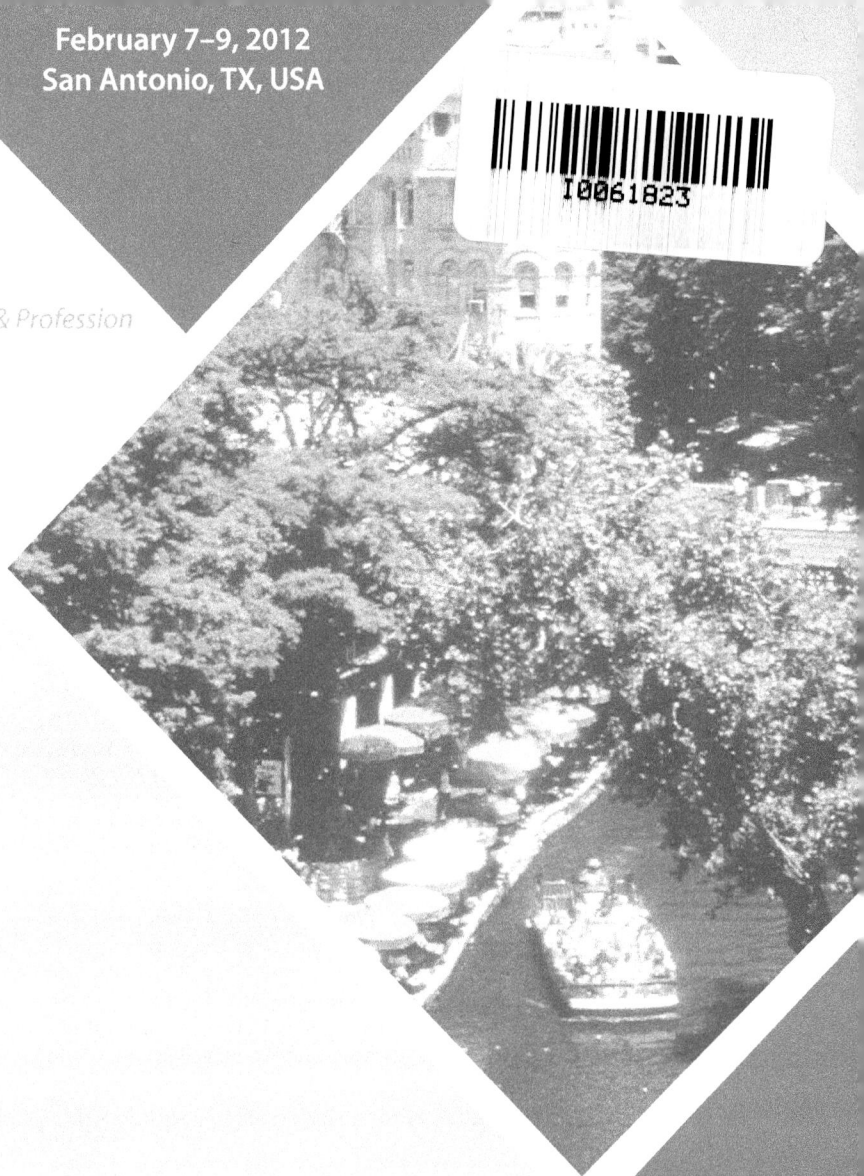

CODASPY'12

Proceedings of the Second ACM Conference on
Data and Application Security and Privacy

Sponsored by:
ACM SIGSAC

Supported by:
Institute of Cyber Security, Center for Education & Research in Information Assurance and Security, & the Cyber Center at Purdue University

**Association for
Computing Machinery**

Advancing Computing as a Science & Profession

The Association for Computing Machinery
2 Penn Plaza, Suite 701
New York, New York 10121-0701

Notice to Past Authors of ACM-Published Articles
ACM intends to create a complete electronic archive of all articles and/or other material previously published by ACM. If you have written a work that has been previously published by ACM in any journal or conference proceedings prior to 1978, or any SIG Newsletter at any time, and you do NOT want this work to appear in the ACM Digital Library, please inform permissions@acm.org, stating the title of the work, the author(s), and where and when published.

ISBN: 978-1-4503-1091-8 (Digital)

ISBN: 978-1-4503-1368-1 (Print)

Additional copies may be ordered prepaid from:

ACM Order Department
PO Box 30777
New York, NY 10087-0777, USA

Phone: 1-800-342-6626 (USA and Canada)
+1-212-626-0500 (Global)
Fax: +1-212-944-1318
E-mail: acmhelp@acm.org
Hours of Operation: 8:30 am – 4:30 pm ET

Printed in the USA

Foreword

It is our great pleasure to welcome you to the second edition of the *ACM Conference on Data and Application Security and Privacy (CODASPY 2012)* which follows the successful first edition (CODASPY 2011) held in February 2011. This conference series has been founded to foster novel and exciting research topics in this arena and to develop directions for further research and development. The initial concept came up in a conversation between the two co-founders when both happened to be at the same meeting. This was followed by discussions with a number of fellow cyber security researchers. Their enthusiastic encouragement persuaded us to move ahead with the always daunting task of creating a high-quality conference.

Data and applications that manipulate data are crucial assets in today's information age. With the increasing drive towards availability of data and services anytime anywhere, security and privacy risks have increased. Vast amounts of privacy-sensitive data are being collected today by organizations for a variety of reasons. Unauthorized disclosure, modification, usage or denial of access to these data and corresponding services may result in high human and financial costs. New applications such as social networking and social computing provide value by aggregating input from numerous individual users and the mobile devices they carry with them and computing new information of benefit to society and individuals. To achieve efficiency and effectiveness in traditional domains such as healthcare there is a drive to make these records electronic and highly available. The need for organizations to share information effectively is underscored by rapid innovations in the business world that require close collaboration across traditional boundaries and the dramatic failure of old-style approaches to information protection in government agencies in keeping information too secret to connect the dots. Security and privacy in these and other arenas can be meaningfully achieved only in context of the application domain. Data and applications security and privacy has rapidly expanded as a research field with many important challenges to be addressed.

In response to the call for papers of CODASPY 2012, a total of 113 papers were submitted from Asia, Australia, Europe and North America. This is a significant increase over the previous year's count of 69. The program committee selected 21 regular research papers which is the same as last year. These papers cover a variety of topics, including privacy of social networks, novel privacy techniques and applications, access control and security of smart appliances and mobile devices. The program committee also selected 10 short papers for presentation. The program is complemented by a key note speech by Giovanni Vigna, as well as a panel (topic not yet decided at press time).

The organization of a conference like CODASPY requires the collaboration of many individuals. First of all, we would like to thank the authors for submitting to the conference and the keynote speaker for graciously accepting our invitation. We express our gratitude to the program committee members and external reviewers for their efforts in reviewing the papers, engaging in active online discussion during the selection process and providing valuable feedback to authors. Our special thanks go to our local arrangement chair Suzanne Tanaka and to our Web master Ram Krishnan. Special thanks also go to Ali Inan for publicizing the conference and Jae Park for assembling the proceedings. Finally, we would like to thank our sponsor, ACM SIGSAC, for their support of this conference.

We hope that you will find this program interesting and that the conference will provide you with a valuable opportunity to interact with other researchers and practitioners from institutions around the world. Enjoy!!

Elisa Bertino
CODASPY'12 General Chair and co-founder
Purdue University, USA

Ravi Sandhu
CODASPY'12 Program Chair and co-founder
University of Texas at San Antonio, USA

Table of Contents

Session 1: Database and Storage Security

Session 2: Security and Privacy for Social Computing

Session 3: Access Control Enforcement

Session 4: Short Papers Session 1

Session 5: Novel Techniques for Access Control

Session 6: Novel Applications of Privacy Techniques

Session 7: Short Papers Session 2

Session 8: Novel Techniques for Data Security and Privacy

Author Index

CODASPY 2012 Conference Organization

General Chair:	Elisa Bertino *(Purdue University, USA)*
Program Chair:	Ravi Sandhu *(University of Texas at San Antonio, USA)*
Proceedings Chair:	Jaehong Park *(University of Texas at San Antonio, USA)*
Local Arrangements Chair:	Suzanne Tanaka *(University of Texas at San Antonio, USA)*
Web Master:	Ram Krishnan *(University of Texas at San Antonio, USA)*
Publicity Chair:	Ali Inan *(Işık University, Turkey)*
Industry Chair:	Dan Thomsen *(Smart Information Flow Technologies, USA)*

Program Committee:

Gail-Joon Ahn *(Arizona State University, USA)*
Vijay Atluri *(Rutgers University)*
Lujo Bauer *(Carnegie Mellon University, USA)*
Elisa Bertino *(Purdue University, USA)*
Barbara Carminati *(University of Insubria, Italy)*
Mauro Conti *(Vrije Universiteit Amsterdam)*
Elena Ferrari *(University of Insubria, Italy)*
Philip Fong *(University of Calgary)*
Gabriel Ghinita *(University of Massachusetts at Boston, USA)*
Murat Kantarciouglu *(University of Texas at Dallas, USA)*
Günter Karjoth *(IBM Research, Switzerland)*
Ram Krishnan *(University of Texas at San Antonio, USA)*
Peng Liu *(The Pennsylvania State University, USA)*
Jaehong Park *(University of Texas at San Antonio, USA)*
Gunther Pernul *(University of Regensburg, Germany)*
Alexander Pretschner *(Karlsruhe Institute of Technology)*
Philippe Pucheral *(University of Versailles, France)*
Indrajit Ray *(Colorado State University)*
Ning Shang *(Qualcomm, USA)*
Elaine Shi *(PARC, USA)*
Larry Shi *(University of Houston, USA)*
Dan Thomsen *(Smart Information Flow Technologies, USA)*
Bhavani Thuraisingham *(University of Texas at Dallas, USA)*
Mahesh Tripunitara *(University of Waterloo, Canada)*
Jaideep Vaidya *(Rutgers University, USA)*
Vijay Varadharajan *(Macquarie University, Australia)*
Shouhuai Xu *(University of Texas at San Antonio, USA)*
Xinwen Zhang *(Hawei, USA)*

Additional reviewers:

Cuneyt Gurcan Akcora
Nicolas Anciaux
Philippe Bonnet
Luc Bouganim
Christian Broser
Eyup Canlar
Jianneng Cao
Chenyun Dai
Jun Dai
Weiqi Dai
Maria Luisa Damiani
Emiliano De Cristofaro
Tao Feng
Earlence Fernandes
Christoph Fritsch
Ludwig Fuchs
Cristiano Giuffrida
Aris Gkoulalas-Divanis
Oliver Gmelch
Michele Guglielmi
Aditi Gupta
Sabri Hassan
Yuan Hong
Ali Inan
Mohammad Islam
Ashish Kamra
Vaibhav Khadilkar
Vivek Krishnan
Mehmet Kuzu
Kyeong-An Kwon
Jonghyuk Lee
Jingqiang Lin
Lei Liu
Ziyi Liu
Weiliang Luo
Luciana Marconi
Jiang Ming

Nabeel Mohamed
Mohamed Nabeel
Michael Netter
Benjamin Nguyen
Robert Nix
Gabriele Oligeri
Stefano Ortolani
Indrakshi Ray
Andreas Reisser
Moritz Riesner
Chun Ruan
Carmen Ruiz Vicente
Iulian Sandu Popa
Yucel Saygin
Alireza Sharifi
Xiaoyan Sun
Mohit Tiwari
Marco Viviani
Guanying Wang
Jun Wang
Michael Weber
Joel Weinberger
Jeffrey Woo
Zhi Xin
Huijun Xiong
Xun Yi
Eunjung Yoon
Qiang Zeng
Zhenxin Zhan
Shengzhi Zhang
Tao Zhang
Bin Zhao
Jun Zhao
Qingji Zheng
Lan Zhou
Yan Zhou

CODASPY 2012 Sponsor & Supporters

Sponsor:

Supporters:

Center for Education and Research
in Information Assurance and Security

CYBER
CENTER

www.purdue.edu/discoverypark/cyber

Secure and Efficient Proof of Storage with Deduplication

Qingji Zheng
Department of Computer Science
University of Texas at San Antonio
qzheng@cs.utsa.edu

Shouhuai Xu
Department of Computer Science
University of Texas at San Antonio
shxu@cs.utsa.edu

ABSTRACT

Both security and efficiency are crucial to the success of cloud storage. So far, security and efficiency of cloud storage have been separately investigated as follows: On one hand, security notions such as Proof of Data Possession (PDP) and Proof of Retrievability (POR) have been introduced for detecting that the data stored in the cloud has been tampered with. On the other hand, the notion of Proof of Ownership (POW) has also been proposed to alleviate the cloud server from storing multiple copies of the same data, which could substantially reduce the consumption of both network bandwidth and server storage space. These two aspects are seemingly quite to the opposite of each other. In this paper, we show, somewhat surprisingly, that the two aspects can actually co-exist within the same framework. This is possible fundamentally because of the following insight: *The public verifiability offered by* PDP/POR *schemes can be naturally exploited to achieve* POW. This "one stone, two birds" phenomenon not only inspired us to propose the novel notion of Proof of Storage with Deduplication (POSD), but also guided us to design a concrete scheme that is provably secure in the Random Oracle model based on the Computational Diffie-Hellman (CDH) assumption.

Categories and Subject Descriptors

C.2.4 [**Communication Networks**]: Distributed Systems; H.3.4 [**Information Storage and Retrieval**]: Systems and Software

General Terms

Security

Keywords

cloud storage, outsourced storage, proof of storage, deduplication, integrity checking, proof of ownership, proof of data possession, proof of retrievability

1. INTRODUCTION

Cloud computing is getting increasingly popular because it can provide low-cost and on-demand use of vast storage and processing resources. The present paper focuses on the security and efficiency of cloud storage, namely that clients outsource their data to cloud storage servers. While cloud storage offers compelling scalability and availability advantages over the current paradigm of "one storing and maintaining its own IT systems and data", it does not come without security concerns. This has led to studies on cloud storage security and efficiency, which are, however, addressed separately as we discuss below.

From the perspective of cloud storage security, there have been two notable notions:

- Proof of Data Possession (PDP): This notion was introduced by Ateniese et al. [2]. It allows a cloud client to verify the integrity of its data outsourced to the cloud in a very efficient way (i.e., far more efficient than the straightforward solution of downloading the data to the client-end for verification). This notion has been enhanced in various ways [8, 3, 15].

- Proof of Retrievability (POR): This notion was introduced by Juels and Kaliski [10]. Compared with PDP, POR offers an extra property that the client can actually "recover" the data outsourced to the cloud (in the flavor of "knowledge extraction" in zero-knowledge proof). This notion has been enhanced and extended in multiple aspects [12, 6, 5, 16].

From the perspective of cloud storage efficiency, deduplication technique has become a common practice of many cloud vendors. This is reasonable especially when there are many duplications in the data outsourced to the cloud (e.g., only 25% of data may be unique according to a survey [1]). As such, the cloud vendor can substantially save storage space by storing a single copy of each data file regardless of the number of clients that outsource it. This explains the term "deduplication". This issue was first introduced to the research community by [9]. Because straightforward deduplication is vulnerable to attacks (e.g., a dishonest client can claim that it has certain data while it does not), Halevi et al. [13] proposed the notion called Proof of Ownership (POW) as well as concrete constructions.

Our contributions. Both the security and efficiency perspectives mentioned above are important and should be offered by a single cloud storage solution, which is a new problem that has not been addressed. In this paper, we tackle this problem by proposing a "2-in-1" notion we call Proof of Data Storage with Deduplication (POSD). Specifically, we introduce the novel concept of POSD, and formalize its functional and security definitions. Moreover, we propose the first efficient POSD scheme and prove its security in the Random Oracle model based on the Computational Diffie-Hellman (CDH) assumption. We also analyze and compare the performance of our scheme and the performance of some relevant PDP/POR/POW schemes, which suggests that our POSD scheme is as efficient as the PDP/POR/POW schemes.

Organization. The rest of the paper is organized as follows. Section 2 briefly reviews the related prior work. Section 3 discusses the notations and cryptographic settings. Section 4 presents the definitions of POSD. Section 5 describes our POSD scheme and its security as well as performance analysis. Section 6 concludes the paper.

2. RELATED WORK

Cloud storage security was not systematically studied until very recently, despite previous investigations for similar problems (cf. [2]). Ateniese et al. [2] introduced the concept of PDP, and Juels et. al [10] proposed the concept of POR, which was improved significantly by Shacham and Waters [12]. The main difference between the two notions is that POR uses Error Correction/Erasure Codes to tolerate the damage to portions of the outsourced data. These solutions are later enhanced in various ways [8, 4, 5, 6, 16].

Data deduplication of ciphertext data in the pre-cloud era was studied in [14, 7]. Data deduplication in the context of cloud computing was recently introduced [9]. Halevi et al. [13] dubbed the term of POW and presented the first systematic study of deduplication in cloud, including several alternative solutions that offer different trade-offs between security and performance.

3. PRELIMINARIES

3.1 Notations

Let ℓ be a security parameter. A function $\varepsilon(\ell)$ is negligible if it is smaller than ℓ^{-const} for any constant $const$ and sufficiently large ℓ.

Let q be an ℓ-bit prime and p a prime such that $q|(p-1)$. Let F be a data file consisting of n blocks, where the ith block F_i is composed of m symbols in $\mathbb{Z}_q$, i.e. $\mathsf{F}_i = (\mathsf{F}_{i1} \cdots, \mathsf{F}_{im})$, where $\mathsf{F}_i \in \mathbb{Z}_q^m$.

Let fid be the identity that uniquely identifies data file F. Let each file be associated with some auxiliary information (i.e. cryptographic tags), denoted by Tag. We consider two variants of Tag: Tag_{int} is the cryptographic information for auditing data integrity, and Tag_{dup} is the cryptographic information for duplication checking.

Let [] denote the optional arguments of a function or algorithm; for example, $\mathsf{Alg}(a, b[, c])$ means that algorithm Alg has two arguments a and b, and optionally a third argument c.

3.2 Cryptographic Setting and Assumptions

Let G and G_T be cyclic groups of prime order q and g be a generator of G. Let $e : G \times G \to G_T$ be a bilinear map, with the following properties: (i) e can be computed efficiently; (ii) for all $(u, v) \in G \times G$, and $a, b \in \mathbb{Z}_q$, $e(u^a, v^b) = e(u, v)^{ab}$; (iii) $e(g, g) \neq 1$.

The standard Computational Diffie-Hellman (CDH) Problem is the following: Given $(g, g^w, h) \in G^3$, where g, g^w, h are selected uniformly at random from G, compute h^w. The CDH Assumption says that no probabilistic polynomial-time (PPT) algorithm can solve the CDH Problem with a non-negligible probability (in ℓ).

The Discrete Log (DLOG) Problem is the following: Given any prime q-order cyclic group G and two random elements g and h, find w such that $\mathsf{g}^w = \mathsf{h}$. The DLOG Assumption says that no PPT algorithm can solve the DLOG Problem only with a non-negligible probability (in ℓ). The DLOG Assumption is weaker than the CDH Assumption.

Let $H_1 : \{0,1\}^* \to G$ and $H_2 : \{0,1\}^* \to \mathbb{Z}_q$ be randomly chosen from the respective families of hash functions. Both H_1 and H_2 are modeled as random oracles.

Let $\mathsf{PRF} : \{0,1\}^\ell \times \{0,1\}^* \to \{0,1\}^\ell$ be a family of secure pseudorandom functions.

4. REQUIREMENTS, MODEL AND DEFINITIONS OF POSD

Requirements. Built on top of [2, 10, 13], we summarize the performance requirements of POSD as:

- A solution should use common functions (e.g., hash functions) so as to allow cross-client data deduplication and cross-client cloud data integrity auditing.

- A solution should consume bandwidth that is substantially less than the size of the data file in question. This prevents the aforementioned trivial solutions.

- A solution should not force the cloud server, when determining whether to conduct a deduplication operation, to retrieve any significant portion of the data file in question. This is plausible because it could be very resource-consuming to load a large data file from secondary storage to memory.

- A solution should only require the client to make a single pass over its data file, while using an amount of memory that is substantially smaller than the size of the data file in question.

As in the cases of PDP/POR and POW, there are trivial solutions to fulfill the functions of POSD. Specifically, a client can download the whole data from the cloud to verify the integrity of its data outsourced to the cloud, and the server can ask the client to upload a data file to show that the client indeed has a copy of the data file before conducting the deduplication operation. However, this trivial solution is not practical because it incurs prohibitive communication overhead. On the other hand, it was also noted in [2, 10, 13] that simple heuristics will not solve the respective problems without shortcomings.

Model participants. We consider a cloud storage service model that involves the following three participants.

(i) Cloud storage server, denoted by S: It provides storage service with relevant assurance procedures, by which the cloud storage clients can check the integrity of their data stored in the cloud and the server can save storage space via data deduplication in a secure fashion.

(ii) Cloud storage clients, denoted by C: A client outsources its data to the cloud in a secure fashion, while allowing the cloud storage server to conduct data deduplication operations. (If a client does not want the server to conduct this operation, this can be achieved via an appropriate contract-level agreement that is out of the scope of the present paper.)

(iii) Third party, denoted by AUDITOR: A client may allow a third party to check the integrity of its data outsourced to the cloud. Moreover, any client, who possesses a data file that is duplicated (i.e., the same data file has been uploaded to the server by another client), can act as an AUDITOR of that specific data file.

Communication channels. If the data file outsourced to the cloud is not confidential, there is no need for private channels. (In this case, secure deduplication still can be relevant because it may be very expensive to eavesdrop the communication during the transfer of a large data file.) In the case the outsourced data files are confidential, we can assume the availability of private communication channels for the execution of certain protocols. This is common to PDP/POR/POW [2, 12, 13] and avoids unnecessary complications in describing the protocols (given that private channels can be implemented using standard techniques in a modular fashion). Note that in order to facilitate deduplication, the data will be stored in plaintext in the cloud, which is the same as in POW [13].

Functional definition. The following definition of POSD is built on the definitions of PDP/POR [2, 12] and POW [13].

Definition 1. (functional definition) A POSD scheme, denoted by Λ, consists of the following tuple of polynomial-time algorithms (KEYGEN, UPLOAD, AUDITINT, DEDUP).

KEYGEN: This is the *key generation* algorithm. It takes as input a security parameter ℓ, and outputs two pairs of public/private keys $(\text{PK}_{int}, \text{SK}_{int})$ and $(\text{PK}_{dup}, \text{SK}_{dup})$, where PK_{int} is made public and SK_{int} is the corresponding private key of a client (this pair of keys may be used for integrity protection/verification purpose), PK_{dup} is made public and SK_{dup} is the private key of the server (this pair of keys may be used for secure deduplication purpose).

UPLOAD: This is the *data uploading* protocol running by a client C and a server S over a private channel so that secrecy of the data is assured. Suppose C wants to upload a new data file F to the cloud, where S can easily determine that F has not be outsourced to the cloud by any client (e.g., by comparing the hash value provided by C against the list of hash values stored by the server). For preprocessing, Client C takes as input a new data file F with a unique identifier fid and the secret key SK_{int}, outputs some auxiliary information Tag_{int} that can be used to audit the integrity of F in the cloud. At the end of the execution, S stores (fid, F, Tag_{int}) received from C as well as possibly some deduplication information Tag_{dup}, which may be produced by the server using SK_{dup}. The server may also keep a hash value of the F's so as to facilitate the detection of data duplications and thus the need of deduplication.

AUDITINT: This is the *data integrity auditing* protocol. It is executed between server S and AUDITOR so that S convinces AUDITOR that integrity of some data file stored in the cloud is assured. The AUDITOR's input includes the data file identifier fid and the corresponding client's PK_{int}. The server's input includes the data file F corresponding to fid and the auxiliary information Tag_{int} associated to F. Essentially, the protocol is of challenge-response type, where AUDITOR sends a challenge chal to the server and the server computes and sends back a response resp. If resp is valid with respect to chal as well as the other relevant information, AUDITOR outputs 1, meaning that the integrity of F is assured, and 0 otherwise. Formally, we can write it as:

$$b \leftarrow (\text{AUDITOR}(\text{fid}, \text{PK}_{int}) \Longleftrightarrow \text{S}(\text{fid}, \text{F}, \text{Tag}_{int}))$$

where $b \in \{0, 1\}$.

DEDUP: This is the *deduplication checking* protocol. It is executed between server S and client C, who claims to possess a data file F (the detection of the need to deduplicate can be fulfilled by C sending the hash value of its data file to S, which can determine whether or not the data file has been in the cloud). This protocol is also essentially of challenge-response type. Basically, S sends a challenge chal to C, which returns a response resp that is produced using data file F and possibly other information. S verifies the validity of resp using possibly Tag_{dup} and PK_{dup}, and outputs 1 if the verification is successful (meaning that the client indeed has data file F) and 0 otherwise. Formally, we can write it as:

$$b \leftarrow (\text{S}(\text{fid}, \text{Tag}_{dup}, [\text{SK}_{dup},]\text{PK}_{dup}) \Longleftrightarrow \text{C}(\text{fid}, \text{F}))$$

where $b \in \{0, 1\}$.

Correctness definition. We require a POSD scheme $\Lambda = $ (KEYGEN, UPLOAD, AUDITINT, DEDUP) to be *correct* if, for honest client and server, the execution of the AUDITINT protocol will always output 1 and the execution of the DEDUP protocol will always output 1.

Security definition. We define security of POSD using games, which specify both the adversary's behavior (i.e., what the adversary is allowed to do) and the winning condition (i.e., under what circumstance we say the attack is successful). At a high-level, we require a POSD scheme to be *server_unforgeable*, which is similar to the security defined by the data possession game in [2], and (κ, θ)_*uncheatable*, which is similar to the security definition in [13].

Intuitively, we say a POSD scheme is *server_unforgeable* if no cheating server can successfully execute the AUDITINT protocol with an honest AUDITOR with a non-negligible probability. Formally, we have:

Definition 2. (server_unforgeability) For POSD scheme $\Lambda = $ (KEYGEN, UPLOAD, AUDITINT, DEDUP), consider the following game between an adversary $\mathcal{A}$ and a challenger, where $\mathcal{A}$ plays the role of the cloud server S while possibly controlling many compromised clients, and the challenger acts as an honest client.

Setup Stage:

- Run algorithm KEYGEN to generate (PK_{int}, SK_{int}) and (PK_{dup}, SK_{dup}). Make PK_{int} and PK_{dup} public, including giving SK_{int} to the respective client and SK_{dup} to $\mathcal{A}$. Note that the SK_{int} of the challenger is not given to $\mathcal{A}$. For any other client, the corresponding SK_{int} may be given to $\mathcal{A}$ as long as it requests (i.e., these clients are compromised by, or collude with, $\mathcal{A}$).

Challenge Stage: At this stage, $\mathcal{A}$ can do anything with respect to the clients other than the challenger. With respect to the challenger, $\mathcal{A}$ does the following.

- $\mathcal{A}$ adaptively chooses a data file $F \in \{0,1\}^*$ for the challenger. The challenger picks a unique identifier fid and runs the UPLOAD protocol with $\mathcal{A}$. At the end of the execution, $\mathcal{A}$ obtains (fid, F, Tag_{int}). The above process may be repeated for polynomial many times. Denote by $\mathcal{Q} = \{(fid, F, Tag_{int})\}$, the set of tuples $\mathcal{A}$ received from the challenger when executing the UPLOAD protocol. Note that the challenger keeps a record of $\mathcal{Q}_{fid} = \{fid\}$, namely the projection of $\mathcal{Q}$ on attribute fid.

- $\mathcal{A}$ can execute AUDITINT with the challenger with respect to any $fid \in \mathcal{Q}_{fid}$, and execute DEDUP with the challenger with respect to some data file (possibly chosen by $\mathcal{A}$). This process can be executed polynomial (in ℓ) number of times.

Forgery Stage:

- The adversary outputs an $fid \in \mathcal{Q}_{fid}$ corresponding to F that was outsourced to the cloud.

The adversary wins the game if for any $F' \neq F$,
$$1 \leftarrow (\text{AUDITOR}(fid, PK_{int}) \Longleftrightarrow \mathcal{A}(fid, F', \cdot)),$$

We say Λ is *server_unforgeable* if the winning probability for any PPT algorithm $\mathcal{A}$ is negligible in ℓ.

Intuitively, we say a POSD scheme is (κ, θ)_uncheatable if given a file F with min-entropy κ, no cheating client, who can find F' containing θ-bit Shannon entropy of F, convinces the server that it has F with a probability non-negligibly more than $2^{-(\kappa - \theta)}$. Formally, we have:

Definition 3. $((\kappa, \theta)$_uncheatability) For a POSD scheme $\Lambda = (\text{KEYGEN}, \text{UPLOAD}, \text{AUDITINT}, \text{DEDUP})$, consider the following game between the adversary $\mathcal{A}$ (who plays the role of the compromised clients) and the challenger (who plays the role of the server and an honest client).

Setup Stage:

- Run algorithm KEYGEN to generate (PK_{int}, SK_{int}) as well as (PK_{dup}, SK_{dup}). Make PK_{int} and PK_{dup} public, including giving PK_{int} and PK_{dup} to the adversary $\mathcal{A}$. For a compromised client, the corresponding SK_{int} is given to $\mathcal{A}$. However, both SK_{dup} and SK_{int} corresponding to the honest client are only given to the challenger. (Note that if the SK_{int} corresponding to the honest client is given to $\mathcal{A}$, $\mathcal{A}$ could use it to authenticate to the server to download the client's any data outsourced to the server.)

- The challenger chooses a data file F of κ-bit min-entropy, and a unique identifier fid. The challenger honestly executes the UPLOAD protocol by playing the roles of both the client and the server, and gives the publicly observable information to the adversary $\mathcal{A}$.

Challenge Stage: At this stage, $\mathcal{A}$ seeks to infer the content of F by running the UPLOAD, AUDITINT and DEDUP protocols with the challenger. In particular, $\mathcal{A}$ may penetrate into the cloud server to learn some portions of F. This is reasonable because stealing the whole F, or any form of its compressed version (because F has enough min-entropy and thus Shannon entropy), could alert the defender about the compromise because of the abnormal use of network bandwidth and/or CPU resources. Moreover, subliminal channels normally do not offer bandwidth compatible to the magnitude of κ. Note that the above adversarial model also accommodates that $\mathcal{A}$ can command the compromised clients to launch some type of guessing attacks with respect to F, which is possible for example when F has a public structure (e.g., Word document or movie file). In any case, suppose $\mathcal{A}$ learned up to θ-bit Shannon entropy of F.

Forgery Stage: $\mathcal{A}$ eventually outputs some F'. $\mathcal{A}$ wins the game if
$$1 \leftarrow (S(fid, Tag_{dup}, [SK_{dup},]PK_{dup}) \Longleftrightarrow \mathcal{A}(fid, F')).$$

We say Λ is (κ, θ)_uncheatable if the winning probability for any PPT algorithm $\mathcal{A}$ is negligible (in ℓ) more than $2^{-(\kappa - \theta)}$. Note that $\kappa - \theta \geq \ell$ would be the most often cases because we mainly deal with large data files, and thus $\mathcal{A}$'s winning probability is effectively required to be negligible in ℓ.

Discussion. In the above security definitions, we did not consider the notion of *fairness*, which was very recently introduced to prevent a dishonest client from legitimately accusing an honest cloud server of tampering its data in the setting of *dynamic* POR [16]. This is because POSD in this paper deals with *static* data, rather than dynamic data where fairness can be reasonably involved [16]. For static data, fairness can be easily achieved by letting a client sign sign F in the UPLOAD protocol or after a successful execution of the DEDUP protocol.

5. POSD **CONSTRUCTION AND ANALYSIS**

5.1 **Basic Ideas**

As discussed above, it is conceptually convenient to think "POSD=PDP/POR+POW" because POSD aims to fulfill the functionalities of both integrity audit and deduplication. In this paper, we focus on the scenario of "POSD=PDP+POW" because of the following. First, POR is more costly that PDP due to its use of Error Correcting/Erasure Codes for fulfilling retrievability. Second, in the DEDUP protocol of POSD (and POW), retrievability is actually not needed because the server already knows F. Nevertheless, the basic ideas are equally applicable to the scenario of "POSD=POR+POW." In what follows we first elaborate the insight that led us to our design.

Relationship between PDP/POR and POW, revisited. From the definition of POSD, we see some similarity between the AUDITINT protocol and the DEDUP protocol. Specifically, both protocols are in a sense for verifying integrity except that one is for data in the cloud-end (i.e., cloud server attests to client) and the other is for data in the client-end (i.e., client attests to cloud server). Because the AUDITINT protocol is the core of PDP/POR, there is some similarity between PDP/POR and POW (as noted in [13]) as well as POSD. However, it is stated in [13] that PDP/POR protocols are not applicable in the setting of POW (and thus POSD) — we call this the "Deduplication Gap" between PDP/POR and POW/POSD— because of the following:

> In PDP/POR, there is a preprocessing step that facilitates that the client can later verify the integrity of its data in the cloud. Whereas, in the setting of POW, a new client possesses a secret data file F, *but no other secrets*.

Halevi et al. [13] correctly excluded the possibility of using PDP/POR based on symmetric key cryptosystems [2, 12] for the purpose of POW (because the new client does not, and should not, know the secret keys). We observe, however, that Publicly Verifiable PDP/POR protocols are actually sufficient for the purpose of POW. As we will see, this is made possible because the client can compute the needed information from F on the fly and without using any secret information.

Why is the public verifiability sufficient to bridge the above "Deduplication Gap"? Conceptually, public verifiability of PDP/POR meaning that a third party, who may be given some *non-secret* information by a client, can verify the integrity of the client's data in the cloud. Putting this into the setting of POW/POSD, we can let the DEDUP protocol be essentially the same as the core PDP/POR protocol by reversing the roles of the client and the server. More specifically, if the AUDITINT protocol is publicly verifiable, it is possible that only the public key PK_{int} is needed for the cloud server and only the data file F (as well as the public parameters, of course) is needed for the client.

5.2 Construction

Recall that q is an ℓ-bit prime and p is another prime such that $q|(p-1)$. G and G_T are cyclic groups of prime order q, and $e : G \times G \to G_T$ is a bilinear map. We use two hash functions (random oracles) $H_1 : \{0,1\}^* \to G$ and $H_2 : \{0,1\}^* \to \mathbb{Z}_q$.

F is a data file consisting of n blocks of m symbols in $\mathbb{Z}_q$, namely $F_i = (F_{i1} \cdots, F_{im})$, where $F_i \in \mathbb{Z}_q^m$ for $1 \le i \le n$. F is uniquely identified by fid.

The POSD scheme is described as follows (in the end of this subsection we will explain some design decisions to help understand our scheme):

KEYGEN: This algorithm generates cryptographic keys as follows:

- Select v_1 and v_2 uniformly at random from $\mathbb{Z}_p^*$ such that the orders of v_1 and v_2 are q (if v_2 is generated from v_1, then the DLOG of v_2 to base v_1 should be erased afterwards). Select s_{j1}, s_{j2} uniformly at random from $\mathbb{Z}_q^*$ for $1 \le j \le m$. Set $z_j = v_1^{-s_{j1}} v_2^{-s_{j2}} \mod p$ for $1 \le j \le m$.

- Let g be a generator of G. Select u uniformly at random from G. Select w uniformly at random from $\mathbb{Z}_q^*$, and set $z_g = g^w$.

- Set $PK_{int} = \{q, p, g, u, v_1, v_2, z_1, \cdots, z_m, z_g\}$ and the client's private key $SK_{int} = \{(s_{11}, s_{12}), \cdots, (s_{m1}, s_{m2}), w\}$. Note that using an appropriate Pseudorandom Function (PRF), we can further reduce the storage at the client-end to constant (i.e., using a single key to the PRF for generating the $s_{11}, s_{12}, \cdots, s_{m1}, s_{m2}, w$).

- Set $PK_{dup} = PK_{int}$ and $SK_{dup} = \text{null}$, where PK_{dup} is also made public.

UPLOAD: This protocol is performed between a client, who is to outsource a data file F to the cloud, and the cloud server as follows:

- For each data block F_i, where $1 \le i \le n$, the client selects r_{i1}, r_{i2} uniformly at random from $\mathbb{Z}_q^*$ and computes:

$$
\begin{aligned}
x_i &= v_1^{r_{i1}} v_2^{r_{i2}} \mod p, \\
y_{i1} &= r_{i1} + \sum_{j=1}^m F_{ij} s_{j1} \mod q, \\
y_{i2} &= r_{i2} + \sum_{j=1}^m F_{ij} s_{j2} \mod q, \\
t_i &= \left(H_1(\text{fid}||i) \cdot u^{H_2(x_i)} \right)^w \quad (\text{in } G).
\end{aligned}
$$

The client sends $(\text{fid}, F, \text{Tag}_{int})$ to the server, where $\text{Tag}_{int} = \{(x_i, y_{i1}, y_{i2}, t_i)_{1 \le i \le n}\}$.

- Upon receiving $(\text{fid}, F, \text{Tag}_{int})$, the server sets $\text{Tag}_{dup} = \text{Tag}_{int}$.

AUDITINT: This protocol is executed between an auditor, which can be the client itself, and the cloud server to verify the integrity of the client's data file F stored in the cloud. Note that the client does not need to give any information to the auditor except the public keys PK_{int} and the data file identifier fid.

- The auditor chooses a set of c elements $I = \{\alpha_1, \ldots, \alpha_c\}$ where α_i is selected uniformly at random from $\{1, \ldots, n\}$, and chooses a set of coefficients $\beta = \{\beta_1, \ldots, \beta_c\}$ where β_i is selected uniformly at random from $\mathbb{Z}_q^*$. The auditor sends $\text{chal} = (I, \beta)$ to the server.

- The server computes:

$$
\mu_j = \sum_{i \in I} \beta_i F_{ij} \mod q
$$

for $1 \le j \le m$, and

$$
\begin{aligned}
Y_1 &= \sum_{i \in I} \beta_i y_{i1} \mod q, \\
Y_2 &= \sum_{i \in I} \beta_i y_{i2} \mod q, \\
T &= \prod_{i \in I} t_i^{\beta_i} \quad (\text{in } G).
\end{aligned}
$$

The server sends $\text{resp} = (\{\mu_j\}_{1 \le j \le m}, \{x_i\}_{i \in I}, Y_1, Y_2, T)$ to the auditor, where $x_i = v_1^{r_{i1}} v_2^{r_{i2}} \mod p$ for $1 \le i \le n$ were generated by the client in the execution of the UPLOAD protocol.

- Upon receiving resp, the auditor parses resp as $\{\{\mu_j\}_{1\le j\le m}, Y_1, Y_2, T, \{x_i\}_{i\in I}\}$, computes

$$X = \prod_{i\in I} x_i^{\beta_i} \mod p,$$

$$W = \prod_{i\in I} H_1(\mathsf{fid}\|i)^{\beta_i},$$

and verifies

$$X \overset{?}{=} v_1^{Y_1} v_2^{Y_2} \prod_{j=1}^{m} z_j^{\mu_j} \mod p$$

$$e(T, g) \overset{?}{=} e(W u^{\sum_{i\in I}\beta_i H_2(x_i)}, z_g) \quad (\text{in } G_T).$$

If both hold, return 1; otherwise, return 0.

DEDUP: This protocol is executed between the client, who claims to have a data file F with identifier fid that was already outsourced to the cloud by another client, and the server. This is a simple variant of the above AUDITINT protocol, where the auditor only needs to know the public keys PK_{int} and the data file identifier fid. Here, we let the cloud server play the role of the auditor (with some minor adaptations because there are some information that is not known to the client in producing the response), who naturally knows PK_{int} and fid.

- The server chooses a set of c elements $I = \{\alpha_1, \ldots, \alpha_c\}$ where α_i is selected uniformly at random from $\{1, \ldots, n\}$, and chooses a set of coefficients $\beta = \{\beta_1, \ldots, \beta_c\}$ where β_i is selected uniformly at random from $\mathbb{Z}_q^*$. The server sends $\mathsf{chal} = (I, \beta)$ to the client.

- The client computes

$$\mu_j = \sum_{i\in I} \beta_i \mathsf{F}_{ij} \mod q$$

for $1 \le j \le m$, and sends $\mathsf{resp} = (\{\mu_i\}_{1\le i\le m})$ to the server.

- The server computes from $\mathsf{Tag}_{dup} = \{(x_i, y_{i1}, y_{i2}, t_i)_{1\le i\le n}\}$:

$$Y_1 = \sum_{i\in I} \beta_i y_{i1} \mod q,$$

$$Y_2 = \sum_{i\in I} \beta_i y_{i2} \mod q,$$

$$W = \prod_{i\in I} H_1(\mathsf{fid}\|i)^{\beta_i},$$

$$X = \prod_{i\in I} x_i^{\beta_i} \mod p,$$

$$T = \prod_{i\in I} t_i^{\beta_i} \quad (\text{in } G).$$

The server verifies

$$X \overset{?}{=} v_1^{Y_1} v_2^{Y_2} \prod_{j=1}^{m} z_j^{\mu_j} \mod p,$$

$$e(T, g) \overset{?}{=} e\left(W u^{\sum_{i\in I}\beta_i H_2(x_i)}, z_g\right) \quad (\text{in } G_T).$$

If both hold, return 1; otherwise, return 0.

Discussion on some design decisions. To help understand our scheme, now we discuss some design decisions we

made to satisfy both the above performance design requirements and the security definitions. First, our UPLOAD and AUDITINT protocols are new. When compared with existing protocols for the similar purpose [2, 12, 8, 5, 6, 16], it has the following significant advantage during the execution of the UPLOAD protocol (a thorough comparison will be present in Section 5.5). Our scheme only requires the client to perform $O(n)$ exponentiation operations plus $O(mn)$ multiplication operations, where n is the number of data blocks and m is number of symbols in each block (i.e., mn is the number of symbols in a data file). In contrast, the referred schemes require the client to perform $O(mn)$ exponentiation operations plus $O(mn)$ multiplication operations. As such, our AUDITINT protocol would be of independent value as it could also be used as the core of PDP/POR protocols.

Second, in our POSD scheme we used $z_j = v_1^{-s_{j1}} v_2^{-s_{j2}}$ for verification, which is reminiscent of the signature scheme in [11]. However, our scheme is not a digital signature scheme because we actually allow a sort of manipulation. On the other hand, we use $z_j = v_1^{-s_{j1}} v_2^{-s_{j2}}$ rather than, for example, $z_j = v_1^{-s_{j1}}$. This is because security of our construction partially relies on the DLOG problem, or more precisely the DLOG of v_2 with respect to base v_1.

Third, in the UPLOAD protocol, the purpose of t_i is to prevent the server from forging any new legitimate tuple of (x_i', y_{i1}', y_{i2}') from a legitimate (x_i, y_{i1}, y_{i2}) and F_i. To see this, let us consider the case without using t_i. Note that (x_i, y_{i1}, y_{i2}) with respect to block F_i satisfies

$$x_i = v_1^{y_{i1}} v_2^{y_{i2}} \prod_{j=1}^{m} z_j^{\mathsf{F}_{ij}} \mod p.$$

Without using t_i, the server can choose r_{i1}' and r_{i2}' from $\mathbb{Z}_q^*$, and set

$$x_i' = x_i v_1^{r_{i1}'} v_2^{r_{i2}'} \mod p,$$
$$y_{i1}' = y_{i1} + r_{i1}' \mod q,$$
$$y_{i2}' = y_{i2} + r_{i2}' \mod q$$

so that (x_i', y_{i1}', y_{i2}') also satisfies

$$x_i' = v_1^{y_{i1}'} v_2^{y_{i2}'} \prod_{j=1}^{m} z_j^{\mathsf{F}_{ij}} \mod p.$$

As another example of attacks, the server can generate (x_i', y_{i1}', y_{i2}') as follows: let $x_i' = x_i z_1 \mod p$, $y_{i1}' = y_{i1}$ and $y_{i2}' = y_{i2}$. During the execution of the UPLOAD protocol, the server may return $\mathsf{F}_i' = \{\mathsf{F}_{i1} + 1, \mathsf{F}_{i2}, \ldots, \mathsf{F}_{im}\}$ by adding one to the first symbol of block F_i. As a consequence, (x_i', y_{i1}', y_{i2}') and F_i' also satisfy

$$x_i' = v_1^{y_{i1}'} v_2^{y_{i2}'} z_1^{\mathsf{F}_{i1}+1} \prod_{j=2}^{m} z_j^{\mathsf{F}_{ij}} \mod p.$$

5.3 Correctness Analysis

With respect to correctness definition, the correctness of

the POSD scheme can be verified as follows:

$$v_1^{Y_1} v_2^{Y_2} \prod_{j=1}^{m} z_j^{\mu_j}$$

$$= v_1^{\sum_{i\in I}\beta_i y_{i1}} v_2^{\sum_{i\in I}\beta_i y_{i2}} \prod_{j=1}^{m}(v_1^{-s_{j1}} v_2^{-s_{j2}})^{\mu_j}$$

$$= v_1^{\sum_{i\in I}\beta_i y_{i1}} v_2^{\sum_{i\in I}\beta_i y_{i2}} \prod_{j=1}^{m}(v_1^{-s_{j1}} v_2^{-s_{j2}})^{\sum_{i\in I}\beta_i F_{ij}}$$

$$= v_1^{\sum_{i\in I}\beta_i(r_{i1}+\sum_{j=1}^{m}F_{ij}s_{j1})} v_2^{\sum_{i\in I}\beta_i(r_{i2}+\sum_{j=1}^{m}F_{ij}s_{j2})}$$

$$\prod_{j=1}^{m}(v_1^{-s_{j1}} v_2^{-s_{j2}})^{\sum_{i\in I}\beta_i F_{ij}}$$

$$= v_1^{\sum_{i\in I}\beta_i r_{i1}} v_2^{\sum_{i\in I}\beta_i r_{i2}}$$

$$= (v_1^{r_{i1}} v_2^{r_{i2}})^{\sum_{i\in I}\beta_i}$$

$$= \prod_{i\in I} x_i^{\beta_i}$$

$$= X.$$

and

$$e(T, g)$$

$$= e\left(\prod_{i\in I} t_i^{\beta_i}, g\right) = e\left(\prod_{i\in I}\left(H_1(\mathsf{fid}||i)u^{H_2(x_i)}\right)^{w\beta_i}, g\right)$$

$$= e\left(\prod_{i\in I}\left(H_1(\mathsf{fid}||i)u^{H_2(x_i)}\right)^{\beta_i}, g^w\right)$$

$$= e\left(\left(\prod_{i\in I}H_1(\mathsf{fid}||i)\prod_{i\in I}u^{H_2(x_i)}\right)^{\beta_i}, z_g\right)$$

$$= e\left(Wu^{\sum_{i\in I}\beta_i H_2(x_i)}, z_g\right).$$

5.4 Security Analysis

Now we prove that the POSD scheme satisfies Definitions 2 and 3.

THEOREM 1. *Assume H_1 and H_2 are hash functions modeled as random oracles, and the* CDH *problem is hard. The* POSD *scheme is* server_unforgeable.

PROOF. We show our proof through a sequence of games between a challenger, who plays the role of an honest client, and adversary $\mathcal{A}$, who acts as the malicious server. The overall proof strategy is: given fid' corresponding to $(\mathsf{F},\mathsf{Tag}_{int})$ stored in the server and a challenge randomly selected by the challenger, if the adversary can pass the verification using $(\mathsf{F}',\mathsf{Tag}'_{int}) \neq (\mathsf{F},\mathsf{Tag}_{int})$, then there is an algorithm that can solve the CDH problem.

Game$_0$: **Game$_0$** is defined as in Definition 2, where the challenger only keeps the relevant public and private keys, and $\mathcal{Q}_{\mathsf{fid}}$, which is the list of the data file identifiers fid's it has used (as mentioned before, a PRF can reduce the storage of the fid's to constant).

Game$_1$: **Game$_1$** is the same as **Game$_0$** except that the challenger keeps $\mathcal{Q} = \{(\mathsf{fid},\mathsf{F},\mathsf{Tag}_{int})\}$,, the list of $(\mathsf{fid},\mathsf{F},\mathsf{Tag}_{int})$ involved in the execution of the UPLOAD protocol. In this case, we prove that if the adversary $\mathcal{A}$ can produce a forgery $(\mathsf{fid}',\mathsf{F}',\mathsf{Tag}'_{int}) \notin \mathcal{Q}$ that can pass the test in the AUDITINT

protocol with respect to the challenger's challenge (I,β), then there is an efficient algorithm that can solve the CDH problem.

The simulator is constructed as follows:

- For generating the keys, the simulator works as follows:

  - Select v_1 and v_2 uniformly at random from $\mathbb{Z}_p^*$ such that the order of v_1 and v_2 is q. Select uniformly at random s_{j1} and s_{j2} from $\mathbb{Z}_q^*$ for $1 \leq j \leq m$. Set $z_j = v_1^{-s_{j1}} v_2^{-s_{j2}} \mod p$ for $1 \leq j \leq m$.
  - Let g be a generator of group G, and select h from G at random. Set $u = g^\gamma h^\eta$, where γ and η are chosen uniformly at random from $\mathbb{Z}_q^*$.
  - Select z_g uniformly at random from group G, which means that the simulator does not know the corresponding w with $z_g = g^w$.
  - Set $\mathrm{PK}_{int} = \{p,q,g,u,h,v_1,v_2,z_1,\ldots,z_m,z_g\}$ and $\mathrm{PK}_{dup} = \mathrm{PK}_{int}$. However, the simulator only knows secrets $\mathrm{SK} = \{(s_{11},s_{12}),\ldots,(s_{m1},s_{m2})\}$ but not the w.

- The simulator model $H_2(\cdot)$ as a random oracle. Given x_i, if x_i has been queried, return $H_2(x_i)$. Otherwise, select η uniformly at random from $\mathbb{Z}_q^*$ and return η. The simulator keeps the list of $(x_i, H_2(x_i))$.

- When the simulator is asked to compute Tag_{int} for data file F, the simulator executes the following: for each data block F_i where $1 \leq i \leq n$, select r_{i1} and r_{i2} uniformly at random from $\mathbb{Z}_q^*$ and computes

$$x_i = v_1^{r_{i1}} v_2^{r_{i2}} \mod p,$$

$$y_{i1} = r_{i1} + \sum_{j=1}^{m} \mathsf{F}_{ij} s_{j1} \mod q,$$

$$y_{i2} = r_{i2} + \sum_{j=1}^{m} \mathsf{F}_{ij} s_{j2} \mod q.$$

Select λ_i uniformly at random from $\mathbb{Z}_q^*$ and set

$$H_1(\mathsf{fid}||i) = g^{\lambda_i} / \left(u^{H_2(x_i)}\right).$$

Thus, we have

$$t_i = \left(H_1(\mathsf{fid}||i)u^{H_2(x_i)}\right)^w = (g^w)^{\lambda_i} = (z_g)^{\lambda_i}.$$

Set the cryptographic tag for block F_i as $(x_i, y_{i1}, y_{i2}, t_i)$ and thus $\mathsf{Tag}_{int} = \{(x_i, y_{i1}, y_{i2}, t_i)_{1\leq i\leq n}\}$. The simulator keeps the list of $(\mathsf{fid}||i, H_1(\mathsf{fid}||i))$. Note that λ_i is unknown to $\mathcal{A}$.

- When $\mathcal{A}$ queries $H_1(\mathsf{fid}||i)$ separately, the simulator operates as follows. If $\mathsf{fid}||i$ has been queried, return $H_1(\mathsf{fid}||i)$. Otherwise, select λ'_i uniformly at random from $\mathbb{Z}_q^*$ and return $h^{\lambda'_i}$. Note that λ'_i is unknown to $\mathcal{A}$.

- The simulator interacts with $\mathcal{A}$ until $\mathcal{A}$ outputs a forgery $(\mathsf{fid}', (I,\beta), \{x_i\}_{i\in I}, Y'_1, Y'_2, T', \{\mu'_j\}_{1\leq j\leq m})$ at the Forgery stage and wins the game, where (I,β) is chosen at random by the simulator.

Suppose $\mathcal{A}$ produces $(\mathsf{fid}', (\mathrm{I}, \beta), \{x_i\}_{i \in \mathrm{I}}, \mathrm{Y}_1', \mathrm{Y}_2', T', \{\mu_j'\}_{1 \leq j \leq m})$ to win **Game**$_1$. This means that $\mathsf{fid}' \in \mathcal{Q}_{\mathsf{fid}}$, but

$$(\{\mu_j'\}_{1 \leq j \leq m}, \{x_i'\}_{i \in \mathrm{I}}, \mathrm{Y}_1', \mathrm{Y}_2', T') \neq (\{\mu_j\}_{1 \leq j \leq m}, \{x_i\}_{i \in \mathrm{I}}, \mathrm{Y}_1, \mathrm{Y}_2, T), \tag{1}$$

where $\mu = \sum_{i \in \mathrm{I}} \beta_i \mathsf{F}_i \mod q$, $\mu' = \sum_{i \in \mathrm{I}} \beta_i \mathsf{F}_i' \mod q$, and $(\mathsf{fid}', \mathsf{F}, \mathsf{Tag}_{int}) \in \mathcal{Q}$ from which $\{x_i\}_{i \in \mathrm{I}}, \mathrm{Y}_1, \mathrm{Y}_2, T$ are computed. The correctness of the scheme implies

$$e(T, g) = e\left(\prod_{i \in \mathrm{I}} H_1(\mathsf{fid}'||i)^{\beta_i} u^{\sum_{i \in \mathrm{I}} \beta_i H_2(x_i)}, z_g\right) \tag{2}$$

Since $\mathcal{A}$ wins in **Game**$_1$, we have

$$e(T', g) = e\left(\prod_{i \in \mathrm{I}} H_1(\mathsf{fid}'||i)^{\beta_i} u^{\sum_{i \in \mathrm{I}} \beta_i H_2(x_i')}, z_g\right). \tag{3}$$

In what follows, we will consider three cases of Eq. (1):

- Case 1: $T \neq T'$.

- Case 2: $T = T'$, but $x_i \neq x_i'$ for some $i \in \mathrm{I}$.

- Case 3: $T = T'$, $x_i = x_i'$ for all $i \in \mathrm{I}$, but $(\mathrm{Y}_1, \mathrm{Y}_2, \{\mu_j\}_{1 \leq j \leq m}) \neq (\mathrm{Y}_1', \mathrm{Y}_2', \{\mu_j'\}_{1 \leq j \leq m})$.

In each case, we will utilize, among other things, Eqs. (2) and (3), to show that the simulator can solve the CDH problem, which means that $\mathcal{A}$ cannot win **Game**$_1$ with a non-negligible probability. This will complete the proof.

Case 1: $T \neq T'$.
In this case, we have

$$e(T/T', g) = e\left(u^{\sum_{i \in \mathrm{I}} \beta_i (H_2(x_i) - H_2(x_i'))}, z_g\right).$$

By substituting u with $g^\gamma h^\eta$, we have

$$e(T/T', g) = e\left((g^\gamma h^\eta)^{\sum_{i \in \mathrm{I}} \beta_i (H_2(x_i) - H_2(x_i'))}, z_g\right).$$

Rearrange the terms, we get

$$T/T' = (g^{w\gamma} h^{w\eta})^{\sum_{i \in \mathrm{I}} \beta_i (H_2(x_i) - H_2(x_i'))}.$$

We claim that

$$\sum_{i \in \mathrm{I}} \beta_i (H_2(x_i) - H_2(x_i')) \neq 0 \mod q.$$

Otherwise, we get $T/T' = 1$, which contradicts the assumption $T \neq T'$. Together with the fact that $z_g = g^w$, we can get

$$h^w = \left((T/T') \cdot z_g^{-\gamma(\sum_{i \in \mathrm{I}}(H_2(x_i) - H_2(x_i')))}\right)^{\frac{1}{\sum_{i \in \mathrm{I}}(H_2(x_i) - H_2(x_i'))}},$$

which means that if $T \neq T'$, the simulator can solve the CDH problem by computing h^w with respect to given g and $z_g = g^w$ for unknown w.

Case 2: $T = T'$, but $x_i \neq x_i'$ for some $i \in \mathrm{I}$.
Because $T = T'$, we have

$$\prod_{i \in \mathrm{I}} H_1(\mathsf{fid}'||i)^{\beta_i} u^{\sum_{i \in \mathrm{I}} \beta_i H_2(x_i)} = \prod_{i \in \mathrm{I}} H_1(\mathsf{fid}'||i)^{\beta_i} u^{\sum_{i \in \mathrm{I}} \beta_i H_2(x_i')}.$$

By arranging the term, we have

$$u^{\sum_{i \in \mathrm{I}} \beta_i (H_2(x_i) - H_2(x_i'))} = 1.$$

As the probability that

$$\sum_{i \in \mathrm{I}} \beta_i (H_2(x_i) - H_2(x_i')) = 0 \mod q$$

is negligible and $u = g^\gamma h^\eta$, we have

$$\begin{aligned} h &= g^{\frac{\sum_{i \in \mathrm{I}} \gamma(H_2(x_i) - H_2(x_i'))}{\sum_{i \in \mathrm{I}} \eta(H_2(x_i) - H_2(x_i'))}} \\ &= g^{\gamma \eta^{-1} \sum_{i \in \mathrm{I}} (H_2(x_i) - H_2(x_i'))}. \end{aligned}$$

This means that the simulator can solve the DLOG of random h with respect to base g, which immediately breaks the CDH assumption.

Case 3: $T = T'$, $x_i = x_i'$ for all $i \in \mathrm{I}$, but $(\mathrm{Y}_1, \mathrm{Y}_2, \{\mu_j\}_{1 \leq j \leq m}) \neq (\mathrm{Y}_1', \mathrm{Y}_2', \{\mu_j'\}_{1 \leq j \leq m})$.
Note that

$$\prod_{i \in \mathrm{I}} x_i'^{\beta_i} = v_1^{\mathrm{Y}_1'} v_2^{\mathrm{Y}_2'} \prod_{j=1}^m z_j^{\mu_j'} \mod p$$

and

$$\prod_{i \in \mathrm{I}} x_i^{\beta_i} = v_1^{\mathrm{Y}_1} v_2^{\mathrm{Y}_2} \prod_{j=1}^m z_j^{\mu_j} \mod p.$$

Because $x_i = x_i'$ for all $i \in \mathrm{I}$, we have

$$v_1^{\mathrm{Y}_1'} v_2^{\mathrm{Y}_2'} \prod_{j=1}^m z_j^{\mu_j'} = v_1^{\mathrm{Y}_1} v_2^{\mathrm{Y}_2} \prod_{j=1}^m z_j^{\mu_j} \mod p.$$

By replacing z_j with $v_1^{-s_{j1}} v_2^{-s_{j2}}$ in the above equation, we get

$$v_1^{\mathrm{Y}_1' - \mathrm{Y}_1 - \sum_{j=1}^m s_{j1}(\mu_j' - \mu_j)} = v_2^{\mathrm{Y}_2 - \mathrm{Y}_2' - \sum_{j=1}^m s_{j1}(\mu_j - \mu_j')} \mod p.$$

Thus, if $(\mathrm{Y}_1, \mathrm{Y}_2, \{\mu_j\}_{1 \leq j \leq m}) \neq (\mathrm{Y}_1', \mathrm{Y}_2', \{\mu_j'\}_{1 \leq j \leq m})$, then the simulator can compute the DLOG of random v_2 with respect to base v_1, which immediately breaks the CDH assumption. $\square$

THEOREM 2. *Assume H_1 and H_2 are hash functions modeled as random oracles, and the CDH problem is hard. The POSD scheme is (κ, θ)-uncheatable with respect to challenge of $c = \frac{n}{\theta - \kappa} \log(2^{\theta - \kappa} + \epsilon)$ blocks in the DEDUP protocol, where κ is the min-entropy of the file F in question, θ is the amount of entropy leaked to or stolen by the adversary, and ϵ is negligible in security parameter ℓ.*

PROOF. According to Theorem 1, given that H_1 and H_2 are hash functions modeled as random oracles, and the CDH problem is hard, our scheme is server_unforgeable. That is, given the challenge $\{\mathrm{I}, \beta\}$ with file identifier fid, the response $\{\mu_1, \cdots, \mu_m, \{x_i\}_{i \in \mathrm{I}}, \mathrm{Y}_1, \mathrm{Y}_2, T\}$ must be computed honestly from $(\mathsf{fid}, \mathsf{F}, \mathsf{Tag}_{int})$, so that

$$\prod_{i \in \mathrm{I}} x_i^{\beta_i} = v_1^{\mathrm{Y}_1} v_2^{\mathrm{Y}_2} \prod_{j=1}^m z_j^{\mu_j} \mod p,$$

$$e(T, g) = e\left(\prod_{i \in \mathrm{I}} H_1(\mathsf{fid}||i)^{\beta_i} u^{\sum_{i \in \mathrm{I}} \beta_i H_2(x_i)}, z_g\right)$$

Without loss of generality, let (I, β) be the challenge with corresponding file identifier fid in the execution of DEDUP. Let $(\mu_1', \cdots, \mu_m')$ be the response from the malicious client and $\{x_i'\}_{i \in \mathrm{I}}, \mathrm{Y}_1', \mathrm{Y}_2', T'$ are computed from Tag_{dup} by the cloud server. Recall that $\mathsf{Tag}_{dup} = \mathsf{Tag}_{int}$, then we have $\{x_i' = x_i\}_{i \in I}, Y_1' = Y_1, Y_2' = Y_2, T' = T$. Therefore, in order to satisfy

$$\prod_{i \in I} x_i'^{\beta_i} = v_1^{Y_1'} v_2^{Y_2'} \prod_{j=1}^m z_j^{\mu_j'} \mod p,$$

$$e(T', g) = e\left(\prod_{i \in I} H_1(\mathsf{fid}||i)^{\beta_i} u^{\sum_{i \in I} \beta_i H_2(x_i')}, z_g\right)$$

we have $\mu_j' = \mu_j, 1 \leq j \leq m$, otherwise we can solve the DLOG problem of random v_2 with respect to base v_1 (see case 3 in the proof of Theorem 1). That is, the malicious client must compute $(\mu_1', \cdots, \mu_m')$ honestly from F. In other words, the malicious client can win the game only if it can figure out the unknown bits entropy in the data blocks specified by the set I.

Let Evnt denote the event that there are c data blocks with unknown bits entropy and the adversary tries to guess the unknown bits entropy in order to cheating successfully. In order to simplify the model, assume that the unknown bits entropy distributes over the data blocks of F uniformly. Meanwhile, because the challenged data blocks are chosen uniformly at random so that we can assume that the unknown bits entropy distributes over F uniformly. Therefore the probability

$$\begin{aligned}
\Pr[\mathsf{Evnt}] &= \frac{1}{2^{c(\kappa - \theta)/n}} \\
&= 2^{c(\theta - \kappa)/n} \\
&= 2^{\log(2^{\theta - \kappa} + \epsilon)} \quad \left(c = \frac{n}{\theta - \kappa} \log(2^{\theta - \kappa} + \epsilon)\right) \\
&= 2^{\theta - \kappa} + \epsilon \\
&= \frac{1}{2^{\kappa - \theta}} + \epsilon.
\end{aligned}$$

This completes the proof. $\square$

5.5 Performance Analysis

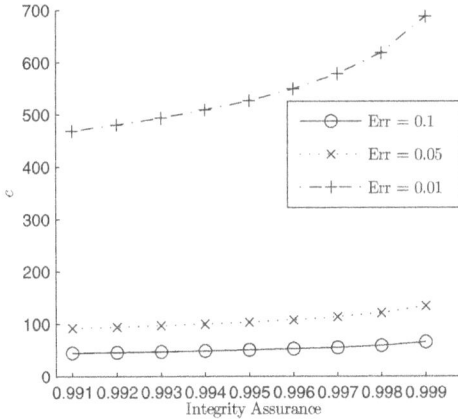

Figure 1: The impact of ERR and integrity assurance on challenge size c

On the size of the challenges. The size of the challenges in the AUDITINT protocol is an important performance parameter. Let ERR be the probability of block being corrupted (i.e., portions of the data modified by the server).

Figure 1 shows the required size of challenges in order to achieve integrity assurance in the interval $[0.991, 0.999]$ under three circumstances: ERR$= 0.1$, ERR$= 0.05$ and ERR$= 0.01$. Consider, for example, the case of ERR$= 0.01$. It only requires to send less than 500 challenges in order to achieve 99.1% integrity assurance, regardless of the size of the data blocks. This also explains the advantage of POR and PDP.

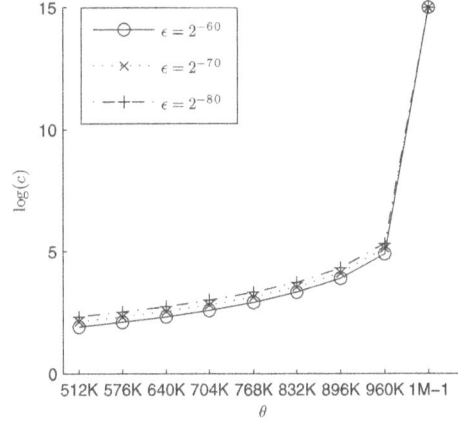

Figure 2: The impact of θ on the challenge size c: $n = 2^{15}$ and $\kappa = 1M$ bits

Theorem 2 shows a lower bound on the number of challenged data blocks in order to fulfill (κ, θ)_uncheatability. In order to illustrate the impact of the lower bound of c with parameters κ, θ, n and ϵ, we consider two cases: one file with small min-entropy (1M bits) and the other with large min-entropy (128M bits). With respect to negligible probability 2^{-80}, Figure 2 shows that given a file of 2^{15} data blocks with 1M bits min-entropy, our scheme can fulfill $(1M, 960K)$_uncheatability by challenging about 2^6 data blocks (or 0.1% portions of the data file).

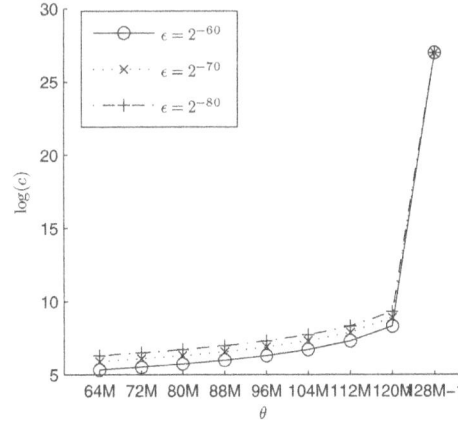

Figure 3: The impact of θ on the challenge size c: $n = 2^{27}$ and $\kappa = 128M$ bits

Figure 3 shows that given a file of 2^{27} data blocks with 128M bits min-entropy, fulfilling $(128M, 120M)$_uncheatability requires to challenge about 2^9 data blocks (or 2^{-18} portions of the data file). This shows that even if the adversary has obtained 93.75% of the data file (e.g., by penetrating into the cloud server in a stealthy fashion and without being detected), the attacker cannot cheat against reasonably small challenges.

Comparison with some relevant schemes. Because POSD is the first scheme that simultaneously allows proof of storage integrity and deduplication, in Table 1 we compare its efficiency to the most efficient PDP scheme in [2], the most efficient POR scheme in [12], and the only existing POW scheme in [13], respectively. The two particular PDP and POR schemes are chosen also because they offer the afore-mentioned *public verifiability*, namely that a third-party can examine the storage integrity on behalf of a client, which is exploited to construct POSD. The POW scheme is the one based on Merkle-tree in [13]; it is chosen because its security is compatible with our POSD scheme (there are more efficient but less secure solutions in [13]). Note that in the client storage, we consider a single file F. In principle, each client can outsource polynomially-many data files to the cloud. In this case, storage of the identifies, fid's, still can be made constant by letting each client use a Pseudo-random Function PRF to generate fid's from its secret key while maintaining a counter.

From the perspective of assuring cloud data storage integrity, we draw the following observations from Table 1. First, our POSD scheme requires $O(n)$ exponentiations for a client to preprocess a data file before uploading it to the cloud. This complexity is substantially smaller than the preprocessing complexity $O(mn)$ exponentiations of the schemes in [2, 12]. Second, our POSD scheme incurs $O((m+c)\ell)$ communication overhead in the audit process, which is higher than the $O(m\ell)$ communication overhead of the PDP and POR schemes. To demonstrate that the extra communication is not significant especially when we deal with large files, let us consider the following realistic example. Suppose a data file consists of 2^{27} blocks of 2^8 symbols (2.5-GB file if $\ell = 160$). Assume that the probability of block corruption is ERR = 0.01. That is, roughly 2^{21} data blocks are corrupted. Suppose we want to achieve 99.5% integrity assurance (i.e., with probability 99.5% the tamperation of a data file is detected), the extra communication overhead in our POSD scheme is only 2^{16} bits (8KB). Moreover, it should be noted that the PDP and POR schemes cannot fulfill deduplication.

From the perspective of secure data deduplication, , we draw the following observations from Table 1. First, our POSD scheme is slightly less efficient than the POW scheme. However, the POW scheme cannot fulfill the auditability of cloud storage security (note that it was well-known that Merkle-tree is not sufficient to fulfill PDP/POR [2, 12, 16]). Second, our POSD scheme incurs smaller communication overhead because $O(m\ell)$ is often much smaller than $O(c\log(n)m\ell)$. Third, the POW scheme is indeed secure in the standard model based on the existence of Collision-Resistant Hash (CRH) functions. However, it cannot fulfill auditability of cloud storage integrity.

6. CONCLUSION

We motivated the need of the cloud storage notion we call proof of storage with deduplication or POSD, to fulfill data integrity and duplication simultaneously. We also presented an efficient POSD scheme, which is proven secure in the Random Oracle model based on the Computational Diffie-Hellman assumption. Compared with the PDP/POR/POW schemes, our scheme is as efficient as theirs.

One interesting future work is to remove the random oracle in the protocol without jeopardizing performance. Another is to seek a different design methodology for such protocols so as to achieve even substantially better performance.

Acknowledgements.

This work was supported in part by an AFOSR MURI grant and a NSF grant.

7. REFERENCES

[1] The digital universe decade - are you ready? International Data Corporation, 2010. http://idcdocserv.com/925.

[2] G. Ateniese, R. Burns, R. Curtmola, J. Herring, L. Kissner, Z. Peterson, and D. Song. Provable data possession at untrusted stores. In *Proceedings of the 14th ACM conference on Computer and communications security*, CCS '07, pages 598–609, New York, NY, USA, 2007. ACM.

[3] G. Ateniese, R. Di Pietro, L. V. Mancini, and G. Tsudik. Scalable and efficient provable data possession. In *Proceedings of the 4th international conference on Security and privacy in communication netowrks*, SecureComm '08, pages 9:1–9:10, New York, NY, USA, 2008. ACM.

[4] G. Ateniese, S. Kamara, and J. Katz. Proofs of storage from homomorphic identification protocols. In *Proceedings of the 15th International Conference on the Theory and Application of Cryptology and Information Security: Advances in Cryptology*, ASIACRYPT '09, pages 319–333, Berlin, Heidelberg, 2009. Springer-Verlag.

[5] K. D. Bowers, A. Juels, and A. Oprea. Proofs of retrievability: theory and implementation. In *Proceedings of the 2009 ACM workshop on Cloud computing security*, CCSW '09, pages 43–54, New York, NY, USA, 2009. ACM.

[6] Y. Dodis, S. Vadhan, and D. Wichs. Proofs of retrievability via hardness amplification. In *Proceedings of the 6th Theory of Cryptography Conference on Theory of Cryptography*, TCC '09, pages 109–127, Berlin, Heidelberg, 2009. Springer-Verlag.

[7] J. R. Douceur, A. Adya, W. J. Bolosky, D. Simon, and M. Theimer. Reclaiming space from duplicate files in a serverless distributed file system. In *Proceedings of the 22 nd International Conference on Distributed Computing Systems (ICDCS'02)*, ICDCS '02, pages 617–, Washington, DC, USA, 2002. IEEE Computer Society.

[8] C. Erway, A. Küpçü, C. Papamanthou, and R. Tamassia. Dynamic provable data possession. In *Proceedings of the 16th ACM conference on Computer and communications security*, CCS '09, pages 213–222, New York, NY, USA, 2009. ACM.

[9] D. Harnik, B. Pinkas, and A. Shulman-Peleg. Side channels in cloud services: Deduplication in cloud

	PDP [2]	POR [12]	POSD (this paper)	POW [13]
total key size	$O(m)$	$O(m)$	$O(m)$	0 (no keys)
use Random Oracle?	yes	yes	yes	no
security assumption	RSA	CDH	CDH	CRH
For integrity audit purpose				
client storage	$O(1)$	$O(1)$	$O(1)$	N/A
server storage	$O(n)$	$O(n)$	$O(n)$	N/A
audit preprocessing comp.	$O(mn)\text{Ex}+O(mn)\text{Mu}$	$O(mn)\text{Ex}+O(mn)\text{Mu}$	$O(n)\text{Ex}+O(mn)\text{Mu}$	N/A
audit computation (client)	$O(c)\text{Ex}+O(cm)\text{Mu}$	$O(c+m)\text{Ex}+O(cm)\text{Mu}$	$O(c)\text{Ex}+O(cm)\text{Mu}$	N/A
audit computation (server)	$O(c)\text{Ex}+O(cm)\text{Mu}$	$O(c)\text{Ex}+O(cm)\text{Mu}$	$O(c)\text{Ex}+O(cm)\text{Mu}$	N/A
audit communication	$O(m\ell)$	$O(m\ell)$	$O((m+c)\ell)$	N/A
integrity assurance	$1-(1-\text{Err})^c$	$1-(1-\text{Err})^c$	$1-(1-\text{Err})^c$	N/A
For deduplication purpose				
dedup preprocessing comp.	N/A	N/A	$O(n)\text{Ex}+O(mn)\text{Mu}$	ECC $+O(n^2)\text{H}$
dedup. computation (client)	N/A	N/A	$O(cm)\text{Mu}$	$O(n^2)\text{H}$
dedup. computation (server)	N/A	N/A	$O(c)\text{Ex}+O(cm)\text{Mu}$	$O(c\log(n))\text{H}$
dedup. communication	N/A	N/A	$O(\ell m)$	$O(cm\ell\log(n))$

Table 1: Efficiency comparison between some PDP, POR, POW and our POSD schemes, where n is the number of blocks of a data file, m is the number of symbols of a data block, c is the number of blocks that will be challenged, Err is the probability of block corruption, Ex represents modular exponentiation operation, Mu represents modular multiplication operation, and N/A indicates that a property is not applicable to a certain scheme.

storage. *IEEE Security and Privacy*, 8:40–47, November 2010.

[10] A. Juels and B. S. Kaliski, Jr. Pors: proofs of retrievability for large files. In *Proceedings of the 14th ACM conference on Computer and communications security*, CCS '07, pages 584–597, New York, NY, USA, 2007. ACM.

[11] T. Okamoto. Provably secure and practical identification schemes and corresponding signature schemes. In *Proceedings of the 12th Annual International Cryptology Conference on Advances in Cryptology*, CRYPTO '92, pages 31–53, London, UK, 1993. Springer-Verlag.

[12] H. Shacham and B. Waters. Compact proofs of retrievability. In *Proceedings of the 14th International Conference on the Theory and Application of Cryptology and Information Security: Advances in Cryptology*, ASIACRYPT '08, pages 90–107, Berlin, Heidelberg, 2008. Springer-Verlag.

[13] B. P. A. S.-P. Shai Halevi, Danny Harnik. Proofs of ownership in remote storage systems. Cryptology ePrint Archive, Report 2011/207, 2011. http://eprint.iacr.org/.

[14] M. W. Storer, K. Greenan, D. D. Long, and E. L. Miller. Secure data deduplication. In *Proceedings of the 4th ACM international workshop on Storage security and survivability*, StorageSS '08, pages 1–10, New York, NY, USA, 2008. ACM.

[15] Q. Wang, C. Wang, K. Ren, W. Lou, and J. Li. Enabling public auditability and data dynamics for storage security in cloud computing. *IEEE Trans. Parallel Distrib. Syst.*, 22:847–859, May 2011.

[16] Q. Zheng and S. Xu. Fair and dynamic proofs of retrievability. In *Proceedings of the first ACM conference on Data and application security and privacy*, CODASPY '11, pages 237–248, New York, NY, USA, 2011. ACM.

Practical Oblivious Storage

Michael T. Goodrich
Dept. of Computer Science
University of California, Irvine
goodrich@ics.uci.edu

Michael Mitzenmacher
Dept. of Computer Science
Harvard University
michaelm@eecs.harvard.edu

Olga Ohrimenko
Dept. of Computer Science
Brown University
olya@cs.brown.edu

Roberto Tamassia
Dept. of Computer Science
Brown University
rt@cs.brown.edu

ABSTRACT

We study *oblivious storage* (OS), a natural way to model privacy-preserving data outsourcing where a client, Alice, stores sensitive data at an honest-but-curious server, Bob. We show that Alice can hide both the content of her data and the pattern in which she accesses her data, with high probability, using a method that achieves $O(1)$ amortized rounds of communication between her and Bob for each data access. We assume that Alice and Bob exchange small messages, of size $O(N^{1/c})$, for some constant $c \geq 2$, in a single round, where N is the size of the data set that Alice is storing with Bob. We also assume that Alice has a private memory of size $2N^{1/c}$. These assumptions model real-world cloud storage scenarios, where trade-offs occur between latency, bandwidth, and the size of the client's private memory.

Categories and Subject Descriptors

K.6.5 [**Management of Computing and Information Systems**]: Security and Protection

General Terms

Algorithms, Security

1. INTRODUCTION

Outsourced data management is a large and growing industry. For example, as of July 2011, Amazon S3 [2] reportedly stores more than 400 billion objects, which is four times its size from the year before, and the Windows Azure service [15], which was started in late 2008, is now a multi-billion dollar enterprise.

With the growing impact of online cloud storage technologies, there is a corresponding growing interest in methods for privacy-preserving access to outsourced data. Namely, it is anticipated that many customers of cloud storage services will desire or require that their data remain private. A necessary component of private data access, of course, is to encrypt the objects being stored. But information can be leaked from the way that data is accessed, even if it is encrypted (see, e.g., [5]). Thus, privacy-preserving data access must involve both encryption and techniques for obfuscating the patterns in which users access data.

1.1 Problem Statement

The classic model for the obfuscation of the access pattern is *oblivious RAM simulation*. We use the related *oblivious storage* model, which has been recently proposed. These models are outlined in the rest of this section.

In the *oblivious random access machine (ORAM)* simulation [8] approach, the client, Alice, is modeled as a CPU with a limited-size cache that accesses a large indexed memory managed by the owner of the data service, Bob. The goal is for Alice to perform an arbitrary RAM computation while completely obscuring from Bob the data items she accesses and the access pattern. Unfortunately, although known ORAM simulations [1, 6, 8, 9, 10, 14, 17, 20, 22] can be adapted to the problem of privacy-preserving access to outsourced data, they do not naturally match the interfaces provided by existing cloud storage services, which are not organized according to the RAM model (e.g., see [4]).

A notable exception to this aspect of previous work on ORAM simulation is a recent paper by Boneh *et al.* [4], who introduce the *oblivious storage (OS)* model. In this model, the storage provided by Bob is viewed more realistically as a collection of key-value pairs and the query and update operations supported by his API are likewise more accurately viewed in terms of operations dealing with key-value pairs, which we also call *items*. An OS solution is *oblivious* in this context if an honest-but-curious polynomial-time adversary is unable to distinguish between the (obfuscated) versions of two possible access sequences of equal length and maximum set size, which are polynomially related, beyond a negligible probability. Although the solution to the OS problem given by Boneh *et al.* is somewhat complicated, it is nevertheless considerably simpler than most of the existing ORAM solution techniques. In particular, it avoids additional details required of ORAM simulations that must deal with the obfuscation of an arbitrary RAM algorithm. Thus, an argument can be made that the OS approach is both more realistic and supports simpler oblivious simulations. The goal of this paper, then, is to explore further simplifications and improvements to achieve practical solutions to the oblivious storage problem.

1.2 Related Previous Work

Research on oblivious simulation of one computational model by another began with Pippenger and Fischer [18], who show that one can obliviously simulate a computation of a one-tape Turing machine computation of length N with an two-tape Turing machine computation of length $O(N \log N)$. That is, they show how to perform such an oblivious simulation with a computational overhead that is $O(\log N)$.

Goldreich and Ostrovsky [8] show that one can perform an oblivious RAM (ORAM) simulation using an outsourced data server and they prove a lower bound implying that such simulations require an overhead of at least $\Omega(\log N)$, for a RAM memory of size N, under some reasonable assumptions about the nature of such simulations. For the case where Alice has only a constant-size private memory, they show how Alice can easily achieve an overhead of $O(N^{1/2} \log N)$, using a scheme called the "square-root solution," with $O(N)$ storage at Bob's server. With a more complicated scheme, they also show how Alice can achieve an overhead of $O(\log^3 N)$ with $O(N \log N)$ storage at Bob's server, using a scheme called the "hierarchical solution."

Williams and Sion [22] provide an ORAM simulation for the case when the data owner, Alice, has a private memory of size $O(N^{1/2})$. They achieve an expected amortized time overhead of $O(\log^2 N)$ using $O(N \log N)$ memory at the external data provider, Bob. Additionally, Williams et al. [23] claim a result that uses an $O(N^{1/2})$-sized private memory and achieves $O(\log N \log \log N)$ amortized time overhead with a linear-sized outsourced storage, but some researchers (e.g., see [17]) have raised concerns with the assumptions and analysis of this result. Likewise, Pinkas and Reinman [17] published an ORAM simulation result for the case where Alice maintains a constant-size private memory, claiming that Alice can achieve an expected amortized overhead of $O(\log^2 N)$ while using $O(N)$ storage space, but Kushilevitz et al. [14] have raised correctness issues with this result as well [14]. Goldreich and Mitzenmacher [9] show that one can achieve an overhead of $O(\log^2 N)$ in an ORAM simulation, with high probability, for a client with constant-sized local memory, and $O(\log N)$, for a client with $O(N^\epsilon)$ memory, for a constant $\epsilon > 0$. Kushilevitz et al. [14] also show that one can achieve an overhead of $O(\log^2 N / \log \log N)$ in an ORAM simulation, with high probability, for a client with constant-sized local memory. Ajtai [1] proves that ORAM simulation can be done with polylogarithmic overhead without cryptographic assumptions about the existence of random hash functions, as is done in the papers mentioned above (and this paper), and a similar result is given by Damgård et al. [6].

The importance of privacy protection in outsourced data management naturally raises the question of the practicality of the previous ORAM solutions. Unfortunately, the above-mentioned theoretical results contain several complications and hidden constant factors that make these solutions less than ideal for real-world use. Stefanov et al. [20] study the ORAM simulation problem from a practical point of view, with the goal of reducing the worst-case bounds for data accesses. They show that one can achieve an amortized overhead of $O(\log N)$ and worst-case performance $O(N^{1/2})$, with $O(\epsilon N)$ storage on the client, for a constant $0 < \epsilon < 1$, and an amortized overhead of $O(\log^2 N)$ and similar worst-case performance, with a client-side storage of $O(N^{1/2})$, both of which have been hidden constant factors than previous ORAM solutions. Goodrich et al. [10] similarly study methods for improving the worst-case performance of ORAM simulation, showing that one can achieve a worst-case overhead of $O(\log N)$ with a client-side memory of size $O(N^\epsilon)$, for any constant $\epsilon > 0$.

As mentioned above, Boneh et al. [4] introduce the oblivious storage (OS) problem and argue how it is more realistic and natural than the ORAM simulation problem. They study methods that separate access overheads and the overheads needed for rebuilding the data structures on the server, providing, for example, $O(1)$ amortized overhead for accesses with $O((N \log N)^{1/2})$ overhead for rebuilding operations, assuming a similar bound for the size of the private memory on the client.

1.3 Our Results

In this paper, we study the oblivious storage (OS) problem, providing solutions that are parameterized by the two critical components of an outsourced storage system:

- N: the number of items that are stored at the server

- M: the maximum number of items that can be sent or received in a single message, which we refer to as the *message size*.

We assume that the objects being outsourced to Bob's cloud storage are all of the same size, since this is a requirement to achieve oblivious access. Thus, we can simply refer to the memory and message sizes in terms of the number of items that are stored. This notation is borrowed from the literature on external-memory algorithms (e.g., see [21]), since it closely models the scenario where the memory needed by a computation exceeds its local capacity so that external storage is needed. In keeping with this analogy to external-memory algorithms, we refer to each message that is exchanged between Alice and Bob as an *I/O*, each of which, as noted above, is of size at most M. We additionally assume that Alice's memory is of size at least $2M$, so that she can hold two messages in her local memory. In our case, however, we additionally assume that $M \geq N^{1/c}$, for some constant $c \geq 2$. This assumption is made for the sake of realism, since even with $c = 3$, we can model Bob storing exabytes for Alice, while she and he exchange individual messages measured in megabytes. Thus, we analyze our solutions in terms of the constant

$$c = \log_M N.$$

We give practical solutions to the oblivious storage problem that achieve an efficient amortized number of I/Os exchanged between Alice and Bob in order to perform put and get operations.

We first present a simple "square-root" solution, which assumes that M is $N^{1/2}$, so $c = 2$. This solution is not oblivious, however, if the client requests items that are not in the set. So we show how to convert any oblivious storage solution that cannot tolerate requests for missing items to a solution that can support obliviously also such requests. With these tools in hand, we then show how to define an inductive solution to the oblivious storage problem that achieves a

Method	I/Os (Number of messages)		Message Size (M)	Client Memory	Server Storage
	Online	Amortized			
Williams *et al.* [23]	$O(\log N \log \log N)$	$O(\log N \log \log N)$	$O(N^{1/2})$	$O(N^{1/2})$	$O(N)$
Shi *et al.* [19]	$O(\log N)$	$O(\log N)$	$O(\log^2 N)$	$O(\log^2 N)$	$O(N \log N)$
Goodrich *et al.* [10]	$O(\log N)$	$O(\log N)$	$O(1)$	N^ν	$O(N)$
Boneh *et al.* [4]	$O(1)$	$O(\log N)$	$N^{1/2}$	$O(N^{1/2})$	$N + 2N^{1/2}$
Our Method $N^{1/2}$	$O(1)$	$O(1)$	$N^{1/2}$	$2N^{1/2}$	$N + N^{1/2}$
Our Method $N^{1/c}$	$O(1)$	$O(1)$	$N^{1/c}$	$cN^{1/c}$	$N + 2\sum_{i=1}^{c-2} N^{(c-i)/c}$

Table 1: **Comparison between selected oblivious storage approaches. Online I/Os refers to the number of accesses performed to retrieve the requested item. Note that additional I/Os may be required before the next request can be processed. Thus, we also give the amortized number of I/Os per request. Message size (M) refers to the number of items that can be transferred in a single I/O. We denote with N the number of items outsourced to the server and with c and ν arbitrary constants such that $c \geq 2$ and $0 < \nu < 1$. The message size, client memory, and server storage are measured in terms of the number of items. Also, we note that the constant factor in the $O(1)$ access overhead for our $N^{1/c}$ method depends on constant c.**

constant amortized number of I/Os for each access, assuming $M = N^{1/c}$. We believe that $c = 2$, $c = 3$, and $c = 4$ are reasonable choices in practice, depending on the relative sizes of M and N.

The operations in these solutions are factored into *access operations* and *rebuild operations*, as in the approach advocated by Boneh *et al.* [4]. Access operations simply read or write individual items to/from Bob's storage and are needed to retrieve the requested item, whereas rebuild operations may additionally restructure the contents of Bob's storage so as to mask Alice's access patterns. In our solutions, access operations use messages of size $O(1)$ while messages of size M are used only for rebuild operations.

An important ingredient in all oblivious storage and oblivious RAM solutions is a method to obliviously "shuffle" a set of elements so that Bob cannot correlate the location of an element before the shuffle with that after the shuffle. This is usually done by using an oblivious sorting algorithm, and our methods can utilize such an approach, such as the external-memory oblivious sorting algorithm of Goodrich and Mitzenmacher [9].

In this paper, we also introduce a new simple shuffling method, which we call the *buffer shuffle*. We show that this method can shuffle with high probability with very little information leakage, which is likely to be sufficient in practice in most real-world oblivious storage scenarios. Of course, if perfectly oblivious shuffling is desired, then this shuffle method can be replaced by external-memory sorting, which increases the I/O complexity of our results by at most a constant factor (which depends on c).

In Table 1, we summarize our results and compare the main performance measures of our solutions with those of selected previous methods that claim to be practical.

1.4 Organization of the Paper

The rest of this paper is organized as follows. In Section 2, we overview the oblivious storage model and its security properties and describe some basic techniques used in previous work. Our buffer shuffle method is presented and analyzed in Section 3. We give a preliminary miss-intolerant square-root solution in Section 4. Section 5 derives a miss-tolerant solution from our square-root solution using a cuckoo hashing scheme. In Section 6, we show how

to reduce the storage requirement at the client. Finally, in Section 7, we describe our experimental results and provide estimates of the actual time overhead and monetary cost of our method, obtained by a prototype implementation and simulation of the use of our solution on the Amazon S3 storage service.

2. THE OBLIVIOUS STORAGE MODEL

In this section, we discuss the OS model using the formalism of Boneh *et al.* [4], albeit with some minor modifications. As mentioned above, one of the main differences between the OS model and the classic ORAM model is that the storage unit in the OS model is an *item* consisting of a key-value pair. Thus, we measure the size of messages and of the storage space at the client and server in terms of the number of items.

2.1 Operations and Messages

Let S be the set of data items. The server supports the following operations on S.

- get(k): if S contains an item, (k, v), with key k, then return the value, v, of this item, else return null.

- put(k, v): if S contains an item, (k, w), with key k, then replace the value of this item with v, else add to S a new item (k, v).

- remove(k): if S contains an item, (k, v), with key k, then delete from S this item and return its value v, else return null.

- getRange(k_1, k_2, m): return the first m items (by key order) in S with keys in the range $[k_1, k_2]$. Parameter m is a cut-off to avoid data overload at the client because of an error. If there are fewer than m such items, then all the items with keys in the range $[k_1, k_2]$ are returned.

- removeRange(k_1, k_2): remove from S all items with keys in the range $[k_1, k_2]$.

The interactions between the client, Alice, and the server, Bob, are implemented with messages, each of which is of size at most M, i.e., it contains at most M items. Thus,

Alice can send Bob a single message consisting of M put operations, each of which adds a single item. Such a message would count as a single I/O. Likewise, the response to a getRange(k_1, k_2, m) operation requires $O(\lceil m/M \rceil)$ I/Os; hence, Alice may wish to limit m to be $O(M)$. Certainly, Alice would want to limit m to be $O(M)$ in most cases, since she would otherwise be unable to locally store the entire result of such a query if it reaches its cut-off size.

As mentioned above, our use of parameter M is done for the sake of practicality, since it is unreasonable to assume that Alice and Bob can only communicate via constant-sized messages. Indeed, with network connections measured in gigabits per second but with latencies measured in milliseconds, the number of rounds of communication is likely to be the bottleneck, not bandwidth. Thus, because of this orders-of-magnitude difference between bandwidth and latency, we assume

$$M \geq N^{1/c},$$

for some fixed constant $c \geq 2$, but that Alice's memory is smaller than N. Equivalently, we assume that $c = \log_M N$ is a constant. For instance, as highlighted above, if Bob's memory is measured in exabytes and we take $c = 3$, then we are reasonably assuming that Alice and Bob can exchange messages whose sizes are measured in megabytes. To assume otherwise would be akin to trying to manage a large reservoir with a pipe the size of a drinking straw.

We additionally assume that Alice has a private memory of size bM, in which she can perform computations that are hidden from the server, Bob. To motivate the need for Alice outsourcing her data, while also allowing her to communicate effectively with Bob, we assume that $b \geq 2$ and $2M < N$.

2.2 Basic Techniques

Our solution employs several standard techniques previously introduced in the oblivious RAM and oblivious storage literature. To prevent Bob from learning the original keys and values and to make it hard for Bob to associate subsequent access to the same item, Alice replaces the original key, k, of an item with a new key $k' = h(r||k)$, where h is a cryptographic hash function (i.e., one-way and collision-resistant) and r is a secret randomly-generated nonce that is periodically changed by Alice so that a subsequent access to the same item uses a different key. Note that Bob learns the modified keys of the items. However, he cannot derive from them the original keys due to the one-way property of the cryptographic hash function used. Also, the uniqueness of the new keys occurs with overwhelming probability due to collision resistance.

Likewise, before storing an item's value, v, with Bob, Alice encrypts v using a probabilistic encryption scheme. E.g., the ciphertext is computed as $E(r||v)$, where E is a deterministic encryption algorithm and r is a random nonce that gets discarded after decryption. Thus, a different ciphertext for v is generated each time the item is stored with Bob. As a consequence, Bob cannot determine whether v was modified and cannot track an item by its value. The above obfuscation capabilities are intended to make it difficult for Bob to correlate the items stored in his memory at different times and locations, as well as make it difficult for Bob to determine the contents of any value.

We distinguish two types of OS solutions. We say that an oblivious storage solution is *miss-intolerant* if it does not allow for get requests that return null. Thus, Alice must know in advance that Bob holds an item with the given key. In applications that by design avoid requests for missing items, this restriction allows us to design an efficient oblivious-storage solution, since we don't have to worry about any information leakage that comes from queries for missing keys. Alternatively, if an oblivious storage solution is oblivious even when accesses can be made to keys that are not in the set, then we say that the solution is *miss-tolerant*.

2.3 Security Properties

Our OS solution is designed to satisfy the following security properties, where the adversary refers to Bob (the server) or a third party that eavesdrops the communication between Alice (the client) and Bob. The adversary is assumed to have polynomially bounded computational power.

Confidentiality. Except with negligible probability, the adversary should be unable to determine the contents (key or value) of any item stored at the server. This property is assured by the techniques described in the previous subsection.

Hardness of Correlation. Except with negligible or very low probability beyond $1/2$, the adversary should be unable to distinguish between any two possible access sequences of equal length and maximum set size. That is, consider two possible access sequences, σ_1 and σ_2, that consist of L operations, get, put, and remove, that could be made by Alice, on a set of size up to N, where L is polynomial in N. Then an oblivious storage (OS) solution has *correlation hardness* if it applies an obfuscating transformation so that, after seeing the sequence of I/Os performed by such a transformation, the probability that Bob can correctly guess whether Alice has performed (the transformed version of) σ_1 or σ_2 is more than $1/2$ by at most $1/N^\alpha$ or a negligible amount, where $\alpha \leq 1$ is a constant[1] that represents a trade-off between efficiency and degree of obfuscation.

Note that N is used above in both the upper bound on the size of Alice's set and also in the probability of Bob correctly distinguishing between two of her possible access sequences.

3. THE BUFFER SHUFFLE METHOD

One of the key techniques in our solutions is the use of oblivious shuffling. The input to any *shuffle* operation is a set, A, of N items. Because of the inclusion of the getRange operation in the server's API, we can view the items in A as being ordered by their keys. Moreover, this functionality also allows us to access a contiguous run of M such items, starting from a given key. The output of a shuffle is a reordering of the items in A with replacement keys, so that all permutations are equally likely. During a shuffle, the server, Bob, can observe Alice read (and remove) M of the items he is storing for her, and then write back M more items, which provides some degree of obfuscation of how the items in these read and write groups are correlated. An additional desire for the output of a shuffle is that, for any item x in the input, the adversary should be able to correlate x with any item y in the output only with probability that

---
[1] We assume $L << N^\alpha$ in this case.

is very close to $1/N$ (which is what he would get from a random guess).

During such a shuffle, we assume that Alice is wrapping each of her key-value pairs, (k, v), as $(k', (k, v))$, where k' is the new key that is chosen to obfuscate k. Indeed, it is likely that in each round of communication that Alice makes she will take a wrapped (input) pair, (k', X), and map it to a new (output) pair, (k'', X'), where the X' is assumed to be a re-encryption of X. The challenge is to define an encoding strategy for the k' and k'' wrapper keys so that it is difficult for the adversary to correlate inputs and outputs.

3.1 Theoretical Choice: Oblivious Sorting

One way to do this is to assign each item a random key from a very large universe, which is separate and distinct from the key that is a part of this key-value pair, and obliviously sort [9] the items by these keys. That is, we can wrap each key-value pair, (k, v), as $(k', (k, v))$, where k' is the new random key, and then wrap these wrapped pairs in a way that allows us to implement an oblivious sorting algorithm in the OS model based on comparisons involving the k' keys. Specifically, during this sorting process, we would further wrap each wrapped item, $(k', (k, v))$, as $(\alpha, (k', (k, v)))$, where α is an address or index used in the oblivious sorting algorithm. So as to distinguish such keys even further, Alice can also add a prefix to each such α, such as "Addr:" or "Addr$i$:", where i is a counter (which could, for instance, be counting the steps in Alice's sorting algorithm). Using such addresses as "keys" allows Alice to consider Bob's storage as if it were an array or the memory of a RAM. She can then use this scheme to simulate an oblivious sorting algorithm.

If the randomly assigned keys are distinct, which will occur with very high probability, then this achieves the desired goal. And even if the new keys are not distinct, we can repeat this operation until we get a set of distinct new keys without revealing any data-dependent information to the server.

From a theoretical perspective, it is hard to beat this solution. It is well-known, for instance, that shuffling by sorting items via randomly-assigned keys generates a random permutation such that all permutations are equally likely (e.g., see [13]). In addition, since the means to go from the input to the output is data-oblivious with respect to the I/Os (simulated using the address keys), the server who is watching the inputs and outputs cannot correlate any set of values. That is, independent of the set of I/Os, any input item, x, at the beginning of the sort can be mapped to any output item, y, at the end. Thus, for any item x in the input, the adversary can correlate x with any item y in the output with probability exactly $1/N$. Finally, we can use the external-memory deterministic oblivious-sorting algorithm of Goodrich and Mitzenmacher [9], for instance, so as to use messages of size $O(M^{1/2})$, which will result in an algorithm that sorts in $O((N/M) \log_{\sqrt{M}}(N/M)) = O((N/M)c^2)$ I/Os. That is, such a sorting algorithm uses a constant amortized number of I/Os per item.

Although oblivious sorting algorithm offers hardness of correlation of $1/N$ between the location of an item in the input and its new location in the output sequence, it requires a fairly costly overhead, as the constant factors and details of this algorithm are somewhat nontrivial. Thus, it would be nice in applications that don't necessarily require perfectly

oblivious shuffling to have a simple substitute that could be fast and effective in practice.

3.2 The Buffer Shuffle Algorithm

So, ideally, we would like a different oblivious shuffle algorithm, whose goal is still to obliviously permute the collection, A, of N values, but with a simpler algorithm. The *buffer-shuffle* algorithm is such an alternative:

1. Perform a scan of A, M numbers at a time. With each step, we read in M wrapped items from A, each of the form $(k', (k, v))$, and randomly permute them in Alice's local memory.

2. We then generate a new random key, k'', for each such wrapped item, $(k', (k, v))$, in this group, and we output all those new key-value pairs back to the server.

3. We then repeat this operation with the next M numbers, and so on, until Alice has made a pass through all the numbers in A.

Call this a single *pass*. After such a pass, we can view the new keys as being sorted at the server (as observed above, by the properties of the OS model). Thus, we can perform another pass over these new key-value pairs, generating an even newer set of wrapped key-value pairs. (This functionality is supported by range queries, for example, so there is little overhead for the client in implementing each such pass.) Finally, we repeat this process for some constant, b, times, which is established in our analysis below. This is the buffer-shuffle algorithm.

3.3 Buffer-Shuffle Analysis

To analyze the buffer-shuffle algorithm, we first focus on the following goal: we show that with probability $1 - o(1)$ after four passes, one cannot guess the location of an initial key-value pair with probability greater than $1/N + o(1/N)$, assuming $M = N^{1/3}$, where N is the number of items being permuted. After we prove this, we discuss how the proof extends to obtain improved probabilities of success and tighter bounds on the probability of tracking so that they are closer to $1/N$, as well as how to extend to cases where $M = N^{1/k}$ for integers $k \geq 3$.

We think of the keys at the beginning of each pass as being in key-sorted order, in $N^{2/3}$ groups of size $N^{1/3}$. Let $P_{i,j}$ be the perceived probability that after i passes the key we are tracking is in group j, according to the view of the tracker, Bob. Note that Bob can see, for each group on each pass, the set of keys that correspond to that group at the beginning and end of the pass, and use that to compute values $P_{i,j}$ corresponding to their perceived probabilities. Without loss of generality, we consider tracking the first key, so $P_{0,1} = 1$.

Our goal will be to show that $P_{i,j} = N^{-2/3} + o(N^{-2/3})$, for $i = 3$ and for all j, conditioned on some events regarding the random assignment of keys at each pass. The events we condition on will hold with probability $1 - o(1)$. This yields that the key being tracked appears to a tracker to be (up to lower order terms) in a group chosen uniformly at random. As the key values in each group are randomized at the next pass, this will leave the tracker with a probability only $1/N + o(1/N)$ of guessing the item, again assuming the bad $o(1)$ events do not occur.

Let $X_{i,k,j}$ be the number of keys that go from group k to group j in pass i. One can quickly check that $X_{i,k,j}$ is 0 with probability near 1. Indeed, the probability that $X_{i,k,j} = c$ is bounded above by

$$\binom{N^{1/3}}{c} \left(N^{-2/3}\right)^c = O\left(N^{-c/3}\right).$$

We have the recurrence

$$P_{i,j} = \sum_k P_{i-1,k} \frac{X_{i,k,j}}{N^{1/3}}.$$

The explanation for this recurrence is straightforward. The probability that the key being tracked is in the jth group after pass i is the sum over all groups k of the probability that the key was in group k, given by $P_{i-1,k}$, times the probability that the corresponding new key was mapped to group j, which is $X_{i,k,j}/N^{1/3}$.

Our goal now is to show that over successive passes that as long as the values $X_{i,k,j}$ behave nicely, the $P_{i,j}$ will quickly converge to roughly $N^{-2/3}$. We sketch an argument for probability $1 - o(1)$ and then comment on how the $o(1)$ term can be reduced to any inverse polynomial probability in a constant number of passes. Our main approach is to note that bounding the $X_{i,k,j}$ corresponds to a type of balls and bins problem, in which case negative dependence can be applied to get a suitable concentration result via a basic Chernoff bound.

THEOREM 1. *When $M = N^{1/3}$, after four passes, Bob cannot guess the location of an initial item with probability greater than $1/N + o(1/N)$.*

PROOF SKETCH: We consider the four passes in succession.

- Pass 1: It is easy to check that with probability $1-o(1)$ (using union bounds and the binomial distribution to bound the number of keys from group 1 that land in every other group) there are up to $c \log N$ groups for which $X_{1,1,j} = 2$ and 0 groups for which $X_{1,1,j} = 3$. Thus, there are $N^{1/3} - O(\log N)$ groups for which $P_{1,j} = N^{-1/3}$ and $O(\log N)$ groups for which $P_{1,j} = 2N^{-1/3}$.

- Pass 2: Our interpretation here (and going forward) is that each key in group j after pass $i-1$ has a "weight" $P_{i-1,j}/N^{1/3}$ that it gives to the group it lands in in pass i; the sum of weights in a group then yields $P_{i,j}$.

  With this interpretation, with probability $1 - o(1)$, there are $N^{2/3} - o(N^{2/3})$ keys at the end of pass 1 with positive weight (of either $N^{-2/3}$ or $2N^{-2/3}$). These keys are rerandomized, so at the end of pass 2, the number of keys with positive weight in a given bucket j is expected to be constant, and again simple binomial and union bounds imply that the maximum number of keys with positive weight in any bucket is at most $c \log N$ with probability $1 - o(1)$. Indeed, one can further show at the end of pass 2 that the number of groups j with $P_{2,j} > 0$ must be at least $\Omega(N^{2/3})$ with probability $1 - o(1)$; this follows from the fact that, for example, if Y_j is the $0/1$ random variable that represents whether a group j received at least one weighted key, then $E[Y_j] > 1/2$, and the Y_j are negatively associated, so Chernoff bounds apply. (See, for example, Chapter 3 of [7].)

- Pass 3: Conditioned on the $1 - o(1)$ events from the first two passes, at the end of the second pass there are $\Omega(N)$ keys with positive weight going into pass 3, and the possible weight values for each key are bounded by $(c' \log N)/N$ for some constant c'. The expected weight for each group after pass 3 is obviously $N^{-2/3}$. The weights of the keys within a group are negatively associated, so we can apply a Chernoff bound to the weight associated with each group, noting that to apply the Chernoff bound we should re-scale so the range of the weights is $[0, 1]$. Consider the first group, and let Z_i be the weight of the ith keys in the first group (scaled by multiplying the weight by $N/(c' \log N)$). Let $Z = \sum_{i=1}^{N^{2/3}} Z_i$. Then

  $$\Pr\left(\left|Z - \frac{N^{1/3}}{c' \log N}\right| \geq N^{1/5}\right) \leq e^{-2N^{1/15}}.$$

  Or, rescaling back, the weight in the first group is within $N^{-4/5}/(c' \log N)$ of $N^{-2/3}$ with high probability, and a union bound suffices to show that this is the same for all groups.

- Pass 4: After pass 3, with probability $1-o(1)$ each key has weight $1/N + o(1/N)$, and so after randomizing, assuming the events of probability $1 - o(1)$ all hold, the probability that any key is the original one being tracked from Bob's point of view is $1/N + o(1/N)$. □

We remark that the $o(1)$ failure probability can be reduced to any inverse polynomial by a combination of choosing constant c and c' to be sufficiently high, and/or repeating passes a (constant) number of times to reduce the probability of the bad events. (For example, if Pass 1, fails with probability p, repeating it a times reduces the failure probability to p^a; the $o(1)$ failure probabilities are all inverse polynomial in N in the proof above.)

Similarly, one can ensure that the probability that any key is the tracked key to $1/N + o(1/N^a)$ for any constant a by increasing the number of passes further, but still keeping the number of passes constant. Specifically, note that we have shown that after the first four passes, with high probability the weight of each key bounded between $N^{-1} - N^{-j}$ and $N^{-1} + N^{-j}$ for some $j > 1$, and the total key weight is 1. We re-center the weights around $N^{-1} - N^{-j}$ and multiply them by N^{j-1}; now the new reweighted weights sum to 1. We can now re-apply above the argument; after four passes we know that reweighted weights for each key will again be $N^{-1} - N^{-j}$ and $N^{-1} + N^{-j}$. Undoing the rescaling, this means the weights for the keys are now bounded $N^{-1} - N^{-j}$ and $N^{-1} + N^{1-2j}$, and we can continue in this fashion to obtain the desired closeness to $1/N$.

Finally, we note that the assumption that we can read in $N^{1/3}$ key-value pairs and assign them new random key values can be reduced to $N^{1/j}$ pairs for any $j \geq 3$. We sketch the proof. Each step, as in the original proof, holds with probability $1 - o(1)$.

In this case we have $N^{(j-1)/j}$ groups. In the first pass, the weight from the shuffling is spread to $\Omega(N^{2/j})$ key-value pairs, following the same reasoning as for Pass 1 above. Indeed, we can continue this argument; in the next pass, where the weight will spread to $\Omega(N^{3/j})$ key-value pairs, and so on, until after $j - 2$ passes there are $\Omega(N^{(j-1)/j})$

keys with non-zero weight with high probability, with one small modification in the analysis: at each pass, we can ensure that each group has less than j weighted keys with high probability.

Then, following the same argument as in Pass 2 above, one can show that after the following pass $\Omega(N)$ keys have non-zero weight, and the maximum weight is bounded above by $(c' \log N)/N$ for some constant c'. Applying the Chernoff bound argument for Pass 3 above to the next pass we find that the weight within each of the $N^{(j-1)/j}$ groups is equal to $1/N + o(1/N)$ after this pass, and again this suffices by the recurrence to show that at most one more pass is necessary for each key-value pair to have weight $1/N + o(1/N)$.

4. A SQUARE ROOT SOLUTION

As is a common practice in ORAM simulation papers, starting with the work of Goldreich and Ostrovsky [8], before we give our more sophisticated solutions to the oblivious storage problem, we first give a simple *square-root* solution. Our general solution is an inductive extension of this solution, so the square-root solution also serves to form a basis for this induction.

In this square-root solution, we assume $M \geq N^{1/2}$. Thus, Alice has a local memory of size at least $N^{1/2}$, and she and Bob can exchange a message of size up to at least $N^{1/2}$ in a single I/O. In addition, we assume that this solution provides an API for performing oblivious dictionary operations where every $\mathsf{get}(k)$ or $\mathsf{put}(k,v)$ operation is guaranteed to be for a key k that is contained in the set, S, that Alice is outsourcing to Bob. That is, we give a miss-intolerant solution to the oblivious storage problem.

Our solution is based on the observation that we can view Alice's memory as a miss-tolerant solution to the OS problem. That is, Alice can store $O(M)$ items in her private memory in some dictionary data structure, and each time she queries her memory for a key k she can determine if k is present without leaking any data-dependent information to Bob.

4.1 Construction

Let us assume we have a miss-tolerant dictionary, $D(N)$, that provides a solution to the OS problem that works for sets up to size N, with at most $O(1)$ amortized number of I/Os of size at most N per access. Certainly, a dictionary stored in Alice's internal memory suffices for this purpose (and it, in fact, doesn't even need any I/Os per access), for the case when N is at most M, the size of Alice's memory.

The memory organization of our solution, $B(N)$, we describe here, consists of two caches:

- A cache, C_0, which is of size M and is implemented using an instance of a $D(M)$ solution.

- A cache, C_1, which is of size $N + M$, which is stored as a dictionary of key-value pairs using Bob's storage.

The extra M space in C_1 is for storing M "dummy" items, which have keys indexed from a range that is outside of the universe used for S, which we denote as $-1, -2, \ldots, -M$. Let S' denote the set of N items from S, plus items with these dummy keys (along with null values), minus any items in C_0. Initially, C_0 is empty and C_1 stores the entire set S plus the M items with dummy keys. For the sake of obliviousness, each item, (k,v), in the set S' is mapped to a

substitute key by a nonce pseudo-random hash function, h_r, where r is a random number chosen at the time Alice asks Bob to build (or rebuild) his dictionary. In addition, each value v is encrypted as $E_K(v)$, with a secret key, K, known only to Alice. Thus, each item (k,v) in S' is stored by Bob as the key-value pair $(h_r(k), E_K(v))$.

To perform an access, either for a $\mathsf{get}(k)$ or $\mathsf{put}(k,v)$, Alice first performs a lookup for k in C_0, using its technology for achieving obliviousness. If she does not find an item with key k (as she won't initially), then she requests the item from Bob by issuing a request, $\mathsf{get}(h_r(k))$, to him. Note that, since k is a key in S, and it is not in Alice's cache, $h_r(k)$ is a key in S', by the fact that we are constructing a miss-intolerant OS solution. Thus, there will be an item returned from this request. From this returned item, $(h_r(k), E_K(v))$, Alice decrypts the value, v, and stores item (k,v) in C_0, possibly changing v for a put operation. Then she asks Bob to remove the item with key $h_r(k)$ from S'.

If, on the other hand, in performing an access for a key k, Alice finds a matching item for k in C_0, then she uses that item and she issues a dummy request to Bob by asking him to perform a $\mathsf{get}(h_r(-j))$ operation, where j is a counter she keeps in her local memory for the next dummy key. In this case, she inserts this dummy item into C_0 and she asks Bob to remove the item with key $h_r(-j)$ from S'. Therefore, from Bob's perspective, Alice is always requesting a random key for an item in S' and then immediately removing that item. Indeed, her behavior is always that of doing a get from C_0, a get from C_1, a remove from C_1, and then a put in C_0.

After Alice has performed M accesses, C_0 will be holding M items, which is its capacity. So she pauses her performance of accesses at this time and enters a *rebuilding* phase. In this phase, she rebuilds a new version of the dictionary that is being maintained by Bob.

The new set to be maintained by Bob is the current S' unioned with the items in C_0 (including the dummy items). So Alice resets her counter, j, back to 1. She then performs an oblivious shuffle of the set $S'' = C_0 \cup S'$. This oblivious shuffle is performed either with an external-memory sorting algorithm [9] or with the buffer-shuffle method described above, depending, respectively, on whether Alice desires perfect obscurity or if she can tolerate a small amount of information leakage, as quantified above. Finally, after this random shuffle completes, Alice chooses a new random nonce, r, for her pseudo-random function, h_r. She then makes one more pass over the set of items (which are masked and encrypted) now stored by Bob (using $\mathsf{getRange}$ operations as in the buffer-shuffle method), and she maps each item (k,v) to the pair $(h_r(k), E_K(v))$ and asks Bob to store this item in his memory. This begins a new "epoch" for Alice to then use for the next M accesses that she needs to make.

4.2 Analysis

Let us consider an amortized analysis of this solution. For the sake of amortization, we charge each of the previous M accesses for the effort in performing a rebuild. Since such a rebuild takes $O(N/M)$ I/Os, provided $M \geq N^{1/c}$, for some constant $c \geq 2$, this means we will charge $O(N/M^2)$ I/Os to each of these previous accesses. Thus, we have the following.

LEMMA 2. *Suppose we are given a miss-tolerant OS solution, $D(N)$, which achieves $O(1)$ amortized I/Os per access for messages of up to size M, when applied to a set of size N/M. Then we can use this as a component, $D(N/M)$,* of a miss-intolerant OS solution, $B(N)$, that achieves $O(1)$ amortized I/Os per access for messages of size up to $M \geq N^{1/c}$, for some constant $c \geq 2$. The private memory required for this solution is $O(M)$.

PROOF SKETCH: The number of amortized I/Os will be $O(1)$ per access, from $D(N)$. The total number of I/Os needed to do a rebuild is $O(N/M)$, assuming M is at least $N^{1/c}$, for some constant $c \geq 2$. There will be N/M items that are moved in this case, which is equal to the number of previous accesses; hence, the amortized number of I/Os will be $O(1)$ per access. The performance bounds follow immediately from the above discussion and the simple charging scheme we used for the sake of an amortized analysis. For the proof of security, note that each access that Alice makes to the dictionary S' will either be for a real item or a dummy element. Either way, Alice will make exactly N/M requests before she rebuilds this dictionary stored with Bob. Moreover, from the adversary's perspective, every request is to an independent uniform random key, which is then immediately removed and never accessed again. Therefore, the adversary cannot distinguish between actual requests and dummy requests. In addition, he cannot correlate any request from a previous epoch, since Alice randomly shuffles the set of items and uses a new pseudo-random function with each epoch. □

By then choosing the messages size, M, appropriately, we obtain the following result.

THEOREM 3. *The square-root solution achieves $O(1)$ amortized I/Os for each data access, allowing a client, Alice, to obliviously store N items in a miss-intolerant way with an honest-but-curious server, Bob, using messages of size $M = N^{1/2}$ and local memory of size $2M$. The probability that this simulation fails to be oblivious is exponentially small for a polynomial-length access sequence, if oblivious sorting is used for shuffling, and polynomially small if buffer-shuffling is used.*

PROOF SKETCH: Plugging $M = N^{1/2}$ into Lemma 2 gives us the complexity bound. The obliviousness follows from the fact that if she has an internal memory of size $M = N^{1/2}$, then Alice can easily implement a miss-tolerant OS solution in her internal memory, which achieves the conditions of the $D(M)$ solution needed for the cache C_0. □

Note that the constant factor in the amortized I/O overhead in the square-root solution is quite small.

Note, in addition, that by the obliviousness definition in the OS model, it does not matter how many accesses Alice makes to the solution, $B(N)$, provided that her number of accesses are not self-revealing of her data items themselves.[2]

5. MISS-TOLERANCE

An important functionality that is lacking from the square-root solution is that it does not allow for accesses to items that are not in the set S. That is, it is a miss-intolerant OS solution. Nevertheless, we can leverage the square-root solution to allow for such accesses in an oblivious way, by using a hashing scheme.

---

[2]An access sequence would be self-revealing, for example, if Alice reads a value and then performs a number of accesses equal to this value.

5.1 Review of Cuckoo Hashing

The main idea behind this extension is to use a miss-intolerant solution to obliviously implement a *cuckoo hashing* scheme [16]. In cuckoo hashing, we have two hash tables T_1 and T_2 and two associated pseudo-random hash functions, f_1 and f_2. An item (k, v) is stored at $T_1[f_1(k)]$ or $T_2[f_2(k)]$. When inserting item (k, v), we add it to $T_1[f_1(k)]$. If that cell is occupied by another item, $(\hat{k}, \hat{v})$, we evict that item and place it in $T_2[f_2(\hat{k})]$. Again, we may need to evict an item. This sequence of evictions continues until we put an item into a previously-empty cell or we detect an infinite loop (in which case we rehash all the items). Cuckoo hashing achieves $O(1)$ expected time for all operations with high probability. This probability can be boosted even higher to $1 - 1/n^s$ by using a small cache, known as a *stash* [12], of size s to hold items that would have otherwise caused infinite insertion loops. With some additional effort (e.g., see [3]), cuckoo hashing can be de-amortized to achieve $O(1)$ memory accesses, with very high probability, for insert, remove, and lookup operations.

In most real-world OS solutions, standard cuckoo hashing should suffice for our purposes. But, to avoid inadvertent data leakage and ensure high-probability performance bounds, let us assume we will be using de-amortized cuckoo hashing.

5.2 Implementing Cuckoo Hashing with a Miss-Intolerant OS Solution

Let us assume we have a miss-intolerant solution, $B(N)$, to the OS problem, which achieves a constant I/O complexity for accesses, using messages of size M.

A standard or de-amortized cuckoo hashing scheme provides an interface for performing $\mathsf{get}(k)$ and $\mathsf{put}(k, v)$ operations, so that get operations are miss-tolerant. These operations are implemented using pseudo-random hash functions in the random access memory (RAM) model, i.e., using a collection of memory cells, where each such cell is uniquely identified with an index i. To implement such a scheme using solution $B(N)$, we simulate a read of cell i with $\mathsf{get}(i)$ operation and we simulate a write of x to cell i with $\mathsf{put}(i, x)$. Thus, each access using $B(N)$ is guaranteed to return an item, namely a cell (i, x) in the memory (tables and variables) used to implement the cuckoo-hashing scheme. Thus, whenever we access a cell with index i, we actually perform a request for (an encryption of) this cell's contents using the obliviousness mechanism provided by $B(N)$.

That is, to implement a standard or de-amortized cuckoo hashing scheme using $B(N)$, we assume now that every (non-dummy) key in Alice's simulation is an index in the memory used to implement the hashing scheme. Thus, each access is guaranteed to return an item. Moreover, because inserts, removals, and lookups achieve a constant number of memory accesses, with very high probability, in a de-amortized cuckoo-hashing scheme (or with constant expected-time performance in a standard cuckoo hashing scheme), then each operation in a simulation of de-amortized cuckoo hashing in $B(N)$ involves a constant number of accesses with very high probability. Therefore, using a de-amortized cuckoo-hashing scheme, we have the following result.

THEOREM 4. *Given a miss-intolerant OS solution, $B(N)$, that achieves $O(1)$ amortized I/O performance with messages of size M and achieves confidentiality and hardness*

Figure 1: Memory layout for $c = 2$. The locations accessed by the user are visualized as gray-filled rectangles.

of correlation, we can implement a miss-tolerant solution, $D(N)$, that achieves $O(1)$ amortized I/O performance and also achieves confidentiality and hardness of correlation.

PROOF SKETCH: The result follows from using a cuckoo hashing interface to hide accesses to $B(N)$ for items that are not there. The hardness of correlation of the resulting OS solution, $D(N)$, depends on the shuffle algorithm used during the rebuild phase of $B(N)$. □

A standard cuckoo-hashing scheme yields instead the following result.

THEOREM 5. *Given a miss-intolerant OS solution, $B(N)$, that achieves expected $O(1)$ amortized I/O performance, with messages of size M, we can implement a miss-tolerant solution, $D(N)$, that achieves $O(1)$ expected amortized I/O performance and also achieves confidentiality and hardness of correlation.*

Our use of cuckoo hashing in the above construction is quite different, by the way, than previous uses of cuckoo-hashing for oblivious RAM simulation [9, 11, 14]. In these other papers, the server, Bob, gets to see the actual indexes and memory addresses used in the cuckoo hashing scheme. Thus, the adversary in these other schemes can see where items are placed in cuckoo tables (unless their construction is itself oblivious) and when and where they are removed; hence, special care must be taken to construct and use the cuckoo tables in an oblivious way. In our scheme, the locations in the cuckoo-hashing scheme are instead obfuscated because they are themselves built on top of an OS solution.

Also, in previous schemes, cuckoo tables were chosen for the reason that, once items are inserted, their locations are determined by pseudo-random functions. Here, cuckoo tables are used only for the fact that they have constant-time insert, remove, and lookup operations, which holds with very high probability for de-amortized cuckoo tables and as an expected-time bound for standard cuckoo tables.

6. AN INDUCTIVE SOLUTION

The miss-tolerant square-root method given in Section 5 provides a solution of the oblivious storage problem with amortized constant I/O performance for each access, but requires Alice to have a local memory of size $2N^{1/2}$ and messages to be of size $N^{1/2}$ during the rebuilding phase (although constant-size messages are exchanged during the access phase). In this section, we show how to recursively apply this method to create a more efficient solution.

For an integer $c \geq 2$, let $D_c(N)$ denote a miss-intolerant oblivious storage solution that has the following properties:

1. It supports a dictionary of N items.

2. It requires local memory of size $cN^{1/c}$ at the client.

3. It uses messages of size $N^{1/c}$.

4. It executes $O(1)$ amortized I/Os per operation (each get or put), where the constant factor in this bound depends on the constant c.

5. It achieves confidentiality and hardness of correlation.

Note that using this notation, the square-root method derived in Section 5 using cuckoo hashing is a $D_2(N)$ oblivious storage solution.

6.1 The Inductive Construction

For our inductive construction, for $c \geq 3$, we assume the existence of a oblivious storage solution $D_{c-1}(N')$. We can use this to build a miss-tolerant oblivious storage solution, $D_c(N)$, using message size $M = N^{1/c}$ as follows:

1. Use the construction of Lemma 2 to build a miss-intolerant OS solution, $B_c(N)$, from $D_{c-1}(N/M)$. This solution has $O(1)$ amortized I/Os per access, with very high probability, using messages of size M and private memory of size $O(M)$ since $D_{c-1}(N/M)$ uses memory of size

$$\left(\frac{N}{M}\right)^{\frac{1}{c-1}} = N^{\frac{1-\frac{1}{c}}{c-1}} = N^{\frac{1}{c}} = M.$$

2. Use the construction of Theorem 4 to take the miss-intolerant solution, $B_c(N)$, and convert it to a miss-tolerant solution. This solution uses an $O(1)$ amortized number of I/Os, with high probability, using messages of size $M = N^{1/c}$, and it has the performance bounds necessary to be denoted as $D_c(N)$.

An intuition of our construction is as follows. We number each level of the construction such that c is the top most and 2 is the lowest level, hence there are $c - 1$ levels. The top level, c, consists of the main memory A_c of size $O(N)$ and uses the rest of the construction as a cache for $O(N/M)$ items which we referred to as $B_c(N)$. This cache is the

Figure 2: Memory layout for $c = 3$. Oblivious solution B_2 and the cache are both used to buffer the items that have been accessed from A_3. B_2 is rebuilt every time the cache is full while A_3 is rebuilt whenever B_2 becomes full.

beginning of our inductive construction and, hence, itself is an OS over $O(N/M)$ items. The inductive construction continues such that level i contains a miss-tolerant data structure A_i and levels $(i - 1), \ldots, 2$ are used as a cache of level i. The construction terminates when we reach level 2 since the size of the cache at level 2 is equal to the message size M which Alice can request using a single access or store in her own memory. We give an illustration of our construction for $c = 2$ and $c = 3$ in Figures 1 and 2, respectively.

THEOREM 6. *The above construction results in an oblivious storage solution, $D_c(N)$, that is miss-tolerant, supports a dictionary of N items, requires client-side local memory of size $cN^{1/c}$, uses messages of size $N^{1/c}$, achieves an amortized $O(1)$ number of I/Os for each get and put operation, where the constant factor in this bound depends on the constant $c \geq 2$. In addition, this method achieves confidentiality and hardness of correlation.*

PROOF SKETCH: The complexity of the solution follows from its inductive construction. A request for an item in $D_c(N)$ requires accesses to $c - 1$ levels where each level i is a miss-intolerant oblivious solution, $D_i(N/M^{c-i})$, with a cuckoo hashing interface. Hence, oblivious access to each level incurs $O(1)$ amortized I/Os and $O(c)$ I/Os in total for $D_c(N)$.

The confidentiality and hardness of correlation of $D_c(N)$ relies on the fact that accesses to each level are made through an oblivious solution which guarantees these properties. □

7. PERFORMANCE

We have built a system prototype of our oblivious storage method to estimate the practical performance of our solution and compare it with that of other OS solutions. In our simulation, we record the number of access operations to the storage server for every original data request by the client. Our prototype specifically simulates the use of Amazon S3 as the provider of remote storage, based on their current API. In particular, we make use of operations get,

put, copy and delete in the Amazon S3 API. Since Amazon S3 does not support range queries, we substitute operation getRange(i_1, i_2, m) of our OS model with m concurrent get requests, which could be issued by parallel threads running at the client to minimize latency. Operation removeRange is handled similarly with concurrent delete operations. We have run the simulation for two configurations of our OS solution, $c = 2$ and $c = 3$. For $c = 3$ we use standard cuckoo hashing for second level cache, B_2. We consider two item sizes, 1KB and 64KB. The size (number of items) of the messages exchanged by the client and server is $M = N^{1/c}$ where N, the number of items in the outsourced data set, varies from 10^4 to 10^6.

7.1 Storage Overhead

The overall storage space (no. of items) used by our solution on the server is $N + 2 \sum_{i=1}^{c-2} N^{(c-i)/c}$, i.e. $N + N^{1/2}$ for $c = 2$ and $N + 2N^{2/3}$ for $c = 3$. For $c = 2$, our method has storage overhead comparable to that of Boneh *et al.* [4] and much smaller than the space used by other approaches.

7.2 Access Overhead

In Table 2, we show the number of I/Os to the remote data repository during the oblivious simulation of N requests. Recall that the number of I/Os is the number of round trips the simulation makes. Thus, the getRange operation is counted as one I/O. In the table, column Minimum gives the number of I/Os performed by Alice to receive the requested item. The remaining I/Os are performed for reshuffling. For $c = 2$, this number is 2 since the client sends a get request to either get an actual item or a dummy item, followed by a delete request. For $c = 3$, this number is slightly higher since Alice needs to simulate accesses to a cuckoo table through an OS interface. We compare our I/O overhead and the total amount of data transferred with that of Boneh *et al.* [4]. They also achieve $O(1)$ request overhead and exchange messages of size $M = N^{1/2}$ with the server. Our new buffer shuffle algorithm makes our approach more efficient in terms of data transfer and the number of operations the user makes to the server.

7.3 Time Overhead

Given the trace of user's operations during the simulation and empirical measurements of round trip times of operations on the Amazon S3 system (see Table 4), we estimate the access latency of our OS solutions in Tables 5 and 6 for 1KB items and 64KB items, respectively.

7.4 Cost Overhead

Finally, we provide estimates of the monetary cost of OS our solution in Table 5 using the pricing scheme of Amazon S3 (see Table 4 and http://aws.amazon.com/s3/pricing/ [3]). Since our results outperform other approaches in terms of number of accesses to the server we expect that our monetary cost will be also lower.

Acknowledgments

This research was supported in part by the National Science Foundation under grants 0721491, 0915922, 0953071, 0964473, 1011840, and 1012060, by NetApp, Inc., and by the Center for Geometric Computing and the Kanellakis Fellowship at Brown University.

References

[1] M. Ajtai. Oblivious RAMs without cryptographic assumptions. In *Proc. ACM Symp. on Theory of Computing (STOC)*, pages 181–190. ACM, 2010.

[2] Amazon. Amazon S3 Service. http://aws.amazon.com/s3-sla/.

[3] Y. Arbitman, M. Naor, and G. Segev. De-amortized cuckoo hashing: Provable worst-case performance and experimental results. In *Proc. Int. Conf. Automata, Languages and Programming (ICALP)*, pages 107–118. Springer, 2009.

[4] D. Boneh, D. Mazières, and R. A. Popa. Remote oblivious storage: Making oblivious RAM practical. Technical report, CSAIL, MIT, 2011. http://dspace.mit.edu/handle/1721.1/62006.

[5] S. Chen, R. Wang, X. Wang, and K. Zhang. Side-channel leaks in Web applications: a reality today, a challenge tomorrow. In *Proc. IEEE Symp. on Security and Privacy*, pages 191–206, 2010.

[6] I. Damgård, S. Meldgaard, and J. B. Nielsen. Perfectly secure oblivious RAM without random oracles. In *Proc. Theory of Cryptography Conference (TCC)*, pages 144–163, 2011.

[7] D. Dubhashi and A. Panconesi. *Concentration of Measure for the Analysis of Randomized Algorithms*. Cambridge University Press, New York, NY, USA, 2009.

[8] O. Goldreich and R. Ostrovsky. Software protection and simulation on oblivious RAMs. *J. ACM*, 43(3):431–473, 1996.

[9] M. T. Goodrich and M. Mitzenmacher. Privacy-preserving access of outsourced data via oblivious RAM simulation. In *Proc. Int. Colloq. on Automata, Languages and Programming (ICALP)*, pages 576–587, 2011.

[10] M. T. Goodrich, M. Mitzenmacher, O. Ohrimenko, and R. Tamassia. Oblivious RAM simulation with efficient worst-case access overhead. In *Proc. ACM Workshop on Cloud Computing Security (CCSW)*, pages 95–100, 2011.

[11] M. T. Goodrich, M. Mitzenmacher, O. Ohrimenko, and R. Tamassia. Privacy-preserving group data access via stateless oblivious RAM simulation. In *Proc. ACM-SIAM Symp. on Discrete Algorithms (SODA)*, 2012. To appear. Preliminary version in http://arxiv.org/abs/1105.4125.

[12] A. Kirsch, M. Mitzenmacher, and U. Wieder. More robust hashing: cuckoo hashing with a stash. *SIAM J. Comput.*, 39:1543–1561, 2009.

[13] D. E. Knuth. *Seminumerical Algorithms*, volume 2 of *The Art of Computer Programming*. Addison-Wesley, Reading, MA, 3rd edition, 1998.

[14] E. Kushilevitz, S. Lu, and R. Ostrovsky. On the (in)security of hash-based oblivious RAM and a new balancing scheme. In *Proc. ACM-SIAM Symp. on Discrete Algorithms (SODA)*, 2012. To appear. Preliminary version in http://eprint.iacr.org/2011/327.

[15] Microsoft Corp. Windows Azure. http://www.microsoft.com/windowsazure.

[16] R. Pagh and F. Rodler. Cuckoo hashing. *Journal of Algorithms*, 52:122–144, 2004.

[17] B. Pinkas and T. Reinman. Oblivious RAM revisited. In T. Rabin, editor, *Advances in Cryptology (CRYPTO)*, volume 6223 of *LNCS*, pages 502–519. Springer, 2010.

[18] N. Pippenger and M. J. Fischer. Relations among complexity measures. *J. ACM*, 26(2):361–381, 1979.

[19] E. Shi, T.-H. H. Chan, E. Stefanov, and M. Li. Oblivious RAM with $O((\log N)^3)$ worst-case cost. In *Proc. ASIACRYPT*, pages 197–214, 2011.

[20] E. Stefanov, E. Shi, and D. Song. Towards Practical Oblivious RAM. In *Proc. Network and Distributed System Security Symposium (NDSS)*, 2012. To appear. Preliminary version in http://arxiv.org/abs/1106.3652.

[21] J. S. Vitter. External sorting and permuting. In M.-Y. Kao, editor, *Encyclopedia of Algorithms*. Springer, 2008.

[22] P. Williams and R. Sion. Usable PIR. In *Proc. Network and Distributed System Security Symposium (NDSS)*, 2008.

[23] P. Williams, R. Sion, and B. Carbunar. Building castles out of mud: practical access pattern privacy and correctness on untrusted storage. In *ACM Conference on Computer and Communications Security (CCS)*, pages 139–148, 2008.

---

[3]Accessed on 9/21/2011

	Minimum/Amortized	
N	$M = N^{1/2}$	$M = N^{1/3}$
10,000	2/13	7/173
100,000	2/13	7/330
1,000,000	2/13	7/416

Table 2: Minimum and amortized number of I/Os to access one item in our OS solution for $c = 2$ and $c = 3$. We simulate a sequence of N accesses on a system that uses four passes of the buffer shuffle algorithm.

	I/O Overhead and Data Transferred (#items)			
N	Boneh *et al.* [4]		Our Method	
	Minimum	Amortized	Minimum	Amortized
10,000	3/9	$13/1.3 \times 10^3$	2/1	$13/1.1 \times 10^3$
100,000	3/10	$17/5.2 \times 10^3$	2/1	$13/3.5 \times 10^3$
1,000,000	3/12	$20/2 \times 10^4$	2/1	$13/1.1 \times 10^4$

Table 3: Minimum and amortized number of I/Os and number of items transferred to access one item. We compare our OS solution for $c = 2$ with that of [4] on a data set with 1KB items. In both solutions the message size is $M = N^{1/2}$ items.

Operation	Price	RTT (ms)	
		1KB	64KB
Get	$0.01/10,000req	36	56
Put	$0.01/1,000req	65	86
Copy	free	70	88
Delete	free	31	35

Table 4: Amazon S3's pricing scheme and empirical measurement of round trip time (RTT) for an operation issued by a client in Providence, Rhode Island to the Amazon S3 service (average of 300 runs).

	$M = N^{1/2}$			$M = N^{1/3}$		
N	Access Time		Total Cost	Access Time		Total Cost
	Minimum	Amortized		Minimum	Amortized	
10,000	67ms	500ms	$55	400ms	8s	$177
100,000	67ms	500ms	$1,744	400ms	12s	$7,262
1,000,000	67ms	500ms	$55,066	400ms	18s	$170,646

Table 5: Estimate of the access time per item and total monetary cost for accessing N items, each of size 1KB, stored on the Amazon S3 system using our OS method for $c = 2$ and $c = 3$.

	$M = N^{1/2}$			$M = N^{1/3}$		
N	Access Time		Total Cost	Access Time		Total Cost
	Minimum	Amortized		Minimum	Amortized	
10,000	91ms	800ms	$55	500ms	12s	$177
100,000	91ms	800ms	$1,744	500ms	18s	$7,262
1,000,000	91ms	800ms	$55,066	500ms	24s	$170,646

Table 6: Estimate of the access time per item and total monetary cost for accessing N items, each of size 64KB, stored on the Amazon S3 system using our OS method for $c = 2$ and $c = 3$.

SENTINEL: Securing Database from Logic Flaws in Web Applications

Xiaowei Li
Department of Electrical
Engineering and Computer
Science
Vanderbilt University
Nashville, TN USA 37203
xiaowei.li@vanderbilt.edu

Wei Yan
Department of Electrical
Engineering and Computer
Science
Vanderbilt University
Nashville, TN USA 37203
wei.yan@vanderbilt.edu

Yuan Xue
Department of Electrical
Engineering and Computer
Science
Vanderbilt University
Nashville, TN USA 37203
yuan.xue@vanderbilt.edu

ABSTRACT

Logic flaws within web applications allow the attackers to disclose or tamper sensitive information stored in back-end databases, since the web application usually acts as the single trusted user that interacts with the database. In this paper, we model the web application as an extended finite state machine and present a black-box approach for deriving the application specification and detecting malicious SQL queries that violate the specification. Several challenges arise, such as how to extract persistent state information in the database and infer data constraints. We systematically extract a set of invariants from observed SQL queries and responses, as well as session variables, as the application specification. Any suspicious SQL queries that violate corresponding invariants are identified as potential attacks. We implement a prototype detection system SENTINEL (SEcuriNg daTabase from logIc flaws iN wEb appLication) and evaluate it using a set of real-world web applications. The experiment results demonstrate the effectiveness of our approach and show that acceptable performance overhead is incurred by our implementation.

Categories and Subject Descriptors

K.6.5 [**Management of Computing and Information Systems**]: Security and Protection—*Unauthorized access*; H.2.7 [**Database Management**]: Database Administration—*Security, integrity, and protection*

General Terms

Design, Experimentation, Security

Keywords

Logic Flaw, Web Application Security, Extended Finite State Machine, SQL Signature, Invariant

1. INTRODUCTION

Database-backed web applications have become a prevalent venue for disseminating information and services. An enormous amount of information is made accessible on Internet through web applications, which interact with the back-end database on behalf of users. While providing great convenience to users, those web applications also attract a large number of security exploits. According to a recent survey [30], the attacks that successfully disclose or tamper sensitive information by compromising vulnerable web applications account for more than 30% of all the cyber attacks. For instance, on June 2010, it was reported that a vulnerability of AT&T website allowed an attacker to harvest the Apple iPAD subscribers' emails by enumerating ICC-ID numbers, which affected over 100,000 Apple customers [1].

In the Web scenario, the front-end web application acts as a single user that interacts with the database. Thus, the database fully trusts the web application, accepts and executes all the queries submitted by the application. As such, the vulnerabilities within web applications may introduce security concerns for the information stored in the database. One class of attacks exploit the application's input validation mechanisms to tamper the intended structure of SQL queries issued by the application, which is well known as SQL injection. Another class of attacks exploit logic flaws within the application, referred to as state violation attacks [10], tricking the application into sending SQL queries at incorrect application states. For example, an attacker may retrieve other users' account information without providing the administrator's credential to the application.

While a large body of literatures focus on fortifying the application's input validation mechanisms, only a few works have attempted to address logic flaws within the web applications. Logic flaws are specific to the functionalities of web applications, thus more difficult to handle. The key to this problem is to derive the application's intended logic (i.e., specification) in a general and automated way. One approach to inferring the application specification is by leveraging program source code. Swaddler [10] establishes statistical models of the application state for each program block using session variables, while Waler [14] characterizes the application logic by associating value-based invariants on function parameters and session variables with each program function. This approach is limited in that they rely on program source code to extract the specification. The inferred specification is highly dependent on how the application is structured and implemented (e.g., the definition of a program function or block). Thus, implementation flaws may result in an inaccurate specification. Another approach infers the application specification by observing and characterizing the application's external behavior. BLOCK [19] observes the web requests/responses between the web application and its users and extracts invariants associated within. While BLOCK, as a black-box approach, is source-code free, its capability is limited since it only observes web requests/responses without taking into account the large amount of information persisted in the database, resulting in an incomplete specification. The persistent information in the database may affect the application's behavior in two ways. First, the application can use persistent objects in the database for maintaining its persistent state across web sessions, while using session variables for managing the state during a session. Second, the persistent objects may embed complex data constraints for web applications. Moreover, BLOCK examines web requests/responses, thus incapable of handling certain state violation attacks that are targeted at the database.

In this paper, we present a black-box approach for automated detection of state violation attacks with a focus on securing the back-end database. To be more specific, we aim to identify and block malicious SQL queries, which are issued in a way that violates the application specification. To derive the application specification in a black-box manner, we have to address the following two issues:

(1) **What external behavior to observe in order to collect sufficient information for specification inference.** Since we focus on securing the database, we observe the interaction between the web application and the database. For the application to utilize persistent objects stored in the database, they have to be returned within SQL responses first. Thus, we collect all the observed SQL queries and responses, as well as the corresponding session variables.

(2) **How to infer the application logic from collected information in a systematic way, so that the application behavior can be characterized adequately.** We model the web application as an extended finite state machine (EFSM). EFSM has been employed for modeling the behavior of complex software [20], since it can capture not only the state transitions but also the data constraints associated with transitions and fits well in the web application scenario. To derive the EFSM, we first construct SQL signatures from observed SQL queries, which represent the output symbols emitted from the EFSM. Then, we extract a set of invariants for each SQL signature from both session variables and SQL responses, which characterize the application state and the associated data constraints when a SQL query is issued. In particular, we leverage a well-known technique (i.e., daikon engine [12]) to derive value-based invariants, including the invariants over variables that are used for indicating the application state and the data constraints. Besides, we extract the dependencies between SQL signatures to infer other data constraints, which are implicitly reflected from previously issued SQL queries. The set of invariants, indexed by SQL signatures, manifest the application specification and are used for evaluating the incoming SQL queries at runtime. Suspicious SQL queries, which violate any invariant associated with their respective signatures, are identified as potential attacks and blocked.

In this paper, we make two major contributions:

(1) We present a black-box approach for deriving the application specification and detecting malicious SQL queries, which exploit application logic flaws. In particular, we characterize the application as an EFSM and systematically utilize the persistent objects in the database for deriving a more complete and accurate specification for web applications, which is missing from existing works.

(2) We implement a prototype detection system SENTINEL and evaluate it with a set of real-world web applications. In particular, SENTINEL is independent of web applications and the database system, and can be easily integrated with existing infrastructures. The experiment results demonstrate the effectiveness of our approach and show that our implementation incurs acceptable performance overhead.

The rest of paper is organized as follows. Section 2 describes an example application and the attacks we focus on in this paper. Then, we present our EFSM model for web applications. Our approach and implementation are illustrated in detail in Section 4 and 5, respectively. Section 6 demonstrates the evaluation of our detection system SENTINEL. Related works are discussed in Section 7. We conclude the paper with future works in the final section.

2. ATTACK

In the area of web application security, the following threat model is usually considered: the attacker is able to manipulate the contents or the sequence of web requests sent to the web application, but cannot directly compromise the server state (i.e., session variables) or the application code. Fig. 1 shows an example application *SimpleOAK*, which is used to illustrate the attacks we address in this paper and demonstrate our system model and approach throughout the paper. A user is first presented with the *index.php* page (the application is at state s_0). After the user inputs correct login credentials, the application will redirect the student to the *user.php* page (the application is at state s_1) and the professor to the *admin.php* page (the application is at state s_2), depending on the role information (i.e., $row['role']$ in *index.php*) retrieved from the database. The *user.php* page shows the student's registrations and grades, as well as the syllabus links for registered courses. The student can only modify his/her own registrations (data constraint c) through the *course.php* page. The *admin.php* page shows all the students' registrations, so that the professor can modify their grades accordingly.

SimpleOAK contains several vulnerabilities. First, the application fails to enforce the correctness of the application state, which allows malicious SQL queries to be issued at an incorrect state. There are two cases of this type of vulnerability in the *SimpleOAK* application.

Case 1: A guest user (i.e., at state s_0) can directly access a student's information (i.e., issuing *Query1* and *Query2* in *user.php*), since the *user.php* page doesn't check if the user has logged in (i.e., whether the session variable $\$\_SESSION['userid']$ is null).

Case 2: A student (i.e., at state s_1) can directly access the professor's page (i.e., issuing *Query3* in *admin.php*) and modify the grades (i.e., issuing *Query4* in *course.php*), since the *admin.php* page fails to verify the application state, which is stored as persistent objects in the database (i.e., whether $row['role']$ in *index.php* is equal to *professor*).

Second, the web application fails to enforce the data constraints (e.g., constraint c) associated with SQL queries,

```php
<?php
include_once("header.php");
if (isset($_GET['logout'])){
    unset($_SESSION['userid']);
    session_destroy();
} else if (isset($_POST['username']) && isset($_POST['password'])){
    $Query0 = mysql_query(sprintf("SELECT * FROM users WHERE login = '%s' AND
password = '%s';", $_POST['username'], $_POST['password']));
    if ($row = mysql_fetch_assoc($Query0)){
        $_SESSION['userid'] = $row['id'];
        if ($row['role'] == "professor"){
            header("Location: admin.php?userid=" . $_SESSION['userid']);
        } else if ($row['role'] == "student"){
            header("Location: user.php?userid=" . $_SESSION['userid']);
        }
    } else { die('Wrong username or password.');}
}?>
<form action="index.php" method="post">
username: <input name="username" type="text"><br>
password: <input name="password" type="password"><br>
<input name="submit" type="submit">
</form></body></html>
```

index.php

```php
<?php
include_once("header.php");
if (isset($_GET['userid'])){
    print("<table><tr><td>Course</td><td>Grade</td><td>Syllabus</td><td>Unregister</td></tr>");
    $Query1 = mysql_query("SELECT * FROM registration WHERE user_id =".
$_GET['userid'].";");
    while ($row = mysql_fetch_assoc($Query1)){
        print("<tr><td>". getCourseName($row['course_id']). "</td><td>". $row['grade'].
            "</td><td><a href=\"./course.php?course_id=". $row['course_id']. "\">link</a>" .
            "</td><td><form method=\"post\" action=\"course.php\">".
            "<input type=\"hidden\" name=\"register_id\" value=" . $row['id'] . ">" .
            "<input type=\"submit\" name=\"action\" value=\"Unregister\"></form></td></tr>");
    }
    print("<table><tr><td>Course</td><td>Register</td></tr>");
    $Query2 = mysql_query("SELECT * FROM course WHERE course.id NOT IN
(SELECT course_id FROM registration WHERE user_id =". $_GET['userid'].")");
    while ($row = mysql_fetch_assoc($Query2)){
        print ("<tr><td>". $row['name']. "</td><td><form method=\"post\" action=\"course.php\">".
            "<input type=\"hidden\" name=\"course_id\" value=" . $row['id'] . ">" .
            "<input type=\"hidden\" name=\"user_id\" value=" . $_GET['userid'] . ">" .
            "<input type=\"submit\" name=\"action\" value=\"Register\"></form></td></tr>");
    }
    print("</table><br><a href=\"./index.php?logout=1\"><b>Logout</b></a>");
}?>
</body></html>
```

user.php

```php
<?php
include_once("header.php");
if (isset($_SESSION['userid'])){
    $Query3 = mysql_query("SELECT * FROM registration;");
    print("<table><tr><td>Name</td><td>Course</td><td>Grade</td></tr>");
    while ($row = mysql_fetch_assoc($Query3)){
        print("<tr><td>". getUserName($row['user_id']).
            "</td><td>". getCourseName($row['course_id']).
            "</td><td><form method=\"post\" action=\"course.php\">".
            "<input type=\"hidden\" name=\"register_id\" value=". $row['id']. ">".s
            "<textarea name=\"grade\">". $row['grade']. "</textarea>".
            "<input type=\"submit\" name=\"action\" value=\"Modify\"></form></td></tr>");
    }
    print("</table><br><a href=\"./index.php?logout=1\"><b>Logout</b></a>");
} else{ die("You are not authorized to view this page"); }
?> </body></html>
```

admin.php

```php
<?php
include_once("header.php");
if (isset($_POST['register_id']) && isset($_POST['grade']) && $_POST['action'] == "Modify") {
    $Query4 = mysql_query("UPDATE registration SET grade=". $_POST['grade'] .
"WHERE id= " . $_POST['register_id']. ";");
    if ($Query4) {
        header("Location: admin.php?userid=" . $_SESSION['userid']);
    } else { die("Fail to update the grade."); }
} else if (isset($_POST['course_id']) && $_POST['action'] == "Register") {
    $Query5 = mysql_query("INSERT INTO registration (user_id, course_id) VALUES
(".$_POST['user_id']. ", ". $_POST['course_id']. ");");
    if ($Query5) {
        header("Location: user.php?userid=" . $_SESSION['userid']);
    } else { die("Fail to register the course.");}
} else if (isset($_POST['register_id']) && $_POST['action'] == "Unregister") {
    $Query6 = mysql_query("DELETE FROM registration WHERE id=" .
$_POST['register_id'].";");
    if ($Query6) {
        header("Location: user.php?userid=" . $_SESSION['userid']);
    } else { die("Fail to unregister the course."); }
} else if (isset($_GET['course_id'])){
    $Query7 = mysql_query("SELECT * FROM course WHERE id =" . $_GET[' course_id'].
";");
    if (res = mysql_fetch_assoc($Query7)){
        print("<h2>". $res['name']."</h2><br>". "<b>Syllabus: </b>". $res['syllabus']."<br>");
    }
}?>
</body><html>
```

course.php

Database Schema

Table: user

user_id	login	password	role
1	howard	helloworld	student
2	john	1234	student
3	larry	admin	professor

Table: course

id	name	syllabus
1	algebra	"difficult"
2	web programming	"easy"

id	user_id	course_id	grade
1	1	2	95
2	1	1	85
3	2	1	68

Table: registration

Figure 1: Example application: *SimpleOAK*

27

which allows the attacker to issue malicious SQL queries by manipulating query parameters.

Case 3: A student is able to view/change another student's registrations.

- View registration: the *user.php* page fails to check the constraint: $\$\_GET['userid'] == \$\_SESSION['userid']$ associated with *Query1* and *Query2*.

- Register a course: the *course.php* page fails to check the constraint: $\$\_POST['userid'] == \$\_SESSION['userid']$ associated with *Query5*.

- Unregister a course: the *course.php* page fails to check if the *user_id* field in the affected row of *registration* table is equal to the session variable $\$\_SESSION['userid']$, when issuing *Query6*.

Case 4: A student can view the syllabus of a course, which he/she hasn't registered, by manipulating the *course_id* parameter in *Query7*. The *course.php* page fails to check the correlation between the student and the course, which exists within *registration* table (i.e., the directed lines in Fig. 1).

To date, there is no automated mechanism that can help developers identify all the above security flaws and detect the corresponding attacks. Developers have to pay extra attention and manually place appropriate checks during development and code auditing.

3. SYSTEM MODEL

We model a web application as an *extended finite state machine (EFSM)* [13], denoted as M. A web application M, as shown in Fig.2, is defined as a seven-tuple: $M = (S, V, I, O, P, U, T)$.

- S denotes the set of application states. A web application maintains its state using either session variables (e.g., $\$\_SESSION['userid']$) or persistent objects (e.g., the *row* column in *user* table) in the database. We refer to the set of session variables and state-related persistent objects as state variables, which collectively characterize the current application state.

- V denotes the set of context variables, which include global variables (e.g., $\$\_SERVER$ variables) and local variables in scope (e.g., $\$row['id']$ in *user.php*), except state variables. They represent the general context of the application's current execution.

- I is the set of input symbols, which include users' web requests (e.g., *GET:user.php?userid=3*) and SQL responses (e.g., $\$Query0$, which contains the response of *Query0*) returned by the database.

- O is the set of output symbols, which include web responses sent to users (e.g., *header("Location:user.php")*) and SQL queries issued to the database (e.g., *Query0*).

- P: $D_S \times D_V \to \{true, false\}$ is the set of data constraints associated with state transitions (e.g., *if ($row['role']==professor)* in *index.php*). D_S and D_V denote the evaluation domains for state variables and context variables respectively.

- U: $D_S \times D_V \to D_S \times D_V$ is the set of update functions, which update state and context variables (e.g., $\$\_SESSION['uerid']=\$row['id']$ in *index.php*).

- T: $S \times I \times P \to S \times O \times U$ defines the state transitions. In a web application, each state transition can be decomposed into two steps: (1) the application accepts the input, executes update functions and possibly transitions to a new state, just before the output symbol is emitted, which can be expressed as T^U: $S \times I \to S \times U$. Whether the application transitions to a new state depends on if state variables are updated. (2) the application evaluates the data constraints over current variables and issues the output symbol if the evaluation returns true, which can be expressed as T^O: $S \times P \to O$. Note here the application state doesn't change in this step. SQL queries may modify state-related persistent objects in the database. However, the application is aware of the state change only after it retrieves those modified persistent objects later. Thus, we regard the application state before and after the output symbol is emitted as the same.

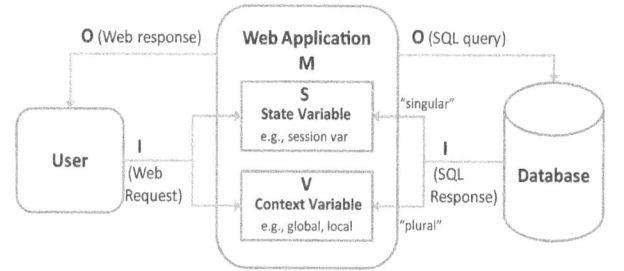

Figure 2: System model of a web application

Fig.3 shows part of the intended EFSM model for *SimpleOAK*, which contains two states and two transitions. First, *SimpleOAK* accepts a POST web request (i_0) at state s_0, which triggers the transition t_0. In the first step t_0^U, the application updates context variables (u_0) and stays at the same state s_0, since no state variables are updated. In the second step t_0^O, the application checks data constraints (p_0) and issues a SQL query to the database (o_0). After the application receives the SQL response from the database (i_1), a new transition t_1 is triggered. It first executes updating functions (u_1) and transitions to a new state s_1, since the state variable $\$\_SESSION['userid']$ is updated to the current user id (i.e., from null to non-null). Then, the application evaluates data constraints (p_1) and returns a web response to the user (o_1).

4. APPROACH

4.1 Approach Overview

Our objective is to detect malicious SQL queries that exploit logic flaws and violate the application specification. From our system model, such violations are manifested during the second step of state transition (i.e., T^O: $S \times P \to O$), when the output symbols (i.e., SQL queries) are emitted. There are two scenarios: (1) the output is emitted when the application is at an incorrect state, which can be captured by characterizing the relationship between the output and the application state (i.e., $S \to O$); (2) the output is emitted when the data constraints are not satisfied, which can be captured by characterizing the relationship between the

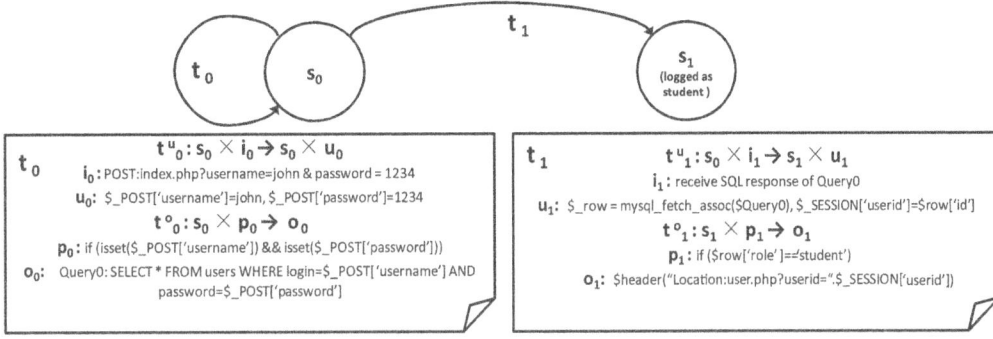

Figure 3: Part of intended EFSM model of *SimpleOAK*

output and data constraints (i.e., $P \to O$). Our approach infers the application specification by observing and analyzing the interactions between the application and the database during attack-free sessions. Then, the inferred specification is used for runtime detection of malicious SQL queries issued by the web application. In the following sections, we first illustrate how we identify the set of output symbols (i.e., O) by constructing SQL signatures from observed SQL queries (Section 4.2). Then, we present how we infer the application specification from collected information, including application state inference (Section 4.3) and data constraint inference (Section 4.4). The inference also captures the first step of state transition (i.e., $T^U : S \times I \to S \times U$), since we utilize updated state variables and context variables triggered by the application input (i.e., either web request or SQL response). The inferred specification is manifested as a set of invariants, indexed by SQL signatures (Section 4.5). Finally, we describe how we evaluate incoming SQL queries and detecting potential attacks at runtime (Section 4.6).

4.2 SQL Signature Construction

Each SQL query is composed of a skeleton structure, which is programmed in the source code, and a set of query parameters, whose values are dynamically fed by the application at runtime. To represent the output with a finite set of symbols, we need to separate the skeleton structure from query parameters, which have unbounded set of values. We extract the skeleton structure of SQL queries in three steps, as shown in Fig.4. First, we identify all the literals in the SQL queries and collect all the observed values for each parameter that assumes a literal. Second, for each parameter, we perform one-sample Komoglov-Smirnov's D Statistics test (KS-test) to determine whether the value domain of the parameter is bounded or not. The KS-test is employed to evaluate whether the number of unique values of the parameter linearly increases with the number of sample sizes. Further details can be found in [18]. Third, for all parameters, if the parameter has a bounded value domain (e.g., *role*), we assume that its value carries implicit meaning for operations, which should be kept within the structure of the query. If the parameter has an unbounded number of values observed (e.g., *user_id*), we replace its value with a place holder token and record the parameter. The resulting string is the skeleton structure of the query (e.g., *SELECT * FROM registration WHERE user_id = <Token>*, where *<Token>* represents a query parameter).

Then, we construct a SQL signature by combining the

skeleton structure of the SQL query and the script name, where the query resides. An example signature is { *user.php, SELECT * FROM registration WHERE user_id = <Token>* }. Each SQL signature represents a unique output symbol that can be issued by the web application.

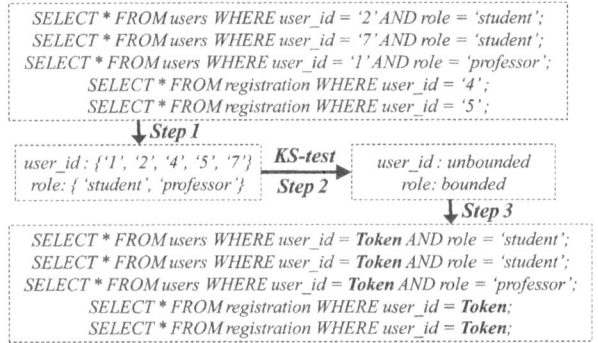

Figure 4: SQL query skeleton structure extraction

4.3 Application State Inference

To infer the relationship between the output and the application state (i.e., $S \to O$), we associate each SQL signature with the set of state variables when a SQL query is issued. First, we have to identify the correct set of state variables to construct the state space S. State variables come from two sources: session variables and persistent objects in the database. Due to the adoption of connection pooling technique [9], which shares SQL connections among different sessions, SQL queries from different sessions cannot be differentiated. We reuse the session id and associate it with each SQL query for indexing the set of session variables.

The state variables that come from persistent objects can only be used by the application after they are retrieved from the database, thus can be observed from SQL responses. However, the SQL response may contain a large amount of objects. Only part of them are actually used in maintaining the application state. As such, we identify three types of SQL responses: (1) Type I: the response is a boolean (i.e., true or false), which applies to UPDATE, INSERT, DELETE queries; (2) Type II: the response of SELECT query, which always contains no more than one row of objects [1]. We say this type of response is "singular", which can

---

[1] If a SELECT query returns a false on error, we consider its response to be zero row of object.

possibly be used for retrieving persistent state information from the database and updating state variables (as shown in Fig.2). For example, $Query0$ in $index.php$ page retrieves the current user information persisted in the database, which determines the current application state (i.e., at either s_0, s_1 or s_2). (3) Type III: the response of SELECT query, which contains variable rows of objects (usually more than one). We say this type of response is "plural", which is used for updating context variables by the application (and inferring data constraints in Section 4.4). For example, $Query1$ in $user.php$ page returns a number of courses the user has registered. We infer the response type for each SQL signature by examining all the responses, returned by SQL queries with the same signature and associate a flag r with each signature to indicate its response type. In particular, we transform the "singular" SQL response into a set of key-value pairs similar to the representation of session variables (e.g., $row['id']$, $row['role']$ in $index.php$).

After collecting all the state variables, we employ a well-known technique (i.e., daikon engine) to extract value-based invariants over state variables, which characterize the application state associated with each signature (Section 4.5.1).

4.4 Data Constraint Inference

To infer the relationship between the output and the data constraints (i.e., $P \rightarrow O$), we extract three types of data constraints P for each SQL signature. First, each SQL signature itself captures part of the data constraints, which are directly encoded within WHERE clauses and automatically enforced (e.g., WHERE course.id NOT IN in $Query2$). Second, we employ daikon engine to infer the mathematical relationship between state variables and context variables (i.e., $|S| \times |V|$), which are fed into SQL queries as query parameters [2]. For example, the variable $\_GET['userid']$ is always equal to the session variable $\_SESSION['userid']$ in $Query1$. Third, data constraints may also be embedded within previously issued SQL queries, since the application implicitly assumes the dependency relationship between SQL queries. We say one SQL query q is dependent on another query q', if the database objects q performs over also satisfy the constraints specified by the WHERE clause of q'. For example, $SimpleOAK$ first retrieves all the registered courses (at least the course id) for one student via $Query1$. Then, the student can view the syllabus of those courses via $Query7$. The application implicitly assumes $Query7$ is dependent on $Query1$, which means that the specified course in $Query7$ always satisfies the constraint within $Query1$ that the course is registered by current student. Since the objects within the SQL response must satisfy the constraints specified by the WHERE clause, instead of analyzing complex WHERE clauses and their logical relationship among different SQL queries, we infer this type of constraint for each signature by evaluating its WHERE clause over previously observed SQL responses. If the WHERE clause of one signature sig is always satisfied by the response of another signature sig', which is always issued earlier and observed during the session, we express such a constraint in the form that sig is dependent on sig' (Section 4.5.2).

4.5 Invariant Extraction

We extract a set of invariants from collected traces to represent the application specification and use them for runtime detection. In the traces, each SQL query t is associated with the following information: a set of query parameters Q, a set of state variables S and its SQL response $Resp$. The SQL queries, as well as relevant information, are grouped by signatures. We extract the following types of invariants for each SQL signature.

4.5.1 Type A: Application state invariant

Type A invariants characterize the application state when SQL queries are issued (i.e., $S \rightarrow O$). For each SQL signature sig, we identify:

A.1: a set of state variables $S_{inv}(sig)$ ($S_{inv}(sig) \subseteq S$) that are always present (i.e., its value is not null). These state variables represent the dimension of the application state. An example in $SimpleOAK$ is $S_{inv}(sig1) = \{\_SESSION['userid'], row['role']\}$, where $sig1 = (user.php, SELECT * FROM registration WHERE user\_id = <Token>)$, which indicates that the application cannot issue $Query1$ at state s_0.

A.2: for a state variable s ($s \in S_{inv}(sig)$) that is always present, its value is drawn from an enumeration set $E(s, sig)$, which indicates the value domain for a specific state dimension. An example in $SimpleOAK$ is $E(row['role'], sig2) = \{'professor'\}$, where $sig2 = (admin.php, SELECT * FROM registration)$, which means that $Query2$ can only be issued when the application is at state s_2.

4.5.2 Type B: Data constraint invariant

Type B invariants characterize the data constraints associated with SQL queries (i.e., $P \rightarrow O$). For each SQL signature sig, we identify:

B.1: the value of a query parameter q ($q \in Q$) is always equal to the value of a state variable that is always present s ($s \in S_{inv}(sig)$). Since the query parameters are drawn from context variables, this type of invariant captures the constraints between the context variables and state variables that the SQL query has to satisfy (i.e., $|S| \times |V|$). An example in $SimpleOAK$ is the value of $Token1$ in $sig3$ is always equal to $\_SESSION['userid']$, where $sig3 = (course.php, INSERT INTO registration (user\_id, course\_id) VALUES (<Token1>, <Token2>))$, which means a student can only register a course for himself.

B.2: the SQL signature sig is dependent on another SQL signature sig', if and only if: a) the skeleton structure of sig' is a SELECT statement; b) sig' has a Type III response type; c) there is always a SQL query with signature sig' issued before a SQL query with signature sig can be issued; d) the WHERE clause of the SQL query with signature sig is always satisfied by the set of objects returned by the previous SQL query with signature sig'. This type of invariant captures the constraints, which are not directly encoded within the WHERE clause of current SQL signature but implicitly specified by previously issued SQL queries.

Several examples in $SimpleOAK$ are: a) the signature $(course.php, UPDATE registration SET grade = <Token1> WHERE id = <Token2>)$ is dependent on $(admin.php, SELECT * FROM registration)$, since the UPDATE query always performs over one of the objects returned by the SELECT statement; b) both the signatures $(course.php, SELECT * FROM course WHERE id = Token)$ and $(course.php, DELETE FROM registration WHERE id = <Token>)$ are

---

[2]We only identify the equality relationship between state variables and context variables here.

```
SigDepLearn(TRACE Γ)
  CandidateSet ← ∅
  BlackList ← ∅
  SessionStore ← empty
  for all queries t IN Γ do
    if a new session then
      SessionStore ← empty
    end if
    Sig ← extractSig(t)
    Cond ← extractWhereClause(t)
    if Cond = null then
      continue
    end if
    for all keys k NOT IN SessionStore do
      Pair ← (Sig, k)
      BlackList.add(Pair)
    end for
    for all keys k IN SessionStore do
      Pair ← (Sig, k)
      if BlackList.exists(Pair) then
        continue
      end if
      if   SessionStore.getRespone(k).eval(Cond)=true
      then
        CandidateSet.add(Pair)
      else
        BlackList.add(Pair)
        if CandidateSet.exists(Pair) then
          CandidateSet.remove(Pair)
        end if
      end if
    end for
    if Sig.getRespType = Type III then
      SessionStore.add(Sig, t.Resp)
    end if
  end for
  return CandidateSet
```

Figure 5: Invariant extraction for SQL signature dependency

dependent on (*user.php, SELECT * FROM registration WHERE user_id = \<Token\>*).

We present an efficient algorithm to extract this type of invariant, as shown in Fig.5. We use a hashtable (i.e., *SessionStore*) to maintain all the objects, carried by SQL responses, during the session. The key of the hashtable is the signature of a SQL query that has a type III response, while the value is the objects within the response. When a type III SQL response is observed, it is added into the hashtable indexed by the signature of the query (i.e., *Sig*). When a SQL query is issued, its WHERE clause (i.e., *Cond*) will be evaluated over those objects maintained in the hashtable. If the clause is satisfied by the response of a previous SQL query, the pair of their signatures is added into a candidate set (i.e., *CandidateSet*). Otherwise, the pair is added into a black list (i.e., *BlackList*) and will not be evaluated anymore. If the dependency relationship between two signatures holds for all the samples in the trace, it becomes one invariant.

4.6 Runtime Detection

Each SQL signature *sig* is associated with a set of invari-ants *Inv(sig)* after invariant extraction. The collection of all the invariants serves as the application specification. For detection, each invariant *inv* is transformed into an evalu-ation function f_{inv}. If the observed SQL query t satisfies the invariant *inv*, f_{inv} returns true. Otherwise, the func-tion returns false. A SQL query is accepted and sent to the database if and only if its signature exists and it satisfies all the invariants associated with the signature. Otherwise, the query is blocked and the application receives an error response. In *SimpleOAK*, all the four attack cases can be detected using corresponding invariants extracted in Section 4.5.

5. IMPLEMENTATION

We implement a prototype detection system SENTINEL for PHP web applications as two components: *Sensor* and *Analyzer*, as shown in Fig.6. *Sensor* is responsible for col-lecting information and communicating with *Analyzer*, while *Analyzer* is responsible for offline training and runtime de-tection. To be more specific, *Sensor* intercepts SQL queries and responses, collects session variable values and script names, and sends them to *Analyzer*. Based on the collected traces, *Analyzer* extracts SQL signatures and infers the set of invariants associated with signatures. At runtime, *Ana-lyzer* evaluates incoming SQL queries and instructs *Sensor* to block malicious queries.

To implement the functionalities of *Sensor*, we modify the *php-mysql* module in PHP interpreter, which provides the connectivity between the web application and the database. Whenever a SQL query is constructed and about to be sent to the database, we capture the query string, identify the script currently being executed (via *$_SERVER['SCRIPT_FILENAME']*), record the current values of session variables and send them to *Analyzer*. In PHP, session variables are by default stored in local files located at */var/lib/php5* and indexed by current session id. When the SQL response is returned from the database, we capture it and also send it to the analyzer. Our extensions to the *php-mysql* module can be dynamically enabled/disabled through an added PHP directive (i.e., mysql:enable_proxy).

Analyzer, the key component of SENTINEL, is imple-mented as a Java Servlet and can be operated in two modes: training and detection, as shown in Fig.7. In the train-ing mode, *Trace Collector* logs all the information received from *Sensor*. After sufficient traces are collected, *Signa-ture Extractor* generates SQL signatures from observed SQL queries. Then, all the information, identified by SQL sig-natures, are fed into *Invariant Extractor*, where we lever-age daikon engine to infer the value-based invariants (i.e., A.1, A.2, B.1). Especially, *Session Manager* is responsible for analyzing sessions and extracting SQL signature depen-dency invariants (i.e., B.2). In the detection mode, when a SQL query is received from *Sensor*, *Signature Extractor* first generates its signature. Then, it is passed to *Detector* for evaluation based on the set of invariants, identified by its signature. Especially, *Session Manager* is responsible for maintaining the observed objects during the session, when a SQL response is received from *Sensor*, and evaluating the query with B.2 invariants. If the query is determined to be safe, *Analyzer* will respond to *Sensor* and allow *Sensor* to forward the query to the database. Otherwise, *Analyzer* will instruct *Sensor* to block the malicious query and *Sensor* will return an error response to the application.

The communication between *Sensor* and *Analyzer* is based on HTTP protocol. *Sensor* composes a web request, which contains collected information, sends it to *Analyzer* and waits for the web response. *Analyzer* processes the web request via *Request Handler*. SENTINEL is independent of web applications and database systems and can be easily integrated with existing infrastructures by just replacing the original *php-mysql* module with our extension version. Although our current prototype works for PHP applications, it can be conveniently extended to handle other platforms as long as the functionalities of *Sensor* (e.g., SQL interception, the interface for communicating with the analyzer) are implemented. Currently, we co-locate *Analyzer* with *Sensor* and the applications, and restrict the access to *Analyzer*. Our implementation has the potential to be deployed as a security service if additional mechanisms for securing the communication between *Sensor* and *Analyzer* (e.g., authenticating *Sensor*) are implemented.

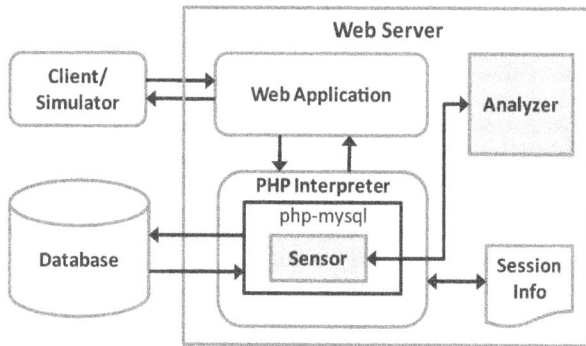

Figure 6: Overview of SENTINEL

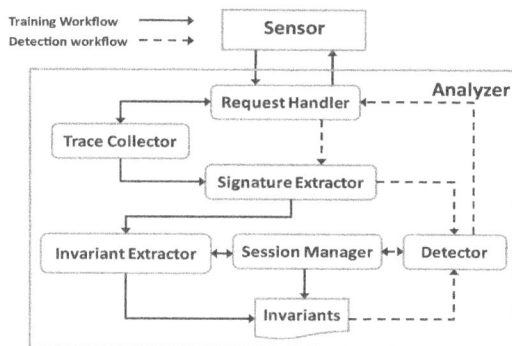

Figure 7: Analyzer component

6. EVALUATION

We evaluate SENTINEL using a set of open-source PHP web applications, as shown in Table 1. (1) Scarf is a conference management system, which is used for managing sessions, papers, users and comments. It has an authentication bypass vulnerability (CVE-2006-5909), which allows the attacker to directly access the administrative functionalities. The page *generaloptions.php* doesn't check if the session variable $_SESSION['privilege']$, which indicates the privilege of current user, is equal to *admin* when retrieving and updating system settings and user accounts stored in the database. (2) Wackopicko [29] is an online photo sharing website that allows users to upload, comment and purchase pictures. It is designed with a number of vulnerabilities, such as cross-site scripting and SQL injection, and used for testing the capabilities of web application vulnerability scanners [11]. In this paper, we focus on the logic vulnerabilities it contains. The first vulnerability allows an attacker to manipulate the *userid* parameter sent to the *sample.php* page and view any users' information, since the application doesn't check whether the *userid* parameter is equal to the id of the user who is currently logged in. The second vulnerability can be exploited by an attacker to view the high-quality versions of arbitrary pictures without purchasing them by manipulating the *picid* parameter sent to the *highquality.php* page. The application uses a database table *own* to maintain the relationship between the pictures and their buyers. However, it fails to check if the current user has purchased a particular picture when retrieving its high-quality version. (3) OpenIT [22] is an IT management system, which consists of a set of modules, such as inventory, help desk, issue tracking, etc. It has a parameter manipulation vulnerability, which allows the attacker to tamper a hidden field that stores the employee id and change other users' information. (4) openInvoice [21] is an invoicing system for keeping track of customers, invoices and items. It has a vulnerability (CVE-2008-6524) that an attacker can exploit to modify the password of an arbitrary user through the *resetpass.php* page.

Table 1: Summary of Evaluated Web Applications

Application	# PHP file	Description	Vulnerability
Scarf	21	Conference management system	Auth bypass (CVE-2006-5909)
Wackopicko	52	Photo sharing website	Parameter manipulation, forceful browsing [29]
OpenIT	25	IT management system	Parameter manipulation [4]
openInvoice	327	Invoicing system	Parameter manipulation (CVE-2008-6524)

We deploy all the web applications on a 2.13GHz Core 2 Linux server with 2GB RAM, running Ubuntu 10.10, Apache web server (version 2.2.16) and PHP (version 5.3.3). The analyzer is hosted by Tomcat 7 on the same machine. To generate traces more efficiently, we build user simulators, which automate the procedure of operating web applications and emulate the interaction between a normal user and the web applications. To build the user simulator, we first identify user roles and their corresponding atomic actions for each application. Those actions include clicking web links, filling in and submitting forms, etc. Then, the user simulator performs a random sequence of atomic actions automatically based on the web application testing tool Selenium WebDriver [26]. To simulate the multi-user scenario, we leverage the information of undergraduate students from a network security class. The user simulator is set up at a 2.83GHz

Core 2 desktop with 8GB RAM running Windows 7 and Firefox4 and connected to the web server using Ethernet.

6.1 Detection Effectiveness

SENTINEL first runs in the training mode to collect traces, extract signatures and infer invariants. Training traces are generated by both manually operating the web applications and running user simulators and don't include attack instances (e.g., SQL injections). Table 2 shows the summary of our training set. In addition to the size of SQL query set, we also report the number of extracted signatures, database fields we observed from SQL queries and responses, likely state variables, as well as each type of inferred invariants. Then, SENTINEL runs in the detection mode. The clean test set is also generated by both manually operating the web applications and running the user simulators. Ten attacks are manually launched against each web application under different circumstances, such as logging as a different user, performing a different sequence of actions before launching the attack, etc. Table 3 shows the summary of our test sets and detection results. We can see that all of the attacks are successfully identified by corresponding invariants. Especially in Wackopicko, the attack, which allows the high-quality versions of arbitrary pictures to be viewed without purchase, is detected by one of the B.2 invariants. To our knowledge, none of the existing techniques can capture this type of logic attack, since they don't take into account the persistent information (i.e., the table *own*) in the database, which reflects part of the application logic. On the other hand, the false positive rate is fairly low. We analyze the false alerts raised by SENTINEL and find that all of them are introduced by the incomplete exploration of user simulators, which is known as an inherent challenge for dynamic analysis techniques. In a nutshell, the detection experiments demonstrate the effectiveness of our approach at detecting malicious SQL queries that violate the intended application logic.

6.2 Performance Overhead

At runtime, SENTINEL intercepts each SQL query and sends it to *Analyzer* for evaluation before forwarding it to the database, which inevitably introduces additional SQL response delay. To evaluate the performance overhead brought by SENTINEL, we measure the averaged SQL response time for running each web application under three circumstances: (1) without SENTINEL; (2) with SENTINEL and *Detector* disabled; (3) with SENTINEL and *Detector* enabled to evaluate each SQL query. Fig. 8 shows the summary of the performance overhead measured for each application. The results are averaged over a number of rounds. We can see that SENTINEL increases SQL response time by a factor of 1.6-4. The performance overhead is introduced mainly through two sources: (1) the communication overhead between *Sensor* and *Analyzer*; (2) the analysis time during which *Analyzer* extracts SQL signature and evaluates the query. While the communication overhead is still acceptable (around 1ms in average), the analysis time is relatively low. Thus, SENTINEL can be integrated with running applications without incurring noticeable performance degradation.

6.3 Discussion

Fingerprint-based techniques have been proposed to defend against SQL injection attacks [18]. Our technique ex-

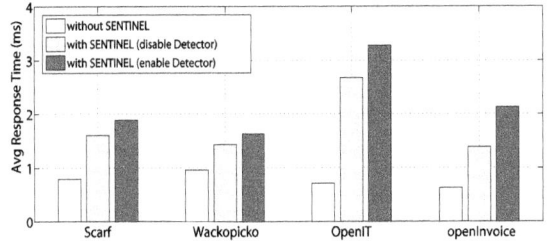

Figure 8: Performance Overhead

tracts SQL signatures to represent the possible output symbols that can be issued by the web application and associates them with invariants, which characterize the application state and data constraints. Similar to fingerprint, our technique has the potential to be employed to mitigate SQL injection attacks, which tamper the SQL query structure captured by the SQL signature. Since we focus on state violation attacks in this paper, we don't evaluate our technique over the detection of SQL injection attacks.

Our technique bears the same limitations as other dynamic analysis techniques. Our collected traces are mostly generated by running user simulators. Due to the fact that the user simulator is incapable of exploring all the possible states of the web application, our inferred invariants can be either incomplete or spurious. The completeness (i.e., coverage) of our technique cannot be directly assessed, as we don't examine the application source code. The attacks that traverse the unexplored state of the application will not be detected by our system, resulting in false negatives. On the other hand, the inferred invariants may be over-restrictive for characterizing the application's behavior, so that normal behaviors are identified as attacks, resulting in false positives. In reality, if real-world traces are available, our technique can be readily applied for characterizing the application behavior more completely and accurately, effectively protecting vulnerable applications.

In this paper, we focus on securing the database access. Thus, we collect SQL queries and extract invariants only for SQL signatures. However, our approach can be extended to handle other types of state violation attacks, such as unauthorized file access, etc. In this case, *Sensor* should be extended to collect relevant sensitive operations, i.e., file I/O system calls, and *Analyzer* establishes models for file access behaviors of the web application.

7. RELATED WORK

Our work is related to two lines of research: web application security and database security.

7.1 Web Application Security

Generally there are two classes of attacks against web applications: input validation attack, which SQL injection belongs to, and state violation attack, which we focus on in this paper.

7.1.1 SQL Injection Attack

A number of techniques have been proposed to defend against SQL injections, such as Prepared Statements [23], etc. AMNESIA [16] statically analyzes the application source

Table 2: Summary of Training Set

Application	SQL queries	Signatures	Database fields	State variables	A.1 Inv	A.2 Inv	B.1 Inv	B.2 Inv
Scarf	4385	95	58	44	1210	457	71	10
Wackopicko	5062	56	57	29	729	52	130	14
OpenIT	5708	50	145	97	1583	401	596	3
openInvoice	8022	113	51	31	746	375	43	2

Table 3: Summary of Detection Result

Application	SQL queries (clean test set)	Blocked queries (false positive)	Attacks	Detected	Invariant violations
Scarf	4694	1	10	10	A.1, A.2
Wackopicko	4984	2	10	10	B.1, B.2
OpenIT	6304	0	10	10	B.1
openInvoice	6585	0	10	10	B.1

code to establish models for the intended structure of each SQL query, while CANDID [3] infers the intended structure of SQL query by dynamically feeding the application with benign inputs and retrofits the vulnerable application in an automatic way. Valeur et al. [28] establish statistical models for characterizing the structure of SQL queries based on collected traces. While there exists a general specification for handling SQL injections, it is difficult to derive such a general specification for addressing state violation attacks. In this paper, we provide a general approach for deriving the intended application logic by observing and characterizing the interaction between the application and the database.

7.1.2 State Violation Attack

The general approach to addressing state violation attacks is to infer the application specification and then identify the discrepancies between the intended application behavior and its runtime behavior (i.e., runtime detection, such as Swaddler [10], BLOCK [19]) or the application implementations (i.e., vulnerability analysis, such as MiMoSA [2], Waler [14], NoTamper [4], WAPTEC [5], [27]). Among these works, Swaddler [10], MiMoSA [2], Waler [14], WAPTEC [5] and [27] all require the application source code for analysis or instrumentation. For example, Swaddler [10] establishes statistical models of the application state for each program block using session variables and detects anomalous states during the application execution. MiMoSA [2] statically extracts an intended workflow graph from the application source code and employs model checking technique to identify vulnerabilities that exist within multi-module interactions. Sun et al. [27] establish per-role sitemaps from source code to identify access control vulnerabilities within web applications. Our approach is completely source code free and thus avoids many issues caused by leveraging source code, including code-quality dependent specification inaccuracy and poor scalability.

BLOCK [19] is a black-box approach to addressing state violation attacks by monitoring the interaction between the application and its users and blocks malicious web requests and responses that violate corresponding invariants. No-Tamper [4] is another black-box approach for detecting parameter tampering vulnerabilities in form processing functionalities of web applications by feeding both benign and malicious input into the application and observing their cor-

responding web responses. Our work addresses two major limitations within the above two existing works in securing the database access: 1) both of them don't take into account the persistent state information for inferring application logic, 2) both of them have limited capability of detecting and blocking attacks that target at the database integrity (e.g., modify or delete data object).

7.2 Database Security

Most database systems currently in use implement role-based access control mechanisms to regulate database accesses. However, when the database is connected to a web application, it cannot differentiate the end users who are actually operating the application and trusts all the queries issued by the application. Thus, if an attacker exploits the web application successfully, he/she can trick the application into sending malicious SQL queries, leading to a "confused deputy" problem [8].

7.2.1 Access Control

A straight-forward approach to addressing the above "confused deputy" problem is to identify the individual users that operate the web application and perform a fine-grained access control for each user. Roichman et al. [24] leverage parameterized views for user identification and implement access control at a finer granularity at the database layer. However, such a "user-based" approach depends on the adoption of parameterized views, which requires retrofitting the entire database system and all the schema. As an alternative approach, Felt et al. [15] propose Diesel to enforce privilege separation between different application modules. The "module-based" approach is only capable of confining the potential damages to a certain vulnerable module and cannot defend against the attacks that exploit the vulnerable module. Our approach neither relies on user identification nor fine-grained access control. Instead, we characterize the application state and data constraints when each SQL query is issued by the application. Our "state-based" approach requires minimal efforts, can be easily integrated with existing systems and effectively identify malicious SQL queries.

7.2.2 Intrusion Detection

Another approach is to build an intrusion detection system (IDS) for database systems. Lee et al. [18] build a signature-based IDS by learning a set of legitimate SQL query fingerprints from database transactions. While the set of fingerprints is exactly the same as the set of SQL signatures we extract from traces, we further associate each SQL signature with invariants to detect state violation attacks. Chung et al. [7], Kamra et al. [17] and Chen et al. [6] establish anomaly-based IDS by deriving user profiles of database accesses from audit logs, while Roichman et al. [25] rely on automatic user identification [24]. However, all of their systems face the same challenge of scaling up to handle a huge number of users. Instead, our approach characterizes the application behavior, not the individual user behavior. Thus, our approach is naturally scalable for handling a large population of users.

8. CONCLUSIONS

In this paper, we present a black-box approach for detecting malicious SQL queries that exploit logic flaws within web applications. We associate a set of invariants with SQL signatures as the application specification, which are inferred from observing the interactions between the application and the database. We use a set of vulnerable web applications for evaluation. The experiment results demonstrate the effectiveness of our approach. We show that very few false positives and acceptable performance overhead are introduced by SENTINEL. In the future, we would like to investigate the techniques for automatically verifying inferred invariants and further suppressing false positives.

9. ACKNOWLEDGMENTS

This work was supported by NSF TRUST (The Team for Research in Ubiquitous Secure Technology) Science and Technology Center (CCF-0424422).

10. REFERENCES

[1] AT&T website breach. http://www.acunetix.com/blog/web-security-zone/articles/analysis-php-attack-apple-information-disclosure/.

[2] D. Balzarotti, M. Cova, V. V. Felmetsger, and G. Vigna. Multi-module vulnerability analysis of web-based applications. In *CCS'07: Proceedings of the 14th ACM conference on Computer and communications security*, pages 25–35, 2007.

[3] S. Bandhakavi, P. Bisht, P. Madhusudan, and V. N. Venkatakrishnan. CANDID: preventing SQL injection attacks using dynamic candidate evaluations. In *CCS'07: Proceedings of the 14th ACM conference on Computer and communications security*, pages 12–24, 2007.

[4] P. Bisht, T. Hinrichs, N. Skrupsky, R. Bobrowicz, and V. N. Venkatakrishnan. NoTamper: automatic blackbox detection of parameter tampering opportunities in web applications. In *CCS'10: Proceedings of the 17th ACM conference on Computer and communications security*, pages 607–618, 2010.

[5] P. Bisht, T. Hinrichs, N. Skrupsky, and V. Venkatakrishnan. WAPTEC: Whitebox Analysis of Web Applications for Parameter Tampering Exploit Construction. In *CCS'11: Proceedings of the 18th ACM conference on Computer and communications security*, pages 575–586, 2011.

[6] Y. Chen and B. Malin. Detection of anomalous insiders in collaborative environments via relational analysis of access logs. In *CODASPY'11: Proceedings of the first ACM conference on Data and application security and privacy*, pages 63–74, 2011.

[7] C. Y. Chung, M. Gertz, and K. Levitt. DEMIDS: A Misuse Detection System for Database Systems. In *Proceedings of the Integrity and Internal Control in Information System*, pages 159–178, 1999.

[8] Confused Deputy Problem. http://en.wikipedia.org/wiki/confused_deputy_problem.

[9] Connection Pooling. http://en.wikipedia.org/wiki/connection_pool.

[10] M. Cova, D. Balzarotti, V. Felmetsger, and G. Vigna. Swaddler: An Approach for the Anomaly-based Detection of State Violations in Web Applications. In *RAID'07: Proceedings of the 10th International Symposium on Recent Advances in Intrusion Detection*, pages 63–86, 2007.

[11] A. Doupe, M. Cova, and G. Vigna. Why Johnny Can't Pentest: An Analysis of Black-box Web Vulnerability Scanners. In *DIMVA'10: Proceedings of the 7th Conference on Detection of Intrusions and Malware and Vulnerability Assessment*, pages 111–131, 2010.

[12] M. Ernst, J. Cockrell, W. Griswold, and D. Notkin. Dynamically Discovering Likely Program Invariants to Support Program Evolution. *IEEE Transactions on Software Engineering*, 27:99–123, 2001.

[13] Extended Finite State Machine. http://en.wikipedia.org/wiki/extended_finite-state_machine.

[14] V. Felmetsger, L. Cavedon, C. Kruegel, and G. Vigna. Toward Automated Detection of Logic Vulnerabilities in Web Applications. In *USENIX'10: Proceedings of the 19th conference on USENIX Security Symposium*, pages 143–160, 2010.

[15] A. Felt, M. Finifter, J. Weinberger, and D. Wagner. Diesel: Applying Privilege Separation to Database Access. In *ASIACCS'11: Proceedings of 6th ACM Symposium on Information, Computer and Communications Security*, pages 416–422, 2011.

[16] W. Halfond and A. Orso. AMNESIA: analysis and monitoring for NEutralizing SQL-injection attacks. In *ASE'05: Proceedings of the 20th IEEE/ACM international Conference on Automated software engineering*, pages 174–183, 2005.

[17] A. Kamra, E. Terzi, and E. Bertino. Detecting anomalous access patterns in relational databases. *The VLDB Journal*, 17:1063–1077, 2008.

[18] S. Y. Lee, W. L. Low, and P. Y. Wong. Learning Fingerprints for a Database Intrusion Detection System. In *ESORICS'02: Proceedings of 7th European Symposium on Research in Computer Security*, pages 264–280, 2002.

[19] X. Li and Y. Xue. BLOCK: A Black-box Approach for Detection of State Violation Attacks Towards Web Applications. In *ACSAC'11: Proceedings of 27th Annual Computer Security Applications Conference*, pages 247–256, 2011.

[20] D. Lorenzoli, L. Mariani, and M. Pezzè. Automatic generation of software behavioral models. In *ICSE'08:*

Proceedings of the 30th international conference on Software engineering, pages 501–510, 2008.

[21] OpenInvoice 0.9 beta. http://sourceforge.net/projects/openinv/.

[22] OpenIT. http://sourceforge.net/projects/openit/.

[23] Prepared Statement. http://php.net/manual/en/pdo.prepared-statements.php.

[24] A. Roichman and E. Gudes. Fine-grained access control to web databases. In *SACMAT'07: Proceedings of the 12th ACM symposium on Access control models and technologies*, pages 31–40, 2007.

[25] A. Roichman and E. Gudes. DIWeDa - Detecting Intrusions in Web Databases. In *Proceeedings of the 22nd annual IFIP WG 11.3 working conference on Data and Applications Security*, pages 313–329, 2008.

[26] SeleniumHQ: Web Application Testing System. http://seleniumhq.org/.

[27] F. Sun, L. Xu, and Z. Su. Static Detection of Access Control Vulnerabilities in Web Applications. In *USENIX'11: Proceedings of the 20th USENIX Security Symposium*, pages 11–11, 2011.

[28] F. Valeur, D. Mutz, and G. Vigna. A Learning-Based Approach to the Detection of SQL Attacks. In *DIMVA'05: Proceedings of the 2nd Conference on Detection of Intrusions and Malware and Vulnerability Assessment*, pages 123–140, 2005.

[29] Wackopicko. https://github.com/adamdoupe/wackopicko.

[30] Web Application Security Statistics. http://projects.webappsec.org/w/page/13246989/web applicationsecuritystatistics.

Stalking Online: on User Privacy in Social Networks

Yuhao Yang[†], Jonathan Lutes[†], Fengjun Li[†], Bo Luo[†], Peng Liu[‡]
† Department of EECS, The University of Kansas, Lawrence, KS, USA
‡ College of IST, The Pennsylvania State University, University Park, PA, USA
{yhyang, jonlutes, fli, bluo}@ku.edu; pliu@ist.psu.edu

ABSTRACT

With the extreme popularity of Web and online social networks, a large amount of personal information has been made available over the Internet. On the other hand, advances in information retrieval, data mining and knowledge discovery technologies have enabled users to efficiently satisfy their information needs over the Internet or from large-scale data sets. However, such technologies also help the adversaries such as web stalkers to discover private information about their victims from mass data.

In this paper, we study privacy-sensitive information that are accessible from the Web, and how these information could be utilized to discover personal identities. In the proposed scenario, an adversary is assumed to possess a small piece of "seed" information about a targeted user, and conduct extensive and intelligent search to identify the target over both the Web and an information repository collected from the Web. In particular, two types of attackers are modeled, namely *tireless attackers* and *resourceful attackers*. We then analyze detailed attacking mechanisms that could be performed by these attackers, and quantify the threats of both types of attacks to general Web users. With extensive experiments and sophisticated analysis, we show that a large portion of users with online presence are highly identifiable, even when only a small piece of (possibly inaccurate) seed information is known to the attackers.

Categories and Subject Descriptors

K.6.5 [**Management of Computing and Information systems**]: Security and Protection; K.4.1 [**Computers and Society**]: Public Policy Issues—*Privacy*

General Terms

Security, Experimentation, Measurement

Keywords

Web, social networks, privacy, attacks

1. INTRODUCTION

The Internet has changed the ways we publish, search and consume information. Even with the static web, a huge amount of personal-related content has been made available online. More recently, various types of online social network (OSN) products have been introduced to the Internet, which further promotes the sharing of personal information. In addition to the great commercial success and social impacts of the OSNs, they also brought new challenges to the research community (e.g., [12, 27, 24]). With enormous number of users and tremendous amount of personal information available over various online social networks, it is critical to ensure that user privacy is well preserved. However, although many researchers have been working on extracting information or learning knowledge from online social networks, very little research effort has been put so far into the study of security and privacy issues until very recently [2, 42, 28, 15, 44, 40, 17, 16, 43, 32].

In online social networks, users voluntarily share personal information within the community under some implicit assumptions that: (1)these information is only accessible to the targeted readers; (2) one's true identity cannot be discovered if he/she only provides limited/incomplete profile information (e.g. an email address and a phone number); (3) a small amount of information is not significant and the disclosure will not hurt one's privacy; and (4) it is very difficult, if not impossible, to collect and link pieces of information scattered over various online social networks or data sets, and associate them to one's real identity. Unfortunately, these assumptions are proven to be either false or at least questionable, in both research literatures and news reports. Several types of privacy attacks in social networks have been proposed, such as the structural re-identification attacks [2, 42, 28, 15, 44, 40], the inference attacks [17, 16, 43], the information aggregation attacks [32, 25], and the traditional attribute re-identification attacks [19, 14]. Although different types of attacks and countermeasures have been proposed in recent literature, only a few of them have been well tested on real data. Moreover, most of the attacks and corresponding protection mechanisms are based on the graph topologies of social networks. Privacy attacks that focus on the attributes are not well studied.

Personal information is scattered over various sources, including online social networks and the general Web. We believe a thorough understanding of the nature of how these information are distributed and retrievable is the key to an effectively defense. This paper takes a first step towards studying private information online, especially the online social networks data. In this paper, we intensively examine the vulnerability of private information in online sources as well as the validity of different types of attribute-based privacy attacks. In particular, we define two types of attackers, *resourceful attacker* and *tireless attacker*, based on their different attack capabilities and strategies. Both types of attackers obtain small amounts of information about their targets, known as seed attributes, from external sources and launch advanced re-identification attacks. The seed information could be non-identifiable attributes, such as names of schools where the target gets degrees. A resourceful attacker is capable of retrieving a large amount of personal information about potential targets from online social network sites and creating his/her own resource database, and re-identifies the target by checking the seed attributes against his/her resource database. On the other hand, a tireless attacker only submits such attributes to search engines, and tirelessly browses and studies the results for clues. We have simulated both types of attacks on our database, with 3 million records collected from an online social network and a phonebook data set, to check their reality and severeness. From the results, we can see that large portions of users with online presence are identifiable even with a small piece of seed information, where the seed information could be inaccurate. Our simulation also shows that it does not require extensive resources or efforts to successfully conduct attributed-based attacks to hurt user's privacy online.

2. RELATED WORKS

In online social networks, users are sometimes either oblivious about their privacy, or concerned but underestimate the privacy risks. Surveys and general discussions on social network privacy and security could be found at [21, 5, 41]. In this paper, we are interested in the nature of user identity and personal information that are voluntarily released to social networks, and how such information could be valuable to attackers. Along this thrust, four types of privacy threats have been discovered in the literature: (1) an individual information item (e.g. an identifiable profile image) may be accessed by adversaries; (2) information items of the same user may be collected from different sources, and aggregated to reveal user privacy; (3) values of hidden information items may be inferred from public information items; and (4) user identities could be recovered from anonymized data sets. We briefly cover them below.

2.1 Private information disclosure

Users give out information to trusted social network community. They also implicitly assume that their information would stay within the community. Unfortunately, this assumption is not always valid. For instance, messages sent to an email-based social network may be archived at a repository and accessible to the open public [11], stalkers may follow people through social networks [9], gadgets and add-ons may access users' profiles [20], code errors reveal user profiles [3], etc. To further understand how people value their secrets and the patterns of information revelation, researches on user behavior study, user education, or policy/legal issues have been proposed [19, 14, 4]. For instance, [19] shows that people value their privacy based on context – i.e., the desirability of the traits in a target group. In this sense, people may be willing to publicize private information if they feel they are "somewhat typical or positively atypical compared

to the target group" [19]. Meanwhile, a study of the Facebook users within the CMU student community shows that, about 80% of the users adopt identifiable or semi-identifiable images in their profile, and less than 2% of the users made use of the privacy settings [14]. In [29, 30], authors proposed a framework that assesses potential privacy risks to a privacy score, which is computed from the sensitivity of the disclosed information and the visibility of such information. Finally, [23] shows that online social networks and applications leak users' personally identifiable information to third parties. In a position paper [37], the author identifies an attack that uses Sybil nodes and search functions to discover hidden social relationships in LinkedIn.

2.2 Information aggregation

When people participate in online social networks, they voluntarily release different types of personal information: name, screen name, telephone numbers, email addresses, locations, etc. Moreover, when users post messages in forums, blogs, and bulletin boards, they also disclose small pieces of private information. However, with the development of information retrieval techniques, adversaries could collect pieces of such personal information of the targeted user [32]. Though a single piece of such information may be harmless, it discloses a significant amount of private information when associated with other pieces of information. Moreover, adversaries could use evidences such as identical email addresses, screen names, similar posts, and attribute/structural re-identification attacks to bridge profiles across different social networks [32, 25]. Particularly, [38, 13, 25] have shown that people are highly identifiable with very little information, which make cross-network aggregations quite feasible. In all cases of information aggregation attacks, private information of the same user from multiple resources is aggregated and severely hurts user privacy.

2.3 Inference attacks

Aside from voluntary disclosure of explicit personal information, [17, 16, 43] study a type of indirect private information inference through social relations. [17, 16] notice that hidden attributes could be inferred from friends' attributes using a Bayesian network. They study the factors that impact inference accuracy, and suggest that selectively hiding social connections or friends' attributes could help preserve privacy. More recently, [43] also focuses on social networks with mixed public and private user profiles. They found that both friendship links and group membership information could be used to infer sensitive hidden attributes. For instance, membership of a local engineer society discloses location information of the user.

2.4 Privacy Threats in Published Social Network Data

When social network data sets are published for various legitimate reasons, user identity and some profile information are often removed to protect the user privacy. Some of the well-known techniques for this purpose includes *k-anonymity* [39, 1], *l-diversity* [33] and *t-closeness* [26]. For instance, in a k-anonymized data set, an individual cannot be distinguished by attributes from other k-1 records. Possibilities of attribute re-identification attacks on publicly available data sets have been studied in [38, 13, 25]. More recently, in [7] authors introduce an attribute-based anonymization method for social network data.

On the other hand, due to the nature of social network data, just anonymizing node attributes is not enough. Graph structure contains significant amount of information which could be utilized to hurt user privacy, i.e. structural re-identification attacks. A good survey on structural anonymization and re-identification attacks could be found at [45]. Notably, [2] first identified the problem that although quasi-identifiers are removed before publishing, node identities could be inferred through graph structure. They show that node identities are vulnerable to both passive and active attacks. In [35], authors introduce a new metric, namely *topological anonymity*, to quantify the level of anonymity using the topology properties of network graph. [44] introduces neighborhood attacks, in which an adversary knows the neighborhood subgraph of the target, and tries to re-identify the user from an anonymized network graph. They propose an approach to further anonymize vertexes by modifying edges to construct isomorphic neighborhoods. In [28], authors define *k-degree anonymity*: in a *k*-degree anonymized graph, each node has the same degree with at least *k* other nodes. They also efficiently propose *k*-degree anonymize graphs with minimal edge additions and deletions. Moreover, [15] models three types of adversary knowledge that could be used to re-identify vertexes from an anonymized social network graph. They tackle the problem through graph generalization – dividing the graph into partitions and publishing summarized partition-level data. *K*-Automorphism is introduced in [46] to defend against multiple attacks. In [18], authors propose a graph anonymization approach that maximally preserves original graph structure and statistical features. Finally, [31] considers social network as a weighted graph, in which edge labels are also considered to be sensitive. They propose to protect sensitive edge labels while keep certain global features of the graph.

3. INFORMATION, VULNERABILITIES AND ATTACKS

3.1 Information and Vulnerabilities

With the Internet explosion, huge amounts of information have been made online. Moreover, advances in information retrieval techniques and Web search engines have enabled easy access to such information. However, large amount of personal information is also exposed to public, not always with the consent of the information owner. In particular, we believe there are three primary channels for personal information disclosure:

Personal information on the general web. In the Web 1.0 era, especially in the early days, personal homepages sometimes contain large amount of personal information. Such information is usually published by owners who are somewhat familiar with the Web. They usually understand the risks better than the novices, hence, the contents may be carefully tailored to protect privacy. On the other hand, some personal information maybe published in sources such as news, employee directories, etc. Overall, this channel is better administered although sensitive information could be disclosed by careless users.

Digitalized public records. With governmental and in-dustrial efforts, a large amount of public records (e.g. phone books) have been digitalized and made available online. Many of them are indexed by commercial search engines, while others require a minimum subscription fee for full access – the barrier is usually low for an adversary to query or even collect the entire databases. Some public information could be highly personal (e.g. salaries of faculty members in public universities).

Online social networks. As online social networks get extremely popular, they become gold mine for adversaries. Large volume of personal information have been collected at social network sites for socialization, career development, and other purposes. As shown in [14], most social network users are poorly protected and their personal information is highly accessible. In this way, social network users may be very vulnerable.

All types of information summarized above are accessible to adversaries, who strive to collect personal information about the targeted users. From the adversaries' perspective, user information could be categorized as (i) private information, (ii) identifiable information, and (iii) non-identifiable information. In the literature, a lot of work has been done on the risks associated with (i) and (ii), and on preventing (i) private information from been disclosed to the Internet. However, seed information obtained by the adversary (from offline) is not always identifiable, hence, the attacker's first objective is to discover the true identity of the target (i.e. from category iii to ii).

3.2 Attacker Models

In this work, we define and simulate two types of attackers, *resourceful attackers* and *tireless attackers*, with different attacking capabilities and strategies.

Resourceful attacker: a *resourceful attacker* is assumed to have enough resource (bandwidth, storage, technique, etc) to construct his/her own database by collecting information from the Web. The database could be constructed in three ways: (1) crawling the general web, extracting personal information from web pages, and storing the data in a local database; (2) implementing a focused crawler to collect data from online public record datasets; (3) crawling online social networks, or downloading research data sets published by social network sites.

In the information retrieval community, many work has been done for entity extraction from the "surface Web", e.g. [6]. However, to populate a local database requires intensive crawling of a significant portion of the surface web, which is very time-consuming. Comparably, collecting information from public records and online social network user profiles is more feasible since the information has been concentrated on such websites. Moreover, considering the user data are usually published in well-structured templates, resourceful attackers can easily implement niche parsers to extract structured personal information. One practical obstacle could be the restriction for massive crawling, which usually violates the terms of use for most online social networks. However, with technical assists, e.g. anonymous routing [8], such crawling is very doable and hard to detect. As such, it is reasonable for us to assume a resourceful attacker has certain technical capability to crawl from typical online data sources.

With the collected databases, resourceful attackers compare his/her external knowledge about the target with information in the database, and search for candidate records for further examination. Meanwhile, if the target is identified from one database, it becomes trivial to use the discovered identity to retrieve more information from other databases. A real-world example for cross-database attacks is given in [25]. The example in [25] is a manually executed attack, but the risk is valid when a resourceful attacker possesses multiple overlapping databases.

Tireless attacker: a *tireless attacker* does not have the resources or techniques to create and maintain a local database. As a compensation, a tireless attacker devotes more time and labor in the attacking process to maximize the chance of success. In particular, a tireless attacker knows some of the attributes of his/her target (seed attributes), and submits such attributes to search engines, and tirelessly browsing and examining the results for clues. Due to the size of the Web, the results returned from search engines are mostly noise, and the attacker needs to be very patient to discover any useful information. The chance of success highly depends on the amount of information provided by the seed attributes. For instance, if the attacker knows that the target get a Bachelor's degree from a large public university and nothing else, it is very unlikely to identify the target in tireless attack. However, if the attacker knows the first name of the target, and the fact that he/she gets a Ph.D. from a small university, the attacker is more likely to discover the true identity (full name) and more personal information of the target.

Meanwhile, a tireless attacker also tries to search or browse in social networks, public records, etc. Furthermore, besides the "brute-force" attack, a tireless attacker can get "smarter" by constructing advanced queries with his/her knowledge about the attacker. For instance, if the attacker knows that the target is currently employed at a university, it is more likely that the target's information will be discovered from webpages within the domain of the university. This type of "advanced search" functions are provided by all major search engines.

4. RESOURCEFUL ATTACKERS

In this section, we focus on two types of privacy attacks (i.e. the re-identification attack and the cross-database aggregation attack) conducted by a resourceful attacker, who is capable of maintaining a private database of a large volume of publicly available online user profiles. In our study, we simulate the power of the resourceful attackers by crawling user data from two publicly available resources, a social networking site and an online phone book data repository, and study the feasibility, difficulty, and the success rate of resourceful attacks with different types of seed attributes.

4.1 Data Collection

To implement a proof-of-concept attacking mechanism, we design niche crawlers to collect data from two resources to simulate the proposed resourceful attacker.

4.1.1 Collecting data from LinkedIn

LinkedIn[1] is a professional online social networking site that provides open access to detailed identifying user profiles. We implemented a specialized crawler to retrieve data

---

[1]http://www.linkedin.com

Table 1: Seed attributes in the resource database created by a resourceful attacker.

Name		Work		Education	
FN	first name	TI	title	S	school name
LN	last name	AF	affiliation	D	degree
		IND	industry	ST	start time
		LO	location	ET	end time
				T	time period

Table 2: Approximate information on attributes.

Attribute	Approximation	Notation
name	initials	$N.in$
school	state	$S.st$
	region	$S.re$
	country	$S.ct$
	continent	$S.cn$

based on the public index of LinkedIn.com, using methods and technologies that are available to any potential resourceful attacker. We collected approximately 9 million (8,943,014) user profiles in total in 10 months. The crawled html profiles are indexed alphabetically by the last name of profile owners and stored in a MySQL database for further offline processing, which includes two major procedures, *data extraction* and *data cleaning*.

Data extraction: The LinkedIn profile contains rich information about one's educational history that is useful in identifying a target. However, the raw data are in html profiles, which need to be extracted to reconstruct corresponding records in the resource database. We implemented a specialized parser to do that. Currently, our parser only extracts data from three fields *name*, *work* and *education* fields, which contain the most useful information for re-identification. In the future, we consider to extend our parser to include more fields such as working experiences. Data from the three fields are further processed and categorized into 11 **seed attributes**, as shown in Table 1. For instance, data in *name* field are segmented as first, middle and last names. Data in *work* field are decomposed to *current title*, *affiliation* (e.g. Software Engineer at XYZ company), *industry* type (e.g. Internet, Higher Education, Research), and current *location* (e.g. San Francisco Bay Area). Similarly, *school name*, *degree* earned, *major*, degree *starting time* and *ending time*, and the entire degree *time period* are extracted from *education* field. Please note that one profile may have multiple education records. Also, not all the profiles contain education information. In some profiles, the education field is either left blank or hidden from non-registered LinkedIn users.

To simulate the attacks where the attacker only had approximate information about the target, we consider two common scenarios. In the first case, the attacker only knows the initial of the target, and in the second case, the attacker only know the approximate location of the school that the target has attended. Therefore, we added four new attributes to our seed attribute table, as shown in Table 2. After cross-checking with the school reference lists, we have successfully added country and continent information to all schools and state information to all the US schools, for 80% of the records.

Data cleaning: The collected data may have redundant or ambiguous contents, which makes data cleaning operations important in data collection. Some of the ambiguity is caused by inaccurate or wrong inputs of careless users, for instance, a user mistakenly includes department name or year of graduation as part of school name. A more common problem resulting in redundant content is that many universities are referred by different names. For example, we noticed University of Cambridge is referred as Cambridge University instead of its formal name in some profiles. We corrected this problem by cross-checking with the school reference lists that contain formal forms for most of the schools. After a quick browsing of the data, we created manually coded heuristic rules to map most of the school names to their formal forms, and removed all the redundant elements and special characters [2].

Another important processing we took in data cleaning is to set aside the schools with less than 3 attendees, which we think are highly likely to be invalid or mistaken entries (proved by later manual check). After all the operations, we successfully obtained about 2,466,721 clean profiles, with 3,417,550 clean education records.

4.1.2 Collecting data from online phone books

Many data sets with private personal information are now publicly available for commercial or administration purposes. Such information is open to public, unless data owners explicitly opt out. Residential phone book data is such a resource, which has been made online through various sources. All the online phone book sites list phone numbers and residential locations for free access. For the registered users, more detailed residential information are also available. Moreover, a few of online phone books even show the names and addresses of the holders as unlisted phone book entries, for instance, while the phone numbers are hidden, the owners' info is displayed on http://www.phonesbook.com.

We assume the resourceful attackers are capable of retrieving all types of online data to enrich their resource databases. Therefore, we crawled residential phone book entries for three regions, two college towns and one state capital city[3], from an online phone book data repository to simulate attackers' knowledge in this category.

After creating his own resource database, the resourceful attacker is capable of launching two types of attacks, the *re-identification attack* and the *cross-network attack*.

4.2 Re-identification attacks

The re-identification attack is to explore the identity (and/or other information-of-interest) of the target by linking or matching the known information about the target to the data in the resource database. In this section, we first simulate a number of re-identification attacks over the crawled LinkedIn data to assess the risk of re-identification attack against profile data that users voluntarily submitted to online social networks. Then, we employ an information theory based approach to theoretically estimate the re-identification risk.

---

[2]Due to lack of referencing lists for high schools and lower level schools, we have to remove all education records at high school level or lower.

[3]City names are anonymized as required by double-blind review policy.

4.2.1 Re-identification attack model

To launch a re-identification attack, the attacker needs to know some information about the target. It is assumed that the attacker obtains such knowledge from external resources. When the attacker obtains offline information about the target, he expresses this knowledge in the form of *seed attributes* that he collects for the resource database.

The attacker's knowledge about each target varies. In some cases, the attacker knows only one seed attribute about the target, e.g. "John has a bachelor's degree". In other cases, the attacker may know more about the target, which can be interpreted as multiple seed attributes, e.g. "John graduated from college in 2004". Sometimes, the knowledge about the target is not accurate. For example, the attacker may only know that "John graduated from a school in Midwest". Since the inaccuracy in the name and school location fields are addressed by the new approximate attributes in Table 2, we can simulate certain inaccurate inputs in attacker's knowledge. For instance, the attacker may know that: "John graduated from a school in Midwest", which indicates Attribute $SchoolRegion = "Midwest"$.

Therefore, we model the attacker's knowledge about a target as an identity-attribute tuple $<I, v_1,..., v_t>$, where I is the identity of the target, and $\{v_1,...,v_t\}$ are the values of the known seed attributes $\{A_1,...,A_t\}$. For instance, the attacker's knowledge "John graduated from college in 2004" can be expressed as:

$$\begin{aligned} Identity: \quad & I = John \\ Attribute \; FirstName: \quad & v_1 = "John" \\ Attribute \; EndTime: \quad & v_2 = "2004" \end{aligned}$$

In the defined resourceful attack model, to re-identify the target, the attacker needs to send the known identity-attribute tuple into the resource database that is built upon the data retrieved from online sources. The severeness of such re-identification attack highly depends on the completeness and identifiability of the records in the resource database. Therefore, the first-step approach towards assessing the risk of such re-identification attack is to study the resource database. In particular, we explore the *identifiability* of the crawled LinkedIn user profiles in our simulated resource database to assess the re-identification risk.

4.2.2 Assessing risk with profile identifiability

The resource database and the seed information are two key components for a successful re-identification. Consider a resource database $\mathbb{D}$ with n records, where each record is associated with one identity. To an attacker, the ideal case for the resource database is that it is large enough to contain records of all the targets and each record contains all information about the target. The ideal case for the seed information is that it is accurate and adequate to distinguish the target from records of others in the database. However, it is very difficult, if not impossible, to meet both conditions in real-world cases. Therefore, for a resourceful attacker, it is important to measure the identifiability of the records in the resource database $\mathbb{D}$.

Definition 1. For a database $\mathbb{D}$ whose scheme is $\mathbb{D}(A_1, ..., A_t)$, we define the **identifiability of a target T in $\mathbb{D}$** as $I_T^{\{v_1,...,v_r\}} = k$, if T cannot be distinguished from other $k-1$ profiles with known seed attributes $\{attr_1,...,attr_r\} = \{v_1,...,v_r\}$, where $r \leq t$.

This definition is similar to the *k-anonymity* concept of privacy in data publishing, but interpreted from the attacker's perspective. For each target whose record is in $\mathbb{D}$, given any adequate and accurate seed information $\{v_1, v_2, ..., v_t\}$, his/her identifiability should be 1, which means he/she is uniquely identified. Typically, since the attacker's seed information is limited, the identifiability of a target, k, is much larger than 1. However, for the attacker, the size of potential profile set (that may contain the target) under this definition is successfully decreased from n to k.

To assess the **identifiability of** $\mathbb{D}$, we further count n_{k-}, which is the number of profiles that cannot be identified from at most k other profiles given seed information $\{attr_1, ..., attr_r\}$. In other words, for every possible value set $\{v_1, ..., v_r\}$ in the seed attribute tuple space $\mathbb{R}^r$,

$$n_{k-} = sum(I_T^{\{v_1,...,v_r\}}), \quad for \quad I_T^{\{v_1,...,v_r\}} < k.$$

Then, we calculate k-or-less proportion $p(k)$ as an indicator of the identifiability of $\mathbb{D}$, where

$$p(k) = \frac{n_{k-}}{n}, \quad for \quad k \in [1, max(k)],$$

and $max(k)$ is the largest k for all possible values of seed attribute tuple $\{attr_1, ..., attr_r\}$.

Next, we select several seed attribute tuples, and assess the identifiability of the resource database with crawled LinkedIn data. First, we simulate the scenario where the attacker only knows a single seed attribute value about the target. Then we measured the k-or-less proportion $p(k)$ for each seed attribute in Table 1. The results of three seed attributes, first name FN, work location LO, and school name S, are shown in Figure 1(a). In the figure, a slowly growing curve indicates better anonymity, since less people are identifiable among smaller sets. As we can see from the figure, users' identifiability shows different patterns for different attribute. Overall, when the adversary only knows one attribute, most people cannot be identified among a relatively large set.

Then, we consider the scenario in which a weaker attacker only knows approximate values of the attributes, as summarized in Table 2. Some of the results are shown in Figure 1(b), when the attacker knows (i) the first and last initials ($N.in$) of the target, but not the name, e.g. the attacker knows "JD", not "John Doe", or (ii) the region where the target goes to school ($S.re$), e.g., "the person went to school in West coast". As we have expected, knowing approximate values on an attribute usually gives the adversary very limited information.

The third type of scenarios that we examine is that the resourceful attacker knows multiple attributes about the target. Figure 1(c) shows the population vs. k-anonymity curves when the resourceful attacker knows (i) first name and affiliation: $<FN, AF>$, e.g. "John works at XYZ company"; (ii) school name and starting time: $<S, ST>$, e.g. "the person went to Stanford in 2001"; and (iii) first name, work location and school name $<FN, LO, S>$, e.g. "John went to Berkeley, and now works at New York". Note that the k axis is scaled to $[1, 100]$. As we can see from the figure, users become very vulnerable when the adversary knows multiple seed attributes.

We also consider the case where the adversary knows approximate information on multiple attributes. The rightmost figure in Figure 2(b) shows the population vs. k-anonymity curve when the attacker knows the states in which

Table 3: Information gain (IG) by knowing a single seed attribute with precise values.

Category	Attribute	IG (bit)
Name	FN	13.348
	LN	16.461
Work	TI	14.433
	AF	12.979
	IND	6.405
	LO	8.011
Education	S	11.8231
	D	1.8336
	ST	5.149
	ET	5.026
	T	7.537

the target goes to school (given that the target goes to at least two schools), e.g. "the person went to school in California and Massachusetts". Obviously, the database is less identifiable under approximate seed information.

4.2.3 Assessing risk using information gain

To quantify the *amount of information* provided by an attribute, we further analyze the problem from a information theory perspective. In our scenario, the goal of the attacker is to identify the particular record which corresponds to the target. Without any prior knowledge, all the records are equally likely to be the target. Hence, to achieve the goal, the average amount of information that the attacker needs to collect (i.e. adversary's expected information gain) is denoted as:

$$E(I(X)) = H(X) = -\log_2 \frac{1}{N}$$

where N is the number of records in the database. In our simulation, $E(I(X)) = 21.23$(bits), i.e. on average, the attacker needs to obtain *21.23 bits* of information in order to identify a target from our database.

When the attacker knows the value v of attribute $attr$, the conditional entropy is denoted as:

$$H(X|attr = v) = -\log_2 \frac{1}{N_{attr=v}}$$

where $N_{attr=v}$ is the number of records that satisfy the condition **attr=v**. On average, the information gain of knowing attribute A is denoted as:

$$\begin{aligned} I(X; A) &= H(X) - H(X|A) \\ &= H(X) - \sum_{v \in V_A} p(A = v)H(X|A = v) \end{aligned}$$

where $H(X|A)$ is the conditional entropy of knowing attribute A. In our settings, an information gain of m bits indicates that the attacker has successfully discovered that the target is among $\frac{N}{2^m} = \frac{2,466,721}{2^m}$ records, on average. In additions, the attacker will need to further obtain $21.23 - m$ bits of information in order to exactly identify the target. Most importantly, if we assume that our data set is a random sample of the general population, attackers' information gain will be the same if he obtains the same attribute in the general population. In that case, $H(X)$ and $H(X|A)$ increases proportionally, while $I(X; A)$ will remain the same (statistically).

(a) Measured k-or-less proportion $p(k)$ using seed attribute tuple with precise values.

seed attribute: first name FN seed attribute: work location LO seed attribute: school S

(b) Measured k-or-less proportion $p(k)$ using seed attribute with approximate values.

seed attribute: initial $N.in$ seed attribute: state $S.st$ seed attribute tuple: $<S.st, S.st>$

(c) Measured k-or-less proportion $p(k)$ using seed attribute tuple with precise values.

seed attribute tuple: $<FN, AF>$ seed attribute tuple: $<S, ST>$ seed attribute tuple: $<FN, LO, S>$

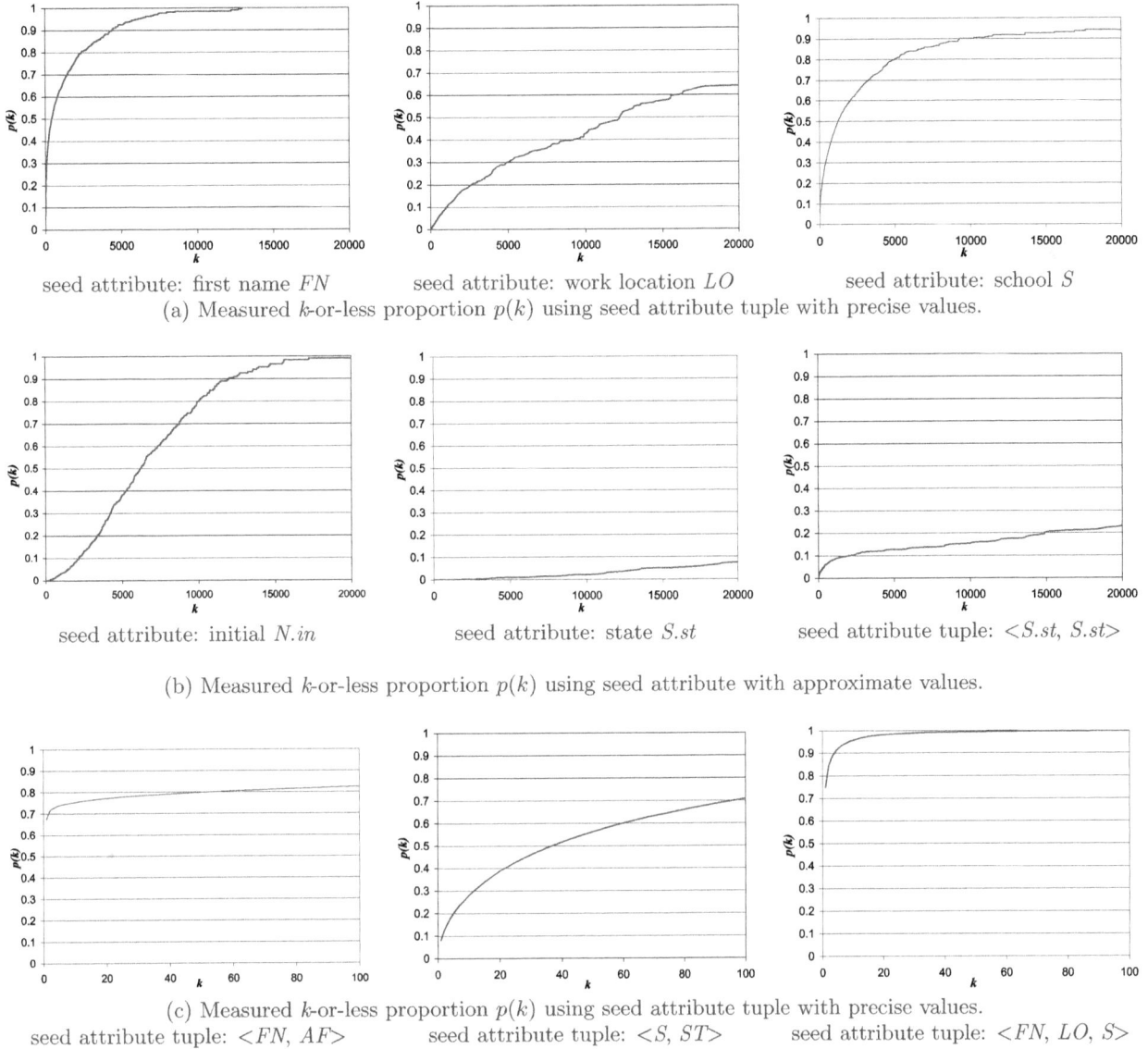

Figure 1: Estimate the risk of *resourceful attacks*.

In Table 3, we show the information gain of the attacker when he/she knows one seed attribute. As we expected, the last name carries the largest amount of information, while first name and school name also carries significant amount of information. However, knowing one attribute alone is not enough for the attacker to identify the target, or to narrow down to a very manageable range. Attribute ln is somehow an exception, which on average narrows the search to less than 30 candidates (i.e. $H(X|A) = 4.77 bit$). When the attacker only know approximate information on an attribute, the information he/she learns from the knowledge is even less, as shown in Table 4.

In the scenario that the attacker knows multiple attributes, the information gain is denoted as:

$$I(X; A_1 A_2) = H(X) - H(X|A_1 A_2)$$

When two attributes A_1 and A_2 are independent, we should

Table 4: Information gain (IG) by knowing seed attribute with approximate values.

Attribute	IG (bit)	Attribute	IG (bit)
$N.in$	8.807	$S.st$	4.795
$S.re$	2.360	$S.ct$	1.853
$S.cn$	1.328		

have:

$$\begin{aligned} I(X; A_1 A_2) &= H(X) - H(X|A_1 A_2) \\ &= H(X) - H(X|A_1) - H(X|A_2) \end{aligned}$$

Table 5 shows the information gain when the attacker knows multiple attributes.

4.3 Cross-database aggregation

As we have introduced, a resourceful attacker is capable of collecting multiple databases from different sources. When

Table 5: Information gain (IG) by knowing multiple seed attributes.

Attributes	IG (bit)	Attributes	IG (bit)
$<FN, S>$	20.316	$<S, ST, ET>$	16.549
$<FN, S.st>$	15.068	$<FN, S.ct>$	12.848
$<FN, ST>$	16.092	$<FN, ST, ET>$	17.362
$<FN, ET>$	15.679	$<D, ST, ET>$	5.685

the attacker identifies the target (i.e. discovers the full name of the target) from one of the databases, it becomes trivial to retrieve relevant records from other databases to learn more about the target.

In our experiments, we simulate cross-database aggregation attack by matching LinkedIn data with online phone book data. We have crawled phone book data for three cities: two college towns and a state capital city. We try to link records from both databases by matching full names. The results are shown in Figure 2. As we can see, approximately 20% of the LinkedIn users from town A could be identified in phone book, while 14% and 14% of the LinkedIn users from town B and town C are re-identified, respectively. According to the literature [25, 13], with known full name and location information, people are very identifiable. We are confident that most of the linked records are true positives (i.e., the two linked records reflect one unique offline identity). For linked records, the attacker will further learn the home address and phone number of the user. In many cases, the attacker also learns the names of the family members of the user.

In cross-database aggregation attacks, when a resourceful attacker identifies a target using attribute-reidentification attacks on one of his databases, it is likely that he can learn more information about the target. In our experiments, we only collected information about users whose phone numbers are listed. As we have mentioned, there are websites (e.g. http://www.phonesbook.com/) that publish addresses of users who opt to exclude their information from the phone book. From our observation, this websites contains 20% more user records than the phone book data set we crawled. Meanwhile, with a small fee, the attacker could subscribe to various databases that collect personal information from public and commercial records. Therefore, a resourceful attacker has great potential to become more powerful than we have demonstrated in this work.

We can also see that the phonebook size is much larger in state capital C, which shows that a relatively larger population who do not have LinkedIn accounts (or configured their accounts as private), but are still visible in the phone book. In this case, although these users are not actively releasing their information online, or are successfully protecting their online identities, unfortunately, their personal information is still accessible from online sources.

5. TIRELESS ATTACKERS

5.1 Tireless Attackers

Tireless attackers do not possess a local database of personal information, as a compensation, they devote their time and energy. In our simulation, the tireless attacker knows some (non-identifiable) attributes about the target. The attacker queries a Web search engine (we use Google in our

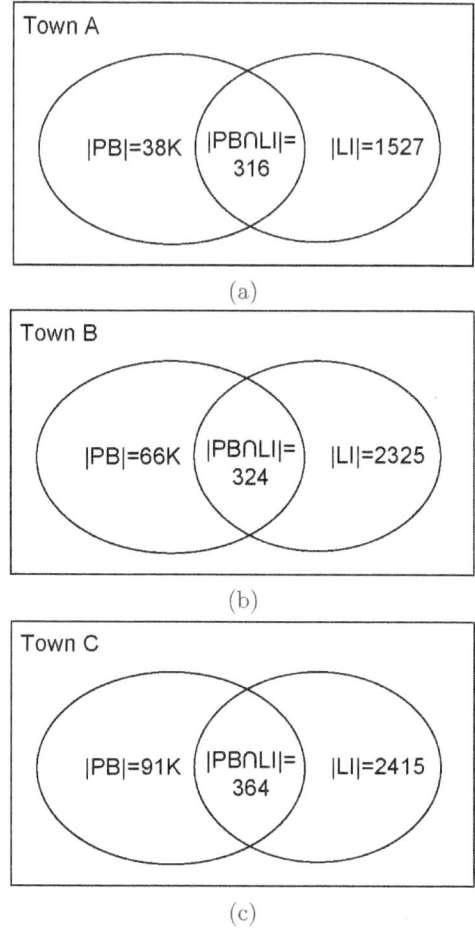

(a)

(b)

(c)

Figure 2: Cross-database aggregation for three cities.

experiments) with the known attributes, and examines the results returned by the search engine for any clue.

To simulate tireless attacks, we have randomly sampled 50,000 users from education and healthcare industry, including faculty, students, researchers, doctors, etc. We simulated tireless attacks on different combinations of known attributes. In Figure 3, we show the success rate when the tireless attacker knows the target's: (1) first name and the name of last school that the target attended $<FN, S>$; (2) last name and school $<LN, S>$; (3) first name and current affiliation $<FN, AF>$; (4) last name and current affiliation $<LN, AF>$; (5) names of two schools, knowing that the target has attended two or more schools $<S, S>$; and (6) school name, degree and year of graduation $<S, D, ET>$. When the full name of the target was discovered in a returned web page in the form of "John Doe" or "Doe, John", we treat the result as *positive*. An attack is successful when at least one positive result is found in the top 200 results returned from the search engine. Please note that in tireless attacks, we exclude all the results from LinkedIn, i.e., an attack is successful only if the target is re-identified from non-LinkedIn sources.

Figure 4 and Figure 5 give more insights on tireless attacks. Figure 4(a) shows a histogram of the number of positive results for successful attacks when the attacker knows

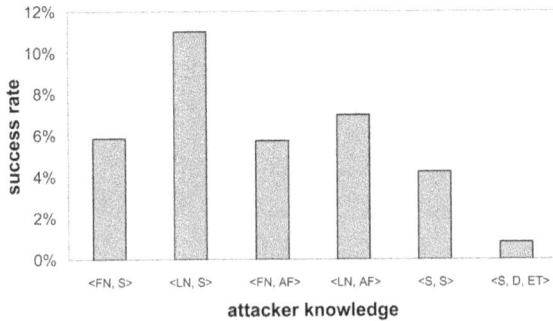

Figure 3: Success rate of tireless attackers.

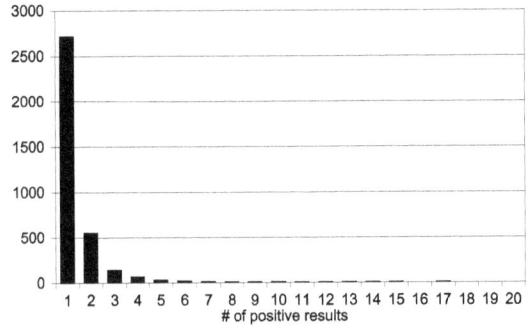

(a) Number of positive results in each successful attack.

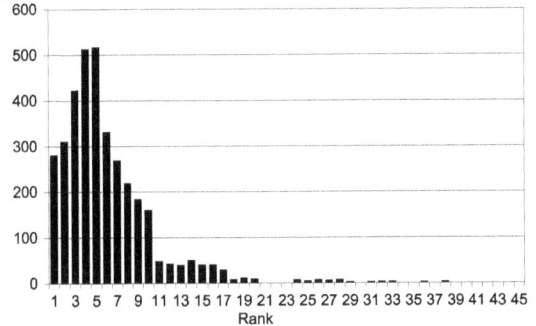

(b) Rank of the first positive result in each successful attack.

Figure 4: Results of successful *tireless attacks* with seed attribute tuple $<FN, AF>$.

the first name and affiliation of the target $<FN, AF>$. Figure 5(a) shows the same histogram for $<FN, S>$ case. We do observe a significant portion of targets who have been re-identified from multiple websites (excluding LinkedIn). Meanwhile, no victim has been re-identified from more than 20 websites. Figure 4(b) and Figure 5(b) show a histogram of the rank of the first positive result for successful attacks of the $<FN, AF>$ and $<FN, S>$ cases, respectively. We observe that most of the positive results came from top 10 results, which indicates that a tireless attacker does not need to be very "tireless" to achieve a successful attack. On the other hand, we also observe that positive results do not always come in top 2 search results.

To further validate the successful attacks, we have manually checked 200 randomly-sampled positive results for each type of attacks. We have discovered that around 70% of them were true positives that also contain further personal information about the target. Meanwhile, we do have some false negatives. For instance, in the $<LN, AF>$ attack, we have found a few pages of conference program committee members. They contain the name of the school, and a person with exactly the same name as the target, but affiliated with a different school or organization. Another major category of false positive appears when the name "Doe, John" is discovered in the context of "Jay *Doe, John* Smith".

Last but not least, when the targets are identified in tireless attacks, we continue the attack by issuing new queries using their identity (i.e. full name) and known attributes. For most of the cases, we can easily discover more sources (again, excluding LinkedIn) that contains further information about the target. A major reason is that we use the LinkedIn user profiles from education and healthcare domains as seeds, and such users are more active on the Internet.

5.2 Smart Tireless Attackers

Regular tireless attackers use a simple textual combination of all the known attributes as the query to be sent to search engines. However, existing web search engines support not only free text queries, but also advanced queries (e.g. Google Advanced Search[4]). Tireless attackers can get smarter by utilizing such functions. In our simulation, when the tireless attacker knows the affiliation of the target (e.g. this person works at XYZ University), it is highly likely that information about the target could be found in the employers' domain (e.g. xyz.edu). A smart attacker first queries

_____
[4]http://www.google.com/advanced_search

the search engine (e.g. Q="XYZ university") to get the official website of the employer, which is usually included in the top 3 returned results. The attacker then issues an advanced query, which contains textual terms and a domain constrain. The textual terms include the other known attributes about the target (e.g. first name "John"), while the domain constrain forces to search within the employer's domain (e.g. "site:xyz.edu").

We simulate smart tireless attacks for the case with seed attribute tuple $<FN, AF>$ (i.e., the attacker knows the first name and current affiliation of the target). We have simulated attacks for 10,000 users, randomly sampled from the 50,000 records that we used for regular tireless attacks. Figure 6 shows the simulation results of such smart tireless attacks. As we can see, the re-identification rate of smart tireless attacks is lower than the re-identification rate of regular tireless attacks. It means that, in at least 50% of the successful regular tireless attacks, the targets are identified from information sources other than websites of their workplaces. When we further look into the successful smart tireless attacks, we observe that most of them are true positives. Moreover, as we can see from Figure 6(b), on average, the rank of the first positive result is higher in smart tireless attacks. Therefore, smart attacks are more effective – less effort is required for the attacker to browse and examine the results. For both regular and smart tireless attacks, we can see that most of the users are either identified in top results, or never identified. It means that when the user is not "highly visible", his/her information is most likely buried in the massive amount of online information and becomes invisible. However, consider the fact that only a small portion of the general population have disclosed their information

(a) Number of positive results in each successful attack.

(b) Rank of the first positive result in each successful attack.

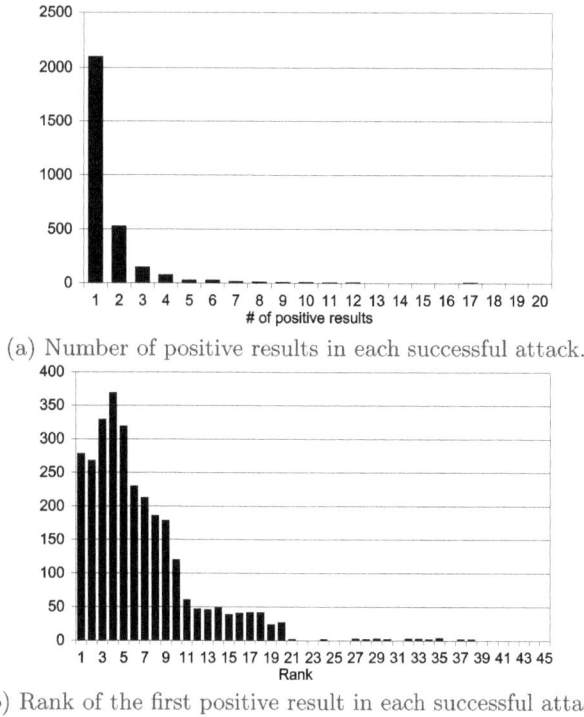

Figure 5: Results of successful *tireless attacks* with seed attribute tuple $<FN, S>$.

(a) Number of positive results in each successful attack

(b) Rank of the first positive result in each successful attack

Figure 6: Results of successful *smart tireless attacks* with seed attribute tuple $<FN, AF>$

on the Web, people with an online presence is still highly distinguishable.

6. ANALYSIS AND REFLECTION

Information. We have observed a large amount of personal information available over the Internet. Each information item may include both identifiable and non-identifiable attributes. Not all such information is published by the owner (of the identity), or with the consent of the owner. For instance, we have observed webpages such as news stories published by the employer. Moreover, the user might be completely unaware that his/her information has been accessible and searchable over the Internet. From the simulation results, we can see that it is very difficult, if not impossible, to completely hide one's online identity in the Internet age.

On the other hand, we have introduced an information-theory-based approach to evaluate the values of personal information items to the attackers. We believe that the results will help users determine the types and amounts of information to be published on personal and social networking sites.

Vulnerability. We have simulated the data collection process of resourceful attackers. We can see that personal information could be easily collected by attackers, especially from social networking or public record sites, where information is published in well-structured templates. On the other hand, automatically and accurately extracting *large amounts* of structured information from free (unstructured) text is not an easy task. Named-entity extraction [10, 6] is a very hard problem. Although we have seen successes in controlled datasets or for popular entities that appear on many web contexts, the general problem of arbitrary entity

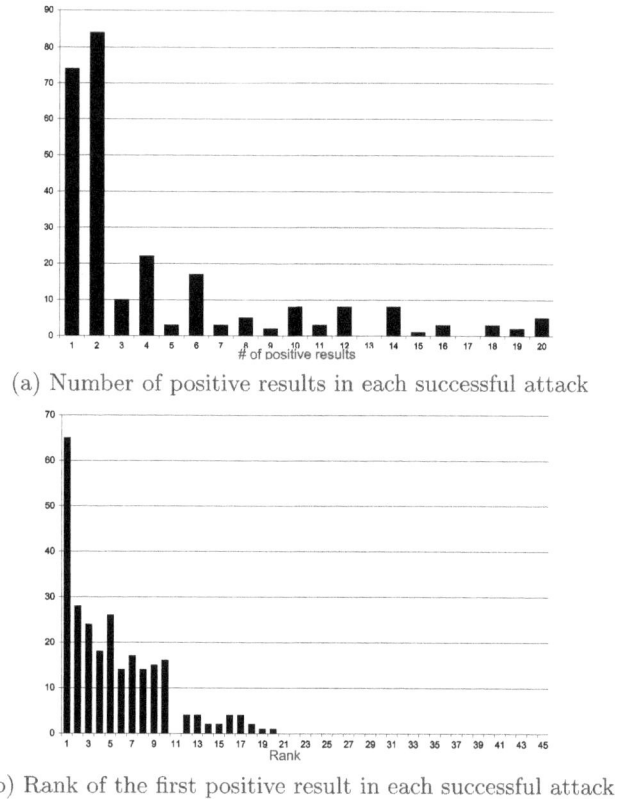

extraction is still far from being solved. In particular, diversity of web documents and limited evidences (e.g. a user's phone number only appears on one webpage) make it very difficult to precisely extract and collect large amounts of entities from the web. However, we have shown that it takes little effort for a human attacker to exploit search engines to locate webpages containing such information.

Next, with the simulation results of resourceful and tireless attackers, we have shown that **people with web presences are highly identifiable**, even with very limited or approximate information. Moreover, information from multiple resources could be linked to provide more information to the attacker. A major reason behind the phenomenon is that many people do not have a web presence, as confirmed by our cross-network aggregation attacks. On the contrary, people with web presence are very likely to appear in multiple sources. In this sense, we have a group of people who are more active on the Web, while the mass majority of the population mostly remain silent online. As a result, the online population becomes very identifiable. There appears to be a dilemma: if we have more people online, the identity of the existing users will be better "shadowed" than they are right now. However, in this way, we may put more people under risk.

Attacks. Recent advances in information retrieval techniques are shown to be a double-bladed sword – they provide great functions to the users, but also reveal their private information to attackers with sufficient capabilities and resources, or strong wills. Intuitively, we can interpret the

46

goal of the attacker as taking a piece of seed information as input against large data that are available online to successfully find a hit.

Ideally, if the seed is precise and adequate and the data is large enough to guarantee that it contains the target, the attack will always succeed. While the results are constrained in reality, the attacker manages to increase his chance and efficiency by meeting the conditions at his most. The first (and often hidden) assumption is that the focused data should be large enough to contain data of a particular target. In the resourceful attack, the focused data is the resource database created by the attacker, which in turn motivates the long-term and multi-source data collection. The second condition that affects the success rate of the attack is the identifiability of the user with the seed information (in terms of either seed attributes or search terms). In the tireless attack, it is assumed implicitly that the related data should be in the high-rank results returned by search engines. This in turn explains why tireless attack is only effective when the target is highly distinct against proper search terms (or combination of search terms). The study of the identifiability will also shed light on how to tailor one's online presence to shadow his identity within an indistinguishable group.

7. CONCLUSION

A large amount of personal information has been made available over the Internet. The advances in information retrieval technologies provide powerful Web search engines to legitimate users. However, they also provide adversaries with a convenient access to the abundant personal information on the Web.

In this paper, we have studied personal information that is disclosed to the Web through various sources, especially through online social networks. We also analyze the vulnerabilities in information and possible attacks. In particular, we have presented two types of attackers: the resourceful attackers and the tireless attackers. We assume that an attacker possesses a small piece of "seed" information about his target. A resourceful attacker searches local database with data collected from various online sources, including social networks and online public records. On the other hand, a tireless attacker queries web search engines with his seed information, and untiringly examines the results. We have simulated both attacks with real data collected from online social networks and phonebook, and quantitatively analyzed the results. From the results, we can see that large portions of users with online presence are very identifiable, even with a small piece of seed information, and the seed information could be inaccurate. We also show that it does not require extensive resources or efforts to successfully conduct such attacks.

8. ACKNOWLEDGEMENTS

Bo Luo was partially supported by NSF OIA-1028098 and University of Kansas General Research Fund 2301420. Peng Liu was partially supported by AFOSR FA9550-07-1-0527 (MURI), ARO W911NF-09-1-0525 (MURI), NSF CNS-0905131 and NSF CNS-0916469.

9. REFERENCES

[1] G. Aggarwal, T. Feder, K. Kenthapadi, R. Motwani, R. Panigrahy, D. Thomas, , and A. Zhu. k-anonymity: Algorithms and hardness. Technical report, Stanford University, 2004.

[2] L. Backstrom, C. Dwork, and J. Kleinberg. Wherefore art thou r3579x?: anonymized social networks, hidden patterns, and structural steganography. In *Proceedings of ACM international conference on World Wide Web*, pages 181–190, 2007.

[3] P. Cashmore. Privacy is dead, and social media hold smoking gun. CNN, October 2009.

[4] J. Caverlee and S. Webb. A large-scale study of myspace: Observations and implications for online social networks. In *Proceedings of the International Conference on Weblogs and Social Media*, 2008.

[5] X. Chen and S. Shi. A literature review of privacy research on social network sites. In *Multimedia Information Networking and Security, 2009. MINES '09. International Conference on*, volume 1, pages 93 –97, nov. 2009.

[6] T. Cheng, X. Yan, and K. C.-C. Chang. Entityrank: searching entities directly and holistically. In *VLDB '07: Proceedings of the 33rd international conference on Very large data bases*, pages 387–398, 2007.

[7] S. Chester and G. Srivastava. Social network privacy for attribute disclosure attacks. In *Advances in Social Networks Analysis and Mining (ASONAM), 2011 International Conference on*, pages 445 –449, july 2011.

[8] R. Dingledine, N. Mathewson, and P. Syverson. Tor: the second-generation onion router. In *USENIX Security Symposium*, 2004.

[9] B. Dubow. Confessions of 'Facebook stalkers'. USA Today, March 2007.

[10] O. Etzioni, M. Cafarella, D. Downey, A.-M. Popescu, T. Shaked, S. Soderland, D. S. Weld, and A. Yates. Unsupervised named-entity extraction from the web: An experimental study. *Artificial Intelligence*, 165(1):91 – 134, 2005.

[11] G. Eysenbach and J. E. Till. Ethical issues in qualitative research on internet communities. *BMJ*, 323:1103–1105, 2001.

[12] L. Garton, C. Haythornthwaite, and B. Wellman. Studying online social networks. *Journal of Computer-Mediated Communication*, 3(1), 1997.

[13] P. Golle. Revisiting the uniqueness of simple demographics in the us population. In *WPES '06: Proceedings of the 5th ACM workshop on Privacy in electronic society*, pages 77–80, New York, NY, USA, 2006. ACM.

[14] R. Gross, A. Acquisti, and I. H. John Heinz. Information revelation and privacy in online social networks (the facebook case). In *Proceedings of ACM workshop on Privacy in the electronic society*, pages 71–80, 2005.

[15] M. Hay, G. Miklau, D. Jensen, D. Towsley, and P. Weis. Resisting structural re-identification in anonymized social networks. *Proc. VLDB Endow.*, 1(1):102–114, 2008.

[16] J. He and W. W. Chu. Protecting private information in online social networks. In *Intelligence and Security Informatics*, pages 249–273, 2008.

[17] J. He, W. W. Chu, and Z. Liu. Inferring privacy information from social networks. In *IEEE*

International Conference on Intelligence and Security Informatics, pages 154–165, 2006.

[18] X. He, J. Vaidya, B. Shafiq, N. Adam, and V. Atluri. Preserving privacy in social networks: A structure-aware approach. In *Web Intelligence and Intelligent Agent Technologies, 2009. WI-IAT '09. IEEE/WIC/ACM International Joint Conferences on*, volume 1, pages 647 –654, sept. 2009.

[19] B. A. Huberman, E. Adar, and L. R. Fine. Valuating privacy. *IEEE Security and Privacy*, 3(5):22–25, 2005.

[20] M. Irvine. Social network users overlook privacy pitfalls. USA Today, April 2008.

[21] P. Joshi and C.-C. Kuo. Security and privacy in online social networks: A survey. In *Multimedia and Expo (ICME), 2011 IEEE International Conference on*, pages 1 –6, july 2011.

[22] V. Kostakos, J. Venkatanathan, B. Reynolds, N. Sadeh, E. Toch, S. A. Shaikh, and S. Jones. Who's your best friend?: targeted privacy attacks in location-sharing social networks. In *Proceedings of the 13th international conference on Ubiquitous computing*, UbiComp '11, pages 177–186, 2011.

[23] B. Krishnamurthy and C. E. Wills. On the leakage of personally identifiable information via online social networks. In *WOSN '09: Proceedings of the 2nd ACM workshop on Online social networks*, pages 7–12, New York, NY, USA, 2009. ACM.

[24] J. Leskovec and E. Horvitz. Planetary-scale views on a large instant-messaging network. In *WWW '08: Proceeding of the 17th international conference on World Wide Web*, pages 915–924, 2008.

[25] F. Li, J. Y. Chen, X. Zou, , and P. Liu. New privacy threats in healthcare informatics: When medical records join the web. In *ACM SIGKDD Workshop on Data Mining in Bioinformatics*, 2010.

[26] N. Li, T. Li, and S. Venkatasubramanian. t-closeness: Privacy beyond k-anonymity and l-diversity. In *Proceedings of the 23rd International Conference on Data Engineering*, pages 106–115, 2007.

[27] Y.-R. Lin, Y. Chi, S. Zhu, H. Sundaram, and B. L. Tseng. Facetnet: a framework for analyzing communities and their evolutions in dynamic networks. In *WWW '08: Proceeding of the 17th international conference on World Wide Web*, pages 685–694, 2008.

[28] K. Liu and E. Terzi. Towards identity anonymization on graphs. In *Proceedings of the 2008 ACM SIGMOD*, pages 93–106, 2008.

[29] K. Liu and E. Terzi. A framework for computing the privacy scores of users in online social networks. In *Data Mining, 2009. ICDM '09. Ninth IEEE International Conference on*, pages 288 –297, dec. 2009.

[30] K. Liu and E. Terzi. A framework for computing the privacy scores of users in online social networks. *ACM Trans. Knowl. Discov. Data*, 5:6:1–6:30, December 2010.

[31] L. Liu, J. Wang, J. Liu, and J. Zhang. Privacy preserving in social networks against sensitive edge disclosure. Technical Report CMIDA-HiPSCCS 006-08, University of Kentucky, 2008.

[32] B. Luo and D. Lee. On protecting private information in social networks: A proposal. In *Workshop on Modeling, Managing, and Mining of Evolving Social Networks - in conjunction with IEEE ICDE*, 2009.

[33] A. Machanavajjhala, D. Kifer, J. Gehrke, and M. Venkitasubramaniam. L-diversity: Privacy beyond k-anonymity. *ACM Trans. Knowl. Discov. Data*, 1(1):3, 2007.

[34] A. Masoumzadeh and J. Joshi. Preserving structural properties in anonymization of social networks. In *Collaborative Computing: Networking, Applications and Worksharing (CollaborateCom), 2010 6th International Conference on*, pages 1 –10, oct. 2010.

[35] L. Singh and J. Zhan. Measuring topological anonymity in social networks. In *GRC '07: Proceedings of the 2007 IEEE International Conference on Granular Computing*, page 770, Washington, DC, USA, 2007. IEEE Computer Society.

[36] A. C. Squicciarini, M. Shehab, and J. Wede. Privacy policies for shared content in social network sites. *The VLDB Journal*, 19:777–796, December 2010.

[37] J. Staddon. Finding "hidden" connections on linkedin an argument for more pragmatic social network privacy. In *Proceedings of the 2nd ACM workshop on Security and artificial intelligence*, AISec '09, pages 11–14, New York, NY, USA, 2009. ACM.

[38] L. Sweeney. Uniqueness of simple demographics in the u.s. population, 2000.

[39] L. Sweeney. k-anonymity: a model for protecting privacy. *Int. J. Uncertain. Fuzziness Knowl.-Based Syst.*, 10(5):557–570, 2002.

[40] X. Ying and X. Wu. Randomizing social networks: a spectrum preserving approach. In *SIAM International Conference on Data Mining (SDM)*, 2008.

[41] C. Zhang, J. Sun, X. Zhu, and Y. Fang. Privacy and security for online social networks: challenges and opportunities. *Network, IEEE*, 24(4):13 –18, july-august 2010.

[42] E. Zheleva and L. Getoor. Preserving the privacy of sensitive relationships in graph data. In *International Workshop on Privacy, Security, and Trust in KDD (PinKDD)*, pages 153–171, 2008.

[43] E. Zheleva and L. Getoor. To join or not to join: The illusion of privacy in social networks with mixed public and private user profiles. In *18th International World Wide Web conference (WWW)*, April 2009. Earlier version appears as CS-TR-4926.

[44] B. Zhou and J. Pei. Preserving privacy in social networks against neighborhood attacks. In *Proceedings of the 24th International Conference on Data Engineering (ICDE)*, April 2008.

[45] B. Zhou, J. Pei, and W. Luk. A brief survey on anonymization techniques for privacy preserving publishing of social network data. *SIGKDD Explor. Newsl.*, 10(2):12–22, 2008.

[46] L. Zou, L. Chen, and M. T. Özsu. k-automorphism: a general framework for privacy preserving network publication. *Proc. VLDB Endow.*, 2:946–957, August 2009.

Measuring Query Privacy in Location-Based Services

Xihui Chen[*]
Interdisciplinary Centre for Security, Reliability
and Trust, University of Luxembourg
xihui.chen@uni.lu

Jun Pang
Computer Science and Communications,
University of Luxembourg
jun.pang@uni.lu

ABSTRACT

The popularity of location-based services leads to serious concerns on user privacy. A common mechanism to protect users' location and query privacy is spatial generalisation. As more user information becomes available with the fast growth of Internet applications, e.g., social networks, attackers have the ability to construct users' personal profiles. This gives rise to new challenges and reconsideration of the existing privacy metrics, such as k-anonymity. In this paper, we propose new metrics to measure users' query privacy taking into account user profiles. Furthermore, we design spatial generalisation algorithms to compute regions satisfying users' privacy requirements expressed in these metrics. By experimental results, our metrics and algorithms are shown to be effective and efficient for practical usage.

Categories and Subject Descriptors

C.2.0 [**Computer-Communication Networks**]: General—*Security and protection*; K.4.1 [**Computers and Society**]: Public Policy Issues—*Privacy*

General Terms

Security, measurement

Keywords

Location based services, query privacy, anonymity, measurement

1. INTRODUCTION

The popularity of mobile devices with localisation chips and ubiquitous access to Internet give rise to a large number of location-based services (LBS). Consider a user who wants to know where the nearest gas station is. He sends a query to a location-based service provider (LBSP) using his smart-phone with his location attached. The LBSP then processes the query and responds with results. Location-based queries lead to privacy concerns especially

---

[*]This work was supported by the FNR Luxembourg under project SECLOC 794361.

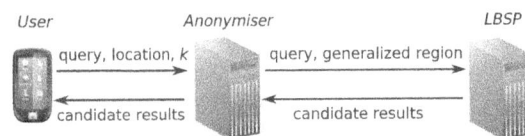

Figure 1: A centralised framework of LBSs

in cases when LBSPs are not trusted. Attackers can cooperate with LBSPs and have access to users' location-related queries. The amount and risk of information leakage from LBS queries have been discussed, for example, in [7, 13]. The analysis mainly focused on information leakage from locations. However, query content itself is also a source of users' privacy leakage. For instance, a query about casinos implies the issuer's gambling habit which the issuer wants to keep secret. Thus besides location privacy, the anonymity of issuers with respect to queries is also important in privacy preservation. Intuitively, *query privacy* is the ability to prevent other parties to learn the issuers of queries. One way to protect query privacy is to anonymise queries by removing users' identities. However, this does not suffice when considering locations which can help reveal users' identities, since attackers can acquire users' locations through a number of ways, e.g., triangulating mobile phones' signals and localising users' access points to Internet. Sometimes, public information such as home addresses and yellow pages can also help obtain users' positions. Therefore, locations within queries are critical in protecting users' query privacy as well. Replacing locations with a generalised area is an alternative to break the linkability between users and their locations, which is called *spatial cloaking* [16, 20].

In the last few years, k-anonymity [24] has been widely used and investigated in the literature on releasing microdata, e.g., medical records. A user is k-anonymous if he is indistinguishable from at least other $k - 1$ users. In the context of query privacy in LBS, k-anonymity can be interpreted as: given a query, any attacker based on the query location cannot identify the issuer with probability larger than $\frac{1}{k}$ [15]. Most of existing works adopt the centralised framework (depicted in Fig. 1), where a trusted agent *anonymiser* is introduced. Users first send their queries to the anonymiser who *anonymises the queries* and *generalises the locations* before sending them to the LBSP. The responses from the LBSP are first sent to the anonymiser and then forwarded to the corresponding users. In the centralised framework, normally it is assumed that the communication channels between users and the anonymiser are secure while the ones between the anonymiser and the LBSP are public.

A common assumption for k-anonymity is that all users have the same probability to issue queries. In other words, a uniform probability distribution is assumed over users with respect to sending any query, which is often not realistic especially when attackers gain more information about the users. Given a specific query, certain users tend to be more likely to issue it when compared to others. For instance, users who love movies are more possible to search for nearing cinemas. For any user in a generalised area satisfying k-anonymity, the probability to be the issuer is no longer $\frac{1}{k}$ in such situations. The case can be worse especially for those users who are more likely than others. Suppose a k-anonymised region of a query from a young person for searching clubs at midnight. If there are only two young people in the generalised region, then they are more likely to be taken as the candidates for the issuer from attackers' view than other users in this region. Therefore, k-anonymity is not a sufficient metric to describe users' privacy requirements when taking into account user profiles, which was addressed first by Shin et al. [26]. Nowadays, the popularity of social networks and more exposure of people's information on Internet provide attackers sources to gather enough background knowledge to obtain user profiles. Besides *passive attacks* in which attackers simply observe the connection between users, attackers can also perform *active attacks*, e.g., by creating new accounts so as to identify users even in an anonymised social network [17]. Wu et al. give a literature study on the existing attacks to obtain users' profiles [33]. Therefore, it is a new challenge to measure and protect users' query privacy in LBSs with the assumption that attackers have the knowledge of user profiles.

Our contributions. In this paper, we extend k-anonymity and propose new metrics to correctly measure users' query privacy in the context of LBSs, which enable users to specify their query privacy requirements in different ways. Furthermore, we design new generation algorithms to compute anonymising spatial regions according to users' privacy requirements. Through experiments, we show that our algorithms are efficient enough to meet users' demands on real-time responses and generate regions satisfying privacy requirements. We also show the different strengths of our metrics which help users choose the correct requirements to achieve a balance between privacy and the quality of service delivered by the LBSP.

Structure of the paper. Sect. 2 gives a brief investigation of related work on measuring anonymity, query privacy and area generalisation algorithms. In Sect. 3, we present our formal framework, the threat model, and the derivation of user profiles. We formally define a number of query privacy metrics in Sect. 4 and develop generalisation algorithms in Sect. 5. In Sect. 6, through experiments we discuss features of the metrics and evaluate the performance of the generalisation algorithms. The paper is concluded in Sect. 7.

2. RELATED WORK

We give a brief literature study on measuring anonymity and on query privacy metrics with focus on k-anonymity. Then we summarise existing region generalisation algorithms.

2.1 Anonymity metrics

In the literature, various ways to measure anonymity have been proposed. Chaum [6] uses the size of an anonymity set to indicate the degree of anonymity provided by a network based on Dining Cryptographers. An anonymity set is defined as the set of users who could have sent a particular message as observed by attackers. Berthold et al. [3] define the degree of anonymity as $\log N$, where N is the number of users. Reiter and Rubin [22] define the degree of anonymity as the probability that an attacker can assign to a user of being the original sender of a message. They introduce metrics like beyond suspicion, probable innocence and possible innocence. Serjantov and Danezis [25] define an anonymity metric

based on entropy and a similar metric is given by Díaz et al. [11] which is normalised by the number of users. Zhu and Bettati [35] propose a definition of anonymity based on mutual information. The notion relative entropy is used by Deng et al. [10] to measure anonymity. Different information-theoretic approaches based on Kullback-Leider distance and min-entropy are proposed [5, 9, 31] to define information leakage or the capacity of noisy channels.

2.2 Query privacy metrics

The concept of k-anonymity was originally proposed by Samarati and Sweeney in the field of database privacy [24]. The main idea of k-anonymity is to guarantee that a database entry's identifier is indistinguishable from other $k-1$ entries. However, this method does not work in all cases. For instance, the fact that an HIV carrier is hidden in k carriers does not help protecting his infection of the virus. Further research has been done to fix this problem [18]. In the context of privacy in LBSs, k-anonymity is first introduced by Gruteser and Grunwald [15]. It aims to protect two types of privacy – *location privacy* and *query privacy*. The former means that given a published query, attackers cannot learn the issuer' exact position while the latter enforces the unlinkability between the issuer and the query. Because of its simplicity, k-anonymity has been studied and refined in many ways. For instance, Tan et al. define *information leakage* to measure the amount of revealed location information in spatial cloaking, which quantifies the balance between privacy and performance [32]. Xue et al. [34] introduce the concept of *location diversity* to ensure generalised regions to contain at least ℓ semantic locations (e.g., schools, hospitals).

Deeper understanding of k-anonymity reveals its drawbacks in preserving users' location privacy. Shokri et al. analyse the effectiveness of k-anonymity in protecting location privacy in different scenarios in terms of adversaries' background information [30], i.e., *real-time location information*, *statistical information* and *no information*. Based on the analysis, they conclude that cloaking (e.g., k-anonymity) is effective for protecting query privacy but not location privacy. They also show its flaws which the adversary can exploit to infer users' current locations. In this paper, we focus on protecting query privacy using cloaking with the assumption that the adversary learns users' real-time locations.

Recently, Shokri et al. design a tool *Location-Privacy Meter* that measures location privacy of mobile users in different attack scenarios [28, 29]. Their work assumes that attackers can utilise user profiles (e.g., mobility patterns) extracted from uses' sample traces to infer the ownership of collected traces. It is in spirit close to our work. They use the incorrectness of attackers' conclusions on users' positions drawn from observations as the privacy metric. In this paper, we focus on users' query privacy with regards to an individual query rather than query histories. Moreover, we make use of users' static and public personal information, such as professions and jobs as user profiles. Considering information such as mobility patterns and query histories is part of our future work.

The work by Shin et al. [26] is most closely related. They describe user profiles using a set of attributes whose domains are discretised into disjoint values. User profiles are represented by *profile vectors* with a bit for each value. Shin et al. propose three new metrics based on k-anonymity by restricting different levels of similarity between profiles of users in generalised regions. This is analogous to our notion of *k-approximate beyond suspicion* which will be discussed in Sect. 4. Compared to Shin et al.'s work [26], we define a more comprehensive set of metrics that can measure query privacy from different perspectives and develop corresponding generalisation algorithms.

2.3 Area generalisation algorithms

The first generalisation algorithm called IntervalCloaking is designed by Gruteser and Grunwald [15]. Their idea is to partition a region into quadrants with equal area. If the quadrant where the issuer is located contains less than k users, then the original region is returned. Otherwise, the quadrant with the issuer is taken as input for the next iteration. The algorithm CliqueCloak [14] is proposed by Gedik and Liu in which regions are generalised based on the users who have issued queries rather than all potential issuers. The major improvement is that this algorithm enables users to specify their personal privacy requirements by choosing different values for k. Mokbel et al. [21, 8] design the algorithm Casper which employs a quadtree to store the two-dimensional space. The root node represents the whole area and each of other nodes represents a quadrant region of its parent node. The generalisation algorithm starts from the leaf node which contains the issuer and iteratively traverses backwards to the root until a region with more than k users is found. Another algorithm nnASR [16] simply finds the nearest k users to the issuer and returns the region containing these users as the anonymising spatial region.

The above algorithms suffer from a particular attack called "outlier problem" [2], where attackers have the generalisation algorithms and users' spatial distribution as part of their knowledge. Intuitively, this happens when some users in a generalised region do not have the same region returned by the algorithm as the issuer. Thus, these users can be removed from the anonymity set, resulting in a set with less than k users. Hence, an algorithm against this attack needs to ensure that for each user in the anonymity set it always returns the same region. Kalnis et al. design the first algorithm called hilbASR that does not have the outlier problem [16]. The algorithm exploits the Hilbert space filling curve to store users in a total order based on their locations. The curve is then partitioned into blocks with k users. The block with the issuer is returned as the generalised region. Mascetti et al. propose two algorithms, dichotomicPoints and grid, which are also secure against the outlier problem [20]. The former iteratively partitions the region into two blocks until less than $2k$ users are located in the region while the latter draws a grid over the two-dimensional space so that each cell contains k users and returns the cell with the issuer. Because of the simplicity of implementation and the relatively smaller area of the generalised regions, we adopt and extend these two algorithms in our algorithm design.

The area of generalised regions is usually used to measure the quality of service responded by LBSPs, as smaller regions lead to more accurate query results and less communication overhead.

3. PRELIMINARIES

In this section, we present a formal framework, define the attacker model subsequently, and discuss how to derive a priori probabilities for users to issue a query based on their profiles.

3.1 A formal framework

Let $\mathcal{U}$ denote a set of users, $\mathcal{L}$ the set of locations (positions), and $\mathcal{T}$ the set of time instances that can be recorded. The granularity of time instances is determined by LBSs. Given a time t, we have a function to map a user to his location at t: $whereis : \mathcal{U} \times \mathcal{T} \to \mathcal{L}$. The user *spatial distribution* at time t can be defined as the set $\{(u, whereis(u,t)) \mid u \in \mathcal{U}\}$, denoted by $dis(t)$. Suppose the set of queries supported by LBSs is represented by $\mathcal{Q}$, e.g., the nearest gas station. Let $Q \subseteq \mathcal{U} \times \mathcal{L} \times \mathcal{T} \times \mathcal{Q}$ be the set of queries from users $\mathcal{U}$ at a specific time. An element in Q is a quadruple $\langle u, whereis(u,t), t, q \rangle$, where $u \in \mathcal{U}$ and $q \in \mathcal{Q}$.

Table 1: Notations

$\mathcal{U}$	set of users
$\mathcal{T}$	set of time instances
$\mathcal{L}$	set of locations
$\mathcal{R}$	set of possible generalised regions
$q \in \mathcal{Q}$	a query supported by the LBS
$\langle u, \ell, t, q \rangle \in Q$	a query issued by u at position ℓ at time t
$\langle r, t, q \rangle \in Q'$	a generalised query sent by the anonymiser
$dis(t)$	spatial distribution of users in $\mathcal{U}$ at time t
$\mathcal{M}(q)$	probability distribution of user to issue q
$u\ell(r,t)$	set of users located in region r at time t
$req(\langle u, \ell, t, q \rangle)$	user u's privacy requirement on $\langle u, \ell, t, q \rangle$
$p(u \mid q)$	probability of u to issue q among users in $\mathcal{U}$
$p(u \mid \langle r, t, q \rangle)$	probability of u to issue $\langle r, t, q \rangle$
$whereis(u,t)$	position of user u at time t
$f(\langle u, \ell, t, q \rangle)$	an algorithm computing generalised queries

Given a query $\langle u, whereis(u,t), t, q \rangle \in Q$, the anonymising server (*anonymiser*) would remove the user's identity and replace his location with a larger area to protect his query privacy. We only consider *spatial generalisation* in this paper as in LBSs users require instant responses. Let $2^{\mathcal{L}}$ be the power set of $\mathcal{L}$ and then we use $\mathcal{R} \subset 2^{\mathcal{L}}$ to denote the set of all possible generalised regions. The corresponding output of the anonymising server can be represented as $\langle r, t, q \rangle$, where $r \in \mathcal{R}$ and $whereis(u,t) \in r$. Suppose the set of generalised queries $Q' \subset \mathcal{R} \times \mathcal{T} \times \mathcal{Q}$. The generalisation algorithm of the aonymiser can be represented as a function $f : Q \to Q'$. For instance, we have $f(\langle u, whereis(u,t), t, q \rangle) = \langle r, t, q \rangle$.

The generalisation algorithm used by the anonymiser to compute generalised queries makes use of current user spatial distribution and might also take users' privacy requirements as part of its input. In our framework, a privacy requirement is represented by a pair – a chosen privacy metric by the issuer and the corresponding specified value (see more discussion in Sect. 4 and 5). We use $req(\langle u, whereis(u,t), t, q \rangle)$ to denote u's requirement on query $\langle u, whereis(u,t), t, q \rangle$.

We use $p(u_j \mid q_i)$ to denote the conditional probability of user u_j to be the issuer when query q_i is observed, and $\sum_{u_j \in \mathcal{U}} p(u_j \mid q_i) = 1$. Variations of users' profiles along with time and positions are out of the scope of this paper, and considered as part of our future work. For the sake of simplicity, in the following discussion we use a probability matrix $\mathcal{M}$, where element $m_{ij} = p(u_j \mid q_i)$. We use $\mathcal{M}(q_i)$ to denote the i-th row of $\mathcal{M}$, the probability distribution over users to issue the query q_i.

Let $u\ell : \mathcal{R} \times \mathcal{T} \to 2^{\mathcal{U}}$ be the function mapping a region to the set of users located in it. In other words, $u\ell(r,t) = \{u \in \mathcal{U} \mid whereis(u,t) \in r\}$. Given a generalised query $\langle r, t, q \rangle$, user u's probability to be the issuer among the users in region r can be computed as follows:

$$p(u \mid \langle r, t, q \rangle) = \frac{p(u \mid q)}{\sum_{u' \in u\ell(r,t)} p(u' \mid q)}$$

We summarise the list of important notations in Tab. 1.

3.2 The attacker model

Through generalising locations, users' query privacy is protected by preventing attackers from re-identifying issuers with high probabilities. Most approaches in the literature (e.g., see [20]) assume that attackers have a global view of users' real-time spatial distribution (*Assumption 1*). This assumption is conservative but possible in real scenarios. There are many ways to gather users' real-time locations. For instance, most people send queries from some fixed positions, e.g., office and home. Referring to address books or other public database, the potential issuers can be identified. We also adopt this assumption in this paper. It is also natural to assume that the attacker controls the communication channel between the anonymiser and the LBS server (see the second part of Fig. 1) (*Assumption 2*). This allows the attacker to acquire any generalised queries forwarded by the anonymiser. Meantime, we assume the anonymiser is trustworthy and users have a secure connection with the anonymiser through SSL or other techniques (see the first part of Fig. 1). The generalisation algorithm used by the anonymiser is assumed to be public (*Assumption 3*). This leads to an additional requirement. For each user in an anonymity set, a plausible algorithm must compute the same area as the one computed for the issuer.

Different from attackers in the literature (e.g., [20, 32, 30]), the attacker in our model has access to an a priori distribution over users with regards to issuing queries (i.e., the probability matrix $\mathcal{M}$) (*Assumption 4*). Thus, instead of assuming a uniform distribution among users for issuing a particular query, the attacker has a precise probabilistic distribution by exploring user profiles obtained, e.g., by available public information [17, 26].

Users may have different privacy requirements for queries dependent on time, positions and sensitivity of queries, which is usually a subjective decision. So we assume that attackers have no knowledge about this requirement decision process (*Assumption 5*). However, attackers can learn users' privacy requirements after observing the generalised queries by the anonymiser (*Assumption 6*). This is realistic as from the features of the generalised queries, attackers can infer the corresponding privacy requirements.

Last but not least, we assume that the attacker cannot link any two queries from the same user (*Assumption 7*). All queries are independent from the attacker's perspectives. This assumption is strong but still realistic as users tend to issue occasional queries and an issuer's identity is always removed by the anonymiser before forwarding the query to the LBSP.

3.3 Deriving probabilities from user profiles

User profiles can be associated with a set of attributes which can be divided into several categories, e.g., contact attributes (zip codes, addresses), descriptive attributes (age, nationalities, jobs) and preference attributes (hobbies, moving patterns) [26]. The values of these attributes can be discretised into a categorical form. For instance, the value of a home address can be represented by the corresponding zone which it lies in. In this way, each attribute has a finite number of candidate values.

Let $\phi_u = \langle a_1, \ldots, a_m \rangle$ be the profile of user u, where m is the number of attributes. Note that a_i is represented by a string of bits, each of which denotes a possible value of the corresponding attribute. We use $|a_i|$ to denote the length of a_i and $\hat{\phi}_u$ to represent the concatenation of the strings of all attributes. Moreover, let $\hat{\phi}_u[j]$ be the j-th bit of $\hat{\phi}_u$. As the values in the domain of any attribute are disjoint, there is at most one bit to be 1 for any a_i (perhaps all zeros because of lack of information). Consider a user profile consisting of two attributes – salary and gender. As the domain of gender consists of two values – *male* and *female* we use two bits to represent them, 01 and 10, respectively. We divide the numerical values of salary into three intervals – '≤ 1000', '$1000-5000$' and '≥ 5000'. Then user profile $\phi_u = \langle 001, 01 \rangle$ means user u is male and has a salary more than 5000, and $\hat{\phi}_u = 00101$.

Each query $q \in Q$ must have a subset of correlated attributes that can be used to deduce the issuer. Furthermore, each value of a relevant attribute has a different weight measuring the probability

that the user issues the given query when having the attribute value. For instance, for the query asking for expensive hotels, the associated attributes should include salary, jobs and age while gender is irrelevant. Among them, a salary is much more relevant than age and moreover, a salary of more than 5000 euros is much more important than one of less than 1000 euros. Therefore, we introduce a relevance vector to express the relation between attributes' values and queries. Let $W(q) = \langle w_1, \ldots, w_n \rangle$ be the relevance vector of query q where $n = \sum_{i \leq m} |a_i|$.

For any $u \in \mathcal{U}$ and $q \in Q$, let $\mathcal{V}(u, q) = \sum_{i \leq n} w_i \cdot \hat{\phi}_u[i]$ be the relevance of user u's profile to query q. Subsequently, we have:

$$p(u \mid q) = \frac{\mathcal{V}(u, q)}{\sum_{u' \in \mathcal{U}} \mathcal{V}(u', q)}$$

4. QUERY PRIVACY METRICS

We propose a number of new metrics (except for k-anonymity) to measure query privacy taking into account user profiles and formally define them using the framework discussed in Sect. 3.

k-**anonymity.** In k-anonymity, a natural number k is taken as the metric of users' query privacy, which is the size of the anonymity set of the issuer. This means, for a given query, there are at least k users in the generalised region including the issuer. Moreover, in order to prevent attacks based on public generalisation algorithms [20], any user in the anonymity set must have the same generalised region for the same query. Similar to the definitions in the literature [27, 20], k-anonymity can be formally defined as follows:

DEFINITION 1. *Let $\langle u, whereis(u, t), t, q \rangle \in Q$ be a query and $\langle r, t, q \rangle \in Q'$ the corresponding generalised query. The issuer u is k-anonymous if*

$$| \{u' \in \mathcal{U} \mid \quad whereis(u', t) \in r \, \wedge$$
$$f(\langle u', whereis(u', t), t, q \rangle) = \langle r, t, q \rangle\} | \quad \geq k$$

Note that in Def. 1, as all users in the anonymity set take r as the generalised region for the query q at time t, they are all k-anonymous. The following proposed new anonymity metrics enjoy the same property.

k-**approximate beyond suspicion.** As discussed in Sect. 1, when user profiles are considered as part of the attacker's knowledge, the size of an anonymity set k cannot be a fair metric for query privacy. Especially for users with high a priori probabilities, they can easily be chosen as candidates of issuers. Inspired by anonymity degrees defined by Reiter and Rubin [22], we come up with the following new privacy metrics.

Beyond suspicion means from the attacker's viewpoint the issuer cannot be more likely than other potential users in the anonymity set to send the query. In other words, users in the anonymity set have the same probability to perform an action. In the context of LBSs, we need to find a set of users in which users are the same likely to send a given query. This set is taken as the anonymity set whose size determines the degree of users' privacy as in k-anonymity. Let $AS : Q' \rightarrow 2^{\mathcal{U}}$ denote the anonymity set of a generalised query. An issuer of query $\langle u, whereis(u, t), t, q \rangle$ is beyond suspicious with respect to the corresponding generalised query $\langle r, t, q \rangle$ if and only if $\forall u' \in AS(\langle r, t, q \rangle)$,

$$p(u \mid \langle r, t, q \rangle) = p(u' \mid \langle r, t, q \rangle)$$

In practice, the number of users with the same probability to send a query is usually small, which leads to a large generalised area with a fixed k. So we relax the requirement to compute an anonymity set consisting of users with *similar probabilities* instead of the exact same probability. Let $\|p_1, p_2\|$ denote the difference between two probabilities and ϵ be the pre-defined parameter describing the largest difference allowed between similar probabilities.

DEFINITION 2. *Let* $\langle u, whereis(u,t), t, q \rangle \in Q$ *be a query and* $\langle r, t, q \rangle \in Q'$ *the corresponding generalised query. The issuer* u *is* k-*approximate beyond suspicious if*

$$| \{ u' \in AS(\langle r,t,q \rangle) \mid \ \|p(u|\langle r,t,q \rangle), p(u'|\langle r,t,q \rangle)\| < \epsilon \ \wedge \\ f(\langle u', whereis(u',t), t, q \rangle) = \langle r,t,q \rangle \} | \ \geq k.$$

Different from k-anonymity, the set of users that are k-approximate beyond suspicious is computed based on the spatial distribution of users with similar probabilities rather than the original distribution involving all users. The users in an anonymity set have similar probabilities and the size of the anonymity set is larger than k. Therefore, k-approximate beyond suspicion can be seen as a generalised version of k-anonymity. If for a specific query $q \in \mathcal{Q}$, any two users have the same probability to issue it (i.e., $\mathcal{M}(q)$ is a uniform distribution), then k-approximate beyond suspicion is equivalent to k-anonymity.

THEOREM 1. *For a given query* $q \in \mathcal{Q}$, *if for any two users* $u_1, u_2 \in \mathcal{U}$ *we have* $p(u_1 \mid q) = p(u_2 \mid q)$, *then* k-*anonymity is* k-*approximate beyond suspicion with respect to* q.

For short, we use k-ABS to denote k-approximate beyond suspicion in the following discussion.

User specified innocence. Two weaker anonymity metrics, *probable innocence* and *possible innocence*, are proposed by Reiter and Rubin as well [22]. An issuer is probably innocent if from the attacker's view the issuer appears no more likely to be the originator of the query. In other words, the probability of each user in the anonymity set to be issuer should be less than 50%. Meantime, possible innocence requires the attacker not be able to identify the issuer with a non-trivial probability. We extend these two notions into a metric with user-specified probabilities (instead of restricting to 50% or non-trivial probability which is not clearly defined). We call the new anonymity metric *user specified innocence* where $\alpha \in [0,1]$ is the specified probability given by the issuer.

DEFINITION 3. *Let* $\alpha \in [0,1]$, $\langle u, whereis(u,t), t, q \rangle \in Q$ *be a query and* $\langle r, t, q \rangle \in Q'$ *the corresponding generalised query. The issuer* u *is* α-*user specified innocent if for all* $u' \in u\ell(r,t)$,

$$p(u' \mid \langle r,t,q \rangle) \leq \alpha \ \wedge \ f(\langle u', whereis(u',t), t, q \rangle) = \langle r,t,q \rangle.$$

Recall that $u\ell(r,t)$ denotes the set of users in region r at time t. It is clear that the anonymity set consists of all users in the generalised area. We abbreviate α-user specified innocence as α-USI.

Intuitively, for a query, an issuer is α-user specified innocent, if the anonymiser generates the same region for any user in the region with the same specified value α. In other words, in the generalised region, the most probable user has a probability smaller than α from the attacker's point of view. With this property, α-USI can also be captured by *min-entropy*, which is an instance of Rènyi entropy [23] and is used to measure the uncertainty of the *one-try* adversary who has exactly one chance to guess the originator in our scenario. Obviously, the best strategy for the adversary is to choose the one with the highest probability. Formally, the *min-entropy* of a variable X is defined as $H_\infty(X) = -\log \max_{x \in \mathcal{X}} p(x)$ where $\mathcal{X}$ is the domain of X. Let U be the variable that stands for the issuer and its domain is $\mathcal{U}$. Then for query $\langle r,t,q \rangle$, the min-entropy of the attacker can be described as $H_\infty(U \mid \langle r,t,q \rangle) = -\log \max_{u \in u\ell(r,t)} p(u \mid \langle r,t,q \rangle)$. It is maximised when the users in region r at time t follow a uniform distribution with regards to issuing query q. It is easy to verify that if a generalised query $\langle r,t,q \rangle$ guarantees the issuer α-user specified innocent, then it also ensures that the corresponding min-entropy is bigger than $-\log \alpha$.

An entropy based metric. Serjantov and Danezis [25] define an anonymity metric based on entropy and Díaz et al. [11] provide a similar metric that is normalised by the number of users in the anonymity set. The concept *entropy* of a random variable X is defined as $H(X) = -\sum_{x \in \mathcal{X}} p(x) \cdot \log p(x)$ where $\mathcal{X}$ is the domain (all possible values) of X. In our context, entropy can also be used to describe the attacker's uncertainty to identify the issuer of a generalised query. Let variable U denote the issuer of query $\langle r,t,q \rangle$. Then the uncertainty of the attacker can be expressed as

$$H(U \mid \langle r,t,q \rangle) = - \sum_{u' \in u\ell(r,t)} p(u' \mid \langle r,t,q \rangle) \cdot \log p(\tilde{u}' \mid \langle r,t,q \rangle).$$

Users can express their query privacy by specifying an entropy value. For a given generalised query $\langle r,t,q \rangle$ and a given value β, we say the issuer is entropy based anonymous with respect to the value β if all users in region r can have r as the generalised region when issuing the same query and the entropy $H(U \mid \langle r,t,q \rangle)$ is not smaller than β.

DEFINITION 4. *Let* $\beta > 0$, $\langle u, whereis(u,t), t, q \rangle \in Q$ *be a query and* $\langle r,t,q \rangle \in Q'$ *the corresponding generalised query. The issuer* u *is* β-*entropy based anonymous if for all* $u' \in u\ell(r,t)$,

$$H(U \mid \langle r,t,q \rangle) \geq \beta \ \wedge \ f(\langle u', whereis(u',t), t, q \rangle) = \langle r,t,q \rangle.$$

For short, we call β-entropy based anonymity β-EBA.

A mutual information based metric. The notion *mutual information* in information theory quantifies the mutual dependence of two random variables. It is usually denoted as $I(X;Y)$ and computed as the difference $H(X) - H(X \mid Y)$ where $H(X \mid Y)$ is the conditional entropy of X when knowing Y. In the context of query privacy, we can use mutual information to evaluate the uncertainty reduced after revealing the generalised query. Before the generalised query is known to the attcker, he only knows that the query q can be issued by a user U in $\mathcal{U}$ with the probability $p(U \mid q)$. So the uncertainty of the attacker can be described as entropy $H(U \mid q)$. After the attacker learns the generalised query, the uncertainty on the issuer can be described as the conditional entropy $H(U \mid \langle r,t,q \rangle)$. Therefore, for a given query q the amount of information gained by the attacker after observing the corresponding generalised query can be computed as

$$\begin{aligned} I(U \mid q; \langle r,t,q \rangle) = &\ H(U \mid q) - H(U \mid \langle r,t,q \rangle) \\ = &\ -\textstyle\sum_{u' \in \mathcal{U}} p(u' \mid q) \cdot \log p(u' \mid q) \\ &\ + \textstyle\sum_{u' \in u\ell(r,t)} p(u' \mid \langle r,t,q \rangle) \cdot \\ &\ \qquad \log p(u' \mid \langle r,t,q \rangle). \end{aligned}$$

Similar to β-EBA, the issuer of query $\langle r,t,q \rangle$ is γ-mutual information based anonymous if $I(U \mid q; \langle r,t,q \rangle)$ is less than γ and all users in region r have it as the generalised region when issuing q.

DEFINITION 5. *Let* $\gamma > 0$, $\langle u, whereis(u,t), t, q \rangle \in Q$ *be a query and* $\langle r,t,q \rangle \in Q'$ *the corresponding generalised query. The issuer* u *is* γ-*mutual information based anonymous if for all* $u' \in u\ell(r,t)$,

$$I(U \mid q; \langle r,t,q \rangle) \leq \gamma \ \wedge \ f(\langle u', whereis(u',t), t, q \rangle) = \langle r,t,q \rangle$$

For short, we call γ-mutual information based anonymity γ-MIA.

5. GENERALISATION ALGORITHMS

In this section, we develop generalisation (or spatial cloaking) algorithms to compute regions satisfying users' privacy requirements in terms of the metrics presented in Sect. 4. As to find a region satisfying k-ABS is similar to compute a region satisfying k-anonymity on a given spatial distribution, we design an algorithm for k-ABS by combining the algorithm grid [20] with the clustering algorithm K-Means [19]. For the other metrics, we design a uniform algorithm based on dichotomicPoints [20] with a newly developed function updateAS to update the intermediate regions.

5.1 An algorithm for k-ABS

To find an area that satisfies k-ABS, we have two main steps. The first is to obtain the spatial distribution of users who have similar probabilities to the issuer. The second step is to run a k-anonymity generalisation algorithm to find a region with at least k users based on the distribution computed at the first step.

The task of the first step can be transformed to the clustering problem. Given $q \in \mathcal{Q}$, we need to cluster the elements in $\mathcal{M}(q)$ such that the users with similar probabilities are grouped together. K-Means is the simplest learning algorithm to solve the clustering problem [19]. The number of clusters is fixed a priori. The main idea is to define K centroids, one for each cluster. In our algorithm, the K centroids are chosen uniformly in $[0, 1]$. Then the points (the elements in $\mathcal{M}(q)$ in our case) are associated to the nearest centroid, resulting in K clusters. The centers of these K clusters are updated as the new centroids. Afterwards, all points need to be binded to the current centroids. This process continues until the centroids remain unchanged between two consecutive iterations. In our case, K is chosen and fixed by the anonymiser. In fact, it defines 'similarity' in the definition of k-ABS in Sect. 4, i.e., ϵ. The larger K is, the smaller ϵ becomes.

For the second step, we use algorithm grid by Mascetti et al. [20] as it generates more regular regions with smaller area compared to others. A two-dimensional space is partitioned into a grid with $\lfloor \frac{N}{k} \rfloor$ cells each of which contains at least k users, where N denotes the number of users in $\mathcal{U}$. A user's position is represented by two dimensions x and y. The algorithm grid consists of two steps. First, users are ordered based on dimension x, and then on y. The ordered users are divided into $\lfloor \sqrt{\frac{N}{k}} \rfloor$ blocks of consecutive users. The block with the issuer enters the second step. The users in this block are then ordered first based on dimension y and then x. These users are also partitioned into $\lfloor \sqrt{\frac{N}{k}} \rfloor$ blocks. Then the block with the issuer is returned as the anonymity set. Details of the grid algorithm can be found in [20].

Alg. 1 describes our algorithm for k-ABS. In general, it takes the user requirement k and the number of clusters K defined by the anonymiser as inputs and gives the generalised region as output. Function K-Means returns the cluster of users with similar probabilities to that of u with respect to query q. Then the function grid outputs a subset of sim_users with at least k users who are located in the rectangular region. The generalised region is computed by function region.

Algorithm 1 A generalisation algorithm for k-ABS.

1: FUNCTION: kABS
2: INPUT: $\langle u, whereis(u,t), t, q \rangle, dis(t), \mathcal{M}(q), K, k$
3: OUTPUT: A region r that satisfies k-ABS
4:
5: $sim\_users :=$ K-Means$(u, q, K, \mathcal{M}(q))$;
6: $AS :=$ grid$(sim\_users, dis(t), k)$;
7: $r :=$ region(AS)

Note that the clustering algorithm does not have to run each time when there is a query coming to the anoymiser. As long as the spatial distribution remains static or does not have big changes, for the queries received during this period, the anonymiser just executes the clustering algorithm once and returns the cluster containing the issuer as output of function K-Means directly.

In Alg. 1, K-Means can terminate in time $\mathcal{O}(N^{K+1} \log N)$ where N is the number of users [1]. The complexity of grid algorithm is $\mathcal{O}(\sqrt{kN} \log \sqrt{kN})$ [20]. Therefore, in general, the complexity of Alg. 1 is $\mathcal{O}(N^{K+1} \log N + \sqrt{kN} \log \sqrt{kN})$. The correctness of Alg. 2 is stated as Thm. 2.

THEOREM 2. *For any $\langle u, \ell, t, q \rangle \in Q$, Alg. 1 computes a generalised region in which the issuer u is k-approximate beyond suspicious.*

5.2 An algorithm for α-USI, β-EBA, γ-MIA

For privacy metrics α-USI, β-EBA, and γ-MIA, we design a uniform algorithm where users can specify which metric to use. Recall that in grid, the number of cells is pre-determined by k and the number of users. Thus it is not suitable to perform area generalisation for metrics without a predefined number k. Instead we use the algorithm dichotomicPoints to achieve our design goal.

The execution of dichotomicPoints involves multiple iterations in each of which users are split into two subsets. Similar to grid, positions are represented in two dimensions x and y, and users are also ordered based on their positions. However, different from grid the orders between axises are determined by the shape of intermediate regions rather than fixed beforehand. Specifically, if a region has a longer projection on dimension x, then x is used as the first order to sort the users. Otherwise, y is used as the first order. Users are then ordered based on the values of their positions on the first order axis and then the second order. Subsequently, users are partitioned into two blocks with the same or similar number of users along the first order axis. The block containing the issuer is taken into the next iteration. This process is repeated until any of the two blocks contains less than $2k$ users. This termination criterion is to ensure security against the outlier problem for k-anonymity (see Sect. 2).

However, in our uniform algorithm, instead of checking the number of users, we takes the satisfaction of users' privacy requirement as the termination criterion, e.g., if all users in the two blocks have a probability smaller than α. When issuing a query $q \in \mathcal{Q}$, the issuer u's privacy requirement $req(\langle u, whereis(u,t), t, q \rangle)$ consists of a chosen metric (i.e., USI, EBA, MIA) and its corresponding value (i.e., α, β, γ). For instance, if a user wants to hide in a set of users with a probability smaller than 20% for issuing a query, then his privacy requirement is specified as (USI, 20%).

In our uniform algorithm, after the determination of the first order axis, we call function updateAS. It takes a set of users and partitions them into two subsets along the first order axis, both of which should satisfy the issuer's privacy requirement and updateAS returns the one containing the issuer as the updated anonymity set. When it is not possible to partition users along the first order axis, i.e., one of the two blocks generatlised by any partition fails the issuer's requirement, the second order axis will be tried. If both tries have failed, updateAS simply returns the original set, which means no possible partition can be made with respect to the privacy requirement. In this situation, the whole algorithm terminates. Otherwise, the new set of users returned by update AS is taken into the next iteration.

Our uniform algorithm is described in Alg. 2. The boolean variable $cont$ is used to decide whether the algorithm should continue. It is set to *false* when the set of users in AS does not satisfy the requirement (line 6) or when AS cannot be partitioned furthermore (line 26). In both cases, the algorithm terminates. The anonymity set AS is represented as a two-dimensional array. After ordering users in AS, $AS[i]$ consists of all users whose positions have the

Algorithm 2 The uniform generalisation algorithm for α-USI, β-EBA, and γ-MIA.

```
1: FUNCTION: uniformDP
2: INPUT: qu = ⟨u, whereis(u,t), t, q⟩, req(qu), dis(t), M(q)
3: OUTPUT: Region r that satisfies req(qu)
4:
5:   AS := U;
6:   cont := check(AS, req(u));
7:   while cont do
8:       min_x := min_{u'∈AS} whereis(u').x;
9:       min_y := min_{u'∈AS} whereis(u').y;
10:      max_x := max_{u'∈AS} whereis(u').x;
11:      max_y := max_{u'∈AS} whereis(u').y;
12:      if (max_x − min_x) ≥ (max_y − min_x) then
13:          first := x;
14:          second := y;
15:      else
16:          first := y;
17:          second := x;
18:      end if
19:      AS' = updateAS(AS, req(qu), first, dis(t), M(q));
20:      if AS' = AS then
21:          AS' = updateAS(AS, req(qu), second, dis(t), M(q));
22:      end if
23:      if AS' ≠ AS then
24:          cont := true;
25:      else
26:          cont := false;
27:      end if
28:  end while
29:  return region(AS);
```

Algorithm 3 The function updateAS.

```
1: FUNCTION: updateAS
2: INPUT: AS, req(qu), order, dis(t), M(q)
3: OUTPUT: AS' ⊆ AS that contains u and satisfies req(qu)
4:
5:   AS := reorder(AS, order);
6:   i := mid(AS, order);
7:   if check(left(i), req(qu)) ∧ check(right(i), req(qu)) then
8:       AS := part(i, u);
9:   else
10:      found := false;
11:      j := 0;
12:      while j ≤ len(order) ∧ ¬found do
13:          if check(left(j), req(qu)) ∧ check(right(j), req(qu))
             then
14:              found := true;
15:              AS := part(j, u);
16:          else
17:              j := j + 1;
18:          end if
19:      end while
20:  end if
21:  return AS;
```

same value on the first order axis. We use len($order$) to denote the size of AS in the dimension denoted by $order$. For instance, in Fig. 2(a), axis x is the first order axis and $AS[3]$ has three users with the same x values. Moreover, len($first$) is 6.

The function updateAS shown in Alg. 3 is critical for our algorithm uniformDP. It takes as input a set of users and outputs a subset that satisfies the issuer's privacy requirement $req(qu)$. It first orders the users and then divides them into two subsets with the same number of users along the first order axis (indicated by the variable $order$). This operation is implemented by the function mid($AS, order$) which returns the middle user's index in the first dimension of AS. If both of the two subsets satisfy $req(qu)$, then the one containing the issuer is returned (implemented by function part(i, u)). Otherwise, an iterative process is started. In jth iteration, the users are partitioned into two sets one of which contains the users in $AS[1], \ldots, AS[j]$ (denoted by left(j)) and the other contains the rest (denoted by right(j)). These two sets are checked against the privacy requirement $req(qu)$. If both left(j) and right(j) satisfy $req(qu)$, the one with issuer u is returned by part(j, u). If there are no partitions feasible after len($order$) iterations, the original set of users is returned.

An example execution of Alg. 2 is shown in Fig. 2. The issuer is represented as a black dot. In Fig. 2(a) the users are first partitioned into two parts from the middle. Assume both parts satisfy $req(qu)$, so the set b_1 is returned as the anonymity set AS for the next iteration. As b_1's projection on axis y is longer, the first order is set to axis y (Fig. 2(b)). If after dividing the users from the middle, the set b_2 does not satisfy $req(qu)$. Thus, the users are partitioned from $AS[1]$ to $AS[4]$ (Fig. 2(c)). Suppose no partitions are feasible. The

first order axis is then switched to axis x. Function updateAS is called again to find a partition along axis x (Fig. 2(d)).

We can see Alg. 2 iterates for a number of times. In each iteration, some users are removed from the previous anonymity set. Operations such as partition and requirement check are time-linear in the size of the anonymity set. The number of iterations is logarithmic in the number of the users. So in the worst case, the time complexity of Alg. 2 is $\mathcal{O}(N \log N)$, where N denotes the number of all users in $\mathcal{U}$. The correctness of Alg. 2 is stated as Thm. 3.

THEOREM 3. *For any query* $\langle u, \ell, t, q \rangle$, *Alg. 2 computes a generalised region that satisfies the issuer u's privacy requirement* $req(\langle u, whereis(u,t), t, q \rangle)$.

Detailed proof of the theorem is given in the appendix.

6. EXPERIMENTAL RESULTS

We have performed an extensive experimental evaluation of the metrics presented in Sect. 4 using the algorithms in Sect. 5. The experiments are based on a dataset with 10,000 users' locations generated by the moving object generator developed by Brinkhoff [4]. Users' locations are scattered in the city of Oldenburg (Germany). As we focus on evaluating our generalisation algorithms, we randomly assign a priori probabilities to users although it is possible to generate user profiles as in [26] and calculate the probabilities using our methodology described in Sect. 3.

We implemented the algorithms using Java and experiments are run on a Linux laptop with 2.67Ghz Intel Core(TM) and 4GB memory. The results discussed in this section are obtained by taking the average of 100 simulations of the corresponding algorithms.

Through experiments, for all the proposed metrics we present the impact of the user specified parameters to the average area of generalised regions, in order to help users determine the right trade-off between privacy protection and the quality of services. Moreover, we illustrate the features of different metrics. In particular, we show that k-ABS gives a better protection than k-anonymity to users, who are potentially more likely to issue a query that others. The other metrics α-USI, β-EBA, γ-MIA are insensitive to users' a priori probabilities. Last, we show our algorithms are efficient

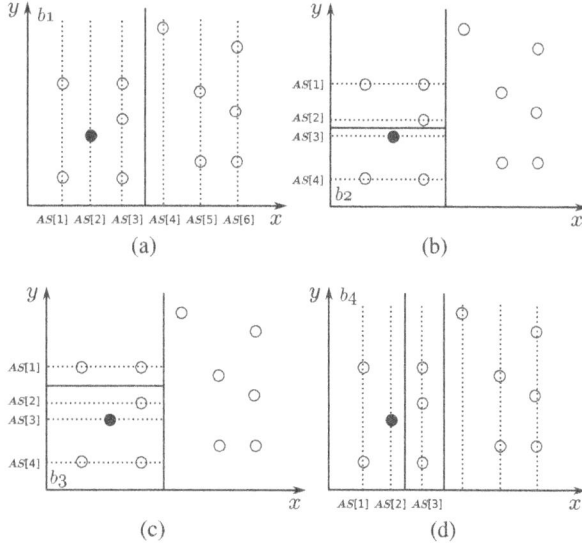

Figure 2: An example execution of our algorithm uniformDP

enough for practical applications which require real-time response by evaluating the average processing time.

6.1 k-ABS

We first address the comparison between k-anonymity and k-ABS and discuss the impact of the parameter K used in the clustering algorithm K-Means (see Alg. 1). In Fig. 3 we show how a user's a posteriori probability ($p(u \mid \langle r, t, q \rangle)$ changes with with respect to k and K. We have selected a user with a relatively high a priori probability so as to compare the performance of both metrics in protecting users who are more likely to issue the query.

First, the user's a posteriori probability decreases as k increases. This is because larger k means more users are in the generalised region. Second, for a given k, the issuer's posteriori probability is normally larger than $\frac{1}{k}$ when k-anonymity is used, but closer to $\frac{1}{k}$ when k-ABS is adopted. This is because that in an anonymity set of k-anonymity, uses have larger differences among their a priori probabilities than the users in an anonymity of k-ABS. Third, in k-ABS, for a given k, the issuer's a posteriori probability is much closer to $\frac{1}{k}$ when more clusters are divided (i.e., bigger K). This can be explained by the observation that more clusters make the users in a cluster containing the issuer become more probable to be the same likely to issue the query.

Fig. 4 shows the average area of generalised regions by Alg. 1. In general, the area becomes larger when k increases. We can also observe that compared to k-anonymity, k-ABS has larger regions for a given value of k. Moreover, when k is fixed the area gets larger when K increases. These observations are all due to the fact that more clusters result in fewer users in each cluster, which in turn leads to larger regions to cover k users.

According to the above observations, the anonymiser can determine an appropriate value of K based on users' a priori distribution for a query (i.e. $\mathcal{M}(q)$) in order to balance users' query privacy and quality of service (smaller area, better quality).

6.2 α-USI

An issuer satisfies α-USI if from the attacker's view each user in the generalised region has a probability smaller than the specified value α to be the issuer.

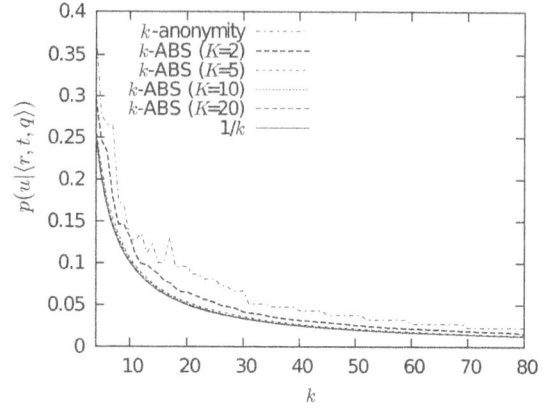

Figure 3: Posterior probabilities (k-ABS)

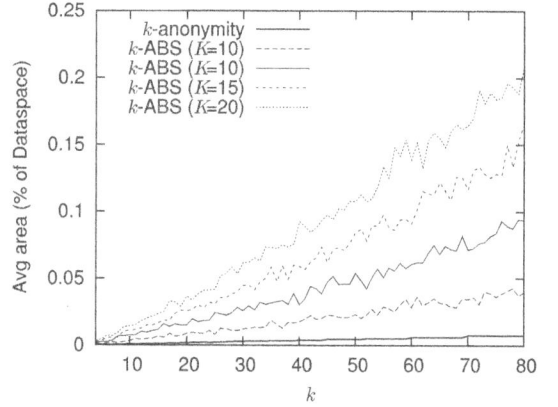

Figure 4: Area of generalised regions (k-ABS)

In Fig. 5, we show that the average a posteriori probabilities of issuers with different a priori probabilities (indicated by lines marked 'high', 'medium' and 'low') and different specified values of α. We use a reference line to indicate the difference between users' requirement (α) and the result of Alg. 2. First, we find that users' a posteriori probabilities are always smaller than α, which shows the correctness of our algorithm. Second, for users with relatively high a priori probabilities, their a posteriori probabilities are closer to their requirements in terms of α. Meanwhile, for the users with low a priori probabilities, the value of α does not have a big influence on users' a posteriori probabilities. This can be explained by the definition of α-USI. A generalised region has to ensure that all users within it have a posteriori probabilities smaller than α (this is required to fix the outlier problem).

Fig. 6 shows changes of generalised regions' area along with α and the impact of users' a priori probabilities. The generalised regions become smaller as α increases. As we can see in Alg. 2, issuers' positions and α determine the generalised regions. Users' a priori probabilities have little impact on the generalisation process. This is also confirmed by experiments. In Fig. 6 users with different levels of a priori probabilities have regions with similar sizes.

Usually, for a given query users have an approximate estimation of their a priori probabilities compared to others, e.g., high or low. The above analysis enables users to estimate their a posteriori probabilities with regards to different values of α. This in turn helps them to choose an appropriate value for α to balance their query privacy and quality of service.

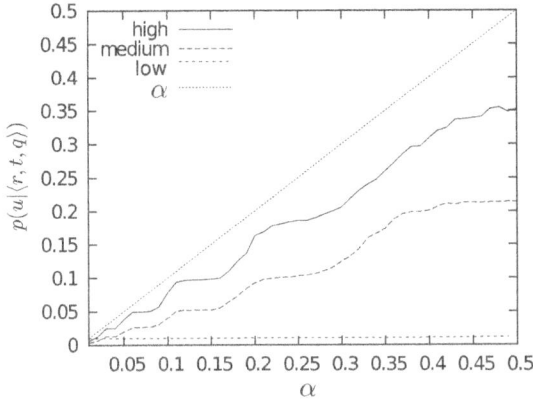

Figure 5: Posterior probabilities (α-USI)

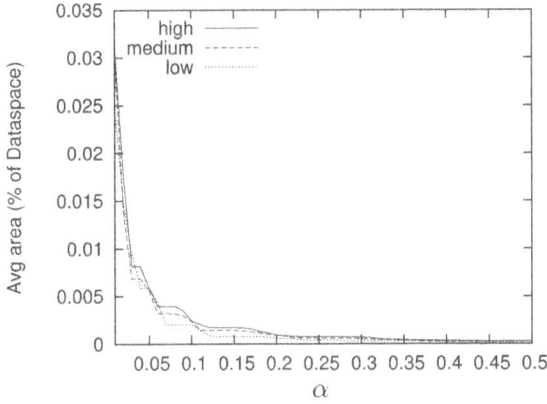

Figure 7: Entropies (β-EBA)

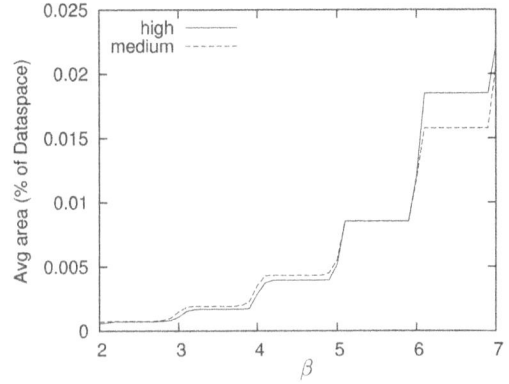

Figure 6: Area of generalised regions (α-USI)

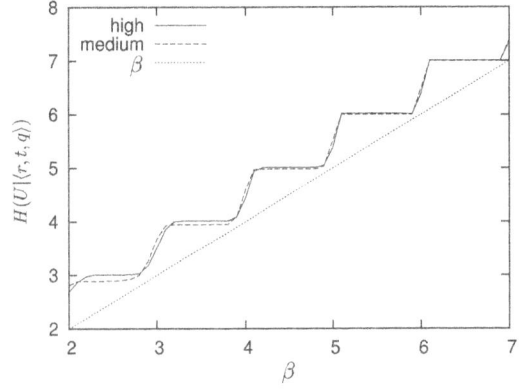

Figure 8: Area of generalised regions (β-EBA)

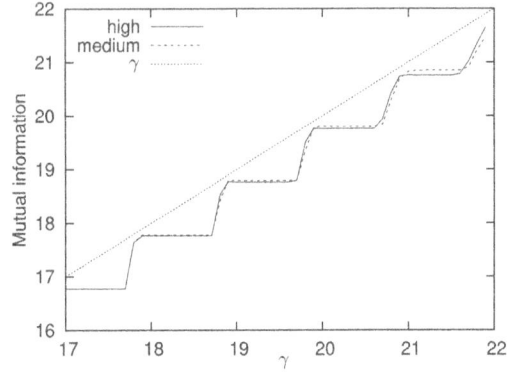

Figure 9: Mutual information (γ-MIA)

6.3 β-EBA and γ-MIA

A generalised region that satisfies β-EBA ensures that the entropy over users in the region is larger than β, while γ-MIA ensures that the amount of uncertainty reduced is less than γ.

In Fig. 7 and Fig. 9, we show that the entropies and mutual information corresponding to the generalised regions by our algorithm satisfy the definitions of β-EBA and γ-MIA. We can observe that users' a priori probabilities do not have impact on the outputs – the two lines for users with high and low a priori probabilities almost coincide. Similar to α-USI, this is because a generalised region is determined by the values β or γ and issuers' positions rather than their a priori probabilities. The values of entropy (resp. mutual information) change sharply when β (resp. γ) is getting close to integers, this is due to the nature of entropy. Similarly, we show how the average area of generalised regions changes along with β and γ in Fig. 8 and Fig. 10, respectively – the area usually gets doubled when β and γ are increased by one.

6.4 Performance analysis

We illustrate the performance of Alg. 1 through Fig. 12. Although the clustering algorithm needs to run only once for a spatial distribution for a given K, we execute it for each query instead in order to test the performance in the worst case when there happens to be only one query issued. As algorithm K-Means has a complexity depending on K, for a given k the computation time increases when K becomes larger. When $K = 5$, the average computation time is about 140ms while it is around 250ms when $K = 20$.

Fig. 11 shows the average computation time of Alg. 2 (for α-USI and β-EBA) and grid (for k-anonymity). In this figure, we use a normalised value $norm$ to compare the performance for different metrics: $norm = k$ for k-anonymity, while $norm = 1/\alpha$ for α-USI and $norm = 2^{\beta}$ for β-EBA, respectively. The computation time of β-EBA (11 – 12ms) is a bit larger than α-USI (about 10ms) because computing entropy is a bit more complex. Furthermore, as $norm$ increases, more time is needed for β-EBA. This is also determined by Alg. 3, where larger k leads to more time to traverse the region in order to find a possible partition. The implementation for γ-MIA is based on the calculation of entropies, so in general the computation time of γ-MIA is almost same as β-EBA.

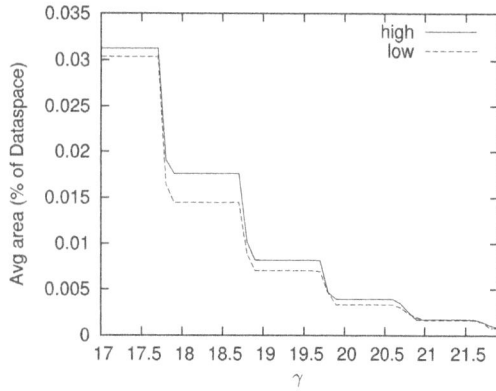

Figure 10: Area of generalised regions (γ-MIA)

We can observe that the computation time of algorithm grid is linear with k (see k-anonymity in Fig. 11), which confirms the results in [20]. However, due to the complexity of the clustering algorithm K-Means used in Alg. 1, the impact of k is not obvious in Fig. 12.

There exist a few ways to improve the efficiency of our implementations such as using a better data structure and reducing redundant computation. With powerful servers deployed in practice, our roposed generalisation algorithms are efficient enough to handle concurrent queries and give real-time responses.

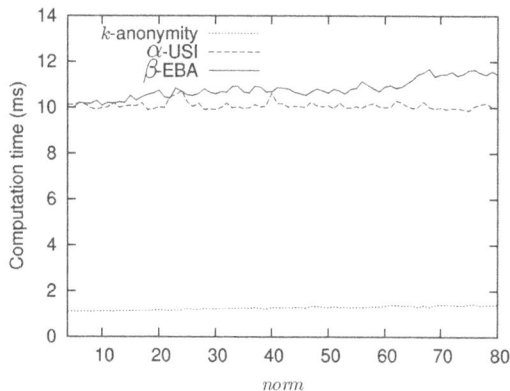

Figure 11: Computation time of the algorithms.

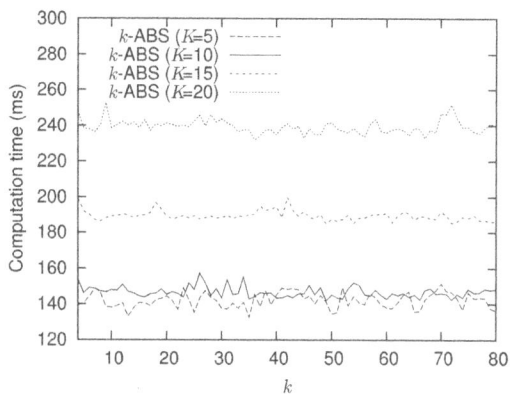

Figure 12: Computation time of the algorithms.

7. CONCLUSION

In this paper, we consider a powerful attacker who can obtain user profiles and has access to users' real-time positions in the context of LBSs. Assuming this stronger attacker model, we propose new metrics to correctly measure users' query privacy in LBSs, including k-ABS, α-USI, β-EBA and γ-MIA. For information theory based metrics, the determination of users' specified values is not intuitive. However, users can use other metrics as references. For instance, k-anonymity corresponds to $\log k$-EBA when the distribution for users to issue a query is (close to) uniform. Spacial generalisation algorithms are developed to compute regions satisfying user's privacy requirements specified in the proposed metrics. Extensive experiments show our metrics are effective in balancing privacy and quality of service in LBSs and the algorithms are efficient to meet the requirement of real-time responses.

Our metrics are not exhaustive, and there exist other ways to express query privacy. For instance, we can use min-entropy to express information leakage [31] in a way analogous to mutual information: $I_\infty(X; Y) = H_\infty(X) - H_\infty(X \mid Y)$. Intuitively, it measure the amount of min-entropy reduced after the attacker has observed a generalised query. It is very interesting to study differential privacy [12] to see how it can be adopted for LBS scenarios.

In future, we want to develop an application for an LBS, making use of the proposed metrics to protect users' query privacy. This can lead us to a better understanding of privacy challenges in more realistic situations. The implementation of our algorithms can also be improved as well, e.g., using a better clustering algorithm for kABS. Another interesting direction is to study a more stronger attacker model, where the attacker, for instance, can have access to mobility patterns of users.

8. REFERENCES

[1] D. Arthur, B. Manthey, and H. Röglin. k-Means has polynomial smoothed complexity. In *Proc. 50th Symposium on Foundations of Computer Science (FOCS)*, pp. 405–414. IEEE CS, 2009.

[2] A. R. Beresford. *Location privacy in ubiquitous computing*. PhD thesis, University of Cambridge, 2005.

[3] O. Berthold, A. Pfiztmann, and R. Standtke. The disadvantages of free mix routes and how to overcome them. In *Proc. Workshop on Design Issues in Anonymity and Unobservability*, LNCS 2009, pp. 30–45. Springer, 2000.

[4] T. Brinkhoff. A framework for generating network-based moving objects. *GeoInformatica*, 6(2):153–180, 2002.

[5] K. Chatzikokolakis, C. Palamidessi, and P. Panangaden. Anonymity protocols as noisy channels. *Information and Computation*, 206(2-4):378–401, 2008.

[6] D. Chaum. The dining cryptographers problem: Unconditional sender and recipient untraceability. *Journal of Cryptology*, 1(1):65–75, 1988.

[7] R. Cheng, Y. Zhang, E. Bertino, and S. Prabhakar. Preserving user location privacy in mobile data management infrastructures. In *Proc. 6th Workshop on Privacy Enhancing Technologies (PET)*, LNCS 4258, pp. 393–412, 2006.

[8] C.-Y. Chow, M. F. Mokbel, and W. G. Aref. Casper*: Query processing for location services without compromising privacy. *ACM Transactions on Database Systems*, 34(4):1–48, 2009.

[9] M. R. Clarkson, A. C. Myers, and F. B. Schneider. Quantifying information flow with beliefs. *Journal of Computer Security*, 17(5):655–701, 2009.

[10] Y. Deng, J. Pang, and P. Wu. Measuring anonymity with relative entropy. In *Proc. 4th Workshop on Formal Aspects in Security and Trust (FAST)*, LNCS 4691, pp. 65–79. Springer, 2007.

[11] C. Díaz, S. Seys, J. Claessens, and B. Preneel. Towards measuring anonymity. In *Proc. 2nd Workshop on Privacy Enhancing Technologies (PET)*, LNCS 2482, pp. 54–68. Springer, 2003.

[12] C. Dwork. Differential privacy. in *Proc. 33rd International Colloquium on Automata, Languages and Programmin (ICALP)*, LNCS 4052, pp. 1-12. Springer, 2006.

[13] J. Freudiger, R. Shokri, and J. P. Hubaux. Evaluating the privacy risk of location-based services. In *Proc. 15th Conference on Financial Cryptography and Data Security (FC)*, LNCS. Springer, 2011.

[14] B. Gedik and L. Liu. Protecting location privacy with personalized k-anonymity: Architecture and algorithms. *IEEE Transactions on Mobile Computing*, 7(1):1–18, 2008.

[15] M. Gruteser and D. Grunwald. Anonymous usage of location-based services through spatial and temporal cloaking. In *Proc. 1st Conference on Mobile Systems, Applications, and Services (MobiSys)*. USENIX, 2003.

[16] P. Kalnis, G. Ghinita, K. Mouratidis, and D. Papadias. Preventing location-based identity inference in anonymous spatial queries. *IEEE Transactions on Knowledge and Data Engineering*, 19(12):1719–1733, 2007.

[17] J. M. Kleinberg. Challenges in mining social network data: processes, privacy, and paradoxes. In *Proc. 13th ACM SIGKDD Conference on Knowledge Discovery and Data Mining (KDD)*, pp. 4–5. ACM, 2007.

[18] N. Li, T. Li, and S. Venkatasubramanian. t-closeness: Privacy beyond k-anonymity and l-diversity. In *Proc. 23rd Conference on Data Engineering (ICDE)*, pp. 106–115. IEEE CS, 2007.

[19] J. B. MacQueen. Some methods for classification and analysis of multivariate observations. In *Proc. 5th Berkeley Symposium on Mathematical Statistics and Probability*, volume 1, pp. 281–297. University of California, 1967.

[20] S. Mascetti, C. Bettini, D. Freni, and X. S. Wang. Spatial generalization algorithms for LBS privacy preservation. *Journal of Location Based Services*, 1(3):179–207, 2007.

[21] M. F. Mokbel, C.-Y. Chow, and W. G. Aref. The new casper: A privacy-aware location-based database server. In *Proc. 23rd Conference on Data Engineering (ICDE)*, pp. 1499–1500. IEEE CS, 2007.

[22] M. K. Reiter and A. D. Rubin. Crowds: Anonymity for web transactions. *ACM Transactions on Information and System Security*, 1(1):66–92, 1998.

[23] A. Rényi. On measures of entropy and information. In *Proc. 4th Berkeley Symposium on Mathematics, Statistics, and Probability*, pp. 547–561. University of California, 1961.

[24] P. Samarati. Protecting respondents' identities in microdata release. *IEEE Transactions on Knowledge and Data Engineering*, 13(6):1010–1027, 2001.

[25] A. Serjantov and G. Danezis. Towards an information theoretic metric for anonymity. In *Proc. 2nd Workshop on Privacy Enhancing Technologies (PET)*, LNCS 2482, pp. 41–53. Springer, 2003.

[26] H. Shin, V. Atluri, and J. Vaidya. A profile anonymization model for privacy in a personalized location based service environment. In *Proc. 9th International Conference on Mobile Data Management (MDM)*, pages 73–80. IEEE CS, 2008.

[27] R. Shokri, J. Freudiger, M. Jadliwala, and J.-P. Hubaux. A distortion-based metric for location privacy. In *Proc. 2009 ACM Workshop on Privacy in the Electronic Society (WPES)*, pp. 21–30. ACM, 2009.

[28] R. Shokri, G. Theodorakopoulos, J.-Y. L. Boudec, and J.-P. Hubaux. Quantifying location privacy. In *Proc. 32nd IEEE Symposium on Security and Privacy (S&P)*. IEEE CS, 2011.

[29] R. Shokri, G. Theodorakopoulos, G. Danezis, and J.-P. Hubaux. Quantifying location privacy: The case of sporadic location exposure. In *Proc. 11th Privacy Enhancing Technologies Symposium (PETS)*, 2011.

[30] R. Shokri, C. Troncoso, C. Díaz, J. Freudiger, and J.-P. Hubaux. Unraveling an old cloak: k-anonymity for location privacy. In *Proc. 2010 ACM Workshop on Privacy in the Electronic Society (WPES)*, pp. 115–118. ACM, 2010.

[31] G. Smith. On the foundations of quantitative information flow. in *Proc. 12th International Conference on Foundations of Software Science and Computation Structures (FOSSACS)*, LNCS 5504, pp. 288–302. Springer, 2009.

[32] K. W. Tan, Y. Lin, and K. Mouratidis. Spatial cloaking revisited: Distinguishing information leakage from anonymity. In *Proc. 11th Symposium on Spatial and Temporal Databases (SSTD)*, LNCS 5644, pp. 117–134. Springer, 2009.

[33] X. Wu, X. Ying, K. Liu, and L. Chen. A survey of algorithms for privacy-preservation of graphs and social networks. In *Managing and Mining Graph Data*, pp. 421–442, 2009.

[34] M. Xue, P. Kalnis, and H. K. Pung. Location diversity: Enhanced privacy protection in location based services. In *Proc. 4th Symposium on Location and Context Awareness (LoCA)*, LNCS 5561, pp. 70–87. Springer, 2009.

[35] Y. Zhu and R. Bettati. Anonymity vs. information leakage in anonymity systems. In *Proc. 25th Conference on Distributed Computing Systems (ICDCS)*, pp. 514–524. IEEE CS, 2005.

APPENDIX

A. PROOF OF THM. 3

PROOF. By Def. 3, Def. 4 and Def. 5, Alg. 2 computes a region r for a query $\langle u, whereis(u,t), t, q \rangle$ that satisfies a constraint related to the issuer's a posteriori probability, entropy, or mutual information. Furthermore, for any $u' \in u\ell(r)$, the algorithm computes the same region. We take α-USI as an example to show the correctness of our algorithm and the proofs of the other two are analogous.

By Def. 3, we have to prove (1) the a posteriori probability of user u is smaller than α, i.e., $p(u \mid \langle r, t, q \rangle) \leq \alpha$; (2) for any $u' \in u\ell(r)$, $f(\langle u', whereis(u',t), t, q \rangle) = \langle r, t, q \rangle$.

(1) At the line 5 of Alg. 2, we set AS to the original user set $\mathcal{U}$ and the algorithm continues only if $\mathcal{U}$ satisfies the issuer's requirement $req(\langle u, whereis u, t, q \rangle)$. Otherwise, it is impossible to return a region satisfying the requirement. The set AS is only reassigned to another set when a partition is made (line 8 or line 15 in Alg. 3). The two sets by the partition satisfy the requirement and the one containing the issuer is assigned to AS. Thus, it is guaranteed that the final region r ensures $p(u \mid \langle r, t, q \rangle) \leq \alpha$.

(2) Let u' be any user in the generalised region r of Alg. 2. Let AS_j and AS'_j be the values of AS in the jth iteration of Alg. 2 of u and u', respectively. We show that $AS_j = AS'$ by induction on the number of iterations, i.e. j.

INDUCTION BASIS: Initially, we suppose $\mathcal{U}$ meets the requirement. Then we have $AS_1 = AS'_1$.

INDUCTION STEP: Assume at jth iteration $AS_j = AS'_j$. We have to show that the algorithm either terminates with AS_j and AS'_j, or enter the next iteration with $AS_{j+1} = AS'_{j+1}$. The equality that $AS_j = AS'_j$ is followed by that $\text{mid}(AS_j, order) = \text{mid}(AS'_j, order)$. There are three possible executions.

Case 1: if $left(i)$ and $right(i)$ of AS_j and AS'_j satisfy the requirements (line 7 of Alg. 3), the part containing the issuer is returned. Thus AS_{j+1} contains u as well as all other users in $u\ell(r)$, including u'. Thus, $AS_{j+1} = AS'_{j+1}$.

Case 2: if the check at line 7 of Alg. 3 fails, then the algorithm switches to find from the beginning the first feasible partition. Suppose the partition is made at the position x for AS_j. Then x is also the right position for AS'_j as $AS_j = AS'_j$. Because of the similar reason in the previous possible execution, the same subset is set to AS_{j+1} and AS'_{j+1}. Thus, $AS_{j+1} = AS'_{j+1}$.

Case 3: if there are no possible partitions, Alg. 3 returns AS_{j+1} and AS'_{j+1} in both cases. Then the first order is changed and Alg. 3 is called again. If one of the first two execution is taken, with the analysis above, we have $AS_{j+1} = AS'_{j+1}$. Otherwise, Alg. 2 terminates with $\text{region}(AS_j)$ and $\text{region}(AS'_j)$ which are equal. $\square$

Revisiting Link Privacy in Social Networks

Suhendry Effendy
effendy@comp.nus.edu.sg

Roland H.C. Yap
ryap@comp.nus.edu.sg

Felix Halim
halim@comp.nus.edu.sg

School of Computing
National University of Singapore
13 Computing Drive, Singapore

ABSTRACT

In this paper, we revisit the problem of the link privacy attack in online social networks. In the link privacy attack, it turns out that by bribing or compromising a small number of nodes (users) in the social network graph, it is possible to obtain complete link information for a much larger fraction of other non-bribed nodes in the graph. This can constitute a significant privacy breach in online social networks where the link information of nodes is kept private or accessible only to closely related nodes.

We show that the link privacy attack can be made even more effective with degree inference. Since online social networks typically have high degree, the link privacy attack becomes quite feasible even with an in-lookahead neighborhood of one (only friends can see a user's links/profile). To reduce the effect of the link privacy attack, we present several practical mitigation strategies – non-uniform user privacy settings, approximation of the node degree information and a non-constant cost model for the attack. All the strategies are able to mitigate the privacy link attack by either reducing the effectiveness of the attack or by making it more expensive to mount. Interestingly, some of the more efficient strategies now become worse than the RANDOM strategy and the effect of a larger neighborhood which would otherwise make the attack even more efficient can be mitigated.

Categories and Subject Descriptors

F.2.2 [**Theory of Computation**]: Analysis of Algorithms and Problem Complexity—*Nonnumerical Algorithms and Problems*; H.2.8 [**Information Systems**]: Database Management—*Database applications*[Data mining]; J.4 [**Computer Applications**]: Social and Behavioral Sciences—*Sociology*

General Terms

Algorithms, Design, Experimentation, Security

Keywords

Privacy, social networks, crawlers

1. INTRODUCTION

Nowadays, online social networks (OSN) are extremely popular with a significant fraction of Internet users using social networks (well over half a billion users) [14]. The social graph of the relationships between users as well as other related data becomes a key asset of the OSN. This is illustrated by the well publicized falling out between Google and Facebook when it comes to sharing the social graph and differences in privacy policies [15]. Most OSNs have privacy controls and policies to protect the information in the social graph from being disclosed to the public or to other users. In fact, such controls and policies are constant evolving in OSNs.

How much information is disclosed to the public or other users depends on the particular OSN. In some OSNs, many users have open profiles where much of the graph information about the relationships of the user to other users (the edges or links) is publicly disclosed, e.g. in Facebook many users have profiles which are open to any other user in Facebook. In other OSNs, the link information may be mostly private. A prime example is LinkedIn where the edges (friend information) is not public and is only disclosed to other friends. In this paper, we are concerned with the second case rather than OSNs where link data is predominantly public where there are less privacy concerns as a large portion of the graph is crawlable from the publicly disclosed information [6].[1]

In this paper, we are concerned on protecting the privacy of the users focusing on mostly private or closed OSNs. We remark that privacy need not only be a concern of the users but it is also a key concern of the OSN sites themselves [15]. The constant evolution of privacy control/policies of OSNs may also be in response to sites protecting privacy of their users and to prevent other entities from stealing or profiting from that information. Privacy policies are usually controlled based on the distance between users in the social graph. For example, a user can only view the link (or other private) information revealed by their friends. The objective of an attacker would be to steal and collect as much information as possible. This may be achieved by hacking into the users' account [9] or by leveraging on weak privacy settings of some users which leak private information about their friends [8].

One might think that a mostly private OSN like LinkedIn, where the only publicly available information is a user and degree public directory, will not suffer from additional privacy leaks. However, a recent paper by Korolova et al [7] shows that the privacy leak can be significant. In this paper, we revisit this problem from two perspectives. Firstly, we show that the privacy leak can be worse than shown in [7] since we used more OSNs (real and also synthetic) which are larger. The effectiveness of privacy attacks depend on

---

[1]Note that in some cases, it may be necessary to be a member of the OSN in order to view more public information. We still consider that to be public.

the attacker's strategies and we show that a straightforward use of inference on the graph based on availability of a public degree directory can substantially magnify the attack. Our experiments suggest that that the effectiveness of the attack is due in part to the high degree of nodes in the social graph.

Secondly, given the importance of privacy both for the OSN as a whole as well as from the individual user's perspective, measures which can reduce the effectiveness of privacy leak attacks are desirable. We present several defense measures motivated by existing OSN features which are practical and fit easily with OSN. Our experiments show that these defenses which are able to mitigate the attacks.

In this paper, we propose that the appropriate property to study the link privacy attack is the in-lookahead neighborhood of the social graph. Our experiments show that the use of degree inference can significantly increase the efficiency of the link privacy attack even for an in-lookahead neighborhood of one, thus, the attack becomes even more feasible. We focus on the in-lookahead neighborhood, rather than the out-lookahead used in [7], because the in-lookahead neighborhood is compatible with user node privacy settings which the out-lookahead neighborhood might not be. We show that by providing a privacy control to users to allow them to set their in-lookahead to a smaller value if so desired, the link privacy attack's efficiency can be reduced, even when only some users change their privacy settings. We also show that abstracting the public degree information can help to reduce the attack's efficiency. Furthermore, it can mislead the attacker's strategy which can become worse than not knowing degree information at all.

The paper is organized as follows. Sec. 2 discuss the related work on OSN privacy. We detailed our graph and the attack model in Sec 3. Sec. 4 presents mechanisms to mitigate against link privacy attacks. We show preliminary empirical results on the effectiveness of link privacy attacks and their mitigation in Sec. 5. Finally, Sec. 6 concludes.

2. RELATED WORK

We revisit the problem of link privacy attack which was introduced by Korolova et al. [7]. In this paper, we investigate a different notion of *lookahead* as detailed in Sec. 3. Our *in-lookahead* model captures the real world model used by real social networks (such as Facebook and LinkedIn). We show that under our more realistic in-lookahead model, the attack is less effective than the uniform *out-lookahead* used in [7, 4]. We also investigate other mitigation strategies to reduce the effectiveness of the link privacy attacks.

Mislove et al. [8] show that users' attributes that are closed can be inferred from their friends and suggest to close the friend list as well for stronger privacy. Since the friend list of the public users are still open, it can be used to infer their friends' attributes. However, the link privacy attack shows that closing the friend list is not sufficient. Becker et al. [2] developed a tool to identify such leakage of information and recommend user actions to mitigate privacy risk.

The goal of the link privacy attack is to discover/reveal as much graph information which was originally private. The method suggested in the original attack is to reveal the node (a user in the social graph is modeled as a node) information by bribing or stealing node credentials [7]. However, other techniques are also possible to obtain the same information such as the social network penetration attack [5].

Anonymization of the social graph by collapsing multiple nodes into an anonymized node [11] is concerned about privacy but is different from the scenario addressed by link privacy attacks which operate on the actual OSN.

While public listings can be used to infer/approximate the degree and other properties of graph [3], we are interested in finding the whole/exact node and link structures of the OSN graph by compromising as few nodes as possible.

3. THE MODEL

This section consist of two parts. We first define the graph model (Section 3.1) and the primary goal of the attack (Section 3.2), then we list several possible attack strategies and discuss a theoretical upper bound of any attack using only neighborhood information. Next, we explain how the attacker can increase the efficiency of an attack by degree inference (Section 3.4).

3.1 Graph Model

Although some online social networks, such as LiveJournal, allow uni-directional relations between users, many others such as Facebook and LinkedIn, require a mutual relationship between users. In this paper, we view an online social network as an undirected graph $G = (V, E)$ where the nodes V are the users and the edges E are the relationships, friendships, connections or links between the users.

An online social network could choose to disclose neighborhood information to a certain extent. We model this using the *in-lookahead* and *out-lookahead* of a node. We say a node has in-lookahead $L = 0$ if the node (the user) is the only one who can see exactly who it links to, i.e. a closed user profile; and a node has in-lookahead $L = 1$ if the user and the friends of the node can see exactly who the node links to. More formally, a node has in-lookahead L if any node whose distance is no more than L can see that node's entire immediate neighborhood. The concept of in-lookahead of a node is that a node restricts what can be seen by *other nodes*.

The dual of in-lookahead is out-lookahead where a node can specify what information the node can access at distance L from itself. In other words, a node has out-lookahead $L = 0$ if only the user itself can see exactly its own links (this should always be possible); and it has out-lookahead $L = 1$ if the user can see exactly who the node links to as well as the friends of the friends which the node links to. In general, a node has out-lookahead L if a user can see all of the edges incident to the nodes within distance L from it.

We say a node u is *covered* when the attacker can see exactly who u links to, and u is *seen* when the attacker cannot see all the links of u links but u connects to at least one of the covered nodes (i.e., the node existence is known because of the covered nodes). We will define these terms further in Section 3.2.

In an in-lookahead model, nodes which will be covered by bribing node u are determined by u neighborhood's in-lookahead (not by u's in-lookahead itself). Figure 1(a) shows an example, bribing node u will cover u itself and also nodes a, d, e because their distance to u is not larger than their in-lookahead. Nodes b, f, g and i are seen because their distance to u is larger than their in-lookahead but they are connected to covered nodes, while nodes c and h are neither covered nor seen by bribing u. In an out-lookahead model, nodes which will be covered by bribing node u are determined only by u's out-lookahead. In the Figure 1(b) example, bribing u will cover u itself and its entire immediate neighbors (a, d, g) because u has out-lookahead of one. Nodes b, e, h are seen because their distance to u is larger than u's out-lookahead but they are connected to covered nodes. Nodes c, f and i are neither covered nor seen by bribing node u alone.

The effect of a user's privacy policy is to restrict what infor-

(a) in-lookahead

(b) out-lookahead

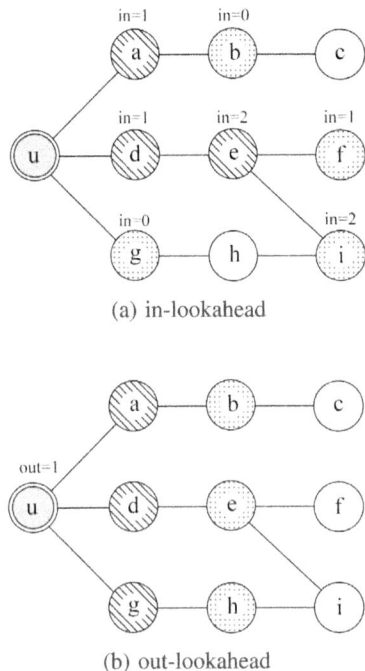

Figure 1: Examples of the in-lookahead and out-lookahead model

mation other nodes in the OSN can access or see. This matches well with the in-lookahead definition. Out-lookahead expresses something rather different from a privacy policy since a node with out-lookahead L unilaterally defines what information is accessible from itself without needing to get permission from other nodes. For example, if an attacker which has a single node can declare that out-lookahead L is the diameter of the social graph, then all nodes can be seen. Thus, out-lookahead is incompatible with privacy policies.

In a uniform out-lookahead environment, each node is able to see nodes whose distance is no more than L from itself, which means that only nodes whose distance is within L from each other can see their links. So a node with out-lookahead L will also have in-lookahead L. Alternatively, when the lookahead is uniform, the out-lookahead model is the same as the in-lookahead model. In [7], the out-lookahead neighborhood is used rather than in-lookahead, but they only consider uniform lookahead environment so it does not matter.

It is common for OSNs to provide some form of user controlled privacy settings. For example, in Facebook user could customize their in-lookahead to "only me" ($L = 0$), "friends" ($L = 1$), "friends of friends" ($L = 2$) or "everyone" ($L = \infty$). LinkedIn on the other hand provides "only me" ($L = 0$) or "friends" ($L = 1$). A uniform lookahead neighborhood is too restrictive an assumption given that OSNs are more likely to provide non-uniform in-lookahead neighborhoods as a mechanism for users to control access to their information. For this reason, in this paper, we investigate the effect of non-uniform neighborhoods and focus only on in-lookahead rather than out-lookahead in subsequent discussion and analysis.

In addition to the connection information, some online social networks, such as LinkedIn, also provides other information like degree information of each node and a public directory which contains all usernames. This additional information enables the attacker to discover the link structure of the social network more eas-

ily. In this paper, we use the fact that degree information and user's existence are known to the attacker.

3.2 Goal of the Attack

The primary goal of the link privacy attack is to discover the complete link structure of all or some nodes in the OSN. Conceptually, the attack is achieved either by maliciously breaking into users' account, either through malware on the user's machine or malware in the OSN [9]. Alternatively the attacker can offer a payment or service in exchange for permission to view the neighborhood structure of a node u in the OSN. By gaining access to user u's account, an attacker immediately learns about all edges incident to nodes whose in-lookahead is no less than their distance from u. We call an attacked node u as a *bribed* node and the action taken by the attacker as bribing node u (even if the information may be obtained through other means). If an attacker has already discovered all incident edges to a node, we call such a node *covered*. An attacker can also learn about the existence of node v that connects to covered node and cannot be covered by u because v's in-lookahead is less than its distance to u, we call this node v as *seen* node. In other words, seen nodes are nodes which are neither covered nor bribed and the attacker knows at least an edge to these nodes.

We follow [7] by measuring the attack's effectiveness using the notion of *node coverage*, i.e. the fraction of nodes whose entire immediate neighborhood is known (i.e. covered nodes). One could also consider measuring the attack's effectiveness using *edge coverage*, i.e. the fraction of edges known to the attacker among all edges that exist in the graph. Using *node coverage*, we consider a node is covered if and only if the attacker knows exactly which node it is connected to and which node it is not connected to, thus this notion accounts for the attacker's knowledge about existing and edges which do not exist. Edge coverage, on the other hand, does not capture negative knowledge about edges. Therefore, throughout the paper, we use node coverage as the evaluation measure. Edge coverage is also more difficult to analyze as it is biased by some nodes having high degree (or large neighborhoods) while others may have low degree (or small neighborhoods).

3.3 Attack Strategies

We define node u's *neighborhood* as a collection of nodes whose in-lookahead is greater or equal to its distance to node u. Each time a node is bribed, the attacker can immediately cover its neighborhood, and we call such nodes *directly-covered*. Another type of covered nodes which involves degree inference will be defined further in Section 3.4.

Naturally, the effectiveness of the attacker will depend on which sets of users are bribed. In this paper, we first revisit some natural attack bribery strategies and comparisons based on [7].

- BENCHMARK: Consider an OPTIMAL strategy whose goal is to have the the minimum number of nodes bribed for maximum coverage. This can be reduced to the set cover problem which is NP-hard which would be impractical for large graphs. Instead, the reference point used is the following greedy approximation which is called BENCHMARK.

  Pick the next uncovered node to bribe among all nodes which will cover the maximum number of nodes not yet covered. For $L \leq 1$, this strategy can be employed if the attacker has the degree information of all nodes. However, for $L > 1$, this strategy requires knowledge of the graph itself as it needs to know how many nodes will be covered if a node is bribed. This means that it is not feasible for the attacker to use BENCHMARK for $L > 1$, thus, it is meant as a point of reference rather than a feasible attack strategy.

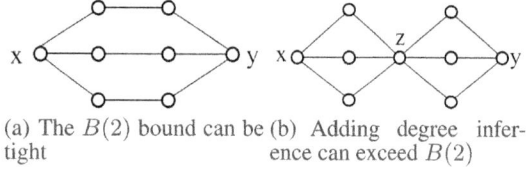

(a) The $B(2)$ bound can be tight   (b) Adding degree inference can exceed $B(2)$

Figure 2: Examples of $B(n)$ on some graphs

- GREEDY: Pick the next uncovered node to bribe among all nodes as one with the maximum *unseen-degree*, i.e., its degree minus the number of incident edges already known by the attacker. In the case of $L \leq 1$, this strategy is equal to BENCHMARK as it only needs information on the degree of all nodes.

- HIGHEST: Pick the next uncovered node to bribe among all nodes as one with highest degree.

- RANDOM: Pick the next uncovered node to bribe among all nodes uniformly at random.

- CRAWLER: Pick the next uncovered node to bribe among all seen nodes as one with the maximum unseen-degree. This strategy is similar to GREEDY except that this strategy only considers seen nodes.

The various strategies require different public information about the OSN graph. The GREEDY, HIGHEST and CRAWLER strategies utilize a public directory with the degree of all nodes, e.g. LinkedIn provides a public degree directory. The BENCHMARK strategy also uses a public degree directory for $L \leq 1$ but needs the entire graph for $L > 1$. The RANDOM strategy only needs a public directory of user names, e.g. Facebook provides a user directory. The CRAWLER strategy has the smallest requirement out of the strategies – a starting node to bribe and degree information for each node.

We conjecture that the effectiveness of the link privacy attack in OSNs is due to the high degree of nodes in the graph. Consider the function $B(m) = \sum_{i=1}^{m} d(u_i)$ where $d(u_i)$ is the degree of the i-th node bribed plus one (thus, it is the neighborhood size of the node bribed) and where nodes u_1 to u_m are selected in non-increasing order of degree.

Let n be the smallest value for $B(n)$ where $B(n) > |V|$. A link privacy attack may use a different sequence of n nodes than $B(n)$. Let $C_S(n)$ be the node coverage given n nodes bribed for strategy S. We first look at the analog of $B(n)$ for $C_S(n)$. Let $D_S(n)$ be the degree sum using $d()$ of the bribed nodes with link privacy attack S, i.e. $D_S(n) = \sum_{i=1}^{n} d(u_i)$ where u_i are the nodes bribed in attack S. The degree sum is an over approximation of $C_S(n)$.

PROPOSITION 1. *Let S be a link privacy attack which bribes nodes $u_1, \ldots, u_n$, then $D_S(n) \geq C_S(n)$.*

The following result shows that $B(n)$ is a reference bound for the node coverage by any attack strategy for $L = 1$.

THEOREM 2. *Given a graph G, $B(n) \geq C_S(n)$ for any link privacy attack S with in-lookahead $L = 1$ which bribes n nodes.*

PROOF. Assume to the contrary that there is a strategy S where $C_S(n) > B(n)$. We make use of the fact that $D_S(n) \geq C_S(n)$, thus we want to show that $D_S(n) > B(n)$ does not hold. Let the set of nodes in graph G be denoted by $U = \{u_1, u_2, \ldots, u_{|V|}\}$.

Without loss of generality, we can assume $d(u_1) \geq d(u_2) \geq \ldots \geq d(u_{|V|})$. By definition, $B(n) = \sum_{i=1}^{n} d(u_i)$, the first n nodes sorted by degree, and we abuse notation to write B to also denote these nodes. Attack S bribes the nodes $U' = \{u'_1, u'_2, \ldots, u'_n\}$ to obtain the nodes covered as $Cs(n)$. We can divide U' into two subsets, $X = \{u_i | u_i \in U \cap U' \wedge i \leq n\}$ and $Y = \{u_i | u_i \in U \cap U' \wedge i > n\}$, so $D_S(n) = \sum_{x \in X} d(x) + \sum_{y \in Y} d(y)$. Now $B(n) = \sum_{x \in X} d(x) + \sum_{z \in B-X} d(z)$ giving $B(n) \geq D_S(n)$ as all degrees in $B - X$ are no smaller than degrees in Y given the ordering for $d(u_i)$. This contradicts the assumption.

□

Thus, $B(n)$ serves as an evaluation for the strategies discussed after bribing n nodes. In the rest of the paper, the value $B(n)$ will be referred to as BOUND.

COROLLARY 3. *Given a graph G, $B(n)$ is larger or equal to the nodes covered by the bribery strategies BENCHMARK, GREEDY, HIGHEST, RANDOM, CRAWLER for in-lookahead $L = 1$.*

Although we could expect that the bound from $B(n)$ to be significantly larger than the node coverage from a particular strategy, this bound is reasonable as it is tight for some graphs.

PROPOSITION 4. *There exist graphs where the value $B(n)$ is the same as the number of nodes covered with some bribery strategy.*

PROOF. Consider the graph in Figure 2(a). As there are 8 nodes, $B(2) = 8$ (selects node x and y) but this is also the same result as the strategy which bribes node x and y. □

We can generalize $B(n)$ to larger in-lookahead, $L > 1$, by replacing the degree with the nodes covered in the neighborhood of the selected node where the sequence of nodes is selected in non-increasing order of their neighborhood size.

Since the degree of nodes in the graph is the significant contributor to the effectiveness of the link privacy attack, we also define the following comparisons which will be used in the experiments:

- AVG: Assume that the number of nodes covered per bribe is equal to the average degree, then $AVG(m) = md_{avg}$ where d_{avg} is the average degree of graph G.

- MED: Assume that the number of nodes covered per bribe is equal to the median degree then $MED(m) = md_{med}$ where d_{med} is the median degree of graph G.

Note that AVG and MED do not serve as any kind of bounds, however, they are less than BOUND, but are used to serve as a simple measure of attack effectiveness.

3.4 Degree Inference

So far, we have considered attack strategies based on [7]. Recall that by bribing a node the attacker immediately covers its neighborhood and is also able to see which nodes are connected to those directly-covered nodes although those nodes are not covered yet (i.e. the seen nodes). The attacker can combine this with degree information (the strategy may already use a public degree directory) to infer that node u is covered without actually covering it by bribing either node u or directly covering it by bribing node v whose in-lookahead neighborhood contains u. Thus, a seen node can be considered as covered if all of its incident edges are known, we call such nodes as *inferred-cover*.

The use of degree inference can be applied to any strategy. To illustrate the additional power by adding degree inference to a bribery strategy, we show that it can be more powerful than a strategy without degree inference.

PROPOSITION 5. *There exist graphs where a bribery strategy using degree inference needs m bribed nodes to cover c nodes but the smallest n where $B(n) \geq c$ has $n > m$.*

PROOF. Consider the graph in Figure 2(b). $n = 2$ is the smallest value where $B(n)$ exceeds the number of nodes in the graph, $B(2) = d(z) + d(x)$. Using degree inference, after bribing node z, we can infer from the degree of x and y that they are also covered, bribing only one node. □

Later, we experimentally study degree inference attacks and compare it to attacks which only consider directly-covered nodes on various graphs. We show in practice that degree inference technique can substantially amplify an attack.

4. ATTACK MITIGATION

Experiments have shown that the threat from the link privacy attack is significant. Due to the effectiveness of node coverage from the bribery attack, the attacker only needs to bribe a small fraction of the nodes to discover a significant fraction of the complete link structure of non-bribed nodes.

In this section, we investigate three mechanisms to reduce the effect of the link privacy attack, namely, a non-uniform in-lookahead environment, reducing the available public degree information, and a non-uniform cost model for the bribes. These mechanisms are motivated by existing features in online social networks.

4.1 Non Uniform In-Lookahead

In a real online social network, the in-lookahead value may vary between nodes. For example, Facebook allows users to customize who can see their profile or list of friends (friends, friends of friends, etc.). LinkedIn is more restrictive but also has a similar mechanism that allow user to control who can see their connection (only me, friends).

Thus, real OSNs do not have uniform in-lookahead which motivates us to study the effect of having non-uniform in-lookahead environment to the link privacy attack. In particular, we analyze the effect of a non-uniform in-lookahead where $k\%$ nodes have in-lookahead $L = 0$ and the remaining $(100-k)\%$ nodes have $L = 1$.

We show that by allowing the user to control their in-lookahead to a smaller L, the effectiveness of the link privacy attack is reduced.

4.2 Degree Abstraction

Having degree information of each node publicly available allows the attacker to discover the link structure more easily by picking the "right" user to bribe, i.e. some strategies and also degree inference make use of a public degree directory such as the one in LinkedIn. This suggests that the OSN which still produces a public degree directory might not release exact degree information in that directory. Rather an approximation of the degree of a node is given which we call here *degree abstraction*.

An example of degree abstraction is LinkedIn. When a user has more than 500 connections (degree > 500) then it is only shown as "> 500" instead of the actual number of connections.

In this paper, we study what happens when the OSN applies some degree abstraction. While there are many possibilities, we use a simple one which is to abstract the degree into a range. For example, a node with degree 17 might be listed publicly as having

Graph	Nodes	Edges	Avg. Degree	Med. Degree	CC
DBLP	801K	6,384K	7.97	4	0.6455
LiveJournal	615K	9,482K	15.42	8	0.3131
Facebook	150K	3,284K	21.89	12	0.2967
WS p=0.1	100K	1,000K	10.00	10	0.4903
PL a=3	100K	872K	8.72	7	0.0009

Table 1: Statistics of the graphs

degree between 11 and 50. We show that with this degree abstraction, several attack strategies are impaired. The experiments show that the effectiveness of the attack is worse than not knowing the degree at all. It also reduces the effect of degree inference.

4.3 Non-Constant Cost Model

In the previous part of the paper, we used the same assumption as [7] that the cost of bribing a node is constant for every node. We now study the case where cost of bribing a node vary depends on the size of its neighborhood. The simplest cost model is that the cost is linear in the amount of information provided by the node being bribed, we call this the *linear cost model*. More precisely, the cost of bribing a node which has m neighborhood size is $m + 1$, i.e. its neighborhood and itself. Note that the cost depends on the amount of information from the bribed node rather than whether that information is useful to the attacker or not.

The linear cost model may be considered to be reasonable for the following reasons. The bribed node can decide that if there is more link information, then it should cost more. From the viewpoint of the OSN itself, it could be a potential business model to also charge for the neighborhood information. In which case, the bribed node should at least pass on the cost to the attacker. This would work even if the attacker compromises a user, the cost would still need to be paid if the OSN charges for it. Other cost models are also possible but in our experiments, we only consider the linear cost model for simplicity. For OSNs with paid premium accounts, this can also be captured with a more specific cost model, e.g. LinkedIn provides several categories of accounts.

5. EXPERIMENTAL EVALUATION

We evaluate the effectiveness of the attack strategies as well as the defenses on real-world online social networks and synthetic small-world graphs.

5.1 Dataset

Our experiments use the following real world OSNs and synthetic graphs. For real online social network data, we use DBLP [12], LiveJournal [13] and Facebook. LiveJournal is a directed graph but in this experiment (as in also other papers), it is treated as an undirected graph. The Facebook graph is obtained by selecting a subgraph of an existing Facebook dataset through a greedy crawl where edges leading to uncrawled nodes are removed to avoid references to nodes not in the graph. Only the largest connected component are used in all the graphs.

We also evaluate using synthetic graphs generated from the following models:

- Random Watts and Strogatz (WS) model: We use the model from [10] to generate a small-world graph. First, we create a ring consisting of all nodes, connecting each node with its nearest neighbors so that each node has degree d. Then for

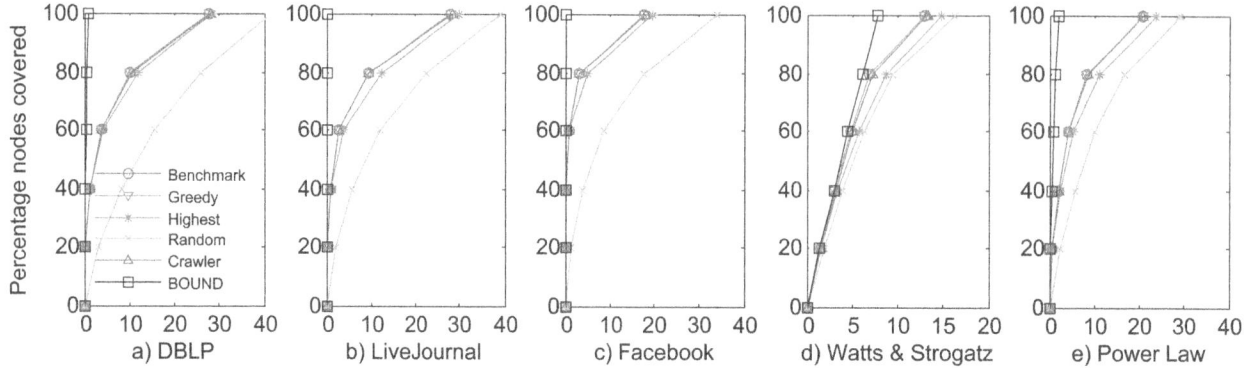

Figure 3: Comparing attack strategies, $L = 1$ (x-axis: percentage of nodes bribed)

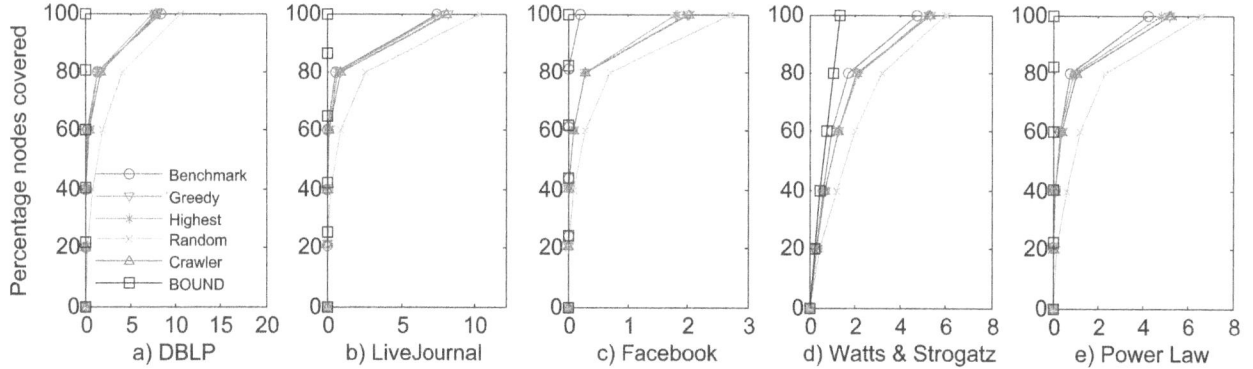

Figure 4: Comparing attack strategies, $L = 2$ (x-axis: percentage of nodes bribed)

each edge, with a probability of p, it is rewired such that one node of the edge is retained and the other end node is selected randomly. The resulting graph has 100,000 nodes with average degree $d_{avg} = 10$.

The purpose of this model is to be able to experiment with small-world graphs whose size and clustering coefficient (CC) can be varied. The graph generated by this model has a near uniform degree and bell-shaped distribution. The clustering coefficient is large and similar to the real social networks used.

- Random power law (PL) model: We use the configuration model in [1] to generate this graph. Basically, the model generates a graph that satisfies a given degree distribution, picking uniformly at random from all such graphs. This model is also used in experiment by [7].

More precisely, we generate a degree distribution that satisfies the power law with $\alpha = 3$ and picking two nodes uniformly at random to form edges of the graph. The resulting graph has 100,000 nodes and a minimum degree $d_{min} = 5$. The graph has some self-loops and multi-edges that are removed without effecting the power law degree distribution.

Since the edges are chosen randomly, the clustering coefficient of this graph is very low.

Table 1 gives the statistics of all graphs used in our experiments.

5.2 Comparing Attack Strategies

The purpose of these experiments is to revisit the experimental results from [7] on a broader range of datasets. A link privacy attack a_1 is considered more efficient than attack a_2 if it needs to

bribe less nodes to attain the same level of node coverage. We evaluate the efficiency of the attack strategies in Section 3.3 on all the datasets. The effectiveness of our link privacy attack experiments confirms the smaller experiments in [7], a small percentage of nodes bribed can lead to high coverage of the graph, consequently, a large privacy leak.

Figure 3 compares the efficiency between strategies for an uniform in-lookahead $L = 1$ environment, while Figure 4 shows it for $L = 2$. As expected, the BENCHMARK strategy has the best efficiency as it needs the smallest number of nodes to be bribed compared to other strategies. However, as mentioned earlier, the BENCHMARK strategy is not a feasible attack for $L > 1$ as it requires the knowledge of the graph itself.

For $L = 1$, GREEDY is the same as BENCHMARK. CRAWLER also shows a similar performance. HIGHEST is not as good as GREEDY but it is close. The performance of RANDOM is further away than all the other strategies, it needs to bribe approximately 10% more nodes than other strategies to have 100% node coverage in the real social network datasets. On the other hand, in the synthetic datasets, it only needs 2-5% more nodes. This shows that the synthetic graphs while having similar trends behave differently from real world OSNs. Furthermore, it appears that having a power law distribution is not a contributing factor. The attack is also effective on the Watts and Strogatz synthetic graph where the degree distribution is approximately uniform. Note also that the Power Law synthetic graph has a low clustering coefficient while the Watts and Strogatz one has a high clustering coefficient. We can also see that in the Watts and Strogatz network, the correspondence between BOUND and the various strategies is much better. These results support our conjecture that the effectiveness of the link privacy attacks is more to do with the degree of the nodes rather than

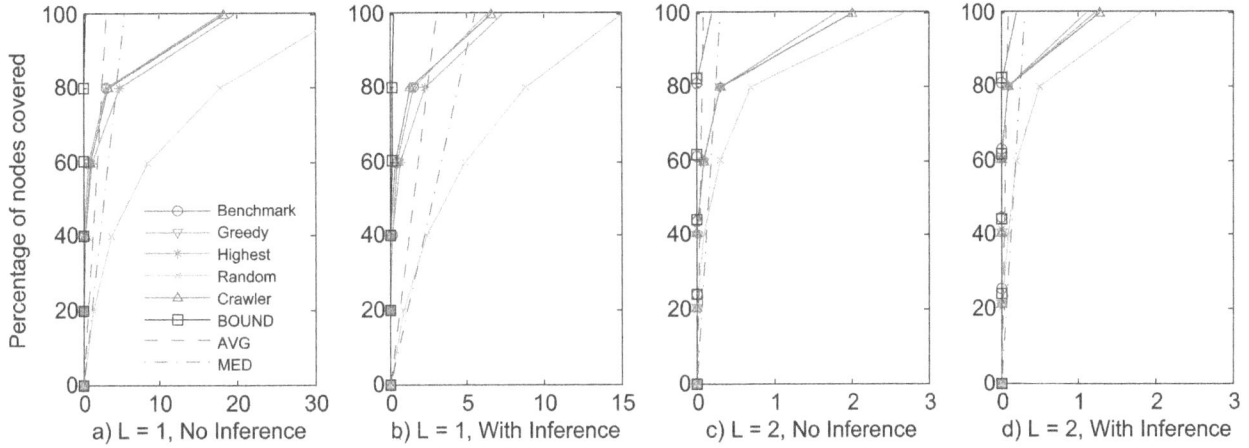

Figure 5: Degree inference, Dataset = Facebook (AVG: assumes the number of nodes covered per bribe is equal to the average degree, MED: assumes the number of nodes covered per bribe is equal to the median degree)

a certain general graph structure. We will look further at this with degree inference.

In $L = 2$, HIGHEST has a slightly better performance than GREEDY and CRAWLER. RANDOM still has the worst performance, but it only differs approximately 2% from other strategies to reach 100% node coverage. This suggests that even without a public degree directory, the link privacy attack still achieves high effectiveness in a $L \geq 2$ environment.

We see that in most cases, BOUND is further away than all the strategies. The exception is in the Watts and Strogatz graph, which may be due to the more uniform degree distribution.

The results show that to obtain a 100% node coverage, the attacker may still need to bribe a significant fraction of nodes, between 10-30%. However, if the attacker is satisfied with 80% node coverage then the amount of nodes bribed is much less. In $L = 1$, to have 80% node coverage the attacker needs at most half of the bribed compared with 100% node coverage, except for the RANDOM strategy which may need two-thirds. Even much less nodes bribed is needed in $L = 2$ to get 80% node coverage, the attacker needs only at most a fifth of the nodes bribed compared to 100% node coverage. In the DBLP, LiveJournal and Facebook datasets with $L = 2$ this is achieved with bribing less than 2% of nodes.

5.3 The Effect of Degree Inference

We now evaluate link privacy attacks where degree inference is employed to amplify the attack's efficiency. In Figure 5, we have only shown degree inference effect on the Facebook dataset as attacks on other datasets have a similar trend.

From Figure 4, we saw that achieving ∼80% coverage in a $L = 2$ environment is already feasible for most attack strategies. We see that degree inference further increases the efficiency of any attack strategies in $L = 1$ by at least 50%. To get 80% coverage in $L = 1$ Facebook dataset, GREEDY strategy needs to bribe 3% of nodes, but with degree inference, this reduces to 1.5%. Thus, the link privacy attack become more feasible even in $L = 1$ with degree inference.

In a $L = 2$ environment, degree inference also makes attacks more efficient, it increases efficiency by at least 50%. Initially the GREEDY strategy needs 0.3% of nodes to achieve 80% coverage and this is reduced to 0.1% with degree inference.

Figure 6 is a zoomed in version of Figure 5 for $L = 1$, while Figure 7 shows the results for the DBLP dataset. In Figure 6, we see that without degree inference, until the attack reaches about

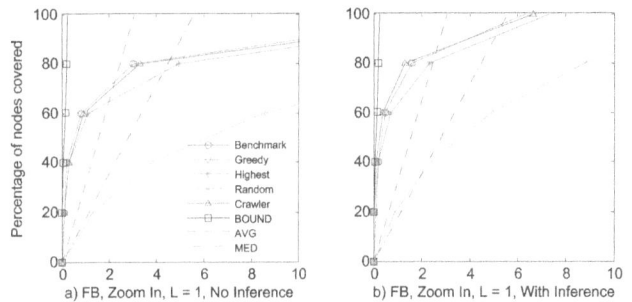

Figure 6: Degree inference (zoomed in), Dataset = Facebook (x-axis: percentage of nodes bribed)

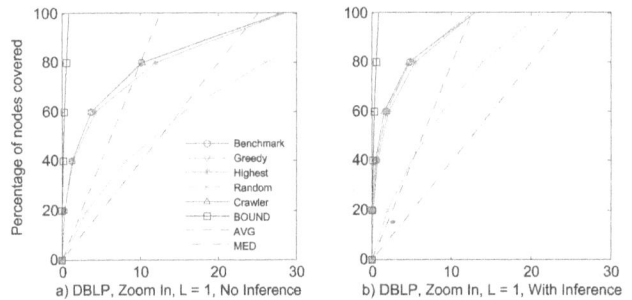

Figure 7: Degree inference (zoomed in), Dataset = DBLP (x-axis: percentage of nodes bribed)

80%, except for RANDOM, the efficiency of other strategies is near AVG or MED, but drops after that. Once degree inference is added, efficiency improves so that all strategies except RANDOM are mostly better than AVG or MED. RANDOM also improves. In the DBLP dataset (Figure 7), efficiency is increased even further to reach AVG. The experiments show that the link privacy attack may be significant even with a $L = 1$ neighborhood.

5.4 Non Uniform In-Lookahead Environments

We now investigate the effect of having an non-uniform in-lookahead environment on the link privacy attack. We pick k% nodes in the graph to have in-lookahead $L = 0$ and the remaining $(100 - k)$% to have $L = 1$ where $k = 10$%, 20% and 30%. A natural

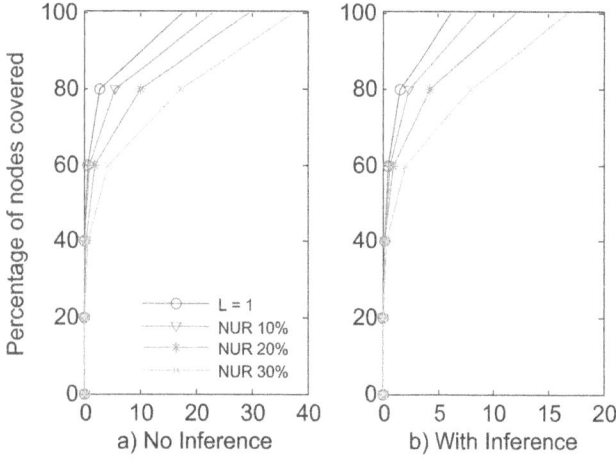

Figure 8: Random non-uniform in-lookahead, Dataset = Facebook, Strategy = GREEDY (x-axis: percentage of nodes bribed, NUR $k\%$ = non0uniform in-lookahead where $k\%$ nodes are $L = 0$ with the random distribution)

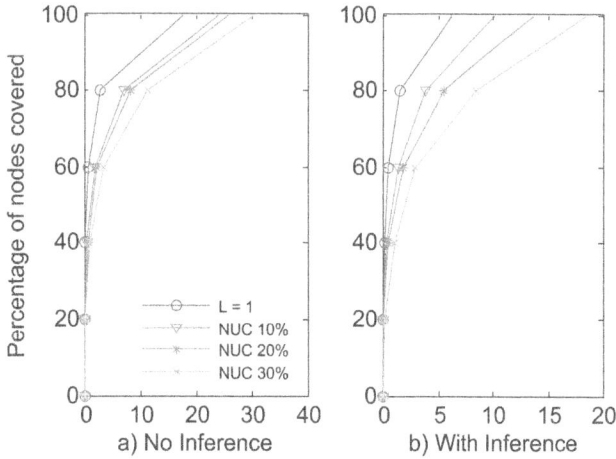

Figure 9: Clustered non-uniform in-lookahead, Dataset = Facebook, Strategy = GREEDY (x-axis: percentage of nodes bribed, NUC $k\%$ = non-uniform in-lookahead where $k\%$ nodes are $L = 0$ with the clustered distribution)

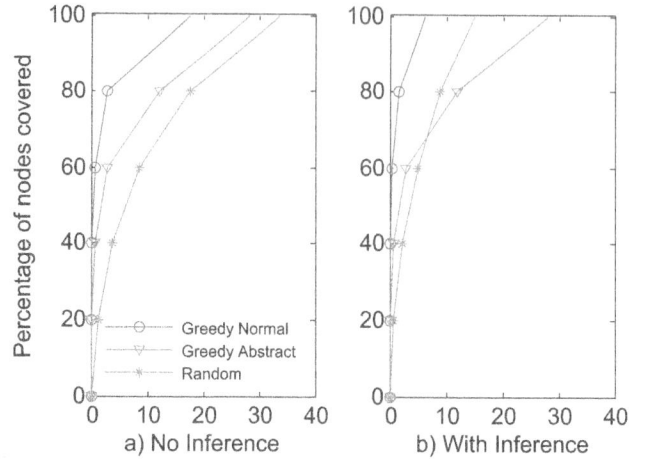

Figure 10: Degree abstraction, Dataset = Facebook, $L = 1$ (x-axis: percentage of nodes bribed)

Environment	Distribution	$\%D$
without degree inference		
$L = 1$	-	+0%
$k = 10\%$	random	+30%
$k = 20\%$	random	+63%
$k = 30\%$	random	+107%
$k = 10\%$	clustered	+37%
$k = 20\%$	clustered	+44%
$k = 30\%$	clustered	+70%
with degree inference		
$L = 1$	-	+0%
$k = 10\%$	random	+44%
$k = 20\%$	random	+100%
$k = 30\%$	random	+177%
$k = 10\%$	clustered	+67%
$k = 20\%$	clustered	+133%
$k = 30\%$	clustered	+200%

Table 2: Effect of non-uniform in-lookahead on the link privacy attack in Facebook using GREEDY ($\%D$ = percentage of increase in bribed nodes relative to an uniform in-lookahead $L = 1$ with the corresponding degree inference)

question that arises is which nodes to pick? As we do not understand yet about the behavior of users toward their privacy setting in real social networks, we have used the following two distributions in our experiments:

- Pick $k\%$ nodes uniformly at random. We call this distribution the *random distribution*.

- Pick $k\%$ nodes at random where adjacent nodes have a higher chance to be picked. This distribution is created in the following fashion. Initially, we create a bag which contains all nodes in the graph, then we pick a node randomly from the bag. For each picked node, we put two copies of its immediate neighbors into the bag, and continue to pick nodes in this fashion until it reaches $k\%$. With this method, if a node is picked then its neighbors have a higher chance to also be picked. We call this the *clustered distribution*.

The rationale behind the clustered distribution is a user who has many friends that care about their privacy control might

also be affected to also pay more attention to his/her own privacy setting.

Figure 8 shows the effect of having an non-uniform in-lookahead with the random distribution in the Facebook dataset with the GREEDY strategy, while Figure 9 shows the clustered distribution for the same dataset and strategy. Other datasets and strategies have a similar trend, and are not shown. We find that having a non-uniform in-lookahead decreases the efficiency of the link privacy attack.

Table 2 contrasts the difference using the $\%D$ column which gives the percentage of increase in bribed nodes relative to baseline which is the number of nodes bribed in an uniform in-lookahead $L = 1$ environment with the corresponding degree inference, i.e. $+x\%$ without degree inference means $x\%$ more nodes need to be bribed compared to the baseline with $L = 1$ and without degree inference. A higher value of k means more nodes have $L = 0$ in-lookahead, which results in more nodes needing to be bribed.

We can see that even for $k = 10\%$, it can decrease the attack's

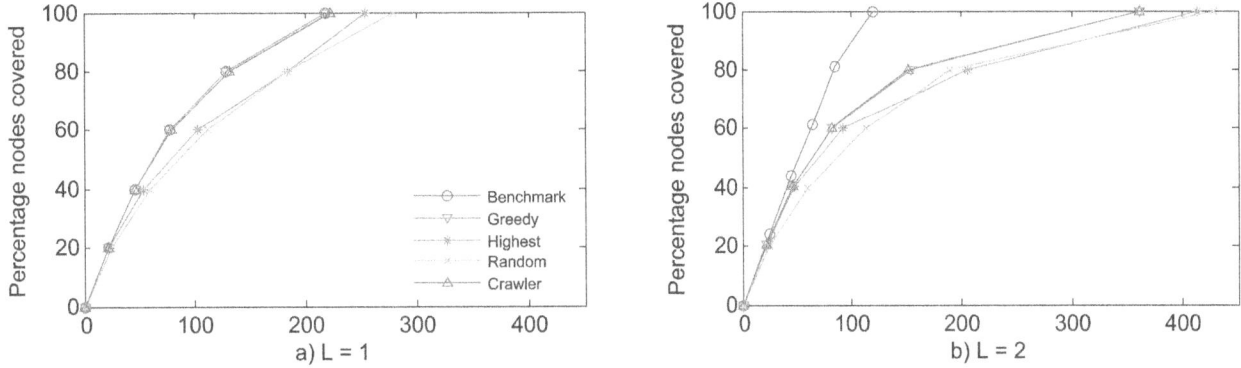

Figure 11: Linear cost model, Dataset = Facebook (x-axis: percentage of cost relative to number of nodes)

efficiency by increasing the number of nodes that have to be bribed by around 30%, and when $k = 30\%$ it can increase the bribed nodes by around 107% with random distribution and $L = 1$. Using non-uniform in-lookahead can also decrease attack's efficiency by even more when degree inference technique is employed. For $k = 30\%$, the attacker needs to bribe 177% more nodes to cover all nodes in the network. This goes up to 200%, which means that three times the number of nodes bribed is needed for the $k = 30\%$ and $L = 1$ clustered distribution. We find then that allowing the user to control their in-lookahead to a smaller L can significantly decrease the efficiency of the link privacy attack even though only some users switch to the $L = 0$ in-lookahead.

5.5 Degree Abstraction

We found degree abstraction to be helpful in mitigating the link privacy attack. We perform the following simple experiment where each node degree is classified into the following four ranges:

- $1 - 10$: for every node whose degree is between 1 and 10.

- $11 - 50$: for every node whose degree is between 11 and 50.

- $51 - 100$: for every node whose degree is between 51 and 100.

- > 100: for every node whose degree is higher than 100.

A reasonable choice of ranges is used so as to not look arbitrary to users of the OSN.

As the GREEDY, HIGHEST and CRAWLER strategies need degree information to work, we use the maximum degree of each range as the degree information needed by those strategies. For example, a node with degree 17 is classified in range 11-50, so we use 50 as degree information of this node. We also employ the degree inference in the same fashion so that it does not overestimate any node as inferred-cover.

Figure 10 shows the effect of degree abstraction on the link privacy attack using the GREEDY strategy on the Facebook dataset. We do not show results on other strategies and datasets as they have a similar trend. When degree inference technique is not employed, degree abstraction is able to decrease the attack efficiency by 60%. What is interesting is that when a degree inference technique is employed, the GREEDY and also other strategies which use degree information, perform worse than RANDOM. This means that it it is better to know nothing at all about the degree rather than using the abstracted degree information. This shows that degree abstraction allows still some useful information for users of the OSN but the degree information becomes less useful to attackers.

5.6 Linear Cost Model

Figure 11 shows the evaluates attacks under the linear cost model on the Facebook dataset. Other datasets have a similar trend, and are not shown. The x-axis is the ratio of bribing cost over number of nodes in the graph given as a percentage. We can see that in $L = 1$, the cost to reach 100% node coverage is approximately 250%, while in $L = 2$, the cost could reach 400%. This is expected because with higher L, the neighborhood size of each node is much higher, hence increasing the bribing cost, but the amount of overlapping information received by the attacker is also increased which means that the attacker may pay multiple times for the same information.

An interesting result found is that the BENCHMARK strategy in $L = 2$ needs less nodes to bribe than in $L = 1$. This is not the case for the other strategies. This suggests that the cost model does not have much affect on the BENCHMARK strategy in $L > 1$. It also means that with a correct strategy, the bribing cost could be reduced in $L > 1$, though it might be clear how to obtain such an attack strategy,

6. CONCLUSION

In this paper we evaluated the vulnerability of social networks to the link privacy attack. We also present the use of degree inference which can substantially amplify an existing strategy not using it. Our results suggest that the efficiency of the attack is due to the high degree of the networks. We propose and evaluate practical mitigation techniques to defend against the attack. We find that by providing degree information, the link privacy attack effectiveness is significantly increased, which means that giving precise degree information may be detrimental. A non-uniform in-lookahead environment and degree abstraction can give a measure of protection to link privacy attacks. We conclude that privacy mechanisms in online social networks ought to allow users to control their in-lookahead to a smaller in-lookahead L and either avoid making public degree information or approximate the information. A more realistic model, of which linear cost is the simplest, also helps in making the attack more expensive. In the constant cost model, the attack is even more effective with a larger L but once the cost model is no longer constant, the effect of the larger L is mitigated by the increased cost.

7. ACKNOWLEDGEMENTS

This work was supported by AcRF grant R-252-000-441-112.

8. REFERENCES

[1] W. Aiello, F. Chung, and L. Liu. A random graph model for power law graphs. In *IEEE Symposium on Foundations of Computer Science*, 2000.

[2] J. Becker and H. Chen. Measuring privacy risk in online social networks. In *Web 2.0 Security Privacy*, 2009.

[3] J. Bonneau, J. Anderson, R. Anderson, and F. Stajano. Eight friends are enough: Social graph approximation via public listings. In *ACM EuroSys Workshop on Social Network Systems*, 2009.

[4] J. Bonneau, J. Anderson, and G. Danezis. Prying data out of a social network. In *International Conference on Advances in Social Network Analysis and Mining*, 2009.

[5] Y. Boshmaf, I. Muslukhov, K. Beznosov, and M. Ripeanu. The socialbot network: When bots socialize for fame and money. In *Annual Computer Security Applications*, 2011.

[6] S. Effendy, F. Halim, and R. Yap. Partial social network disclosure and crawlers. In *International Conference on Social Computing and its Applications*, 2011.

[7] A. Korolova, S. N. R. Motwani, and Y. Xu. Link privacy in social networks. In *Conference on Information and Knowledge Management*, 2008.

[8] A. Mislove, B. Viswanath, P. Gummadi, and P. Druschel. You are who you know: Inferring user profiles in online social networks. In *ACM International Conference on Web Search and Data Mining*, 2010.

[9] K. Thomas and D. Nicol. The koobface botnet and the rise of social malware. In *Malicious and Unwanted Software (MALWARE), 2010 5th International*, 2010.

[10] D. Watts and S. Strogatz. Collective dynamics of 'small-world' networks. *Nature*, 1998.

[11] E. Zheleva and L. Getoor. Preserving the privacy of sensitive relationships in graph data. In *KDD Workshop on Privacy, Security, and Trust in KDD*, 2008.

[12] DBLP. http://informatik.uni-trier.de/~ley/db (July 7, 2011).

[13] SNAP: LiveJournal social network. http://snap.stanford.edu/data/soc-LiveJournal1.html.

[14] Search Engine Journal, 2011. http://www.searchenginejournal.com/wp-content/uploads/2011/08/20110824SocialMediaBlack.pdf.

[15] Technology Review, 2011. http://www.technologyreview.com/Wire/20825/.

On Practical Specification and Enforcement of Obligations

Ninghui Li, Haining Chen, Elisa Bertino
Purdue University, Department of Computer Science
305 N. University Street, West Lafayette, IN 47907,USA
{ninghui, chen623, bertino}@cs.purdue.edu

ABSTRACT

Obligations are an important and indispensable part of many access control policies, such as those in DRM (Digital Rights Management) and healthcare information systems. To be able use obligations in a real-world access control system, there must exist a language for specifying obligations. However, such a language is currently lacking. XACML (eXtensible Access Control Markup Language), the current *de facto* standard for specifying access control policies, seems to integrate obligations as a part of it, but it treats obligations largely as black boxes, without specifying what an obligation should include and how to handle them. In this paper we examine the challenges in designing a practical approach for specifying and handling obligations, and then propose a language for specifying obligations, and an architecture for handling access control policies with these obligations, extending XACML's specification and architecture. In our design, obligations are modeled as state machines which communicate with the access control system and the outside world via events. We further implement our design into a prototype system named ExtXACML, based on SUN's XACML implementation. ExtXACML is extensible in that new obligation modules can be added into the system to handle various obligations for different applications, which shows the strong power of our design.

Categories and Subject Descriptors

D.4.6 [**Security and protection**]: Access controls

General Terms

Security, Languages

Keywords

XACML, Obligation Policy, Architecture

1. INTRODUCTION

Obligations are an important part of many access control policies. For example, some policies permit resources to be accessed

provided that the data subjects whose data is accessed will be notified after the access, and some policies require data to be deleted within some days of access.

A trend in access control is to use a common formal language for specifying access control policies, so that separation of policy specification from enforcement mechanism can be better achieved, and the policy evaluation and enforcement mechanism can be reused cross different systems. XACML is emerging as a *de facto* standard for specifying access control policies in many settings.

To be able to use obligations in a real-world access control system, there must exist a language for specifying obligations. Such a language is currently lacking. Even though XACML appears to make obligations an integral part of access control policies, the XACML standard does not specify what an obligation element ought to contain and how to handle it. The standard states that the Policy Enforcement Point (PEP) should not enforce the decision of the Policy Decision Point (PDP) if the decision is accompanied by obligations that the PEP does not know how to handle. Without a common language for specifying obligations, any policy that returns obligations simply causes the policy's decision to be ignored or contradicted by the PEP.

This paper aims at developing a language for specifying obligations and an architecture that extends the XACML architecture for handling access control policies with these obligations. Integrating obligations in the processing of access control presents several challenges that have not been adequately addressed in the literature.

First, many types of obligations exist, and one cannot anticipate all types of obligations when designing the language to specify obligations; thus, the design must be extensible to support new types of obligations. Second, failures in discharging some obligations may affect the decision the PEP makes on a request, causing the PEP to deny the request even when the PDP returns a `Permit` decision for the request. Third, the PEP's decision may in turn affect which obligations should be carried out. This mutual interaction between obligations and PEP decisions must be carefully thought out.

We examine these issues and introduce a design that meets these challenges. We choose a simple yet extensible architecture, allowing new types of obligations to be added by adding appropriate system components for handling particular types of messages. Our key ideas are as follows. We model an obligation as a state machine that communicates with the PEP using events. The PEP manages the lifecycle of obligations. An obligation includes rulesets to specify its responses to input events. These responses include changing its state in response to events, which informs the PEP about what course of actions it should take regarding the request, and generating events, which inform the environment about what actions must be taken to fulfill the obligation. Some of these actions are deployment specific. These deployment specific actions are implemented by obligation modules. Multiple obligation modules can be attached to the PEP, each implementing some actions. These obligation modules communicate with the PEP and the obligations through an event interface.

We come up with a concrete design to extend XACML with support for obligations. In our design, we reuse the elements for rules in policies for rules in obligations. We have implemented our design into a prototype system named ExtXACML, based on SUN's XACML implementation [17]. ExtXACML consists of a PDP, a PEP, a Timer, an Access Management Interface (AMI), and different obligation modules. Among these components, the PDP and the PEP are deployment-independent, while the AMI and the obligation modules are application-specific. Thus we implemented the AMI and the obligation modules for a specific application shown in Section 5.1. ExtXACML can handle access control policies with different kinds of obligations, including obligations before, during or after accesses to resources, obligations performed by systems or users, and their combinations. Furthermore, ExtXACML is extensible in that new obligation modules can be added into the system to handle various obligations for different applications. All of these features show the strong power of our proposed design.

The rest of the paper is organized as follows. Overview of obligation handling in XACML is given in Section 2. After the challenges concerning specification and handling of obligations are discussing in Section 3, we discuss our design for both obligation specification and an architecture to enforce obligations to meet the challenges in Section 4. In Section 5, we show an application and the implementation of a prototype system called ExtXACML for the application. Related work is presented in Section 6. Section 7 concludes this paper and outlines our future work.

2. OVERVIEW OF OBLIGATION HANDLING IN XACML

In this section, we describe and analyze how XACML handles policy combining and obligations. Our descriptions are based on XACML 2.0 [18], and the high-level ideas remain accurate for the current draft of XACML 3.0 [19].

Rules, Policies, and Policy-sets. XACML defines three levels of policy elements: rules, policies, and policy-sets. A *rule* is the most basic policy element; it has three main components: a *target*, a *condition*, and an *effect*. The target defines a set of subjects, resources and actions that the rule applies to; the condition specifies restrictions on the attributes in the target and refines the applicability of the rule; the effect is either Permit, in which case we call the rule a *permit rule*, or Deny, in which case we call it a *deny rule*. If a request satisfies both the rule target and rule condition, the rule *is applicable* to the request and yields the decision specified by the effect element together with a set of (possibly empty) obligations and advice; otherwise, the rule *is not applicable* to the request and yields the decision NotApplicable.

A *policy* consists of four main components: a *target*, a *rule-combining algorithm (RCA)*, a set of *rules*, and *obligations*. The policy target decides whether a request is applicable to the policy and it has similar a structure as the rule target. The RCA specifies how the decisions from the rules are combined to yield one decision. The obligations element consists of a set of obligations, which represent functions to be executed in conjunction with the enforcement of an authorization decision.

A *policy-set* also has four main components: a *target*, a *policy-combining algorithm (PCA)*, a set of *sub-policies*, and *obligations*. A sub-policy can be either a policy or a policy-set. The PCA specifies how the results of evaluating the sub-policies are combined to yield one decision.

In XACML, a rule, a policy, or a policy-set returns one of the following four decisions for each request: P (Permit), D (Deny), NA (NotApplicable), and IN (Indeterminate). The value IN occurs when there is a policy evaluation error.

Policy Combining Algorithms. XACML has six standard PCAs. They are *"Deny-overrides"*, *"Ordered-deny-overrides"*, *"Permit-overrides"*, *"Ordered-permit-overrides"*, *"First-applicable"* and *"Only-one-applicable"*. Ordered-deny-overrides and ordered-permit-overrides are the same as deny-overrides and permit-overrides, respectively, except that rules and policies have to be evaluated in the order they appear.

XACML "Permit-overrides" PCA has the preference $P > D > IN > NA$. That is, when any sub-policy permits the request, the policy as a whole permits it. When no sub-policy permits the request, and at least one denies it, the policy as a whole denies it. Otherwise, when there is an error somewhere, the policy reports error on the request. Otherwise, the policy is non-applicable. The "Deny-overrides" PCA uses the preference $D > P > NA$; in addition, it treats IN as always equivalent to D. That is, whenever a sub-policy returns IN, the policy would return deny. The "First-applicable" PCA returns the effect of the first applicable sub-policy as the result if no errors occur. Whenever an error occurs, the policy returns IN. The "Only-one-applicable" PCA returns the effect of the unique policy in the policy-set that applies to the request. If there are more than one applicable policies, the PCA reports the conflict by returning IN. Furthermore, if an error occurs during evaluation of any policy, the PCA also returns IN.

Obligations in XACML An obligation in XACML has two required attributes: ObligationID and FulfillOn. In addition, an obligation may have other attribute assignments, which the PEP is supposed to interpret. The FulfillOn attribute takes value of either Permit or Deny. When combining sub-policies, one also needs to determine how the obligations with these sub-policies are combined. XACML 2.0 handles obligations as follows [18].

> A policy or policy set may contain one or more obligations. When such a policy or policy set is evaluated, an obligation SHALL be passed up to the next level of evaluation (the enclosing or referencing policy, policy set or authorization decision) only if the effect of the policy or policy set being evaluated matches the value of the FulfillOn attribute of the obligation.

In other words, an obligation will be returned by the PDP if it is associated with a policy whose decision contributes to the final decision made by the PDP, and the obligation's FulfillOn attribute equals the final decision.

3. COMPLEXITIES IN OBLIGATIONS SPECIFICATION AND HANDLING

Designing a language for specifying obligations is challenging, because one needs to support multiple types of obligations, and because one has to consider issues such as what to do if processing an obligation fails, and what happens when the PEP makes a decision that is different from the PDP's decision. In this section, we explore these complexities.

3.1 Different Types of Obligations

There are different types of obligations. Based on when the actions required by an obligation must be performed relative to the actual access of resources, the $UCON_{ABC}$ model introduced the concepts of pre-obligation, and ongoing-obligation [12, 16, 13]. Another type of obligations which is not included in the UCON model is post-obligation.

Perhaps the most common type of obligations is that of post-obligations, which specify actions required to be performed after accesses to resources have occurred. Such post-obligations have been widely considered in many areas such as Digital Rights Management (DRM) system, healthcare information system, etc. For example, a policy in a healthcare information system may require that a patient record be deleted within 30 days after a treatment. A member of an online music store has to pay monthly metered payment at the end of each month for continuous music services.

Pre-obligations are obligations that should be fulfilled before the usage of resources is allowed. An example is that whoever wants to access a digital library has to provide his or her name and email address. In this case, if the user fails to fulfill the obligation to provide sufficient information, he or she will be denied to access the digital library.

Ongoing-obligations need to be fulfilled during the usage of resources. One example is to require a user to keep certain advertising windows open while accessing some service. The user may be allowed to access the service in the beginning, but if the user fails to fulfill the ongoing-obligation, the service will be terminated.

There also exist obligations that do not naturally fall in the taxonomy of pre-, post-, and ongoing- obligations. An example that has both pre- and post- component is to require a user to agree to provide usage log information before listening to some music, and to report the usage log after listening.

Some obligations may be required even when a request is to be denied, and there is no access. For example, a security management policy may specify that a denied request is considered to be a security violation, and hence auditing and logging must be performed.

Obligations may also be useful when the policy evaluation encounters an error. For example, evaluating a policy may encounter an error because some important attribute is lacking, and the policy evaluation result should notify the user to provide the required information. Obligation is a natural mean for such purpose.

A language for obligations should support all these different usages of obligations.

3.2 Interactions

In addition to different timings of enforcement, obligations also differ in that the required actions need to be performed by different subjects. Some actions, such as logging and notification, can be performed by the access control component with simple extensions. Other actions can be performed only by other components of the system, such as those requiring data to be removed after a certain period of time. Other actions must be performed by users. For instance, a patient must agree on the consent of an operation before the doctor is allowed to perform the operation.

We thus separate the *Access Control Component* (ACC) from the rest of the system, which we call the *External Environment* (EE). We now consider what kinds of interaction between the ACC and the EE are needed. At a basic level, for each access request there needs to be one round-trip communication between the EE and the ACC. When encountering an access request, the EE gives control to the ACC, which will make the decision whether the request should be authorized. The ACC should then inform the EE about the decision. The existence of obligations, however, causes this interaction between the ACC and the environment to be more complex.

While some obligations can be fulfilled by the ACC, many obligations cannot, and require the EE to perform some actions. Besides, the ACC needs to know whether the obligations are fulfilled

to make decisions on permitting the request or not. Consider a pre-obligation example, in which the user must accept a license agreement before being allowed to access. In this example, the ACC has to wait for events from the EE's user-interface component to know whether the required action has been performed. Furthermore, such events may occur in an asynchronous fashion. In other words, the existence of obligations forces the ACC to have more complicated, often asynchronous communications with the EE.

Supporting the full life cycle of obligations also raises challenges, as the lifetime of obligations may be much longer than that of accesses. Some obligations may require actions to be performed long before the access has taken place. Examples include requiring data subjects to be notified after data has been accessed within 30 days of the access, requiring data to be deleted within a certain timeframe, and so on. The policy may also require followup actions to take place when these obligations are violated. To support these obligations, the system needs to monitor events regarding these obligations and to record whether these obligations are fulfilled or violated.

3.3 How Obligations Affect the PEP Decisions

When the PDP returns a decision together with obligations, the PEP does not always follow the same decision as the PDP. The PEP's decision on a request will be affected by the obligations. More specifically, the PEP's decision can be affected by whether the PEP understands the obligations or not, and whether the attempt to fulfill the obligation succeeds or not.

To illustrate the potential pitfalls in such interactions, we first examine XACML's design. XACML has three kinds of PEPs: Base PEP, Deny-Biased PEP, and Permit-biased PEP. Their behavior, inferred from the XACML standard, is summarized in Table 1.

Some behaviors in Table 1 can be quite surprising. For example, both a Base PEP and a Permit-biased PEP will permit a request when the PDP returns `Deny` accompanied by obligations that the PEP does not understand or is unwilling or unable to discharge. This is inferred from the following description in Section 7.1.1 of XACML 2.0 and Section 7.2 of XACML 3.0.

> If the decision is "Deny", then the PEP SHALL deny access. If obligations accompany the decision, then the PEP shall deny access only if it understands, and it can and will discharge those obligations.

We find the behavior of a base PEP permitting a request when the PDP returns Deny rather disturbing. First, this violates the "Fail-safe Default" principle [15], which says that a protection mechanism should deny access by default, and grant access only when explicit permission exists. Second, this also violates the "Psychological Acceptability" principle [15]. We believe the majority of policy authors do not anticipate that the inability to discharge an obligation associated with a "Deny" decision will cause the request to be permitted. Third, as there is no clear way to predict whether a PEP "can and will" discharge all obligations, this makes the outcome of access control policies rather unpredictable. Furthermore, this may prove to be a loophole exploitable by an adversary. If an adversary can create errors causing a PEP to fail to discharge an obligation, the adversary can potentially gain access. For example, suppose that a policy says that an access should be denied with an obligation to notify the system administrator about the access via email (perhaps because the access indicates active intrusions), and the adversary can cause the email mechanism to fail, the adversary may be able to gain access.

Along these arguments, Deny-biased PEP appears the only reasonable choice. We point out that if one wants to enforce a policy

PDP decision	Permit (will discharge obligations)	Permit (cannot discharge obligations)	Deny (will discharge obligations)	Deny (cannot discharge obligations)	Not Applicable	Indeterminate
Base PEP	Permit	Deny	Deny	Permit	undefined	undefined
Deny-Biased PEP	Permit	Deny	Deny	Deny	Deny	Deny
Permit-Biased PEP	Permit	Permit	Deny	Permit	Permit	Permit

Table 1: PEP Behaviors in XACML

that permits all requests unless a particular policy-set S_1 denies it, one can still achieve this goal under a Deny-biased PEP, by wrapping first S_1 and then a policy that permits all requests in another policy set that uses First-Applicable PCA. Hence using only Deny-biased PEP will not reduce the overall expressive power.

In summary, we believe that while the inability to fulfill obligations can cause the PEP to reach a decision different from the PDP's decision, the only allowable change of decision is from a Permit to Deny.

We also observe that the requirement that the PEP follows the PDP's decision only if the PEP "understands, and can and will discharge those obligations" requires more clarifications. Does this mean that the PEP must wait until the obligations are either fulfilled or violated to make its decision, or that the PEP can decide so long as it knows how to discharge the obligations (but the process of discharging the obligation may still fail)?

We believe the right answer is "it depends". Some obligations must be fulfilled before the decision is returned; for example, a request may be authorized only if the user has first completed a registration step. Some obligations only need to be processed after the decision has been made and the requested access has occurred. Consider, for example, an obligation that requires the system to log the duration of the access afterwards. The action cannot be carried out before the request is permitted. Suppose that after the access, the system fails to log, either because of failure in obtaining the necessary information or because of failure in writing the log (e.g., the storage device becomes full). From the policy's point of view, the obligation is not discharged and should be recorded as such; however, the request is permitted rather than denied.

In summary, there are different kinds of obligations, some should be processed before the request can be permitted, and failure to fulfill them means the decision should change from Permit to Deny. For other obligations, their fulfillment does not affect the decision of the request. A language for specifying obligations should be able to allow all these possibilities.

3.4 Which Obligations to Discharge

In XACML, obligations can be FulfillOn Permit or Deny. However, the decisions of PDP and PEP are not always the same. Hence it is not obvious what obligations need to be discharged. For example, suppose that the PDP returns Permit, together with several obligations that are FulfillOn Permit, and the PEP is unable to discharge one of the obligations, either because the PEP does not understand some parts of the obligation or because the processing of the obligation results in an error. As a result, the PEP needs to deny the request. In this situation, several questions naturally arise.

If the PEP needs to deny the request, should the other obligations that are fulfilled on permit be processed? One may argue "Yes" because the PDP's decision is Permit. One may also argue "No" because the PEP's decision is Deny rather than Permit. The answer to this question is not specified in XACML. We believe that the correct answer is that it depends. It is plausible that some obligations should still be processed because the PDP has decided to authorize the request, which may be a sufficient condition to trigger the obligations. It is equally plausible that some obligations no longer need to be processed, because the PEP will deny the request due to the failure in obligation processing.

If the PEP needs to deny the request, should obligations that are FulfillOn Deny be processed? In XACML, these obligations are not returned by the PDP to the PEP, because the PDP's decision is Permit; hence the PEP will not see these obligations and thus cannot process them. However, one may argue that it is desirable that certain obligations must be performed whenever an access is denied, no matter what reasons caused the deny to occur. Hence our answer to the question is again that it depends. Some deny-related obligations do not need to be processed because the PDP does not decide to deny the request. Others need to be processed because the PEP will deny the request. The language should meet the needs of flexibilities.

3.5 Which Obligations to Return

Obligations are included in policies, which are evaluated by the PDP. Given a request, the PDP computes a decision and associated obligations. How to determine which obligations should be returned is a non-trivial question. XACML has obligations that are fulfilled either on Permit or on Deny. Furthermore, all obligations that are returned by the PDP are treated as mandatory, i.e., the PEP must handle all obligations. We raise the following questions regarding this design.

Should there be optional obligations? In XACML, all obligations that are returned by the PDP are mandatory. However, one may want to use obligations to specify actions that are desirable, but not essential. For example, certain logging may be desirable, but can be omitted when the system is under a heavy-load. XACML 3.0 has a concept called advices, which appear to be optional obligations.

Should there be obligations that are FulfillOn Indeterminate? In XACML, obligations are FulfillOn either Permit or Deny. However, a PDP may return Indeterminate, to indicate an error during policy evaluation. Different kinds of errors may require different actions to be taken by the requester (e.g., in case of missing attribute information) or by the system administrator (e.g., in case of policy errors). Obligations are the natural mean to serve this need. Currently, XACML uses Status for dealing with errors. However, the Status element simply shows the error information in a text fashion, without the ability to inform different entities the need for more actions.

Should there be obligations that are fulfill-on-applicable? Some policies may want certain obligations (such as logging) fulfilled so long as the policy is found applicable to a request, no matter whether the final decision is Permit or Deny. For example, so long as there is an attempt to access some private information, such as medical information or credit history information, it may be desirable that the data subject be notified and that the attempt be logged. For this purpose, we need obligations that must be discharged whenever a policy's target matches the request.

4. DESIGN OF OBLIGATION SPECIFICATION AND PROCESSING

We have examined the diverse kinds of obligations. A language for specifying obligations should be able to handle all these diversities without presenting an overly complex design that confuses policy authors who need to specify obligations. In this section, we present our design for specifying obligations and handling them.

4.1 Architecture Design

One important challenge in specifying obligations is that what an obligation requires the system or users to perform depends upon specific applications and policy requirements in the system, which can be quite diverse, as illustrated by the many examples in Section 3. This means that the logic for handling obligations must be extensible.

One architecture that supports this extensibility requirement is to implement application-specific modules for handling obligations and "plug" these modules into the PEP, so that the PEP simply passes obligations to these modules, without the need to have any logic for handling obligations or understanding the lifecycles of obligations. The design of XACML implies such architecture, because XACML does not specify how the PEP handles obligations. This design, however, is problematic. The main reason is that the lifecycle of obligations is intricately intertwined with the PEP's decision on a request. Some obligations must be fulfilled before a request is to be permitted. Some obligations must continuously monitor the system progress during an access, and suspend or revoke the access when they are violated. Forcing obligation handling outside the PEP and into a separate obligation handling component will greatly complicate the interface between them, decreasing the performance. This also wastes the opportunity to implement the logics for managing obligation lifecycles and interactions with PEP decisions only once. Implementing these logics only once ensures that they are correctly implemented and consistent across all obligations, helping policy authors to write policies that use obligations.

Hence we choose the design that the PEP implements the obligation lifecycle logics, the obligation modules handle application-specific behaviors, and the PEP and the obligation modules use an event mechanism to communicate with each other. Figure 1 shows our proposed architecture.

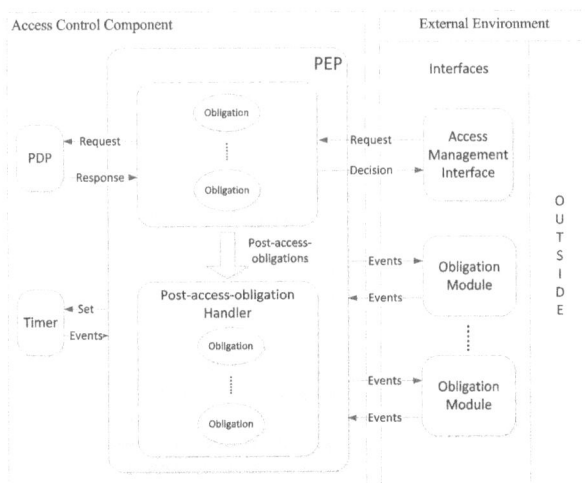

Figure 1: Proposed architecture

Architecturally, the overall system is divided into two parts: an Access Control Component (ACC), and an External Environment (EE). The EE is where applications are executed, and the ACC helps the EE to manage access control to resources. The ACC can be implemented independently of any particular deployment. One reference implementation can be used in all deployments. Code in the EE, however, needs to know what applications are used in the deployment and how to interact with them.

The ACC has a PEP, a PDP, and a Timer. Here we focus on runtime policy enforcement, and do not directly deal with policy administration issues, as they are orthogonal to the focus of the paper. Hence we omit some components in XACML architecture, such as the Policy Administration Point (PAP). The PEP receives access requests, consults the PDP for a decision, handles any associated obligations, and makes the final decision about the request. It also needs to manage obligations, sometimes even after an access request has long completed. Because of this, we divide the PEP into two parts: the main PEP part, dealing with actions associated with access requests, and the post-access-obligation handling part, maintaining obligations that need processing after the request has long completed. The former needs access to the PDP and generally needs to make timely decisions. The performance requirement for the latter is lower.

The EE needs to interact with the ACC. In order to do so, it needs to have interface components, which include an Access Management Interface (AMI) and zero or more Obligation Modules. The AMI is where access requests occur in the system. The exact form of AMI is deployment-dependent. In the simplest form, the AMI will be code snippets before each request, which will invoke the PEP for access decisions. In other deployments, the AMI may also control ongoing access sessions and consult with the PEP to control these sessions. One might argue that the AMI is really the PEP, since the access decision is enforced by the AMI. We take the view that any policy enforcement component must consist of two parts. One part is deployment-dependent; it knows what operations on resources are subject to policy control, and which codes perform these operations. The other part is deployment-independent; it evaluates access control policies, manages obligations, and makes the final decision on a request. We separate these two parts, calling the former AMI, and the latter PEP.

The obligation modules implement application-specific obligation-handling functionalities (such as notifying users, and writing to logs). These modules interact with the PEP through an event interface. Each module registers itself with the PEP to receive certain kinds of events, then performs the actions requested in these events, and often reports the status of these actions back to the PEP and the obligations via events. There may be multiple obligation modules, each handling one family of related obligation actions. For example, one obligation module can handle logging and auditing, another can handle user interactions, and yet another can handle requirements about notifying data subjects.

4.2 Obligations as State Machines

Conceptually, each obligation is a state machine that interacts with the outside world through events. The state space of all obligations is pre-determined in our approach. At any time, it is in one of the states in Table 2. We organize these states into six stages, which are described below.

Stage 1: pre-decision. An obligation in this stage means that this obligation wants certain actions to be performed before the PEP makes the decision; the PEP cannot issue the decision on a request if any mandatory obligation is in the *pre-decision* stage.

Pre-obligations, which require certain conditions to be satisfied before a request can be permitted, would start in this stage. Un-

state name	stage	meaning
pre-decision	1	the obligation needs processing before the PEP makes decisions;
pre-satisfied	2	the pre-decision part of the obligation has been satisfied;
pre-failed	2	the pre-decision part of the obligation has failed; if this obligation is mandatory, then the PEP must deny the request; if an obligation wants to force a PEP to deny a request even though the PDP permits it, the obligation should enter this state;
pre-session	3	waiting for the event indicating that an access session has started;
during-session	4	waiting for the event indicating that an access session has stopped;
monitor-satisfied	4	this obligation wants to monitor the access session, and the access session can be permitted to proceed;
monitor-unsatisfied	4	this ongoing obligation is currently unsatisfied (but may become satisfied later), and the current access session must be either terminated, or temporarily put on hold until the obligation switches to the *during-access-satisfied* state;
monitor-terminate	4	this ongoing obligation has been violated so that the current access session must be terminated;
post-access	5	the obligation is waiting for additional events from the external environment;
fulfilled	6	the processing of the obligation has completed, and the obligation is fulfilled;
violated	6	the processing of the obligation has completed, and the obligation is violated;
ended	6	the processing of the obligation has ended before it reaches its natural completion state;

Table 2: States of an obligation.

til they move onto later stages, the PEP should not permit the request. Obligations that are associated with a PDP decision other than `Permit` may also start here. For example, if a policy identifies a request as coming from an active attacker, the policy may require switching on certain automatic auditing and tracing functionalities before denying the request (which may alert the attacker).

Stage 2: decision. An obligation in this stage means that from this obligation's point of view, the PEP is free to go ahead and issues its decision about the request; furthermore, the obligation wants to be notified about the PEP's decision via an event. An obligation may start in this stage if it does not need any processing before the PEP's final decision.

Stage 3: pre-session. An obligation enters this stage only when the obligation is notified that the PEP decides to permit the request, and the obligation wants to be notified when the access session starts.

Stage 4: during-session. An obligation enters this stage only when there is an ongoing access session, and the obligation either wants to control the session, or wants to be notified when the session terminates.

Stage 5: post-access. An obligation enters this stage if it needs further processing, independent of whether there is an access session, or whether an access session has ended or not. A post obligation that requires notifying data subjects after access will be in this state waiting for an event telling whether the notification has occurred. An obligation that requires a denied access to be logged with a proof of logging will also be in this state waiting for the event confirming logging.

Stage 6: completed. The processing of the obligation has completed.

The allowed transitions between states in different stages are given in Figure 2. We note that an obligation does not have to go through all these stages. An obligation must start at either Stage 1 or Stage 2, and must end in Stage 6 . Stages 3 and 4 can only be entered when the access request is permitted by the PEP, and Stage 4 can be entered only when there actually is an access session. Stage 5 is often needed when an obligation wants to be notified about whether certain processing required by the obligation succeeds.

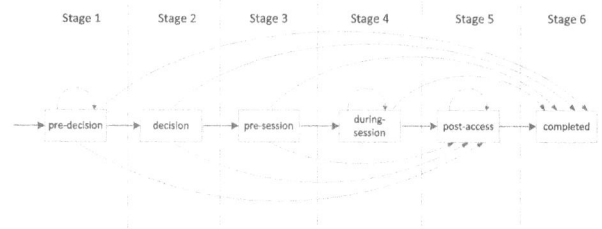

Figure 2: Obligation stage transitions.

4.3 Events and Obligations

An obligation needs to specify its behaviors on different events. We choose to reuse the syntax for rules in XACML policies to specify an obligation's behavior on events. More specifically, an obligation associates with each state a sequence of rules. When an event is delivered to an obligation, the PEP finds the rule sequence associated with the current state of the obligation, and then evaluates this rule sequence on the event, while providing other context information from the current request. If a rule is evaluated to be true, then the effect of the rule specifies the next state the obligation should go to, and optionally events for the PEP and the external environment.

An obligation in our approach is thus similar to an XACML policy. An XACML policy takes in a request (which can be viewed as an input event), and uses a ruleset to evaluate the request to derive a decision (which can be viewed as the resulting state) and optionally some associated obligations (which can be viewed as output events). Obligations generalize XACML policies in that they can be evaluated on events other than requests and in that they have states and may use different rulesets in different states.

We introduce the notion of *event families* to group related events together. Each event belongs to one event family. We have three predefined event families. These events are not handled or created by any external obligation modules, but by the PEP itself. The events in these families are given in Table 3. These three families are explained below.

- *PEP-notification.* These are related to the status of handling the access request. They are generated by the PEP for obligations. All obligations are required to be prepared to handle

76

event family	event name	meaning	stage
PEP-notification	obligation-interrupt	The PEP wants the obligation to leave the current state so that the PEP can proceed to the next step; the obligation should move away from the current state.	Stages 1-5
PEP-notification	obligation-abort	The PEP either does not know how to handle the obligation, or has encountered error(s) while evaluating the obligation, and is about to discard the obligation. This event gives the obligation a chance to deal with this failure in a graceful fashion.	Stages 1-5
PEP-notification	PDP-permit	The PDP returned Permit. The PEP plans to permit the request (provided that the necessary obligations are satisfied).	Stage 1
PEP-notification	PDP-permit-PEP-deny	The PDP returned Permit; however, the PEP has decided to deny the request, perhaps because some other mandatory obligations processed earlier have already failed.	Stage 1
PEP-notification	PDP-deny	The PDP returned Deny. The PEP plans to deny the request.	Stage 1
PEP-notification	PDP-indeterminate	The PDP returned Indeterminate. The PEP plans to deny the request.	Stage 1
PEP-notification	PEP-permitted	The PEP has permitted the request.	Stage 2
PEP-notification	PEP-denied	The PEP has denied the request.	Stage 2
PEP-session	access-session-started	The access session has started.	Stage 3
PEP-session	access-session-ended	The access session has ended.	Stage 4
Timer	timer-request	An event generated by evaluating an obligation, informing the PEP that the obligation wants to receive a particular Timer event, as specified in this request.	Stages 1-5
Timer	timer-cancel	An event generated by evaluating an obligation, informing the PEP that the obligation wants to cancel an earlier Timer request.	Stages 1-5
Timer	timer	An event generated by the PEP to an obligation, which has set a timer via an earlier request.	Stages 1-5

Table 3: Pre-defined events
Column 1 gives the event family name; column 2 the event name, and column 4 the stage(s) in which the event may occur.

events in this family. This family is the only such required event family.

- *PEP-session.* These events are generated by the PEP when the PEP can get information about the ongoing access sessions. They are generated by the PEP for obligations. An obligation which wants to perform actions based on the starting and ending of access sessions should request to receive events of this family, and be prepared to handle them.

- *Timer.* These events are sent between the PEP and the obligations. Obligations that request time-dependent actions should be prepared to handle events in this family.

Beyond these three families, new families can be defined for different kinds of functionalities that are needed by obligations. For example, one could define an event family for logging, which may include one event for requesting to create a log entry, and optionally another event for notification for the success/failure of the logging. For another example, an event family can be created for user interaction in a specific application.

Each obligation module understands one or more event families, and registers itself with the PEP on these event families. When obligations generate events in these families, the obligation module will receive these events from the PEP. The obligation module may send events targeting obligations back to the PEP; these events should be in the event families the module registers itself on.

Similarly, each obligation also specifies what event families it requires. This specification serves at least two purposes. First, it helps the PEP to filter which events to deliver to the obligation. For example, if an obligation does not want to control the access session, it will not include the PEP-session family in the list, and the PEP will not deliver session-related events to the obligation.

Second, it enables the PEP to quickly check whether it is able to handle the obligation. If for one event family listed here, no obligation module has registered to handle it, then the PEP knows that it cannot handle this obligation, and must consider these obligations as violated.

All events have some common fields, such as Event Id, Obligation Id, and Message (which explains the event to humans using text). Within one event family, there can be multiple types of events. For example, the timer event family has three types of events: timer-request events, timer-cancel events, and timer events. (See Table 3 for their meanings.) A timer-request event in addition has fields including the specification of the timer, which is in one of two forms, either a specific time in future, or a time duration which specifies a timer that expires after that duration. A timer-cancel or timer event in addition has a field including the Event Id of the corresponding time-request event.

4.4 The Schema of Obligation.

An obligation has the following elements:

- *FulfillOn.* This field helps determine when an obligation should be returned by the PDP together with the decision. It can take the following values: permit, deny, error, and applicable. Their effects will be discussed in Section 4.5.

- *a boolean variable indicating whether the obligation is optional.* Its default value is no. An optional obligation can be ignored. If the PEP does not understand the obligation, or does not want to process it for performance or other considerations, it can ignore the obligation, considering it as fulfilled.

- *a list of event families that this obligation needs.* This specifies what events this obligation would like to receive and is going to generate.

- *a starting state, which is either pre-decision or pre-satisfied.*

- *optional state variables, and their initial values.* These variables enable an obligation to store additional necessary state information; they can be defined using the existing data types in XACML.

- *one or more rulesets, each associated with one state.* Processing of an obligation is always triggered by an event, and when the PEP needs to process an obligation, it evaluates the ruleset associated with the current state of the obligation. Each ruleset includes one or more rules which are evaluated in a first-applicable manner.

  - Each rule is similar to a rule in XACML policy, and it has a target, a condition, and an effect. Both the target and the condition are predicates, which may refer to fields in the event triggered the processing, the context associated with the request, and state variables within the obligation. If both the target and the condition are satisfied, then the effect is returned.

  - The effect contains

    * *the next state*, which will tell which state the obligation should be in after the processing
    * a (possibly empty) list of assignments to the state variables, which will change the values of these variables
    * a (possibly empty) list of events (which can be Obligation-type events, Timer-request events or Timer-cancel events) to be sent out

In the Appendix 10.2, we give the BNF syntax for obligations, as well as the XML encoding for an example obligation.

4.5 PDP's Obligation Handling Logic

The PDP needs to determine what obligations are to be returned together with the policy decision. Each obligation has a FulfillOn field. Recall that in XACML, this field can take two values: permit and deny. In our design, we keep the semantics of these two values, but add two new values: error and applicable. These effects are summarized in the Table below.

	Condition under which the obligation will be returned by the PDP
permit	when the current policy permits the request, and this contributes to the PDP returning permit for the request.
deny	when the current policy denies the request, and this contributes to the PDP returning deny for the request.
error	when the current policy results in IN, and this contributes to the PDP returning IN for the request
applicable	when the current policy's target matches the request; this obligation will be returned even if current policy's decision disagrees with the PDP's decision.

An obligation whose FulfillOn attribute is `Permit` or `Deny` is treated exactly the same as in XACML. This helps compatibility with current XACML semantics. An obligation whose FulfillOn attribute is error will be returned when the policy directly containing the obligation returns `Indeterminate` for the request, and so is every parent policy and the PDP as a whole. By allowing obligations to accompany `Indeterminate`, we allow more flexible behaviors when policy errors occur. For example, the obligation may inform users what should be provided to gain access, or inform the system administrators about the error via emails.

An obligation whose FulfillOn is "applicable" is returned when the policy directly containing the obligation *does not* return NA. This enables a policy to "force" an obligation up the policy hierarchy, no matter what the PDP's decision of the request will be.

4.6 PEP's Obligation Handling Logic

The PEP maintains a current state for each obligation it is processing. The PEP processes an obligation by sending an event to it. The PEP will choose the ruleset corresponding to the current state that the obligation is in, and then will evaluate the ruleset against the event, the context of the request with which the obligation is associated, and the state variables. How the PEP handles obligations is shown in the pseudo-code in Algorithm 1. In part I, the PEP obtains the PDP decision together with obligations, and initializes the values of PEP_decision and Permit_to_Deny accordingly. In part II, the PEP notifies all obligations, i.e., pre-obligations, that require processing before the final PEP decisions are made. In part III, the PEP waits until all obligations move past pre-decision stage. In part IV, the PEP can finally issue its decision on the request, and can notify obligations about the decision. In part V, the PEP handles obligations, i.e., ongoing-obligations and post-obligations, after the decision.

For the sake of space limitation and clarity, Algorithm 1 is simplified by leaving out details to address some issues. One issue is how to deal with optional obligations. We use the following approach. After Part I, a routine is called to determine how each optional obligation is to be handled. There are three possibilities. An optional obligation may be *discarded*, meaning that the PEP simply ignores it. An optional obligation may be *attempted*, meaning that the PEP will try to fulfill it; however, any failure in fulfillment will *not* affect the PEP decision. Or it may be *turned to mandatory*, meaning that the PEP commits to fulfill this obligation and treats it as a mandatory one.

In Algorithm 1, the PEP needs to wait for all obligations to move beyond the pre-decision stage to make the final decision. However, it is possible that one obligation refuses to move on. This may occur because the obligation itself is erroneous, or because it is waiting for an external event that has not arrived yet. To avoid delaying a decision indeterminately, the PEP may need to set a timer for itself for how long to wait for obligations to move on. When the timer is fired, the PEP sends an "obligation-interrupt" event to force it to leave the current state. An obligation can decide what to do when receiving such an event. It can directly move to the the final stage, such as the *violated* state. It can also move to a later, but not final, stage, and request follow-up actions because of this failure.

The obligations' state changes must follow the logic we lay out in Section 4.2. For example, an obligation should never move from a later stage to an earlier stage, and an obligation in the decision stage, after receiving an PEP-notification event, should not stay in this stage, and so on. After evaluating each obligation, the PEP should check that the obligation's new state is within the allowed logic. When encountering such a logic error with an obligation, the PEP should send an "obligation-abort" event to the obligation. After that, the PEP discards the obligation.

In Algorithm 1 we also omitted codes to deal with obligations that want to monitor the access session. These obligations will be in stages 3 and 4. The logic, however, is straightforward. When the PEP knows that an access session has started, it notifies all obligations in the pre-session state (Stage 3). When any mandatory obligation is in the monitor-unsatisfied state, the PEP must suspend the access session. When any mandatory obligation is in the monitor-terminate state, the PEP must terminate the access session. When all mandatory obligations that are in Stage 4 are in the monitor-satisfied state, the access session can be resumed or continued. When the access session ends, the PEP notifies all obligations in Stage 4 using an access-session-ended event, and expects all obligations to move to Stages 5 or 6.

4.7 Meeting the Challenges

We now briefly discuss how our design for obligation handling, as specified above, meet the challenges we identified in Section 3. First, obligations are state machines and contain rules that can process events. This supports pre-, post-, ongoing- obligations, and any combination of them. This also enables obligations to perform different post actions depending on the state of what happens during the pre and/or ongoing stages.

Second, our architectural choices of implementing the obligation lifecycle logic in the PEP, while using obligation modules to handle application-specific actions enable the PEP to make access decisions and process obligations based on the status of obligations in the system, and at the same time, provide the extensibility necessary for diverse kinds of obligations.

In our design, failure to fulfill mandatory obligations may cause the PEP to deny a request when the PDP returns `Permit`; however, failure to fulfill obligations can never cause the PEP to permit a request when the PDP returns `Deny`. Also note that in our design, one obligation can perform different actions based on whether the PEP's final decision is `Permit` or `Deny`. This enables an obligation that is returned with a PDP `Permit` decision to easily deal with the case that the PEP needs to deny the request. We also allow forced obligations, as well as obligations helping to deal with policy evaluation errors.

5. IMPLEMENTATION

In this section, we first describe a concrete example of using our design, and then our implementation of the design.

5.1 Application

We use as example an obligation that combines a pre-obligation, an ongoing-obligation, and a post-obligation. In order to use an application called MusicPlayer to listen to the latest songs, a user has to accept the license agreement within 60 seconds. After listening to every 6 songs, the user needs to watch an Ad which will go away by itself after 5 seconds. If the user watches the Ad for less than 5 seconds, the access will be stopped. The access information will be logged after the obligation is completed, no matter whether the obligation is fulfilled or violated.

The state transition diagram of this obligation is shown in Figure 3. Initially, the obligation is in the *pre-decision* state. After the obligation receives a "PDP-permit" event, it stays in the *pre-decision* state, and sends two events. One event asks the user to accept the license agreement; the other is a timer-request event specifying a timer duration of 60 seconds.

If the user does not accept the agreement within 60 seconds, the PEP will send a timer event to the obligation, and the obligation will enter the *pre-failed* state. The PEP now must deny the request and notify the obligation about the decision, causing the obligation to enter the *post-access* state, while sending out an event requiring the PEP to log the access information. After receiving an event confirming logging, the obligation goes to the *violated* state.

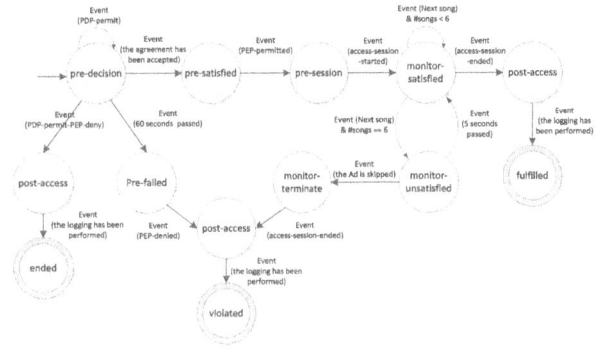

Figure 3: State transitions of a combining obligation

If the user does accept the agreement within 60 seconds, the obligation will receive an event from the external environment (i.e., an external event) indicating that the user has done so. The obligation enters the *pre-satisfied* state, and then upon receiving the "PEP-permitted" event, the obligation enters the *pre-session* state. Later the obligation is triggered by a "access-session-started" event and enters the *monitor-satisfied* state. The obligation receives an event whenever a new song is played, and uses a state variable to record the number of songs that have been played currently. If an external event indicating that the next song is played comes and the value of the state variable is still less than 6, the obligation stays in the *monitor-satisfied* state. If the number reaches 6, the obligation enters the *monitor-unsatisfied* state, as well as generating an event requiring the user to watch an Ad for 5 seconds. If the user has watched the Ad for 5 seconds, the obligation goes back to the *monitor-satisfied* state. If the user does not do so, the obligation goes to the *monitor-terminate* state, forcing the PEP to terminate the access. The obligation then moves to the *post-access* state, to deal with the post-access logging requirement.

The user might actively terminate the access. When the obligation is in the *monitor-satisfied* state and receives an "access-session-ended" event, it enters the *post-access* state. Finally, the obligation enters the *fulfilled* state, completing the transitions.

5.2 Implementation

Following the design in Section 4, we have implemented a prototype system called ExtXACML, based on SUN's XACML implementation [17]. The architecture of ExtXACML is shown in Figure 1. Note that the PEP, the PDP and the Timer are general ones for a XACML system, while the AMI and the Obligation modules are application-specific. We implemented the AMI and the Obligation modules for the application described in Section 5.1.

AMI is the component that interacts with users. Via AMI, a user can start a request asking for listening to songs, play the next song, terminate the access actively, and exit the system.

There are two Obligation modules in the implementation. *MusicPlayerUIObligationModule* deals with user interactions. It shows the license agreement and notifies the obligation about the user's action. It also shows an Ad for 5 and records whether the user has closed it within 5 seconds. *LogObligationModule* logs the access information no matter the access is allowed or denied. The former module requires actions from the user, while the latter needs a system action. In other applications, there might be other Obligation modules for notifying administrators, and sending emails, etc. ExtXACML is extensible in that new Obligation modules can be added into the system to handle various obligations for different applications.

These Obligation modules register themselves to the PEP to receive certain kinds of events, and send events targeting specific obligations back to the PEP, which then sends them to appropriate obligations. For example, the MusicPlayerUIObligationModule informs the PEP that it wants to receive and handle events in the Obligation-music-player-UI family.

The PDP evaluates requests based on the policies loaded, and then returns a PDP decision, together with a (possibly empty) list of obligations. We use the PDP implementation in SunXACML.

The PEP is the main component of ExtXACML. After the PEP receives a request, it assigns a request Id to this request, calls the PDP to evaluate the request, and obtains the result. If the list of obligations is empty, the PEP can directly decide whether the request is allowed or not on the basis of the PDP decision. Otherwise, the next step is to deal with the obligations whose fulfillment might affect the final PEP decision, which is shown in Algorithm 1. The PEP keeps a state for each obligation, recording request Id, subject Id, action Id, the result returned from the PDP, the obligation's current state, and a (possibly empty) list of state variables. The only state variable used in the MusicPlayer example is the number of songs that have been played since the last Ad. When events come, the obligation rules will be evaluated, the state will be updated, and some other events will be sent out.

Our implementation needs to deal with timers. In particular, ExtXACML supports two forms of timer, either a specific time in future or a time duration, and it sets or cancels a timer via events from the timer event family. We use the java.util.Timer class to implement this. Also, while we reuse the code in SunXACML for evaluating rulesets in obligations, we need to extend the mechanisms for obtaining context information. XACML uses AttributeSelector and AttributeDesignator for this purpose. ExtXACML adds two new selectors, EventAttributeSelector and StateVariableSelector, to fetch necessary information from events and state variables for evaluating obligation rules.

6. RELATED WORK

Various obligation concepts have been studied in literature, most of which focus on theoretical analysis. The UCON$_{ABC}$ model first introduced the notions of pre-obligation and ongoing-obligation , respectively [12, 16, 13, 21]. Katt et al. extended obligations in the UCON model to inlude post-obligations. Bettini et al. [2, 1, 3] formalized obligations and investigated mechanisms for monitoring obligations. If obligations are not fulfilled, the system will take compensatory actions, which range from decreasing the trustworthiness of the user, replacing unfulfilled obligations with (perhaps more costly) alternatives, etc. Heimdall [4] is a prototype obligation monitoring platform which tracks the fulfillment of pending obligations. Its policy language xSPL supports time constraints in obligations. Irwin et al. [5, 14, 6] introduced the notion of *accountability* of obligations, which analyzes whether the reason that some obligations are not fulfilled is due to user negligence or insufficient authorization. Recently several policy languages have been proposed to support the specification of obligations in security policies, such as XACML [18], EPAL [9], KAoS [20], Ponder [11] and Rei [7].

Our approach differs from these prior approaches in the following ways. First, our model of an obligation as a state machine interacting with the outside world through events is more powerful and expressive. In existing work, an obligation specifies that on some condition one event ought to happen, which is typically a certain subject must perform a certain action. It is satisfied if that single event occurs, and violated otherwise. Our model allows an obligation to specify that certain sequences of events must occur, with possibly different timing constraints for these events, and with later events possibly dependent upon earlier ones. Our model also allows an obligation to generate events that cause external effect during the lifecycle of the obligation, allowing, for example, sending a reminder when certain actions have not occurred by certain times. Second, we examine the intricate interactions between obligation status and the decision on a request and allow obligations to affect the PEP's decision in any desirable way. Finally, we introduce an extensible architecture to enforce obligations. This includes an XML-based specification language for obligations, and an prototype implementation of PEP's obligation handling functionalities.

Zhang et al. [21] and Katt et al. [8] also use state machines to model obligation enforcement. However, they use a state machine to model the behaviors of the PEP, rather than individual obligations. In their model, each obligation still specifies a single desired event. In our approach, the state of the PEP is modeled implicitly in the algorithm the PEP uses to handle requests and obligations.

Lischka [10] proposes XOML (eXtensible Obligation Markup Language), which allows users to dynamically define and negotiate obligations between the PDP and the PEP in a distributed environment. Obligations specified in this language have a unique obligation Id and a list of parameters. This goes one step beyond XACML's current approach of treating an obligation as a blackbox; however, such obligations still cannot be enforced by the PEP.

7. CONCLUSIONS AND FUTURE WORK

Handling obligations in practical access control systems requires addressing several challenges. For example, there are different types of obligations, and failures of fulfilling these obligations might affect the PEP's decision made on a request. Furthermore, the PEP's decision might also affect which obligations should be carried out and how they should behave.

To meet these challenges, we have proposed a language for specifying obligations. In this language, an obligation is modeled as a state machine which communicates with the PEP and the external environment via events, and includes rulesets to specify its responses to input events. This allows one to specify sophisticated obligations. We have also introduced an architecture for handling access control policies with those obligations, extending XACML's specification and architecture. We designed a simple yet extensible architecture which allows new types of obligation to be included by adding new obligation modules. Based on SUN's XACML implementation, we implemented our design into a prototype system called ExtXACML for a specific application. Our prototype is extensible in that new obligation modules can be attached to handle different types of obligations.

Although obligations are deployment-dependent, it is still possible to build libraries for some commonly used obligations, such as logging access information and notifying administrators via emails. One future direction is to define event families for these kinds of obligations and implement the obligation modules.

Our model of obligations can be viewed as a generalized version of access control policies. One can view them as special cases of dynamic policies, i.e., policy objects that can be dynamically created and that can create other policy objects as the effects of evaluating them. Such dynamic policies can be modeled as state machines that use rulesets to process input events, and generate output events, possibly accompanied by other policy objects. Such dynamic policies may also be useful to model stateful access control policies, administrative policies for selecting appropriate access control policies for a request, policies for data objects dynamically created from combining multiple protected objects, and so on. We plan to explore interesting aspects of dynamic policies, e.g., their formal specification, enforcement mechanism, practical applications, etc.

8. ACKNOWLEDGMENTS

The work reported in this paper was partially supported by the Air Force Office of Scientific Research MURI Grant FA9550-08-1-0265, and by the National Science Foundation under Grant No. 0905442.

9. REFERENCES

[1] C. Bettini, S. Jajodia, X. Wang, and D. Wijesekera. Obligation monitoring in policy management. In *Proceedings of the 3rd International Workshop on Policies for Distributed Systems and Networks (POLICY'03)*, 2003.

[2] C. Bettini, S. Jajodia, X. S. Wang, and D. Wijesekera. Provisions and obligations in policy management and security applications. In *Proceedings of the 28th international conference on Very Large Data Bases*, pages 502–513, 2002.

[3] C. Bettini, S. Jajodia, X. S. Wang, and D. Wijesekera. Provisions and obligations in policy rule management. *J. Netw. Syst. Manage.*, 11:351–372, 2003.

[4] P. Gama and P. Ferreira. Obligation policies: An enforcement platform. In *Proceedings of the Sixth IEEE International Workshop on Policies for Distributed Systems and Networks*, 2005.

[5] K. Irwin, T. Yu, and W. H. Winsborough. On the modeling and analysis of obligations. In *Proceedings of the 13th ACM conference on Computer and communications security*, CCS '06, pages 134–143, 2006.

[6] K. Irwin, T. Yu, and W. H. Winsborough. Assigning responsibility for failed obligations. *IFIP International Federation for Information Processing*, 263:327–342, 2008.

[7] L. Kagal, T. Finin, and A. Joshi. A policy language for a pervasive computing environment. In *Proceedings of the 4th IEEE International Workshop on Policies for Distributed Systems and Networks*, POLICY '03, 2003.

[8] B. Katt, X. Zhang, R. Breu, M. Hafner, and J.-P. Seifert. A general obligation model and continuity: Enhanced policy enforcement engine for usage control. In *Proceedings of the 13th ACM symposium on Access control models and technologies*, pages 123–132, 2008.

[9] I. Z. R. Laboratory. The enterprise privacy authorization language (EPAL 1.1). Avaiable at http://www.zurich.ibm.com/pri/projects/epal.html.

[10] M. Lischka. Dynamic obligation specification and negotiation. In *12th IEEE/IFIP Network Operations and Management Symposium (NOMS 2010)*, pages 155–162, Osaka, Japan, Apr. 2010. IEEE.

[11] E. L. N. Damianou, N. Dulay and M. Sloman. The ponder policy specification language. In *Proc. Policy 2001: Workshop on Policies for Distributed Systems and Networks*, pages 18–39, 2001.

[12] J. Park and R. Sandhu. Towards usage control models: Beyond traditional access control. In *Proceedings of the seventh ACM symposium on Access control models and technologies*, pages 57–64, 2002.

[13] J. Park and R. Sandhu. The UCON$_{ABC}$ usage control model. *ACM Trans. Inf. Syst. Secur.*, 7(1):128–174, February 2004.

[14] M. Pontual, O. Chowdhury, W. H. Winsborough, T. Yu, and K. Irwin. Toward practical authorization-dependent user obligation systems. In *Proceedings of the 5th ACM Symposium on Information, Computer and Communications Security*, ASIACCS '10, 2010.

[15] J. H. Saltzer and M. D. Schroeder. The protection of information in computer systems. *Proceedings of the IEEE*, 63(9), 1975.

[16] R. Sandhu and J. Park. Usage control: A vision for next generation access control. In *Inter. Workshop on Mathematical Methods, Models and Architectures for Computer Networks Security*, 2003.

[17] Sun. Sun's XACML implementation. Avaiable at http://sunxacml.sourceforge.net/index.html.

[18] X. TC. Extensible access control markup language (XACML) version 2.0. *OASIS Standard*, 2005. Avaiable at http://www.oasis-open.org/committees/xacml/.

[19] X. TC. Extensible access control markup language (XACML) version 3.0 (draft). 2010. Avaiable at http://www.oasis-open.org/committees/xacml/.

[20] A. Uszok, J. Bradshaw, R. Jeffers, N. Suri, P. Hayes, M. Breedy, L. Bunch, M. Johnson, S. Kulkarni, and J. Lott. KAoS policy and domain services: Toward a description-logic approach to policy representation, deconfliction, and enforcement. In *Proceedings of the 4th IEEE International Workshop on Policies for Distributed Systems and Networks*, POLICY '03, 2003.

[21] X. Zhang, F. Parisi-Presicce, R. Sandhu, and J. Park. Formal model and policy specification of usage control. *ACM Trans. Inf. Syst. Secur.*, 8(4):351–387, November 2005.

10. APPENDICES

10.1 PEP Obligation Handling Logic

How the PEP handles obligations is shown in Algorithm 1.

10.2 Obligation Schema and Example

The obligation schema in BNF form is shown as follows.

```
< Obligations > := < Obligation >*
< Obligation > := < InitialState >< EventFamilies > [StateVariables]
                    < StateRuleSets >
Attributes: ObligationId, FulfillOn, IsOptional
< InitialState > := ("pre − decision"|"pre − satisfied")
< EventFamilies > := < EventFamily >+
< StateVariables > := < StateVariable >+
< StateVariable > := < AttributeValue >
Attributes: StateVariableId, DataType
< StateRuleSets > := < StateRuleSet >+
< StateRuleSet > := < State >< RuleSet >
< State > := ("pre − decision"|"pre − satisfied"|"pre − failed"|"pre −
            session"|"during − session"|"monitor − satisfied"|
            "monitor − unsatisfied"|"monitor − terminate"|"post −
            access"|"fulfiled"|"violated"|"ended")
< RuleSet > := < Rule >+
< Rule > := [Target][Condition] < Effect >
Attributes: RuleId
< Effect > := < NextState > [StateVariableAssignments][Events]
< NextState > := ("pre−decision"|"pre−satisfied"|"pre−failed"|"pre−
            session"|"during − session"|"monitor − satisfied"|
            "monitor − unsatisified"|"monitor − terminate"|
            "post − access"|"fulfiled"|"violated"|"ended")
< StateVariableAssignments > := < StateVariableAssignment >+
< StateVariableAssignment > := < AttributeValue >
Attributes: StateVariableId, DataType
< Events > := < Event >+
< Event > := < EventType >< Message > [Timer][ObligationFamily]
Attributes: EventId, EventFamilyId, ObligationId, TimerRequestEventId (option-
al)
< Timer > := < StartTime > | < TimeDuration >
```

Note that the EventFamilies element includes a list of event family which the obligation can handle, such as PEP-notification event family, PEP-session event family, Timer event family, different kinds of obligation related event families, and so on. One example of obligation related families is the event family for the

Algorithm 1 Pseudo-code of PEP obligation handling logic (simplified version)

PEP_decide(*Request*)

1: {*Part I: Obtain PDP decision and obligations, and initialize.*}
2: (PDP_decision, Obligations) ← evaluate(Policy, Request);
3: **if** PDP_decision == Permit **then**
4:     PEP_decision ← May_Permit;
5: **else**
6:     PEP_decision ← Deny;
7: **end if**
8: Permit_to_Deny ← **false**;
9:
10: {*Part II: Notify all obligations that require processing before decisions are made.*}
11: **for all** obligation Ob that is in pre-decision state **do**
12:     evaluate(Ob, event(PDP_decision));
13:     **if** Ob.state == pre-failed **and** PEP_decision == May_Permit **then**
14:         PEP_decision ← Deny;
15:         Permit_to_Deny ← **true**;
16:         **break**;
17:     **end if**
18: **end for**
19: **if** Permit_to_Deny == **true then**
20:     **for all** obligation Ob that is in pre-decision state **do**
21:         evaluate(Ob, event(PDP-permit-PEP-deny));
22:     **end for**
23: **end if**
24:
25: {*Part III: Wait until all obligations move past pre-decision stage.*}
26: **while** at least one obligation in pre-decision state **do**
27:     wait for Ext_event, event from the external environment;
28:     Ob = the obligation that Ext_event is directed to;
29:     evaluate(Ob, Ext_event);
30:     **if** Ob.state == pre-failed **and** PEP_decision == May_Permit **then**
31:         PEP_decision ← Deny;
32:         **for all** obligation Obp still in pre-decision state **do**
33:             evaluate(Obp, event(PDP-permit-PEP-deny));
34:         **end for**
35:         break;
36:     **end if**
37: **end while**
38:
39: {*Part IV: Decide the request, and notify obligations about the decision.*}
40: **if** PEP_decision == May_Permit **then**
41:     PEP_decision ← Permit;
42: **end if**
43: decide_request(PEP_decision);
44: **for all** obligation Ob in decision stage **do**
45:     evaluate(Ob, event(PEP-decision);
46: **end for**
47:
48: {*Part V: handles obligations after the decision.*}
49: **while** at least one obligation not in completed stage **do**
50:     wait for Ext_event, event from the external environment;
51:     Ob = the obligation that Ext_event is directed to;
52:     evaluate(Ob, Ext_event);
53: **end while**

logging obligation. This family includes events like Obligation-logging events, Obligation-logging-done events, and Obligation-logging-fail events.

In the following, an example is shown for illustrating how to specify obligations in XML.

```xml
<Obligations>
  <Obligation ObligationId="accept-watchAd-log" FulfillOn="Permit" IsOptional="false">
    <InitialState>pre-decision</InitialState>
    <EventFamilies>
      <EventFamily EventFamilyId="PEP-notification"></EventFamily>
      <EventFamily EventFamilyId="PEP-session"></EventFamily>
      <EventFamily EventFamilyId="Timer"></EventFamily>
      <EventFamily EventFamilyId="Obligation-music-player-UI"></EventFamily>
      <EventFamily EventFamilyId="Obligation-logging"></EventFamily>
    </EventFamilies>
    <StateVariables>
      <StateVariable StateVariableId="number"
          DataType="http://www.w3.org/2001/XMLSchema#integer">
        <AttributeValue>0</AttributeValue>
      </StateVariable>
    </StateVariables>
    <StateRuleSets>
      <StateRuleSet>
        <State>pre-decision</State>
        <RuleSet RuleSetId="pre-decision-rulset">
          <ObligationRule ObligationRuleId="rule1">
            <Condition FunctionId="urn:oasis:names:tc:xacml:1.0:function:and">
              <Apply
                  FunctionId="urn:oasis:names:tc:xacml:1.0:function:anyURI-equal">
                <AttributeValue
                    DataType="http://www.w3.org/2001/XMLSchema#anyURI"
                    >accept-watchAd-log</AttributeValue>
                <EventAttributeSelector EventField="ObligationId"
                    DataType="http://www.w3.org/2001/XMLSchema#anyURI"/>
              </Apply>
              <Apply
                  FunctionId="urn:oasis:names:tc:xacml:1.0:function:anyURI-equal">
                <AttributeValue
                    DataType="http://www.w3.org/2001/XMLSchema#anyURI"
                    >PEP-notification</AttributeValue>
                <EventAttributeSelector EventField="EventFamilyId"
                    DataType="http://www.w3.org/2001/XMLSchema#anyURI"/>
              </Apply>
              <Apply
                  FunctionId="urn:oasis:names:tc:xacml:1.0:function:string-equal">
                <AttributeValue
                    DataType="http://www.w3.org/2001/XMLSchema#string"
                    >PDP-permit</AttributeValue>
                <EventAttributeSelector EventField="EventType"
                    DataType="http://www.w3.org/2001/XMLSchema#string"/>
              </Apply>
            </Condition>
            <ObligationEffect>
              <NextState>pre-decision</NextState>
              <Events>
                <Event EventId="obligation-accept"
                    EventFamilyId="Obligation-music-player-UI"
                    ObligationId="accept-watchAd-log">
                  <EventType>Obligation-accept-agreement</EventType>
                  <ObligationFamily>Accept</ObligationFamily>
                  <Message>Please accept the license agreement</Message>
                </Event>
                <Event EventId="timer-request-sixty-seconds"
                    EventFamilyId="Timer"
                    ObligationId="accept-watchAd-log">
                  <EventType>timer-request</EventType>
                  <Timer>
                    <TimerDuration>PT60S</TimerDuration>
                  </Timer>
                  <Message>The obligation should be fulfilled within 60 seconds</Message>
                </Event>
              </Events>
            </ObligationEffect>
          </ObligationRule>
          ......
        </RuleSet>
      </StateRuleSet>
      ......
    </StateRuleSets>
  </Obligation>
  ......
</Obligations>
```

Deriving Implementation-level Policies for Usage Control Enforcement*

Prachi Kumari
Certifiable Trustworthy IT Systems
Karlsruhe Institute of Technology
Germany

Alexander Pretschner
Certifiable Trustworthy IT Systems
Karlsruhe Institute of Technology
Germany

ABSTRACT

Usage control is concerned with how data is used after access to it has been granted. As such, it is particularly relevant to end users who own the data. System implementations of access and usage control enforcement mechanisms, however, do not always adequately reflect end user requirements. This is due to several reasons, one of which is the problem of mapping concepts in the end user's domain to technical events and artifacts. For instance, semantics of basic operators such as "copy" or "delete", which are fundamental for specifying privacy policies, tend to vary according to context. For this reason they can be mapped to different sets of system events. The behaviour users expect from the system, therefore, may differ from the actual behaviour. In this paper we present a translation of specification-level usage control policies into implementation-level policies which takes into account the precise semantics of domain-specific abstractions. A tool for automating the translation has also been implemented.

Categories and Subject Descriptors

H.4 [**Information Systems Applications**]: Miscellaneous

General Terms

Security

Keywords

Security and privacy, policy enforcement, usage control, semantics, user vs. system requirements

1. INTRODUCTION

Access and usage control systems provide means to specify and enforce policies about who can access data and how.

*Support by the Google Research Award "Towards Operational Privacy" is gratefully acknowledged.

At the level of *end users*, a policy is a set of rules specified using abstract vocabularies such as "this picture may not be printed" or "this address may not be distributed." We refer to these rules as specification-level policies. The set of actions, subjects and objects that are used in such policies differs according to the domain context. Within each domain, policies must be defined and enforced at different levels of abstraction, including the operating system [1], windows manager [2], virtual machine [3], etc. Every specification-level policy hence needs to be mapped to a set of implementation-level policies, usually one per layer of abstraction. This is because the data that is to be protected comes in different representations: as file, as window content, object attributes, etc. Eventually, all these representations boil down to some representation in memory, but it is often more convenient and simpler to perform protection at higher levels of abstraction [4].

Usage control policies can in general be enforced in two ways. *Detective enforcement* aims at detecting violations of a policy. In case of a violation, usually a compensating, correcting, or notifying action is taken. In contrast, *preventive enforcement* aims at avoiding policy violations [5]. The subject of this paper is the derivation of implementation-level policies from abstract specification-level policies for preventive enforcement of usage control requirements. There are two major challenges in enforcement: firstly, to keep track of all representations of the same data at different layers of abstractions. For instance, if a picture downloaded from a web-based social network site (WBSN) is to be protected, then the window content, the cache file, and the browser-internal representation, as well as their copies, need to be protected. The second challenge is to translate the policy specified for abstract data with abstract actions into implementation-specific policies at different layers of abstraction.

The problem of addressing different representations of the same data in the system without explicitly listing them has been tackled elsewhere [6]. For enforcement of usage control policies, a set of layer-specific enforcement and data flow tracking mechanisms is configured by a data-oriented policy language. The respective data flow tracking model keeps track of the connections between various representations of data across different levels of abstraction. In this line of research, the authors expect the policies to exist and have not addressed the problem of deriving them. In this paper, we tackle the derivation of implementation-level policies.

One major issue in the derivation of policies is that there is not one single "correct" semantics for actions like "copy" or "delete." To address this problem, two questions need to be answered: the first one concerns the domain-specific semantics of actions, that is, how an action on a data affects other associated data in the domain. For example, "does deleting a profile in a social network mean deleting all posts and links from other profiles also?" The second question is about the technical semantics of actions. That is, how is an action at the abstract level translated into technical events that are eventually performed, e.g., "does copying a picture mean taking screenshots also or only coping the corresponding jpeg files? Does deleting a file mean throwing away the key or deleting the FAT entry or randomly overwriting the hard disk's sectors several times?" Finding answers to both sets of questions is fundamental to the derivation of policies. This is because, in the absence of clear semantics of basic operators (viz. copy and delete), it is impossible to define policies for basic privacy requirements regarding dissemination, retention or deletion of data, that leave no room for misinterpretation. In general, it is not possible to directly intercept/check/detect/monitor if a copying or deletion event has happened or is currently happening.

The other challenge in the derivation of policies is methodological. Although there exist many methodologies for recording, analyzing and understanding user requirements, we do not know of a well-defined framework that facilitates the translation of these requirements into implementation-level policies in a systematic way. Typically, this translation is a manual exercise which can result in implementations that, at different levels of abstraction, permit events that should not be allowed to happen and/or forbid events that should be allowed. Also, in the absence of a well-defined translation methodology, this tedious and lengthy process cannot be automated. Similar problems arise whenever user requirements are transformed into system requirements.

In this paper, we address these issues in the context of usage control policies. We provide a framework for precisely defining the semantics of the actions specified in domain-specific policies that, at the same time, takes into account the underlying technology. We also present methodological guidance in order to automate the translation of policies. The complete process requires human intervention in two roles: the first one is an "end user" who is expected to be well-versed in the domain-specific terminology but is oblivious to the corresponding technical details, which are taken care of by the more sophisticated "power user." For this, we present a meta-model of the data-processing system that reflects the specification and translation of policy elements from abstract to technical levels. We do this in three steps: (1) define a domain model to describe obligations on future data usage; (2) map high-level domain-specific abstractions to low-level technical representations; (3) define enforcement mechanisms for every technical representation.

End users define policies using high level domain-specific terminology. The mapping from high level domain-specific abstractions to low-level technical representations and the definition of enforcement mechanisms [7,8] is provided by the second role, the power user. Policies are then automatically translated to rules that are sufficiently technical to configure enforcement mechanisms.

One example use is from the social network domain: Alice wants her friends to be able to view the pictures she posts in her profile. In contrast, they should not be able to make local copies of those pictures on their machines. Alice can specify the policy "never copy picture" using one of the policy templates described later in this paper, *without knowledge of any technical policy specification language.* By means of the domain model and the mappings provided by the power user, this policy is mapped to more technical policies at various levels of abstraction. The power user also decides on the mode of enforcement (inhibition, modification, execution). Finally, sets of implementation-specific executable rules are generated, one per layer of abstraction. The enforcement of the policy itself is tackled elsewhere [9] and is outside the scope of this paper.

One crucial assumption in this paper is the static system structure. In deriving implementation-level policies from specification-level usage control policies, we have deliberately not considered the adaptive nature of systems. Though unrealistic, this assumption is reasonable in order to simplify the problem and achieve initial results.

Problem. In sum, we tackle two problems in this paper. The first concerns the lack of semantics of events in usage control policies. The second concerns the problem of transforming abstract policies to their technical counterparts in an automated manner. In the larger context, through this work we try to fill the gap between user and system requirements for domain-specific applications.

Solution. We present a framework and a tool for defining the semantics of events that takes into account the different representations of data and its potential flow through a technical system. Our solution comprises both the technical and the methodological aspects of deriving technical policies from more abstract policies.

Contribution. We are not aware of methodologies for translating specification-level usage or access control policies into implementation-level policies that configure usage or access control mechanisms at different abstraction levels.

Organization. §2 puts our work in context. §3 presents the domain meta-model and, as an example, a WBSN instantiation of it. §4 describes the translation of policies. §5 describes the tool we implemented for automating policy translations. §6 backs our proposed framework through several examples. §7 concludes by discussing limitations, further refinements and future work. Appendix A describes the translation of future-time specification-level obligational formulas to the past-time conditions of implementation-level policies.

2. RELATED WORK

The subject of this paper is the derivation of implementation-level policies from specification-level policies using a domain meta-model that is instantiated to define the technical semantics of domain-specific abstractions in high-level usage control policies. The general problem addressed is the translation of user requirements into system requirements.

Often, user requirements are not adequately translated into system requirements which results in systems with functionalities that are not desired while missing out on the desired ones [10]. The gap between these two types of requirements has been a major problem in the domain of requirement engineering [11–13] and although a lot of work has been done on understanding, eliciting, analyzing user requirements [14] and translating them into system requirements for different application domains [15, 16], it remains one of the prominent topics in software engineering research [10, 17].

In the context of security, modeling vulnerabilities, failures and countermeasures [18–21], security requirements and their potential conflicts with other functional and non-functional requirements, application of standards [22, 23], access control policies and requirements [24,25] and policy description languages [7, 26–28] have been mainly addressed.

In terms of derivation/refinement of policies from the business to the technology level, the focus has been on the derivation of role-based access control policies. In this line of work, Yee and Korba have presented two approaches for semi-automatic derivation, one relies on third-party surveys of user perceptions of data privacy and the other on retrieval from a community of peers [29]; Young and Anton [30] have proposed a commitment (obligations) analysis methodology to derive software requirements from privacy policies; Su et al. have proposed a policy refinement methodology based on resource hierarchies [31]; Bandara et al. have presented a methodology based on system goals [32]; Guerrero et al. have proposed an ontology-based approach [33]; and Udupi et al. have presented an automated, domain independent approach based on data classification [34]. Lodderstedt et al. specify RBAC policies in UML and translate them to code or deployment files [35] and do not consider the semantics of atomic actions or resources. Aziz et al. [36] have proposed a resource hierarchy meta-model for translating domain-specific elements in XACML policies at the level of virtual organizations to generate corresponding XACML resource-level policies. This is similar to our work in terms of the approach. However, the policies are refined from the abstract level (users, resources and applications) to the logical level (user ids, resource addresses and computational commands like read/write); further technical representations of policy elements in concrete systems are not considered. Besides, the policy refinement literature concerns access control privacy policies only. To the best of our knowledge, the translation of usage control policies has not been investigated.

Usage control, which extends the concept of data protection beyond access control [37, 38], puts constraints upon further usage of data after access is granted. Usage control enforcement, for various policy languages [7, 26–28, 39], has been done at different layers of abstraction [1–4] in the system. However, in all these enforcement cases, policies are supposed to exist and their derivation from end user requirements to enforcement mechanisms has not been addressed.

Though all the work cited above makes some kind of distinction between high-level abstract and low-level concrete data and actions, they have not defined precise frameworks that can guide the derivation from top to bottom. In this context, many architecture frameworks have been proposed that differentiate among business, data, application, and technical infrastructure layers in enterprise settings; the prominent ones being the Zachman framework [40] and the Open Group Architecture Framework (TOGAF) [41]. Of these, the Zachman framework focuses on the classification of various architectural artifacts. The three initial perspectives of "what", "how" and "where" for information systems architecture [42] are part of our domain meta-model at the second and third layers.

3. THE FRAMEWORK

Specification-level policies describe *what* must and must not happen throughout the execution of a system. Implementation-level policies refine them by stating *how* they will actually be enforced. This paper addresses the problem of automatically deriving the latter from the former.

Specification-level policies consist of domain-specific abstractions (that is, data and actions) and constraints. Examples include never-copy-picture, delete-document-after-30-days, etc. We need, firstly, to define the meaning of data and actions. Secondly, because specification-level policies tend to be formulated in terms of the *future* usage of data, we need to transform the constraints into enforceable conditions that are defined on the *past* (as explained elsewhere [7]; otherwise, the system would need to be able to look into the future. For a special subset of properties, it is in fact possible to detect the policy's violation at the earliest moment in time [43]. However, since we are concerned with *preventive* enforcement, we do not rely on these approaches). To address the first challenge, we present a meta-model where the meaning of high-level abstractions of data and actions is provided by mapping them to their possible technical representations. The second challenge, the translation of constraints, is essentially the problem of deriving past-time rules to configure enforcement mechanisms. Our mechanisms consist of a description of when they are applicable (triggering event and a condition); and the respective actions to be taken in that case. Mechanisms are hence of the event-condition-action format. Different mechanisms may correspond to one obligation at different levels of abstraction.

We address all these issues step-by-step in the next sections. We start by addressing the problem of defining the semantics of data and actions in specification-level policies.

3.1 Data and Containers

In order to enforce usage control policies specified for data, we must be able to differentiate between data and actions, and their technical representations. At the end user's level, data is an abstract concept with an intuitive set of actions relevant to it. The end user can therefore specify usage control policies only in those abstract terms. At the system level, data comes in different concrete representations called the containers (files, pixmaps, memory regions, network packets etc.). The mappings between data and containers tell which set of data is potentially stored in which container at runtime [6]. Extending this concept of distinction between data and its representation, we present a meta-model of the domain that includes the distinction among user-intelligible high-level actions on data like "delete profile" and "copy picture" (layer 1), corresponding technical events on containers (which we call transformers) (layer 2), and the specific implementations of these transformers and containers (layer 3). Mappings between various components at different layers in the meta-model provide the semantics of high level actions on data in terms of a set of corresponding technical events at various levels of abstraction.

3.2 The Domain Meta-Model

Our domain meta-model is shown in Figure 1. It consists of three layers: the platform-independent layer that is to be defined and used by the end user; the platform-specific layer that is to be defined and used by the power user; and the implementation-specific layer, also to be defined and used by the power user, that reflects the technicalities of the system on which the policies are to be deployed.

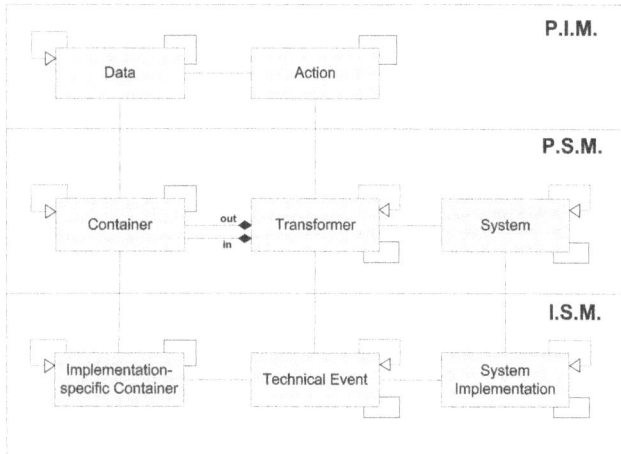

Figure 1: Domain meta-model

The platform-independent (PIM) layer corresponds to the abstract *data* and the set of intuitive *actions*. Associations and generalization-specialization relationships among data define the abstract data model of the application domain and capture the scenario when in a domain, certain data are seen as aggregation of or associated with (set of) other data or as generalization/specializations of other data. For example, a profile is associated with all blogposts that a specific user posts in a blog-domain, an album is an aggregation of all pictures posted by a specific user in a WBSN-domain etc. The specification of such relationships can also help define semantics of actions on one data in terms of a set of actions on other data. For example, deleting the profile means also deleting all associated posts, or denying copies of the album means that no picture in the album can be copied irrespective of the difference in the technical representations of the two. Generalization-specialization relationships among data at the PIM layer also define the semantics of an action on one data in terms of actions on another data at the platform-specific layer. For example, if a blog account is a *specialization of* a general account, then the technical semantics of actions like copy and delete for a blog account is the same as for the general account.

The platform-specific (PSM) layer corresponds to all possible representations of data, known as *containers*, and the set of *transformers* that read and write data between these containers at different layers of abstraction in the *system*. Transformers can be seen as functions that use sets of (atomic and/or complex) events in corresponding systems to transform the containers when certain actions are performed on data; e.g. screenshot in the windowing system, copy & paste in the web browser, copy file in the file system, etc. Containers, transformers and systems can be associated with and/or generalize sets of other containers, transformers and systems. For instance, a database can be seen as a specialization of a file; copy file transformers are associated with a set of transformers for opening, reading, writing and closing a file, and a WBSN system is spread across multiple layers of abstractions over many servers and client machines.

As there is more than one way of implementing different

systems, multiple implementations of containers and transformers exist. This is shown in the third layer of our meta-model, the implementation-specific layer (ISM). Mappings between data and containers, and, actions and transformers specify the semantics of actions on data in terms of sets of transformers applied to sets of containers; e.g. semantics of "copy picture" in the context of a WBSN are given by screenshot in the windowing system, copy & paste in the web browser, copyfile in the operating system. Mapping containers and transformers to their implementations specifies the semantics of action on data in terms of low-level technical implementations; e.g. the semantics of "copy picture" is given by "getImage on a drawable object" in the X11 windowing system, "cmd_copy on an html image object" in the Mozilla Firefox web browser, and "sequence of open, read, write and close system calls on file" in a Unix operating system. For illustration, we instantiate our meta-model for the case of a WBSN in the next subsection.

3.3 A Social Network Example

For space reasons, only parts of the complete domain model are shown in Figure 2. The classes of the meta model (data, container) that are instantiated by a class of the WBSN domain model are indicated as stereotypes (« ») on top of the class name (WBSN data, WBSN container).

The PIM layer domain model contains copy, delete etc. actions for the classes of payload and traffic data. Profile information, pictures, posts, comments and other data posted by end users is payload data; all data generated by browsing activities of end users, e.g. links clicked, profiles visited etc. are traffic data. A detailed data model of WBSN is given in [44].

WBSN Containers are specialized into web browser container, windowing system container, operating system containers etc. which are further specialized as DOM element, window, file and other containers. Copy&paste, screenshot, CopyFile and other transformers transfer data between these containers. The system is a generalization of logical systems (i.e. layers of abstraction like web browser, windowing system, operating system etc.), physical hosts/locations (e.g. caches, backups and other servers, client machines etc.) and applications that span over both logical and physical systems (e.g. social network, mail systems, ERP systems etc.). These systems and their implementations evolve over time. However, in this paper we treat them as static. We reiterate that we have done this deliberately - in order to simplify the problem. The dynamic nature of distributed systems is part of our ongoing work.

At the ISM layer, specific implementations include a Firefox web browser, the X11 windowing system, an OpenBSD operating system with corresponding containers and transformers. For the Facebook implementation of social network, various logical systems shown at the ISM layer are deployed at hundreds of physical locations.

The definition of the domain models and the mappings provides the semantics of data (in terms of its structure and the containers that contain the data) and actions (in terms of technical events) in specification-level policies. The next step is the translation of constraints. We begin with an overview of the complete process of specifying and deriving the policies, followed by the details.

P.I.M.

Profile | Post | Picture | Comment | ...

Copy | Delete | ...

Payload Data | Traffic Data

<<Data>> WBSN Data | <<Action>> WBSN Action

P.S.M.

Copy&Paste | Screenshot | CopyFile | ...

DOM element | Web browser container
Window | Windowing system container
File | Operating system container
...

<<Container>> WBSN Container | in out | <<Transformer>> WBSN Transformer | <<System>> WBSN System

Application | Logical System | Physical Host

Social Network | Operating System | Windowing system | Backup Server | ...

I.S.M.

HTML element | Drawable | Unix File | ...

<<Implementation-specific Container>> WBSN Implementation-specific Container | <<Technical Event>> WBSN Technical Event | <<System Implementation>> WBSN System Implementation

Facebook | Firefox | X11 WS | OpenBSD | ...

Copy_cmd | getImage | Open | ...

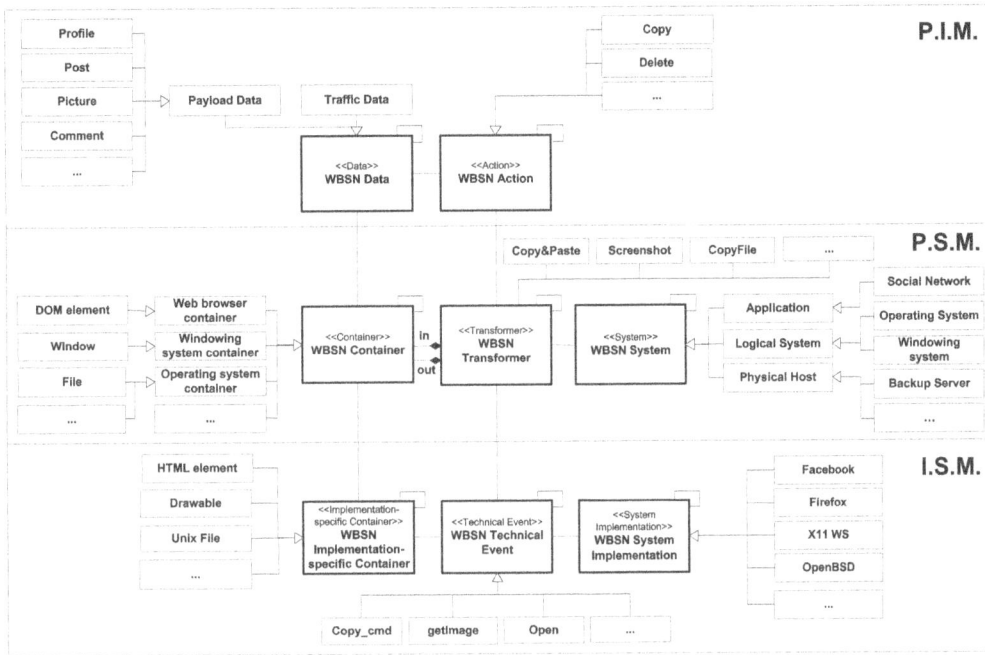

Figure 2: WBSN Domain Model, an instance of Fig. 1

3.4 Overview of Policy Specification and Translation

Figure 3 shows the sequences of steps for the systematic specification and translation of specification-level policies to implementation-level policies. The first flow chart describes the tasks performed by the power user for the definition of the domain model and the policy templates and the translation of policies specified using these templates. The second flow chart describes the end user tasks for specification of policies (and also their translation, in case he opts not to use the templates). In the complete process, end user tasks start only after all the tasks are completed by the power user. The initial steps are about defining the three domain mod-

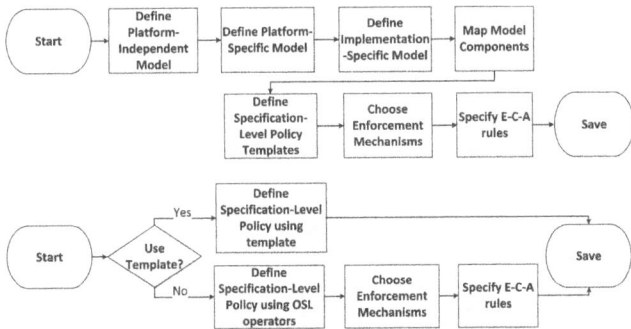

Start → Define Platform-Independent Model → Define Platform-Specific Model → Define Implementation-Specific Model → Map Model Components → Define Specification-Level Policy Templates → Choose Enforcement Mechanisms → Specify E-C-A rules → Save

Start → Use Template? — Yes → Define Specification-Level Policy using template → Save
— No → Define Specification-Level Policy using OSL operators → Choose Enforcement Mechanisms → Specify E-C-A rules → Save

Figure 3: Policies Specification and Translation

els because this provides the vocabulary for specifying PIM policies and their translations to the ISM layer: string representations of data, actions and their technical implementations are used in specification and implementation-level policies. The platform-independent domain model is defined in the *first step*. In the *second* and the *third steps*, the

platform and implementation -specific models of the application are defined. In the *fourth step*, high level components from the PIM level are mapped to PSM level technical representations (§5). As the implementation-specific model is a refinement of the platform-specific model, the definition of ISM components includes the mapping to PSM-level counterparts and is not a separate step in the process. In the *fifth step*, when the power user creates specification-level policy templates (§5), he is also required to define the further translation of the resulting policies. In sum, when the PIM policy (or template) is saved, multiple XML representations of the PIM policy are generated, each corresponding to one specific layer of abstraction in the ISM model and containing implementation-specific representations of the abstract data and action specified in the PIM policy. In the *sixth step*, enforcement strategies corresponding to every XML PIM-policy are chosen. Finally, executable event-condition-action rules are defined in the *seventh step*. Usually, the power user defines classes of policies as templates. The end user specifies PIM policies using the available templates. As their translation is already defined by the power user, the policies are automatically translated when the end user saves them. The end user can also specify PIM policies without templates, using standard OSL operators. In that case, he must decide upon the enforcement mechanisms and define the corresponding ECA rules.

In a nutshell, the meta-model from Figure 1 is instantiated to three-layered domain models and the mappings between the layers for the application context (as in Figure 2). In the subsequent steps, the specification-level policy, the enforcement strategies and the event-condition-action rules for enforcement are defined; they can be generated for template classes of policies. In the next section we go into the details of policy specification and translation.

4. POLICY SPECIFICATION AND TRANSLATION

Specification-level policies stipulate what must or must not happen to data in the future. Hence they contain obligations in future time temporal logic. In our framework, we specify obligations in OSL, a policy specification language that combines the classical propositional operators with future time temporal and cardinality operators such as *until*, *always*, *after*, *within*, *during*, *repmax* etc. Intuitively, $until(a, b)$ is true if a is true until b eventually becomes true or b never becomes true; the *always* operator is intuitive, $after(n, a)$ is true if a becomes true after n time steps; *within* and *during* are intuitive. The cardinality operator $repmax(n, a)$ specifies that a must be true at most n times in the future. For space reasons, we do not describe all OSL operators here. For the complete syntax and semantics, see [6, 7].

Usually, a high-level action in a policy is expressed in terms of a sequence of corresponding low level events. In certain cases, this might not be the best approach. Let us for instance consider the policy of denying picture copies at the operating system level; this means that a sequence of system calls that result in a copy of the picture are denied. But infinitely many sequences of system calls can achieve the same result and coming up with a list of them has a high chance that we miss out a few of them. Alternatively, if all such sequences might start with a particular system call (e.g. in any case, a file must be opened to be copied), blocking this particular system call (the first in the sequence) might seem a solution. The problem with this approach is that this particular system call starts many other sequences, some being required features of the system. Blocking any other "main" system call of the sequence requires the sequence to be precisely identified and enumerated. Thus it turns out that expressing the semantics of high level action in terms of a sequence of low level events might not be the best approach in some cases. Especially when actions of the form copy and delete are concerned, the user wants to make sure that specific situations must or must not occur in the system, that is, the system must or must not be in specific states. For this, state-based policies have been introduced in [6]. State-based policies refine actions in policies in terms of states that the system must or must not enter. As the mappings between data and containers define the states of a system, this means that the data must be restricted to or must never enter specific containers. For this, operators like *isNotIn*, *isCombinedWith* and *isOnlyIn* are used. Thus specification level policies can be enforced both as event-based policies and state-based policies. In Section 6 we show example policies for both cases.

Figure 4 shows how the meta-model fits into the big picture of usage control policies and how components from one relate to the other. An OSL policy consists of a set of obligational *formulas*. An obligational formula consists of a logical expression which is a set of state-based and event-based operators. Complex policies contain nested formulas; hence, formulas can also be operands in a policy. The other operands include action with data as its parameter, both of which are string representations of the classes in the PIM domain model. End user policies are specified using templates which contain these string representations, hence they apply to classes and not specific instances of data. Note that

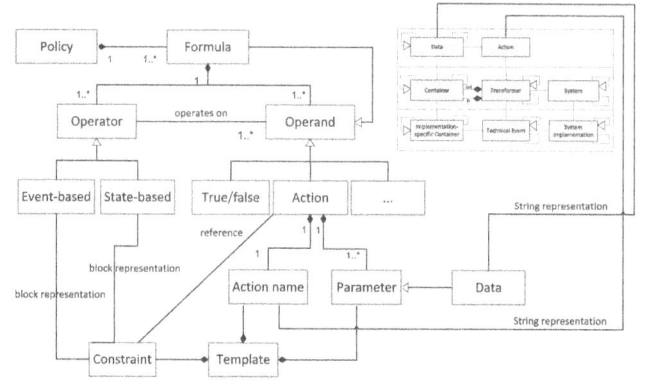

Figure 4: The big picture

graphical templates are defined in order to hide OSL from the end user; end users may, but are not expected to express policies in OSL. So the templates are designed to consist of data, action and constraints as representations of OSL operators. Constraints can also be expressed in terms of actions that trigger the policy; hence actions are shown to be referenced in constraints (in concrete syntax these are XPath constructs containing reference to trigger event).

The specific kind of preventive enforcement (inhibition, modification, execution) needs to be prescribed by the power user as one specification-level policy can be enforced in many ways. For instance, let us consider the requirement "picture must not be copied without notification" in a WBSN domain. At the abstract level, preventive enforcement by *inhibition* of this requirement means that all actions of the type copy are blocked; preventive enforcement by *modification* means that the picture is allowed to be copied but the resulting image at the destination is for instance, replaced by another picture (for instance, showing an error); and preventive enforcement by *execution* means that the picture is allowed to be copied but the owner is notified about the action. Abstractly, these enforcement mechanisms are parameterized event-condition-action (ECA) rules where the rule is triggered provided that the *Event* takes place and the *Condition* evaluates to true. The *Action* specifies how precisely inhibition, delay, modification, or execution take place [8]. For instance, let us consider again the above requirement. To show the ECA rules corresponding to different enforcement strategies, we use these propositions with picture as p: $attemptCopy(p)$ denotes that an attempt to copy picture has been made, $copy(p)$ denotes that a picture is copied, $notifyAdmin(p)$ states that a notification about the picture should be sent to the administrator, $adminNotified(p)$ means that the administrator has already been notified about the picture.

Enforcement by execution means that whenever the picture is copied, a notification is sent to the administrator.

```
Event: copy(p)
Condition: true
Action: EXECUTE notifyAdmin(p)
```

Enforcement by modification means that whenever there is an attempt to copy the picture and a notification has not been sent, the picture is replaced by another predefined picture "error.jpg"(using function *replaceByError(p)*).

```
Event: attemptCopy(p)
Condition: not(adminNotified(p))
Action: MODIFY replaceByError(p)
```

Enforcement by inhibition means that whenever there is an attempt to copy the picture and a notification has not been sent, the attempt is blocked.

```
Event: attemptCopy(p)
Condition: not(adminNotified(p))
Action: INHIBIT
```

Implementation-level policies are encoded in XML with an Event declaration part, a Condition part, and an Action part (ECA pattern). The event declaration part is the trigger of the implementation-level policy, and represents the request for the execution of an action. The trigger event can be underspecified, that is, all the parameters need not be declared here. It is possible to reference the trigger event of implementation-level policies in the conditions and action parts using XPath expressions. When a trigger event matching the event declaration part of an implementation-level policy is received, and the condition part evaluates to true, the action part of the mechanism is evaluated. Our language allows the specification of implementation-level policies that inhibit/prevent the intended action and might also execute arbitrary actions before the requested action is executed. In case the action allow is specified, it is possible to specify modifications in the parameters values or to delay the execution of the action.

Deciding about the enforcement strategy and the translation of future time obligations to their past forms are the two basic requirements for deriving implementation-level policies from specification-level policies. We present the translation of future time obligations to past time conditions in Appendix A. In the next section we give an overview of the automation of the translation and the implemented tools.

5. AUTOMATION OF POLICY SPECIFICATION AND TRANSLATION

In Section 3.4, we have introduced the methodology for a systematic derivation of implementation-level policies from specification-level policies. The first four tasks of the power user define the semantics of domain specific abstractions in technical terms. The last three tasks describe the translation of an OSL policy into ECA rules. Based on this, policies are translated from the PIM to ISM layer in the meta-model when the end user specifies them using templates. If the end user specifies policies without predefined templates, the translation is semi-automatic. The complete process cannot be fully automated in this case because of the following reasons:

1. Definition of enforcement mechanisms needs human intervention for at least every class of specification-level policy, as one specification-level policy can be enforced in many different ways.

2. Complex obligations may need to be decomposed into subconditions each of which is then mapped to the *condition* part of a separate ECA rule. Decomposition may be required to get rid of nested temporal formulas, whose translation cannot be automatically achieved. A trivial (and fully automatic) solution of this problem

is to turn each subformula of the specification-level policy into one ECA rule.

We have implemented two editors, to be used by two roles of users (the end user and the power user), for specification and translation of policies according to the meta-model described in Section 3. In this section, we describe these tools through examples from the domain of WBSN applications. However, *the tools are generic and can be used for any domain-specific application* (in the next section we also show some examples for Android-based smart phone applications) as all domain data is stored separately in databases and XML files and the domain can be changed by modifying the contents of them.

At the PIM level, end users are not supposed to be adept in any technical policy specification language. Yet, they should be able to specify usage control policies. We address this problem by means of our *end user tool* which enables the user to specify PIM policies by editing templates in a drag and drop interface. *Templates* consist of constraints that abstract the syntax of the different OSL operators. Additionally, they contain placeholders for string representations of data and actions. Thus in a template, a policy is made up of data, action and constraint blocks. Constraints are represented by rounded rectangles, actions by rectangles and data by double ellipses. The solid arrow is from the operator to the operand and the dotted arrow is from action to its object parameter value. The specific actions and data are specified by the end user by dragging and dropping these values from the palette. Additional parameter values for actions (sender, receiver, location, purpose, currency etc.) are specified by choosing the option from the right-click context menu. To begin with, we have specified five templates for describing usage control policies, as most of the policies relevant for end users of WBSN applications can be specified through them. Creating new templates is not difficult and can be done later also.

The five templates can specify policies of the form "**never do X**;" "**no X until Y**;" "**X always implies Y**;" "**do X within N duration**;" "**X can be repeated maximum N times**." Figure 5 shows an example template for a policy of the form "**never do X**" on the left and an example policy specified using that template on its right.

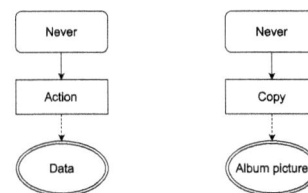

Figure 5: Pictures in albums must not be copied

It appears more convenient for an end user to state "album picture must not be copied" using the template than to formally express it in OSL as the obligational formula:

$$always(\underline{not}(E_{fst}(Copy, \{(object, albumpicture)\}))).$$

Thus, templates enable less sophisticated end users to specify usage control policies without the knowledge of any policy specification language. We strengthen this argument by help of further examples of templates and corresponding policies.

Figure 6 shows the graphical representation of the policy mentioned earlier in Section 4, "picture must not be copied without notification" which is of the form "**no X until Y**" and can be formally expressed in OSL as the obligation

$$until(\underline{not}(E_{fst}(Copy, \{(object, Albumpicture)\})),$$
$$E_{fst}(Send, \{(object, Notification)\}))$$

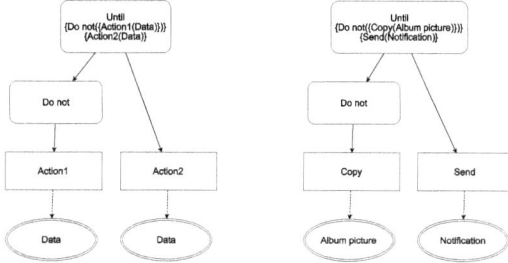

Figure 6: No copy without notification

Figure 7 shows the graphical representation of the obligation

$$always(\underline{implies}(E_{fst}(Delete, \{(object, Profile)\}),$$
$$E_{fst}(Delete, \{(object, \{Album, Blogpost, Song, Video\})\}))))$$

which is of the form "**X always implies Y**" and in general defines the meaning of action on one data in terms of same or other action(s) on (other) data; the specific example states that deleting a profile also means deleting all albums, blogposts, songs and videos posted in the profile.

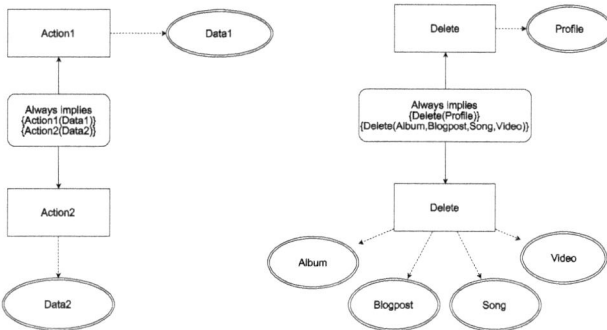

Figure 7: Deleting profile means deleting all other data

The simplification of specifying OSL policies is obvious in the above examples. If the end user is knowledgable about OSL, he can also write these policies using our editor. In that case, further definition of the enforcement mechanisms is also taken care of by the end user.

The *power user tool* is used to define the abstract (PIM) and concrete (PSM & ISM) domain models and the respective mappings. It provides two sets of functionalities: one for the definition of different domain models and the other for mapping the elements across models. Domain-specific models for PIM, PSM and ISM layers can be defined, modified and deleted using this tool and their components are mapped to each other by links; for instance, by connecting

"picture" from the PIM layer to "file, DOM element, window content" from the PSM layer. The abstract model provides domain-specific vocabulary for specifying PIM policies and the mappings achieve the automatic translation of abstract policy components to their concrete counterparts in the specified policies. Syntactical transformation from OSL to ECA rules is specified by the power user using predefined templates .

In the next section we present some examples of implementation-level policies derived from specification-level policies. These policies have been defined and shown to be enforced in [4, 6, 9] and other related work where they are assumed to exist and have not been derived from user requirements. We show their derivation here as a proof of concept of our work.

6. DERIVATION OF POLICIES BY EXAMPLES

We start with the example policy from the use case in Section 1, "picture must not be copied" whose graphical specification is shown in Figure 5. Figure 2 shows the semantics of data and action of this policy, where the concrete model of the WBSN domain includes three layers of abstraction in client machines: the web browser, the windowing system and the operating system. Implementation-level policies for the three levels of abstraction are shown below.

```
<!-- For Firefox Web Browser -->
<controlMechanism>
 <id>Browser_CopyPaste</id>
 <triggerEvent>
  <id>copy</id>
   <parameter name="obj" value="img_profile" type="dataUsage"/>
   <parameter name="isTry" value="true"/>
 </triggerEvent>
 <condition> <true /> </condition>
 <actions> <inhibit/> </actions>
</controlMechanism>

<!-- For X11 Windowing System -->
<controlMechanism>
 <id>X11_Screenshot</id>
 <triggerEvent>
  <id>GetImage</id>
   <parameter name="obj" value="0x1a00005" type="dataUsage"/>
   <parameter name="isTry" value="true"/>
 </triggerEvent>
 <condition> <true /> </condition>
 <actions>
  <allow>
    <modify>
     <parameter name="planeMask" value="0x0" />
    </modify>
  </allow>
 </actions>
</controlMechanism>

<!-- For Windows Operating System -->
<controlMechanism>
 <id>OS_Restrict_File_Usage</id>
 <triggerEvent>
  <id>open</id>
   <parameter name="obj" value="cacheFile" type="dataUsage"/>
   <parameter name="isTry" value="true"/>
 </triggerEvent>
 <condition>
  <XPathEval>
   /triggerEvent/parameter[@name='PNAME']/@value!='c:\\Firefox\\firefox.exe
   '
  </XPathEval>
 </condition>
 <actions> <inhibit/> </actions>
</controlMechanism>
```

The policy is enforced at the web browser and the operating system levels by inhibition (we make an exception to our simple inhibition rule at the OS level by allowing the web browser (specifically, Mozilla Firefox) to open the picture so that the end user can (only) view the picture in a web browser) and at the windowing system level by modification. Here, the choice of the enforcement strategy is implementation-driven. For the X11 windowing system, inhibiting screenshots altogether (sending an empty response) results in an error message from the server. So it is better to enforce the policy as modifying the trigger event instead of inhibiting it: we modify the request for screenshot on a drawable by changing the *planeMask* value from 0xffff (meaning every plane is included) to 0x0 (no plane included) resulting in a black rectangle at the destination.

We have already discussed the problem and the solution of expressing high-level actions like copy and delete in terms of sequences of low level events (Section 4). So in the next example, we show a high-level policy translated into a state-based low level policy. In the use case from the WBSN, the end user wants that his friends should be able to play his songs, make local copies, but they should not be able to distribute it further. The abstract policy is, "song must not be distributed." At the specification level, this requirement is expressed using the policy template of Figure 5 with action as distribute and data as song. Figure 8 shows an instantiation of the domain meta-model for the corresponding concrete representations at the OS-level.

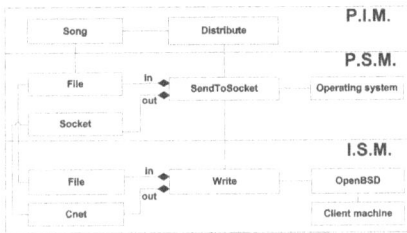

Figure 8: Semantics of "distribute song"

At the OS level, distributing data over the network is interpreted by the power user as writing data in a specific container to the socket descriptor. "song.mp3" and "Net" are names for containers at runtime. In particular, "Net" is a reserved name for the container "Cnet" that stands for "the network". The requirement can be formally expressed in OSL as

isNotIn(*song.mp3, Net*)

We choose to enforce the policy by inhibition. Hence the mechanism is triggered whenever a write system call sends the song (the data) stored in "song.mp3" over the network, i.e. to a socket descriptor.

```
<controlMechanism>
 <id>OS_Disclosure_example</id>
 <triggerEvent>
  <id>write</id>
   <parameter name="isTry" value="true"/>
 </triggerEvent>
 <condition>
  <not>
   <isNotIn data="song.mp3">
    <containers>
     <container>Net</container>
    </containers>
   </isNotIn>
  </not>
 </condition>
 <actions> <inhibit/> </actions>
</controlMechanism>
```

Our third example is from the domain of smart phone applications for Android phones: pictures taken at certain locations must be blurred when viewed outside the premises. This requires that the concrete representations of pictures taken from the camera must be identified when saved in the

system, these representations must be tainted when the picture is taken at the specified location and, when the location of viewing the pictures is not the same, the representations must be temporarily blurred before being displayed. Therefore location is a key parameter of action in this case. At the PIM layer, tainting is captured by "flagging" a picture. Figure 9 shows the specification of two policies in the end user tool.

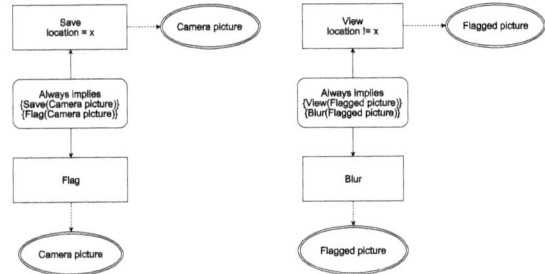

Figure 9: Blur picture when viewed outside the original location

Both the policies are specified using the template shown in Figure 7. The first policy (on left) stipulates that when a camera picture taken at location x is saved, it should be flagged:

$$always(implies(E_{fst}(Save, \{(object, Camerapicture), (location, x)\}),$$
$$E_{fst}(Flag, \{(object, Camerapicture)\})))$$

The second policy stipulates that when there is an attempt to view the flagged picture 'outside' a specific location ('negateLocation' parameter value set to true), the picture must be blurred:

$$always(implies(T_{fst}(View, \{(location, x), (negateLocation, true),$$
$$(object, Flaggedpicture)\}), E_{fst}(Blur, \{(object, Flaggedpicture)\})))$$

with T_{fst} denoting an 'intended' action. Figures 10 and 11 show the semantics of data and action in the two policies using domain models. At the implementation layer, pictures taken from the camera are identified by a special taint mark (0x00080 in our case) and are tainted with another taint mark (0x10000) when they are saved as files at the OS level.

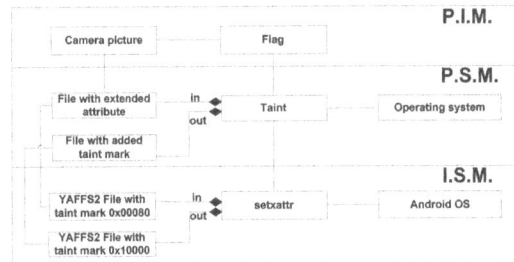

Figure 10: Semantics of "flag camera picture"

Viewing a flagged picture means reading the file with taint marking 0x10000 at the OS level.

We enforce both policies by modification. At runtime, when a picture taken by camera (identified with the taint mark 0x00080=128) at the location x (location=49.445626, 7.760339; checked in the trigger event part)is written to the

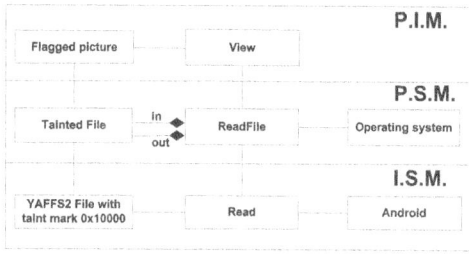

Figure 11: Semantics of "view flagged picture"

file system, the trigger is modified with parameter value 0x10000 (=65536). When there is an attempt to read the file with taint marking 65536 and the location is *not equal to* x (checked by the last parameter of location in trigger event part; when this flag is set to true, the evaluation is negated), the event is blocked.

```
<!-- Adds taint 0x10000 for pictures taken at given location -->
<controlMechanism>
 <id>TaintPictures</id>
 <triggerEvent>
  <id>OSFileSystem.write</id>
  <parameter name="taint" value="128" />
  <parameter name="location" value="49.445626;7.760339;50;true;false"/>
 </triggerEvent>
 <condition> <true /> </condition>
 <actions>
  <allow>
   <modify>
    <parameter name="data" value="taint$65536" />
   </modify>
  </allow>
 </actions>
</controlMechanism>

<!-- When not at the given location, files with taint marking 0x10000 =
     65536 are blurred upon access-->
<controlMechanism id="BlurPictures">
 <triggerEvent id="OSFileSystem.read" />
  <parameter name="taint" value="65536" />
  <parameter name="location" value="49.445626;7.760339;50;true;true" />
 </trigger>
 <condition> <true /> </condition>
 <actions>
  <allow>
   <modify>
    <parameter name="data" value="blur$5" />
   </modify>
  </allow>
 </actions>
</controlMechanism>
```

7. CONCLUSIONS AND FUTURE WORK

The problem we address in this paper is the systematic derivation of usage control policies from specification-level to implementation-level taking into account the technical semantics of high level actions like copy and delete for all the different representations of data. Specification-level policies are specified using abstract terminology and hence must be translated into more technical policies that can be enforced at different layers of abstraction in the system. In this direction, our contribution is twofold: on one hand we present a framework that allows us to define the semantics of actions in terms of elements of application-specific domain models and translates the policies from their specification level syntax to event-condition-action (ECA) format; and on the other hand, we provide methodological guidance for the specification and translation of policies so that the complete process, which is cumbersome when manually done, can be automated.

For the precise semantics of actions in usage control policies, we present a domain meta-model that has three layers

which correspond to abstract data and actions (PIM layer) and their various representations (PSM layer) and implementations of these representations in the real world (ISM layer) (§3). The idea is to map abstract entities from the specification-level policies to their technical counterparts to define the semantics of actions on data in terms of transformers that write/read to/from the containers in which data is stored. After this, enforcement strategies are decided upon and the specification-level policy, which is expressed in OSL in our framework, is transformed into sets of ECA rules (§4). As a result of translation, a set of implementation level policies is generated for one specification level policy: usually, one implementation-level policy per layer of abstraction. By means of several examples, we have shown the applicability of our methodology (§6).

To automate the process, we have two roles: an end user and a more sophisticated power user. We have implemented two editors to be used by them. In one editor, the power user defines the three domain models and maps the components from these models to each other (§5). The end user then uses the string representations of the classes of the abstract domain model to specify policies in the second editor. The end user specifies policies in an interactive drag and drop user interface using templates, which abstract standard OSL operators and thus make it possible for an end user to describe requirements without knowing any technical policy specification language.

This is however a first step towards the complete solution of deriving implementation-level policies from specification-level policies that configure usage control mechanisms at different levels of abstraction. There is a deliberately introduced limitation of our work - we have not considered the dynamic structure of systems while translating policies. We have assumed that the system architecture is static and has been specified in the very beginning. This means that the sets of all possible containers and the transformers and their implementations are known beforehand. In the first step of our work this assumption is reasonable as it helps us in reducing the complexity of the problem. However, in the real world, systems change over time. Services and applications are added/ removed and physical hosts change location. In that case, many of the mappings between the components of different models might become invalid and new mappings need to be specified. To address this issue, we need a policy management system where manager components take care of registering and de-registering details to handle the dynamic case. This is work in progress and so we do not discuss details of it here.

Another limitation on the solution is posed by the evolution of specification-level policies in a distributed setup where receivers of data transform themselves into senders of data over time, and so the policies that they attach with data might evolve with this change [45]. In our present solution, we have not considered this aspect of the problem.

Finally, a fundamental concern is about the usability of policy-specification tools in general: though we have introduced templates to abstract both technical semantics and syntax of usage control policies, these requirements tend to be complex and end users might not be capable of understanding and specifying them at all. An approach in that case would be to let data protection officers or any other trusted authority specify these policies for particular domains.

8. REFERENCES

[1] M. Harvan and A. Pretschner. State-based Usage Control Enforcement with Data Flow Tracking using System Call Interposition. In *Proc. 3rd Intl. Conf. on Network and System Security*, pages 373–380, 2009.

[2] A. Pretschner, M. Buechler, M. Harvan, C. Schaefer, and T. Walter. Usage control enforcement with data flow tracking for x11. In *Proc. 5th Intl. Workshop on Security and Trust Management*, pages 124–137, 2009.

[3] L. Desmet, W. Joosen, F. Massacci, K. Naliuka, P. Philippaerts, F. Piessens, and D. Vanoverberghe. The S3MS.NET Run Time Monitor: Tool Demonstration. *ENTCS*, 253(5):153–159, 2009.

[4] P. Kumari, A. Pretschner, J. Peschla, and J. Kuhn. Distributed data usage control for web applications: a social network implementation. In *Proc. 1st ACM Conf. on Data and application security and privacy*, pages 85–96, 2011.

[5] D. Povey. Optimistic security: a new access control paradigm. In *Proc. 1999 workshop on New security paradigms*, NSPW '99, pages 40–45. ACM, 2000.

[6] A. Pretschner, E. Lovat, and M. Buechler. Representation-independent data usage control. In *Proc. 6th Intl. Workshop on Data Privacy Management*, 2011.

[7] M. Hilty, A. Pretschner, D. Basin, C. Schaefer, and T. Walter. A policy language for distributed usage control. In *Proc. ESORICS*, pages 531–546, 2008.

[8] A. Pretschner, M. Hilty, D. Basin, C. Schaefer, and T. Walter. Mechanisms for Usage Control. In *Proc. ACM Symp. on Information, Computer & Communication Security*, pages 240–245, 2008.

[9] E. Lovat and A. Pretschner. Data-centric multi-layer usage control enforcement: A social network example. In *Proc. ACM Symp. on Access Control Models and Technologies*, 2011.

[10] J. Beatty and J. Hulgan. Experiences with a requirements object model. Lecture Notes in Comput. Sci., pages 104–117. Springer Berlin / Heidelberg, 2009.

[11] M.E.C. Hull, K. Jackson, and J. Dick. *Requirements Engineering, 2nd Ed.* Springer, 2005.

[12] G. Kotonya and I. Sommerville. *Requirements engineering: processes and techniques.* Worldwide series in computer science. 1998.

[13] I. Bray. *An Introduction to Requirements Engineering.* Addison Wesley, aug 2002.

[14] M. Jackson. *Software requirements & specifications: a lexicon of practice, principles and prejudices.* ACM Press/Addison-Wesley, New York, USA, 1995.

[15] C.A. Gunter, E.L. Gunter, M. Jackson, and P. Zave. A reference model for requirements and specifications - extended abstract. In *Proc. 4th Intl. Conf. on Requirements Engineering, 2000*, 2000.

[16] K.L. Heninger. Specifying software requirements for complex systems: New techniques and their application. *IEEE Trans. on Software Engg.*, SE-6(1):2 – 13, jan. 1980.

[17] B.H.C. Cheng and J.M. Atlee. Research directions in requirements engineering. *Future of Software Engineering*, pages 285–303, 2007.

[18] J. McDermott and C. Fox. Using abuse case models for security requirements analysis. ACSAC '99, 1999.

[19] Bruce Schneier. Attack trees, 1999.

[20] G. Sindre and A.L. Opdahl. Eliciting security requirements by misuse cases. In *Proc. 37th Intl Conf. on Technology of Object-Oriented Languages and Systems*, pages 120 –131, 2000.

[21] W. E. Vesely, F. F. Goldberg, N. H. Roberts, and D. F. Haasl. *Fault Tree Handbook.* U.S. Nuclear Regulatory Commission, 1981.

[22] G. Elahi. Security requirements engineering: State of the art and practice and challenges, 2008.

[23] J. Wilander and J. Gustavsson. Security requirements - a field study of current practice. In *E-Proc. Symposium on Requirements Engineering for Information Security*, 2005.

[24] Q. He and A.I. Antón. Requirements-based access control analysis and policy specification. *Information & Software Technology*, 51:993–1009, June 2009.

[25] G. Neumann and M. Strembeck. A scenario-driven role engineering process for functional rbac roles. In *Proc. 7th ACM symp. on Access control models and technologies*, SACMAT '02, pages 33–42, 2002.

[26] R. Iannella (ed.). Open Digital Rights Language v1.1, 2008. http://odrl.net/1.1/ODRL-11.pdf.

[27] Multimedia framework (MPEG-21) – Part 5: Rights Expression Language, 2004. ISO/IEC standard 21000-5:2004.

[28] N. Damianou, N. Dulay, E. Lupu, and M. Sloman. The Ponder Policy Specification Language. In *Proc. Workshop on Policies for Distributed Systems and Networks*, pages 18–39, 1995.

[29] G. Yee and L. Korba. Semiautomatic derivation and use of personal privacy policies in e-business. *IJEBR*, 1(1):54–69, 2005.

[30] J. Young. Commitment analysis to operationalize software requirements from privacy policies. *Requirements Engineering*, 16:33–46, 2011.

[31] L. Su, D. Chadwick, A. Basden, and J. Cunningham. Automated decomposition of access control policies. In *Proc. 6th IEEE Intl. Workshop on Policies for Distributed Systems and Networks*, pages 6–8, 2005.

[32] A.K. Bandara, E.C. Lupu, J. Moffett, and A. Russo. A goal-based approach to policy refinement. In *Proc. 5th IEEE Workshop on Policies for Distributed Systems and Networks*, pages 229–239, 2004.

[33] A. Guerrero, V.A. Villagrá, J.E. López de Vergara, A. Sánchez-Macián, and J. Berrocal. Ontology-based policy refinement using swrl rules for management information definitions in owl. In *DSOM*, pages 227–232, 2006.

[34] Y.B. Udupi, A. Sahai, and S. Singhal. A classification-based approach to policy refinement. In *Proc. 10th IFIP/IEEE Intl Symp. on Integrated Network Management*, 2007.

[35] T. Lodderstedt, D. Basin, and J. Doser. Secureuml: A uml-based modeling language for model-driven security. In *UML*, pages 426–441, 2002.

[36] B. Aziz, A.E. Arenas, and M. Wilson. Model-based refinement of security policies in collaborative virtual organisations. ESSoS, pages 1–14, 2011.

[37] A. Pretschner, M. Hilty, and D. Basin. Distributed usage control. *Commun. ACM*, 49(9):39–44, 2006.

[38] J. Park and R. Sandhu. The UCON ABC usage control model. *ACM Trans. on Information and System Security*, 7(1):128–174, 2004.

[39] X. Zhang, J. Park, F. Parisi-Presicce, and R. Sandhu. A logical specification for usage control. In *Proc. SACMAT*, pages 1–10, 2004.

[40] C. O'Rourke, N. Fishman, and W. Selkow. *Enterprise architecture using the Zachman Framework*. Course Technology, 2003.

[41] The Open Group. TOGAF Version 9. The Open Group Architecture Framework. 2009.

[42] J. A. Zachman. A framework for information systems architecture. *IBM Syst. J.*, 26:276–292, September 1987.

[43] O. Kupferman and M.Y. Vardi. Model checking of safety properties. *Formal Methods in System Design*, 19(3):291–314, 2001.

[44] P. Kumari. Requirements analysis for privacy in social networks. In *Proc. 8th Intl. Workshop for Technical, Economic and Legal Aspects of Business Models for Virtual Goods*, 2010.

[45] A. Pretschner, F. Schütz, C. Schaefer, and T. Walter. Policy evolution in distributed usage control. *Electr. Notes Theor. Comput. Sci.*, 244:109–123, 2009.

APPENDIX

A. FUTURE TO PAST TRANSLATION

As mentioned in the start of Section 3, in order to be evaluated in the condition part of an ECA rule, every obligation expressed in future time OSL formula must be translated to its past form. Specification-level usage control obligations are described in language Φ^+ (+ for future). It is a temporal logic with explicit operators for cardinality and permissions. We distinguish between purely propositional (Ψ) and temporal and cardinality operators (Φ^+) [6]. The intuitive semantics of these opeartors are given in Section 4.

$\Psi ::= \underline{true} \mid \underline{false} \mid E(Event) \mid T(Event) \mid \underline{not}(\Psi) \mid \underline{and}(\Psi, \Psi) \mid \underline{or}(\Psi, \Psi) \mid \underline{implies}(\Psi, \Psi)$

$\Phi^+ ::= \Psi \mid \underline{not}(\Phi^+) \mid \underline{and}(\Phi^+, \Phi^+) \mid \underline{or}(\Phi^+, \Phi^+) \mid \underline{implies}(\Phi^+, \Phi^+) \mid \underline{until}(\Phi^+, \Phi^+) \mid \underline{after}(\mathbb{N}, \Phi^+) \mid \underline{within}(\mathbb{N}, \Phi^+) \mid \underline{during}(\mathbb{N}, \Phi^+) \mid \underline{always}(\Phi^+) \mid \underline{repmax}(\mathbb{N}, \Psi) \mid \underline{replim}(\mathbb{N}, \mathbb{N}, \mathbb{N}, \Psi) \mid \underline{repuntil}(\mathbb{N}, \Psi, \Phi^+)$

Mechanisms, or ECA rules, are specified in a past temporal logic Φ^-.

$\Phi^- ::= \Psi \mid \underline{not}^-(\Phi^-) \mid \underline{and}^-(\Phi^-, \Phi^-) \mid \underline{or}^-(\Phi^-, \Phi^-) \mid \underline{implies}^-(\Phi^-, \Phi^-) \mid \underline{since}^-(\Phi^-, \Phi^-) \mid \underline{before}^-(\mathbb{N}, \Phi^-) \mid \underline{within}^-(\mathbb{N}, \Phi^-) \mid \underline{during}^-(\mathbb{N}, \Phi^-) \mid \underline{always}^-(\Phi^-) \mid \underline{repmax}^-(\mathbb{N}, \Psi) \mid \underline{replim}^-(\mathbb{N}, \mathbb{N}, \mathbb{N}, \Psi) \mid \underline{repsince}^-(\mathbb{N}, \Psi, \Phi^-)$

Informal semantics of these operators are as follows: $since^-(a, b)$ is true if a has been true ever since b happened; $before^-(n, a)$ is true if a was true n time steps ago; $within^-$, $during^-$ and $always^-$ are intuitive. The cardinal operator $repmax^-(n, a)$ specifies that a has been true at most n times in the past; $replim^-(l, m, n, a)$ specifies a lower (l) and an upper limit (m) upon repetitions of a in the last n timesteps; and $repsince^-(n, a, b)$ specifies that a has been true at most

n times since b became true. For formal semantics of both future and past operators, see [6].

For translating specification-level obligations into conditions of implementation-level policies, we assume that there is a special proposition $START$ that denotes the moment in time when the future-time formula has to hold, that is, when the policy is deployed. This can be an activation event, the universally valid proposition *true*, or any other propositional formula described in OSL.[1] The translation function τ from specification-level obligational formulas to the conditions of implementation-level policies is inductively defined as follows:

1. Propositions $\phi \in \Psi$ remain unchanged: $\tau(\phi)$ is transformed into ϕ.

2. $\tau(\phi \wedge \psi)$ is transformed into $\tau(\phi) \wedge \tau(\psi)$; $\tau(\neg\phi)$ is transformed into $\neg\tau(\phi)$; all other propositional operators can be expressed by virtue of conjunction and negation.

3. $\tau(\underline{always}(\phi))$ for $\phi \in \Psi$ is transformed into the condition $before^-(1, \tau(\phi) \underline{since}^- START) \wedge \neg\tau(\phi)$; the rule is applicable if ϕ has been true at every time-step since START except in the current time step.

4. $\tau(\phi \underline{until} \psi)$ for $\phi, \psi \in \Psi$ is transformed into the condition $before^-(1, \tau(\phi \wedge \neg\psi) \underline{since}^- START) \wedge \tau(\neg\phi \wedge \neg\psi)$; the rule is applicable if, ϕ has been true (and ψ false) at every time step since START but in the current time step, both ϕ and ψ are false.

5. $\tau(\underline{within}(n, \phi))$ for $\phi \in \Psi$ is transformed into the condition $before^-(n, START) \wedge during^-(n, \tau(\neg\phi))$; the rule is applicable if START was true n time steps ago and in the past n time steps, ϕ has been false at every time step.

6. $\tau(\underline{during}^-(n, \phi))$ for $\phi \in \Psi$ is transformed into the condition $before^-(n, START) \wedge \neg during^-(n, \tau(\phi))$; the rule is applicable if START was true n time steps ago and in the past n time steps, ϕ has been false at least once.

7. $\tau(\underline{after}(n, \phi))$ for $\phi \in \Psi$ is transformed into the condition $before^-(n, START) \wedge \neg\tau(\phi)$; the rule is applicable if START was true n time steps ago and in the current time step, ϕ is false.

8. $\tau(\underline{repuntil}(n, \psi, \phi))$ for $\phi \in \Psi$ is transformed into the condition $(\neg\tau(\phi) \underline{since}^- START) \wedge \neg repsince^-(n-1, \psi, START) \wedge \psi$; the rule is applicable if ϕ has not been true since $START$ (via $\neg\tau(\phi)\underline{since}^- START$); if furthermore, there have been at least n occurrences of the propositional formula ψ (via $\neg repsince^-(n-1, \psi, START)$); and if there is another occurrence of the propositional formula ψ in the current step (where usually one distinguished proposition will correspond to the triggering event; this translates into a respective desired event in the transformation of ψ). Note that the semantics of $\underline{since}^-$ includes the current time step.

9. $\tau(\underline{repmax}(n, \psi))$ is transformed via the equivalence with the respective *repuntil* operator: $repmax(n, \psi) = \underline{repuntil}(n, \psi, \underline{false})$

---

[1] The rule is assumed to be applicable at the *first* violation of the obligational formula; further violations are not considered.

Discovering Access-Control Misconfigurations: New Approaches and Evaluation Methodologies

Lujo Bauer   Yuan Liang
Carnegie Mellon University
{lbauer,yliang}@cmu.edu

Michael K. Reiter   Chad Spensky
UNC Chapel Hill
{reiter,cspensky}@cs.unc.edu

ABSTRACT

Accesses that are not permitted by implemented policy but that share similarities with accesses that have been allowed, may be indicative of access-control policy misconfigurations. Identifying such misconfigurations allows administrators to resolve them before they interfere with the use of the system. We improve upon prior work in identifying such misconfigurations in two main ways. First, we develop a new methodology for evaluating misconfiguration prediction algorithms and applying them to real systems. We show that previous evaluations can substantially overestimate the benefits of using such algorithms in practice, owing to their tendency to reward predictions that can be deduced to be redundant. We also show, however, that these and other deductions can be harnessed to substantially recover the benefits of prediction. Second, we propose an approach that significantly simplifies the use of misconfiguration prediction algorithms. We remove the need to hand-tune (and empirically determine the effects of) various parameters, and instead replace them with a single, intuitive tuning parameter. We show empirically that this approach is generally competitive in terms of benefit and accuracy with algorithms that require hand-tuned parameters.

Categories and Subject Descriptors

D.4.6 [**Security and Protection**]: Access controls; K.6.5 [**Security and Protection**]: Authentication; H.2.0 [**Information Systems**]: Security, integrity, and protection

General Terms

Security, Performance, Human Factors

Keywords

Access control, machine learning, misconfiguration

1. INTRODUCTION

Access-control policy often exhibits patterns across users and the resources they access, partly due to the use of groups and roles

(perhaps only implicitly) in policy creation. These patterns are evidenced in the accesses allowed in the system. If a user is permitted access to most of the same resources that other users access, then the few exceptions might represent *misconfigurations*, i.e., potential accesses that are consistent with *intended* policy but that are denied by the policy actually *implemented* in the system. Reactive access control, in which failed access attempts cause an administrator to be prompted to modify policy [6, 18], can help restore access after such failures. However, in many contexts (e.g., health information systems), the latency associated with such interventions may be unacceptable. Even when the cost of erroneously denying or delaying a single access is not as high, repeatedly denying access can severely inhibit the usability of an access-control system, and thus encourage users to circumvent it. As such, eliminating misconfigurations that erroneously deny access is essential in many contexts. Unfortunately, with few exceptions (e.g., [8, 7]), these kinds of misconfigurations have not been widely studied.

In this paper, we focus on identifying these access-control policy misconfigurations before they interfere with legitimate accesses. We improve upon previous work in several ways. We revisit the methodology for evaluating misconfiguration prediction algorithms and applying them to real systems. Prior work in which predictions were made on the basis of observed accesses evaluated these predictions by comparing them to intended policy. Any prediction that matched intended policy contributed to the measured *benefit*—the fraction of intended policy that was uncovered through predicted misconfigurations—and *accuracy*—the fraction of predicted misconfigurations that were consistent with intended policy. This included predictions that were consistent with already implemented policy and so were not indicative of misconfigurations at all.

We develop a richer framework that considers, in addition to exercised policy, the implemented policy that is deducible from observed accesses and correct predictions. This makes it possible to eliminate predictions that are already implemented from contributing to benefit and accuracy. Our framework allows us to more realistically evaluate misconfiguration prediction algorithms, and we show empirically that the actual benefits of misconfiguration prediction as cast in previous work are substantially overestimated. Fortunately, our framework makes it possible to improve misconfiguration prediction by making deducible policy available to the prediction engine. Our evaluation shows that through this we can recover much of the benefit and accuracy that previously appeared to be achievable.

We also recast the previous approaches to prediction so that they can be used effectively in different settings. Specifically, we remove the need for an administrator to tune multiple parameters until she achieves a desired balance between accuracy and benefit in a new setting. Our method enables an administrator to chose a desired balance β, and ensures that $\frac{Benefit}{Accuracy} \approx \beta$ with no additional tuning, while maximizing benefit and accuracy subject to this constraint. The difficulties of achieving this with some previous approaches, e.g., the approach of Bauer et al. [7], derive from their use of *association rule mining* [2], by which the access logs are analyzed to extract *association rules* of the form $x \Rightarrow y$, where x and y denote sets of resources. Informally, such a rule means that a user with access to x typically has access to y, as well, and so would be used to predict that y should be accessible to users who can access x. This approach is parameterized by the required *support* for (or fraction of all users with access to) x and y, and the required *confidence* of the rule (the fraction of users with access to x who also can access y). Rules are used as predictors of misconfigurations only when their confidence and support exceed these thresholds. While increasing the required confidence or support generally increases accuracy and decreases benefit, how to incrementally adapt these two parameters to ensure $\frac{Benefit}{Accuracy} \approx \beta$, while maximizing benefit and accuracy, was unresolved.

To address this problem, we adopt an approach that combines confidence and support into a single parameter called *predictive accuracy* and that uses a Bayesian framework to determine the contributions of support and confidence to the expected accuracy of a rule [17]. Collapsing support and confidence into a single parameter allows us to rank rules according to predictive accuracy and then to issue predictions in this order. This provides a way to ensure $\frac{Benefit}{Accuracy} \approx \beta$ while providing good benefit and accuracy. We have scaled this approach to experiments involving tens of thousands of users or resources, making it potentially applicable, for example, for access control to physical or virtual resources in hospitals or to personal data in a social network.

To summarize, the contributions of our paper are: (1) A new framework for evaluating misconfiguration prediction algorithms and applying them to real systems, which reveals that previous evaluations overestimated the benefit of misconfiguration prediction but also makes it possible to largely recover the accuracy and benefit of prediction. (2) A new approach to configuring misconfiguration prediction algorithms that obviates the need for laborious hand-tuning of parameters, thus making it more feasible to apply misconfiguration prediction in different settings.

2. RELATED WORK

Several works use data-mining or machine-learning techniques to analyze access-control policies. Firewalls were an early target for automated policy analysis, and a number of tools were developed for the empirical analysis of firewall policies (e.g., [5, 14, 20, 3, 21, 1]). These tools typically enable an administrator to verify that a set of policies is consistent, or that a policy obeys desired properties. Another approach incorporates similar techniques in policy-specification tools, which use the output of the analysis directly to help an administrator specify policy that meets desired goals [10]. More closely related are works that use rule mining or Bayesian inference to analyze router policies and automatically find misconfigurations (e.g., [13, 9, 12]). Similarly to firewall analysis, these approaches take as input configuration files and detect discrepancies between configurations, e.g., user accounts without passwords, or router interfaces using private IP addresses. These works differ from ours in a number of ways, perhaps most notably in that they focus on finding inconsistencies in static policies. In contrast, we analyze policy as it is revealed in accesses over time, which gives rise to our analysis of policy in an incremental fashion, the basis for several of our innovations.

Our work is also similar to that of Das et al., who analyze access-control policy for file servers to detect inconsistencies between the permissions given to users who appear to be peers [8]. Das et al.'s

	|A							
	a	b	c	d	e	f	g	h
1	x	x	x	x	x	x	x	x
2	x	x	x		x	x		
3					x	x	x	x
4							x	
5					x	x		x
6	x	x	x	x				
7	x	x	x					
8				x				

Figure 1: Relation R for a sample database

system takes as input both low-level file-system policy (which user can access which file) and metadata, such as group membership information separate from the low-level policy, and identifies misconfigurations that either deny legitimate accesses or allow erroneous ones. In contrast, we focus on misconfigurations that prevent legitimate accesses, and our algorithm does not require access to policy or metadata sets other than what can be observed from a sequence of accesses. Like Bauer et al.'s approach [7], the performance of Das et al.'s system depends on hand-tuning certain parameters; a main focus of our work is to render such tuning unnecessary.

Our approach to detecting misconfigurations has some similarity to role mining (e.g., [19, 11, 15, 16]), which seeks to distill from a low-level policy a collection of roles that can represent the same policy more abstractly. Since the goal of role mining is to find a better representation of policy that exists, role mining algorithms take as input a whole policy, rather than processing a possibly partial policy incrementally, as we do. Also, the specific goal in role mining is to find commonalities between users that may be indicative of shared role membership, while in our approach we focus on the inconsistencies between users to detect misconfigurations and cause the policy to be amended.

3. ASSOCIATION RULE MINING

Association rule mining is a method for finding relationships in databases that has been widely studied in the data-mining community. It involves using statistical measures to generate association rules of the form $x \Rightarrow y$, where x and y can be any sets of resources. We utilize these rules to identify misconfiguration in an access-control environment. The rules that we consider are of the form *"Permission to access resources a, b, and c $\Rightarrow$ Permission to access to resource d."* For every user with permission to access a, b, and c, this rule would result in a prediction that that user should have access to resource d. An administrator could then either reject or grant this access. We consider a prediction to be *helpful* if the administrator grants a user Alice access to d and *incorrect* if the administrator denies access.

3.1 Confidence and Support

Rule mining is typically performed on a "database" representing a binary relation $R \subseteq O \times A$ between *objects* O and *attributes* A. (In our case, O is a set of users, A is a set of resources that users access, and oRa means that user o accessed resource a.) The *support* of $x \subseteq A$, denoted $\mathsf{S}(x)$, is defined as $|\{o \in O : \forall a \in x, oRa\}|/|O|$, i.e., the fraction of objects related to all elements of x. The *confidence* of a rule $x \Rightarrow y$, denoted $\mathsf{C}(x \Rightarrow y)$, is defined as $\mathsf{S}(x \cup y)/\mathsf{S}(x)$, or, intuitively, the fraction of objects related to x that are also related to y.

Rule mining algorithms seek to identify "high quality" rules, and to do so, typically prune rules using two parameters, min_sup and min_conf. Generally speaking, a rule mining algorithm will identify rules $x \Rightarrow y$ such that $\mathsf{S}(x \cup y) \geq min\_sup$ and $\mathsf{C}(x \Rightarrow y) \geq min\_conf$, and so higher values of min_sup and min_conf yield higher quality rules. For example, consider the sample database shown in Figure 1, where $O = \{1, 2, 3, 4, 5, 6, 7, 8\}$ and $A = \{a, b, c, d, e, f, g, h\}$. Here, $\mathsf{S}(\{b, d\}) = 3/8$ and $\mathsf{C}(\{d\} \Rightarrow \{b\}) = 3/4$, and so the rule $\{d\} \Rightarrow \{b\}$ would be generated if $min\_conf \leq 3/4$ and $min\_sup \leq 3/8$.

3.2 Predictive Accuracy

Both min_sup and min_conf have an impact on the quality of the rules that are generated. Unfortunately, it is often unclear how the two parameters together should be tuned to achieve desired performance. To simplify this issue, in this paper we adopt a method for combining confidence and support into a single measure called *predictive accuracy* [17].

Informally, the predictive accuracy of a rule is the expected value for its true accuracy given the confidence c of the rule and the support s that its precondition enjoys. This value is denoted

$$
\begin{aligned}
&\mathsf{PA}(c, s) \\
&= \mathbb{E}(\mathsf{A}(x \Rightarrow y) \mid \mathsf{C}(x \Rightarrow y) = c, \mathsf{S}(x) = s) \\
&= \sum_a a \mathbb{P}\left(\mathsf{A}(x \Rightarrow y) = a \mid \mathsf{C}(x \Rightarrow y) = c, \mathsf{S}(x) = s\right) \quad (1)
\end{aligned}
$$

where $\mathsf{A}(x \Rightarrow y)$ is the true accuracy of the rule $x \Rightarrow y$ and the expectation is taken with respect to choice of association rule $x \Rightarrow y$ uniformly at random from among all possible rules. Using Bayes' rule, (1) can be rewritten

$$
\begin{aligned}
&\sum_a a \frac{\mathbb{P}\left(\mathsf{C}(x \Rightarrow y) = c \mid \mathsf{A}(x \Rightarrow y) = a, \mathsf{S}(x) = s\right)}{\mathbb{P}\left(\mathsf{C}(x \Rightarrow y) = c \mid \mathsf{S}(x) = s\right)} \cdot \mathbb{P}\left(\mathsf{A}(x \Rightarrow y) = a \mid \mathsf{S}(x) = s\right) \\
&= \sum_a a \frac{\mathbb{P}\left(\mathsf{C}(x \Rightarrow y) = c \mid \mathsf{A}(x \Rightarrow y) = a, \mathsf{S}(x) = s\right)}{\mathbb{P}\left(\mathsf{C}(x \Rightarrow y) = c \mid \mathsf{S}(x) = s\right)} \cdot \mathbb{P}\left(\mathsf{A}(x \Rightarrow y) = a\right) \quad (2)
\end{aligned}
$$

where

$$
\mathbb{P}\left(\mathsf{A}(x \Rightarrow y) = a \mid \mathsf{S}(x) = s\right) = \mathbb{P}\left(\mathsf{A}(x \Rightarrow y) = a\right)
$$

since the underlying accuracy of a rule $x \Rightarrow y$ is independent of the support $\mathsf{S}(x)$ that its precondition x enjoys. The factor

$$
\mathbb{P}\left(\mathsf{C}(x \Rightarrow y) = c \mid \mathsf{A}(x \Rightarrow y) = a, \mathsf{S}(x) = s\right)
$$

is the probability of cs "successes" (yielding confidence c) out of s "trials" with a per-trial "success probability" of a, and so this value can be computed using the binomial distribution. Similar reasoning enables computing

$$
\begin{aligned}
&\mathbb{P}\left(\mathsf{C}(x \Rightarrow y) = c \mid \mathsf{S}(x) = s\right) \\
&= \sum_a \mathbb{P}\left(\mathsf{C}(x \Rightarrow y) = c \mid \mathsf{A}(x \Rightarrow y) = a, \mathsf{S}(x) = s\right) \\
&\qquad \cdot \mathbb{P}\left(\mathsf{A}(x \Rightarrow y) = a\right)
\end{aligned}
$$

provided that we can compute $\mathbb{P}\left(\mathsf{A}(x \Rightarrow y) = a\right)$, which is also needed for (2). Of course, since the only approximation we have for $\mathsf{A}(x \Rightarrow y)$ is $\mathsf{C}(x \Rightarrow y)$, we take

$$
\mathbb{P}\left(\mathsf{A}(x \Rightarrow y) = a\right) \approx \mathbb{P}\left(\mathsf{C}(x \Rightarrow y) = a\right) \quad (3)
$$

This yields the the following calculation of (1):

$$
\mathsf{PA}(c, s) \approx \frac{\sum_a a B(cs; s, a) \mathbb{P}\left(\mathsf{C}(x \Rightarrow y) = a\right)}{\sum_a B(cs; s, a) \mathbb{P}\left(\mathsf{C}(x \Rightarrow y) = a\right)} \quad (4)
$$

where $B(k; N, p)$ is the probability of exactly k successes in N independent trials, each with success probability p. An implication

of this formulation is that to approximate the predictive accuracy of a rule, we need to compute $\mathbb{P}\left(\mathsf{C}(x \Rightarrow y) = a\right)$, i.e., the probability with which a rule, drawn uniformly at random from all possible rules, has confidence a. Scheffer [17] suggested estimating this probability through sampling.

While support and confidence are used to calculate the predictive accuracy, we need not choose predictions by placing conditions on confidence and support explicitly (e.g., the thresholds min_sup or min_conf). As we will discuss in §4, by ranking rules in decreasing order of their predictive accuracy, we are able to make predictions in a way that maintains $\frac{Benefit}{Accuracy} \approx \beta$.

4. MISCONFIGURATION PREDICTION FRAMEWORK

In this section we detail our framework for evaluating misconfiguration prediction (§4.1), which we argue is more encompassing than previous approaches. We then describe our method for guiding predictions to strike a desired balance between accuracy and benefit (§4.2).

4.1 Model and Definitions

Our method for finding misconfigurations uses records of actual system accesses. Let a *policy atom* be a user-resource pair (u, r). We denote the sequence of *unique* accesses in the system as $a_1, a_2, \ldots$ (i.e., $a_{\ell+1} \notin \{a_1, \ldots, a_\ell\}$) where each a_ℓ is a policy atom. Each access a_ℓ occurs at a distinct, integral logical time $\mathsf{time}(a_\ell) \in \mathbb{N}$. Logical times are totally ordered and are assigned so that $\mathsf{time}(a_\ell) < \mathsf{time}(a_{\ell+1})$. The *exercised policy* at time t is $Exercised_t = \{a_\ell : \mathsf{time}(a_\ell) \leq t\}$.

In addition to actual accesses, additional policy might be *deduced* on the basis of information conveyed in accesses (or, as we will see below, in the results of misconfiguration predictions). For example, an access (u, r) might be accompanied by a credential that demonstrates that u has access to other resources besides r. (For example, this credential might show that u is in a group that has access to other resources.) For this reason, we define $Deduced_t$ to be the set of policy atoms that can be deduced from $Exercised_t$. In particular, $Exercised_t \subseteq Deduced_t$. We also assume that $Deduced_t \subseteq Deduced_{t+1}$, i.e., over time, more policy can be revealed, but previously existing policy is not invalidated. (Relaxing this assumption, e.g., to support revocation of policy, is possible and would not significantly impact our evaluation framework.) We stress that some contents of $Deduced_t$ might not be visible to our prediction engine, due to lack of integration between the prediction engine and the access-control system; e.g., the credentials accompanying an access might not be made available to the prediction engine. Hence, we define a set $Visible_t \subseteq Deduced_t$ that is the set of policy atoms visible to the prediction engine at time t. We do not generally require that $Visible_t = Deduced_t$ (we will discuss this more below), though we do presume that $Visible_t \subseteq Visible_{t+1}$, i.e., that the system never "forgets" information that it used in previous predictions, and that $Exercised_t \subseteq Visible_t$.

The job of our system is to issue *predictions* of what might be a misconfiguration, based on the accesses seen in the system so far. Like an access, each prediction is a policy atom (u, r) and is made at a logical time $t \in \mathbb{N}$. However, predictions need not be issued at times distinct from each other, and generally they will not be. So, predictions $p_1, p_2, \ldots$ are only partially ordered by their logical times; specifically, $\mathsf{time}(p_\ell) \leq \mathsf{time}(p_{\ell+1})$. Let $Predictions_t = \{p_\ell : \mathsf{time}(p_\ell) \leq t\}$. A prediction p_ℓ is made by enumerating some number of association rules (with confidence less than one) in decreasing order of their predictive accuracies (see §4.2), computed

t	Exercised	Deducible	No Deduction New Rule(s)	No Deduction New Prediction(s)	Lazy Deduction New Rule(s)	Lazy Deduction New Prediction(s)	Eager Deduction New Rule(s)	Eager Deduction New Prediction(s)
9	(u3, r6)	(u3, r2)	r6 ⇒ r7 r6 ⇒ r4	(u3, r7), ~~(u5, r4)~~	r6 ⇒ r7 r6 ⇒ r4	(u3, r7), ~~(u5, r4)~~	r2 ⇒ r4 r2 ⇒ r6 r6 ⇒ r2 r6 ⇒ r4 r6 ⇒ r7	(u5, r2), (u2, r6), (u2, r7), ~~(u2, r4)~~, ~~(u5, r4)~~
10							r2, r6 ⇒ r7	(u3, r7)
11	(u3, r9)	(u5, r9)	r6, r7 ⇒ r4 r6, r7 ⇒ r9	(u5, r9)	r6, r7 ⇒ r4 r6, r7 ⇒ r9	(u5, r9)	r2, r6, r7 ⇒ r9	(u2, r9)
12	(u3, r10)	(u5, r10)	r6, r7, r9 ⇒ r4 r6, r7, r9 ⇒ r10	(u5, r10)	r6, r7, r9 ⇒ r4 r6, r7, r9 ⇒ r10	(u5, r10)	r2, r6, r7, r9 ⇒ r10	(u2, r10)
13	(u2, r6)	(u2, r7) (u2, r9) (u2, r10)	r6 ⇒ r7 r6 ⇒ r9 r6 ⇒ r10 r6 ⇒ r4	(u2, r7), (u2, r9), (u2, r10), (u5, r2), (u3, r2), ~~(u2, r4)~~	r6 ⇒ r7 r6 ⇒ r9 r6 ⇒ r10 r6 ⇒ r4	(u2, r7), (u2, r9), (u2, r10), (u3, r2), (u5, r2), ~~(u2, r4)~~		

Figure 2: A portion of the access log of the real dataset (described in §5.1) and resulting predictions (with $\beta = 20$, see §4.2), where users are denoted u1, u2, . . .; resources are denoted r1, r2, . . .; and the log is pictured beginning at $t = 9$ with $Exercised_8 = Visible_8 = \{(u1, r1), (u2, r2), (u1, r3), (u3, r4), (u4, r5), (u5, r6), (u5, r7), (u6, r8)\}$. Underlined atoms were added to $Helpful_t$ and canceled atoms were added to $Incorrect_t$.

using $Visible_t$ for $t = \text{time}(p_\ell)$; i.e., the object set O is the users in $Visible_t$ and the attribute set A is the resources in $Visible_t$. Each rule $x \Rightarrow \{r\}$ derived in this way yields a prediction p_ℓ of policy atom (u, r) at time $t = \text{time}(p_\ell)$ if and only if (i) $\forall r' \in x : (u, r') \in Visible_t$; (ii) $(u, r) \notin Visible_t$; and (iii) $(u, r) \notin Predictions_{t-1}$. In other words, a rule will lead to a prediction for a user u if and only if user u has accessed all the resources in the precondition x of the rule but not resource r, and if the prediction has not already been made.

In a real system, each prediction would need to be judged, presumably by a human administrator (e.g., [8, 7]). For our evaluation, we determine the correctness of each prediction relative to an *intended policy*, *Intended*, which is a set of policy atoms; intuitively, the intended policy is the ideal (though perhaps not implemented) policy in the system. We will discuss how we instantiate *Intended* in our datasets in §5.1, but for now, we simply stipulate that $Deduced_t \subseteq Intended$ for all times t. Among the predictions that are consistent with intended policy, those that are not already deduced are *helpful*; we define these inductively as $Helpful_0 = \emptyset$ and $Helpful_{t+1} = Helpful_t \cup (Predictions_{t+1} \cap (Intended \setminus Deduced_t))$. The *incorrect* predictions can be defined more straightforwardly: $Incorrect_t = Predictions_t \setminus Intended$. We assume that our prediction system is informed of the result when it makes predictions, i.e., whether the prediction was correct, incorrect or already deducible. As such, $Helpful_t \subseteq Visible_{t+1}$ and $Predictions_t \cap Deduced_t \subseteq Visible_{t+1}$. This means that all predictions at time t are resolved prior to predictions at time $t + 1$, though we stress this is a modeling simplification and is not necessary in practice.

In §5, we will evaluate the performance of this approach in three types of systems.

No deduction.

In a system with "no deduction" (ND), we define $Deduced_{t+1} = Visible_{t+1} = Exercised_{t+1} \cup Helpful_t$. This is the setting in which previous proposals for misconfiguration prediction based on accesses have been evaluated [7]. A system permitting no deduction based on previous accesses might be, e.g., one in which every access permission is demonstrated using a distinct per-resource capability. In such systems, it cannot be deduced that policy allows any accesses other than those that have already been exercised.

Eager deduction.

In an "eager deduction" (ED) system, we stipulate that $Visible_{t+1} = Deduced_{t+1}$, but generally $Visible_{t+1} \supseteq Exercised_{t+1} \cup Helpful_t$. That is, we expect that it is possible to deduce more than just what has been observed or predicted, and all such deductions are "eagerly" exploited to improve predictions. An example of an ED system would be one that reasons using credentials presented in previous accesses and gathered from previous predictions (e.g., as would be possible in a proof-carrying authorization system [4]) and then imports these into the prediction engine.

Lazy deduction.

In a "lazy deduction" (LD) system, $Visible_{t+1} = Exercised_{t+1} \cup Helpful_t \cup (Predictions_t \cap Deduced_t)$, but we permit $Visible_{t+1} \subseteq Deduced_{t+1}$. As such, there are deductions that are not visible to the prediction algorithm (the meaning of "lazy"), but that are still relevant in measuring its success, as defined below. Specifically, a lazy system is one in which deducible policy that has not been exercised or predicted can nevertheless be consulted to "filter" predictions before they are posed to a human. We expect most practical systems to be eager, lazy, or in between.

Figure 2 illustrates a small portion of an access log from our real dataset described in §5.1, including the access that occurred in each time step ("Exercised") and the additional policy atoms that were deducible based on information accompanying that access ("Deducible"). As shown in this figure, ND counts all of (u5, r9) at $t = 11$, (u5, r10) at $t = 12$, and (u2, r7), (u2, r9), (u2, r10), and (u3, r2) at $t = 13$ as helpful, even though these can be deduced as already part of implemented policy at times $t = 11$, 12, 13, 13, 13, and 9, respectively. As such, LD does not count these as helpful. Because ED incorporates deducible facts when predicting misconfigurations, it uncovers policy more effectively, e.g., finding (u2, r6) at time $t = 9$ before it is exercised at $t = 13$ (and thus rectifying this potential misconfiguration before that access).

The measures of success that we produce for our system are intuitively the precision and recall of its predictions, which we call *accuracy* and *benefit*. Our definition of accuracy is natural:

$$Accuracy_t = \frac{|Helpful_t|}{|Helpful_t \cup Incorrect_t|}$$

Then, the accuracy *Accuracy* is simply $Accuracy_t$ at the maximum value of t in the execution. Note that the denominator of $Accuracy_t$

is the size of $Helpful_t \cup Incorrect_t$ and not of $Predictions_t$; the difference is predictions that were already deducible by the time they were made. These predictions are not helpful, but would presumably not be passed to a human, since their truth can be deduced already (and so are not "incorrect"). Similarly, benefit is defined

$$Benefit_t = \frac{|Helpful_t|}{|Intended|}$$

and then the benefit $Benefit$ is simply $Benefit_t$ at the maximum value of t in the execution. When interpreting $Benefit$ it is important to recognize that $Benefit$ can never reach 1, since some policy atoms must be exercised before others can be predicted. Thus, it is important to interpret $Benefit$ relative to the maximum value of $Benefit$ that an algorithm could achieve in a given scenario. We show this in §5.

4.2 Algorithm for Enforcing Benefit vs. Accuracy Ratio

There is a tension between benefit and accuracy: seeking to maximize accuracy typically involves making only those predictions that are very likely to be correct, which results in a lower benefit. On the other hand, maximizing benefit is achieved by making predictions more indiscriminately, and hence lowering accuracy. In previous approaches to misconfiguration identification, instantiating the prediction algorithm with different parameters led to results on different points of the spectrum from higher accuracy/lower benefit to lower accuracy/higher benefit. However, the relationship between different parameter sets and different points on this spectrum both was ad-hoc and varied across environments, and so the parameters needed to be tuned by trial and error, which is likely not possible in real-world applications, to achieve the desired tradeoff between benefit and accuracy.

As discussed in §1, a contribution of this paper is a method for ensuring $\frac{Benefit}{Accuracy} \approx \beta$ across a wide range of scenarios, with no additional parameter tuning. A prediction engine can track $Accuracy_t$ over time but, because it does not know $Intended$, it cannot track $Benefit_t$ precisely. So, instead, our method tracks

$$Visible\text{-}Benefit_t = \frac{|Helpful_t|}{|Visible_t|}$$

since $Visible_t$ is the engine's closest approximation to $Intended$ and one that should approach $Intended$ over time. The prediction engine can thus compute

$$\frac{Visible\text{-}Benefit_t}{Accuracy_t} = \frac{|Helpful_t \cup Incorrect_t|}{|Visible_t|} \quad (5)$$

and monitor for the event in which this ratio drops below the target value β. That is, in the absence of predictions, $Visible_t$ will grow over time as new accesses are exercised (and t incremented), thus causing (5) to drop below β. Once that occurs, the prediction engine can issue predictions, adding each to $Helpful_t$, $Incorrect_t$ or $Visible_t$ once it is resolved, until (5) climbs above β. At this point, it suspends making further predictions until (5) falls below β. Since an incorrect prediction is added to $Incorrect_t$ and has no effect on $Visible_t$, and since a helpful prediction is added to both $Helpful_t$ and $Visible_t$, predictions can continue indefinitely only if they are always already deducible (and so have no effect) or helpful.

Once predictions are solicited as a result of (5) falling below β, they are derived at the same logical time t by enumerating rules (ignoring those with confidence 1) in decreasing order of their predictive accuracies based on visible policy $Visible_t$, until enough of these predictions are resolved to suspend predictions and allow logical time $t + 1$ to begin. The only exception is if rule generation exhausts all rules with nonzero predictive accuracy, in which

case time $t + 1$ is begun anyway—in particular, with $Visible_{t+1}$ incorporating the resolutions to predictions at time t before doing so—and predictions continue until (5) again exceeds β or no new predictions are generated.

5. RESULTS

In this section we empirically evaluate our approach to applying misconfiguration prediction algorithms to real systems. The goals of our evaluation are twofold.

First, we seek to show that prior evaluations tended to overestimate the benefit of misconfiguration prediction in real systems. These prior evaluations considered only "no deduction" (ND) systems, which we believe are less likely to occur in practice than "lazy deduction" (LD) and "eager deduction" (ED) systems (as described in §4.1). In §5.2 we show that using an ND methodology to evaluate an LD system tends to significantly overestimate the benefit that is achieved by misconfiguration prediction. In §5.3, we examine the addition of *annotations*—extra group or role information that accompanies accesses—into the prediction engine to recover some of the benefit, but we find this offers only incremental improvement. However, we show in §5.4 that by moving to an ED configuration, where the prediction engine can leverage all information deducible from past accesses, benefit can be more substantially increased (though still not to the levels promised by an ND evaluation).

Second, we evaluate our method for guiding predictions to strike a desired balance between accuracy and benefit (§4.2), which we call Ratio. We show that Ratio performs competitively, in terms of the benefit and accuracy that it achieves, with traditional association-rule-mining algorithms that require hand-tuning of min_conf and min_sup settings in order to achieve good performance. We perform this comparison on ND, LD, and ED systems (§5.2–5.4), and in each case we compare against the "best" settings of min_conf and min_sup (which vary and must be determined independently for each system). We also show that Ratio succeeds in ensuring the desired tradeoff between benefit and accuracy (§5.6), whereas the results of tuning min_conf and min_sup are often unintuitive and can only be determined empirically.

5.1 Datasets

To evaluate the misconfiguration prediction technique of §4.2 in the ND, LD and ED models, we require datasets for which we can construct *exercised policy*, *deduced policy*, and *intended policy*, as described in §4.1. None of these can be derived from implemented policies as represented in, e.g., file access-control lists or firewall rules, since implemented policies do not reveal which parts are exercised or, thus, what deductions those accesses permit. Moreover, implemented policies might not accurately reflect intended policy; indeed, our thesis is that by observing exercised policy, we can predict misconfigurations in implemented policy to bring it closer to intended. Fortunately, we have gained access to a dataset of exercised, deduced, and intended policies for a deployed system, and we augment this with numerous synthetic datasets. We detail both types of datasets below.

Real dataset.

The dataset generated by a real system is a variant of the dataset used in a previous work on misconfiguration detection [7]. The system from which the data was drawn is a discretionary access-control system deployed in an office environment for controlling access to physical space. The system allows users to specify access policy both via roles and by directly delegating to individuals. The dataset encompasses a sequence of 26,383 accesses observed over 1,113 days, during which the system was used by 38 users and protected 35 resources. The *exercised policy* against which we test is the subsequence of this access log constructed by removing all duplicate accesses (i.e., for any principal and resource, only the first access by that principal to that resource is kept), and in this case comprises 247 unique accesses. Each access in the dataset is annotated with the policy information (e.g., role assignments or delegations) that made that access possible. We use these annotations to construct $Deduced_t$, i.e., the set of accesses we know to be possible at time t, for all times t covered by exercised policy. More specifically, $Deduced_t$ is produced via an algorithm that accumulates annotations into a knowledge base, and then attempts to infer all consequences of the facts present in this knowledge base (i.e., all accesses enabled by the knowledge base). Each annotation (or policy fragment) in this dataset was represented as a formula in an authorization logic, and the inference method was forward chaining; however, many other representations of policy would work equally well. Finally, the corresponding *intended policy* was constructed by surveying the users of the system to learn what policy they had created or were willing to create that had not been observed during system operation (e.g., because it was not required for any of the accesses observed). For the rest of the paper we will refer to this dataset as the *real* dataset.

Synthetic datasets.

A practical algorithm for misconfiguration detection should perform well on a variety of datasets. The single real dataset that we obtained is unlikely to be representative of datasets that would be generated in other real settings. Beyond differences in scale and density, policies in different datasets could be organized very differently. More specifically, the real dataset we used describes an environment where a large fraction of the allowed accesses are to resources to which everyone has access, which we expected could overstate the benefit of our approach.

To evaluate our system more thoroughly than is possible with just this one dataset, we created a range of *synthetic* datasets. Our goal was for our synthetic datasets to contain a mix of role- or group-based policy and direct person-to-person delegations, on the grounds that the former would be similar to real organizational access-control policies and the latter would inhibit prediction but typically occurs in practical systems. We also wanted the datasets to span a wider range in terms of the number of groups or roles, their sizes, and the depth of group or role hierarchies. As with the real dataset, we wanted each synthetic dataset to have exercised, deduced, and intended policy components.

Roughly speaking, the intended policy of each dataset was created via the following algorithm. First, we create a set of users and a set of resources, and allow some of those users direct access to some resources. With some prespecified probability, we then allow each user who has access to a resource to create a role, and probabilistically assign to that role some resources and some users. We iteratively repeat this process on all users who received access to a resource in the previous round of policy creation. At each iteration, we probabilistically decide whether to continue to the next iteration or discontinue role creation. Role creation terminates either by such a probabilistic choice, or because a target policy density has been reached. After creating role-based policy in this manner, we optionally augment it with direct delegations to achieve the desired mix of role-based and directly delegated policy. The direct delegations are created straightforwardly: we pick a target user and a resource to which she does not have access, and cause a user who does have access to that resource to delegate this access to the target. The algorithm is parameterized by probabilities that guide

every step of the policy-creation process (whether to create another role, whether to add another user to a role, whether to iterate on role creation), but even repeatedly running the algorithm with the same set of parameters causes it to generate a wide range of policies. The algorithm guards against creating degenerate policies or overly permissive ones; the synthetically generated datasets that we employ here had densities ranging between 30% and 45%, and averaging 35%, where density is the percent of possible policy atoms contained in intended policy.

Once intended policy has been created in this manner, we use it to randomly generate the sequence of accesses that comprises the exercised policy. The exercised policy is complete with respect to the intended policy; i.e., at the maximum t, $Exercised_t = Intended$. As with the real data, each access is annotated with the policy (e.g., group or role information) that enabled it. Once exercised policy is generated, we use it to compute $Deduced_t$, for every t within scope of the exercised policy, using the same process as for the real dataset.

In §5.2–5.4, we present results using the real dataset described above, deferring treatment of the synthetic datasets until §5.5. We do so both to simplify §5.2–5.4 and because unlike the real dataset, the synthetic datasets permit us to additionally measure the impact of varying amounts of *chaff* on misconfiguration prediction. Here, chaff refers to direct delegations that do not conform to the structure (groups and roles) used in the generation of the remainder of the policy; i.e., 5% chaff implies that 5% of the possible accesses is enabled by direct delegations, and the remainder is enabled by group- or role-based policy. Unless otherwise specified, results for our synthetic datasets were based on 5% chaff. Also unless otherwise stated, we use synthetic datasets with 50 users and 50 resources, with 50 users and 70 resources, and with 70 users and 50 resources. For each of these three sets of parameters describing the number of users and resources, we generated 10 data sets; the results we show in §5.5 are averages over the 30 datasets, 10 of each parameter set. Though we obtained similar results for much larger synthetic datasets, here we focus on these smaller datasets, which made it easier to evaluate the relative performance of different facets of our approach, across many parameter sets and many datasets per parameter.

5.2 No Deduction Versus Lazy Deduction

We first examine the benefit and accuracy of our system using the ND model, which is the model in which previous work was evaluated [7]. Figure 3(a) shows plots of benefit (*Benefit*) and accuracy (*Accuracy*) achieved in an ND evaluation for the real dataset. In the Ratio curves, each point corresponds to a different value of β. Each other curve plots the benefit and accuracy of a traditional rule-mining algorithm with min_sup indicated in the legend and with min_conf varied; each point corresponds to a different setting of min_conf.[1]

An immediate observation from this figure is the impressive benefit and accuracy of misconfiguration identification in the ND model. As we have contended previously, however, the ND model, by setting $Deduced_{t+1}$ to be simply $Exercised_{t+1} \cup Helpful_t$, precludes any deductions being made from the evidence of access-control policy that might have accompanied policy atoms. This is why so many predictions in Figure 2 (e.g., $(u3, r2)$ at $t = 13$) are counted as helpful in the ND model even though they were already deducible (for $(u3, r2)$, at time $t = 9$).

Perhaps the easiest way to take this additional information into

---

[1] We used $\beta \in \{.05, .15, .25, .4, .55, .7, .9, 1.2, 1.6, 2.2, 20\}$ and $min\_conf \in \{.01, .1, .2, .3, .4, .5, .6, .7, .8, .9, .95\}$.

100

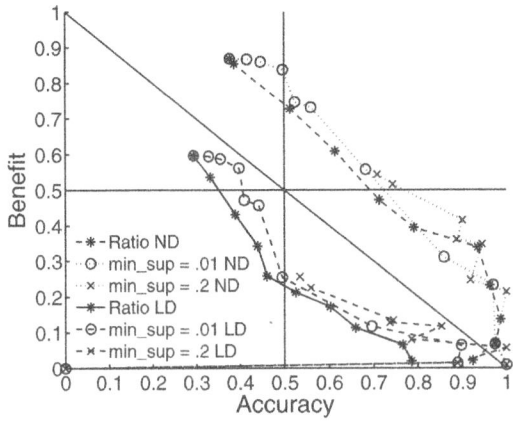

(a) No Deduction vs. Lazy Deduction

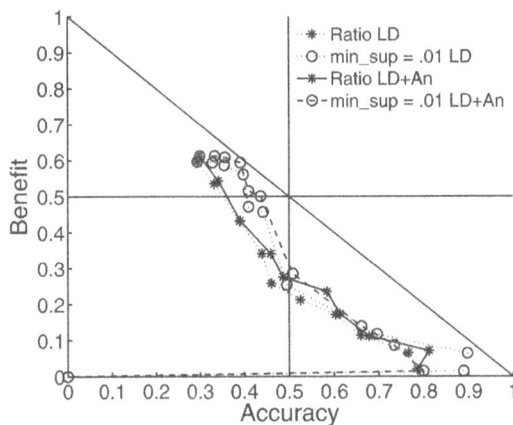

(b) Lazy Deduction with annotations

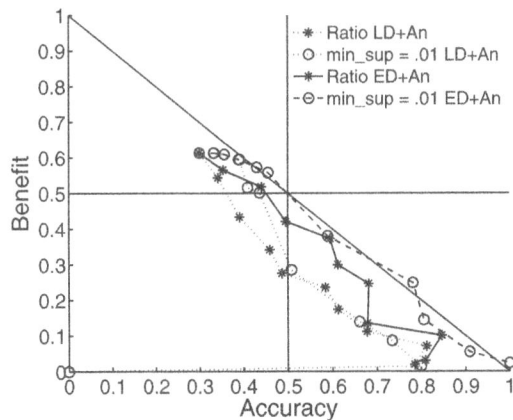

(c) Eager Deduction with annotations

Figure 3: Achieved benefit and accuracy on real dataset in ND, LD, and ED configurations

account is to use it to "filter out" predictions that can be proved to be correct before they reach a human administrator—the LD model. In doing so, the curves marked LD in Figure 3(a) result. A notable lesson from these new curves is that the ND model sub-

stantially overestimates the effectiveness of misconfiguration prediction when deduction is possible.

More specifically, on the real dataset the highest benefit provided by any prediction algorithm evaluated in the ND case is 86.8%; the more realistic view represented by LD reveals the maximal benefit to be a much lower 59.6%. This maximal attained benefit of 59.6% indicates that many of the predictions credited as correct in the ND case were, in fact, already deducible by the time they were made, and hence were not indicative of misconfigurations. In fact, we can say for certain that this benefit of 59.6% is the maximum that could be achieved by any prediction algorithm operating in an LD case, because this is the highest value reached by a tuning of the naive algorithm that is so biased towards attaining high benefit that it makes every prediction for which there is *any* statistical evidence. This highest attainable benefit can be increased somewhat by allowing the prediction algorithm access to more information, as we will show in §5.3–§5.4.

Also evident in Figure 3(a) is that ND can overstate accuracy, again because the highest-ranked association rules tend to be already deduced. In this case, the comparison with LD reveals that many of the predictions that contribute to ND's high accuracy are redundant with what can be deduced and that the non-redundant predictions, which are the only ones made by LD, are much less accurate. For example, using the Ratio method on the real data with $\beta = .7$, accuracy falls from 79.1% in ND to 46.1% in LD (and benefit declines from 39.5% to 25.8%). We will show in §5.3–§5.4 that much of this accuracy can also be recovered by giving the prediction algorithm access to more information.

Another take-away message from Figure 3(a) is that Ratio is competitive with the various tunings of traditional rule-mining based on min_sup and min_conf, typically trailing the best such curve by at most a few percentage points in each of benefit and accuracy. One exception is that the distance between the best min_sup LD curve and "Ratio LD" curve grows when the parameters (min_conf or β, respectively) are configured to strongly emphasize accuracy over benefit. However, these highest-accuracy configurations yield very few predictions, and so this gap in accuracy reflects only a small number of incorrect predictions by Ratio.

Figure 3(a) also shows the dramatic differences that can result from different values of min_sup as min_conf is varied. (For example, $min\_sup = .2$ attains a maximum benefit far below that of $min\_sup = .01$.) This motivates the move to our Ratio method to achieve a desired balance of $\frac{Benefit}{Accuracy}$. The extent to which the Ratio method accomplishes this is evaluated in §5.6.

5.3 Utilizing Annotations

A middle ground between an LD system and fully incorporating all deductions into the prediction engine (an ED system, evaluated in §5.4) is importing *annotations* into the prediction engine (i.e., into $Visible_t$) in the form of name of groups or roles to which a user has been demonstrated to belong in the course of gaining access to resources. For example, in our datasets we can extract group memberships from some of the credentials that accompany accesses.

We model annotations in our framework by adding new "resources" denoting groups and roles into the resource set. When a new credential stating a user's membership in the group or role is observed, this is realized as a new policy atom—a new element of exercised policy. During rule generation, these "resources" can appear only in x for a rule $x \Rightarrow y$. This permits rules like "Membership in Students $\wedge$ access to Student Lounge $\Rightarrow$ access to Computer Lab". (We do not further reason about what other resources those group memberships might permit users to access, which is the additional power of deduction that ED systems use.)

The intuition behind including annotations is that it increases the potentially predictable misconfigurations. For example, while two users u, u' may have no actual resources that they have both accessed, knowing that they are both in a particular group (i.e., have "accessed" the corresponding group "resource") can be leveraged to infer a misconfiguration. As such, a system employing annotations has a higher potential for uncovering misconfigurations than those that do not.

Figure 3(b) shows the gains that result from incorporating annotations in our framework. Each graph shows Ratio in an LD analysis, both with and without annotations, as well as traditional rule mining with $min\_sup = .01$ in comparable evaluations. (Other values of min_sup were comparable or worse.) The gains offered by the inclusion of annotations are noticeable but modest, for both Ratio and traditional rule mining. For example, when making predictions on the real dataset using Ratio with $\beta = .7$, accuracy improved from approximately 46.1% to 48.7%, and benefit from 25.7% to 27.6%.

5.4 Eager Deduction

The previous section showed modest gains through introducing annotations that could be directly extracted from access credentials and added to exercised policy. Next, we examine the power of incorporating all deducible policy atoms into $Visible_t$ as soon as those atoms can be deduced, i.e., an ED system. The additional information this offers to the prediction engine results in substantially improved benefit and accuracy over that offered by LD and annotations alone, as shown in Figure 3(c). This benefit derives, we believe, simply from the engine using more complete information. For example, in Figure 2, ED's prediction of $(u2, r6)$ at $t = 9$, before it is exercised at $t = 13$, follows from the rule $r2 \Rightarrow r6$, which is generated from the combination of the deducible atom $(u3, r2)$ and the exercised atom $(u3, r6)$. Because LD predicts $(u3, r2)$ at $t = 13$, only after $(u2, r6)$ is exercised, it fails to predict $(u2, r6)$ in a helpful fashion. Due to such cases, using Ratio with $\beta = .7$, LD with annotations achieved a benefit of 27.6% and accuracy of 48.7%, while under ED with annotations this improved to 37.3% benefit and 59.5% accuracy. This represents a 35% increase in benefit and a 22% increase in accuracy. Note that the maximum benefit achievable on the real dataset by any algorithm in an ED configuration with annotations is 61.2%, and so at $\beta = .7$ over 60% of the possibly identifiable misconfigurations were, in fact, correctly identified.

Two additional points are worth noting in Figure 3(c). First, Ratio again remains competitive with traditional rule mining (for which $min\_sup = 0.01$ is again the best of the min_sup values we tried). As discussed in §5.2, the points at configurations emphasizing higher accuracy represent very few predictions, and so while the gaps in accuracy at such configurations are large and favor traditional rule mining, they represent few actual predictions.

Second, in comparing Figures 3(c) and 3(a), we see that an ED system, despite its improvements over LD, does not fully regain the benefit and accuracy promised by the original ND analysis. For example, the $\beta = .7$ parameter mentioned previously exhibits a decrease in accuracy from 79% to 59% and a decrease in benefit from 39% to 37%. We nevertheless believe that the results in Figure 3(c) are compelling evidence of the utility of misconfiguration prediction in systems where misconfigurations need to be avoided.

5.5 Results on Synthetic Datasets

Figures 4(a)–4(c) show plots analogous to those of Figures 3(a)–

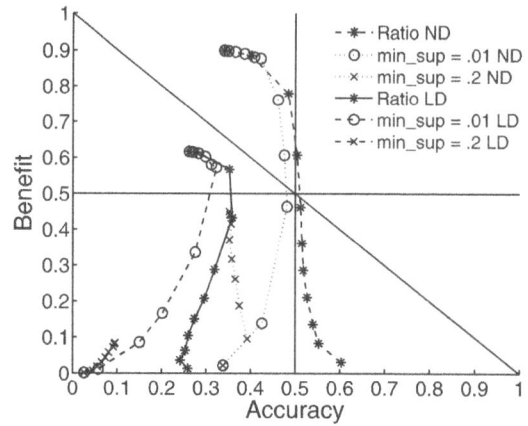

(a) No Deduction vs. Lazy Deduction

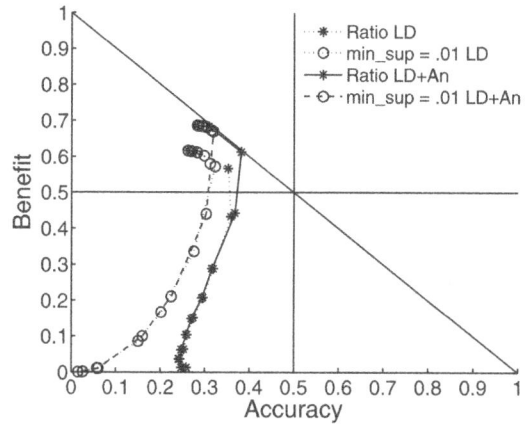

(b) Lazy Deduction with annotations

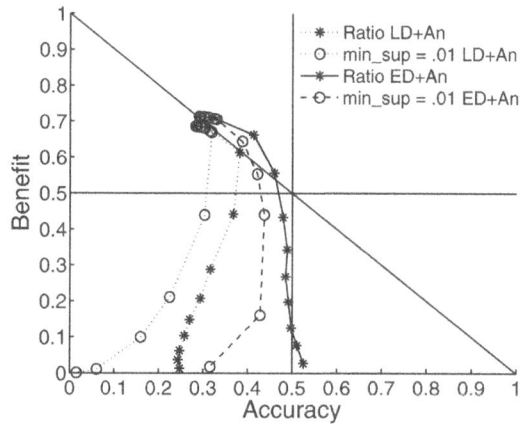

(c) Eager Deduction with annotations

Figure 4: Achieved benefit and accuracy on synthetic datasets (averaged over 30 datasets) in ND, LD, and ED configurations

3(c). The primary difference between the methodologies for producing these figures is that each point in Figures 4(a)–4(c) is an average over all synthetic datasets described in §5.1. Recall that Figures 3(a)–3(c) are the results for a single dataset.

To avoid redundant discussion, we will not recount each experiment or the commonalities of results with those of §5.2–§5.4, except to note that these graphs support the conclusions drawn out in

§5.7. That said, the results of Figures 4(a)–4(c) appear to support our decision to evaluate on both real and synthetic datasets. As we conjectured, the real dataset yields results different from those obtained on the synthetic datasets. Evaluating on both yields a better understanding of how the different approaches perform in a range of settings that we believe to be realistic. For example, including annotations increased benefit more significantly in the synthetic datasets (Figure 4(b)) when parameters were tuned to maximize benefit, owing to additional predictions that annotations allowed to be uncovered. However, accuracy was worse on average in the synthetic datasets, particularly when tuned to maximize accuracy. Again, though, due to the few predictions made in these cases, the significance of this difference is unclear.

As previously mentioned, to cover a large range of parameter settings and enable us to report averages of many runs, we focused our evaluation on smaller datasets to produce Figures 4(a)–4(c). We also experimented with larger datasets to a degree and, interestingly, found the achieved benefit and accuracy tended to increase with the size of the dataset. For example, at $\beta = .9$ and 15% density, the benefit and accuracy increased by $\sim 23\%$ as the datasets grew from 50 users and resources to 250 users and resources. However, because these results were based on fewer datasets, we naturally must have less confidence in these results.

As discussed in §5.1, synthetic datasets also permit us to evaluate the impact of chaff (direct delegations) on misconfiguration prediction. Figure 5 shows the average benefit and accuracy achieved by different techniques on synthetic datasets with 0% and 10% chaff, versus the 5% chaff represented in the datasets in Figure 4. Each test was done using Eager Deduction with annotations. Generally these results suggest that Ratio is at least as robust to increasing chaff as traditional rule-mining methods, and perhaps is more so. Of course, by increasing the percentage of (random) chaff in the dataset, identifying any policy misconfigurations with association rule mining becomes increasingly difficult and, in the limit, untenable with any technique.

5.6 Enforcing the Target Ratio

Recall that the primary motivation for the Ratio algorithm is to ensure that $\frac{Benefit}{Accuracy} \approx \beta$ for a given β. To examine the extent to which Ratio succeeds at accomplishing this, we show in Figure 6 the values of $(Accuracy, Benefit)$ at the end of each evaluation of misconfiguration prediction, for both real and synthetic datasets and for the parameter values we considered. Figure 6(a) shows that Ratio is able to provide predictable ratio values for all of our datasets, while traditional rule-mining (Figure 6(b)) provides no such predictability. So, an administrator using Ratio can confidently set β at the birth of the system and achieve a long-term performance that will satisfy the chosen β. It is worth noting that in our real dataset, where $Exercised_t \subset Intended$ at the final time t, the finishing points still exhibit the behavior sought by the Ratio algorithm.

5.7 Discussion

The evaluation in §5.2–§5.6 yields several high-level conclusions. First, our framework, which allows a more realistic evaluation of misconfiguration identification, reveals that previously reported results overestimated the effectiveness of misconfiguration identification for some realistic settings (§5.2). Second, much of this apparent loss can be regained through allowing the inference algorithm access to policy annotations and deducible policy (§5.3–§5.4). With these enhancements, the measured benefit of misconfiguration identification is substantial (Figure 3(c)). Third, our algorithm succeeds in maintaining the desired ratio between benefit

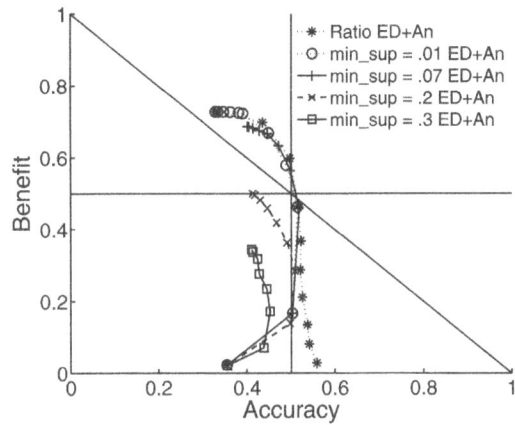

(a) 0% chaff (Eager)

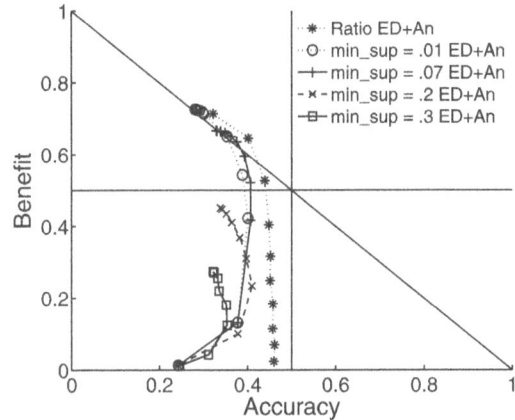

(b) 10% chaff (Eager)

Figure 5: Effects of increased chaff on misconfiguration prediction on synthetic datasets

and accuracy for all our datasets (§5.6). While evaluation on our synthetic datasets (§5.5) illustrates some differences in achieved benefit and accuracy versus the real dataset, both types of datasets support these three conclusions.

6. CONCLUSION

Policy misconfigurations that interfere with legitimate accesses impede the usability (and thus security) of access-control systems. Fortunately, accesses in a system often exhibit patterns that are indicative of intended policy, and access logs can be leveraged to identify policy misconfigurations before they cause harm.

In this paper, we improve the state of the art in identifying such misconfigurations in two ways. First, we provide a new method by which administrators can strike a desired balance between benefit (which measures how many misconfigurations are detected) and accuracy (which measures false positives in such detection), and we show empirically that this method is effective. Second, we develop a new methodology for evaluating and deploying misconfiguration-detection systems, and we apply this methodology to several misconfiguration algorithms on both a real dataset and a collection of synthetic datasets. Our methodology allows previous results in misconfiguration detection to be interpreted more realistically, revealing some potential flaws in earlier analyses. Our methodology also shows that by harnessing data available in most practical access-

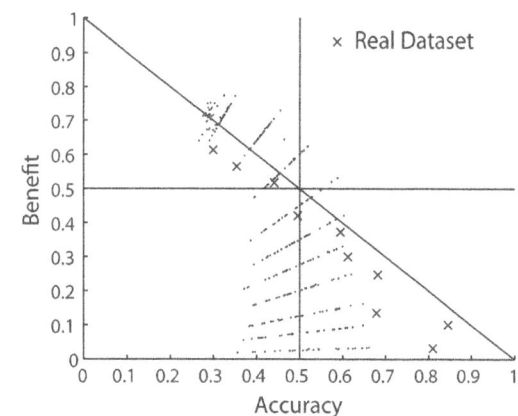

(a) Ratio Method

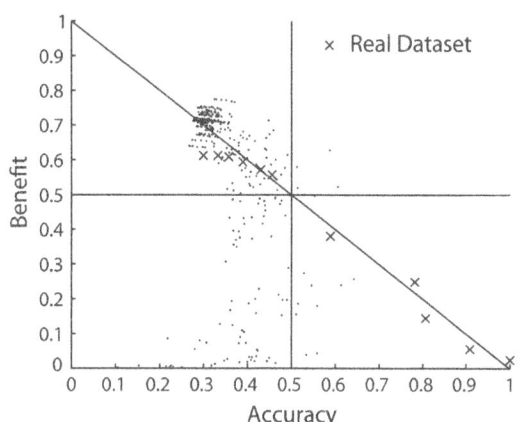

(b) $min\_sup = .01$

Figure 6: Scatter plot of ($Accuracy$, $Benefit$) for Ratio and traditional rule mining over 31 datasets, with control parameter (β in 6(a), min_conf in 6(b)) varied

control systems, the benefit and accuracy of misconfiguration detection can be largely recovered.

7. ACKNOWLEDGMENTS

This work was supported by NSF grant 0756998; by Carnegie Mellon CyLab under Army Research Office grant DAAD19-02-1-0389; and by ONR grants N000141010155 and N000141010343.

8. REFERENCES

[1] M. Abedin, S. Nessa, L. Khan, E. Al-Shaer, and M. Awad. Analysis of firewall policy rules using traffic mining techniques. *International Journal of Internet Protocol Technology*, 5:3–22, Apr. 2010.

[2] R. Agrawal, T. Imielinski, and A. Swami. Mining association rules between sets of items in large databases. In *ACM SIGMOD International Conference on Management of Data*, pages 207–216, May 1993.

[3] E. S. Al-Shaer and H. H. Hamed. Discovery of policy anomalies in distributed firewalls. In *23rd INFOCOM*, March 2004.

[4] A. W. Appel and E. W. Felten. Proof-carrying authentication. In *6th ACM Conference on Computer and Communications Security*, 1999.

[5] Y. Bartal, A. J. Mayer, K. Nissim, and A. Wool. Firmato: A novel firewall management toolkit. In *1999 IEEE Symposium on Security and Privacy*, May 1999.

[6] L. Bauer, S. Garriss, J. M. McCune, M. K. Reiter, J. Rouse, and P. Rutenbar. Device-enabled authorization in the Grey system. In *Information Security: 8th International Conference, ISC 2005*, volume 3650 of *Lecture Notes in Computer Science*, pages 431–445, Sept. 2005.

[7] L. Bauer, S. Garriss, and M. K. Reiter. Detecting and resolving policy misconfigurations in access-control systems. *ACM Transactions on Information and System Security*, 14(1), May 2011.

[8] T. Das, R. Bhagwan, and P. Naldurg. Baaz: A system for detecting access control misconfigurations. In *19th USENIX Security Symposium*, Aug. 2010.

[9] K. El-Arini and K. Killourhy. Bayesian detection of router configuration anomalies. In *2005 ACM SIGCOMM Workshop on Mining Network Data*, August 2005.

[10] T. Jaeger, A. Edwards, and X. Zhang. Policy management using access control spaces. *ACM Transaction on Information and System Security*, 6(3):327–364, 2003.

[11] M. Kuhlmann, D. Shohat, and G. Schimpf. Role mining—revealing business roles for security administration using data mining technology. In *8th ACM Symposium on Access Control Models and Technologies*, June 2003.

[12] F. Le, S. Lee, T. Wong, H. Kim, and D. Newcomb. Detecting network-wide and router-specific misconfigurations through data mining. *IEEE/ACM Transactions on Networking (TON)*, 17(1):66–79, 2009.

[13] F. Le, S. Lee, T. Wong, H. S. Kim, and D. Newcomb. Minerals: Using data mining to detect router misconfigurations. In *MineNet '06: 2006 SIGCOMM Workshop on Mining Network Data*, pages 293–298, 2006.

[14] A. Mayer, A. Wool, and E. Ziskind. Fang: A firewall analysis engine. In *2000 IEEE Symposium on Security and Privacy*, May 2000.

[15] I. Molloy, H. Chen, T. Li, Q. Wang, N. Li, E. Bertino, S. Calo, and J. Lobo. Mining roles with semantic meanings. In *13th ACM Symposium on Access Control Models and Technologies*, pages 21–30, 2008.

[16] I. Molloy, N. Li, T. Li, Z. Mao, Q. Wang, and J. Lobo. Evaluating role mining algorithms. In *14th ACM Symposium on Access Control Models and Technologies*, pages 95–104, 2009.

[17] T. Scheffer. Finding association rules that trade support optimally against confidence. *Intelligent Data Analysis*, 9(4):381–395, 2005.

[18] G. Stevens and V. Wulf. Computer-supported access control. *ACM Trans. Comput.-Hum. Interact.*, 16:12:1–12:26, September 2009.

[19] J. Vaidya, V. Atluri, and Q. Guo. The role mining problem: Finding a minimal descriptive set of roles. In *12th ACM Symposium on Access Control Models and Technologies*, 2007.

[20] A. Wool. Architecting the Lumeta firewall analyzer. In *10th USENIX Security Symposium*, 2001.

[21] L. Yuan, J. Mai, Z. Su, H. Chen, C.-N. Chuah, and P. Mohapatra. FIREMAN: A toolkit for FIREwall modeling and ANalysis. In *2006 IEEE Symposium on Security & Privacy*, 2006.

Comparison-Based Encryption
for Fine-grained Access Control in Clouds

Yan Zhu[1,2], Hongxin Hu[3], Gail-Joon Ahn[3], Mengyang Yu[1,2], Hongjia Zhao[1,2]

[1] Institute of Computer Science and Technology, Peking University, Beijing, 100871, China
[2] Beijing Key Laboratory of Internet Security Technology, Peking University, Beijing, 100871, China
[3] Laboratory of Security Engineering for Future Computing (SEFCOM), Arizona State University,
Tempe, Arizona, 85281, USA
{yan.zhu,myyu,zhaohj}@pku.edu.cn; {hxhu,gahn}@asu.edu

ABSTRACT

Access control is one of the most important security mechanisms in cloud computing. However, there has been little work that explores various comparison-based constraints for regulating data access in clouds. In this paper, we present an innovative comparison-based encryption scheme to facilitate fine-grained access control in cloud computing. By means of forward/backward derivation functions, we introduce comparison relation into attribute-based encryption to implement various range constraints on integer attributes, such as temporal and level attributes. Then, we present a new cryptosystem with dual decryption to reduce computational overheads on cloud clients, where the majority of decryption operations are executed in cloud servers. We also prove the security strength of our proposed scheme, and our experiment results demonstrate the efficiency of our methodology.

Categories and Subject Descriptors

D.4.6 [**Operation Systems**]: Security and Protection—*Access controls, Cryptographic controls*; E.3 [**Data Encryption**]: Public key cryptosystems

General Terms

Security, Theory, Verification

Keywords

Access Control, Cryptography, Integer Comparison, Dual Decryption, Attribute-Based Encryption, Cloud

1. INTRODUCTION

The emerging cloud-computing paradigm is rapidly gaining momentum as an alternative to traditional information technology due to the reason that it provides an extensible and powerful environment for growing amounts of services and data. One fundamental aspect of this paradigm shifting is that data storage and processing are being outsourced into the cloud. However, cloud computing is also facing many challenges for data security as the users outsource their sensitive data to clouds, which are generally beyond the same trusted domain as data owners.

To address such a problem, access control is considered as one of critical security mechanisms for data protection in cloud applications. Unfortunately, traditional data access control approaches usually assume that data is stored in a trusted data server for all users. This assumption however no longer holds in cloud computing since the data owners and cloud servers are very likely to be in different domains. Hence, attribute-based encryption (ABE) has been introduced into cloud computing to encrypt outsourced sensitive data in terms of access policy on attributes describing the outsourced data, and only authorized users can decrypt and access the data [5, 9, 10, 12, 14, 20]. Since the access control policy of every object is embedded within it, the enforcement of policy becomes an inseparable characteristic of the data itself. This is in direct contrast to most currently access control systems, which rely upon a trusted host to mediate access and maintain policies.

Challenges. Although there have been some attempts to construct fine-grained access control systems in clouds, existing work lacks a systematic mechanism to support a complete comparison relation, $<, >, \leq, \geq$, in policy specification. In particular, to realize integer comparisons in ABE, Bethencourt *et al.* [5] proposed a naive approach, called as BSW's scheme, by using Bitwise-comparison operators based on AND/OR operators. However, this scheme has following shortcomings:

- It cannot support dual comparative expressions, where two range-based comparative constraints must be embedded into the outsourced files as well as the user's private key. For example, we cannot generate a user's private key with a range $4 \leq Month \leq 10$, which is particularly useful for representing fine-grained policies.

- It cannot support efficient cryptographic comparison methods. In Bitwise-comparison, the sizes of user's key and ciphertext are very large because the integer must be split into bits, and this causes higher computational costs of both encryption and decryption.

- All algorithms in existing scheme are run in a stand-alone mode, and the overheads of running those algorithms are big due to the sophisticated bilinear pairing operations, especially for decryption. Hence, such a system is unsuitable for lightweight cloud clients, such as mobile devices, in a cloud environment.

To address those limitations, it is critical to investigate a more comprehensive solution to enable fine-grained expressions of range constraints in ABE-based systems.

Contributions. In this paper, we attempt to construct a new cryptosystem to explore richer attribute expressions in access control policies, especially for range constraints, and efficient support for lightweight clients in clouds.

Our contributions in this work are summarized as follows:

- We define and construct two new cryptographic functions, forward and backward deviation functions, to solve integer comparison problem. By avoiding complex bitwise comparison, our comparison method incorporates the expression of integer range in user's private key, as well as enables the security based on one-way function.

- We present a novel comparison-based encryption (CBE) scheme to enable fine-grained access control in cloud computing, which not only provides O(1) size of private-key and ciphertext for each range attribute, but also supports the provable security under RSA and CDH assumption.

- We introduce a cryptosystem with key delegation and dual decryption structure to reduce computational overheads on lightweight devices by shifting the majority of decryption operations to cloud servers. We prove that this structure is secure against various chosen derivation-key attacks.

- We implement a prototype of CBE system to evaluate our proposed approach. Our experimental results not only validate the efficiency of our scheme and algorithms, but also verify that the decryption overheads is effectively apportioned over cloud servers and clients.

This paper is organized as follows. We define the basic notation in Section 2. In Section 3, we introduce the framework of CBE cryptosystem and corresponding security requirements. Section 4 shows how the CBE scheme can be constructed. In Section 5, we discuss how to apply CBE for achieving fine-grained access control in clouds. Section 6 gives the security analysis of our scheme. We evaluate the performance of our scheme in Section 7. Finally, we overview the related work in Section 8, and conclude this paper in Section 9.

2. PRELIMINARIES

First, we establish the notation used in this paper. In many practical scenarios, the users may be restricted to access resources at a predefined level, range or period. For example, a user wishes to send an important notice which remains valid until a certain date, or a university permits the plumbers to check water-pipe into some areas during the first three days of each month. Hence, *range (or period) constraints* are used to specify the exact intervals during which an action can be enabled or disabled for a certain resource. We can represent the constraint by an integer attribute A_t with interval $[t_i, t_j]$, where $[t_i, t_j]$ is a range (or interval) denoting the lower (e.g. beginning time) and upper (e.g. ending time) bounds for the instants in A_t.

On the other hand, in order to realize comparison-based access control, a user is also assigned a digital certificate (called *access privilege*) which includes an integer attribute A_t. For example, as the definition in the X.500 standard, we assume that each user is assigned a licence with a time interval $[t_a, t_b]$ for a certain attribute A_t. Specially, given a range constraint $[t_i, t_j]$ and an access privilege $[t_a, t_b]$ on the same attribute A_t, we must satisfy the following criterion:

DEFINITION 1 (COMPARISON CRITERION). *Given an access constraint $t_i \leq A_t \leq t_j$ for the protected resources and a privilege $t_a \leq A_t \leq t_b$ in the user's certificate, secure data access control must guarantee that the user can be permitted to access the resources if and only if $[t_i, t_j] \cap [t_a, t_b] \neq \emptyset$.*

This requirement is necessary for integer or level attributes in attribute-based access control, in which we define the policy with range constraints to specify the exact intervals during which an event can be enabled or disabled by matching the user's certificate. Further, we introduce this requirement into attribute-based encryption to define the comparison criterion of integer or level attributes.

3. COMPARISON-BASED ENCRYPTION

3.1 Definition of Fine-grained Access Control with Comparison

In mathematics, the ordering imposed on a set of elements U is said to be a *total ordering relation* or *chain* if and only if every two elements are comparable in U. The set of integer, ordered usually by the $\leq, \geq$ (or $<, >$) relations, is totally ordered as the subsets of natural numbers and rational numbers. It is obvious that some attributes, such as level, time, and position location, also satisfy the total ordering relation or monotone, which can be mapped into consecutive integers. So that we consider the values of these attributes as a countable set constituted in the range $[0, Z]$, $U = \{t_1, \cdots, t_T\} \subseteq [0, Z]$. Based on this ordering relation on U, we define an attribute-based access control with comparison operations as follows:

- $\mathcal{A}$: the set of attributes $\mathcal{A} = \{A_1, \cdots, A_m\}$;

- $A_k(t_i, t_j)$: the range constraint of attribute A_k on $[t_i, t_j]$, i.e., $t_i \leq A_k \leq t_j$;

- $\mathcal{P}$: the access control policy expressed as a Boolean function on AND/OR logical operations, generated by the grammar: $\mathcal{P} ::= A_k(t_i, t_j)|\mathcal{P}$ AND $\mathcal{P}|\mathcal{P}$ OR $\mathcal{P}$; and

- $\mathcal{L}$: the access privilege assigned into the user's certificate, generated by $\mathcal{L} ::= \{A_k(t_a, t_b)\}_{A_k \in \mathcal{A}}$.

3.2 Framework of CBE Cryptosystem

With the focus on comparison-based access control and dual-decryption mechanism in cloud environment, a comparison-based encryption (CBE) consists of six algorithms as follows:

- Setup($1^\kappa, \mathcal{A}$): Takes a security parameter κ as input, outputs the master key MK and the public-key $PK_\mathcal{A}$;

- GenKey($MK, u_k, \mathcal{L}$): Takes the user's ID number u_k as the input, the access privilege $\mathcal{L}$ and MK, outputs the user's private key $SK_\mathcal{L}$;

- Encrypt($PK_A, \mathcal{P}$): Takes a comparable access policy $\mathcal{P}$ and PK as input, outputs the ciphertext header $\mathcal{H}_\mathcal{P}$ and a random session key ek;

- Delegate($SK_\mathcal{L}, \mathcal{L}'$): Takes a private key $SK_\mathcal{L}$ and a specified privilege requirement $\mathcal{L}'$ as input, outputs a derivation key $\widetilde{SK}_{\mathcal{L}'}$ if each attribute in $\mathcal{L}$ and $\mathcal{L}'$ satisfies the above-mentioned comparison criterion;

- Decrypt1($\widetilde{SK}_{\mathcal{L}'}, \mathcal{H}_\mathcal{P}$): Takes a user's private key $\widetilde{SK}_{\mathcal{L}'}$ and a ciphertext header $\mathcal{H}_\mathcal{P}$ as input, outputs a new ciphertext header $\widetilde{\mathcal{H}}_\mathcal{P}$ if $\mathcal{L}'$ satisfies the constraint of $\mathcal{P}$; and

- Decrypt2($SK_\mathcal{L}, \widetilde{\mathcal{H}}_\mathcal{P}$): Takes a user's private key $SK_\mathcal{L}$ and a ciphertext header $\widetilde{\mathcal{H}}_\mathcal{P}$ as input, outputs a session key ek which can be used to decrypt the stored data.

With the help of this framework, a workflow of CBE-based cryptosystem for clouds is depicted in Figure 1. For sake of clarity, the operations on the data are not shown in the framework since data owner could easily employ traditional symmetric key cryptosystem to encrypt and then outsource data with the help of a random session key ek.

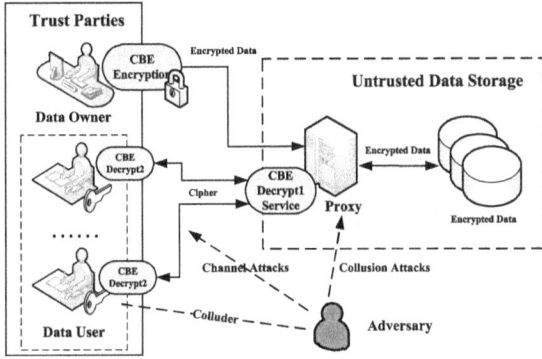

Figure 1: Workflow of CBE-based Cryptosystem for Clouds.

- First, the system manager establishes a CBE cryptosystem by invoking the *Setup* algorithm, and then assigns a private key $SK_\mathcal{L}$ on a specified access privilege $\mathcal{L}$ to each user in this system by the *GenKey* algorithm;

- For each file needing to store in the cloud, the data owner specifies an access control policy $\mathcal{P}$ to encrypt data by using the *Encrypt* algorithm before it leaves from the cloud client;

- Anytime a user can send a request to the proxy to access a stored file in the cloud.

1. After obtaining the policy $\mathcal{P}$ embedded in ciphertext header $\mathcal{H}_\mathcal{P}$, the proxy extracts the necessary privilege $\mathcal{L}'$ from $\mathcal{P}$ and sends $\mathcal{L}'$ to the user.

2. The user invokes the *Delegate* algorithm to generate a temporary derivation key $\widetilde{SK}_{\mathcal{L}'}$ for $\mathcal{L}'$ and returns it to the proxy.

3. The proxy makes use of $\widetilde{SK}_{\mathcal{L}'}$ to convert $\mathcal{H}_\mathcal{P}$ into a new $\widetilde{\mathcal{H}}_\mathcal{P}$ by using the *Decrypt*1 algorithm and sends it to the user.

4. The user invokes the *Decrypt*2 algorithm to decrypt $\widetilde{\mathcal{H}}_\mathcal{P}$ to get the session key ek.

To reduce the user's decryption overheads, decryption in this framework is converted into an interactive decryption protocol consisted by three algorithms: Delegate, Decrypt1, and Decrypt2.

3.3 Security Requirements

In our framework, we are concerned with the security risks from data users or service providers as follows:

Data users: In our framework, the malicious users cannot observe the encrypted data stored in outsourced storages, thus they cannot directly attack to the ciphertext header $\mathcal{H}_\mathcal{P}$. However, the malicious users could try to make use of the *Delegate* algorithm to access files. To do so, they can change the range of his privileges independently or cooperatively. We are certainly more concerned with the second case, which is called *collusion privilege attack*.

Another attack is based on the fact that the malicious users can increase their capabilities of attack by observing the derivation keys from channel. It is a potential threat because the derivation keys, directly derived from the valid private keys, involves enough information of access privileges. Based on this threat, we define a security game to describe *key security under chosen derivation-key attacks* (KS-CDA):

Setup: The challenger runs the Setup algorithm and gives the public parameters to the adversary.

Learning: The adversary is allowed to choose a range attribute A_t and query the *Delegate* algorithm with the polynomial number of users $u_{k_1}, \cdots, u_{k_s}$ with any interval $A_t[t_{k_i}, t_{k'_i}] \in \mathcal{L}_k$. The challenger responds the corresponding keys $\{\widetilde{SK}_{\mathcal{L}_k}\}$ to the adversary.

Challenge: The challenger sends a challenge private key $SK_{\mathcal{L}^*}$ of user u^* to the adversary, where $A_t[t_i, t_j] \in \mathcal{L}^*$ and the user u^* is not queried before.

Response: The adversary outputs a private key $SK_{\mathcal{L}'}$ corresponding to u^*. If this key is valid and $\mathcal{L}'$ has more privileges than $\mathcal{L}^*$, the adversary wins this game.

Proxy: Similarly to the solution proposed in [20], we just consider the "Honest but Curious" proxy server assumption, that is, the proxy will honestly follow our proposed algorithms in general, but try to find out as much secret information as possible based on the inputs. More specifically, we assume the attacker is more interested in the stored data (by obtaining the session key to decrypt the data) and the user's private key than other secret information.

Further, attackers will also try to obtain as much prior knowledge as possible to help them break the encryption or forge the private key. To better evaluate this attack, we also define a security game to describe the *semantical security under chosen derivation-key attacks* (SS-CDA):

Setup: The challenger runs the Setup algorithm and gives the public parameters to the adversary.

Learning: The adversary is allowed to choose a range attribute A_t and query the *Delegate* algorithm with the polynomial number of users $u_{k_1}, \cdots, u_{k_s}$ with any interval $A_t[t_{k_i}, t_{k'_i}] \in \mathcal{L}_k$. The challenger responds the corresponding keys $\{\widetilde{SK}_{\mathcal{L}_k}\}$ to the adversary.

Challenge: The challenger sends a challenge ciphertext $\mathcal{H_P}^*$ to the adversary, where all $A_t[t_i, t_j] \in \mathcal{P}$ are queried before.

Response: The adversary outputs a session key ek^* corresponding to $\mathcal{H_P}^*$. If this key is valid, the adversary wins this game.

In our framework, the proxy need not to keep track of all access queries, or the system works in an anonymous manner. Therefore, we consider that the attackers also work in an anonymous environment.

4. CONSTRUCTION OF CBE SCHEME

In this section, we propose a novel construction for integer comparison to overcome the limitations of BSW's CP-ABE scheme. We first give the background on composite order bilinear groups. Then, we present two key constructions: forward and backward derivation functions. Finally, we present the construction of our CBE scheme based on those techniques.

4.1 Composite Order Bilinear Map

We set up our systems using bilinear pairings introduced by Boneh and Franklin [6, 7]. We define a bilinear map group system $\mathbb{S} = (N = pq, \mathbb{G}, \mathbb{G}_T, e)$, where $N = pq$ be the RSA-modulus, p, q are two large primes, $\mathbb{G}$ and $\mathbb{G}_T$ are two cyclic groups with order $n = sp'q'$ [1], and e be a computable bilinear map $e : \mathbb{G} \times \mathbb{G} \to \mathbb{G}_T$ with the following properties:

- Bilinearity: for any $g, h \in \mathbb{G}$ and all $a, b \in \mathbb{Z}$, $e(g^a, h^b) = e(g, h)^{ab}$;

- Non-degeneracy: $e(g, h) \neq 1$ whenever g and h are the generators of group $\mathbb{G}$; and

- Computability: $e(g, h)$ is efficiently computable.

In this system, we make N public and keep n, s, p', q' secret.

Let $\mathbb{G}_s$ and $\mathbb{G}_{n'}$ denote the subgroups of order s and $n' = p'q'$ in $\mathbb{G}$, respectively. We note that when $g \in \mathbb{G}_s$ and $h \in \mathbb{G}_{n'}$, $e(g, h)$ is the identity element in $\mathbb{G}_T$. To see this, suppose w denote a generator of $\mathbb{G}$, then $w^{n'}$ generates $\mathbb{G}_s$ and w^s generates $\mathbb{G}_{n'}$. Hence, for some k_1, k_2, $g = (w^{n'})^{k_1}$ and $h = (w^s)^{k_2}$, we have

$$e(g, h) = e((w^{n'})^{k_1}, (w^s)^{k_2}) = e(w^{k_1}, w^{k_2})^{sn'} = 1.$$

This orthogonality property of $\mathbb{G}_s$ and $\mathbb{G}_{n'}$ will be used to implement the comparison mechanism in our constructions.

4.2 Forward/Backward Derivation Functions

CBE scheme utilizes "one-way" property to represent the total ordering relation of integers. This means that given the integer relation $t_i \leq t_j$ and two corresponding values v_{t_i}, v_{t_j}, there exists an efficient algorithm to obtain v_{t_j} from v_{t_i}; however, it is hard to compute v_{t_i} from v_{t_j}. Based on this idea, we formally define the forward and backward derivation functions.

---

[1] Without loss of generality, we have $n = sn' = s_1 s_2 p' q' | lcm(p+1, q+1)$, $n' = p'q' | n$, $s = s_1 s_2$, $p = 2p's_1 - 1$, $q = 2q's_2 - 1$, and s_1, s_2, p', q', p, q are some secret large primes.

Let comparable variables be denoted as a countable set $U = \{t_1, t_2, \cdots, t_T\}$ constituted from the discrete consecutive integers with total ordering $0 \leq t_1 \leq t_2 \leq \cdots \leq t_T \leq Z$, where Z is the maximum integer. In order to construct a cryptographic algorithm for integer comparison, we use a cryptographic map $\psi : U \to V$, where $V = \{v_{t_1}, \cdots, v_{t_T}\}$ is a set of cryptographic values. It is obvious that ψ must be an order-preserving map, that is a map such that if $t_i \leq t_j$ in U implies there exists a partial-order relation $\preceq$ to ensure $v_{t_i} \preceq v_{t_j}$ in V, where $v_{t_i} = \psi(t_i)$ and $v_{t_j} = \psi(t_j)$. In order to setup this kind of relation over V, we consider the partial-order relation in V as the "one-way" property in cryptography, which is defined as a forward derivation function:

DEFINITION 2 (FORWARD DERIVATION FUNCTION, FDF). *Given a function $f : V \to V$ based on a set $(U, \leq)$, it is called a forward derivation function if it satisfies the conditions:*

- ***Easy to compute:*** *the function f can be computed in a polynomial-time, if $t_i \leq t_j$, i.e., $v_{t_j} \leftarrow f_{t_i \leq t_j}(v_{t_i})$;*

- ***Hard to invert:*** *it is infeasible for any probabilistic polynomial (PPT) algorithm to compute v_{t_i} from v_{t_j} if $t_i < t_j$.*

Similarly, we also define a function $\bar{f}$ for the derivation in opposite direction, which is called *Backward Derivation Function* (BDF). In order to avoid interference between f and $\bar{f}$, we use a different sign $\bar{\psi} : U \to \bar{V}$, and then the BDF $\bar{f}$ is defined as follows:

DEFINITION 3 (BACKWARD DERIVATION FUNCTION, BDF). *Given a function $\bar{f} : \bar{V} \to \bar{V}$ based on a set $(U, \leq)$, it is called a forward derivation function if it satisfies the conditions:*

- ***Easy to compute:*** *the function $\bar{f}$ can be computed in a polynomial-time, if $t_i \geq t_j$, i.e., $\bar{v}_{t_j} \leftarrow \bar{f}_{t_i \geq t_j}(\bar{v}_{t_i})$;*

- ***Hard to invert:*** *it is infeasible for any probabilistic polynomial (PPT) algorithm to compute $\bar{v}_{t_i}$ from $\bar{v}_{t_j}$ if $t_i > t_j$.*

4.3 Cryptographic Construction of FDF/BDF

The cryptography construction for integer comparisons is constructed based on forward/backward derivation functions. This construction is built on a special multiplicative group $\mathbb{G}_{n'}$ of RSA-type composite order $n' = p'q'$, where p', q' are two large primes. First, we choose two different random generators $\varphi, \bar{\varphi}$ in a group $\mathbb{G}_{n'}$, where $\varphi^{n'} = \bar{\varphi}^{n'} = 1$. Next, we choose two different random λ and μ in $\mathbb{Z}_{n'}^*$, where the order of λ, μ are sufficiently large in $\mathbb{Z}_{n'}^*$.

Based on RSA cryptography system, we define two mapping functions $(\psi(\cdot), \bar{\psi}(\cdot))$ from an integer set $U = \{t_1, \cdots, t_T\}$ into $V = \{v_{t_1}, \cdots, v_{t_T}\}$ and $\bar{V} = \{\bar{v}_{t_1}, \cdots, \bar{v}_{t_T}\}$ as follows:

$$v_{t_i} \leftarrow \psi(t_i) = \varphi^{\lambda^{t_i}} \in \mathbb{G}_{n'},$$
$$\bar{v}_{t_i} \leftarrow \bar{\psi}(t_i) = \bar{\varphi}^{\mu^{Z-t_i}} \in \mathbb{G}_{n'}.$$

where, φ^{λ^t} denotes $\varphi^{(\lambda^t)}$ rather than $(\varphi^\lambda)^t$. Note that, the values, $w_{t_i} = \lambda^{t_i}$ and $\bar{w}_{t_j} = u^{Z-t_j}$, can only be computed in the integer $\mathbb{Z}$ if n' are unknown. Next, according to the definition of $\psi(\cdot)$ and $\bar{\psi}(\cdot)$, it is easy to define the FDF $f(\cdot)$ and BDF $\bar{f}(\cdot)$ as

$$v_{t_j} \leftarrow f_{t_i \leq t_j}(v_{t_i}) = (v_{t_i})^{\lambda^{t_j - t_i}} \in \mathbb{G}_{n'},$$
$$\bar{v}_{t_j} \leftarrow \bar{f}_{t_i \geq t_j}(\bar{v}_{t_i}) = (\bar{v}_{t_i})^{\mu^{t_i - t_j}} \in \mathbb{G}_{n'}.$$

It is easy to show that $(\varphi^{\lambda^{t_i}})^{\lambda^{t_j-t_i}} = \varphi^{\lambda^{t_j}} = v_{t_j} \in \mathbb{G}_{n'}$ and $(\bar{\varphi}^{\mu^{Z-t_i}})^{\mu^{t_i-t_j}} = \bar{\varphi}^{\mu^{Z-t_j}} = \bar{v}_{t_j} \in \mathbb{G}_{n'}$. But it is intractable to obtain v_{t_i} from v_{t_j} for $t_i \leq t_j$ under the RSA assumption that λ^{-1} and μ^{-1} cannot be efficiently computed based on the secrecy of n' [2].

4.4 Proposed CBE Scheme

We use the above-mentioned FDF/BDF functions to construct an efficient CBE scheme with the range comparisons on integer attributes, as follows:

- $Setup(1^\kappa, \mathcal{A}) \to (MK, PK_{\mathcal{A}})$: Given a bilinear map system $\mathbb{S}_N = (N = pq, \mathbb{G}, \mathbb{G}_T, e(\cdot, \cdot))$ of composite order $n = sn'$ and two subgroups $\mathbb{G}_s$ and $\mathbb{G}_{n'}$ of $\mathbb{G}$. This algorithm chooses the random generators $w \in \mathbb{G}$, $g \in \mathbb{G}_s$, and $\varphi, \bar{\varphi} \in \mathbb{G}_{n'}$, as well as two random $\lambda, \mu \in \mathbb{Z}_n^*$ as described in Section 4.3. Thus, we have $e(g, \varphi) = e(g, \bar{\varphi}) = 1$ but $e(g, w) \neq 1$. Additionally, the setup algorithm employs a hash function $H : \{0,1\}^* \to \mathbb{G}$, mapping any attribute described as a binary string to a random group element. Next, the setup algorithm chooses two random exponents $\alpha, \beta \in \mathbb{Z}_n^*$ and set $h = w^\beta$, $\eta = g^{1/\beta}$, $\zeta = e(g, w)^\alpha$. Finally, the setup algorithm outputs the public key

$$PK = (\mathbb{S}_N, g, h, \zeta, \eta, w, \varphi, \bar{\varphi}, \lambda, \mu, H(\cdot))$$

and the master key $MK = (g^\alpha, \beta, p, q, n')$.

- $GenKey(MK, u_k, \mathcal{L}) \to SK_{\mathcal{L}}$: Given a user u_k with license $\mathcal{L}$ on a set of attributes $S = \{A_t\} \subseteq \mathcal{A}$, the GenKey algorithm first chooses a unique integer τ_k to distinguish the different users. Assume that the user u_k is assigned a range attribute $A_t \in \mathcal{L}$ with the constraint $A_t[t_a, t_b]$, this algorithm chooses a random $r \in \mathbb{Z}$ and sets the user's attribute key as

$$(D_t, D'_{t_a}, \bar{D}'_{t_b}, D''_t)_{A_t[t_a, t_b]} = (g^{\tau_k} H(A_t)^r, (v_{t_a})^r, (\bar{v}_{t_b})^r, w^r),$$

where $v_{t_a} = \varphi^{\lambda^{t_a}} \in \mathbb{G}_{n'}$ and $\bar{v}_{t_b} = \bar{\varphi}^{\mu^{Z-t_b}} \in \mathbb{G}_{n'}$. The private key is

$$SK_{\mathcal{L}} = (D = g^{(\alpha+\tau_k)/\beta}, \{(D_t, D'_{t_a}, \bar{D}'_{t_b}, D''_t)\}_{A_t[t_a, t_b] \in \mathcal{L}}).$$

- $Encrypt(PK_{\mathcal{A}}, \mathcal{P}) \to (\mathcal{H}_{\mathcal{P}}, ek)$: Given an access policy tree $\mathcal{T}$ over access policy $\mathcal{P}$, the ciphertext can be composed of a ciphertext header

$$\mathcal{H}_{\mathcal{P}} = (\mathcal{T}, C = h^s, \{((\bar{E}_{t_i}, E'_{t_i}), (E_{t_j}, E'_{t_j}))\}_{A_t[t_i, t_j] \in \mathcal{T}})$$

and a session key $ek = \zeta^s = e(g^\alpha, w)^s$, where

$$((\bar{E}_{t_i}, E'_{t_i}), (E_{t_j}, E'_{t_j}))_{A_t[t_i, t_j]}$$
$$= (((\bar{v}_{t_i}w)^x, H(A_t)^x), (((v_{t_j}w)^y, H(A_t)^y)),$$

where s is a main secret in $\mathbb{Z}_N$ for this tree $\mathcal{T}$, $\Delta_s(A_t) = x + y$ is the secret share of s in the tree $\mathcal{T}$ for an attribute A_t (see BSW's scheme).

- $Delegate(SK_{\mathcal{L}}, \mathcal{L}') \to \widetilde{SK}_{\mathcal{L}'}$: Given the private key $SK_{\mathcal{L}}$ and a specified $\mathcal{L}'$, this algorithm checks whether each attribute $A_t \in \mathcal{L}'$ holds $t_a \leq t_j$ and $t_b \geq t_i$ for $A_t[t_a, t_b] \in \mathcal{L}$ and $A_t[t_i, t_j] \in \mathcal{L}'$. If so, it computes

$$D'_{t_j} \leftarrow f_{t_a \leq t_j}(D'_{t_a}) \cdot D''_t = f_{t_a \leq t_j}(v_{t_a}^r) \cdot w^r = v_{t_j}^r \cdot w^r,$$
$$\bar{D}'_{t_i} \leftarrow f_{t_b \geq t_i}(\bar{D}'_{t_b}) \cdot D''_t = \bar{f}_{t_b \geq t_i}((\bar{v}_{t_b})^r) \cdot w^r = \bar{v}_{t_i}^r \cdot w^r,$$

---

[2]The secrecy of n' is similar to that of Euler's totient function $\phi(N)$ for RSA-type $N = pq$.

where,

$$f_{t_a \leq t_j}(v_{t_a}^r) = (\varphi^{r\lambda^{t_a}})^{\lambda^{t_j-t_a}} = \varphi^{r\lambda^{t_j}} = v_{t_j}^r,$$
$$f_{t_b \geq t_i}(\bar{v}_{t_b}^r) = (\bar{\varphi}^{r\mu^{Z-t_b}})^{\mu^{t_b-t_i}} = \bar{\varphi}^{r\mu^{Z-t_i}} = \bar{v}_{t_i}^r.$$

Next, it chooses a random $\delta \in \mathbb{Z}$ and computes $\widetilde{SK}_{\mathcal{L}'} = \{\widetilde{D}_t, \widetilde{D}'_{t_j}, \widetilde{D}'_{t_i}\}_{A_t \in \mathcal{L}'}$, where, $\tau'_k = \tau_k + \delta$, $r' = r + \delta$,

$$\widetilde{D}_t = D_t \cdot (gH(A_t))^\delta = g^{\tau_k+\delta} H(A_t)^{r+\delta} = g^{\tau'_k} H(A_t)^{r'},$$
$$\widetilde{D}'_{t_j} = D'_{t_j} \cdot (v_{t_j}w)^\delta = (v_{t_j}w)^{r+\delta} = (v_{t_j}w)^{r'},$$
$$\widetilde{D}'_{t_i} = \bar{D}'_{t_i} \cdot (\bar{v}_{t_i}w)^\delta = (\bar{v}_{t_i}w)^{r+\delta} = (\bar{v}_{t_i}w)^{r'}.$$

Finally, it outputs $\widetilde{SK}_{\mathcal{L}'}$ as the derivation key for $\mathcal{L}'$.

- $Decrypt1(\widetilde{SK}_{\mathcal{L}'}, \mathcal{H}_{\mathcal{P}}) \to \widetilde{\mathcal{H}}_{\mathcal{P}}$: Given the private key $\widetilde{SK}_{\mathcal{L}'}$ and a ciphertext header $\mathcal{H}_{\mathcal{P}}$, this algorithm also check whether each range attribute $A_t[t_i, t_j] \in \mathcal{L}'$ is consistent with $A_t[t_i, t_j] \in \mathcal{P}$. If true, the secret share $\Delta_s(A_t)$ of s over $\mathbb{G}_T$ is reconstructed by using

$$F_1 \leftarrow \frac{e(\widetilde{D}_t, E_{t_j})}{e(\widetilde{D}'_{t_j}, E'_{t_j})} = \frac{e(g^{\tau'_k} H(A_t)^{r'}, (v_{t_j}w)^x)}{e((v_{t_j}w)^{r'}, H(A_t)^x)}$$
$$= \frac{e(g^{\tau'_k}, (v_{t_j}w)^x) \cdot e(H(A_t)^{r'}, (v_{t_j}w)^x)}{e((v_{t_j}w)^{r'}, H(A_t)^x)}$$
$$= e(g^{\tau'_k}, v_{t_j}^x) \cdot e(g^{\tau'_k}, w^x) = e(g^{\tau'_k}, w)^x,$$

$$F_2 \leftarrow \frac{e(\widetilde{D}_t, \bar{E}_{t_i})}{e(\widetilde{D}'_{t_i}, E'_{t_j})} = \frac{e(g^{\tau'_k} H(A_t)^{r'}, (\bar{v}_{t_i}w)^y)}{e((\bar{v}_{t_i}w)^{r'}, H(A_t)^y)}$$
$$= \frac{e(g^{\tau'_k}, (\bar{v}_{t_i}w)^y) \cdot e(H(A_t)^{r'}, (\bar{v}_{t_i}w)^y)}{e((\bar{v}_{t_i}w)^{r'}, H(A_t)^y)}$$
$$= e(g^{\tau'_k}, \bar{v}_{t_i}^y) \cdot e(g^{\tau'_k}, w^y) = e(g^{\tau'_k}, w)^y,$$

$$F_t = F_1 \cdot F_2 = e(g^{\tau'_k}, w)^{\Delta_s(A_t)},$$

where, $e(g^{\tau'_k}, v_{t_j}^x) = e(g^{\tau'_k}, \bar{v}_{t_i}^y) = 1$ due to $g^{\tau'_k} \in \mathbb{G}_s$ and $v_{t_j}^x, \bar{v}_{t_i}^y \in \mathbb{G}_{n'}$. Next, the value $T = e(g^{\tau'_k}, w)^s$ is computed from $\{e(g^{\tau'_k}, w)^{\Delta_s(A_i)}\}_{A_i \in \mathcal{T}}$ by using the aggregation algorithm (see BSW's scheme). Finally, the new ciphertext header $\widetilde{\mathcal{H}}_{\mathcal{P}} = (C, T)$ is returned.

- $Decrypt2(SK_{\mathcal{L}}, \widetilde{\mathcal{H}}_{\mathcal{P}}) \to ek$: After receiving $\widetilde{\mathcal{H}}_{\mathcal{P}} = (C, T) = (w^{\beta s}, e(g^{\tau'_k}, w)^s)$, the decryptor uses the secret δ to compute $D' = D \cdot \eta^\delta = g^{(\alpha+\tau_k)/\beta} g^{\delta/\beta} = g^{(\alpha+\tau_k+\delta)/\beta} = g^{(\alpha+\tau'_k)/\beta}$. Next, the session key is computed by

$$ek = \frac{e(C, D')}{T} = \frac{e(g^{(\alpha+\tau'_k)/\beta}, (w^\beta)^s)}{e(g^{\tau'_k}, w)^s} = e(g^\alpha, w)^s.$$

For improving the efficiency, the output of this algorithm is a random session key ek instead of a plaintext because this key can be used to encrypt the object files using symmetrical-key cryptosystem.

Note that, it is also easy to combine $Decrypt1$ and $Decrypt2$ into one decryption algorithm, so that we can directly use that to decrypt the ciphertexts by using private keys.

Table 1: Attribute lists for employee's working hours.

People	Period-of-Validity	Job	Level	Day	Hour
Anderaon	2009/01-2011/06	Manager,	4	Mon.-Fri.	9:00AM-14:00PM
Grant	2010/04-2010/12	Accountant	3	Thu.-Fri.	10:00AM-16:00PM
Kidman	2010/04-2011/06	Engineer	2	Mon.-Fri.	9:00AM-16:00PM
Coolidge	2010/01-2010/12	Retailer	2	Mon.-Wed.	9:00AM-16:00PM
Jones	2010/08-2010/12	Retailer	1	Mon.-Sat.	10:00AM-17:00PM

Table 2: Schedule for outsourced storage systems.

Files	Period-of-Validity	Job	Level	Day	Hour
Tech. Archive	2009/11-2010/03	Engineer	≥ 3	Mon.-Fri.	9:00AM-16:00PM
		Manager	≥ 4	(All)	16:00PM-9:00AM
Sales Record	2010/01-2010/03	Accountant OR Manager	≥ 3	Thu.-Fri.	(All)
Salary History	2010/05-2010/11	Manager	≥ 4	Mon.-Fri.	9:00AM-16:00PM
Service Log	2009/06-2010/04	Retail	≥ 1	Mon.-Fri.	9:00AM-16:00PM
		Engineer	≥ 3	(All)	16:00PM-9:00AM
Contact Info.	2010/11-2011/05	(All)	≥ 1	Mon.-Sat.	9:00AM-16:00PM

5. CBE FOR FINE-GRAINED ACCESS CONTROL IN CLOUDS

In this section, we demonstrate the usability of our CBE scheme for fine-grained access control in the cloud-based application systems. Especially, we discuss how our CBE scheme can be used to support various temporal constraints, including simple temporal constraints and periodic constraints.

5.1 Fine-grained Access Control in Clouds

Cloud-based service relieves the client's burden for storage management and maintenance by providing a comparably low-cost, scalable, location-independent platform. However, the fact that clients no longer have physical possession of data, indicates that they are facing a potentially formidable risk for abusing, coping, missing or corrupting data. Hence, an important issue for outsourced storage systems is to design an efficient approach to prevent the data stored at remote servers from unauthorized access.

The CBE scheme provides exactly an effective approach to regulate outsourced sensitive data, which enables only authorized users to access data based on the various attributes. We next give an example to show how CBE scheme can provide a fine-grained access control in clouds. We assume that a small business company, which has many retailers distributed across US, constructs their data centers using CBE on a platform as a service (PaaS) environment, e.g., Google's App Engine or Amazon's Elastic. These retailers may use the mobile handheld devices to access the data centers.

According to the employee's working hours, Table 1 illustrates a simple schedule for some employees, which consists of five attributes: Period-of-Validity, which is a time attribute on month basis; Job, which is a string attribute to denote employee's position; Level, which is an integer attribute to denote secret level for documents; Day and Hour, which are two period attributes to denote working days and hours. The system manager assigns the attribute values into the employee's private key by using CBE scheme.

In this example, the manager wishes to define the access policies to protect each component of their business information: Technique Archive, Sales Record, Salary History, Service Log, Contact Information. An access policy can be viewed as a description of attributes, which is used to match the attribute values in the employee's private key. As illus-

trated in Table 2, these attributes describe various functions and temporal constraints for these business information.

A document, like a technique archive, reposits the core technology of latest products, which is being manufactured in 2009/11-2010/03. Its policy therefore stipulates that only engineers with Level ≥ 3 can view this document during regular working hours (at 9:00AM-16:00PM from Monday to Friday), as well as the managers can view it at other times. Another example is the sales-record from 2010/01 to 2010/03, which can be accessed by accountant or manager with Level ≥ 3 from Thursday to Friday. As described above, these policies are represented as follows:

Technique Archive: *(2009/11 $\leq$ Period-of-Validity $\leq$ 2010/03) **AND** (((Engineer) **AND** (Level $\geq$ 3) **AND** (Monday$\leq$ Day $\leq$ Friday) **AND** (9:00AM $\leq$ Hour $\leq$ 16:00PM)) **OR** ((Manager) **AND** (Level $\geq$ 4) **AND** (16:00PM $\leq$ hour $\leq$ 9:00AM)))*

Sales Record: *(2010/01 $\leq$ Period-of-Validity $\leq$ 2010/03) **AND** (Accountant OR Manager) **AND** (Level $\geq$ 3) **AND** (Thursday$\leq$ Day $\leq$ Friday)*

It is obvious that our CBE construction can effectively implement these access policies by using integer comparison and temporal constraints. After the documents are encrypted in accordance with the above policies, only Manager Anderaon can access the technique archive, and Engineer Kidman cannot view it due to his invalid Period-of-Validity. Similarly, both Manager Anderaon and Accountant Grant can access Sales Record. The above-mentioned example implements the protection of encrypted files by using the attribute matching between ciphertext-policy and user's private key. In order to ensure the security of secrets in these files, the session key (see Figure 2) must be renewed whenever these files are updated, so that the employees whose private keys had lapsed cannot access them.

5.2 File Structure Based on CBE

In the CBE scheme, since the access control policy is embedded within each protected object, the enforcement of policy becomes an inseparable characteristic of the data itself. This is in direct contrast to most currently available systems, which depend on a trusted host to govern the data access and maintain policies. Such a file header $H_{\mathcal{P}}$ is shown in Figure 2, in which "Cipher" consists of constant-size C, "Access Policy" consists of $\mathcal{T}$, and "Encrypted Attribute List" denotes the attribute set $\{(E_{t_i}, E'_{t_i}), (E_{t_j}, E'_{t_j})\}$ in CBE-type ciphertext. In this case, the number of users is not limited. Moreover, no file needs be changed to permit the access of existing files for a new user.

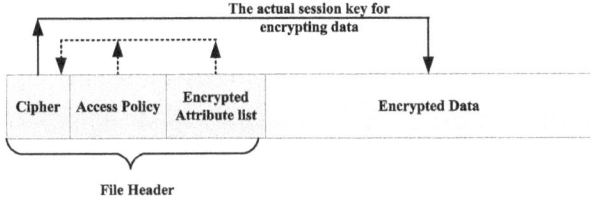

Figure 2: File structure based on CBE scheme.

5.3 Supporting Temporal Constraints with CBE

In this subsection, we illustrate how our CBE scheme can be utilized to construct various temporal constraints, enabling fine-grained access control in clouds.

5.3.1 Simple Temporal Constraint

In order to realize the temporal constraint on the single time axis, we need a function to convert the time into a nonnegative integer in $[0, Z]$. For instance, the function

$$f_1(Y, M) := 12 \cdot (Y - 2000) + M$$

transforms (Year, Month) into an integer and its inversion still holds, where $Z = 600$ if the cryptosystem can be used for 50 years. Similarly, we define a function $f_2(Y, M, D) := 365 \cdot (Y - 2000) + 31 \cdot M + D$ to transform (Year, Month, Day).

For a simple temporal system (or called a single temporal coordinate system), we categorize the relationships between constraints and permissions into four cases:

1. The encryptor uses the current time t'_c (time-stamp) to encrypt a file. Any user can decrypt it if and only if $t_1 \leq t'_c \leq t_2$, where $[t_1, t_2]$ is the granted time range. This means that we need to check $(t_1 \leq t'_c)$ and $(t'_c \leq t_2)$ by using $v_{t'_c} \leftarrow f_{t_1 \leq t'_c}(v_{t_1})$ and $\bar{v}_{t'_c} \leftarrow \bar{f}_{t'_c \leq t_2}(\bar{v}_{t_2})$;

2. The encryptor assigns a period of validity $[0, t']$ to encrypt a file. Any user can decrypt it if and only if $(t_1 \leq t' \leq t_2)\mathrm{OR}(t_1 \leq t_2 \leq t')$ for a licence $[t_1, t_2]$. This means that we just need to check $(t_1 \leq t')$ by using $v_{t'} \leftarrow f_{t_1 \leq t'}(v_{t_1})$, as shown in Figure 3;

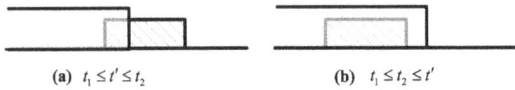

(a) $t_1 \leq t' \leq t_2$ **(b)** $t_1 \leq t_2 \leq t'$

Figure 3: The range relations on $[0, t] \bigcap [t_1, t_2]$.

3. The encryptor assigns a period of validity $[t', T]$ to encrypt a file. Any user can decrypt it if and only if $(t_1 \leq t' \leq t_2)\mathrm{OR}(t' \leq t_1 \leq t_2)$ for a licence $[t_1, t_2]$. This means that we just need to check $(t_2 \geq t')$ by using $\bar{v}_{t'} \leftarrow \bar{f}_{t' \leq t_2}(\bar{v}_{t_2})$, see Figure 4;

4. The encryptor assigns a period of validity $[t'_1, t'_2]$ to encrypt a file. Any user can decrypt it if and only if $[t_1, t_2] \bigcap [t'_1, t'_2] \neq \emptyset$. This includes four cases: 1) $t_1 \leq t'_1 \leq t_2 \leq t'_2$; 2) $t'_1 \leq t_1 \leq t'_2 \leq t_2$; 3) $t'_1 \leq t_1 \leq t_2 \leq t'_2$; and 4) $t_1 \leq t'_1 \leq t'_2 \leq t_2$. We can synthesize these cases into

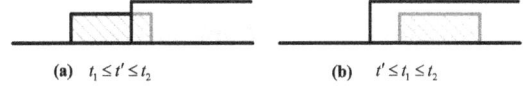

(a) $t_1 \leq t' \leq t_2$ **(b)** $t' \leq t_1 \leq t_2$

Figure 4: The range relations on $[t, T] \bigcap [t_1, t_2]$.

a simple format: $((t_1 \leq t'_2)$ AND $(t'_1 \leq t_2))$. This means that we need to check $((t_1 \leq t'_2)$ AND $(t'_1 \leq t_2))$ by using $v_{t'_2} \leftarrow f_{t_1 \leq t'_2}(v_{t_1})$ and $\bar{v}_{t'_1} \leftarrow \bar{f}_{t'_1 \leq t_2}(\bar{v}_{t_2})$, as depicted Figure 5;

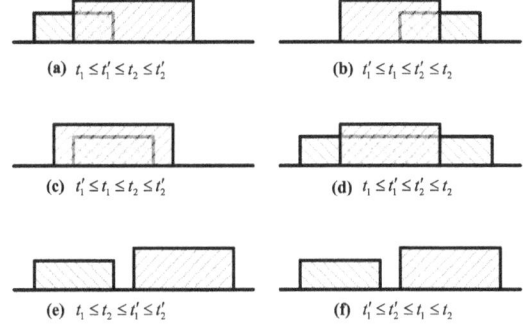

(a) $t_1 \leq t'_1 \leq t_2 \leq t'_2$ **(b)** $t'_1 \leq t_1 \leq t'_2 \leq t_2$

(c) $t'_1 \leq t_1 \leq t_2 \leq t'_2$ **(d)** $t_1 \leq t'_1 \leq t'_2 \leq t_2$

(e) $t_1 \leq t_2 \leq t'_1 \leq t'_2$ **(f)** $t'_1 \leq t'_2 \leq t_1 \leq t_2$

Figure 5: The range relations on $[t'_1, t'_2] \bigcap [t_1, t_2]$.

For four afore-mentioned cases, we show corresponding cryptographic operations in Table 3, in which each case can be implemented by using at most two derivation operations. Hence, with the help of f and $\bar{f}$, we can realize the simple temporal constraint in an attribute-based cryptosystem.

5.3.2 Periodic Constraint

Periodic constraints are another important way for expressing temporal constraints. Alien from the common constraints with continuous-time range, this kind of constraints can be divided into some intervals. That is, given a set of time $U = \{t_1, \cdots, t_T\}$, the permitted time is defined as $U_p = \bigcup_{i=I}[t_{i_b}, t_{i_e}]$, where I is an index set, each index $i \in I$ corresponds to an interval $U_i = [t_{i_b}, t_{i_e}]$, and $U_i \bigcap U_j = \emptyset$ for different $i, j \in I$. By the same token, we also extend the granted time in licence to periodic expression, that is, $U_g = \bigcup_{j=J}[t_{j_b}, t_{j_e}]$, where J is an index set of granted intervals. It is easy to see that a user can also be authorized if and only if $U_p \bigcap U_g \neq \emptyset$ in terms of Definition 1.

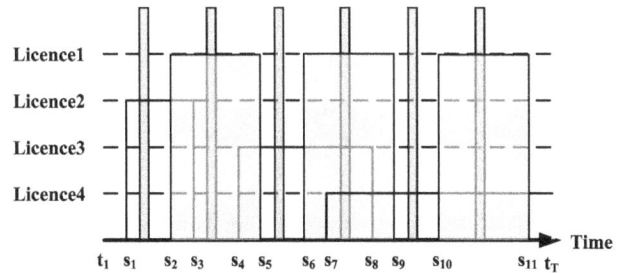

Figure 6: An example for periodic time.

In Figure 6, we show some examples for periodic constraints. We assume that a policy assigns the permission during periodic intervals on blue boxes. The black lines above the time axis indicate the users' granted-times in their

Table 3: Cryptographic operations for deferent cases.

	Cases	Logical Representations	Cryptographic Operations
1	$t_1 \leq t'_c \leq t_2$	$(t_1 \leq t'_c) \wedge (t'_c \leq t_2)$	$v_{t'_c} \leftarrow f_{t_1 \leq t'_c}(v_{t_1})$ and $\bar{v}_{t'_c} \leftarrow \bar{f}_{t'_c \leq t_2}(\bar{v}_{t_2})$
2	$[0, t']$	$(t_1 \leq t')$	$v_{t'} \leftarrow f_{t_1 \leq t'}(v_{t_1})$
3	$[t', T]$	$(t_2 \geq t')$	$\bar{v}_{t'} \leftarrow \bar{f}_{t' \leq t_2}(\bar{v}_{t_2})$
4	$[t'_1, t'_2]$	$(t_1 \leq t'_2) \wedge (t'_1 \leq t_2)$	$v_{t'_2} \leftarrow f_{t_1 \leq t'_2}(v_{t_1})$ and $\bar{v}_{t'_1} \leftarrow \bar{f}_{t'_1 \leq t_2}(\bar{v}_{t_2})$

licenses. The intersection portions of these lines indicate intervals in which permission-licence assignments are valid. For example, when the licence$_1$ is assigned to the regular intervals on pink boxes, the licence is activated every other blue interval. The other licences are kind of like licence$_1$.

The aforementioned construction can be used to realize periodic constraints by using OR logical to connect each interval $[t_{i_b}, t_{i_e}]$. Obviously, this kind of exhaustion method is not a perfect solution for large index sets I, J because this method needs to search all intervals. Here, we propose a simple method handling multiple attributes to address this problem as follows: periodic is represented by logic combination of multiple range attributes, where each attribute can be defined by a notation in calendar, such as Hours, Days, Weeks, Months, and Years. For example, $(Months[3, 5])$ and $(Years[2009, 2011])$.

TIME&DAY	Monday	Tuesday	Wednesday	Thursday	Friday	Saturday	Sunday
00:00-08:59							
09:00-10:59	Stu/Fac/Sta	Stu/Fac/Sta	Stu/Fac/Sta	Stu/Fac/Sta	Stu/Fac/Sta	Stu/Fac/Sta	
11:00-12:59	Stu/Fac/Sta	Stu/Fac/Sta	Stu/Fac/Sta	Stu/Fac/Sta	Stu/Fac/Sta	Stu/Fac/Sta	
13:00-14:59							
15:00-16:59	Stu/Fac/Sta	Stu/Fac/Sta	Stu/Fac/Sta	Stu/Fac/Sta	Stu/Fac/Sta		
17:00-18:59	Stu/Fac/Sta	Stu/Fac/Sta	Stu/Fac/Sta	Stu/Fac/Sta	Stu/Fac/Sta		
19:00-20:59							
21:00-22:59	Fac	Fac	Fac	Fac	Fac	Repairmen	
23:00-23:59	Fac	Fac	Fac	Fac	Fac	Repairmen	

Figure 7: An example for library schedule in a university.

In Figure 7, we show several examples on two attributes: Weeks (W) and Hours (H). We make use of a table to describe all combinations between weeks and hours, i.e., $(w_i, h_j) \in W \times H$, where $W \times H$ denotes Cartesian product on weeks and hours, $w_i \in W$ and $h_j \in H$. Assume that this figure is a schedule for a library in a university. The grey parts denote the working hours for students (Stu), faculties (Fau), and staffs (Sta) every week, i.e., $((W[1, 5]) \wedge ((H[9, 13]) \vee (H[15, 19]))) \vee ((W[6, 6]) \wedge (H[9, 13]))$, in which the students, faculties, and staffs obtain admissions to enter the library. The orange parts denote the time in which only faculties are permitted to enter the library every week, i.e., $((W[1, 5]) \wedge (H[21, 24]))$. Finally, the cyan parts denote the repairman's working hours for installing and maintaining the equipments every week, i.e., $((W[6, 6]) \wedge (H[21, 24]))$.

6. SECURITY ANALYSIS

We now briefly analyze the security of CBE scheme.[3] First, we describe the hardness assumptions used in our

---

[3]The details of the security analysis are omitted in this paper due to the space limitation.

scheme: Given a bilinear map group system $\mathbb{S}_N = (N = pq, \mathbb{G}, \mathbb{G}_T, e(\cdot, \cdot))$ with composite order n. The security of TACE scheme is constructed on three basic assumptions:

DEFINITION 4 (RSA ASSUMPTION). *Given an RSA public key (N, e) and a ciphertext $C = M^e \in \mathbb{G}_{n'}$, it is intractable to compute the plaintext M.*

DEFINITION 5 (CO-CDH ASSUMPTION). *For two random $x, y \in \mathbb{Z}_n^*$, given a quadruple $(G_1, G_1^x, G_2, G_2^y) \in \mathbb{G}^4$, it is intractable to compute G_2^{xy}.*

DEFINITION 6 (BILINEAR CO-CDH ASSUMPTION). *For two random $x, y \in \mathbb{Z}_n^*$, given a quintuple $(G_1, G_1^x, G_1^y, G_2, G_2^y) \in \mathbb{G}^5$, it is intractable to compute $e(G_1^y, G_2^{xy})$.*

Since this scheme is constructed based on BSW's CP-ABE scheme, CBE scheme remains semantically secure against chosen plaintext attack (IND-CPA) [5]. In addition, we introduce forward and backward derivation functions $(f, \bar{f})$ into CBE scheme. It is easy to find that one-way property of f and $\bar{f}$ can be guaranteed under the RSA assumption: given an RSA public key (N, e) and a ciphertext $C = M^e \in \mathbb{G}_{n'}$, it is infeasible to compute M. This is based on the fact that it is intractable to compute n, n' and $\frac{1}{e}$ (mod n') by factoring large number $N = pq$.

6.1 Security for Collusion Privilege Attacks

We depend on the confidentiality of r to guarantee the security of scheme against collusion privilege attacks. For sake of clarity, we only consider the collusion attacks by two adversaries to analyze all possible cases. For example, two users, u_i and u_j, intend to transfer the u_i's range attribute key $(D_t^{(i)}, D_{t_a}'^{(i)}, \bar{D}_{t_b}'^{(i)}, D_t''^{(i)})$ into the u_j's the attribute key $(D_t^{(j)}, D_{t_{a'}}'^{(j)}, \bar{D}_{t_{b'}}'^{(j)}, D_t''^{(j)})$ due to $t_a < t_{a'} < t_{b'} < t_b$, that is,

$$(D_t^{(i)}, D_{t_a}'^{(i)}, \bar{D}_{t_b}'^{(i)}, D_t''^{(i)}) = (g^{\tau_i} H(A_t)^r, v_{t_a}^r, \bar{v}_{t_b}^r, w^r),$$
$$(D_t^{(j)}, D_{t_{a'}}'^{(j)}, \bar{D}_{t_{b'}}'^{(j)}, D_t''^{(j)}) = (g^{\tau_j} H(A_t)^{r'}, v_{t_{a'}}^{r'}, \bar{v}_{t_{b'}}^{r'}, w^{r'}).$$

It is easy to find following two approaches to collude a new private key with more privileges:

1. $(\boxed{D_t^{(j)}}, D_{t_a}'^{(i)}, \bar{D}_{t_b}'^{(i)}, D_t''^{(i)}) = (g^{\tau_j} H(A_t)^r, v_{t_a}^r, \bar{v}_{t_b}^r, w^r),$

2. $(D_t^{(j)}, \boxed{D_{t_a}'^{(j)}, \bar{D}_{t_b}'^{(j)}}, D_t''^{(j)}) = (g^{\tau_j} H(A_t)^{r'}, v_{t_a}^{r'}, \bar{v}_{t_b}^{r'}, w^{r'}).$

We called them as CPA-I and CPA-II attacks, respectively.

For CPA-I attacks, we can prove the following theorem (see the proof in Appendix A):

THEOREM 1. *Given a CBE cryptosystem over the RSA-type elliptic curve system $\mathbb{S}_N$, it is intractable to extract the values g^{τ_k} or $H(A_t)^r$ from the user's key $SK_{\mathcal{L}} = (D_t = g^{\tau_k} H(A_t)^r, D_{t_a}' = v_{t_a}^r, D_{t_b}' = \bar{v}_{t_b}^r, D'' = w^r)$ under computational Co-Diffie-Hellman (Co-CDH) assumption.*

This theorem shows that the colluders cannot forge a new key by exchanging $g^{\tau k}$ or $H(A_t)^r$ from some known private-keys. Hence, our scheme can resist the CPA-I type attacks.

For CPA-II attacks, the attackers try to replace $(v_{t_a'}^{r'}, \bar{v}_{t_b'}^{r'})$ by $(v_{t_a}^{r'}, \bar{v}_{t_b}^{r'})$ according to $(v_{t_a}^r, \bar{v}_{t_b}^r)$, where $t_a < t_{a'} < t_{b'} < t_b$. However, the confidentiality of r and r' can guarantee the security of scheme against this attack in terms of the following theorem (see the proof in Appendix B).

THEOREM 2. *Given a multi-tuple* $(N, \varphi, \lambda, t_i, (\varphi^r)^{\lambda^{t_i}})$ *over the RSA-type elliptic curve system* $\mathbb{S}_N$, *where* $r \in_R \mathbb{Z}$. *It is intractable to compute* $(t_j, (\varphi^r)^{\lambda^{t_j}})$ *with* $t_j < t_i$ *for all PPT algorithms under the RSA assumption.*

6.2 Security for KS-CDA Attacks

In addition to collusion attack, chosen derivation-key attack (CDA) is a more easy-to-implement approach to break our CBE scheme, in which the adversary only needs to eavesdrop the channel via the proxy server. In this way, the adversary can obtain as much prior knowledge as possible from the stolen derivation keys, and attempt to forge a new private-key with the help of a known private-key.

Our scheme can prevent the CDA attack from two aspects: 1) the derivation key retains the user's unique identity τ_k, so that other users cannot use this key according to Theorem 1, and 2) a new random variant σ is also introduced into the derivation key to wrap the original private key under the Diffie-Hellmen assumption. Hence, we prove that our scheme is KS-CHA secure under the Bilinear co-CDH assumption (see the proof in Appendix C) as follows:

THEOREM 3. *Given a RSA-type elliptic curve system* $\mathbb{S}_N = (N = pq, \mathbb{G}, \mathbb{G}_T, e(\cdot, \cdot))$ *with order* $n = sn'$, *CBE cryptosystem over* $\mathbb{S}_N$ *is key secure against chosen derivation-key attacks (KS-CDA) under the Bilinear co-CDH assumption on* $\mathbb{G}$ *even if the secret* s *and* n' *is known.*

6.3 Security for SS-CDA Attacks

When a "honest but curious" service provider tries to reveal the encrypted contents, it can explore potential security issues of our scheme. First, we consider the ciphertext-only attack. We will present our CBE scheme is as strong as the BSW's scheme. In order to demonstrate that the cloud service providers cannot compromise the ciphertext without private keys, we compare the difference between the ciphertext of our scheme and that of BSW's scheme in Table 4.

Table 4: Difference between our CBE scheme and BSW's scheme

Scheme	Ciphertext		
BSW's scheme	$g^{(\alpha+\tau_k)/\beta}$	$g^{\tau k} H(A_l)^r$	w^r
Our scheme	$g^{(\alpha+\tau_k)/\beta}$	$g^{\tau k} H(A_l)^r$	$(v_{t_a} w)^r$

It is easy to find that the different between them is merely the value $v_{t_a}^r$ which is introduced into ciphertexts. In fact, our scheme is compatible with BSW's CP-ABE scheme for string-based matching. Hence, our scheme can be considered as an extension of BSW's scheme in this point. Thus, our scheme remains the same security properties as of BSW's scheme, i.e., semantically secure against chosen plaintext attack (IND-CPA) [5]. This means that the cloud service providers cannot obtains the contents of ciphertexts without the knowledge of private keys.

Next, we analyze whether the derivation keys $\{\widetilde{SK}_{\mathcal{L}'}\}$ observed by the adversary (or proxy) increase the adversary's advantage against our scheme. Although $\{\widetilde{SK}_{\mathcal{L}'}\}$ are delegated from the private key $\{SK_{\mathcal{L}}\}$, it cannot be used to decrypted the ciphertexts because 1) they contain only part of information of the private-keys, and 2) the random δ is used to avoid revealing the decryption information to the adversary. In order to verify the validity of this method, we prove that any (polynomial) number of derivation keys observed by the adversary cannot increased the advantage of attacks under the Bilinear co-CDH assumption. This theorem is described as follows (see the proof in Appendix D):

THEOREM 4. *Given a RSA-type elliptic curve system* $\mathbb{S}_N = (N = pq, \mathbb{G}, \mathbb{G}_T, e(\cdot, \cdot))$ *with order* $n = sn'$, *CBE cryptosystem over* $\mathbb{S}_N$ *is semantically secure against chosen derivation-key attacks (SS-CDA) under the Bilinear co-CDH assumption on* $\mathbb{G}$ *even if the secret* s *and* n' *is known.*

7. PERFORMANCE EVALUATION

In this section, we evaluate the performance of our CBE scheme. We first examine the complexity of our CBE scheme. Then, we discuss the parameter generation for a specific level of security. We also demonstrate the computational cost of performing comparison operations in our experiments.

7.1 Complexity Analysis

In this subsection, we will analyze the complexity of our CBE scheme. For simplification, we give several notations to denote the time for various operations in our scheme. $E(\mathbb{G})$ and $E(\mathbb{G}_T)$ are used to denote the exponentiation in $\mathbb{G}$ and $\mathbb{G}_T$, respectively. B is used to denote the bilinear pairing $e : \mathbb{G} \times \mathbb{G} \to \mathbb{G}_T$. We neglect the operations in $\mathbb{Z}_N$, the hash function $H : \{0, 1\}^* \to \mathbb{G}$ and the multiplication in $\mathbb{G}$ and $\mathbb{G}_T$, since they are much more efficient than exponentiation and paring operations. In Table 5, we analyze the computation and communication complexity for each phase, where $|\mathcal{T}|$ denotes the number of the leaf nodes in the tree, S denotes the set of attributes of encryptor and decryptor, and $l_{\mathbb{Z}_n}, l_{\mathbb{G}}, l_{\mathbb{G}_T}$ denote the length of elements in $\mathbb{Z}_n^*, \mathbb{G}, \mathbb{G}_T$, respectively.

In the tradition cryptosystem, decryption is an algorithm executed by a single party. But decryption in our scheme is converted into an interactive decryption protocol consisting with three algorithms: Delegate, Decrypt1, and Decrypt2. Although the sum of overheads of these algorithms is slightly larger than that of one single algorithm, we try to shift the mainly computational overheads of decryption into cloud servers, which have more computing power. In Table 5, the overheads of Decrypt1 are far larger than the sum of the other algorithms as a result that the bilinear pairing operation consumes more memory usage and CPU time than other operations. In addition, the sum of communication overheads of three algorithms is also consistent with that of one single algorithm. In particular, the output of Decrypt1 in a cloud server is a fixed data package size.

7.2 Parameter Generation

The security of CBE scheme is based on the RSA and CDH assumptions. Thus, we define the security parameters as follows: Let $N = pq$ be the RSA-modulus, we construct

Table 5: Performance Analysis of CBE Scheme

	Computation Complexity	Communication Complexity
Setup	$1 \cdot B + 3 \cdot E(\mathbb{G})$	$6 \cdot l_{\mathbb{G}} + 1 \cdot l_{\mathbb{G}_T} + 2 \cdot l_{\mathbb{G}}$
KeyGen	$(1 + 5|S|) \cdot E(\mathbb{G})$	$(1 + 4|S|) \cdot l_{\mathbb{G}}$
Encrypt	$(1 + 4|\mathcal{T}|) \cdot E(\mathbb{G}) + 1 \cdot E(\mathbb{G}_T)$	$4|\mathcal{T}| \cdot l_{\mathbb{G}} + 1 \cdot l_{\mathbb{G}_T}$
Delegate	$(1 + 7|S|) \cdot E(\mathbb{G})$	$3|S| \cdot l_{\mathbb{G}}$
Decrypt1	$2|S| \cdot B + |\mathcal{T}| \cdot E(\mathbb{G}_T)$	$1 \cdot l_{\mathbb{G}} + 1 \cdot l_{\mathbb{G}_T}$
Decrypt2	$1 \cdot B + 1 \cdot E(\mathbb{G})$	

DCOE scheme using composite order bilinear groups based on RSA-type Cryptosystem $\mathbb{S}_N$ over elliptic curve (EC) [8]. To ensure the security of $\mathbb{S}_N$, we assume that $\#E_p(a,b) = p + 1$ and $\#E_q(a,b) = q + 1$. Hence, there exists a group $\mathbb{G}_{N_n}$ of order $N_n = lcm(p+1, q+1)$ in $\mathbb{S}_N$. According to the above theorem, we define $n = s_1 s_2 p' q'$, $p + 1 = 2s_1 p'$ and $q + 1 = 2s_2 q'$, where p', q' are two sufficiently large primes and $|p'| = |q'| = 512$ bits. Such that, we can generate a bilinear map system $\mathbb{S}_N = (N, \mathbb{G}, \mathbb{G}_T, e(\cdot, \cdot))$ of composite order n, where $\mathbb{G}$ is a subgroup of order n in $\mathbb{G}_{N_n}$ due to $n|N_n$. Further, there exists the subgroup $\mathbb{G}'$ of order $n' = p'q'$ in $\mathbb{G}$, where $n'|n$. These parameters guarantee that our CBE system is secure against the cycling attack.

Finally, given two random generators $g, w \in \mathbb{G}$, we require that the Discrete Logarithm problems on $g' = g^{n'}$ and $w' = w^s$ are difficult in $\mathbb{G}$, that is, two orders, $ord_n(g')$ and $ord_n(w')$, are also sufficiently large. This is also the precondition of the Co-Diffie-Hellman assumption. On the other hand, it is easy to find that the DDH problem is easy in $\mathbb{G}$ because there exists a bilinear map $e : \mathbb{G} \times \mathbb{G} \to \mathbb{G}_T$. Hence, the CDH assumption holds under the above-mentioned parameters. Beyond this, the security of CBE scheme also depends on the Discrete Logarithm assumption in $\mathbb{G}_s$ where the length of $|s|$ is at less 160 bit.

7.3 Experimental Results

We have implemented our scheme on an experimental cloud computing environment (called M-Cloud). We simulated the encryption service and the storage service by using two local IBM servers with two Intel Core 2 processors at 2.16 GHz and 500M RAM running Windows Server 2003 and 64-bit Redhat Enterprise Linux Server 5.3, respectively. These two servers were connected into the M-Cloud via 250 MB/sec of network bandwidth. The storage server was responsible for managing a 16TB storage array based on Hadoop distributed file system (HDFS) 0.20 cluster with 8 worker nodes located in our laboratory. Using GMP and PBC libraries, we have developed a cryptographic library upon which our CBE systems can be constructed. This C library contains approximately 5,500 lines of code and has been tested on both Windows and Linux platforms.

We show the practical computational costs of algorithms for our scheme in Figure 8 under the effective calculation length is $L = 2048$-bits. In this example, for a certain comparison range $[1, Z]$, we generate a secret-key with licence $[t_1, t_2]$, where $t_1 \in_R [1, Z/4]$ and $t_2 \in_R [3Z/4, Z]$; and a message is encrypted by the time $t \in_R [Z/4, 3Z/4]$. So, we ensure that $\max(t - t_1, t_2 - t) \geq Z/4$. As the value of Z is changed from 4 to 65,536, the computational costs should keep pace with the growth of comparison ranges. However, this kind of growth is not significant by comparison with bilinear operations.

Our experimental results are showed in Figure 8, where

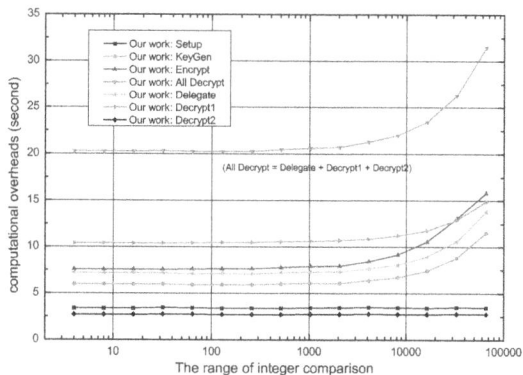

Figure 8: Computational costs of our scheme under different comparison range (the effective calculation length is $L = 2048$-bits).

the curve "All Decrypt" depicts the sum of operation overheads of Delegate, Decrypt1, and Decrypt2 in our scheme. It is obvious that the decryption overhead is well decomposed into these three algorithms, and the overhead of Decrypt1 is the largest of all algorithms. Also, the overhead of Delegate is slightly less than that of KeyGen algorithm, and Decrypt2 has a constant overhead (without regard to the growth of length of data). Hence, these experimental results verify our theoretical analysis in Section 7.1, that is, the decryption overheads can be effectively apportioned over cloud servers and clients.

8. RELATED WORK

In recent years, cryptographic access control [11, 13] has been introduced as a new access control paradigm to manage dynamic data sharing systems. It relies exclusively on cryptography to provide confidentiality and integrity of data managed by the systems, and is particularly designed to run in an untrusted or hostile environment which lacks of trust knowledge and global control [13]. Hence, attribute-based encryption (ABE) is proposed to realize a fine-grained attribute-based access control mechanism. Since Sahai and Waters [16] introduced ABE as a new means for encrypted access control in 2005, ABE has received much attention and many schemes have been proposed in recent years, such as, ciphertext-policy ABE (CP-ABE) [5, 9, 12] and key-policy ABE (KP-ABE) [10, 14].

One part of cryptographic access control focuses on time-based access control. There are a variety of applications requiring time-based access control. For example, a web-based electronic newspaper company could offer several types of subscription packages, covering different topics. Each user may decide to subscribe to one package for a certain period of time (e.g., a week, a month, or a year). Time control is of particular significance and has been concerned in access control [2, 3, 4]. In [3], the authors gave a temporal access control model and [2, 4] described applications in database systems and secure broadcasting. There have been plentiful time-bound key assignment schemes to set up the period of validity for the cryptographic key [19, 1, 17]. For example, Tzeng [19] used Lucas function and one-way hash function to achieve temporal control for cryptographic key assignment in hierarchical access control and provide the applications in secure broadcasting and cryptographic key backup.

In the context of ABE, there has been little work on studying time control or integer comparison mechanisms. Even though Bethencourt et al. [5] gave a bitwise-matching method to implement integer comparison based on CP-ABE scheme, this method unfortunately is not efficient enough for practical applications. In addition, Time-specific encryption (TSE) [15] and multi-dimensional range queries over encrypted data (MRQED) [18] are, in essence, constructed on the similar bitwise approach with BSW's CP-ABE scheme, which makes use of a policy tree (consists of 0/1 branches) on equal matching to realize the integer comparison.

9. CONCLUSIONS AND FUTURE WORK

In this paper, we have presented a novel comparison-based encryption scheme to support fine-grained access control in cloud computing. We also prove the security of our proposed scheme and demonstrate the efficiency of our scheme with experimental evaluation. As part of future work, we would extend our work to explore more efficient construction of CBE, the efficient CBE-oriented pairings, as well as the formal methods of security analysis for general binary relation. We will also optimize our solution to improve the performance of integer comparisons.

10. ACKNOWLEDGMENTS

The work of Y. Zhu, Y. Yu and H. Zhao was supported by the National Natural Science Foundation of China (Project No.61170264 and No.10990011) and the NDRC under Project "A cloud-based service for monitoring security threats in mobile Internet". This work of G.-J. Ahn and H. Hu was partially supported by the grants from US National Science Foundation (NSF-IIS-0900970 and NSF-CNS-0831360) and Department of Energy (DE-SC0004308).

11. REFERENCES

[1] G. Ateniese, A. D. Santis, A. L. Ferrara, and B. Masucci. Provably-secure time-bound hierarchical key assignment schemes. In *ACM Conference on Computer and Communications Security*, pages 288–297, 2006.

[2] E. Bertino, C. Bettini, E. Ferrari, and P. Samarati. A temporal access control mechanism for database systems. *IEEE Trans. Knowl. Data Eng.*, 8(1):67–80, 1996.

[3] E. Bertino, P. A. Bonatti, and E. Ferrari. Trbac: A temporal role-based access control model. *ACM Trans. Inf. Syst. Secur.*, 4(3):191–233, 2001.

[4] E. Bertino, B. Carminati, and E. Ferrari. A temporal key management scheme for secure broadcasting of xml documents. In V. Atluri, editor, *ACM Conference on Computer and Communications Security*, pages 31–40. ACM, 2002.

[5] J. Bethencourt, A. Sahai, and B. Waters. Ciphertext-policy attribute-based encryption. In *IEEE Symposium on Security and Privacy*, pages 321–334, 2007.

[6] D. Boneh and M. Franklin. Identity-based encryption from the weil pairing. In *Advances in Cryptology*

(*CRYPTO'2001*), volume 2139 of LNCS, pages 213–229, 2001.

[7] D. Boneh, E.-J. Goh, and K. Nissim. Evaluating 2-dnf formulas on ciphertexts. In J. Kilian, editor, *TCC*, volume 3378 of *Lecture Notes in Computer Science*, pages 325–341. Springer, 2005.

[8] S. D. Galbraith and J. F. McKee. Pairings on elliptic curves over finite commutative rings. In *10th IMA International Conference of Cryptography and Coding, Cirencester, UK, December 19-21, 2005, Proceedings*, pages 392–409, 2005.

[9] V. Goyal, A. Jain, O. Pandey, and A. Sahai. Bounded ciphertext policy attribute based encryption. In *ICALP (2)*, pages 579–591, 2008.

[10] V. Goyal, O. Pandey, A. Sahai, and B. Waters. Attribute-based encryption for fine-grained access control of encrypted data. In *ACM Conference on Computer and Communications Security*, pages 89–98, 2006.

[11] A. Harrington and C. D. Jensen. Cryptographic access control in a distributed file system. In *SACMAT*, pages 158–165. ACM, 2003.

[12] L. Ibraimi, Q. Tang, P. H. Hartel, and W. Jonker. Efficient and provable secure ciphertext-policy attribute-based encryption schemes. In *ISPEC*, pages 1–12, 2009.

[13] A. V. D. M. Kayem. *Adaptive Cryptographic Access Control for Dynamic Data Sharing Environments*. Ph.d thesis, Queeną́s University Kingston, Ontario, Canada, October 2008.

[14] R. Ostrovsky, A. Sahai, and B. Waters. Attribute-based encryption with non-monotonic access structures. In *ACM Conference on Computer and Communications Security*, pages 195–203, 2007.

[15] K. Paterson and E. Quaglia. Time-specific encryption. In J. Garay and R. De Prisco, editors, *Security and Cryptography for Networks*, volume 6280 of *Lecture Notes in Computer Science*, pages 1–16. Springer Berlin / Heidelberg, 2010.

[16] A. Sahai and B. Waters. Fuzzy identity-based encryption. In *EUROCRYPT*, pages 457–473, 2005.

[17] A. D. Santis, A. L. Ferrara, and B. Masucci. New constructions for provably-secure time-bound hierarchical key assignment schemes. In *SACMAT*, pages 133–138, 2007.

[18] E. Shi, J. Bethencourt, T. H. H. Chan, D. Song, and A. Perrig. Multi-dimensional range query over encrypted data. In *Security and Privacy, 2007. SP'07. IEEE Symposium on*, pages 350–364, may 2007.

[19] W. Tzeng. A time-bound cryptographic key assignment scheme for access control in a hierarchy. *IEEE Trans. on Knowledge and Data Engineering*, 14(1):182–188, 2002.

[20] S. Yu, C. Wang, K. Ren, and W. Lou. Achieving secure, scalable, and fine-grained data access control in cloud computing. In *INFOCOM*, pages 534–542, 2010.

APPENDIX

A. PROOF OF CPA-I ATTACK RESISTANT

PROOF. First, let $g^{\tau k} = w^\xi$, $H(A_t) = w^k$, $v_{t_a} = w^{k_1}$ and $\bar{v}_{t_b} = w^{k_2}$ in $\mathbb{G}$, so we use the same generator w to denote $SK_\mathcal{L}$ as $D_t = g^{\tau k} H(A_t)^r = w^{\xi+kr}$, $D_{t_a} = v_{t_a}^r = w^{k_1 r}$, $\bar{D}_{t_b} = \bar{v}_{t_b}^r = w^{k_2 r}$, and $D_t = w^r$ in $\mathbb{G}$. Such that, we convert the theorem into the problem: it is intractable to extract the values (w^ξ, w^{kr}) from $(w, w^r, w^k, w^{k_1}, w^{k_2}, w^{k_1 r}, w^{k_2 r}, w^{\xi+kr})$. It is obvious that two unknown k_1, k_2 have no concern with this problem, such that the above problem is reduced into $(w, w^r, w^k, w^{\xi+kr}) \rightarrow (w^\xi, w^{kr})$.

Assume that there exists a PPT algorithm $\mathcal{A}$ that can breaks this problem. Given a Co-CDH problem $(G_1, G_1^x, G_2, G_2^y) \rightarrow G_2^{xy}$, we can construct an efficient algorithm $\mathcal{B}$ to solve this Co-CDH problem according to the algorithm $\mathcal{A}$ as follows:

(1) $\mathcal{B}$ invokes the algorithm $\mathcal{A}$ on input $(w = G_1, w^r = G_1^x, w^k = G_2^y, w^{\xi+kr} = G_2^z)$, where z is a random integer;

(2) If the output of algorithm $\mathcal{A}$ is (R_1, R_2), $\mathcal{B}$ checks whether

two equations $R_1 \cdot R_2 = G_2^z$ and $e(G_1, R_2) = e(G_1^x, G_2^y)$ hold. If not, $\mathcal{B}$ repeats step (1);

(3) $\mathcal{B}$ computes $G_2^{xy} = R_2$ and returns it as output.

The output of algorithm $\mathcal{B}$ is valid because the input of $\mathcal{A}$ satisfies $r = x$, $w^{kr} = (G_2^y)^r = G_2^{xy} = R_2$, $e(G_1, R_2) = e(G_1, G_2^{xy}) = e(G_1^x, G_2^y)$, and $G_2^z = w^{\xi + kr} = R_1 \cdot R_2$.

This means that the algorithm $\mathcal{B}$ is a PPT algorithm to solve Co-CDH problem only if $\mathcal{A}$ is also a PPT algorithm. But it is well-known that the Co-CDH problem is hard for any PPT algorithms, hence this contradicts the hypothesis. $\square$

B. PROOF OF CPA-II ATTACK RESISTANT

PROOF. Seeking a contradiction, we assume that there exists a PPT algorithm $\mathcal{A}$ that can get a $(t_j, (\varphi^r)^{\lambda^{t_j}})$ under above input $(N, \varphi, \lambda, t_i, (\varphi^r)^{\lambda^{t_i}})$, where $t_j < t_i$. We can use the algorithm $\mathcal{A}$ to construct a PPT algorithm $\mathcal{B}$ that can break the RSA problem over elliptic curve: given the public-key $(\mathbb{G}, N, e)$ and a ciphertext C to compute the plaintext $M = C^{e^{-1}}$. The algorithm $\mathcal{B}$ is described as follows:

(1) Given a RSA problem $(\mathbb{G}, N, e)$, $\mathcal{B}$ invokes the algorithm $\mathcal{A}$ on input $(N, \varphi, \lambda = e, t_i, C)$, where t_i is randomly chosen in integer set and $\varphi = C^{r'}$ is a random element in $\mathbb{G}$;

(2) If the algorithm $\mathcal{A}$ returns a solution (t_j, R), $\mathcal{B}$ first checks if $R^{\lambda^{t_i - t_j}} = C$ (or $\varphi = R^{r'\lambda^{t_i - t_j}}$) and $t_i - t_j - 1 \geq 0$ (or $t_i - t_j > 0$). If not, $\mathcal{B}$ repeats step (1);

(3) $\mathcal{B}$ computes computing $M = R^{e^{t_i - t_j - 1}} \in \mathbb{G}$ in terms of $R^{\lambda^{t_i - t_j}} = C = M^\lambda$, and returns the ciphertext M.

In the algorithm $\mathcal{B}$, we cannot know the secret $r = \frac{1}{\lambda^{t_i} r'}$ (mod n') for unknown n' (because of the actual difficulty of factoring large number $N = pq$), event through $\varphi = C^{r'}$ and r' is known. This means that the algorithm $\mathcal{B}$ is a PPT algorithm to solve RSA problem only if $\mathcal{A}$ is also a PPT algorithm. But it is well-known that the RSA problem is hard for any PPT algorithms, hence this contradicts the hypothesis. $\square$

C. PROOF OF KS-CDA RESISTANT

PROOF. Assume that there exists a PPT algorithm $\mathcal{A}$ that can breaks this problem over $\mathbb{S}_N$ with the known s, n'. Given a Co-CDH problem $(G_1, G_1^x, G_2, G_2^y) \to G_2^{xy}$ in $\mathbb{G}$, we can construct an efficient algorithm $\mathcal{B}$ to solve this Co-CDH problem according to the algorithm $\mathcal{A}$ as follows:

(1) **Setup**: $\mathcal{B}$ follows the *Setup* algorithm to get the elements $(g, h, \xi, \lambda, \mu)$ and then sets $w = G_2$, $\varphi = G_2^{k_1} \in \mathbb{G}_{n'}$, $\bar{\varphi} = G_2^{k_2} \in \mathbb{G}_{n'}$, where α, β, k_1, k_2 are known by $\mathcal{B}$, $s|k_1$, and $s|k_2$. Therefore, $\mathcal{B}$ sends $PK = (\mathbb{S}_N, g, h, \zeta, w, \varphi, \bar{\varphi}, \lambda, \mu)$ to the adversary $\mathcal{A}$ and $H(\cdot)$ can be obtained by the random Oracle query of $\mathcal{B}$.

(2) **Learning**: $\mathcal{A}$ chooses a range attribute A_t and query Delegate algorithm with the polynomial number of users $u_{k_1}, \cdots, u_{k_s}$ with any time interval $A_{t_i}[t_{k_i}, t_{k_i'}] \in \mathcal{L}_i$. For each query, $\mathcal{B}$ chooses two random τ_i, σ_i and $H_i \in \mathbb{G}$ and sets $r_i = y$, and then computes

$$\widetilde{D}_{t_i} = (g^{\tau_i} H(A_t)^{r_i})^{\sigma_i} = (g^{\tau_i} G_2^{xy})^{\sigma_i} = H_i^{\sigma_i},$$
$$\widetilde{D}'_{t_{k_i}} = (v_{t_{k_i}} w)^{r_i \sigma_i} = (G_2^{yk_1 \lambda^{t_{k_i}}} G_2^y)^{\sigma_i} = (G_2^y)^{\sigma_i(k_1 \lambda^{t_{k_i}} + 1)},$$
$$\widetilde{D}'_{t_{k_i'}} = (\bar{v}_{t_{k_i'}} w)^{r_i \sigma_i} = (G_2^{yk_2 \lambda^{(Z - t_{k_i'})}} G_2^y)^{\sigma_i} = (G_2^y)^{\sigma_i(k_2 \lambda^{(Z - t_{k_i'})} + 1)},$$

and sends these derivation keys $\widetilde{SK}_{\mathcal{L}_i} = \{(\widetilde{D}_{t_i}, \widetilde{D}'_{t_{k_i}}, \widetilde{D}'_{t_{k_i'}})\}$ to the adversary $\mathcal{A}$. Note that, $H(A_t) = G_2^x$ and $\widetilde{SK}_{\mathcal{L}_i}$ is anonymous for $\mathcal{B}$ because τ_i is unknown.

(3) **Challenge**: $\mathcal{B}$ chooses two random τ^*, r^* and defines $r_i =$

$\frac{r^*}{z}$ which is unknown by $\mathcal{B}$. And then it computes $D^* = g^{(\alpha + \tau^*)/\beta}$,

$$D_t^* = g^{\tau^*} H(A_t)^{r^*} = g^{\tau^*} (G_1^x)^{r^*},$$
$$D'^*_{t_i} = v_{t_i}^{r^*} = G_2^{k_1 \lambda^{t_i} \frac{r^*}{z}} = G_1^{k_1 r^* \lambda^{t_i}},$$
$$D'^*_{t_j} = \bar{v}_{t_j}^{r^*} = G_2^{k_2 \lambda^{Z - t_j} \frac{r^*}{z}} = G_1^{k_2 r^* \lambda^{Z - t_j}},$$
$$D''^*_t = w^{r^*} = G_2^{\frac{r^*}{z}} = G_1^{r^*}.$$

Hence, $\mathcal{B}$ sends $SK_{\mathcal{L}} = (D^*, (D_t^*, D'^*_{t_a}, D'^*_{t_b}, D''^*_t)\}$ as a challenge private key to $\mathcal{A}$, where $\mathcal{L} = A_t[t_i, t_j]$.

(3) **Response**: If the output of algorithm $\mathcal{A}$ is $(\mathcal{L}_i, SK_{\mathcal{L}_i})$, where $SK_{\mathcal{L}_i} = (D^*, (D_{t_i}^*, D'^*_{t_{k_i}}, D'^*_{t_{k_i'}}, D''^*_t))$ and $A_{t_i}[t_{k_i}, t_{k_i'}] \in \mathcal{L}_i$, $\mathcal{B}$ checks whether the equations

$$D'^*_{t_{k_i}} = G_2^{yk_1 \lambda^{t_{k_i}}}, D'^*_{t_{k_i'}} = G_2^{yk_2 \lambda^{(Z - t_{k_i'})}}, D''^*_t = G_2^y$$

and $e(G_1, D_{t_i}^*/g^{r^*}) = e(G_1^x, G_2^y)$ hold. If not, $\mathcal{B}$ repeats step (1), Else, $\mathcal{B}$ computes $G_2^{xy} = D_{t_i}^*/g^{r^*}$ and returns it as output.

The output of algorithm $\mathcal{B}$ is valid because the input of $\mathcal{A}$ satisfies $D_{t_i}^* = g^{r^*} G_2^{xy}$. This means that the algorithm $\mathcal{B}$ is a PPT algorithm to solve Co-CDH problem only if $\mathcal{A}$ is also a PPT algorithm. But it is well-known that the Co-CDH problem is hard for any PPT algorithms, hence this contradicts the hypothesis. $\square$

D. PROOF OF SS-CDA RESISTANT

PROOF. Assume that there exists a PPT algorithm $\mathcal{A}$ that can breaks this problem over $\mathbb{S}_N$ with the known s, n'. Given a Bilinear Co-CDH problem $(G_1, G_1^x, G_1^y, G_2, G_2^y) \to e(G_1^y, G_2^{xy})$, we can construct an efficient algorithm $\mathcal{B}$ to solve this Co-CDH problem according to the algorithm $\mathcal{A}$ as follows:

(1) **Setup**: $\mathcal{B}$ chooses a random integer θ and defines $\alpha = xy, \beta = \frac{\theta}{z}$, where $z = \log_{G_1} G_2$ is unknown. $\mathcal{B}$ chooses the random integers λ, μ, k_1, k_2 to computes $g = G_1^{n'}$, $h = w^y = G_1^\theta$, $w = G_2$, $\zeta = e(G_1^x, G_2^y) = e(G_1, G_2)^{xy}$, $\varphi = G_2^{k_1}$, and $\bar{\varphi} = G_2^{k_2}$, where $s|k_1$ and $s|k_2$. So that $\mathcal{B}$ generates $PK = (\mathbb{S}_N, g, h, \zeta, w, \varphi, \bar{\varphi}, \lambda, \mu)$ and sends it to $\mathcal{A}$. $H(\cdot)$ can be obtained by the random Oracle query of $\mathcal{B}$.

(2) **Learning**: $\mathcal{A}$ can send the polynomial number of *Delegate* queries with any time interval $\mathcal{L}_i = \{A_{t_i}[t_{k_i}, t_{k_i'}]\}$. For each query, $\mathcal{B}$ chooses the random τ_i, σ, r_i and computes

$$\widetilde{D}_{t_i} = (g^{\tau_i} H(A_{t_i})^{r_i})^\sigma = G_1^{\sigma \tau_i} G_2^{\sigma k_i r_i},$$
$$\widetilde{D}'_{t_{k_i}} = (v_{t_j}^{r_i} \cdot w^{r_i})^\sigma = G_2^{\sigma r_i(k_1 \lambda^{t_{k_i}} + 1)},$$
$$\widetilde{D}'_{t_{k_i'}} = (\bar{v}_{t_i}^{r_i} \cdot w^{r_i})^\sigma = G_2^{\sigma r_i(k_2 \lambda^{(Z - t_{k_i'})} + 1)},$$

where $H(A_{t_i}) = G_2^{k_i}$ and k_i is random integer. Finally, $\mathcal{B}$ returns $\widetilde{SK}_{\mathcal{L}_i} = \{\widetilde{D}_{t_i}, \widetilde{D}'_{t_{k_i}}, \widetilde{D}'_{t_{k_i'}}\}_{A_{t_i}[t_{k_i}, t_{k_i'}] \in \mathcal{L}_i}$ to $\mathcal{A}$.

(3) **Challenge**: $\mathcal{B}$ sets $s = y$ and chooses a random a and $G_2^b = G_2^y/G_2^a$, where $w^s = G_2^y$ and $s = a + b$. Such that, $\mathcal{B}$ computes $h^s = (G_1^y)^\theta$, and

$$\bar{E}_{t_i} = (\bar{v}_{t_i} w)^a = (G_2^a)^{(k_2 \mu^{Z - t_i} + 1)}, \quad E'_{t_i} = H(A_t)^a = (G_2^a)^{k_i},$$
$$E_{t_j} = (v_{t_j} w)^b = (G_2^b)^{(k_1 \lambda^{t_j} + 1)}, \quad E'_{t_j} = H(A_t)^b = (G_2^b)^{k_i}.$$

$\mathcal{B}$ outputs $\mathcal{H}_{\mathcal{P}}^* = (\mathcal{T}, h^s, \{((\bar{E}_{t_i}, E'_{t_i}), (E_{t_j}, E'_{t_j}))\}_{A_t[t_i, t_j] \in \mathcal{T}})$ as the challenge ciphertext to $\mathcal{A}$.

(4) **Response**: $\mathcal{A}$ outputs a session key ek^* to $\mathcal{B}$, and $\mathcal{B}$ also outputs it as result.

If the output of algorithm $\mathcal{A}$ is valid, $\mathcal{B}$ is also valid because $ek^* = e(g^\alpha, w^s) = e(G_1^{xy}, G_2^y) = e(G_1^y, G_2^{xy})$. This means that the algorithm $\mathcal{B}$ is a PPT algorithm to solve Co-CDH problem only if $\mathcal{A}$ is also a PPT algorithm. But it is well-known that the Co-CDH problem is hard for any PPT algorithms, hence this contradicts the hypothesis. $\square$

Relationship-Based Access Control:
Its Expression and Enforcement Through Hybrid Logic

Glenn Bruns
Bell Labs, Alcatel-Lucent
Glenn.Bruns@alcatel-lucent.com

Philip Fong   Ida Siahaan
University of Calgary
{pwlfong, isriaha}@ucalgary.ca

Michael Huth
Imperial College London
M.Huth@imperial.ac.uk

ABSTRACT

Access control policy is typically defined in terms of attributes, but in many applications it is more natural to define permissions in terms of relationships that resources, systems, and contexts may enjoy. The paradigm of relationship-based access control has been proposed to address this issue, and modal logic has been used as a technical foundation.

We argue here that hybrid logic – a natural and well-established extension of modal logic – addresses limitations in the ability of modal logic to express certain relationships.

We identify a fragment of hybrid logic to be used for expressing relationship-based access-control policies, show that this fragment supports important policy idioms, and demonstrate that it removes an exponential penalty in existing attempts of specifying complex relationships such as "at least three friends". We also capture the previously studied notion of *relational* policies in a static type system.

Categories and Subject Descriptors

D. Software [**D.4 OPERATING SYSTEMS**]: D.4.6 Security and Protection Subjects: Access controls

General Terms

Security

Keywords

Access-control models, Hybrid Logic, Relationship-based Access Control

1. INTRODUCTION

Access control is typically specified and enforced in terms of attributes: authenticated properties that must be possessed by the requester of a resource, the context of the request or the resource itself in order to grant access.

But there are many applications in which the decision of granting access should not primarily be based on attributes

(e.g. whether a VPN connection is on or off) but rather on relationships that resources, systems, and contexts may enjoy. For example, a teenager may want to share pictures from a concert only with friends who actually went to the event. Expressing such policies through attributes is hard to do even within a monolithic and closed system, and is simply not feasible in distributed and open systems.

The paradigm of relationship-based access control [12, 10, 8] has been proposed to address this shortcoming of attributes. This research gives us a first understanding of appropriate *semantic* notions for relationship-based access control (see e.g. [8]). Yet, despite the initial progress reported in [10], it is less clear what appropriate syntactic counterparts these policies should have.

Ideally, a policy language for relationalship-based access control should be

- expressive enough to capture important policy idioms
- not so expressive as to make reasoning intractable
- intuitive for expressing and enforcing access control,
- formal, to support policy analysis, implementation, and optimization, and
- based on robust mathematical foundations.

Recent work [8, 10] has proposed the use of modal logics as such a mathematical foundation. We entirely agree with the spirit of that proposal, that a policy be specified as a formula of some logic. But the work in [10] already recognized that modal logic alone cannot express some pertinent relationships. Features that appear to be lacking include:

- the ability to bind a node to a principal in a relationship graph
- graded variants of modalities, e.g. "at least four friends"
- the ability to evaluate sub-policies from the perspective of a named principal, and
- the ability to *efficiently* compute a policy decision by evaluating a formula on a relationship graph.

The latter point is crucial, since existing attempts to realize the aforementioned features appear to do so at the expense of losing efficieny of policy evaluation.

We argue here that a natural and well-established extension of modal logic – *hybrid logic* [3] – can overcome these shortcomings and provide a robust mathematical foundation for relationship-based access control.

A key contribution of this paper is the recognition that fragments of hybrid logic are well-suited to the needs of relationship-based access control. Another key contribution of this paper is the demonstration that our proposed use of hybrid logic eliminates a known exponential penalty incurred in expressing important policy idioms such as "at

$$t ::= n \mid x$$
$$\phi ::= t \mid p \mid \neg\phi \mid \phi_1 \wedge \phi_2 \mid \langle i \rangle \phi \mid \langle -i \rangle \phi \mid$$
$$\qquad @_t \phi \mid \downarrow x\, \phi$$

Figure 1: The syntax of a simple hybrid logic HL, where n ranges over *Nom*, x ranges over *Var*, p ranges over *AP*, and i ranges over *I*.

least two colleagues" in existing modal logics for relationship-based access control [10].

As further evidence of the utility of hybrid logic, we also devise a fragment of this hybrid logic that gives rise only to policies whose access-control decisions depend only on the connectedness structure between the owner and the requester of a resource in a network graph.

Outline of paper.

We present a hybrid logic suitable for access control in Section 2. We explain, in Section 3, how this hybrid logic can be used for an access-control model based on relationships. Section 4 is devoted to examples of useful policy idioms written in this hybrid logic. A local model-checking algorithm for policy decisions is given in Section 5. In Section 6, a type system is developed for a fragment of our hybrid logic and it is shown that type-safe such formulas determine so-called *relational* policies. Related work is reflected upon in Section 7. A paper summary and remarks about future work conclude the paper in Section 8.

2. HYBRID LOGIC

We define the syntax and semantics of hybrid logic, with a view towards its application in policy-based access control.

Syntax.

We take as given a set *Nom* of *nominal* symbols, an infinite set *Var* of *variable* symbols, a set *I* of *label* symbols, and a set *AP* of *propositional* symbols. Nominals and variables allow us to bind nodes in relationship graphs to principals. Labels represent the different relationships present in that graph. Using these sets of symbols, we define formulas of a hybrid logic HL in Fig. 1. Other logical symbols can be derived in the usual way. For example,

$$[i]\phi \stackrel{\text{def}}{=} \neg\langle i \rangle \neg\phi \qquad \phi \vee \psi \stackrel{\text{def}}{=} \neg(\neg\phi \wedge \neg\psi)$$
$$\bot \stackrel{\text{def}}{=} p \wedge \neg p \qquad \top \stackrel{\text{def}}{=} p \vee \neg p$$

express a must modality for label i, disjunction, falsity, and truth (respectively).

Semantics.

We define models for HL, which express relationship graphs for access control, as well as valuations, which map variables to nodes in relationship graphs.

DEFINITION 1. *1. A model M of HL is a triple*

$$(S, \{R_i \subseteq S \times S \mid i \in I\}, V) \tag{1}$$

where S is a non-empty set of nodes, R_i a binary relation on S for all $i \in I$, and $V: (Nom \cup AP) \to 2^S$ a total function with $V(n)$ a singleton for all n in Nom.

2. A valuation $g: Var \to S$ is a total function. For some such g, we write $g[x \mapsto s]$ for the valuation that maps x to s, and maps t to $g(t)$ if $t \neq x$.

$$
\begin{array}{llll}
M, s, g & \models & x & \stackrel{\text{def}}{=} & s = g(x) \\
M, s, g & \models & n & \stackrel{\text{def}}{=} & V(n) = \{s\} \\
M, s, g & \models & p & \stackrel{\text{def}}{=} & s \in V(p) \\
M, s, g & \models & \neg\phi & \stackrel{\text{def}}{=} & M, s, g \not\models \phi \\
M, s, g & \models & \phi_1 \wedge \phi_2 & \stackrel{\text{def}}{=} & M, s, g \models \phi_1 \text{ and } M, s, g \models \phi_2 \\
M, s, g & \models & \langle i \rangle \phi & \stackrel{\text{def}}{=} & M, s', g \models \phi \text{ for some } (s, s') \in R_i \\
M, s, g & \models & \langle -i \rangle \phi & \stackrel{\text{def}}{=} & M, s', g \models \phi \text{ for some } (s', s) \in R_i \\
M, s, g & \models & @_n \phi & \stackrel{\text{def}}{=} & M, s^*, g \models \phi \text{ where } V(n) = \{s^*\} \\
M, s, g & \models & @_x \phi & \stackrel{\text{def}}{=} & M, g(x), g \models \phi \\
M, s, g & \models & \downarrow x\, \phi & \stackrel{\text{def}}{=} & M, s, g[x \mapsto s] \models \phi \\
\end{array}
$$

Figure 2: Satisfaction relation $M, s, g \models \phi$ specifying that formula ϕ of hybrid logic HL is true in node s of model M under valuation g.

The intuition behind function V is that $V(p)$ is the set of nodes at which p is true, and that $V(n)$ is the set containing the unique node in the relationship graph of M "named" n by V. Valuations g are total functions from variables to nodes. Note that attributes of principals can be expressed in models of HL through propositions in set AP.

The meaning of formulas in HL is defined by a satisfaction relation $M, s, g \models \phi$, defined inductively in Figure 2.

Each nominal and variable is true at a single node. The meaning of nominals is specified through function V; the meaning of variables through valuation g. Propositions, on the other hand, are true at zero, one, or more nodes.

The meanings of conjunction and negation are standard, as is the meaning of the modalities. Formula $\langle i \rangle \phi$ holds at s if there is some R_i-successor s' of s such that ϕ holds at s'. Dually, $\langle -i \rangle \phi$ holds at s if there is some R_i-predecessor $\tilde{s}$ of S such that ϕ holds at $\tilde{s}$.

We now discuss the *hybrid* operators of HL. Intuitively, $@_t \phi$ jumps to the node named by t, whereas $\downarrow x\, \phi$ binds the current node to variable x. Formally, formula $@_t \phi$ says that ϕ holds at the unique node identified by t with respect to function V (if t is a nominal) or valuation g (if t is a variable). Formula $\downarrow x\, \phi$ holds at node s if ϕ holds at s, but where now valuation g is updated so that x identifies s.

Notational conventions.

Operator $\downarrow x$ is a binding operator with the usual notions of free and bound variables. We fix some notation for satisfaction checks.

DEFINITION 2. *Let ϕ be a formula of HL.*

1. If ϕ contains no free variables, we write $M, s \models \phi$ for any $M, s, g \models \phi$, as the evaluation of latter expression is independent of the choice of valuation g.

2. If ϕ contains only free variables $x_1, \ldots, x_n$, we write $M, s, [x_1 \mapsto s_1, \ldots, x_n \mapsto s_n] \models \phi$ for any $M, s, g[x_1 \mapsto s_1, \ldots, x_n \mapsto s_n] \models \phi$, as the evaluation of the latter expression is again independent of the choice of g.

3. If ϕ is the Boolean combination of formulas of the form $@_t \psi$, we write $M, g \models \phi$, as then either $M, s, g \models \phi$ is true at all nodes s or false at all nodes s.

We now use our hybrid logic HL to define an access-control model, focusing on the policy-decision point of such a model.

3. ACCESS-CONTROL MODEL

We outline here an archetypical model for relationship-based access control that uses hybrid logic for expressing access-control policies.

Protection state.

A protection state is simply a model M of HL in which the elements of S denote principals. The binary relations R_i represent interpersonal relations tracked by the access-control system. Each label i in I identifies one type of relationship (e.g., "parent"), such that (s_1, s_2) is in R_i iff principals s_1 and s_2 participate in a relationship of type i. In short, $(S, \{R_i \mid i \in I\})$ represents a directed, poly-relational social network. The valuation V specifies attributes of the principals. Each propositional symbol p in AP denotes an attribute. If a principal s in S has the attribute p, then s is in $V(p)$. Similarly, globally significant principals (e.g., trusted authorities) are identified by nominals via V.

Fragment of HL for specifying access-control policies.

Principals own resources and seek access on resources. We associate with each object *obj* a formula ϕ in HL that expresses a relationship between two parties: the *owner* and the *requester*. Then the requester is permitted access to *obj* if the owner and requester are in the relationship specified by ϕ. This approach has been suggested in [8] already, for a different logic, and it is what makes the access-control model *relationship-based*.

We propose to use two distinguished variables own and req to denote the principal who is the owner and the requester of the implicit object, respectively.

DEFINITION 3. *Let* HL(own, req) *be the set of formulas of* HL *that*

- *contain at most* own *and* req *as free variable, and*
- *are Boolean combinations of formulas of form* $@_{\text{own}} \phi$ *and* $@_{\text{req}} \psi$.

We refer to formulas of HL(own, req) as *policies*. A common policy pattern is a conjunction

$$@_{\text{own}} \phi \wedge @_{\text{req}} \psi \tag{2}$$

This specifies an access-control policy of the resource owner own via two sub-policies. Sub-policy $@_{\text{own}} \phi$ represents the perspective of the owner in the protection state, while $@_{\text{req}} \psi$ represents the requester's perspective. Note that (2) is consistent with using only one such perspective. For example, dropping the second conjunct amounts to choosing ψ to be $\top$ and so the righthand conjunct is redundant.

Authorization decision.

The access-control system arrives at an authorization decision as follows. Given a protection state (i.e., a model) M, a requesting principal r has permission to access an object *obj* in *Obj* that is controlled by principal o according to a policy *pol* in HL(own, req) iff the following condition holds:

$$M, [\text{own} \mapsto o, \text{req} \mapsto r] \models pol \tag{3}$$

Intuitively, the only free variables own and req of formula *pol* of HL(own, req) get bound to the principals named by the owner and requester, respectively, and this formula is then evaluated with those bindings.

Thus, checking whether an access is granted amounts to checking the satisfaction of a HL(own, req) formula with respect to a valuation. We discuss a local model-checking algorithm for HL(own, req) below.

Policy functions.

Through the semantics of hybrid logic, which has been defined as a satisfaction relation, every policy ϕ in HL(own, req) induces a *policy function*, which maps protection states to binary *permission relations*.

DEFINITION 4. *1. A policy function P is a total function $M = (S_M, \dots) \mapsto P(M)$ from models M to binary relations $P(M) \subseteq S_M \times S_M$.*

2. The policy function induced by a policy ϕ of HL(own, req), *written* p$[\phi]$, *is defined as follows:*

$$\mathsf{p}[\phi] = \{(o, r) \in S_M \times S_M \mid M, [\text{own} \mapsto o, \text{req} \mapsto r] \models \phi\}$$

The intuition behind policy functions is that a requester r can access an object of owner o in protection state M if (o, r) is in $P(M)$ – and is denied access if (o, r) is not in $P(M)$. Note that a policy function maps a collection of relations (plus a mapping for nominals and propositions) over a set of principals to a single permission relation over the same set.

4. EXAMPLE POLICIES

We now provide example policies, starting with basic ones.

Basic policies.

If the owner of an object defines the policy to be

$$@_{\text{own}} \langle friend \rangle \text{req} \tag{4}$$

then every friend of the resource owner is granted access to that resource. Note that this policy specifies no constraints from the perspective of the requester. Similarly, the formula

$$@_{\text{own}} \langle friend \rangle (\text{req} \vee \langle friend \rangle \text{req}) \tag{5}$$

captures a "friend or a friend of a friend" policy. The formula

$$@_{\text{own}} (\langle teammate \rangle \text{req} \wedge \langle friend \rangle \text{req}) \tag{6}$$

specifies that all friends who are teammates get access. This example already hints at the usefulness of hybrid logic. The use of the variable req allows us to refer to some principal who is *both* a teammate and a friend of the owner.

If req behaved like a normal proposition that could be true at zero or more nodes, then we could not capture this semantic conjunction in the logic; the existential quantification of $\langle i \rangle$ does not distribute through conjunction.

The policies we have specified so far are variants or adaptations of policies written the logic E of [10]. To see the true benefits of using HL, we write more complex policies next.

More complex policies.

Consider a teacher who wants to confine access to her picture to friends who are teachers, but who also wants to grant access to only those friends of such friends who are not taught by friends. This is hard to express in English, but there is a true case of an English teacher who had to resign because her picture could be seen by student friends of friends – unbeknownst to her. Hybrid logic can express

119

such a policy unambiguously. One possible formula is

$$@_{\mathsf{own}} (\langle friend \rangle (\mathsf{req} \wedge isTeacher) \vee$$
$$\langle friend \rangle (isTeacher \wedge \langle friend \rangle \mathsf{req} \wedge$$
$$\neg \langle student \rangle \mathsf{req})) \quad (7)$$

Note that this formula is indeed in $\mathsf{HL}(\mathsf{own}, \mathsf{req})$. The first disjunct specifies that access is granted if the requester is a friend who is a teacher, where $isTeacher$ is in AP. The second disjunct specifies that access is granted if the requester is a friend of a teacher friend of the owner, but where the requester is also not a student of that teacher friend.

We point out that this policy does not prevent the scenario where access is granted to *some* student of a teacher friend, since the may modality is an existential quantification.

This policy also illustrates the utility of propositions (attributes), as we here want to express that a friend is *some* teacher, not necessarily the teacher or student of the owner or requester. This property could be expressed through $\langle teacher \rangle \top$, someone is a teacher if they teach someone. But such an encoding becomes ackward for unary relations such as $isDiabetic$, so we do include propositions in our logic HL.

Dual policies.

The last example illustrates that we can compose negative and positive permissions. For example, the policy

$$@_{\mathsf{own}} \langle friend \rangle (\mathsf{req} \wedge \neg Alice) \quad (8)$$

says access is granted to all friends, except to *Alice*, a principal that is a nominal in *Nom*. Note that this policy makes no assumption about whether or not *Alice* is actually a friend.

The policy expressed in (8) serves also as an example for how one might "dualize" a policy written from the perspective of one of the principals into an equivalent one written from the perspective of the other principal. The policy

$$@_{\mathsf{req}} (\langle -friend \rangle \mathsf{own} \wedge \neg Alice) \quad (9)$$

is intuitively equivalent to that in (8), but of form $@_{\mathsf{req}} \phi$.

Graded modalities.

A nice feature of hybrid logic is that it allows us to express so called *graded* may modalities [3] as syntactic sugar of the logic. To see this let n be a positive natural number, and let $\langle i \rangle_n$ be the corresponding graded may modality for label i. The intuition of $\langle i \rangle_n \phi$ is that it holds in node s iff there are *at least* n many R_i-successors of s at which ϕ holds.

For example, a policy that grants access if there are at least 3 friends of the owner who satisfy ϕ can be specified as

$$@_{\mathsf{own}} \langle friend \rangle_3 \phi \quad (10)$$

To see that $\langle i \rangle_n \phi$ is expressible in HL, take $n+1$ many variables $x, y_1, y_2, \ldots y_n$ that do not occur in ϕ and define

$$\langle i \rangle_n \phi \stackrel{\text{def}}{=} \downarrow x \langle i \rangle \downarrow y_1 (\phi \wedge \quad (11)$$
$$@_x \langle i \rangle \downarrow y_2 (\neg y_1 \wedge \phi \wedge$$
$$@_x \langle i \rangle \downarrow y_3 (\neg y_1 \wedge \neg y_2 \wedge \phi \wedge$$
$$\cdots$$
$$@_x \langle i \rangle \downarrow y_n (\neg y_1 \wedge \neg y_2 \wedge \cdots \wedge \neg y_{n-1} \wedge \phi)) \ldots)$$

This standard encoding says that at the current node, named x, there is some R_i-successor y_1 of x that satisfies ϕ, and there is some R_i-successor y_2 of x that is different from

y_1 and satisfies ϕ, and so on. This clearly renders the desired semantic effect of having at least n many R_i-successors of the currrent node that satisfy ϕ.

Graded modalities give us the ability to count exactly as well. To specify that there are exactly n R_i-successors that satisfy ϕ, we may write

$$\langle i \rangle_{=n} \phi \stackrel{\text{def}}{=} \langle i \rangle_n \phi \wedge \neg \langle i \rangle_{n+1} \phi \quad (12)$$

One can model a rudimentary trust level in a network of friends by asking whether the requester is connected to the owner by a path of *friend* labels of length at most k. We can specify such policies inductively for $k \geq 1$ as

$$\mathsf{depth}[friend, 1] \stackrel{\text{def}}{=} \langle friend \rangle \mathsf{req} \quad (13)$$
$$\mathsf{depth}[friend, k+1] \stackrel{\text{def}}{=} \mathsf{depth}[friend, k] \vee$$
$$\langle friend \rangle \mathsf{depth}[friend, k]$$

We can combine this trust mechanism with graded modalities to express a policy that grants access if there are at least two colleagues who have sufficient trust in the requester:

$$@_{\mathsf{own}} \langle colleague \rangle_2 \mathsf{depth}[friend, 3] \quad (14)$$

Next, let us now consider a policy cf_k based on common friends. It grants access to the owner, to his friends, and to those who have at least $k > 0$ common friends. Through graded may modality, we can express this in $\mathsf{HL}(\mathsf{own}, \mathsf{req})$ as

$$\mathsf{cf}_k \stackrel{\text{def}}{=} @_{\mathsf{own}} (\mathsf{req} \vee \langle friend \rangle \mathsf{req} \vee \langle friend \rangle_k \langle friend \rangle \mathsf{req}) \quad (15)$$

The leftmost disjunct specifies that the owner has access, the second disjunct says that friends of the owner have access, and the third disjunct says that access is granted to requesters who have at least k many friends in common with the owner. The encoding assumes that R_{friend} is symmetric. If not, the last modality should be an inverse one.

Here is an example policy of $\mathsf{HL}(\mathsf{own}, \mathsf{req})$ that has non-dual subpolicies from the perspective of owner and requester:

$$@_{\mathsf{own}} (\langle friend \rangle \mathsf{req} \wedge \langle friend \rangle_3 \top) \wedge @_{\mathsf{req}} \langle friend \rangle_5 \neg \mathsf{own} \quad (16)$$

This policy grants access if the requester is a friend of the owner, the owner has at least three friends (counting or not counting the requester), and if additionally the requester has at least five friends other than the owner. Intuitively, in order to express this policy in $\mathsf{HL}(\mathsf{own}, \mathsf{req})$ we seem to require both operators $@_{\mathsf{req}}$ and $@_{\mathsf{own}}$ as the policy involves a form of counting in both nodes named by **own** and **req**.

5. LOCAL MODEL CHECKING

In our setting, we are given a model M as protection state, and a policy *pol* in $\mathsf{HL}(\mathsf{own}, \mathsf{req})$ as specification of access control. We then wish to decide whether M, [own $\mapsto o$, req $\mapsto r$] $\models$ *pol* for specified nodes o and r.

This form of evaluation is a kind of *local* model checking. The term "local" is used because the intuition is that the model M is explored only as needed from the nodes of interest, those named by **own** and **req**. Local model checking is a good fit for our needs as only those portions of the model that are potentially needed to make an access-control decision are explored.

Description of algorithm.

We now describe our local model-checking algorithm for $\mathsf{HL}(\mathsf{own}, \mathsf{req})$. Its pseudo-code is depicted in Figure 3. The

```
MC(s,g,φ) {
  case {
    φ is x : return (areEqual(s,g(x)));
    φ is n : return (isElem(s,V(n)));
    φ is p : return (isElem(s,V(p)));
    φ is ¬ψ : return (!MC(s,g,ψ));
    φ is ψ₁ ∧ ψ₂ : return (MC(s,g,ψ₁) && MC(s,g,ψ₂));
    φ is ⟨i⟩ψ : return MCmay(s,g,ψ,i,fwd);
    φ is ⟨-i⟩ψ : return MCmay(s,g,ψ,i,bwd);
    φ is @ₙ ψ : let t = hd(V(n)) in return MC(t,g,ψ);
    φ is @ₓ ψ : let t = g(x) in return MC(t,g,ψ);
    φ is ↓x ψ : let h = g[x ↦ s] in return MC(s,h,ψ);
  }
}

MCmay(s,g,φ,i,direction) {
  if (direction == fwd) { X = [ s' |  (s,s') in R_i ];
  } else              { X = [ s' |  (s',s) in R_i ]; }
  for (all s' in X) {
      if (MC(s',g,φ)) { return true; }
  }
  return false;
}

policyDecision(o,r,φ) {  // φ in HL(own,req)
  let g = [own ↦ o, req ↦ r] in {
    return MC(o,g,φ);
  }
}
```

Figure 3: Local model checking algorithm for HL.

model M is implicit but its structure and local nodes and valuations are explicit in the code.

The algorithm MC has as argument a local node s, a valuation g, and a formula ϕ of HL. Its body is a case analysis of the top-level operator of ϕ. We assume that $V(n)$ and $V(p)$ are implemented as lists, that isElem is a membership test for such lists, that hd returns the first element of a non-empty list, and that areEqual can check for node equality.

The algorithm does a recursive decent until it encounters formulas that are variables, nominals, or propositions. The cases of the forward and backward modalities require a call to a sub-routine MCmay.

Routine MCmay first computes the set of all R_i-successors or predecessors of node s, where that choice is decided by an inspection of a parameter value that indicates whether the modality is a forward one $\langle i \rangle$ or a backward one $\langle -i \rangle$.

It then iterates through all these nodes until one of them makes the formula true, in which case it does return true. If no such node makes the formula true, it returns false.

A genuine implementation of algorithm MC would *not* pre-compute the sets X, but would generate new elements of X on demand until either a witness for truth has been found, or all elements of X are revealed not to be such witnesses. Also, to make this efficient each reached node would keep a hash table of subformulas it has already evaluated so that each subformula is evaluated at most once in each node.

We can use that local model-checking algorithm to implement a policy decision point in policyDecision. It takes as input a node o representing the owner of the object, a node r representing the requester of that object, and a formula ϕ of HL(own,req) representing the access-control policy. Then it creates the valuation that binds own and req to o and r, respectively. Finally, it returns the result of the local model check on ϕ under valuation g.

6. RELATIONAL POLICIES

Previous work [2, 10] has noted that what distinguishes relationship-based access control from traditional access-control paradigms is its extensive use of *relational policies*. Intuitively, a relational policy is one in which the authorization decision is based *solely* on how owner and requester are connected to one another (e.g., friend, friend-of-friend, etc). Therefore, a relational policy does not base its authorization decision on the requester's identity (e.g., John can access), attributes (e.g., managers can access), or social positions (e.g., all those who have at least 100 friends can access).

The goal of this section is to identify a syntactic fragment of the logic HL(own, req) that captures relational policies. This then allows policy developers to efficiently verify that their policy specifications determine relational policies.

Relational policies.

We begin by formalizing what it means for a policy function to be relational. We first define some auxiliary concepts that use only the binary relations R_i of models.

DEFINITION 5. *Fix models* $M = (S_M, \{R_i^M \subseteq S_M \times S_M \mid i \in I\}, V_M)$ *and* $N = (S_N, \{R_i^N \subseteq S_N \times S_N \mid i \in I\}, V_N)$.

1. *These models are* isomorphic via *a bijection* $f: S_M \to S_N$, *if, for all* $i \in I$: $(s,t) \in R_i^M$ *iff* $(f(s), f(t)) \in R_i^N$.

2. *Nodes* s, t *of* S_M *are* connected, *written* $s \overset{M}{\leftrightsquigarrow} t$, *if either* $s = t$, *or inductively, there is an* s' *in* S_M *with* $(s, s') \in R_i^M \cup (R_i^M)^{-1}$, *for some* $i \in I$, *and* $s' \overset{M}{\leftrightsquigarrow} t$.

3. *The* shared component *of nodes* s, t *in* M, *written* $\mathsf{SC}(M, s, t)$, *is the relational structure* $(S, \{R_i \subseteq S \times S \mid i \in I\})$ *defined as follows:*

$$S \overset{\text{def}}{=} \{s, t\} \cup \{s' \in S_M \mid s \overset{M}{\leftrightsquigarrow} s', s' \overset{M}{\leftrightsquigarrow} t\}$$
$$R_i \overset{\text{def}}{=} R_i^M \cap (S \times S)$$

There are two parts to what it means to be a relational policy function. First, the policy function must be *topology-based*: it must consume neither attribute information (i.e., valuations are not considered) nor "identity information" (i.e., isomorphic labeled graphs cannot be distinguished) when an authorization decision is made.

DEFINITION 6. *A policy function* P *is* topology-based *if, for all models* M *and* N, *and all bijections* $f : S_M \to S_N$, *whenever* M *and* N *are isomorphic via* f, *then* $P(N) = \{(f(s), f(t)) \mid (s, t) \in P(M)\}$.

Second, the policy function must be *local*: changes in permission to a model must reflect a change in connectivity between the owner and requester.

DEFINITION 7. *A policy function* P *is* local *iff, for all models* M *and* N, *and all* $s, t \in S_M \cap S_N$, *we have that*

$$\mathsf{SC}(M, s, t) = \mathsf{SC}(N, s, t) \text{ implies } P(M)(s, t) = P(N)(s, t).$$

The definition of "local" demands that any change in an access decision must imply that either s and t have gone from being disconnected to being connected (or vice versa), or the shared component of s and t have been altered.

Such a requirement ensures that any change of authorization decision is not caused merely by the social positions of the requester or the owner (i.e., where exactly they are in the relational structure). We note that this definition of local-ness is equivalent to the one given in [10].

121

$$\psi \ ::= \ \top \ | \ \bot \ | \ x \ | \ \neg\psi \ | \ \psi_1 \wedge \psi_2 \ | \ \psi_1 \vee \psi_2 \ |$$
$$\langle i \rangle \psi \ | \ \langle -i \rangle \psi \ | \ [i]\psi \ | \ [-i]\psi \ | \ @_x \psi \ | \ \downarrow\! x\, \psi$$
$$\phi \ ::= \ \top \ | \ \bot \ | \ @_{\mathsf{own}} \psi \ | \ @_{\mathsf{req}} \psi \ | \ \neg\phi \ | \ \phi \wedge \phi \ | \ \phi \vee \phi$$

Figure 4: Syntax of candidate formulas for a relational fragment of HL(own, req), with x from *Var*.

Example. The following formulas express local policies:

$$@_{\mathsf{own}} (\langle\mathsf{child}\rangle\mathsf{req} \wedge [\mathsf{child}]\mathsf{req}) \qquad (17)$$

$$@_{\mathsf{own}} \langle\mathsf{friend}\rangle(\mathsf{req} \wedge \langle\mathsf{spouse}\rangle\top) \qquad (18)$$

Formula (17) demands the requester to be the *only* child of the owner. Formula (18) requires the requester to be a *married* friend of the owner.

The following formulas express policies that are not local:

$$@_{\mathsf{req}} \langle\mathsf{spouse}\rangle\top \qquad (19)$$

$$@_{\mathsf{own}} [\mathsf{child}]\mathsf{req} \qquad (20)$$

Formula (19), which is a relaxation of (18), requires the requester to be married. It is not local as a change of authorization decision only requires the introduction (or elimination) of a spouse edge in the neighbourhood of the requester, which may otherwise be disconnected from the owner.

Formula (20), which is a relaxation of (17), grants access either if the owner has no child, or if the requester is the only child. The following explains why it is not a local policy. Suppose we start with a model M in which the owner has no child, and the requester is disconnected from the owner. The requester has access in M. Now the owner gives birth to a child, resulting in a new model N, in which the owner is incident to a child edge. The requester loses his or her access in protection state N, but the owner and the requester remain disconnected. **(End of Example.)**

We can now define the technical notion of relational policy.

DEFINITION 8. *A policy function is relational iff it is both topology-based and local.*

A relational fragment of HL(own, req).

It is easy to show that every formula in HL(own, req) expresses a topology-based policy. To obtain relational policies, the challenge is to ensure that formulas are constructed to express *only* local policies. To better appreciate the nature of this challenge, observe the following:

PROPOSITION 1. *The family of local policies contains* $\mathsf{p}[\top]$ *and* $\mathsf{p}[\bot]$ *and is closed under boolean combinations.*

Thus complex local policies can be built up from primitive ones using the boolean connectives offered by HL(own, req). It is the modal operators $\langle i \rangle$ and $\langle -i \rangle$ that may break local-ness of policies. The reason is that, in general, local-ness is not preserved by relational composition.

Suppose P_1 and P_2 are policy functions. We write $P_1 \circ P_2$ to denote the policy function P such that $P(M) = \{(s, t) \in S_M \times S_M \mid \exists s' \in S_M : (s, s') \in P_1(M), (s', t) \in P_2(M)\}$. Even though policy functions P_1 and P_2 may both be local, $P_1 \circ P_2$ need not be local. An example is when P_2 is $\mathsf{p}[\top]$. Thus $\langle i \rangle \psi$ may not be local even if ψ is local. This is illustrated by formula (19).

We define a relational fragment of HL(own, req) to ensure that modal operators preserve local-ness. This relational fragment is obtained in two steps. First, we constrain the syntax of HL(own, req) by the grammar in Figure 4. Second, we impose a type system (Figure 5) to further constrain formula construction, such that only properly typed formulas belong to the fragment.

DEFINITION 9. *The hybrid logic fragment* HL_{rel} *contains those formulas ϕ as defined in Figure 4 such that:*
- *For all subformulas $@_{\mathsf{own}} \psi$ of ϕ, we have ψ : Local(req).*
- *For all subformulas $@_{\mathsf{req}} \psi$ of ϕ, we have ψ : Local(own).*

We now explain the two steps of restricting HL(own, req) in turn. First, the syntax of ϕ in Figure 4 reiterates the requirement of HL(own, req), that policy formulas are boolean combinations of subformulas of the form "$@_{\mathsf{own}} \psi$" or "$@_{\mathsf{req}} \psi$". As long as these subformulas express local policies, then Proposition 1 ensures that ϕ is local.

Second, the inference rules in Figure 5 involve two type judgments of form "ψ : Local(x)" and "ψ : OC(x)", where x is typically either own or req. Intuitively, the derivation of judgment ψ : Local(req) means ψ can be used within $@_{\mathsf{own}}$ to form a local policy. Similarly, the derivation of judgment ψ : Local(own) ensures that $@_{\mathsf{req}} \psi$ is a local policy. The judgment based on label OC(x) is for typing subformulas ψ that are "*owner-checkable (OC)*" as defined in [10]. Although OC formulas are not local, they can be combined with local formulas in a conjunction to yield local formulas.

THEOREM 1 (TYPE SOUNDNESS). *If ψ : Local(req), then $\mathsf{p}[@_{\mathsf{own}} \psi]$ is a local policy. Similarly, if ψ : Local(own), then $\mathsf{p}[@_{\mathsf{req}} \psi]$ is a local policy.*

To see an application of this theorem, consider the policy in (18) of form $@_{\mathsf{own}} \psi$. The first conjunct type checks as Local(req), the second one as OC(req). So their conjunction and also ψ both type check as Local(req). Theorem 1 ensures the policy itself is local. The policy in (17) can be type checked in a similar fashion.

An attempt to type check the policy of form $@_{\mathsf{own}} \psi$ in (19), however, fails: our type system can assign type OC(own) to ψ but this cannot be lifted to type Local(own). Policy (20) fails to type check to Local(req) for a similar reason.

The encoding of graded modalities $\langle i \rangle_n \phi$ given in (11) will type check to Local(x) so long as ϕ type checks to Local(x).

Our typing rules can also type check the depth-first search tree encoding of finitary relational policies [10, Appendix A].

In summary, we have identified a relational fragment HL_{rel} via a grammar and a type system. This allows policy developers to efficiently verify whether the policy formula under development is indeed relational.

7. RELATED WORK

Modal logics for access control.

Access-control logics for distributed systems can be interpreted as modal logics, with Kripke-style, possible-world semantics. In ABLP [1], every principal is a modality, and states in a model are epistemic states. ICL and its variants [11] can be compiled into formulas in the modal logic S4. Following [8, 10], HL(own, req) formulas are interpreted against models that capture principal attributes and social

$$\frac{\psi : \mathsf{Local}(x)}{\psi : \mathsf{OC}(x)} \quad \text{(O-Sub)}$$

$$\overline{\top : \mathsf{OC}(x)} \quad \text{(O-Top)}$$

$$\overline{\bot : \mathsf{OC}(x)} \quad \text{(O-Bot)}$$

$$\overline{y : \mathsf{OC}(x)} \quad \text{(O-Var)}$$

$$\frac{\psi : \mathsf{OC}(x)}{\neg\psi : \mathsf{OC}(x)} \quad \text{(O-Not)}$$

$$\frac{\psi_1 : \mathsf{OC}(x) \qquad \psi_2 : \mathsf{OC}(x)}{\psi_1 \vee \psi_2 : \mathsf{OC}(x)} \quad \text{(O-Or)}$$

$$\frac{\psi_1 : \mathsf{OC}(x) \qquad \psi_2 : \mathsf{OC}(x)}{\psi_1 \wedge \psi_2 : \mathsf{OC}(x)} \quad \text{(O-And)}$$

$$\frac{\psi : \mathsf{OC}(x)}{\langle i\rangle\psi : \mathsf{OC}(x)} \quad \text{(O-May)}$$

$$\frac{\psi : \mathsf{OC}(x)}{[i]\psi : \mathsf{OC}(x)} \quad \text{(O-Mus)}$$

$$\frac{\psi : \mathsf{OC}(x) \qquad y \neq x}{@_y\,\psi : \mathsf{OC}(x)} \quad \text{(O-At)}$$

$$\frac{\psi : \mathsf{OC}(x) \qquad y \neq x}{\downarrow y\,\psi : \mathsf{OC}(x)} \quad \text{(O-Dow)}$$

$$\overline{\bot : \mathsf{Local}(x)} \quad \text{(L-Bot)}$$

$$\overline{x : \mathsf{Local}(x)} \quad \text{(L-Var)}$$

$$\frac{\psi_1 : \mathsf{Local}(x) \qquad \psi_2 : \mathsf{Local}(x)}{\psi_1 \vee \psi_2 : \mathsf{Local}(x)} \quad \text{(L-Or)}$$

$$\frac{\psi_1 : \mathsf{OC}(x) \qquad \psi_2 : \mathsf{Local}(x)}{\psi_1 \wedge \psi_2 : \mathsf{Local}(x)} \quad \text{(L-And1)}$$

$$\frac{\psi_1 : \mathsf{Local}(x) \qquad \psi_2 : \mathsf{OC}(x)}{\psi_1 \wedge \psi_2 : \mathsf{Local}(x)} \quad \text{(L-And2)}$$

$$\frac{\psi : \mathsf{Local}(x)}{\langle i\rangle\psi : \mathsf{Local}(x)} \quad \text{(L-May)}$$

$$\frac{\psi : \mathsf{Local}(x) \qquad y \neq x}{@_y\,\psi : \mathsf{Local}(x)} \quad \text{(L-At)}$$

$$\frac{\psi : \mathsf{Local}(x) \qquad y \neq x}{\downarrow y\,\psi : \mathsf{Local}(x)} \quad \text{(L-Dow)}$$

Figure 5: A type system for formulas from Fig. 4, identifying polices that are local. The typing rules for inverse modalities $\langle -i\rangle$ and $[-i]$, which closely parallel O-May, O-Mus and L-May, are omitted for brevity.

networks. The nodes of a model denote principals, modalities correspond to relationship types, and accessibility relations express interpersonal relations.

Modal logics for relationship-based access control.

In [10], a modal logic E for relationship-based access control was developed as an extension and improvement of a similar modal logic B [8]. So we focus our discussion on E here.

Its abstract syntax is given by

$$\phi ::= \top \mid p \mid \neg\phi \mid \phi_1 \wedge \phi_2 \mid \langle i\rangle\phi \mid \langle -i\rangle\phi \mid \downarrow p\,\phi \mid \phi_1 \otimes \phi_2$$

where p ranges over a set of propositional symbols with a reserved symbol a, and i ranges over a set of labels. In [10], the operator $\downarrow p$ is actually written $@_p$ but we chose the former notation here, as it will aid our comparative discussion.

The models for E are similar to those for HL. Semantically, propositions are treated in E like nominals in hybrid logic: they are true in exactly one node. Symbol a represents the requester of an access. The semantics of the $\downarrow p$ operator is actually that of the $\downarrow n$ operator in hybrid logic, except that $\downarrow \mathsf{a}\,\phi$ is interpreted as $\bot$. Intuitively, $\downarrow p\,\phi$ identifies p with the owner of the object.

Lastly, operator $\phi \otimes \psi$ holds if one can separate model M into two parts of node sets that only overlap for the owner and requester, and where ϕ holds in one of these parts and ψ holds in the other one.

This operator crucially increased the expressiveness of B so that, e.g., thresholds on the number of specific successors of a node can be expressed. Since one can encode graded modalities and similar counting mechanisms in HL, we do not need to add such an operator to our logic.

We view this fact as a big advantage of using HL instead of E. For $\phi \otimes \psi$ incurs a seemingly unavoidable exponential penalty, since there are exponentially many partitions of the set of nodes that need to be considered in its evaluation. The evaluation of HL over models, however, is linear in the size of the model and formula with appropriate caching in place.

Another advantage of HL is the greater flexibility of atomic formulas: HL offers nominals, variables, and propositions (i.e. attributes). Further, the operator $@_t$ is very useful as it specifies where a policy should be evaluated. In fact, by promoting HL(own, req) we suggest most policies would be Boolean combinations of policies of form $@_t\,\psi$.

Hybrid logics for access control.

We are not aware of much other work on using hybrid logic for access control. But in [5], a logical framework is used to design an authorization logic for time-dependent access-control decisions. The logic contains a variant of the $@_t$ operator, $A@I$, which allows the relativization of the truth of proposition A to the time interval I.

Local-ness in ReBAC policies.

Local-ness ensures that change of authorization decision is due to a change in "connectivity" between the owner and the requester of an object. The notion was originally formulated in [2] (an extension of [9]), in which a local policy is one such that, if there is a change of authorization decision due to the introduction of one new edge, then the new edge must be connected to both the owner and the requester. The definition was based on social networks that are undirected graphs, with no edge labels.

In [7], the definition was generalized to account for the introduction of "one or more" edges. The two definitions can be shown to be equivalent. In [10], the definition was adapted to account for social networks that are directed and poly-relational, such that the definition in [7] is merely a special case. In this work we adopt a formulation of local-ness that makes explicit the kind of graph structures that local policies cannot distinguish. One can show that this new formulation is equivalent to that of [10].

8. CONCLUSIONS AND FUTURE WORK

In this paper we have proposed the use of hybrid logic for the specification and enforcement of access-control decisions in the relationship-based approach to access control.

Concretely, we presented a fragment of hybrid logic that is customized to the needs of relationship-based access control. We demonstrated that the models of that hybrid logic are appropriate as models of protection states in relationship-based access control. We showed how the semantics of hybrid logic on such models gives meaning to access-control policies written in that logic.

Then we discussed how this semantics can be implemented as a policy-decision point, via a local model-checking algorithm. Next, we featured numerous examples of policies and showed how they can be elegantly specified in our hybrid logic. Importantly, we showed how hybrid logic can express graded modalities such as "at least three friends".

To understand better connections with related work, we identified an attribute-free fragment of our hybrid logic, via a static type system, in which only policies can be specified that are *relational* in a technical sense from the literature.

We then discussed related work and how our approach improves on it. Let us finally point out future work.

Heterogeneous protection state.

It would be beneficial to let nodes model either *subjects or objects*, so that relationships can also be expressed between subjects and objects. An example of the sort of policy one could then write in HL is

$$@_{\mathsf{req}} \langle sameFloor \rangle \mathsf{resc} \wedge @_{\mathsf{own}} \langle collaborator \rangle \mathsf{req} \wedge$$
$$@_{\mathsf{resc}} \, isPrinter \wedge @_{\mathsf{file}} \, isPDF$$

This says that a print job should be granted those requesters req who are on the same floor as the resource resc, and where additionally the resource resc is a printer, the file file to be printed is in PDF format, and the owner own is a collaborator of the requester req.

Policy composition.

One may think of policies written in HL as just one aspect of control to resources. Different aspects of controlling access could then be combined. For example, in [8] there is a mechanism for determining an appropriate context for evaluating a policy function, where the context is an appropriate model for that policy. Since policies ϕ in HL determine policy functions as well, one can readily use the protection model of [8] with our hybrid logic HL.

Another example is when we have an attribute-free language, e.g. HL with empty AP. Then we may treat each HL policy as a "rule", and then combine rules in a PBel style policy composition language [4], perhaps with rules from other policy languages that refer to attributes.

Footprint of policy evaluation.

Our local model-checking algorithm can be made to run linearly in the size of the model. This low complexity is little comfort for social networks graphs with hundreds of millions of nodes. But policies used by people in social networks ap-

pear to have a small footprint, meaning that only few nodes and edges of the social relationship graph are reached and computed upon during local model checking. We illustrate this point with a Facebook style policy.

In Facebook, access policies are given by fixed options such as Everyone, Friends of Friends, Only Friends, and Customize [6]. The default policy is Everyone which involves no relations. Policies commonly use the options Only Friends or Customize. In the option Customize the owner builds lists of groups or lists of friends that are granted or denied access.

In contrast, option Friends of Friends, specified in (5), grants access to all friends and friends of friends. Its evaluation may visit all friends-of-friends nodes. But its equivalent policy

$$@_{\mathsf{own}} \langle friend \rangle (\mathsf{req} \vee \downarrow x \, @_{\mathsf{req}} \langle friend \rangle x)$$

only explores the owner's friends nodes.

Acknowledgments

We thank Ian Hodkinson for having pointed out to us a wealth of literature on hybrid logic and for always having been willing to discuss technical issues.

9. REFERENCES

[1] M. Abadi, M. Burrows, B. Lampson, and G. Plotkin. A calculus for access control in distributed systems. *ACM Transactions on Programming Languages and Systems*, 15(4):706–734, Sept. 1993.

[2] M. Anwar, Z. Zhao, and P. W. L. Fong. An access control model for Facebook-style social network systems. Technical Report 2010-959-08, Department of Computer Science, University of Calgary, July 2010. Submitted for review.

[3] C. Areces and B. ten Cate. Hybrid logics. In P. Blackburn, J. van Benthem, and F. Wolter, editors, *Handbook of Modal Logic*. Elsevier, 2007.

[4] G. Bruns and M. Huth. Access control via Belnap logic: Intuitive, expressive, and analyzable policy composition. *ACM Trans. Inf. Syst. Secur.*, 14(1):9, 2011.

[5] H. DeYoung. A logic for reasoning about time-dependent access control policies. Senior Research Thesis CMU-CS-08-131, School of Computer Science, Carnegie Mellon University, 20 May 2008.

[6] Facebook, 2011. http://www.facebook.com/about/privacy/your-info-on-fb#controlprofile.

[7] P. W. L. Fong. Preventing Sybil attacks by privilege attenuation: A design principle for social network systems. In *Proc. of the 2011 IEEE Symposium on Security and Privacy (S&P'11)*, pages 263–278, Oakland, CA, USA, May 2011.

[8] P. W. L. Fong. Relationship-based access control: protection model and policy language. In *CODASPY*, pages 191–202, 2011.

[9] P. W. L. Fong, M. Anwar, and Z. Zhao. A privacy preservation model for Facebook-style social network systems. In *Proc. of the 14th European Symp. on Research In Comp. Sec. (ESORICS'09)*, volume 5789 of *LNCS*, pages 303–320, Saint Malo, France, Sept. 2009.

[10] P. W. L. Fong and I. Siahaan. Relationship-based access control policies and their policy languages. In *SACMAT*, pages 51–60, 2011.

[11] D. Garg and M. Abadi. A modal deconstruction of access control logic. In *FOSSACS'2008*, volume 4962 of *LNCS*, pages 216–230, 2008.

[12] C. E. Gates. Access control requirements for Web 2.0 security and privacy. In *Proc. of IEEE Web 2.0 Privacy and Security Workshop (W2SP'07)*, Oakland, California, May 2007.

Bounding Trust in Reputation Systems with Incomplete Information

Xi Gong
North Carolina State
University
xgong2@ncsu.edu

Ting Yu
North Carolina State
University
tyu@csc.ncsu.edu

Adam J. Lee
University of Pittsburgh
adamlee@cs.pitt.edu

ABSTRACT

Reputation mechanisms represent a major class of techniques for managing trust in decentralized systems. Quite a few reputation-based trust functions have been proposed in the literature for use in many different application domains. However, in many situations, one cannot always obtain all of the information required by the trust evaluation process. For example, access control restrictions or high collection costs might limit one's ability to gather every possible feedback that could be aggregated. Thus, one key question is how to analytically quantify the *quality* of reputation scores computed using *incomplete information*.

In this paper, we start a first effort towards answering the above question by studying the following problem: given the existence of certain missing information, what are the worst and best trust scores (i.e., the bounds of trust) a target entity can be assigned by a given reputation function? We formulate this problem based on a general model of reputation systems, and then examine the ability to bound a collection representative trust functions in the literature. We show that most existing trust functions are monotonic in terms of direct missing information about the target of a trust evaluation, which greatly simplifies this process. The problem of trust bounding with the presence of indirect missing information is much more complicated. We show that many well-known trust functions are not monotonic regarding indirect missing information, which means that a case-by-case analysis needs to be conducted for each trust function in order to bound an entity's trust.

Categories and Subject Descriptors: C.2.4 [Computer-Communication Networks]: Distributed Systems—*Distributed applications*; K.4.4 [Computer and Society]: Electronic Commerce—*Security*

General Terms: Security

Keywords: Reputation, trust, missing information

1. INTRODUCTION

Large-scale decentralized systems—e.g., P2P networks and online auction communities—allow entities from different security domains to interact and conduct business with each other in an ad-hoc manner. Such systems offer significant advantages in terms of service variety, availability, and robustness. As a priori trust relationships do not typically exist between entities, establishing trust at runtime is a key problem in the design of trustworthy decentralized systems. Reputation mechanisms are a prominent technique for trust management in these types of systems. In a reputation system, once a transaction is finished, the participants issue feedback that evaluates the service or behavior of one another during the transaction. Before a new transaction starts, one may first assess an entity's trustworthiness based on the feedback provided by other entities. This process can be viewed as the application of a so-called *trust function* that takes as input the feedbacks from an entity's past transactions (and possibly those of other related parties), and outputs a trust value to indicate its trustworthiness.

Quite a few trust functions have been proposed in the literature. Some are based on generic models of decentralized systems, while some others target specific applications domains. The designs of these trust functions may thus differ greatly with respect to methodologies for trust inferences as well as protocols for information collection. However, existing work largely overlooks the problem of missing information and its impact on trust evaluation. In large-scale decentralized systems, there are many reasons that one may not always be able to access all the information required by a trust function. For example, some entities may impose access control restrictions regarding how feedbacks they issue can be accessed by others in order to mitigate potential privacy concerns. In other situations, especially in P2P networks, feedbacks are stored in a distributed manner among multiple entities. Some entities may not be online at the time of trust evaluation, and thus the feedbacks stored by these entities may be unavailable. Sometimes, even if all necessary feedbacks are retrievable, it may be too costly to collect them all. As a result, it is not uncommon to evaluate an entity's trust based upon incomplete information.

A natural question is thus how to quantify the quality of an entity's trustworthiness score when it is computed using incomplete information. There are several ways to formulate the above question. For example, if we can make reasonable assumptions about the distribution of the missing feedback information, we could perhaps compute the 95% confidence interval for a participant's trustworthiness. In this paper, we study a deterministic version of this problem that makes no assumptions regarding the distribution of missing information: given the range of possible values taken by missing information, what are the possible trust scores for an entity? In particular, we are interested in establishing the worst- and best-possible trustworthiness ratings for a target entity.

Answering this problem can help us make better decisions in decentralized systems. For instance, suppose our policy is to conduct a transaction with an entity if its trustworthiness is over 0.8. If the bounds of its trustworthiness can be established as $[0.8, 0.9]$, then it is safe to do business with that entity, even if some information is missing. For sampling based approaches to dealing with missing information, this bound can guide us to decide whether it is appropriate to stop sampling. A wide bound (e.g., $[0.2, 1]$) suggests the current degree of sampling is insufficient, resulting in the large uncertainty about the target's trustworthiness. On the other hand, a narrow bound (e.g., $[0.85, 0.9]$) indicates diminishing returns for further sampling. This paper presents our first effort towards exploring the above trust bounding problem. Our contributions can be summarized as follows:

- We present a general model of reputation assessment, categorize the possible types of missing information, and formally define the trust bounding problem.

- We develop the notion of *monotonicity* as it relates the evaluation of trust functions using incomplete information. This provides a generic method for bounding an entity's trustworthiness given any monotonic trust function. We further argue that monotonicity regarding direct missing information should be a property of any reasonable trust function.

- We study the monotonicity of a large set of representative trust functions from the literature. We find that, technically, monotonicity proofs for trust functions based on weighted recommendations or direct topology information are relatively easy. On the other hand, monotonicity proofs for trust functions based on matrix iterations are particularly challenging.

- We show that monotonicity in general does not hold for indirect missing information by providing concrete examples of existing trust functions in the literature. This suggests that the trust bounding problem has to be studied in a case-by-case manner for specific trust functions.

The rest of this paper is organized as follows. In Section 2, we give a general model of reputation systems, categorize the possible types of missing information, and formally define the trust bounding problem. In Section 3, we propose a classification of trust functions based on their design principles. Section 4 then introduces the monotonicity property of trust functions and discusses its relation to trust bounding. In Sections 5, we analyze the monotonicity of several representative trust functions with respect to a single missing edge with known topology in the trust graph. We report on related work in Section 6, and conclude in Section 7.

2. PROBLEM DEFINITION

In this section, we first provide a general model for reasoning about reputation systems. We then categorize the types of missing information that may exist within such a system. Finally, we formalize the trust bounding problem.

2.1 A General Model For Reputation System

In decentralized systems, entities interact with each other through transactions, which may include monetary interactions, retrieving information from a website, file downloads, and the like. Without loss of generality, we assume that a transaction is uni-directional, i.e., there is a clear distinction between a service provider and a service consumer. Note that a service provider in one transaction may be a consumer in another transaction. A *feedback* is a report issued by a consumer about a provider after a transaction. It can be denoted as a four-tuple (c, s, r, t), indicating that consumer c issues a feedback about provider s with a rating r at time t. In practice, a rating r may be multi-dimensional, covering multiple aspects (e.g., product quality, customer service, shipping speed, etc.) of a transaction. The value for a rating may also be taken from any total ordered domain. Some examples include 0 to 5 stars, a binary positive/negative vote, or a choice from a scale ranging from poor to excellent. For simplicity, in this paper we focus on binary positive/negative votes; as we will see later, such a setting is compatible with the design of most existing trust functions.

Though multiple transactions may happen between a pair (c, s) of consumer and provider, most trust functions in the literature consider only an aggregate of these transactions (e.g., the ratio of positive or negative transactions among all the transactions). We call such an aggregation the *opinion* of c over s, or c's *local trust* of s. The information in a reputation system can be modeled as a *trust graph*.

DEFINITION 1 (TRUST GRAPH). *Given a set of principals P and a totally ordered domain of weights W, a trust graph is a weighted directed graph $G = \langle P, E \rangle$. The edge (c, s, w) in the set $E \subseteq P \times P \times W$ encodes the local opinion w that the consumer c has for the service provider s.*

Figure 1 shows an example trust graph.

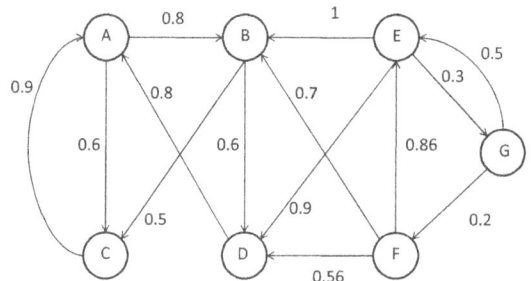

Figure 1: An Example Trust Graph

Although the specific design of trust functions in the literature may differ significantly, most can be abstracted into a common form.

DEFINITION 2 (TRUST FUNCTION). *Given a trust graph $G = \langle P, E \rangle$ and a totally ordered domain W, a trust function $F : G \times P \times P \to W$ is a function that takes as input trust graph and a pair of entities u and v, and computes the extent of u's trust in v.*

Intuitively, given the feedback information stored in a trust graph, F computes the trustworthiness of v from u's point of view. For some trust functions (e.g., [5]) $F(G, u, v) =$

$F(G, u', v)$ for any $u, u' \in P$. In general, however, it is often the case that $F(G, u, v) \neq F(G, u', v)$ if $u \neq u'$.

2.2 Types of Missing Information

There can be several types of missing information within the trust graph observed by a principal in the system. For instance, there may be one or more missing feedbacks between one or more pairs of entities. Alternately, there may be entire pieces of the topology that are unknown. To help make a more systematic analysis later, we now categorize the possible missing information scenarios.

- **Single missing edge weight, known topology.** Having known topology of the trust graph means that we can explicitly enumerate all of the possible paths from any pair of nodes in the trust graph. In this scenario, missing information is restricted to some subset of the feedbacks between one pair of principals, which results in a missing edge weight. This missing information may be due, for example, to restrictions imposed by individual principals. For instance, we may know that there are a total of 10 transactions between Alice and Bob, but Alice only makes the feedbacks of 6 of these interactions accessible. As a result, we cannot know Alice's *exact* opinion of Bob.

- **Set of missing edges, known topology.** This situation is a generalization of the above single-edge case. This may occur, for instance, as a result of a principal's access controls. For instance, if Bob requests feedback reports from Alice, she may provide him with a subset of her reports for multiple principals. Thus Bob might know everyone with whom Alice has interacted, but have incomplete weight values for each.

- **Unknown topology.** In this case, not only can edge *weights* be missing, but perhaps entire *edges* may be missing from some principal's view of the trust graph. For example, a subgraph of the complete trust graph G may not be accessible at all due to restrictions imposed by security policies of a domain. Note that missing edges also imply missing weights on those edges.

2.3 The Trust Bounding Problem

Given the above possible types of missing information, we are interested in bounding the possible trust values that can be assigned to some target principal v in the system by some source principal u. We formalize the *trust bounding problem* as follows:

DEFINITION 3 (EXTENDS, $\sqsupseteq$). *Let $\perp$ denote an unknown edge weight. Given two trust graphs $G = \langle P, E \rangle$ and $G' = \langle P', E' \rangle$, we say that G' extends G if and only if (i) $P \subseteq P'$ and (ii) $(u, v, w) \in E' \leftrightarrow [(u, v, w) \in E \vee (u, v, \perp) \in E \vee \nexists w' \in W : (u, v, w') \in E]$. We denote by $G' \sqsupseteq G$ the fact that G' extends G.*

Informally, a trust graph G' extends a trust graph G if and only if (i) it contains a superset of G's vertices, and (ii) all edges in G' already exist in G, provide a weight for an edge with an unknown weight in G, or connect two vertices that are unconnected in G.

DEFINITION 4 (TRUST BOUNDING PROBLEM). *Given a partial trust graph $G = \langle P, E \rangle$, a trust function F, a source*

principal u, and a destination principal v, the trust bounding problem *is to compute the pair $\langle min_{G' \sqsupseteq G} F(G', u, v), max_{G' \sqsupseteq G} F(G', u, v) \rangle$.*

In this paper, as a first effort, we restrict our discussion to the case of a single missing edge weight in the trust graph. That is, given the range of possible values taken by this single missing edge, what are the possible trust scores for an entity? In particular, we are curious about establishing the worst- and best-possible trustworthiness of the entity.

DEFINITION 5 (SINGLE EDGE TRUST BOUNDING PROBLEM). *Given a trust graph $G = \langle P, E \rangle$, a trust function F, and a single edge $(u, v, w) \in E$ for which the weight w is unknown, the* single edge trust bounding problem *is to compute the pair $\langle min_w F(G, u, v), max_w F(G, u, v) \rangle$.*

3. TYPES OF TRUST FUNCTIONS

We have surveyed a large set of representative trust functions in the literature and have observed that although the specific functions may differ from each other greatly, their underlying design principles can be categorized into three major classes. We now discuss each class and several representative trust functions, which will be helpful during our later analysis of the trust bounding problem.

3.1 Recommendation Based Functions

The idea of this class of trust functions can be explained with the help of the following formula.

$$t_{uv} = \sum_{j \in S} w_{uj} \cdot t_{jv}. \tag{1}$$

When an entity u wants to evaluate the trust of another entity v but has not had any direct interactions with v, she can ask for opinions from a set $S \subseteq P$ of witnesses j who have directly interacted with v. These opinions are denoted as t_{jv}, and are combined using weights w_{uj} which represent u's belief in j's opinion. The following are two representative examples from this class of functions.

Managing the Dynamic Nature of Trust (MDNT) [11]. The trust function in this work can be summarized as the following formula.

$$Rep(u, v) = \sum_{i=1}^{N} WTV(i) \Diamond Rep(i, v)$$
$$+ \beta \times \sum_{j=1}^{M} Trustworthiness(j, v)/M. \tag{2}$$

The meaning of the formula is as followed. Suppose entity u want to evaluate the reputation of entity v. Then she asks for opinions from her witness neighborhood which consists of i's. $WTV(i)$ depicts the correctness of entity i in historical recommendations. $\Diamond$ allows some flexibility in the choice of a concatenation function. In addition, u collects opinions from M entities whose WTV's is unknown to her. So she assigns them the same weight in the recommendation, reflected by taking an arithmetic mean of the opinions from these M entities. Finally, a positive changeable parameter β is used to adjust the impact of these entities. In this function, WTV plays an important role in generating the weights of the witnesses. After each transaction, the source entity s rates the quality of the service from t and compares it with the recommendations received from the witness entities. The difference is stored for the witness's record. After a long time period, many records are collected to evaluate whether a witness entity is a good recommender, and the evaluation result is represented by WTV.

Credence [12]. Credence is a distributed reputation mechanism for P2P file sharing systems. In Credence, users manually provide positive/negative votes indicating the authenticity of a downloaded file. Historical records of an entity's recent votes are stored. In this context, we can consider a file as the v entity in a feedback (u, v, r, t). When a file's authenticity or quality needs to be evaluated, a vote is raised among the neighbors of u. The final trust for the file is computed by taking a weighted average of the neighbor entities' opinions.

The weights of the neighbors depend on the statistical correlation between the vote history of u and that of each of its neighbors, which is computed using the following formula:

$$\theta_{uv} = (P - UV)/\sqrt{U(1-U)V(1-V)}. \qquad (3)$$

where U (respectively V) is the fraction of votes from u (respectively v) with positive intention, and P is the fraction of such pairs that agree with both votes having positive intention. θ is called coefficient of correlation, and takes value in $[-1, 1]$. It's not hard to prove that a value of θ being close to 1 implies a strong agreement between the pair and a value close to -1 indicates a strong disagreement between the pair. Moreover, when θ_{uv} is close to 0, the pair can be considered as being irrelative or independent. Then, θ_{uv} can be taken in formula 1 to compute weight.

$$t_{uv} = \sum_{j \in S} \frac{\theta_{jv}}{\sum_j \theta_{jv}} \cdot Vote_{jv}. \qquad (4)$$

where S is the set of voters.

As we can see from the above two examples, the key to this type of trust functions lies in the definition of weights. In [11] weights are computed based upon the correctness of historical recommendations made by a witness, while in Credence the weights depend on the statistical correlation between the voting history of the source entity and that of the witness. A key observation is that a specific opinion is used either in computing a witness' weight(WTV and θ) or in the opinion of a witness(Rep, $Trustworthiness$ and $Vote$), but not both. As we will see, this property allows us to derive a general method to reason the monotonicity of this type of trust functions and simplify the trust bounding problem.

3.2 Topology Based Functions

This class of trust functions makes explicit use of the topology of a trust graph when calculating trust score. When an entity u wants to evaluate another entity v with whom it has not interacted with directly, it finds paths from u to v in G. A concatenation algorithm is then used to derive the strength of these paths. The final trust is achieved from a weighted aggregation over all such paths. This class of functions bears some similarity to the class of recommendation based trust functions. Nevertheless, the pivotal difference is that the weight on a single edge may contribute to both the strength of a path and the weight of that path in an aggregation. Representative examples of this class of trust functions include the trust function proposed in the NICE system [6] and the Beta Reputation System [3].

NICE [6]. After each transaction in the NICE system, the client u signs a cookie stating the quality of the transaction with the server v, which later can be used to prove the trustworthiness of v to others. Two functions are then proposed to calculate the trust that u should have for v. One function computes the weight of the strongest path, while the other function computes the weighted sum of the strongest disjoint paths from u to v. In the process of inferring trust along a path, the minimum weight of any edge along the path is taken as the strength of the path. If the "strongest path" function is used, it is obvious to find the path with the highest score. If instead the "weighted sum" function is used, the weight on the first-hop edge starting from u is defined as the weight of the path.

Beta Reputation Systems[3]. The Beta Reputation System is another standard topology based trust function. It assumes that the feedback for every transaction is a binary outcome $\{1, 0\}$, where 1 represents a positive feedback and 0 represents a negative feedback. It first aggregates feedbacks locally to get two inputs for an entity v. r_v^u represents the amount of positive feedbacks for v provided by u, while s_v^u represents the amount of negative feedbacks for u. The quantities r_v^u and s_v^u are then used as shape parameters for a beta distribution. By plugging them in $\varphi(p|r_v^u, s_v^u)$ we get

$$\varphi(p|r_v^u, s_v^u) = \frac{\Gamma(\alpha + \beta)}{\Gamma(\alpha)\Gamma(\beta)} p^{(\alpha-1)}(1-p)^{(\beta-1)}, \qquad (5)$$
$$0 \leq p \leq 1, \alpha > 0, \beta > 0.$$

Then it derives the expected value from the distribution and converts it into a more straightforward expression.

$$(E(\varphi(p|r_v^u, s_v^u)) - 0.5) * 2 = \frac{r_v^u - s_v^u}{r_v^u + s_v^u + 2} \in [-1, 1]. \qquad (6)$$

where $E(\varphi(p|r_v^u, s_v^u)) = \frac{r_v^u + 1}{r_v^u + s_v^u + 2}$ is the expected value.

Moreover, the author proposes specific formulas to aggregate and concatenate opinions from multiple entities. When an entity wants to evaluate the trust of another entity, it can compute the trust score of the target following the aggregation and concatenation formulas provided that it can find some paths to the target entity through the trust graph.

3.3 Matrix Based Functions

This final class of trust functions take the adjacency matrix of a trust graph as input, and iteratively apply various matrix operators until convergence to derive each entity's trust. The Path Algebra [9], PeerTrust [13], and EigenTrust [5] schemes are all representative examples of this class of trust functions.

Path Algebra [9]. Path Algebra assumes that feedbacks have been aggregated into opinions in the range $[0, 1]$. The basic intuition is then similar to that of NICE. Specifically, Path Algebra defines two basic functions: concatenation and aggregation. A concatenation function computes the strength of path from the source u to the target v (intuitively it concatenates the opinion on each edge of the path to form the strength of the whole path). And an aggregation function aggregates the strengths of multiple paths to form the final trust. The choice of these functions can be left open to specific applications. Typical concatenation functions include multiplication and minimization, while typical aggregation functions can be maximization, minimization, and average.

Unlike NICE—which explicitly enumerates paths from u to v—Path Algebra requires repetitive combination of the concatenation and aggregation functions until the result converges. This is achieved through a process similar to matrix multiplication. Specifically, given a row $(a_1, \ldots, a_n)$ and a column $(b_1, \ldots, b_n)$ of a matrix, Path Algebra first computes $c_i = C(a_i, b_i)$ where C is the concatenation function, and then aggregates all c_i using the aggregation function. When the combination of minimization (concatenation) and maximization (aggregation) is chosen, the computation is equivalent to finding a strongest path between each pair of entities. As an instance, Zhao et al implemented VectorTrust [15] which uses maximization to aggregate and multiplication to concatenate.

PeerTrust [13]. PeerTrust derives a matrix $\mathbf{A}$ that is based on complaint records reported by entities in the system.

$$\mathbf{A} = (a_{v,u}) = \begin{cases} \frac{C(v,u)}{I(v)} & \text{if } I(v) \neq 0 \\ 0 & \text{if } I(v) = 0 \end{cases} \quad (7)$$

In the above equation, $C(v, u)$ denotes the aggregate number of complaints (negative feedbacks) that entity v receives from entity u, and $I(v)$ represents the amount of transactions that v has. PeerTrust then executes the following operations on the above matrix, where $t_1 = (1, 1, \ldots, 1)^T$:

$$\text{Repeat: } t_{n+1} = \mathbf{1} - \mathbf{A}t_n;$$

$$\text{Until we get a converged } t_n.$$

In the converged vector, each element corresponds to the trust of an entity, independent of the source of the trust evaluation. As such, we call the resulting trust scores *global trust scores*.

EigenTrust [5]. In EigenTrust, a user u rates her transaction with service provider v as either positive ($tr(v, u) = 1$) or negative ($tr(v, u) = -1$). Then EigenTrust defines

$$s_{vu} = \text{ sum of } tr(v, u)\text{'s} = sat(v, u) - unsat(v, u);$$

$$c_{vu} = \frac{max(s_{vu}, 0)}{\sum_u max(s_{vu}, 0)};$$

where $sat(v, u)$ and $unsat(v, u)$ are the number of satisfactory and unsatisfactory transactions that v received from u respectively.

Moreover, EigenTrust computes a matrix $\mathbf{C} = [c_{vu}]$ and performs the following operations on this matrix:

$$\text{Repeat: } t_{n+1} = \mathbf{C}^T t_n;$$

$$\text{Until we get a converged } t_n.$$

where n denotes the number of participants in the community and $t_1 = (\frac{1}{n}, \frac{1}{n}, \ldots, \frac{1}{n})^T$.

EigenTrust computes a global trust score for each entity. However, unlike PeerTrust, it ensures a normalization of trust. That is at each step, EigenTrust ensures that the summation of all the elements in t equals 1.

4. MONOTONICITY DEFINITION

Clearly, trust bounding is a nontrivial problem. Enumerating all possible weight assignments for missing edge values would be too expensive, especially in the event of a continuous weight domain. To simplify this process, we now explore

a property of certain trust functions that we call *monotonicity*. We focus, in particular, on monotonicity with respect to a single edge variable.

DEFINITION 6 (MONOTONICITY, SINGLE EDGE CASE). *Consider a trust function F. Let G be a trust graph with a single undefined edge $(x, y, \perp)$, and let $G(w)$ denote the extension of G with the edge (x, y, w). Given a pair of principals u and v, we say that F is* positively monotonic to a single edge variable *with regard to u and v if for every such G and for every pair of edge weights w and w' we have that $F(G(w), u, v) \geq F(G(w'), u, v)$ whenever $w \geq w'$.*

Negative monotonicity can be similarly defined. It is not hard to see that if a trust function $F(G, u, v)$ is monotonic to an edge variable (either positively or negatively), then we can easily compute the minimum of $F(G, u, v)$ by simply evaluating F over extensions of G in which the missing edge variable is assigned the maximum and minimum possible weights.

This property can be similarly applied to the case of multiple undefined edges. Specifically, if F is monotonic to each edge variable with regard to u and v, the bounds of $F(G, u, v)$ can be straightforwardly obtained by taking the minimum and maximum of each variable respectively.

Given the above observation, the question of trust bounding can thus be answered easily if we can establish the monotonicity property of a trust function regarding certain edge variables. To distinguish the roles of different edges, we further define direct edges and indirect edges.

DEFINITION 7 (DIRECT AND INDIRECT EDGES). *Consider a trust graph $G = \langle P, E \rangle$, a source principal u, a target principal v, and an edge $e = (x, y, w)$. The edge e is said to be a direct edge with respect to the target principal v if and only if $y = v$. Otherwise, e is said to be an indirect edge with respect to the target principal v.*

Next we examine the monotonicity of existing trust functions regarding these two types of edges.

5. ANALYSIS RESULTS

5.1 Monotonicity: Direct Edge Weights

We first focus on the case of direct edge variables. We argue that a well-designed trust function should be positively monotonic to a direct edge variable. To understand the intuition behind this assertion, suppose we want to bound $F(G, u, v)$. A direct edge variable $w_{s,v}$ represents the entity s's opinion of v. Intuitively, positive opinions should improve an individuals overall reputation, although the absolute degree of improvement may depend on the reputation of the individuals contributing opinions. However, a *positive* opinion should not cause a reputation to *decrease*. One may wonder whether negative trust inferences may happen: i.e., Alice distrusts Bob so much that if Bob thinks highly of a person, Alice will take the opposite opinion. Although this may happen in real human communities, this behavior is dangerous in online decentralized systems, as it opens the door to easy trust manipulations. That is, although it would be hard for an attacker to be trusted by everybody, it would be very easy for the attacker to be distrusted by most entities. If we allow negative trust inference, such an attacker may (easily) accrue a bad reputation with the sole purpose of positively rating trusted services in an effort to decrease the overall reputation of that service. Positive monotonicity prevents this type of attack.

Recommendation Based Functions. It is not hard to show that this class of functions is monotonic with respect to a direct edge weight $w_{u,v}$. The essential reason is due to the observation that was mentioned previously: a direct edge weight only contributes to the local trust of a witness u for some target entity v, but not to the weight of the witness when her opinion is considered by others. Thus, when the value of a direct edge variable increases, the weighted trust can only change in one direction, depending on the weight on the witness u. In most recommendation-based trust functions, weights are nonnegative. Therefore, they are all positively monotonic to a direct edge variable, which is consistent with our argument above.

The only exception is Credence, whose weights on witnesses' local trust can be in the range $[-1, 1]$. Therefore, Credence could be negatively monotonic to $w_{u,v}$ if the weight of u is negative (i.e., u's voting records are negatively correlated with that of the source of the trust evaluation). As discussed above, this property allows an attacker to manipulate through negative trust inferences. Specifically, it could vote negatively on well-known high quality items, causing a strong negative correlation between itself and the source of a trust evaluation, so that its vote on the target entity or item would have a much higher impact on the final trust. One may wonder whether the effect would be the same when the attacker tries to form a strong positive correlation with the source. The different is that by voting negatively on well-known high quality items, an attacker can have a strong negative correlations with multiple honest entities. Thus, one manipulation of his voting history can be used to attack multiple entities. On the other hand, form a strong positive correlation with one entity usually does not result in the same with another honest entity, thus limiting the manipulation power of an attacker.

Topology Based Functions. This class of trust functions is also monotonic regarding direct missing information. A direct edge weight $w_{u,v}$ only positively monotonically affects the strength of a path, but not the weight of the path. Since the common functions to combine the strengths of multiple paths (e.g., MAX, AVG) are all monotonic to the strengths of individual paths, we can easily see that $w_{u,v}$'s impact to the final trust score is also positively monotonic.

Take NICE as an example. If an entity a wants to evaluate the trust of another entity v, it first computes the strength of the possible (disjoint) paths from a to v. Obviously, the edge weight $w_{u,v}$ will only affect the strength of one specific path p. And since $u \neq a$ (otherwise, a has direct experience with v and can use its local trust directly), $w_{u,v}$ would not affect p's weight. (In NICE, the weight of a path is determined by the weight of its first hop.) Since the weight of a path is nonnegative, the trust function is positively monotonic to a direct edge variable.

Matrix Based Functions. Matrix based trust functions are more complex to analyze than the prior two classes of trust functions. Due to their usage of specific iteration operations, it is difficult to provide a general proof of monotonicity. Therefore, we chose three representative matrix based trust functions—Path Algebra, PeerTrust, and EigenTrust—and make a case-by-case analysis.

The positive monotonicity of Path Algebra regarding direct edge variables is relatively easy to establish. Note that all the elements in the matrix are nonnegative, and both of the concatenation and the aggregation functions described in [9] are positively monotonic. For each iteration, the matrix operation can be viewed as a composition of the concatenation and aggregation function. This implies that any feasible combination of possible such functions gives a positively monotonic trust function. We omit the formal proof due to its simplicity.

PeerTrust is more complicated to analyze than Path Algebra, since subtraction is used during the computation. As such, the transient trustworthiness of the entities may fluctuate between iterations. However, after the computation converges, a positive monotonicity property can be observed. A full proof of PeerTrust's monotonicity exists in the full version of this paper.

EigenTrust is one of the most influential trust functions in the literature. Although the general principle of Eigen-Trust is similar to that of PeerTrust, EigenTrust involves a normalization process that makes its analysis much more challenging. Specifically, EigenTrust is based on a stochastic matrix derived from the feedbacks in a system, such that the sum of each row must be 1. Therefore, we cannot apply the approach used to prove the monotonicity of PeerTrust to analyze EigenTrust, because standard matrix inverse does not existing for a stochastic matrix. To date, we have been unable to establish a proof of the monotonicity for EigenTrust. However, we cannot find a counterexample either. We have conducted extensive simulations over various reputation system settings, and all the results suggest that EigenTrust is positively monotonic to direct edge variables. Figure 2(b) shows how the final trust score of one entity changes when varying a direct edge weight from 0 to 1 in a small decentralized system. Figure 2(a) compares the temporary trust score of this after each iteration of the algorithm.

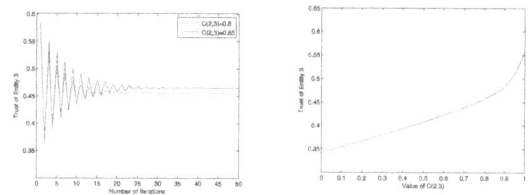

(a) The change of trust score after each iteration (b) Monotonicity shape

Figure 2: Simulation observation on EigenTrust

5.2 Monotonicity: Indirect Edge Weights

Recommendation Based Functions. Recommendation based functions are not always monotonic regarding indirect edge weights. Whether monotonicity holds mainly depends on how weights are computed. For example, Credence computes the weight of a witness based on the correlation between historical ratings of the source of trust evaluation and those of the witness. In this context, a witness sharing similar votes with the source is assigned a higher weight in the aggregation of local trust. For this trust function, monotonicity is not guaranteed. For instance, consider the case where the rating on an entity v by the source u is 0.5. If a witness s has a rating for v that is close to 0.5, it achieves a high weight. However, a lower rating like 0.1 or a higher rating like 0.8 for v would lower the weight assigned to s, causing a non-monotonic change of the final trust score.

Compared to *Credence*, MDNT [11] computes the weight of a witness based on its historically correction record. After each transaction, the source entity of the evaluation will compare the quality of the service with the recommendations gathered before the transaction. A witness will get a positive feedback if his recommendation is matches the source entity's experience, and a negative feedback otherwise. After a period of time, every recommender establishes a history about the accuracy of his recommendations. Witnesses with higher correction rates will be assigned higher weights. For this trust function, monotonicity holds regarding an indirect edge variable, but the function may be negatively monotonic.

Note that even if a trust function is not monotonic to an edge variable, it does not mean that we cannot solve the trust bounding problem efficiently. It simply means that we need to study the specific design of such trust functions in a case-by-case manner. For example, even though Credence is not monotonic, given the voting history of the source of trust evaluation $(r_1, \ldots, r_n)$ and that of a witness $(r'_1, \ldots, x_i, \ldots, r'_n)$, it is not hard to compute when the correlation between these two vectors is minimized and maximized (i.e., when they have the same or opposite direction in the multi-dimensional space that two vectors are in).

Topology Based Functions. Topology based functions are not always monotonic regarding indirect missing information either. In contrast to a direct edge weight, an indirect edge weight w_e may affect both the strength of a path and the weight of the path; this may lead to a non-monotonic polynomial function of w_e. Below is a concrete example of the reputation system introduced in NICE [6].

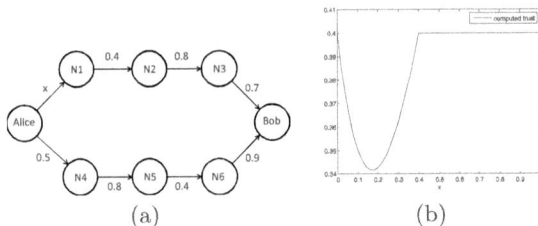

(a)   (b)

Figure 3: An example showing NICE is non-monotonic

As shown in figure 3(a), Alice wants to evaluate the trustworthiness of Bob. She first computes the strength of paths connecting to Bob with the weights of the edges in the paths. Then she uses *weighted sum of strongest disjoint paths* to merge the computed trust ratings. The two disjoint paths in the figure are $path_1 = \{Alice \rightarrow N_1 \rightarrow N_2 \rightarrow N_3 \rightarrow Bob\}$ and $path_2 = \{Alice \rightarrow N_4 \rightarrow N_5 \rightarrow N_6 \rightarrow Bob\}$. The weight on $Alice \rightarrow N_1$ is missing. Following the NICE algorithm, the strength of a path is the minimum weight of all its edges. And the weight of a path is the weight of its first hop from Alice. Therefore, we have the strength of $path_1$ as

Table 1: A summary of the monotonicity of our surveyed trust functions

Class	Function	Direct	Indirect
Recommendation	MDNT	Yes	Yes
	Credence	No	No
Topology	NICE	Yes	No
	Beta	Yes	Yes
Matrix	Path Algebra	Yes	Yes
	PeerTrust	Yes	Yes
	EigenTrust	Uncertain	No

$\min\{x, 0.4\}$ and the strength of $path_2$ as 0.4. The weights of these two paths are x and 0.5, respectively. Then the final trust score of Bob from Alice's point of view can be expressed as in equation 5.2.

$$t_{Alice \rightarrow Bob} = \begin{cases} \frac{x^2 + 0.2}{x + 0.5} & \text{when } x \leq 0.4 \\ \frac{0.4x + 0.2}{x + 0.5} & \text{when } x > 0.4 \end{cases} \quad (8)$$

The parabola-shape curve in Figure 3(b) indicates that this trust function is not monotonic.

Matrix Based Functions. As for Matrix based functions, we can show that the trust functions defined by Path Algebra are also positively monotonic to indirect edge variables. We can also derive a rigorous proof of monotonicity with respect to indirect edge variables for the PeerTrust trust function. For the details of the proof please refer to the full paper. However, for the EigenTrust trust function, no monotonic cases happened based upon our simulation results.

Table 1 summarizes the observations that we have made regarding the monotonicity of our candidate trust functions with respect to direct and indirect missing information.

6. RELATED WORK

Quite a few trust functions and reputation systems have been proposed in the literature over the last decade; for excellent surveys of these results, see [2, 4]. However, to the best of our knowledge, our work is the first to study the trust evaluation when certain information is missing in a reputation system. Next, we briefly overview recent research on securing reputation-based trust management.

Much work has been done specifically to prevent attacks in P2P systems. Zhang et al. [14] suggests that trust functions are effective when assuming that the service providers behave consistently, i.e., they always try their best to provide good services. However, a reputation system can be easily manipulated when an attacker adapts its behavior to take advantage of a trust function. Therefore, the authors propose a statistics based algorithm to test whether the transaction history of a service provider is compatible with that of an honest entity. They also develop a scheme that combines the above test with trust functions to force an attacker to behave relatively consistently, and thus increasing the cost of manipulation. In [1], Damiani et al. identify three attacks specific to reputation based systems, namely Pseudospoofing, ID Stealth and Shilling. The authors design a protocol called *XRep* which defends against all of the above attacks.

Many other works investigate defences against manipulation and other adversary activities in reputation systems with a more general system setting. For example, CORE [8] only takes positive values of indirect ratings to prevent denial of service attacks that use malicious negative feedbacks against reliable entities. *TrustGuard* [10] combats malicious oscillatory behaviors with a strategic oscillation guard based on Proportional-Integral-Derivative controller. The system confines feedback to unforgeable transaction proofs and separates out dishonest feedbacks with a similarity measure to rate the reliability of a feedback. To prevent malicious entities subverting the system by reporting false trust values, a secure EigenTrust is implemented with the help of distributed hash table. It asks multiple entities to compute the trust value for an entity and then pick up the correct trust from non-malicious entities and eliminate the conflicts arising from malicious entities by a majority vote. In NICE, cookies are assigned to infer the trust of the target entity. However, a malicious entity may discard the cookie with a low value to hide his past misbehavior. Lee et al. propose to use negative cookies, which are feedbacks with low ratings. These cookies are stored by the issuer instead of by the target so that they cannot be discarded by the target.

7. CONCLUSION AND FUTURE WORK

Due to the decentralized nature of reputation systems, it is common that only a subset of feedback reports might be available at the time of a given trust function invocation. As such, it is important to examine the *quality* of reputation scores that can be obtained using incomplete information. In this paper, we initiate a first effort to investigate mechanisms for quantifying the effects of missing information. We formally define the trust bounding problem, which sets out to derive the minimum and maximum trust score of an entity when considering all possible values of the missing information. We identify two different types of missing information, and study the monotonicity properties of representative trust functions from the literature. Our investigation shows that most existing trust functions are monotonic with respect to *direct* missing information for the target of a trust evaluation, and thus the trust bounding problem can be easily solved in that context. On the other hand, the impact of *indirect* missing information on trust functions is more complicated. We have identified trust functions that are monotonic to indirect missing information, as well as some other functions that are not.

This work represents only a first step toward dealing with missing information in reputation systems. Many interesting avenues of follow-up work still remain to be explored. For instance, EigenTrust is one of the most well-known and influential trust functions in the literature, yet we cannot establish any formal proofs of its monotonicity regarding direct missing information due to its unique normalization process. One promising approach would be to leverage group inverses [7] as a mathematical tool to reveal the connection between the entries in an approximately inverse matrix and a variable in the original matrix. Formally establishing the monotonicity of EigenTrust would help better understand the properties of other matrix-based trust functions. Another interesting direction is to consider a probabilistic interpretation of the reputation quality problem (as mentioned in Section 1), and investigate various sampling techniques to accurately and efficiently estimate an entity's trustworthiness. This could lead to reliable distributed algorithms for reputation sampling in distributed systems. The samples collected could be used as input to existing trust functions, thereby producing reliable assessment metrics from unreliable primitives.

8. REFERENCES

[1] E. Damiani, S. D. Capitani, S. Paraboschi, F. Violante, and D. E. I. Politecnico. A Reputation-Based Approach for Choosing Reliable Resources in Peer-to-Peer Networks. In *Proceedings of the 9th ACM CCS*, pages 207–216, 2002.

[2] K. Hoffman, D. Zage, and C. Nita-Rotaru. A survey of attack and defense techniques for reputation systems. In *ACM Computing Surveys*, volume 42, pages 1–31, Dec. 2009.

[3] A. Jøsang and R. Ismail. The Beta Reputation System. In *Proceedings of the 15th Bled eCommerce Conference*, 2002.

[4] A. Jøsang, R. Ismail, and C. Boyd. A survey of trust and reputation systems for online service provision. In *Decision Support Systems*, volume 43, pages 618–644, Mar. 2007.

[5] S. D. Kamvar, M. T. Schlosser, and H. Garcia-Molina. The Eigentrust algorithm for reputation management in P2P networks. In *WWW Conference Series*, pages 640–651, 2003.

[6] S. Lee, R. Sherwood, and B. Bhattacharjee. Cooperative peer groups in NICE. In *Proceeding of the INFOCOM 2003*, 2003.

[7] C. D. Meyer. The role of the group generalized inverse in the theory of finite markov chains*. *Review Literature And Arts Of The Americas*, 17(3), 1975.

[8] P. Michiardi and R. Molva. CORE: A collaborative reputation mechanism to enforce node cooperation in mobile ad hoc networks. In *Proceedings of the 6th CMS*, pages 107–121, Deventer, The Netherlands, 2002.

[9] M. Richardson, R. Agrawal, and P. Domingos. Trust management for the semantic web. In *Proceeding of the ISWC*, 2003.

[10] M. Srivatsa, L. Xiong, and L. Liu. TrustGuard: Countering vulnerabilities in reputation management for decentralized overlay networks. In *Proceedings of the 14th WWW conference*, 2005.

[11] E. S. Staab. The Pudding of Trust Editor's Perspective. *IEEE Intelligent Systems*, 3(4):19(5):74–88, 2004.

[12] K. Walsh and E. Sirer. Experience with an object reputation system for peer-to-peer filesharing. In *Proceedings of the 3rd NCDI conference*, 2006.

[13] L. Xiong and L. Liu. Building trust in decentralized peer-to-peer electronic communities. *Electronic Commerce Research*, 2002.

[14] Q. Zhang, W. Wei, and T. Yu. On the modeling of honest players in reputation systems. *Journal of Computer Science and Technology*, 24:808–819, 2009.

[15] H. Zhao and X. Li. VectorTrust: trust vector aggregation scheme for trust management in peer-to-peer networks. *The Journal of Supercomputing*, pages 1–25, 2011.

The Privacy in the Time of the Internet: Secrecy vs Transparency

Murillo Pontual
The University of Texas at San Antonio
mpontual@cs.utsa.edu

Andreas Gampe
The University of Texas at San Antonio
agampe@cs.utsa.edu

Omar Chowdhury
The University of Texas at San Antonio
ochowdhu@cs.utsa.edu

Bazoumana Kone
The University of Texas at San Antonio
bazoumana.kone@utsa.edu

Md. Shamim Ashik
The University of Texas at San Antonio
sashik@cs.utsa.edu

William H. Winsborough
The University of Texas at San Antonio
wwinsborough@acm.org

ABSTRACT

In the current time of the Internet, specifically with the emergence of social networking, people are sharing both sensitive and non-sensitive information among each other without understanding its consequences. Federal regulations exist to mandate how sensitive information (*e.g.*, SSN, health records, *etc.*) of a person can be shared (or, used) by organizations. However, there are no established norms or practices regarding how information that is deemed to be not sensitive may be used or shared. Furthermore, for the sake of transparency, different organizations reveal small amounts of non-sensitive information (*i.e.*, photos, salaries, work hours, size of the houses, *etc.*) about their clients or employees. Although such information seems insignificant, the aggregation of it can be used to create a partial profile of a person which can later be used by malicious parties for robbery, extortion, kidnapping, *etc.* The goal of this work is to create awareness by demonstrating that it is plausible to create such a partial profile of a person just by crawling the Internet. For this, we have developed an open source framework that generates batch crawlers to create partial profiles of individuals. We also show empirical comparisons of the amount of information that can be gathered by using free and also paid websites.

Categories and Subject Descriptors

K.4.1 [**Computers and Society**]: Public Policy Issues

General Terms

Security, Experimentation

Keywords

Privacy, Internet, Transparency, Social Networking, Information Sharing

1. INTRODUCTION

In the age of Internet, organizations are heavily dependent on computer information systems for using, sharing, and safe-guarding critical information about their clients and employees. Organizations are expected to keep a certain degree of transparency in their functions. Transparency in this case serves several important purposes, such as, creating accountability, building public confidence and trust, and also creating informed stakeholders.

Federal regulations [1, 2] mandate how the organizations can use or share critical private information of individuals. These regulations carry the force of law and violations of them bring in the threat of severe punishment. To maintain a certain degree of transparency, the organizations release some not-so-sensitive information (*e.g.*, name, photo, salary, rent or mortgage, address, office hours, *etc.*) of their clients and employees to the Internet. There is no established norm or custom based on which one can decide how to use or share this information.

This not-so-sensitive information might seem very insignificant with respect to compromising privacy of an individual. However, we argue that this not-so-sensitive information can be aggregated to create a partial profile of an individual, which can then be used by malicious parties to kidnap, extort, rob, *etc.*, the individual (for examples see [3]). This semi-complete profile can also be sold in the black-market.

Social networking [4, 5, 6, 7] has received a lot of attention concerning breaches of privacy of its users [8, 9, 10]. With the emerging trend of social networking, more people are voluntarily sharing not-so-sensitive information (*e.g.*, address, name, email, phone number, pictures, location, *etc.*) with each other without the proper understanding of its implications. Previous work [8, 9, 10, 11, 12] has attempted to create awareness among social networking users by showing the different privacy vulnerabilities that are inherent to these social networking websites, for example by using vacation messages to create lists of vulnerable homes [13] or harvesting email addresses for spamming [12].

As discussed above, previous work is more specifically concentrated on the privacy implications of social networking websites. However, our goal is more general in the sense that we want to create awareness by demonstrating that individuals share a lot more than they need to on the Internet. In this work, we attempt to show the feasibility of aggregating information related to a person by crawling the Internet.

We also try to provide a framework that can be used to generate batch crawlers that can crawl for information in the web.

Contributions. Our **first contribution** is designing and developing an open source framework that creates batch crawlers for different websites in the Internet. The framework learns from a monitored run performed by a user and creates a crawler that imitates the observed behavior on the target website. The tool saves the search results as HTML files which are later processed semi-automatically to gather the data.

After developing the tool, we used it for crawling information about 6000 employees of The University of Texas at San Antonio (UTSA) from the websites White Pages, Intelius, Texas Tribune, *etc.*, [14, 15, 16, 17, 18]. We also calculated probabilities of finding a person's address, age, size of the house, *etc.*, given the name of the person. This is our **second contribution**.

We then bought a subscription for the payed website Net Detective [19] and crawled it for the same information. We compared the information gathered from Net Detective and the free websites. We found out that the information gathered from Net Detective is limited compared to the free websites. A comparison of the availability of the information gathered from the different sources constitutes our **third contribution**.

Road map. The remainder of this paper is organized as follows. Section 2 provides some examples necessary to understand our contributions. Section 3 explains our framework. Section 4 presents the availability of the information collected in free websites. Section 5 presents a comparison of the availability of the information gathered from free and paid sources. Section 6 discusses related work. Section 7 discusses future work and concludes.

2. MOTIVATION

More and more people are sharing public information over the Internet. This trend contrasts with past behaviors, where people did not feel so comfortable about having their information made public, or even being stored in a central database. Several studies (see [3]) before the meteoric rise of the internet in the late nineties indicated that the majority of Americans felt not in control of their information and was against sharing by the government or companies. However, this started to change with the popularization of social networks (*e.g.*, Facebook, Myspace, Orkut, etc.). Several studies [12, 20, 3] have shown that people are unaware of the dangers of making their personal information public over social networks. For instance, according to Garfinkel [3], in a typical social network, 90.8% of the profiles contain photos, 87.8% have a date of birth, 50.8% contain the home address, and 39.9% phone numbers.

Furthermore, not only people are releasing their information, but also governments around the world are making their citizens' personal information public. For example, in Sweden the income tax returns are publicly available over the Internet [21], whereas in Texas, since 1973, by the Texas Public Information Act [14], all the public employees' records are made public.

What kind of harm not-so-sensitive information can bring to a person when it is made publicly available over the Internet will depend on a set of factors, for example, the economical situation of the person, the type of the job the person has, where the person lives, *etc.* For instance, in a developing nation that has many cases of robbery and kidnapping, publishing salaries and addresses is not a good idea.

Given the above motivation we are going to present a few examples that illustrate the dangers of having not-so-sensitive information made public. The following examples were collected from [3, 20, 21].

1. **Direct Marketing** is an advertising technique that utilizes personal information to communicate directly to the customer. Although direct marketing is not a threat *per se*, it can be very aggressive and annoying to the customers.

2. **Stalking, Kidnapping and Theft** are a category of threat where the not-so-sensitive information may be used to harm a person in a real-life situation. An extreme example was the murder of two doctors involved in abortion clinics after their information was made public on a website.

3. **Identity Theft** is the act of impersonating another's identity. There are two ways that one can impersonate another person: one can steal a person's identity in real life, or one can steal a person's virtual identity (*e.g.*, faking a Facebook profile of someone else). With a real-life stolen identity, a perpetrator might for example open new or access existing bank accounts and do monetary damage. A virtual identity can be used for social engineering-based attacks, advertising, slander, cyber-bullying etc.

4. **Phishing, Spam, and Scams** are social engineering techniques that attempt to deceive naive users to release some of their sensitive information (*e.g.*, a credit card number) by making them believe they are communicating with a trustworthy entity. If coupled with identity theft that gains enough information to convince the victim, this is more successful than the generic 419 fraud.

5. **Harm to Reputation** can happen depending on what type of information is made public about a person. A popular example is the screening of applicants by future employers, which today includes Facebook accounts. Here, a person may harm herself. Other examples include vengeful ex-relations sharing personal data, as for example Rate Your Boyfriend [22].

3. DATA ACQUISITION

Most public information is available in the form of online databases. Mainly form-based websites are used to access and search for data. In the age of "Web 2.0", many providers heavily utilize Javascript and AJAX technologies for a smoother user experience without visible HTTP reloads.

To collect the information for our study, we need to access the data stored in the online databases. However, for the number of people we investigate, a manual acquisition is unfeasible. Thus, an automatic way is necessary. Standard crawler software is not applicable to our case: Searching in such a database does not equate to following links in the form-displaying document.

As a solution, we developed our own crawler framework that is targeted towards form-based sites and supports Javascript and AJAX. The framework is actually a crawler-generator, as we want to crawl many different databases, which each differ in the way forms are designed, search data is entered, and the search submitted.

The framework is implemented as a Java library that models a pipeline for the information retrieval, and uses HtmlUnit [23], which is intended for use with unit testing frameworks. The decision for HtmlUnit was mainly guided by the strong support for Javascript.

We divide the search into five different steps, as shown in Figure 1. The different steps are:

1. Log into the website. Online databases might require an account to access the information. In such cases, we manually register to create an account in that website. After creating the account, the crawler can log into the website to perform any searches. When an account is not required to perform searches, we skip this step.

2. Find the search site. The search form might be on a subpage of the website. For any search, the crawler should navigate to the search page.

3. Perform the search. This includes filling in the form fields and submitting the query.

4. Iterate over results. If the result set of a search is too large, most websites paginate the result. For completeness, the crawler needs to be able to follow pagination links and save all search results to disk.

5. After all searches are completed, the crawler should cleanly log out from the website.

These five steps are connected in a standard order, represented by solid lines in Figure 1. The crawler will loop the pagination step for all sub-pages generated by a query, and will loop steps two through four for all queries.

The dashed lines represent abnormal flow. In case the Internet connection breaks down, the crawler is logged out, or other unusual behavior, the process is repeated from step one.

The pipeline is parameterized by information specific to each crawled website. The Login step requires the address of the login page, as well as the way a login is performed, i.e., which information to put into forms and submit for a login. The Search step usually just needs the address of the search page. The Form Data step needs to know how to split up search information and fill the right form fields. Finally, it needs to submit the search form. The Pagination step needs to recognize pagination links. They are usually formatted in a straight-forward manor. Logging out is usually performed by visiting a certain page.

The most interesting configuration point is step three. On this example the two main problems can be explained: First, the original search parameter (in our case a single name string) needs to be split up for the different search parameters, e.g., first and last name, middle initial, and so on. Second, it is necessary to write that information into the right form fields.

In many cases, the input to the crawler does not have the same structure as the form input on a website. For example, the Texas government employee salary database, as made available, identifies persons by a single string consisting of the first name, the middle initial, and the last name, separated by spaces, whereas those parts are represented by different form fields on most search pages. As we want our crawler framework to be as general as possible, we have to address those structural differences. Our current solution is a lightweight adoption of a technique presented in [24]. The input is tokenized and substrings of tokens can be referenced. For simplicity of the implementation, currently a regular expression is used to correctly split the search strings into tokens under the consideration of a middle initial.

As a result, search information can be stated by information descriptors, which are either string literals, e.g., static login information, or token+substring identifiers. e.g., "#1" for the first token, i.e., the first name, and "#2[1:1]" for the first character of the second token, i.e., the middle initial.

To write the split-up information into the right form fields, we employ a mapping from field identifiers to information descriptors. In most cases, form fields can be uniquely and easily identified by the name tag. In rare cases, further tag information (e.g., the id tag) or even the field type are necessary. Note that not all fields in a form will be mapped, as to not disturb some possible data transfer of the website, like session information.

To ease the use of the framework, i.e., providing the pipeline stages with the right information, we developed a graphical tool that collects the data by monitoring a sample run performed by the user. To this end, we designed an embedded web browser. For a simplified implementation, the instrumentation is done via Javascript event hooks intercepting mouse clicks and URL changes. The form information is collected as plain Javascript helper objects in an array. The clicked form field is also stored as a special element of the array. Finally, the array is serialized to JSON and sent to a small server running in the monitor, which deserializes and stores all interactions.

4. EMPIRICAL EVALUATION

In this section, we summarize our data collection process, sources of data, and also the analysis process of the data collected. We also provide the scope of the data aggregated from different sources.

Table 1: Sources of information (websites)

Data Set	Size	Homonyms Ratio
Texas Tribune	554,790	1:1.132
UTSA Employees	6,316	1:1.0006
White Pages	133,344	1:25.244
Housing	6,596	1:2.956
Net Detective	43,229	1:8.264
Facebook	30,170	1:9.203
Total	750,591	–

4.1 Information Sources

In this study, we have collected more than 750,000 publicly available records containing personal not-so-sensitive information (e.g., name, salary, home address, work department, etc.). The first column of table 1 lists the websites

Figure 1: Crawler Pipeline

from which we gathered these information. In the rest of this paper, we call these websites *sources, datasets* or *databases* interchangeably. The Texas Tribune [18] is a website from which we collected 667,000 records of government employees from the state of Texas. Typically, these employees are affiliated with public schools, counties, universities, *etc.* A snapshot of an employee record contains the following information: the job title, the public agency where the employee works, the department where the employee is affiliated, the employee gender, the date when the employee was hired, and the employee's annual salary. According to the website, they exclude employees that earn less than $20,000 from their database . Furthermore, when an employee has multiple positions, the salary field contains the sum of all the salaries of such employee, whereas the order fields (*e.g.*, title, agency, and department) contain the information about the highest paid job that such employee hold. The data records are updated periodically according to the Texas Tribune, however, the period is not made available on the website.

The source UTSA employees depicts a subset of the Texas Tribune dataset, containing 6,596 employee records from the University of Texas at San Antonio (UTSA). It contains the same information that was collected from the Texas Tribune website. As presented in the introduction, the goal of this paper is to discover the amount of publicly available information about an individual in the Internet . To this end, in this paper we use the names of the UTSA's employees as inputs to harvest more information in another websites (figure 2 depicts the usage of the names of UTSA's employees as an aggregator to collect more information in other websites).

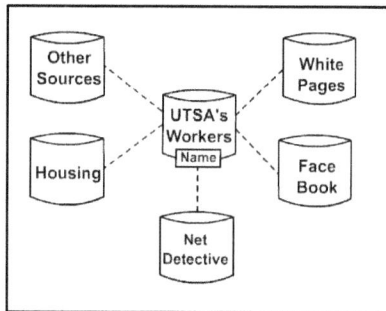

Figure 2: Aggregation method

The White Pages website [16] comprises of the following pieces of information: name, aliases, home address, phone number, relatives, and date of birth (DOB). We have collected 133,344 records of personal not-so-sensitive information by using the names of the UTSA's employees and San Antonio city as inputs to the White Pages engine, .

House Almanac (presented in table 1 as Housing) [17] is a website that contains housing information about some of

the cities of Texas (*e.g.*, Austin, Dallas, Houston, and San Antonio). Then, we used San Antonio resident UTSA's employee names to collect housing information for them. We gathered 6,596 records containing the following information: address, co-owner names, subdivision, date of purchase, size, and market price.

Net Detective [19] on the other hand is a paid service that contains the following information about an individual: name, address, aliases, criminal records, phone number, *etc.* We crawled 43,229 records of San Antonio resident UTSA employees from this website. Section 5 contains a more in depth discussion about the information gathered from this website.

We utilized the Facebook engine to crawl for information from the Facebook website. We collected 30,170 records of UTSA employees from Facebook. Each such record contains whether an individual has a Facebook account and the weblink for his profile provided that he has an account. According to [12], a typical Facebook profile contains the following information: name, gender, employers, current city, interests, activities, relationship status, relatives, email, etc. So, our goal when checking whether a given UTSA employee has a Facebook account is a proof of concept that someone can combine the information gathered in free websites (*e.g.*, White Pages, House Almanac, *etc.*) with the information available in Social Networks (*e.g.*, Facebook , Twitter, *etc.*) to build a comprehensive profile about a person.

All the information collected from the sources presented in table 1 comprises of 24 different pieces of information. Together they form a personal profile that details what information is publicly available about a person over the Internet. In addition to that, we have also categorized these pieces of information into 4 main groups, namely, personal information, job information, residence information, and educational information. The categories and respective data items are summarized in Table 2. It is expected that the amount of not-so-sensitive information about an individual will grow to be more complete if we enhance our datasets to contain for information sources.

Table 2: Categories & data items

Personal	Name, aliases, date of birth, age, citizenship, relatives, personal photos, gender
Job	Agency, department, job title, hire date, salary, work phone, work address, email, work history
Residence	Address, subdivision, house size, purchase date, market price, home phone, photos
Education	Degree level, educational history

In table 5 we present an example profile. Note that, not all of the information present in a profile can be acquired from the sources presented in table 1. Information such images, email address, educational information *etc.* were additionally collected from other sources (*e.g.*, Google, personal websites, Yahoo, *etc.*). Since, our study is limited among the employees of the University of Texas of San Antonio, a good source of information about them were available at the university's official website. We found individual curriculum vitae, class pages, department pages, *etc.*, which were also rich sources of information. Note that, in our example profile we intentionally left out the image field. In section 4.3, we present a more comprehensive study about how this information were gathered.

Finally, we consider homonyms ratio that tells us the number of persons sharing the same name in a dataset. We present the homonyms ratio of the different sources we used, in table 1. This is a rough measure of the difficulty of creating an individual's profile. Recall that we use names of individuals as the matching criterion to aggregate information collected from multiple sources. When a name is too common (*i.e.*, the number of homonyms is too high), one cannot be sure which of the individuals the information belongs to. By inspecting homonyms ratio presented in table 1, we can see that in the Texas Tribune dataset, for each unique employee's name we have 1.132 entries. This a low level of homonyms. The UTSA employees dataset almost does not have homonyms (2 among 6300), and can be used as a good aggregator set. On the other hand, the White Page dataset contains a higher number of homonyms, for each unique name there are 25.244 records. The housing dataset contains a medium number of homonyms, for each unique name, there are approximately 3 records. The Net Detective dataset has approximately 8 records per unique name. Whereas, the Facebook dataset contains 9 records per unique name.

4.2 Analysis

Recall that the goal of this work is to gather as much information as possible about a person from the Internet. With the insights gained above, that on average a name is not unique, we compute the probability of finding certain pieces of information about *any* person with a given name.

To compute the probability to find any information, we count the number of records from a data source that include the data, excluding duplicates as defined by the name. For example, the White pages data source contains age information for some of the records. We count all search results that have the age information, i.e., the age is not given as "unknown", disregarding multiple records for the same name. For instance, the three data records ("John Smith",unknown), ("John Smith",30) and ("John Smith",35) count as one hit for the name "John Smith". We then divide the count by the number of all unique names to compute the percentage of unique names with information, which we consider as an approximation of the probability of finding information given a name.

Table 3 summarizes the probabilities for the different pieces of information associated with a name. We studied the following kinds of information: home address, housing price and size, age, home phone, and Facebook account. However, we should note that the UTSA dataset also implicitly contains information about the gender, hiring date, salary and job description of all persons. Thus the probability of finding this information is trivially 1 for our dataset and omitted for clarity.

The first entry presented in Table 3 is the probability of finding a home address given a name. By inspecting the table, one can see that the probability is very high, 83.6%. However, in addition to the address if one wants to find more details (*i.e.*, house price, house size, house subdivision, date of purchase) about the house associated with a name, then the probability is lower, around 35.3%. The probability for finding the age or date of birth of a specific name is 59.6%. The probability finding the home-phone is 75.0%. Finally, the probability of finding home address, home phone, and age associated with a name is 52.5%. If in addition, one wants to find the age, address, home phone, house price, and house size information associated with a name, then the probability is 26.3%. Recall that, we have a dataset of UTSA employees containing the following information: salary, job title, name, hire date, and gender. Now, if we find any information (*e.g.*, address, age, home phone, *etc.*) then we will also get the information residing in the UTSA dataset.

Finally, given a name, we calculate the probability of finding a Facebook account with that name. Previous studies [20, 12] have shown that people tends to release a lot of personal information over social network websites. They also provided probabilities of finding different fields of the Facebook profile given an email. Once we calculate the probability of a person having a Facebook account, we can reuse the previous work to gather information from Facebook and aggregate the information we collected from the free websites. Including information from Facebook will enable one to create a more detailed (*e.g.*, interests, personality, location, languages, *etc.*) profile of a person.

Our input dataset (UTSA's employees) contained full names including middle initials. A first search was performed using the full information available. If the result is non-empty, that is, Facebook found an account under the full name (in table 3 we call this Facebook full names), we can assume with high probability that this account is for the person searched for. In our study, 25.4% of the dataset had a match with the full name. However, many people do not regularly use their middle initials and omit them in online accounts. Thus, we performed a second search dropping all initials (in table 3 we call this Facebook short names). This potentially results in more matches, but reduces the probability that a search result actually corresponds to the person in question. In such cases, further investigation of the Facebook profile is necessary to increase the confidence in a match. In our study, 39.1% of the dataset had a match with the short name. Overall, the probability of finding a Facebook account given a name (either short or long) is 59.0%.

Table 3: Probabilities of finding personal information from free websites

Properties	Prob.
Address	0.836
Housing price and size	0.353
Address, housing price and size	0.340
Age	0.596
Home phone	0.750
Address, age and home phone	0.525
Address, age, home phone, housing price, size	0.263
Facebook total	0.590
Facebook full names	0.254
Facebook short names	0.391

4.3 Profile Creation

Several interesting properties are hard to collect with automated crawlers, because the search might rely on non-structured websites or complex search results that cannot automatically be analyzed. These include: personal photos, email addresses, relatives, citizenship, work history, house photos, and educational history. To investigate how likely it is to find this information, we manually collected this information for 31 randomly selected UTSA employees, using Google, the UTSA website, Intelius, Yahoo People Search and other sources. The data is shown in Table 4.

The probability of finding personal pictures and email addresses based on a name is very high, 90.3% and 100%, respectively. This results from our selection of UTSA employees, which usually have a work website that contains a picture and address. Equally high is the probability for finding relatives. Many websites like Intelius or Yahoo People Search contain such information. Furthermore, personal documents like dissertations contain family information. The probability of finding a citizenship is around 22.5%. Usually, one can get this information on resumes. The probability of finding where a person had worked before is 87.0%. Multiple sources, most prominently LinkedIn, helps in gathering this information. Online maps are excellent tools for house photos. We used Google Maps, which resulted in a near-perfect probability of finding images of the house or apartment complex. Last, educational history is common to find in our target group (90.3%), since it is contained in resumes.

Table 4: Probability of finding other information

Property	Probability
Personal Photos	0.903
Relatives	1.000
Citizenship	0.225
Work History	0.870
House Photos	1.000
Educational History	0.903
Email address	1.000

4.4 Study Limitations

All the probabilities computed in this section considered that given a name one can find some information about the name. However, we cannot guarantee that when we aggregate data from different sources, the aggregation will result in a profile that is related to exactly the same person we have queried for. In fact, since each dataset contains more than one record per unique name, the probability that we get gives us only the chance of finding a match between the name and desirable information. Although, this is not ideal, one can try to find clues in other websites to increase the confidence in a match. For instance, the housing dataset contains information about the owners of a house, in this case, this information usually contains the names of a couple. As the White Pages dataset also contains names of relatives of an individual, one can use the spouse name to narrow down the search result and increase the confidence of a match.

In addition to this, we use as our aggregator dataset the names of the UTSA's employees. By doing this, we also got the job title, gender, salary, and hire date. However, we understand that not all state governments and organizations

release this type of information over the Internet. Two opposite examples are Sweden and Brazil. In Sweden, personal tax return information about every citizen is made available online for public use. This of course includes job titles and salaries, and with a history search also hiring dates. Brazil, on the other hand, while having a very efficient tax system, does not release any information publicly. To bridge this gap in release policies, we note that usually third-party information providers are available. For example, the Glassdoor [25] website provides average salaries for a diverse range of companies in the US. This information can be used to approximate missing data points. In that sense, we feel our approach can be successfully extended to different types of users, even though they do not work in a country, state, or company that publishes all of their information publicly available online.

5. COMPARISON WITH PAID ALTERNATIVE

The Net Detective website is a paid service that claims to offer more than 1.1 billion records about people around the world, and 231, 461, 546 records for US residents. However, the amount of records that could be collected from it when using the name of UTSA's employees is around 1/4 of the size of what we could collect from the White Pages records (see table 1). During the course of our study, they charged $29.00 for unlimited access for 3 years. Their website advertises that one can find the following pieces of information about a person: people searches, criminal records, sex offender list, arrest records, phone records, address records, social security records, public records, birth, marriage, divorce, and death records. However, what we found was a different story. The $29.00 subscription only allowed us to check for home address, date of birth, and home phone. They charged an additional $10.00 non-refundable processing fee for 3 days of accessing other additional information. We did not pay this fee considering it to be a scam as they did not live upto their initial promise of providing the information that comes with the $29.00 subscription fee.

5.1 Analysis

We follow the same methodology described in section 4 to compute the probability of getting information about individuals from the Net Detective website. Table 6 summarizes these probabilities. Given a name, the chance of getting a full home address containing zip code, state, city, and street is 82.8% which is very similar to the probability for White Pages (83.6%). The probability of finding a date of birth in Net Detective is 35.7%, whereas it is 59.6% for White Pages. Similarly, the probability of finding a home phone is 68.7%, which is less than that of the White Pages (75.0%). Finally, the probability of finding these 3 information together is 27.7%, which is 52.2% for the White Pages. To conclude, we felt that this site is not a good alternative to collect public information about people. In an approximation, the information we gather from the Net Detective service was a subset of the information we collected from the free service of White Pages.

6. RELATED WORK

David Brin is one of the first researchers to study the relation of privacy and its relationship with modern soci-

Table 5: Profile Example

Personal Information			
Name	Alice Eve	Alias	Ali Eve
DOB	10/09/2007	Age	42
Citizenship	American	Relatives	Bob Eve (Husband)
Gender	Female		
Job Information			
Company	UTSA	Job Tittle	Secretary
Hire Date	11/12/2005	Salary	$45,000.00
Work Phone	(210) 444-4444	Email	asmith@utsa.edu
Work History	UT Tyler, secretary 2004 - 2005		
Residence Information			
Address	111 Flower Street, 78221	Subdivision	Flower
Size	1200 Sq feet	Date Purchase	06/02/2006
Current Price	$130,000.00	Phone	(210) 222-2222
Educational Information			
Degree	B.A. in Geography	History	Bachelor in Geography, UT Tyler - 2000-2003

Table 6: Probabilities of finding personal information in the Net Detective website

Property	Probability
Address	0.828
Age	0.357
Home phone	0.687
Address, age and home phone	0.277

eties [21]. In his opinion, the only viable option is to make all personal sensitive information public, in his words "A transparent society". In similar lines, Garfinkels [3] shows how our society is already becoming a transparent society. These two books are more philosophical, whereas our work is more practical. We collect real public data to see how much information can one gather about a person via the Internet. In other words - how transparent is our society.

Many researchers have been studying the impact of social networks on the reputation and privacy of its users. In particular, Jin et al. [26] presents techniques for detecting whether a user profile in a social network is cloned, whereas Solove [20] shows more ethical and philosophical issues about the topic. In contrast, the scope of our work is broader and it discusses how someone can learn about others over the Internet (not restricted to social networks). In that sense our research is complimentary with [20, 26].

Harvesting information on databases is a well known topic in the literature, and it has raised a lot of discussions about ethical questions [27, 28, 29, 30]. However, few researchers have presented techniques for harvesting personal information over Social Networks. In particular, Polakis et al. [12] present a comprehensive study how someone using an email address as input can crawl personal information on Facebook, and other social networking websites. On the other hand, Krishnamurthy et al. [31] point several techniques that can be used to leak sensitive personal information from social networks. The work in [12] is the one that is more similar to ours. Nevertheless, where that work is concentrated on using Facebook profiles given an email to harvest personal information, we use a series of free websites to gather other types of information that were not considered in [12]. In that sense, our work is complimentary also to their work.

In a previous section, we have described how personal information gathered from the Internet can be used by malicious parties for different purposes. One of the threats that has received more attention from the researchers is the Spam attack [32, 33]. Compared to our work, both researchers focus more in defining how spammers act, and how they collect the information that will be used to send Spam emails, whereas the scope of our work is more general.

7. CONCLUSION AND FUTURE WORK

In this work, we observe that with the growing popularity of social networking websites, people are sharing not-so-sensitive information (e.g., location, images, employer name, phone number, email address, home address, personal websites, etc.) among each other without understanding the consequences. Furthermore, for the sake of transparency organizations also release some information of their customers or employees that is deemed to be not-so-sensitive (e.g., name, salary, home address, work department, etc.). However, individuals are not fully aware of all the information that is available about them on the Internet and even if they are aware, consider this information to be insignificant. Although the individual pieces of information seem harmless, the aggregation of this information can be used against the individual for kidnapping, robbery, extortion, spamming, phishing, direct marketing, etc. We show that it is possible and feasible to aggregate this information about a large number of people just by crawling the Internet. To this end, we have developed a framework that creates batch crawlers that imitate and automate a user's interaction with a website to crawl information about many individuals. We used the framework to crawl a multitude of *free* and *public* data sources like social networking sites, and also included a paid alternative. The crawled data was then used to compute the probabilities to find certain kinds of not-so-sensitive information that together can potentially become dangerous. Included in the analysis is also a surprising comparison of the free and for-pay alternatives: it turns out that the available free information is already stronger than the paid-for version.

The result of this study is a number of significant probabilities of finding sets of certain kinds of information. For example, the probability to find all of the gender, salary, address and housing price of a person is greater than one in three. While we do not intend to give advice or suggest social norms, we believe those numbers should be taken seriously. Internet users should be aware of the potential side effects and amount of publicly released data, because only informed netizens can make informed decisions about their behaviour, the sharing of information, and the associated risks on the Internet. From our experiments, we realized that without significant resources (except for time) and with the right tools, gathering not-so-sensitive information about many individuals is not that challenging.

Future work. As our future work, we intend to perform a comprehensive user study that will expose individuals to our findings. Namely, we are interested in the reactions of participants to the amount and detail of information that is available about them on the Internet, and whether there should be federal regulations that would mandate the amount of not-so-sensitive information that can be revealed by organizations for the sake of transparency. A small-scale pilot study seems to confirm our suspicions about the average Internet user: it revealed that the participants were usually astonished by the amount of personal information that was available on the Internet about them. Furthermore, we want to extend our analysis for other countries (*e.g.*, Brazil, Sweden, *etc.*) and compare their views with respect to privacy to the views taken in US.

8. REFERENCES

[1] "Health resources and services administration," 1996, health Insurance Portability and Accountability Act, Public Law 104-191.

[2] "Federal trade commission, How to comply with the children's online privacy protection rule," 1999, public Law.

[3] S. Garfinkel, *Database nation: the death of privacy in the 21st century.* Sebastopol, CA, USA: O'Reilly & Associates, Inc., 2001.

[4] "Facebook," http://www.facebook.com.

[5] "Myspace," http://www.myspace.com.

[6] "Orkut," http://www.orkut.com.

[7] "Hi5," http://www.hi5.com.

[8] K. Thomas, C. Grier, and D. M. Nicol, "unfriendly: multi-party privacy risks in social networks," in *Proceedings of the 10th international conference on Privacy enhancing technologies.* Berlin, Heidelberg: Springer-Verlag, 2010, pp. 236–252.

[9] D. Freni, C. Ruiz Vicente, S. Mascetti, C. Bettini, and C. S. Jensen, "Preserving location and absence privacy in geo-social networks," in *Proceedings of the 19th ACM international conference on Information and knowledge management.* New York, NY, USA: ACM, 2010, pp. 309–318.

[10] A. L. Young and A. Quan-Haase, "Information revelation and internet privacy concerns on social network sites: a case study of facebook," in *Proceedings of the fourth international conference on Communities and technologies.* New York, NY, USA: ACM, 2009, pp. 265–274.

[11] A. Ho, A. Maiga, and E. Aimeur, "Privacy protection issues in social networking sites," in *Computer Systems and Applications, 2009. AICCSA 2009. IEEE/ACS International Conference on,* may 2009, pp. 271 –278.

[12] I. Polakis, G. Kontaxis, S. Antonatos, E. Gessiou, T. Petsas, and E. P. Markatos, "Using social networks to harvest email addresses," in *Proceedings of the 9th annual ACM workshop on Privacy in the electronic society,* ser. WPES '10. New York, NY, USA: ACM, 2010, pp. 11–20.

[13] "Please Rob Me," http://pleaserobme.com/.

[14] "Texas Public Information Act-1973," https://www.oag.state.tx.us/open/.

[15] "Intelius," http://www.intelius.com/.

[16] "White Pages," http://www.whitepages.com/.

[17] "House Almanac," http://www.housealmanac.com/.

[18] "Texas Tribune," http://www.texastribune.org/.

[19] "Net Detective," https://www.netdetective.com/.

[20] D. J. Solove, *The Future of Reputation: Gossip, Rumor, and Privacy on the Internet.* New Haven, CT, USA: Yale University Press, 2007.

[21] D. Brin, *The Transparent Society: Will Technology Force Us to Choose Between Privacy and Freedom?* Perseus Books Group, Jun. 1999.

[22] "Rate Your Boy Friend," http://www.rateyour-boyfriend.com/.

[23] "Htmlunit," http://htmlunit.sourceforge.net/.

[24] S. Gulwani, "Automating string processing in spreadsheets using input-output examples," in *Proceedings of the 38th annual ACM SIGPLAN-SIGACT symposium on Principles of programming languages,* ser. POPL '11. New York, NY, USA: ACM, 2011, pp. 317–330.

[25] "Glassdoor," http://www.glassdoor.com/.

[26] L. Jin, H. Takabi, and J. B. Joshi, "Towards active detection of identity clone attacks on online social networks," in *Proceedings of the first ACM conference on Data and application security and privacy,* ser. CODASPY '11. New York, NY, USA: ACM, 2011, pp. 27–38.

[27] H. T. Tavani, "Informational privacy, data mining, and the internet," *Ethics and Inf. Technol.,* vol. 1, pp. 137–145, January 1998.

[28] L. Van Wel and L. Royakkers, "Ethical issues in web data mining," *Ethics and Inf. Technol.,* vol. 6, pp. 129–140, June 2004.

[29] M. S. Olivier, "Database privacy: balancing confidentiality, integrity and availability," *SIGKDD Explor. Newsl.,* vol. 4, pp. 20–27, December 2002.

[30] A. Narayanan and V. Shmatikov, "How to break anonymity of the netflix prize dataset," *CoRR,* vol. abs/cs/0610105, 2006, informal publication.

[31] B. Krishnamurthy and C. E. Wills, "On the leakage of personally identifiable information via online social networks," in *Proceedings of the 2nd ACM workshop on Online social networks,* ser. WOSN '09. ACM, 2009, pp. 7–12.

[32] C. Kreibich, C. Kanich, K. Levchenko, B. Enright, G. M. Voelker, V. Paxson, and S. Savage, "On the spam campaign trail," in *Proceedings of the 1st Usenix Workshop on Large-Scale Exploits and Emergent Threats.* Berkeley, CA, USA: USENIX Association, 2008, pp. 1:1–1:9.

[33] M. B. Prince, B. M. Dahl, L. Holloway, A. M. Keller, and E. Langheinrich, "Understanding how spammers steal your e-mail address: An analysis of the first six months of data from project honey pot," in *CEAS,* 2005.

Cookie-based Privacy Issues on Google Services

Vincent Toubiana   Vincent Verdot   Benoît Christophe

Bell Labs Research
Alcatel-Lucent Bell Labs France
Route de Villejust, 91620 Nozay, France
firstname.lastname@alcatel-lucent.com

ABSTRACT

With the success of Web applications, most of our data is now stored on various third-party servers where they are processed to deliver personalized services. Naturally, we must be authenticated to access this personal information, but the use of personalized services only restricted by identification could indirectly and silently leak sensitive data. We analyzed *Google Web Search* access mechanisms and found that the current policy applied to session cookies could be used to retrieve users' personal data. We describe two attack schemes based on the Google's "SID cookie". First, we show that it permits a *session fixation* attack in which the victim's searches are recorded in the attacker's Google Web Search History. The second attack leverages the search personalization (based on the same SID cookie) to retrieve a part of the victim's click history and even some of her contacts. We implemented a proof of concept of the latter attack on the Firefox Web browser and conducted an experiment with ten volunteers. Thanks to this prototype we were able to recover up to 80% of the user's search click history.

Categories and Subject Descriptors

H.2 [**DATABASE MANAGEMENT**]: Security, integrity, and protection

General Terms

Security

1. INTRODUCTION

Over the last few years, Google's core service "Search" was enhanced through feature deployments, new User Interface and display optimizations. One major improvement regarding the quality of search results was the personalization of ranking algorithms. Personalized search results are ranked according to the user's context (*e.g.* localization and language), profile (search history), social networks and other characteristics extracted from various Google's services. Via

the Google Dashboard, users can view and possibly edit any data that was collected by their use of Google services. This recorded information may be very sensitive, so the access to this interface naturally requires an authentication.

However, while the direct access to users' data is subject to a strict security policy, using personalized services (which may leak this same personal information) is not. Indeed, some Web applications like Google Search only verify the (unsecured) user's session ID to render personalized features. Such a session can be hijacked by simply capturing the corresponding "SID cookie". Unlike cookies used to authenticate the user, the SID cookie may be sent cleartext, *i.e.* unprotected. Furthermore, this cookie is sent whenever the user accesses to a service hosted on `google.com`, increasing attack opportunities. In this paper we show how the SID cookie could be misused by an attacker, providing non expressly granted access to Google Search personalized results and history.

We study two attack schemes that exploit the current Google's privacy policy regarding personalized services (*i.e.* unauthenticated access). More specifically, we hijack an SID cookie to circumvent Google protection and access a user's personal data who — possibly forced by the attacker — transmitted her cookie in clear text. We emphasize the risk of using unauthenticated personalized services over a shared network with the following contributions.

1. The study of a *session fixation* attack in which the victim's searches are directly recorded in the attacker's Google Web Search History.

2. The description of an *information leakage* attack that uses the unprotected SID cookie to retrieve the victim's visited search results and a list of her contacts.

3. A proof of concept, based on the browser extension "Firesheep", and a tool we used to evaluate the impact of the *information leak*.

The remaining of this paper is organized as follows. Section 2 describes Google's architecture and services relevant to the understanding of the proposed attacks. Section 3 presents the *session fixation* attack, explains how it can be easily deployed and lists practical limitations. Then we detail the second attack using the same SID cookie to retrieves user's click history and contacts in Section 4. An implementation of this latter attack is proposed in Section 5 along with statistics showing how seriously a Google account's click history could be compromised. Finally section 6 discusses measures deployed in 2011 to counter these attacks and section 7 concludes this paper.

2. GOOGLE SERVICE SESSION

Google provides more than twenty different services, covering most of people needs over the Web. With a single Google account, a user can access to all of these applications even those hosted on different domains (*e.g.* YouTube or Blogger). Only a couple of cookies are used to help users navigating smoothly between these services.

2.1 Google.com cookies

At least three cookies are systematically sent by the user's browser to Google servers when accessing a service under the `google.com` domain.

- PREF: this cookie carries the preferences for the browser currently accessing the service. These preferences refer to the interface, the language, the number of results returned by a search, etc. It is specific to a browser and not bound to any account.

- SID: this non-secured session cookie is transmitted to Google servers to identify the user and personalize the provided services. In the particular case of Search, this identification will trigger results personalization. Even if the user is not logged in, best effort personalization of search results can be performed based on the recent search history.

- SSID: this secured session cookie provides access to services that contains user data and personal information like *Gmail, Google Calendar, Google Contacts*, etc.

It is our understanding that unlike the SSID cookie transmitted through encrypted connection, the SID cookie has only an identification purpose and so cannot be used to authenticate a user and does not have any security purpose. On the other hand, the SSID cookie is sent only over encrypted connections and is required for services providing access to users' data and personal information.
In our study, we focus on the SID cookie and the information leakage that results of subsequent service personalization.

2.2 Setting up the Attack

The SID cookie is valid over the whole Google domain, so it is sent to every Web application hosted by Google (`*.google.com`). Some services, such as *Gmail*, are only available via a secured HTTPS connection, whereas others can be accessed through a clear, unsecured, connection (HTTP) that is the case of *Google Search* and other services listed in Table 1.

The SID cookie is sent every time a request to a service under the (`google.com`) domain is sent, even if the page content cannot be personalized (*e.g* privacy policy, terms of services). This cookie is sent to many URLs, however it is enough for one of this URL not to be accessible through a secure HTTPS connection to compromise it.

2.2.1 *Bypassing HTTPS enforcement policy*

HTTPS-Everywhere [4] is a browser extension that, redirects a user to the secured version of the requested service (when available) to prevent traffic interception. Unfortunately this approach suffers from several drawbacks:

- First, not every service is yet available through HTTPS. For instance, *Google Alerts* remains only accessible through HTTP.

- Second, the list of services available through HTTPS has to be maintained. Some services are already available in HTTPS but not yet redirected. A list of such services is reported in Table 1.

- Finally, some services are redirected while not yet available. As a result these services can not be reached by HTTPS-Everywhere users.

Due to these flaws, even HTTPS-Everywhere users could be redirected to a URL where they would have to send their SID cookies in clear text.

2.2.2 *Intercepting the SID cookie*

Whenever a user accesses to one of the URLs listed in Table 1, her vulnerable SID cookie is exposed and so is her personal information. The objective of the attacker is to force the victim to exchange this cookie with unsecured services over a shared network, and so easily capture the cookie. Here are some examples.

- The attacker can setup an open access point using the same wireless network name than an existing local hotspot (*e.g.* fast-food restaurant name) and include in the welcome page an hidden iframe pointing to an unsecured Google service. When connected, the browser will send to the rogue access point the valid SID cookie in clear text.

- In an open wireless network, the attacker could also spoof the access point's physical address (MAC) and respond to a victim's HTTP GET request by any Web page including the hidden iframe just like in the previous case.

3. SESSION FIXATION ATTACK

In a session fixation attack [8], the victim is somehow forced to log in a session controlled by the attacker. Then, all subsequent operations she will perform will be associated to the attacker's account. In the case of Web Search, modifying the victim's SID cookie "on-the-fly" enables the attacker to transparently trace every search request. This section describes how this attack can be easily and silently performed.

3.1 The handy user interface flaw

A condition for a session fixation attack to succeed is that the victim should not notice that she is logged in the attacker account otherwise she would not perform any operation.

With the new Google's top bar [12], the email address no longer appears in the upper right corner of the search page. Instead, is now displayed the user's profile name (see Figure 1). Unlike the email address, this pseudonym is not unique: users are free to choose whatever "display name" they want. So, by simply looking at the Google Search page, you cannot know which account is actually logged in — although you should still be able to know the user's identity. As an example, Figure 1 shows the same display name "Vincent T" used by two different users.

If the attacker knows the victim's profile name, he can set the same pseudonym to another account and then make her using it to capture Web searches into his Web Search History. Because the victim sees her name on the top of the page (as usual), she cannot realize her searches are hijacked. If she clicks on the profile name and so expands the

URL not available in HTTPS		URL not redirected to HTTPS	
Specialties	Service	Specialties	Service
google.com/blogsearch	picasa.google.com	google.com/sitesearch	investor.google.com
google.com/dirhp	maps.google.com	google.com/transparencyreport	desktop.google.com
google.com/alerts	knol.google.com/k	google.com/adsense/support	
google.com/mobile	webaccelerator.google.com	google.com/insights/search	
google.com/nexus	sketchup.google.com	google.com/prdhp	
google.com/analytics	books.google.com	google.com/appsstatus	
google.com/postini	video.google.com	google.com/chromebook	
google.com/chrome	scholar.google.com	google.com/patents	
google.com/wallet	gears.google.com		
google.com/ads/preference			
google.com/baraza			
google.com/imghp			

Table 1: List of URLs that for the victim to send in clear its cookie

account options, she may see that the email address does not correspond to hers. In that case she will be aware of the attack but unfortunately, she will not be able to delete already logged queries as the Web Search History requires an authentication and so the attacker's credentials.

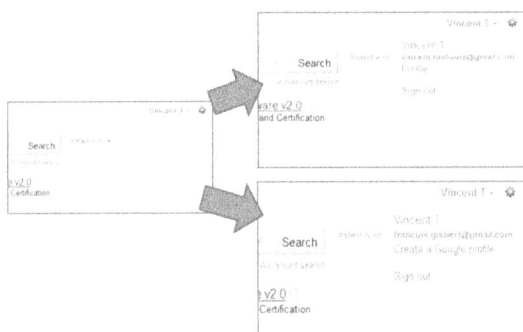

Figure 1: A pseudonym used by two different accounts

3.2 Session Phishing

Figure 2 gives an overview of the attack where the the victim's SID (VCT) is overwritten by the attacker's one (ATCK). In this session fixation attack, the attacker must first discover the victim's Google profile name. Because it is displayed on top of every page returned by Google to a logged user, the attacker can easily obtain it by listening to the network exchanges between the victim's browser and the Google servers. Note that the name is displayed in many Google applications: *Gmail, Google Talk, Blogger*, etc. Once the attacker knows the profile name, he quickly sets the same name to his Google account (or any account he controls). Then he replaces the victim's SID cookie by his own.

Following the introduction of *Google+*, the top bar has been updated to integrate several features. In addition to the user name, user's picture now also appears in the bar. Because this picture can be downloaded by the attacker, he can also fool the victim by having the same picture in addition to having the same name.

For this attack to succeed, the attacker must intercept and modify the requests exchanged between the target's browser and the Google servers. We described in the previous section

how the victim can be trapped "thanks" to the new Google's user interface. In the next two sections, we describe two different situations regarding if the target is logged in or not to her Google's account when the attack is performed.

3.2.1 The user is logged in

Once the attacker forced his target to send a request to a Google service (cf. 2.2) and configured an account, he overwrites the victim's SID cookie with his own. Therefore, the attacker has to perform a *man-in-the-middle attack*, either by creating a rogue access point or by spoofing a valid one's MAC address. Once the attacker is placed between his target and the Google servers, he appends to the response — sent by a Google service to the victim's browser — the header "Set-Cookie: SID=ATTACKER_SESSION_ID".

Because it receives an updated cookie from a supposed `google.com` host, the browser replaces the SID cookie with the new one. Now every search query issued by the victim will be associated to the attacker's session and will appear in his Web Search History. The attacker also knows the victim's email address and so can associate these searches to her identity.

3.2.2 The user is logged out

If the victim is not logged in an account, the attacker cannot overwrite an existing session by using her pseudonym. However, the attacker can set as profile name the words usually displayed when no one is logged. For instance, on the US Google Web page, it is "Sign in". When the victim will be logged in the attacker's session, the only indicator that could raise her suspicion is the tiny arrow next to the words "Sign in", cf. Figure 3. As long as the target does not overwrite her session ID cookie — by logging to her account — the attack remains active.

3.3 Limitations

At the time of writing, we observe that this attack is not applicable on the encrypted version of Google Search (service available at `https://www.google.com`). Furthermore, if the victim is simultaneously logged to an authenticated Google service such as *Gmail*, she could suspect of an attack as she will be asked to re-enter her credentials every time the session cookie is modified.

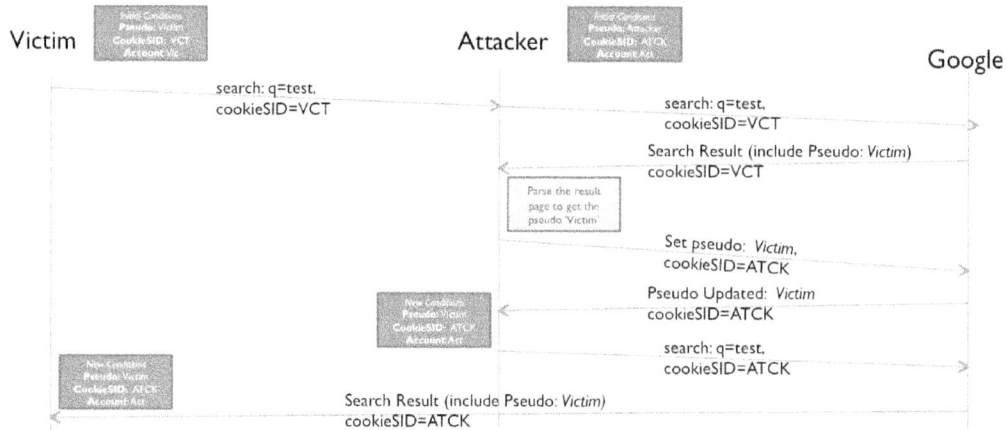

Figure 2: Session fixation attack overview

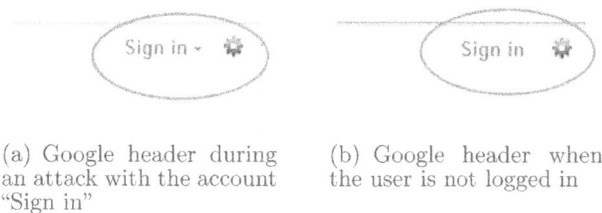

(a) Google header during an attack with the account "Sign in"

(b) Google header when the user is not logged in

Figure 3: Comparison of the top bar used with the "Sing In" pseudonym and the top bar displayed to unlogged users

4. PERSONALIZED SEARCH ATTACK

The search results provided to users who enabled Google Web Search History are personalized and colored based on their previous interactions. One advantage of this feature is the ability to see the websites a user previously visited in the Google's search results. Furthermore, frequently visited pages are more likely to be high ranked. In 2009, Google also started to consider social network indicators as part of the inputs used to improve the search algorithm. "Social Search" now up-ranks results that user's contacts shared publicly via *Google Buzz*, *Twitter* and other social networks.

The personalized search algorithm is based on private data held in the user's account. As such, it can be considered as a controlled information leakage. In [2], authors suggest that this information leakage can be used to know some of the results a user clicked on. At the time of writing this flaw has not yet been fixed as considered hard to exploit: an attacker must know what the victim searched for and then compare the personalized and un-personalized results. Similarly, the visited-link coloration feature/vulnerability [2] is not addressed as considered innocuous regarding the benefits it offers.

However, since these flaws have been reported, Google introduced new features that could be used to improve the efficiency of attacks based on this information leakage. This section shows how these features could be misused to compromise users' click history.

4.1 New Google features

In this section we list the features that make the *information leak* attack more critical. These features could be misused to render this attack "non-destructive" and significantly reduce the number of queries to be issued to retrieve the previously clicked search results (and so harder to detect).

4.1.1 Google Instant

With *Google Instant* results are displayed as the user is typing his query and before he even completes it. This prediction is based on what the user is typing and, if available, personalized query suggestions.

Google Instant results are ranked and colored just like the result list provided to the user when he actually clicks on the "Search" button. However, the query typed in the search box is not recorded in Web Search History unless he interacts with the page or remains idle more than three seconds. If the attacker keeps interacting with the *Google Instant* search box, none of the queries will be logged in the target's history, and the attack will remain silent and non-destructive (*i.e.* it does not affect the victim Web Search History).

4.1.2 Google Search filters

Visited Results

Collecting a user's visited links via random regular searches may take a very long time as the result pages mix visited and unvisited hyperlinks. However, an update of the Google Search interface introduced new filters. For instance, the "Visited" one filters out unvisited results (see Figure 4). By enabling this filter, the information leakage becomes critical: only visited links remain listed as search results, partly disclosing the user's click history.

This filter enabled, Google may also display what search request led to the visited page. Until June 2011, every server provided this information occasionally, but a recent update of the search interface now hides this information.

Social

With the "Social" filter, pages commented, twitted or shared via a social platform are displayed. The user's social network is built up according to his Gmail contacts and possibly other social applications such as Twitter, Livejournal,

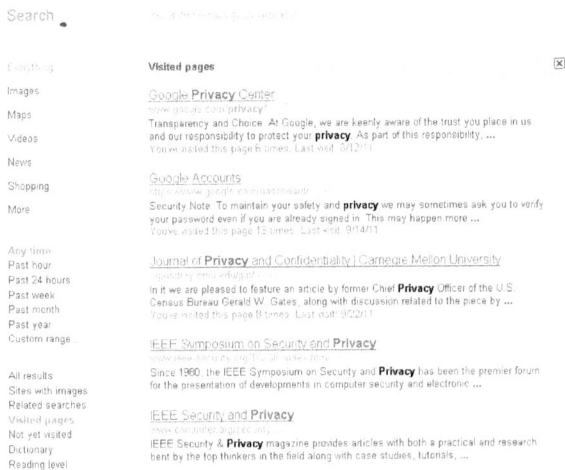

Figure 4: List of visited search results for the keyword "privacy"

etc (once linked to his Google account). This filter does not only provide the list of shared links, but also the connections that exist between the user and his social peers. Moreover, the user's Gmail contacts that should be treated as strictly private data is exposed and so could be used for blackmailing, phishing or spamming attacks. While we did not investigated how many contacts this attack may compromise, it appears that people who share a lot of information or belong to a large social network, are very likely to be listed in the "Social" search result page.

In addition to the list of *Gmail* contact, *Google+* users will also receive links that have been shared by people in their Circles whether or not these contacts belong to exposed Circles. Consequently, information about the victim private Circles could also be leaked and retrieved through the "Social" filter.

4.2 Capturing the victim's data

The sole prerequisite to run this attack is to capture the SID cookie of a user with Web Search History enabled. SID cookies are not marked "secured" and so are usually sent cleartext. If the victim uses a secure connection (HTTPS), the attacker could use the iframe injection described in Section 2 to force her to send the SID cookie cleartext. Once the cookie has been intercepted, the attack is launched by opening a window on Google Search with the "Visited" filter enabled.

To start the attack, we use a list of 15 terms composed of domain extension (`.com`, `.net`, `.org`, `.us`, `.edu`, `.fr`, `.co`), words and acronyms likely to appear in URLs (`.jsp`, `.asp`, `.php`, `.html`, `index`, `www`) and popular websites (`google`, `facebook`). Then, depending on the host associated to the cookie, the attacker may obtain a list of search requests the victim previously issued. We implemented two versions of the attack, as described in the following sections.

4.2.1 Silent approach

If the "Search for" feature is enabled, a background process parses the proposed "Instant" results while the program enters keywords. As the keywords are entered letter by letter, previously searched queries are likely to be proposed.

When a new "old" query is displayed, it is appended to the list of queries to be typed next by the program. Even if not all the user's previous queries can be retrieved using this process, a large portion of her interests can be inferred from this set of information.

4.2.2 Destructive approach

Selecting appropriate keywords to be part of the query list could provide a similar result. However, to maximize the chance of finding all the visited links, the program should not only parse the first page of results, but browse all of them. We implemented a prototype that parses the result page and then clicks on "Next" to display and parse the following and so until the last page. This process — almost as effective in term of number of visited link retrieved — is more efficient in terms of submitted queries. Another feature of this second approach is that –with *Google Instant* disabled – the attacker can set his Google PREF cookie to display 100 results per page instead of 10. Because the PREF cookie is browser specific – and not linked to the currently used Google Account – the attacker search preferences won't be mirrored on the victim browser. The list of retrievable clicked URLs can therefore be browsed very quickly. However, this attack is destructive; as the program interacts with the result pages, queries entered during the attack will appear in the victim's Web Search History.

We conducted an experiment that we analyzed in section 5 and which shown that on average, 40% of the click history could be compromised. For Google users who search only occasionally from their account, up to 80% of the click history could be retrieved using this method.

5. IMPLEMENTATION AND EVALUATION

In order to validate the applicability of our attack and to illustrate its easy deployment, we implemented a proof of concept as a Firefox extension and another extension to measure the number of visited links that were retrievable. Both tools are available online [1] and we describe them in this section. We then detail and analyze our experiment results.

5.1 Extending Firesheep

In October 2010, the Firefox extension Firesheep [1] was released and emphasized the simplicity of session hijacking. This extension monitors network interfaces to capture cookies corresponding to sessions established on popular Web Service websites like Facebook, Google and Twitter. Once a cookie is captured, the extension provides an access to the account related to the hijacked session.

We extended Firesheep to implement our attack. Thanks to the Firehseep modularity, we easily added a module performing an attack on the session hijacked.

As a result, when a Google SID cookie is captured, the account name appears in the Firesheep sidebar. Double clicking on it starts the attack ; double clicking again displays the retrieved list of visited links.

5.2 Measurement methodology

This section describes how we conducted our experiment without compromising the privacy of users who volunteered.

---

[1] see http://unsearcher.org/sid-cookie-attack

5.2.1 Silent attack

We started by using the version of the attack based on the "Search for" feature. We measured the number of recorded links retrieved and the number of links that were not retrieved every time a new query was typed. Due to time constraints, we have only evaluated this attack on a limited set of users. The results of this experiment are analyzed in section 5.3.1.

5.2.2 Destructive attack

After Google removed the "Search for" feature, we implemented the destructive attack scheme and evaluated it on an extended set of users.

We asked ten users to run the test on their Google accounts, we provided them with an extension that downloads their Web Search History and then simulates the attack from their accounts. The extension — developed for this experiment — and the corresponding instructions have been publicly released [2] to let users evaluate which portion of their click history can be exposed. The extension extracts from a user Web Search History the clicks recorded since 1st January 2011 and then issues some queries from the user's account with the "Visited" filter activated and the number of displayed results set to 100.

5.3 Result Analysis

We summarize the result of the two sets of experiment in Table 2. Because the two experiments have been conducted at different points in time, volunteers Web Search History — and Google ranking algorithm — are likely to have been modified between these two experiments. Therefore no conclusion can be drawn from a comparison of the two experiment results.

5.3.1 Silent attack

The result of the first experiment — conducted in June 2011 while "Search for" information was still available — is illustrated in Figure 5. During the simulated attack, between 183 and 203 queries were typed for each users, meaning that at least 168 queries were retrieved. The number of search queries that have been retrieved for each of the user are surprisingly similar considering the disparity in the number of clicked results.

Google only provided a subset of the query which results were visited, some queries were missing and most listed links were not associated to a query. Recall that Google previously fixed Google Suggest information leakage [2] which exposed the list of "clicked" queries. A limit on the number of queries displayed in the list of visited results might have been imposed to prevent an attacker from recovering this list through another vector.

In the results depicted in Figure 5 a similar number of links are retrieved for the first 15 queries which are the same for every user. Then, for the user with the less visited links (User 7), the curve follows a slower progression that can have two possible explanations. First, the listed results have already been listed previously and are ignored. Second, the number of links that can be extracted from Google Instant results increase with the length of the typed query. If *Users*

9 and 10 types longer queries than *User 7*, more results can potentially be extracted per query. For *Users 9 and 10* the attack provides similar results with more than 400 links retrieved when only 50 query are typed. Despite the disparity between the numbers of links clicked, a similar number of links were retrieved. This result suggests that there is a limitation on the number of links that may appear in the search results.

Although the main attack vector (the "Search for" feature) is no longer available, user interest can still be used and inferred from keywords appearing in visited links titles or even estimated from aggregated information provided by *Google Trends* [3].

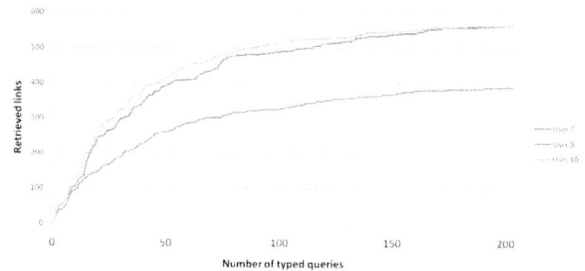

Figure 5: Silent Approach: Number of links retrieved as a function of the number of search in the Web Search History

5.3.2 Destructive attack

We simulated the destructive attack on a set of ten volunteers who visited between 88 and 3059 search results between January and July 2011 (this experiment has been conducted in July 2011). For these users, between 72 and 467 links were retrieved counting for 82% to 11% of the links recorded in their Web Search History over the considered period. We also recorded the total number of links that the attack retrieved independently of the date they were visited.

The attack provides similar results for the three users with the more visited links in their search history. For these three users who visited more links (Users 8, 9 and 10), a similar number of visited links were retrieved (between 628 and 644) although the number of clicks in the Web Search History varied from 1340 and 3059.

Figure 6 depicts the ratio of retrieved query as a function of the number of query submitted. We decided to use suffix and file extensions in our search term list as they are very likely to appear in the URL of visited links and will return many search results. For instance, the query .com will return the list of visited links with the .com suffix.
The objective is to recover a large portion of the victim visited search results with the smallest set of search queries. Limiting the number of queries that will appear in the Web Search History reduces the risk that the victim detect the attack. A detected attack is likely to result in the purge of the victim Web Search History and would prevent any further exploitation of the SID cookie by the attacker.

Four queries — with no associated visited search results — are likely to remain unnoticed in victims Web Search History and are enough to retrieve a large part of the clicked

---

[2]The extension is available at `http://unsearcher.org/Test%20Flaw/ad@monitor.xpi`

[3]Available at `http://trends.google.com/websites`

USER	U1	U2	U3	U4	U5	U6	U7	U8	U9	U10	Avg
Links (since Januray 2011)	88	111	211	426	625	812	1148	1340	2521	3059	1034
Found (since Januray 2011)	72	69	145	133	199	320	372	429	467	351	256
Query 1	66%	15%	41%	4%	16%	12%	23%	21%	12%	07%	22%
Query 2	68%	50%	60%	26%	19%	23%	28%	26%	16%	09%	33%
Query 4	72%	62%	66%	29%	24%	34%	31%	29%	17%	10%	37%
Query 15	82%	62%	69%	31%	32%	39%	32%	32%	19%	11%	41%
Found	338	69	359	137	315	541	425	628	644	640	410
Time	2m22	1m40	2m40	1m48	2m13	4m27	3m36	4m14	3m48	4m	3m06
(Silent exp) Links Total	NA	NA	NA	NA	NA	NA	639	NA	2850	2190	NA
Links Retreived	NA	NA	NA	NA	NA	NA	391	NA	567	565	NA
Ratio	NA	NA	NA	NA	NA	NA	61%	NA	26%	20%	NA

Table 2: Summary of the experiment results

results. For all users, the attack submitted the 15 queries in less than 5 minutes.

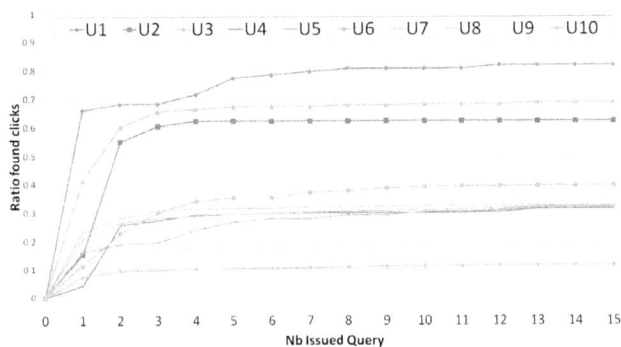

Figure 6: Destructive Approach: Result for the 10 users'

6. COUNTERMEASURE

In **February 2011**, we informed Google Security Team of our discovery. By **June 2011** the "Search for" optimization that we used in the first version of the information leakage attack was disabled. Finally in **October 2011**, Google made the "Visited" search filter only available through HTTPS thus highly reducing the exposure of "click-history". At the same time, Google started to make HTTPS connections to its search engine the default, this definitive solution to preventing all the attacks described in this paper.

While the most critical vulnerability has been addressed, some information may still leaks through Google Search personalization in countries where HTTPS is not already used by default. In this section we overview existing solutions that have been proposed to protect Web Search privacy and evaluate them against the two attacks. Finally, we discuss alternative to HTTPS that Google could have deployed to limit the exposure of users' data.

6.1 Client-side solutions

Installing the HTTPS-Everywhere browser extension enforces the HTTPS policy and prevents session fixation. Because some services are not available on HTTPS, users remain vulnerable to the information leakage attack. Similarly, browser extensions that anonymize user searches block the transmission of identifying cookies when searching on Google. Therefore, anonymization solution like Private Web Search [10] and Google Sharing [9] should effectively prevent clicked links to be recorded in users Web Search History. However, these browser extensions disable personalization features and so negatively impact the user experience. Following a contractual/policy based approach, Unsearch [11] leverages "Google Instant" to let users enjoy Google's personalized results without having their search requests and subsequent clicked results recorded in their Web Search history.

Nevertheless these mechanisms do not provide a flawless protection and some cookies may still be unsecurely transferred, e.g. when the HTTPS version of a service is not available or when using other Google services than *Search*. Indeed, requests sent to other Google services are not supposed to be anonymized, thus SID cookies could be intercepted using the scheme described in Section 2.2. Therefore, the attacker could retrieve the victim's *Gmail* and *Google Plus* contacts in addition to links that were clicked during unsecured searches.

Private Information Retrieval solutions like [3] and [6] focus on preventing the disclosure of user searches by mixing real and decoy queries. Both solutions neither apply to protect clicked results nor provide a protection against attacks described in this paper. TrackMeNot (TMN, [5]) obfuscates users' search requests and so the corresponding history by automatically issuing *pseudo-random* queries. TrackMeNot also protects click history by randomly clicking on search results. Therefore TMN offers an effective protection against the information leakage attack by injecting bogus clicked links in users web search history. Thus, an attacker cannot identify which links were actually clicked by the user. Furthermore, due to the Web history's length limitation, a part of the users' activity will be eventually dropped.

6.2 Changes in the Google services

In the rest of this section we suggest other mechanisms could also offer a protection specific to the attacks we described.

6.2.1 Enforcing access to search filters

The information leakage highly relies on the availability of the "visited" and "social" filters that hide search results that would be irrelevant for the attacker. Google should enforce the access control to these search filters: a user without a valid pair of SSID *and* SID cookies shall not be able to set these filters. Google could enforce such access policy by adding a secured token to URLs activating search filters, these tokens should be transmitted through HTTPS only to prevent any interception. This idea can be implemented by displaying search filter links in a secured iframe like the one used to display *Google Plus* notifications. This solution enforces neither the integrity of search results nor the confidentiality, but it suffices to assure the authentication of the user enabling the search filter.

6.2.2 Generalizing shared links

An even simpler solution could be applied to prevent user's contacts disclosure through the "social filter". *Google Plus* users can organize their social contacts in *Circles*. Currently, "social search" results show shared links along with the name of the contact who shared it and his comments if applicable. We believe that providing the circle name instead of the full contact identity would be sufficient for the end-user.

We propose to replace the name of the sharer by the smaller *circle* he belongs to. For such solution to be efficient, the link should not be associated to any comment otherwise *de-anonymization* would be trivial. This solution would not only protect the privacy of users whose SID cookie has been compromised, but would also accurately matches the privacy expectation of users sharing links on social networks [7]. While this temporary solution does not prevent the information leakage, it makes its exploitation more complicated and detectable.

7. CONCLUSION

We presented two attacks that leverage the two-level cookie based access policy. By exploiting the different access rights that are attached to each cookie we show that an attacker can force his victim to have her searches recorded in his Web Search History. We have described an information leakage attack, implemented a proof of concept and evaluated the number of links visited over the last six months that could be exposed. We also described measures that Google took to prevent such attacks.

8. ACKNOWLEDGEMENT

We thank our colleagues and friends who accepted to take part to the evaluation of the flaw. We also thank members of the NYU Privacy Research Group especially Helen Nissenbaum who provided useful feedbacks. We thank Claude Castelluccia, Jessica Staddon and members of the Google Security Team for fruitful and productive conversations.

9. REFERENCES

[1] Eric Butler. Firesheep, 2010. http://codebutler.com/firesheep.

[2] Claude Castelluccia, Emiliano De Cristofaro, and Daniele Perito. Private information disclosure from web searches. In *Proceedings of the 10th international conference on Privacy enhancing technologies*, PETS'10, pages 38–55, Berlin, Heidelberg, 2010. Springer-Verlag.

[3] Christopher W. Clifton and Mummoorthy Murugesan. Providing privacy through plausibly deniable search. April 2009.

[4] Electronic Frontier Foundation. Https everywhere. https://www.eff.org/https-everywhere.

[5] Daniel C. Howe and Helen Nissenbaum. Trackmenot: resisting surveillance in web search. In *I. Kerr, C. Lucock, V. Steeves (Eds.), Lessons from the Identity Trail: Privacy, Anonymity and Identity in a Networked Society*, pages 409–428, Oxford UK, 2009. Oxford University Press.

[6] A. Solanas J. Domingo-Ferrer and J. Castelli-Roca. Preserving user's privacy in web search enginesh(k)-private information retrieval from privacy-uncooperative queryable databases. *Online Information Review*, 3(4), 2009.

[7] Andrew Swerdlow Jessica Staddon. Public vs. publicized: Content use trends and privacy expectations, 2011.

[8] Mitja Kolsek. Session fixation vulnerability in web-based applications, December 2002. http://www.acrossecurity.com/papers/session_fixation.pdf.

[9] Thoughtcrime Labs. Google sharing. http://www.googlesharing.net.

[10] Felipe Saint-Jean, Aaron Johnson, Dan Boneh, and Joan Feigenbaum. Private web search. In *WPES '07: Proceedings of the 2007 ACM workshop on Privacy in electronic society*, pages 84–90, New York, NY, USA, 2007. ACM.

[11] TMN Team. Unsearch. https://chrome.google.com/webstore/detail/jojanedhfpmmjlkakmkhkgalbaokiphp.

[12] Alma Whitten. The freedom to be who you want to be..., February 2011. http://googlepublicpolicy.blogspot.com/2011/02/freedom-to-be-who-you-want-to-be.html.

Refinement-based Design of a Group-centric Secure Information Sharing Model

Wanying Zhao, Jianwei Niu, William H. Winsborough
The University of Texas at San Antonio
One UTSA Circle, San Antonio, Texas, USA 78249
{wzhao, niu}@cs.utsa.edu, wwinsborough@acm.org

ABSTRACT

This paper presents a formal, state machine-based specification (*stateful specification*) of a group-centric secure information sharing (g-SIS) model. The stateful specification given here is a refinement of a prior specification that is given in first-order linear temporal logic (FOTL). Such FOTL specification defines authorization based solely on group operations, but gives little guidance regarding implementation. The current specification is the result of a second step in a multi-step design process that separates concerns and provides multiple opportunities to detect unintended policy characteristics. We show that our stateful specification is consistent with the prior FOTL specification by using a combination of model-checking and manual techniques.

Categories and Subject Descriptors

D.4.6 [**Operating Systems**]: Security and Protection – Access controls

General Terms

Security

Keywords

Access Control, Formal Specification, Formal Verification, System Refinement, Secure Information Sharing

1. INTRODUCTION

As a society, we enjoy a great opportunity to make information much more highly available than it has been historically. This can facilitate emergency preparedness by supporting rapid dissemination of information concerning immanent natural or man-made threats or response requirements. Information sharing can also support more general publish/subscribe relationships, as well as enable collaborations that otherwise might require physical proximity. However, all these applications require that some degree of access

control (AC) be enforced over shared information. This requirement has sometimes been dubbed, "share, but protect."

Information can be shared between individuals, as with limited access blogs or forums, or between representatives of various kinds of organizations. In the latter case, the metaphor of a secure meeting room may be apt. Participants may be working toward some specific goal, such as designing a new product, arriving at an acquisition or merger agreement, or conducting a joint military operation.

Group-centric secure information sharing (g-SIS) [7] is a recently introduced AC model that brings users and information together in a group to provide for access. It is a simple, yet flexible sharing framework suited for use in highly dynamic environments. The g-SIS framework defines authorizations in terms of action histories involving *group operations* (namely, user join, user leave, object add, and object remove). The temporal order in which those operations occur determines whether a user is authorized to access an object. One particular g-SIS policy, presented by Krishnan *et al.*, is given by what is called the π *specification* [8], and is expressed in many-sorted, first-order linear temporal logic (FOTL)[1]. However, the FOTL specification is highly abstract. It would be difficult for security systems' stakeholders to comprehend and implement a AC system directly from it.

To alleviate users efforts, we develop a separate specification of authorization policy, which is given in terms of attributes and data structures that record appropriate information to enable efficient authorization decisions. The π specification was the first step in the multi-step design process. Our current specification is the result of a second step in the multi-step design process that bridges the gap between abstract FOTL specification and enforcement model. The current specification introduces and maintains data structures that summarize sufficient information about the history of group operations to enable authorization decisions to be made directly from the data structure values. This in and of itself is a significant step toward generating a specification from which a developer could implement. However, it is not the last. Later steps, not undertaken here, will address distribution, communication, latency issues, *etc.*

The specification we present here is given by a state machine (SM). The notion of an SM differs from that of a conventional finite state machine only in that the number of

---

[1]FOTL resembles the more familiar propositional linear temporal logic (PLTL) that is used in model checkers. The differences are analogous to those between many-sorted first-order predicate calculus and propositional logic. [2]

(reachable) states is potentially countably infinite. An SM is intuitive and expressive, yet programming-language neutral. To provide a shorthand by which to contrast these two approaches to specification, we call the FOTL specification a *stateless specification* and an SM-based specification a *stateful specification*. Our stateful specification is a *refinement* of the stateless π specification in the sense that our specification is consistent with the π specification, but provides additional detail.

We develop a combination of methodologies to formally verify that a stateful specification and its corresponding stateless specification are consistent (refinement equivalent). We use a model checking tool, NuSMV [3], to verify if a state machine specification consisting of a single user and a single object within a group satisfies the stateless specification expressed in temporal logic. As the g-SIS system can have unbounded numbers of objects, users, and groups, we develop a manual reasoning technique to generalize automated model checking results to infinite universes.

Our contributions are as follows. First, we present our stateful specification and its data structures. Our specification also shows how to handle requests to perform group operations, and how to filter out requests to perform illegal operations. We also provide invariants that relate the values of the data structures in the SM to the histories under which the data structure have those values. Second, we show a soundness result, which says that any sequence of group operations accepted by the stateful specification causes the SM to arrive at the same authorization decisions as are arrived at by the π specification. Thirdly, we show a completeness result. Specifically, we show that every sequence of group operations that satisfies the π specification is accepted by our SM. (We already know from soundness that the authorization decisions agree.)

The rest of the paper is organized as follows. Section 2 summarizes the key elements of the prior g-SIS policy given by the stateless π specification. Section 3 presents our stateful specification of that policy. Section 4 demonstrates that our stateful specification is consistent with the stateless π specification in the sense outlined above. Section 5 discusses how to handle requests to perform group operations that are illegal. Section 6 discusses factors that limit scalability of our design and on-going work seeking to mitigate those factors. Section 7 discusses related work and section 8 presents our conclusions and discusses our future work.

2. BACKGROUND ON G-SIS AND THE π SPECIFICATION

As discussed in the introduction, g-SIS supports four basic group operations—join, leave, add, and remove—and the π specification considers *strict* and *liberal* variants of each. Let us summarize the intuition of each of these eight operations. When a user joins a group by Strict Join (SJ), only objects added to the group after join time are accessible. When Liberal Join (LJ) is used, the user can additionally access objects added previously by using Liberal Add (LA). When a user leaves a group by Strict Leave (SL), the user loses all access previously granted by membership in the group. When Liberal Leave (LL) is used, the user retains access to those objects granted by his membership immediately prior to leave time. If an object is added to a group by Strict Add (SA), only users who joined the group prior to add

time can access the object; users joining later do not receive access. When Liberal Add (LA) is used, users joining later via Liberal Join also receive access. If an object is removed from a group by Strict Remove (SR), all users lose access to it. When Liberal Remove (LR) is used, users who had access to the object at remove time retain access. Since π specification supports read-only operation, the "access" in following sections of this paper is read access.

2.1 g-SIS Language

The π specification is expressed in a form of linear temporal logic, specifically many-sorted FOTL, determining whether a user is permitted to access an object in a given group based on the history of group operations at each point in time. The temporal operators of FOTL used in this paper and their intuitive meanings are summarized in Table 1.

As mentioned above, the π system supports the eight group operations that are represented by *action predicates* in $\mathcal{A} = \{\text{SJ}, \text{LJ}, \text{SL}, \text{LL}, \text{SA}, \text{LA}, \text{SR}, \text{LR}\}$. Authorization is represented by the *authorization predicate*, Authz.

Sorts enable us to distinguish users from objects, *etc.* They resemble very simple types. For users, objects, and groups, we denote the corresponding sorts by U, O, and G. We also use, respectively, the variables u, o, and g, possibly with subscripts. Sorts are assigned when a variable is quantified: $\forall u : U.\phi$. The semantic values over which a variable ranges depend on the variable's sort and are drawn from a set that is called the *carrier* of that sort. For the sorts identified above we denote the corresponding carriers by $\mathcal{U}$, $\mathcal{O}$, and $\mathcal{G}$, respectively. We use the following metavariables to range over individuals: $\mathbf{u} \in \mathcal{U}$, $\mathbf{o} \in \mathcal{O}$, and $\mathbf{g} \in \mathcal{G}$. We denote the collection of carriers by $\mathcal{C} = \langle \mathcal{G}, \mathcal{U}, \mathcal{O} \rangle$. In general, these carriers may be finite or countably infinite.

We use $\Omega_{\mathcal{C}}$ to denote the set of finite interpretations of action and authorization predicates over the carriers in $\mathcal{C}$. An *interpretation*, ι, is a function mapping each predicate in the language to a relation over the appropriate carriers. Although they need not be so, the relations in the interpretations we use are finite, reflecting the fact that at any point in time, only a finite number of users, objects and groups have been introduced to the system. In our context an interpretation for π maps predicates to relations of the following types: $[\![\text{SJ}]\!]\iota, [\![\text{LJ}]\!]\iota, [\![\text{SL}]\!]\iota, [\![\text{LL}]\!]\iota \subset \mathcal{U} \times \mathcal{G}$. $[\![\text{SA}]\!]\iota, [\![\text{LA}]\!]\iota, [\![\text{SR}]\!]\iota, [\![\text{LR}]\!]\iota \subset \mathcal{O} \times \mathcal{G}$, and $[\![\text{Authz}]\!]\iota \subset \mathcal{U} \times \mathcal{O} \times \mathcal{G}$. Each $\kappa \in \Omega_{\mathcal{C}}^{\omega}$ is an infinite sequence of interpretations called a *trace*. For each $i \in \mathbb{N}$, we write $[\![\text{SJ}]\!]\kappa_i \subseteq \mathcal{U} \times \mathcal{G}$ to denote the relation associated with SJ by κ_i. If $\langle \mathbf{u}, \mathbf{g} \rangle \in [\![\text{SJ}]\!]\kappa_i$, this means user $\mathbf{u}$ does a Strict Join of group $\mathbf{g}$ at position i. Similarly, $\langle \mathbf{u}, \mathbf{o}, \mathbf{g} \rangle \in [\![\text{Authz}]\!]\kappa_i$ indicates that user $\mathbf{u}$ is authorized to access object $\mathbf{o}$ in group $\mathbf{g}$ at position i.

Let us now outline what it means for a trace to satisfy an FOTL formula. Here we illustrate the construction just below by giving the most important semantic rules. To handle variables, we need the notion of an *environment* η, which assigns to each variable an element of the carrier corresponding to the variable's sort. The statement that, at index i, κ satisfies ϕ under environment η, written $\kappa, i, \eta \models \phi$, is defined inductively on the structure of ϕ. For example, $\kappa, i, \eta \models \text{SJ}(u, g)$ holds if $\langle \eta(u), \eta(g) \rangle \in [\![\text{SJ}]\!]\kappa_i$. For temporal operators "since": $\kappa, i, \eta \models \phi_1 \mathcal{S} \phi_2$ holds if there exists $k \in \mathbb{N}$ such that $0 \leq k \leq i$ and $\kappa, k, \eta \models \phi_2$, and for all $j \in \mathbb{N}$ such that $k < j \leq i$, $\kappa, j, \eta \models \phi_1$. Other temporal operators can be found in [2]. For example of an-

Table 1: Intuitive summary of temporal operators

Operator	Read as	Explanation
$\ominus$	Previous	($\ominus$ p) means that formula p held in the previous state.
$\diamondsuit$	Once	($\diamondsuit$ p) means that formula p held at least once in the past.
$\mathcal{S}$	Since	(p $\mathcal{S}$ q) means that q happened in the past and p held continuously from the state following the last occurrence of q to the present.
$\boxminus$	Historically	$\boxminus$ p means p holds at all states preceding (and including) the current state.
$\square$	Henceforth	$\square$ p means p will continuously hold in all future states starting from the current state.

other rule, $\kappa, i, \eta \models \exists u : U.\phi$ if there exists $\mathbf{u} \in \mathcal{U}$ such that $\kappa, i, \eta[u \mapsto \mathbf{u}] \models \phi$. For a formula ϕ, ϕ is satisfied by a trace κ, written $\kappa \models \phi$, if $\kappa, 0, \eta \models \phi$ for all environments η. The complete semantics of the g-SIS language can be found in [7]

2.2 The π Specification

The π specification defines three *well formedness* requirements that every trace must satisfy at every state. Requirement τ_0 states that no user can join and leave a given group at the same time and no object can be added to and removed from the same group at the same time. Requirement τ_1 states that no user can both strictly and liberally join or leave a given group at the same time and similarly for objects. Requirement τ_2 says that no user can join a group that he currently belongs to and that he cannot leave a group unless he currently belongs to it. It also expresses the analogous requirements for objects.

The π specification determines at each point in time whether a user is permitted access to an object via a given group, based on the history of group operations involving the user and object with respect to that group. The π specification is given as follows:

$$\pi : \forall u : U.\forall o : O.\forall g : G.$$
$$\square((\text{Authz}(u, o, g) \leftrightarrow \lambda_1(u, o, g) \vee \lambda_2(u, o, g)) \wedge$$
$$\bigwedge_{0 \le j \le 2} \tau_j(u, o, g))$$

in which $\lambda_1(u, o, g)$ and $\lambda_2(u, o, g)$ defined by

$\lambda_1(u, o, g)$:
$$(\neg \text{SL}(u, g) \wedge \neg \text{SR}(o, g)) \, \mathcal{S} \, [(\text{SA}(o, g) \vee \text{LA}(o, g)) \wedge$$
$$((\neg \text{LL}(u, g) \wedge \neg \text{SL}(u, g)) \, \mathcal{S} \, (\text{SJ}(u, g) \vee \text{LJ}(u, g)))]$$
$\lambda_2(u, o, g)$:
$$(\neg \text{SL}(u, g) \wedge \neg \text{SR}(o, g)) \, \mathcal{S} \, [\text{LJ}(u, g) \wedge$$
$$((\neg \text{SR}(o, g) \wedge \neg \text{LR}(o, g) \, \mathcal{S} \, \text{LA}(o, g)))]$$

The second subformula (involving the τ's) says that traces satisfying the π specification must be well formed. The two subformulas, λ_1 and λ_2 correspond to two cases in which a user is authorized for access to an object. In case (a), handled by λ_1, the user joins the group before or at the same time as the object is added; in case (b), handled by λ_2, the object is added before the user joins. In case (a), authorization does not depend on whether the join and add are strict or liberal because the user is already a member when the object is added. The right-hand subformula of λ_1 (in square brackets) formalizes the requirement that the user is in the group when the object is added. The left-hand subformula permits authorization to continue after liberal leave or liberal remove. Case (b) allows for authorization when both the join and the add are liberal. The right-hand subformula of λ_2 (in square brackets) formalizes the requirement that the

object is in the group when the user joins. As it does in λ_1, the left-hand subformula permits authorization to continue after liberal leave or liberal remove. Note that in any trace κ such that $\kappa \models \pi$, the interpretation of Authz is uniquely determined at each κ_i by the history of interpretations of the action predicates leading up to that point in the trace. In particular, $\mathbf{u}$ is authorized for access to $\mathbf{o}$ via $\mathbf{g}$ at step $i \in \mathbb{N}$ just in case $\langle \mathbf{u}, \mathbf{o}, \mathbf{g} \rangle \in [\![\text{Authz}]\!]\kappa_i$.

3. STATEFUL G-SIS SPECIFICATION

This section begins by introducing the construction of the state machine designed for stateful specification, followed by defining the data structures, and the invariants that identify historical conditions under which each value of each data structure is assumed. We then present the general formula that defines authorization in the stateful g-SIS specification based on the data structure values. We then show the transition relations for each data structure that would maintain the invariants correctly as group operations were performed. To illustrate the stateful specification, we use a case study to show data structure value updates and authorization decisions in the end of this section.

3.1 Our Stateful Specification and its Relationship to the Stateless Specification

Our stateful specification is a deterministic SM that we call $M_\pi^{\mathcal{C}}$, which produces authorization decisions identical to those made by traces that satisfy the π specification. The notion of a state machine we use is standard. It corresponds to the familiar notion of a finite state machine, with the difference being that, depending on the size of the carriers, the state space is not necessarily finite. A state machine is given by $M = \langle Q, q^0, \Sigma, \delta \rangle$. Q is a (possibly infinite) set of machine states [2], $q^0 \in Q$ is a distinguished start state, Σ is an alphabet, and $\delta \subset Q \times Q \times \Sigma$ is a deterministic transition relation. Given any sequence $\sigma \in \Sigma^\omega$, we define the *run of M induced by σ*, if it exists, to be the unique sequence $\rho \in Q^\omega$ of machine states defined inductively as follows. The initial state is $\rho_0 = q^0$ and for each $i \in \mathbb{N}$, $\delta(\rho_i, \rho_{i+1}, \sigma_{i+1})$. (This kind of SM ignores σ_0.) If there comes a point in σ at which no transition is defined, σ is *rejected* by M; otherwise it is accepted and the induced run ρ is well defined.

Our stateful specification $M_\pi^{\mathcal{C}}$ has the form $M_\pi^{\mathcal{C}} = \langle Q_\pi, q_\pi^0, \Sigma_{\mathcal{C}}, \delta_\pi \rangle$. The alphabet $\Sigma_{\mathcal{C}}$ is the set of interpretations of the action predicates in $\mathcal{A}$ (see section 2.1). Each state in Q_π is an assignment of values to each of the data structures introduced below in section 3.2. The initial state q_π^0 and the transition relation δ_π are also presented in section 3.2.

Note that the only difference between $\Omega_{\mathcal{C}}$ and $\Sigma_{\mathcal{C}}$ is that elements of the former interpret the authorization predicate

---

[2] In section 4 we will show that we verify the model with countably infinite carrier by using combination of model checking technique and manual proofs.

151

Authz, as well as the predicates in $\mathcal{A}$. We call each $\sigma \in \Sigma_{\mathcal{C}}^{\omega}$ an *action sequence*. An action sequence σ can be obtained from a trace κ by projecting each element of the trace, κ_i, onto the action predicates. In this case we write $\sigma = \kappa\!\restriction_{\mathcal{A}}$. Because τ_0, τ_1, and τ_2 do not use Authz, $\kappa\!\restriction_{\mathcal{A}}$ is well formed just in case κ is well formed. As noted at the end of the previous section, for any $\kappa \in \Omega_{\mathcal{C}}^{\omega}$ such that $\kappa \models \pi$, the interpretation of Authz at κ_i is uniquely determined by the prefix of $\sigma = \kappa\!\restriction_{\mathcal{A}}$ of length $i+1$. Put another way, for each well formed action sequence σ, there is a unique κ such that $\sigma = \kappa\!\restriction_{\mathcal{A}}$ and $\kappa \models \pi$. The run of $M_{\pi}^{\mathcal{C}}$, ρ, induced by a given $\sigma \in \Sigma_{\mathcal{C}}^{\omega}$ maintains the data structures contained in each ρ_i so that their values can be used to make authorization decisions without the need to consult σ. In section 4 we will show that (1) given any action sequence σ, there is a run of $M_{\pi}^{\mathcal{C}}$, ρ, induced by σ if and only if σ is well formed and (2) ρ generates exactly the same authorization decisions as does the unique κ such that $\sigma = \kappa\!\restriction_{\mathcal{A}}$.

3.2 Data Structures and Invariants

This section presents the data structures used by $M_{\pi}^{\mathcal{C}}$. The design process we used was organized by simultaneously specifying invariants that characterize properties of the history up to any given point in σ and relating those properties to values assumed by the data structures at that point. We knew we needed certain combinations of data structure values to indicate that either λ_1 or λ_2 was satisfied. We developed natural-seeming data structures for representing when this is the case, as well as corresponding invariants that together entailed λ_1 or λ_2. Table 2 summarizes the data structures of $M_{\pi}^{\mathcal{C}}$, each of the values they can take on, and the temporal invariants under which each of those values is assumed.

Boolean-valued data structures CurrUserMem$(\mathbf{u}, \mathbf{g})$ and CurrObjMem$(\mathbf{o}, \mathbf{g})$ represent, respectively, whether user $\mathbf{u}$ and object $\mathbf{o}$ are current members of group $\mathbf{g}$. The structures Join_Type$(\mathbf{u}, \mathbf{g})$, Leave_Type$(\mathbf{u}, \mathbf{g})$, Add_Type$(\mathbf{o}, \mathbf{g})$ and Remove_Type$(\mathbf{o}, \mathbf{g})$ record that the most recent join, leave, add, and remove events for the respective users, objects and groups were strict or liberal. Their possible values are L, S, and NULL, representing respectively liberal, strict, and the case in which no such event has yet occurred.

Recall that when a user (resp., object) experiences a liberal leave (resp., remove), users continue to have access to the objects to which they had access prior to these events. We use PrevAuthz$(\mathbf{u}, \mathbf{o}, \mathbf{g})$ to record whether $\mathbf{u}$ was authorized for $\mathbf{o}$ via $\mathbf{g}$ at the time the most recent liberal leave and/or liberal remove occurred. (This is needed to handle correctly the left-hand subformulas of each of λ_1 and λ_2.)

Recall that when an object is added prior to a user joining, if either of these actions is strict, the user does not gain access to the object. To make authorization decisions correctly in this case, the stateful specification uses timestamps (not shown in Table 2—see use in definition of Authz_DS, section 3.3); the structures Join_TS$(\mathbf{u}, \mathbf{g})$ and Add_TS$(\mathbf{o}, \mathbf{g})$ record timestamps associated with the most recent join of $\mathbf{u}$ and add of $\mathbf{o}$, respectively. For simplicity, we assume here that timestamps are simply natural numbers with 0 representing that the event has not occurred, and with other values increasing monotonically with time (*e.g.*, the current index in the action sequence). Thus, the case in which the object add precedes the user join can be identified simply by comparing the associated timestamp values. This is the

mechanism used in the authorization decisions made by the stateful specification, presented in the next section.

Timestamps are a natural solution in an implementation because their values can be established in a distributed, decentralized manner[3]. However, they are not conducive to verification via model checking because, theoretically, they grow without bound as the system runs. Model checking can be applied directly only to finite state machines. To overcome this, we use a standard technique called *abstraction* [4] wherein the unbounded structure is replaced by a bounded one that contains only the information that is essential to the state machine. Specifically, we introduce a structure JoinT_LE_AddT$(\mathbf{u}, \mathbf{o}, \mathbf{g})$, shown in Table 2, which takes on the value 1 when $\mathbf{u}$ joined before or at the same time as $\mathbf{o}$ was added. (If $\mathbf{u}$ or $\mathbf{o}$ has been a group member multiple times, the structure reflects the most recent join and add.) If the add occurred first, the value is 0. Three additional values represent the cases in which one or both of the actions have never occurred: No_Join, No_Add, and NULL, the latter indicating that neither has occurred. We use abstraction JoinT_LE_AddT for verification (in model checking) purpose only.

For all $\mathbf{u} \in \mathcal{U}$, $\mathbf{o} \in \mathcal{O}$ and $\mathbf{g} \in \mathcal{G}$, for all well formed action sequence $\sigma \in \Sigma_{\mathcal{C}}^{\omega}$, and for all $i \in \mathbb{N}$, letting ρ be the run induced by σ, the invariants listed in Table 2 hold. Due to space limit, here we just explain the first invariant in the table as an example. At a given point i, the value of CurrUserMem$(\mathbf{u}, \mathbf{g})$ is 1 if user $\mathbf{u}$ never leaves group $\mathbf{g}$ since the last time he joined $\mathbf{g}$. Otherwise, the value is 0. Note that each of the invariants has been verified by using model checking. As we discuss further in section 4, because the formulas being model checked refer to group operations involving only one user and/or object and group, it is sufficient to check that the formulas hold for very small carriers containing only one element each. This enables us to convert the formulas to propositional form, making them amenable to model checking. The invariants also assist in designing the transition relations that we will introduce in section 3.4.

3.3 Stateful Specification of Authorization

In this section, we show how authorization decisions are made based on the data structures we introduced in the previous section. We denote the function that yields these authorization decisions by Authz_DS, which is defined as follows. (Because Authz_DS is not itself a data structure, in the following, ρ_i can be viewed as a parameter to the function, much as when a method is invoked on an object in object oriented programming.) For all $\mathbf{u} \in \mathcal{U}$, $\mathbf{o} \in \mathcal{O}$ and $\mathbf{g} \in \mathcal{G}$, for all well formed action sequence $\sigma \in \Sigma_{\mathcal{C}}^{\omega}$, and for all $i \in \mathbb{N}$, letting ρ be the run induced by σ, we define ρ_i.Authz_DS by

$$
\rho_i.\text{Authz\_DS}(\mathbf{u}, \mathbf{o}, \mathbf{g})
$$
$$
= \begin{cases} 1 & \text{if} \quad \rho_i.\phi_1(\mathbf{u}, \mathbf{o}, \mathbf{g}) = 1 \text{ and} \\ & \qquad \rho_i.\phi_2(\mathbf{u}, \mathbf{o}, \mathbf{g}) = 1 \text{ and} \\ & \qquad \rho_i.\phi_3(\mathbf{u}, \mathbf{o}, \mathbf{g}) = 1 \\ 0 & \text{otherwise} \end{cases}
$$

---

[3]Issues such as clock synchronization and appropriate management of latency will be introduced in later steps of the design process, and are not handled here.

Table 2: Data Structures, Values, and Invariants. Boolean value "true" is represented by 1, "false", by 0

$$\rho_i.\text{CurrUserMem}(\mathbf{u},\mathbf{g}) = \begin{cases} 1 & \text{if } \sigma, i, [u \mapsto \mathbf{u}, g \mapsto \mathbf{g}] \models \neg(\text{SL}(u,g) \vee \text{LL}(u,g)) \, \mathcal{S} \, (\text{SJ}(u,g) \vee \text{LJ}(u,g)) \\ 0 & \text{otherwise} \end{cases}$$

$$\rho_i.\text{CurrObjMem}(\mathbf{o},\mathbf{g}) = \begin{cases} 1 & \text{if } \sigma, i, [o \mapsto \mathbf{o}, g \mapsto \mathbf{g}] \models \neg(\text{SR}(o,g) \vee \text{LR}(o,g)) \, \mathcal{S} \, (\text{SA}(o,g) \vee \text{LA}(o,g)) \\ 0 & \text{otherwise} \end{cases}$$

$$\rho_i.\text{Join\_Type}(\mathbf{u},\mathbf{g}) = \begin{cases} L & \text{if } \sigma, i, [u \mapsto \mathbf{u}, g \mapsto \mathbf{g}] \models \neg\text{SJ}(u,g) \, \mathcal{S} \, \text{LJ}(u,g) \\ S & \text{if } \sigma, i, [u \mapsto \mathbf{u}, g \mapsto \mathbf{g}] \models \neg\text{LJ}(u,g) \, \mathcal{S} \, \text{SJ}(u,g) \\ \text{NULL} & \text{if } \sigma, i, [u \mapsto \mathbf{u}, g \mapsto \mathbf{g}] \models \boxminus\neg(\text{LJ}(u,g) \vee \text{SJ}(u,g)) \end{cases}$$

$$\rho_i.\text{Leave\_Type}(\mathbf{u},\mathbf{g}) = \begin{cases} L & \text{if } \sigma, i, [u \mapsto \mathbf{u}, g \mapsto \mathbf{g}] \models \neg\text{SL}(u,g) \, \mathcal{S} \, \text{LL}(u,g) \\ S & \text{if } \sigma, i, [u \mapsto \mathbf{u}, g \mapsto \mathbf{g}] \models \neg\text{LL}(u,g) \, \mathcal{S} \, \text{SL}(u,g) \\ \text{NULL} & \text{if } \sigma, i, [u \mapsto \mathbf{u}, g \mapsto \mathbf{g}] \models \boxminus\neg(\text{LL}(u,g) \vee \text{SL}(u,g)) \end{cases}$$

$$\rho_i.\text{Add\_Type}(\mathbf{o},\mathbf{g}) = \begin{cases} L & \text{if } \sigma, i, [o \mapsto \mathbf{o}, g \mapsto \mathbf{g}] \models \neg\text{SA}(o,g) \, \mathcal{S} \, \text{LA}(o,g) \\ S & \text{if } \sigma, i, [o \mapsto \mathbf{o}, g \mapsto \mathbf{g}] \models \neg\text{LA}(o,g) \, \mathcal{S} \, \text{SA}(o,g) \\ \text{NULL} & \text{if } \sigma, i, [o \mapsto \mathbf{o}, g \mapsto \mathbf{g}] \models \boxminus\neg(\text{LA}(o,g) \vee \text{SA}(o,g)) \end{cases}$$

$$\rho_i.\text{Remove\_Type}(\mathbf{o},\mathbf{g}) = \begin{cases} L & \text{if } \sigma, i, [o \mapsto \mathbf{o}, g \mapsto \mathbf{g}] \models \neg\text{SR}(o,g) \, \mathcal{S} \, \text{LR}(o,g) \\ S & \text{if } \sigma, i, [o \mapsto \mathbf{o}, g \mapsto \mathbf{g}] \models \neg\text{LR}(o,g) \, \mathcal{S} \, \text{SR}(o,g) \\ \text{NULL} & \text{if } \sigma, i, [o \mapsto \mathbf{o}, g \mapsto \mathbf{g}] \models \boxminus\neg(\text{LR}(o,g) \vee \text{SR}(o,g)) \end{cases}$$

$$\rho_i.\text{PrevAuthz}(\mathbf{u},\mathbf{o},\mathbf{g}) = \begin{cases} 1 & \text{if } \sigma, i, [u \mapsto \mathbf{u}, o \mapsto \mathbf{o}, g \mapsto \mathbf{g}] \models \neg(\text{SL}(u,g) \vee \text{SR}(o,g)) \, \mathcal{S} \\ & [\ominus\text{Authz}(u,o,g) \wedge ((\text{LL}(u,g) \vee \text{LR}(o,g)) \wedge \neg\text{SL}(u,g) \wedge \neg\text{SR}(o,g))] \\ 0 & \text{otherwise} \end{cases}$$

$$\rho_i.\text{JoinT\_LE\_AddT}(\mathbf{u},\mathbf{o},\mathbf{g}) = \begin{cases} 1 & \text{if } \sigma, i, [u \mapsto \mathbf{u}, o \mapsto \mathbf{o}, g \mapsto \mathbf{g}] \models \neg(\text{SJ}(u,g) \vee \text{LJ}(u,g)) \, \mathcal{S} \\ & ((\text{SA}(o,g) \vee \text{LA}(o,g)) \wedge \diamondplus(\text{SJ}(u,g) \vee \text{LJ}(u,g))) \\ \text{No\_Join} & \text{if } \sigma, i, [u \mapsto \mathbf{u}, o \mapsto \mathbf{o}, g \mapsto \mathbf{g}] \models \boxminus\neg(\text{SJ}(u,g) \vee \text{LJ}(u,g)) \wedge \diamondplus(\text{SA}(o,g) \vee \text{LA}(o,g)) \\ \text{No\_Add} & \text{if } \sigma, i, [u \mapsto \mathbf{u}, o \mapsto \mathbf{o}, g \mapsto \mathbf{g}] \models \boxminus\neg(\text{SA}(o,g) \vee \text{LA}(o,g)) \wedge \diamondplus(\text{SJ}(u,g) \vee \text{LJ}(u,g)) \\ \text{NULL} & \text{if } \sigma, i, [u \mapsto \mathbf{u}, o \mapsto \mathbf{o}, g \mapsto \mathbf{g}] \models \boxminus(\neg(\text{SJ}(u,g) \vee \text{LJ}(u,g)) \wedge \neg(\text{SA}(o,g) \vee \text{LA}(o,g))) \\ 0 & \text{otherwise} \end{cases}$$

in which ϕ_1, ϕ_2, and ϕ_3 are as given by

$\rho_i.\phi_1(\mathbf{u},\mathbf{o},\mathbf{g})$

$$= \begin{cases} 1 & (\rho_i.\text{Join\_Type}(\mathbf{u},\mathbf{g}) = L \\ & \wedge\rho_i.\text{Add\_Type}(\mathbf{o},\mathbf{g}) = L)\vee \\ & ((\rho_i.\text{Join\_TS}(\mathbf{u},\mathbf{g}) \leq \rho_i.\text{Add\_TS}(\mathbf{o},\mathbf{g})) \wedge \\ & (\rho_i.\text{Join\_TS}(\mathbf{u},\mathbf{g}) \neq 0) \wedge (\rho_i.\text{Add\_TS}(\mathbf{o},\mathbf{g}) \neq 0))\vee \\ & (\rho_i.\text{PrevAuthz}(\mathbf{u},\mathbf{o},\mathbf{g}) = 1\wedge \\ & (\rho_i.\text{Join\_TS}(\mathbf{u},\mathbf{g}) > \rho_i.\text{Add\_TS}(\mathbf{o},\mathbf{g})) \\ 0 & \text{otherwise} \end{cases}$$

$\rho_i.\phi_2(\mathbf{u},\mathbf{o},\mathbf{g})$

$$= \begin{cases} 1 & (\rho_i.\text{CurrUserMem}(\mathbf{u},\mathbf{g}) = 1)\vee \\ & (\rho_i.\text{Leave\_Type}(\mathbf{u},\mathbf{g}) = L\wedge \\ & \rho_i.\text{PrevAuthz}(\mathbf{u},\mathbf{o},\mathbf{g}) = 1) \\ 0 & \text{otherwise} \end{cases}$$

$\rho_i.\phi_3(\mathbf{u},\mathbf{o},\mathbf{g})$

$$= \begin{cases} 1 & (\rho_i.\text{CurrObjMem}(\mathbf{o},\mathbf{g}) = 1)\vee \\ & (\rho_i.\text{Remove\_Type}(\mathbf{o},\mathbf{g}) = L\wedge \\ & \rho_i.\text{PrevAuthz}(\mathbf{u},\mathbf{o},\mathbf{g}) = 1) \\ 0 & \text{otherwise} \end{cases}$$

Let us summarize the intuition behind ϕ_1, ϕ_2, and ϕ_3, each of which must be true for $\mathbf{u}$ to have access to $\mathbf{o}$ via $\mathbf{g}$. Formula ϕ_1 ignores the question of whether $\mathbf{u}$ and $\mathbf{o}$ are currently members of $\mathbf{g}$; that issue is handled by ϕ_2 and ϕ_3. Formula ϕ_1 is true if any of the following three cases

holds: the most recent join and add were both liberal; $\mathbf{u}$ joined before or at the same time as $\mathbf{o}$ was added; $\mathbf{u}$ joined after $\mathbf{o}$ was added, but the last time they were both in $\mathbf{g}$, $\mathbf{u}$ had access to $\mathbf{o}$. Formula ϕ_2 requires that $\mathbf{u}$ is currently a member of $\mathbf{g}$ unless $\mathbf{u}$'s the most recent leave was liberal and $\mathbf{u}$ had access $\mathbf{o}$ immediately prior to leaving. Formula ϕ_3 states for $\mathbf{o}$ the same requirement that ϕ_2 states for $\mathbf{u}$.

Note that neither ϕ_2 nor ϕ_3 depends on the most recent join or add type because the π specification uses what is called *lossless* versions of join and add [8]. This means that when $\mathbf{u}$ joins $\mathbf{g}$ or $\mathbf{o}$ is added to $\mathbf{g}$, this never causes $\mathbf{u}$ to lose access $\mathbf{o}$ if $\mathbf{u}$ had access immediately prior to the join or add operations. This intuition is stated formally in the π specification. So if $\mathbf{u}$ to had access to $\mathbf{o}$ via $\mathbf{g}$ prior to the join (respectively, add), then the access will be retained at least until the subsequent leave (respectively, remove—whichever comes first).

3.4 Transition Relations

We present transition relations of data structures used by M_π^C. To illustrate, here we show initial states and transition relations of two data structures: CurrUserMem and PrevAuthz.

For all $\mathbf{u} \in \mathcal{U}$ and $\mathbf{g} \in \mathcal{G}$, the initial value of CurrUserMem$(\mathbf{u},\mathbf{g})$ is assigned as 0, as we assume that when the system starts, no user is in any group. To express the state transition relation, we use the convention that values of structures in the destination state are denoted by adding primes to the structure names; unprimed names refer to the structures' values in the source state. The state transition relation for CurrUserMem is given by following.

$$((\text{CurrUserMem}(\mathbf{u}, \mathbf{g}) = 1) \wedge (\text{SL}'(\mathbf{u}, \mathbf{g}) \vee \text{LL}'(\mathbf{u}, \mathbf{g})) \wedge$$
$$(\text{CurrUserMem}'(\mathbf{u}, \mathbf{g}) = 0)) \vee$$
$$((\text{CurrUserMem}(\mathbf{u}, \mathbf{g}) = 0) \wedge (\text{SJ}'(\mathbf{u}, \mathbf{g}) \vee \text{LJ}'(\mathbf{u}, \mathbf{g})) \wedge$$
$$(\text{CurrUserMem}'(\mathbf{u}, \mathbf{g}) = 1)) \vee$$
$$(\neg(\text{SJ}'(\mathbf{u}, \mathbf{g}) \vee \text{LJ}'(\mathbf{u}, \mathbf{g}) \vee \text{SL}'(\mathbf{u}, \mathbf{g}) \vee \text{LL}'(\mathbf{u}, \mathbf{g})) \wedge$$
$$(\text{CurrUserMem}'(\mathbf{u}, \mathbf{g}) = \text{CurrUserMem}(\mathbf{u}, \mathbf{g})))$$

Note that the formula defining the transition relation for CurrUserMem is false when a user attempts to leave a group to which he does not belong. This reflects the fact that there is no legal transition in this case and that the action sequence is rejected by M_π^C. This is appropriate because such an action sequence is not well formed.

For all $\mathbf{u} \in \mathcal{U}$, $\mathbf{o} \in \mathcal{O}$ and $\mathbf{g} \in \mathcal{G}$, the initial value of PrevAuthz$(\mathbf{u}, \mathbf{o}, \mathbf{g})$ is 0, as no action occurred in the past and previously $\mathbf{u}$ is not authorized to access $\mathbf{o}$. The state transition relation for PrevAuthz is given by following.

$$(((\text{LL}'(\mathbf{u}, \mathbf{g}) \vee \text{LR}'(\mathbf{o}, \mathbf{g})) \wedge \neg\text{SL}'(\mathbf{u}, \mathbf{g}) \wedge \neg\text{SR}'(\mathbf{o}, \mathbf{g}))$$
$$\wedge (\text{PrevAuthz}'(\mathbf{u}, \mathbf{o}, \mathbf{g}) = \text{Authz\_DS}(\mathbf{u}, \mathbf{o}, \mathbf{g})) \vee$$
$$((\text{SL}'(\mathbf{u}, \mathbf{g}) \vee \text{SR}'(\mathbf{o}, \mathbf{g})) \wedge (\text{PrevAuthz}'(\mathbf{u}, \mathbf{o}, \mathbf{g}) = 0)) \vee$$
$$(\neg(\text{LL}'(\mathbf{u}, \mathbf{g}) \vee \text{LR}'(\mathbf{o}, \mathbf{g}) \vee \text{SL}'(\mathbf{u}, \mathbf{g}) \vee \text{SR}'(\mathbf{o}, \mathbf{g}))$$
$$\wedge (\text{PrevAuthz}'(\mathbf{u}, \mathbf{o}, \mathbf{g}) = \text{PrevAuthz}(\mathbf{u}, \mathbf{o}, \mathbf{g})))$$

Recall that we use PrevAuthz$(\mathbf{u}, \mathbf{o}, \mathbf{g})$ to record whether $\mathbf{u}$ was authorized for $\mathbf{o}$ via $\mathbf{g}$ at the time the most recent liberal leave and/or liberal remove took place. The PrevAuthz$'(\mathbf{u}, \mathbf{o}, \mathbf{g})$ value in the destination state of transition relation depends on the Authz_DS$(\mathbf{u}, \mathbf{o}, \mathbf{g})$ value in the source state. As defined in 3.3, the Authz_DS$(\mathbf{u}, \mathbf{o}, \mathbf{g})$ value can be computed by values of all data structures on the source state.

3.5 Case Study

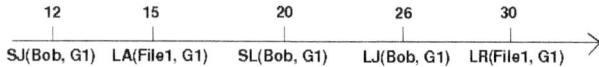

Figure 1: Case Study

In this section we present a case study to show how data structures are updated in stateful specification and how authorization is determined in a given point by using data structure values.

We assume that each user, object and group have their respective unique identifier in the system. Assume that we have a research group G_1. Although there may be many users and objects in G_1, in our case study, we only consider user Bob and object $File_1$ in G_1.

In the initial state, the data structures are assigned values as following,

- CurrUserMem$(Bob, G_1) = 0$,
- Join_Type$(Bob, G_1) = \text{NULL}$,
- Leave_Type$(Bob, G_1) = \text{NULL}$,
- Join_TS$(Bob, G_1) = 0$,
- CurrObjMem$(File_1, G_1) = 0$,
- Add_Type$(File_1, G_1) = \text{NULL}$,
- Remove_Type$(File_1, G_1) = \text{NULL}$,

- Add_TS$(File_1, G_1) = 0$,
- PrevAuthz$(Bob, File_1, G_1) = 0$.

As shown in figure 1. Bob joins G_1 by SJ at timestamp 12. It causes the following data structures to be updated, and other data structures remain unchanged since initial assignment.

- CurrUserMem$(Bob, G_1) = 1$,
- Join_Type$(Bob, G_1) = S$,
- Join_TS$(Bob, G_1) = 12$.

At timestamp 15, $File_1$ is added to G_1 by LA, It causes the following data structures to be updated, and other data structures remain unchanged.

- CurrObjMem$(File_1, G_1) = 1$,
- Add_Type$(File_1, G_1) = L$,
- Add_TS$(File_1, G_1) = 15$.

Bob leaves G_1 by SL at timestamp 20, the following data structures are updated.

- CurrUserMem$(Bob, G_1) = 0$,
- Leave_Type$(Bob, G_1) = S$,

Note that we only listed the data structure values that are updated and different from the values in previous state.

Suppose we need to make a authorization decision for Bob to read $File_1$ in G_1 at this state (at timestamp 20). According to Authz_DS defined in section 3.3, the value is determined by the values of data structures at this state. We compute that Authz_DS$(Bob, File_1, G_1) = 0$. (As $\phi_2 = 0$).

At timestamp 26, Bob rejoins G_1 by LJ. The following data structures are updated as:

- CurrUserMem$(Bob, G_1) = 1$,
- Join_Type$(Bob, G_1) = L$,
- Join_TS$(Bob, G_1) = 26$.

At timestamp 30, $File_1$ is removed from G_1 by LR. The following data structures are updated.

- CurrObjMem$(File_1, G_1) = 0$,
- Remove_Type$(File_1, G_1) = L$,
- PrevAuthz$(Bob, File_1, G_1) = 1$.

Because an LR occurs, PrevAuthz needs to be updated. Note that the PrevAuthz is based on the value of Authz_DS in the previous state, that is, at timestamp 26. (Because no group action for Bob or $File_1$ occurred and no data structure were updated since then.) In the previous state, Join_Type$(Bob, G_1) = L$, Add_Type$(File_1, G_1) = L$, CurrUserMem$(Bob, G_1) = 1$, CurrObjMem$(File_1, G_1) = 1$. So we get Authz_DS$(Bob, File_1, G_1) = 1$. (All ϕ_1, ϕ_2 and ϕ_3 have value 1.) According to the transition relation of PrevAuthz, PrevAuthz$(Bob, File_1, G_1)$ is updated to 1 based on Authz_DS value in the previous state.

Consider we need to make a authorization decision for Bob to read $File_1$ in G_1 at timestamp 35. The Authz_DS$(Bob, File_1, G_1)$ is determined by the values of data structures at this state. Because no group action for Bob or $File_1$ ever occurred since timestamp 30, all data structure value remain unchanged since then. Because Remove_Type$(File_1, G_1) = L$ and PrevAuthz$(Bob, File_1, G_1) = 1$, the Authz_DS gets the value 1. (All ϕ_1, ϕ_2 and ϕ_3 have value 1.)

The PrevAuthz records authorization decision at the time the most recent leave or remove occurs. Whenever authorization decision is to be made, we do not need to refer to the entire event history. Instead, we use the data structures that summarized the event history information to make an authorization decision.

In contrast, stateless specification contains no such data structures to provide summarized event history information, every action in the history need to be kept track of. And whenever a authorization decision is to be made, the entire trace need to be inspected. Since there may be only LR and LL in the group, and the overlapping membership period for user and object can be arbitrarily far in the past.

In the current design step, we assume that the timestamps are managed by a global clock. Clock synchronization and latency issues will be addressed in later steps of development process, but not in this paper.

4. THE REFINEMENT EQUIVALENCE OF STATELESS AND STATEFUL POLICY

The correctness requirements of the stateful specification $M_\pi^{\mathcal{C}}$ are (1) that for all action sequence $\sigma \in \Sigma_{\mathcal{C}}^\omega$, $M_\pi^{\mathcal{C}}$ accepts σ if and only if σ is well formed and (2) the stateless Authz and the stateful Authz_DS agree at each step i. We refer to the "only if" part of (1) together with (2) as *soundness*. We refer to the "if" part of (1) as *completeness*.

We introduce a distinguished collection of small carriers, $\mathcal{C}_{sm} = \langle \mathcal{G}_{sm}, \mathcal{U}_{sm}, \mathcal{O}_{sm} \rangle$, in which each carrier contains exactly one element. As we argue just below Lemma 4.1, both soundness and the correctness of our invariants hold for arbitrary carriers if they hold for $\mathcal{C}_{sm}$. This enables us to use model checking to verify these results by converting FOTL formulas interpreted over $\mathcal{C}_{sm}$ to PLTL formulas. We have verified the following lemma by using the NuSMV model checker [3].

LEMMA 4.1 (SMALL-CARRIER SOUNDNESS). *Let* $\mathcal{U}_{sm} = \{u\}$, $\mathcal{O}_{sm} = \{o\}$, $\mathcal{G}_{sm} = \{g\}$, *and* $\mathcal{C}_{sm} = \langle \mathcal{U}_{sm}, \mathcal{O}_{sm}, \mathcal{G}_{sm} \rangle$. *For all traces* $\kappa \in \Omega_{\mathcal{C}_{sm}}^\omega$, *if a run* ρ *of* $M_\pi^{\mathcal{C}_{sm}}$ *is induced by* $\kappa \restriction_A$, *then (1)* κ *is well formed and (2) if* $\kappa \models \pi$, *then for all* $i \in \mathbb{N}$, $\langle \mathbf{u}, \mathbf{o}, \mathbf{g} \rangle \in [\![\text{Authz}]\!]\kappa_i$ *if and only if* $\rho_i.\text{Authz\_DS}(\mathbf{u}, \mathbf{o}, \mathbf{g})$.

The lemma generalizes to large carriers for two reasons. First, by inspecting the formula, in the π specification, Authz($\mathbf{u}, \mathbf{o}, \mathbf{g}$) depends only on group operations involving these individuals. Second, the transition relations for each data structure in $M_\pi^{\mathcal{C}}$ refer to only one user and/or object and to one group, both with respect to the data structure indices and with respect to the group operations. It follows from these observations that in both the stateless and the stateful specification the authorization of a given user for a given object via a given group is independent of group operations involving any other users, objects, or groups. Hence, the size of the carriers is immaterial to the validity of the proof. Thus we have the following.

THEOREM 4.2 (SOUNDNESS OF ARBITRARY CARRIERS). *Given an arbitrary collection of countable carriers* $\mathcal{C} = \langle \mathcal{G}, \mathcal{U}, \mathcal{O} \rangle$, *for all traces* $\kappa \in \Omega_{\mathcal{C}}^\omega$, *if a run* ρ *of* $M_\pi^{\mathcal{C}}$ *is induced by* $\kappa \restriction_A$, *then (1)* κ *is well formed and (2) if* $\kappa \models \pi$, *then for all* $\langle \mathbf{u}, \mathbf{o}, \mathbf{g} \rangle \in \mathcal{U} \times \mathcal{O} \times \mathcal{G}$ *and for all* $i \in \mathbb{N}$, $\langle \mathbf{u}, \mathbf{o}, \mathbf{g} \rangle \in [\![\text{Authz}]\!]\kappa_i$ *if and only if* $\rho_i.\text{Authz\_DS}(\mathbf{u}, \mathbf{o}, \mathbf{g})$.

We have verified the following lemma for the small carrier case using model checking. The result generalizes to large carriers for the same reasons discussed above.

LEMMA 4.3 (CORRECTNESS OF INVARIANTS). *For a system with carriers* $\mathcal{C} = \langle \mathcal{G}, \mathcal{U}, \mathcal{O} \rangle$, *the invariants of all data structures are all satisfied.*

For completeness proof, we need to show that every trace that satisfies the stateless specification can be generated by the SM. From theorem 4.2, we know that every time the stateless specification confirms Authz, the stateful specification also confirms Authz_DS, and vise versa. So for completeness, we need only prove that every trace that satisfies the well formed constraints is accepted by the SM. Since it can not be proved by using model checking, we show completeness by using manual proof techniques instead. This manual proof makes use of lemma 4.3.

THEOREM 4.4 (COMPLETENESS). *For a system with carriers* $\mathcal{C} = \langle \mathcal{G}, \mathcal{U}, \mathcal{O} \rangle$, *any well formed action sequence* $\sigma \in \Sigma_{\mathcal{C}}^\omega$ *induces a run* ρ *of* $M_\pi = \langle Q_\pi, q_\pi^0, \Sigma_{\mathcal{C}}, \delta_\pi \rangle$.

Consider any well formed action sequence σ. The proof shows by induction on $i \in \mathbb{N}$ that $M_\pi^{\mathcal{C}}$ has a transition defined for each σ_i, as needed to complete the proof. The body of the proof then is an extensive case analysis based on the possible machine states and σ_i. The invariants associated with each possible machine state are combined with the well formedness requirements to show that a transition exists in all cases. Due to space constraints, the complete proof could be found in our technical report [12].

5. REFINING THE SPECIFICATION TO HANDLE ACTION REQUESTS

The action sequence provided as input to a given run of $M_\pi^{\mathcal{C}}$ is provided by the environment in which $M_\pi^{\mathcal{C}}$ is deployed. An implementation of an AC system cannot reject an ill-formed action sequence, as halting the system is unacceptable. In this section, we discuss informally an aspect of the stateful specification that refines the π specification, namely the treatment of group-operation *requests*. The stateful specification augments $M_\pi^{\mathcal{C}}$ with an input/output SM that acts as a transducer, converting an input action-request sequence into a well formed action sequence, which is then provided as input to $M_\pi^{\mathcal{C}}$.

Ensuring that the output of the filter SM is a legal action sequence is straightforward. (As part of our work with the model checking, we generated a filter SM and verified that it satisfies this requirement. For this purpose, our model-checking code nondeterministically generates arbitrary request sequences.) Slightly more interesting is the problem of ensuring that for each legal action sequence, there exists a request sequence that causes the filter SM to generate the given action sequence. This can be ensured by requiring that when presented with a set of requests that, taken together, are all legal, the filter SM does not drop any of them. Together, these two requirements are sufficient in the sense that the action sequences that can be generated by the filter SM are exactly the well formed action sequences. However, these requirements do not uniquely specify the filter SM. Consider the case in which a single user requests to perform both a liberal and a strict join on the same group at the same time. The simplest behavior in this case is to drop both requests. However other options exist: ask the user which one to perform; apply a predefined policy that selects between the two; or flip a coin and drop one on that basis.

6. LIMITATIONS OF SCALABILITY

The limitation of our stateful specification concerns PrevAuthz. First, the structure is inherently centralized, as information is kept in it for each $\langle \mathbf{u}, \mathbf{o}, \mathbf{g} \rangle$ tuple. Second, each time a user operation is performed on a group $\mathbf{g}$, the value of the structure must be updated for all tuples involving that user and group and similarly for each object operation. There are environmental conditions in which these limitations may not be a major problem, namely when the system is not highly distributed and/or the rate of authorization queries greatly exceeds the rate of group operations. In particular, PrevAuthz enables authorization queries to be answered in constant time. Nevertheless, a less centralized approach would often be desirable. An alternative would be use timestamps to maintain with each user and object the history of group operations in which it participates. Authorization of a user for an object could then be decided by comparing the histories of each. The problem with this approach is that, the overlapping membership periods for the user and object can be arbitrarily far in the past (when no SL or SR has been performed). Thus the local histories can grow without bound, as can the time required to make authorization decisions. In future work, we would like to develop a hybrid approach combining these two approaches.

7. RELATED WORK

Many research efforts have been made towards developing security systems by leveraging formal methods. In particular, model checking has been increasingly employed to reason about security properties in access control systems, such as Role-Based Access Control Models (RBAC) and trust management systems. Schaad *et al.* [9] verified separation of duty properties in RBAC systems using NuSMV. Other work [5, 6, 11] also supports the use of formal tools to verify properties of security policies.

FOTL specification of security and privacy systems can exhibit a high-level of complexity, leading to difficulty in the assessment admission of system behavior and in the development of enforcement. One notable technique that is closely related to our work is the development of small model theorem [13] in the verification of parameterized systems. The small model theorem reduces the problem of reasoning about infinite-state system to the verification of a finite-state system, which can then be model checked.

Stepwise refinement techniques have been used in the design of security systems to improve the correctness. In Sprenger *et al.* [10], the refinement could help designers to master the complexity of both models and proofs by focusing on individual design aspects at each step. Alur *et al.* develop a framework of secrecy and preservation of secrecy for labeled transition systems via refinement [1]. It is unclear if their approach is scalable to handle unbounded attributes as the π specification is expressed in FOTL.

8. CONCLUSION AND FUTURE WORK

We presented a stateful g-SIS specification that is a refinement of the prior stateless π specification [8]. By using a combination of model checking and manual proofs, we show that our stateful specification makes authorization decisions identical to those made by the π specification. These steps bring us a significant step closer to our ultimate goal of constructing a specification that can be implemented by a security non-expert. In the future, we plan to address the problems that arise in handling the communication latency and extend our design to support read-write stateful specification.

Acknowledgements

Jianwei Niu is supported in part by NSF awards CNS-0964710, THECB NHARP 010115-0037-2007, and the University of Texas at San Antonio research award TRAC-2008.

9. REFERENCES

[1] R. Alur and S. Zdancewic. Preserving secrecy under refinement. In *ICALP qŕ06, volume 4052 of LNCS*, pages 107–118, 2006.

[2] A. Barth, A. Datta, J. C. Mitchell, and H. Nissenbaum. Privacy and contextual integrity: Framework and applications. In *SP '06*, pages 184–198, 2006.

[3] A. Cimatti, E.M.Clarke, F. Giunchiglia, and M. Roveri. NuSMV: A new symbolic model checker. *International Journal on Software Tools for Technology Transfer*, 2(4):410–425, 2000.

[4] E. M. Clarke, O. Grumberg, and D. E. Long. Model checking and abstraction. *TOPLAS*, 16(5):1512–1542, 1994.

[5] M. Drouineaud, M. Bortin, P. Torrini, and K. Sohr. A first step towards formal verification of security policy properties for RBAC. In *Proceedings of Fourth International Conference on Quality Software*, pages 60–67, 2004.

[6] S. Jha, N. Li, M. Tripunitara, Q. Wang, and W. Winsborough. Towards formal verification of role-based access control policies. *IEEE Trans. Dependable Secur. Comput.*, 5(4):242–255, 2008.

[7] R. Krishnan, J. Niu, R. Sandhu, and W. H. Winsborough. Group-centric secure information sharing models for isolated groups. *ACM Trans. Infor. Syst. Secur.*, 14(3), 2011.

[8] R. Krishnan, R. Sandhu, J. Niu, and W. Winsborough. Foundations for group-centric secure information sharing models. In *SACMAT*, pages 115–124, 2009.

[9] A. Schaad, V. Lotz, and K. Sohr. A model-checking approach to analysing organisational controls in a loan origination process. In *SACMAT '06*, pages 139–149, 2006.

[10] C. Sprenger and D. Basin. Developing security protocols by refinement. In *Proceedings of the 17th ACM conference on Computer and communications security*, CCS '10, pages 361–374. ACM, 2010.

[11] N. Zhang, M. Ryan, and D. P. Guelev. Synthesising verified access control systems through model checking. *Journal of Computer Security*, 16(1):1–61, 2008.

[12] W. Zhao, J. Niu, and W. H. Winsborough. Refinement-based design of a group-centric secure information sharing model. Technical Report CS-TR-2011-16, UTSA, 2011.

[13] L. D. Zuck and A. Pnueli. Model checking and abstraction to the aid of parameterized systems (a survey). *Computer Languages, Systems & Structures*, 30(3-4):139–169, 2004.

Risk-Based Security Decisions Under Uncertainty

Ian Molloy
IBM Research TJ Watson
Hawthorne, NY, USA
molloyim@us.ibm.com

Luke Dickens
Imperial College
London, UK
lwd03@doc.ic.ac.uk

Charles Morisset
Security Group, IIT-CNR
Pisa, Italy
charles.morisset@iit.cnr.it

Pau-Chen Cheng
IBM Research TJ Watson
Hawthorne, NY, USA
pau@us.ibm.com

Jorge Lobo
IBM Research TJ Watson
Hawthorne, NY, USA
jlobo@us.ibm.com

Alessandra Russo
Imperial College
London, UK
ar3@doc.ic.ac.uk

ABSTRACT

This paper addresses the making of security decisions, such as access-control decisions or spam filtering decisions, under uncertainty, when the benefit of doing so outweighs the need to absolutely guarantee these decisions are correct. For instance, when there are limited, costly, or failed communication channels to a policy-decision-point. Previously, local caching of decisions has been proposed, but when a correct decision is not available, either a policy-decision-point must be contacted, or a default decision used. We improve upon this model by using learned classifiers of access control decisions. These classifiers, trained on known decisions, infer decisions when an exact match has not been cached, and uses intuitive notions of utility, damage and uncertainty to determine when an inferred decision is preferred over contacting a remote PDP. Clearly there is uncertainty in the predicted decisions, introducing a degree of risk. Our solution proposes a mechanism to quantify the uncertainty of these decisions and allows administrators to bound the overall risk posture of the system. The learning component continuously refines its models based on inputs from a central policy server in cases where the risk is too high or there is too much uncertainty. We have validated our models by building a prototype system and evaluating it with requests from real access control policies. Our experiments show that over a range of system parameters, it is feasible to use machine learning methods to infer access control policies decisions. Thus our system yields several benefits, including reduced calls to the PDP, reducing latency and communication costs; increased net utility; and increased system survivability.

Categories and Subject Descriptors

D.4.6 [**Security and Protection**]: Access controls; H.4 [**Information Systems Applications**]: Miscellaneous; D.2.8 [**Software Engineering**]: Metrics—*complexity mea-sures, performance measures*; H.4.2 [**Types of Systems**]: Decision support

General Terms

Management, Security, Theory

Keywords

Access Control, Risk, Decision, Classification

1. INTRODUCTION

A security decision is a decision made by a security system in order to address a potential threat. In general, the problem can be stated as follows: the environment submits a request to interact with the system, and the system decides if this interaction should be *allowed* or *denied*. A well-known example of security decision systems are access control modules, in charge of allowing or denying accesses done by users over resources. Similarly, a firewall is responsible for allowing or denying a particular network connection, and a spam filter denies (i.e. drops) e-mails classified as spam. These different systems, although achieving different purposes, follow a similar PEP/PDP architecture, a Policy Enforcement Point (PEP), defined at the application level, forwards each access request made within an application to a Policy Decision Point (PDP), which analyses this request and returns an authorization decision—allow or deny.

Although usually associated with the XACML [9] access control language, this architecture can clearly be adapted to any decision based system, where the policy simply denotes the classification of interactions with the system into the allowed ones and the denied ones. In some solutions, such as [7,11,16], a PDP is commonly implemented as a dedicated authorization server, where a PDP is located on a different node than the PEPs. While facilitating the enforcement of a consistent policy throughout the system, this architecture relies on the PEP being able to contact the PDP to query decisions, and therefore suffers from a single point of failure. In particular, key factors that affect the performance of the PEP are latency of the communication with the PDP, reliability and survivability of this connection (and the PDP itself), as well as the aggregated impact of communication costs (which can include contacting a human to perform the authorization). For example, in several contexts, such as mobile applications, these costs may be prohibitive.

A number of approaches have been proposed to address these issues, one common theme is to *cache* security decisions at the PEP, such that the PEP does not have to forward the same request more than once to the PDP. This is known as *authorization recycling* [5, 30] and is exact: either the PEP finds the request-decision pair in the history, or it forwards the request to the PDP. Recently, others have been exploring the tradeoff between efficiency and accuracy in an access control context. For example, Ni et al. [17] have used a machine-learning algorithm to build a classifier of policy decisions from past request-decision pairs. Once the classifier is *accurate enough*, it is used it as a local decision point. As with any machine learning approach, the classifier has a degree of uncertainty with every decision, and can be incorrect even if it has a high accuracy. Thus, every decision made with such a classifier is inherently associated with a *risk* of the decision being wrong, either incorrectly allowing or denying some requests.

In this paper, we build on the fact that machine-learning can be successfully used to predict local decisions [17], and we claim that the measurable uncertainty provided by the classifier can be translated to a measure of risk for making a decision, when utility values for accesses are available. We first propose a model defining a very general policy with which to make decisions: when the utility of the local decision is high with respect to its risk, enact the local decision, otherwise defer to the central PDP. Our claim is validated by several experiments showing that we can increase the utility of the system compared to the risk-free approach of [17]. Although our approach relies on the existence of utility values, which can be challenging to accurately define, it must be pointed out that the actual utility value of an access is not important, the decision mechanism simply needs to be able to *compare* two (potentially weighted) values. Hence, the values we have chosen for the experiments are not relevant as such, however we have considered different distributions of the values, and we show that our approach is better for these distributions than simply ignoring even conservative approximations of those values.

Intuitively, we have built a distributed decision system to test this principle: local decision points determine whether the tradeoff of the uncertainty and utility associated with a local decision is favorable and defer to the central PDP for a binding decision if not. This is a general framework that allows us to explore the balance between avoiding potential errors in local decisions, and the desire to limit reliance on the central PDP. We present three methodologies for making decisions: *Expected Utility*, a risk neutral approach that weighs expected gains and damage equally; *Risk Adjusted Utility*, a pessimistic version of expected utility, where we penalise the uncertainty about damage more heavily; and *Independent Risk Constraints*, which augments expected utility with independent risk thresholds, where we reject high utility decisions when they are outweighed by their associated risk.

To validate this system, we have used data from a large corporation used to grant entitlements and permissions to system administrators. Our classifiers are initially untrained and in the beginning always consult the central PDP. Over time, the classifiers are trained using the central PDP's decisions thus improving accuracy and reducing the uncertainty, yielding fewer queries. In our experiments, we focus on the risk adjusted utility measure due to space constraints and because it provides a more conservative view of risk. An

empirical evaluation of Risk Adjusted Utility at different significance levels and how it compares to Expected Utility is given in Section 5.3 together with other experimental results. Compared with an implementation of simple caching algorithm, our results show that our learning based approach reduces the queries to PDP by as much as 75% and increases the system utility by eight fold when the cache hit ratio is low, and has almost identical performance to the caching algorithm when the hit ratio is high.

Our results from this dataset show that machine-learning can be viably used for informing distributed access control decisions. The accuracy and robustness of our approaches are high, and more conservative measure of risk may be applied when appropriate. We believe these techniques can generalize to other use cases and domains, including information sharing in military and coalition environments; financial applications like credit card processing; and load balancing services like Netflix or document repositories. Compared to pure machine-learning solutions, our methods estimate the uncertainty of each classification, allowing one to minimize the pitfalls of using approximate decisions. Further, our solution avoids the higher communication costs of naive caching solutions, when the access control policy is too large to fit into the cache or locality of reference is poor.

This paper is organized as follows. Section 2 briefly discusses traditional access control systems. Section 3 discusses the architecture of access control systems based on our approach. We present in Section 4 different techniques to assess the risk and uncertainty of local access control decisions. An experiment and evaluation of our approach, applied on different scenarios, is presented in Section 5. Section 6 concludes this paper.

Related Work

Caching access control decisions has been already implemented [7, 11, 16]. The framework for policy evaluation presented in [3] uses a caching mechanism and is shown to dramatically decrease the evaluation time of access control requests. Clearly, caching approaches are only valid when the cache is consistent, that is, returns the same decision as the central PDP; techniques to ensure strong cache consistency are proposed in [32]. In the context of distributed systems, each node can build its own cache in collaboration with the other nodes, thus improving the accuracy of each cache [31].

Such caching methods return a local decision on a request only if this *exact* request has been previously submitted and answered. In the context of the Bell-LaPadula model [14], Crampton et al. [5] present a method to calculate a previously unseen decision using the history of submitted requests, their responses, and the formal rules governing Bell-LaPadula. A similar approach for the RBAC model [8] is presented in [30] and an extension to Bloom filters is used in [25]. These inference techniques require knowledge of the underlying access control model, and are most efficient for hierarchical and structured access control models. Inference algorithms have also been proposed based on the relationship of subjects and objects in a database [18, 19], but the structure of the subject/object space still needs to be known.

An experiment of using machine-learning for making access control decisions is proposed in [17], where the authors note that there is a probability that the classifier can return a decision different than the one that would be returned from the central PDP. A notion of risk in access control is introduced in [4, 15, 33], where the notion of an access to be either allowed or denied is blurred, and each access is instead associated with a potential utility and damage. We reuse these notions here, in order to calculate the potential utility and damage of each access.

2. TRADITIONAL DECISION SYSTEM

A *security decision system* is a mechanism that grants or denies requests made by the environment, to perform some interaction with the system. The system follows a *policy*, which classifies each request and returns a decision about it. Such a mechanism usually consists of two parts: the *Policy Decision Point* (PDP), which analyzes a request and decides whether it should be granted or not; and the *Policy Enforcement Point* (PEP), to which the access request is submitted and the PDP's decision is enforced. The PDP's decisions are assumed to be always *correct*.

For instance, an access control mechanism usually describes a request as a triple (s, o, a), meaning that the subject $s \in \mathcal{S}$ asks to access the object $o \in \mathcal{O}$ according to the access mode $a \in \mathcal{A}$. There are several commonly used access control models, such as the the Bell-LaPadula model [14] and the RBAC model [8]. Similarly, a spam filter considers a request to be a simple e-mail that needs to be classified. In both cases, the PDP returns a decision to the PEP, such as **allow** or **deny**. More complex decisions exist, for instance XACML [9] decisions can also denote that the policy is not applicable to the request or that there is not enough information available to correctly evaluate the request. The policy decision can also include mitigations and/or obligations. For instance, when a user requests read access to a picture, the policy might require that the picture's resolution be downgraded before granting access. While our approach can handle any set of possible decisions, in this paper we restrict the *atomic* decisions, denoted $\mathcal{D}_{atm}$, to be the set {**allow**, **deny**}.

In today's networked world, decisions systems are commonly distributed, meaning the PDP is not local to where decisions must be enforced: thus each node of the system requires its own PEP. As described in Section 1, it is not always possible or desirable for a PEP to contact the PDP, and to fully replicate the PDP on each node could be too difficult and costly for deployment and management. This paper describes an architecture, which can make decisions locally even when the *correct* decision is not known with certainty, and controls the level of uncertainty of local decisions—described in terms of utility and risk.

This approach is not tied to a particular model, but it fits well with requests characterised by sets of attributes, as such requests are well-suited for learning-based techniques. For instance, we can cite attribute-based access control [2, 29], where each subject and object is associated with some attributes and the policy is defined using these attributes.

3. UNCERTAIN DECISION

We assume that there is at least one *oracle* node containing the full policy, called the *central* PDP; and a *correct local decision* is one that agrees with the central policy. Each node has a local PDP consisting of three entities: a decision-proposer (or proposer), which returns a *guess* of the correct decision and a measure of the uncertainty; a risk-assessor (or assessor), which determines whether the decision is taken lo-

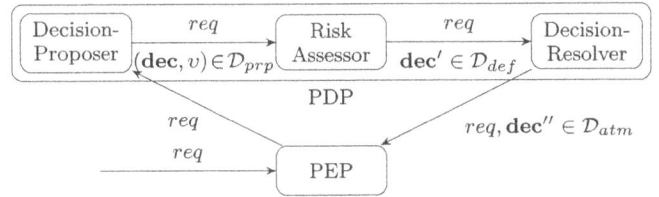

$\mathcal{D}_{atm}$:   Atomic decisions, *e.g.* {**allow**, **deny**}
$\mathcal{D}_{prp}$:   Proposals, *e.g.* $\mathcal{D}_{atm} \times [0, 1]$
$\mathcal{D}_{def}$:   Deferrable decisions, *e.g.* $\mathcal{D}_{atm} \cup \{\textbf{defer}\}$

Figure 1: Architecture of a local node

cally or deferred to the central PDP; and a decision-resolver (or resolver), which returns an enforceable decision. A PEP passes requests to the proposer, and enforces the decision from the resolver. Figure 1 depicts the architecture of a local nodel decision system.

3.1 Decision-Proposer

A decision-proposer takes an access request as an input, and returns a *proposal* (**dec**, v), where **dec** $\in \mathcal{D}_{atm}$ is a "guess" of the correct decision for this request, and v is a measure of uncertainty about **dec** being correct; v can take a number of forms, depending on how the decision-proposer predicts decisions. In its simplest form v is a probability, and the set of all possible proposals $\mathcal{D}_{prp}$ is given by $\mathcal{D}_{atm} \times [0, 1]$. In this setting a proposal (**allow**, p) means that **allow** is the correct decision with probability p; (**allow**, p) is logically equivalent to (**deny**, $1 - p$) if $\mathcal{D}_{atm} = \{\textbf{allow}, \textbf{deny}\}$.

The measure v can also be a pair (α, β); where $\alpha, \beta \in [1, \infty]$ are parameters of a beta distribution [1], Beta$(\mu | \alpha, \beta)$; this captures our uncertainty about the value of the probability p that **dec** is correct, and μ is a variable approximating p. The beta distribution fits well with our learning based approach and gives finer control over risk estimation—see Section 4.

A proposer may be a simple caching algorithm which stores a given number of requests together with the corresponding correct decisions from the central PDP. In this setting, a proposal is a pair (**dec**, p) $\in \mathcal{D}_{atm} \times [0, 1]$. If the policy never changes then cached decisions are always correct. So, if the decision for a request has been cached then **dec** is that decision and $p = 1$ indicating complete certainty; otherwise **dec** is randomly chosen and $p = 0.5$ indicating complete uncertainty. If the policy is periodically updated, then there is a probability that a cached decision no longer agrees with the central policy. For instance, if 10% of central decisions change every hour, then a decision cached an hour ago could be assigned a 0.9 probability of being correct.

Ni et al. have shown in [17] that machine-learning techniques can be successfully used to propose a decision. In this case, the proposer is mainly a classifier produced by a machine-learning algorithm, which treats a decision as a class and assigns a request to a class based on the request's attributes. The learning process uses an input set of requests whose corresponding correct decisions are known, and relies on the assumption that two requests close to each other are likely to have the same decision. Of course, this assumption does not hold for every policy, and it is actually quite simple to build a policy violating it. However, this assumption has been empirically shown to hold in [17].

We extend this assumption here by claiming that the uncertainty related to the classifier can also be used as a meaningful measure of risk. Roughly speaking, as it will be detailed in Section 5.2, a Support Vector Machine (SVM) [26] classifies decisions by splitting the space of all decisions with an hyperplane. As illustrated in Figure 2, we follow the intuition that the farther a decision is from the hyperplane, the more accurate it is. Here again, this assumption is not always true, and it is clearly possible to build a classifier violating it, but we show in this paper that this assumption holds for some concrete, realistic policies. Hence, the proposals in our model are of the form $(\mathbf{dec}, \alpha, \beta)$, where α and β are computed from the numbers of correct and incorrect assignments made by the classifier. The computation of these numbers is given in Section 5.2.

3.2 Risk Assessor

A risk-assessor (or assessor) takes a request and a proposal and returns a *deferrable decision*. The assessor must determine whether a decision can be made locally, based on the proposal, or should be deferred to the central PDP. Hence, the risk assessor can return any decision in the set of deferrable decisions, $\mathcal{D}_{def} = \mathcal{D}_{atm} \cup \{\mathbf{defer}\}$, where $\mathbf{defer}$ is the decision to contact the central PDP. Note that, deferrable decisions are no longer associated with uncertainty. In other words, the role of the risk-assessor is to transform the uncertainty in a proposal into a firm decision.

A trivial definition for a risk-assessor is to fix an uncertainty threshold below which all decisions are deferred to the central policy, and above which all the decisions are taken locally. However, in general, different requests have different potential impacts on the system. Some requests have high potential utility for the system, and wrongly denying them might cause big loss of utility, and some requests have high potential damage, and wrongly allowing them is a threat to the integrity and survival of the system. Another parameter to consider is the cost of contacting the central PDP, which is important in some situations. The risk-assessor can also take a *risk appetite*, which controls the degree that the decisions are *risk-averse*; a risk-averse decision maker is willing to accept a lower expected utility if there is more certainty about the consequences of a decision. More details on the risk assessor are given in Section 4.

3.3 Decision Resolver

A decision resolver takes a request and a deferrable decision, $\mathbf{dec}_d \in \mathcal{D}_{def}$ and returns an atomic decision, $\mathbf{dec}_a \in \mathcal{D}_{atm}$. Typically, $\mathbf{dec}_a = \mathbf{dec}_d$ if $\mathbf{dec}_d \in \mathcal{D}_{atm}$; otherwise, the resolver defers the request to the central PDP.

4. ASSESSING LOCAL DECISIONS

In this section, we consider how the risk-assessor takes a proposal from the decision-proposer, and returns a firm decision. By design in our system, the proposer's suggested decision may conflict with the decision that would have been made if passed to the central policy. If a request that would be allowed by the central PDP is denoted as *valid*, then there can be two kinds of errors that the local PDP can make: false-allows (allowing an invalid request) and false-denies (denying a valid request). These errors can have negative consequences: a false-allow can result in the leakage of

information, corruption of information, or privilege escalation; a false-deny can result in disruption of service, breach of service level agreements (SLA), and other consequences such as damaged reputation. Further, making a correct decision leads to gains and benefits.

Ideally, a decision system should enable as many appropriate requests as possible, and so our primary concern is to maximize the number and value of these requests—subject to limiting costs and damages. This trades off the potential gains of each security decision, against the costs and damages that may result from poor decisions. Consider an assessor deciding whether to locally allow or deny a request, or to pass this decision on to a central PDP. The assessor has a ternary choice to make: whether to allow the request locally, **allow**; to deny locally, **deny**; or to defer the decision to the central PDP, **defer**. We assume that the central PDP is an *oracle*, and always gives the correct decision. If the assessor decides **allow**, then either the request is valid (a true-allow) and the system makes a gain, g, because an appropriate interaction has been made; or the request is invalid and the decision has caused some amount of damage, d_A, due to an inappropriate interaction being made. Likewise, if the assessor decides **deny**, then either the request was invalid, **deny** is the correct decision and nothing additional happens (i.e. a gain of 0), or the request was valid and the **deny** decision is incorrect, and a damage, d_D, is incurred for a false-deny. If the assessor decides to **defer** and the request is valid, then the central PDP will grant the request and the system will make a gain, g, but incur a cost, c. In this paper we will assume that this gain and this cost are constant. If the decision is **defer** and request is not valid then the central PDP will deny the request and there will be no gain and again a contact cost, c. As the central PDP is an oracle, it never makes an incorrect decision, so there is no damage associated with this.

These gains, costs and damages are shown in Table 1 (a). In general, the gains, costs and damages can be probability distributions over potential values. For instance, in some cases, wrongly allowing a request only implies the probability of an attack. For simplicity in our examples, we assume these to be fixed, known values unless otherwise stated. Standard gains and costs (negative gains) are kept separate from damage, which is assumed to be associated with rare and costly negative impacts; this distinction becomes important, when we consider risk measures in Sections 4.2 and 4.3 and when considering probability distributions over these values. The impacts presented in Table 1 (a) are not the most general that could be conceived, but are sufficiently rich to be of interest. For example, there may be a gain associated with denying an invalid request, e.g., an increase in system reputation, or a damage in allowing a valid request, e.g., increasing the number of copies of a document.

All of the approaches described in this paper make a trade-off between the uncertainties in classification and in estimation of these gains and damages. To apply our methodology to a real example, we must be able to (approximately) compute these gains and damages or find probability distributions over them. We note here that there are many applications and domains where these gains and damages can be estimated either empirically or analytically. For example, in financial service transactions like credit cards, these costs may be estimated easily or provided a priori by some agreement. Other examples include cases where fine grained

Table 1

(a) Outcome Gains and Damage				
	Request Valid		Request Invalid	
	gain	damage	gain	damage
allow	g	0	0	d_A
deny	0	d_D	0	0
defer	$g-c$	0	$-c$	0

(b) Expected utilities		
	$U(\cdot\|\mathbf{allow},p)$	$U(\cdot\|\mathbf{deny},p')$
allow	$\mathbf{E}(pg-(1-p)d_A)$	$\mathbf{E}((1-p')g-p'd_A)$
deny	$\mathbf{E}(-pd_D)$	$\mathbf{E}(-(1-p')d_D)$
defer	$\mathbf{E}(pg-c)$	$\mathbf{E}((1-p')g-c)$

Table 1: **When gains, costs and damages are incurred and their influence on utility.**

service level agreements are defined a priori. We discuss further details in Section 4.4.

4.1 Expected Utility

In the simplest case, the proposer can return one of two kinds of answers, e.g. $(\mathbf{allow},p)$ or $(\mathbf{deny},p')$. The first response, $(\mathbf{allow},p)$ means that the proposer has classified the request as an allow with probability p that this is correct, i.e. that the request is valid. Likewise, $(\mathbf{deny},p')$ means that the proposer has classified the request as a deny with probability p' that the request is invalid.

The expected utility for a decision, $\mathbf{dec} \in \mathcal{D}_{def}$, is the expected gain of each outcome (request valid or invalid) minus the expected damage, and these utilities are shown in Table 1(b). In this approach, we assume a risk neutral posture, meaning deferrable decisions are based purely on the expected utility, $U(\cdot)$, for each decision. The assessor simply returns the decision corresponding to the highest utility.

There are cases where the assessor may not defer but return a decision contrary to the proposer's. For example, when the proposer returns $(\mathbf{allow},p)$ given a request where $d_A \gg d_D$, $d_D < c$ and $g \approx c$, then it may occur that $U(\mathbf{defer}) < U(\mathbf{deny})$. Since our goal is to execute the central policy as faithfully as possible, our system always defers to the central PDP in these cases. Hence, given a request req and a decision proposer δ returning a decision and a probability, the expected utility assessor, ρ_{eu}, is defined as:

$$\rho_{eu}(req) = \begin{cases} \mathbf{allow} & \text{if } \delta(req) = (\mathbf{allow},p) \wedge \\ & U(\mathbf{allow}) \geq U(\mathbf{defer}) \\ \mathbf{deny} & \text{if } \delta(req) = (\mathbf{deny},p) \wedge \\ & U(\mathbf{deny}) \geq U(\mathbf{defer}) \\ \mathbf{defer} & \text{otherwise} \end{cases}$$

Thus in this approach, we directly use the certainty of the decision to compute the expected utility and choose the decision with the highest utility. However, this approach can lead to rare but significant damages due to incorrect decisions. Because while the probability of an incorrect decision may be very small to produce a small expected damage, the value of damage can be significant. In the following approaches we will try to explicitly account for the risk of such significant damage.

4.2 Risk Adjusted Utility

In some cases, such as when using machine-learning techniques, the proposer returns a tuple $(\mathbf{dec},\alpha,\beta)$, where $\mathbf{dec} \in \{\mathbf{allow},\mathbf{deny}\}$ and where $\alpha,\beta \in [1,\infty]$ are the parameters of a beta distribution [1], thus describing uncertain knowledge about the probability of a correct classification.

Here we focus just on the **allow** case, and assume that the assessor can return either **allow** and **defer**. If the proposer returns $(\mathbf{allow},\alpha,\beta)$, we take $\frac{\alpha}{\alpha+\beta}$, the expectation of

the beta distribution, as the *expected probability* that this decision is correct and denoed by p. The risk adjusted utility assumes that any uncertainty in the utility is dominated by the damage term, this can be when the damage is fixed, known and very large (the case we examine here), or if there is a probability distribution over damage with high variance. Based on this assumption, we use the expected values of gain and cost, but are pessimistic when considering the impact of damage and use the *expected shortfall* at some significance value of n, which we denote by $\mathbf{ES}_n(\cdot)$. Intuitively, the expected shortfall considers the average of the worst $100n\%$ of outcomes. For example, an expected shortfall for $n = 0.05$ uses the average damage in the worst 5% of universes. For the sake of exposition, we do not give here the definition of $\mathbf{ES}_n(\cdot)$, and we refer to [6] for further details. Risk adjusted utility for various decisions and proposer outputs is shown in Table 2 (a).

Given a request req and a proposer δ returning a proposal $\delta(req)$, the risk adjusted utility assessor, ρ_{au}, is defined as:

$$\rho_{au}(req) = \begin{cases} \mathbf{allow} & \text{if } \delta(req) = (\mathbf{allow},\alpha,\beta) \wedge \\ & \tilde{U}(\mathbf{allow}) \geq \tilde{U}(\mathbf{defer}) \\ \mathbf{deny} & \text{if } \delta(req) = (\mathbf{deny},\alpha',\beta') \wedge \\ & \tilde{U}(\mathbf{deny}) \geq \tilde{U}(\mathbf{defer}) \\ \mathbf{defer} & \text{otherwise} \end{cases}$$

This approach differs from the risk-neutral approach from the previous section by taking a risk averse approach which mitigates against very large damages.

4.3 Independent Risk Constraints

Our second risk method, called *independent risk constraints*, uses the standard expected utility to rank the decisions in order of risk neutral preference, and then reject any which do not satisfy our risk constraint(s). Given a proposition $(\mathbf{dec},\alpha,\beta)$, we calculate the expected utilities as they appear in Table 1 (b) using $p = \frac{\alpha}{\alpha+\beta}$ for the probability of **allow**, and $p' = \frac{\alpha}{\alpha'+\beta'}$ for the probability of **deny**. The risk, $R(\cdot)$, is calculated independently by taking a pessimistic view of the utility, and is the expected shortfall, at significance n, of the inverse of the utility. The risks for each decision and proposer output are shown in Table 2 (b).

The decision making process involves, for each deferrable decision $\mathbf{dec} \in \mathcal{D}_{def}$, a threshold $t(U(\mathbf{dec}))$, that depends on the utility of the decision. We first find the expected utilities and risks as shown in Tables 1 (b) and 2 (b), then rank the decisions according to their utilities, and choose the first decision for which risk is below the corresponding threshold. Notice that **defer** carries zero risk and will always be risk acceptable. Given request req and decision proposer δ returning proposal $\delta(req)$, the independent risk assessor,

	$\tilde{U}(\cdot\,\vert\textbf{allow},\alpha,\beta)$	$\tilde{U}(\cdot\,\vert\textbf{deny},\alpha',\beta')$
allow	$\textbf{E}(pg)+\textbf{ES}_n(-(1-p)d_A)$	–
deny	–	$\textbf{ES}_n(-(1-p')d_D)$
defer	$\textbf{E}(pg-c)$	$\textbf{E}((1-p')g-c)$

	$R(\cdot\,\vert\textbf{allow},\alpha,\beta)$	$R(\cdot\,\vert\textbf{deny},\alpha',\beta')$
allow	$-\textbf{ES}_n(pg-(1-p)d_A)$	–
deny	–	$-\textbf{ES}_n(-(1-p')d_D)$
defer	$-\textbf{ES}_n(pg-c)$	$-\textbf{ES}_n((1-p')g-c)$

Table 2: Risk Adjusted Utilities and Risks for various decisions given proposer outputs.

ρ_{ic}, is defined as:

$$\rho_{ic}(req)=\begin{cases}\textbf{allow} & \text{if} \begin{pmatrix}\delta(req)=(\textbf{allow},\alpha,\beta)\wedge\\ U(\textbf{allow})\geq U(\textbf{defer})\wedge\\ R(\textbf{allow})\leq t(U(\textbf{allow}))\end{pmatrix}\\ \textbf{deny} & \text{if} \begin{pmatrix}\delta(req)=(\textbf{deny},\alpha',\beta')\wedge\\ U(\textbf{deny})\geq U(\textbf{defer})\wedge\\ R(\textbf{deny})\leq t(U(\textbf{deny}))\end{pmatrix}\\ \textbf{defer} & \text{otherwise}\end{cases}$$

More generally still we may not always have a decision with zero risk, and hence we may need some way to resolve a decision when all decisions exceed the risk threshold. Further, one may wish to be able to override a decision whose risk is greater than the threshold by compensating for the additional aggregate risk. For example, additional risk mitigating measures, risk escrow services, or bounding the aggregate risk and limiting its distribution [15] have been proposed as compensation mechanisms. This is an orthogonal research problem and the most appropriate technique is a subject of future research.

Both risk methods have their advantages and disadvantages. For instance, risk adjusted utility behaves more like standard expected utilities, and there is always a clearly defined decision for the assessor. Conversely, the independent risk assessor keeps the two measures, utility and risk separate, which allow us to define multiple risk thresholds at different significance levels. However, we do not necessarily know how to deal with situations where all decisions violate the risk constraint(s).

4.4 Estimating Utility with Uncertainty

The instantiation of the parameters in order to address a real-world situation is a complex task, as it requires one to evaluate the damage and utility associated with access control entities. In some instances, all values are easily derivable and in a common set of units. For example, when processing credit card transactions, all values are in currencies, and rates are agreed upon a priori through formal contracts. Consider the Visa Debit Processing Service [27, 28]: the damage from a false allow is the transaction amount, plus a *Chargeback Fee*, e.g., a fixed amount of $15 or a percentage, e.g., 5%; the gain is the profit margin for the items sold, minus any processing fees, e.g., 20% the value of the transaction; the contact cost is an *Authorisation Fee*, a fixed value to process the transaction or a percentage (or both), e.g., $1 or 3%; and the damage of false deny can be estimated as a fixed fraction of the gains from customers that do not have alternative forms of payment.

In many scenarios, the actual value of gains, losses, and damages may be given in different units, e.g., currency, reputation, and physical assets, and may themselves be uncertain. Our discussion above assumes these measures are point estimates in a common set of units, for example currency, where there is further uncertainty in such a conversion.

We suggest the same techniques used to calculate the risk of making an incorrect decision described in Section 4.2 can be applied to selecting conservative, risk-adjusted conversion rates and handling the uncertainty in value distributions. If one obtains a probability density function (PDF) over values, say human life to dollars, the expected value can be used for gains, while a pessimistic value can be used for damages, resulting in conservative estimates. For example, if we take US household income as an estimator, then the median income, around $34–55K, is the expected and the top 5%, $157K, might be used for the risk.

Clearly, our method will work best when these values are known, such as in credit card processing use case. When these values have distributions over some ranges, our approach is sound as long as such distributions are conservative, over-estimating damages and losses while under-estimating gains. Further, note that we are being conservative here by taking the pessimistic probability and the pessimistic damage (the worst $n\%$ of the worst $n\%$).

5. EXPERIMENTAL EVALUATION

In this section, we describe our prototype system and experimental results. To evaluate the usefulness of risk-based decision making, we devise a simple decentralized access control system consisting of a single local risk-based policy enforcement and decision point, and a central policy decision point that we call the *oracle*. In our experiments, users submit requests, which are locally evaluated and an estimate of the uncertainty calculated as described in Section 4.2. By evaluating potential risks and gains, the system determines when decisions can be made locally, and when the oracle must be queried at a cost. We run the system over a large number of requests, e.g., 100,000, logging the request, decisions, and uncertainty. After which, we compare these decisions with the oracle policy, and aggregate the net utility of the system, including any gains, costs and damages incurred during operation. Hence, for each set of parameters, we present two graphs, one for the number of central queries given the number of transactions for each technique (the lower the better), and one for the (accumulated) utility given the number of transactions for each technique (the higher the better).

For clarity, we distinguish between *standard* damage (for a false-allow) and loss (damage of a false-deny) in the following detailed description of our experiments.

5.1 Experimental Setup

The oracle is considered infallible, and always returns correct results. The oracle contains a real access control policy from a system that provisions administrative access to a commercial system obtained from a corporation. The policy consists of 881 permissions and 852 users with 25 attributes

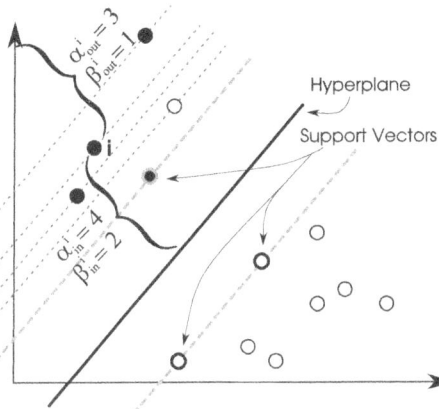

Figure 2: A Support Vector Machine classifier & (α,β) calculation for uncertainty. The dark points are correctly classified.

describing each user; there are 6691 allowed requests. We do not have access to actual permission usage logs, e.g., requests or frequency of permission use, and instead simulate incoming requests by sampling from the full policy, obtaining both valid (allow) and invalid (deny) requests. Users are selected uniformly and randomly, and permissions are selected from a multinomial distribution where all allowed permissions are independently and identically distributed, as are all denied permissions, but the probability of selecting an allowed permission is a tunable system parameter. For example, while a uniform sampling of single permissions at random may return a valid transaction 0.9% of the time (the density of the user-permission relation), we can generate sample requests with an arbitrary frequency of valid requests, e.g. 30%, 50% or 80%. This allows us to model different scenarios, such as a system under attack (mostly invalid requests), or normal usage (mostly valid requests).

5.2 Classifiers

Our experimental prototype is implemented in Python, and uses PyML for support vector machines[1] [26], which we use for our classifier. A support vector machine (SVM) is a supervised learning method for classification and regression. Each input is represented as a point in a k-dimensional space. Given a set labeled points as the training set, an SVM finds a hyperplane (normal unit vector $\mathbf{w}$ and offset b from the origin) that separates the two classes by maximizing the minimal distance between any point and the hyperplane. As illustrated on Figure 2, the class of an unlabeled point $\mathbf{x}$ is determined by which side of the hyperplane it is on, i.e., $\text{sign}(\mathbf{w} \cdot \mathbf{x} - b)$.

An SVM is a linear classifier, however a kernel can be applied first to allow non-linear classification. Kernels may result in over fitting when the number of input data points is too small, e.g., less than or equal to the degree of a polynomial kernel. To prevent this, we do not train the SVM until a sufficient number of data points are specified and cached. We use both polynomial (degree four) and radial bias function (RBF) kernels.

Each PDP based on an SVM will store a small number of data points (requests and decisions) in a cache for later

retraining. Before predicting the decision using an SVM, we first check to see if the point is in the cache. When it is, we return the known decision with zero uncertainty (assuming a static policy). When a new request is deferred to the oracle, the request and the oracle's decision are stored in the cache so that the SVM may be (re)trained. When the number of samples exceeds the size of the cache a new SVM is trained and the point correctly classified and projected farthest from the hyperplane is discarded. Thus the cache contains the points that most closely define the support vectors.

Intuitively there is less uncertainty in the classification of a point the farther away it is from the hyperplane ($distance = |\mathbf{w} \cdot \mathbf{x} - b|$), and the uncertainty is high between the support vectors (the points closest to the hyperplane). As explained in Section 4.2, the uncertainty of a classification is represented by a beta distribution with parameters α and β. To determine this uncertainty for a point i, we first set α_i and β_i to 1. Then for each point in the cache that is at the same distance or closer to the hyperplane than i, α_i is incremented by 1 if this point is correctly classified by the SVM, otherwise β_i is incremented by 1. For example, in Figure 2, $\alpha_i = \alpha_{\text{in}}^i = 4$, $\beta_i = \beta_{\text{in}}^i = 2$, assuming i is correctly classified. The hyperplane itself has $\alpha = \beta = 1$. The intuition for this method is to be conservative and only consider the points with equal or less certainty than i has. Further explanation and empirical evaluation is given in the Appendix.

In our setting, there are $|\mathcal{O} \times \mathcal{A}|$ SVM classifiers, one per permission, trained on subjects $s \in \mathcal{S}$. An alternative implementation is to define a single classifier whose input is $\mathcal{S} \times \mathcal{O} \times \mathcal{A}$, however, based on the results from [17], some object-right requests have more uncertainty than others. To simplify calculating the uncertainty of the classified requests, we choose to define a classifier per permission.

Our data points represent users. We map a user to a k-dimensional space by converting their attributes into binary vectors. For example, consider a *Department* attribute of a company that has three values: R&D, Sales, and Marketing. These are represented by the binary vectors $\langle 0, 0, 1 \rangle$, $\langle 0, 1, 0 \rangle$, and $\langle 1, 0, 0 \rangle$, respectively. The final k-bit vector for a user is the concatenation of all attributes. In the remainder of this paper when we refer to a subject $s \in \mathcal{S}$, we are referring to a point in some k-dimensional space.

We implement several baseline PDPs to compare against the risk-based PDP: a local PDP that will always defer to the central PDP (**Default PDP**), and a first-in-first-out cache (**FIFO Cache**), such that if the request is not in the cache, the oracle is queried. We use two FIFO cache sizes: (E) the size of the FIFO cache is equal to the total memory of the SVMs; (Inf) the FIFO cache is unbounded.

We also implement three learning-based PDPs: the first one (**SACMAT'09**) is a PDP consistent with the approach in [17], where we train an SVM for each permission and accept any decision they return, i.e., we assume there is zero uncertainty. The second one (**Seeded SVM**) is a PDP where an SVM is constructed for each permission and seeded with n random users granted the permission, and m random users not granted the permission. We train and test on the $n + m$ users and we use $n = m = 10$. Finally, the third one (**Unseeded SVM**) uses an untrained SVM created for each permission. Before the SVMs can be trained a minimum number of allow and deny decisions must be specified by querying the oracle. The cache of an unseeded SVM is the same as a seeded SVM.

---

[1]PyML provides a wrapper for libSVM

5.3 Evaluation Results

In our experiments, we first compare our general approach with a default policy that always contacts the central PDP, and the two FIFO caches, the bounded size cache (the same as all SVMs combined), and the unbounded (see previous section for details). For these experiments we restrict ourselves to the seeded SVM settings and evaluate the results against the scenarios described in Figure 3 (cc = the cost of contacting the central PDP; g = the gains for true-allow, d = the damage of false-deny, l = the loss of false-allow. For space limitations we only show tables where true-denies have 0 gain and 0 loss). The figure shows that regardless of the parameters our approach behave well, i.e. calls to the central PDP are reduced (in some cases as much as 75% – see Figure 3(a)) and the utility is better than in any of the other standard approaches. This confirms the independence of our approach from the setting of the parameters making it applicable to many situations.

Performance impact of the ratio of valid requests.

We evaluate this for two reasons. First, the ratio in a typical deployment is unknown. Second, [17] shows that SVMs result in more false-denies than false-allows, so varying the ratio may reveal useful insights. We found that the sampling rate of valid versus invalid requests impacts the rate of cache hits for the FIFO implementations, greatly affecting their performance. When the number of cache hits was low, for example, by sampling more invalid requests, we explore a larger amount of the possible request space, resulting in more cache misses before a hit is returned. Conversely, at a high rate of valid requests, a larger fraction of the valid sampled requests reside in the cache (in part due to the smaller sampling size because the fraction of allowed requests is so low). The higher number of false-denies also results in increased uncertainty, causing the SVMs to be retrained more frequently, and thus deferring more requests. The results are shown in Figure 4.

Impact of completely trusting the classifiers.

Ni et al. [17] did not evaluate the uncertainty of classifier outputs. Here, the false-allows and false-denies can result in devastating losses. To illustrate this, we use the decision resolver (SACMAT'09) described earlier which accepts any predicted decision, regardless of the risk. Figure 5 illustrates the potential decrease in utility from a small number of false-positives in the classifier.

Impact of high communication cost.

We set the cost to contact the oracle to be five-times the gains from allowing a valid request, and set the damage to be four-times the communication costs. This type of scenario may correspond to a military setting where communication is expensive, e.g., requiring a satellite link, or where radio usage should be minimized to avoid triangulation by the enemy. The results, shown in Figure 6, illustrate that while our risk-based approach outperforms the FIFO caches and reduces queries by 65%, it cannot keep the utility positive. However, it should be noted that the FIFO caches lose over three-times more utility due to the communication costs.

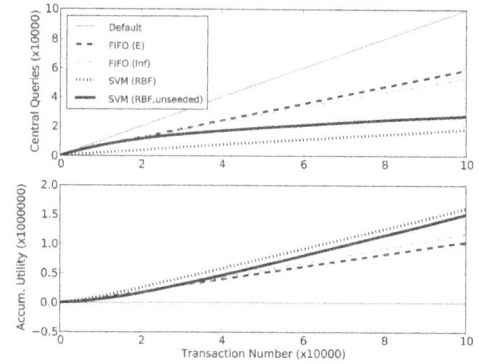

(a) Small cc, $g = 2cc$, $d = l = 2g$

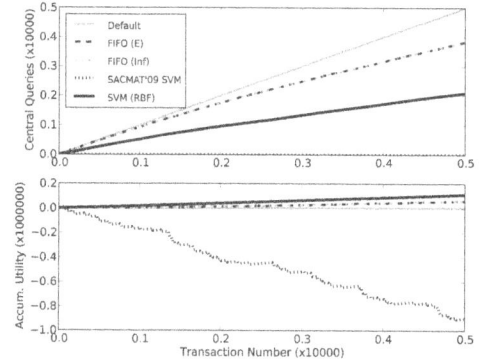

(b) Small cc, $g = 4cc$, $d = 10g$, $l = 0$

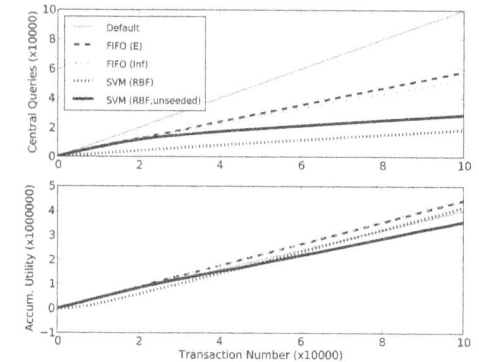

(c) Small cc, $g = 10cc$, $d = 2cc$, $l = 10g$

Figure 3: Evaluation under different system parameters.

Credit Card Scenario.

We approximate the credit card scenario described in Section 4.4 assuming the retailer to be a supermarket chain. Supermarket operating profit margins are very low, with the most profitable chains making about 4% and many losing money [20–23]. We assumed a 2% profit[2] on bills of $100 for the experiments[3], so the gain is set to be $2. We assume that 90% of the transactions are valid requests and the damage

---

[2] Assuming this profit already considers the transaction fee.
[3] Average weekly bill of a family of 4 is over $250 in the US.

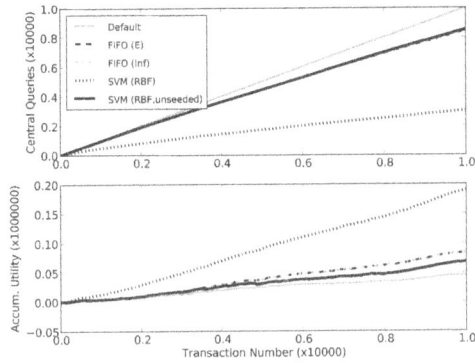

(a) 30% Valid Requests

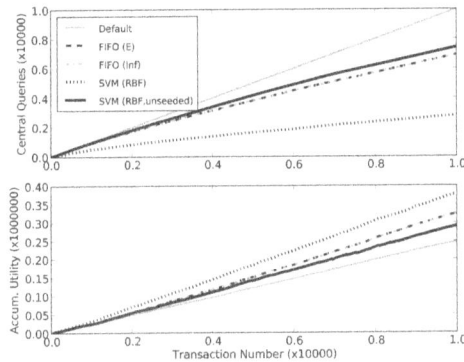

(b) 50% Valid Requests

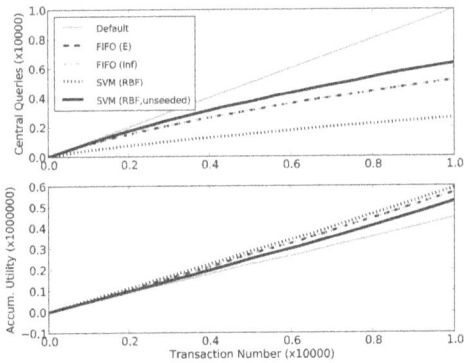

(c) 70% Valid Requests

Figure 4: Risk-based classifiers outperform traditional caching with high cache-miss rates.

for a false-allow is $25. We set the loss due to a false-deny equal to the gain, this is a conservative estimate since it does not consider the effects of customer dissatisfaction. The cost of contacting the central PDP, i.e. the transaction fee, was set to $1. The results shown in Figure 7 clearly shows the benefits of the risk-based approach against the basic cache approaches.

Flexibility and Power of Risk Adjusted Utility.

We compare different choices of the significance value n on the access control data. Figure 8 shows this method us-

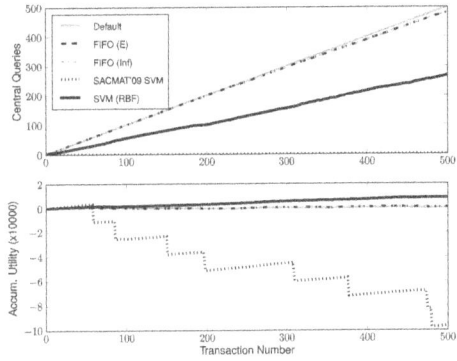

Figure 5: The impact of not evaluating classifier risk.

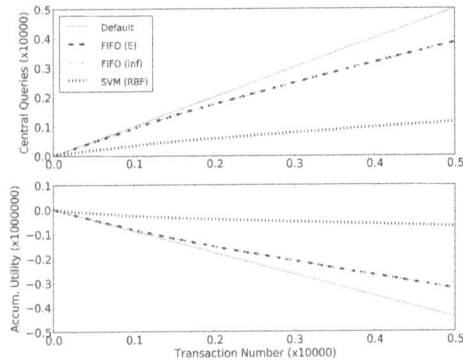

Figure 6: Communication costs is 5 times the gains, and damages are 10 times the gains.

ing three values of significance 99% 97% and 95%, which basically ignore only the most optimistic assessments of the probability, and are hence risk averse postures. These are compared with the expected utility approach, with a risk neutral posture, and the finite sized cache – which could be regarded as a highly risk averse posture, i.e. I only decide locally if I have seen the exact request before. In this example the cost of an incorrect allow is high, but it pays to make decisions locally if you can be sure. Notice that the expected utility method actually acquires utility most greedily, and over a long time-scale we could expect it to outperform the other methods. However, it is liable to jolts of negative utility, as can be seen at around transaction 1500. The risk adjusted utility approaches avoid this jolt by being pessimistic and deferring the decision under these conditions. Notice also that the lower the significance value n, the lower the gradient of the utility curve, this shows that more caution corresponds to a safer, but less successful, operation. The very risk averse method of caching performs the worst in this case, showing that too much caution can be undesirable too.

Non–Access Control Policies.

We now move from access control models and show how our risk–based approach can be applied to other types of security policies. There are many security applications where a policy specifying which actions are allowed is impractical. For example consider a web browser and a policy that states a user should not visit malicious web sites that con-

165

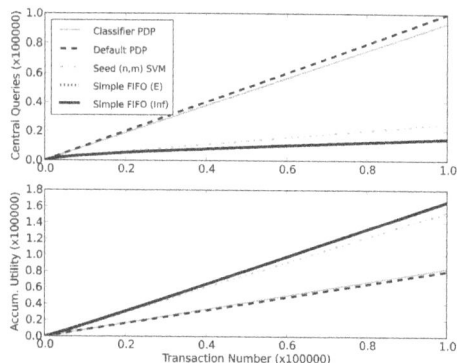

Figure 7: Emulation of credit card cost in a supermarket.

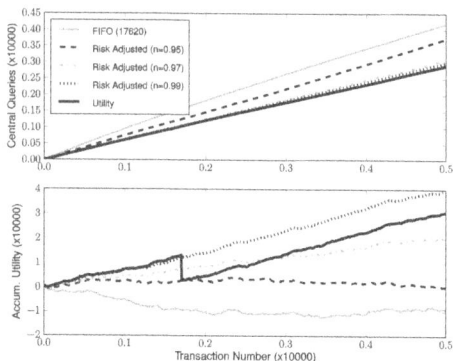

Figure 8: The Risk Adjusted Utility method with different significance values n, the set of features for the request was reduced to artificially increase the possibility of misclassification.

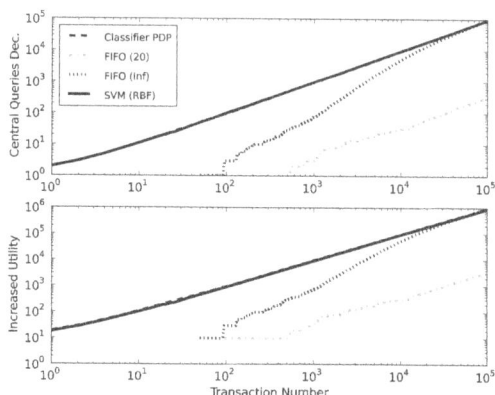

Figure 9: Performance improvement compared to the Default PDP on the web-spam dataset.

reaches that of our approach. In real-world scenarios, this is impractical.

In addition to spam and access control, our techniques could equally apply to areas of botnet detection [10], malware [13], etc. In general, the risk-adverse framework presented in this paper is applicable to a wide range of security applications where the correctness or arbitrary decisions can be approximated.

6. CONCLUSION AND FUTURE WORK

This paper presents a new learning and risk-based architecture for a local PDP, where a decision is first proposed with a known level of uncertainty. The tradeoff of the uncertainty and utility associated with this decision is then assessed, determining whether the decision can be taken locally or the central PDP should be contacted. We defined three different risk methodologies, namely *Expected Utility*, *Risk Adjusted Utility*, and *Independent Risk Constraints*, each representing a different risk perspective. The main contribution of this paper is to reinforce the assumption that machine-learning can be used to make security decisions (as already demonstrated in [17]) and to validate the intuitive assumption that the uncertainty of a classifier can be used as an accurate measure of risk. Clearly, our approach depends on the definition of utility values (see Section 4.4), however, as Kephart recently stated [12], the definition of such values is an effort required from field experts in order to provide more flexible and autonomous security systems.

Our approach was validated using data from a large corporation, and consistently performed better in experiments than a naive caching mechanism, in a number of different scenarios. In the best case, we reduce the number of queries to the central PDP by as much as 75% and saw an eight-fold increase in the system utility. Such improvements occurred when the cache hit rate is low.

We would like to compare our work with other inference techniques cited in Section 1. We also need to consider dynamic access control policies, where a decision for a given request might change over time. In this context, the uncertainty returned by the decision-proposer must combine the uncertainty due to classifier error with the uncertainty due to possible updates to the policy. Finally, additional research is needed to better determine when a classifier should

tain spam, phishing attacks, or other malware. Each web page must be manually inspected to ensure it is legitimate before access can be granted, and due to the rate at which content is added, a white list cannot be generated without adversely impacting usability and utility.

We apply our risk framework to a web spam dataset from Yahoo! Research[4]. This dataset contains many precomputed features from the content of web pages, e.g., the number of unique words, visible words, word length, etc., and links, e.g., in-degree out-degree, page rank, etc. These features are not exhaustive, and we are not suggesting we have developed a new technique to detect spam. In fact, there is no prior indication the SVM parameters selected are optimal for the task of detecting spam, but rather that our risk framework can produce a measurable improvement at efficiently mitigating the exposure. We refer to [24] for a state-of-the-art approach for efficiently detecting web spam. We measure the improvement of several methods compared to the default policy of always asking a human to classify the web page. The results are plotted in Figure 9 on a log-log plot. It can be seen that our approach significantly outperforms the FIFO cache. In fact, it's not until the infinite FIFO cache becomes exhaustive that its performance

---

[4]http://barcelona.research.yahoo.net/webspam/datasets/uk2007/

be retrained and when a given sample should be discarded, particularly challenging when dealing with dynamic policy changes.

7. REFERENCES

[1] C. M. Bishop. *Pattern Recognition and Machine Learning (Information Science and Statistics).* Springer, 2007.

[2] P. Bonatti and P. Samarati. Regulating service access and information release on the web. In *Proceedings of the 7th ACM conference on Computer and communications security*, CCS '00, pages 134–143, New York, NY, USA, 2000. ACM.

[3] K. Borders, X. Zhao, and A. Prakash. Cpol: high-performance policy evaluation. In *Proceedings of the 12th ACM conference on Computer and communications security*, CCS '05, pages 147–157, New York, NY, USA, 2005. ACM.

[4] P.-C. Cheng, P. Rohatgi, C. Keser, P. A. Karger, G. M. Wagner, and A. S. Reninger. Fuzzy multi-level security: An experiment on quantified risk-adaptive access control. In *IEEE Symposium on Security and Privacy*. IEEE Computer Society, 2007.

[5] J. Crampton, W. Leung, and K. Beznosov. The secondary and approximate authorization model and its application to Bell-LaPadula policies. In *Proceedings of 11th ACM Symposium in Access Control Models and Technologies*, pages 111–120, 2006.

[6] E. Eberlein, R. Frey, M. Kalkbrener, and L. Overbeck. Mathematics in Financial Risk Management. *Jahresbericht der Deutschen Mathematiker Vereinigung*, 109:165–193, 2007.

[7] Entrust. GetAccess design and administration guide, September 1999.

[8] D. F. Ferraiolo and D. R. Kuhn. Role-based access control. In *Proceedings of the 15th National Computer Security Conference*, pages 554–563, 1992.

[9] S. Godik and T. Moses. Oasis extensible access control markup language (XACML). OASIS Committee Secification cs-xacml-specification-1.0, November 2002, http://www.oasis-open.org/committees/xacml/, 2002.

[10] G. Gu, R. Perdisci, J. Zhang, and W. Lee. Botminer: clustering analysis of network traffic for protocol- and structure-independent botnet detection. In *Proceedings of the 17th conference on Security symposium*, pages 139–154. USENIX Association, 2008.

[11] G. Karjoth. Access control with IBM Tivoli Access Manager. *ACM Trans. Inf. Syst. Secur.*, 6:232–257, May 2003.

[12] J. Kephart. The utility of utility: Policies for self-managing systems. In *Policies for Distributed Systems and Networks, International Workshop, POLICY'11 Pisa, Italy*, 2011. To appear.

[13] A. Lanzi, D. Balzarotti, C. Kruegel, M. Christodorescu, and E. Kirda. Accessminer: Using system-centric models for malware protection. *CCS '10: Proceedings of the 17th ACM conference on Computer and communications security*, pages 399—419, Jul 2010.

[14] L. LaPadula and D. Bell. Secure Computer Systems: A Mathematical Model. *Journal of Computer Security*, 4:239–263, 1996.

[15] I. Molloy, P.-C. Cheng, and P. Rohatgi. Trading in risk: Using markets to improve access control. In *NSPW*, 2008.

[16] Netegrity. Siteminder concepts guide, 2000.

[17] Q. Ni, J. Lobo, S. B. Calo, P. Rohatgi, and E. Bertino. Automating role-based provisioning by learning from examples. In B. Carminati and J. Joshi, editors, *SACMAT*, pages 75–84. ACM, 2009.

[18] S. Rizvi, A. Mendelzon, S. Sudarshan, and P. Roy. Extending query rewriting techniques for fine-grained access control. In *Proceedings of the 2004 ACM SIGMOD international conference on Management of data*, SIGMOD '04, pages 551–562, New York, NY, USA, 2004. ACM.

[19] A. Rosenthal and E. Sciore. Administering permissions for distributed data: factoring and automated inference. In *Proceedings of the fifteenth annual working conference on Database and application security*, DAS'01, pages 91–104, Norwell, MA, USA, 2002. Kluwer Academic Publishers.

[20] Safeway Inc. Annual report for the fiscal year ended January 3, 2009. http://http://www.sec.gov/Archives/edgar/data/86144/000119312509043434/d10k.htm.

[21] Supervalu Inc. Annual report for the fiscal year ended February 28, 2009. http://www.sec.gov/Archives/edgar/data/95521/000095015209004223/c50531e10vk.htm.

[22] The Great Atlantic & Pacific Tea Company Inc. Fiscal 2008 Annual Report to Stockholders. http://www.sec.gov/Archives/edgar/data/43300/000139843209000171/ex13.txt.

[23] The Kroger Co. ANNUAL REPORT for the fiscal year ended January 31, 2009. http://www.sec.gov/Archives/edgar/data/56873/000110465909021710/a09-1837_110k.htm.

[24] K. Thomas, C. Grier, J. Ma, V. Paxson, and D. Song. Design and evaluation of a real-time url spam filtering service. *IEEE Symposium on Security and Privacy*, pages 1–16, Mar 2011.

[25] M. V. Tripunitara and B. Carbunar. Efficient access enforcement in distributed role-based access control (RBAC) deployments. In *Proceedings of the 14th ACM symposium on Access control models and technologies*, SACMAT '09, pages 155–164. ACM, 2009.

[26] V. N. Vapnik. *Statistical Learning Theory*. Wiley-Interscience, Sep 1998. ISBN 9780471030034.

[27] Visa Debit Processing Service | Transaction Processing | Authorization Processing. http://www.visadps.com/services/authorization_processing.html.

[28] Card-Present | Merchants | Visa USA. http://usa.visa.com/merchants/risk_management/card_present.html.

[29] L. Wang, D. Wijesekera, and S. Jajodia. A logic-based framework for attribute based access control. In *Proceedings of the 2004 ACM workshop on Formal methods in security engineering*, FMSE '04, pages 45–55, New York, NY, USA, 2004. ACM.

[30] Q. Wei, J. Crampton, K. Beznosov, and M. Ripeanu. Authorization recycling in rbac systems. In *Proceedings of the 13th ACM symposium on Access*

control models and technologies, SACMAT '08, pages 63–72, New York, NY, USA, 2008. ACM.

[31] Q. Wei, M. Ripeanu, and K. Beznosov. Cooperative secondary authorization recycling. In *Proceedings of the 16th international symposium on High performance distributed computing*, HPDC '07, pages 65–74, New York, NY, USA, 2007. ACM.

[32] M. Wimmer and A. Kemper. An authorization framework for sharing data in web service federations. In W. Jonker and M. Petkovic, editors, *Secure Data Management*, volume 3674 of *Lecture Notes in Computer Science*, pages 47–62. Springer, 2005.

[33] L. Zhang, A. Brodsky, and S. Jajodia. Toward Information Sharing: Benefit And Risk Access Control (BARAC). *Seventh IEEE International Workshop on Policies for Distributed Systems and Networks (POLICY'06)*, 0:45–53, 2006.

APPENDIX

Calculating α and β

Whenever the assessor defers a request, we get a new labeled point. For each labeled point, we know which side of the hyperplane the classifier placed it and how far away (a distance measured in the potentially non-linear feature space implicitly mapped up to by the classifier). We divide our collection of labeled points J, into the set J^+ of positively classified and the set J^- of negatively classified points. For each point in $i \in J^+$, we say that the distance from the hyperplane is $d(i)$ and the central PDPs labeling of the point (the true class) is $correct(i) \in \{valid, invalid\}$. The values α^i_{in}, β^i_{in}, α^i_{out}, and β^i_{out} are then defined by how many valid points are closer, invalid points are closer, valid points are farther away and invalid points are farther away from the hyperplane respectively. More formally:

$$\alpha^i_{\text{in}} = | \{j \mid d(j) <= d(i), correct(j) = valid, j \in J^+\} | + 1$$
$$\beta^i_{\text{in}} = | \{j \mid d(j) <= d(i), correct(j) = invalid, j \in J^+\} | + 1$$
$$\alpha^i_{\text{out}} = | \{j \mid d(j) >= d(i), correct(j) = valid, j \in J^+\} | + 1$$
$$\beta^i_{\text{out}} = | \{j \mid d(j) >= d(i), correct(j) = invalid, j \in J^+\} | + 1$$

Figure 2 graphically illustrates how these values are calculated for an example point i. A similar definition applies to α^i_{in}, β^i_{in}, α^i_{out} and α^i_{out} for $i \in J^-$.

We use the above values to define three methods – in, out and inout, to evaluate the accuracy of the classifier. Each method finds parameters for a beta-distribution, α^i and β^i, which estimates the probability that i is correctly classified locally, based on evidence in terms of labeled points.

in : We use $\alpha^i = \alpha^i_{\text{in}}$ and $\beta^i = \beta^i_{\text{in}}$ to look at the region between the hyperplane and point i, and assume that i is similar to a point sampled randomly from that region. This can be considered a conservative method, as only points closer to the hyperplane than i are considered.

out : We look at all possible regions from some point j and going away from the hyperplane, such that j is closer to the hyperplane than i. We then choose the most favourable region, i.e. the one with the best expected probability. It is like saying that i was sampled from that region, which is justified by seeing that i appears in each region considered. Formally, if $i \in J^+$, we use

$$\alpha^i = \alpha^{j^*}_{\text{out}} \text{ and } \beta^i = \beta^{j^*}_{\text{out}} \text{ for the point}$$
$$j^* = \operatorname*{arg\,max}_{j \in J^+, d(j) < d(i)} \frac{\alpha^j_{\text{out}}}{\alpha^j_{\text{out}} + \beta^j_{\text{out}}}$$

inout : We simply set $\alpha^i = \alpha^i_{\text{in}}$ and $\beta^i = \beta^i_{\text{out}}$ and hence count all positive examples closer to the plane than i and all negative examples further away. This lacks a probabilistic justification, but can be considered a rough and ready way to evaluate 'how far' a point is from the hyperplane. This method relies on having a good classifier and assumes a regular and well behaved structure on the space of requests.

Figure 10 shows how these three methods performed against basic caching with infinite queue on an example based on the access control data. As can be seen, the *in* method performs the best, the *out* method less well and the *inout* method approximately on par with caching (the unseeded SVM with the *in* method is included for comparison). In other experiments, the *in* always performed at least as well as the other methods, and often better. We therefore use the *in* method in the remaining experiments in this paper where needed.

Acknowledgement

This research was partially supported by the EU FP7-ICT project NESSoS (Network of Excellence on Engineering Secure Future Internet Software Services and Systems) under the grant agreement n. 256980, by the EU-funded project CONNECT and sponsored by the U.S. Army Research Laboratory and the U.K. Ministry of Defence and was accomplished under Agreement Number W911NF-06-3-0001. The views and conclusions contained in this document are those of the author(s) and should not be interpreted as representing the official policies, either expressed or implied, of the U.S. Army Research Laboratory, the U.S. Government, the U.K. Ministry of Defence or the U.K. Government. The U.S. and U.K. Governments are authorized to reproduce and distribute reprints for Government purposes notwithstanding any copyright notation hereon.

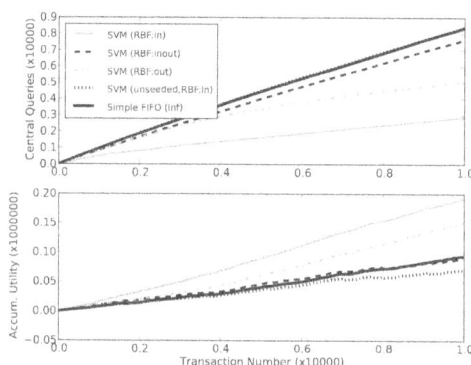

Figure 10: The different alpha-beta methods, in, out and inout were compared on the access control data using the secure-store group of utility values, i.e. $g = 4 * c$, $d_A = 10 * g$ and $d_D = 0$ with 30% of valid requests.

Quantitative Access Control with Partially-Observable Markov Decision Processes

Fabio Martinelli
Security Group, IIT-CNR
Pisa, Italy
fabio.martinelli@iit.cnr.it

Charles Morisset
Security Group, IIT-CNR
Pisa, Italy
charles.morisset@iit.cnr.it

ABSTRACT

This paper presents a novel access control framework reducing the access control problem to a traditional decision problem, thus allowing a policy designer to reuse tools and techniques from the decision theory. We propose here to express, within a single framework, the notion of utility of an access, decisions beyond the traditional allowing/denying of an access, the uncertainty over the effect of executing a given decision, the uncertainty over the current state of the system, and to optimize this process for a (probabilistic) sequence of requests. We show that an access control mechanism including these different concepts can be specified as a (Partially Observable) Markov Decision Process, and we illustrate this framework with a running example, which includes notions of conflict, critical resource, mitigation and auditing decisions, and we show that for a given sequence of requests, it is possible to calculate an optimal policy different from the naive one. This optimization is still possible even for several probable sequences of requests.

Categories and Subject Descriptors

D.4.6 [**Security and Protection**]: Access Controls; K.6.5 [**Management of Computing and Information Systems**]: Security and Protection

General Terms

Design, Security, Theory

Keywords

Access Control, AC-MDP, AC-POMDP, AC-DP

1. INTRODUCTION

Within an information system, the access control mechanism is in charge of controlling accesses done by subjects of the system (*e.g.* users, processes, etc) over objects of the

system (*e.g.* files, processes, etc), and to deny those specified as non secure, according to a policy. For instance, in a military setting, a top-secret file should only be accessed by users with the appropriate credentials. In general, the workflow of an access control mechanism can be defined in four steps: intercepting accesses; collecting information relative to accesses; making a decision about accesses; enforcing accordingly accesses. The XACML [31] architecture defines different sub-systems responsible for these tasks: the Policy Enforcement Point (PEP) intercepts the accesses and enforces them, the Context Handler harvests the information relative to the entities involved in the access and to the current state of the system, and the Policy Decision Point (PDP) returns a decision, potentially with some obligations that the PEP needs to follow when enforcing the access.

On the one hand, the methodology for making access control decisions usually follows a binary vision of the world, where an access control policy classifies each access as either "good" or "bad". Lampson [26] laid the basis of most modern access control systems, by introducing a set of subjects, a set of objects, a set of access modes, and the notion of access matrix, which extensively defines what access rights have subjects over objects. An access is "good" if it belongs to the matrix, and "bad" otherwise. An equivalent approach is to classify the states of the system as secure or not, and to make sure that only secure states are reachable. For instance, the Bell-LaPadula model [27] introduces the notions of simple-security and *-security, which state that the information can only flow up, with regard to a lattice of levels of security. Numerous access control policies have been defined in the last decades, refining in different ways the concept of access control matrix, but usually keeping the binary division between "good" and "bad" accesses.

Furthermore, most access control systems are usually designed as *interactive* systems, taking the current environment and a single access request, and allowing it if the access is "good", denying it otherwise. However, allowing an access might lead to denying another one later on, that would have been allowed otherwise. If the latter access is "better" than the former access, then intuitively there is a loss of *utility*. For instance, consider an exclusive resource, that can be accessed by at most one user. If the system grants the access to Alice who pays only $100 for it, then Bob, who would pay $500 for it, cannot access it. Hence, if the system *knows* (or can predict) that Bob will ask to access the resource, it might be "better" to deny the access to Alice. In general, it might be possible to *optimize* the decision process for a sequence of requests, while taking into account some uncertainty, for instance whether Bob will actually ask the access or not, or if the payment from Alice is fraudulent.

On the other hand, modern information systems, such as social networks, can be open, distributed and dynamically updated [25]. In this context, it can be hard for the Context Handler to harvest accurate and up-to-date information [24, 19]. Moreover, the effect of decisions on the system are not always entirely predictable, as errors can happen. Dealing with uncertainty might therefore be required when making access control decision, which leads to the problem of risk-based access control [8, 20, 21, 33].

Hence, we claim that the problem of specifying an access control policy can be seen as first associating utility values with accesses and/or states (instead of simple "bad" or "good" values) and then optimizing the decision making process for a sequence of requests while taking into account uncertainty over the next request in the sequence, the effect of each decision and the current state of the system. In other words, the access control decision problem can be reduced to a *decision* problem, and analysed in a *quantitative* way. In order to perform such an analysis, we present here a formalisation of the access control problem using (Partially-Observable) Markov Decision Processes (POMDP) [3, 37].

This formalisation is done in an incremental way, and we introduce three main decision processes, such that each one is a generalization of the previous one:

- An *Access Control Decision Process (AC-DP)* works with deterministic transitions and known sequences of requests, such that an optimal policy can be derived for this sequence, according to utility values associated with each transition. When the sequence of requests is limited to a single request, this process is semantically close to traditional access control mechanisms.
- An *Access Control Markov Decision Process (AC-MDP)* adds a dimension of uncertainty, by considering probabilistic transitions instead of deterministic ones. Hence, an AC-MDP deals with probabilistic sequences of requests and with uncertain effects of decisions.
- An *Access Control Partially Observable Markov Decision Process (AC-POMDP)* adds another dimension of uncertainty, by considering, in addition to probabilistic transitions, uncertainty over the current state.

An AC-DP is just an instance of an AC-MDP, which is in turn just an instance of an AC-POMDP, and in general, it follows that the optimal policy of a process is given by Equation (6), in Section 4. Hence, the main contribution of this paper is two-fold:

- First, we present a clear and illustrated framework for defining access control systems as decision processes, thus paving the way for using techniques from decision theory in the context of access control.
- Second, this framework is presented as a methodological guide for a policy designer, for which the burden is shifted from specifying each authorized access in each possible case to first specifying the utility values of accesses and states, regardless of the uncertainty, and then to specify the uncertainty of the system. The optimal policy is then defined (or approximated) by solving the corresponding system of equations of the POMDP.

Note that we reuse the notations introduced by Cassandra in [5], and we extend them in order to include access control concepts.

Organisation

The rest of this paper is organized as follows: Section 2 introduces the concept of AC-DP, Section 3 adds probabilistic transitions to define the concept of AC-MDP, Section 4 considers probabilistic states in order to define the concept of AC-POMDP. We discuss the limitations of our framework in Section 5 and we sketch some future works and conclude in Section 6.

Related Work

To the best of our knowledge, Markov Decision Processes have not yet been used in the context of access control systems. However, the problem of dealing with risk and uncertainty for access control systems has been already studied in the literature. For instance, Aziz *et al.* [2] refine a policy to a more restrictive one, in order to deal with threats.

Risk is often considered as an input to the system, that must stay below a certain threshold. Cheng *et al.* introduce in [8] the Fuzzy Multi-Level Security model, where each access is associated with a level of risk, and the final decision of the authorization mechanism is given according to some predefined risk thresholds. Diep *et al.* extend this approach in [13] by considering costs in terms of availability, integrity and confidentiality for each decision, and use thresholds for each corresponding risk.

Some approaches aim at calculating the risk from the environment. For instance, Ni *et al.* introduce in [33] fuzzy security parameters that can be inferred from traditional parameters, hence introducing a notion of uncertainty directly into the parameters of the system, while Chen and Crampton present in [7] a way to calculate the risk for a RBAC model, using intuitive notions of competence and distance between users, roles and permissions. The probabilistic change of security attributes is considered by Krautsevich *et al.* in [20], who model this change using a Markov chain.

Dealing with uncertainty requires quantitative techniques, and therefore accesses must be associated with a utility value. Some models use these notions, for instance Krautsevich *et al.* extend in [22] the auto-delegation mechanism [11] with probabilistic availability, reusing some notions of utility functions previously introduced in [19]. Similarly, Molloy *et al.* present in [30] a model to predict and make local decisions under uncertainty, where the system needs to choose between taking a decision locally or defer it to a central server, according to the utility of the access and the cost of communicating with the server.

Beyond the scope of access control, several pieces of work use the concept of Markov Decision Process (MDP) in the context of security. For instance, Kreidl introduces in [23] a simple MDP with only three states (normal, under attack and failure) and three decisions (wait, defend and reset), which analyses the cost of defending countermeasures against the cost of an intrusion.

Similarly, He *et al.* present in [14] an analysis of the operational costs and the negative and positive impact of security countermeasures using Domain Partitional Markov Decision Processes, which partition the network into several security domains, each domain coming with its own MDP. This work, as the previous one, mostly focuses on the detection of intrusions and the decisions needed when some are discovered.

Finally, Singh *et al.* use in [36] an MDP to make channel assignments for network devices. This problem can be considered as a special instance of an access control problem, where the devices ask to access channels, with a specific policy stating that any device can access a channel, but the more devices use a given channel, the lower is the utility for this channel. Hence, our approach can be seen as a more general approach, where the policy is not constrained. Moreover, we also consider decisions beyond allow/deny.

2. AC-DP

Cassandra gives in [5] the example for a decision process of a robot trying to survive in a real-world environment: the robot observes the environment, detects an obstacle or not, and decides which direction to move to. It can also decides to take *autonomous* decisions, for instance about auditing and fixing itself. Because the robot can predict, with some uncertainty, how the environment or itself will react to its actions, it can *optimize* the actions it takes, rather than simply making a decision with respect to the current environment. Intuitively, we want to follow an analogous approach to describe an access control decision process, that is, a process taking an environment and a request, and making a decision (such as allow or deny) about this request, which leads to a new environment and a new request to control, for which a new decision needs to be made.

In this section, we make two assumptions: the effect of a decision is deterministic, and the exact sequence of future requests is known and finite. Such assumptions are well-suited for closed systems working in batch-mode or dealing with complex tasks. For instance, the queries to a database often consist of nested sub-queries, which, in terms of access control, translates to having nested access requests (*e.g.* one for each table accessed by the query). Similarly, the permission to execute a program is implied by the permission of accessing each resource accessed by this program. Note that it is always possible to consider a sequence to be reduced to a single request, in order to work in a traditional setting. However, we claim (and we will illustrate) that knowing the sequence of requests might allow the decision process to make better decisions. We consider in the following sections systems for which these assumptions do not hold.

Hence, a decision process is a labelled transition system, where each state represents the state of the system together with the current request to control, and each transition represents a decision made by the controller. In order to define such a system, we expect the policy designer to provide the specification of a state, as a composition of some security information and a request (Section 2.1); the transition function (Section 2.2) and the utility and reward function (Section 2.3). Using this information, we can define the notion of AC-DP (Section 2.4). These different concepts are illustrated with a running example, that we extend along the paper in order to illustrate the expressivity of our framework.

2.1 System State

As described in Figure 1, we consider the following situation: the environment (consisting of users, processes, etc) submits access requests to the access control decision process, which makes a decision for each request. More precisely, at time t_i, the environment submits a request r_i, leading the decision process to analyse a state σ_i, which consists of the request r_i and some security information, and makes a decision d_i. This decision and the next request from the

environment leads to a new state, from which a new decision can be made, and so on. Our objective is to model the access control decision process, which can be seen as a state machine, where states contains requests from the environment and security information, and where transitions are decisions. Intuitively, this state machine will correspond in the following sections to a Markov Decision Process.

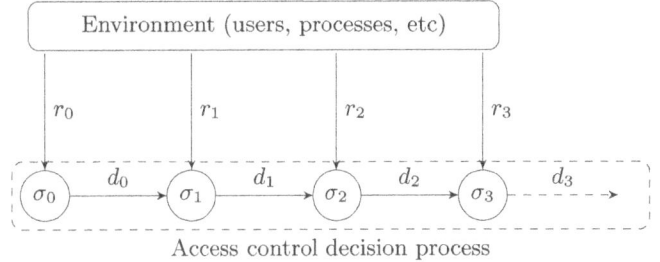

Figure 1: Global system

Hence, we define an *access control state* in two parts: the security information, *i.e.* all the information required to make an access control decision, and the access request that needs to be controlled. Writing $\mathcal{I}$ for the set of security information and $\mathcal{R}$ for the set of access requests, we therefore define the set of access control states as $\Sigma = \mathcal{I} \times \mathcal{R}$. Furthermore, we write $\mathcal{A}$ for the set of *decisions*, and it follows that an access control policy is a function $\delta : \Sigma \rightarrow \mathcal{A}$, that is, a function that takes a state including a request to be controlled, and returns a decision about this request. Finally, we define a special request ϵ, such that for any security information ι, the state (ι, ϵ) represents the state where no request needs to be evaluated.

Running Example

In order to illustrate the different concepts we present in this paper, we introduce a running example. Let us consider a system with a set $\mathcal{S}$ of subjects and a set $\mathcal{O}$ of objects, such that an access is a pair $(s, o) \in \mathcal{S} \times \mathcal{O}$ (we deliberately omit the access mode, for the sake of simplicity). A subject can be either registered or not, which is denoted by a function $\mathbf{reg} : \mathcal{S} \rightarrow \{0, 1\}$. Similarly, an object can be either confidential or not, which is denoted by the function $\mathbf{cf} : \mathcal{O} \rightarrow \{0, 1\}$. When no confusion can arise, given a subject s_i and an object o_j, we will write $\mathbf{reg}_i$ and $\mathbf{cf}_j$ for $\mathbf{reg}(s_i)$ and $\mathbf{cf}(o_j)$, respectively. The security information part of a state (ι, r) is therefore a triple $\iota = (\mathbf{reg}, \mathbf{cf}, m)$, where $m \subseteq \mathcal{S} \times \mathcal{O}$ is the set of accesses previously granted. The point of this set is to enable the definition of conflicts between accesses, as we will see when defining the reward function in Section 2.3. The set of decisions is (at this stage) $\mathcal{A} = \{\mathbf{allow}, \mathbf{deny}\}$.

2.2 Transition Function

As we said above, a decision process is a labelled transition, where each transition corresponds to the execution of a particular decision, and therefore the policy designer must also specify the *transition function* $\mathcal{T} : \Sigma \times \mathcal{A} \rightarrow \Sigma$, such that given a state σ and a decision a, $\mathcal{T}(\sigma, a)$ stands for the state obtained from σ by executing the decision a.

Since a state consists of some security information ι and a request r, the transition function $\mathcal{T}$ can be split into two independent transition functions $\mathcal{T}_\iota : \Sigma \times \mathcal{A} \to \mathcal{I}$ and $\mathcal{T}_r : \Sigma \times \mathcal{A} \to \mathcal{R}$, such that given a state σ and a decision a, $\mathcal{T}(\sigma, a) = (\mathcal{T}_\iota(\sigma, a), \mathcal{T}_r(\sigma, a))$. These two transition functions represent both aspects of the transformation of a state.

Indeed, the function $\mathcal{T}_\iota$ is responsible for describing the effect over the security information of making a decision about a request. Such a function is intuitively equivalent to traditional transition functions in access control systems, where a state only contains the security information part.

The function $\mathcal{T}_r$ is on the contrary responsible for returning the following request that needs to be controlled. In general, following the setting described in Figure 1, this function is controlled by the environment. However, we assume at this stage that the decision process knows its definition. When only a single request is known, we define $\mathcal{T}_r(\sigma, a) = \epsilon$, for any state σ and any decision a. In practice, we could directly include a concrete sequence of requests in the state, and remove requests from this sequence as the system controls them. However, such a concrete structure does not bring much in the decision process and tends to obfuscate the exposition of the framework, so we leave the concrete definition of the function $\mathcal{T}_r$ to be done at the implementation level.

Running Example

Although the function $\mathcal{T}_r$ changes for each sequence of requests, we can define the transition function $\mathcal{T}_\iota$, which simply adds the requested access when it is allowed, ans does nothing otherwise:

$$\mathcal{T}_\iota((\mathbf{reg}, \mathbf{cf}, m), \epsilon, a) = (\mathbf{reg}, \mathbf{cf}, m)$$
$$\mathcal{T}_\iota((\mathbf{reg}, \mathbf{cf}, m), (s, o), \mathbf{allow}) = (\mathbf{reg}, \mathbf{cf}, m \cup \{(s, o)\})$$
$$\mathcal{T}_\iota((\mathbf{reg}, \mathbf{cf}, m), (s, o), \mathbf{deny}) = (\mathbf{reg}, \mathbf{cf}, m)$$

2.3 Utility and Reward Function

An important aspect of a decision process is the ability to give a *utility value* to a decision or a state. In other words, it is possible to express the interest for the system of making a given decision in a given state, and we introduce an *utility domain* $\mathcal{U}$. The general idea is that when confronted with several decision to make, the controller chooses the one offering the best utility.

For instance, a very simple utility domain is the set $\{\mathbf{good}, \mathbf{bad}\}$. Such a set follows the traditional intuition behind access control policies, but provides little flexibility. For instance, if every possible decision in a given state is associated with the utility $\mathbf{bad}$, the controller does not know which one to choose. Hence, we usually consider richer utility domains, such as $\mathbb{R}$, which can provide finer-grained decisions. Note that it is possible to say that a negative value is equivalent to $\mathbf{bad}$, while a positive one is equivalent to $\mathbf{good}$, however, if the system has to choose between two decisions leading to different negative utility values, it can choose the "best" solution between two bad options.

The policy designer must then specify a *reward function* $\mathcal{W} : \Sigma \times \mathcal{A} \times \Sigma \to \mathcal{U}$, such that given two states σ_i and σ_j, and a decision a, $\mathcal{W}(\sigma_i, a, \sigma_j)$ stands for the reward of making the decision a in the state σ_i and arriving in the state σ_j, and we write w_{ij}^a for such a reward. The reward function $\mathcal{W}$ can be defined in many different ways, for instance by associating a utility value for reaching a particular state σ_j, or by giving the utility value of taking the decision a for a request r.

Intuitively, the reward function encodes the security policy of the system, and can also include notions such as the principle of least privilege or the separation of duties. In the first case, the policy designer can simply specify a state where a user accesses a resource with exactly the required privileges with a higher reward than a state where, all other things being equal, the same user accesses the resource with non necessary privileges. In the second case, the policy designer can associate a negative reward with a state where a same user is performing two operations that should normally executed by two different users.

If there is no access request to control, then the decision taken by the process is irrelevant, and therefore there should not be any reward associated with such a situation. Hence, we have the following assumption:

$$\forall \sigma_i, \sigma_j \in \Sigma \; \forall \iota \in \mathcal{I} \; \forall a \in \mathcal{A} \quad \sigma_i = (\iota, \epsilon) \Rightarrow w_{ij}^a = 0 \quad (1)$$

Note that the reward w_{ij}^a does not depend on the transition function $\mathcal{T}$, which is the reason why the state σ_j is explicit in the definition of $\mathcal{W}$. However, given a state σ_i and a decision a, since we consider in this section that the transition function is deterministic, there is a single state σ_j reachable, namely $\mathcal{T}(\sigma_i, a)$. For the sake of the exposition (and to be consistent with the notations introduced in the following sections), we introduce the value q_i^a, which indicates the reward for executing the decision a from the state σ_i, and which is defined by $q_i^a = \mathcal{W}(\sigma_i, a, \mathcal{T}(\sigma_i, a))$.

Clearly, defining the function $\mathcal{W}$ for a concrete system might be a complex task [12], and this has been recently considered by Kephart [18] as a challenge that needs to be addressed by the security community. A traditional approach, inherited from the finance world, where decision mechanisms have been used for a long time, is to associate a pecuniary value with each access. For instance, Symantec revealed in its 2011 survey [40] that "20% of businesses lost at least \$195,000 as a result of cyber-attacks". Hence, a state identifying the violation of a security property could be associated with a negative reward of \$195,000. Moreover, once pecuniary values have been associated with some entities, markets techniques can be used to derive more dynamic values [29].

The aim of this framework is not to define concrete utility values, but rather to provide the tools to take advantage of them. As we discuss in Section 5, we acknowledge the fact that it is a challenging task (and so is defining an actual policy in general), but we believe that a framework such as the one presented here can help the policy designer to define accurate and meaningful values.

Running Example

We first associate each access (s_i, o_j) with a value using the function rew_1, which is defined in Table 1.

$rew_1(s_i, o_j)$	$\mathbf{reg}_i = 0$	$\mathbf{reg}_i = 1$
$\mathbf{cf}_j = 0$	4	6
$\mathbf{cf}_j = 1$	-10	10

Table 1: Rewards for single accesses

Note that these values are arbitrary: they represent the intuitive idea that giving a confidential object to a non-registered subject is "bad", and otherwise, giving an access

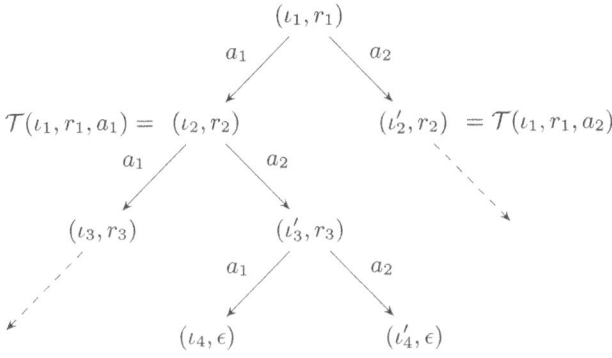

Figure 2: Example of AC-DP for the sequence $r_1; r_2; r_3$ and for the set of decisions $\mathcal{A} = \{a_1, a_2\}$

to a registered subject has a high value (because she potentially knows best how to use it), and granting an access to a confidential object has high value (because they potentially have more useful information).

In order to model the fact that an object should not be accessed by more than one user, we introduce the reward function rew_2 expressed over sets of accesses, such that $rew_2(m) = -100$ if there exists an object o and two different subjects s and s' such that (s, o) and (s', o) belong to m, and $rew_2(m) = 0$ otherwise.

The reward function $\mathcal{W}$ is defined from the functions rew_1 and rew_2. Given two states $\sigma_i = (\mathbf{reg}, \mathbf{cf}, m, r)$ and $\sigma_j = (\mathbf{reg}', \mathbf{cf}', m', r')$, we define:

$$w_{ij}^a = \begin{cases} 0 & \text{if } r = \epsilon \text{ or } \sigma_j \neq \mathcal{T}(\sigma_i, a) \\ rew_2(m') & \text{if } a = \mathbf{deny} \\ rew_1(s, o) + rew_2(m') & \text{if } r = (s, o) \text{ and } a = \mathbf{allow} \end{cases}$$

When there is no request to control (*i.e.* when $r = \epsilon$), there is no reward. Similarly, the reward for arriving in a state σ_j that is different from the one obtained using the transition function is null, as it is impossible (this situation will change when we consider later on probabilistic transitions). Otherwise, we always consider the reward associated with the resulting set of accesses[1] (*i.e.* $rew_2(m')$), and if we grant the access, we also add the reward associated with this particular access (*i.e.* $rew_1(s, o)$).

2.4 AC-DP

Intuitively, a decision process takes some security information and a request, and returns which decision to take. The choice of this decision is made by a policy, whose aim is to maximise the utility value.

DEFINITION 1. *An Access Control Decision Process (AC-DP) is tuple $\langle \Sigma, \mathcal{A}, \mathcal{T}, \mathcal{W} \rangle$, where $\Sigma = \mathcal{I} \times \mathcal{R}$ is a set of access control states, $\mathcal{A}$ is a set of decisions, $\mathcal{T} : \Sigma \times \mathcal{A} \to \Sigma$ is a transition function and $\mathcal{W} : \Sigma \times \mathcal{A} \times \Sigma \to \mathcal{U}$ is a reward function.*

Figure 2 illustrates an AC-DP for the sequence of requests $r_1; r_2; r_3$ and the set of decisions $\mathcal{A} = \{a_1, a_2\}$: from the

---

[1]Clearly, when the access is denied, we have $m = m'$, and therefore we could equivalently consider $rew_2(m)$.

initial state (ι_1, r_1), the proces can either choose a_1 or a_2, leading respectively to (ι_2, r_2) and (ι_2', r_2) (for the sake of the illustration, we did not consider here the case where the request r_1 would need to be evaluated again, however such situations are covered in the following with the introduction of mitigations techniques). The process keeps going on until reaching states where the request to be controlled is ϵ, such as the states (ι_4, ϵ) and (ι_4', ϵ). In this particular example, we can see that there are 2^3 paths possible.

The policy defines which path to choose, and in order to specify the policy, we define the *value* of a policy δ to be the sum of the rewards accumulated by the AC-DP when starting from a given state and by choosing the decisions returned by the policy. This value is given by the *value function* $V^\delta : \Sigma \to \mathcal{U}$ of a policy δ, which is defined as:

$$V^\delta(\sigma_i) = q_i^{\delta(\sigma_i)} + \beta \cdot V^\delta(\mathcal{T}(\sigma_i, \delta(\sigma_i))) \tag{2}$$

where $0 \leq \beta \leq 1$ is a discounting factor. This factor is used to potentially attach less importance to the rewards obtained in the future.

A policy δ^* is said to be *optimal* if, and only if, for any state σ_i and any other policy δ, $V^{\delta^*}(\sigma_i) \geq V^\delta(\sigma_i)$. From Equation (2), we can define the optimal policy as:

$$\delta^*(\sigma_i) = \arg\max_{a \in \mathcal{A}} [q_i^a + \beta \cdot V^{\delta^*}(\mathcal{T}(\sigma_i, a))] \tag{3}$$

where $\arg\max$ stands for the function returning one element maximizing the formula. Note that this definition is potentially recursive, since the decision selected by δ^* from σ_i depends on the value of the policy for $\mathcal{T}(\sigma_i, a)$, which can be equal to σ_i. Moreover, if the set of spaces is infinite (for instance by considering an infinite number of subjects and/or objects), it might not be possible to define an optimal policy.

It is worth observing that when only single request are considered instead of sequences of request, *i.e.* when $\mathcal{T}_r(\sigma, a) = \epsilon$, for any state σ and any decision a, then the value of a policy is simply the reward associated with taking the decision indicated by this policy. Indeed, in this case, in Equation (2), the request of the state $\mathcal{T}(\sigma_i, \delta(\sigma_i))$ is equal to ϵ, and following Equation (1), we can deduce that $V^\delta(\mathcal{T}(\sigma_i, \delta(\sigma_i))) = 0$. Moreover, if the utility domain is defined as $\{\mathbf{good}, \mathbf{bad}\}$, then the reward function is semantically equivalent to a traditional policy, classifying each transition into the good ones and the bad ones. Hence, any traditional access control policy can be easily expressed in our framework.

Running Example

Let $\mathcal{S} = \{s_1, s_2\}$, such that s_1 is registered while s_2 is not, *i.e.* $\mathbf{reg}_1 = 1$ and $\mathbf{reg}_2 = 0$, and $\mathcal{O} = \{o_1, o_2\}$ such that o_1 is confidential and o_2 is not, *i.e.* $\mathbf{cf}_1 = 1$ and $\mathbf{cf}_2 = 0$. Let us also consider the sequence of requests (s_2, o_1), (s_2, o_2), (s_1, o_2). We implement this sequence by defining the initial state $\sigma_0 = (\mathbf{reg}, \mathbf{cf}, \emptyset, (s_2, o_1))$, and the request transition function $\mathcal{T}_r$, such that for any ι and for any decision a:

$$\mathcal{T}_r(\iota, (s_2, o_1), a) = (s_2, o_2)$$
$$\mathcal{T}_r(\iota, (s_2, o_2), a) = (s_1, o_2)$$
$$\mathcal{T}_r(\iota, (s_1, o_2), a) = \epsilon$$

Because of the function rew_2, the accesses (s_2, o_2) and (s_2, o_1) cannot be both accepted at the same time, otherwise the system would get a reward of -100. Let us call

$\delta_1:$	$(\emptyset,(s_2,o_1))$	$\xrightarrow{\text{deny}}$	$(\emptyset,(s_2,o_2))$	$\xrightarrow{\text{allow}}$	$(\{(s_2,o_2)\},(s_1,o_2))$	$\xrightarrow{\text{deny}}$	$(\{(s_2,o_2)\},(s_1,o_1))$	$\xrightarrow{\text{allow}}$	$(\{(s_1,o_1),(s_2,o_2)\},\epsilon)$
			$\downarrow$		$\downarrow$		$\downarrow$		$\downarrow$
			reward $= 0$		reward $= 4$		reward $= 0$		reward $= 10$
$\delta_2:$	$(\emptyset,(s_2,o_1))$	$\xrightarrow{\text{deny}}$	$(\emptyset,(s_2,o_2))$	$\xrightarrow{\text{deny}}$	$(\emptyset,(s_1,o_2))$	$\xrightarrow{\text{allow}}$	$(\{(s_1,o_2)\},(s_1,o_1))$	$\xrightarrow{\text{allow}}$	$(\{(s_1,o_1),(s_1,o_2)\},\epsilon)$
			$\downarrow$		$\downarrow$		$\downarrow$		$\downarrow$
			reward $= 0$		reward $= 0$		reward $= 6$		reward $= 10$

Table 2: Policy examples

δ_1 the naive policy allowing an access if the associated reward is positive, and denying it otherwise. We can see on Table 2 that $V^{\delta_1}(\sigma_0) = 14$ (we consider in this example a discounting factor $\beta = 1$). This policy is however not optimal: indeed, let us consider the policy δ_2 only allowing accesses from registered users, and denying all others. As shown on Table 2, we have $V^{\delta_2}(\sigma_0) = 16$, and it follows $V^{\delta_2}(\sigma_0) > V^{\delta_1}(\sigma_0)$. The policy δ_2 is not optimal either, since if only unregistered users ask for accesses, then this policy will get a value of 0, while another policy allowing the accesses to non-confidential files obtains a higher value.

This simple example illustrates the fact that the policy always selecting the decision returning the best *immediate* reward is not always optimal, and that when the sequence of requests is known, it can be worth inspecting it in order to find the best policy for this state. For finite sequences of requests, the number of possibilities to consider is finite for a given state, and the best policy can be calculated using Equation (3).

Extended Running Example

In the previous example, we have shown that an AC-DP is able to consider sequences of requests in order to find the best policy for a given state. We now show that an AC-DP is also able to choose between two "bad" situations. In order to illustrate this case, we add a new reward function rew_3 defined over sets of accesses, that states that the object o_1 is a critical resource and needs to be accessed, such as the medical record of a patient currently having a heart attack. We define $rew_3(m) = rew_2(m') + 50$ if there exists a subject s such that (s,o_1) belongs to m and $rew_2(m)$ otherwise, and we redefine the reward function $\mathcal{W}$ as follows:

$$w_{ij}^a = \begin{cases} 0 & \text{if } r = \epsilon \text{ or } \sigma_j \neq \mathcal{T}(\sigma_i,a) \\ rew_3(m') & \text{if } a = \textbf{deny} \\ rew_1(s,o) + rew_3(m') & \text{if } a = \textbf{allow} \end{cases}$$

Consider now the state $\sigma_1 = (\textbf{reg},\textbf{cf},\emptyset,(s_2,o_1))$. Based on the new reward function, we can calculate that $q_1^{\textbf{allow}} = 50 - 10 = 40$, while $q_1^{\textbf{deny}} = 0$. In other words, it is more interesting for the system to allow this access, even though the access itself has a negative reward. However, with the state $\sigma_2 = (\textbf{reg},\textbf{cf},\{(s_1,o_1)\},(s_2,o_1))$, that is, the state where s_1 is already accessing o_1 and where s_2 asks to access it, we have $q_2^{\textbf{allow}} = 50 - 100 - 10 = -60$, and $q_2^{\textbf{deny}} = 50$, and in this case it is more interesting to deny this access. Note that this property would still hold without rew_2.

The fact that the system might need to allow "bad" accesses leads to using mitigation strategies, that are, roughly speaking, methods to limit the exposure of an access. For instance, the resolution of a picture can be downgraded, a monitoring system can be enforced, etc. Such techniques usually have a cost, that we express here in terms of re-

duced utility, both for positive values (reduced gains) and negative values (reduced losses).

For the sake of this example, we extend the previous definition for a state, such that a state σ is now a tuple $(\textbf{reg},\textbf{cf},m,\textbf{mit})$, where $\textbf{reg}$, $\textbf{cf}$ and m are defined as before, and where $\textbf{mit} = 1$ if mitigations procedures are enforced, and $\textbf{mit} = 0$ otherwise. Moreover, we introduce a new decision $\textbf{mitigate}$, such that executing this decision set the value of $\textbf{mit}$ to 1. This decision has the particularity not to change the request to be controlled. More formally, we define:

$$\mathcal{T}_t((\textbf{reg},\textbf{cf},m,\textbf{mit}),r,\textbf{mitigate}) = (\textbf{reg},\textbf{cf},m,1)$$
$$\mathcal{T}_r((\textbf{reg},\textbf{cf},m),r,\textbf{mitigate}) = r$$

We define a new reward function rew_4 returning the utility of accesses when mitigation techniques are enforced, such that $rew_4(s,o)$ is equal to half the value of $rew_1(s,o)$. The reward function is modified such that, given two states $\sigma_i = (\textbf{reg},\textbf{cf},m,\textbf{mit})$ and $\sigma_j = (\textbf{reg}',cf',m',\textbf{mit}')$, for any decision a, we have:

$$w_{ij}^a = \begin{cases} 0 & \text{if } r = \epsilon \text{ or } \sigma_j \neq \mathcal{T}(\sigma_i,a) \\ & \quad \text{or } a = \textbf{mitigate} \\ rew_3(m') & \text{if } a = \textbf{deny} \\ rew_4(s,o) + rew_3(m') & \text{if } a = \textbf{allow} \text{ and } \textbf{mit}' = 1 \\ rew_1(s,o) + rew_3(m') & \text{if } a = \textbf{allow} \text{ and } \textbf{mit}' = 0 \end{cases}$$

Note that this reward function only considers the mitigation status for new accesses, and not old ones, implying that an access granted while mitigation techniques are enforced will always be mitigated, even if these techniques are suspended in the future. Clearly, a concrete implementation might require a finer-grained mitigation management, but this specification suffices to illustrate the usage of mitigations.

Indeed, consider the state $\sigma_3 = (\textbf{reg},\textbf{cf},\emptyset,0,(s_2,o_1))$, which is equivalent to the previous state σ_1 with no mitigation techniques enforced. Clearly, we have $q_3^{\textbf{allow}} = 40$ and $q_3^{\textbf{deny}} = q_3^{\textbf{mitigate}} = 0$. Hence, the naive policy would still be to directly allow the access (s_2,o_1). However, if we define $\sigma_4 = (\textbf{reg},\textbf{cf},\emptyset,1,(s_2,o_1))$, we have $\mathcal{T}(\sigma_3,\textbf{mitigate}) = \sigma_4$ and $q_4^{\textbf{allow}} = 45$. In this case, we can observe that the most interesting policy is for the AC-DP to make an *autonomous* decision, that is to start mitigation techniques, before allowing a "bad" access.

3. MARKOV DECISION PROCESS

The notion of AC-DP presented in the previous section assumes that transitions between states are *deterministic*, that is, given a state and a decision, the process knows exactly what is the next state. However, in general, it is not always possible to know the exact sequence of requests. Moreover, the effect of a decision over the security information might be non predictable, for instance for hybrid systems involving hardware, where faults can happen. This section introduces the notion of Access Control Markov Decision Process (AC-MDP), which is a Markov Decision Process where the state is an access control state.

Roughly speaking, an AC-MDP is an AC-DP with *probabilistic* transitions. Hence, the main novelty of this section is the introduction of the probability function $\mathcal{P} : \Sigma \times \mathcal{A} \times \Sigma \to [0,1]$, which replaces the transition function $\mathcal{T}$.

3.1 AC-MDP

DEFINITION 2. *An Access Control Markov Decision Process (AC-MDP) is a tuple $\langle \Sigma, \mathcal{A}, \mathcal{P}, \mathcal{W} \rangle$, where $\Sigma = \mathcal{I} \times \mathcal{R}$ is a set of access control states, $\mathcal{A}$ is a set of decisions, $\mathcal{P} : \Sigma \times \mathcal{A} \times \Sigma \to [0,1]$ is the probability function, such that $\mathcal{P}(\sigma_i, a, \sigma_j)$ stands for the probability of reaching the state σ_j by executing the decision a from the state σ_i, and $\mathcal{W} : \Sigma \times \mathcal{A} \times \Sigma \to \mathcal{U}$ is the reward function, such that $\mathcal{W}(\sigma_i, a, \sigma_j)$ stands for the reward associated with executing the decision a from the state σ_i and arriving in the state σ_j. When no confusion can arise, we write p_{ij}^a and w_{ij}^a for $\mathcal{P}(\sigma_i, a, \sigma_j)$ and $\mathcal{W}(\sigma_i, a, \sigma_j)$, respectively.*

We write q_i^a for the immediate reward for executing the decision a in the state σ_i:

$$q_i^a = \sum_j p_{ij}^a \cdot w_{ij}^a$$

As for an AC-DP, a *policy* is a function $\delta : \Sigma \to \mathcal{A}$, which returns for each state the decision to execute, in other words, given a state with an access request to control, the policy returns the decision to be made for this request. Given a policy δ and a state σ_i, the value function V^δ is calculated as follows:

$$V^\delta(\sigma_i) = \sum_j p_{ij}^{\delta(\sigma_i)} [w_{ij}^{\delta(\sigma_i)} + \beta \cdot V^\delta(\sigma_j)]$$

which can be simplified to:

$$V^\delta(\sigma_i) = q_i^{\delta(\sigma_i)} + \beta \sum_j p_{ij}^{\delta(\sigma_i)} V^\delta(\sigma_j) \tag{4}$$

The definition of the optimal policy is refined to:

$$\delta^*(\sigma_i) = \arg\max_{a \in \mathcal{A}} [q_i^a + \beta \sum_j p_{ij}^a V^{\delta^*}(\sigma_j)] \tag{5}$$

In a similar way that an AC-DP splits the transition function $\mathcal{T}$ into $\mathcal{T}_r$ and $\mathcal{T}_\iota$, the probability function $\mathcal{P}$ can be split into the probability functions $\mathcal{P}_r$ and $\mathcal{P}_\iota$, as we describe now.

3.2 Probabilistic Request Sequence

In some cases, even if we do not know with certainty the sequence of requests, it might be possible to know the probability of a such a sequence to occur. Indeed, attack patterns and behavioral analyses of users can determine the likelihood of a given request to be submitted after another given one. For instance, it might be observed that a user who is denied an access to a object might try to access a similar object, or might ask her supervisor to access the object for her. Similarly, relationships between different objects/subjects can give some indication of the relationship between the access requests. For instance, a user accessing a master LaTeX file is likely to request to access some files included in the master file.

Assuming that the transition function $\mathcal{T}_\iota$ is defined, the policy designer can provide a function giving the conditional probability of a request r to be the next one, knowing the current state σ and the decision taken a, and we write $\mathcal{P}_r(r \mid \sigma, a)$ for this probability. Given two states $\sigma_i = (\iota, r)$ and $\sigma_j = (\iota', r')$, we define:

$$p_{ij}^a = \begin{cases} 0 & \text{if } \iota' \neq \mathcal{T}_\iota(\sigma_i, a) \\ \mathcal{P}_r(r' \mid \sigma_i, a) & \text{otherwise} \end{cases}$$

In practice, this probability function can be used to encode the availability of subjects, by stating that a subject with a low probability to be available has also a low probability to submit a request. The decision to allow a request with a low reward depends then on the probability that a request with the same goal (for instance accessing a critical resource) but a higher reward will be submitted in the future, knowing that denying the access can lead to negative penalties while waiting for the other request.

Running Example

Without prior knowledge of the environment, it can be hard to define the function $\mathcal{P}_r$, especially if the subjects submitting the requests are human beings, whose behavior cannot be always accurately predicted. However, in some cases, we can try to approximate this behavior. For instance, we can say that if an access is already in the set of current accesses, then the corresponding request will not be submitted again, and that the distribution of probabilities for other accesses is uniform.

Given a set of requests $\mathcal{R}$ (including ϵ), a state $\sigma = (\mathbf{reg}, \mathbf{cf}, m, \mathbf{mit}, r)$ and a decision a, we first define the function α which returns the requests that are possible after executing the decision a:

$$\alpha(\sigma, a) = \begin{cases} \{r\} & \text{if } a = \mathbf{mitigate} \text{ or } r = \epsilon \\ \mathcal{R} \setminus (m \cup \{r\}) & \text{if } a = \mathbf{allow} \text{ and } r \neq \epsilon \\ \mathcal{R} \setminus m & \text{otherwise} \end{cases}$$

Note that since the request ϵ is never added to the set of curent accesses m, we clearly have that ϵ is always a possible request. The definition of the function $\mathcal{P}_r$ is then simply:

$$\mathcal{P}_r(r \mid \sigma, a) = \begin{cases} 0 & \text{if } r \notin \alpha(\sigma, a) \\ 1/\mathbf{card}(\alpha(\sigma, a)) & \text{otherwise} \end{cases}$$

where **card** denotes the set cardinality function.

For instance, let us consider the running example of Section 2.4, without mitigation, and, for the sake of clarity, let us consider restrict our attention to the only object o_1. In this case, we have $\mathcal{R} = \{\epsilon, (s_1, o_1), (s_2, o_1)\}$, and for the state $\sigma_2 = (\mathbf{reg}, \mathbf{cf}, \emptyset, 0, (s_2, o_1))$, we have:

$\mathcal{P}_r(r \mid \sigma_2, a)$	$r = (s_1, o_1)$	$r = (s_2, o_1)$	$r = \epsilon$
$a = \mathbf{allow}$	1/2	0	1/2
$a = \mathbf{deny}$	1/3	1/3	1/3

Figure 3 illustrates the corresponding AC-MDP, without the unreachable states, *i.e.* the states for which the probability to reach them from a different state is null. An edge of this automaton represents the probability of the process to move from one state to another for a given decision. For instance, the process can move from the state σ_4 to σ_3 with the decision **deny** with a probability 1/2.

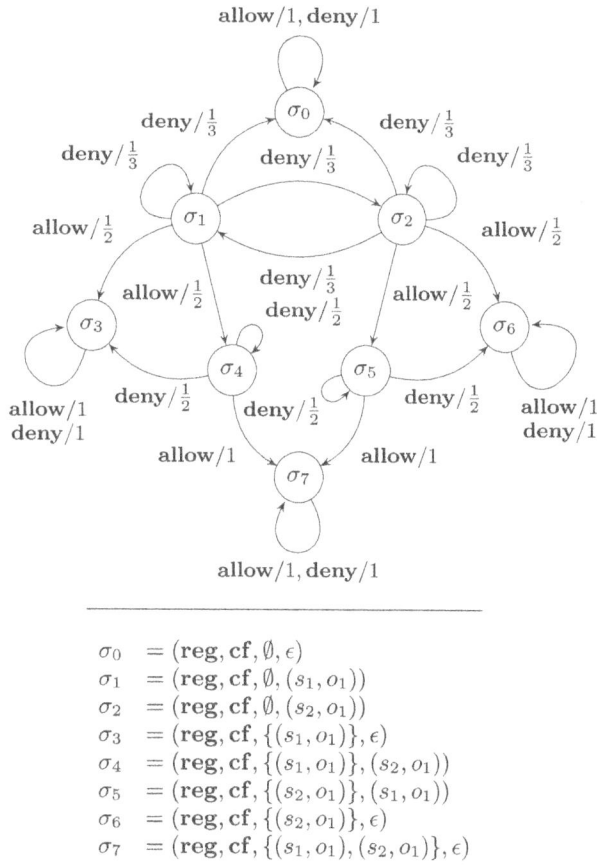

$$\sigma_0 = (\mathbf{reg}, \mathbf{cf}, \emptyset, \epsilon)$$
$$\sigma_1 = (\mathbf{reg}, \mathbf{cf}, \emptyset, (s_1, o_1))$$
$$\sigma_2 = (\mathbf{reg}, \mathbf{cf}, \emptyset, (s_2, o_1))$$
$$\sigma_3 = (\mathbf{reg}, \mathbf{cf}, \{(s_1, o_1)\}, \epsilon)$$
$$\sigma_4 = (\mathbf{reg}, \mathbf{cf}, \{(s_1, o_1)\}, (s_2, o_1))$$
$$\sigma_5 = (\mathbf{reg}, \mathbf{cf}, \{(s_2, o_1)\}, (s_1, o_1))$$
$$\sigma_6 = (\mathbf{reg}, \mathbf{cf}, \{(s_2, o_1)\}, \epsilon)$$
$$\sigma_7 = (\mathbf{reg}, \mathbf{cf}, \{(s_1, o_1), (s_2, o_1)\}, \epsilon)$$

Figure 3: AC-MDP without unreachable states, and for $\mathcal{S} = \{s_1, s_2\}$, $\mathcal{O} = \{o_1\}$, $\mathcal{A} = \{\mathbf{allow}, \mathbf{deny}\}$

3.3 Probabilistic ι modification

In general, the access control mechanism is only a component of the information system, and cannot entirely control that the decisions it takes are actually enforced by the system. For instance, in Section 2, we extended the running example to include mitigation techniques, which limit the exposure of the system when granting an access. However, in practice, there might exist a non null probability that these techniques are not enforced. Consider for example a mitigation technique consisting in videotaping the room in which the access is physically done: if the video-camera is not properly functioning, then although the access control mechanism can return the **mitigate** decision, the mitigation techniques are in practice not enforced.

Regardless of the decisions returned by the access control mechanism, leaks can also occur, and an access can be added to the set of current accesses even if it is not allowed. In other words, the decision process must take into account the fact that it controls a concrete system, which might not be perfect and where errors can occur. Of course, such considerations make it harder for the access control mechanism to take a decision, and being too pessimistic might lead to a too conservative approach, where all accesses are denied. However, including them might allow the policy designer to analyse worst case scenarios, and to study the behavior of the system in such cases.

Similarly than for the probability function $\mathcal{P}_r$, the policy designer can specify a probability function $\mathcal{P}_\iota$, such that $\mathcal{P}_\iota(\iota \mid \sigma, a)$ stands for the probability of the security information to be equal to ι when executing the decision a from the state σ. Assuming that the transition function $\mathcal{T}_r$ is defined, given two states $\sigma_i = (\iota, r)$ and $\sigma_j = (\iota', r')$, we define:

$$p_{ij}^a = \begin{cases} 0 & \text{if } r' \neq \mathcal{T}_r(\sigma_i, a) \\ \mathcal{P}_\iota(\iota' \mid \sigma_i, a) & \text{otherwise} \end{cases}$$

Running Example

In order to illustrate the function $\mathcal{P}_\iota$, we assume that the only non deterministic part concerns the execution of mitigation techniques, such that there exists a probability p_f that these techniques are not enforced even though the decision is **mitigate**. Hence, given two states $\sigma_i = (\iota, r)$ and $\sigma_j = (\iota', r')$, and the function $\mathcal{T}_\iota$ defined in Section 2.2, we define:

$$\mathcal{P}_\iota(\iota' \mid \sigma_i, a) = \begin{cases} 1 & \text{if } a \neq \mathbf{mitigate} \text{ and } \mathcal{T}_\iota(\sigma_i, a) = \iota' \\ p_f & \text{if } a = \mathbf{mitigate} \text{ and } \iota = \iota' \\ 1 - p_f & \text{if } a = \mathbf{mitigate} \text{ and } \mathcal{T}_\iota(\sigma_i, a) = \iota' \\ 0 & \text{otherwise} \end{cases}$$

Since the reward associated with the **mitigate** decision is null, this function $\mathcal{P}_\iota$ will not change the decision process, since if the mitigation enforcement fails, the process knows it, and can decide to ask for them again. In Section 4, we introduce uncertainty over the states, where the actual state of the system cannot be fully observed, and therefore it will no longer be possible to know if the mitigation enforcement fails or not.

3.4 General Probabilistic Transition

In general, if the policy designer specifies the function $\mathcal{P}_\iota$ and $\mathcal{P}_r$, given two states $\sigma_i = (\iota, r)$ and $\sigma_j = (\iota', r')$, we can directly define:

$$p_{ij}^a = \mathcal{P}_\iota(\iota' \mid \sigma_i, a) \cdot \mathcal{P}_r(r' \mid \sigma_i, a)$$

Note that an AC-DP is just a particular instance of an AC-MDP, where the probability functions are deterministic. Indeed, given the transition functions $\mathcal{T}_r$ and $\mathcal{T}_\iota$, we can easily define:

$$\mathcal{P}_r(r' \mid \sigma, a) = \begin{cases} 1 & \text{if } r' = \mathcal{T}_r(\sigma, a) \\ 0 & \text{otherwise} \end{cases}$$

$$\mathcal{P}_\iota(\iota' \mid \sigma, a) = \begin{cases} 1 & \text{if } \iota' = \mathcal{T}_\iota(\sigma, a) \\ 0 & \text{otherwise} \end{cases}$$

In this case, we can observe that Equation (4) can be simplified in order to obtain Equation (2).

4. PARTIALLY-OBSERVABLE MARKOV DECISION PROCESS

As we described in Section 3, an access control decision process might need to take into account uncertainty over the sequence of requests and the exact consequences of each decision. When this uncertainty can be estimated through the functions $\mathcal{P}_r$ and $\mathcal{P}_\iota$, respectively, then the process can take a decision by quantitatively analyzing the potential outcomes.

Another degree of uncertainty that should be considered is the uncertainty over the *current* state of the process. Indeed, although an AC-MDP can handle uncertainty in the future, it also assumes that the current state is known. However, this is not always the case in practice, especially in open and distributed systems, where information is collected from different, potentially unreliable sources. For instance, the meta-information about a file can be corrupted during a transfer, and the exact sensitivity of this file might not be known. Similarly, the exact location of a user might be imprecise, and only an estimation of her probable locations might be provided.

We release this assumption in this section by introducing the notion of an Access Control Partially Observable Markov Decision Process (AC-POMDP), which is a Partially Observable Markov Decision Process [37] where the state is an access control state. An AC-POMDP extends an AC-MDP by considering a probability distribution $\pi : \Sigma \to [0,1]$ over states and a set Θ of observations.

DEFINITION 3. *An Access Control Partially Observable Markov Decision Process is a tuple $\langle \Sigma, \mathcal{A}, \mathcal{P}, \Theta, \mathcal{C}, \mathcal{W} \rangle$ where $\Sigma = \mathcal{I} \times \mathcal{R}$ is a set of access control states, $\mathcal{A}$ is a set of decisions, $\mathcal{P} : \Sigma \times \mathcal{A} \times \Sigma \to [0,1]$ is the probability function, such that $\mathcal{P}(\sigma_i, a, \sigma_j)$ stands for the probability of reaching the state σ_j by executing the decision a from the state σ_i, Θ is a set of observations, $\mathcal{C} : \mathcal{A} \times \Theta \times \Sigma \to [0,1]$ is the observation model, such that $\mathcal{C}(a, \theta, \sigma_j)$ stands for the probability that we observe θ when we are in state σ_j and our last decision was a, and $\mathcal{W} : \Sigma \times \mathcal{A} \times \Sigma \to \mathcal{U}$ is the reward function, such that $\mathcal{U}$ is a utility domain and $\mathcal{W}(\sigma_i, a, \sigma_j)$ stands for the reward associated with executing the decision a from the state σ_i and arriving in the state σ_j. When no confusion can arise, we write p_{ij}^a, $c_{j\theta}^a$ and w_{ij}^a for $\mathcal{P}(\sigma_i, a, \sigma_j)$, $\mathcal{C}(a, \theta, \sigma_j)$ and $\mathcal{W}(\sigma_i, a, \sigma_j)$, respectively.*

We write q_i^a for the immediate reward for executing the decision a in the state σ_i:

$$q_i^a = \sum_{j,\theta} p_{ij}^a \cdot c_{j\theta}^a \cdot w_{ij}^a$$

One of the most well-known examples for the use of POMDPs is the Tiger example given by Cassandra *et al.* [6], where there are two doors, and behind one of them there is a tiger, the goal of the process being to choose which door to open, and to preferably avoid the tiger. Since it is not known behind which door the tiger is, the process can decide to listen, instead of choosing directly a door. Listening leads to collect an *observation* indicating, with some uncertainty, behind which door the tiger is. Intuitively, the more the process listens, the more certain it becomes about the location of the tiger. However, listening has a cost, and the more the process listens, the lower the final reward will be. Hence, the aim of the process is to find the best trade-off between listening and choosing a door.

Instead of knowing the actual state, the process knows a probability distribution over the possible current states, and we call the *belief state* such a probability distribution. More formally, a belief state is a function $\pi : \Sigma \to [0,1]$, such that $\pi(\sigma_i)$ represents the probability for the system to be in the current state σ_i. When no confusion can occur, we write π_i for $\pi(\sigma_i)$. In general, it can be hard to calculate such a belief state at any time. In practice, assuming that the initial belief state is known, we can calculate the following ones inductively. Indeed, given a decision a, an observation

θ and a belief state π, we can calculate the following belief state π_j' using Baye's rule:

$$\pi_j' = \frac{\sum_i \pi_i \cdot p_{ij}^a \cdot r_{j\theta}^a}{\sum_{i,j} \pi_i \cdot p_{i,j}^a \cdot r_{j\theta}^a}$$

Given a decision a, an observation θ and a belief state π, we write $T(\pi, a, \theta)$ for the new belief state where each component is calculated according to the previous formula. A policy is now a function from belief state to decisions, and the definition of the value function of a policy δ is:

$$V^\delta(\pi) = \sum_i \pi_i q_i^{\delta(\pi)} + \beta \sum_{i,j,\theta} \pi_i p_{ij}^{\delta(\pi)} c_{j\theta}^{\delta(\pi)} V^\delta(T(\pi, \delta(\pi), \theta))$$

The optimal policy can therefore be calculated by:

$$\delta^*(\pi) = \arg \max_{a \in \mathcal{A}} \sum_i \pi_i q_i^a + \beta \sum_{i,j,\theta} \pi_i p_{ij}^a c_{j\theta}^a V^{\delta^*}(T(\pi, a, \theta))$$

$$(6)$$

Solving a POMDP is in general complex, and there exist several algoritms to approximate this function. The aim of this paper is not to provide an actual solution, but to reduce the access control problem to a known problem, and we refer to [5] for more details about solving algorithms.

Running Example

We describe here an example inspired by the tiger one, where the registration of subjects is uncertain, that is, given a subject s_i, it is not certain whether $\mathbf{reg}_i = 0$ or $\mathbf{reg}_i = 1$. Such situation typically happens in open systems, when no authentication is required. In order to make some decision, the process might need to know if the subject is registered or not. We therefore introduce, for each subject s_i a new decision $\mathbf{check}_i$, which can raise one of the two observations θ_r^i and θ_n^i, respectively meaning that it has been observed that the subject s_i is registered or not. We consider here that only the decision $\mathbf{check}_i$ can bring an observation about the registration of subjects, and thus we also introduce an observation $\theta_\emptyset$, which stands for the null observation. Hence, given a state $\sigma_j = (\mathbf{reg}, \mathbf{cf}, m, \mathbf{mit}, r)$, we define the function $\mathcal{C}$ for each observation in $\Theta = \{\theta_r^i, \theta_n^i, \theta_\emptyset\}$ as follows:

$$\mathcal{C}(a, \theta_r^i, \sigma_j) = \begin{cases} 0.9 & \text{if } a = \mathbf{check}_i \text{ and } \mathbf{reg}_i = 1 \\ 0.1 & \text{if } a = \mathbf{check}_i \text{ and } \mathbf{reg}_i = 0 \\ 0 & \text{otherwise} \end{cases}$$

$$\mathcal{C}(a, \theta_n^i, \sigma_j) = \begin{cases} 0.9 & \text{if } a = \mathbf{check}_i \text{ and } \mathbf{reg}_i = 0 \\ 0.1 & \text{if } a = \mathbf{check}_i \text{ and } \mathbf{reg}_i = 1 \\ 0 & \text{otherwise} \end{cases}$$

$$\mathcal{C}(a, \theta_\emptyset, \sigma_j) = \begin{cases} 1 & \text{if } a \neq \mathbf{check}_i \\ 0 & \text{otherwise} \end{cases}$$

Note that we illustrate the fact that an observation does not necessarily bring complete certainty over the current state. For instance, we specify that if the subject s_i has been observed to be registered, *i.e.* the system observes θ_r^i, then there is still a probability 0.1 that the subject is not actually registered.

5. DISCUSSION

The framework we have presented in the previous sections allows a policy designer to express, under the same formalism, the rewards associated with each decision, the uncertainty related to the execution of such decisions, the uncertainty related to the current knowledge of the system state, and to calculate the according optimal policy.

The first point that needs to be discussed is whether the optimal policy should be calculated beforehand, for each possible state, or at run-time, for the current state of the system. Clearly, there is no definitive answer to this question, as both approaches can be complex. Indeed, there is potentially a large number of states, including many states that will never be reached, especially in the case of AC-PODMPs, since the policy needs to be calculated for each possible state distribution. On the other hand, calculating the optimal policy for a particular state can be too complex for systems with limited resources, such as mobile devices.

Different techniques could be used to address this problem, for instance by investigating the general solutions for solving POMDPs, such as [15, 35, 38, 39]. Indeed, although finding the optimal solution of a POMDP is PSPACE-complete for finite-horizons [34] (*i.e.* for a finite sequence of requests) and undecidable for infinite horizons [28], it is sometimes possible to calculate approximate solutions, and some interesting complexity boundaries, with respect to the error margin, can be found in [16]. Moreover, access control systems have specific properties, and some analysis might lead to simplify the problem in some cases. For instance, in some systems, a request to release an access can be always accepted, regardless of the context. Similarly, the optimal policy for a sequence of independent requests (for instance accessing objects in different security domains) can be the sequence of optimal decisions for each individual request. Identifying such sequences of requests can thus simplify the problem.

In practice, many systems can be intuitively abstracted to a smaller system, with a limited number of subjects/objects, as expressive as the original one. For instance, consider the matrix based security model, as described by Lampson [26]: an access is granted if the corresponding right belongs to the matrix, and denied otherwise; although a concrete system can contain a large number of subjects and/or objects, each security situation can be clearly reduced to a system with a single subject s and two objects o_1^r and o_2^r for each access right r, such that s has the right r over o_1^r and not the right r over o_2^r. The number of states for such a reduced model is quite limited, and therefore a global calculation can be considered beforehand. However, the problem of reducing systems is not trivial in general, and it might not be possible to automate this process. Since a reduced model must be as expressive as the concrete model, we also must be able to compare them [41, 17].

The second point that can raise discussion is the definition of the reward function. Indeed, it might be hard in general to specify the actual reward for a specific decision or state. As we said in Section 2.3, although it is sometimes possible to define the pecuniary cost in a given context, it is not always straight-forward to define concrete utility values. It would be therefore useful to specify a language providing basic constructs allowing to characterize the reward function, such that the actual values can be inferred. In particular, one could consider defining on the one hand priorities between subjects, objects, accesses, states, and on the other hand conflictual and strictly forbidden situations. Moreover, thresholds of uncertainty can be included.

An important question is the benefit of our approach compared to the traditional one. Indeed, the reward function might seem more complex to define compared to a standard access control policy, and the quantification of the uncertainty of the system might not be straight-forward. However, we believe that the resulting decision process can provide a better accuracy, especially in complicated cases, for instance when there are only "bad" outcomes for a given request (*i.e.* both denying and allowing this request would have a negative impact). Moreover, our incremental approach allows a policy designer to start from a standard policy, and to extend it according to the context.

6. CONCLUSION - FUTURE WORKS

We have presented in this paper a framework representing an access control problem as a decision problem, and using the well-known notion of (Partially-Observable) Markov Decision Process to represent an access control decision process. We have introduced the concepts of Access Control Decision Process (AC-DP, Section 2), with no uncertainty involved; of Access Control Markov Decision Process (AC-MDP, Section 3), with uncertainty about the future states of the system; and of Access Control Partially Observable Markov Decision Process (AC-PODMP), which adds uncertainty about the current state of the system. Each of these processes is a generalization of the previous one, with increasing uncertainty, and the general equation for defining an optimal policy for an AC-POMDP is given by Equation (6). In other words, if the policy/system designer is able to provide all the different parameters of this equation (*i.e.* the state description, the reward function and the uncertainty parameters), we can calculate automatically the optimal policy of the system.

These processes have been illustrated by a simple yet expressive example, and several interesting observations have been made throughout the paper:

- Knowing the sequence of requests allows the system to make more optimal decisions than knowing a single request (running example of Section 2.4).
- Mitigation decisions are considered at the same level than standard decisions (extended running example of Section 2.4).
- Attack patterns and statistical user behavior can be modeled through probabilistic sequences of requests (running example of Section 3.2).
- Probabilistic failure of security mechanisms can be taken into account (running example of Section 3.3).
- Uncertainty over states and autonomous measures are also considered (running example of Section 4).

It is worth emphasizing that our approach, by providing a quantitative analysis, allows the process to make *autonomous* decisions, such as the enforcement of mitigation techniques or the auditing of subjects/objects. We thus shift from a traditional view where the access control mechanism is an interactive, passive system, which takes access requests and acts accordingly, to a more dynamic view, where the access control mechanism is an active system, which inspects the current state of the system and takes the appropriate measures in order to reach an optimal utility.

A clear limitation of our approach is that it relies on the one hand on the definition of the reward function, which, as we discussed in the previous section, has yet to be defined for most access control systems and is not trivial, and on the other on the definition of the actual uncertainty of the system. Indeed, the calculation of the probability function $\mathcal{P}$ and of the observation model $\mathcal{C}$ can be quite complex in practice, at it might be hard to give concrete values for them. However, we believe that the lack of these values is partly due to the absence of incentive for defining them. In other words, collecting such values is pointless without tools to analyze and treat them. We think that by providing a quantitative access control framework, such as the one presented in the paper, field experts will gain interest in these techniques and provide ways to collect and/or observe the utility and uncertainty values, in a similar way that finance expert have been providing models for markets in order to use decision processes. Moreover, we hope that specifying the use of MDPs and POMDPs in an access control context will help building a bridge between the access control community and the decision theory community.

Several leads need to be considered in the future. Firstly, MDPs and POMDPs have been well studied in the literature, and as we discussed in the previous Section, we need to investigate how existing resolution techniques, such as [15, 35, 38, 39], can apply to the access control problem. Secondly, as mentioned in the previous Section, a specific language for the definition of the reward function could be helpful for the policy designer. Clearly, it could be useful to start from existing policy languages, such as XACML [31], by adding the notion of reward instead of directly using the decisions. Moreover, languages for defining workflow satisfiability problems [9, 42] can also provide a good source of inspiration, as they deal with conflict and priority issues.

Thirdly, the concept of *risk strategy* needs to be made explicit in the framework. Indeed, in Section 2.4, we use the maximum function in order to get the optimal value for the policy in Equation (3). In practice, the policy designer might want to use a finer-grained choice, according to the desired risk exposure. For instance, gaining with certainty $200 has the same expected gain than gaining $600 with a chance of $1/2$ and to a loss of $200 with a chance of $1/2$. However, intuitively, a risk averse process will choose the former while a system trying to reach the highest possible gain will choose the latter. Hence, there is a need for defining a risk strategy, also including the aggregated risk or the uncertainty over the uncertainty, for instance when probability distribution functions are used instead of simple probabilities.

Finally, complex environments, where it is not always possible to define a single rule to classify accesses or states, require policy composition languages [32, 4, 10]. Situations with only bad outcomes are usually dealt with by composing *exception* policies [1, 11]. With our approach, the notion of exception should be directly included in the reward function, as we did in the running example of Section 2.3. Hence, it would be interesting to look at the composition of reward functions in a way analogous to policy composition, and in particular, to find out under which conditions the composition of two optimal policies is also an optimal policy.

Acknowledgements

This research was supported by the EU FP7-ICT project NESSoS (Network of Excellence on Engineering Secure Future Internet Software Services and Systems) under the grant agreement n. 256980 and by the EU-funded project CONNECT.

7. REFERENCES

[1] C. Ardagna, S. Capitani Di Vimercati, T. Grandison, S. Jajodia, and P. Samarati. Regulating exceptions in healthcare using policy spaces. In *Proceeedings of the 22nd Annual IFIP WG 11.3 Working Conference on Data and Applications Security*, pages 254–267, Berlin, Heidelberg, 2008. Springer-Verlag.

[2] B. Aziz, S. N. Foley, J. Herbert, and G. Swart. Reconfiguring role based access control policies using risk semantics. *J. High Speed Networks*, 15(3):261–273, 2006.

[3] R. Bellman. A markovian decision process. *Indiana Univ. Math. J.*, 6:679–684, 1957.

[4] G. Bruns and M. Huth. Access-control policies via belnap logic: Effective and efficient composition and analysis. In *CSF '08: Proceedings of the 2008 21st IEEE Computer Security Foundations Symposium*, pages 163–176. IEEE Computer Society, 2008.

[5] A. R. Cassandra. Optimal policies for partially observable markov decision processes. Technical report, Brown University, Providence, RI, USA, 1994.

[6] A. R. Cassandra, L. P. Kaelbling, and M. L. Littman. Acting Optimally in Partially Observable Stochastic Domains. In *Proceedings of the Twelfth National Conference on Artificial Intelligence (AAAI-94)*, volume 2, pages 1023–1028, Seattle, Washington, USA, 1994. AAAI Press/MIT Press.

[7] L. Chen and J. Crampton. Risk-aware role-based access control. In *Proceedings of 7th International Workshop on Security and Trust Management*, 2011. To appear.

[8] P.-C. Cheng, P. Rohatgi, C. Keser, P. A. Karger, G. M. Wagner, and A. S. Reninger. Fuzzy multi-level security: An experiment on quantified risk-adaptive access control. In *Proceedings of the 2007 IEEE Symposium on Security and Privacy*, pages 222–230, Washington, DC, USA, 2007. IEEE.

[9] J. Crampton. A reference monitor for workflow systems with constrained task execution. In *Proceedings of the 10th ACM Symposium on Access Control Models and Technologies*, pages 38–47, 2005.

[10] J. Crampton and M. Huth. An authorization framework resilient to policy evaluation failures. In D. Gritzalis, B. Preneel, and M. Theoharidou, editors, *ESORICS*, volume 6345 of *Lecture Notes in Computer Science*, pages 472–487. Springer, 2010.

[11] J. Crampton and C. Morisset. An auto-delegation mechanism for access control systems. In *Security and Trust Management - 6th International Workshop, STM 2010, Athens, Greece, September 23-24, 2010, Revised Selected Papers*, volume 6710 of *Lecture Notes in Computer Science*, pages 1–16. Springer, 2011.

[12] G. Cybenko. Why johnny can't evaluate security risk. *IEEE Security and Privacy*, 4:5, January 2006.

[13] N. N. Diep, L. X. Hung, Y. Zhung, S. Lee, Y.-K. Lee, and H. Lee. Enforcing access control using risk assessment. In *Proceedings of the Fourth European Conference on Universal Multiservice Networks*, pages 419–424. IEEE Computer Society, 2007.

[14] H. He, Y. Shuping, and P. Wu. Security decision making based on domain partitional markov decision process. In *Information Engineering and Computer*

Science, 2009. ICIECS 2009. International Conference on, pages 1 –4, dec. 2009.

[15] K. Hsiao, L. P. Kaelbling, and T. Lozano-Pérez. Grasping pomdps. In *in Proc. IEEE Int. Conf. on Robotics and Automation*, pages 4685–4692, 2007.

[16] D. Hsu, W. S. Lee, and N. Rong. What makes some pomdp problems easy to approximate? In J. Platt, D. Koller, Y. Singer, and S. Roweis, editors, *Advances in Neural Information Processing Systems 20*, pages 689–696. MIT Press, Cambridge, MA, 2008.

[17] M. Jaume and C. Morisset. Towards a formal specification of access control. In P. Degano, R. Kusters, L. Vigano, and S. Zdancewic, editors, *Proceedings of the Joint Workshop on Foundations of Computer Security and Automated Reasoning for Security Protocol Analysis*, pages 213–232, 2006.

[18] J. Kephart. The utility of utility: Policies for self-managing systems. In *Policies for Distributed Systems and Networks, International Workshop, POLICY'11 Pisa, Italy*, 2011. To appear.

[19] L. Krautsevich, A. Lazouski, F. Martinelli, and A. Yautsiukhin. Influence of attribute freshness on decision making in usage control. In *Proceedings of the 6th International Workshop on Security and Trust Management*. Springer, 2010.

[20] L. Krautsevich, A. Lazouski, F. Martinelli, and A. Yautsiukhin. Risk-aware usage decision making in highly dynamic systems. In *Proceedings of The Fifth International Conference on Internet Monitoring and Protection*. IEEE, 2010.

[21] L. Krautsevich, A. Lazouski, F. Martinelli, and A. Yautsiukhin. Risk-based usage control for service oriented architecture. In *Proceedings of the 18th Euromicro International Conference on Parallel, Distributed and Network-Based Computing*. IEEE, 2010.

[22] L. Krautsevich, F. Martinelli, C. Morisset, and A. Yautsiukhin. Risk-based auto-delegation for probabilistic availability. In *Proceedings of the 4th SETOP International Workshop on Autonomous and Spontaneous Security*. LNCS, 2011. to appear.

[23] O. P. Kreidl. Analysis of a markov decision process model for intrusion tolerance. In *Proceedings of the 2010 International Conference on Dependable Systems and Networks Workshops (DSN-W)*, DSNW '10, pages 156–161. IEEE Computer Society, 2010.

[24] R. Krishnan, J. Niu, R. S. Sandhu, and W. H. Winsborough. Stale-safe security properties for group-based secure information sharing. In *Proceedings of the 6th ACM Workshop on Formal Methods in Security Engineering, FMSE 2008, Alexandria, VA, USA*, pages 53–62. ACM, 2008.

[25] P. Kumari, A. Pretschner, J. Peschla, and J.-M. Kuhn. Distributed data usage control for web applications: a social network implementation. In *First ACM Conference on Data and Application Security and Privacy, CODASPY 2011, San Antonio, TX, USA, February 21-23, 2011, Proceedings*, pages 85–96, 2011.

[26] B. Lampson. Protection. In *Proceedings of the 5th Annual Princeton Conference on Information Sciences and Systems*, pages 437–443, Princeton University, 1971.

[27] L. LaPadula and D. Bell. Secure Computer Systems: A Mathematical Model. *Journal of Computer Security*, 4:239–263, 1996.

[28] O. Madani, S. Hanks, and A. Condon. On the undecidability of probabilistic planning and infinite-horizon partially observable markov decision problems. In *Proceedings of AAAI '99/IAAI '99*, pages 541–548, Menlo Park, CA, USA, 1999. American Association for Artificial Intelligence.

[29] I. Molloy, P.-C. Cheng, and P. Rohatgi. Trading in risk: Using markets to improve access control. In *NSPW 2008, 15th ACM New Security Paradigms Workshop, Lake TAhoe, CA, USA, September 22-25, 2008, Proceedings*, New York, NY, USA, 2008. ACM.

[30] I. Molloy, L. Dickens, C. Morisset, P.-C. Cheng, J. Lobo, and A. Russo. Risk-based access control decisions under uncertainty. Technical Report RC25121, IBM Watson, September 2011.

[31] T. Moses. eXtensible Access Control Markup Language TC v2.0 (XACML), Feb. 2005.

[32] Q. Ni, E. Bertino, and J. Lobo. D-algebra for composing access control policy decisions. In W. Li, W. Susilo, U. K. Tupakula, R. Safavi-Naini, and V. Varadharajan, editors, *ASIACCS*, pages 298–309. ACM, 2009.

[33] Q. Ni, E. Bertino, and J. Lobo. Risk-based access control systems built on fuzzy inferences. In *Proceedings of the 5th ACM Symposium on Information, Computer and Communications Security*, pages 250–260, New York, NY, USA, 2010. ACM.

[34] C. Papadimitriou and J. N. Tsitsiklis. The complexity of markov decision processes. *Math. Oper. Res.*, 12:441–450, August 1987.

[35] J. Pineau, G. J. Gordon, and S. Thrun. Anytime point-based approximations for large pomdps. *J. Artif. Intell. Res. (JAIR)*, 27:335–380, 2006.

[36] J. P. Singh, T. Alpcan, P. Agrawal, and V. Sharma. A markov decision process based flow assignment framework for heterogeneous network access. *Wirel. Netw.*, 16:481–495, February 2010.

[37] R. D. Smallwood and E. J. Sondik. The Optimal Control of Partially Observable Markov Processes Over a Finite Horizon. *Operations Research*, 21(5), 1973.

[38] T. Smith and R. G. Simmons. Heuristic search value iteration for pomdps. In *Proceedings of the 20th Conference in Uncertainty in Artificial Intelligence, July 7-11 2004*, pages 520–527, 2004.

[39] M. T. J. Spaan and N. A. Vlassis. Perseus: Randomized point-based value iteration for pomdps. *J. Artif. Intell. Res. (JAIR)*, 24:195–220, 2005.

[40] Symantec. State of security survey, 2011. http://www.symantec.com/content/en/us/about/media/pdfs/symc_state_of_security_2011.pdf.

[41] M. Tripunitara and N. Li. Comparing the expressive power of access control models. In *SIGSAC: 11th ACM Conference on Computer and Communications Security*. ACM SIGSAC, 2004.

[42] Q. Wang and N. Li. Satisfiability and resiliency in workflow systems. In *Proceedings of 12th European Symposium on Research in Computer Security*, pages 90–105, 2007.

Role Engineering: From Theory to Practice

Nino Vincenzo Verde
Department of Mathematics
University of Roma Tre
nverde@mat.uniroma3.it

Jaideep Vaidya
MSIS Department and CIMIC
Rutgers University
jsvaidya@cimic.rutgers.edu

Vijay Atluri
MSIS Department and CIMIC
Rutgers University
atluri@rutgers.edu

Alessandro Colantonio
Bay31 GmbH, Switzerland
alessandro@bay31.com

ABSTRACT

Role Based Access Control (RBAC) is the de facto standard in access control models, and is widely used in many applications and organizations of all sizes. However, the task of finding an appropriate set of roles, called role engineering, remains the most challenging roadblock to effective deployment. In recent years, this problem has attracted a lot of attention, with several bottom-up approaches being proposed, under the field of role mining. However, most of these theoretical approaches cannot be directly applied to large scale datasets, which is where they are most necessary. Therefore, in this paper, we look at how to make role mining *practical* and *usable* for actual deployment. We propose a six steps methodology that makes role mining scalable without sacrificing on utility and is agnostic to the actual role mining technique used. The experimental evaluation validates the viability of our approach.

Categories and Subject Descriptors

D.4.6 [**Operating Systems**]: Security and Protection—*Access controls*; H.2.8 [**Database Management**]: Database Applications—*Data Mining*; K.6.5 [**Management of Computing and Information Systems**]: Security and Protection

General Terms

Security

Keywords

Role-Based Access Control, RBAC, Role Engineering, Role Mining

1. INTRODUCTION

In computer security, access control mechanisms are crucial design elements that aim at mediating requests to data and services. Among all models proposed in the literature, *role-based access control* (RBAC) [1] has become the norm for managing permissions within commercial applications [29]. The high-level formalism and the simplicity of its design made it an attractive and pragmatic choice for implementing access control. Under RBAC, a role is a set of permissions, while users acquire the permissions to perform system functions only when they are assigned to specific roles. Because of the intuitiveness of RBAC, security policies can be easily defined by business users that do not usually have all the needed IT knowledge.

The roles definition phase, also known as *role engineering*, has been largely recognized as the most expensive task in deploying RBAC [20]. Interestingly, role design determines RBAC's cost. When there are hundreds or thousands of users within an organization, with individual functions and responsibilities to be accurately reflected in terms of access permissions, only a well-defined role engineering process allows for significant savings of time and money while protecting data and systems [3]. Usually, role engineering approaches can be categorized as: *top-down* and *bottom-up*. The former generally ignores existing permissions, and carefully decomposes business processes into elementary components, identifying which access permissions are necessary to carry out specific tasks in order to formulate roles. The latter aims at extracting roles from the existing access permissions [16]. Top-down analysis has been recognized as the costliest part for deploying RBAC as it requires a significant amount of analysis of the business processes, and moreover it has to be performed mainly manually [9]. For this reason, and also because the complexity of this task grows with the introduction of new and more complicated information systems, bottom-up approaches are largely preferred to top-down approaches. Indeed, they can be easily automated by resorting to data mining techniques, thus leading to what is usually referred to as *role mining*.

In recent years, various role-definition approaches have been proposed, where each of them bears in mind a different aspect of the problem [18]. Many of these works proved that the role mining problem is reducible to well-known NP-hard problems, and several heuristic algorithms have been proposed. However, such algorithms have a complexity that is not linear compared to the number of users or permissions to analyze [2, 25, 11]. When dealing with large organizations, such algorithms are not practically useful. Indeed, the number of elicited candidate roles as well as the running time become an issue, especially when the role engineering task is periodically and frequently performed as part of the life-cycle of roles [3]. To overcome these limitations, role mining products such as Oracle Identity Analytics[1] or Bay31 Role Designer[2] use a *Divide et Impera* approach. For example, Oracle Identity Analytics separates large numbers of users into more manageable groups, called "waves", for the purpose of defining roles. This is accomplished by first dividing users into business units based on their managers, departments, divisions, or other attributes. Then, these business units are grouped into waves (usually four to six business units per wave), which are independently analyzed using role mining, clustering and categorization algorithms. The Bay31 Role Designer allows a "role engineering campaign" manager to delegate parts of the overall role analysis to different people. Each of these people contributes their particular knowledge of the business and Role Designer combines it all to form a coherent set of business role. To identify the subsets of data to analyze, the product uses a partitioning approach inspired by the recent work of Colantonio et al. [5]. In particular, using an index referred to as "entrustability", the access data is divided into smaller subsets that are homogeneous from a business perspective. Instead of performing a single bottom-up analysis on the entire organization, each subset is analyzed independently. This eases the attribution of business meaning to roles elicited by any existing role mining algorithm, and reduces the problem complexity.

The main drawback of the afore mentioned *Divide et Impera* approaches is that it is impossible to find roles that spread across several partitions. Yet, such roles can be very useful to system administrators. For instance, it is likely that users spreading across different partitions (e.g., different organization units) have common entitlements that simply permit access to top-level resources (i.e., to resources at their entry points). A so called "structural" role might control access to an application's entry point, whereby a user could only open that application if he or she had been assigned to a structural role that grants that access. Conversely, "functional" roles are defined as controlling access to resources within applications. The role engineering process should include the definition of both structural roles and functional roles [10].

The main objective of this paper is to offer an approach that essentially provides practical and usable solutions to the role mining problem, improving the scalability of the role mining solutions while eliciting structural roles. Hence, overcoming the main limitation of existing *Divide et Impera* approaches. We focus on making the role mining problem tractable by reducing the problem size without sacrificing on utility and accuracy. The proposed approach does this by effectively compressing the original access control dataset, analyzing the compressed dataset to identify interesting portions, and reconstructing the portions of the original dataset that are worth investigating. Scalability is assured by targeted partitioning that ensures that the created sub-problems focus only on the interesting portions of the original dataset—and are therefore orders of magnitude smaller than the original one. At this point, *any* existing role mining algorithm can be used to analyze user-permission assignments within these subsets. Thus, our approach is ag-

nostic to the specific role mining methodology used, namely it can be used in conjunction with them to enhance their scalability.

The remainder of the paper is organized as follows: in Section 2 we briefly overview related work. We present the six steps that compose our methodology in Section 3, detailing the corresponding algorithms and their computational analysis. A running example is used to aid the exposition. Then, the viability of the proposed approach is extensively demonstrated in Section 4, showing the results of several tests on real, and synthetic data. Finally, Section 5 provides concluding remarks, and explores future work.

2. RELATED WORK

Coyne [9] first described the problem of role engineering, and presented the concepts of a top-down approach. Successive work [21, 19] also followed the same top-down approach though the process of discovering roles was different. However, in all of these approaches, existing permissions are not taken into consideration at all. Nowadays, instead, the use of bottom-up techniques is considered more opportune. This is mainly due to the fact that top-down analysis is a very time-consuming activity, and also because many organizations that are switching to RBAC find themselves with a collection of several legacy and standard security systems on different platforms that provide "conventional" access control [16]. During the past years several algorithms explicitly designed for bottom-up role engineering have been proposed [22, 25, 11, 28, 23, 24, 12, 17]. It is now well known that the role mining problem is NP-hard [23] and that the solutions to many other well-known NP-hard problems, such as graph vertex coloring, clique partition, binary matrix factorization, bi-clustering can be used to develop a good solution [6, 11].

Typically, a large organization may easily have several thousands users, and hundreds of thousands of access permissions. While many heuristics have been proposed in the literature, they are not efficient when dealing with very large datasets. Recently, Colantonio et al. [5], proposed an approach that makes the role mining feasible when dealing with such huge datasets. In particular, using an index referred to as "entrustability", they propose to divide the access data into smaller subsets that are homogeneous from a business perspective. Instead of performing a single bottom-up analysis on the entire organization, each subset is analyzed independently. This eases the attribution of business meaning to roles elicited by any existing role mining algorithm, and reduces the problem complexity. However, using this approach it is not possible to find roles that extend across several partitions, even if it is clear that such roles can be very useful to the system administrators. Let us suppose, for example, that "intranet access", "web-proxy access" and "mail access", are three permissions that should be granted to all the users. Analyzing the partitions independently, a role that handles these three permissions will be probably duplicated in many partitions, resulting in a role that involves the permissions "intranet access", "web-proxy access", "mail access" and "HR software" inside the subset that regards the HR department, and "intranet access", "web-proxy access", "mail access" and "Print Invoice" inside the subset that regards the Accounting department. In very large datasets it is important to figure out if it is possible to create organizational roles, that involves many users, and in this case also many partitions.

---

[1] http://www.oracle.com/us/products/middleware/identity-management/oracle-identity-analytics/index.html
[2] http://www.bay31.com/role_designer

The focus of this paper is on making the role mining problem tractable by reducing the problem size, but also allowing the elicitations of organizational roles.

3. PROPOSED APPROACH

Our approach relies on the fact that it is possible to significantly reduce the computational burden of role mining while still maintaining utility by judiciously partitioning, locally analyzing, and recombining the given data. We can thus decompose our approach into six successive steps, as shown in Figure 1. In the first step the original dataset is decomposed into several partitions. In step 2, similar clusters of users are identified within each partition. In step 3, we develop a significantly smaller set of representative users that represent each cluster. Thus, steps 1-3 can be viewed as the process of building a compressed dataset. In the fourth step, the compressed dataset is evaluated to find portions that are interesting to analyze. In step 5, the corresponding portions of the original dataset are rebuilt. Once these interesting portions are identified, in step 6, role engineering can be carried out over these portions. Note that any existing (or new) role mining algorithm can be used at this point. Indeed, our methodology does not rely on any specific role mining algorithm, and is agnostic to the specific mining approach taken. We now describe in detail each individual step. Figure 2 depicts a small access control dataset of 12 users, 10 permissions, and 51 user-permission assignments that is used to explain each step. Rows represents users, columns represents permissions, while a black cell indicates that the user has the corresponding permission granted. Note that the users and permissions have been automatically permuted to aid in the exposition (this is not necessary for any of the steps, it is simply to give a more intuitive picture of the approach [8]). Table 1 summarizes the main definitions used in the rest of the paper.

Step 1. Partitioning

In this step, the original dataset is decomposed into several disjoint subsets. This is similar to past work [5, 7] that also attempts to make analysis of large scale data feasible. However, in all prior approaches, each partition is analyzed independently, without searching for the roles that extend across different partitions. On the contrary, in our approach, the subsequent steps specifically focus on the identification of all roles.

Partitioning can be done in many ways – for example, by utilizing business information, following some other rule of thumb, or even at random. However, it has been shown that using business information is typically preferable to the others since it generates more meaningful roles [5]. Business information includes both user and permission attributes – any of these can be used. For example, it is possible to partition users by the country they are working in, or by organizational branches. Formally, given $U \subseteq USERS$, the partition of UP induced by U is defined as the set:

$$\{\langle u, p \rangle \in UP : u \in U\} \tag{1}$$

Similarly, the access control dataset can be partitioned using permission attributes as well. In this case, a subset $P \in PERMS$ induces the partition

$$\{\langle u, p \rangle \in UP : p \in P\}$$

For the sake of clarity, in the following we will only consider partitions induced by users attributes, though either way above is fine. The bold dotted line between users U_10 and U_3 in Figure 2a represents a partitioning based on some business information that splits the users into the two partitions $\{U\_7, U\_6, U\_12, U\_9, U\_8, U\_11, U\_10\}$(Partition 1) and $\{U\_3, U\_4, U\_5, U\_2, U\_1\}$ (Partition 2) as depicted in Figure 2b.

Step 2. Identification of Clusters

In step 2, we analyze each partition independently, trying to identify clusters of users, from which representative users will be picked. Since each partition is analyzed independently, the memory load is correspondingly reduced and it is also easily possible to parallelize this step.

To identify clusters, we use the well known clustering algorithm: *Partitioning Around Medoids* (PAM) [15, 26]. This is similar to the k-means clustering algorithm except that medoids are used instead of means and dissimilarities are used instead of distances. The "medoid" of a cluster is that object whose average dissimilarity to all the other objects in the cluster is minimal. PAM is used within each partition to identify the clusters of users. This algorithm has two key properties:

1. It is less subject to outliers than other clustering algorithms;

2. It performs clustering with respect to any specific distance metric.

These properties make it especially suitable for access control data since outliers are quite prevalent in these datasets and can cause major security violations, and the notion of user distance is not well defined. We now introduce the specific distance metric that is used to evaluate the similarity of two users – the Jaccard Coefficient [14]:

$$J_u(u_1, u_2) = \frac{|perms(u_1) \cap perms(u_2)|}{|perms(u_1) \cup perms(u_2)|}. \tag{2}$$

where $u_1, u_2 \in USERS$. Now, the distance or dissimilarity between two users u_1 and u_2 is defined as:

$$D(u_1, u_2) = 1 - J_u(u_1, u_2). \tag{3}$$

We now describe the basic PAM algorithm [15], and then discuss our modified heuristic for it. The PAM algorithm proceeds in five steps:

1. Randomly select k initial medoids.
2. Associate each user to the closest medoid.
3. The cost of a configuration is defined as the sum of the distances of each non-medoid to its closest medoid. Now, for each medoid, and for each non-medoid, the cost of the new configuration achieved after swapping the two, is computed.
4. The configuration minimizing the cost is selected, and the previous two steps repeated until no further improvement is possible.
5. The set of medoids, and their associated objects, are finally returned.

The computational cost of this algorithm is $O(k(n-k)^2)$, where k is the number of medoids, and $n-k$ is the number of non-medoids. Usually $k \ll n$, therefore the factor

Table 1: Summary of the main definitions

$PERMS$	The set of all the access permissions
$USERS$	The set of the users
$UP \in USERS \times PERMS$	The set of the existing user-permission assignments to analyze
$perms\colon USERS \to 2^{PERMS}$	identifies the permissions assigned to a given user
$users\colon PERMS \to 2^{USERS}$	identifies users assigned to a permission

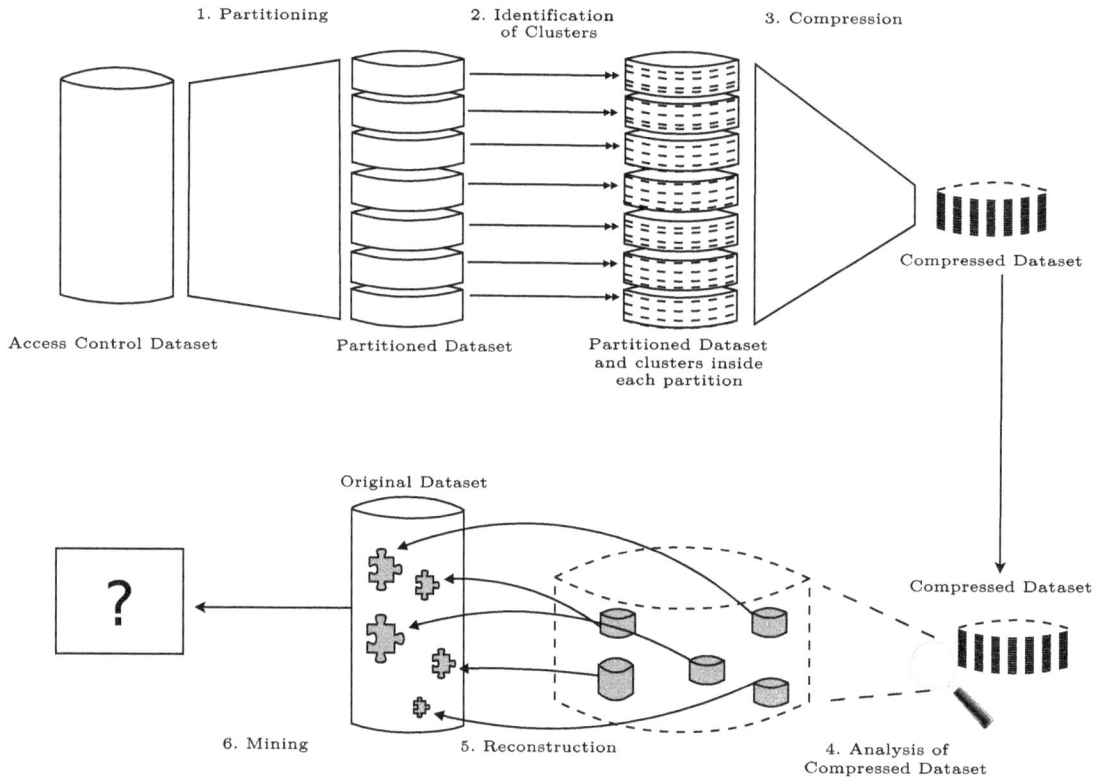

Figure 1: The Proposed Methodology at a glance

of k can be ignored, and $n - k \approx n$. Therefore, the computational cost is really $O(n^2)$, i.e., quadratic with respect to the number of users. The quadratic cost is due to the fact that all possible swaps of medoid and non-medoid objects are considered before selecting the one minimizing the overall cost.

Since the number of users is typically quite high, to reduce the cost of the basic algorithm described above, we propose a modified heuristic presented in Algorithm 1, where instead of checking all possible swaps, a small number of random swaps are chosen, and a swap carried out immediately if the new cost is lower than the current cost. Thus, an additional parameter to the algorithm is s, the number of tentative swaps executed.

The computational cost of Algorithm 1 is $O(sk(n - k))$, where s is the number of tentative swaps, k is the number of medoids, and n is the number of users. Asymptotically the algorithm leads to a local minimum when s grows. Our experimental results (in Section 4), show that very good results can be achieved even with very small values of s.

A key parameter for clustering is the number of medoids (i.e., number of clusters) that are being searched for in each partition. One way of selecting this is through comput-

---

Algorithm 1 Heuristic Partitioning Around Medoids

1: **procedure** HEURISTICPAM(Set of Users $USERS$, number of swaps s, number of medoids k)
2: $\quad MEDOIDS$ = Randomly selected $u_1, \ldots, u_k \in USERS$;
3: $\quad$ **for** $i = 0 \ldots s$ **do**
4: $\quad\quad$ Randomly select $u \in USERS : u \notin MEDOIDS$;
5: $\quad\quad$ Calculate the cost c of the new configuration, where u and its medoid are swapped;
6: $\quad\quad$ **if** $c <$ cost of the old Configuration **then**
7: $\quad\quad\quad$ Swap u and its medoid;
8: $\quad\quad$ **end if**
9: $\quad$ **end for**
10: $\quad$ **return** $MEDOIDS$
11: **end procedure**

---

ing the silhouette coefficients [15], that is a measure of how tightly grouped all the data in the clusters are. Algorithm 1 is executed using different values of k, the silhouette coefficients are computed in each case, and the number of medoids giving the maximum silhouette coefficient chosen. However,

(i) Partition1

(i) Partition1

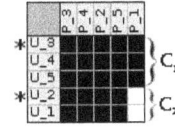

(ii) Partition2

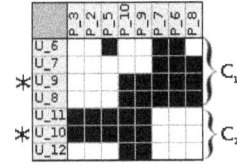

(ii) Partition2

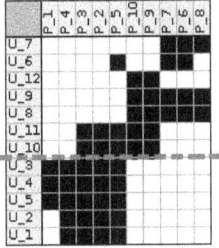

Figure 2a: Original UPA Matrix

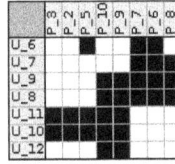

Figure 2b: Partitioning

Figure 2c: Clusters Identification

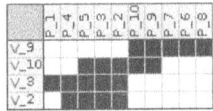

Figure 2d: Compressed Dataset

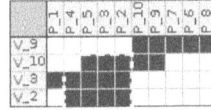

Figure 2e: Analysis of Compressed Dataset

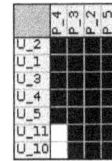

Figure 2f: Reconstruction of the Interesting Portion

Figure 2: An expository example.

computing the silhouette coefficient for different k is a very time consuming process, and in the experimental section we will use a given percentage of users in each partition as medoids. Our results show that high quality results can be achieved by simply selecting only 5% of users as medoids.

Figure 2c shows the result obtained by applying Algorithm 1, with $k = 2$, in both of the partitions depicted in Figure 2b. The clusters identified are highlighted with curly braces and the corresponding medoids are denoted with an asterisk: thus, C_1 containing the users U_6, U_7, U_8, U_9 (with medoid U_9) and C_2 containing the users U_10 and U_11, U_12 (with medoid U_10) are discovered in Partition 1. Similarly, U_1, U_2 (with medoid U_2) and U_3, U_4, U_5 (with medoid U_3) are identified in Partition 2.

Step 3. Compression

After identifying the user clusters (and associated medoids), we analyze each of the clusters in order to create a new compressed dataset. In this dataset, each cluster is represented by just one (virtual) user. The binarization procedure described in Algorithm 2 is used to identify the permissions to grant to this virtual user. Essentially, given a cluster of users U, and a binarization threshold t, each permission $p \in PERMS$ is granted to the virtual user if and only if $\text{support}_U(p) \geq t$, where support_U indicates the percentage of users possessing the permission p within the cluster U. Thus, the resulting compressed dataset contains one user

for every cluster of users identified in Step 2. Further, the virtual user does not necessarily have the same permissions as the medoid. Indeed, the threshold t plays a key role in determining this: for example, when $t = 1$, only the permissions shared by all the the users in the cluster will be granted to the virtual user, where as with $t = 0$ all the permissions that are granted to at least one user in the cluster will be granted. In the experimental validation, we experiment with different values for the threshold, and provide some guidance on how this can be chosen.

Algorithm 2 Binarization Procedure

1: **procedure** BINARIZATIONPROCEDURE(ClusterOfUsers clust, threshold t)
2:    create new user *virtualUser*;
3:    **for** Permission $p \in PERMS$ **do**
4:       **if** $\text{support}_U(p) \geq t$ **then**
5:          Grant p to *virtualUser*
6:       **end if**
7:    **end for**
8:    **return** *virtualUser*
9: **end procedure**

Note that as before, this step can also be fully parallelized thus guaranteeing a noticeable speed-up of the overall analysis. Further, the kind of compression that we perform will not cause the presence of unauthorized permissions inside the final list of roles, indeed the roles will be elicited only after analyzing the compressed dataset (Step 4) and rebuilding portions of the original one (Step 5). Figure 2d illustrates Step 3 in the context of our example. The compressed dataset is formed of four virtual users, each corresponding to one of the clusters highlighted in Figure 2c. The threshold used was $t = 0.5$, i.e., only those permissions that are supported by at least half of the users of the cluster are granted to the virtual user. For example, the virtual user V_9 represents the cluster U_9, U_6, U_7, U_8, and is granted the permissions P_10, P_9, P_7, P_6 and P_8. This is correct, since only those permissions are also owned by at least two of the users in the cluster. The virtual users V_10, V_3 and V_2 are also generated in the same way from the corresponding user clusters.

Step 4. Analysis of Compressed Dataset

After the prior three steps are completed, a compressed dataset has been built that effectively summarizes the original dataset. Now, we analyze this compressed dataset in order to discover portions of the original dataset that are worth inspecting.

Note that access control datasets can be represented as (often, sparse) binary matrices, where rows represents users, columns represents permissions, and a 1 in a cell indicates the presence of a user-permission assignment, while a 0 represents the absence. If we consider such a matrix, the portions worth inspecting are composed of "dense" and "large" subsets of rows and columns, since they allow us to find roles that can handle many user-permission assignments. Due to the use of the binarization procedure (Algorithm 2), there may exist permissions in the original user clusters that have not been granted to the corresponding virtual users because of low support. However, these should still be potentially taken into consideration.

To do so, we use the maximal pseudo-bicluster tool that has been introduced in [4]. A pseudo-bicluster is a pattern that can be seen as a superset of any interesting role. We can then focus the role mining on a subset of these patterns, that identifies portions of the dataset (in this case our compressed dataset) that are worth successively analyzing.

For the sake of clarity, below we first contextualize the definitions of pseudo-bicluster, and maximal pseudo-bicluster within the role based access control domain [4].

DEFINITION 1 (PSEUDO-BICLUSTER). *Given the user-permission assignments UP to analyze, a pseudo-bicluster B is a pair $\langle U, P \rangle : U \subseteq USERS, P \subseteq PERMS$ such that at least one user has all the permissions P granted, and at least one permission is granted to all the users U, formally:*

$$\exists u \in U, \exists p \in P, P \subseteq perms(u), U \subseteq users(p).$$

where the functions perms and users have been defined in Table 1.

For a given pseudo-bicluster $B = \langle U, P \rangle$ we also denote with $\hat{U} \subseteq U$ the set of users that have all of and only those permissions $p \in P$ granted, and with $\hat{P} \subseteq P$ the set of permissions that are granted to all of and only the users $u \in U$, that is:

$\forall u \in \hat{U}, \forall p \in P : u$ has the permission p granted in UP

$\forall p \in \hat{P}, \forall u \in U : u$ has the permission p granted in UP.

DEFINITION 2 (MAXIMAL PSEUDO-BICLUSTER). *Let $B = \langle U, P \rangle$ be a pseudo-bicluster of the user-permission assignments set UP. It is also a maximal pseudo-bicluster if:*

$$\nexists \text{ a pseudo-bicluster } B' = \langle U', P' \rangle \ : \ \hat{U} \times \hat{P} \subset \hat{U}' \times \hat{P}'.$$

In other words, a maximal pseudo-bicluster $B = \langle U, P \rangle$ is a pseudo-bicluster to which we cannot add any other user such that it has all of and only the permissions P granted, nor can we add any other permission that is granted to all of and only the users U. It is important to notice that the more *dense* a maximal pseudo-bicluster $B = \langle U, P \rangle$ – i.e., almost all the users $u \in U$ have almost all the permissions $p \in P$ granted – the more likely that the pattern represented by B is interesting from the role mining perspective. Thus, dense Maximal Pseudo-Biclusters are preferable because the users and the permissions involved are likely to be more similar. Also, Maximal Pseudo-Biclusters that involve many users and many permissions are preferable because they can be potentially managed with "large" roles. Thus, the following measure captures both of these points for a given maximal pseudo-bicluster:

DEFINITION 3 (RELEVANCE). *The relevance of a Maximal Pseudo-Bicluster $B = \langle U, P \rangle$ is defined as:*

$$\varrho(B) = |\hat{U}| \times |\hat{P}|$$

Since $\hat{U} \in U$ and $\hat{P} \in P$, it turns out that $\varrho(B) < |U| \times |P|$. It means that a Maximal Pseudo-Bicluster that involves few users and few permissions cannot have a high relevance. Further, the relevance of B reaches the maximum when $\hat{U}$ is equal to U, and $\hat{U}$ is equal to P. Indeed, in that case all the users and the permissions of the Maximal Pseudo-Bicluster can be managed with just one role. Since the relevance of a Maximal Pseudo-Bicluster is an absolute value, we use the normalized version:

DEFINITION 4 (NORMALIZED RELEVANCE). *The normalized relevance of a Maximal Pseudo-Biclusters $B = \langle U, P \rangle$ is defined as:*

$$\overline{\varrho}(B) = \frac{\varrho(B)}{|UP|}$$

where $UP \in USERS \times PERMS$ is the set of the existing user-permission assignments.

It can be shown that $0 < \overline{\varrho}(B) \leq 1$, indeed $\varrho(B)$ is always greater than 0 and lower than, or equal to $|UP|$. Maximal Pseudo-Biclusters that have a high normalized relevance correspond to those portions of a dataset that when inspected are likely to have roles that can be used to manage many user-permission assignments. Therefore, in this step, we search for the maximal Pseudo-Biclusters having high normalized relevance within the compressed dataset. Note that since the virtual users many not have some of the permissions granted, the maximal pseudo-bicluster may not correspond to a single role, but it does narrow the search area when looking for large roles. Several strategies are possible to select the maximal Pseudo-Biclusters – for example, we can select in descending order of size, up to a fixed number, or we can take a given percentage of the existing maximal Pseudo-Biclusters. Once this subset has been selected, we can proceed to Step 5.

With respect to our expository example (Figure 2), when the compressed dataset shown in Figure 2d is analyzed to identify (and order) maximal pseudo-biclusters, three maximal pseudo-biclusters are identified with the same maximum normalized relevance. The first is composed of the virtual users V_10, V_3, V_2, and the permissions P_4, P_5, P_3, P_2. Its normalized relevance is equal to $3/51$, indeed $|\hat{U}| = 1$, $|\hat{P}| = 3$ and $|UP| = 51$. The second Maximal Pseudo-Biclusters with the same relevance is composed of the virtual user V_9, and the permissions P_10, P_9, P_7, P_6, P_8. In this case, it involves only one user, and if we are searching for roles that extend across partitions, it can be discarded. The third Maximal Pseudo-Biclusters is identified by the virtual users V_10, V_3, V_2, and the permissions P_5, P_3, P_2, P_10 and P_9. This Maximal Pseudo-Bicluster identifies another area that should be further analyzed in the original dataset.

Step 5. Reconstruction

Once the maximal pseudo biclusters with high normalized relevance have been identified, we now recover the portions of the original dataset that these maximal pseudo biclusters correspond to. This phase can be seen as the expansion of the portions highlighted in the previous step. Algorithm 3 depicts the reconstruction procedure. We assume that a hash map has been maintained (in the prior steps), that, given a virtual user, returns the original users from which the virtual user has been built (i.e., gives the association of virtual users to user clusters). Now, the idea is simple. We start by creating a new Maximal Pseudo-Cluster (Line 2) with no users assigned, and then, using the hash map, we gradually add the original users into the bicluster (Line 3-5). The procedure returns the new maximal pseudo-bicluster. Thus, it identifies an area of the original dataset that is worth inspecting. Therefore, for each maximal pseudo-bicluster selected in Step 4, we reconstruct the corresponding original pseudo-bicluster, and each of them identifies a given subset of the original dataset. Compared with the original dataset, these subsets involve only few users and few permissions. So, they are easier to analyze using any role mining algorithm, and this analysis can even be executed in parallel.

Figure 2f shows the result of the reconstruction of the Maximal Pseudo-Bicluster highlighted in Figure 2e. The Maximal Pseudo-Bicluster involves the virtual users V_10, V_3 and V_2. Looking at Figure 2c, it can be seen that they respectively identify the sets: $\{U\_11, U\_10, U\_12\}$, $\{U\_3, U\_4, U\_5\}$ and $\{U\_2, U\_1\}$. For these users, only the permissions P_4, P_5, P_3, P_2 are taken into consideration for the reconstruction, indeed only these permissions belong to the highlighted Maximal Pseudo-Bicluster. It can be seen that, even if the permission P_1 is granted to U_3, U_4, U_5, it will not be considered in the reconstruction phase. Further, the portion of the original dataset that we rebuild is effectively an area where we can find meaningful roles that involves users belonging to different partitions. Also, it has to be considered, that this portion of the original matrix involves the 51% of all the original user-permission assignments, but only 4 permissions out of 10, and 7 users out of 12. This gain will increase when thousands of users and permissions are involved in the original dataset, and with the sparsity of the dataset.

Algorithm 3 Reconstruction of the Original Portions

1: **procedure** RECONSTRUCT(MaximalPseudoBicluster $B = \langle U, P \rangle$)
2:     create new MaximalPseudoBicluster $B' = \langle \emptyset, P \rangle$;
3:     **for** User $u \in U$ **do**
4:         B'.Add($HashMap(u)$)
5:     **end for**
6:     **return** B'
7: **end procedure**

Table 2: Properties of the real Datasets analyzed

DATASET	USERS	PERMISSIONS
HP Customers	10021	277
HP Apj	2044	1164
HP Americas Small	3477	1587
HP Americas Large	3485	10127

Step 6. Mining

Once the interesting portion of the dataset is reconstructed, any role mining mining algorithm can be used to actually discover the roles. In effect, our procedure is completely agnostic to the actual role mining methodology used and serves to zoom attention to the interesting areas of the original dataset. Therefore, Step 6 of our methodology corresponds to the independent analysis of the reconstructed portions. Since the analysis is executed independently, it can be also executed in parallel, thus further reducing the runtime complexity.

4. EXPERIMENTAL EVALUATION

We now experimentally validate our approach. To do this, we have evaluated our approach on several datasets of differing characteristics, both real and synthetic. We first discuss these datasets, then introduce the evaluation strategy, and finally present the results achieved.

4.1 Datasets

Our primary case study has been carried out on a large private organization that has more than two thousand users, more than six thousand permissions, and a total of more than 100,000 user-permissions assignments. In order to preserve the privacy of the organization it is not possible to reveal more information about the activities performed by the users, the applications used, and the corresponding permissions granted. However, we actually had detailed data on this dataset, including both user and permission attributes such as "Job Title", "Cost Center", "Division", "Organizational Unit", "Application" etc. Without using any compression, the binary matrix representing all of these user-permissions assignments requires almost 12Gb of space. Using other (sparse representation) data structures this requirement can be reduced, but even considering only 2 bytes to store each one of the 100,000 user-permission assignments (1 byte to store the user index, and 1 byte for the permission index), roughly 200Mb of memory space is required. Indeed, this dataset is not the largest that we had available, but we chose it because it was still possible to analyze it using the standard approaches. Thus, we use this dataset to compare the performance of our methodology, with respect to a traditional approach that performs the analysis of the whole dataset. Note that with larger datasets traditional analysis becomes even more infeasible. Indeed, larger datasets in our possesion were impossible to analyze, both because computational time and memory required.

To execute the first step of our methodology, we used a business attribute that was at our disposal, that is the "Job Title". As per this attribute, a total of 95 different partitions have been created during the "Partitioning" step.

In order to confirm the effectiveness of our methodology we analyzed also several other access control datasets that are publicly available [11]. In particular, we analyzed all the dataset at our disposal with more than 1000 users. A description of their main properties can be found in Table 2. Since no business information is available for these datasets, we executed the Step 1 randomly partitioning the users in a number of partitions equal to the 1% of the number of users.

To complete the evaluation, we applied our methodology to synthetic datasets as well. Each dataset has been generated using the following procedure. We created an empty matrix composed by 10000 rows and 1000 columns. In each matrix, a given number n of subsets of rows and columns have been randomly chosen. Each subset of rows, and each subset of columns, counts a number of elements that are proportional to $100 \times x^2$ and $20 \times x^2$, where x is a random number uniformly chosen between 0 and 1. The elements of the matrix that belongs to one of such subsets are set to 1, while the other ones are set to 0. Using this procedure we generated different binary matrices, and we used them as access control datasets that have 10000 users, and 1000 permissions. In other words, we granted a permission to a specific user if, and only if, the corresponding cell in the matrix was set to 1.

4.2 Experiments Setup

In the following, we will report on several experiments that have been executed to evaluate the performance of our methodology. In particular, since our approach does not depend on any particular role mining algorithm, we will execute our experiments searching for a general pattern inside our data: the maximal biclusters [4]. These patterns are related to the concept of closed itemsets [27], that are used in the discovery of association rules, strong rules, correlations, sequential rules, episodes, multidimensional patterns, and many other important tasks [13].

In order to estimate the performance achieved, we will compare the results with and without utilizing our approach. In particular, given the datasets described in Section 4.1, we will search for maximal biclusters, and we will compare this list of actual maximal biclusters with the maximal biclusters generated by using our methodology. Since each maximal bicluster identifies a set of users and a set of permissions, we use two similarities indexes as metrics: the similarity of two sets of users, and the similarity of two sets of permissions that are defined in the following.

DEFINITION 5. (SIMILARITY OF TWO SETS OF USERS)

$$Sim_u (U_1, U_2) = \frac{|U_1 \cap U_2|}{|U_1 \cup U_2|} \qquad (4)$$

where $U_1, U_2 \subseteq USERS$

DEFINITION 6. (SIMILARITY OF TWO SETS OF PERMIS-

SIONS)

$$Sim_p (P_1, P_2) = \frac{|P_1 \cap P_2|}{|P_1 \cup P_2|} \qquad (5)$$

where $P_1, P_2 \subseteq PERMS$

Given the two lists of maximal biclusters, each element of the first list is compared with all the elements in the second list. Among all these pairs, the highest user and permission similarities are taken into consideration, and the arithmetic mean of all the similarities (that we indicate with "Users Similarity" and "Permissions Similarity") is the index that we use to compare the two lists of maximal biclusters . In summary, given the list of maximal biclusters generated by our six-steps methodology and the one generated by considering the whole dataset, high "Users Similarity" means that the two lists of roles are very similar considering the users to role assignments. While, high "Permission Similarity" means that the two lists of roles are very similar considering the permission to role assignments. If the "Users Similarity" and the "Permission Similarity" calculated as above are both equal to one, then the accuracy of our six steps methodology is maximal, indeed it is able to elicit the same list of maximal biclusters generated analyzing the dataset as a whole.

4.3 Results

We first discuss the results achieved on our case study and then look at the results with the other datasets. Figure 3 reports the "Permissions Similarity" achieved. The number of swaps s used in Step 2 has been set equal to 100. The compression ratio used to determine the number of medoids in each partition is depicted on the x-axis, while the values of users and permissions similarities are reported on the y-axis. The results for different binarization thresholds are reported. In particular, it can be noticed that in all the cases the Permission Similarity is always greater than 90%(Figure 3(a)). It indicates that we loose only around 10% of precision when adopting our methodology, independent of the selected binarization threshold.

As showed in Figure 3(b), the User Similarity is instead more sensitive. This is mainly due do the fact that we are using a compression that involves users instead of permissions. A low binarization threshold allows us to achieve better results, indeed the best users similarity is reached when the binarization threshold is equal to 0.6. In this case, using only around 5% of the users as medoids, we achieve an User Similarity higher than the 60%. When the binarization threshold is higher, we reach however outstanding results: Using the 25% of users, in all the cases the users similarity is greater than the 60%, even when the binarization threshold is 1.

The complexity of Algorithm 1 is $O(sk(n-k))$, therefore, a higher number of swaps s requires more effort. Figure 4, like Figure 3(b), reports users and permissions similarities, but in this case the number of swaps executed in Algorithm 1 is equal to 1000, that is ten times the case illustrated in Figure 3(b). It can be seen that both the User Similarity and the Permission Similarity, are not markedly different from the results achieved in Figure 3. Therefore, already 100 swaps can be considered sufficient to achieve good results. Figure 5 compares the effort needed to search the maximal biclusters without our methodology, with the effort needed to execute our methodology with 100 and 1000 swaps. The effort is shown as a percentage: $x\%$ effort indicates that our

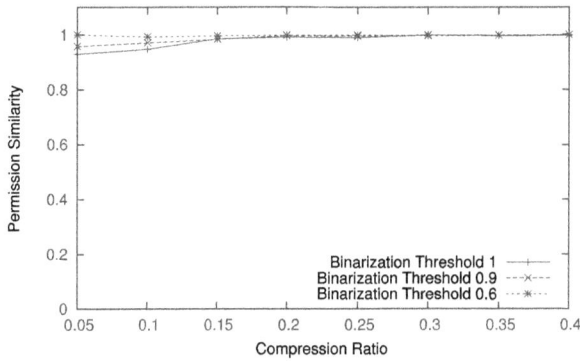

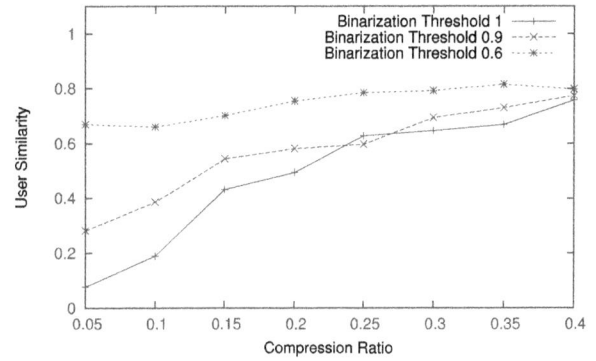

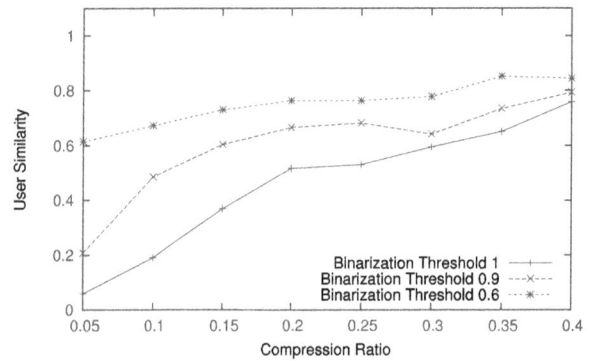

(a) Permission Similarity   (b) User Similarity

Figure 3: **Users and Permissions Similarity of the actual list of maximal biclusters, and the one built using our six step methodology.** $s = 100$

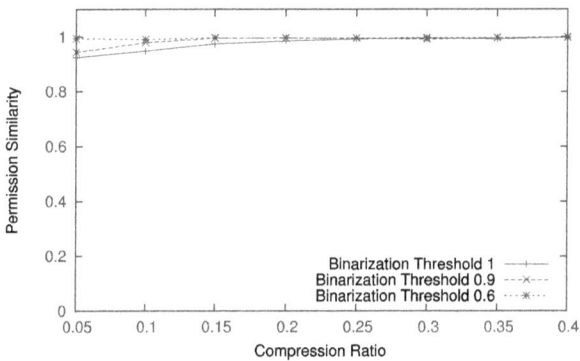

(a) Permission Similarity   (b) User Similarity

Figure 4: **Users and Permissions Similarity of the actual list of maximal biclusters, and the one built using our six step methodology.** $s = 1000$

methodology requires only $x\%$ of the computational time required without it. Figure 5(a) shows that the effort required is always less than the 7% when $s = 100$. With only 5% of users as medoids, the effort is even less than 5%.

The most important outcome of our six step methodology can be seen by analyzing Figure 5(a), and Figure 3 together. It turns out that it is possible to achieve the 100% of *Permission Similarity*, and the 80% of *User Similarity* with less than the 7% of effort. This largely confirms the effectiveness and the efficiency of the proposed framework.

As discussed above, we also analyzed several other access control datasets that are publicly available [11]. In the following experiments, the threshold t has been set to 0.6, and the value s to 100. Figure 6(a) shows the *Permission Similarity* achieved when analyzing the four dataset described in Table 2, while Figure 6(b) shows the *User Similarity*. It can be seen that HP AMERICAS LARGE is the dataset that had the worst performance. This is mainly due to the fact that this dataset has a larger number of permissions than users. In cases like this, it is better to apply our methodology trying

to compress permissions instead that the number of users. In all the other cases the permission similarity is higher than 80% when the compression ratio is higher then 0.05, and the users similarity is higher than 60% when the compression ratio is higher than 0.25. It is worth noticing that the results are slightly worse than in the real case illustrated in figures 3(a) and 3(b). This is mainly due to the fact that for the public datasets we do not have at our disposal any business information to drive the partitioning step, leading to assigning users randomly to the different partitions, and therefore users that are not similar at all are likely assigned to the same partitions.

Figures 6(c) and 6(d) shows the *Permission Similarity* and the *User Similarity* of the datasets that we randomly generated using the procedure described in Section 4.1. Even in this case the results are similar to the real datasets that we previously analyzed: the permissions similarity is always higher than the users similarity, and a users similarity higher than roughly the 60% can be achieved when the compression ratio is higher than 0.25.

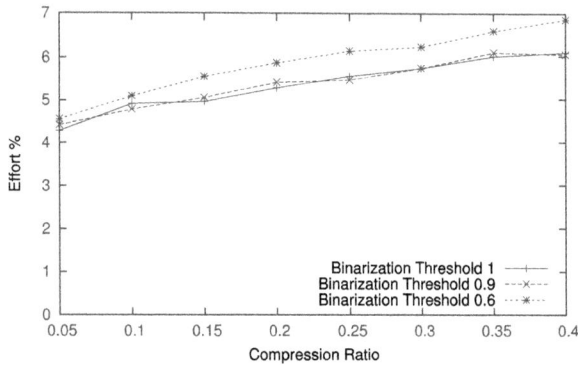

(a) Effort with s=100   (b) Effort with s=1000

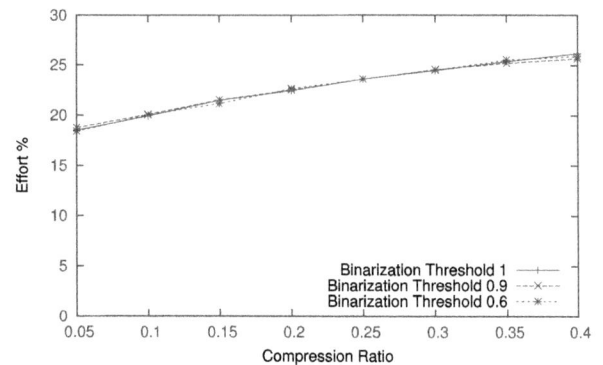

Figure 5: Percentage of Effort when using our methodology

5. CONCLUSIONS AND FUTURE WORK

In this paper, we have tackled the problem of making role mining practical and feasible. Our primary contribution is to develop an approach that can effectively reduce the computational workload, parallelize the effort, while retaining maximal utility and accuracy. An additional advantage is that our approach is agnostic to the specific role mining methodology used, and therefore can be used in conjunction with any specific technique already developed or yet to be developed. We have validated our approach on both real and synthetic datasets and demonstrated its viability. In the future, we plan to look at utilizing more semantics to further reduce the workload, and explore the use of automated techniques towards making the process more transparent and usable to security administrators.

6. ACKNOWLEDGMENTS

The work of Atluri was supported by the National Science Foundation, while working at the Foundation. Any opinion, finding, and conclusions or recommendations expressed in this material are those of the author and do not necessarily reflect the views of the National Science Foundation.

7. REFERENCES

[1] ANSI/INCITS 359-2004, Information Technology – Role Based Access Control, 2004.

[2] A. Colantonio, R. Di Pietro, and A. Ocello. A cost-driven approach to role engineering. In *Proc. ACM SAC*, pages 2129–2136, 2008.

[3] A. Colantonio, R. Di Pietro, and A. Ocello. *Role Mining in Business—Taming Role-Based Access Control Administration*. World Scientific Publishing Co. Inc, 2011.

[4] A. Colantonio, R. Di Pietro, A. Ocello, and N. V. Verde. ABBA: Adaptive bicluster-based approach to impute missing values in binary matrices. In *Proc. ACM SAC*, pages 1027–1034, 2010.

[5] A. Colantonio, R. Di Pietro, A. Ocello, and N. V. Verde. Mining business-relevant RBAC states through decomposition. In *Proc. IFIP SEC*, volume 330 of *IFIP International Federation for Information Processing*, pages 19–30. Springer, 2010.

[6] A. Colantonio, R. Di Pietro, A. Ocello, and N. V. Verde. Taming role mining complexity in RBAC. *Computers & Security*, 29:548–564, 2010.

[7] A. Colantonio, R. Di Pietro, A. Ocello, and N. V. Verde. A new role mining framework to elicit business roles and to mitigate enterprise risk. *Decision Support Systems*, 50:715–731, 2011.

[8] A. Colantonio, R. Di Pietro, A. Ocello, and N. V. Verde. Visual role mining: A picture is worth a thousand roles. *IEEE Transactions on Knowledge and Data Engineering*, 99(PrePrints), 2011. To appear.

[9] E. J. Coyne. Role-engineering. In *Proc. ACM RBAC*, pages 15–16, 1995.

[10] E. J. Coyne and J. M. Davis. *Role Engineering for Enterprise Security Management*. Artech House, Dec. 2007.

[11] A. Ene, W. Horne, N. Milosavljevic, P. Rao, R. Schreiber, and R. E. Tarjan. Fast exact and heuristic methods for role minimization problems. In *Proc. ACM SACMAT*, pages 1–10, 2008.

[12] M. Frank, A. P. Streich, D. Basin, and J. M. Buhmann. A probabilistic approach to hybrid role mining. In *Proc. ACM CCS*, pages 101–111, 2009.

[13] J. Han and M. Kamber. *Data Mining: Concepts and Techniques*. Morgan Kaufmann, 2nd edition, 2006.

[14] P. Jaccard. Etude comparative de la distribution florale dans une portion des Alpes et des Jura. *Bulletin del la Société Vaudoise des Sciences Naturelles*, 37:547–579, 1901.

[15] L. Kaufman and P. J. Rousseeuw. *Finding Groups in Data: An Introduction to Cluster Analysis*. John Wiley, 1990.

[16] M. Kuhlmann, D. Shohat, and G. Schimpf. Role mining – revealing business roles for security administration using data mining technology. In *Proc. ACM SACMAT*, pages 179–186, 2003.

[17] H. Lu, J. Vaidya, and V. Atluri. Optimal boolean matrix decomposition: Application to role engineering. In *Proceedings of the 24th IEEE International Conferene on Data Engineering, ICDE '08*, pages 297–306, 2008.

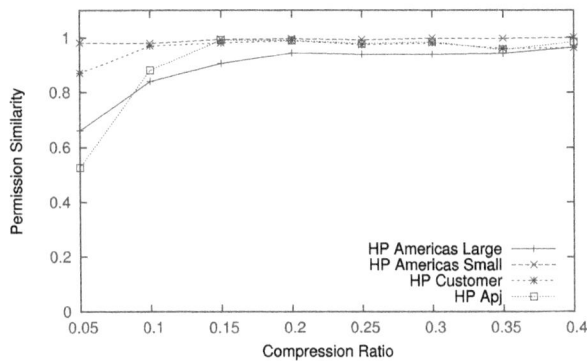

(a) Permission Similarity

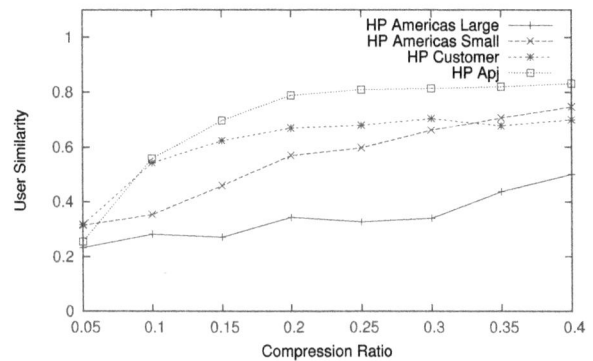

(b) User Similarity

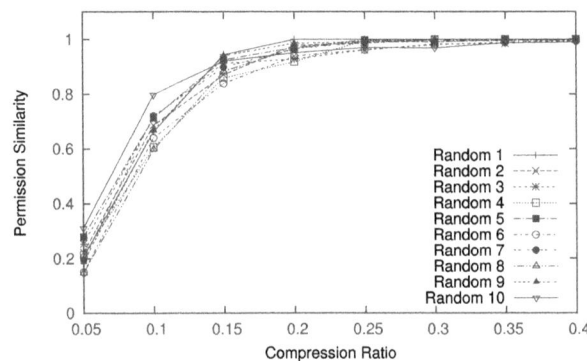

(c) Permission Similarity

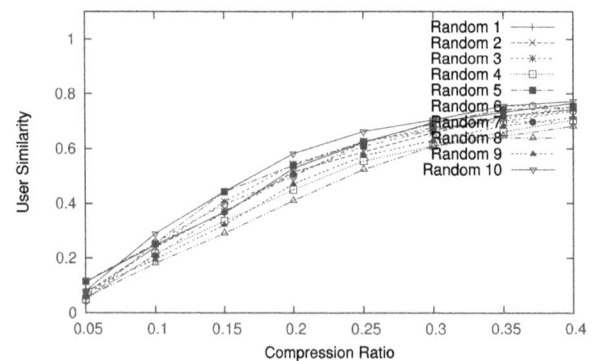

(d) User Similarity

Figure 6: Analysis of several datasets. Since for these datasets no business information are available, we randomly partitioned the users during Step 1, creating a number of partitions equal to the 1% of the number of users. In this simulation $s = 100$ and $t = 0.6$.

[18] I. Molloy, N. Li, T. Li, Z. Mao, Q. Wang, and J. Lobo. Evaluating role mining algorithms. In *Proc. ACM SACMAT*, pages 95–104, 2009.

[19] G. Neumann and M. Strembeck. A scenario-driven role engineering process for functional RBAC roles. In *Proc. ACM SACMAT*, pages 33–42, 2002.

[20] A. C. O'Connor and R. J. Loomis. 2010 economic analysis of role-based access control. Technical report, National Institute of Standards and Technology (NIST), 2010.

[21] H. Röckle, G. Schimpf, and R. Weidinger. Process-oriented approach for role-finding to implement role-based security administration in a large industrial organization. In *Proc. ACM RBAC*, volume 3, pages 103–110, 2000.

[22] J. Schlegelmilch and U. Steffens. Role mining with ORCA. In *Proc. ACM SACMAT*, pages 168–176, 2005.

[23] J. Vaidya, V. Atluri, and Q. Guo. The role mining problem: finding a minimal descriptive set of roles. In *Proc. ACM SACMAT*, pages 175–184, 2007.

[24] J. Vaidya, V. Atluri, Q. Guo, and N. Adam. Migrating to optimal RBAC with minimal perturbation. In *Proc. ACM SACMAT*, pages 11–20, 2008.

[25] J. Vaidya, V. Atluri, and J. Warner. RoleMiner: mining roles using subset enumeration. In *Proc. ACM CCS*, pages 144–153, 2006.

[26] M. van der Laan, K. Pollard, and J. Bryan. A new partitioning around medoids algorithm. *Journal of Statistical Computation and Simulation*, 73(8):575–584, 2003.

[27] M. J. Zaki and C.-J. Hsiao. Efficient algorithms for mining closed itemsets and their lattice structure. *IEEE Transactions on Knowledge and Data Engineering (TKDE)*, 17(4):462–478, 2005.

[28] D. Zhang, K. Ramamohanarao, and T. Ebringer. Role engineering using graph optimisation. In *Proc. ACM SACMAT*, pages 139–144, 2007.

[29] N. Zhang, M. Ryan, and D. P. Guelev. Synthesising verified access control systems through model checking. *J. Comput. Secur.*, 16(1):1–61, 2008. IOS Press.

Privacy Streamliner: A Two-Stage Approach to Improving Algorithm Efficiency

Wen Ming Liu and Lingyu Wang
Concordia Institute for Information Systems Engineering, Concordia University
Montreal, QC H3G 1M8, Canada
{l_wenmin,wang}@ciise.concordia.ca

ABSTRACT

In releasing data with sensitive information, a data owner usually has seemingly conflicting goals, including privacy preservation, utility optimization, and algorithm efficiency. In this paper, we observe that a high computational complexity is usually incurred when an algorithm conflates the processes of privacy preservation and utility optimization. We then propose a novel *privacy streamliner* approach to decouple those two processes for improving algorithm efficiency. More specifically, we first identify a set of potential privacy-preserving solutions satisfying that an adversary's knowledge about this set itself will not help him/her to violate the privacy property; we can then optimize utility within this set without worrying about privacy breaches since such an optimization is now simulatable by adversaries. To make our approach more concrete, we study it in the context of micro-data release with publicly known generalization algorithms. The analysis and experiments both confirm our algorithms to be more efficient than existing solutions.

Categories and Subject Descriptors

H.2.7 [**Database Management**]: Database Administration—*security, integrity, and protection*; K.6.m [**Management of Computing and Information Systems**]: Miscellaneous—*Security*

General Terms

Security, Theory, Algorithms

Keywords

Privacy Preservation, Micro-Data Disclosure, *l*-Diversity

1. INTRODUCTION

In many privacy-preserving applications ranging from micro-data release [9] to social networks [7, 20], a major challenge is to keep private information secret while optimizing the utility of disclosed or shared data. Recent studies further reveal that utility optimization may actually interfere with privacy preservation by leaking additional private information when algorithms are regarded as public knowledge [25, 29]. Specifically, an adversary can determine

a guess of the private information to be invalid if it would have caused the disclosed data to take a different form with better utility. By eliminating such invalid guesses, the adversary can then obtain a more accurate estimation of the private information.

A natural solution to this problem is to simulate the aforementioned adversarial reasoning [18, 25, 29]. Specifically, since knowledge about utility optimization can assist an adversary in refining his/her mental images of the private information, we can first simulate such reasoning to obtain the refined mental images, and then enforce the privacy property on such images instead of the disclosed data. However, it has been shown that such approaches are inherently recursive and deemed to incur a high complexity [29].

In this paper, we observe that the interference between privacy preservation and utility optimization actually arises from the fact that those two processes are usually mixed together in an algorithm. On the other hand, we also observe a simple fact that *to meet both goals does not necessarily mean to meet them at exactly the same time*. Based on such observations, we propose a novel *privacy streamliner* approach to decouple the process of privacy preservation from that of utility optimization in order to avoid the expensive recursive task of simulating the adversarial reasoning.

To make our approach more concrete, we study it in the context of micro-data release with publicly known generalization algorithms. Unlike traditional algorithms, which typically evaluate generalization functions in a predetermined order and then release data using the first function satisfying the privacy property, a generalization algorithm under our approach works in a completely different way: The algorithm starts with the set of generalization functions that can satisfy the privacy property for the given micro-data table; it then identifies a subset of such functions satisfying that knowledge about this subset itself will not assist an adversary in violating the privacy property (which is generally not true for the set of all functions, as we will show later); utility optimization within this subset then becomes simulatable by adversaries [12], and is thus guaranteed not to affect the privacy property. We believe that this general principle can be applied to other similar privacy preserving problems, although developing the actual solution may be application-specific and non-trivial.

The contribution of this paper is twofold. First, our privacy streamliner approach is presented through a general framework that is independent of specific algorithmic constructions or utility metrics. This allows our approach to be easily adapted to a broad range of applications to yield efficient solutions. We demonstrate such possibilities by devising three generalization algorithms to suit different needs while following exactly the same approach. Second, our algorithms provide practical solutions for privacy-preserving micro-data release with public algorithms. As confirmed by both

A Micro-Data Table t_0

Name	DOB	Condition
Ada	1985	flu
Bob	1980	flu
Coy	1975	cold
Dan	1970	cold
Eve	1965	HIV

The Disclosure Sets

Name	Condition									
	t_{01}	t_{02}	t_{03}	t_{04}	t_{05}	t_{06}	t_{07}	t_{08}	t_{09}	t_{10}
Ada	flu	cold	flu	cold	flu	cold	flu	cold	HIV	HIV
Bob	flu	cold	flu	cold	HIV	HIV	flu	cold	flu	cold
Coy	cold	flu	cold	flu	cold	flu	HIV	HIV	cold	flu
Dan	cold	flu	HIV	HIV	cold	flu	cold	flu	cold	flu
Eve	HIV	HIV	cold	flu	flu	cold	cold	flu	flu	cold

Table 1: The Motivating Example

complexity analysis and experimental results, those algorithms are more efficient than existing algorithms.

The rest of this paper is organized as follows. We first build intuitions through an example in the remainder of this section. We then present our main approach and supporting theoretical results in Section 2. Section 3 devises three generalization algorithms by following the approach. Section 4 experimentally evaluates the efficiency and utility of our algorithms. We discuss the possibilities for extending our approach and the practicality of the approach in Section 5. We then review related work in Section 6, and finally conclude the paper in Section 7.

Motivating Example

The left table in Table 1 shows a micro-data table t_0 to be released. To protect individuals' privacy, the *identifier* Name will not be released. Also, the identifiers are partitioned into *anonymized groups*, with the *quasi-identifier* DOB inside each such group modified to be the same value [22] (in this paper, we will only consider generalization and leave suppression [15] and bucketization [26] for the future work). For simplicity, we will focus on the partitioning of identifiers while omitting the modification of quasi-identifiers. For this particular example, we assume the desired privacy property to be that the highest ratio of a *sensitive value* Condition in any anonymized group must be no greater than $\frac{2}{3}$ [19].

By our *privacy streamliner* approach, we need to start with all partitions of the identifiers that can satisfy the privacy property. In this example, any partition that includes $\{Ada, Bob\}$ or $\{Coy, Dan\}$ will violate the privacy property, since the two persons inside each of those groups share the same condition. It can be shown that there are totally 9 partitions satisfying the privacy property, as shown below. We will refer to the set of such identifier partitions as the *locally safe set (LSS)*.

$$P_1 = \{\{Ada, Coy\}, \{Bob, Dan, Eve\}\},$$
$$P_2 = \{\{Ada, Dan\}, \{Bob, Coy, Eve\}\},$$
$$P_3 = \{\{Ada, Eve\}, \{Bob, Coy, Dan\}\},$$
$$P_4 = \{\{Bob, Coy\}, \{Ada, Dan, Eve\}\},$$
$$P_5 = \{\{Bob, Dan\}, \{Ada, Coy, Eve\}\},$$
$$P_6 = \{\{Bob, Eve\}, \{Ada, Coy, Dan\}\},$$
$$P_7 = \{\{Coy, Eve\}, \{Ada, Bob, Dan\}\},$$
$$P_8 = \{\{Dan, Eve\}, \{Ada, Bob, Coy\}\},$$
$$P_9 = \{\{Ada, Bob, Coy, Dan, Eve\}\}$$

It may seem to be a viable solution to start optimizing data utility inside the LSS, since every partition here can satisfy the privacy property. However, such an optimization may still violate the privacy property, because it is not simulatable by adversaries [12] unless if we assume the LSS to be public knowledge (that is, adversaries may know that each identifier partition in the LSS can satisfy the privacy property for the unknown table t_0). Unfortunately, this

knowledge about LSS could help adversaries to violate the privacy property. In this case, it can be shown that adversaries' mental image about the micro-data table would only include t_{01} and t_{02} shown in the right table in Table 1. In other words, adversaries can determine that t_0 must be either t_{01} or t_{02}. Clearly, the privacy property is violated since *Eve* is associated with *HIV* in both cases.

Since the LSS may contain too much information to be assumed as public knowledge, we turn to its subsets. In this example, it can be shown that by removing P_7 from the *LSS*, the disclosure set becomes $\{t_{01}, t_{02}, t_{03}, t_{04}\}$. The privacy property is now satisfied since the highest ratio of a sensitive value for any identifier is $\frac{1}{2}$. We call such a subset of the LSS the *globally safe set (GSS)*. Optimizing data utility within the GSS will not violate privacy property, because the GSS can be safely assumed as public knowledge and the optimization is thus simulatable by adversaries.

However, there is another complication. At the end of utility optimization, one of the generalization functions in the GSS will be used to release data. The information disclosed by the GSS and that by the released data is different, and by intersecting the two, adversaries may further refine their mental image of the micro-data table. In this example, since the adversaries' mental image about the micro-data table in terms of the GSS is $\{t_{01}, t_{02}, t_{03}, t_{04}\}$, adversaries know both *Ada* and *Bob* must be associated with either *flu* or *cold*. Now suppose the utility optimization selects P_3, then from the released table, adversaries will further know that either *Ada* or *Eve* must have *flu* while the other has *HIV*. Therefore, adversaries can now infer that *Ada* must have *flu*, and *Eve* must then have *HIV*.

To address this issue, we will further confine the utility optimization to a subset of the GSS. In this example, if we further remove P_3, P_6, P_8 from the GSS, then the corresponding mental image of adversaries will contain all the 10 tables (from t_{01} to t_{10}). It can be shown that now the privacy property will always be satisfied regardless of which partition is selected during utility optimization. Taking P_1 as an example, from its corresponding generalized table, adversaries may further refine their mental image about t_0 as the first six tables (from t_{01} to t_{06}), but the highest ratio of a sensitive value is still $\frac{1}{2}$. We call such a subset of identifier partitions the *strongly globally safe set (SGSS)*. The SGSS allows us to optimize utility without worrying about violating the privacy property.

Therefore, the key problem in applying the privacy streamliner approach is to find the SGSS. The naive solution of directly following the above example to compute the LSS, GSS, and eventually SGSS is clearly impractical due to the large solution space. In the rest of this paper, we will present more efficient ways to directly construct the SGSS without first generating the LSS or GSS.

2. THE MODEL

We first give the basic model in Section 2.1. We then introduce the concept of *l-candidate* and *self-contained property* in Section 2.2. Finally, we prove that the SGSS can be efficiently constructed using those concepts in Section 2.3. Table 2 summarizes our notations.

$t_0, t, t(id, q, s)$	Micro-data table
$\mathcal{I}, \mathcal{Q}, \mathcal{S}$	Projection $\Pi_{id}(t), \Pi_q(t), \Pi_s(t)$
R_{iq}, R_{qs}, R_{is}	Projection $\Pi_{id,q}(t), \Pi_{q,s}(t), \Pi_{id,s}(t)$
$C(.|t), C_i(.|t)$	A color of table t
$S^C(.|t)$	The set of colors in t
$P(.|t), P_i(.|t)$	A identifier partition of table t
$S^P(.|t)$	A set of identifier partitions of t
$ss^l(.|t)$	Locally safe set (LSS) of t
$ss^g(.|t)$	Globally safe set (GSS) of t
$ss^s(.|t)$	Strongly globally safe set (SGSS) of t

Table 2: The Notation Table

2.1 The Basic Model

We denote a micro-data table as $t_0(id, q, s)$ where id, q, and s denote the *identifier*, *quasi-identifier*, and *sensitive value*, respectively (each of which may represent multiple attributes). Denote by $\mathcal{I}, \mathcal{Q}, \mathcal{S}$ the set of identifier values $\Pi_{id}(t_0)$, quasi-identifier values $\Pi_q(t_0)$, and sensitive values $\Pi_s(t_0)$ (all projections preserve duplicates, unless explicitly stated otherwise). Also, denote by R_{iq}, R_{qs}, R_{is} the projections $\Pi_{id,q}(t_0), \Pi_{q,s}(t_0), \Pi_{id,s}(t_0)$, respectively.

As typically assumed, $\mathcal{I}, \mathcal{Q}$, and their relationship R_{iq} may be known through external knowledge, and $\mathcal{S}$ is also known once a generalization is released. Further, we make the worst case assumption that each tuple in t_0 can be linked to a unique identifier value through the corresponding quasi-identifier value. Therefore, both R_{is} and R_{qs} need to remain secret to protect privacy. Between them, R_{is} is considered as the private information and R_{qs} as the utility information.

We say a micro-data table t_0 is *l-eligible* if at most $\frac{|t_0|}{l}$ tuples in t_0 share the same sensitive value. We call the set of all identifier values associated with the same sensitive value s_i a *color*, denoted as $C(t_0, s_i)$ or simply C_i when t_0 and s_i are clear from the context. We use $S^C(t_0)$ or simply S^C to denote the collection of all colors in t_0.

EXAMPLE 1. *The left-hand side of Table 3 (the right-hand side will be needed for later discussions) shows a micro-data table t_0 in which there are two colors: $C_1 = \{id_1, id_2\}$ and $C_2 = \{id_3, id_4\}$, so $S^C = \{C_1, C_2\}$.* ⊡

R_{qs}

id	q	s
id_1	q_1	s_1
id_2	q_2	s_1
id_3	q_3	s_2
id_4	q_4	s_2
$\mathcal{I}$	$\mathcal{Q}$	$\mathcal{S}$

$P_1 = \{\{id_1, id_3\}, \{id_2, id_4\}\}$
$P_2 = \{\{id_1, id_4\}, \{id_2, id_3\}\}$
$P_3 = \{\{id_1, id_2, id_3, id_4\}\}$
$P_4 = \{\{id_1, id_2\}, \{id_3, id_4\}\}$

Table 3: An Example

We denote by $ss^l(t_0)$, $ss^g(t_0)$, and $ss^s(t_0)$ the *locally safe set (LSS)*, *globally safe set (GSS)*, and *strongly globally safe set (SGSS)* for a given t_0, respectively (those concepts have been illustrated in Section 1).

EXAMPLE 2. *Continuing Example 1 and assuming the privacy property to be 2-diversity [19], it can be shown that $ss^l(t_0) =$*

$\{P_1, P_2, P_3\}$ *and* $P_4 \notin ss^l$ *where* P_1, P_2, P_3, P_4 *are shown on the right-hand side of Table 3. Further,* $\{P_1, P_3\}$ *and* $\{P_2, P_3\}$ *are both GSS and SGSS.* ⊡

We have previously given a sufficient condition for the SGSS, namely, the *l-cover* property [31]. In other words, a set of identifier partitions S^P is a SGSS with respect to l-diversity if it satisfies l-cover (however, no concrete method is given there to satisfy this property, which is the focus of this paper). Intuitively, l-cover requires each color to be indistinguishable from at least $l-1$ other sets of identifiers in the identifier partition. If no ambiguity is possible, we also refer to a color C together with its $l-1$ covers as the l-cover of C. As these concepts are needed later in the proofs of our main results discussed in Section 2.3, we repeat them in Definition 4 and 5 shown in Appendix A (note the remaining content of this paper can be understood without those definitions).

2.2 l-Candidate and Self-Contained Property

We first give a necessary but not sufficient condition for l-cover, namely, *l-candidate*. As formally stated in Definition 1, subsets of identifiers can be candidates of each other, if there exists one-to-one mappings between those subsets that always map an identifier to another in a different color. We will prove later that any collection of subsets of identifiers can be l-cover for each other only if they form an l-candidate.

DEFINITION 1 (l-CANDIDATE). *Given an l-eligible micro-data table t_0, we say*

- $ids_1 \subseteq \mathcal{I}$ *and* $ids_2 \subseteq \mathcal{I}$ *are candidate for each other, if*

  - $ids_1 \cap ids_2 = \emptyset$ *and* $|ids_1| = |ids_2|$, *and*

  - *there exists a bijection* $f : ids_1 \rightarrow ids_2$, *such that every* $id \in ids_1$ *and* $f(id) \in ids_2$ *are from different colors.*

- $ids_1, ids_2, \ldots, ids_l \subseteq \mathcal{I}$ *form a l-candidate, if for all* $(1 \leq i \neq j \leq l)$, ids_i *and* ids_j *are candidates for each other.*

- *Denote by* $Can^l(.|t_0) = (can_1, can_2, \ldots, can_{|S^C|})$ *a sequence of* $|S^C|$ *l-candidates each* can_i *of which is the l-candidate for the color* C_i *in* t_0 *(note that there is exactly one l-candidate for each color in the sequence, and* $Can^l(.|t_0)$ *is not necessarily unique for* t_0*).*

EXAMPLE 3. *In the table shown on the left-hand side of Table 3, the two colors $C_1 = \{id_1, id_2\}$ and $C_2 = \{id_3, id_4\}$ are candidates for each other, and they together form a 2-candidate $\{C_1, C_2\}$. Also, we have that $Can^l(.|t_0) = (\{C_1, C_2\}, \{C_1, C_2\})$ (note that $Can^l(.|t_0)$ denotes the sequence of l-candidates and we use the indices in the multiset to present the order in the remainder of this paper, and if no ambiguity is possible, we shall not distinguish the notations between a collection and a sequence). In this special case, it has two identical elements, the first one for C_1 and the second one for C_2, since both colors have the same l-candidate.* ⊡

Next we introduce the *self-contained* property in Definition 2. Informally, an identifier partition is self-contained, if the partition does not break the one-to-one mappings used in defining the l-candidates. Later we will show that the self-contained property is sufficient for an identifier partition to satisfy the l-cover property and thus form a SGSS.

DEFINITION 2 (SELF-CONTAINED PROPERTY AND FAMILY SET). *l*-candidates. All the proofs can be found in the Appendix B due to *Given a micro-data table t_0 and a collection of l-candidates Can^l, we say*

- *an anonymized group G in an identifier partition P is self-contained with respect to Can^l, if for every pair of identifiers $\{id_1, id_2\}$ that appears in any bijection used to define Can^l, either $G \cap \{id_1, id_2\} = \emptyset$ or $G \cap \{id_1, id_2\} = \{id_1, id_2\}$ is true.*

- *an identifier partition P is self-contained if for each $G \in P$, G is self-contained.*

- *a set S^P of identifier partitions is self-contained, if for each $P \in S^P$, P is self-contained; we also call such a set S^P a* family set *with respect to Can^l.*

Next we introduce the concept of *minimal self-contained identifier partition* in Definition 3 to depict those identifier partitions that not only satisfy the self-contained property but have anonymized groups of minimal sizes. Intuitively, for any given collection of *l*-candidates Can^l, a minimal self-contained identifier partition may yield optimal data utility under certain utility metrics (we will discuss this in more details later).

DEFINITION 3 (MINIMAL SELF-CONTAINED PARTITION).
Given a micro-data table t_0 and a collection of l-candidates Can^l, an identifier partition P is called the minimal self-contained partition *with respect to Can^l, if*

- *P satisfies the self-contained property with respect to Can^l, and*

- *for any anonymized group $G \in P$, no $G' \subset G$ can satisfy the self-contained property.*

EXAMPLE 4. *In Example 3, assume the bijections used to define l-candidate for C_1 in Can^l are $f_1(id_1) = id_3$ and $f_1(id_2) = id_4$ while for C_2 are $f_2(id_3) = id_1$ and $f_2(id_4) = id_2$, then the identifier partitions P_1 and P_3 shown in the left-hand side of Table 3 satisfy the self-contained property, whereas P_2 does not. Also, P_1 is the minimal self-contained identifier partition, and $\{P_1\}$, $\{P_3\}$, $\{P_1, P_3\}$ are all family sets.*

Similarly, assume the bijections used to define *l*-candidate for C_1 in Can^l are $f_1(id_1) = id_4$ and $f_1(id_2) = id_3$ while for C_2 are $f_2(id_3) = id_2$ and $f_2(id_4) = id_1$, then the identifier partitions P_2 and P_3 satisfy the self-contained property, whereas P_1 does not. Also, P_2 is the minimal self-contained identifier partition, and $\{P_2\}$, $\{P_3\}$, $\{P_2, P_3\}$ are all family sets. Finally, assume $f_1(id_1) = id_3$, $f_1(id_2) = id_4$ and $f_2(id_3) = id_2$, $f_2(id_4) = id_1$, then in this case only P_3 satisfies self-contained property, whereas P_1 and P_2 do not. It is clearly evidenced by this example that, given micro-data table, its minimal self-contained partition is determined not only by the Can^l, but also the corresponding bijections. In this paper, we focus on deriving Can^l and constructing minimal self-contained partitions as well as family sets based on the bijections. Therefore, unless explicitly stated otherwise, Can^l is referred to itself together with the corresponding bijections in the remainder of this paper.

2.3 Main Results

In this section, we first prove that the self-contained property and *l*-candidate provide a way for finding identifier partitions that satisfy the *l*-cover property, and then we prove results for constructing

space limitations.

First, in Lemma 1, we show that a minimal self-contained identifier partition always satisfies the *l*-cover property.

LEMMA 1. *Given an l-eligible micro-data table t_0, every minimal self-contained partition satisfies the l-cover property. Moreover, for each color C, its corresponding l-candidate in Can^l is also an l-cover for C (that is, C together with its $l-1$ covers).*

In Lemma 2, we prove that an anonymized group in any self-contained identifier partition must either also be a group in the minimal self-contained partition, or be a union of several such groups. This result will be needed in later proofs.

LEMMA 2. *Given any l-eligible t_0, a collection of l-candidates Can^l and its corresponding minimal self-contained partition $P^{lm} = \{ids_1, ids_2, \ldots, ids_k\}$, any self-contained identifier partition P satisfies that $\forall (G \in P)$, either $G \cap ids_i = \emptyset$ or $G \supseteq ids_i$ $(i \in [1, k])$ is true.*

Based on Lemma 1 and 2, we now show that similar results hold for any self-contained identifier partition and any family set, as formulated in Theorem 1.

THEOREM 1. *Given an l-eligible t_0 and the l-candidates Can^l, we have that*

- *any self-contained identifier partition P satisfies the l-cover property. Moreover, for each color in t_0, the corresponding l-candidate in Can^l is also the l-cover for P.*

- *any family set S^{fs} satisfies the l-cover property. Moreover, for each color in t_0, the corresponding l-candidate in Can^l is also the l-cover for S^{fs}.*

Based on the above results, once the collection of *l*-candidates is determined, we can easily construct sets of identifier partitions to satisfy the *l*-cover property. Therefore, we now turn to finding efficient methods for constructing *l*-candidates. First, Lemma 3 and 4 present conditions for subsets of identifiers to be candidates for each other.

LEMMA 3. *Given an l-eligible t_0, any $ids \subseteq \mathcal{I}$ that satisfies $|ids| = |C|$ and $ids \cap C = \emptyset$ is a candidate for color C.*

LEMMA 4. *Given an l-eligible t_0, any $ids_1, ids_2 \subseteq \mathcal{I}$ satisfying following conditions are candidates for each other:*

- *$|ids_1| = |ids_2|$ and $ids_1 \cap ids_2 = \emptyset$, and*

- *the number of all identifiers in $ids_1 \cup ids_2$ that belong to the same color is no greater than $|ids_1|$.*

Based on Lemma 3 and 4, we now present conditions for constructing *l*-candidates of each color in Theorem 2. We will apply those conditions in the next section to design practical algorithms for building the SGSS.

THEOREM 2. *Given an l-eligible t_0, each color C together with any $(l-1)$ subsets of identifiers $\{ids_1, ids_2, \ldots, ids_{l-1}\}$ that satisfy following conditions form a valid l-candidate for C:*

- *$\forall (x \in [1, l-1])$, $|ids_x| = |C|$ and $ids_x \cap C = \emptyset$;*

- *$\forall ((x, y \in [1, l-1]) \wedge (x \neq y))$, $ids_x \cap ids_y = \emptyset$;*

- *the number of all identifiers in $\cup_{x=1}^{l-1} ids_x$ that belong to the same color is no greater than $|C|$.*

3. THE ALGORITHMS

In this section, we design three algorithms for constructing l-candidates for colors and analyze their complexities. It is important to note that there may exist many other ways for constructing l-candidates based on the conditions given in Theorem 2. This flexibility allows us to vary the design of algorithms to suit different needs of various applications, because different l-candidates will also result in different SGSSs and hence algorithms more suitable for different utility metrics. We demonstrate such a flexibility through designing three algorithms in the following.

To simplify our discussions, we say an identifier is *complete* (or *incomplete*) if it is (or is not) included in any l-candidate; similarly, we say a color is *complete* (or incomplete) if it only includes complete identifiers (or otherwise); we also say a set of identifiers is *compatible* (or *incompatible*) with an identifier id, if there does not exist (or exists) identifier in that set that is from the same color as id; finally, given any color, an identifier from other colors is said to be *unused* with respect to that color if it has not yet been selected as a candidate for any identifier in that color. Table 4 summarizes the notations used in the algorithms.

n	The number of (incomplete) tuples in t_0
C_i	The ith color, or the set of (incomplete) identifiers in the ith color
n_c	The number of (incomplete) colors in t_0
S^C	The sequence of (incomplete) colors in t_0
n_i	The number of (incomplete) tuples in color C_i
can_{ia}	The set of $(l-1)$ identifiers selected for identifier id_{ia} in color C_i
can_i	l-candidate for color i
Can^l	The collection of l-candidates

Table 4: Notations for Algorithms

3.1 The RIA Algorithm (Random and Independent)

The main intention in designing the RIA algorithm is to show that, based on our results in Theorem 2, l-candidate can actually be built in a very straightforward way, although its efficiency and utility is not necessarily optimal. In the RIA algorithm, to construct the l-candidates for each color C_i, $(l-1)$ identifiers can_{ia} are selected randomly and independently for each identifier id_{ia} in C_i. The only constraint in this selection process for any color is that the same identifier will not be selected more than once. Clearly, designing such an algorithm is very straightforward. Roughly speaking, for each identifier id_{ia} in any color C_i, RIA randomly selects $(l-1)$ identifiers from any other $(l-1)$ colors that are not selected by other identifiers in C_i, and then form l-candidate can_i for C_i from the can_{ia} of each identifier.

The RIA algorithm is shown in Table 5. RIA first set $Can^l = \phi$ (line 1). Then, Given the l-eligible table t_0, RIA iteratively constructs l-candidate for all its colors (line 2-9). In each iteration, RIA first repeatedly selects $(l-1)$ identifiers can_{ia} for each identifier $id_{i,a}$ in color C_i. These identifiers are from $(l-1)$ different colors and not be used yet by the other identifier in current color. Then RIA builds the $(l-1)$ candidates for current color. To construct the wth candidate, RIA selects the wth identifier from each can_{ia} for each identifier $id_{i,a}$ in color C_i. Consequently C_i, together with its $(l-1)$ candidates, form the l-candidate, can_i, for color C_i. Finally, all the can_i for each color form the set Can^l of l-candidates, and RIA terminates and returns Can^l.

The computational complexity of RIA algorithm is $O(l \cdot n)$ since: since: first, for each color, each of its identifiers costs exactly $(l-1)$ many constant times (line 4-6) to select its $(l-1)$ identifiers, and there are n_i identifiers in the color, so totally $(l-1) \times n_i$. Then,

Input: an l-eligible Table t_0, the privacy property l;
Output: the set Can^l of l-candidates for each color;
Method:
1. Let $Can^l = \emptyset$;
2. **For** $i = 1$ to n_c
   // Iteratively construct l-candidate for each color C_i
3. **For** $a = 1$ to n_i
   // Iteratively select the $l-1$ number of identifiers for each identifier $id_{i,a}$ in color C_i
4. Randomly select $l-1$ different colors S_{ia}^C from $S^C \backslash \{C_i\}$;
5. Randomly select one *unused* identifier from each color in S_{ia}^C;
6. Form can_{ia} by collecting the previously selected $l-1$ identifiers in any order;
7. **For** $i = 1$ to n_c
8. **For** $w = 1$ to $l-1$
   // Create the l-candidate can_i for C_i based on the $can_{ia}(a \in [1, n_i])$
9. Create in can_i its wth candidate: $\bigcup_{a=1}^{n_i}$ (the wth identifier in can_{ia});
10. Let $Can^l = \{can_i : 1 \le i \le n_c\}$;
11. **Return** Can^l;

Table 5: The RIA Algorithm

based on these identifiers, it takes $(l-1) \times n_i$ many times to create its l-candidate. There are totally n_c many colors in the micro-table. Finally it takes n_c many times to create the set of l-candidates. Therefore, in totally its computational complexity is $O(\sum_i^{n_c}(2 \times (l-1) \times n_i) + n_c) = O(l \times n)$, because the size of all colors adds up to be n, and $n_c \le n$. Note that once an identifier select same identifier which was selected by the previously considered identifier in the color, RIA must reselect other identifier for that identifier. During the analysis of computational complexity, we ignore the time of solving such conflicts in colors and identifiers in line 4 and line 5 respectively. It is reasonable for most cases in the real life that $n_i \times (l-1) \ll n$, since in such case the probability of conflicts is very low. Note that the RIA algorithm only builds the l-candidates. In order to obtain the self-contained identifier partition and hence the SGSS (as shown in Theorem 1), we still need to merge the can_{ia}'s that share the common identifiers (which actually has a higher complexity than $O(l \times n)$, but we will not further discuss it since our intention of introducing the RIA algorithm is not due to its efficiency).

3.2 The RDA Algorithm (Random and Dependent)

The RDA algorithm aims at general-purpose data utility metrics that only depends on the size of each anonymized group in an identifier partition, such as the well known *Discernibility Metric (DM)* [4]. As we shall show through experiments, our RDA algorithm will produce solutions whose data utility by the DM metric is very close to that of the optimal solution, since the RDA algorithm can minimize the size of most anonymized groups in the chosen identifier partition.

Roughly speaking, for the color C_i that has the most incomplete identifiers, the algorithm randomly selects $(l-1)$ identifiers can_{ia} for each of its identifiers id_{ia}, one from each of the next $(l-1)$ colors with the most incomplete identifiers, until the number of incomplete colors is less than l. For the remaining identifiers, the

Input: an l-eligible Table t_0, the privacy property l;

Output: the set Can^l of l-candidates for each color;

Method:

1. **Let** n_c be the number of colors in t_0;
2. **Let** S^C be the sequence of the colors in the non-increasing order of their cardinality;
3. **Let** C_i, n_i ($i \in [1, n_c]$) be the ith color and its cardinality;
4. **While** ($n_c \geq l$)
   // Construct l-candidate for the color in which most number of incomplete identifiers
5.   Determine the color C_i which has most number of incomplete identifiers;
6.   **For** $a = 1$ to n_i
7.   **If**($id_{i,a}$ is *complete*)
8.   **Skip** to check the next identifier in current color;
   // Iteratively select the $l - 1$ number of identifiers for each identifier $id_{i,a}$ in color C_i
9.   Randomly select $l - 1$ *incomplete* identifiers from $l - 1$ different colors in S^C with most *incomplete* identifiers;
10.   Form can_{ia} by collecting the previously selected $l - 1$ identifiers in any order;
11.   Remove the *complete* colors from S^C, and recalculate n_c;
12.   Reorder the colors in S^C based on their number of *incomplete* identifiers;
13.   **If** ($n_c < l$) **Break**;
14. **While** ($S^C \neq \emptyset$)
15.   Select any *incomplete* identifier $id_{j,b}$ from the color $C_j \in S^C$ with the most number of *incomplete* identifiers;
16.   Select any $l - 1$ identifiers from the *compatible* can_{ia} with the minimal cardinality;
17.   Form can_{jb} by collecting the previously selected $l - 1$ identifiers in any order;
18.   **If** (color C_i is *complete*) Remove it from S^C;
19. **For** $i = 1$ to n_c
20.   **For** $w = 1$ to $l - 1$
   // Create the l-candidate can_i for C_i based on the $can_{ia}(a \in [1, n_i])$
21.   Create in can_i its wth candidate: $\bigcup_{a=1}^{n_i}$(the wth identifier in can_{ia});
22. **Let** $Can^l = \{can_i : 1 \leq i \leq n_c\}$;
23. **Return** Can^l;

Table 6: The RDA Algorithm

algorithm simply selects any $l - 1$ identifiers as their candidates from any compatible can_{ia}. The key difference from the RIA algorithm is that the RDA algorithm will not consider an identifier once it has selected its candidates, or been selected as a candidate, in most cases. This difference not only improves the data utility by minimizing the size of anonymized groups in the identifier partition, but also ensures the sets of candidates selected for different identifiers to be disjoint, which eliminates the need for the expensive merging process required by the RIA algorithm.

The RDA algorithm is shown in Table 6. Compared to RIA algorithm, RDA simply skips and does not reselect the $l - 1$ identifiers for the $l - 1$ candidates if the identifiers have been selected (line 7-8), and ensures that each identifier is not selected as candidates (line 9). Specifically, RDA algorithm first sets n_c, C_i, n_i, and S^C to be the number of colors, the ith color and its cardinality, and the sequence of colors in the non-increasing order of cardinality in t_0 respectively (line 1-3). Then, RDA iteratively selects $l - 1$ identifiers $can_{i,a}$ for each identifier $id_{i,a}$ in color C_i until the number of incomplete colors is less than l (line 4-13). Here C_i is the color which has the most number of incomplete identifiers in S^C. In each iteration, RDA first selects one incomplete color with most incomplete identifiers (line 5). Then for each of its incomplete identifiers, RDA forms can_{ia} by randomly selecting $(l - 1)$ incomplete identifiers from $(l - 1)$ different colors in S^C (line 9-10), and removes the completed colors from S^C, recounts n_c, and reorders the colors in S^C in the non-increasing order of the number of incomplete identifiers (line 11-12). Next, RDA forms can_{ia} for the remainder identifiers (line 14-18). In each iteration, RDA first selects any in-

complete identifier $id_{j,b}$ from the color C_j with the most number of incomplete identifiers (line 15) , and then forms can_{jb} by collecting any $l - 1$ identifiers from any compatible can_{ia} with smallest size (line 16-17). Finally, all the can_i for each color form the set Can^l of l-candidates, and RDA terminates and returns Can^l (line 19-23).

Note that, we can derive the minimal self-contained partition directly through the bijections in the l-candidates. In other words, each can_{ia} is a transient group (see proof of Lemma 1) for minimal self-contained partition, furthermore, it is the anonymized group in minimal self-contained partition when the intersection between any two can_{ia} is empty. Actually, the construction of the set of l-candidate based on can_{ia}s (Line 19-22 in RDA algorithm) is only used to prove its existence. Therefore, in order to ensure that can_{ia}s are disjoint, line 16-17 can be replaced by: Append $id_{j,b}$ to its compatible can_{ia} with the minimal cardinality. Since can_{ia}s are disjoint, the merge process in Table 9 can be bypassed. This will reduce the computational complexity and improve the data utility under certain type of utility measures based on the size of the QI-groups, such as DM.

Furthermore, we show that the computational complexity of Line 9-12 is linear in l. First, the remainder colors in S^C are incomplete, and we can also design certain additional data structure to store the incomplete identifiers in each incomplete color and record the cardinality. Therefore, Line 9-10 can be processed in time linear in l. Second, since after Line 9-10, only $l - 1$ colors (besides color C_i) are affected and their cardinality is only reduced by 1, Line 11-12 also can be processed in time linear in l with the assistance of additional structure. Based on previous discussions, the computational complexity of RDA algorithm is $O(n)$. First, Line 1-3 runs in $O(n)$ time by applying bucket sort (Additionally, $n_c << n$ holds for general cases in real world). Second, from Line 4-17, each identifier in the micro-data table is considered once all through the process with the assistance of additional data structure. We will evaluate utility of the RDA algorithm through experiments in the next section.

3.3 The GDA Algorithm (Guided and Dependent)

For both the RIA and RDA algorithms, we have assumed that the utility metric is independent of the actual quasi-identifier values. Our intention of designing the GDA algorithm is to demonstrate how our approach also allows designing algorithms that optimize data utility based on actual quasi-identifier values. For this purpose, assuming the quasi-identifier is composed of attributes $q_1, q_2, \ldots, q_d$, we assign an integer *weight* $weight_i$ to each attribute $q_i (i \in [1, d])$, and a rank $rank \in [1, |q_i|]$ to each value of the attribute q_i. Given any tuple t_a in the micro-data table t_0 and its value of each quasi-identifier attribute $t_a[q_i]$, we define its *weighted-rank* as $wr_a = \sum_{i=1}^{d} (weight_i \times rank(t_a[q_i]))$. Given any two tuples t_a and t_b, we define their *QI-distance* as $d_{ab} = |wr_a - wr_b|$. Also, given a tuple t_a and a set of tuples t_B, we define the *average QI-distance* as $d_{aB} = \frac{\sum_{b \in t_B} (d_{ab})}{|t_B|}$. Intuitively, a smaller QI-distance indicates that placing the two tuples into the same anonymized group will produce better data utility (for example, patients from the same geographical region should be grouped together).

Roughly speaking, for each incomplete identifier $id_{i,a}$ in the color C_i with the most incomplete identifiers, the algorithm determines $l - 1$ incomplete colors that can minimize the QI-distance between their first incomplete identifier with the largest weighted-rank and $id_{i,a}$, and then selects these $l - 1$ identifiers to be the $l - 1$ candidates for $id_{i,a}$, until the number of incomplete colors is less than l. For each remainder identifier $id_{j,b}$, GDA selects $(l - 1)$ identifiers from its compatible can_{ia} which has the smallest average QI-distance from $id_{j,b}$.

The GDA algorithm is shown in Table 7. Given a micro-data table t_0 and an integer l, GDA first initialize the following: Set n_c, C_i, n_i, and S^C to be the number of colors, the ith color and its cardinality, and the sequence of colors in the non-increasing order of cardinality in t_0 respectively (line 1-3); Compute the weighted-rank for each identifier (tuple) based on its quasi-identifier information (line 4); Sort the identifiers inside a color in ascending order of their weighted-rank values (line 5). After that, GDA iteratively constructs can_{ia} for each identifier in the micro-table t_0 (line 6-11). In each iteration, GDA repeatedly selects $l - 1$ identifiers can_{ia} for each identifier $id_{i,a}$ in color C_i. For each identifier $id_{i,a}$, we select the $l - 1$ best colors among the whole set of colors other than C_i itself. To judge the best colors, we compare the QI-distance between the QI-attributes of $id_{i,a}$ and the first identifier in each color which is not yet mapped to any identifier in C_i. The less the QI-distance is, the better the identifier is. Finally, all the can_i for each color forms the set Can^l of l-candidates, and GDA terminates and returns Can^l (line 12-16). From the description above, the selection of l-candidate for each color is further decided by the selection of $l - 1$ identifiers for each of its identifier, which in turn are selected based on the QI-distance, it is, the local optimization. Therefore, the transient groups are expected to be closer with regard to the QI-attributes, which may increase the data utility. However, this approach cannot assure the size of the anonymized group since there

may exists many merges when construct the locally-minimal partition based on such set of l-candidates.

The computational complexity of GDA algorithm is $O(n \log n)$ since after sorting each color based on the weighted-rank values, each identifier is processed only once throughout the process of building l-candidates. Since this algorithm aims at minimizing the average QI-distance inside each anonymized group, we will evaluate its data utility in the next section based on such a quasi-identifier value-dependent metric.

3.4 The Construction of SGSS

Remind that our ultimate objective is to construct strongly globally safe set (SGSS) in which the data utility is optimized later. Once Can^l has been constructed by RIA, RDA, or GDA algorithm, in this paper we adopt the approach based on the corresponding bijections in Can^l to building the minimal self-contained partition and then the SGSS.

More specifically, for RDA and GDA algorithms, each can_{ia}, created in step 10 in Table 6 and in step 9 in Table 7 respectively, forms an anonymized group. Then we simply append the $id_{j,b}$, in step 15 in Table 6 and in step 11 in Table 7 respectively, to the selected can_{ia}. Similarly, for RIA algorithm, each can_{ia} created in step 6 in Table 5 forms an anonymized group, and we then merge the resultant anonymized groups which have common identifiers to be disjoint sets. The algorithms in the literature to achieve disjoint sets are applicable for our problem and the details are omitted here.

For the experiments in Section 4, we integrate the process in building the minimal self-contained partitions into the algorithms of constructing Can^l for RDA and GDA algorithms.

4. EXPERIMENTS

In this section, we evaluate the efficiency and utility of our proposed algorithms through experiments. To compare our results to that reported in [28], our experimental setting is similar to theirs. We adopt two real-world datasets, OCC and SAL, at the Integrated Public Use Micro-data Series [21]. Each dataset contains 600k tuples. The domain sizes of the six chosen attributes of both datasets are shown in Table 8. Among these, we select four attributes, *Age*, *Gender*, *Education*, and *Birthplace*, as the QI-attributes for both datasets, and we select *Occupation* and *Income* as the sensitive attribute for OCC and SAL, respectively. For our experiment, we adopt the *MBR* (*Minimum Bounding Rectangle*) function (similar to that in [28]) to generalize QI-values within the same anonymized group once we obtain an identifier partition using our algorithms. As mentioned before, the RIA algorithm is only introduced to demonstrate how simple an algorithm can be by following our approach, we will not evaluate its performance, but only focus on the RDA and GDA algorithm. In fact, in these two algorithms, each can_{ia} forms an anonymized group (transient group), and for the remainder identifiers shown in step 6 in Table 6 and step 7 in Table 7 are simply appended in the selected compatible anonymized groups (Step 19-22 in Table 6 and step 12-15 in Table 7 are used to represent the l-candidates). All experiments are conducted on a computer equipped with a 1.86GHz Core Duo CPU and 1GB memory.

Attribute	Age	Gender	Education	Birthplace	Occupation	Income
Domain Size	79	2	17	57	50	50

Table 8: Description of OCC and SAL Datasets

We evaluate computational complexity using execution time, and evaluate data utility of the released table using two measurements:

199

Input: an l-eligible table t_0, the privacy property l;
Output: the set Can^l of l-candidates for each color;
Method:
1. **Let** n_c be the number of colors in t_0;
2. **Let** S^C be the sequence of the colors in the non-increasing order of their cardinality;
3. **Let** C_i, n_i $(i \in [1, n_c])$ be the ith color and its cardinality;
4. Compute the weighted-rank for each tuple in the table t_0;
5. Sort the tuples in each color in ascending order of their weighted-rank values;
6. **While** $(n_c \geq l)$
7.   **Let** C_i be the color with the most incomplete identifiers;
8.   **For** each incomplete identifier $id_{i,a}$ in C_i
9.   Create can_{ia} by selecting $l - 1$ *incomplete* identifiers from the first $l - 1$ colors that minimize the QI-distance between their first and $id_{i,a}$;
10.   **For** each incomplete identifier $id_{j,b}$
11.   Create can_{jb} by selecting $l - 1$ identifiers with minimal QI-distance from compatible can_{ia} with the least average QI-distance;
12. **For** $i = 1$ to n_c
13.   **For** $w = 1$ to $l - 1$
         // Create the l-candidate can_i for C_i based on the $can_{ia}(a \in [1, n_i])$
14.   Create in can_i its wth candidate: $\bigcup_{a=1}^{n_i}($ the wth identifier in $can_{ia})$;
15. **Let** $Can^l = \{can_i : 1 \leq i \leq n_c\}$;
16. **Return** Can^l;

Table 7: The GDA Algorithm

Discernibility Metric (DM) [4] and Query Workload Error (QWE, which is a utility metric that depends on quasi-identifier values) [14].

4.1 Computation Overhead

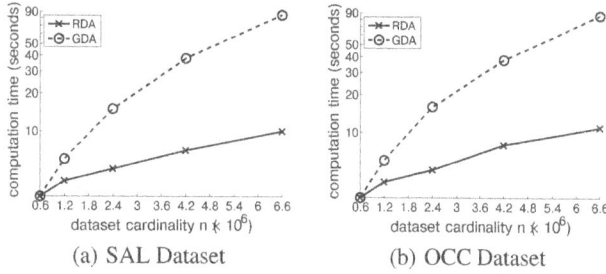

(a) SAL Dataset   (b) OCC Dataset

Figure 1: Execution Time vs. Dataset Cardinality n

Figure 1 illustrates the computation time of both of our algorithms on both datasets against the dataset cardinality n. We generate n-tuple datasets by synthesizing $\frac{n}{600k}$ copies of OCC, SAL respectively (Reminder that both OCC and SAL contain 600k tuples). We set $l = 8$ for this set of experiments, and conduct the experiment 100 times and then take the average. From the results, it is clear that both of our algorithms are practically efficient, and the computation time increases slowly with n. The RDA algorithm is slightly more efficient than GDA. This is because, when selecting candidates for each identifier, RDA considers the $l - 1$ colors with the most incomplete identifiers while GDA considers the $l - 1$ colors whose incomplete identifiers have the least QI-distances. Therefore, the more complex computation required by the GDA algorithm results in slightly more overhead than RDA. *Comparing to Results in [28]* In contrast to the results reported in [28], both of our algorithms are more efficient, while the RDA algorithm requires significantly less time than that in [28]. Although not reported here due to space limitations, we have also

investigated the computation time against l as well as the number of QI-attributes. Both algorithms are insensitive to these two parameters. This is as expected since the computation complexity of both algorithms only depends on the cardinality of dataset n.

4.2 Data Utility

We first conduct a set of experiments on the original SAL and OCC dataset to evaluate the utility of released tables measured by the *DM* metric. Figure 2 shows the DM cost (the lower cost the better utility) of each algorithm against l. From the results, we can see that the DM cost of our RDA algorithm is very close to the optimal cost (calculated using a separate algorithm), while the DM cost of the GDA algorithm is only slightly higher than the optimal cost. This is as expected, because the RDA algorithm is specifically designed for a general-purpose utility metric that aims to minimize the size of each anonymized group regardless of actual quasi-identifier values, whereas the GDA algorithm will attempt to minimize the QI-distance (the assignment of weight and rank for the GDA algorithm is described below).

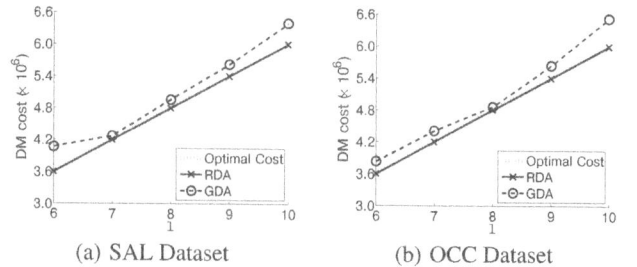

(a) SAL Dataset   (b) OCC Dataset

Figure 2: Data Utility Comparison: DM Cost vs. l

Following [28], we then evaluate the query workload error (QWE) by answering count queries. The intention is to compare our algorithms with a utility metric that depends on the actual quasi-identifier values. For this purpose, predicates on QI-attributes are constructed on *Age*, *Gender*, with an *and* operations between them, and with an *and* operations between all the QI-attributes, respectively. We set *weight* to be 1,10000,1, and 1 for *Age*, *Gender*, *Education*, and *Birthplace*, respectively. By processing 1000 randomly-generated queries for each type of predicates, we intend to investigate how well the released table preserves the R_{qs} relation. For each query, we first obtain its accurate answer *acc* from the original micro-data table, and then adopt the approximation technique in [14] to compute the approximate answer *app* from the released table output by our algorithms. The error of an approximate answer is formulated as $\frac{|acc-app|}{max\{acc,\delta\}}$ [28], where δ is set to 0.5% of the dataset cardinality. Then, the average error of all queries is taken as the QWE.

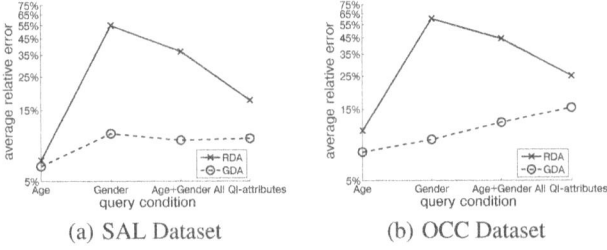

(a) SAL Dataset   (b) OCC Dataset

Figure 3: Data Utility Comparison: Query Accuracy vs. Query Condition($l = 6$)

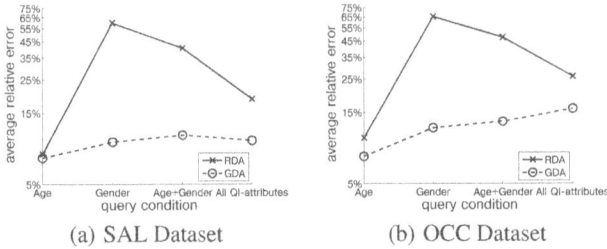

(a) SAL Dataset   (b) OCC Dataset

Figure 4: Data Utility Comparison: Query Accuracy vs. Query Condition($l = 7$)

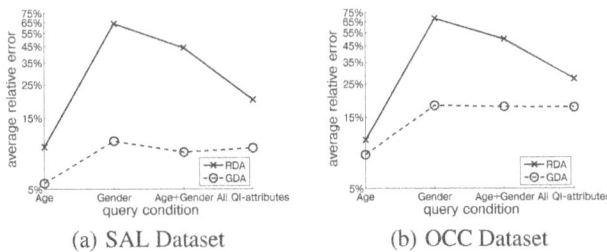

(a) SAL Dataset   (b) OCC Dataset

Figure 5: Data Utility Comparison: Query Accuracy vs. Query Condition($l = 8$)

Figures 3, 4, 5, 6, and 7 show the average relative error against different types of predicates for $l = 6, 7, 8, 9$ and 10 respectively. Compared to RDA, GDA now has better utility, which is as expected since GDA does consider the actual quasi-identifier values in generating the identifier partition, as mentioned in Section 3.

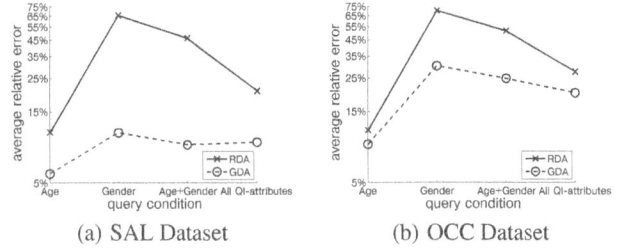

(a) SAL Dataset   (b) OCC Dataset

Figure 6: Data Utility Comparison: Query Accuracy vs. Query Condition($l = 9$)

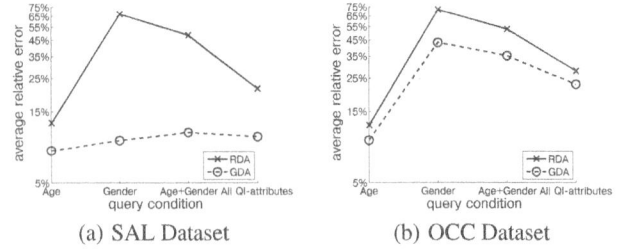

(a) SAL Dataset   (b) OCC Dataset

Figure 7: Data Utility Comparison: Query Accuracy vs. Query Condition($l = 10$)

Particularly, the average relative error for querying on SAL and OCC with *Gender* as the only query condition for $l = 8$ is reduced from 64%, 69% (of RDA) to 10%, 18%, respectively. Finally, although not reported here due to space limitations, the utility result of our algorithms measured by QWE are close to the results reported in [28] (no result based on DM was reported there).

5. DISCUSSION

Possible Extensions In this paper, we have focused on applying the self-contained property on l-candidates to build sets of identifier partitions satisfying the l-cover property, and hence to construct the SGSS. However, there may in fact exist many other methods to construct the SGSS, which will lead to potential directions of future work. First, there are different ways for building the l-candidates for each color. As discussed above, theoretically any subset of $\mathcal{I}$ satisfying the constraints shown in Lemma 3 can be a valid candidate for a color, and $l - 1$ such subsets together with that color will form a valid l-candidate for that color if they satisfy the constraints shown in Theorem 2. Second, once l-candidates are given, there still exist different ways, including applying the self-contained property, for constructing sets of identifiers to satisfy the l-cover property. Third, even the l-cover property is not necessarily the only valid way for directly building the SGSS. Finally, although we have focused on l-diversity and the utility measures DM and QWE, the principle of decoupling utility optimization from privacy preservation can potentially be applied to other privacy applications to yield efficient solutions.

Practicality of Our Approach We have demonstrated the practicality of our approach by showing through complexity analysis and experiments that our proposed algorithms are efficient enough to be applied to real world applications. It is important to note that it would be unfair to compare the performance of our algorithms to many existing algorithms that ignore the issue of privacy breaches caused by adversarial knowledge about algorithms [23, 10]. As to utility, as discussed earlier, our proposed algorithms produce results comparable to existing methods. We believe the flexibility of our approach may lead to other algorithms with further improved utility. For the QWE metric, note that our experiments only evaluate the QWE cost on the minimal self-contained partition. The utility may be increased by fine-tuning the weight information for each quasi-identifier, and by optimizing among the family set. We will conduct more experimental comparisons in terms of performance and utility between our algorithms and the traditional approaches in our future work.

The Focus on Syntactic Privacy Principles We have focused on syntactic privacy principles and methods, such as l-diversity and generalization, in this paper. However, the general approach of decoupling utility optimization from privacy preservation is not necessarily limited to such a scope. In particular, one interesting issue is to consider its applicability to differential privacy [6], which is being accepted as one of the strongest privacy models and extended to privacy preserving data publishing [17]. On the other hand, since most existing approaches that ensure differential privacy are random noise-based and are suitable for specific types of statistical queries, we have regarded this direction as future work.

6. RELATED WORK

The privacy preserving issue has received significant attentions in many different domains, including micro-data release [9, 22, 6], mobile network [8], social network [7, 20], and other web applications [3, 5]. In the context of privacy-preserving micro-data release, since the introduction of the k-anonymity concept [22], much effort has been made on developing efficient privacy-preserving algorithms [1, 2, 22, 13], Meanwhile many other models are also proposed to enhance the k-anonymity model, such as l-diversity [19], t-closeness [16], differential privacy [6], and so on. In particular, differential privacy [6] aims to achieve the goal that the probability distribution of any disclosed information should be similar enough regardless of whether that disclosed information is obtained using the real database, or using a database without any one of the existing records. Our future work will attempt to apply the proposed approach to other domains and privacy properties.

While many existing work assume the released generalization to be the only source of information available to an adversary, recent work [29, 25] show that this is actually not the case. In addition to the information that can be obtained from the actual released generalization, adversaries may also infer more information about private data by reasoning about how the generalization algorithm optimizes the data utility while satisfying the privacy property. With such extra inferred information, the adversary may eventually violate the privacy property. In the work of [29] [25], the authors discover the above problem and correspondingly introduce models and algorithms to address the issue. However, the method in [25] is still vulnerable to algorithm-based disclosure [11], whereas the one in [29] incurs a prohibitive complexity. To improve the efficiency, a so-called exclusive strategy is proposed in [30] to penalize the cases where a recursive process is required to compute the adversarial mental image about the micro-data table. More generally, a k-jump strategy is proposed in [18] to penalize such cases where with more control in the sense that only k, instead of all, generalization functions will be skipped. Despite the improved efficiency, most of those methods are still impractical due to the high complexity.

We have previously reported the preliminary idea of our proposed approach and the concept of l-cover in [31], which has been reviewed in Section 1 and Section 2.1 to make our paper more self-contained. However, no concrete methods for building identifier partitions that can satisfy the l-cover property was reported in [31], which is the main focus of this paper. Finally, the authors of [28] introduce algorithms that share the same spirit with our algorithms, and can achieve similar performance (more precisely, their algorithms are slightly less efficient than ours since their time complexity is $O(n^2 log n)$). In fact, under slight modification, their algorithms, such as ACE algorithm which is originally intended to publish dynamic datasets[27], can be regarded as another instantiation of our model and approach. This further confirms the correctness and flexibility of our approach.

7. CONCLUSION

In this paper, we have proposed a *privacy streamliner* approach for privacy-preserving applications. We reported theoretical results required for instantiating this approach in the context of privacy-preserving micro-data release using public algorithms. We have also designed three such algorithms by following the proposed approach, which not only yield practical solutions by themselves but also reveal the possibilities for a large number of algorithms that can be designed for specific utility metrics and applications. Our experiments with real datasets have proved our proposed algorithms to be practical in terms of both efficiency and data utility. Our future work will apply the proposed approach to other privacy-preserving applications and privacy properties in order to develop efficient algorithms.

Acknowledgment

The authors thank the anonymous reviewers for their valuable comments. The authors also thank Prof. Xiaokui Xiao (Nanyang Technological University, Singapore) for his help regarding experiments. This material is based upon work partially supported by Natural Sciences and Engineering Research Council of Canada under Discovery Grant N01035, Fonds de recherche sur la nature et les technologies, and Canada Graduate Scholarship.

8. REFERENCES

[1] Gagan Aggarwal, Tomás Feder, Krishnaram Kenthapadi, Rajeev Motwani, Rina Panigrahy, Dilys Thomas, and An Zhu. k-anonymity: Algorithms and hardness. Technical report, Stanford University, 2004.

[2] Gagan Aggarwal, Tomás Feder, Krishnaram Kenthapadi, Rajeev Motwani, Rina Panigrahy, Dilys Thomas, and An Zhu. Anonymizing tables. In *ICDT '05*, pages 246–258, 2005.

[3] Michael Backes, Goran Doychev, Markus Dürmuth, and Boris Köpf. Speaker recognition in encrypted voice streams. In *ESORICS '10*, pages 508–523, 2010.

[4] Roberto J. Bayardo and Rakesh Agrawal. Data privacy through optimal k-anonymization. In *ICDE '05*, pages 217–228, 2005.

[5] Shuo Chen, Rui Wang, XiaoFeng Wang, and Kehuan Zhang. Side-channel leaks in web applications: A reality today, a challenge tomorrow. In *IEEE Symposium on Security and Privacy '10*, pages 191–206, 2010.

[6] Cynthia Dwork. Differential privacy. In *ICALP (2)*, pages 1–12, 2006.

[7] Philip W. L. Fong, Mohd Anwar, and Zhen Zhao. A privacy preservation model for facebook-style social network systems. In *ESORICS '09*, pages 303–320, 2009.

[8] Julien Freudiger, Mohammad Hossein Manshaei, Jean-Pierre Hubaux, and David C. Parkes. On non-cooperative location privacy: a game-theoretic analysis. In *CCS '09*, pages 324–337, 2009.

[9] B. C. M. Fung, K. Wang, R. Chen, and P. S. Yu. Privacy-preserving data publishing: A survey of recent developments. *ACM Computing Surveys*, 42(4):14:1–14:53, June 2010.

[10] Benjamin C. M. Fung, Ke Wang, and Philip S. Yu. Top-down specialization for information and privacy preservation. In *ICDE '05*, pages 205–216, 2005.

[11] Xin Jin, Nan Zhang, and Gautam Das. Algorithm-safe privacy-preserving data publishing. In *EDBT '10*, pages 633–644, 2010.

[12] K.Kenthapadi, N.Mishra, and K.Nissim. Simulatable auditing. In *PODS*, pages 118–127, 2005.

[13] Kristen LeFevre, David J. DeWitt, and Raghu Ramakrishnan. Incognito: Efficient fulldomain k-anonymity. In *SIGMOD '05*, pages 49–60, 2005.

[14] Kristen LeFevre, David J. DeWitt, and Raghu Ramakrishnan. Mondrian multidimensional k-anonymity. In *ICDE '06*, page 25, 2006.

[15] L.H.Cox. Suppression, methodology and statistical disclosure control. *J. of the American Statistical Association*, pages 377– 385, 1995.

[16] Ninghui Li, Tiancheng Li, and Suresh Venkatasubramanian. t-closeness: Privacy beyond k-anonymity and l-diversity. In *ICDE '07*, pages 106–115, 2007.

[17] Ninghui Li, Wahbeh H. Qardaji, and Dong Su. Provably private data anonymization: Or, k-anonymity meets differential privacy. *CoRR*, abs/1101.2604, 2011.

[18] Wen Ming Liu, Lingyu Wang, and Lei Zhang. k-jump strategy for preserving privacy in micro-data disclosure. In *ICDT '10*, pages 104–115, 2010.

[19] Ashwin Machanavajjhala, Daniel Kifer, Johannes Gehrke, and Muthuramakrishnan Venkitasubramaniam. L-diversity: Privacy beyond k-anonymity. *ACM Trans. Knowl. Discov. Data*, 1(1):3, 2007.

[20] Arvind Narayanan and Vitaly Shmatikov. De-anonymizing social networks. In *IEEE Symposium on Security and Privacy '09*, pages 173–187, 2009.

[21] Steven Ruggles, Matthew Sobek, J. Trent Alexander, Catherine Fitch, Ronald Goeken, Patricia Kelly Hall, Miriam King, and Chad Ronnander. Integrated public use microdata series: Version 3.0. http://ipums.org, 2004.

[22] Pierangela Samarati. Protecting respondents' identities in microdata release. *IEEE Trans. on Knowl. and Data Eng.*, 13(6):1010–1027, 2001.

[23] Ke Wang, Philip S. Yu, and Sourav Chakraborty. Bottom-up generalization: A data mining solution to privacy protection. In *ICDM '04*, pages 249–256, 2004.

[24] Raymond Chi-Wing Wong and Ada Wai-Chee Fu. *Privacy-Preserving Data Publishing: An Overview*. Morgan and Claypool Publishers, 2010.

[25] Raymond Chi-Wing Wong, Ada Wai-Chee Fu, Ke Wang, and Jian Pei. Minimality attack in privacy preserving data publishing. In *VLDB '07*, pages 543–554, 2007.

[26] Xiaokui Xiao and Yufei Tao. Anatomy: simple and effective privacy preservation. In *VLDB '06*, pages 139–150, 2006.

[27] Xiaokui Xiao and Yufei Tao. M-invariance: towards privacy preserving re-publication of dynamic datasets. In *SIGMOD '07*, pages 689–700, 2007.

[28] Xiaokui Xiao, Yufei Tao, and Nick Koudas. Transparent anonymization: Thwarting adversaries who know the algorithm. *ACM Trans. Database Syst.*, 35(2):1–48, 2010.

[29] Lei Zhang, Sushil Jajodia, and Alexander Brodsky. Information disclosure under realistic assumptions: privacy versus optimality. In *CCS '07*, pages 573–583, 2007.

[30] Lei Zhang, Lingyu Wang, Sushil Jajodia, and Alexander Brodsky. Exclusive strategy for generalization algorithms in micro-data disclosure. In *DBSec '08*, pages 190–204, 2008.

[31] Lei Zhang, Lingyu Wang, Sushil Jajodia, and Alexander Brodsky. L-cover: Preserving diversity by anonymity. In *SDM '09*, pages 158–171, 2009.

Appendix

A. DEFINITIONS OF COVER, L-COVER AND THEIR EXAMPLE

DEFINITION 4 (COVER). *We say $ids_1, ids_2 \subseteq \mathcal{I}$ are cover for each other with respect to a set $S^P \subseteq ss^l$, if*

- $ids_1 \cap ids_2 = \emptyset$, *and*
- *there exist a bijection $f : ids_1 \rightarrow ids_2$ such that for any $ids_x \in P_i$, $P_i \in S^P$, there always exists $P_j \in S^P$ satisfying $ids_x \setminus (ids_1 \cup ids_2) \cup f(ids_x \cap ids_1) \cup f^{-1}(ids_x \cap ids_2) \in P_j$ [31].*

DEFINITION 5 (L-COVER). *We say a set $S^P \subseteq ss^l$ satisfies the l-cover property, if every color C has at least $l - 1$ covers $ids_i (i \in [1, l-1])$ with the bijections f_i satisfying that*

- *for any $id \in C$, each $f_i(id)$ $(i \in [1, l-1])$ is from a different color, and*
- *for any $ids_x \in P$ and $P \in S^P$, we have $|ids_x \cap C| = |ids_x \cap ids_i| (i \in [1, l-1])$ [31].*

EXAMPLE 5. *Continuing Example 2 and considering $S^P = \{P_1, P_3\}$, the colors $C_1 = \{id_1, id_2\}$ and $C_2 = \{id_3, id_4\}$ provide cover for each other, since for C_1 we have $f_1(id_1) = id_3$ and $f_1(id_2) = id_4$, and for C_2 we have $f_2(id_3) = id_1$ and $f_2(id_4) = id_2$. Further, S^P satisfies the l-cover property where $\{C_1, C_2\}$ is the l-cover of both C_1 and C_2.*

Similarly, for $S^P = \{P_2, P_3\}$, C_1 and C_2 provide cover for each other since for C_1 we have $f_1(id_1) = id_4$ and $f_1(id_2) = id_3$, and for C_2 we have $f_2(id_3) = id_2$ and $f_2(id_4) = id_1$. Further, S^P also satisfies the l-cover property. $\square$

B.1. PROOF OF LEMMA 1

PROOF. To prove the lemma, we first show the procedure *l-candidate-to-P^{lm}* in Table 9 based on the self-contained property to construct its minimal self-contained partition.

Input: an l-eligible table t_0, a collection of l-candidates Can^l
Output: the minimal self-contained partition;
Method:
1. Create a set of anonymized groups $S^G = \emptyset$;
2. **For** each color C_i
3.   **For** each $id_{i,a} \in C_i$
4.   Create in S^G a anonymized group
        $G_{i,d} = \{id_{i,a}\} \bigcup_{u=1}^{l-1} \{f_{i,u}(id_{i,a})\}$;
5. Merge the anonymized groups which have common identifiers to build minimal self-contained partition (P^{lm});
6. **Return** P^{lm};

Table 9: procedure: *l-candidate-to-P^{lm}*

Then, we show that $P^{lm} \in ss^l$. As shown in Table 9, to satisfy the self-contained property, for each identifier $id_{i,a}$ in each color C_i, the identifiers to which $id_{i,a}$ is mapped in each of the l-1 candidates should be in the same final anonymized group. We call such set of identifiers ,$G_{i,a} = \{id_{i,a}\} \bigcup_{u=1}^{l-1} \{f_{i,u}(id_{i,a})\}$, for a^{th} identifier in color C_i is *transient group*. Obviously, each transient group itself satisfies entropy l-diversity. Furthermore, based on the Definition 2, for any color C_i in the micro-data table, if an identifier $id_{i,a}$ in C_i is in the final anonymized group, then its whole transient group $G_{i,a}$ will be in the final anonymized group. In other words, in any final anonymized group G, the ratio of any identifier in any C_i associated with the sensitive value S_i equals to $\frac{|n_{C_i}|}{|n_{C_i}| \times l + \delta}$ where $\delta \geq 0$ and $|n_{C_i}|$ is the number of identifiers from color C_i in the anonymized group. Therefore, it is less than or equal to $\frac{|n_{C_i}|}{|n_{C_i}| \times l} = \frac{1}{l}$. Thus, each anonymized group in minimal self-contained partition satisfies l-diversity, so does the minimal self-contained partition. We have thus proved that $P^{lm} \in ss^l$.

Next, consider the $l-1$ covers for each color $C_i \in S^C$. Without loss of generality, we rewrite its corresponding l-candidate as $can_i^l = \{C_i, ids_{i,1}, ids_{i,2}, \ldots, ids_{i,l-1}\}$ so that C_i is the first element, we show that for the set of identifier partition P^{lm} ($|P^{lm}| = 1$), $ids_{i,1}, ids_{i,2}, \ldots ids_{i,l-1}$ are $l-1$ covers of C_i. By Definition 4, C_i and $ids_{i,u}(u \in [1, l-1])$ should satisfy following two conditions:

- $C_i \cap ids_{i,u} = \emptyset$, and

- there exists a bijection $f_{i,u} : C_i \to ids_{i,u}$ satisfying that for any $ids_x \in P^{lm}$, $ids_{x'} = ids_x \setminus (C_i \cup ids_{i,u})) \cup f_{i,u}(ids_x \cap C_i) \cup f_{i,u}^{-1}(ids_x \cap ids_{i,u}) \in P^{lm}$.

The first condition is satisfied by the definition of l-candidate. For the second condition, let the bijection $f_{i,u}$ be the corresponding bijection for $ids_{i,u}$ in the l-candidate can_i^l. It is obvious that $ids_{x'} = ids_x$. Therefore, the second condition also holds.

Finally, we further show that the previous $l-1$ covers of C_i satisfy the following three conditions defined in the definition of l-cover.

- $\forall (u \neq w), ids_{i,u} \cap ids_{i,w} = \emptyset$, and

- $\forall (id \in C_i)$, each $f_{i,u}(id)$ $(u \in 1, l-1])$ is from different color.

- $\forall (ids \in P^{lm}), |ids \cap C_i| = |ids \cap ids_{i,u}|$ $(u \in [1, l-1])$.

The first two conditions follow directly from the definition of l-candidate. The last condition is satisfied by the property of self-contained. In other words, given such P^{lm}, all colors have their l-covers, therefore, P^{lm} satisfies l-cover property. Thus we have proved the lemma. $\square$

B.2. PROOF OF LEMMA 2

PROOF. We prove by contradiction. First assume that there exist $G \in P$ and $ids_i \in P^{lm}$, such that $G \cap ids_i \neq \emptyset$ and $ids_i - G \neq \emptyset$. Then, due to $ids_i - G \neq \emptyset$, there must exist identifier $id_o \in ids_i$ such that $id_o \notin G$. Assume that $id_o \in G'$, where $(G' \in P) \wedge (G' \neq G)$. Moreover, due to $G \cap ids_i \neq \emptyset$, there also exists identifier $id_i \in ids_i$ such that $id_i \in G$. Thus there exist id_o and id_i which is a pair of identifiers for some bijection in Can^l, and $G \cap \{id_o, id_i\} = \{id_i\}$ and $G' \cap \{id_o, id_i\} = \{id_o\}$. However, By definition of *self-contained*, it has the following transitive property. That is, if $\{id_1, id_2\}, \{id_2, id_3\}, \ldots, \{id_{a-1}, id_a\}$ each pair satisfies that there exists bijections for the set of l-candidates such that $f_{i-1,i}(id_{i-1}) = id_i$ or $f_{i,i-1}(id_i) = id_{i-1}$. Then for any self-contained anonymized group G, either $G \cap \bigcup_{i=1}^{a}(id_i) = \emptyset$ or $G \supseteq$

$\bigcup_{i=1}^{a}(id_i)$. Thus by definition, since $id_o \in ids_i$ and $id_i \in ids_i$, $\forall (G \in P), G \cap \{id_o, id_i\} = \emptyset$ or $G \cap \{id_o, id_i\} = \{id_o, id_i\}$.

Therefore, neither G nor G' satisfies self-contained, so does P, leading to a contradiction. $\square$

B.3. PROOF OF THEOREM 1

PROOF. *First, we prove that any self-contained identifier partition P satisfies l-cover property.*

We first show that $P \in ss^l$. Note that the privacy model l-diversity satisfies the monotonicity property. That is, for any two anonymized groups G_1 and G_2 satisfying l-diversity, the final anonymized group derived by merging all tuples in G_1 and in G_2 satisfies l-diversity [24]. Based on Lemma 2, each anonymized group G in P satisfies $G = \bigcup_{X \subseteq \{1,2,\ldots,k\}} ids_X$. Therefore, each anonymized group G satisfies l-diversity, so does P.

Then we have proved that, given the l-candidate can_i^l of certain color C_i, the $can_i^l \setminus \{C_i\}$ are, the $l-1$ covers of C_i for P, similar to the proof of Lemma 1.

Finally, the set of $l-1$ set of identifiers $can_i^l \setminus \{C_i\}$ are $l-1$ covers of color C_i which satisfy the three conditions of l-cover definition.

Second, we prove any family set satisfies the l-cover property.

We first show that $\forall (P \in S^{fs}), P \in ss^l$. Since the privacy model l-diversity satisfies the monotonicity property [24], based on the definition of family set, it is clear that the table generalization corresponding to each identifier partition in S^{fs} satisfies l-diversity.

Similar with previous proofs, for each color $C_i \in S^C$ and its corresponding l-candidate $can_i^l = \{C_i, ids_{i,1}, ids_{i,2}, \ldots, ids_{i,l-1}\}$, we have proved that for the family set S^{fs}, $ids_{i,1}, ids_{i,2}, \ldots, ids_{i,l-1}$ are the $l-1$ covers of C_i. Moreover, these $l-1$ covers of C_i satisfy the three conditions of l-cover. This completes the proof. $\square$

B.4. PROOF OF LEMMA 3

PROOF. By the definition 1, C and ids should satisfy the following two conditions:

- $C \cap ids = \emptyset$ and $|C| = |ids|$;
- there exists a bijection $f : C \to ids$, such that $\forall (id \in C)$, id and $f(id)$ are from different colors.

The first condition follows directly from the condition of the lemma. Since $|C| = |ids|$, there must exist bijection $f : C \to ids$. Moreover, since $C \cap ids = \emptyset$, $\forall (id_x \in ids), id_x \notin C$, by the definition of color, id_x has sensitive value other than it of color C. In other words, id_x must belong to the other color C' other than C. Therefore, The second condition is also satisfied, which completes the proof. $\square$

B.5. PROOF OF LEMMA 4

PROOF. The first constraint in the lemma respectively guarantees the first condition of definition 1. Consider the second condition. Since $|ids_1| = |ids_2|$, there must exist bijections between ids_1 and ids_2. Assume that the second condition of definition 1 does not hold. Then there must exist at least $|ids_1| + 1$ number of identifiers in $ids_1 \cup ids_2$ with identical sensitive value, which is in contradiction with the second constraint in lemma. Therefore, the second condition of definition 1 also satisfies. Since the two conditions both hold, the proof is complete. $\square$

B.6. PROOF OF THEOREM 2

PROOF. To prove the theorem, we should show that any two sets of identifiers from the sets C and ids_x $(x \in [1, l-1])$ are candidate for each other. The fact that C and each ids_x $(x \in [1, l-1])$ are candidate follows the Lemma 3, while the fact any two ids_x, ids_y $((x, y \in [1, l-1]) \wedge (x \neq y))$ are candidate follows the Lemma 4. This completes the proof. $\square$

Privacy Analysis using Ontologies

Martin Kost
kost@informatik.hu-berlin.de

Johann-Christoph Freytag
freytag@informatik.hu-berlin.de

DBIS Group
Humboldt-Universität zu Berlin
Berlin, Germany

ABSTRACT

As information systems extensively exchange information between participants, privacy concerns may arise from potential misuse. Existing design approaches consider non-technical privacy requirements of different stakeholders during the design and the implementation of a system. However, a technical approach for privacy analysis is largely missing.

This paper introduces a formal approach for technically evaluating an information system with respect to its designed or implemented privacy protection. In particular, we introduce a system model that describes various system aspects such as its information flow. We define the semantics of this system model by using ontologies. Based on the system model together with a given privacy ontology, and given privacy requirements we analyze the modeled system to detect privacy leakages and to calculate privacy indicators. The proposed method provides a *technical* approach to check whether a system conforms to the privacy requirements of the stakeholders or not.

Categories and Subject Descriptors

D.2.1 [**Software Engineering**]: Requirements/Specifications; I.6.4 [**Simulation and Modeling**]: Model Validation and Analysis

General Terms

Design, Security, Verification

1. INTRODUCTION

Pervasive or ubiquitous computing is rapidly developing. Several services are already available by devices such as locators, routing systems, intelligent travel guides, or personal devices. Concurrently, the resulting pervasive environments offer new opportunities of abuse. Very often, components exchange data, which might raise privacy concerns. Adversaries might combine observed data to extract personal information and to identify the corresponding individuals.

In consequence, data protection authorities [4] call for the use of a Privacy-by-Design (PbD) approach to integrate privacy requirements into the overall design process. A PbD approach must ensure that privacy criteria are considered during all phases of the design and the implementation of a system. Several researchers already contributed towards a better technical support for PbD. Spiekermann and Cranor identify and contrast two approaches: privacy-by-architecture and privacy-by-policy [26]. Gürses et al. single out data minimization as the fundamental principle for PbD [10]. Kargl et al. describe a privacy policy enforcement system based on a protected distributed perimeter [15]. In [18], Kung et al. generally describe a PbD process applied to ICT (Information and Communication Technologies) applications based on the three principles of minimization, enforcement, and transparency. Despite all of these efforts, a comprehensive support for privacy requirements engineering, implementation, and verification is largely missing.

The challenge is therefore to come up with a technical privacy analysis approach which checks if a system conforms to privacy requirements defined by different stakeholders. Up to now, privacy analysis is mostly performed by hand in a process driven manner; e. g., manual review of non-technical specifications such as business processes, or code inspections. It is only applied to systems and applications in an isolated manner instead of performing a global analysis over all interactive systems together. The analysis results are subjective and therefore not comparable. Existing privacy preserving solutions, e. g., pay-as-you-drive insurance [27], are application and domain specific; the applied privacy analysis approaches cannot be reused easily. Today's privacy analysis approaches are not applicable to complex systems because they do not reflect technical details resulting from system design and implementation.

In summary, this paper makes the following contributions: 1.) Introducing a formal/technical approach for analyzing the information flow of a system in order to evaluate how the user's privacy is protected; 2.) Defining and calculating technical indicators for privacy evaluation; 3.) Analyzing privacy risk using technical privacy indicators; 4.) Automatically detecting violations of given (individual) privacy requirements; 5.) Performing privacy analysis in an application independent manner using domain specific semantics in form of ontologies. Using our approach potentially results in ICT systems that better implement the privacy requirements of different stakeholders.

The remainder of this paper is structured as follows: Section 2 presents an example scenario of the ITS (Intelligent Transportation Systems) domain to elaborate and describe open issues of existing approaches for privacy analysis. Section 3 introduces our technical approach of privacy analysis. Therefore, this section describes technologies and concepts, which may be used to create privacy requirements and to describe system models that define information necessary for performing the proposed analysis. We discuss expected results of the analysis in form of privacy violations, indicators, and given guarantees. Further, we integrate necessary process steps into the development process of applications. Section 4 explains how to express the required system models and privacy concepts using ontologies. Section 5 discusses how an implementation of our approach may use privacy ontologies for performing the technical privacy analysis of a system. Section 6 discusses related work.

2. OPEN PRIVACY ISSUES IN ITS

In this section, we elaborate and describe open issues of existing design approaches that only integrate a non-technical privacy analysis process. Within the project FP7 PRECIOSA project [3], we investigated several ITS applications such as emergency call, electronic tolling, pay as you drive insurance, online navigation, intersection collision detection, and more to derive common privacy requirements. Thereby, we applied a non-technical and a technical privacy analysis. Exemplary, we apply a non-technical privacy analysis process to a selected ITS scenario and highlight the shortcomings of the analysis result. We perform the following steps to apply a non-technical privacy analysis: First, we describe the overall scenario and its required functionalities. Second, we develop an abstract process description. Finally, we evaluate privacy principles to setup non-technical privacy requirements. Based on the analysis result, we identify open issues that result from the technical realization of the designed ITS scenario.

2.1 ITS Scenario and Process Description

The selected scenario supports ITS safety: Vehicles send beacon messages containing the current vehicle position to Roadside Units (RSUs) enabling services such as traffic monitoring and some safety applications like intersection collision warnings. Data processors, i.e., the RSU and the Traffic Control Center (TCC), process personal information including the current location of every car and therefore of every driver. Thus, (on behalf of the data controller) the application designer or the data protection supervisor has to identify general privacy requirements that are application or domain independent as well as domain specific ones.

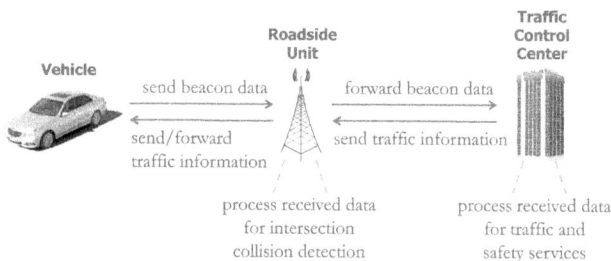

Figure 1: Business Process of ITS Scenario.

Privacy Principle	Resulting Privacy Requirements
1. *Purpose Specification*	**Beacon data** will only be used with the **purpose** of intersection collision detection, traffic monitoring, traffic control, and to **inform about critical events**;
2. *Consent*	The vehicle driver has to **agree** with the use of his/her beacon data for the **specified purposes**; if the driver revokes his agreement the data will no longer be used;
3. *Limited Collection*	**Beacon data** will be **limited** for communication, storage, and collection **to the minimum** necessary for accomplishing the specified purposes;
4. *Limited Use*	RSU and TCC execute **only** those **operations** on the beacon data that are **consistent** with the **purposes** for which the data was collected, stored, and communicated;
5. *Limited Disclosure*	**Beacon data** will **not** be **communicated** outside the system for purposes other than those for which the driver gave his/her consent;
6. *Limited Retention*	Beacon data will be **retained** by the system only **as long as necessary**;
7. *Accuracy & Context Preservation*	Beacon data stored by the system will always be **accurate, up-to-date**, and never be decoupled from its **context** and **purpose**;
8. *Security*	Beacon data will be protected by appropriate **security measures** against unauthorized use;
9. *Openness*	The driver will be able to **access all information** that is stored in the system which is **related** to him/her;
10. *Compliance*	The driver will—directly or indirectly—be able to **verify** the **compliance** of the system with the above principles;

Table 1: Application of Privacy Principles.

Given the above-described scenario, the application designer identifies the application requirements and develops an abstract process description (see Figure 1). In our example, the ITS scenario consists of three actors which communicate with each other; these are vehicles, RSUs, and a TCC. The RSU acts as a mediator between vehicles and the TCC. Furthermore, the RSU calculates events of impacting collisions. It requires every vehicle to send its location and a time stamp periodically using a short time interval. The TCC requires additional information such as road condition; e.g., slippery road segments, to monitor the traffic. Monitoring the traffic includes detecting and communicating critical events, or predicting and controlling the traffic flow; e.g., detect emerging traffic jams in order to avoid them.

2.2 Non-technical Privacy Analysis

Application designers evaluate the developed abstract process description of their application in order to identify privacy issues. Non-technical privacy analyses such as *Privacy Impact Assessment* [20] take privacy principles and regulations as input to create a set of questions. The answers form privacy impact assessments that assist managers and decision-makers to avoid or mitigate privacy risks and to determine the best design choice. In Table 1, we exemplary

Technical Aspects	Resulting Privacy Issues
1. **Complexity**: processing and combining plenty of non personal information;	1. May **produce personal identifiable information**;
2. **Adding** (the processing of) technical **information** such as IDs, time, and location;	2. May lead to **tracking** of individuals; e. g., location tracking profiles;
3. **Optimization** of costs and performance leads to consolidation of infrastructure such as data stores and data tables;	3. **Violation of isolation principle** may arise if components implement multiple applications or communicate with other components;
4. **Refining design** decisions which extends the information flow; gathering current vehicle location via mobile phone instead of using smart devices to raise reliability in regions with sparse infrastructure or because of energy consumption limits;	4. **New personal information is processed** to get current location of vehicle—may require other (configuration of) PETs (Privacy Enhancing Technologies); e. g., anonymization;
5. **Caching** of intermediate results; e. g., the mobile phone data, because of performance issues;	5. Raises issue of **limited retention** which could not be detected beforehand;

Table 2: New Privacy Issues resulting from Implementation.

select and evaluate ten privacy principles (based on [5] and [14]) to derive privacy requirements.

Afterwards, the application designer takes the abstract process description and the identified application requirements to design a formal system model. Thereby, he derives technical privacy requirements from the identified non-technical privacy requirements in Table 1. For instance, we may derive the requirement to exchange vehicle ids, e. g., license plates, with dynamic pseudonyms; or we may limit the data which is sent to vehicles as warning messages; for instance, by obfuscating the event location with an obfuscation range of 20 meters.

2.3 Arising technical Privacy Issues

After designing the system model, designers and developers spend several iterations implementing and redesigning the software model. During these iterations they identify new technical requirements, modify existing ones, and implement the modifications. Up to now, these iterations usually do not consider identifying and refining privacy requirements. In Table 2, we give some examples how an implementation may introduce new privacy issues that are impossible or at least difficult to detect beforehand.

Based on our evaluation, we conclude that a technical analysis should provide the following functionalities in order to address the identified privacy issues of Table 2:

- Identifying personal information—to detect privacy issues 1 and 4 of Table 2;

- Identifying personal identifiers—to detect 1;

- Identifying possible combining non-personal information to personal information and operations which create personal information—to detect 1, 2, and 3;

- Identifying operations which operate on personal information—to detect 5;

- Identifying components which perform operations on personal information (potentially collecting these information)—to detect 3 and 5;

- Identifying privacy threats in form of single operations or operation sequences which violate privacy requirements—to detect 2;

- Calculating additional privacy indicators such as values of privacy metrics for processed data—to detect 4;

- Checking a system model for its conformance with privacy requirements defining constraints on its design, deployment, and behavior such as obligations to use specific (configured) components/PETS—to detect 3.

In general, it is difficult to detect privacy-violating processing of personal information because information has several serialization forms. There exist different data type definitions, attribute names etc. for the same information. Information may be combined in different ways to derive new information that might be sensitive or identifying. We may describe location information using different a.) GPS formats, b.) expansions such as postal code, city name, or street name, c.) sights, d.) event bound locations, e.) persons which may be related to locations by different identifying information; for instance, a.) complete name, b.) nickname, c.) social role such as trainer of a football club, d.) relationships among (groups of) people such as living partners or teacher and their students at some school and more. To address these challenges we derive the following requirements for performing a technical privacy analysis:

1. **consider** the **concepts** behind the processed data items—abstract from data formats in the system model;

2. **classify** the **concepts** and **consider their relationships** such as generalization, part-of, equivalence;

3. **create** and **evaluate rules** to derive indirect and complex privacy aspects from described relationships.

In this section, we identified open privacy issues that result from realizing technical aspects of an information system. To address these issues we derived necessary functionalities and requirements that a technical privacy analysis must realize. We need to integrate different technologies in order to implement/support the derived functionalities. In addition, we have to coordinate the use of the functionalities by sophisticated process steps that must be integrated into the development lifecycle.

3. TECHNICAL PRIVACY ANALYSIS

In the previous section, we elaborated essential functionalities and requirements of a technical privacy analysis. Based on these results we propose technologies and concepts for realizing these functionalities and we coordinate necessary process steps. The described approach bases on work carried out within the two research projects FP7 PRECIOSA [3] and DESWAP [2]. First, we describe the general idea of our approach to support the assessment of privacy. Next, we describe methods that we may use to derive privacy requirements. We use these requirements to detect privacy violations by evaluating the system model. In addition we introduce privacy indicators to detect vulnerabilities of the system and to support the transparency of realized privacy

Figure 2: Privacy Assessment Cycle.

protection mechanisms. In order to evaluate a system regarding privacy we model system aspects; e. g., aspects describing the processing of data or the composition of the system. We introduce model elements for describing simple system models that comprise the most relevant aspects. In order to use a technical privacy analysis we must coordinate necessary process steps and integrate them into existing development processes. Further, we discuss the privacy guarantees we may get by applying the formal privacy analysis. At the end of this section, we describe how to define a common privacy vocabulary in order to addresses the requirements identified at end of Section 2.3.

3.1 Supporting Privacy Assessment

Our approach aims to analyze systems formally with respect to the implementation of privacy criteria. Therefore, we realize a *privacy assessment cycle* as shown in Figure 2. This cycle involves two groups of stakeholders: those with an interest in privacy protection, and those responsible for design and implementation. The former stakeholders identify their privacy needs on a non-technical level; e. g., using a PIA process [20]. The resulting privacy requirements include privacy criteria such as user preferences and privacy regulations. The latter stakeholders use these non-technical privacy requirements to translate them into technical privacy statements, to carry out the design and implementation of a system, and to evaluate the resulting system behavior and properties in order to calculate privacy indicators, i. e., evidence that the high-level privacy statements are met.

We suggest using a technical method for evaluating and verifying formally the implemented privacy protection solution with respect to the specified requirements. When applied during system design and system development, this approach could significantly increase the acceptance of the system by users.

3.2 Deriving Privacy Requirements

Our approach is based on the evaluation of specified privacy requirements. In general, it is a challenging task to specify requirements that reflect the interests of the stakeholders appropriately. In existing development processes, the application/system engineers often work together with the stakeholders for setting up and refining non-technical application requirements. Next, the engineers together with domain experts translate the non-technical into technical requirements. Requirements engineering technologies assist engineers for setting up and translating such requirements.

In particular, goal-driven requirements engineering employs goals (enhanced with descriptions of scenarios and purposes) to elicit, specify, analyze, and validate requirements [16]. The authors He and Anton applied this approach to privacy in the area of access control and permissions [12]. While restricted to Role Based Access Control (RBAC), they

provide a foundation that can be adapted to other privacy protection mechanisms as well. High-level privacy policies and requirements are expressed in the form of authorization rules. Major concepts to define privacy protection elements are purpose, condition, obligation, and context. Context constraints define restrictions on data purpose and privacy preferences such as the recipient of data or data retention period.

The creation of formal descriptions that define privacy constraints involves further aspects such as failures of a system or vulnerabilities. A goal-oriented approach is proposed by [7] including a risk analysis based on an attack/adversary model. This model is used to identify countermeasures and calculate the probability of the execution of an attack and its success. Attack trees are an established method for modeling security threats [21]. They have already been successfully utilized for the modeling of attacks on inter-vehicle communication systems [6].

Still open is the issue of formulating privacy requirements while addressing the requirements identified in Section 2.3 and to evaluate the effectiveness of applied realizations such as enforced access control policies.

3.3 Detecting Violations of Privacy Requirements

Privacy requirements may define constraints on systems and applications at different points in the development life cycle such as design, implementation, deployment, and runtime. In addition different groups of stakeholders define domain independent, domain specific, or application specific requirements. For instance, privacy principles are general (domain independent) requirements that engineers may consider for every application. As well as domain independent requirements, we must support to express application specific privacy requirements that were derived by refining domain independent requirements.

In our approach, we specify privacy requirements in form of privacy constraints. Privacy constraints are logical expressions that define conditions on properties derived from the system model. By evaluating privacy constraints for a given system model we detect privacy violations. We detect different forms of violations; e. g.:

- unrestricted or unpermitted operations on personal information;

- the violation of individual privacy preferences; e. g., out-of-range-values of privacy metrics or the violation of access control constraints;

- the absence of required security mechanisms such as encryption;

- the violation of privacy principles such as limited retention or data minimalisation, i. e., the identification of unnecessary computation of information which exceeds the assigned purposes.

We give a simplified example of the privacy principle *limited retention* formulated as privacy constraint:

> Violation of Limited Retention :=
>   creation of permanent data D *and*
>   (no obligation defined for removing D *or*
>   no remove operation is following)

We formulated the following user defined constraint in form of a privacy policy. The policy defines permissions to execute operations on selected data of the user. Thereby, the permissions are bound to a defined context that has to match with the context of the request. In our example, the context defines that the data can only be processed on a server node by the traffic state application. The policy permits to query the data and to retrieve the result if certain anonymity is guaranteed. We may get the required anonymity either by formulating a query that produces the required anonymity or by applying an anonymization function on the query result.

```
Context(node-type='server' and
    requestor='TrafficStateApp')
{
  Permit process-query On location, trafficstate,
    vehicle-type As query-result
  Permit retrieve On query-result With
    (k-anonymity > 10)
  Permit TableAnonymization(metric='k-anonymity',
    anonymity-value='10') On query-result
    Retrieve=true
}
```

3.4 Defining and Evaluating Indicators

Privacy indicators describe privacy aspects of the system such as identified personal information, combined personal information, operations on personal information, and components that perform such operations. Additionally, privacy indicators may consist of privacy metrics to calculate quantitative values such as degree of anonymity.

Privacy indicators are selected system properties that are domain or application independent. On the detailed/technical level, these indicators may reflect properties directly described by the system model. The selected properties mostly describe aspects of the performed data processing and the composition of the system. We use logic rules and metrics to calculate and to derive new indicators from the system model and other indicators. We further abstract system details to derive indicators that describe general system properties such as the number of performed operations on personal information or the number of components involved in executing a privacy relevant functionality. In this way, we may abstract the indicators up to non-technical indicators describing aspects such as privacy risk or the compliance of privacy principles.

Example of defining an architectural constraint that uses privacy indicators to restrict a distributed storing of personal information:

> PI := personal information
> NPPI := nodes containing components that process PI
> NSPI := nodes containing components that store PI
>
> if sizeof(NPPI) > 1 then
>   define constraint: NSPI $\leq$ 1

Example of a privacy indicator that describes the compliance of privacy principles:

> Violations of Privacy Principles :=
> {Violation of Limited Retention,
> Violation of Purpose Specification, ...}

Compliance of Privacy Principles :=
forall v *in* Violations of Privacy Principles: v = false;

Example of a simplified privacy indicator that calculates a privacy risk:

$$Privacy\ Risk := \frac{1}{Privacy\ Risk\ Aspects} \cdot$$
$$\left(\frac{Number\ of\ violated\ Privacy\ Principles}{Number\ of\ Privacy\ Principles} + \right.$$
$$\frac{NumViolPrcplFunc}{(NumPerfFunc * NumPrcpl)} +$$
$$\frac{Number\ of\ Operations\ on\ Personal\ Information}{Number\ of\ Operations} +$$
$$\frac{Average\ of\ (Anonymity\ of\ Processed\ Data\ Set}{Size\ of\ Processed\ Data\ Set} +$$
$$\frac{Average\ of\ (Anonymity\ of\ Stored\ Data\ Set}{Size\ of\ Stored\ Data\ Set} +$$
$$\left. \frac{Number\ of\ Vulnerabilities}{(NumPerfOpPI + NumCompExcOpPI)} \right)$$

where:

NumViolPrcplFunc := Number of violated Privacy Principles of performed Functionalities
NumPerfFunc := Number of performed Functionalities
NumPrcpl := Number of Privacy Principles
NumPerfOpPI := Number of performed Operations on Personal Information
NumCompExcOpPI := Number of Components which execute operations on Personal Information

By evaluating the calculated privacy indicators we may a.) detect and address privacy leakages; e. g., the publication of personalized location information, b.) calculate the privacy risk or privacy implications such as privacy nudges [1], which result from using the system, c.) select and configure appropriate PETs; e. g., an anonymization function to obfuscate location information, and d.) evaluate the effect of integrating PETs regarding given privacy requirements.

3.5 Modeling Data Processing

We model system aspects especially the data processing (as part of the system model) to get the information necessary for performing a technical privacy analysis. Privacy requirements directly or indirectly describe the permitted and unpermitted information flow that we consider as the processing of personal information. In order to evaluate whether a system model violates given privacy requirements the system model has to comprise the data processing performed within the system. Besides detecting privacy violations and privacy threats, we also want to identify vulnerabilities that describe points at which privacy threats may occur. The used data processing model includes the description about a.) *components* which operate on data, b.) *operations* performed by these components, c.) *data* items as input and output of the operations, and d.) the *information flow* of the performed operations. Figure 3 illustrates a graphical representation of the data processing model. We started our investigations with this simple system model that may be extended to consider additional system and privacy aspects.

Besides structural and operational system information we need data classifications to evaluate privacy aspects; e. g., to identify personal information. Ideally, designers together

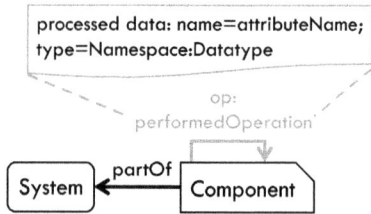

Figure 3: Model of Data Processing—Agenda.

with domain experts annotate the system model by mapping data types with corresponding entries of standardized *data classifications*. Such classifications may be defined using taxonomies or (domain specific) ontologies. Object identification mechanisms as applied to information integration may assist designers to define correct mappings. Alternatively, designers and domain experts may use their own data classification. In consequence they have to prove the suitability of the applied classifications.

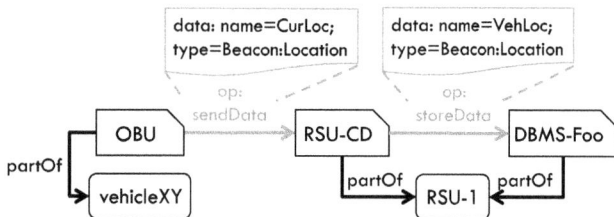

Figure 4: ITS scenario—Model of Data Processing.

The described data processing models may be derived from UML diagrams as part of a system specification, from declarative query, data flow languages, or other system specifications or may be created by hand. With Figure 4, we partially illustrate the data processing model of the ITS scenario described in Section 2. The sample scenario consists of the two systems *vehicleXY* and *RSU-1* which communicate with each other using their embedded components *OBU* (on board unit) and *RSU-CD* (RSU communication device). Additionally, the roadside unit integrates the database management system DBMS-Foo as a component for storing the received beacon data.

3.6 Applying Formal Analysis

Figure 5 illustrates how we support development processes by integrating formal analysis. During the *translation* phase, high level requirements are translated into technical requirements. These requirements are used in the *realization* phase to create a formal system description and identified related *constraints*. The *analysis and verification* phase uses a formal system description to assure that *constraints* are met. In the case of constraint violations a *revision* phase takes place which leads to a modification of the technical requirements or of the formal system description, i.e., a redesign of the system.

The envisioned ontology-based development process includes the following privacy enhancing phases:

1. **Identification:** *Identifying high-level privacy requirements* derived from general privacy principles; e.g., using approaches such as PIA [20]. The resulting requirements are typically described in an informal way.

Tools supporting this phase are often limited; e.g., to structured forms.

2. **Translation**: *Mapping the abstract high-level requirements to a detailed formal description of privacy requirements* that can then be related to attributes of a *formal system model*.

3. **Realization:** *Realizing the formal requirements and formally modeling the system*, including its structure and information flows.

4. **Analysis and Verification:** *Matching the formal privacy requirements to the formal system model* to either verify that a given system satisfies the privacy requirements, or to assist a designer in changing the system to meet the privacy requirements. Therefore, the analysis must show at which points privacy requirements are violated and must indicate how to redesign the system structurally or to integrate and to configure existing PETs.

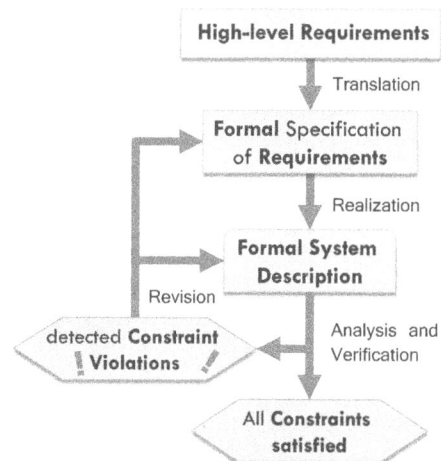

Figure 5: Development Process supporting formal analysis.

3.7 Giving Privacy Guarantees

The goal of applying a technical privacy analysis is to improve the implemented protection of privacy in the analyzed system. In addition to identify vulnerabilities of the system and to calculate indicators which support the transparency of applied privacy protection mechanisms, we want to give privacy guarantees for the analyzed system model. In the following, we describe prerequisites, possible guarantees, and limits of using our approach for giving privacy guarantees. To apply a technical privacy analysis our approach requires 1.) to provide a complete description of necessary system and privacy aspects in form of a system model, 2.) to consider domain specific aspects for creating the system model, privacy requirements, and privacy indicators, 3.) to provide a correct classification of processed data, 4.) to appropriately translate stakeholders privacy criteria into technical privacy requirements. Our suggested technical privacy analysis guarantees 1.) to detect operations on personal information and quasi identifiers, 2.) to localize components which store personal information and execute operations on personal information, 3.) to detect violations of given privacy principles, 4.) to detect violations of given (domain specific) privacy requirements (of different stakeholders), and 5.) combined with a policy enforcement, we guarantee the realization of user defined privacy preferences. Thereby, the quality of the given guarantees depends on the quality of the used system model and privacy statements. We have to address problems such as ambiguous defined concepts (e.g., synonyms, homonyms, and domain specific concepts), constraints, and relationships as well as misinterpretations. The use of a standard privacy vocabulary improves the acceptance, flexibility, interoperability, and quality of the analysis results.

3.8 Defining a common Privacy Vocabulary

As identified in previous sections – especially in Section 2.3 – we have to address the following requirements: 1.) we require a language to formulate privacy requirements, system models, and privacy indicators; 2.) we must deal with ambiguous concepts (e.g., synonyms, homonyms, and domain specific concepts), constraints, and relationships; 3.) we must abstract the used data formats in the system model to consider the concepts behind the processed data items; 4.) we must classify the concepts and consider relationships between them such as generalization, part-of, equivalence; 5.) we must create and evaluate rules to derive indirect and complex privacy aspects from the described relationships. We use standard ontology languages to define a common privacy vocabulary combined with standard reasoning technologies based on description logic to address these requirements.

Significant work is already available in ontology-based engineering. An overview is provided by [9]. Lee and Gandhi present a framework supporting ontology-based requirements engineering to predict, control, and evolve system behavior [19]. Hartig et al. show how to integrate an ontology-based analysis in a component-based software design process [11].

An ontology-based privacy analysis and verification method is further justified by two specific needs. First, capturing of privacy requirements necessitates the manipulation of a wealth of concepts on privacy, privacy protection, security, storage protection, and others. Second, many constraints related to privacy are domain specific. Therefore, our work includes: a categorization of the different forms of privacy requirements and the presentation of domain specific privacy ontologies. These contributions are further detailed in the following Section 4.

4. DESCRIBING PRIVACY CONCEPTS

We perform privacy analysis on information systems to evaluate the implementation of privacy requirements and to calculate privacy indicators. The result may form the basis for a verification of the analyzed system. Thus, we need a formal and unambiguous description of system models, the technical requirements, and metrics for calculating privacy indicators. As mentioned in Section 3.8 we must base our analysis on well defined (ideally standardized) modeling languages and vocabularies. *Ontologies* provide in part such foundation. The use of ontologies allows us to abstract from implementation issues to identify and to define basic concepts for describing privacy aspects in a domain independent manner. We extend such basic concepts by domain dependent aspects as necessary, and define logic based rules

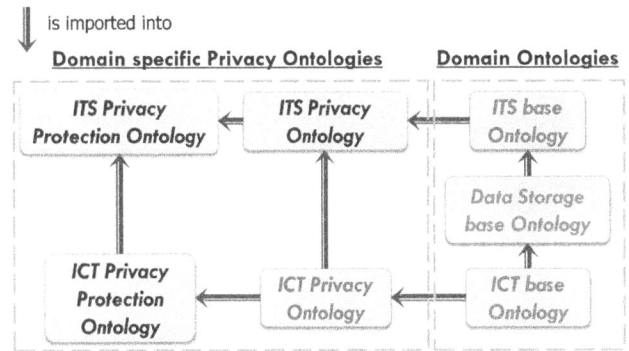

Figure 6: Dependencies between Partial Ontologies.

to derive new system properties and to check for consistency. We implemented our approach using common ontology technology and provide a privacy ontology framework which is available at `http://preciosa.informatik.hu-berlin.de/ontology/`.

4.1 Perspectives and Application Domains

In general, complex systems involve different stakeholders; e.g., users, manufacturers, and legal stakeholders [23, 24] such as data subjects, data processors, data controllers, and legal agencies. Every stakeholder comes with a different background and expectations resulting from their expertise, their cultural background, their interests, and other factors. Regarding privacy, we must identify the relevant domains and model those parts that reflect the concerns and interests of all stakeholders involved.

As an example, we use the domain of ITS to demonstrate how to apply our approach. In the following, we identify the relevant domains for ITS together with privacy related domains and describe their relationships. We describe those by identifying all necessary domain concepts and defining them in the appropriate ontologies. In each domain, we identify only those concepts that are required for privacy analysis. Additionally, we limit our ontologies to those terms that are necessary to define the fundamental concepts in an unambiguous manner. Those might be further refined and extended if necessary. In a second step, we then relate concepts of different domains with the same meaning by (non-automatically) defining mappings between those resulting in a comprehensive ITS Privacy Ontology.

We use the following sources to develop the identified domain ontologies: models of classical authentication and authorization [13], security ontologies [25], the knowledge extracted from specific privacy domains as privacy protection for data storage or communication, and knowledge extracted from legal documents [23, 24].

First, we define basic concepts of the ICT domain and represent them in the *ICT base Ontology*. Subsequently, we relate those terms by defining mappings between terms of different domains with the same meaning to include privacy relevant aspects. Figure 6 illustrates the domain ontologies and their relationships. For example, the *ICT base Ontology* defines fundamental concepts such as *Information, Data, System*, and others for describing concepts of the ICT domain. The *Policy base Ontology* contains the description of fundamental policy concepts such as *Policy, PolicyStatement, Context, Entity, Permission, Condition*, and others.

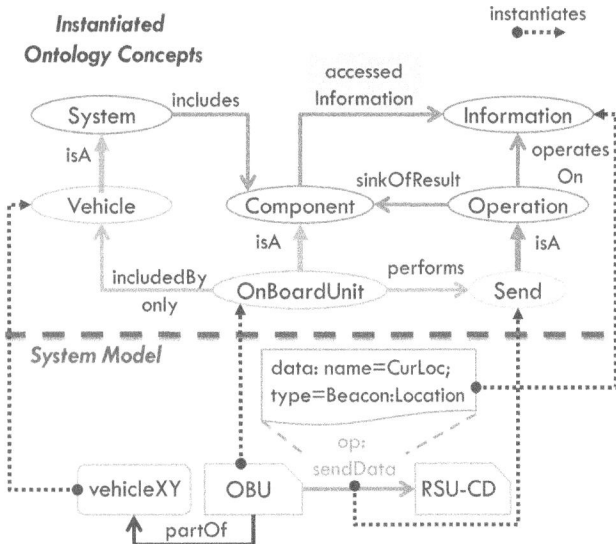

Figure 7: ITS Scenario—System based Description.

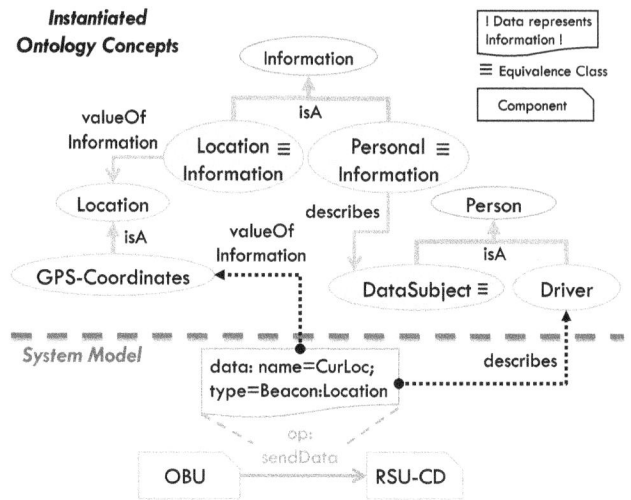

Figure 8: ITS Scenario—Information based Description.

Then, with the *ICT Privacy Ontology* we combine the *ICT base Ontology* and the *Policy base Ontology* and expand the set of definition by some privacy concepts such as *Data-Controller, DataProcessor, DataSubject, PersonalInformation*, and others.

4.2 Base Ontologies

We designed the ontologies to analyze a system regarding different privacy aspects. Therefore, the base ontology (see Figure 10 in the Appendix) defines the semantics of the data processing model which we introduced in Section 3.5. A *Component* as part of a *System* may access *Information* by processing information or creating a result item. We classify and specialize operations (with domain specific ontologies) to evaluate more precisely the effects which result from their execution. Further, we distinguish between Information and *Data* (which represents information) to address the issue that information may have several forms of serialization. We introduce the concept of *ComplexInformation* to model information which is composed of other information. For instance, we introduce address information which is composed of location information such as city, postal code, street, and more. In Section A we describe parts of the ICT Base Ontology, the ICT Privacy Ontology, and the ICT Privacy Protection Ontology to illustrate the definition of concepts and the integration of additional concepts from other domains.

4.3 Defining Indicators and Requirements

The privacy ontologies define privacy indicators as described in Section 3.4 by using logic based rules. A reasoning tool may evaluate those in order to derive new information and to check for consistency.

We define rules—as part of the ontologies—which we evaluate to infer information about the described system model. These rules evaluate system information thus deriving information about privacy relevant aspects. For instance, we characterize information as personal identifiers by evaluating statements which relate information uniquely to individuals (such as the object property *identifies* does). Furthermore,

we define equivalence classes and refine concepts such as *Information* and *Operation* by defining hierarchies to classify individuals regarding their privacy relevance. For instance, we define *ssid* as a personal identifier and *address information* as personal identifier as well as personal information. We use equivalence classes and property chains to detect privacy threats; e. g., components which perform operations that operate on information which have been classified as personal or identifying.

4.4 Extending Vocabulary by Domain specific Concepts

The *ICT Privacy Protection Ontology* provides a basic vocabulary for describing information flows and privacy criteria to model the application of privacy protection mechanisms in ICT. For completeness, we also model the data storage domain, the communication domain, and the ITS domain by corresponding ontologies. The *ITS base Ontology* imports concepts from the *ICT base Ontology*. In addition, the ontology includes fundamental concepts of ITS such as *Location, Localization, LocationTracking, Vehicle, RSU*, and more. Expanding the base ontologies by ITS concepts leads to a vocabulary which we use to adequately describe system models (especially its processing of information) and (privacy) requirements in the context of ITS. The used modularization and refinement approach may be adapted by other application domains.

4.5 Describing the ITS Scenario

We illustrate the use of privacy ontologies by the ITS scenario which we introduced in Section 2. Figures 7 and 8 partially describe the system model of the scenario as well as the relationships between the model elements and concepts defined in the ITS ontology. In Figure 7 we illustrate how we translate the elements of the described system model (see Figure 4) into instantiations of the ontologies. The illustrated system model consists of the system vehicle *vehicleXY* and the two components: the OnBoardUnit *OBU* which is *partOf* the *vehicleXY* and the communication device *RSU-*

CD. The OBU sends data about the current location to the RSU.

In Figure 8 we illustrate the mapping of the processed data to corresponding ontology concepts. Since the processed data is of type *Beacon:Location* this data represents information that *describes* a specific *Driver*. Furthermore, ITS domain includes a mapping from data of type *Beacon:Location* to the concept *GPX* representing a format for describing location information using *GPS-Coordinates*. Assuming that all drivers are identifiable a *Driver* becomes a *DataSubject* allowing us to infer the following information: 1) All three components process *LocationInformation*; 2) the information processed becomes personal information because the equivalence class *PersonalInformation* comprises *Information* which itself describes a *DataSubject*.

Our ontology framework consists of nine base ontologies, eight domain ontologies (such as ITS, data storage, communication) and four application specific ontologies. Those define about 380 concepts and 150 object properties. We use the Web Ontology Language (OWL) to describe all ontology statements, Protégé to edit and to visualize them, and Pellet to validate and reason about them. The description logic expressivity is SRIQ(D) if we include the definition of the object properties *identifies*, *consistsOf*, *partOf*, and *memberOf* as transitive. Otherwise the expressivity is ALCRIQ(D).

5. PERFORMING PRIVACY ANALYSIS USING ONTOLOGIES

So far, we described the main contribution of the paper in form of an approach for enhancing the software development process with formal privacy analysis by using ontologies for describing privacy related aspects of a predefined system model. In the following, we describe how to apply the ontology based privacy analysis and illustrate its application by the introduced ITS scenario.

5.1 Instantiating Privacy Ontologies

We use reasoning tools for evaluating the system model by inferring about the given axioms and rules. Therefore, we need a description of the system model and given privacy requirements in form of ontology statements. Usually, designers create system models using standard modeling languages such as UML and modeling tools. We have to translate these system models and given privacy requirements into ontology statements. Therefore, we map the required information with instances of ontology concepts. In particular, we map those parts of the system model which we described in Section 3.5 as part of the data processing model. Based on this mapping, we transform the selected elements to instances of the corresponding concepts in the target ontology by using transformation rules (Figure 9). Besides structural and operational system information we must define data classifications to evaluate privacy aspects (e. g., to identify personal information). Therefore, designers annotate the system model by *data classifications* which map data types of the system to corresponding (domain specific) ontology concepts (as described in Section 3.5).

As a result of executing the described transformation we get the required information expressed by instances of the *ICT base Ontology* or domain specific ontologies. These instances now become instances of the privacy extended ontologies such as the *ICT Privacy Ontology* and the domain

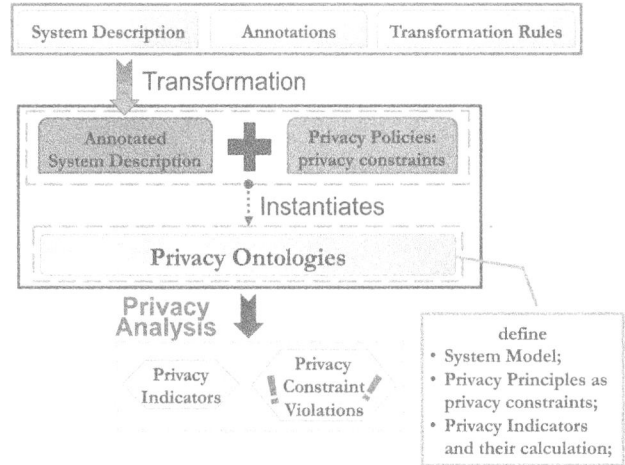

Figure 9: Transform System Model for Ontology based Privacy Analysis.

specific privacy ontologies. We can use these extended ontologies to evaluate privacy specific aspects of the system.

5.2 Analyzing the Annotated System Model

After transforming the annotated system model we use reasoning tools to perform the privacy analysis. Thereby, the reasoner evaluates the ontology statements in form of defined instances, axioms, and rules to infer new information and to check for inconsistencies. Thus, we classify the information regarding its type and privacy aspects by using hierarchies and selected classes such as *PersonalInformation*, we derive new information such as localization of information, check given privacy constraints, and detect vulnerabilities and privacy threats. In this way, we realize the following required functionalities: 1.) evaluating in an implementation independent way the specified a.) information flow and b.) the realization of the given privacy requirements, 2.) calculating privacy indicators which describe a.) detected/identified privacy issues, b.) inferred (new) privacy requirements by evaluating general privacy rules/patterns, c.) values of privacy metrics; e. g., to describe privacy risk, 3.) verifying that all identified privacy issues have been addressed by applying appropriate measures such as PETs or redesign patterns.

The current implementation of our analysis is limited because we use common ontology techniques. The implementation of the analysis does not support probabilistic privacy and does not consider the order and time of operation sequences. Probabilistic privacy is important because privacy has a statistical nature. Traditionally (as in security), the information flow is considered as black and white. We only check if a specific information flow has occurred which we classify as a violation. In privacy analysis, we must consider the probabilities with that an event may occur; e. g., that an adversaries successfully obfuscate information, infer personal information, or relates individuals with sensitive information. Thus, we need to extend formal methods to assure statistical guarantees rather black-and-white correctness guarantees. Probabilistic ontologies may be a good solution to combine our approach with statistical methods. As well as probabilistic privacy, the aspects of time and order introduce a new complexity for evaluating systems. To detect privacy threats effectively we must consider time intervals and the order of operation sequences. Most ontology techniques do not support directly time aspects and the order of sequences.

5.3 Analyzing the ITS Scenario

We address the identified privacy issues of Table 2 in Section 2.3 by evaluating rules which describe possible combinations of ITS data to derive personal information (privacy issues 1 and 2), considering technical information (privacy issues 2, 3, and 5), and considering the system composition (privacy issues 3 and 4).

Applying our privacy analysis approach to the ITS scenario described in Section 2 we detect several privacy constraint violations. One type of violation concerns the privacy principles such as limited retention and limited use. Regarding the store operation of the system model we miss specifications (e. g. in form of a specified remove operation) which realize the limited retention principle. Furthermore, the processing of data is not bound to a purpose which might also trigger a privacy violation rule. To address such privacy violations we may revise the system model by adding specifications limiting the use of the data to a specific context, e. g., defined by the constraints $Purpose = CollisionDetection$ and $SystemType = RSU$, and defining a retention time such as $Retention = 3 \; Minutes$. Furthermore, we may define individual privacy preferences; e. g., to limit the communication range and to transmit only obfuscated location information. In the same way, we evaluate its realization by the system model.

5.4 Evaluation

In order to determine the effort of using our approach we identified the requirements for performing the proposed technical privacy analysis in Section 3.7. Most of these requirements are the same requirements for performing an obligatory (non-technical) privacy analysis (as described in Section 2.2) or are based on its results. We may invest additional effort to create the required formalization in form of a system model and necessary domain ontologies. If we apply our analysis to another application of the same domain, we may reuse the domain ontologies and the results of the analyses become comparable. Furthermore, we circumvent to analyze systems by hand, which is an error-prone process; e. g., manual review of non-technical specifications, or code inspections. As for non-technical privacy analysis, the quality of the results depends on the quality of the used descriptions in form of the system model and privacy statements. The use of a standard privacy vocabulary improves the acceptance, flexibility, interoperability, and quality of the analysis results. The evaluation of completeness criteria is out of scope of this paper. Currently, a catalog/collection which contains a (in-)formal description of known privacy leakages is not available. Therefore, we miss completeness criteria evaluating our approach.

6. RELATED WORK

While the private impact assessment process [20] provides guidelines on how to elicit high-level privacy statements, no guidance is provided on how to translate those statements into technical requirements. Model checking mechanisms process a model of a system and test automatically whether this model meets a given specification [8]. As most verification techniques, model checking explores all possible system states making it appropriate for infinite state space systems. M. Tschantz and J. Wing provide a comprehensive overview about formal methods to model and evaluate privacy aspects identify challenges concerning models, logics, languages, or tools [28]. In [13], the authors provide a privacy ontology which is based on privacy principles of the legal perspective. The authors aim to support the building and evaluation of privacy-aware applications. To the reader it is not clear how to apply the mentioned ontology for evaluating a real system because the approach does not integrate information about a system model. In [22], the authors suggest to use a privacy ontology to derive the level of privacy for e-commerce applications. The process of describing and evaluating applications regarding privacy is done by designing and evaluating P3P policies in combination with the proposed privacy ontology. The approach is restricted to the e-commerce domain and is not integrated into existing development processes. We propose the missing comprehensive approach to evaluate a system regarding the implementation of stakeholder's privacy criteria.

7. CONCLUSION

In this paper, we describe a new approach using ontologies to evaluate a system model regarding its realization of given privacy requirements. We describe how to integrate and use existing techniques for supporting the privacy assessment of systems. Therefore, we extend the development process of applications and systems by technical privacy analysis and verification. We implemented our approach using common ontology technology and provide a privacy ontology framework[1].

In future work, we plan to apply the technical privacy analysis for selected use cases to evaluate its benefits. To make the evaluation results transparent we require the creation of benchmarks for technical privacy analysis. In addition, we investigate in detail what kind of privacy guarantees we can give for a given set of conditions. We plan to introduce a formalism to prove the correctness of such guarantees. Furthermore, we want to provide tools and guidelines to support the application of the introduced privacy analysis approach. For instance, in order to support designers in creating a formal system description we require declarative (query and policy) languages; statements in these languages express the processing of information and its requirements, respectively. Statements of this language must reference the concepts of the introduced (privacy) ontologies. Therefore, we directly express and analyze the intended information flow and the implementation of the specified privacy requirements resulting in a simplification of the mapping into ontology instances. In addition, components which execute such language statements might monitor and control the intended information processing thereby monitoring and enforcing the specified privacy statements [15, 17].

8. ACKNOWLEDGMENTS

This paper describes results based on work carried out within the FP7 PRECIOSA project [3] for which we acknowledge the support of the European Commission DG INFSO.

---

[1]http://preciosa.informatik.hu-berlin.de/ontology/

9. REFERENCES

[1] Carnegie mellon cylab - project nudging users towards privacy. http://www.cylab.cmu.edu/index.html.

[2] DESWAP (Development Environment for Semantic Web APplications) project., 2007.

[3] PRECIOSA (Privacy Enabled Capability in Co-operative Systems and Safety Applications) FP7 project., 2010.

[4] A. Cavoukian (Information & Privacy Commissioner Ontario, Canada). Privacy-by-design. http://www.privacybydesign.ca/.

[5] R. Agrawal, J. Kiernan, R. Srikant, and Y. Xu. Hippocratic databases. In *28th VLB Conference*, Hong Kong, China, 2002.

[6] A. Aijaz, B. Bochow, F. Dötzer, A. Festag, M. Gerlach, R. Kroh, and T. Leinmüller. Attacks on inter-vehicle communication systems - an analysis. In *3rd Int. Workshop on Intelligent Transportation (WIT 2006)*, March 2006.

[7] Y. Asnar, P. Giorgini, and J. Mylopoulos. Goal-driven risk assessment in requirements engineering. *Requirements Engineering*, 2010.

[8] E. M. Clarke and E. A. Emerson. Synthesis of synchronization skeletons for branching time temporal logic. In *In Logic of Programs: Workshop*. Springer-Verlag, 1981.

[9] D.Gasevic, N.Kaviani, and M.Milanovic. Ontologies and software engineering. In S. Staab and R. Studer, editors, *Handbook on Ontologies*. Springer Publishing Company, 2009.

[10] S. F. Gürses, C. Troncoso, and C. Diaz. Engineering privacy by design. In *Computers, Privacy & Data Protection*, 2011.

[11] O. Hartig, M. Kost, and J.-C. Freytag. Automatic component selection with semantic technologies. *Proc.s of the 4th Int. Workshop on Semantic Web Enabled Software Engineering (SWESE) at ISWC*, 2008.

[12] Q. He and A. I. Anton. A framework for modeling privacy requirements in role engineering. *Proc.s of the 9th Int. Workshop on Requirements Engineering: Foundation for Software Quality (REFSQ'03)*, 2003.

[13] M. Hecker and T. Dillon. Privacy support and evaluation on an ontological basis. In *Proc. of the IEEE 23rd Internat. Conf. on Data Engineering Works.*, Washington, DC, USA, 2007. IEEE Computer Society.

[14] ISO TC 204/SC/WG 1. Intelligent transport systems – system architecture – privacy aspects in its standards and systems. Technical report, ISO, 2008.

[15] F. Kargl, F. Schaub, and S. Dietzel. Mandatory Enforcement of Privacy Policies using Trusted Computing Principles. In *Intelligent Information Privacy Maangement Symposium, AAAI Spring Symposium Series*, Stanford, 2010. AAAI.

[16] E. Kavakli. Goal oriented requirements engineering: a unifying framework. *Requirements Engineering Journal, Springer-Verlag London*, 6, 2002.

[17] M. Kost, B. Wiedersheim, S. Dietzel, F. Schaub, and T. Bachmor. PRECIOSA PeRA: Practical enforcement of privacy policies in intelligent transportation systems. In *Proc. of the Demo. Session at the Fourth ACM Conf. on Wireless Network Security*, 2011.

[18] A. Kung, J.C.Freytag, and F.Kargl. Privacy-by-design in its applications. In *2nd Int. Workshop on Data Security and PrivAcy in wireless Networks*, Lucca, 2011.

[19] S. W. Lee and R. A. Gandhi. Ontology-based active requirements engineering framework. *Asia-Pacific Software Engineering Conf.*, 0, 2005.

[20] I. Linden Consulting. Privacy impact assessment. http://www.ico.gov.uk/for_organisations/data_protection/topic_guides/privacy_impact_assessment.aspx, 2007.

[21] S. Mauw and M. Oostdijk. Foundations of attack trees. In D. Won and S. Kim, editors, *ICISC*, volume 3935 of *Lecture Notes in Computer Science*. Springer, 2005.

[22] E. C. Michael Hecker, Tharam S. Dillon. Privacy ontology support for e-commerce. *IEEE Internet Computing*, 12, 2008.

[23] E. Parliament and of the Council of 24 October 1995. Directive 95/46/ec of the european parliament and of the council of 24 october 1995 on the protection of individuals with regard to the processing of personal data and on the free movement of such data, online (access july 31, 2009), 1995.

[24] T. E. PARLIAMENT and T. C. O. T. E. UNION. Directive 2010/40/eu of the european parliament and of the council. *Official Journal of the European Union*, L 207/1, 2010.

[25] M. Schumacher. Security engineering with patterns: Toward a security core ontology. *Springer-Verlag*, LNCS 2754, 2003.

[26] S. Spiekermann and L. Cranor. Privacy engineering. *IEEE Transactions on Software Engineering*, 35(1), January/February 2009.

[27] C. Troncoso, G. Danezis, E. Kosta, and B. Preneel. Pripayd: privacy friendly pay-as-you-drive insurance. In *WPES '07: Proc.s of the 2007 ACM workshop on Privacy in electronic society*, New York, NY, USA, 2007. ACM.

[28] M. Tschantz and J. Wing. Formal methods for privacy. In A. Cavalcanti and D. Dams, editors, *FM 2009: Formal Methods*, volume 5850 of *Lecture Notes in Computer Science*. Springer Berlin / Heidelberg, 2009.

APPENDIX

A. PRIVACY ONTOLOGIES

As described in Section 4.2 we designed the ontologies to analyze a system regarding different privacy aspects. The base ontology (see Figure 10) defines the semantics of the data processing model which we introduced in Section 3.5. A *Component* as part of a *System* (object property *includes*) may access *Information* by processing information (object property *operatesOn*) or creating a result item (object property *creates*). To detect information which was accessed by a component (object property *accessedInformation*) we define two corresponding property chains. We classify and specialize operations (with domain specific ontologies) to evaluate more precisely the effects which result from their execution. Further, we distinguish between Information and *Data* (which represents information) to address the issue that information may have several forms of serialization. We introduce the concept of *ComplexInformation* to model information which is composed of other information. For instance, we introduce address information which is composed of location information such as city, postal code, street, and more.

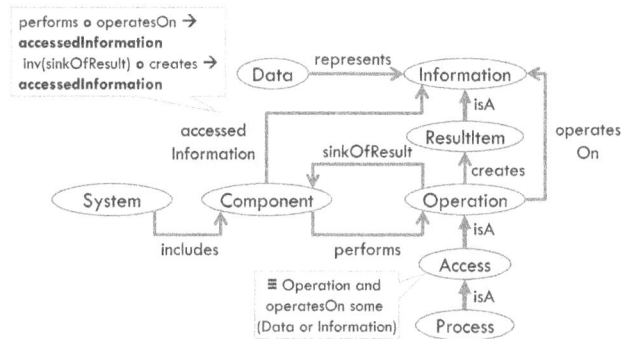

Figure 10: Data Processing Model in ICT ontology.

In Figure 11 we describe parts of the ICT Base Ontology, the ICT Privacy Ontology, and the ICT Privacy Protection Ontology to illustrate the definition of concepts and the integration of additional concepts from other domains. The *ICT base Ontology* defines general concepts such as *Threat, Information, Identifier, Mechanism, ProtectionMechanism, Component*, and *ProtectionComponent* and their relationships. Based on these definitions, other ontologies define additional concepts, relationships, and axioms. For instance, the *ICT Protection Ontology* defines concepts such as *Privacy Threat, Pseudonym, Pseudonymization, Anonymization, AccessControl, PrivacyProtectionMechanism*, and *PrivacyProtectionComponent*. In addition, this ontology defines relationships which model the following statements. Privacy protection components implement some privacy protection mechanisms which protect against specific privacy threats. Pseudonymization, anonymization, and access control are privacy protection mechanisms.

For more information about the ontologies and examples for detecting privacy leakages we refer to the homepage (http://preciosa.informatik.hu-berlin.de/ontology).

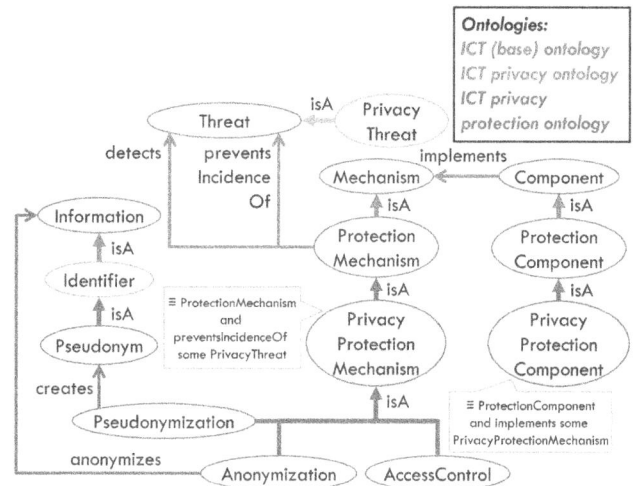

Figure 11: ICT Privacy Protection Ontology.

S2A: Secure Smart Household Appliances

Yuxin Chen
Department of Computer Science
Swiss Federal Institute of Technology (ETHZ)
Zurich, Switzerland
yuxin.chen@inf.ethz.ch

Bo Luo
Department of EECS
The University of Kansas
Lawrence, KS, USA
bluo@ku.edu

ABSTRACT

Security protection is an integral component for smart homes; however, smart appliances security has received little attention in the research community. Household appliances become very vulnerable if we introduce smart functions without proper security protection. In particular, smart access functions enable users to operate devices remotely. Meanwhile, smart devices are are also designed to support residential demand response, i.e. postpone non-urgent tasks to non-peak hours. However, remote adversaries could utilize such functions to manipulate smart appliances' operations without physically touching them. Such interferences, if not properly handled, could damage the smart devices, disturb owners' life or even harm the households' physical security.

In this paper, we present S2A, a security protection solution to be embedded in smart appliances. First, a SUP model is developed to quantify penalties from device security, usability and electricity price. We employ multi-criteria reinforcement learning to integrate the three factors to determine an optimal operation strategy. Next, to leverage the risk of forged control commands or pricing data, we present a realtime assessment mechanism based on Bayesian inference. Risk indices are further integrated into the SUP model to serve as weighting factors of corresponding decision criteria. Evaluation shows that S2A ensures appliances security while providing good usability and economical efficiency.

Categories and Subject Descriptors

K.6.5 [**Management of Computing and Information systems**]: Security and Protection—*Physical Security*

General Terms

Security, Design

1. INTRODUCTION

As the next-generation standard for power generation and transmission, advanced computation and telecommunication capabilities are introduced into smart devices to constitute a large-scale smart grid network, and to support "smart" functions, such as large sale load balancing, dynamic pricing, smart consumption. Unfortunately, most of the advanced functions, especially those on the power consumption side (i.e., smart home side), are not yet implemented in the pilot projects. Security concern is one of the major obstacles that prevent broad industrial adoption of such smart functions.

Smart appliances are envisioned to receive control commands and electricity prices from the network. Embedded control systems have been installed in household appliances. Manufactures are starting to build appliances with remote access functions (a.k.a. smart access). For instance, LG products with THINQ technology were demonstrated at CES 2011. General Electronics (GE) has been working with Tendril to connect GE household products over Zigbee wireless networks. Such smart access capabilities enable owners to remotely monitor and operate their devices using phones, tablets, or through designated websites. On the other hand, smart meters are designed to receive realtime electricity pricing (RTP) and pass on to household devices [14], which optimizes energy consumptions based on RTP [34]. However, smart appliances are not yet equipped with *smart security protection mechanisms* to defend against cyber attacks. For instance, they follow remote control commands without verifying the authenticity of such commands. In this context, if we introduce "smart" functions to electrical appliances without proper security protection, they become more vulnerable than conventional devices. Adversaries could manipulate or intervene smart appliances' operations remotely, without physically touching them. More severely, when compromised devices are set to work in abnormal conditions for an extended period of time, they could be physically damaged, and even compromise environmental safety. For instance, overheating electric motors are shown to be a root cause of insulation failures, which is very dangerous to the users. In this paper, instead of focusing on the traditional security notions of *confidentiality*, *integrity* and *availability*, we focus on the *operational or physical safety* of smart devices. Therefore, the security goal of the S2A approach is to ensure the physical safety of the smart devices, preventing them from working in abnormal conditions, when the smart control environment becomes unreliable.

In this paper, we present S2A (secure smart appliances), a security protection mechanism for smart appliances. S2A is an embedded software solution, which employs machine learning technologies to provide smart and flexible protections for smart household appliances. First, for an individual smart appliance, the S2A models heterogeneous notions of device security (S), usability (U), and electricity pricing (P) into homogeneous benefit (or penalty) functions. We then employ multi-criteria reinforcement learning (MCRL) to integrate all three factors to determine the optimal operation strategy, which aims to maximize usability and minimize both security penalties and electricity costs. Next, to leverage the risk of fake control commands or forged pricing data, we propose a real-time risk assessment and re-weighting mechanism. We invoke Bayesian inference approaches to evaluate the trustworthiness of input from each channel, and adjust the parameters for MCRL criteria accordingly. Through security analysis and simulation results, we show that our solution ensures appliance security, while maintaining usability and economical efficiency of power consumption.

Our contributions are: (1) we introduce a comprehensive security protection for smart household devices. Our solution integrates usability, electricity pricing, and device security to maximize the overall benefit (or minimize overall penalty). (2) By employing machine learning methods, S2A provides an effective and reliable security protection. Moreover, compared with the conventional security notion, which is black-or-white, S2A seamlessly integrates risk assessment into decision algorithms, without making a verdict of "safe" or "under attack". (3) We propose a flexible approach, in which degree of protection and quality of service is based on resources (e.g. historical data) and capabilities.

2. RELATED WORK

Smart grids are envisioned as the next generation power system [50, 16, 40, 48]. Some vision/introductory papers can be found at [25, 11, 35, 6]. Existing research projects mostly focus on the "power grid" side (i.e. the macro grid), for example, large scale dynamic load balancing, reliability and recovery, power market [45, 24, 38, 32]. On the other end of the spectrum, smart meters are being implemented [22], and smart meter communication systems are being deployed [41, 42, 1, 39]. Meanwhile, smart appliances are proposed to improve user experience and cost efficiency: realtime retail pricing (RTP) introduces dynamically changing electricity prices that reflect the realtime supply-vs-demand trend [4, 5]. RTP is delivered to smart meters and then household appliances. With the built-in intelligence, smart appliances could move non-urgent tasks to off-peak hours to enhance economic efficiency of power usage [10]. Recently, [34] introduces a reinforcement learning approach to identify a relatively optimal time to start tasks. Tasks from the queue are picked to execute based on RTP and the length of wait. On the other hand, systems have been designed to enable remote monitor and control for household appliances through smart meters [47, 20, 36, 46].

Security and privacy protection is an important and challenging component in smart grids [26, 19]. A comprehensive survey is provided at [2]. In particular, [30, 31] studied the security requirements in the overall smart grid framework and presented security technologies to fulfill such requirements. [44] presents a conceptual framework to protect power grid automation systems. [7] points out security requirements and threats related to smart meters. [3] analyzes external intrusions, and introduces specification-based detection approach as a potential solution. [27, 28] show

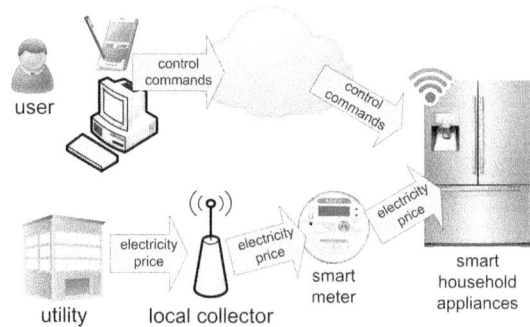

Figure 1: Smart appliances receive control commands and realtime electricity pricing from remote.

that adversaries could attack the advanced metering infrastructure to manipulate power usage for energy theft.

Most of the above-mentioned security protection approaches focus on the power grid, from generators to distributers to smart meters. Meanwhile, security issues related to household appliances have been lightly studied in the context of ubiquitous computing and home-area networks [23, 33]. They mostly concern about wireless communication security, authentication and privacy issues. For instance, [21] shows that in-home activities could be inferred from realtime energy consumption data. However, to our best knowledge, there has not been any work on protecting appliances' physical security, especially at the presence of untrustworthy external inputs (control commands and prices).

3. PROBLEM AND SOLUTION OVERVIEW

3.1 Smart Household Devices

Smart devices receive users' control commands and realtime pricing (RTP) from the network. As shown in Figure 1, utility distribution companies broadcast realtime electricity prices to households. Various proposals have been suggested in the literature. The more popular approach is to employ wired communication from utility companies to neighborhood collector devices, and wireless communications (e.g. wireless mesh) to further deliver to smart meters. Smart meters then send RTP information to compatible smart appliances via home-area WiFi. Meanwhile, manufactures such as LG and GE are starting to introduce remote control functions to smart appliances. In their design, users send control commands via a designated website or a mobile app. The commands go though the Internet to be delivered to the appliances, which connect to the Internet through household WiFi. There are also proposals that such commands could be delivered via smart meters.

3.2 The Threat Model

In a large scale open platform with many stakeholders, from the viewpoint of a smart device, it cannot assume absolute security of all the external peer(s). When adversaries penetrate into the control systems or temper with the communication channel, they could inject forged inputs (control commands and/or RTP data) into household smart devices, who may not be able to verify the authenticity and validity of such inputs. The interferences, if not properly handled, could affect the owner's regular lifestyle, or even cause serious physical damages. Let us look at some examples:

Example 1: Electric vehicles (EV) are designed to optimize the economical efficiency of power consumption, i.e., charge the battery when the electricity price is low, and (optionally) provide power to the household or the grid when the price is high (a.k.a. vehicle-to-grid [17, 18]). An intruder may send forged pricing data to trick EV to operate improperly to cause financial losses to the owner, to affect the load balancing of the power grid, or even mess up with the grid to achieve financial advantages. □

Example 2: Battery life of electric vehicles heavily rely on proper use and maintenance. An intruder may send forged fluctuant pricing to trick EV battery to constantly switch between charge and discharge for a relatively long period (e.g. start and stop charging 10 times per hour for 10 hours). This attack will seriously damage the battery, and even cause hazardous conditions when the battery gets overheated. □

Example 3: An adversary could penetrate into the remote control systems or home-area networks to obtain control of household appliances. Such interference could affect the owner's regular lifestyle, or even cause serious physical damages. When an adversary sets all the exothermic devices in a household to maximum heat level simultaneously, the room temperature rises significantly. More dangerously, the circuit gets overloaded, and the risk of fire increases. □

In this paper, we consider the situation where *smart devices (excluding smart meters) receive potentially harmful inputs from ostensibly legitimate sources.* We do not consider smart meters, since they are usually located outside of the household, and they are physically insecure. On the other hand, a mal-functioning smart meter will not directly threat household safety. In our settings, each smart appliance in the residence functions as an agent that has an embedded control unit to manage its own operations. We assume that smart devices are physically secure since they are usually located inside the household. We also assume that the embedded control systems are not compromised: the control logic is relatively less complicate; they only receive limited information (control and price) from designated sources; software updates usually require physically touching the device (e.g. using a USB drive). Therefore, it is not easy to hack into the kernels of the smart devices remotely.

The goal of the paper is to protect the operational security of household smart devices in the presence of potentially harmful inputs from information (and command) distribution channels. We also aim to maintain usability (QoS) and economical efficiency. In particular, we study two channels that may take suspicious inputs: *user control commands (UCC)* and *realtime pricing (RTP)*. Meanwhile, based on the duration and frequency of suspicious inputs, we consider two types of threats: *Threat 1. sporadic incidents* and *Threat 2. continuous attacks.* Continuous active attacks are potentially more damaging, and may not be handled by existing rule-based security protection mechanisms.

Please note that smart meters have essentially different capabilities and functionalities than household appliances. Our threat models and countermeasures are not applicable on smart meters. Some related works on smart meter security are summarized in Section 2.

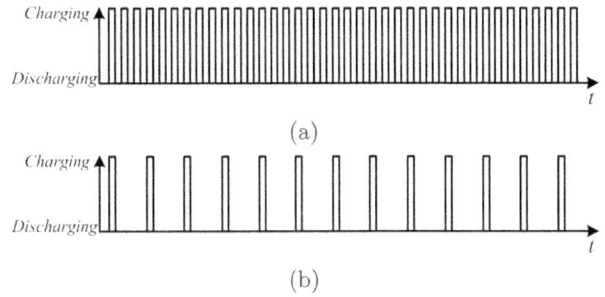

Figure 2: Battery charging system under active attack: (a) forged control commands that rapidly switch between charging and discharging; (b) chargers operations with rule-based protection.

3.3 Rule-based Security Protection

At present, most of the household appliances, including smart devices, are equipped with embedded security protection mechanisms that are usually rule-based. For instance, when an air conditioner is switched off, its internal security protection mechanism will keep it off for n minutes before it could be restarted. Similarly, when a smart car stops charging, it will mandatorily wait for m minutes to avoid immediate recharging to protect the battery. Some devices use sensors to obtain status information, and security rules are based on sensor inputs. For example: an electronic motor should stop for n minutes when the motor temperature is higher than x degrees. However, the rules are mostly designed to protect the device against users' misuse. They provide minimum protection, and do not consider future consequences. In particular, they can hardly protect the devices against active attacks, especially continuous attacks.

Example 4: Figure 2 gives an example of a battery charging system under active attack. Aimed to damage the battery, the attacker sends forged control commands that rapidly switch between charging and discharging. The embedded rule-based protection mechanism enforces an interval of t minutes between two charges, to protect the battery against transient power line faults. As shown in Figure 2 (b), for continuous attacks, such protection mechanism will only increase charging interval to t. However, without more complicate security protection mechanism, the battery is still damaged after an extended period of time. □

3.4 Solution Overview

In this paper, we propose the S2A framework, as an embedded software solution to protect operational security of smart household appliances against misuses and forged inputs. The goals are: (1) ensure appliances' security, (2) maintain usability, and (3) reduce energy costs. Typically, smart appliances need to make appropriate tradeoffs between ensuring usability (e.g. user wants to start the dishwasher) and minimizing energy cost (e.g. smart dishwasher wants to wait for low electricity price). Such requirements usually lead to a complicate optimization problem, which is difficult, if not impossible, to solve with rule-based methods.

We propose a two-phase solution, which enables smart devices to learn to protect themselves, without requesting any support from "supernodes" or smart meters. In the first phase, we aim to achieve an optimized and fine-grained operational strategy. The SUP model considers security penalties, usability penalties, as well as economical benefits. In the second phase, we assess the trustworthiness of each input channel by comparing the instant input with historical data. Since user commands and RTP demonstrate very different patterns in the regular working conditions, different intrusion detection mechanisms are invoked accordingly. We do not provide a verdict of "safe" or "under attack (forged input)". Instead, the security assessments are seamlessly feedback to the SUP model as weight factors of the corresponding penalty (or benefit) functions.

4. THE S2A FRAMEWORK

4.1 Overview of the S2A Framework.

Figure 3 demonstrates the S2A framework. As shown, our solution constitutes two major components (tiers): the SUP module and the realtime risk assessment module.

Tier 1: The SUP model. Tier 1 considers the basic scenario of S2A framework, in which an appliance is an independent device without any knowledge to external historical information or environmental information. Note that we assume a short operation log is available, which records a queue of user requests to use the device, and recent history of on-off operations. In the basic S2A solution, we define a SUP model to capture security, usability and electricity price. In SUP, a security function $s(t)$ is defined to model the operational penalty for the physical safety of smart electrical devices; a usability penalty function $u(t)$ is defined to model the frustration of users (similar to [34]) when they wait for the delayed operations; and finally real-time electricity price is received by smart pricing $p(t)$. When a user requests a S2A-enabled device to operate, SUP balances all three penalties to make a smart operation plan, so that: the device always works in a safe working mode; the user will not be very unhappy because of long wait; and the total cost of electricity to complete the task is relatively low. In our solution, we employ multi-criteria reinforcement learning (MCRL) to make real-time operational decisions based on three criteria: $s(t)$, $p(t)$, and $p(t)$.

Tier 2: Real-time risk assessment for SUP. In the second tier of the S2A framework, we consider the trustworthiness of the user requests and the electricity pricing information. To protect smart appliances in the presence of suspicious control commands or price data, we use Bayesian inference (RRA-RTP and RRA-UCC in Figure 2) to assess the credibility of the inputs, i.e. the likelihood of tampered control commands or forged electricity prices. Note that we only evaluate the validity of remote data, not physical operations on the device (e.g. pushing a button on the washer is always considered to be a valid control command). The Bayesian inference modules takes current inputs to compare with historical data, and generates two risk indexes R_p and R_u, which measure the trustworthiness of the control commands and electricity prices, respectively. Unlike conventional intrusion detection approaches, we do not provide a verdict on whether the system is under attack or not. Instead, the risk factors are seamlessly integrated into SUP. For instance, the risk index for user command (R_U) is sent back to the SUP model to serve as weighting factor for the usability penalty. In this way, when forged inputs are de-

tected at tier 2, its risk factor increases, and the corresponding weight factor for the suspicious input channel decreases, to fade out the suspicious input.

Override Rules. To improve user experience and to give users better control, especially in unusual circumstances, the following override rules are enabled in S2A.

(1). In S2A, the user may force the task to be conducted without any delay, i.e. force usability functions to override smart-pricing functions. As a reference, in [34], user could press "start" button twice to instantly start the operation, without waiting for low electricity price. However, security penalty is still in place to ensure device security.

(2). For security purposes, we assume that the device could be turned off at anytime. That is, there is no security penalty if the user intends to turn the devices off.

(3). When users request legitimate but unusual operations from remote, the operation could appear to be highly suspicious to the realtime risk analysis module. To prevent any legitimate requests from being denied or deferred, we introduce an additional task verification process, which is independent from the routine verification. Risk assessment could be overridden by additional validation, so that critical (and irregular) task will not be delayed. Technically, we enforce an extra authentication to verify the identity of the requestor. For verified tasks, we increase the weight for usability and decrease the weight for smart pricing. Once again, security penalty is still in place.

4.2 The SUP Model

Overview. The core of the S2A framework is an SUP model. For a smart appliance without long time memory, we first identify its operational states Ω (i.e., the total reward/penalty gained by leaving the previous states), and model state transitions as a set of actions A. For simplicity of description, we only consider the case that appliances are either ON or OFF. Hence, we have four types of actions: $A = \{\langle OFF{\rightarrow}OFF\rangle, \langle OFF{\rightarrow}ON\rangle, \langle ON{\rightarrow}ON\rangle, \langle ON{\rightarrow}OFF\rangle\}$. We model the process as a multi-objective Markov decision process (MMDP) that considers the following three criteria, and define penalty functions for each action w.r.t. each criterion. Note that we can easily add more modes (e.g., use four modes: high, mid, low, off) by adding penalty functions. Our learning algorithms takes general MMDP, with no restrictions on number of states or actions.

Security Criterion. A *security penalty function* $s(A, t) \in R^+$ is defined to denote the penalty of performing action A at time t. At high level, security penalty $s()$ quantifies the potential of damaging the device (e.g. overheat the battery) and/or harming the environment (e.g. burn down the house). We only enforce penalties for turning on the device ($\langle OFF{\rightarrow}ON\rangle$) or keeping on the device ($\langle ON{\rightarrow}ON\rangle$). $s(\langle ON \rightarrow ON\rangle, t)$ and $s(\langle OFF \rightarrow ON\rangle, t)$ cannot coexist since the current state is either ON or OFF. For simplicity of description, we use $s(t)$ when there is no confusion. A larger $s(t)$ indicates that the current working condition is not desirable, and pushes the decision against turning or keeping the device on.

The parameters of the penalty function are defined by the manufacture of the appliance, based on the operational and security characteristics of the device. In our model, each device is equipped a built-in function generator $G_s(oper)$,

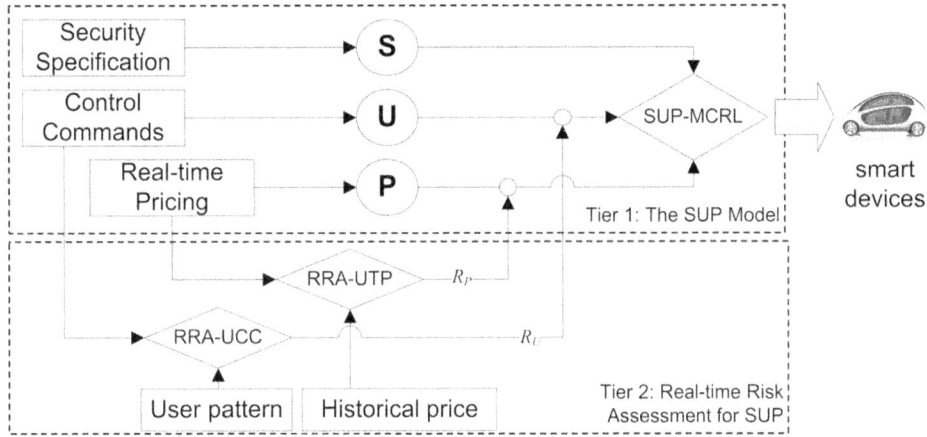

Figure 3: The S2A Framework: SUP-MCRL: the security-usability-pricing model with multi-criteria reinforcement learning; RRA-RTP: realtime risk analysis on realtime electricity pricing; RRA-UCC: realtime risk analysis on users' control commands; R_P and R_U: risk factors.

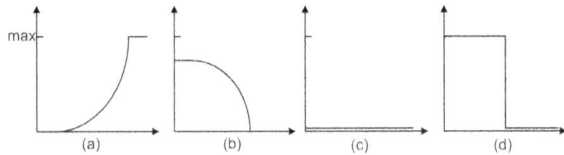

Figure 4: Examples of security penalty functions

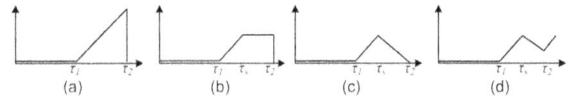

Figure 5: Examples of usability penalty functions

which constructs penalty functions based on pre-defined rules, device states and recent operations. $G_s(oper)$ is triggered to refresh $s(t)$ whenever an operation is performed (i.e. at state change: $\langle OFF \rightarrow ON rlangle$ or $\langle ON \rightarrow OFF \rangle$). For "smarter" appliances, the security penalty is generated on-the-fly from sensor inputs (e.g. heat, environmental temperature, etc). When the security penalty reaches MAX, it cannot be surpassed by other penalty functions – the device should remain off until security penalty drops.

Example 5: Some devices cannot operate for more than a pre-defined period of time – they need to stop and cool down. When the appliance is first switched on, $G_s(oper)$ generates a security penalty function for keeping the device on ($\langle ON \rightarrow ON \rangle$). In this case, $s(t)$ demonstrates an increasing pattern (Figure 4 (a)). When it is switched off before reaching maximum penalty, $G_s(oper)$ refreshes $s(t)$ to $s(t, \langle OFF \rightarrow ON \rangle)$, which requires the device to keep off for a while, and then starts to decrease (Figure 4 (b)). On the other hand, some devices (e.g. batteries) cannot switch between on and off frequently. There could be no security penalty for keep charging (Figure 4 (c)), but the penalty function for $\langle OFF \rightarrow ON \rangle$ reaches maximum value once the device is turned off, hence preventing it from being switched on until a waiting period (Figure 4 (d)). □

Usability Criterion. A smart appliance receives user request $c(t) \in R^+$ indicating his/her desire to run the devices at time t. Such a control command, however, does not necessarily start the device instantly, but rather specifies a reservation with the S2A system to run the device at an optimal (possibly later) time to balance user utility with other factors, such as economical efficiency and system security. With the user reservation at time t_0, a certain quantity

$c(t_0) = e_0$ of electricity is requested for the operation, otherwise $c(t_0) = 0$, indicating that there is no reserved energy use at t_0. User reservations are stored in a FIFO *pending energy queue* $\mathbf{q}_i = \{\langle t_0, e_0 \rangle, \langle t_1, e_1 \rangle, \ldots\}$.

In the SUP model, we capture *usability penalty* with a penalty function $u(A, t) \in R^+$, which denotes the expected usability penalty when we take action A at time t. When the requested task is delayed ($\langle ON \rightarrow OFF \rangle$ or $\langle OFF \rightarrow OFF \rangle$) due to high electricity price or active security protection, usability penalty ($u(t)$) starts to increase. Meanwhile, there is no usability penalty for turning on or keeping on the device. In practice, $u(t)$ cannot be detected on-the-fly, rather, it is calculated from a pre-defined usability penalty model, which is based on characteristics of the appliance's usage and user-centric analysis results. Note that $s(t)$ represents the appliance's perception (guess) of users' dissatisfaction. When the operation pauses at time t_0 ($\langle ON \rightarrow OFF \rangle$), the appliance immediately knows that task completion will be postponed. Hence, the penalty $s(t)$ starts to increase at t_0.

Example 6: Figure 5 shows some simple examples of usability penalty function $u(t)$. In Figure 5 (a), the task is paused at τ_1, where the penalty function for $\langle OFF \rightarrow OFF \rangle$ starts to increase linearly. In Figure 5 (b), the delayed task is restarted at time τ_s, the expected completion time stops changing. Hence, usability penalty (for $\langle ON \rightarrow OFF \rangle$) keeps static, until the task is completed at τ_2. Meanwhile, if the user is aware of the task progress, the dissatisfactory level could decrease when s/he knows that the task is in progress and is expected to finish soon (Figure 5(c)). Last, as shown in Figure 5 (d), user frustration may increase again when the task is paused at τ_2, before its completion. □

In S2A, the usability model is pre-built in the smart device by its manufacturer. $u(t)$ is generated when a new task

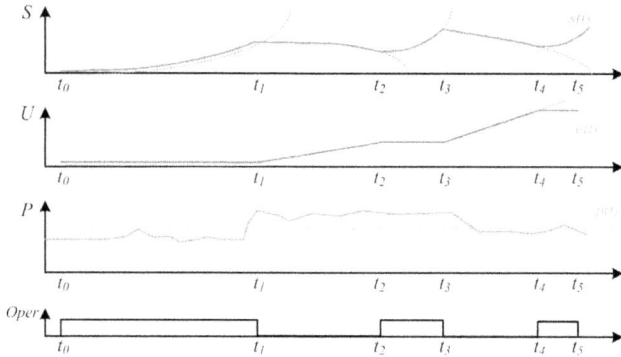

Figure 6: Example of a smart appliance operating under SUP model.

is picked from the task queue. It is refreshed when the operation of the appliance changes. In general, $u(t)$ increases (usually nonlinearly) for $\langle \text{OFF} \rightarrow \text{OFF} \rangle$, and stays stable or decreases when the task is progressing ($\langle \text{ON} \rightarrow \text{OFF} \rangle$). The model also takes in the recent working history and environmental parameters, so that $u(t)$ is adjusted to users' everyday life. Different appliances will also have different patterns for usability penalty in different conditions. For instance, users are less concerned when a smart car is being charged at night; but s/he may want the task to complete soon if the car is plugged-in in the morning. In this paper, we model $u(t)$ as an abstract function. Usability and user behavior modeling problems are studied in the human factors research community. Usability in the context of dynamical electricity pricing has been studied in the context of residential demand response (RDS), e.g. [34, 15, 12].

Smart Pricing Criterion. Smart appliances are designed to receive realtime retail electricity prices (RTP) from the distributor. In the SUP model, realtime price is provided by a function $p(t) \in R^+$. Data from world-wide pilot projects have shown different patterns of electricity pricing. Most of them demonstrates a daily revolving pattern, which peaks in early evening, decreases later into the night, and increases in the morning. Currently, our model only considers electricity cost. With reasonable modifications, it could be expanded to include more complicate cost models, which consider costs from multiple sources.

The SUP Model. The SUP model integrates all the criteria described above to minimize three factors: security penalty, usability penalty, and total expense for the task. Before discussing the detailed learning algorithm, we show an intuitive example on how the SUP model works.

Example 7: As shown in Figure 6, the user submits a request at time t_0 to an S2A embedded device. Since the electricity price $p(t)$ is low, the appliance starts instantly (note that the dashed line in P plot represents average electricity price, not a decision threshold – there is no preset decision threshold for each penalty function). We assume that this device cannot continuously operate for a very long period of time. Security penalty starts to increase gradually. At t_1, there is a sharp raise of electricity price. Meanwhile, $u(t)$ is very low at t_1 – there has not been any delay until t_1. At t_1, the SUP model decides to pause the job. Starting from t_1,

usability penalty starts to grow since the completion time is expected to be postponed (we use a linear function to model usability penalty in this example, however, real-world usability model is usually non-linear). Security penalty reduces as the device is off. At t_2, the SUP model decides to switch the device on, based on the increasing usability penalty and decreasing security penalty. At t_3, due to very high security penalty (e.g. the motor it very hot), the device is turned off again. The device cools down until t_4, when it is restarted to get the task done at t_6. □

5. THE ALGORITHMS

In this section, we describe the core algorithms to support smart protection in the S2A framework. First, we introduce multi-criteria reinforcement learning (MCRL) to determine the optimal operational strategy for the SUP model. Next, we introduce Bayesian-based realtime risk assessment, and seamlessly integrates risk indices into the SUP model.

5.1 MCRL for SUP

The core problem in the SUP model is to learn an optimal operational behavior for a smart appliance in the presence of dynamic preferences/penalties introduced by multiple objectives. In SUP, a device is an independent agent, which learns an approximately optimal strategy through trail and error interactions with the environmental variables. The *pending energy* is defined as the amount of energy that is required to finish the task. When the input power to the device is stationary, its pending energy is directly proportional to the remaining time to finish the task. The *environment* of a smart appliance is described by a deterministic multi-objective Markov decision process (MMDP) $\langle \Omega, A, f, \vec{\rho} \rangle$, where Ω is the finite set of discrete states, A is the set of actions, $f : \Omega \times A \rightarrow \Omega$ is the state transition function, and $\vec{\rho}$ is the vector-based penalty function $\vec{\rho} : \Omega \times A \rightarrow \mathbb{R}^n$. The state signal $x_k \in \Omega$ describes the environment at each discrete time-step k. In SUP, x_k encodes the device's current working status (i.e., whether the device is on or off), the current pending energy, the pricing information, the cumulative delay of the task, and the duration since the last operation (i.e., how long has the device been on or off), etc. The learning agent can alter the state at each time step by taking actions $a_k \in A$ of keeping on/off or turning off/on a device accordingly. As a result of the action a_k, the environment changes its state from x_k to $x_{k+1} \in \Omega$ according to the state transition rules given by $f : x_{k+1} = f(x_k, a_k)$. The agent then receives immediate vector-valued penalties of taking the action a_k on the basis of multiple evaluating objectives, which is completely determined by the current state and action: $\vec{\phi}_{k+1} = \vec{\rho}(x_k, a_k)$.

In the SUP settings, each of the penalty criterions is associated with a weight in accordance with its reliability. Given a weight vector $\vec{w} = (w_1, \ldots, w_n)$ and an MMDP, a new MDP with vector-valued penalty functions is created when multiplying each penalty $\rho_i(x, a)$ of type i with w_i. For a constant weight vector $\vec{w}$, the goal of the learning agent is to minimize the expected discounted penalty:

$$\Phi_k = E\{\sum_{j=0}^{\infty} \gamma^j \vec{\phi}_{k+j+1} \cdot \vec{w}\} \quad (1)$$

where $\gamma \in [0, 1)$ is the discount factor. It can be regarded as encoding increasing uncertainty about the penalties that will be received in the future. Such discounted penalty compactly represents the penalty accumulated in the long run, and measures a policy's long-term performance.

For deterministic SUP models, the behavior of an agent is described by its policy $\pi : \Omega \rightarrow A$, which specifies how the agent chooses its actions given the state. The vector-based *action-value function*, $\vec{Q}^\pi : \Omega \times A \rightarrow \mathbb{R}^n$, is the expected return of a state-action pair given the policy π: $\vec{Q}^\pi(x,a) = E\{\sum_{j=0}^{\infty} \gamma^j \vec{\phi}_{k+j+1} . * \vec{w} | x_k = x, a_k = a, \pi\}$, and the optimal Q-function is defined as $\vec{Q}^*(x,a) = \min_\pi \vec{Q}^\pi(x,a)$. It satisfies the Bellman optimality equation

$$\vec{Q}^*(x,a) = \vec{\rho}(x,a) + \gamma \min_{a'} \vec{Q}^*(\pi(x,a),a'), \ \forall a' \in A \quad (2)$$

where $a' = \text{argmin}_{a'}[\vec{w} \cdot \vec{Q}^*(\pi(x,a),a')]$.

The formula is derived from the original Q-Learning[43], with vector-based representation of the immediate and expected discounted penalty function. The current estimate of $\vec{Q}^*$ is updated using estimated samples of the right-hand side of Equation 2. These samples are computed using actual experience with the task, in the form of weighted penalty vectors and pairs of subsequent states x_k, x_{k+1}:

$$\begin{aligned}\vec{Q}_{k+1}(x_k,a_k) &= \vec{Q}_k(x_k,a_k) + \\ \alpha_k[\vec{\phi}_{k+1} &+ \gamma \vec{Q}_k(x_{k+1},a') - \vec{Q}_k(x_k,a_k)]\end{aligned} \quad (3)$$

where $a' = \text{argmin}_{a'}[\vec{w} \cdot \vec{Q}_k(x_{k+1},a')]$.

In variable-penalty settings, we employ an efficient variable-transfer algorithm derived from [29]. Since the immediate penalty at each time step is a linear combination of different penalty factors (e.g., usability penalty, electricity cost), and the Q-value function (long term penalty) is based on the sums of the immediate penalties, we can infer that the *expected discounted penalty* of policy π starting from state x: $\vec{w} \cdot \vec{Q}^\pi(x,a)$ is also linear in penalty weights.

In variable-penalty reinforcement learning, each weight vector corresponds to an individual Markov decision process. All the MDPs share the same transition dynamics (i.e., same states, same actions, same transition function, etc. One example is that delaying a task will always increase user frustration), but are linear in a set of penalty features. Thus, given a new weight vector $\vec{w}_{new}$ and a starting state x_k, one can approximate the optimal policy π_{new} for the new weight vector based on the already learned policy set $\mathcal{C}$, simply by selecting the one with minimum expected discounted penalty $\pi_{new} = \text{argmin}_{\pi \in \mathcal{C}} Q^\pi(x_k,a')$, where $a' = \text{argmin}_{a'}[\vec{w}_{new} \cdot \vec{Q}^\pi(x_k,a')]$.

SUP-MCRL is presented in Algorithm 1. In step 11, the agent tests all actions in all states with nonzero probability, which is an exploration-exploitation tradeoff problem. The agent uses the Boltzmann exploration strategy, which in state x selects action a with probability

$$Probability(x,a) = \frac{e^{1/(\tau \vec{w} \cdot \vec{Q}(x,a))}}{\sum_{a'} e^{1/(\tau \vec{w} \cdot \vec{Q}(x,a'))}} \quad (4)$$

where $\tau > 0$ controls the randomness of the exploration. When $\tau \rightarrow 0$, this is equivalent with greedy action selection. When $\tau \rightarrow \infty$, actions are random. When $\tau \in (0,\infty)$, actions with lower penalties are more likely to be selected.

5.2 Real-time Risk Assessment (RRA) for SUP

The above model assumes that all the inputs are valid. However, the control commands and price data could be

---

Algorithm 1 Multi-Criteria Reinforcement Learning for SUP

$i \leftarrow 1$
$c \leftarrow 0$
$\mathcal{C} \leftarrow \emptyset$
$\pi_{init} \leftarrow \emptyset$
repeat
  Obtain the current weight vector $\vec{w}$ and the starting state x_k
  if $\mathcal{C} \neq \emptyset$ **then**
    Compute $\pi_{init} \leftarrow \vec{w} \cdot \vec{Q}^\pi(x_k,a')$
    Initialize the Q-function vectors of the states
  end if
  Learn the new policy π' through vector Q-Learning
  if ($\mathcal{C} = \emptyset$) or $\vec{w} \cdot Q^{\pi_{init}}(x_k,a') - (\vec{w} \cdot Q^{\pi'}(x_k,a'') > \gamma)$ **then**
    $\mathcal{C} \leftarrow \mathcal{C} \cup \pi'$
    $c \leftarrow 0$
    $i \leftarrow i + 1$
  else
    $c \leftarrow c + 1$
  end if
until $c \geq \frac{1}{\epsilon} \ln \frac{(i+1)^2}{\delta}$
return $\mathcal{C}$

---

fake since the input channels from remote sources are vulnerable. Assuming (trusted) historical data is available, we can further evaluate the trustworthiness of current inputs by comparing them with the reference data. Due to the different characteristics of smart pricing signals and remote user control commands, we evaluate different input channels with different models. In particular, real-time pricing signals mostly show a periodical pattern that repeats daily; while the user control commands are more likely to be scattered over a certain period of a day and usually conform to diversiform distributions. The RRA scheme estimates anomalies when the new patterns are not in accordance with a historic norm, and generates two risk indexes, indicating the belief (for RTP) and the confidence (for remote use control commands) that the input sources are trustworthy, respectively.

5.2.1 RRA-RTP

The smart pricing signal p in S2A is represented in terms of stochastic variables that are time indexed. Suppose RTP circulates in periods of T. Rather than serializing real-time pricing data continuously over time, we model the current pricing by exploiting the periodical structure of historic pricing information, and extracting each RTP p_t^d at time t ($t = 1, ..., T$) as a distinct stochastic process, which evolves over the index of changing cycles d. For instance, if electricity pricing data changes/evolves daily, the pricing sequence at midnight could be modeled as random variables that are indexed with dates, as these pricing variables are more closely correlated and easier to be inferred.

For real-time risk assessment of smart pricing inputs, we choose a Hidden Markov Model (HMM), where the hidden states correspond to the working conditions $z_{1:T}$ of an appliance (i.e., time-indexed states indicating whether the appliance is under attack), and the observable states correspond to the real-time pricing states $p_{1:T}$ (and any other states that we could measure). Such Dynamic Bayesian Network (DBN) encodes the joint probability distribution over those stochastic variables that capture the evolution of the dynamic working conditions. In particular, we adopt the following state transition model P_t and observation model P_o:

$$z_t \sim P_t(\hat{z}_t|z_{t-1})$$
$$p_t \sim P_o(\hat{p}_t|\mathbf{p}_t^{hist}, z_t)$$

where $\hat{z}_t$ and $\hat{p}_t$ are the predicted states, $\mathbf{p}_t^{hist}$ denotes the historic pricing vector at time t, $p_t \in \mathbb{R}^+$ is the real-time pricing signal, and $z_t \in \{True, False\}$ denotes the unknown hidden states. The parameters of the conditional probability functions are known matrices that could be obtained or learned from the S2A system. Although we only consider smart pricing signals as observable states for discussion simplicity, it is worth mentioning that our RRA-RTP algorithm is also applicable for DBNs with multi-dimensional observation states with minor modification.

The aim of the analysis is to compute the posterior distribution of the hidden states $P(z_{0:t}|p_{1:t})$. Since the observation model could be non-Gaussian distribution (i.e., daily electricity pricing may change significantly with seasons), we employ a *particle filtering* (PF) algorithm [37] to approximate the probability distribution of the hidden variables. The basic idea is to establish a posterior probability distribution of the hidden variable by utilizing a large number of random samples. The samples are propagated over time in a sequential importance sampling step and a subsequent resampling step: (1) The SIS step generates samples from a specific probability distribution and computes their associate weight. (2) The resampling step then multiplies and/or discards these samples to automatically concentrate them in regions of interest of the state-space of the hidden variables.

Given N particles $\{z_{0:t-1}^{(i)}\}_{i=1}^{N}$ at time $t-1$ approximately distributed according to the distribution $P(z_{0:t-1}^{(i)}|p_{1:t-1})$, particle filters enable us to compute N particles $\{z_{0:t}^{(i)}\}_{i=1}^{N}$ approximately distributed according to the posterior $P(z_{0:t}^{(i)}|p_{1:t})$ at time t. As we cannot sample from the posterior directly, the PF update process is achieved by an appropriate importance proposal distribution $Q(z_{0:t})$, from which we can generate samples:

$$Q(\hat{z}_{0:t}|p_{1:t}) = Q(\hat{z}_t|z_{0:t-1}, p_t)P(z_{0:t-1}|p_{1:t-1})$$

The samples from $Q(\cdot)$ must be weighted by the importance weights

$$w_t = \frac{P(\hat{z}_{0:t}|p_{1:t})}{Q(\hat{z}_{0:t}|p_{1:t})} \propto \frac{P_o(p_t|\mathbf{p}_t^{hist}, \hat{z}_t)P_t(\hat{z}_t|z_{0:t-1})}{Q_t(\hat{z}_t|z_{0:t-1}, p_{1:t})} \quad (5)$$

where $Q_t(\cdot|\cdot)$ denotes the choice of proposal distribution. To simplify the calculation, one can adopt the transition prior as proposal distribution (i.e., $Q_t(\cdot|\cdot) = P_t(\cdot|\cdot)$) [13]. In this case, the weights are given by the likelihood function

$$w_t = P_o(p_t|\mathbf{p}_t^{hist}, \hat{z}_t)$$

The detailed algorithm is shown in 2.

5.2.2 RRA-UCC

The patterns of user control commands are highly user-dependent, and may be non-revolving. Such characteristics make it infeasible to construct a probabilistic graphical model as we did in RRA-RTP for anomaly inference. Instead, we formulate a *frequentist approach* to assess the reliability of remote control signals, using observed frequencies and statistical hypothesis testing. With historic data, any

---

Algorithm 2 RRA-RTP with Particle Filtering

---
for $t = 1$ to T **do**
  For $i = 1, ..., N$, sample from the transition priors $\hat{z}_t^{(i)} \propto P_t(z_t|z_{t-1}^{(i)})$, and set

$$\hat{z}_{0:t}^{(i)} \leftarrow (\hat{z}_t^{(i)}, z_{0:t-1}^{(i)})$$

  For $i = 1, ..., N$, evaluate and normalize the importance weights

$$w_t^{(i)} \propto P_o(p_t|\mathbf{p}_t^{hist}, z_t^{(i)})$$

  Multiply/Discard particles with respect to high/low importance weights $w_t^{(i)}$ to obtain N particles $\{z_{0:t}^{(i)}\}_{i=1}^{N}$.
end for

---

given (daily) UCC input can be considered as one of an infinite sequence of possible repetitions of the same experiment, each capable of producing statistically independent results.

In RRA-UCC, we integrate two complementary risk assessment schemes to detect anomalies in task starting time (e.g. remotely start the bread maker at 1am) and anomalies in task frequency (e.g. switch smart car charging on and off 10 times in a minute), respectively. In our settings, smart appliances have pre-built default distribution patterns of starting times, whose parameters are learned from the usage in the household. Normally, the UCC distribution prototype of appliances is a sum of N Gaussians in the form

$$f(x) = \sum_i a_i \exp(-\frac{(x - \mu_i)^2}{2\sigma_i^2}).$$

For instance, a smart dishwasher is embedded with a UCC prior in the form of three Gaussian distributions. In a household where residents do not eat breakfast, the first Gaussian will show a weak (or none) peak. Given the number of Gaussians in the prior distribution, we can easily obtain the parameters of each component distribution by multi-Gaussian fitting techniques (e.g.,[49]). The mean values μ_i are clustering centers of the user control commands. The confidence level α_t of an incoming command $c(t)$ appearing at time t is then evaluated according to the ith Gaussian with the nearest mean value: $\alpha_t = f_i\{(t - \mu_i)/\sigma_i^2\}$, where $i = \text{argmin}_i (t - \mu_i)$. Next, to detect operation frequency anomalies, we explore the periodical control command interval distributions in a household. The basic idea is that, the intervals between adjacent operations within a certain period should conform to the historic norm. Suppose that a significant repeating cycle of an appliance's behavior is T (generally T should be $n \in \mathbb{N}^+$ days). At time t, appliance A receives a remote control command $c(t)$. We obtain all the intervals between UCCs in $[t - T, t]$, and compare its distribution with the distributions of intervals in time slices $[t - 2T, t - T], ..., [t - mT, t - (m - 1)T]$ from historic clean data using non-parametric statistical testing approaches (i.e., Kolmogorov-Smirnov Test [9]). Then we select the historic time slice(s) where UCC intervals are most similarly distributed with the current time window $[t-T, t]$, and retrieve the statistical test results α_f (i.e., the p-value of K-S test) as a measurement of trustworthiness of the current operation frequency.

The frequentist approach gives a confidence level with a frequency probability interpretation and/or a pre-experiment interpretation. Such probabilities are combined as the risk

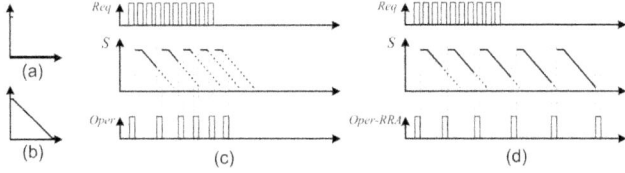

Figure 7: Real-time risk assessment for UCC of smart car charging system.

assessment of the user control command:

$$R_u = f(\alpha_t) + g(\alpha_f) \qquad (6)$$

where $f(\cdot)$ and $g(\cdot)$ are monotone increasing functions.

Example 8: We consider a smart car, which could be remotely controlled to start and stop charging. In Figure 7, (a) and (b) are security penalty functions for the charging system: users can start charging at anytime, but need to wait for a while to restart charging after stopping it. An adversary, taking over the control, can send many consecutive charging requests. In the basic SUP model w/o risk detection, usability penalty increases as the later tasks are being hold by the security function. The increasing $u(t)$ penalty will force charging to restart soon after the security function drops below MAX. Restart interval will decrease with higher usability penalty. On the other hand, with RRA, it is detected that the requests are unusual. With more requests received, weight for $u(t)$ will decrease significantly, so that usability will have very small impact in operational decision making. Therefore, recharging interval will increase to a level that will not hurt physical security of the battery. □

6. SECURITY ANALYSIS

Objective. From security perspective, the goal of the S2A approach is to ensure that: (1) the smart device shall not work in extreme state; and (2) the smart device shall not work in abnormal state for a long period. It is acceptable that a device may need to work in abnormal mode for a short while in special circumstances, or while the risk assessment components are in the process of detecting an intrusion.

Threat model. We assume that smart devices are physically secure since they are usually located inside the house. We also assume that their control systems are not compromised – the control logic is relatively less complicate, and they only receive limited information (control and price) from designated sources; therefore, it is not easy to hack into the kernels of smart devices. Devices are under two types of threats: (a) improper operational requests from legitimate users; and (b) faked operational requests or electricity prices from attackers. Threat (a) is usually once-only, while threat (b) could be continuous and more risky.

Baseline security. In response to threat (a), physical security of each individual appliance is protected by security penalty function $s(t)$ in S2A. $s(t)$ defines the penalty of turning on or keeping on the appliance at time t. It cannot be overridden by other factors. However, it could be suppressed when the usability penalty is high (e.g. the task had been held for a long time), so that the appliance may work at non-favorable mode for a short period of time. Both $s(t)$ and $u(t)$ are generated by mechanisms embedded in smart

appliances. Manufactures should set a very high security penalty (e.g. infinite) when the device is approaching extreme status. Moreover, to ensure security objective (1) described above, $s(t)$ cannot be surpassed when it reaches max – the device must be switched off. Therefore, with a properly designed security function, the device is guaranteed not to work in extreme state. The baseline security assurance applies for both threat (a) and (b).

Response to continuous attacks. Tier 2 of the S2A framework is to identify abnormal inputs, especially continuous abnormal inputs. Forged pricing data (or legitimate but unstable data) is detected by the RRA-RTP component. The RRA-RTP model employs HMM, so that the current risk assessment will affect the next assessment; therefore, the risk index will propagate continuously. When pricing information demonstrates unusual patterns for an extended period of time, RRA-RTP will detect increasing risk, and the weight for $p(t)$ will continuously decrease. In this way, price factor will become too weak to disturb the normal operations of the device. On the other hand, fake user input will be detected by RRA-UCC. A one-time fake command may not be detected if the command history does not demonstrate a strong pattern, or the fake command falls in the pattern. Meanwhile, when the attacker sends multiple commands in a short period of time (e.g. "start battery charging" - "stop charging" - "start charging" - etc.), the high frequency abnormalities are always accurately detected. The weight for usability factor decreases accordingly, and the system sees less need to fulfill such requests. S2A ensures that the smart device will not work in extreme mode in any condition; and also ensures that the smart device will not work in abnormal mode for a long period, with the presence of continuous attacks (faked operational requests or electricity prices).

False positives. Traditional intrusion detection systems (IDS) strive to reduce false positives and false negatives. Conceptually, *false negatives* are undetected anomalies. As we have shown, since we do not label the input data with a binary decision (safe or abnormal), unusual inputs will always be penalized in the second tier of the SUP model. On the other hand, *false positives* are normal inputs (that appears to be suspicious) that are mistakenly labeled as anomalies. Again, since we do not enforce a decision boundary, such inputs are not classified as anomalies. As they carry patterns that are different from regular ones, they will be somehow penalized (i.e. weights will be reduced) in the SUP model. However, the degree of the penalties are lower than the "true negatives". More importantly, the existence of the usability criterion effectively balances the (wrong) penalties, so that users will not become extremely dissatisfied.

Comparison with rule-based security protection. In some appliances, security protection is provided by rule-based decision (e.g. the motor should stop after continuous operation for 5 minutes, or the device has to remain off for 3 minutes before turned on again). Compared with rule-based decision method, we provide fine-grained security protection – SUP starts protection before reaching the extremely critical point (i.e., the rule-based decision boundary), but also allows a certain level of compromise at the strong demands from other factors. Moreover, in the presence of continuous active attacks, we provide better security by dropping attacker inputs, instead of working at minimum-protection

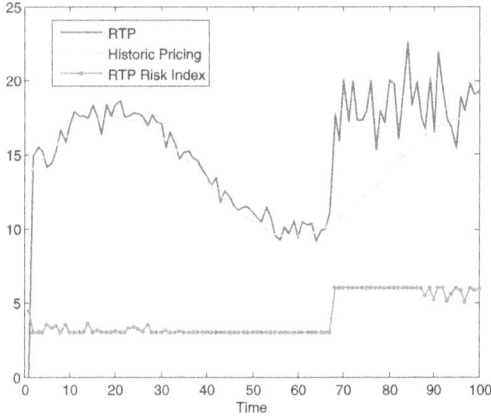

Figure 8: Real-time risk assessment for realtime pricing: RRA-RTP

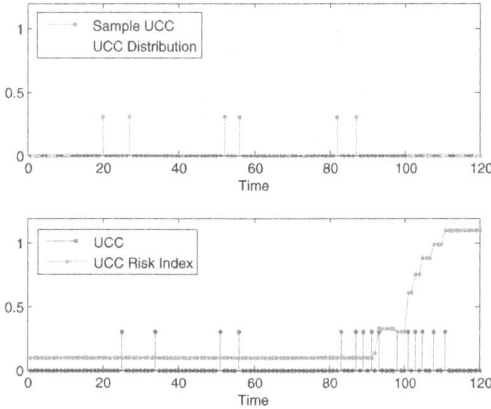

Figure 9: Real-time risk assessment for user control commands: RRA-UCC

conditions (as shown in Example 4 in Section 3). On the other hand, when we take smart pricing and remote control into consideration, the system becomes too complicated to be handled by rule-based models.

7. EXPERIMENTAL RESULTS

To demonstrate the effectiveness of the S2A approach, we first generated synthetic usage and pricing data based on heuristic assumptions, and tested S2A with these data. Note that our S2A framework could take arbitrary form of UCC and RTP inputs; as well as arbitrary form of security and usability penalties. In our simulation, the Q-value of a state-action pair converges after approximately 150 learning steps. In real world applications, however, the Q-table of a smart appliance is usually pre-trained by manufacturer, so that it would adapt to new conditions faster and more accurate.

For RRA-RTP, we implement Algorithm 2 with 1000 particles. The observation model P_o is set to be the weighted sum of historic mean RTP and white noises, where the weights are derived from the current states z_t in the HMM. As is shown in Figure 8, historical pricing (dashed line) follows a periodic pattern that revolves daily. The solid blue line denotes realtime pricing, and the red dots indicates the risk indexes (R_p) generated by RRA-RTP. As shown, RTP devi-

ates away from the historic distribution starting from time point 68. The anomalies are detected and R_p increases correspondingly. On the other hand, Figure 9 shows the real-time risk assessments of user control commands. The upper plot shows the UCC distribution pattern, which is learned from historical control commands. The lower figure denotes real-time user control commands and the corresponding risk indexes generated by our algorithm. As we can see, slight offsets of request time will not immediately affect the risk assessment. However, clear unusual patterns (starting at time 90) are effectively detected. The risk index increases when we have higher confidence that the received control commands demonstrate an abnormal pattern.

We have tested S2A for different alternations of user commands, electricity pricing and security penalty patterns. Figure 10 demonstrates part of the experiment, which contains a complete use case. In this experiment, we adopt a scenario that the device cannot work for a long time (e.g. a motor). As shown in the first plot, a request is made at time point 4829 (middle of X-axis). It is put on hold due to high RTP (plot 4), and usability penalty starts to increase (plot 3). At approximately time 4840, usability penalty surpasses RTP penalty, the job starts to be processed, and the security penalty increases. S and P together stop the operation at time 4842, and waited until time 4848, when RTP drops to very low. From 4848 to the end of the task, the security penalty has stopped the operation twice, to force the motor to cool off. Overall, the task was completed with balanced considerations of S, U, and P.

8. CONCLUSION & FUTURE WORK

In this paper, we present S2A, a two-stage security protection framework for smart household appliances. We first introduce a Security–User–Price (SUP) model to capture three key factors, and present a multi-criteria reinforcement learning (MCRL) approach to integrate all three factors to dynamically determine an optimal operational strategy for the smart device. Furthermore, we present two risk assessment approaches based on statistical inferences. They evaluate the trustworthiness of users' remote control commands as well as the pricing information received through smart grid communication systems. The realtime risk indices are seamlessly incorporated into the SUP model to serve as weighting factors of the corresponding penalty functions, therefore ensures device security under active attacks. Through security analysis and experimental results, we show that S2A protects the device security of smart appliances, while maintaining usability and economic efficiency.

We have presented the S2A model in the paper, however, deploying the model on smart appliances still requires a lot of research and engineering efforts. First, it is nontrivial to define security functions for different types of smart devices. For appliances with sensors to monitor device status, it is also challenging to quantify (usually non-linear) sensor inputs and assess risks. On the other hand, it requires intensive human and behavior studies to observe usage habits of different devices and construct usability functions from the observed patterns. That is, the model still needs to be equipped with application-specific parameters to demonstrate best performance. Finally, it is important and effective to enable collaborations between smart devices for situational awareness and better risk assessment.

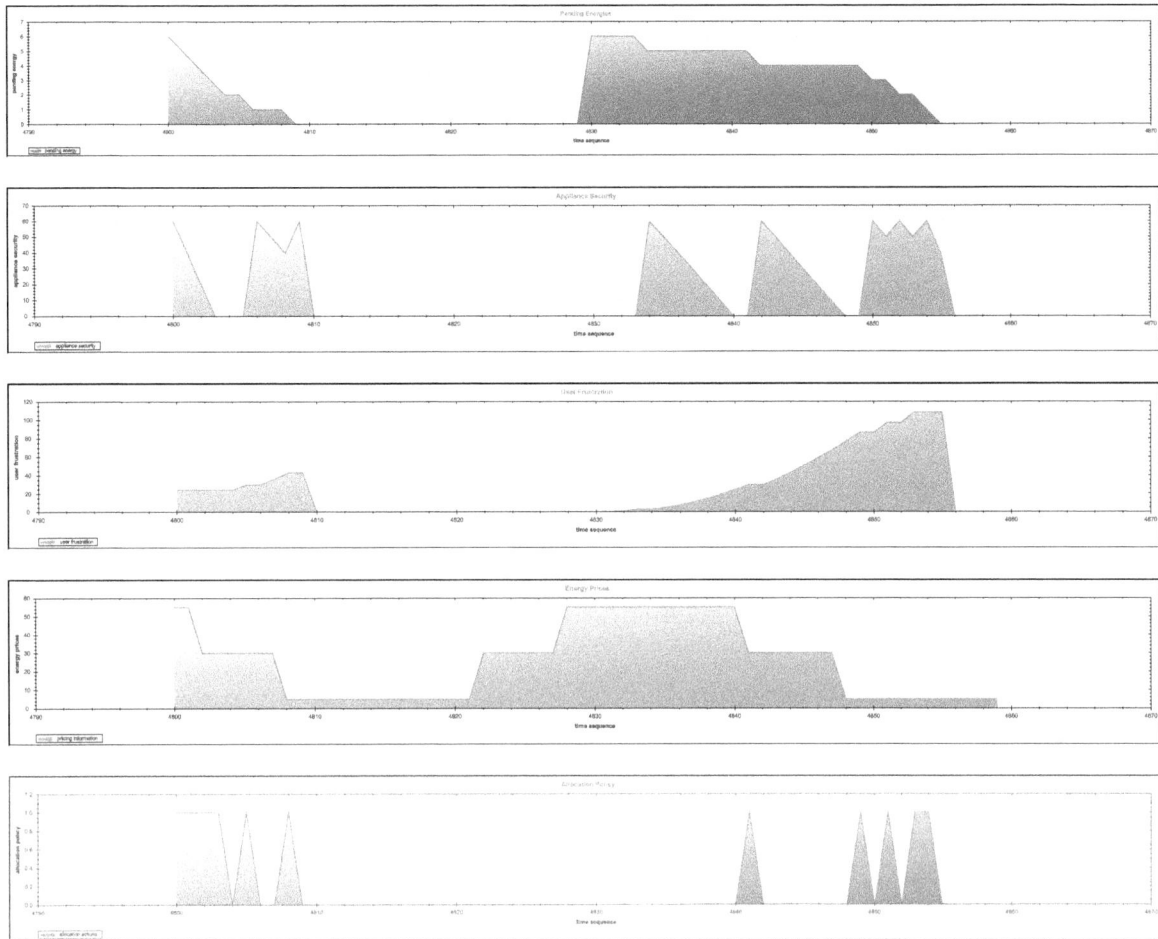

Figure 10: Sample results for S2A. From top to bottom: pending energy, appliance security penalty, usability penalty, smart pricing, and energy allocation actions.

9. ACKNOWLEDGEMENTS

Bo Luo was partially supported by NSF OIA-1028098 and University of Kansas General Research Fund 2301420. The authors would like to thank the anonymous reviewers for their constructive suggestions to improve the manuscript.

10. REFERENCES

[1] A. Aggarwal, S. Kunta, and P. Verma. A proposed communications infrastructure for the smart grid. In *Innovative Smart Grid Technologies (ISGT)*, 2010.

[2] T. Baumeister. Literature review on smart grid cyber security. Technical Report CSDL-10-10, Department of Information and Computer Sciences, University of Hawaii, Honolulu, Hawaii 96822, Dec. 2010.

[3] R. Berthier, W. Sanders, and H. Khurana. Intrusion detection for advanced metering infrastructures: Requirements and architectural directions. In *IEEE SmartGridComm*, pages 350 –355, oct. 2010.

[4] S. Borenstein. The long-run efficiency of real-time electricity pricing. *The Energy Journal*, 26(3), 2005.

[5] S. Borenstein. The redistributional impact of non-linear electricity pricing. Working paper 602, Regulation2point0, 2010.

[6] A. Bose. Smart transmission grid applications and their supporting infrastructure. *Smart Grid, IEEE Transactions on*, 1(1):11 –19, june 2010.

[7] F. Cleveland. Cyber security issues for advanced metering infrasttructure (ami). In *IEEE Power and Energy Society General Meeting*, pages 1 –5, july 2008.

[8] F. Cohen. The smarter grid. *Security Privacy, IEEE*, 8(1):60 –63, jan.-feb. 2010.

[9] W. J. Conover. *Practical Nonparametric Statistics*. John Wiley & Sons, December 1998.

[10] Q. Dam, S. Mohagheghi, and J. Stoupis. Intelligent demand response scheme for customer side load management. In *IEEE ENERGY 2008*, 2008.

[11] H. Farhangi. The path of the smart grid. *Power and Energy Magazine, IEEE*, 8(1):18 –28, 2010.

[12] A. Faruqui and S. George. Quantifying customer response to dynamic pricing. *The Electricity Journal*, 18(4):53 – 63, 2005.

[13] N. Gordon, D. Salmond, and A. Smith. Novel approach to nonlinear/non-gaussian bayesian state estimation. *Radar and Signal Processing, IEE Proceedings F*, 140(2):107 –113, apr 1993.

[14] A. B. Haney, T. Jamasb, and M. G. Pollitt. Smart metering and electricity demand: Technology,

economics and international experience. Technical report, Faculty of Economics, University of Cambridge, 2009.

[15] K. Herter, P. McAuliffe, and A. Rosenfeld. An exploratory analysis of california residential customer response to critical peak pricing of electricity. *Energy*, 32(1):25 – 34, 2007.

[16] A. Johnson. The history of the smart grid evolution at southern california edison. In *Innovative Smart Grid Technologies (ISGT)*, pages 1 –3, jan. 2010.

[17] W. Kempton and J. Tomic. Vehicle-to-grid power fundamentals: Calculating capacity and net revenue. *Journal of Power Sources*, 144(1):268 – 279, 2005.

[18] W. Kempton and J. Tomic. Vehicle-to-grid power implementation: From stabilizing the grid to supporting large-scale renewable energy. *Journal of Power Sources*, 144(1):280 – 294, 2005.

[19] H. Khurana, M. Hadley, N. Lu, and D. Frincke. Smart-grid security issues. *Security Privacy, IEEE*, 8(1):81 –85, jan.-feb. 2010.

[20] Y. Kim, T. Schmid, Z. M. Charbiwala, and M. B. Srivastava. Viridiscope: design and implementation of a fine grained power monitoring system for homes. In *Ubicomp '09*, 2009.

[21] M. A. Lisovich, D. K. Mulligan, and S. B. Wicker. Inferring personal information from demand-response systems. *IEEE Security and Privacy*, 8:11–20, 2010.

[22] S.-W. Luan, J.-H. Teng, S.-Y. Chan, and L.-C. Hwang. Development of a smart power meter for ami based on zigbee communication. In *PEDS*, 2009.

[23] J. marc Seigneur, C. D. Jensen, S. Farrell, E. Gray, and Y. Chen. Towards security auto-configuration for smart appliances. In *in Proceedings of the Smart Objects Conference*, pages 03–45, 2003.

[24] M. Masoum, P. Moses, and S. Deilami. Load management in smart grids considering harmonic distortion and transformer derating. In *Innovative Smart Grid Technologies (ISGT)*, 19-21 2010.

[25] S. Massoud Amin and B. Wollenberg. Toward a smart grid: power delivery for the 21st century. *Power and Energy Magazine, IEEE*, 3(5):34 – 41, sept.-oct. 2005.

[26] P. McDaniel and S. McLaughlin. Security and privacy challenges in the smart grid. *Security Privacy, IEEE*, 7(3):75 –77, may-june 2009.

[27] S. McLaughlin, D. Podkuiko, and P. McDaniel. Energy theft in the advanced metering infrastructure. In *Critical Information Infrastructures Security*. 2010.

[28] S. McLaughlin, D. Podkuiko, S. Miadzvezhanka, A. Delozier, and P. McDaniel. Multi-vendor penetration testing in the advanced metering infrastructure. In *ACSAC*, 2010.

[29] N. Mehta, S. Natarajan, P. Tadepalli, and A. Fern. Transfer in variable-reward hierarchical reinforcement learning. *Machine Learning*, 73(3):289–312, 2008.

[30] A. Metke and R. Ekl. Smart grid security technology. In *Innovative Smart Grid Technologies*, 2010.

[31] A. R. Metke and R. L. Ekl. Security technology for smart grid networks. *Smart Grid, IEEE Transactions on*, 1(1), june 2010.

[32] K. Moslehi and R. Kumar. Smart grid - a reliability

perspective. In *Innovative Smart Grid Technologies (ISGT)*, pages 1 –8, 19-21 2010.

[33] H. Nakakita, K. Yamaguchi, M. Hashimoto, T. Saito, and M. Sakurai. A study on secure wireless networks consisting of home appliances. *Consumer Electronics, IEEE Transactions on*, 49(2):375 – 381, may 2003.

[34] D. O'Neill, M. Levorato, A. Goldsmith, and U. Mitra. Residential demand response using reinforcement learning. In *IEEE SmartGridComm*, 2010.

[35] F. Orecchini and A. Santiangeli. Beyond smart grids - the need of intelligent energy networks for a higher global efficiency through energy vectors integration. *International Journal of Hydrogen Energy*, 2011.

[36] D. Petersen, J. Steele, and J. Wilkerson. Wattbot: a residential electricity monitoring and feedback system. In *CHI*, 2009.

[37] B. Ristic, S. Arulampalam, and N. Gordon. *Beyond the Kalman Filter: Particle Filters for Tracking Applications*. Artech House, 2004.

[38] B. D. Russell and C. L. Benner. Intelligent systems for improved reliability and failure diagnosis in distribution systems. *Smart Grid, IEEE Transactions on*, 1(1):48 –56, june 2010.

[39] T. Sauter and M. Lobashov. End-to-end communication architecture for smart grids. *IEEE Transactions on Industrial Electronics*, 58(4), 2011.

[40] S.-Y. Son and B.-J. Chung. A korean smart grid architecture design for a field test based on power it. In *Transmission Distribution Conference Exposition: Asia and Pacific, 2009*, pages 1 –4, oct. 2009.

[41] V. Sood, D. Fischer, J. Eklund, and T. Brown. Developing a communication infrastructure for the smart grid. In *Electrical Power Energy Conference (EPEC), 2009 IEEE*, pages 1 –7, oct. 2009.

[42] G. Srinivasa Prasanna, A. Lakshmi, S. Sumanth, V. Simha, J. Bapat, and G. Koomullil. Data communication over the smart grid. In *IEEE International Symposium on Power Line Communications and Its Applications*, 2009.

[43] C. J. C. H. Watkins and P. Dayan. Q-learning. *Machine Learning*, 8:279–292, 1992.

[44] D. Wei, Y. Lu, M. Jafari, P. Skare, and K. Rohde. An integrated security system of protecting smart grid against cyber attacks. In *Innovative Smart Grid Technologies, 2010*, pages 1–7. IEEE, 2010.

[45] X. Wei, Z. Yu-hui, and Z. Jie-lin. Energy-efficient distribution in smart grid. In *SUPERGEN*, 2009.

[46] M. Weiss and D. Guinard. Increasing energy awareness through web-enabled power outlets. In *MUM*, 2010.

[47] M. Weiss, F. Mattern, T. Graml, T. Staake, and E. Fleisch. Handy feedback: connecting smart meters with mobile phones. In *Ubicomp '09*, 2009.

[48] P. Wolfs and S. Isalm. Potential barriers to smart grid technology in australia. In *Australasian Universities Power Engineering Conference*, 2009.

[49] D. Xu, L. Yang, and Z. He. Overcomplete time delay estimation using multi-gaussian fitting method. In *IEEE VLSI Design and Video Technology*, 2005.

[50] Z. Zhang. Smart grid in america and europe: Similar desires, different approaches (part 1). *Public Utilities Fortnightly*, 149(1), 2011.

Protecting Health Information on Mobile Devices

Musheer Ahmed and Mustaque Ahamad
Georgia Tech Information Security Center (GTISC)
School of Computer Science, Georgia Institute of Technology
{musheer, mustaq}@cc.gatech.edu

ABSTRACT

Mobile applications running on devices such as smart phones and tablets will be increasingly used to provide convenient access to health information to health professionals and patients. Also, patients will use these devices to transmit health information captured by sensing devices in settings like the home to remote repositories. As mobile devices become targets of security threats, we must address the problem of protecting sensitive health information on them. We explore key threats to data on mobile devices and develop a security framework that can help protect it against such threats. We implemented this framework in the Android operating system and augmented it with user consent detection to enhance user awareness and control over the use of health information.

Our framework can be used to enforce security policies that govern access to sensitive health data on mobile devices. Physicians and patients using our framework can install third-party healthcare applications with the guarantee that sensitive medical information will not be sent without their knowledge even when these applications are compromised. We describe the key mechanisms implemented by our framework and how they can enforce a security policy. We also discuss our early experience with the framework.

Categories and Subject Descriptors

D.4.6 [**Operating Systems**]: Security and Protection—*Information flow controls*

General Terms

Security

Keywords

Security; Mobile Devices; Healthcare Data Protection

1. INTRODUCTION

Mobile devices like smart phones have evolved from being simple calling units to sophisticated computing devices with rich functionality. They are easily available and always connected which makes them highly attractive for accessing medical data at any location and during emergencies. Such timely and convenient access could improve healthcare quality and reduce costs but it introduces the problem of protection of health data on mobile devices. Since health data could be highly sensitive, it must be secured to build user trust and meet regulatory requirements.

Unfortunately, mobile devices are known to be vulnerable to a wide variety of security threats [5] and they are becoming increasing targets of malware authors [1]. Studies have shown that medical data disclosure is already the second highest breach category [11]. Thus, if such data is accessed on mobile devices, we need to protect it against attacks that would exploit mobile device vulnerabilities. There are several challenges that must be addressed for secure health information access on mobile devices. Because such devices are popular platforms for running a variety of applications, we must ensure that sensitive data does not flow to untrusted applications. Also, such data must not be allowed to flow outside of the device to untrusted hosts. Explicit user consent can be useful when it is not clear if certain data sharing should be permitted. In this case, we need to securely capture and process user input to avoid malware scripted events that can attempt to mimic user actions.

In this paper, we explore security mechanisms that provide a framework for enforcing security policies that are inspired by health information security and privacy principles, including use limitation, security safeguards, and patient awareness [15]. Our security framework can help protect sensitive medical data against unsafe and unintended uses on mobile devices. We implement this framework on the Android operating system by building on its existing data protection features. Our security enhanced framework helps prevent third-party healthcare applications from leaking sensitive medical information even when they become infected by malware. These third-party healthcare applications do not require any modifications to work with our framework.

Explicit patient consent plays an important role in how medical information is shared. Unfortunately sophisticated malware can script events to fool healthcare applications into believing that user consent has been obtained. To counter such attacks, we also explore a secure consent detection mechanism for mobile platforms which helps distinguish between user initiated actions and scripted malware actions. This mechanism could be highly effective in preventing unintended disclosure of medical information. Since it is only activated when necessary, it does not consume significant amount of resources. Our policy enforcement and user consent detection mechanisms can support security policies that will be deployed to meet the requirements for a high-quality mHealth system [14].

We make the following contributions in this work:

- We introduce the concept of a constrained application for the Android platform which can be used to safeguard sensitive data and prevent its flow to unauthorized entities. A constrained application's sensitive data can be protected even in the presence of attacks that can successfully compromise the application.

- We identify the mechanisms necessary to support constrained application execution on Android and explore how these mechanisms can be implemented.

- We propose and describe how a user consent detection mechanism can help distinguish actual user input from scripted events that can be generated by malware. Such secure consent can enable user awareness and control over how health information is shared.

- We use sample health applications and a security policy to demonstrate how sensitive health data can be securely accessed on mobile devices.

Although the mechanisms proposed by us can help protect sensitive data for a variety of applications, we make certain assumptions that make them particularly useful for health applications. Our approach requires tagging of sensitive data which is easier when it is accessed for a small number of trusted repositories. We also rely on user consent which is well accepted in the healthcare domain. Finally, user consent based override is well suited for health applications where "break-the-glass" scenarios allow exceptions to security policies in case of emergencies.

The rest of the paper is organized as follows. Section 2 provides the motivation for the problem explored in the paper and outlines security policy requirements. We discuss our research approach in Section 3. Section 4 describes the implementation details of our framework and Section 5 provides an evaluation of our framework. Sections 6 discusses related research and we conclude the paper in Section 7.

2. MOBILE DEVICE DATA SECURITY: MOTIVATION AND REQUIREMENTS

The motivation for securing health data accessed on mobile devices comes from two observations. First, mobile devices offer a convenient way for users to access information. Second, since such devices can run a variety of applications which can communicate with each other and external entities, patients and healthcare providers are naturally concerned about unauthorized disclosure of health data. Such disclosure could have serious consequences on patients, ranging from medical identity theft to blackmail or discrimination. If a health application captures and stores new data into medical records maintained in a remote repository, unauthorized updates could corrupt the medical history of a patient which could have serious consequences for future diagnosis or treatment. Because of these reasons, healthcare regulations such as the Health Insurance Portability and Accountability Act (HIPAA) and Health Information Technology for Economic and Clinical Health (HITECH) Act address privacy and security of health information when it is accessed by entities engaged in healthcare related activities. These outline rules that apply to doctors, pharmacists, medical insurance and billing agents to name a few who fall in the category of covered entities. We briefly discuss two relevant rules which help us understand the need for protecting health data when it is accessed on mobile devices.

The HIPAA privacy rule protects all individually identifiable health information held or transmitted by a covered entity. Disclosures can only be made for specific purposes or situations such as the treatment, payment or other healthcare related operation. The privacy rule requires covered entities to maintain reasonable technical data safeguards to prevent intentional or unintentional use or disclosure of protected health information [12]. The HIPAA security rule requires a covered entity to ensure the confidentiality, integrity, and availability of health information that it creates, receives, maintains, or transmits. The covered entities must also protect against reasonably anticipated threats, hazards and disclosures that are not permitted by the privacy rule [13]. As healthcare professionals access sensitive patient medical data on mobile devices, regulatory requirements will apply to these devices as well. To secure data as mandated for covered entities or desired by patients, it becomes vital for us to understand the threats faced by electronic health information on a mobile device.

Unintended disclosures of protected health information could happen on mobile devices due to malware infections. Malicious software is known to install itself on computing devices through some vulnerability in an application or by using social engineering techniques to trick the user. Such malware, once installed on the device, could obtain sensitive information stored on the device or from other applications and can send it to untrusted applications or remote malicious entities.

Another threat comes from application developers who do not take appropriate measures to ensure data security. This could leave the data vulnerable to violations of confidentiality and integrity. Already, there is evidence that many applications share data with external entities without explicit consent of owners of devices where such applications run [3]. Although the operating system could be the target of attacks, we focus on more common attacks that target applications.

Finally, devices could be stolen or used when left unattended which would eventually lead to disclosure of sensitive medical information. Other work has explored techniques like data encryption and remote monitoring of access to data to counter this threat and we will not address it in this work [8].

2.1 Mobile Device Data Security Policies

Based on the security and privacy requirements of electronic health information and the relevant threats in a mobile environment, we can now outline key features of security policies that can be used to ensure proper use of health data on mobile devices. Mobile devices are commonly used by a single user and operate under user control. Therefore, their security policies are different from other platforms. The security policy on these devices typically does not rely on identity credentials but deals with information sharing or exchange decisions based on the context of an action. More specifically, the policy must prevent disclosure of sensitive information by mediating its movement outside the authorized application's boundary. Security policies for mobile devices can be divided into two categories. For mobile devices that are used by healthcare professionals such as doctors and nurses, the policy may be specified by the healthcare enterprise. If the enterprise is a covered entity, such a policy may capture regulatory and compliance requirements. Although the device is in the control of a user, the policy may be 'locked down' and the enterprise may enforce that no changes are made to it by the user. A user may also access her or his health data on a mobile device and may choose to share it with other entities. In this case, the policy is defined by the user of the device. Our goal is to develop mechanisms that can support a variety of such policies. To motivate these mechanisms, we first start by outlining key requirements of such policies.

2.2 Requirements

Mobile device security policies primarily focus on sharing of health data between applications on the device or exchange of data with remote entities. We will now describe framework mechanisms that are necessary to enforce a variety of such policies to meet the needs of healthcare applications. We will use a sample third-party mobile healthcare application called Sana Mobile [20] to illustrate key features of our security framework. Sana is an open-source remote telemedicine platform which collects patient data from procedures performed by health workers and uploads this information for a doctor to review. Doctors can then send their diagnosis to health workers through the mobile application.

Our mobile device data security framework must monitor and prevent disclosure of sensitive health information to unauthorized parties that include untrusted applications running on the device and remote services. It should also stop transfer of sensitive health data to insecure storage devices. We also want a user to be able to allow or deny certain health data sharing requests. We discuss each of these in detail.

2.2.1 *Controlling Remote Communication*

Healthcare applications like Sana must be able to communicate with external entities over several channels such as the Internet and Bluetooth. These channels allow transfer of data and hence need to be secured. Sana could connect to a Blood Pressure Monitor via Bluetooth and read the user's blood pressure and pulse reading. This could then be uploaded to a repository in a doctor's office via the Internet. However, all information accessed by an application like Sana may not be sensitive. In particular, information downloaded from a public health advice portal need not be protected. Thus, we need to ensure fine-grain control over the sharing of application state by tracking access to sensitive health data by Sana. The security policy enforcement engine must also mediate requests for sending data over network channels by Sana. It must detect data flow on both incoming and outgoing channels and the source of incoming data itself could be useful in deciding if the data is sensitive (e.g., data is received from an electronic medical record repository).

For the Internet channel, the framework should be aware of all connections made by the application and monitor those specifically rather than all open connections on the device. The framework should allow communication with trusted external entities and prevent it when it involves unauthorized entities. One can take an approach that keeps a list of trusted entities which could include the user's PHR and EHR repositories or offices of healthcare providers. The policy enforcement engine allows flow of health data between Sana and these trusted entities and data received from them is marked as sensitive. It is possible to seek user input before communication is disallowed and it can be allowed when explicitly permitted by the user. Obviously, one challenge is to determine what remote entities are trusted. We believe that since health data only needs to be shared with a limited number of external entities which do not change frequently, such lists can be built with user input without imposing excessive burden on users.

2.2.2 *Preventing Data Sharing with other Applications*

As with every other mobile application, Sana could share information with other applications. However, sharing between a healthcare application and other untrusted applications could lead to disclosure of sensitive health information. Thus, we need to monitor inter-process communication channels and place safeguards to prevent such disclosures. The policy enforcement framework must detect flow of sensitive data between Sana and other applications and can respond in one of two ways. It could disallow the data sharing and notify the user. This is meaningful because a healthcare application must avoid interacting with other potentially unsafe applications and should typically include all required functionality within itself. Another response would be to notify the user and allow the user to decide if such sharing should be allowed. In this case, interactions between the healthcare application and other applications must be explicitly consented for by the user of the device. The policy enforcement does not monitor communication of untrusted applications and any data that is allowed to be shared with them must be viewed as non-sensitive.

2.2.3 *Controlling Insecure Data Storage*

Apart from sharing health information with other applications or sending it to remote entities, Sana can also store data permanently on the mobile device's main memory or an external memory card. Usually, mobile operating systems provide data protection and separation between applications on the device's main memory. However, sometimes an application could be allowed to share data on the file system with other applications which could lead to a disclosure of sensitive information.

Similar to data sharing, the policy enforcement framework must detect operations performed on files containing sensitive information and respond in multiple ways. The framework could prevent untrusted applications from reading files that are owned by healthcare applications. This is because untrusted applications should not need access to sensitive information. The framework could also prevent storage of sensitive information on the file system and require the application to connect to a remote repository for storing sensitive information. This provides a higher degree of security but is more restrictive for the application. Another response would be to notify the user and allow the user to decide if the particular file operation should be allowed. In this case, explicit consent of the user of the device must be required for all operations performed on files containing sensitive information. The policy enforcement does not monitor files of untrusted applications and any files that are allowed to be accessed with such applications must be viewed as non-sensitive.

Another concern is that external memory such as an SD card can be inserted into other devices which can read all stored data and this could also lead to disclosure of health information. Hence, our policy enforcement framework must mediate all external storage requests of sensitive data made by Sana. It can either disallow requests that want to store information on the external memory or it can notify the user when such an attempt is made. Such a notification would allow the user to decide if the action in question is safe and would not lead to disclosure of health data. Again, once the user allows storage of some information that comes from Sana, it should be viewed as non-sensitive.

Finally, some mobile devices can be connected to other computing devices via USB and data from certain memory locations of the mobile device can be accessed by the computing device. This could also lead to a loss of sensitive information. Hence, the policy enforcement framework must prevent applications from storing sensitive information to such memory locations or explicit user consent should be obtained to sanitize this information before it can be stored at such a location.

2.2.4 User Consent Detection

We take an approach where user consent is sought in case the policy enforcement engine suspects that potentially sensitive data may flow to untrusted applications, remote entities or even to a storage device. This is motivated by healthcare regulation that give patients and healthcare providers the ability to decide if sharing of medical information needs to occur. In the previous sections, we discussed mechanisms which notify the user of a potential disclosure of healthcare information and require him to decide if the particular action should be allowed or blocked. However, this notification and user response cannot be captured within a simple dialog prompt due to the sophistication of current malware. Such malware is capable of executing scripted actions on the device as though the user generated a response. Hence, we require a secure mechanism which will help differentiate automated malicious activity from genuine user activity. This is termed as user consent detection. The policy enforcement framework must use user consent detection whenever input from the user is required regarding a particular action. Once activated, the framework should display a prompt to the user detailing the action which caused it, and request the user to accept or deny the communication.

3. APPROACH

We will now discuss the design of a framework which will enforce the security goals outlined in the previous section. We rely on a set of assumptions to build a trusted mobile device platform for secure handling of medical data. We assume the operating system on the mobile device is trusted. This includes the kernel and layers below applications. We also assume a third party mobile healthcare application runs on the device and accesses electronic health information.

This application downloads and facilitates meaningful sharing of sensitive health data when valid credentials are provided by the user. We do not assume that the health application is trusted. It may be compromised by a malware infection and it may coexist and share non-sensitive information with other untrusted applications.

Since security of sensitive data relies on proper enforcement of a security policy, the enforcement engine must be part of the trusted computing base. Also, we assume that the operating system is trusted and add mechanisms to it to implement the enforcement engine functionality. We also advocate that applications that handle sensitive health information must be treated differently by our framework compared to other untrusted applications that do not deal with sensitive information. We term the the applications which deal with sensitive information as *constrained applications* because their behavior is constrained in order to achieve security goals. Policy enforcement must only apply to constrained applications and only to data that is deemed sensitive. No restrictions are placed on other applications unless they try to interact with constrained applications. Applications can be declared as constrained by the application developer in the manifest file or by the user at the application installation screen, which could appear as a checkbox along with other permissions that the application requires. We also assume that certain system applications that implement limited functionality can also be trusted. We use one such application, the background service, that is used to support user awareness and control of how data is accessed on the device.

3.1 Tagging Sensitive Data

We do not assume that all data in a constrained application is sensitive. A healthcare application may contain publicly available information such as symptoms of a disease and these may not require our additional data safeguards. If such non-sensitive data is not allowed to be shared, it may interfere with the normal functioning of an application. Thus, to support secure access only for data that is sensitive in a constrained application, we must be able to distinguish it from other non-sensitive information within the application. This can be done in multiple ways, one is to maintain a list of all specific sensitive data locations within the application. This list would need to be updated every time sensitive information enters the application and the list would need to be traversed every time data tries to leave the application. Such a design choice may not be scalable and would expand the list size greatly if we track information flows.

Our other option is to tag memory locations which contain sensitive information. This does not require us to maintain a master list of all sensitive information locations within the application and anytime data tries to leave the application, we will only need to check its memory location tag. Hence, this design choice is more scalable. Another point to consider is that information within a constrained application may be of different levels of sensitivity which may need to be accommodated by the policy being enforced.

We must tag all incoming data with a label describing its level of sensitivity or mark it as non-sensitive information. We also need to maintain tags properly as sensitive information flows across memory locations. Data tagging can be done in multiple ways. All incoming data could be classified by the source itself and include the nature and sensitivity level of the information as metadata. Another method would be to classify data on the device based on the sensitivity level of the source repository from which the information comes. The device could be pre-populated with a list of trusted private repositories which contain sensitive information and a list of public repositories which contain publicly accessible non-sensitive information. A private repository could be classified by the highest level of sensitivity of the data it contains. All incoming data from a repository connected via a communication channel such as the Internet will be tagged with its specific sensitivity level. In case the application connects to a previously unknown repository, the user can be prompted to define its sensitivity level.

Apart from external sources, data can also enter the constrained application through other channels such as the file system and the external memory card. Data read from files containing sensitive information should be tagged with its level of sensitivity. Whenever new data on a memory card is accessed by a constrained application, the user could be prompted to choose whether the entire memory card or only certain folders and files contain sensitive information. The level of granularity can be left at the convenience of the user. All sensitive information that is loaded from the memory card is tagged by our framework.

Finally, data input by the user into an application could also be sensitive. Our framework must provide two modes of data entry into the constrained application. A sensitive data entry mode, which can be selected from our service application, tags all user input as sensitive. The regular data entry mode is used to input non-sensitive information. One could argue that sensitive data can also come from other applications, but such applications should also be marked as constrained in the first place. We will discuss how tracking of tagged data can be used in this case. Collaborating constrained applications could be allowed to share sensitive information but explicit consent must be obtained from the user first when tagged data crosses application boundaries.

3.2 Monitoring Tagged Data Flow

Once information has been tagged, we must allow it to move freely within the constrained application. As tagged information flows, we need to track it. We achieve this by using TaintDroid [3]. TaintDroid is an information flow tracking system that taints data within the Android operating system. For example, if a tagged data item is copied into another part of memory, TaintDroid tags the memory locations where the data is copied. We chose TaintDroid because it can provide an efficient solution for tracking the flow of sensitive health information in an application. If any data from tagged memory tries to leave the constrained application, we must ensure that such transfer does not violate the security policy of the application. If tagged information is being sent to an external repository via a communication channel, the policy enforcement engine must check if the external repository is at the same or higher sensitivity level as the information itself. Only when this is the case, the information is allowed to leave the device. If the external repository contains only public information and does not contain any sensitive information, then a default data security policy can be enforced. The user will be prompted to provide the sensitivity level of any newly connected external repositories. If the user chooses not to provide the level or when it is lower than the data, communication is disallowed.

Tagged information can also be stored on the file system. Files stored on the mobile device's main memory must be tagged with the highest level of sensitivity of the information contained along with the constrained application that created the file. Applications can also store tagged information on a memory card. The first time an application attempts to store tagged information on a memory card, the user is alerted about the risk of sensitive data disclosure if the memory card is removed from the mobile device and used elsewhere. The user can then choose to allow storage request or deny requests made by the application. Similarly, tagged information that is detected at the inter-process communication between two applications will be subjected to the constrained application's security policy. In the next Section, we explore a concrete implementation of mechanisms that can support these policies.

4. MECHANISMS FOR SUPPORTING CONSTRAINED APPLICATIONS

We chose the Android mobile operating system to explore the implementation of constrained applications and security policies that can be used to govern access to sensitive health data. We chose this system because it is open source and an emerging healthcare platform for which several healthcare applications have already been developed. Similar implementations can be done on other mobile operating systems. Before we discuss our implementation, we briefly describe some relevant details of the Android operating system. At the base of the Android operating system lies the Linux kernel which provides core system functionality. Above this layer are the libraries, application framework, dalvik virtual machine and application layers.

All Android applications require an `ApplicationManifest.xml` file. This file contains information about the application which is required by the Android operating system before it can run the application's code. This includes amongst others the permissions required by the application to access protected parts of the API, interactions with other applications and permissions required by other applications to interact with its components. These permissions are declared statically at install time. Hence, even though these permissions could provide some degree of protection against data breaches, they cannot be tailored at run-time. In addition, the permission model which exists in Android is coarse-grain and cannot fully enforce the fine-grain tagged data policies we explore. Permissions such as those required to access the Internet grant the application unchecked access and do not allow us to restrict the application to communicate with a subset of known safe or user consented repositories.

Finally, while certain features such as internal data storage within the device's memory may seem private to the application, exceptional cases exist which can allow sharing of this data with another application or the data can be made public. Hence, the security features provided by Android are insufficient to enforce the security policies required to protect sensitive healthcare information. However, once we add our mechanisms to the Android operating system, such policies can be enforced.

We implemented our framework on a Google Nexus One phone running Android 2.1. We used the TaintDroid [3] framework for tagged data tracking and built our mechanisms over it. For our particular implementation, we as-

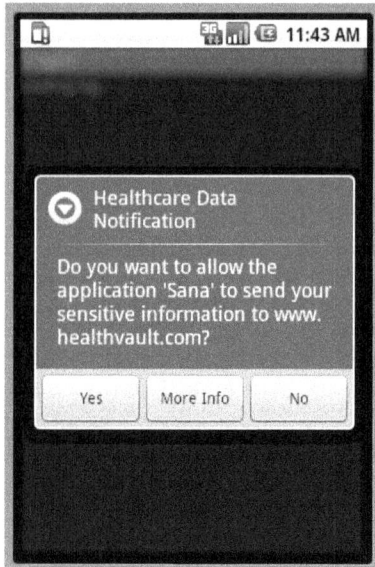

Figure 1: A prompt generated by our framework.

sume that data tagging occurs based on the nature of the source repository or based on explicit user input. We will also assume a single level of sensitivity while describing this section. In other words, we will consider data to be either sensitive or non-sensitive. However, our framework can accommodate 32 levels of sensitivity for data.

The most significant challenge we faced in implementing this framework was understanding the internal interactions of the relevant parts of Android. The Android kernel is a modified Linux kernel for which sufficient documentation exists. However, our mechanisms reside in layers above the kernel for which we did not have sufficient documentation. These layers document the exposed APIs which can be used by the applications that run above them but their internal interactions are not described. This required considerable time on our part to understand these internal interactions before we could enhance the system to include our data protection mechanisms. The middle layers of the Android operating system also include code in several different programming languages. The interactions between code written in these languages and movement of data across them required native code to be implemented within the operating system. Our external data flow mediation was implemented in the dalvik virtual machine in about 400 lines of Java code. Our inter-process communication mediation was implemented in the binder library in about 200 lines of C++ code. Our user consent detection mechanism was implemented in the framework layer in about 250 lines of code.

4.1 Background Service

Much of our framework functionality for enforcing a security policy resides within the Android operating system but we also use a background service to support user interactions required for security policy enforcement. This service launches automatically when the device is powered on and listens for any communication from the operating system. Whenever user input is required, a dialog prompt is displayed to the user above any currently active application

as shown in Figure 1. The background service is only used to display prompts and the response is detected by our user consent detection mechanism which is able to distinguish between scripted responses by malware and actual user input. We describe this mechanism in detail in a later section.

4.2 Security Policy Enforcement Engine

Our policy enforcement engine implements mechanisms that can support several policies. We currently use a simple syntax for policy specification and illustrate it via an example but it is possible to utilize more advanced policy specification languages. Our framework implementation allows the structure and source of policy files to be easily changed without affecting the rest of the framework. Our current implementation uses policy files stored on the device. However, the policy files could also be downloaded from an external trusted source. As shown in Figure 2, we maintain a separate policy engine within the virtual machine and at the binder library. This is because the external or network communication channel policy enforcement needs to happen within the dalvik virtual machine while the inter-process communication channel enforcement needs to be done within the binder library. Although a single policy engine could enforce both, we decided to avoid the Java-native transition overhead [9] by including two instances of the policy engine. This also allows us to change the policy structure and complexity of either the network or inter-process communication channels without affecting the other.

Policies for different constrained applications are stored separately which allows our enforcement engine to quickly locate the policies that belong to a particular application. Our policies follow the syntax: `DESTINATION:CONTEXT:ACTION`. The `CONTEXT` for a policy rule is optional and only defined if necessary. Examples of `CONTEXT` include `LOCATION`, `SENSITIVITY_LEVEL` and `TIME`. The following are example policy rules for a constrained application on our framework:

```
www.healthvault.com::allow
www.myphr.com:confidential,0800-1700:allow
com.healthapp.sample:1700-0800:deny
```

The first rule allows information to flow between this application and the www.healthvault.com repository regardless of any other context for the action. The next rule allows information to flow between this application and the www.myphr.com repository only if the sensitivity level of the data is confidential or lower and between 08:00 and 17:00 hours. The last rule denies this application from communicating via IPC to the application belonging to the package name com.healthapp.sample between 17:00 and 08:00 hours. Similarly, a variety of policies can exist for an application within our framework. A policy may include a large number of such rules.

4.3 Controlling External Data Flow

To secure network communication channels, we implement complete mediation for external communication requests over the Internet. It also became apparent that a similar mechanism could be put into place as well for other communication channels such as Bluetooth. Our communication channel data mediation monitors all incoming and outgoing data between the constrained application and external entities.

On the Android operating system, every application runs within its own dalvik virtual machine. This virtual machine runs above the kernel layer. Even though data movement between applications and external communication channels is first processed in the kernel, we implemented our mediation within the virtual machine as we are able to use TaintDroid tag values at this layer. It was not possible for us to determine the taint tags within the kernel based on the existing TaintDroid taint framework and the notion of an application does not exist at the kernel.

Whenever a connection is made between an external entity and an application, our framework first checks if this application is constrained based on the process that engages in the network transaction. If the application is constrained, the policy engine will then determine if the location has been previously been classified as trusted or untrusted. For preclassified locations, then the policy engine will determine if this location is a private repository containing sensitive information. If so, all the incoming information from this repository will be tagged as sensitive. If the location is a public repository, then all incoming information will not be tagged as sensitive. Tags for data coming from locations for which the policy does not contain any classification yet will be defined by the user. The user will be prompted by our background service of the current connection and will be asked to classify this new external location. The user's response will be captured by our user consent detection mechanism.

We also discussed that we can classify data from the same external location as non-sensitive and a number of sensitivity levels based on the metadata from the location itself. This can support finer granularity of data protection and would prevent any non-sensitive information from a private repository to be falsely tagged as sensitive. However, in our current implementation, we assumed that the external repository does not provide such a classification of the data it sends to the device. This is the current case with all existing third-party applications. The sensitivity classification is performed on the device based on the source of the information. We can also use other techniques such as text-mining to determine if the received data contains sensitive information and create a tag based on it. This is currently not implemented in our framework.

When information tries to leave the device to an external location, our framework first determines if the application is constrained. For constrained applications, the taint tag of the information that is leaving the device will determine if it is sensitive or not. Non-sensitive information is allowed to leave the device to any external location. However, if the information is sensitive, our policy enforcement engine will check if a policy exists for the type of data and the external location. If no policy exists, the user will be asked to define one using the background notification service and our user consent detection mechanism. Information flowing out of non-constrained applications will not be mediated.

4.4 Controlling Communication with Untrusted Applications

Before we discuss our policy enforcement mechanism for inter-process communication, we will discuss some pertinent details of the Android operating system. All inter-process communication between applications in separate dalvik virtual machines takes place through the Binder library. Binder

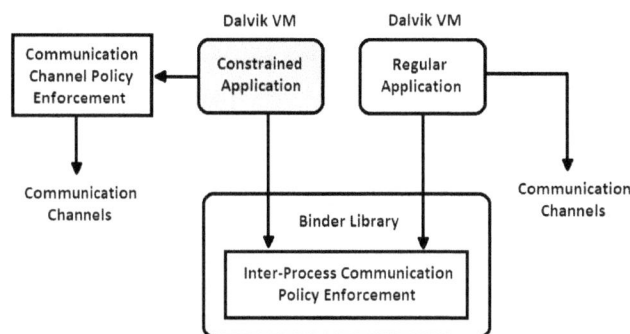

Figure 2: Policy enforcement framework.

is a custom Android protocol which uses the core concepts of OpenBinder. The binder kernel module is a very low-level protocol where it is difficult to extract taint tags. Hence, we implement our policy enforcement engine for inter-process communication at a higher layer built on top of the kernel module in the binder library. Binder uses Parcel as a marshaling protocol that writes primitive types into transaction buffers. These binder transactions can either be one-way or two-way involving a request parcel and a response parcel.

Our framework intercepts the parcels between two communicating applications within the Binder system. At this point, we are able to determine which two applications are communicating. We then check if either of the communicating processes is a constrained application. If none of them is constrained, we allow the communication to proceed. Otherwise we check the parcel objects to detect if either the request or the subsequent response within a transaction contains any information tagged as sensitive. Our framework enforces a policy only if any one of the communicating processes is constrained and the information it is sharing within the parcel message is tagged as sensitive. However, a devious receiver in an IPC transaction could unpack the variables within the parcel message in a different way to acquire its value without the taint tag. To prevent this, TaintDroid taints the entire parcel message as sensitive even if only a few variables within the parcel message are actually sensitive. This could potentially introduce false positives within the application and we will explore it in the future.

We discovered while implementing our framework that at launch time, an application communicates with the `system _server` process which provides core system services. This communication is vital for the launched application and hence the `system_server` is allowed to bypass our enforcement engine's mediation at the IPC even if a false positive is detected during a binder transaction with a constrained application. However, for all other transactions involving constrained applications, the parcels are checked to determine if they contain any sensitive information. If a policy does not already exist between a constrained application and the application it is communicating with, the user is allowed to provide a policy rule for the current transaction. This is done by generating a user prompt using our background service and activating the user consent detection mechanism.

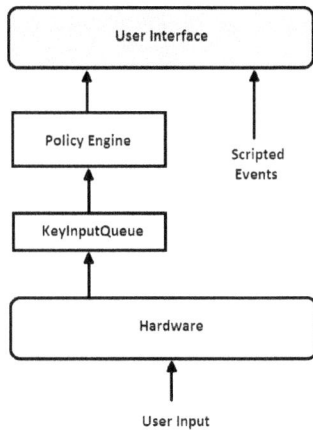

Figure 3: User consent detection mechanism.

4.5 User Consent Detection

As mentioned in previous sections, our enforcement engine generates prompts for the user to define policy rules when one does not exist to determine if certain data flows should be allowed. However, if such prompts can be intercepted by malware, it can define policy rules which could lead to a breach of sensitive information. To prevent such a situation, our framework must be able to distinguish between actual user input and potentially malicious scripted events.

We first studied how user input events are generated within the Android operating system. Hardware input such as touchscreen presses are first received at the kernel which translates them into actions at the application layer. Each individual touch to the phone screen is received as a sequence of raw codes from the touchscreen driver. These key presses are stored in a `KeyInputQueue`, shown in Figure 3, which eventually reach the application as events. We extract the x and y co-ordinates of the touchscreen press on the device from this queue. Retrieving the information at this level allows us to be oblivious to the touchscreen hardware drivers present below as all drivers input their key presses to this queue. This also provides the flexibility of working above different hardware drivers without requiring any changes to our consent detection mechanism. At the same time, our experiments verified that we are below the level at which scripted actions generate events for the operating system. Thus, this enables us to easily distinguish malware scripted actions and actual user input. However, data isolation between different applications complicates this process. The data from hardware drivers can only be accessed by the `system_server` process within the framework layer and is isolated from other applications running within the dalvik virtual machine. To allow the policy engine within the virtual machine to receive the x and y co-ordinates of each touchscreen press, we created a system service which exports only these co-ordinates to the dalvik virtual machine. This is done by using the Android Interface Definition Language(AIDL) to define an interface which different processes agree upon to communicate with each other via IPC.

When user consent detection needs to occur, the background service of our framework launches a notification which details the triggering action. The user is asked to select a button on the screen to allow or deny the action. The x and y co-ordinates generated from the drivers are compared to those corresponding to the allow or deny buttons on the screen. The positions of the allow or deny buttons generated by our background service remain constant for each device and hence the x and y ranges for each button are known beforehand. Based on the response given by the user, the action is permitted or blocked.

Apart from the co-ordinates, we can also retrieve the pressure of each touchscreen press, the area of the finger used to touch the screen and the duration of each press from the hardware driver. All of this information can be used to create user specific profiles similar to a hardened password [16] which provides a stronger guarantee that the owner of the device has responded to the prompt rather than any other user. However, this is not implemented within our framework.

5. EVALUATION

Our framework includes additional checks when communication takes place between applications or when an application exchanges data with an external entity. This could have some performance impact on the applications. To understand this, we present an evaluation of our framework in the following subsections. We outline the factors which could affect performance and discuss the expected trends. We also provide performance measurements of delays introduced by our framework for a sample application. Following that, we also modify an existing third-party healthcare application to include malicious functionality and evaluate the response of our framework to its actions.

5.1 Performance Analysis

To understand performance overheads of our policy enforcement, we examine the sources of overhead which could potentially be added by our framework. Since we use Taint-Droid for taint tracking of sensitive data, one source of overhead could be the taint tracking mechanism. However, it has been reported that TaintDroid introduces only 14% performance overhead and 4.4% memory overhead on a CPU-bound microbenchmark. This overhead is not significant for third-party healthcare applications such as Sana which are used to access health information.

The next source of overhead comes from the security policy and its enforcement. Since we do not store the policy in memory, our framework will not consume significant amounts of additional memory even if a large number of policy files exist on the device. Also, security policy decisions need to occur infrequently, storing these policies in memory is not as important. However, the drawback of reading a policy file is that policy enforcement decisions may take longer if the size and complexity of the file increases. This is obvious as the files need to be parsed to extract the relevant policy before its rules can be enforced.

Additional overhead could arise due to data movement between the binder library and the dalvik virtual machine. This is due to the cost associated with the Java-native transition to provide the parameters required by the policy engine and to return the policy decision [9]. As mentioned earlier, native code transition is required as the dalvik virtual machine is mainly in Java while the binder library layer is mainly in C++. We avoided such a situation by providing separate policy engines for IPC and network communication.

Communication	TaintDroid	Policy Enforcement framework
Upload	161.66 ms	181.83 ms
Download	18.20 ms	49.38 ms
Local Sharing	16.69 ms	18.53 ms

Table 1: Performance Evaluation Results

5.1.1 Performance Metrics

To evaluate the performance of our framework, we developed a healthcare application which has the ability to upload, download and locally share a patient's health information. We then measured the time taken to perform these actions on the application in the presence and absence of our framework on the mobile device. First, we measured the time elapsed between the user pressing a button on the application to upload data to a repository to the data actually being written to a socket. Next, we measured the time elapsed between the user pressing a button on the application to download data from a repository to the time the data is placed into a receive buffer from the socket. Finally, we measured the time elapsed between the user pressing a button on the application to share this information with another application and the time it takes to perform the IPC transaction. We summarize our findings for average times taken for the above actions in Table 1.

Our experimental results show that our policy enforcement mechanism added a 20.17 ms overhead while sending data on the network and a 31.18 ms overhead while receiving data. The overhead added by our policy enforcement for IPC transactions was found to be 1.84 ms. This proves that our policy enforcement framework adds acceptable overhead for mobile applications for a policy similar to the one described in Section 4.2.

5.2 Threat Analysis

To demonstrate the functionality of our framework and to explore the security provided by it, we downloaded and used an open-source third party healthcare application called Sana Mobile. We created different variants of this application each of which includes a different hidden malicious functionality. Each variant of this application represents a situation where a breach of sensitive healthcare information may occur. We allowed these applications to execute over the modified Android operating system and observed our framework's response which we discuss below.

5.2.1 Malware Infected Applications

The Android market is an online software store which allows users to browse and install third-party applications. These applications provide useful features to the user and can sometimes be downloaded for free from the market. However, recent studies have shown that these applications can steal sensitive user information without the user's knowledge [3]. At install time, users are shown a list of permissions such as Internet access requested by the application. However, they cannot control what information is sent on the Internet and what subset of remote servers are allowed to receive this information. This requires that the user trust application developers to not send sensitive information on the device to any malicious or unauthorized remote servers.

Apart from this, genuine applications which do not contain any malicious functionality are known to be vulnerable due to variety of reasons such as design flaws and coding er-

rors. To patch these vulnerabilities, developers release updates. User devices which are not regularly updated with these patches could be exploited to harm the user and the device. Hence, even if malicious functionality is not originally included within the application, vulnerabilities can be exploited to steal sensitive information on the device.

Our first variant of Sana imitates both malicious applications and also vulnerable applications which are exploited by malware. We install this variant on a device running our framework and assess our framework's response to its malicious behavior. When the user installs this variant on the device, he or she would check a box on the permissions screen to indicate that the application will deal with sensitive information. Our framework will now tag information flowing into this application from external locations that are defined to be sensitive and check and enforce policy rules on the flow of such information at the application's exit points. This variant contains hidden functionality which periodically uploads sensitive information gathered by the application into a remote malicious server using the Internet as the communication channel. We run this remote malicious server on a desktop and monitor the incoming connections.

When this application first connects to its private repository to download sensitive healthcare information, the user is prompted that a connection has been made to an external location which is not known to be trusted. The user then indicates through the user prompt generated by our framework that the external location contains sensitive information and data from it is tagged as sensitive. When this application tries to discretely connect to the remote malicious server for the first time, our framework looks for a previously defined policy for this application. When no existing policy is found, the user is prompted to allow or deny the Sana application request to send information tagged as sensitive to the malicious server. The user is then aware that the application is sending sensitive information to a remote unknown server which the user did not initiate. He or she would then deny this action, preventing the loss of sensitive information. Our framework then enters a policy for this particular application which would deny sending any sensitive information to that particular malicious server. All future requests by this application to send sensitive information to that malicious server are subsequently blocked. This successfully prevents a data breach from occurring.

5.2.2 Insecure Programming Practices

Application developers do not always make the most secure choices while developing software. Such insecure design choices could later be exploited for malicious purposes. Our next variant of Sana imitates an insecure design choice which could potentially be exploited by malware. We added a background service to Sana which launches at phone boot time and continues to run in the background even if the application is not active. This background service periodically connects to a private repository containing sensitive information such as communication from a doctor, lab test results etc. Whenever new health information pertaining to the user of the device is available on the repository, the background service downloads this information and sends this data to Sana.

Since Sana is an open source application, all the services launched by it can be found in the ApplicationManifest.xml file including the background service we added. We then created a separate weather application with hidden malicious functionality. As the name suggests, the weather application displays weather information to the user. But this application also requests permissions to bind to the background service of Sana. This can be easily done by adding a `service` tag within the `ApplicationManifest.xml` file of the weather application. Within this `service` tag, the weather application specifically requests permissions to bind to the Sana's background service. Once this permission has been requested in the manifest file, Android will allow the weather application to bind to the service. Although Android will display the required permissions to the user at install time, the service permissions are not shown to the user. The user is completely unaware that the weather application is maliciously binding to Sana's background service.

The weather application can now conveniently bind to the background service periodically and collect sensitive health information from our variant's background service. When this weather application binds to our variant and tries to download this information, an IPC transaction is initiated. Our framework checks to see if any one of the communicating applications is constrained. Once it determines that the Sana variant is constrained, it checks every parcel request and response between these applications to assess if they contain any sensitive information. This is done by checking the tags of the parcels in every transaction. When the background service responds to the malicious weather application by sending sensitive information, our framework detects a parcel containing sensitive information being sent from a constrained application and immediately checks if a previous policy rule exists. If one does not exist, which is the case here, the user is notified of this transaction through a prompt generated by the background service. The user consent detection framework is activated to capture the response of the user. Thus, our framework is able to successfully prevent loss of sensitive information via IPC.

5.2.3 Malicious Scripted Actions

Our third variant emulates a malicious application which is aware that the user will be prompted to confirm any potential disclosure of sensitive information such as that provided by our framework. As an attempt to subvert this process, this variant inserts scripted events into the operating system to hijack any such prompts and prevent the user from being notified of potential disclosures. This scripted input can automatically select the button on the prompt which will allow the breach of sensitive information to occur.

When this variant tries to steal sensitive information from the device, our policy enforcement engine detects sensitive information leaving a constrained application and triggers a prompt detailing the action from the background service and the user consent detection mechanism is activated. This prompt will wait for input from the user to either allow or deny the particular action in question. At this point, the variant quickly responds to the prompt by inserting simulated key events. However, our user consent detection mechanism ignores any such event and looks at the `KeyInputQueue` where actual hardware key events are present. Scripted events are not inserted in this queue and can be used to easily distinguish between actual user generated hardware events and potentially malicious scripted events. Our framework extracts the x and y co-ordinates of the touchscreen press by the user and is able to determine which

specific button was selected at the prompt generated by our background service. When the user responds to block this unknown movement of sensitive data outside the constrained application, our consent detection mechanism notifies the policy enforcement framework which inserts the appropriate policy into the application's policy file. Thus, this mechanism helps defeat any attempts at subverting our policy enforcement by using scripted actions.

6. RELATED WORK

Mobile operating systems have traditionally been lacking in providing comprehensive data security. However, the Android operating system includes significant improvements in security over other mobile operating systems. One of these improvements is the notification of all permissions required by applications at install-time to the user. These permission labels grant the application access to phone assets. Even though such a process provides greater transparency, its success largely depends on user understanding of its implications. Issues such as these have led to the emergence of systems such as Kirin [4] - an install-time permission validation service, Saint [18] - a framework for developers to provide install-time and runtime interface policies and Apex [17] - a framework that allows users to selectively grant permissions to applications. However, none of these have focused on our goal of protecting sensitive data against the threats we consider in this paper. Other work has addressed how to implement SELinux enforcement policies on Android [21]. This only affects the underlying Linux kernel and such a mechanism cannot mediate inter-component communication at the application layer.

As mentioned earlier, TaintDroid [3] is an information flow tracking system for the Android operating system. We used its tainting mechanism to specifically taint only sensitive information within an application. We then used its taint tracking mechanism to mediate sensitive data flow if it tries to leave the application and enforce our security policies. HiStar [22] is another information flow system which provides strict information flow control and prevents private data from being leaked. However, HiStar creates a more restrictive environment for applications by denying any component which reads tainted files access to the network. In our framework, we allow any constrained application's component that reads sensitive information to send this information on the network but only to a subset of known trusted external entities allowed by the security policy.

Previous work has addressed how to prevent privacy breaches of medical information from adversaries within the medical domain and outside [7]. Research done by Gardner et al. [6] shares a common goal of protecting medical records on smart phones. However, they focus on creating a cryptographic secret sharing scheme which controls access to medical information. On the other hand, we develop a security policy enforcement framework which helps protect medical data against a variety of threats in a mobile environment.

Research has been done to detect user consent on personal computers and use that to block malicious network traffic [2, 10, 19]. These systems operate under the assumption that processes which initiate outbound network connections shortly after receiving user input are user intended. We do not make such an assumption and use raw input received at the hardware to determine if an action is user intended. Our framework also detects user consent for local actions on the device whereas other systems do this only for network activity.

7. CONCLUSION

As mobile devices support richer and highly connected applications, it is inevitable that medical information would be accessed and meaningfully shared on them. Due to the sensitive nature of this data and the vulnerable mobile environment, we must secure health information against potential threats which could lead to unauthorized disclosure. We develop a framework to support policies based on security and privacy needs of health data. We detail the mechanisms required to support such policies on applications which deal with medical information, which we term as constrained applications, on the Android platform. We also implemented a user consent detection system which helps us differentiate malicious scripted events from user initiated actions. However, in the future we would like to explore other techniques such as text-mining to determine the sensitivity level of information received by the constrained application. We also want to develop methods to capture the context of sensitive information which will help the users make better policy decisions. We will also explore how other data governance policies can be supported by our mechanisms.

Acknowledgments

This work was supported by the NSF CISE NetSE grant 0905493. Any opinions, findings, conclusions or recommendations expressed in this publication are those of the authors and do not necessarily reflect the views of the National Science Foundation.

8. REFERENCES

[1] A. Bose and K. Shin. On mobile viruses exploiting messaging and bluetooth services. In *Securecomm and Workshops*, 2006.

[2] W. Cui, R. Katz, and W. Tan. BINDER: An extrusion-based break-in detector for personal computers. In *Proc. USENIX Security*, 2005.

[3] W. Enck, P. Gilbert, B. Chun, L. Cox, J. Jung, P. McDaniel, and A. Sheth. Taintdroid: An information-flow tracking system for realtime privacy monitoring on smartphones. In *Proceedings of OSDI*, 2010.

[4] W. Enck, M. Ongtang, and P. McDaniel. On lightweight mobile phone application certification. In *Proceedings of the 16th ACM conference on Computer and communications security*. ACM, 2009.

[5] J. Friedman and D. Hoffman. Protecting data on mobile devices: A taxonomy of security threats to mobile computing and review of applicable defenses. *Information, Knowledge, Systems Management*, 7(1), 2008.

[6] R. Gardner, S. Garera, M. Pagano, M. Green, and A. Rubin. Securing medical records on smart phones. In *Proceedings of the first ACM workshop on Security and privacy in medical and home-care systems*, pages 31–40. ACM, 2009.

[7] R. Gardner, S. Garera, A. Rubin, A. Rajan, C. Rozas, and M. Sastry. Protecting patient records from unwarranted access. *Future of Trust in Computing*, pages 122–128, 2009.

[8] R. Geambasu, J. John, S. Gribble, T. Kohno, and H. Levy. Keypad: an auditing file system for theft-prone devices. In *Proceedings of the sixth conference on Computer systems*, pages 1–16. ACM, 2011.

[9] Google. Designing for performance. http://developer.android.com/guide/practices/design/performance.html.

[10] R. Gummadi, H. Balakrishnan, P. Maniatis, and S. Ratnasamy. Not-a-bot: improving service availability in the face of botnet attacks. In *NSDI '09: Proceedings of the 6th USENIX symposium on Networked systems design and implementation*, 2009.

[11] R. Hasan and W. Yurcik. A statistical analysis of disclosed storage security breaches. In *Proceedings of the second ACM workshop on Storage security and survivability*. ACM, 2006.

[12] HHS. Summary of the hipaa privacy rule. http://www.hhs.gov/ocr/privacy/hipaa/understanding/summary/index.html.

[13] HHS. Summary of the hipaa security rule. http://www.hhs.gov/ocr/privacy/hipaa/understanding/srsummary.html.

[14] D. Kotz, S. Avancha, and A. Baxi. A privacy framework for mobile health and home-care systems. In *Proceedings of the first ACM workshop on Security and privacy in medical and home-care systems*, 2009.

[15] Markle. The architecture for privacy in a networked health information environment. http://www.markle.org/sites/default/files/P1_CFH_Architecture.pdf.

[16] F. Monrose, M. Reiter, and S. Wetzel. Password hardening based on keystroke dynamics. *International Journal of Information Security*, 1(2):69–83, 2002.

[17] M. Nauman, S. Khan, and X. Zhang. Apex: extending Android permission model and enforcement with user-defined runtime constraints. In *Proceedings of the 5th ACM Symposium on Information, Computer and Communications Security*. ACM, 2010.

[18] M. Ongtang, S. McLaughlin, W. Enck, and P. McDaniel. Semantically Rich Application-Centric Security in Android. In *2009 Annual Computer Security Applications Conference*. IEEE, 2009.

[19] B. Payne. Improving host-based computer security using secure active monitoring and memory analysis. 2010.

[20] Sana. Sana mobile. http://www.sanamobile.org/.

[21] A. Shabtai, Y. Fledel, and Y. Elovici. Securing Android-Powered Mobile Devices Using SELinux. *IEEE Security and Privacy*, 2009.

[22] N. Zeldovich, S. Boyd-Wickizer, E. Kohler, and D. Mazières. Making information flow explicit in histar. In *Proceedings of the 7th symposium on Operating systems design and implementation*, pages 263–278. USENIX Association, 2006.

Efficient Run-time Solving of RBAC User Authorization Queries: Pushing the Envelope

Alessandro Armando
DIST Univ. of Genova, Italy &
Fondazione Bruno Kessler,
Trento, Italy

Silvio Ranise
Fondazione Bruno Kessler,
Trento, Italy

Fatih Turkmen
DISI Univ. of Trento, Italy &
Fondazione Bruno Kessler,
Trento, Italy

Bruno Crispo
DISI Univ. of Trento, Italy

ABSTRACT

The *User Authorization Query (UAQ) Problem* for Role-Based Access Control (RBAC) amounts to determining a set of roles to be activated in a given session in order to achieve some permissions while satisfying a collection of authorization constraints governing the activation of roles. Techniques ranging from greedy algorithms to reduction to (variants of) the propositional satisfiability (SAT) problem have been used to tackle the UAQ problem. Unfortunately, available techniques suffer two major limitations that seem to question their practical usability. On the one hand, authorization constraints over multiple sessions or histories are not considered. On the other hand, the experimental evaluations of the various techniques are not satisfactory since they do not seem to scale to larger RBAC policies.

In this paper, we describe a SAT-based technique to solve the UAQ problem which overcomes these limitations. First, we show how authorization constraints over multiple sessions and histories can be supported. Second, we carefully tune the reduction to the SAT problem so that most of the clauses need not to be generated at run-time but only in a pre-processing step. Finally, we present an extensive experimental evaluation of an implementation of our techniques on a significant set of UAQ problem instances that show the practical viability of our approach; e.g., problems with 300 roles are solved in less than a second.

Categories and Subject Descriptors

D.4.6 [**Operating Systems**]: Security and Protection—*Access controls, verification*

General Terms

Security, Algorithms, Verification

1. INTRODUCTION

The *User Authorization Query (UAQ) Problem* for Role-Based Access Control (RBAC) is the problem of determining a set of roles to be activated in a given session in order to achieve a given set of permissions while satisfying all constraints governing the activation of roles (e.g., mutual exclusion of roles) [6]. In many cases, one is interested in finding an optimal solution, i.e. a solution that minimizes (or maximizes) the set of active roles or permissions in accordance with the least privilege principle.

Approaches to solving the UAQ problem are given in [6]. A first approach is based on a greedy search for a set of roles covering the needed permissions that also tries to minimize the additional permissions these roles may have. If any solution is found, then it is checked whether it satisfies all constraints. If the check succeeds, then the set of roles is returned as a solution, otherwise the request is rejected. The approach is very efficient, but incomplete since the greedy search algorithm does not explore the space of possible solution but stops as soon as one is determined. A complete approach, based on a simple generate-and-test strategy is also discussed. The idea is to enumerate all the subsets of the set of roles assigned to the user and stop as soon as one is found that provides the needed permissions and satisfies all constraints. The problem with this second approach is that in the worst-case, the first step can be asked to generate 2^n solutions, where n is the number of roles assigned to the user associated with the session.

By borrowing ideas from constraint satisfaction, [5] puts forward a number of alternative, more efficient procedures: a variety of search algorithms based on the Davis-Putnam-Logemann-Loveland (DPLL) algorithm and a procedure based on a reduction of the UAQ problem to the MAXSAT problem and leverages off-the-shelf propositional satisfiability (SAT) solvers. The same paper provides also a comparative experimental analysis between the proposed procedures. The experiments indicate that the greedy search procedure proposed in [6] is very likely to reject requests that have a solution. Moreover, the experiments indicate that the SAT-based procedure scales better than the DPLL-based procedures when optimal solutions are sought, whereas the DPLL-based procedures scale better than the SAT-based procedure when an exact solution is wanted. However, the experiments indicate that the time needed to solve the UAQ problem is in the order of seconds even for relatively simple problems. For instance, finding a minimal solution to UAQ problems with 33 roles takes more than 7 seconds in average. These results seem to question more than confirming the practical usefulness of techniques for solving the UAQ problem that are available in the literature.

In this paper we improve the SAT-based procedure of [5] in a number of ways:

1. We show that the procedure can be extended to handle a wider class of constraints spanning over the session history as well as over multiple sessions belonging to the same user.

2. We demonstrate that most of the encoding into SAT need not to be generated at run-time, but can be computed once for all as a pre-processing step. As we will see later in the paper, this has important consequences on the performance and hence on the practical usability of the approach.

3. We have implemented the SAT-based procedure presented in this paper using state-of-the-art SAT solvers. Furthermore, we have carried out a thorough experimental analysis obtained by running our implementation against a wide range of UAQ problems. The results indicate that the improved procedure described in this paper not only tackles a wider class of constraints, but also outperforms the procedure presented in [5]. More importantly, the experiments indicate that our technique can quickly solve UAQ problems of real-world complexity: problems with 300 roles are solved in less than 1 second in average.

Plan of the paper. Section 2 briefly recalls the basic notions underlying RBAC, defines the types of dynamic constraints that we consider in the context of UAQ problem. Section 3 explains how to reduce instances of the UAQ problem to (variants of) the SAT problem, how propositional assignments can be mapped back to solutions of the original UAQ problem instance, and how all this is integrated with some key optimizations in our use of the solver. Section 4 discusses our experimental settings, the generation of UAQ problem instances, the results of an implementation of our SAT-based solver, and a comparison with the approach in [5]. Section 5 concludes the paper.

2. PROBLEM DEFINITION

RBAC [3] regulates access through roles. Roles in a set R associate permissions in a set P to users in a set U by using a *user-assignment relation* $UA \subseteq U \times R$ and a *permission-assignment* relation $PA \subseteq R \times P$. If $(u, r) \in UA$, then a *user u is a member of role r*. The set of roles R is endowed with a hierarchy relation, i.e. a partial order $\succeq \subseteq R \times R$ where $r_1 \succeq r_2$ means that r_1 is *more senior than* r_2 for $r_1, r_2 \in R$. A user u *has permission p* iff there exist roles $r, r' \in R$ such that $r \succeq r'$, $(u, r) \in UA$, and $(r', p) \in PA$. An *RBAC policy* is a tuple $RP = (U, R, P, UA, PA, \succeq)$. All the RBAC policies considered in this paper are assumed to be *finite*, i.e. U, R, and P have finite cardinality (and thus UA, PA, and $\succeq$ have finite cardinality too).

A *session* allows a user to activate a sub-set of the roles that the user is assigned to according to the UA relation. Formally, let S be a set of sessions, $user : S \to U$ is a function that associates each session $s \in S$ with the corresponding user, and a *state* is a function $\rho : S \to 2^R$ that associates

each session with a subset of the roles assigned to $user(s)$ by the UA relation, i.e. if $r \in \rho(s)$ then $(user(s), r) \in UA$. If $r \in \rho(s)$, then a *role r is active in session s at state ρ*. If $u \in U$, then S_u denotes the set of sessions associated with u, i.e. $S_u = \{s \in S : user(s) = u\}$. We assume, for the sake of simplicity, that sessions pre-exist and that the user associated with each session is known in advance. A *history* of an RBAC policy RP is a sequence $H = [\rho_0, \ldots, \rho_k]$ of states of RP, where $k \geq 0$ and ρ_i is obtained from ρ_{i-1} by activating or deactivating one or more roles in some session $s \in S$ and all the remaining sessions are left unmodified (i.e. $\rho_i(s') = \rho_{i-1}(s')$ for all $s' \in (S \setminus \{s\})$, for $i = 1, \ldots, k$). If $H = [\rho_0, \ldots, \rho_{k-1}]$, then $H@\rho_k$ denotes $[\rho_0, \ldots, \rho_{k-1}, \rho_k]$.

2.1 Constraint Specifications

Mutual Exclusive Role (MER) constraints are used to reduce the possibility or impact of frauds. Thus RBAC policies are often enriched with mutually exclusive role constraints. Usually MER constrains are classified as static MER (SMER) and dynamic MER (DMER) based on their enforcement type. SMER constraints ensure that a user is not assigned conflicting roles and hence constrain the applicability of administrative actions affecting the user-assignment relation UA. DMER constraints ensure that a user does not activate conflicting roles. In this paper we focus on DMER constraints and therefore we will not consider SMER constraints any more.

DMER constraints are defined on a set rs of roles and are variants of the same constraint type which vary depending on the way they are enforced. Formally, given an RBAC policy $(U, R, P, UA, PA, \succeq)$, a set $rs \subseteq R$, and $1 \leq n < |rs|$, we define the following types of constraints:

- SS-DMER(rs, n): single-session dynamic MER;

- MS-DMER(rs, n): multi-session dynamic MER;

- SS-HMER(rs, n): single-session history-based MER; and

- MS-HMER(rs, n): multi-session history-based MER.

We will also consider role activation constraints referring to cardinality restrictions on the concurrent or sequential activations of a given role. Formally, let $r \in R$ and $t \geq 2$, we define

- CARD(r, t): cardinality constraint.

Given an RBAC policy $(U, R, P, UA, PA, \succeq)$, a history $H = [\rho_0, \ldots, \rho_k]$, and a constraint c, we say that H *satisfies* c (in symbols, $H \models c$) iff

- $[\rho_0, \ldots, \rho_k] \models$ SS-DMER(rs, n) iff for all $s \in S$, $|rs \cap \rho_i(s)| < n$ for $i = 0, \ldots, k$;

- $[\rho_0, \ldots, \rho_k] \models$ MS-DMER(rs, n) iff for all $u \in U$, $|rs \cap \bigcup_{s \in S_u} \rho_i(s)| < n$ for $i = 0, \ldots, k$;

- $[\rho_0, \ldots, \rho_k] \models$ SS-HMER(rs, n) iff for all $s \in S$, $|rs \cap \bigcup_{i=1}^{k} \rho_i(s)| < n$;

- $[\rho_0, \ldots, \rho_k] \models$ MS-HMER(rs, n) iff for all $u \in U$, $|rs \cap \bigcup_{i=1}^{k} \bigcup_{s \in S_u} \rho_i(s)| < n$;

- $[\rho_0, \ldots, \rho_k] \models$ CARD(r, t) iff $|\{s \in S : r \in \rho_i(s)\}| < t$ for $i = 0, \ldots, k$.

We say that H *satisfies* a finite set C of constraints (in symbols, $H \models C$) iff H satisfies c, for each $c \in C$.

Given an RBAC policy $(U, R, P, UA, PA, \succeq)$ and a finite set C of constraints of the types listed above, we will speak of an *RBAC policy with constraints* (or, simply, an *RBAC policy*) to denote the tuple $(U, R, P, UA, PA, \succeq, C)$. A history H is *valid with respect to the RBAC policy* $(U, R, P, UA, PA, \succeq, C)$ iff $H \models C$; the RBAC policy is usually omitted when it is clear from the context. In the rest of this paper, we will consider valid histories only.

2.2 The User Authorization Query Problem

Given an RBAC policy $(U, R, P, UA, PA, \succeq, C)$, define $\pi(r) = \{p \in P|$ there exists $r \succeq r'$ and $(p, r') \in PA\}$, i.e. the set of permissions assigned to role r. If $Q \subseteq R$, then we define $\pi(Q) = \bigcup_{r \in Q} \pi(r)$.

DEFINITION 2.1. *Let* $RP = (U, R, P, PA, UA, C)$ *be an RBAC policy and* $H = [\rho_0, \ldots, \rho_{k-1}]$ *be a history of RP. A User Authorization Query (UAQ) for RP is a tuple* (s, P_{lb}, P_{ub}, obj), *where* $s \in S$, $P_{lb} \subseteq P_{ub} \subseteq P$, *and* $obj \in \{$any, min, max$\}$. *The UAQ Problem associated with* (s, P_{lb}, P_{ub}, obj) *and* H *is the problem of extending* H *to a new (valid) history* $H@\rho_k$, *where the RBAC state* ρ_k *of RP is called the* solution *(of the UAQ problem), such that* $P_{lb} \subseteq \pi(\rho_k(s)) \subseteq P_{ub}$ *and*

- *if* $obj = $ min, *then for every RBAC state* ρ'_k *such that* $P_{lb} \subseteq \pi(\rho'_k(s)) \subseteq P_{ub}$ *we have* $\pi(\rho_k(s)) \subseteq \pi(\rho'_k(s))$;

- *if* $obj = $ max, *then for every RBAC state* ρ'_k *such that* $P_{lb} \subseteq \pi(\rho'_k(s)) \subseteq P_{ub}$ *we have* $\pi(\rho'_k(s)) \subseteq \pi(\rho_k(s))$.

Notice that $\rho_k(s') = \rho_{k-1}(s')$ *for all* $s' \in S \setminus \{s\}$.

If Q is a set of propositions, then $\sum Q < n$ is a proposition that holds iff at most $n - 1$ of the propositions in Q hold.

THEOREM 2.1. *Let* $RP = (U, R, P, PA, UA, C)$ *be an RBAC policy and* $H = [\rho_0, \ldots, \rho_{k-1}]$ *a history of RP. A state* ρ_k *of RP is a solution of the UAQ* (s, P_{lb}, P_{ub}, obj) *for RP iff it satisfies the following conditions:*

1. for each $r \in R$, if $r \in R$ and $(user(s), r) \notin UA$, then $r \notin \rho_k(s)$;

2. for each $p \in P$, if $p \in P_{lb}$, then $p \in \pi(\rho_k(s))$;

3. for each $p \in P$, if $p \in (P \setminus P_{ub})$, then $p \notin \pi(\rho_k(s))$;

4. for each $r, r' \in R$ and $p \in P$, if $r \in \rho_k(s)$ and $(p, r') \in PA$ with $r \succeq r'$, then $p \in \pi(\rho_k(s))$;

5. for each $p \in P$, if $p \in \pi(\rho_k(s))$, then there exist $r, r' \in R$ such that $r \in \rho_k(s)$, $r \succeq r'$, and $(p, r') \in PA$;

6. if $MER(rs, n) \in C$, where MER is SS-DMER, MS-DMER, SS-HMER, or MS-HMER, then $\sum \{\chi_k(r, s) : r \in rs\} < n$, where $\chi_k(r, s)$ is defined in Table 1.

7. if CARD$(r, t) \in C$ and $|\{s' \in S \setminus \{s\} : r \in \rho_{k-1}(s')\}| = t - 1$, then $r \notin \rho_k(s)$.

Additionally, if $obj = $ min ($obj = $ max), then consider only those $\rho_k(s)$ such that $\pi(\rho_k(s))$ is minimal (maximal, resp.) w.r.t. set inclusion.

3. A SAT-BASED PROCEDURE FOR SOLVING UAQ PROBLEMS

Let $RP = (U, R, P, PA, UA, C)$ be an RBAC policy, $H = [\rho_0, \ldots, \rho_{k-1}]$ a history of RP, and (s, P_{lb}, P_{ub}, obj) a UAQ problem for RP. Since RP is finite and only finitely many sessions are active at any given time instant, the UAQ problem can be reduced to a SAT problem as follows. Preliminarily, we introduce the following propositional variables:

- $\overline{p}$ to represent the statement "$p \in \pi(\rho_k(s))$," for each $p \in P$;

- $\overline{r}$ to represent the statement "$r \in \rho_k(s)$," for each $r \in R$;

- $\overline{Y_r(s)}$ to represent the statement "$r \in \rho_{k-1}(s)$" (called *Yesterday statement*, or *Y-statement* for short) for each $r \in R$, $s \in S$, and $k \in \mathbb{N}$;

- $\overline{O_r(s)}$ to represent the statement "$r \in \rho_{<k}(s)$" (called *Once statement*, or *O-statement* for short) for each $r \in R$, $s \in S$, and $k \in \mathbb{N}$, where $\rho_{<k}(s)$ abbreviates $\bigcup_{i=1, \ldots, k-1} \rho_i(s)$.

The key idea of the approach rests on the observation that most of the clauses in the encoding can be computed off-line and only a small number of (unit) clauses need to be computed at runtime. The set of clauses that can be statically generated is $\mathcal{C}(s)$, defined as the smallest set of propositional clauses such that

1. for each $r \in R$ if $(user(s), r) \notin UA$ then $\neg \overline{r} \in \mathcal{C}(s)$;

2. for each $p \in P$ and $r \in R$ such that $(p, r') \in PA$ with $r \succeq r'$, $(\neg \overline{r} \vee \overline{p}) \in \mathcal{C}(s)$;

3. for each $p \in P$, $(\neg \overline{p} \vee \bigvee \{\overline{r} : $ exists $r' \in R, r \succeq r', (p, r') \in PA\}) \in \mathcal{C}(s)$;

4. for each $MER(rs, n) \in C$, where MER is SS-DMER, MS-DMER, SS-HMER, or MS-HMER, the CNF of the following propositional formulae is in $\mathcal{C}(s)$:

   (a) $\sum \{\overline{\chi_k(r, s)} : r \in rs\} < n$,
   (b) $(\overline{\chi_k(r, s)} \leftrightarrow \overline{\chi}_k(r, s))$,

   where $\overline{\chi_k(r, s)}$ is a new propositional variable and the formula $\overline{\chi}_k(r, s)$ is defined in Table 1;

5. if CARD$(r, t) \in C$ and $|\{s' \in S \setminus \{s\} : r \in \rho_{k-1}(s')\}| = t - 1$, then $\neg \overline{r} \in \mathcal{C}(s)$.

This propositional encoding is used in the program UAQ-solve of Figure 1 to solve instances of the UAQ problem. It consists of a preprocessing phase (lines 13-18) followed by a loop that reads one UAQ problem at a time (line 21) and tackles it by calling an external PMAX-SAT solver (line 34), which is capable of finding a propositional assignment that satisfies all those clauses labelled as *hard* together with the maximum (or minimum) number of clauses marked as *soft*. The use of a PMAX-SAT solver allows us to handle the UAQ instances (s, P_{lb}, P_{ub}, obj) where $obj \in \{$min, max$\}$. These instances require to find the minimal and maximal, respectively, set of permissions associated to session s between P_{lb} and P_{ub} (lines 22-33). Indeed, when no clauses are marked as soft, the PMAX-SAT solver behaves as a "standard" SAT

Table 1: Definition of $\chi_k(rs, s)$

Constraint	$\chi_k(s, r)$	$\overline{\chi}_k(s, r)$
SS-DMER	$r \in \rho_k(s)$	$\overline{r}$
MS-DMER	$r \in \rho_k(s)$ or $r \in \rho_{k-1}(s')$ for some $s' \in S_{user(s)} \setminus \{s\}$	$\overline{r} \vee \bigvee_{s' \in S_{user(s)} \setminus \{s\}} \overline{Y_r(s')}$
SS-HMER	$r \in \rho_k(s)$ or $r \in \rho_{<k}(s)$	$\overline{r} \vee \overline{O_r(s)}$
MS-HMER	$r \in \rho_k(s)$ or $r \in \rho_{<k}(s')$ for some $s' \in S_{user(s)}$	$\overline{r} \vee \bigvee_{s' \in S_{user(s)}} \overline{O_r(s')}$

solver and it is possible to handle those UAQ problem instances for which $obj =$ any. It is possible to extract a solution of the original UAQ problem from a propositional assignment satisfying the set of clauses sent to the PMAX-SAT solver (line 34 of Figure 1) in UAQ-solve(). To see how, define $\rho_k(s) = \{r \in R : \overline{r(s)}$ is in $\pi\}$ and $\rho_k(s') = \rho_{k-1}(s')$ for every $s' \in S \setminus \{s\}$. This functionality is encapsulated in the procedure print-solution (at line 38) in Figure 1.

The correctness of UAQ-solve() derives from Theorem 2.1 and the following observations. First, conditions 1.–7. of Theorem 2.1 can be effectively translated into propositional logic by quantifier instantiation of the universal and existential quantifiers over roles and permissions as they range over the finite sets R and P, respectively. Second, items 1, 2, 3, and 5 of the encoding used to generate the set $\mathcal{C}(s)$ of clauses are the propositional encoding of conditions 1, 4, 5, and 7 of Theorem 2.1, respectively. Third, item 4 of the encoding takes into account condition 6 of Theorem 2.1 via the definition of $\overline{\chi}_k(r, s)$ in Table 1 (see also procedure add-YO-clauses() in Figure 1). Fourth, the remaining conditions (namely, 2 and 3) of Theorem 2.1 are handled at lines 24-27 in Figure 1.

THEOREM 3.1. *Let*

- $RP = (U, R, P, PA, UA, C)$ *be an RBAC policy,*

- *UAQ-solve() be in a state obtained by submitting a sequence* $[q_1, \ldots q_n]$ *of UAQ problem instances* ($n \geq 1$), *and*

- $\hat{H} = [\hat{\rho}_1, \ldots, \hat{\rho}_n]$ *be a sequence of states such that* $\hat{\rho}_i$ *is the solution returned by the procedure to the UAQ problem instance* q_i, *for each* $i = 1, \ldots, n$.

Then, $\hat{H}$ *is a (valid) history of* RP. *Moreover, if a new UAQ problem instance* q *is submitted to* UAQ-solve(), *then the procedure returns a solution* $\hat{\rho}$ *iff* $\hat{\rho}$ *is a solution to* q.

Although we have assumed that the set S of sessions is fixed over histories, our technique can be extended to handle the dynamic creation of sessions. For lack of space, we do not show here the changes in the encoding to accomodate this extension.

4. EXPERIMENTAL EVALUATION

We present a thorough experimental evaluation of our approach obtained by running an implementation of UAQ-Solve in Figure 1 on several synthetic UAQ problems.

In the literature (see, e.g., [1]), several dimensions have been identified to characterize RBAC policies, such as the number of users, roles, permissions, and sessions. In our

Table 2: Experimental Settings

$|U|$	$|R|$	$|P|$	$|S_u|$	$|C_t|$	$|H|$
100	40 - 300	80	10	5	100
80	50	60	2 - 50	5	100
100	60	80	10	5	10 - 100

framework, also the length of histories plays a significant role for the evaluation of authorization queries because of HMER constraints. Since there are several reasonable values for each one of the parameters listed above, we explain the rationale underlying our choices in Section 4.1. Then, we explain our method to generate valid histories of increasing length in Section 4.2 where we use the capability of solving UAQ problems to ensure the validity of histories. Finally, we discuss our findings on several synthetic instances of the UAQ problem and compare with the approach presented in [5] when considering only SS-DMER constraints in Section 4.3.

4.1 Dimensions of the UAQ problem

Recall from Definition 2.1 that a UAQ problem instance (s, P_{lb}, P_{ub}, obj) is defined in terms of a RBAC policy $RP = (U, R, P, PA, UA, C)$ and a (valid) history $H = [\rho_0, \ldots, \rho_{k-1}]$ of RP. Thus, there are several dimensions that should be taken into account to generate problem instances for the UAQ problem. Here, we discuss various dimensions that determine the underlying RBAC policy RP, the length of the history H, and the choice of session s with the sets P_{lb} and P_{ub} of permissions.

Table 2 provides the values for various components of an RBAC policy RP (namely the number of users $|U|$, roles $|R|$, permissions $|P|$, sessions per user $|S_u|$, constraints per type $|C_t|$) and the length $|H|$ of histories that we have considered in the experiments. In the columns $|R|$, $|S_u|$, and $|H|$, a range $m - M$ of values (where m and M are the minimum and maximum values, respectively) corresponds to the three plots that will be discussed in Section 4.3, where the performances for increasing numbers of roles and sessions, and longer histories, respectively, are measured. We do not show a plot for increasing numbers of users since few (unit) clauses are added to $\mathcal{C}(s)$ because of the set U of users (recall item 1 at the beginning of Section 3). Since $|S_u|$ represents the number of sessions per user, in order to compute $|S|$, it is sufficient to multiply it by the number $|U|$ of users (hence, there is a linear dependence between the number of users and the number of sessions). Similarly, in order to obtain the total number of constraints C in the underlying RBAC policy RP, one must multiply the value in column $|C_t|$ by

```
1   procedure add-YO-clauses()
2     foreach s ∈ S and r ∈ R
3       if Y[s,r] then
4         HC := HC∪{Y_r(s)};
5       else
6         HC := HC∪{¬Y_r(s)};
7       if O[s,r] then
8         HC := HC∪{O_r(s)};
9       else
10        HC := HC∪{¬O_r(s)};
11
12  program UAQ-Solve()
13    foreach s ∈ S
14      C[s] := C(s); // initialization
15    foreach r ∈ R and s ∈ S
16      Y[s,r] := false; // Yesterday
17      O[s,r] := false; // Once
18    add-YO-clauses();
19    // beginning of on−line phase
20    while(true)
21      read(s,P_lb,P_ub,obj); // reading UAQ problem
22      HC := C(s); // hard constraints
23      SC := ∅;   // soft constraints
24      foreach p ∈ P_lb
25        HC := HC ∪ {p̄};
26      foreach p ∈ (P \ P_ub)
27        HC := HC ∪ {¬p̄};
28      if obj=min then
29        foreach p ∈ (P_ub \ P_lb)
30          SC := SC ∪ {¬p̄};
31      if obj=max then
32        foreach p ∈ (P_ub \ P_lb)
33          SC := SC ∪ {p̄};
34      Res := PMAX-SAT-Solve(HC,SC);
35      if Res=UNSAT then
36        print "No solution.";
37      else
38        print-solution(Res);
39        foreach r ∈ R
40          if r̄ ∈ Res then
41            Y[s,r] := true;
42            O[s,r] := true;
43          else
44            Y[s,r] := false;
45        add-YO-clauses();
```

Figure 1: SAT-based solver for the UAQ Problem

4, which is the number of distinct MER constraint types considered in this paper. (We have not considered CARD constraints in our experiments for the sake of simplicity; their addition is straightforward and does not change our findings in Section 4.3.) For example, a setting with $|U| = 100$, $|S_u| = 2$, and $|C_t| = 4$ gives $|S| = 200$ and $|C| = 16$ for the RBAC policy RP. Each one of the four types of MER constraints has the form $\text{MER}(rs, n)$, where rs is a sub-set of the set R of roles and n is a positive less than or equal the cardinality of rs. In our experiments, rs is a randomly selected sub-set of R containing 3 roles and n is randomly chosen among the values of 2 and 3. The relation PA in

the RBAC policy RP is a randomly chosen subset of $R \times P$ while the generation of the relation UA has been designed so as to augment the chances to violate some of the MER constraints as follows. First, we randomly extract a sub-set rs_{sub} of the set rs of roles of a randomly selected MER constraint among those available in C. Then, we associate a user u to all the roles in rs_{sub} plus some randomly selected roles from $R \setminus rs_{sub}$. We repeat these two steps for each user u in U. The role hierarchy $\succeq$ of the RBAC policy RP is not considered in our experiments since it can be compiled away in a pre-processing step by distributing the permissions to each role.

For the RBAC policy RP, the values of the first five columns in Table 2 were inspired from those discussed in [1]. Unfortunately, no value for the number of sessions is provided although [1] takes into consideration multiple sessions.

The generation of valid histories takes a substantial amount of time because, as we will describe in Section 4.2, it requires to solve a number of instances of the UAQ problem which is equal to the length of a history. As a consequence, to keep the amount of time required by history generation reasonable, we were able to consider RBAC policies categorized as "Literature" in [1]. Notice also that [1] considers only the problem of enforcing RBAC policies and not the UAQ problem as done here.

We are left with the discussion of our choices for (s, P_{lb}, P_{ub}, obj) to complete the description of the dimensions of the UAQ problem. The session s is randomly selected from the set S of sessions. Concerning P_{lb} and P_{ub}, we randomly select a set $perms \subseteq P_u$ of permissions and then let

1. $P_{lb} = P_{ub} = perms$ if $obj = \text{any}$,

2. $P_{lb} = perms$ and $P_{ub} = P_u$ if $obj = \text{min}$, and

3. $P_{lb} = \emptyset$ and $P_{ub} = perms$ if $obj = \text{max}$;

where P_u is the set of permissions that can be acquired by the user u, associated to session s, if all his/her roles are activated, i.e. $P_u = \{p \mid \exists r \in R \text{ s.t. } (u, r) \in UA \text{ and } (r, p) \in PA\}$. Case 1 means that user u wants to activate a set of roles associated with the exact set $perms$ of permissions. Case 2 implies that at least the permissions in $perms$ should be available in the session s of user u. Case 3 is used when the principle of least privilege must be ensured, as no permission outside $perms$ should be available to user u in session s. Case 1 is called "exact match" in [5] where it is shown equivalent to the UAQ problem defined in [6]. Cases 2 and 3 were also solved in [5] albeit considering only what we call SS-DMER constraints in this paper (for a comparison, see Section 4.3).

4.2 Generation of valid histories

Since sessions and histories play a key role in the satisfaction of MER constraints, we are required to generate histories with multiple sessions in a flexible way to evaluate the efficiency of our approach. We have implemented a procedure to do this as follows; see also Figure 2. The core is the function generate which takes as input a session s and a sub-set $perms$ of the set P of permissions, while using the sets U, S, and P togheter with the relations PA and UA (these last elements are assumed to be chosen as explained in Section 4.1). The function generate solves the UAQ problem instance $(s, perms, perms, \text{any})$ by using a modified version of the procedure UAQ-Solve in Figure 1, called UAQ-Solve^r,

```
function OneSession(s)                          function OneStep(H@ρ)
1   P_u ← {p | ∃r ∈ R s.t. (u,r) ∈ UA and (r,p) ∈ PA}    1   μ ← AllSessions(S)
      where u is the user of session s          2   if μ = fail then
2   let perms be a randomly selected sub-set of P_u    3       if H = [] then return fail
3   return generate(s, perms)                   4       else return OneStep(H)
                                                5   else return H@ρ@(ρ ⊕ μ)
function AllSessions(S_a)
1   if S_a = ∅ then return fail                 function AllSteps(H, b)
2   else begin                                  1   if |H| < b then return AllSteps(OneStep(H), b)
3       randomly pick a session s ∈ S_a         2   else return H
4       μ ← OneSession(s)
5       if μ ≠ fail then return μ               At the top level, invoke AllSteps([→ ∅], n) with n ≥ 1
6       else S_a' ← S_a \ {s}; return AllSessions(S_a')
7   end
```

Figure 2: History generation

and returns either fail, when the problem is unsolvable, or a new state (i.e. a finite mapping $\rho : S \to 2^R$ associating each session to a set of roles), when the problem is solvable. The main difference between UAQ-Solve^r and UAQ-Solve is that, when the UAQ problem is solvable, the former does not compute the new state by using the first solution returned by the SAT solver as the latter would do. Rather, UAQ-Solve^r computes the new state from a randomly selected solution among those available; this is easy to implement since most available SAT solvers support mechanisms to enumerate one after the other all satisfying assignements of a set of clauses. This is done with the aim of having some variety in the generated histories, i.e. every pairs of consecutive states in a generated history should differ in the set of roles that are activated in a given session whereas all the others remain the same.

Before describing in more detail all the functions in Figure 2, we introduce some notions. The singleton mapping associating a session s with a set rs of roles is written as $\{s \mapsto rs\}$, the mapping ρ' such that $\rho'(s_1) = \rho(s_1)$ for each session $s_1 \neq s$ and $\rho'(s) = rs$ (for some set rs of roles) is denoted by $\rho \oplus \{s \mapsto rs\}$, and $\to \emptyset$ is the abbreviation for the mapping that associates each session with the empty set of roles. The variable μ ranges over singleton mappings. The empty history is written as $[]$, and the length of a history H is denoted by $|H|$ (indeed, $|[]| = 0$).

To generate a history of length n, we invoke the function AllSteps on the history containing just $\emptyset$ and the second parameter set to n. This is a recursive function that returns a history of length n after n calls to itself. The function OneStep is invoked on the actual history $H@\rho$ (notice that, initially, $[]@(\to \emptyset)$) which tries to return a history with one additional state appended at the end, by recursively invoking itself and the function AllSessions. The latter is capable of returning either fail or a singleton mapping $\mu = \{s \mapsto rs\}$ for some session s (among those in input) such that $\rho(s) \neq rs$ for a given state ρ. Then, it is tested (line 2) if AllSessions has returned fail in which case OneStep backtracks and tries to extend history H (instead of $H@\rho$) when H is not empty (line 4); otherwise, it reports failure (line 3). If AllSessions has not returned with failure, then μ is a singleton mapping and OneStep appends at the end of $H@\rho$ the mapping $\rho \oplus \mu$. In this way, the recursive call of AllSteps has extended the input history with one new state that introduces a change (e.g., a new active role) to one of the sessions. We now

consider the function AllSessions which, in turn, calls the function OneSession. We start to describe the latter, which takes a session as input, establishes to which user u belongs (line 1), computes the set P_u of permissions associated to u according to the relation UA, and then randomly selects a sub-set $perms$ of P_u. At this point, generate is invoked on s and $perms$. This allows us to compute valid histories that correspond to activations and deactivations of roles by a certain user u in a given session s as explained above. We emphasize that the use of randomization tries to make histories more heterogeneous, considering several possible activations and deactivations patterns. Finally, we describe the function AllSessions which takes a set $S_a \subseteq S$ of sessions as input and randomly picks one among them, say s when S_a is not empty (line 3); otherwise it reports failure (line 1). Then, OneSession is invoked on s and if it returns a singleton mapping μ, this is also returned by AllSessions (line 6); otherwise (i.e. when OneSession returns fail) AllSessions is invoked recursively on the set of remaining sessions, i.e. all those in S_a except s.

In our implementation, we have used the Sat4J library[1] to implement generate. This is so because we can sacrifice a bit the efficiency of SAT solving in favour of a seamless integration (via the available API) within the Java application implementing the functions in Figure 2

4.3 Results

We have implemented the procedure UAQ-solve in Figure 1 in Java. Third party tools have been integrated to leverage state-of-the-art SAT encoding and solving techniques. Concerning the former, we have used the routines described in [4] for the compact encoding of Boolean cardinality constraints derived from the various types of DMER constraints, which put restrictions on the number of Boolean variables that are allowed to be true at the same time. This has been used in the implementation for the generation of the initial set $\mathcal{C}(s)$ of clauses at line 14 of UAQ-solve. Concerning SAT solving, we have chosen the QMaxSAT solver [2] to implement the PMAX-SAT-solve function invoked at line 34 of UAQ-solve. We have chosen QMaxSAT because it performed quite well in the latest MaxSAT evaluation and because of its efficiency on the sets of clauses generated by our encoding.

Our implementation was run on a large set of synthetic

---

[1]http://www.sat4j.org/

UAQ problem instances obtained by randomly generated RBAC policies (see Section 4.1) and randomly generated histories (see Section 4.2). According to the values in Table 2, we consider three scenarios: (a) increasing number of roles (first line of the table) from 40 up to 300 with a step of 10, (b) increasing number of sessions (second line of the table) from 160 to 4000 (recall that $|S| = |S_u| \times |U|$) with a step of 2, and (c) increasing history length (third line of the table) from 10 to 200 with a step of 5.

All the experiments have been conducted on a computer with Intel Xeon 3.20 GHz CPU and 4 GB RAM running Linux. The three plots below show the behaviour of our implementation on the three scenarios. In all plots, the x-axis reports increasing values of one of the dimension in Table 2— namely, $|R|$ for (a), $|S_u|$ for (b), and $|H|$ for (c) whereas the y-axis shows the timings of our implementation of UAQ-solver in milliseconds. For the two plots corresponding to scenario (b) and (c), the y-axis adopts a standard scale to report the timings. Instead, for the plot describing the behaviour in scenario (a), the y-axis adopts a log-scale. In all experiments, each point in the y-axis is obtained from the median value of the overall timings of UAQ-solve over 10 randomly selected pairs of values for P_{lb} and P_{ub} for given RBAC policy, history, and session s. This choice was made to reduce the variance in solving an instance (s, P_{lb}, P_{ub}, obj) of the UAQ problem when P_{lb} and P_{ub} are randomly selected. This phenomenon is particularly acute in scenario (a) when obj is either min or max. All the points in the plots include the time needed to generate the set of propositional clauses and that taken by the solver to establish satisfiability or unsatisfiability. Now, we analyse each of the three scenarios in detail. In the plots, lines labelled with 'EXACT' refer to UAQ instances (s, P_{lb}, P_{ub}, obj) where $P_{lb} = P_{ub} = perms$ and $obj = $ any, for those with 'MAX' we set $P_{lb} = perms$, $P_{ub} = P_u$, and $obj = $ min, and for those with 'MIN' we set $P_{lb} = \emptyset$, $P_{ub} = perms$, and $obj = $ max for some randomly selected sub-set $perms$ of P_u, which is the whole set of permissions that can be acquired by the user u associated to session s. (The choice of P_{lb} and P_{ub} for the various objectives of the UAQ problem was explained in Section 4.1.)

(a) Increasing number of roles. Figure 3 shows the plot for scenario (a), i.e. when the number of roles increases from 40 to 300. The time necessary for encoding and solving each

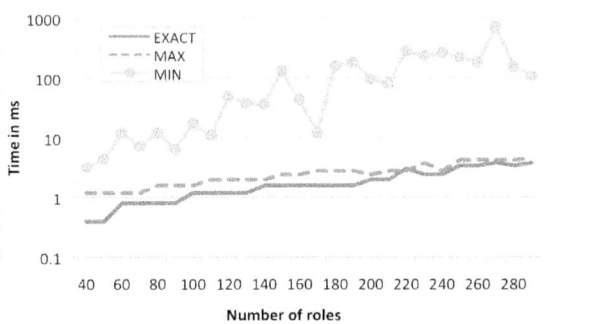

Figure 3: Increasing number of roles

UAQ instance is less than 10 milliseconds up to 300 roles for $obj \in \{$any, max$\}$. When $obj = $ min, there is a degradation in performance since, while the time taken for the generation of the clauses remains the same, the time taken

for the solution of the generated PMAX-SAT problem increases significantly, as expected. However, we observe that the timings in this case are still below 1 second. Furthermore, notice that for most of the RBAC policies classified as 'Literature' by the authors of [1], the number of roles is not larger than 250 and our choice of 300 as the maximum number of roles is compliant with this indication. Interestingly, for such a number of roles, our technique gives a performance of about 200 milliseconds.

(b) Increasing number of sessions. Figure 4 shows the plot for scenario (b), i.e. when the number of sessions per user

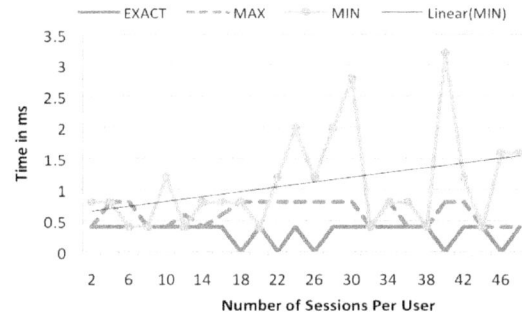

Figure 4: Increasing number of sessions per user

increases from 2 to 50 (and the corresponding number of sessions goes from 160 up to 4000). In this case, regardless of the type of satisfiability problem that must be solved, the performances stay below 3.5 milliseconds and there is no significant degradation when $obj = $ min. We can conclude that increasing the number of sessions per user does not have a significant impact on the performance of our technique.

(c) Increasing history length. Figure 4 shows the plot for scenario (c), i.e. when the history length increases from 10 to 200. In this case, regardless of the type of satisfiability

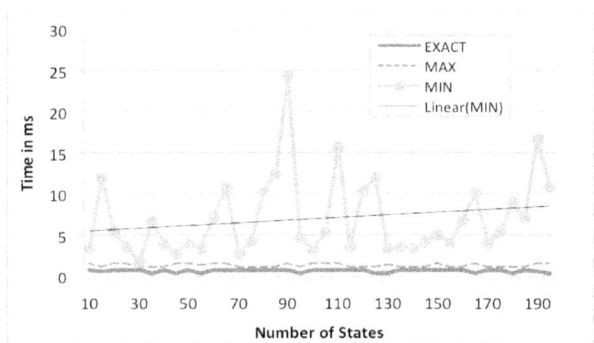

Figure 5: Increasing history length

problem that must solved, the performances stay below 25 milliseconds and there is only a slight degradation for $obj = $ min. In fact, solving the UAQ problem instances always takes less than 2 milliseconds for $obj \in \{$any, max$\}$ and goes up to (almost) 25 milliseconds when $obj = $ min. We can conclude that increasing the history length has almost no impact on the performance of our technique.

4.3.1 Comparison with the SAT-based procedure of Wickramaarachchi, Qardaji, and Li

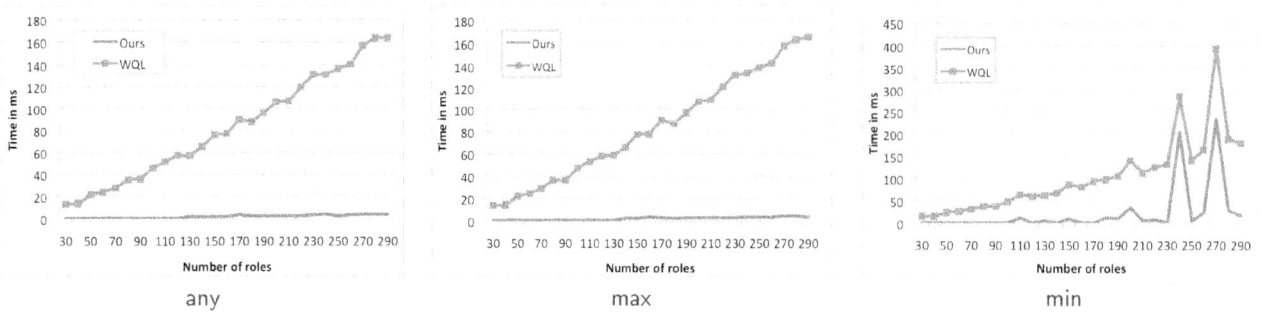

Figure 6: Comparison with the SAT-based procedure of Wickramaarachchi, Qardaji, and Li (2009)

Since the UAQ problem considered in [5] can be seen as an instance of the one defined here when only SS-DMER and CARD constraints are considered, it is interesting to compare the performances of the two approaches. To this end, we have implemented the SAT encoding proposed in [5] and used the same MaxSAT solver (QMaxSAT) previously mentioned for the sake of a fair comparison. Moreover, the set of roles used in the comparison represents all the roles of the system R rather than the user's roles in the UA relation and the first step (i.e. item 1 in Section 3) is applied by both techniques. We believe that this not only makes two approaches in line but also provides an additional optimization in SAT solving by providing more information to the solving process. This can be easily observed from the figures presented in this section and the ones available in [5].

We have considered a similar set of experiments as the ones performed in [5] with some larger number of roles. More precisely, we consider $30 \leq |R| \leq 300$, $|U| = 50$, $|P| = 80$, $|C| = 5$ (recall that we only consider SS-DMER constraints), and use the approach described in Section 4.1 to randomly generate a suitable RBAC policy. We did not report the number of sessions and the length of the history since they are not relevant to establish the satisfiability of SS-DMER constraints. Similar to the experiments in Section 4.3, we take the median value over 10 randomly selected pairs of values of P_{lb} and P_{ub} for the given RBAC policy.

Figure 6 reports the results of the experiments for any (corresponding to the 'exact match' case of [5]), max, and min cases as defined at the end of Section 4.1 for our approach (lines labelled "Ours") and that of [5] (lines labelled "WQL"). In the any and max cases, the timings of our approach are less than 20 milliseconds and in the min case, it is less than 250 milliseconds. Instead, the approach presented in [5] grows linearly, up to around 160 milliseconds in the any and max cases, and up to 400 milliseconds for the min case. Clearly, our technique outperforms that in [5] in the any and max cases while the difference is less striking for the min case. As for the results reported above, the degradation in the performance in our approach is due to the longer running times taken by the solver to handle the min case. The time needed to generate the encoding remains negligible in our approach while it grows almost linearly for increasining number of roles [5]. The key to explain the superiority of our approach is in the observation that most of the clauses in solving UAQ problems can be computed off-line (line 14 of Figure 1) and only a small number of (unit) clauses need to be computed at runtime (see procedure add-YO-clauses of Figure 1 and the definition of $\overline{\chi}_k(r,s)$ in Table 1).

5. CONCLUSIONS

We have described a carefully tuned SAT encoding to solve instances of the UAQ problem which overcomes the main limitations of previously available techniques. In particular, we have extended the types of authorization constraints that can be taken into consideration to DMER constraints whose scope of applicability can accommodate multiple sessions and histories. An important feature of our reduction to SAT is the generation of a large part of the propositional clauses in a pre-processing phase and leave at run-time only the addition of simple (unit) clauses so that the time required for the encoding is greatly reduced. We have also presented an extensive experimental evaluation that show the practical viability of our technique and its superiority to the one presented in [5].

Acknowledgements. This work was partially supported by the "Automated Security Analysis of Identity and Access Management Systems (SIAM)" project funded by Provincia Autonoma di Trento in the context of the "team 2009 - Incoming" COFUND action of the European Commission (FP7). We thank Maurizio Festi and Andrea Mongera for the information about Trento Uni. authorization system.

6. REFERENCES

[1] Marko Komlenovic, Mahesh V. Tripunitara, and Toufik Zitouni. An empirical assessment of approaches to distributed enforcement in role-based access control (rbac). In *CODASPY*, pages 121–132, 2011.

[2] Miyuki Koshimura. Qmaxsat: Q-dai maxsat solver. In *http://sites.google.com/site/qmaxsat/*, 2011.

[3] R. Sandhu, E. Coyne, H. Feinstein, and C. Youmann. Role-Based Access Control Models. *IEEE Computer*, 2(29):38–47, 1996.

[4] Carsten Sinz. Towards an optimal cnf encoding of boolean cardinality constraints. In *Principles and Practice of Constraint Programming (CP)*, pages 827–831, 2005.

[5] Guneshi T. Wickramaarachchi, Wahbeh H. Qardaji, and Ninghui Li. An efficient framework for user authorization queries in rbac systems. In *SACMAT*, pages 23–32, 2009.

[6] Yue Zhang and James B. D. Joshi. Uaq: a framework for user authorization query processing in rbac extended with hybrid hierarchy and constraints. In *SACMAT*, pages 83–92, 2008.

A Model-Theoretic Approach to Data Anonymity and Inference Control

Konstantine Arkoudas
Telcordia Research
One Telcordia Drive
Piscataway, NJ 08854
konstantine@research.telcordia.com

Akshay Vashist
Telcordia Research
One Telcordia Drive
Piscataway, NJ 08854
vashist@research.telcordia.com

Abstract

In secure data management the inference problem occurs when data classified at a high security level becomes inferrible from data classified at lower levels. We present a model-theoretic approach to this problem that captures the epistemic state of the database user as a set of possible worlds or models. Privacy is enforced by requiring the existence of $k > 1$ models assigning distinct values to sensitive attributes, and implemented via model counting. We provide an algorithm mechanizing this process and show that it is sound and complete for a large class of queries.

Categories and Subject Descriptors

H.2.7 [**Database Administration**]: Security, Integrity, and Protection

General Terms

Security

Keywords

privacy, inference control, data anonymity, model theory, model finding, SMT, SMT solving

1. BACKGROUND

The *inference problem* in databases occurs when sensitive information is disclosed indirectly, via a series of ostensibly secure answers to queries. Even though each individual query answer may be properly authorized for disclosure (i.e., the user's clearance level may permit her to receive the answer), the answers may nevertheless collectively compromise sensitive information, in that the user may be able to infer from them information that she is not authorized to have, particularly when she combines the answers with some additional knowledge, e.g., metadata such as integrity constraints or functional dependencies, or domain-specific knowledge.

The problem has attracted a great deal of attention; see [4] for an overview of the work in this field up until 2002. Most approaches fall into two camps, static and dynamic. Static approaches [8, 15, 3, 13] analyze a database prior to querying and try to detect potential inferences that could result in leaks of sensitive information. When such inferences are identified, the database is modified in order to eliminate them; typically the security levels of various attributes are raised accordingly. This usually results in over-classification: large portions of the data are classified as sensitive, and overall data availability is thereby reduced, making the database less useful. As a simple example, consider a company database with three attributes, *Name*, *Job*, and *Salary*. Suppose that we wish to keep secret the association between names and salaries, but freely disclose the association between names and jobs, and between jobs and salaries. Given a functional dependency $Job \rightarrow Salary$, it is clear that the user could come to infer salaries from jobs. For instance, even though the system may not directly tell us Alice's salary, it might tell us that Alice is an engineer, and it might also tell us that engineers make 90K. It is then trivial for the user to infer Alice's salary. In the static approach (as advocated, e.g., by [17]), the solution would be to make the *Job* attribute sensitive once and for all. This means that the system would not disclose Alice's job to anyone who is not authorized to view it.

Dynamic (or "auditing") approaches [6, 2, 7, 12, 16, 11], by contrast, attempt to detect and block potential inferences of sensitive information at query time. If no inference is detected, the regular answer to the query can be released. But if it is determined that compromising inferences could be made on the basis of the answer (and other knowledge, such as previous answers, metadata, etc.), then the answer is not released; it is withheld, or suppressed, or generalized, etc. Dynamic approaches have the benefit of being considerably more precise than static approaches. Overall, data is more available under a dynamic approach because there is no need to be overly conservative ahead of time. The main drawbacks of dynamic approaches have been incompleteness and inefficiency. Incompleteness means that only a very restricted class of inferences could be detected; and their detection was computationally expensive. In this paper we present an approach to inference detection that is complete with respect to a significantly larger class of inferences than previously tackled, and promises to be practical owing to the use of highly efficient off-the-shelf model finders.

Given that the issue at hand is inference, it would appear

that logic-based techniques such as theorem proving might be of use. Indeed, theorem proving techniques could be used to tackle the inference problem, roughly along the following lines: For any given time point $t \geq 1$, let $A_t = \{a_1, \ldots, a_t\}$ be the answers to the queries that the user has posed up to time t. Further, let B be a set of background knowledge that the user can be reasonably expected to have. For instance, B could be a set of functional dependencies. Now let q_{t+1} be a new query and let a_{t+1} be the answer to it. An inference-blocking system will decline to disclose a_{t+1} if $A_t \cup B \cup \{a_{t+1}\} \vdash p$, where p is a sensitive proposition. Typically p is an atomic sentence revealing the value of a sensitive attribute for an individual, such as $salary(Tom) = 70K$.

There are two main drawbacks to this approach. First, usually there is no single proposition p that we need to protect but many. At least in principle, this could be handled, e.g., by formulating a disjunctive proposition $p_1 \vee \cdots \vee p_n$ containing *all* the propositions that we need to protect and checking whether

$$A_t \cup B \cup \{a_{t+1}\} \vdash p_1 \vee \cdots \vee p_n. \quad (1)$$

Depending on the richness of the logic and the particular theorem-proving technology deployed, this may be practical to a certain extent. But there is a second problem here, namely, that the answer a_{t+1} might result in a *partial* information disclosure. That is, it might not allow the user to deduce a particular sensitive proposition, but it may nevertheless provide helpful information in that it might eliminate certain alternatives, thereby narrowing the pool of possible values for a sensitive attribute of some individual. The upshot is that a security breach may occur even though (1) does not hold. For instance, suppose that company rank is a sensitive attribute, and that rank is either E, F, G, or H; and that the user knows that the rank of a certain employee x is either F, G, or H. Actually, it is F. If the new query answer allows the user to eliminate H as a possibility, it is clear that it has given her *some* sensitive information, even though she still does not quite know the actual value, F.

In what follows we propose a model-theoretic approach to inference detection that allows for a more natural formulation of the problem and for much finer security-policy specification and inference control. We model the epistemic state of the user as a set of possible worlds, i.e., as a set of data *models*. The user's knowledge is expressed in a multi-sorted first-order logic that is propositionalized (restricted to a finite domain) over a slice of the database universe, and the models in question are models of this knowledge, in the standard sense of mathematical logic. We introduce a new notion of *anonymity signatures*, which allow us to precisely specify which data associations we wish to protect, and we then require, roughly, that for each tuple of values for the so-called "identifying attributes" of an anonymity signature, there should be at least k distinct values for the corresponding sensitive attribute of the signature that are consistent with what the user knows at the time of the query, where k is a tunable parameter that can be given different values for different anonymity signatures. For instance, if $k = 2$ and the sensitive attribute is salary, then for any individual u in the database there must be at least two distinct values v_1 and v_2 such that $salary(u) = v_1$ and $salary(u) = v_2$ are both consistent with what the user can be expected to know at the time, namely with $A_t \cup B \cup \{a_{t+1}\}$. This condition can be decided by finding two distinct models for

$A_t \cup B \cup \{a_{t+1}\} \cup \{salary(u) = v\}$ that differ on the values they assign to v. This is somewhat similar to the idea of k-anonymity [9] in that the user is not able to distinguish between v_1 and v_2 on the basis of $A_t \cup B \cup \{a_{t+1}\}$. In the case of k-anonymity, however, the indistinguishability holds among rows in the actual database, not among arbitrary values of sensitive attributes. Moreover, in our case it is not necessary to require that the data itself must be k-anonymous, only that *the epistemic state of the user* should be consistent with k distinct values for any given sensitive attribute of any identifiable individual. The approach we propose here allows us to treat partial information disclosures in a model-theoretic fashion, and to mechanize inference detection and control by using state-of-the-art model builders to do a form of model counting.

2. INFORMATION SYSTEMS

We define an *information system* S as a finite set of objects $\mathcal{U}$ and a finite set of attribute names (or simply *attributes*) $\mathcal{A}$. We call $\mathcal{U}$ the *universe* of S. We use the letters u and A as variables ranging over $\mathcal{U}$ and $\mathcal{A}$, respectively. Associated with each attribute name $A \in \mathcal{A}$ is a unique computable domain of values $V(A)$, the set of values for the attribute A. We write $\mathcal{V}$ for the union of all $V(A)$, $A \in \mathcal{A}$. We assume that a fixed subset of the attributes are designated as *sensitive*; these are the attributes whose privacy we wish to protect (though we will refine this considerably soon). A *model* or *possible world* w of an information system is an assignment of a unique value to each attribute and object. More precisely, a possible world of S is a function $w : \mathcal{A} \times \mathcal{U} \to \mathcal{V}$ with $w(A, u) \in V(A)$ for each $A \in \mathcal{A}$, $u \in \mathcal{U}$. When the world w is obvious or immaterial, we write $A(u)$ as a shorthand for $w(A, u)$.

A possible world of an information system can be depicted in tabular format. Consider, e.g., the table: [1]

	Name	Salary
u_1	Tom	50K
u_2	Mary	70K
u_3	Peter	40K

This table can be viewed the following possible world:

$$w(Name, u_1) = Tom, \ w(Salary, u_1) = 50K,$$
$$w(Name, u_2) = Mary, \ w(Salary, u_2) = 70K,$$
$$w(Name, u_3) = Peter, \ w(Salary, u_3) = 40K$$

A *state* M of an information system S is a non-empty set of possible worlds of S. The term "state" is meant to invoke the notion of an agent's *epistemic state*. In particular, the set of worlds in M are all and only the worlds that are considered possible on the basis of what is known by the agent in question. We need to model the user's epistemic state in order to control it properly. When the interaction first starts, the user's state will contain very many possible worlds because the user will be under-informed at that point. As the user obtains more and more answers to her queries, her epistemic state narrows: many possible worlds

---

[1] In this paper we will only be concerned with one information system, i.e., with one data table at a time. Our work can be easily extended to handle multiple tables, although, as shown by [5], a database with multiple tables can be transformed into one with a single "universal" table; see also [19, section 2].

are eliminated and hence the state's information content increases. Essentially, we want to ensure that the epistemic state doesn't narrow too much along the sensitive dimensions. The objective, in other words, will be to ensure that at any given time during the interaction, the user's state has several possible worlds of a certain kind in it. This will be made precise shortly.

3. A LOGIC FOR INFORMATION SYSTEMS

In this section we present the syntax and semantics of a logic for reasoning about information systems (essentially database tables). We will be concerned with a first-order language L consisting of a finite set of sorts S, where S contains a distinct sort ind (for the universe of the information system) along with m distinct sorts $\mathsf{a}_1, \ldots, \mathsf{a}_m$, where each a_i corresponds to an attribute name. For each sort $\mathsf{s} \in \mathsf{S}$, the language also contains a (possibly empty) collection of constant symbols, C_{s}. We write c_{s} as a typical constant of sort s. The language has a number of sorted function and relation symbols. Each function symbol has a unique sort profile associated with it, of the form $\mathsf{s}_1 \times \cdots \times \mathsf{s}_n \to \mathsf{s}$, $n > 0$, and each relation symbol also has a unique sort profile, of the form $\mathsf{s}_1 \times \cdots \times \mathsf{s}_n$. There is an identity symbol $=^{\mathsf{s}}$ with profile $\mathsf{s} \times \mathsf{s}$ for every sort s. We usually drop the sort superscript and simply write $=$. At minimum there are m function symbols $a_1, \ldots, a_m$, where a_i corresponds to attribute A_i and has profile $\mathsf{ind} \to \mathsf{a}_i$. Finally, for each sort s there is a countably infinite set of variables X_{s} of sort s, where for any two distinct sorts s_1 and s_2, X_{s_1} and X_{s_2} are disjoint. We write x_{s} as a typical variable of sort s. Terms t of sort s are defined as follows: any variable or constant of sort s is a term of sort s; and if $t_1, \ldots, t_k$ are terms of sorts $\mathsf{s}_1, \ldots, \mathsf{s}_k$, respectively, and f is a function symbol with profile $\mathsf{s}_1 \times \cdots \times \mathsf{s}_k \to \mathsf{s}$, then $f(t_1, \ldots, t_k)$ is a term of sort s. Nothing else is a term of sort s. If we wish to emphasize that a term t is of sort s, we may write t^{s} instead of just t. The atomic formulas of this logic are of the form $R(t_1^{\mathsf{s}_1}, \ldots, t_k^{\mathsf{s}_k})$ for R with profile $\mathsf{s}_1 \times \cdots \times \mathsf{s}_k$. We also have the usual Boolean combinations, universal quantifications $\forall x_{\mathsf{s}} . \phi$, and existential quantifications $\exists x_{\mathsf{s}} . \phi$.

Since the sorts are fixed for a given information system, a language of the kind we have described here is completely determined by its constant, function, and relation symbols. We may omit sort information from constants and variables when the sorts are obvious or immaterial. We define $\phi[t/x]$ as the formula obtained from ϕ by replacing every free occurrence of x by t. We write $\phi(x_1, \ldots, x_n)$ for a formula that has $x_1, \ldots, x_n$ as its free variables.

An interpretation I for such a language is given with respect to an information system $S = (\mathcal{U}, \mathcal{A})$. In particular, the sort ind is mapped to the universe $\mathcal{U}$, while each sort a_i is mapped to $V(A_i)$. We write s^I for the set that interprets the sort s. Constants are interpreted as usual: each constant c_{s} is mapped to a unique element c^I in s^I. A function symbol $f : \mathsf{s}_1 \times \cdots \times \mathsf{s}_n \to \mathsf{s}$ is assigned a corresponding function $f^I : \mathsf{s}_1^I \times \cdots \times \mathsf{s}_n^I \to \mathsf{s}^I$. This means that each attribute symbol $a_i : \mathsf{ind} \to \mathsf{a}_i$ is mapped to a unique function $a_i^I : \mathcal{U} \to V(A_i)$. Also, each relation symbol R with profile $\mathsf{s}_1 \times \cdots \times \mathsf{s}_n$ is interpreted by a unique relation $R^I \subseteq \mathsf{s}_1^I \times \cdots \times \mathsf{s}_n^I$. The interpretation of each equality symbol $=^{\mathsf{s}}$ is always the identity relation on s^I.

A variable assignment ρ for an interpretation I is a functional finite set of ordered pairs of the form (x_{s}, v) where

$v \in \mathsf{s}^I$. We write $\rho[x_{\mathsf{s}} \mapsto v]$, for $v \in \mathsf{s}^I$, for the assignment that is identical to ρ except that it maps x_{s} to v; and we write $\rho[x_1 \mapsto v_1, \ldots, x_n \mapsto v_n]$ as a shorthand for $(\cdots (\rho[x_1 \mapsto v_1]) \cdots)[x_n \mapsto v_n]$. Also, $[x_1 \mapsto v_1, \ldots, x_n \mapsto v_n]$ is understood as $\emptyset[x_1 \mapsto v_1, \ldots, x_n \mapsto v_n]$. We use this notation for any finite function, not just for variable assignments. The denotation of a term t with respect to a given interpretation I and assignment ρ, denoted $I_\rho(t)$, is defined by structural recursion: if t is a constant symbol c, then $I_\rho(t) = c^I$; if t is a variable x, then $I_\rho(t)$ is the value assigned to x by ρ, viewing the latter as a function (we assume that x is in the domain of ρ); and if t is of the form $f(t_1, \ldots, t_n)$, then $I_\rho(t)$ is $f^I(I_\rho(t_1), \ldots, I_\rho(t_n))$.

We write $I \models_\rho \phi$ to mean that the interpretation I satisfies the formula ϕ with respect to ρ. This satisfaction relation is defined by the usual structural induction. We say that I satisfies ϕ, written $I \models \phi$, iff $I \models_\rho \phi$ for every assignment ρ.

We have seen that an interpretation I is given with respect to an information system S. Yet only some parts of I are truly dependent on the given S, while others are invariant across many different information systems. For instance, if the language contains the integers as a sort and the less-than ($<$) relation on them as a relation symbol, then the interpretation of that sort and the corresponding relation presumably do not change across different information systems. If we factor out these invariant parts, we may then understand an interpretation I as encoding a possible world w of an information system. That is, the truly important parts of I are the functions a_i^I that map each object u in the underlying universe to a particular attribute value in $V(A_i)$. This fixes a data table for the underlying system. Thus, we may understand an interpretation as a possible world of the underlying information system, writing, e.g., $w \models_\rho \phi$ to mean that the interpretation I corresponding to w (obtained from w in tandem with the invariant parts, such as the relations and functions corresponding to symbols such as $<$ and $+$) satisfies ϕ with respect to ρ. And if M is a state (a collection of models), we will write $M \models_\rho \phi$ to mean that $w \models_\rho \phi$ for *every* $w \in M$. Likewise, $M \models \phi$ will means that $M \models_\rho \phi$ holds for every ρ. Assuming a fixed invariant part for I, we understand a *model for* a formula $\phi(x_1, \ldots, x_n)$ as a pair $(w, (v_1, \ldots, v_n))$ consisting of a world w as well as values v_i from the appropriate domains for the variables $x_1, \ldots, x_n$, such that $w \models_{[x_1 \mapsto v_1, \ldots, x_n \mapsto v_n]} \phi(x_1, \ldots, x_n)$.

In what follows we will assume a unique naming convention to the effect that for any language L associated with an information system S; for any element $z \in \mathcal{V} \cup \mathcal{U}$; and for any interpretation I of L; L contains a unique constant symbol $\bar{z}$ (of the appropriate sort) whose denotation under I is z, i.e., $\bar{z}^I = z$. Finally, for any formula ϕ and finite set Σ of constants of sort ind, we define *the propositionalization of ϕ w.r.t. Σ*, written $\phi \upharpoonright \Sigma$, as the formula obtained from ϕ by skolemizing all existential quantifications, followed by expanding every universal quantification $\forall x_{\mathsf{ind}} . \psi$ into the conjunction of all $\psi[c/x_{\mathsf{ind}}]$, for $c \in \Sigma$.

4. ANONYMITY SIGNATURES

Fix an information system S. An *anonymity signature* for S is an ordered pair

$$((A_1, \ldots, A_p), A) \qquad (2)$$

where $(A_1, \ldots, A_p)$ is a sequence of attributes of S and A

is a sensitive attribute of S. We refer to $A_1, \ldots, A_p$ as the signature's *identifying attributes* and to A as the signature's *sensitive attribute*. Intuitively, a sequence of values $v_1, \ldots, v_p$, with $v_i \in V(A_i)$, either uniquely identifies an individual or makes it very likely that an individual can be identified, perhaps with the aid of additional information. For instance, a combination of a name and a social security number would uniquely identify any individual working in the United States. But as shown by [9], there are other combinations of attributes, which, while not necessarily uniquely identifying by themselves, would typically make it very easy to identify an individual when augmented with some publicly available external information. For instance, armed just with a zip code, gender, and a birth date, we can often (around 87% of the time) uniquely identify any individual in this country according to [9, p. 19]. Our definition of anonymity signatures is flexible enough to handle any sequence of attributes deemed to be identifying attributes. The objective is that for any tuple of values $(v_1, \ldots, v_p)$ given for the identifying attributes $A_1, \ldots, A_p$ in a signature of the form (2), the user should not be able to determine the corresponding value for the sensitive attribute A.

By taking advantage of the logic we specified above for a given language L, we can allow for a more flexible form of anonymity signature: we can define an anonymity signature as a *triple* instead of a pair, where the first two elements are as before, except that they are now expressed more formally as attribute sorts, and the third new element is a formula $\phi(x)$ of one free variable ranging over ind: $((s_1, \ldots, s_p), s, \phi(x))$. The idea here is that we only wish to protect the value of the sensitive attribute s (for a given tuple of values for the identifying attributes) for those individuals x for which ϕ holds. Suppose, e.g., that we have attributes *Job* and *Salary*, and we wish to protect the relationship from *Job* to *Salary* but only for managers. We can specify this with the following anonymity signature: $((\mathsf{job}), \mathsf{salary}, job(x) = manager)$ where job and salary are attribute sorts; *job* is an attribute function symbol; and *manager* is an attribute value. We can now define an *anonymity policy* for an information system S as a finite set of anonymity signatures of the above form, expressed in some logic L for S. To make policies more flexible, we may assume that each anonymity signature has a unique positive integer k associated with it.

5. AN ALGORITHM FOR INFERENCE CONTROL

Fix an information system S, a language L for it (as specified in section 3), and the invariant part of some interpretation I for L. We now describe our general algorithm for inference detection and control. First, some notational conventions: For any n terms $t_1, \ldots, t_n$ of the same sort, we define $distinct(t_1, \ldots, t_n)$ as the conjunction stating that any two terms t_i and t_j with $i \neq j$ are distinct. Also, in what follows w_0 will refer to the "real world," namely, the world corresponding to the actual database. Although the user does not have direct access to that world, our algorithm does, and we take advantage of that fact. By a *constant mapping* τ we mean a finite function from constant symbols of sort ind to the universe $\mathcal{U}$ of S. Our algorithm will maintain a dynamically growing set of such constant symbols $\mathcal{C}$ and a corresponding mapping $\tau : \mathcal{C} \mapsto \mathcal{U}$.

Next, let $\sigma = ((\mathsf{a}_1, \ldots, \mathsf{a}_p), \mathsf{a}, \phi(x))$ be an anonymity signature, and let c be a constant symbol in $\mathcal{C}$. We define $N_\sigma(c, \tau)$ as follows:

$$N_\sigma(c, \tau) = \phi[c/x] \bigwedge_{i=1}^{p} a_i(c) = \overline{w_0(A_i, \tau(c))}$$

where c is in the domain of τ (A_i is the attribute name in $\mathcal{A}$ corresponding to the function symbol a_i). We call $N_\sigma(c, \tau)$ the *identifying sentence* for c w.r.t. σ and τ. Our algorithm is parameterized over a finite set of formulas B containing a priori knowledge about the database, which must be consistent with the real world.

A key part of the algorithm is step 6, where we compute what we call the existential and universal "closures" of the query answer. Intuitively, these closures capture the logical content of the query answer, A; we explain them with the aid of an example. Consider a database called `Personnel` with the following contents:

	Name	*Age*	*Salary*	*Job*
u_1	Albert	28	50K	Receptionist
u_2	Betty	25	60K	Engineer
u_3	Calvin	35	70K	Engineer

(This example is taken from [12, p. 22].) Now consider the following SQL query:

```
select Name, Age
from Personnel
where Age < 30;
```

The answer to this query is a set of tuples, namely, (*Albert*, 28) and (*Betty*, 25). As indicated in step 5, we introduce fresh constant symbols to refer to the individuals corresponding to the tuples in this answer. In this case, since we have two tuples, we introduce two fresh constants, let's say c_4 and c_5, with c_4 corresponding to u_1 and c_5 to u_2 (we keep track of this correspondence in the mapping τ). Now, what information does this answer convey? More precisely, exactly what does this answer tell us, in logical terms? It tells us two things: (1) There are two individuals in the information system, one whose name is *Albert* and whose age is 28; and one whose name is *Betty* and whose age is 25. Since c_4 and c_5 are (fresh) names for these individuals, we can express this information by the following conjunction:

$$name(c_4) = Albert \wedge age(c_4) = 28 \wedge$$
$$name(c_5) = Betty \wedge age(c_5) = 25$$

We call this the *existential closure* of the answer. We write $EC(A)$ to denote the existential closure of any query answer A. (2) The answer also tells us that these are the *only* individuals whose age is less than 30. More precisely:

$$\forall x_{\mathsf{ind}} \cdot age(x_{\mathsf{ind}}) < 30 \Rightarrow x_{\mathsf{ind}} = c_4 \vee x_{\mathsf{ind}} = c_5$$

We call this the *universal closure* of the answer. Since we do not want to have unrestricted quantifiers in our formalization, we propositionalize this closure by replacing x_{ind} by every constant symbol *previously* introduced by our algorithm. For instance, suppose that the previously introduced constants are c_1, c_2, and c_3. Then the universal closure of this answer will be expressed by the following three formulas: $age(c_i) < 30 \Rightarrow c_i = c_4 \vee c_i = c_5$, $i = 1, 2, 3$. In general, for any two sets of constants C and C' and any selection

- Set $\mathcal{C} \leftarrow \emptyset$, $\Gamma \leftarrow \emptyset$, $\tau \leftarrow \emptyset$, *violations* $\leftarrow$ *false*.

- While *violations* = *false*, do:

  1. Set $\mathcal{C}' \leftarrow \mathcal{C}$, $\Gamma' \leftarrow \Gamma$, $\tau' \leftarrow \tau$.
  2. Receive a query Q from the user.
  3. Let ϕ_Q be the selection condition of Q (this could be the constant *true*).
  4. Let A be the answer to Q, consisting of a sequence of m tuples corresponding to m individuals $u_1, \ldots, u_m$ in $\mathcal{U}$.
  5. Let $c_1, \ldots, c_m$ be fresh constant symbols and set $\tau \leftarrow \tau[c_1 \mapsto u_1, \ldots, c_m \mapsto u_m]$.
  6. Set $\Gamma \leftarrow \Gamma \cup UC(\mathcal{C}, \phi_Q, \{c_1, \ldots, c_m\}) \cup EC(A) \cup distinct(c_1, \ldots, c_m)$.
  7. Set $\mathcal{C} \leftarrow \mathcal{C} \cup \{c_1, \ldots, c_m\}$.
  8. For each anonymity signature $\sigma = ((\mathsf{a}_1, \ldots, \mathsf{a}_p), \mathsf{a}, \phi(x))$ with degree k, do:
     - For each constant $c \in \mathcal{C}$, construct the following *anonymity predicate* for c:
       $$\psi_c(x) \equiv \neg N_\sigma(c, \tau) \vee \left[a(c) = x \wedge x \neq \overline{w_o(A, \tau(c))} \right]$$
     - Let $\mathcal{C} = \{c_1, \ldots, c_n\}$. Define $\psi(x_1, \ldots, x_n)$ as the conjunction
       $$\psi_{c_1}(x_1) \wedge \cdots \wedge \psi_{c_n}(x_n)$$
       where $x_1, \ldots, x_n$ are distinct fresh variables.
     - For $j = 2, \ldots, k$: Try to find a model $(w_j, (v_{1_j}, \ldots, v_{n_j}))$ for
       $$B \cup \Gamma \cup \{\psi(x_1, \ldots, x_n) \wedge \bigwedge_{i=1}^{n} \bigwedge_{j' < j} x_i \neq v_{i_{j'}}\}.$$
       If successful, continue; otherwise set *violations* $\leftarrow$ *true* and go to step 9.
  9. If *violations* = *false*, return A. Otherwise, suppress A and set $\mathcal{C} \leftarrow \mathcal{C}'$, $\Gamma \leftarrow \Gamma'$, $\tau \leftarrow \tau'$, *violations* $\leftarrow$ *false*.

Figure 1: A model-theoretic algorithm for inference detection and control.

condition ϕ, we define

$$UC(C, \phi, C') = \{\phi(c) \Rightarrow \bigvee_{c' \in C'} c = c' \mid c \in C\}$$

The set C can be thought of as containing all previously introduced constants (for previous query answers), while C' can be viewed as the set of new constants (corresponding to the latest query answer).

Thus, with every new query answer, the user's slice of the universe keeps expanding—new constant names are introduced to denote the individuals corresponding to the answer's tuples. (Some of these new constants, of course, might denote individuals named by previously introduced constants.) The reasoning that our algorithm models is carried out with respect to this dynamically expanding universe. It is this restriction to a finite (but dynamically expanding) slice of the universe that makes the algorithm practical. The restriction is sensible because the user reasons about the information that she has received, which pertains only to the individual tuples in the query answers.

It should be noted that both loops in the algorithm are essentially constant-time. First, on step 8: in practice there is often only one anonymity signature of interest, so this outer loop will often be executed only once. Then, on the third step inside step 8 ("For $j = 2, \ldots, k$"): This inner loop will be iterated only $k - 1$ times. In particular, if $k = 2$,

then the loop will only be executed once. Thus, if there is only one anonymity signature with degree $k = 2$, there will be no iteration at all—the procedure becomes a straight-line algorithm in that case. The case $k = 2$, in fact, corresponds essentially to (1), the theorem-proving formulation.

Note the importance of naming: the presence of the identifying sentence $N_\sigma(c, \tau)$ in the definition of the anonymity predicate

$$\psi_c(x) \equiv \neg N_\sigma(c, \tau) \vee \left[a(c) = x \wedge x \neq \overline{w_o(A, \tau(c))} \right]$$

is significant, because we do not want to preclude the release of a sensitive attribute value *as long as the corresponding individual is not identifiable.*

The correctness of the algorithm is perhaps easier to see in the case of $k = 2$. Let us say that a model-finding algorithm is *sound* iff it never produces an incorrect answer, namely: if it claims that a given set of formulas has no model, then the set in question is indeed unsatisfiable; and if it outputs a putative model for a given set of formulas, then that answer is indeed a model for the given formulas. And such an algorithm is *complete* iff it always terminates and produces an output, for any given (finite) set of formulas.

Theorem 1: *Assume there is only one anonymity signature σ with degree $k = 2$, and assume the algorithm in fig. 1 uses a sound and complete model finder in step 8. Then the* variable violations *becomes* true *iff the value of the sensitive attribute for at least one individual in the query answers has been leaked, i.e., iff there is a constant $c \in C$ such that*

$$B \cup \Gamma \models N_\sigma(c, \tau) \wedge a(c) = \overline{w_o(A, \tau(c))}.$$

PROOF: In one direction, suppose that *violations* becomes *true* for some query. Since $k = 2$, the loop variable $j = 2$ in step 8 must have only assumed the value 2, which means that the model finder was unable to find a model for

$$B \cup \Gamma \cup \{\psi(x_1, \ldots, x_n)\}. \tag{3}$$

By the model finder's soundness, it follows that (3) is unsatisfiable, which is to say that

$$B \cup \Gamma \models \neg\psi(x_1, \ldots, x_n). \tag{4}$$

But ψ is just a conjunction of ψ_{c_i} for $i = 1, \ldots, n$, where n is the total number of constant symbols introduced up to that point. Hence, by (4) and De Morgan's we get

$$B \cup \Gamma \models \bigvee_{i=1}^{n} \neg\psi_{c_i}(x_i). \tag{5}$$

Therefore, there is some $i \in \{1, \ldots, n\}$ such that

$$B \cup \Gamma \models \neg\psi_{c_i}(x)$$

and this, in turn, means precisely that

$$B \cup \Gamma \models N_\sigma(c_i, \tau) \wedge a(c_i) = \overline{w_o(A, \tau(c_i))}. \tag{6}$$

The converse direction is immediate: if (6) holds for some c_i then $B \cup \Gamma \cup \psi_{c_i}(x)$ is unsatisfiable for some i, hence $B \cup \Gamma \cup \psi(x_1, \ldots, x_n)$ is unsatisfiable. Therefore, by the model finder's completeness and soundness, it follows that the attempt to find a model on step 8 will fail, and therefore that *violations* will be set to *true*. ∎

Both the result and the proof generalize to any number of anonymity signatures and any $k > 1$: *violations* becomes *true* iff, for some $c \in C$, there are fewer than $k - 1$ models for $B \cup \Gamma \cup \{\psi_c(x)\}$ assigning distinct values to x.

Of course, there is no sound and complete model-finding algorithm for unrestricted first-order logic, so, as given, the procedure in figure 1 is not quite mechanically computable. However, there are sound, complete, and highly efficient model finders for quantifier-free fragments of first-order logic combining various useful theories that arise in practice [10]. Such a model-finder would be more than complete enough for practical purposes, since most queries encountered in practice are expressible in such a fragment, including statistical queries such as sums, counts, and averages. A look at step 8 shows that a model finder is invoked on:

$$B \cup \Gamma \cup \{\psi(x_1, \ldots, x_n) \wedge \bigwedge_{i=1}^{n} \bigwedge_{j' < j} x_i \neq v_{i_{j'}}\}.$$

From this input, only B, in general, may not be quantifier-less. However, for most sets of background knowledge that arise in practice, such as functional dependencies and integrity constraints, B can be propositionalized in a way that makes it amenable to SMT model finding, by computing $\phi \upharpoonright C$ for every $\phi \in B$.

6. EXAMPLE

In this section we illustrate our algorithm with an example. We present code from our preliminary implementation of the algorithm, using Yices [1] as our model finder. The example revisits the `Personnel` database example of section 5. We first introduce a domain `Ind` for the universe of the information system, and datatypes `Name` and `Job` for the different names and jobs that appear in the database:

```
(define-type Ind)
(define-type Name (datatype Albert Betty Calvin))
(define-type Job (datatype Receptionist Engineer))
```

We can now introduce the attribute functions that give the age, name, salary, and job of a given individual:

```
(define age::(-> Ind int))
(define name::(-> Ind Name))
(define salary::(-> Ind int))
(define job::(-> Ind Job))
```

Let us say that we wish to protect the association between names and salaries, so suppose there is one anonymity signature $((Name), Salary, true)$ with a degree of anonymity $k = 2$. Suppose the user starts the interaction by making the following query Q:

```
select Name, Age from Personnel where Age < 30
```

Thus, the selection condition here is $\phi_Q(x) = age(x) < 30$. The answer to this query returns the two tuples $(Albert, 28)$ and $(Betty, 25)$. We introduce two fresh constant symbols c_1 and c_2 to refer to the individuals corresponding to these tuples, with the mapping $\tau = \{c_1 \mapsto u_1, c_2 \mapsto u_2\}$, and we `assert` that these are distinct: `(assert (not (= c1 c2)))`. We then assert the existential closure of this answer:

```
(assert (and (= (name c1) Albert)
             (= (age c1) 28)
             (= (name c2) Betty)
             (= (age c2) 25)))
```

Since there are no previously introduced constants, there is no universal closure for this answer. Thus, we have now reached step 8 of the algorithm, and we proceed to construct the anonymity predicates for c_1 and c_2. The anonymity predicate for c_1 is as follows:

$$\psi_{c_1}(x) \equiv \neg N_\sigma(c_1, \tau) \vee [salary(c_1) = x \wedge x \neq 50]$$

where $N_\sigma(c_1, \tau) \equiv name(c_1) = Albert$, and hence

$$\psi_{c_1}(x) \equiv name(c_1) \neq Albert \vee [salary(c_1) = x \wedge x \neq 50].$$

Likewise, the anonymity predicate for c_2 is:

$$\psi_{c_2}(x) \equiv name(c_2) \neq Betty \vee [salary(c_2) = x \wedge x \neq 60].$$

Accordingly, the total anonymity predicate $\psi(x_1, x_2)$ is the conjunction of

$$name(c_1) \neq Albert \vee [salary(c_1) = x_1 \wedge x_1 \neq 50]$$

and $name(c_2) \neq Betty \vee [salary(c_2) = x_2 \wedge x_2 \neq 60]$. Moving to the last part of the algorithm, since in this case $k = 2$, all we now need to do is to find a model for $\psi(x_1, x_2)$. The model finder succeeds with the following result: `(= x1 62)`, `(= x2 61)`. This means that, for all the user knows at this point, the salary of c_1 (Albert) could be 62K and the salary of c_2 (Betty) could be 61K, and therefore the answer to this first query does not compromise the security policy and can be safely released.

Suppose the user continues with the query

```
select Age, Salary from Personnel where Age = 28
```

which returns the single tuple $(28, 50K)$. We introduce a new constant symbol c_3, and we update τ to map c_3 to u_1. The existential closure of this answer is simply the conjunction of (= (age c3) 28) and (= (salary c3) 50). Since at this point there are previously introduced constants (c_1 and c_2), we need to compute and assert the universal closure of this answer. This closure is the conjunction of

$$age(c_i) = 28 \Rightarrow c_i = c_3$$

for $i = 1, 2$. At this point we are ready to try to find a model for the predicate $\psi(x, y)$ that we defined above. This time, however, the model finder reports that the current context is unsatisfiable. Thus, the answer would be withheld[2] and we would retract the assertions due to the second query and continue with the top-level loop.

7. CONCLUSIONS

Let A be a sensitive attribute, such as the results of someone's medical tests, or the balance in someone's bank account, etc.; and let v be the actual value of A, i.e., $A = v$. What does it mean to say that an agent x doesn't know the value of A? We suggest the following answer: It means that there is at least one other value $v' \neq v$ such that $A = v'$ is *consistent with what x knows*. Suppose, e.g., that A represents the results of a cancer biopsy for Alice, so that there are only two possible values for A: 0 (negative) and 1 (positive). Suppose that the actual value v is 0, i.e., the result is negative. What does it mean to say that x does not know this information? According to our answer, it means that there is another value v', distinct from v, such that $A = v'$ is consistent with what x knows. In this case, of course, $v' = 1$. That is, to say that x doesn't know the value of A is to say that $A = 1$ is consistent with what x knows.

Suppose that x is a user querying a database and accumulating answers to those queries over time. Let us write K_x to denote the set of all answers that x has received so far; and let B be a set of pertinent background knowledge that x might have a priori (we often have $B = \emptyset$). We may then say that the answers given to x do not "leak" the value of A iff there is some v' such that

$$K_x \cup B \cup \{A = v', v' \neq v\} \qquad (7)$$

is consistent, i.e., satisfiable. Therefore, we may determine whether the answers reveal the value of A by trying to find a model for the set (7). This simple observation is the main idea behind our approach.

Alternatively, we may test whether the value of A has been disclosed by testing whether $K_x \cup B \models A = v$. This is the theorem-proving approach, and it's the dual of the model-finding approach. To say that the answers K_x leak the value of A is simply to say that $K_x \cup B$ entails $A = v$.

Thus, to say that the answers *do not* leak the value of A is to say that the entailment does not hold, i.e., that

$$K_x \cup B \not\models A = v,$$

and this, in turn, is precisely to say that the set $K_x \cup B \cup \{A = v', v' \neq v\}$ is satisfiable. In some sense, this duality means that model-finding captures ignorance while theorem-proving captures knowledge. Since I know something iff I am not ignorant of it, it seems to matter little for practical purposes which method we choose to determine whether x can know the value of A.

However, as we have seen, the model-theoretic approach has a distinct advantage: It allows for a natural formulation of one's *degree* of ignorance, which is precisely the sort of thing that we might want to control when conveying private data. That there are varying degrees of ignorance is clear. For example, the query answers given to x may not reveal the exact age of a person p, but they may narrow it down to between 30 and 35. In that case x is *less* ignorant than she would be if she only knew that p's age lies between 20 and 60. Thus, writing A_p for p's age, the sets

$$K_x \cup B \cup \{A_p = 30\}, \dots, K_x \cup B \cup \{A_p = 35\}$$

are all consistent, i.e., satisfiable. Another way of putting this is to say that the set $K_x \cup B \cup \{A_p = v\}$ has 6 distinct models that assign different values to v. If there were more such models, x would be more ignorant about A_p; and if there were fewer such models, x would be less ignorant.

More precisely, let us say that two models M_1 and M_2 *agree* on an attribute A iff they both assign the same value to A. Let us write $M_1 \equiv_A M_2$ to denote this relation. This is clearly an equivalence relation. Now, the answers K_x result in complete lack of ignorance about the value of an attribute A i.e., in actual knowledge, when the class of all models of $K_x \cup B \cup \{A = v\}$ is partitioned into *exactly one* equivalence class modulo $\equiv_A$, corresponding to $k = 1$. Ignorance with degree $k = 2$ occurs when the relation $\equiv_A$ partitions the set of all models of $K_x \cup B \cup \{A = v\}$ into two equivalence classes. Ignorance with degree $k = 3$ occurs when there are three distinct equivalence classes for $\equiv_A$; and so on. This intuitive theoretical formulation can be applied in practice by using efficient model finders to do the required model counting. Our framework allows the designer of the data's security policy to set the desired degree of ignorance to any $k > 1$. Subsequently, our algorithm will never divulge any information that might reduce the recipient's degree of ignorance below that specified threshold.

The exact degree of ignorance for a given sensitive attribute depends both on our security needs and on the type of the attribute. Clearly, if the attribute is boolean-valued then $k = 2$ is the only possibility. If the attribute is categorical but with a larger number of possible values, or if it is an integer- or real-valued attribute, then there are many more choices for k, depending on how much ignorance we want to maintain. Note that in some cases it is not only the number k of distinct attribute values in an anonymity signature that is important; the distribution of the values may also be important for our security policy. In other words, we may want to control not just the degree of the user's ignorance, but its semantics as well. In the case of salary, for example, it may suffice to check that there are only $k = 2$ distinct values v_1 and v_2 consistent with what the user has been told, as long as v_1 and v_2 are far enough, e.g., $|v_1 - v_2| > 20$. By con-

---

[2]Note that it is not necessary for the algorithm to completely withhold a query answer when a leak is detected. The answer could also be appropriately modified (e.g., generalized). The logical content of the new answer would then be extracted and added to Γ' for the next iteration (see figure 1). In this paper we have chosen to suppress the answer only to simplify the presentation.

trast, even if we check that there are $k = 5$ distinct values, $v_1, \ldots, v_5$, if these happen to be very close to one another and to the real value, then their mere existence may not be too reassuring. Our approach readily accommodates such cases simply by associating an extra constraint with each anonymity signature, a constraint relating the actual distinct values required by the corresponding anonymity predicate. For instance, in the case of salary, we set $k = 2$ and introduce the additional constraint $|v_1 - v_2| > 20$.

Like almost all dynamic approaches to this problem, our method is not intended to handle collusion. It is designed to prevent a single user, over the course of one or multiple interactive sessions with a database, from inferring sensitive information. The few approaches that do handle collusion (e.g., [14]) are extremely logically incomplete, i.e., they can only capture a very restricted class of inferences (mostly different sequences of foreign key relationships that connect the same entities). There are no sound and complete methods for the inference problem in general, particularly in the presence of arbitrary background knowledge, since inference in the general case is undecidable. Nevertheless, the method we have described here, by using SMT solving, is complete enough to handle most queries likely to be encountered in practice. Of course, even for those queries, the problem is theoretically intractable. Like SAT solvers, however, state-of-the-art SMT solvers are extremely well-engineered systems that tend to be highly efficient in practice. Initial experiments with our preliminary implementation of this algorithm show that cutting-edge SMT solvers can handle query histories with thousands of records in a second or two.

Finally, our approach offers the advantage of efficient verifiability, which means that it is not necessary for the inference control to take place on the database server side. As noted by [18], this has been a major bottleneck preventing dynamic auditing algorithms from being deployed in practice, since there may be hundreds or thousands of users querying the database simultaneously. The most computationally expensive part of our algorithm by far is the model finding, and that can be farmed out to the client (user) side. If and when the requisite models are found, they can be shipped back to the database server and checked to verify that they are indeed models; this checking can be done in linear time.

8. ACKNOWLEDGMENTS

We thank Dr. Shoshana Loeb and Dr. Ritu Chadha for many useful discussions on data privacy.

9. REFERENCES

[1] B. Dutertre and L. de Moura. The Yices SMT Solver. Tool paper, available online from yices.csl.sri.com/tool-paper.pdf.

[2] D. Denning. Commutative filters for reducing inference threats in multilevel database systems. In *IEEE Symposium on Security and Privacy*, pages 134–146, 1985.

[3] D. G. Marks. Inference in MLS Database Systems. *IEEE Trans. on Knowl. and Data Eng.*, 8:46–55, 1996.

[4] C. Farkas and S. Jajodia. The inference problem: a survey. *SIGKDD Explor. Newsl.*, 4:6–11, December 2002.

[5] Hinke, Thomas H. and Delugach, Harry S. and Wolf, Randall P. ILIAD: an integrated laboratory for inference analysis and detection. In *Proceedings of the ninth annual IFIP TC11 WG11.3 working conference on Database security IX : Status and prospects*, pages 333–348, London, UK, 1996. Chapman & Hall, Ltd.

[6] J. Biskup and P. A. Bonatti. Controlled query evaluation for enforcing confidentiality in complete information systems. *International Journal of Information Security*, 3:14–27, 2004.

[7] J. M. Kleinberg and C. H. Papadimitriou and P. Raghavan. Auditing Boolean attributes. *Journal of Computer and System Sciences*, 66:244–253, 2003.

[8] L. J. Buczkowski. Database Inference Controller. In D. L. Spooner and C. Landwehr, editor, *Database Security III: Status and Prospects*, pages 311–322, 1990.

[9] L. Sweeney. Foundations of Privacy Protection from a Computer Science Perspective. In *Proceedings, Joint Statistical Meeting, AAAS*, Indianapolis, IN, 2000. dataprivacylab.org/projects/disclosurecontrol/paper1.pdf.

[10] L. De Moura and N. Björner. Satisfiability Modulo Theories: Introduction and Applications. *Communications of the ACM*, 54(9):69–77, September 2011.

[11] P. D. Stachour and B. M. Thuraisingham. Design of LDV: A Multilevel Secure Relational Database Management System. *IEEE Transactions on Knowledge and Data Engineering*, 2:190–209, 1990.

[12] R. W.-M. Yip. *A Data Level Database Inference Detection System*. PhD thesis, University of California Davis, 1998.

[13] S. Dawson and S. De Capitani di Vimercati and P. Lincoln and P. Samarati. Minimal data upgrading to prevent inference and association attacks. In *Proceedings of the eighteenth ACM SIGMOD-SIGACT-SIGART symposium on Principles of database systems*, PODS '99, pages 114–125. ACM, 1999.

[14] J. Staddon. Dynamic Inference Control. In *DMKD*, pages 94–100, 2003.

[15] T. H. Hinke. Inference aggregation detection in database management systems. In *Proceedings of the 1988 IEEE conference on Security and privacy*, pages 96–106. IEEE Computer Society, 1988.

[16] M. B. Thuraisingham. Security checking in relational database management systems augmented with inference engines. *Computers & Security*, 6(6):479–492, 1987.

[17] Tzong-An Su and Gultekin Özsoyoglu. Data Dependencies and Inference Control in Multilevel Relational Database Systems. In *IEEE Symposium on Security and Privacy '87*, pages 202–211, 1987.

[18] Y. Yang and Y. Li and R. H. Deng. New Paradigm of Inference Control with Trusted Computing. In *IFIP Workshop on Database Security*, pages 243–258, 2007.

[19] R. W. Yip and K. N. Levitt. Data Level Inference Detection in Database Systems. In *In Proc. of the 11th IEEE Computer Security Foundations Workshop*, pages 179–189, 1998.

Towards End-to-End Secure Content Storage and Delivery with Public Cloud

Huijun Xiong§, Xinwen Zhang†, Danfeng Yao§, Xiaoxin Wu†, Yonggang Wen‡

§ Virginia Tech, Blacksburg, VA, USA, {huijun, danfeng}@cs.vt.edu
† Huawei Technologies, {xinwen.zhang, wuxiaoxin}@huawei.com
‡ Nanyang Technological University, Singapore, ygwen@ntu.edu.sg

ABSTRACT

Recent years have witnessed the trend of leveraging cloud-based services for large scale content storage, processing, and distribution. Security and privacy are among top concerns for the public cloud environments. Towards end-to-end content security, we propose and implement *CloudSeal*, a scheme for securely sharing and distributing content via the public cloud. CloudSeal ensures the confidentiality of content in the public cloud environments with flexible access control policies for subscribers and efficient content distribution via content delivery network.

CloudSeal seamlessly integrates symmetric encryption, proxy-based re-encryption, *k*-out-of-*n* secret sharing, and broadcast revocation mechanisms. These algorithms allow CloudSeal to cache the major part of a stored cipher content object in the delivery network for content distribution, while keeping the minor part in the cloud storage for key management. The separation of subscription-based key management and confidentiality-oriented proxy-based re-encryption policies uniquely enables flexible and scalable deployment of the solution as well as strong security for cached content in the network. We have implemented CloudSeal on Amazon Web Services, including EC2, S3, and CloudFront. Through experimental evaluation, we demonstrate the end-to-end efficiency and scalability of CloudSeal.

Categories and Subject Descriptors

C.2.0 [**Computer-Communication Networks**]: General—*Security and protection*; K.6.5 [**Management of computing and Information Systems**]: Security and Protection—*Authentication, unauthorized access*.

General Terms

Algorithms, Security

Keywords

cloud computing, cloud storage, proxy-based re-encryption, security, confidentiality, content distribution

1. INTRODUCTION

Recent advance of Internet and information technology has shown two significant trends. First, media content has become the main Internet traffic. As predicated by Cisco, video streaming will consume approximately 90% of Internet traffic in 2015 [18]. Second, utilizing elastic cloud computing and storage resources has become the trend for enterprises and consumer-oriented commercial services. Large scale content processing, storage, and distribution via public cloud infrastructures become promising for quality-guaranteed and cost-efficient media streaming services. Despite the increasing usage of cloud in applications and services, security issues have been the top concerns for cloud computing [6, 22]. Among them, how to maintain the confidentiality and privacy of outsourced content in the public cloud remains a challenging task. The security requirement becomes more complex with flexible content processing and sharing among a large number of users through cloud-based applications and services.

Previous work has addressed such problems in conventional distributed environments [20, 34]. For large scale cloud-based content sharing and distribution services, there are new requirements beyond this. First, the content security should be realized by the content provider who uses public cloud services, instead of the cloud service provider [7, 28]. A content provider needs to encrypt her content with keys that are out of the reach of the cloud provider. Second, the access control policies should be flexible and distinguishable among users with different privileges to access the content. Each piece of content may be shared by different users or groups, and users may belong to multiple groups. Third, the number of redundant copies of the content cached in the content delivery network should be minimum in order to preserve efficiency of content distribution via the content delivery network. A user may earn benefits from the cache of encrypted content in the content delivery network of other users who have the same privilege. Multicast security [14] aims to address the confidentiality of content sharing with dynamic user groups. However, conventional multicast and broadcast involve only two types of entities: multicast/broadcast center and users. The content center belongs to the content provider or is fully trusted by the content provider. Their setting differs from our cloud-based model, which involves a semi-honest cloud provider to assist the content provider and the users. The earlier proxy-based encryption scheme for secure file systems [8] seems to work with semi-honest servers, but it fails to consider frequent key revocation problem, which is required by cloud-based data sharing systems. Therefore, we need a system with stronger content security guarantees and more flexible user and key management mechanisms.

In this paper, we propose CloudSeal, an end-to-end solution for secure content storage and delivery via the public cloud. By end-to-end, we mean that the content is encrypted at cloud-based storage and delivery channels. Only authorized end users or the content provider can decrypt it. CloudSeal ensures content confidentiality and content forward and backward security. CloudSeal applies dual encryption algorithms on the original plaintext of the content and uploads encrypted content to the cloud to protect content confidentiality. Then, CloudSeal seamlessly integrates proxy-based encryption and k-out-of-n secret sharing mechanisms to guarantee content forward and backward security. A proxy is employed in the cloud to transform encrypted content stored in the cloud storage to the delivery network or directly to the subscribers. The content provider updates re-encryption keys for legitimate groups and enforces shared secret keys among authorized subscribers, with which the content retrieved from the cloud can be decrypted.

Besides these security properties, CloudSeal further enables efficient content distribution and flexible content access control mechanisms. CloudSeal splits the ciphertext of the content stored in the cloud into two parts, so that the proxy only re-encrypts a very small part of ciphertext, and the large portion remains unchanged. The proxy guarantees two important properties of the content: 1) the content to be downloaded by the subscribers is always encrypted with the latest re-encryption key; 2) there is only *one* copy of the content stored in the content delivery network. These features enable the efficient cache mechanism during content distribution and achieve fast content distribution. For flexible content access control mechanisms, CloudSeal separates the distribution of the subscribers' decryption key from that of the content to enforce flexible authorization policies. Only authorized users can obtain the latest decryption key, and the content provider maintains the control of issuing new keys. We design k-out-of-n secret sharing and broadcast revocation protocols to renew the shared secret key in a scalable fashion.

We have implemented CloudSeal with Amazon Web Services (AWS), including EC2 (proxy service), S3 (cloud storage), and CloudFront (content delivery). With extensive experimental evaluation, we have demonstrated that Cloud-Seal achieves content distribution efficiency with the support of flexible user management.

The rest of the paper is organized as follows. We present the overview of CloudSeal and its design goals in the next section, and the details of its design in Section 3. Section 4 describes our prototype and evaluation results. We discuss related work in Section 5 and conclude in Section 6.

2. MODEL AND SYSTEM GOALS

Figure 1 shows a three-layer architecture for a typical content storage and distribution system over the public cloud infrastructure: a centralized *storage service* provided by a *cloud provider*, a *content delivery network (or service)* to accelerate content distribution over public network, and end

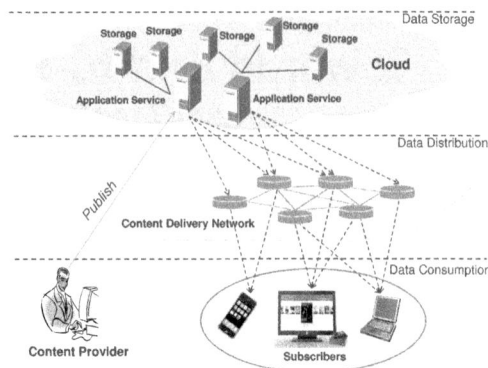

Figure 1: Schematic drawing of data flow in cloud-based storage and delivery services.

users with variant devices as *subscribers (content consumers or clients)*. A *cloud provider* provides two cloud-based services: storage and content delivery. A *content provider* utilizes these two services to store, share, and distribute her content to multiple subscribers. The content provider and subscribers can access content via a cloud-based *application service*, which reads and manages the content stored in the storage service via cloud storage APIs. The application service is an application deployed in the cloud by the content provider or a third party. The content provider can use multiple cloud-based services from different cloud service providers to host her application service, content storage service, and content delivery service. For example, Netflix [3] uses Amazon EC2 and S3 for content processing and storage, and uses multiple content delivery services such as Limelight, Level 3, and Akamia.

2.1 Trust Model and Assumption

CloudSeal trusts the content provider. The cloud service provider is *honest but curious*; that is, it follows the protocol and operations defined in CloudSeal, but it may actively attempt to gain the knowledge of the content. The content delivery service is also semi-trusted: it also may attempt to sniff content distributed and cached in the network, but it honestly performs all the operations and satisfies the quality of services, e.g., as specified in a service level agreement between the content provider and the delivery service provider. In addition, the cloud infrastructure (hardware and software) may be exploited by attackers who aim to obtain content [26].

CloudSeal aims to protect the content with large size and leverages public cloud for storage and content distribution. We assume that a subscriber does not store any cleartext and ciphertext of the content permanently in her local device. Instead, she downloads the content from the cloud and the content distribution network when she wants to access. We further assume that a subscriber does not re-disseminate decrypted content and her share of secrets to unauthorized parties.

2.2 Design Goals

We summarize the security objectives and system objectives of CloudSeal as follows.

- CloudSeal should ensure content confidentiality in the cloud storage and content delivery network even under the collusion between the cloud provider and the revoked subscribers.

- CloudSeal should support dynamic group-based user authorization, i.e., a user may choose to join or leave a group, or to be revoked from a group by the content provider at any time. Only authorized users are able to obtain the cleartext of protected content stored in cloud or cached in network at any system state.

- CloudSeal should support flexible security policies including forward and backward security.

  - For *forward security*, a user cannot access content published before she joins a group.
  - For *backward security*, a user cannot access content that is published after she leaves or is revoked from a group.

For forward and backward security, CloudSeal can be configured to support either or both. For example, a user may be allowed to access any movie that has been released before she subscribes, but cannot access any content after being revoked. For another example, a family content sharing application may allow a family friend to only access shared photos published during a certain period.

Beyond these security objectives, CloudSeal aims to achieve the following system and network performance requirements.

- CloudSeal should preserve the efficiency of content delivery network. In particular, it is desirable for the network to store a single copy of encrypted content at each system state.

- CloudSeal should support light-weight end storage cost. Only a small amount of storage should be required at the content provider side and the subscriber side to sustain user and key management of CloudSeal.

- CloudSeal should not affect user experiences at device side. The overhead of security mechanisms should be acceptable.

3. CLOUDSEAL SCHEME DETAILS

This section presents the overview, algorithms, and security analysis of CloudSeal in details. A preliminary scheme of CloudSeal is presented in [33].

3.1 Overview

Figure 2 shows the architecture of CloudSeal with three types of players: *cloud provider*, *content provider*, and *subscriber*.

- *Cloud Provider* provides two public cloud services: *storage service* for content storing and *content delivery* for content distribution. It also provides virtual infrastructure to host application services, which can be used by the content provider to manipulate the content stored in the cloud, or by the content subscribers to retrieve the content.

- *Content Provider* provides content to groups of subscribers, as well as user management. It uses cloud-based service from the cloud provider to store and distribute content.

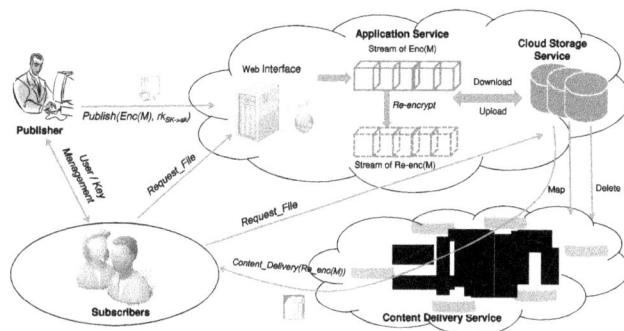

Figure 2: CloudSeal overview.

- *Subscriber* is able to access the content stored in the cloud if she successfully subscribes to the content provider. The subscriber can decrypt delivered content and consume it with local software.

The application service provides web interfaces for the content provider to publish and manipulate content in the cloud, as well as for subscribers to retrieve content from the cloud. The content can be directly accessed by consumers from the cloud storage service via storage APIs provided by the cloud service provider, or be cached in the delivery network once it has been accessed to save bandwidth and communication cost for the sake of high efficient content distribution.

To protect the content stored in the public cloud from being accessed by unauthorized parties, CloudSeal provides several cryptographic tools for the content provider to ensure that only authorized subscribers are able to obtain the decryption keys. The content provider preprocesses cleartext locally by calling CloudSeal Enc function and then publishes the processed content to the public cloud-based storage. Enc function performs dual encryption on the content with symmetric encryption as the first level of encryption and then proxy-based encryption as the second level of encryption. The dual encryption scheme enables CloudSeal to protect content confidentiality as well as outsource flexible access control policies. To delegate different access control mechanism, the content provider distributes corresponding re-encryption keys rk to the application service in the cloud. The application service transforms the ciphertext in the cloud by calling Re_Enc function with rk so that subscribers can decrypt them with the shared secret key uk. When an update happens in the user group, e.g., a user joins or leaves the group, the content provider updates the content re-encryption key rk stored in the application service to invalidate previous version of the content. Specifically, the content provider calls Re_key to generate a new delegation key for the application service. Then the application service produces new ciphertext by executing Re_Enc on the original cipher content in the cloud with the new re-encryption key rk. The small part of the resulting new cipher content is stored in the cloud storage service and the main part is cached in the delivery network to accelerate content distribution. During the re-encryption process, only a small part of the ciphertext of the content needs to be updated. The main part remains unchanged and can be persistently cached within the delivery network. When accessing a content, a client has to obtain all parts from cloud and distribution network in order to decrypt and render the content. This feature seamlessly achieves security objectives and efficient content distribution together.

For user management, CloudSeal has operations of `User Revocation` and `User Subscription`. CloudSeal supports a group of users' access to a set of encrypted content (or a channel) by sharing a secret key uk within the group. When a user joins the group, the content provider issues her shares of future secret keys as well as the current secret key. When a user leaves or is revoked from the group, the content provider broadcasts this user's share of the new decryption key to the entire group so that the remaining users are able to generate the new decryption key autonomously.

3.2 Preliminary

Bilinear Maps [10, 11]: Let $\mathbb{G}$, $\mathbb{G}_T$ be two multiplicative cyclic groups of prime order r, we say $\hat{e}$ is an admissible bilinear map if: (1) computative actions in $\mathbb{G}$ and $\mathbb{G}_T$ are efficient; (2) for all $\alpha, \beta \in \mathbb{Z}_r$ of prime order r, $\hat{e}(g^\alpha, g^\beta) = \hat{e}(g,g)^{\alpha\beta}$; (3) $\hat{e}$ is non-degenerate, which means that not all pairs in $\mathbb{G} \times \mathbb{G}$ are sent to the identity in $\mathbb{G}_T$ by $\hat{e}$.

Secret Sharing [24, 29]: A k-out-of-n threshold secret sharing scheme is that a secret $S \in \mathbb{Z}_r$ shared by n users can be recovered, if the number of the secret shares exceeds the threshold k. The scheme utilizes a random polynomial P of degree $k - 1$, where $P(x) \in \mathbb{Z}_r$ and $P(0) = S$. Given any k shares $< x_0, P(x_0) >, ..., < x_{k-1}, P(x_{k-1}) >$, one can use Lagrange interpolation formulas as follows to recover $P(0)$:

$$P(0) = \sum_{i=0}^{k-1} \lambda_i P(x_i), \text{ where } \lambda_i = \prod_{j \neq i} \frac{x_j}{x_j - x_i} \quad (1)$$

Proxy-based Re-encryption [8]: A proxy-based re-encryption algorithm transforms ciphertext c_{k1} to ciphertext c_{k2} with a key $rk_{k1 \to k2}$ without revealing the corresponding cleartext, where c_{k1} and c_{k2} can only be decrypted by different key $k1$ and $k2$, respectively. $rk_{k1 \to k2}$ is a re-key issued by another party, e.g., the originator of ciphertext c_{k1}.

3.3 CloudSeal Operations

CloudSeal operations involve in two planes: data plane and control plane. In the *data plane*, we describe the operations on the content, including *system setup, content publishing, proxy re-encryption,* and *content retrieving*. In the *control plane*, we present user management including *user revocation* – when a user leaves or is revoked from a group and *user subscription* – when a new user joins a group. Our scheme applies the dual encryption scheme to protect content confidentiality and uniquely bridges the proxy-based re-encryption scheme proposed by Ateniese *et al.* [8] and the secret sharing scheme in [24]. Table 1 shows the notation we use in this paper.

System Setup is called by the content provider to prepare the cryptographic system for content encryption and re-encryption. The content provider first chooses system public parameters *params*, namely $g \in \mathbb{G}$ and a bilinear map $\hat{e}$. It chooses a proxy secret key $SK \in \mathbb{Z}_r$ and public key $PK = g^{SK} \in \mathbb{G}$. The content provider keeps SK secret. The content provider chooses an integer k and a list L of polynomials of degree $k - 1$ with coefficients randomly chosen from $\mathbb{Z}_r$, which are kept secret. The number of users who can be revoked at the same time is $k - 1$. The content

Table 1: Notation.

Term	Notation
PK	content provider's public key
SK	content provider's secret key
uk, uk'	shared secret key for a group
$rk_{SK \to uk}$	re-encryption key
k	number of shares to recover uk
P	polynomial formula
x_i	user i's ID
$P(x_i)$	polynomial value of user i
M	original content
h	temporary secret of content provider

provider then chooses a random number from $\mathbb{Z}_r$ as the initial uk. This setup is performed by the content provider for each group of users.

Content Publishing is run by the content provider to publish its content to the public cloud. The content provider performs the dual encryption scheme as follows. First she encrypts the content M with a symmetric data encryption key DEK to produce ciphertext $C(M, DEK)$. Then she further encrypts the content $C(M, DEK)$ with the secret key SK and *params* as shown in Algorithm 1. The resulting encrypted content has three components (u_{SK}, w, v), which are stored in the cloud-based storage service by the application service via cloud APIs. u_{SK} depends on the random secret h and content provider's secret key SK, w depends on the random secret h and the data encryption key DEK, and v depends on both h and the content. Usually, u_{SK} and w are much smaller than v.

Algorithm 1: *Enc(params, M, SK, DEK)*
1: Content provider chooses a random secret $h \in \mathbb{Z}_r$;
2: Content provider chooses symmetric data encryption key DEK and encrypts the content M to obtain ciphertext $C(M, DEK)$;
3: Let Z denote $\hat{e}(g, g)$; Compute $u_{SK} = g^{SK \cdot h}$ and $Z^h = \hat{e}(g, g^h) = \hat{e}(g, g)^h \in \mathbb{G}_T$.
4: Content provider outputs ciphertext of content M: $(u_{SK}, w, v) = (g^{SK \cdot h}, DEK \cdot Z^h, C(M, DEK) \cdot Z^h)$.

Content Retrieving is for subscribers to access content stored in the public cloud. Two algorithms - *Re_Key* and *Re_Enc* - are involved in this process. Using *Re_Key* algorithm, the content provider generates a content re-encryption key $rk_{SK \to uk}$ with her secret key SK and the current decryption key uk. Details are shown as follows.

Algorithm 2: *Re_Key(params, SK, uk)*
1: Given *params*, SK and uk, the content provider computes $rk_{SK \to uk} = g^{uk/SK}$.

Upon request, the application service obtains the newest $rk_{SK \to uk}$ from the content provider and re-encrypts the target cipher content (u_{SK}, w, v) with the following *Re_Enc* algorithm.

Algorithm 3: *Re_Enc((u_{SK}, w, v), rk_{SK \to uk}, params)*
1: The proxy calculates $u_{uk} = \hat{e}(rk_{SK \to uk}, u_{SK})$ $= \hat{e}(g^{uk/SK}, g^{SK \cdot h}) = \hat{e}(g, g)^{uk \cdot h} = Z^{uk \cdot h}$;
2: The proxy outputs re-encrypted content (u_{uk}, w, v).

The re-encryption is only performed on u_{SK}. Because u_{SK} is independent of the content M, CloudSeal saves the processing time and storage I/O cost of the application service and storage service.

After this, the application service stores cipher content (u_{uk}, w, v) in the cloud storage service and allows the download. For each cipher content, w and v can be cached in the content delivery network, while u_{uk} cannot be cached. Since the size of u_{uk} is small, this operation does not affect the efficiency of content delivery.

When the system state is changed, e.g., a user joins or leaves or is revoked from the group, the shared secret key is updated from uk to uk'. Once the new secret key is updated to authorized users (explained next), the content provider generates the re-key $rk_{SK \to uk'}$ by running Re_Key algorithm and sends the re-key to the application service for content re-encryption with Re_Enc algorithm. The new cipher content is $(u_{uk'}, w, v)$. The user then downloads $u_{uk'}$ from the cloud storage, w and v from the content delivery network.

After a user obtains the encrypted content (u_{uk}, w, v), she follows Algorithm 4 below to decrypt the cipher with her current secret key uk. The user either obtains the secret key uk from the content provider when she first joins or computes it (described in User Revocation next).

Algorithm 4: $Decrypt((u_{uk}, w, v), uk)$

1: Given $u_{uk} = (Z^{uk \cdot h})$ and uk, the subscriber computes $u_{uk}^{1/uk} = Z^h$;

2: The subscriber calculates $DEK = w/Z^h$, and $C(DEK, M) = v/Z^h$;

3: The subscriber decrypts $C(DEK, M)$ with DEK;

4: The subscriber outputs original content M.

User Revocation happens when a subscriber leaves a group or is revoked by the content provider. It requires key revocation operations in the group. Our key revocation process is based on the k-out-of-n threshold secret sharing scheme. We consider the following two cases.

- *Case I:* There are $k-1$ users to be revoked at one time. The content provider revokes $k-1$ users with shares $P(x_1), P(x_2), ..., P(x_{k-1})$, respectively. The content provider broadcasts the shares of secrets and identities of these users $< x_1, P(x_1) >, < x_2, P(x_2) >, ..., < x_{k-1}, P(x_{k-1}) >$ to the entire group. Each user x in the group combines her share of secret $< x, P(x) >$ with these $k-1$ shares, to interpolate the new secret key $uk' = P(0)$. For example, $k = 2$, $P'(0)$ can be calculated by $\frac{x}{x - x_1} P'(x_1) + \frac{x_1}{x_1 - x} P'(x)$ according to Equation 1. The content provider uses uk' as the new shared secret key to generate re-encryption key for non-revoked users.

- *Case II:* There are t users to be revoked, where $t < k - 1$. The content provider performs the revocation by sending the t shares of secret and additional $k-t-1$ shares of the secret of polynomial P. These additional shares are values different from any existing users.

Polynomial P is then removed from the list L. If the list L is empty, the content provider adds new polynomials, as well as computes and distributes corresponding secret shares to current subscribers (for future interpolation purposes).

User Subscription happens when a user joins a group. Successful subscription authorizes a user's access to protected content. To prevent new users from accessing content published before they join (for forward security), the key revocation process is required to be executed as follows.

- Upon receiving join requests from t new users, the content provider obtains the first polynomial P' on list L, and calculates key $uk' = P'(0)$; uk' is sent to the new users in secure channels.

- The content provider assigns each new user a unique identity $x_i \in \mathbb{Z}_r$ and her share of secret from polynomial $P'(x_i)$, along with x_i's values from the other polynomials on list L. The content provider sends these polynomial values, except for $P'(x_i)$, to the new users respectively for future key updating through secure channels.

- The content provider broadcasts new users' share of secret $< x_i, P'(x_i) >$ to the current group members for new key generation. If $t < k - 1$, the content provider generates $k - t - 1$ more share of the secret with P' and sends them to the entire group. These $k - t - 1$ shares of the secret are different from any existing values. P' is removed from the list L.

For each current group member x_j, upon receiving $< x_1, P'(x_1) >, < x_2, P'(x_2) >, ..., < x_{k-1}, P'(x_{k-1}) >$ from the content provider, she calculates the new key with her share of secret $P'(x_j)$ for P' that was received when x_j joined earlier. This user can recover the new secret key $uk' = P'(0) = b$ by calculating $P'(0)$ with its share and received share.

3.4 Security Analysis

CloudSeal aims to protect content confidentiality and user access control (forward and backward security). We briefly discuss them next.

3.4.1 Content Confidentiality

CloudSeal performs two types of encryption algorithms to the content before outsourcing it. One is symmetric encryption algorithm to protect the confidentiality of the original content. The other is the *first-level encryption algorithm* in [8] executed on the resulting ciphertext from the symmetric encryption to enable flexible user access control of the ciphertext. Although we use the same secret parameter h for all blocks of a content to speed up the *first-level encryption algorithm*, CloudSeal is as strong as the symmetric encryption algorithm that is applied on the original plaintext of the content. Therefore, CloudSeal achieves the confidentiality of the encrypted content exposed in the public cloud. Furthermore, in any system state, the cloud service provider or an attacker cannot decrypt the cipher content with only re-encryption keys $rk_{SK \to uk}$.

CloudSeal leverages the dual encryption scheme and uses the same h for all blocks of a content to achieve security and performance at the same time. Several approaches may be alternatives. However they either fail to fulfill the security goals of CloudSeal, or cannot achieve the efficiency of encryption and content distribution for the practical usage. For example, one approach is to distribute DEK via a secure channel to individual users, instead of be encapsulated within the content. This solution cannot support forward and backward security objectives without invaliding cached content in the network and re-publishing content with a new DEK. Furthermore, any leakage of the DEK can compromise the confidentiality of the content permanently, unless the content provider invalidates the cache and re-encrypts and re-distributes it. Sole proxy-based re-encryption algorithm with different secret parameter h for each data block of a big file is too slow for encryption at the content provider side.

3.4.2 Forward and backward security

CloudSeal is designed to protect content forward and backward security. When a user joining or leaving event happens in a group, the content provider issues a new re-encryption key for this group to the application service, then requires the application service to alter the content to be delivered with the newest re-encryption key, and finally updates the entire group with the new group information. For a join event, the content provider sends her the latest decryption key and her shares of secrets for future key update. Consequently, a new user cannot decrypt the old content with the new decryption key, and a revoked user cannot decrypt new content with her old keys. Note that Cloud-Seal does not prevent a user from sharing decrypted content or decryption keys to unauthorized users. A digital rights management tool, such as the Microsoft DRM component in Netflix [25], can be used to solve this problem, which is out of the scope of CloudSeal.

3.4.3 Collusion Resistance

Collusion between delegatees and the proxy is one weakness of many proxy-based re-encryption algorithms. The goal of collusion resistance in such systems is to prevent the recovery of a delegator's secret keys by combination of the issued re-encryption key and delegated decryption keys. CloudSeal utilizes the proxy-based re-encryption scheme proposed in [8], which has been proven to be collusion resistant. This guarantees that the secret key of a content provider is secure even with a user or the cloud provider obtains both re-encryption key and the user's decryption key. With this algorithm, CloudSeal ensures that the entire outsourced content cannot be compromised and the content provider preserves the control of security policies by issuing of different re-encryption keys to different authorized groups of subscribers.

Besides security properties for content sharing and delivery via public cloud, CloudSeal uniquely achieves content distribution efficiency. When a group state changes, only a small part of the cipher content needs to be re-encrypted in cloud, while most of the content objects can be cached in the delivery network and shared by users. The separation of content operations (data plane) and user management operations (control plane) further enables flexible and scalable deployment of CloudSeal in the public cloud and network environment.

4. IMPLEMENTATION & EVALUATION

In this section, we first present the implementation of CloudSeal with Amazon Web Services (AWS), and then evaluate its system and network performance.

4.1 System Implementation

Content sharing applications with public cloud. We spent nontrivial efforts to build a simulated content sharing service based on three AWS services [1]: Elastic Compute Cloud (EC2) service to host an application service for subscribers, Simple Storage Service (S3) to store the cipher content for content providers, and Content Delivery Service

(CloudFront) to distribute content. Amazon EC2 provides a virtual environment and allows developers to launch virtual machine instances with various operating system and applications. Amazon S3 is a cloud-based storage system, which stores data in *buckets* and allows write, read, and delete operations on them. Amazon CloudFront provides high-speed content delivery service by automatically caching content in the nearest edge locations and delivering the cache to end users. To achieve security enhancement of this service, we extend its functionality with algorithms and protocols aforementioned in CloudSeal.

We implement the application service as a website written by PHP and host it with an Apache server running in an Amazon Linux EC2 instance. In order to directly store and manipulate the content in S3, we create a `connection object` with Python library `boto` [2], which calls the function *boto.connect_s3(s3.key, s3.ID)* to establish connections between the EC2 instance and S3 storage. *s3.key* and *s3.ID* are the key and identifier number of Amazon S3 instances assigned when created.

Our content is stored in the buckets of Amazon S3, which assigns each bucket with a global unique name and each file a URL composing with bucket name and file name. We use this URL as a content object in the application service web page. For example, file *video1.mp4* is stored in bucket *bucket1*, the access URL to that file is `http://s3.amazonawa.com/bucket1/video1.mp4`. Applications can use HTTP or BitTorrent-like protocols to access data stored in Amazon S3. Our application service uses HTTP protocol. Users can request files by file names from the file list stored in the application service with `HTTP GET` request. For each published content, we create two buckets in S3: one is for the originally published cipher content $<u_{SK}, w, v>$ from the content provider, which is not updated once stored, and the other for the cipher content $<u_{uk}, w, v>$ to be delivered, which is updated once a user joins or leaves. Although both buckets can be made publicly readable to users, we set `private` permission to the original published one since only the content provider and the application service need to access them. The other content bucket is `publicly` readable to all users. To avoid storage redundancy, only u_{SK} of the cipher content is stored, as the other part $<w, v>$ is the same as the public bucket. This part is so small that we cache them on EC2 to facilitate the cryptographic operations.

CloudSeal with its cryptographic tools. We implement aforementioned data plane cryptographic algorithms (*Enc*, *Re_Key*, *Re_Enc*, and *Decrypt*) based on cryptographic functions from the OpenSSL library [4] and the pairing-based cryptographic library (PBC) [5] with independent native processes. We choose Advanced Encryption Standard (AES) with 16 bytes key as our symmetric encryption algorithm and implement the `CFB` mode of `AES` to randomize the ciphertext of each data block of a file. For pairing-based encryption, instead of mapping an arbitrary M to a certain field $\mathbb{G}_T$, we map the elements in $\mathbb{G}_T$ to byte array in C language and use `XOR` operation in our implementation to produce w and v. This approach accelerates the encryption operation for the content provider. For key updating, we choose random linear polynomial formula so that only one user can be revoked with a single re-encryption operation.

We further develop a web application as the administrative service to assist the content provider for the user and key management on EC2 instance. This service enforces the cryptographic tools running on the same EC2 instance as the application service. When a user signs up in a group with the administrative service, the service updates current decryption key of the group and assigns this key and a share of future decryption keys to the new user. It updates the entire group with the new user's share. When a user decides to leave the group, the user sends `Leave` message to the administrative service. The service again updates the current decryption key and distributes the share of secret of the revoked user. When an update happens in a group, the administrative service blocks any new file downloading activities in this group. Then it calculates the new key and distributes the revocation information to the remaining users, and then re-encrypts the content and stores it back on EC2 with the newest decryption key. After this, this group can start downloading files. In order to keep the up-to-date decryption key, the user periodically checks the administrative service to see whether or not there is a revocation by sending `Update_Checking` HTTP requests to the server. Once there is a revocation, remaining users send `GET_Update_Info` packets to get the newly revocation information and update her decryption key accordingly. As we integrate the administrative service into the HTTP server of the application service to measure the key and user management mechanisms, the user needs to actively pull the update information from the service, instead of passively receiving message from the service. We plan to realize the administrative service with an XMTP (XML MIME Transformation Protocol) server in the future, with which users can receive push notification from the server.

4.2 Experimental Evaluation

To confirm that CloudSeal achieves the performance objectives (cf. Section 2.2), we sought to answer the following questions to demonstrate that the security mechanisms from cryptographic algorithms in CloudSeal bring acceptable costs to end-to-end performance.

1. What is the overhead of cryptographic operations including content encryption by the content provider and the content decryption by the subscribers?

2. What is the overhead of the re-encryption operations including content re-encryption by the application service in the cloud? Will the application service become performance bottleneck due to the overhead?

3. What is the affect of content delivery network to the cloud-based content distribution?

We have conducted a number of experiments to evaluate CloudSeal in the system and cloud levels in May, 2011. We examine the host-based efficiency of the cryptographic algorithms with different pairing types and the user management costs for communication and storage. We further conduct experiments on Amazon public cloud environment to evaluate efficiency of different cloud services of CloudSeal with two EC2 types (small, and medium) and different data distribution mechanisms (with or without CloudFront).

4.2.1 Efficiency of Algorithms and Protocols

Computation Cost. To show the performance at the content provider side and the subscriber side with cryptographic operations, we conduct content encryption (by content provider) and decryption (by content consumer) tests

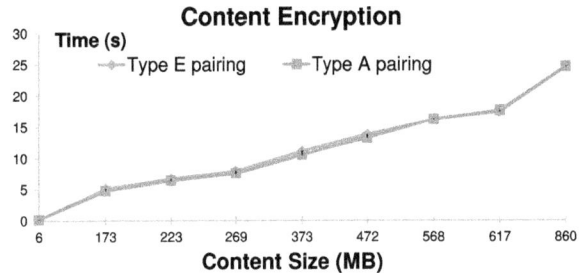

Figure 3: Overhead of encryption operations with different pairing types.

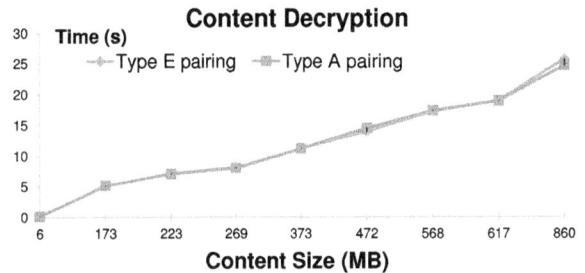

Figure 4: Overhead of decryption operations with different pairing types.

locally on a desktop with Intel Duo CPU 2.93GHz, 4GB RAM, SUMSUNG 7200RPM, and CentOS 2.6. The encryption time consists of symmetric encryption with CFB mode, pairing operation, and `XOR` operations. The decryption time includes key generation, symmetric decryption, pairing operations, and `XOR` operations. We choose two symmetric pairings from the pairing based library [5], including Type E pairing *e.param* and Type A pairing *a.param*, to examine the impact from different pairing types to CloudSeal according to the scheme of CloudSeal. The symmetric key length is 16 bytes. The length of pairing-based master key and decryption key is 20 bytes for both pairing types.

We put 9 different sizes of files in the desktop and run the encryption and decryption algorithms 20 times on each file to compute the average processing time. As shown in Figure 3 and Figure 4, encryption and decryption time increase along with the content size, while there is a tiny difference between the two symmetric pairing types. For content decryption at consumer side, it takes less than 30 seconds to decrypt a 800MB video file.

Communication Cost. We investigate the communication cost caused by a group update, e.g., a user joins or is revoked. Recall that the degree of the polynomials is the number of users who can be revoked simultaneously. For example, a degree 2 polynomial implies that the content provider can revoke two users at one time. Assume we choose a degree d polynomial and we need B bytes to send one user's revoking information, if we have r users remain in the group, each revocation causes $d * B * (r + d)$ bytes traffic in the network with our broadcasting mechanism, where $(r + d)$ is the total number of users in the group. Suppose there are 100 users in one group, d equals to 2, and B is 40 bytes according to our implementation, the total amount for one update in CloudSeal is around $8KB$.

Table 2: Re-encryption Time (Seconds) of 600MB Content on Different Amazon EC2 Instances.

Pairing	Key Length (Bytes)	Small EC2	Medium EC2
TypeE	20	0.00007425	0.000071
TypeA	20	0.00007925	0.000077

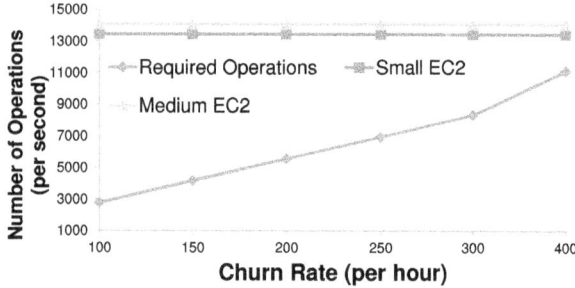

Figure 5: Number of required re-encryption operations with different churning rates

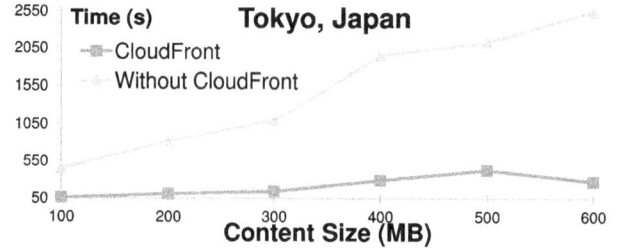

Figure 6: Downloading time for content delivery with storage center at Tokyo.

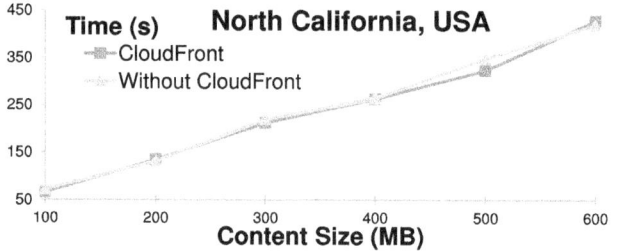

Figure 7: Downloading time for content delivery with storage center at N. California.

Storage Cost. We further look into the storage cost for the key management at both content provider side and subscriber side. In order to sustain system state, the content provider needs to keep current user secret key and a list of polynomials in terms of sets of coefficient for future system update. In our implementation, 20 bytes are enough to represent user secret key or each coefficient of polynomials. The average amount of storage cost for each group at content provider side is 6KB given 100 polynomials of degree 2. This cost is small enough to support a large number of groups of subscribers in the service. For subscribers, they only need to keep their own values of the list of polynomials with total amount of $2KB$ for 100 polynomials of degree 2.

4.2.2 Application Service Performance

We evaluate Amazon EC2 service on two different instance types: small and medium, located in AWS North California data center. The small EC2 instance consists of one core CPU with 1 ECU and 1.7GB memory, and the medium EC2 instance has two core CPU with 5 ECUs and 1.7GB memory. An ECU provides the equivalent CPU capacity of 1.0-1.2 GHz 2007 Opteron or 2007 Xeon processor. We focus on examining the re-encryption algorithm efficiency on Amazon EC2, which is the only operation on cipher content by the application service. We run each experiment 20 times and report the average running time.

As Table 2 shows, the operation on the small EC2 instance is slightly slower than that on the medium instance, which implies that computation ability of CPU has positive impact on cloud performance for our application services. Comparing with previous encryption and decryption time shown in Figure 3 and Figure 4, the re-encryption time on same size of content is significantly shorter.

CloudSeal can serve multiple groups, each having a different set of authorized users. As a centralized component, the application service can be a bottleneck for performance, especially for the content re-encryption operations for all groups. Suppose there are 100 similar groups, each with maximum 100 subscribers and 1000 content objects. We adjust the churn rate of a group to estimate the required re-

encryption operations of the application service. The churn rate varies from 100 users per hour to 400 users per hour, which indicates the number of subscribers who join or leave the group per hour. From Table 2, we can calculate that, with the small EC2 instance, the application service can handle at most $1/0.00007425 = 13468$ re-encryption operations per second and with the medium EC2 instance, the application service can perform $1/0.000071 = 14084$ operations per second. Figure 5 demonstrates that with either small EC2 instance or medium EC2 instance, the number of re-encryption operations per second performed by the application service is much larger than the required operations per second along with different churn rate in the system. This indicates that the application service is adequate in providing revocation induced content re-encryption operations for groups for large churn frequencies. Furthermore, with elastic computing resources, the content provider can allocate more computing instances for the application service in an on-demand manner. Therefore, re-encryption operation in cloud will not be a bottleneck to the system's performance. Besides, as elapsed time for re-encryption operation is unrelated with the size of content, frequent revocation will not add large overhead on our system.

4.2.3 Content Delivery Efficiency

For content delivery network performance, we evaluate content delivery time with Amazon CloudFront. Four elements can affect the delivery efficiency: whether the CloudFront service is enabled, the locations of end consumers, deployed CloudFront edge servers, and the location of the content storage center. In our experiment, we store our content in two different Amazon S3 data centers: North California, USA and Tokyo, Japan. To initiate content delivery action, we develop a customized client with Python to continuously request files from one bucket stored in Amazon S3. We run 5 clients at North California, USA to leverage cache in local edge location. Each client requests 20 files and we measure the time of downloading all of them. As shown in Figures 6 and 7, without using CloudFront, the content delivery time in North California is much smaller than that in Tokyo. When the CloudFront is used, the delivery speed for content stored in Tokyo can be significantly improved by almost 10 times, while there is no obvious improvement for that in North California. We conjecture that this is because our client application is close to the North California S3 data center. Therefore the download speed does not change much when CloudFront is used.

Comparing the time for content delivery with the time of cryptographic operations (encryption, decryption, and re-encryption) shown in Figure 3, Figure 4, and Table 2, the cryptographic time is at least 40 times faster than the content delivery time. Therefore, the security mechanisms implemented in our prototype bring accesptable overhead.

In summary, our evaluation presents the efficiency of CloudSeal in content processing and content delivery. At subscriber side, CloudSeal brings acceptable decryption time. The overhead of CloudSeal does not affect user's experience. At the cloud side, the application service is not the bottleneck of the system and supports the efficient content re-encryption operations. Our system performs well when scaling up to a large number of subscribers. CloudSeal preserves the efficiency of content distribution of the content delivery network with a smaller overhead for cryptographic operations.

5. RELATED WORK

Several security solutions have been recently developed for securing data in cloud [9, 23, 27, 36]. With similar security concerns in outsourcing data to untrusted cloud service, authors in [16, 21, 31, 35, 37] have proposed several solutions. For example, Yu et al. [35] proposed an attribute based access control policy to securely outsource sensitive user data to the cloud. In their approach, data is encrypted by a symmetric key while the access to this symmetric key is controlled by KP-ABE algorithm [17]. To manage dynamic user groups, they delegate *rekey* operations to the cloud and let the cloud server update users' secret keys and re-encrypt data without revealing the underlying plaintext. CloudSeal is different from their approach in that: CloudSeal only allows a content provider to perform the `Re_Key` operation, and the proxy re-encryption is performed directly on part of the cipher content. Directly applying their approach to solve our problem of content delivery may not be practical, as their ciphertext is customized for different users. In comparison, as CloudSeal supports on-demanding data re-encryption operations, our design brings performance advantage for large scale content cached in content delivery network.

Secure storage system is an important application of proxy re-encryption algorithms [8, 19]. CloudSeal is based on the scheme proposed in [8], where the authors implemented an encrypted file storage system with an access control server in charge of data access according to proxy re-encryption schemes. When a client requests data from a block store, it firstly asks the access control server to re-encrypt the block with its public key and the system master key, such that it can decrypt the block with its own secret key. Access control server can deny re-encryption operation if the client is not authorized. In comparison, we consider user revocation

problem in CloudSeal and also the real time efficiency of the system.

Secure multicast communication [12, 13, 14, 15, 32, 38] and conditional access systems [30] address similar security problems as ours in distributing content to dynamic user groups and key management. Proxy re-encryption algorithm and k-out-of-n mechanisms have been used to solve these problems. For example, researchers in paper [15] proposed proxy re-encryption based secure multicast mechanisms to achieve scalability and containment. Several proxies (routers), usually during the content transmission, transitively convert ciphertext data with re-encryption keys assigned when building a multicast network. When a user is to be revoked or a proxy (router) is off the network, corresponding proxy re-encryption keys and group secret keys need to be updated. The problem solved by CloudSeal is different from them due to the cache properties in content delivery network, which requires more efficient and flexible secure content delivery and user management mechanisms.

The security mechanism and supported access control policies of CloudSeal differ from what Netflix adopts [25] in several aspects. First, the goal of CloudSeal is to protect the security of outsourcing content for the content provider, rather than to prevent digital rights of the content on subscribers' device in Netflix, which uses Microsoft DRM on subscriber side to ensure end-to-end content security and digital rights management, e.g., to prevent further dissemination of protected content by an end user. Second, the access control of CloudSeal supports various groups of subscribers with different privileges for different shared content, while Netflix currently supports only one (unlimited) plan for their video streaming service. Third, CloudSeal encrypts the content when storing in public cloud and distributing via content delivery network. Netflix only encrypts the content at the edge of the content delivery network.

6. CONCLUSION AND FUTURE WORK

We designed and implemented CloudSeal, an end-to-end content confidentiality protection mechanism for large scale content storage and distribution systems over the public cloud infrastructure. By leveraging advanced cryptographic algorithms including symmetric encryption, proxy-based re-encryption, threshold secret sharing, and broadcast revocation, CloudSeal addresses unique challenges of efficient cipher content transformation, cipher content caching in the delivery network, and scalable user and key management. Through the prototype implemented on Amazon EC2, S3, and CloudFront, our experimental evaluation demonstrates that CloudSeal achieves the efficiency and avoids possible performance bottleneck. For future work, we plan to extend our current design to support an open service, where each user can publish content and delegate group membership control with our broadcast revocation library.

7. ACKNOWLEDGEMENTS

We thank the anonymous referees for providing valuable reviews. We especially thank Qingji Zheng for his constructive comments on the algorithms and Wei Zhu for his help in implementation.

8. REFERENCES

[1] Amazon Web Services. http://aws.amazon.com.

[2] boto: Python interface to amazon web services. http://code.google.com/p/boto/.

[3] Netflix on Amazon's Cloud. http://www.techflash.com/seattle/2010/05/netflix_on_amazon_cloud.html.

[4] OpenSSL Cryptography and SSL/TLS Tookit, http://www.openssl.org/.

[5] Pairing-based cryptography (pbc) library. http://crypto.stanford.edu/pbc/

[6] Cloud Computing, an IDC update, 2010.

[7] AWS Customer Agreement http://aws.amazon.com/agreement/, 2011.

[8] G. Ateniese, K. Fu, M. Green, and S. Hohenberger. Improved Proxy Re-encryption Schemes with Applications to Secure Distributed Storage. *ACM Trans. Inf. Syst. Secur.*, 9:1–30, February 2006.

[9] E. Bertino, F. Paci, R. Ferrini, and N. Shang. Privacy-preserving Digital Identity Management for Cloud Computing. *IEEE Data Eng. Bull.*, 2009.

[10] D. Boneh and M. K. Franklin. Identity-based Encryption from the Weil Pairing. In *CRYPTO '01*.

[11] D. Boneh, B. Lynn, and H. Shacham. Short Signatures from the Weil Pairing. In *Proc. of ASIACRYPT '01*.

[12] B. Briscoe. MARKS: Multicast Key Management using Arbitratily Revealed Key Sequences. In *Proceedings of NGC'99*.

[13] B. Briscoe. Nark: Receiver-based Multicast Non-repudiation and Key Management. In *Proceedings of EC'99*.

[14] R. Canetti, J. Garay, G. Itkis, D. Micciancio, M. Naor, and B. Pinkas. Multicast Security: A Taxonomy and Some Efficient Constructions. In *INFOCOM '99*.

[15] Y.-P. Chiu, C.-L. Lei, and C.-Y. Huang. Secure Multicast Using Proxy Encryption. In *Information and Communications Security*, Lecture Notes in Computer Science. 2005.

[16] R. Chow, P. Golle, M. Jakobsson, E. Shi, J. Staddon, R. Masuoka, and J. Molina. Controlling Data in the Cloud: Outsourcing Computation without Outsourcing Control. In *Proceedings of CCSW '09*.

[17] V. Goyal, O. Pandey, A. Sahai, and B. Waters. Attribute-based Encryption for Fine-grained Access Control of Encrypted Data. In *Proc. of ACM CCS*, 2006.

[18] Cisco Inc. Cisco Visual Networking Index: Forecast and Methodology, 2010-2015. White paper, Cisco., 2011.

[19] M. Kallahalla, E. Riedel, R. Swaminathan, Q. Wang, and K. Fu. Plutus: Scalable Secure File Sharing on Untrusted Storage. In *Proceedings of FAST*, 2003.

[20] Y. Koglin, D. Yao, and E. Bertino. Secure Content Distribution by Parallel Processing from Cooperative Intermediaries. *IEEE Transactions on Parallel and Distributed Systems*, 2008.

[21] D. Lin and A. Squicciarini. Data Protection Models for Service Provisioning in the Cloud. In *Proceeding of ACM SACMAT '10*.

[22] Lockheed Martin, LM Cyber Security Alliance. Awareness, Trust and Security to Shape Government Cloud Adoption. White paper, Cisco, 2010.

[23] M. Nabeel, N. Shang, J. Zage, and E. Bertino. Mask: A System for Privacy-preserving Policy-based Access to Published Content. In *Proceedings of SIGMOD '10*.

[24] M. Naor and B. Pinkas. Efficient Trace and Revoke Schemes. In *Proceedings of the 4th International Conference on Financial Cryptography*, 2001.

[25] Pomelo, LLC Tech Memo. Analysis of Netflix's Security Framework for *Watch Instantly* Service, 2009.

[26] T. Ristenpart, E. Tromer, H. Shacham, and S. Savage. Hey, You, Get Off of My cloud! Exploring Information Leakage in Third-Party Compute Clouds. In *Proceedings of CCS*, 2009.

[27] R. Sandhu, R. Boppana, R. Krishnan, J. Reich, T. Wolff, and J. Zachry. Towards A Discipline of Mission-aware Cloud Computing. In *Proceedings of the 2010 ACM workshop on Cloud computing security workshop*, CCSW '10.

[28] Cloud Security Alliance. Security Guidance for Critical Areas of Focus in Cloud Computing V2.1, 2009. https://cloudsecurityalliance.org/csaguide.pdf.

[29] A. Shamir. How to Share A Secret. *Commun. ACM*, 22, November 1979.

[30] P. Traynor, K. R. B. Butler, W. Enck, and P. McDaniel. Realizing Massive-Scale Conditional Access Systems Through Attribute-Based Cryptosystems. In *NDSS*, 2008.

[31] W. Wang, Z. Li, R. Owens, and B. Bhargava. Secure and Efficient Access to Outsourced Data. In *Proceedings of CCSW '09*.

[32] C. K. Wong, M. Gouda, and S. S. Lam. Secure Group Communications Using Key Graphs. *IEEE/ACM Trans. Netw.*, 8, February 2000.

[33] H. Xiong, X. Zhang, W. Zhu, and D. Yao. Cloudseal: End-to-End Content Protection in Cloud-based Storage and Delivery Services. In *Proceedings of Securecomm*, 2011.

[34] D. Yao, Y. Koglin, E. Bertino, and R. Tamassia. Decentralized Authorization and Data Security in Web Content Delivery. In *Proc ACM Symp. on Applied Computing (SAC)*, 2007.

[35] S. Yu, C. Wang, K. Ren, and W. Lou. Achieving Secure, Scalable, and Fine-grained Data Access Control in Cloud Computing. In *INFOCOM'10*.

[36] S. Zarandioon, D. Yao, and V. Ganapathy. K2C: Cryptographic Cloud Storage With Lazy Revocation and Anonymous Access. In *Proceedings of Securecomm*, 2011.

[37] L. Zhou, V. Varadharajan, and M. Hitchens. Enforcing role-based access control for secure data storage in the cloud. *The Computer Journal*, 2011.

[38] S. Zhu, C. Yao, D. Liu, S. Setia, and S. Jajodia. Efficient Security Mechanisms for Overlay Multicast based Content Delivery. *Comput. Commun.*, 30:793–806, February 2007.

SecDS : A Secure EPC Discovery Service System in EPCglobal Network

Jie Shi, Darren Sim, Yingjiu Li, Robert Deng
School of Information Systems, Singapore Management University, Singapore 178902
{jieshi,darren.sim.2009,yjli,robertdeng}@smu.edu.sg

ABSTRACT

In recent years, the Internet of Things (IOT) has drawn considerable attention from the industrial and research communities. Due to the vast amount of data generated through IOT devices and users, there is an urgent need for an effective search engine to help us make sense of this massive amount of data. With this motivation, we begin our initial works on developing a secure and efficient search engine (SecDS) based on EPC Discovery Services (EPCDS) for EPCglobal network, an integral part of IOT. SecDS is designed to provide a bridge between different partners of supply chains to share information while enabling them to find who is in possession of an item. The most important property of SecDS is: while efficiently processing user's search, it is also secure. In order to prevent unauthorized access to SecDS, an extended attribute-based access control model is proposed and implemented such that information belonging to different companies can be protected using different policies.

Categories and Subject Descriptors

D.4.6 [**Security and Protection**]: Access controls; H.4 [**Information Systems Applications**]: Miscellaneous

General Terms

Design, Security

Keywords

EPC Discovery Service, Access Control, EPCglobal Network, Internet of Things

1. INTRODUCTION

As an integral part of future Internet, Internet of Things (IOT) has drawn considerable attention from the industrial and research communities around the world. Through IOT, we can look forward to a world where physical objects and virtual data interact [12], generating mass amount of data that will exceed that of what we have on the world-wide-web (WWW) today. There is an urgent need for a relevant search engine, to help us make sense of this data, just as how BING and Google are helping us navigate through the trillion-page Internet today.

EPCglobal network [7] is an important part of IOT. As a global standard RFID data sharing infrastructure, EPCglobal network is made up of Electronic Product Code (EPC) [10], EPC Information Services (EPCIS) [11], EPC Discovery Service (EPCDS) [9], amongst others.

In EPCglobal network, each physical product is associated with an RFID tag, represented by a unique EPC. This EPC can be retrieved from the RFID tags wirelessly via RFID readers as it transits between locations without contact-of-sight. These read events are usually processed by a middleware [8], and are stored locally at each supply chain partner's location-centric EPCIS [24]. With dynamic churn rates of partners and EPCIS, EPCDS becomes a unifying figure, helping partners locate information about a product in the supply chain. Through EPCglobal Network, participants can avoid information blackouts, and reaping the benefits of the RFID promise.

As the search and discovery component of EPCglobal network, EPCDS is designed with the intention of providing a bridge between supply chain partners, allowing them to share information, getting a step closer to achieving an automated supply chain. Due to the sensitivity and high value of the data transacted in EPCDS, a suitable access control mechanism is required. In this paper, we attempt to design and implement a secure and efficient EPCDS (SecDS) with an effective and efficient access control mechanism.

The road to achieve this is paved with the following challenges: (1) information transacted through EPCDS is constantly increasing, while churn rates of users is highly dynamic. This dynamism makes access control policies highly complex. (2) Each partner publishes information independently to EPCDS applying a myriad of access control policies. This disparate collection of access control policies in EPCDS makes it difficult to process, manage and maintain these policies effectively. Adding to this complexity, partners may not know of the existence of all participants in the supply chain. These made traditional access control mechanisms based on identity of users unsuitable. (3) As EPCDS is introduced to increase the visibility of RFID- related objects [9], it is important to support visibility policies (e.g. event information of an EPC is only allowed to be accessed by these partners who have handled the product with this

EPC). It is thus necessary to provide an efficient approach to specify and enforce these policies.

This paper presents the design and implementation of a secure EPCDS system — SecDS. Our contributions are summarized as follows:

- An extended attribute based access control (ABAC) model is proposed for SecDS that enriches the expressiveness of access control policies, while supporting visibility policies.

- We design and implement SecDS where this extended ABAC model is enforced without compromising on the efficiency of users' queries.

We begin with a description of background and motivations for our work in the following section. The extended ABAC model is presented in Section 3 and the implementation of SecDS is introduced in Section 4. Section 5 summarizes our experimental work and finally we introduce related works, conclude the paper, and describe future works.

2. BACKGROUND AND MOTIVATION

2.1 EPCglobal Network

As an important part of Internet of Things, EPCglobal network is a global standard for RFID supply chain networks providing a platform for trading partners to share product information [7]. As a participant of the EPCglobal Network, a company publishes event information of products into the EPCglobal Network, to share with each other. These information gives EPCglobal Network participants visibility of the location and movement of objects within supply chains.

The architecture of EPCglobal Network is described in the standard document [7], which is made up of many components, such as EPC Discovery services (EPCDS), EPC Information Services (EPCIS), and EPC Object Naming Services (EPC ONS). While EPCDS provides query service for serial-level information, EPC ONS provides search service for class-level information [9].

The information in EPCDS is published by EPCISes and searched by users. When a product with RFID tag passes through a supply chain, event information is obtained by RFID readers in each company and transmitted to its EPCIS. When an EPCIS captures event information about an EPC for the first time, it publishes this information into the EPCDS. When a user searches for information about a product with a given EPC, he first issues a query to EPCDS to get the addresses of EPCISes which handled the product with the given EPC. Next, the user queries each EPCIS by using the addresses returned by EPCDS to find the detailed event information. These processes are based on the Directory Look-up design [12], which SecDS complies to.

Based on the description above, we are aware that EPCDS mainly stores information published from EPCISes. When EPCDS uses relational databases as storage engine, the tables are illustrated in Table 1. In Table 1(a), the column **Time** represents when the product (with EPC) is handled, the column **PubisherId** represents the ID of the user who published the entry, and the column **CompanyId** represents the company associated with the record. Tables 1(b) and 1(c) store the information of users and companies. However, these tables only enumerate the basic attributes, while

other additional attributes used to provide precise query are left out for clear presentations.

As shown in Table 1(a), EPCDS stores the information of when, where and what products are handled by a company, which expose business information of companies. To prevent unauthorized access of such sensitive information, a suitable access control mechanism should be implemented in the EPCDS, as highlighted in the corresponding standard and related research work [7, 15].

In Example 2.1, we list many access control policies which should be supported in EPCDS. This example will be used throughout this paper.

EXAMPLE 2.1. *Suppose there exist two production Pro_1 and Pro_2 respectively with EPCs urn:epc:id:sgtin:4049588:-083309.61157415873 [1] and urn:epc:id:sgtin:4049588:083309.-89605325977. For production Pro_1, it comes from manufacturer M1 and is moved to distributor D2 and then shipped to retailer R1. Similar to Pro_1, production Pro_2 is passed through manufacturer M1, distributor D1, and retailers R1 and R2. All of these companies immediately published information (shown in Table 1(a)) to EPCDS when they handle these productions.*

However, the information in Table 1(a) cannot be released without any restriction. Different companies define different access control policies to protect their information. In the following, four representative policies are enumerated:

- *pol_1 (defined by security administrator of manufacturer M1): For the information about any product handled after 2011-01-01, it is allowed to access by the users of these companies who also handle this production and are distributor companies.*

- *pol_2 (defined by security administrator of distributor D1): For the information about any product whose EPC likes urn:epc:id:sgtin:4049588:083310.* (these production are valuable), it is only allowed to access by the users of manufacturer M1, distributor D1, and retailer R1 who are all partners.*

- *pol_3 (defined by security administrator of distributor D1): For the information about the product whose EPC doesn't like urn:epc:id:sgtin:4049588:083310.*, it is allowed to access by the users of these companies who also handle this production.*

- *pol_4 (defined by security administrator of retail R1): For the information about any product handled after 2011-03-01, it is allowed to access by the users of these companies who handle this production before the time R1 handles.*

2.2 Visibility Policy

For two different EPCISes a, b and an EPC e, the data in EPCDS reflects two possible relationships between a and b: they are both in the supply chain of e or they are not. These relationships can be used to specify access control policies. In Example 2.1, policies pol_1, pol_3 and pol_4 all use these relationships to specify access control policies, which

---

[1] The EPC number here is represented by a SGTIN notation that is why the "urn:epc:id:sgtin" is used, and then comes the company prefix(4049588), item reference(083309), and serial number (61157415873)

(a) EPCDS-records

ID	EPC	Time	PublisherId	CompanyId
1	urn:epc:id:sgtin:4049588:083309.61157415873	2011-01-15 11:00	U1001	C101
2	urn:epc:id:sgtin:4049588:083309.89605325977	2011-01-20 14:30	U1001	C101
3	urn:epc:id:sgtin:4049588:083309.89605325977	2011-01-23 12:00	U1002	C102
4	urn:epc:id:sgtin:4049588:083309.61157415873	2011-02-01 10:00	U1003	C103
5	urn:epc:id:sgtin:4049588:083309.89605325977	2011-02-05 16:00	U1004	C104
6	urn:epc:id:sgtin:4049588:083309.61157415873	2011-02-10 15:30	U1004	C104
7	urn:epc:id:sgtin:4049588:083309.89605325977	2011-02-15 14:00	U1005	C105

(b) User-Companies

UserId	Name	CompanyId
U1001	Bob	C101
U1002	Andy	C102
U1003	John	C103
U1004	Peter	C104
U1005	Jack	C105

(c) Companies

CompanyId	Name	Role	URI
C101	M1	Manufacturer	http://www.m1.com
C102	D1	Distributor	http://www.d1.com
C103	D2	Distributor	http://www.d2.com
C104	R1	Retailer	http://www.r1.com
C105	R2	Retailer	http://www.r2.com

are expressed as "who also handle this product". Because the access control policies specified by these relationships directly affect the visibility of the location and movement of objects within supply chains, we call them *visibility policy*.

In [19], the authors also considered visibility policies, but their work is related to supply chain, and cannot be used in EPCDS. Following their work, we considered three kinds of visibility policies: *whole-stream policy*, *up-stream policy* and *down-stream policy*.

DEFINITION 2.2. *(whole-stream policy for EPC e defined by company p)* *The event information published by company p of EPC e, is allowed to access by users of any companies who also publish event data of EPC e.*

DEFINITION 2.3. *(up-stream policy for EPC e defined by company p)* *The event information published by company p of EPC e, is allowed to access by users of any companies who also publish event data of EPC e before the time when p publishes event data of EPC e.*

DEFINITION 2.4. *(down-stream policy for EPC e defined by company p)* *The event information published by company p of EPC e, is allowed to access by users of any companies who also publish event data of EPC e after the time when p publishes event data of EPC e.*

Based on the schema of Table 1(a), for a record of an EPC e belonging to company c_1 which is protected by the whole stream policy, up-stream policy or down-stream policy, any user u_2 belonging to company c_2 is allowed to access this record if the following corresponding SQL predicate is satisfied:

- **whole-stream policy**:
  *exist (select * from EPCDS-records T where T.companyId $= c_2$ and T.EPC $= e$)*

- **up-stream policy**:
  *exist (select * from EPCDS-record T where T.companyId $= c_2$ and T.EPC $= e$ and T.Time $< t$)*

- **down-stream policy**:
  *exist (select * from EPCDS-record T where T.companyId $= c_2$ and T.EPC $= e$ and T.Time $> t$)*

where t is the time when c handles the EPC e.

Due to the complexity of visibility policy, traditional access control models (DAC, MAC, and RBAC) are not suitable for SecDS. In next section, we will extend attribute based access control model to protect the information in SecDS.

3. ATTRIBUTE-BASED ACCESS CONTROL FOR SECDS SYSTEM

Different from traditional access control models (DAC, MAC and RBAC), attribute based access control (ABAC) policies are defined based on attributes of subjects and objects [30].

3.1 Attributes

In SecDS, subjects are users while objects are event information in the table *EPCDS_records*.

- *Subject Attributes*: A subject is a user, who takes actions on event information in SecDS. Each subject is associated with a set of attributes which define the identity and characteristics of the subject. Such attributes may include the subject's identifier, name, country and so on. As a subject represents a company in SecDS, the attributes of a company are also considered as attributes of a subject belonging to it.

- *Object Attributes*: Objects are event information published from EPCISes. Naturally, object attributes will contain *EPC*, *Time*, and so on, which are the columns of table *EPCDS_records*.

- *Visibility Attribute*: To support visibility policy, we set visibility attribute which takes one of the following three values: *whole-stream*, *up-stream* and *down-stream*.

3.2 ABAC Authorization Language

An authorization language (AUL) is used to define who is allowed to perform what operations on what data. In this paper, we only focus on query operations; therefore AUL does not contain operations. The ABAC authorization language (AUL) is shown as follows:

AUL:=object_condition ∧ subject_condition
| object_condition ∧ visibility_condition
| object_condition ∧ subject_condition ∧ visibility_condition

where *subject_condition*, *object_condition* and *visibility_condition* are all boolean conditions for subject attributes, object attributes and visibility attributes respectively. All these conditions are constructed by the rules shown in Figure 1.

```
condition := expression | condition op condition
             | (condition op condition)
expression := attribute comp value |
             attribute comp attribute |
             attribute comp {value_set}
op := and | or
comp := < | > | =| <= | >= | [NOT] LIKE | [NOT] IN
value_set := value | value, value_set
```

Figure 1: Condition Language

EXAMPLE 3.1. *The access control policies described in Example 2.1 are specified in Table 2 according to the authorization language in Figure 1.*

Expressiveness: The authorization language of SecDS is semantically richer and more expressive. Firstly, as an extension of ABAC, this AUL inherits the expressiveness from ABAC which encompasses the functionality of identity based access control, such as DAC and MAC, and R-BAC [30]. Secondly, while conforming to the standards of EPCDS, this AUL supports visibility policies which are not considered in other access control models.

4. SECDS SYSTEM

4.1 Architecture of SecDS System

Before introducing the implementation approach, we first provide the architecture of SecDS as shown in Figure 2.

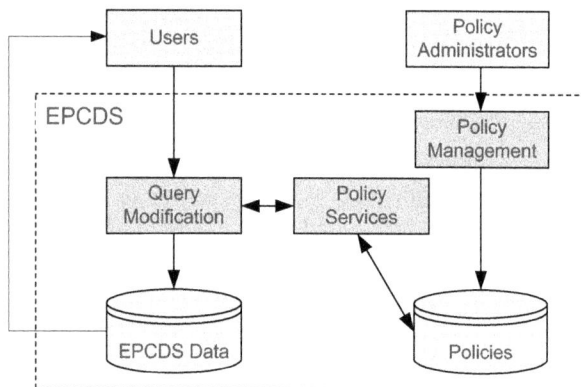

Figure 2: Architecture of SecDS system

SecDS contains the following components: Data Storage Server, Policies Storage Server, Policy Management, Policy

Service, and Query Modification. Data Storage Server stores the event information published from EPCISes and some auxiliary information, while Policies Storage Server stores access control policies. Policy Management, Policy Service and Query Modification components are related to access control. We will focus on these three components in the following sections.

4.2 Policy Management

Policy Management Component (PMC) is used by policy administrator to manage access control policies. There are two different types of policies in SecDS system. First is global policy which is defined by the security administrator of SecDS. Second is local policy which is defined by the security administrator of each EPCIS. The local policy is used to control users' query. Other types of accesses from users, such as publishing data and querying data, are controlled under global policy.

Query operation is the most important access in SecDS, while access control policy over query operation is the most complicated policy. In the following, we only consider local policies which are defined by security administrators of different EPCISes to protect their published data.

For managing local policies, PMC provides services for security administrator of each EPCIS to create, modify and delete their access control policies. We take creation of access control policies as an example to illustrate the process in PMC.

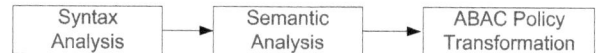

Figure 3: Process of creating policy in policy management component

As shown in Figure 3, there are three steps for creating policies in PMC: Syntax Analysis, Semantic Analysis, and ABAC Policy Transformation. The Syntax Analysis and Semantic Analysis make sure syntax and semantic of newly created access control policies are correct, which are similar to the corresponding components in most access control systems.

In order to reduce the cost of users' queries, ABAC policies are transformed into fine-grained access control (FGAC) policies which use SQL predicates to express users' privilege [1, 22, 25, 5, 28, 27]. In FGAC policy, it assigns a predicate to a user to express which data is allowed to access by the user. FGAC policy is a special case of ABAC policy where the attributes of object are the columns of relational tables and the attribute of subject is user's ID.

The transformation of an ABAC policy into FGAC policies can be taken in two steps. First, an ABAC policy is divided into three different predicates: subject predicate, object predicate and visibility predicate, which contain subject attributes, object attributes, and visibility attributes, respectively. Second, PMC finds all users in SecDS which satisfy the subject predicate, and then assigns the object predicate and visibility predicate to these users. The transformation is similar to the technique given in [17]. In the following, we take an example to further illustrate the ABAC policy transformation.

ID	Name	Predicate	Creator	CompanyId
1	pol_1	$Time > 2011\text{-}01\text{-}01 \land (Visibility =$ whole-stream $\land Role =$ Distributor$)$	C1001	C101
2	pol_2	EPC LIKE urn:epc:id:sgtin:4049588:083310:* $\land Name$ IN (M1, D1, R1)	C1002	C102
3	pol_3	EPC NOT LIKE urn:epc:id:sgtin:4049588:083310:* $\land Visibility =$ whole-stream	C1002	C102
4	pol_4	$Time > 2011\text{-}03\text{-}01 \land Visibility =$ up-stream	C1004	C104

Table 2: ABAC policy table.

UserID	ABACPolicy	ObjectPredicate	Visibility	Creator	CompanyId
U1002	pol_1	TIME > 2011-01-01	whole-stream	U1001	C101
U1003	pol_1	TIME > 2011-01-01	whole-stream	U1001	C101
U1001	pol_2	EPC LIKE urn:epc:id:sgtin:4049588:083310:*	NULL	U1002	C102
U1002	pol_2	EPC LIKE urn:epc:id:sgtin:4049588:083310:*	NULL	U1002	C102
U1004	pol_2	EPC LIKE urn:epc:id:sgtin:4049588:083310:*	NULL	U1002	C102
0	pol_3	EPC NOT LIKE urn:epc:id:sgtin:4049588:083310:*	whole-stream	U1002	C102
0	pol_4	TIME > 2011-03-01	up-stream	U1004	C104

Table 3: FGAC policy table.

EXAMPLE 4.1. *Consider the tables in Table 1 and the ABAC policies in Example 3.1. Policy pol_1 can be divided into the following three parts:*

- *Subject Predicate: role = Distributor;*

- *Object Predicate: TIME > 2011-01-01;*

- *Visibility Predicate: visibility = whole-stream.*

Then, by using subject predicate, we construct the following SQL statement where the subject predicate is added in the WHERE clause:

```
SELECT UseId FROM User-Companies UC, Companies C
WHERE  UC.companyId = C.CompanyId and
       Role = Distributor;
```

After executing the above SQL statement the results $\{U1002, U1003\}$ is returned. Then, the first two records in Table 3 are constructed. All policies in Example 3.1 are transformed into FGAC policies in the table 3. The users' IDs are both 0 in the last two records in Table 3, which means these policies should be checked for all users' queries. When there is no subject predicate in an ABAC policy, the user ID in the record stored the transformed FGAC policy is 0.

ABAC Policy Transformation has both advantages and disadvantages. It improves the efficiency of users' queries but increases the complexity of policy management. While supporting flexible and highly expressive access control policies, attribute based access control takes more time to make access decision. In ABAC system, it needs to determine whether a user satisfies an ABAC policy. This will take time if there are many ABAC policies and users as explained clearly in [17]. After transforming ABAC policies into F-GAC polices, the cost of determining where a user satisfies an ABAC policy is relatively easy by checking the user's query against relevant FGAC policies. However, as stated in [17], the work of maintaining the consistence between ABAC policies and transformed FGAC policies is cumbersome since there are many situations to be taken into account such as values of users' attributes being changed, ABAC policies being added, deleted or updated, and users being added,

deleted, or updated. We adapt the approaches proposed in [17] to solve these problems. In a nut shell, we improve the query performance at the cost of policy management.

4.3 Policy Service

The **Policy Service Component (PSC)** interacts the **Query Modification Component (QMC)** in access control. There are two types of services in PSC: FGAC Policy Searching Service (FPSS) and FGAC Policy Combining Service (FPCS). When a user issues a query, QMC knows which companies' data is required to access by this query and then sends the current user's ID and these companies' IDs to P-SC. PSC first calls FPSS to search in the FGAC policy table for the FGAC policies that are assigned to this user and are created by the companies with the given companies' IDs. Then, PSC invokes FPCS to combine the returned FGAC policies into a single predicate before return it to QMC.

The implementation of FPSS is simple. First, when getting the current user's ID and many companies' IDs, FPSS constructs an SQL query to search in the FGAC policy table for all FGAC policies which are assigned to this user and created by these companies. Then FPSS sends these FGAC policies to FPCS.

Upon receiving a set of FGAC policies from FPSS, FPCS combines these policies into one single predicate. Before introducing combination algorithm, we first revisit visibility policy.

In section 2.2, we already mentioned that what SQL predicates are equal to whole-stream policy, up-stream policy and down-stream policy. However, for understanding easily, in those predicates we directly used the values of EPC and time. These predicates cannot be used in our query modification algorithm. So, we further transform these predicates into SQL predicates which can be directly used in query modification algorithm.

In the following SQL predicates, $T1$ represents the table same to T, which are both table $EPCDS\_records$; u_1 represents the current user's ID who belongs to company c_1.

- **Whole-stream policy:**
  exist (select 1 from $T1$ where $T1.companyId = c_1$ and $T.EPC = T1.EPC$)

- **Up-stream policy**:

  exist (select 1 from T1 where T1.companyId = c_1 and T.EPC = T1.EPC and T1.Time < T.Time)

- **Down-stream policy**:

  exist (select 1 from T1 where T1.companyId = c_1 and T.EPC = T1.EPC and T1.Time > T.Time)

There are three steps taken to combine any FGAC policies.

Step 1: Each FGAC policy is transformed into one predicate:

- If an FGAC policy consists of a visibility predicate only, the visibility predicate is transformed into an EXIST SQL predicate as described above.

- If an FGAC policy consists of an object predicate as described above, there is no need of any transformation.

- If an FGAC policy is made up of a visibility predicate and an object predicate, the two predicates are combined into one predicate in the following steps. First, the visibility predicate is transformed into EXIST SQL predicate; then the object predicate is moved into the WHERE clause of the EXIST SQL predicate with connector AND.

Step 2: A predicate is added for each FGAC policy to ensure that this policy only protect the data of the company which creates this policy without affecting any other companies' data. The predicate is "companyId = C_X", which we call *own predicate*, where C_X is the ID of the company which creates this policy. Let pd_1 denote the predicate constructed in **step 1**. If pd_1 is an EXIST SQL predicate, the *own predicate* is added to the WHERE clause of pd_1 with connector AND; if pd_1 is just an object predicate, the *own predicate* is combined directly with pd_1 by using AND connector.

Step 3: Assume that after **step 1** and **step 2**, two policies are transformed into predicates pd_2 and pd_3, respectively. A connector OR is used to combine two FGAC policies in three cases:

- When pd_2 and pd_3 are both EXIST SQL predicates, the predicate belonging to WHERE clause of pd_2 is moved into the WHERE clause of pd_3 with OR connector.

- If one of predicates pd_2 and pd_3 is EXIST SQL predicate (assuming pd_2 is an EXIST SQL predicate, and pd_3 is a common predicate), pd_3 is moved into the WHERE clause of pd_2 with connector OR.

- If pd_2 and pd_3 are both common predicates , pd_2 and pd_3 are combined directly with connector OR.

The use of *own predicate* in **step 2** and OR connector in **step 3** ensures that all ABAC policies created by one EPCIS take no effect on any other companies' data. By using OR to combine two FGAC policies, it is potential to increase users' privileges while creating new policies [1]. For further restricting users' privilege, a security administrator can revise existing policies instead of writing a new one. The detailed combination algorithm is shown in Algorithm 1. The complexity of this algorithm is $O(N)$ where N is the number of policies which are combined.

Algorithm 1 Policy combination algorithm

Input: *poicySet : pSet*;
Output: *combinedpolicy : cp*

1: cp = NULL
2: **for** $i = 1$ to $pSet.Length$ **do**
3:     $tempply = pSet[i]$;
4:     get object predicate *objp* from *tempply*
5:     get visibility policy *visp* from *tempply*
6:     get publisher ID *pubId* from *tempply*
7:     combine *objp* and *visp* to form predicate *pred*
8:     form an own predicate using *pubId* and add the formed own predicate to *pred* with AND
9:     combine predicates *pred* and *cp* with OR and then give the combined predicate to *cp*
10: **end for**
11: **return** cp

EXAMPLE 4.2. *Consider the FGAC policies in Table 3. Suppose the user with userId U1003 submits a query to search for the information about EPC = urn:epc:id:sgtin:40495-88:083309.89605325977 in Table 1(a). First, QMC gets the set of companies' IDs {C101, C102, C104, C105}, which publish the EPC information , and sends the set to FPSS. Then FPSS executes the following query to get FGAC policies:*

```
SELECT * From FGAC_TABLE WHERE (UserID = U1003 or
UserId = 0) AND CompanyId IN (C101, C102,
C104, C105);
```

In Table 3, UserId = 0 means all users' accesses should be controlled by this policy. The results are the second, sixth and seventh records in Table 3.

Then FPCS combines the three policies into one single predicate. For the second records in Table 3, the object predicate is TIME > 2011-01-01, and visibility is whole-stream. The visibility policy is transformed into EXIST predicate as follows:

```
EXIST (SELECT 1 FROM EPCDS_records T1 WHERE
T1.companyId = C103 and T.EPC = T1.EPC)
```

The object predicate and the own predicate companyId = C101 are both added to the WHERE clause of the above predicate with AND so as to form the predicate item 1 shown below. The transformed predicates for the sixth and seventh records in Table 3 are shown in the following items 2 and 3, respectively. Finally, items 1, 2 and 3 are combined into the following item 4 as the final predicate.

1. *pred1 = EXIST (SELECT * FROM EPCDS_records T1 WHERE (T1.CompanyId = C103 AND T.EPC = T1.EPC AND T.TIME > 2011-01-01) AND T.CompanyId = C101);*

2. *pred2 = EXIST (SELECT * FROM EPCDS_records T1 WHERE (T1.CompanyId = C103 AND T.EPC = T1.EPC AND T.EPC NOT LIKE urn:epc:id:sgtin:404-9588:0083310:*) AND T.CompanyId = C102).*

3. *pred3 = EXIST (SELECT * FROM EPCDS_records T1 WHERE (T1.CompanyId = C103 AND T.EPC = T1.EPC AND T1.TIME < T.TIME AND T.TIME > 2011-03-01) AND T.CompanyId = C104).*

Algorithm 2 Query Modification Algorithm

Input: *originalQuery* : Q; *userId*;
Output: *modifiedQuery* : Q'

1: form a query to get the set *comIdSet* of company IDs who have the data queried by Q;
2: send *comIdSet* and *userId* to PSC to get the combined predicate *pred*
3: construct a view using *pred* and Table *EPCDS_records*
4: replace Table *EPCDS_records* with the view in Q to get Q'
5: **return** Q'

---

*4. pred4 = EXIST (SELECT * FROM EPCDS_records T1 WHERE ((T1.CompanyId = C103 AND T.EPC = T1.EPC AND T.TIME > 2011-01-01) AND T.Publisher = C101) OR ((T1.CompanyId = C103 AND T.EPC = T1.EPC AND T.EPC NOT LIKE urn:epc:-id:sgtin:4049588:0083310:*) AND T.CompanyId = C-102) OR ((T1.CompanyId = C103 AND T.EPC = T1.EPC AND T1.TIME < T.TIME AND T.TIME > 2011-03-01) AND T.Company = C104)).*

4.4 Query Modification

The basic idea of query modification is that before being processed, user queries are transparently modified to ensure that users can access only what they are authorized to access [28]. Query modification is widely used in databases to enforce fine-grained access control which is also demonstrated as a scalable and efficient technique [22, 25, 28].

As aforementioned, ABAC policies in SecDS are transformed into FGAC policies, so that we can use query modification technique to enforce FGAC policies in SecDS.

Algorithm 2 shows our query modification algorithm. At the beginning, the original query is modified using "CompanyId" to replace the select target in the original query. The modified query is executed to return all company IDs who have the queried data. Then, the set of company IDs and the current user ID are sent to Policy Service Component to get a combined predicate. A temporary view is constructed using the returned predicate and *EPCDS_records*. Finally, the view is used to replace table *EPCDS_records* in the original query to form the finial modified query which will be executed instead of the original query.

EXAMPLE 4.3. *Suppose that user U1003 queries for the information about EPC urn:epc:id:sgtin:4049588:083309.896-05325977. The original query Q1 is constructed and modified into Q2 to get all companies whose data is requested to access. After sending the user's ID and the set of companies' IDs to Policy Services Component, PSC returns the combined predicate pred4 in Example 4.2. Finally, the returned predicate pred4 is used to form a view which replaces the table EPCDS_records to form the final modified query Q3.*

- *Q1: SELECT * FROM EPCDS_record WHERE EPC = urn:epc:id:sgtin:4049588:083309.89605325977;*

- *Q2: SELECT companyId FROM EPCDS_record WHERE EPC = urn:epc:id:sgtin:4049588:083309.89605325977;*

- *Q3: SELECT * FROM (SELECT * FROM EPCDS_record T WHERE pred4) WHERE EPC = urn:epc:id:sgtin:4049588:083309.89605325977.*

Security: We assume that SecDS is a trusted server where a secure authentication mechanism is implemented. The query modification algorithm determines the security property of SecDS. In [28], a criterion with three properties is proposed for enforcing fine-grained access control policies in databases; one of these properties is *secure*. The *secure* property is defined as having no information leaked to adversaries under access control policy. It is also stated that the algorithm in [22], which constructs temporary views to replace the tables in user's query, is secure, because the information to which the user is not allowed to access, is filtered out in the constructed temporary views. As only row-level policies are used, our query modification algorithm is a special case of the algorithm given in [22], which supports both row-level and cell-level policies.

5. EXPERIMENTS

We implemented a prototype of SecDS system. Rigorous experiments conducted on the prototype show that SecDS is practical. The average query response time is about 260ms in a setting of 50,000 supply chains, 300 EPCISes, on average 20 EPCISes being involved in each supply chain and on average 10 policies being evaluated for each query. Details of our experiments are given in an extended version of this paper.

6. RELATED WORK

EPCglobal network provides a platform for trading partners to share their product information [10], where EPCIS and EPCDS play an important role for increasing data visibility [11, 9]. There are lots of work focusing on how to implement EPCIS and EPCDS for providing traceability and increasing visibility [2, 13, 14, 20, 24]. However, the information in EPCIS and EPCDS is sensitive which should be protected.

In [15], the authors proposed and implemented a fine grained access control mechanism to protect the information in EPCIS, where query modification technique is used. However, the access control policy for EPCIS is simpler than that of EPCDS. This is because access control policies for an EPCIS are defined by the administrator of this EPCIS only, but the policies for EPCDS are defined by different security administrators of different companies. The access control approach designed for EPCIS cannot be directly applied for EPCDS.

Li el. at. proposed a semantic access control for RFID-enabled supply chains. Since it is not conform to the EPCglobal network, it cannot be used for EPCDS [23].

In [29], Yan et. al. considered an different situation where the EPCDS is an untrusted server, and they proposed a pseudonym-based design to mitigate the adversary's attack. Their work is also not conform to EPCglobal network and is not practical in real world applications.

Rigorous effort has been made in the research community on the security and privacy aspects of RFID systems e.g. [6, 18, 16]. However, these work mainly target at RFID communication systems, rather than EPC discovery services. To the best of our knowledge, SecDS is the first secure and efficient EPC discovery service system with suitable access control mechanism.

Since access control mechanism for EPCDS should support complex policies such as visibility policies, traditional access control models such as DAC, MAC, RBAC and TR-BAC [4, 3, 26] may not suitable. Attribute based access control (ABAC) [21, 30] is adapted in this paper to meet the requirements of access control for EPCDS.

7. CONCLUSION

This paper described SecDS, a search engine based on EPCDS for EPCGlobal network. SecDS is not only efficient in processing users' search queries, but also secure and expressive in enforcing various data protection. We analyzed the requirements of access control for EPCDS and proposed an extended attribute based access control model to meet the requirements. In order to maintain efficiency, we proposed an approach of transforming ABAC policies to FGAC policies, and using query modification techniques to implement these FGAC policies. In future, we will consider how to further enhance the performance of SecDS.

8. REFERENCES

[1] R. Agrawal, P. Bird, T. Grandison, J. Kiernan, S. Logan, and W. Rjaibi. Extending relational database systems to automatically enforce privacy policies. In *ICDE*, pages 1013–1022, 2005.

[2] S. Beier, T. Grandison, K. Kailing, and R. Rantzau. Discovery services-enabling rfid traceability in epcglobal networks. In *COMAD*, pages 214–217, 2006.

[3] E. Bertino, P. A. Bonatti, and E. Ferrari. Trbac: A temporal role-based access control model. *ACM Trans. Inf. Syst. Secur.*, 4(3):191–233, August 2001.

[4] E. Bertino and R. Sandhu. Database security-concepts, approaches, and challenges. *IEEE Trans. Dependable Secur. Comput.*, 2:2–19, January 2005.

[5] S. Chaudhuri, T. Dutta, and S. Sudarshan. Fine grained authorization through predicated grants. In *ICDE*, pages 1174–1183, 2007.

[6] R. H. Deng, Y. Li, M. Yung, and Y. Zhao. A new framework for rfid privacy. In *ESORICS*, pages 1–18, 2010.

[7] EPCglobal. http://www.gs1.org/epcglobal.

[8] EPCglobal. Application level events (ale) standard. http://www.gs1.org/gsmp/kc/epcglobal/ale.

[9] EPCglobal. *Data Discovery (DD JRG) Requirements Document, 17 August, 2009, Version 0.0.25.*

[10] EPCglobal. Electronic product code. http://www.gs1.org/gsmp/kc/epcglobal/tds.

[11] EPCglobal. Epc information services. http://www.gs1.org/gsmp/kc/epcglobal/epcis.

[12] A. C. B. Evangelos A. Kosmatos, Nikolaos D. Tselikas. Intergrating rfids and smart objects into a unified internet of things architecture. *Advances in Internet of Things*, 1(1):5–12, 2011.

[13] S. Evdokimov, B. Fabian, S. Kunz, and N. Schoenemann. Comparison of discovery service architectures for the internet of things. In *Proceedings of the 2010 IEEE International Conference on Sensor Networks, Ubiquitous, and Trustworthy Computing*, pages 237–244, 2010.

[14] C. Floerkemeier, M. Lampe, and C. Roduner. Facilitating rfid development with the accada prototyping platform. In *IEEE International Conference on Pervasive Computing and Communications*, 2007.

[15] E. Grummt and M. Müller. Fine-grained access control for epc information services. In *Proceedings of the 1st international conference on The internet of things*, IOT'08, pages 35–49, 2008.

[16] GSI. Rfid security & privacy lounge. http://www.avoine.net/rfid/index.php.

[17] S. Jahid, C. A. Gunter, I. Hoque, and H. Okhravi. Myabdac: compiling xacml policies for attribute-based database access control. In *CODASPY*, pages 97–108, 2011.

[18] A. Juels. Rfid security and privacy: a research survey. *IEEE Journal on Selected Areas in Communications*, 24(2):381–394, 2006.

[19] F. Kerschbaum. An access control model for mobile physical objects. In *SACMAT*, pages 193–202, 2010.

[20] C. Kürschner, C. Condea, O. Kasten, and F. Thiesse. Discovery service design in the epcglobal network: towards full supply chain visibility. In *Proceedings of the 1st international conference on The internet of things*, IOT'08, pages 19–34, 2008.

[21] B. Lang, I. T. Foster, F. Siebenlist, R. Ananthakrishnan, and T. Freeman. A flexible attribute based access control method for grid computing. *Journal of Grid Computing*, 7(2):169–180, 2009.

[22] K. LeFevre, R. Agrawal, V. Ercegovac, R. Ramakrishnan, Y. Xu, and D. DeWitt. Limiting disclosure in hippocratic databases. In *VLDB*, pages 108–119, 2004.

[23] Z. Li, C.-H. Chu, and W. Yao. Semantic Access Control for RFID-enabled Supply Chains. In *Workshop on RFID Security – RFIDSec Asia'10*, February 2010.

[24] J. Muller, J. Oberst, S. Wehrmeyer, J. Witt, A. Zeier, and H. Plattner. An aggregating discovery service for the epcglobal network. In *Proceedings of the 2010 43rd Hawaii International Conference on System Sciences*, pages 1–9, 2010.

[25] S. Rizvi, A. Mendelzon, S. Sudarshan, and P. Roy. Extending query rewriting techniques for fine-grained access control. In *SIGMOD*, pages 551–562, 2004.

[26] P. Samarati and S. D. C. di Vimercati. Access control: Policies, models, and mechanisms. In *FOSAD*, pages 137–196, 2000.

[27] J. Shi and H. Zhu. A fine-grained access control model for relational databases. *Journal of Zhejiang University - Science C*, 11(8):575–586, 2010.

[28] Q. Wang, T. Yu, N. Li, J. Lobo, E. Bertino, K. Irwin, and J.-W. Byun. On the correctness criteria of fine-grained access control in relational databases. In *VLDB*, pages 555–566, 2007.

[29] Q. Yan, R. H. Deng, Z. Yan, Y. Li, and T. Li. Pseudonym-based rfid discovery service to mitigate unauthorized tracking in supply chain management. In *International Symposium on Data, Privacy, and E-Commerce,*, pages 21–26, 2010.

[30] E. Yuan and J. Tong. Attributed based access control (abac) for web services. In *IEEE International Conference on Web Services*, pages 561–569, 2005.

Identifying Native Applications with High Assurance *

Hussain M. J. Almohri
almohri@vt.edu

Danfeng (Daphne) Yao
danfeng@cs.vt.edu

Dennis Kafura
kafura@cs.vt.edu

Department of Computer Science
Virginia Tech
Blacksburg, VA, USA

ABSTRACT

Main stream operating system kernels lack a strong and reliable mechanism for identifying the running processes and binding them to the corresponding executable applications. In this paper, we address the identification problem by proposing a novel secure application identification model in which user-level applications are required to present identification proofs at run time to be authenticated to the kernel. In our model, applications are supplied with unique secret keys. The secret key of an application is registered with a trusted kernel at the installation time and is used to uniquely authenticate the application. We present a protocol for the secure authentication of applications. Additionally, we develop a system call monitoring architecture that uses our model to verify the identity of applications when making designated system calls. Our system call monitoring can be integrated with existing mandatory access control systems to enforce application-level access rights. We implement and evaluate a prototype of our monitoring architecture in Linux as device drivers with no modification of the kernel. The results from our extensive performance evaluation shows that our prototype incurs low overhead, indicating the feasibility of our approach for cryptographically identifying and authenticating applications in the operating system.

Categories and Subject Descriptors

D.4.6 [**Operating Systems**]: Security and Protection—*Access controls*

General Terms

Security

Keywords

Operating system, malware, cryptography, application authentication, process identification

*This work has been supported in part by NSF grant CAREER CNS-0953638 and ARO grant STIR-450080.

1. INTRODUCTION

Operating system kernels often enforce minimal restrictions on the applications permitted to execute, resulting in the ability of malicious programs to abuse system resources. Stealthy malware running as stand-alone processes, once installed, can freely execute enjoying the privileges provided to the user account running the process. However, kernels are not designed to detect malicious behaviors, or identify malicious processes at runtime.

A well-known approach to protecting systems from malicious activities is through the deployment of mandatory access control (MAC) systems. Such systems often provide the kernel with access monitoring mechanisms as well as policy specification platforms. The user decides on the policies and the various access rights on system resources. Existing MAC systems such as SELinux [17], grsecurity [1], and AppArmor [8] enable the user (or the system administrator) to express detailed and powerful policies. These solutions are often implemented using the Linux Security Modules [26] to monitor access to selected system resources, and apply the specified policies to the corresponding processes.

In this paper, we point out that the existing MAC-based based approaches to application authorization alone are not sufficient for defeating modern malware. That is, the kernel must have secure mechanisms for authenticating and identifying processes, beyond the simple and easy-to-forge process ID (PID) or process name based identification. Thus, a critical problem in detecting malicious activities in the user-space is the ability to strongly identify processes at runtime and bind them to appropriate application identities. The identification of processes is a necessary step to prevent malicious processes to achieve their goals by benefiting from the access rights of legitimate processes.

Although providing useful security solutions, existing MAC systems do not explicitly address the problem of application identification. In [25], the authors present an extension to the Singularity operating system to define applications as first-class entities. The extension provides a language for the specification of application-level access rights. However, the proposed method combines the identity of the application (using application name) with the user's access rights and does not provide an explicit application identification model. Another approach is to identify malicious processes through the use of behavioral analysis. One may attempt to identify malicious processes through an anomaly-detection based approach by conducting analysis on process behaviors. However, this approach suffers from advanced and newly discovered attacks that are capable of bypassing the detection scope [21].

Our goal is to securely identify processes at runtime and distinguish legitimate processes from undesired (and perhaps malicious) ones. Such a secure identification must provide high assurance in detecting and preventing the execution of malicious processes.

We present a novel identification model in which applications are identified and authenticated with high assurance. A privileged legitimate application is associated with a strong identity used to authenticate itself to the kernel. Using our identification model, we achieve the following:

- **Application identification.** Applications with registered identities, can authenticate to the trusted kernel in order to provide proofs of identity. The kernel can prove the identity of legitimate applications, relying on the uniqueness of application identities and a secure in-host authentication protocol.

- **Application monitoring.** Our identification model enables the design and implementation of a sophisticated system call monitoring architecture that is used to enforce *application-level* access rights.

Contributions. We present our secure application identification model using which the kernel can identify and authenticate the running processes. We present the design of a modified challenge-response protocol to securely authenticate applications. Moreover, we design and implement a system call monitoring architecture to monitor the execution of the processes through their interactions with monitored system calls. We use standard benchmarks to evaluate the performance of our implementation and show that our system is feasible to implement without a significant performance penalty.

2. THE AUTHENTICATED APPLICATION FRAMEWORK

A major step in enforcing application-level access rights on the running processes is to identify a process and properly bind it to the corresponding application. Existing mandatory access control (MAC) systems such as AppArmor and SELinux use installation paths and process names to identify processes and enforce appropriate access rights. However, such an identification mechanism is weak. That is because the installation path and the process name are dynamic concepts and are subject to change by the user or by an attacker. Thus, to guarantee secure access control enforcement, a MAC system needs to rely on a strong identification model.

In the diagram of Figure 1, we present a high-level conceptual process of protection against malware that can effectively identify legitimate processes and enforce application-level access rights with the assistance of a mandatory access control system. In this process, three major components need to participate. First, a classification component decides on the legitimacy of the executable code. Next, an identification component must register legitimate applications identified in the first step and prove their identities to the following component. Finally, access policies are specified and used to monitor the execution of a process and enforce access rights within a mandatory access control system. While the classification of applications and policy spec-

ification are critical steps, we realize the lack of a proper identification and binding mechanism that can complete the protection process. Hence, throughout this paper we present our solution for the identification component in the form of the following steps:

1. **Application key registration.** We generate a unique secret key for each legitimate application.

2. **Application authentication.** We use the provided application key to securely authenticate the application code which contains the key and produce identity tokens.

3. **Execution monitoring.** We monitor the execution of the processes to limit the activities of unauthenticated ones.

4. **Identification and binding.** We identify a registered application process using generated identity tokens and bind them to the corresponding application access rights.

We introduce the design and implementation of the *Authenticated Application* (A2) framework to address the four steps required to provide strong identification of applications. The core idea of A2 is a novel identification model that is based on sharing unique symmetric keys between every installed application (that runs in the form of stand-alone processes) and the kernel. The strengths of this model is based on the cryptographic properties of symmetric keys generated by the key generators for standard encryption functions. The design of A2 is driven by the following security goals:

1. Providing unforgeable identities that can be used by mandatory access control systems verify the legitimacy of the processes.

2. Enabling effective application-level access rights at the system call usage level.

To achieve our security goals, we define an application key as follows:

DEFINITION 1. *An application key is a string of characters s of length l generated by a cryptographic key generation function $f : l \rightarrow s$ such that with an appropriate length l, s is always unique and is computationally hard to guess.*

Each application key is generated using a trusted kernel helper (discussed in Section 2.4) and is used for a single application. Every process created by an application must be able to use the key to authenticate itself to the kernel. Application keys can be generated using secure symmetric encryption key generation functions such as AES [20].

2.1 Threat Model

Our basic trusted components are the kernel code and kernel's memory region. We assume that kernel does not contain any malicious code. Further, we assume that confidentiality and integrity of the kernel's memory is preserved. We assume that legitimate applications may be vulnerable and thus allow downloading malicious code. However, legitimate applications may not contain malicious code and a malware cannot misuse a legitimate application without running as a stand-alone process. Specifically, malicious code running within the boundary of a legitimate process (such as

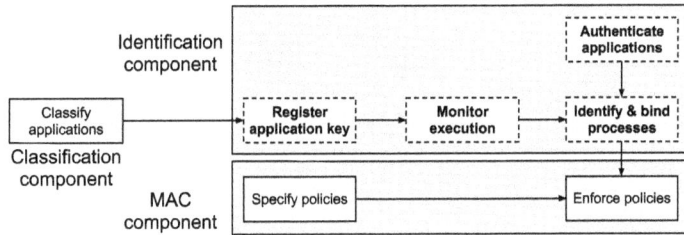

Figure 1: Conceptual process of protection against malware.

a malicious browser script or extension) is out of the scope of our work. Moreover, we assume the hardware, the installed firmware and standard operating system APIs are trusted. We also assume that an attacker has no physical access to the machine and does not know the user's credentials.

A2 is used to fundamentally distinguish legitimate processes from malicious ones. Although the identification model itself is not a malware detection method, it can be used to boost the security guarantees of MAC systems as well as application sandboxing solutions. Later in Section 2.5 we discuss the integration of our application identities with an existing a MAC system.

2.2 Design Overview

In A2, each legitimate application is supplied with a secret key that is only accessible by the application code and the kernel. At the time of creating a process, the application's secret key is used by the process to authenticate itself to the kernel. Once the process is securely authenticated, the kernel can assure its identity relying on the strong properties [4] of the cryptographic hash functions.

In the identification model of A2, applications are recognized as individual principals. Keyed applications are the most privileged applications while unregistered applications (that are unable to identify themselves) are restricted and considered potentially malicious. This identification mechanism provides a secure sandbox for the potentially malicious processes and isolates them from authenticated processes. It is necessary to allow the creation of any process regardless of its identity. This is to enable any application to authenticate itself at runtime in order to provide proof of identity. In addition, this strategy results in uncovering stealthy malware as soon as it interacts with the kernel through a monitored system call.

The A2 framework consists of three main components: *Trusted Key Registrar*, *Authenticator* and *Service Access Monitor (SAM)* depicted in Figure 2. We implement the Authenticator and SAM as Linux kernel modules without modifying the kernel (see Section 3). We describe the functions of our components in the following.

Trusted Key Registrar is a kernel helper responsible for installing a key for the application and registering the application with the kernel. The application interacts with the trusted key registrar to receive a secret key. The trusted key registrar stores the same key and registers it for the corresponding application within a secure storage to be used for the authentication of the processes at runtime.

Authenticator is responsible for authenticating a process when it first loads. The Authenticator generates iden-

tity tokens (defined in Section 2.3.1) based on a token generation protocol.

Service Access Monitor (SAM) is responsible for verifying the tokens at runtime and enforce application-level access rights. Since the tokens are maintained by the Authenticator, SAM realizes its task by coordinating with the Authenticator through a shared data structure. SAM enforces application-level access rights based on a user-specified application policy.

2.3 Secure Authentication of Applications

In order to identify a running process and bind it to the corresponding application [1], the process must be able to prove its identity to the trusted kernel using the application's secret key. The authentication is summarized in three generic steps. First, the kernel needs to send a random nonce to the application process. The process produces the hash-based message authentication code (HMAC) using the nonce and the secret key and returns the nonce back to the kernel. The kernel regenerates the HMAC and compares it to the value returned by the application.

Implementing the authentication protocol in kernel is not trivial. A technical challenge is how to support the secure communication between an application and the kernel in an efficient way. The first design choice is that the kernel directly accesses the application's key and verifies its identity provided that the key is stored in a predefined location. However, this method does not provide the security level that is needed in order to establish a strong identification. The location of the key can be either defined in memory or the file system. Defining the key in the memory imposes additional risk to stealing the key as well as causing complexity of maintaining the key location. The alternative design would be separating the key in a restricted key storage to be used by the kernel at the authentication time. This design choice is not adequate since it is not possible to securely bind a running process to the correct key file at runtime. Therefore, we use an authentication protocol that can be executed on a socket file between the process and the kernel. This method can be realized using a memory-based socket (or a shared memory region) such as the /proc file system [13]. The advantage of using the /proc file system is that it is conveniently accessible by kernel device drivers and is under the complete control of the kernel. More details on the implementation can be found in Section 3.

2.3.1 Token Generation Protocol

Our authentication protocol is used to generate identity

---

[1] A piece of executable code that runs in at least one stand-alone process.

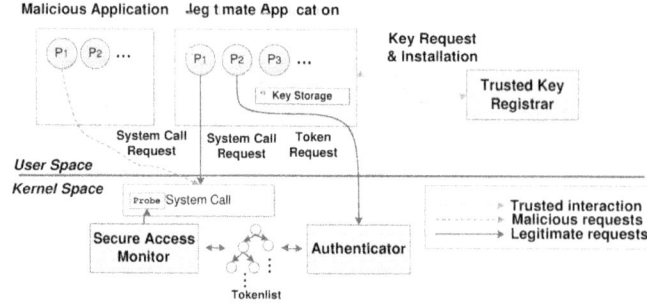

Figure 2: The access to selected system calls is monitored by A2. P_i denotes an application process.

tokens for legitimate applications. The identity tokens are later used to identify the processes when interacting with the kernel through the system calls. The identity tokens are needed since the authentication and verification of identity are separated in A2. That is, the authentication is only performed at the time of creating a new process. When the created process accesses a monitored system call, the identity verification takes places by searching for an identity token. Beside providing the needed security, the separation of authentication and identity verification improves the system call monitoring overhead (see Section 3.2).

Our token generation protocol (TGP) is used to authenticate individual processes based on the keys of the corresponding applications. TGP follows a standard challenge-response authentication protocol used in secure data communications over a network. We modify the standard protocol to include necessary kernel-side verifications as well as including token generation steps.

TGP is used to prove the identity of a process to the kernel. TGP must assure that no process can impersonate other processes using a replay attack provided that the application keys remains secret. Further, a registered application process must be able to successfully authenticate itself, if it was not previously authenticated. TGP also assures that no process can launch a denial of service attack on the kernel. Thus, we say that the identity of a process is proved if the process has a key with compliance to Definition 1 and successfully executes TGP such that a token is generated.

In the following, we formally define a *registered application*, an *identity token* and the *Authenticator*:

DEFINITION 2. *A registered application is a piece of executable code that runs in the form of one or more stand-alone processes and is issued a secret key by the kernel.*

DEFINITION 3. *An identity token is a tuple* (app, pid) *where* app *is the name of a registered application and* pid *is the kernel process ID of the process created by* app.

The identity token is unique and binds to a single process. It is valid until the termination of the process and is generated by the Authenticator but it is readable by the Secure Access Monitor.

DEFINITION 4. *The Authenticator is a kernel module that implements the token generation protocol and is responsible for creating and maintaining identity tokens for registered applications.*

Let A denote the Authenticator module and p be a user process where p.pid is p's process identification and p.app is p's application name. The function malicious(p) would log p as malicious and may take any necessary action depending on the security policies. Additionally, tgenerate(p) is a function to generate a token tk for the process p. Finally, arequest(p.app) is a function used by p to send an authentication request to A. The steps of TGP are as follows. In each step the actions of (if there is any) A and p are specified.

Token Generation Protocol:

1. p: Sends arequest(p.app) to A.

2. A: Receives and verifies the request:

   2.1 Verifies if the requesting application has a registered key. Otherwise, malicious(p).

   2.2 Verifies if p has already established a token. If so, malicious(p).

   2.3 A Limits the authentication requests in order to prohibit the applications to flood the kernel intentionally or due to an unintended software bug. Thus, A verifies if count(p) < limit(p). If the limit check was failed, malicious(p). Each application has a specified limit of simultaneous requests. This is set as part of A's verification policy.

   2.4 Generates a random nonce s and sends it to p. Additionally, A sets a timer t for the string to expire if there was no response from p. The time frame to expire t needs to be very short as this authentication is performed without networking inaccuracies. We only need the timer for the case that the process crashed or was killed and did not continue the authentication.

3. p: Generates the hash-based message authentication code (HMAC) $h = \mathrm{HMAC}(s, \text{p.pid}, k)$ (where k is p's secret key) and sends it to A.

4. A: If t has expired, the authentication request is discarded. If p is still executing, it will be terminated to prevent a race condition.

5. A: Computes $h' = \mathrm{HMAC}(s, \text{p.pid}, k)$. If $h = h'$, then tk = tgenerate(p). tk is valid until the termination of p. Otherwise, malicious(p).

6. A: Stores tk in a data structure tlist that is only readable by the verification module (i.e. SAM).

278

TGP prevents replay attacks since $h = \mathrm{HMAC}(s, \mathtt{p.pid}, k)$ may not be accepted if received from any process other than p. Denial of service attacks are also prevented since TGP limits the number of requests that may be received from a single process in Step 2.3. Further, code injection attacks are avoided in TGP. An attacker can write a malicious code to the shared memory socket. The code may be read either by p or A. However, since the communication between p and A has a definite length (either the length of the request, or the nonce or the HMAC), exploiting a buffer overflow is avoided by verifying the string length.

2.3.2 Tokens Storage

The tlist is a data structure that is maintained by the Authenticator. Authenticator can only allow read access to tlist to be used by a verification module inside the kernel. In systems with heavily use of various types of software (especially multi-process software), tlist may grow relatively large. It is not efficient to store the tlist in a sequential list. That is because, the tlist will be frequently searched for tokens at the time of system call monitoring by the verification module. Therefore, it is beneficial to make use of binary search trees, which on average reduce the time of searching to O(log n) where n is the number of tokens in the list. Binary search trees take longer time for the insert operation compared to a normal sequential list (O(log n) as opposed to O(1)). However, our insert operation is not as critical as the search since the insert is less frequent than the search. Linux kernel include an API for red-black trees [3] (a balanced binary search tree), that can be used for maintaining the tlist . Red-black trees are used for the organization of virtual memory but are available to other Linux kernel functions or modules. These trees provide a search as efficient as that of the binary search trees.

Using the tlist data structure to store the tokens is necessary to avoid modifying the stock Linux kernel. While the performance penalty is modest (see Section 3.2), it is possible to modify the kernel to store the tokens in the process control block. Using the latter design choice, both search and insertion time remain constant. We further discuss this in Section 3.

2.4 Application Key Registration

Prior to performing any authentication, it is necessary for the kernel to generate and register the secret keys for legitimate applications. In this section, we present the key registration and revocation steps.

The secret key must be registered by the kernel at the installation time and must be stored in the application's code. To protect the key from being stolen by static analysis of the executable code, A2 restricts read access to executable codes by any application. Further, the installed key is only associated with one installation instance and is not valid once the application is re-installed.

To register the key, we design a trusted key registrar that is used to register applications' keys in the kernel and the application. The trusted registrar exchanges the key information with the application in a secure system state. The trusted registrar itself is authenticated and identified through the TGP protocol with a special key installed manually. The steps taken by the trusted registrar are as follows:

1. The application is started for the first time and requests a key from the trusted registrar.

2. The trusted registrar verifies if the application was previously issued a key and if the application is designated legitimate either by the user or after an application certification process.

3. If verification passed, the trusted registrar generates k and sends it back to the application. Otherwise, the application is removed and reported as malicious.

4. The application accepts k and stores it in its executable code.

As depicted in Figure 1, the original identity of the application is determined as part of a binary classification and certification process. The purpose of this certification is to verify the legitimacy of the application at the first place. To allow the installation of the application, the trusted registrar decision is based on the user's permission as well the result of the certification process. If either give a negative answer, the trusted registrar would not issue a key for the application. Existing binary analysis and certification solutions such as BitBlaze [23] can be utilized for this purpose.

2.5 Verification of Identities

Our token generation protocol is used to securely authenticate running processes and generate identity tokens. These identity tokens are used by the Secure Access Monitor to validate application access rights at runtime and authorize the use of system calls accordingly. SAM's main functionality is to monitor designated system calls and verify the identity of processes for other cooperating kernel components such as a MAC system. The system call monitoring mechanism assists a MAC system to enforce its specified policies using the provided identity verification. Our monitoring mechanism is general enough to monitor any desired kernel function.

Our identity tokens are integrated with existing MAC systems. For instance, we modified AppArmor to make use of the identity tokens generated by the Authenticator and verified by SAM. Using the identity tokens, AppArmor can strongly bind a process to the application profile and enforce appropriate access rights. Further details on the integration of a MAC system with our framework are left for future work.

2.6 Security Analysis

In this section we present the properties of the A2 framework. We discuss in detail the security guarantees that are achieved using our identification model.

Strong application identities. Our presented application identification model is strong since it uses cryptographic keys that are kept secret and protected by the A2 framework. The secret key of an application is unforgeable as it is computationally hard for a malware to find the key. Moreover, the token generation protocol enables transparent and secure communication between applications and the kernels relying on the properties of the cryptographic hash functions.

Application isolation and access rights. In the A2 framework, we fully sandbox undesired processes. This sandboxing relies on the fact that malicious applications fail to authenticate to the kernel and thus are prevented from using most critical system calls. Moreover, such processes are exposed to the kernel when trying to interact with it without the presence of a valid token. This makes A2 a powerful tool to find malware that was dropped by other applications by various means such as through drive-by-download. Although a legitimate application such as a web browser may allow malware to be downloaded, A2 prevents the downloaded malicious code to reach its ultimate goal.

Key protection. Application binaries provide secure storages for application keys. To protect the secret key from being revealed to other applications, A2 restricts read access to registered application binaries. In principle, malware can also steal a key from application's memory at runtime, using a buffer overflow. However, as we restrict the activities of unidentified processes, such an attack cannot be achieved.

Scope of A2. A2 is capable of identifying interpreted programs running as stand-alone processes. For instance, a Java executable runs as a separate process named Java. In this case, the program can have a unique key and be registered in the installation time. Each program can authenticate itself independently using our framework. Other interpreted languages such as Adobe Action Script and Word document macros are out of the scope of our model.

Programs that are executed as part of other programs (for example using `execve`) are also identifiable using A2. In our model, a process does not inherit its access rights from its parent process or the application that was responsible for ordering the execution. For example, programs often run using a shell terminal. It is the responsibility of the process to perform the authentication and identify itself.

We further discuss a detailed analysis of our security model in our technical report [2].

3. PROTOTYPE

We realize a prototype of the A2 framework in the Linux Operating System (Debian 2.6.32). The two main components of A2 (Authenticator and SAM) are developed as kernel device drivers (modules). Due to limited space, the details on the implementation of the trusted registrar is left as a future work.

3.1 Implementation

The Authenticator module uses the Linux kernel Cryptographic API [6] to perform the HMAC operations using a number of supported hashing algorithms. The Authenticator communicates with the user space using the `/proc` file system, which is a memory-based file system controlled by the kernel. A protocol file is created by the Authenticator in the `/proc` file system and is made accessible to all running processes. The protocol remains secure since the communication is performed using the HMAC (Section 2.3.1).

SAM and the Authenticator communicate via a shared data structure in the memory that holds the valid tokens. This data structure is only visible to SAM and the Authenticator. To verify a process' identity, SAM searches through a list of valid tokens that are maintained by the Authenticator. We currently, implement the list of tokens as a sequential list. In our future implementations we are providing two options for storing the tokens. One is through the use of a red-black tree discussed in Section 2.3.2. Alternatively, Authenticator can store the token in the Process Control Block (PCB). The latter design would eliminate the search overhead but requires a modification to the kernel.

To avoid the need to modify the kernel, SAM uses the `kprobe` API to hook into system calls and monitor process activities. Although the probes introduce extra overhead, the produced overhead does not cause considerable latencies

to application's functionality, limited by an upper-bound of 3 times more overhead (see Section 3.2).

3.2 Performance Evaluation

The strong security guarantees provided by our A2 framework incur computational and management overhead in the operating system. In order to assess the efficiency of our framework, we answer the following questions in our experiments:

- What is the system call overhead caused by A2 as a result of verifying application's identity at the time of making system calls?
- How does A2 impact the overall system performance?

In our evaluation, we design a micro-benchmark to assess the system call overhead. In order to assess the overall system performance penalty due to A2, we use the lmbench micro-benchmark [19]. For our analysis we used a VirtualBox virtual machine (VM) with ubuntu 10.04 (32-bit) installed on it. We allowed the VM to use up to 1 GB of memory. At the time of our analysis a normal load of user programs were launched. In addition to answering the questions mentioned earlier, we experiment with two open-source keyloggers and our key stealer malware to test A2's functionality against undesired software.

To measure the overhead caused by SAM on handling the system calls we designed a set of programs to make extensive use of a collection of system calls. We let SAM to monitor a collection of seven system calls containing frequently used system calls such as `read` and less frequently used system calls such as `getpid`.

Each of our benchmarking programs are given a system call and a number of iteration. We set each program to make calls to the specified system calls for 150,000 iterations. The programs do not perform any other tasks. We measure the time spent in kernel for the system calls made by each program in three experimental settings. First, we measure the system without running any of our kernel modules. Next, we run A2 modules, without performing any verifications by SAM (i.e. searching the `tlist`). In the final experiment, SAM verifies the `tlist` with a total of 300 stored tokens. The results of our experiments are shown in Figure 3. On average, the system call overhead is 3 times more than the baseline latency.

Based on our experimental results, the major latency is caused by the installed `probes` in the kernel functions. That is because, the average extra latency caused by the verification of the `tlist` (that already contains a total of 300 tokens) is 29.03%.

We measured the overall system performance downgrade due to A2, in another set of three experiments. For these experiments, we used the lmbench micro-benchmark [19]. This benchmark provides performance analysis for various system functions such as networking and file system. We include the results for signal handler, pipe communications, UNIX socket transactions, process creation and termination using `fork` and `exit`, and process creation using `execve`. As shown in Figure 4, the extra latencies caused by A2 modules are not significant. On average, there is an increase of 26.76% in processing time and the maximum latency is for UNIX socket transactions for an overhead of 54.65%.

Our results show efficient system call performance without a significant penalty due to our monitoring architecture.

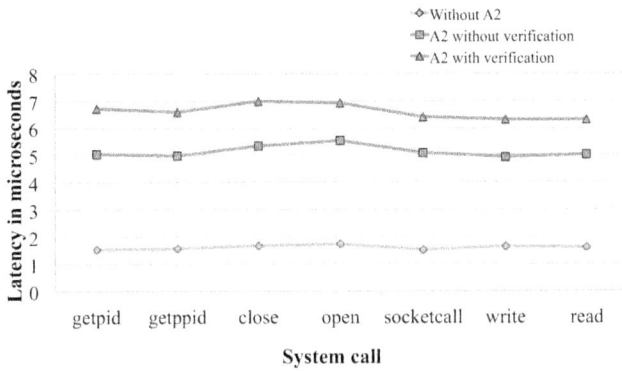

Figure 3: System call overhead measured in three experiments: No A2 modules running, A2 without any verification, and A2 running and performing verification on a list of 300 tokens.

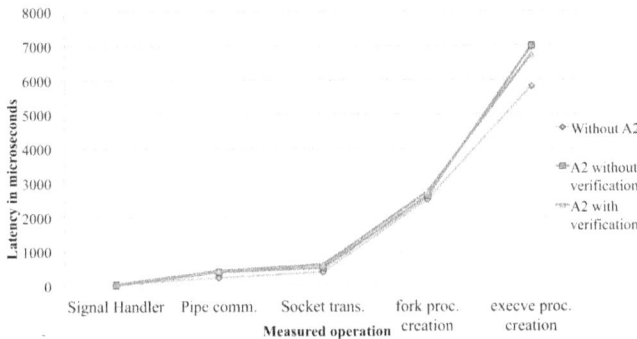

Figure 4: The latency caused by A2 modules for UNIX socket transactions and process creations.

While performing the experiments inside a virtual machine with limited resources, we did not notice the imposed latencies as end users. Moreover, the token generation protocol does not impose further performance penalties as it is not part of the monitoring process. This protocol is only executed once at the time of creation of a process and the generated identification token can be subsequently used in the system call monitoring process.

4. RELATED WORK

Techniques for protection against malware include the use of mandatory access control (MAC) systems, virtual machine monitors (VMM) to isolate untrusted software, application sandboxing, and a variety of other approaches such as hardware-based protection. In the following, we describe how A2 is related and compared to the mentioned approaches.

SELinux is a policy-based MAC system [17], which does not have a strong application identification mechanism that is independent of a particular user identity and does not rely on dynamic features such as a process ID. Grsecurity [1] is a policy specification platform similar to SELinux with a simplified specification language that suffers from the same identification problem. A more usable MAC solution is de-

scribed in [16]. A cryptographic-based MAC system is the authenticated system call work by Rajagopalan et al. [22], which is closed in spirit to our A2 framework. The presented work in the authenticated system call is limited to providing identities (the HMAC) to individual function calls to system calls in an application. Thus, it does not provide an identity to the application itself. Moreoever, Jaeger et al. did pioneering work in kernel-based control of program behaviors, including regulating downloaded executable content [10] and general-purpose policy enforcement through intercepting inter-process communication [9].

As described in Section 2, the identification model provided as part of the A2 framework is complementary to existing MAC-based solutions. We provide strong and secure identification of running processes, which is a critical step before proper application-level access rights can be enforced. A2 can integrate with application-level policy-based MAC systems as described in Section 2.5.

Isolation using virtual machine monitors and application sandboxing has been addressed in a number of projects. VMM-based solutions such as [15, 12] make use of VMM to provide high-assurance isolation and thus monitoring of untrusted software. We do not implement the components of A2 within a VMM to avoid the semantic gap introduced. This semantic gap prevents A2 from close monitoring of the process activities as well as proper identification of the processes. Nevertheless, A2 can also be integrated with VMM-based solutions to provide high assurance on the identity of processes within untrusted environments.

Application sandboxing solutions such as Vx32 [7], UserFS [14], and BLADE [18] are used to isolate undesired code from being executed to maintain integrity and confidentiality of the execution environment. The A2's identification mechanism enables strong and clear sandbox of undesired code that runs as stand-alone processes. Techniques similar to the ones described in the cited literature can be used to further automate the decision on legitimacy of executable code before the application registration step (Section 2.4).

Other approaches for protecting system resources against unauthorized applications include signature-based malware detection (proved to be ineffective against zero day attacks) [5], integrity preserving based on information flow such as PRIMA [11], and Trusted Platform Module [24]. These approaches provide valuable security solutions. However, our security model differs in providing provable identity to native applications.

5. CONCLUSIONS AND FUTURE WORK

We presented a novel identification model that provides strong and unforgeable application identities and binds the processes to their corresponding applications at runtime. Our identification model is combined with our system call monitoring architecture that verifies identities of the processes. This model resolves the problem of detecting the identity and the origins of running processes inside a kernel. In the A2 framework, malicious processes are completely isolated to prevent them from attacking other processes or achieving any attack goals.

Our evaluation results indicate the feasibility of using cryptography for the purpose of identifying running processes. We achieve this result by separating the authentication from the monitoring. Therefore, there is virtually no performance penalty due to the use of cryptographic functions.

6. REFERENCES

[1] grsecurity. http://www.grsecurity.net/.

[2] H. M. J. Almohri, D. Yao, and D. Kafura. Identifying native applications with high assurance. Technical Report, Department of Computer Science, Virginia Tech, 2011.

[3] D. P. Bovet and M. Cesati. *Understanding the linux kernel*. O'Reilly, 2006.

[4] J. A. Buchmann and J. A. Buchmann. Cryptographic Hash Functions. In S. Axler, F. W. Gehring, and K. A. Ribet, editors, *Introduction to Cryptography*, Undergraduate Texts in Mathematics, pages 235–248. Springer New York, 2004.

[5] M. Christodorescu, S. Jha, S. Seshia, D. Song, and R. Bryant. Semantics-aware malware detection. In *Proceedings of the 2005 IEEE Symposium on Security and Privacy*, pages 32–46, may 2005.

[6] J.-L. Cooke and D. Bryson. Strong cryptography in the Linux kernel. In *Proceedings of the 2003 Linux Symposium*, pages 139–144, 2003.

[7] B. Ford and R. Cox. Vx32: lightweight user-level sandboxing on the x86. In *Proceedings of the 2008 USENIX Annual Technical Conference*, pages 293–306, Berkeley, CA, USA, 2008. USENIX Association.

[8] Z. M. Hong Chen, Ninghui Li. Analyzing and comparing the protection quality of security enhanced operating systems. In *Proceedings of the 16th Annual Network & Distributed System Security Symposium*, 2009.

[9] T. Jaeger, J. Liedtke, and N. Islam. Operating system protection for fine-grained programs. In *Proceedings of the 7th USENIX Security Symposium*, 1998.

[10] T. Jaeger, A. D. Rubin, and A. Prakash. Building systems that flexibly control downloaded executable content. In *Proceedings of the 6th USENIX Security Symposium*, July 1996.

[11] T. Jaeger, R. Sailer, and U. Shankar. PRIMA: policy-reduced integrity measurement architecture. In *Proceedings of the 11th ACM symposium on Access control models and technologies*, SACMAT '06, pages 19–28, New York, NY, USA, 2006. ACM.

[12] X. Jiang, X. Wang, and D. Xu. Stealthy Malware Detection and Monitoring Through VMM-based "out-of-the-box" Semantic View Reconstruction. *ACM Transactions on Information Systems Security*, 13:12:1–12:28, March 2010.

[13] M. T. Jones. Access the Linux kernel using the /proc filesystem, 2006. *http://www.ibm.com/developerworks/linux/library/l-proc.html*.

[14] T. Kim and N. Zeldovich. Making Linux protection mechanisms egalitarian with UserFS. In *Proceedings of the 19th USENIX conference on Security*, pages 13–27, Berkeley, CA, USA, 2010. USENIX Association.

[15] B. Li, J. Li, T. Wo, C. Hu, and L. Zhong. A VMM-based system call interposition framework for program monitoring. In *Proceedings of the 16th IEEE International Conference on Parallel and Distributed Systems*, ICPADS '10, pages 706–711, Washington, DC, USA, 2010. IEEE Computer Society.

[16] N. Li, Z. Mao, and H. Chen. Usable mandatory integrity protection for operating systems. In *Proceedings of the 2007 IEEE Symposium on Security and Privacy*, pages 164–178, may 2007.

[17] P. Loscocco and S. Smalley. Integrating flexible support for security policies into the Linux operating system. In *Proceedings of the 2001 USENIX Annual Technical Conference*, Berkeley, CA, 2001. USENIX Association.

[18] L. Lu, V. Yegneswaran, P. Porras, and W. Lee. BLADE: an attack-agnostic approach for preventing drive-by malware infections. In *Proceedings of the 17th ACM conference on Computer and communications security*, CCS '10, pages 440–450, New York, NY, USA, 2010. ACM.

[19] L. McVoy and C. Staelin. lmbench: portable tools for performance analysis. In *Proceedings of the 1996 annual conference on USENIX Annual Technical Conference*, pages 23–23, Berkeley, CA, USA, 1996. USENIX Association.

[20] NIST. Announcing the advanced encryption standard (AES). Federal Information Processing Standards Publication 197, November 2006.

[21] C. Parampalli, R. Sekar, and R. Johnson. A practical mimicry attack against powerful system-call monitors. In *Proceedings of the 2008 ACM symposium on Information, computer and communications security*, ASIACCS '08, pages 156–167, New York, NY, USA, 2008. ACM.

[22] M. Rajagopalan, M. A. Hiltunen, T. Jim, and R. D. Schlichting. System call monitoring using authenticated system calls. *IEEE Transactions on Dependable and Secure Computing*, 3:216–229, July 2006.

[23] D. Song, D. Brumley, H. Yin, J. Caballero, I. Jager, M. G. Kang, Z. Liang, N. James, P. Poosankam, and P. Saxena. BitBlaze: A new approach to computer security via binary analysis. In *Proceedings of the 4th International Conference on Information Systems Security*, ICISS'08, pages 1–25, Berlin, Heidelberg, 2008. Springer-Verlag.

[24] D. Stefan, C. Wu, D. Yao, and G. Xu. Knowing where your input is from: Kernel-level provenance verification. In *Proceedings of the 8th International Conference on Applied Cryptography and Network Security (ACNS)*, pages 71–87. Springer-Verlag, 2010.

[25] T. Wobber, A. Yumerefendi, M. Abadi, A. Birrell, and D. R. Simon. Authorizing applications in singularity. In *Proceedings of the 2nd European Conference on Computer Systems*, EuroSys '07, pages 355–368, New York, NY, USA, 2007. ACM.

[26] C. Wright, C. Cowan, S. Smalley, J. Morris, and G. Kroah-Hartman. Linux security module framework. In *Proceedings of the 11th Ottawa Linux Symposium*, 2002.

An Information Theoretic Privacy and Utility Measure for Data Sanitization Mechanisms

Mina Askari, Reihaneh Safavi-Naini, Ken Barker
Department of Computer Science
University of Calgary, Calgary, Canada
{maskari, rei, kbarker}@ucalgary.ca

ABSTRACT

Data collection agencies publish sensitive data for legitimate purposes, such as research, marketing and *etc.*. Data publishing has attracted much interest in research community due to the important concerns over the protection of **individuals privacy**. As a result several sanitization mechanisms with different notions of privacy have been proposed. To be able to measure, set and compare the level of privacy protection, there is a need to translate these different mechanisms to a unified system. In this paper, we propose a novel information theoretic framework for representing a formal model of a mechanism as a noisy channel and evaluating its privacy and utility. We show that deterministic **publishing property** that is used in most of these mechanisms reduces the privacy guarantees and causes information to leak. The great effect of adversary's background knowledge on this metric is concluded. We also show that using this framework we can compute the sanitization mechanism's preserved utility from the point of view of a data user. By using the specifications of a popular sanitization mechanism, *k*-anonymity, we analytically provide a representation of this mechanism to be used for its evaluation.

Categories and Subject Descriptors

K.4.1 [**Computers and Society**]: Public Policy Issues— *Privacy*

General Terms

Security, Measurement

Keywords

Privacy, Utility, Sanitization Mechanism, Information Theory

1. INTRODUCTION

The explosive growth of collecting, storing and publishing of private information about individuals or organizations by government, statistical and business agencies, health networks and social networking systems together with public desire of receiving and analyzing these data, raises a significant concern for the privacy of individuals in the published datasets. The importance of this concern has expedited the emergence of several sanitization mechanisms to be used by data collectors who have collected personal data and want to publish them for new data users. A data sanitization system aims to transform original sensitive data so that the data are useful while the privacy is preserved. Usually a notion of privacy is attached to a sanitization mechanism based on the adversary's ability in identifying an individual in a published dataset (identity disclosure) [29] or disclosure of the users' sensitive information (attribute disclosure)[18][20] with or without adversary's access to some external data. Achieving privacy via sanitization comes at the cost of information loss and/or utility.

Although these metrics are useful within a sanitization mechanism, most of them are individual and data related that makes it hard to evaluate sanitization mechanisms and compare them in general. In addition, the adversarial models in the evaluations are often not appropriately formalized. A common approach in privacy literature to evaluate the effectiveness of any emerging or popular privacy preserving mechanism is to use some data examples and show that privacy issues such as inferring one individual's sensitive attribute, or change in the prior belief of an adversary about the sensitive attribute after observing the published data, still is remained. Theses ad hoc and scenario-based approaches cannot be used to evaluate any arbitrary sanitization mechanism or compare the results of the evaluation. To be able to measure, set and compare the level of privacy protection and utility of sanitization mechanisms, it is necessary to quantify the privacy and utility of such mechanisms within a unified and generic formal framework. In this paper, we propose an information theoretic framework for representing a formal model of a mechanism as a noisy channel and use it for evaluating privacy and utility of such mechanisms.

In our framework, a sanitization mechanism can be analogized to a noisy channel in which some information is sent by a sender over a communication channel to the receiver who tries to reconstruct the original information. The quality of this communication depends upon how accurately the receiver is able to recover the information (even in the presence of errors) from the transferred data. We consider a sanitization mechanism as an information theoretic channel and the inference of private information is regarded as a hypothesis-testing problem, whereas the adversary is analogous to the receiver who wants to reconstruct the original data after their transformation through the sanitization mechanism. Hence, the quality of the privacy provided by a sanitization mechanism depends on how unsuccessful the adversary is in reconstructing the input dataset. What makes a collected dataset valuable for analysis is the knowledge that exists in that dataset. We quantify the application-independent utility of a sanitization mechanism first by defining an information theoretic utility definition for any given dataset using joint statistical properties of that dataset. We then use this utility definition to measures the amount of utility degradation between any input and output dataset. The expected value of the utility degradation is used as a measure of utility for the mechanism. The associated expected degradation provides a measure of utility of the sanitized data, in the intuitive sense that low degradation approximately preserves the values of the original data, and their joint statistical properties. This is the first time that the utility of a mechanism is defined over all possible usage of a mechanism.

We include two different types of background knowledge for our evaluation. The first type is the amount of information an adversary has about original dataset that will affect the privacy measure. The ability of a given adversary in accurately guessing the original dataset depends on adversary's knowledge. We model this knowledge as a probability distribution over datasets. This type of background knowledge has been recognized in literature and we adapted it for our specific model. We also include the amount of information the data user already has about the dataset that will affect the utility of the released dataset for that specific user. To the best of our knowledge this is the first time that this type of background knowledge is considered for a utility metric. After representing the sanitization mechanism by a channel's matrix, based on this representation and background knowledge of the **adversary**, the privacy of the mechanism and based on this representation and the background knowledge of the **data user**, the utility of the mechanism are computed.

By using the proposed framework, we provide a formal representation of k-anonymity as a popular generalization-based sanitization mechanism to be used to evaluate its privacy and utility. In k-anonymity a set of *quasi-identifier* attributes are recognized [29]. Quasi-identifiers are attributes which can be combined and linked to external data to identify individuals. Then generalization, and/or suppression operations are applied on quasi-identifier values. We show that deterministic **publishing property** that is used in most of these mechanisms reduces the privacy guarantees and causes information to leak. We also show the utility that these mechanisms preserve in the published dataset from the point of view of a neutral data user is high for the mechanisms that output less distorted datasets with higher probability.

Contributions

To the best of our knowledge this is the first general analytical framework for measuring both privacy and utility of sanitization mechanisms using information theory, which includes representation of the datasets and sanitization mechanisms and modeling the adversary and user's background knowledge. The proposed framework is general enough to formally express different sanitization mechanisms in the literature and specific enough to include the details of each mechanism to compute the privacy and utility of them.

Our second main contribution is the representation of k-anonymity, a popular generalization method, as a channel matrix. Representation of k-anonymity as the sanitization method has the challenge of providing a realistic setting for this mechanism. We use a global-recoding full-domain approach to cover a wide range of algorithms. We chose global recoding algorithm since its low time complexity and high quality results make it more likely to be used in practice.

Paper organization

The rest of this paper is organized as follows. In next section we will describe how this work relates to existing literature and how it is distinct from previous work (Section 2). The description of our information theoretic model is provided in Section 3 where we define the representation of the datasets, modeling the sanitization mechanisms as noisy channels and representation of the adversary and data user's background knowledge. In Section 4, we then show in detail how to compute the privacy and utility of such models. In Section 5, a formal representation for k-anonymity as a popular sanitization mechanism with realistic settings is shown. Finally, Section 6 provides the conclusion and suggests multiple future directions and improvements to this work.

2. RELATED WORK

Ensuring privacy in data publishing, is a challenging problem, and has been studied extensively in the past [8][29][18]. A notion of privacy is attached to most of these sanitization mechanisms to show the effectiveness of these methods. Lambert [14] provides a formal description of the risk and harm of possible disclosures, and discusses how to evaluate a dataset in terms of these risks and harms. Dalenius [4] poses the problem of re-identification in sanitized census records and introduces the notion of *quasi-identifiers*. Sweeny [29] introduced a popular method in data publishing known as *k-anonymity*. Based on this definition, a table satisfies *k-anonymity* if every record in the table is indistinguishable from at least *k - 1* other records with respect to every set of quasi-identifier attributes. The *k-anonymity* property aims at protecting against *identity disclosure* (that the adversary could uniquely identify a **victim**'s record from the quasi-group), and does not guarantee protection against *attribute disclosure* (the adversary may not precisely identify the record of a victim, but could infer its sensitive values from the published data). This problem has been recognized by several authors [19][27] and the notion of ℓ-*diversity* [20] was developed to address this problem. Observing that when the overall distribution of a sensitive attribute is skewed diversity does not prevent attribute linkage attacks led Li *et al.* [18] to propose *t*-closeness in which the distribution of a sensitive attribute in any quasi-group should be close to the distribution of the attribute in the overall table and the distance between these distributions should be no more than a threshold *t*. Dwork [9][10] proposes a new model called ϵ-*differential* privacy that requires that the disclosure of any individual's privacy should not substantially (bounded by ϵ) increase as a result of participating in a statistical database. In this model, privacy disclosure is compared with and without the record owner's data in the dataset, while in previous works the comparison was between the prior probability and the posterior probability before and after accessing the dataset.

Achieving privacy via sanitization comes at the cost of losing information. For example, for the mentioned t-closeness, enforcing t-closeness would greatly degrade the data utility because it requires the distribution of sensitive values to be the same in all quasi-groups and this would significantly damage the correlation between quasi identifier and sensitive attributes. Information loss and utility metrics try to measure/keep the data quality of the sanitized data during or after the sanitization process. When the purpose of publishing data is unspecified, similarity between the original data and the anonymized data is considered as information loss and can be used during the sanitization process. For example, for k-anonymity, average size of equivalence classes [17] and discernibility [13] are two generic metrics which take equivalence class size into account to measure utility of a sanitized dataset.

To define more reliable utility measures in the context of data applications such as data mining and queries, other metrics such as information-gain-privacy-loss ratio [12] considering a specific mining task have been proposed. Since in most cases, the data publisher does not know how the published data will be analyzed by the recipient, using a utility metric that only targets some specific workloads, will result in a poor dataset for other purposes. Sramka *et al.*[28] developed a general data mining framework that considers the tradeoff between the privacy and utility measure not in the process of anonymization but after the sanitization process. The defined utility and privacy measures depend on dataset and sanitization mechanism and are independent of the data mining task that will be performed on the data. The proposed privacy and utility measures in our information theoretic framework are not tied to any specific sanitization mechanism or dataset. It is not a method to be used during the sanitization process, rather to model and evaluate the sanitization mechanisms based on their specifications.

Information-theoretic measures play a crucial role in sanitization mechanisms [6][7][22][18][11][1]. Reviewing the literature, however, we realize that most of the current information theoretic metrics are used during the sanitization process and are related to random perturbation techniques. In [6][7], for example, the privacy risk is measured as the mutual information between perturbed key attributes and sensitive attributes. The conditional entropy has also been used in this context. Chatzikokolakis *et al.*[2] considers randomized protocols for hiding private information as noisy channels in anonymous protocols. They use this model to define the degree of anonymity for an anonymity protocol. Sankar *et al.*[24] model the databases as a sequence of values. In this abstract universal database model, sanitization is a problem of mapping a set of database entries to a different set subject to specific utility and privacy requirements. Privacy requirements are specified using entropy, while utility requirements are expressed using rate-distortion theory. This method cannot be used to model the existing sanitization mechanisms in order to evaluate them, rather to show regions of privacy-utility tradeoff for databases.

3. PROBLEM MODELING

Given a **dataset** as an input, the objective of a sanitization mechanism is to release a modified (sanitized or anonymized) version of this dataset such that the released version does not allow an adversary to confidently derive the sensitive information of any individual (who is present in that table), and yet, the released dataset can be used to analyze the statistical patterns or other useful information in original dataset. To achieve this goal a sequence of specific operations (such as suppressing identifiers, noise addition or generalization) are done on data prior to publishing them. To be able to provide a general framework to evaluate the effectiveness of these mechanisms, in terms of privacy and utility, we aim to quantify the privacy and utility of such mechanisms within a unified and generic formal framework.

To develop our framework, we model sanitization mechanisms as noisy channels. In a noisy communication channel, there is a set of possible inputs $a \in A$ that are sent through the channel from the source (Figure 1). In these channels, for an input a that is sent to channel, several outputs $o \in O$ may be observed in destination (Figure 2). Suppose that $\mathbb{P}(a)$ is the probability distribution of inputs to a noisy communication channel. The conditional probability $\mathbb{P}(o|a)$ or **Channel's Matrix** is assigned to such noisy channels such that it gives the conditional probability of observing output o when a is the input (Figure 2).

At destination, observing an output o, the receiver should decide what input was sent to the destination. The quality of this communication depends upon how accurately the receiver is able to recover the information (even in the presence of errors) from the transferred data. Assume that function f is a guess function or decision function $f : O \rightarrow A$ that observing an output o, decides that input $f(o)$ was sent at the source. In a noisy channel, the goal is to compute the error probability of possible decision functions and compute an upper bound for such an error probability. The best strategy for the receiver is to apply the MAP (Maximum *A posteriori* Probability) criterion, which says that one should choose the input with the maximum conditional probability given the observation ($f(o) = a_1$ iff $\max_a \mathbb{P}(a|o) = \mathbb{P}(a_1|o)$).
Best decision function means that it results in the smallest probability of guessing the wrong hypothesis. The probability of error, in this case, is also called *Bayes risk*. When the distribution of input is known, error probability for a given noisy channel (with a channel's matrix assigned to it) is computable. The challenge in this area is to compute the maximum error probability for the MAP method, over all possible input distributions.

We consider a sanitization mechanism as an information theoretic channel and the inference of private information is regarded as a hypothesis-testing problem, whereas the adversary is analogous to the receiver who wants to reconstruct the original data after their transformation through the sanitization mechanism. We assume that **input is the dataset** (in the form of a table) to be kept hidden, the **output is the sanitized table** and the **matrix represents the conditional probability of having a sanitized table for different inputs**. If we consider a dataset (represented as a table T) as an input to such a model, we may observe one or several possible released tables (output) which are the anonymized versions of the dataset based on the characteristics of the sanitization mechanism. It is also possible that one or several input tables are sanitized to the same output table (source of privacy for a sanitization mechanism).

Having modeled a privacy protocol as an information channel (computing the channel's matrix), the privacy of the protocol is then measured as the expected value of guessing the

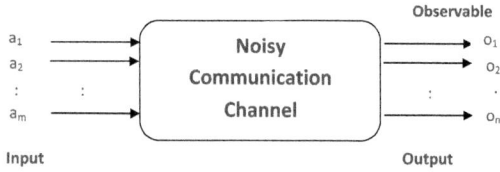

Figure 1: Noisy Channel Model

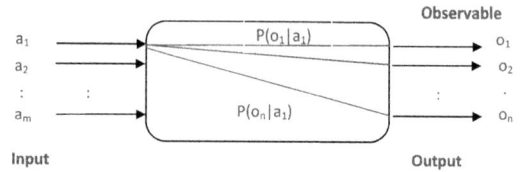

Figure 2: Channel's Matrix for Different Outputs

wrong input by the adversary using the MAP method. In subsection 4.1, we show how to compute probability of error.

3.1 Channel's Matrix

To compute the channel's matrix for a sanitization mechanism, we will first specify the input set T that contains all possible tables T_1 with r records and the set of outputs T' that contains all possible released tables T'_1 of size r. We assume that there is a conditional probability (channel's matrix) $\mathbb{P}(T'|T)$, that is derived based on the characteristics of the sanitization mechanism and represents the possibility of releasing table T' by sanitization mechanism if the input table is T. If the sanitization mechanism is known, then the channel's matrix can be derived. It is not unrealistic to assume that adversary is aware of sanitization mechanism as it has been shown before [31][30]. In Section 5, we will show that how we use the characteristics of k-anonymity to compute such channel's matrix and how we use the assumptions of the algorithm to compute the probability distribution $\mathbb{P}(T'|T)$.

3.2 Conditions of Attack

In previous works, the adversary is given a sanitized table T' generated from a **single** data table T, and the quasi identifier for some target individuals that their information are in the released table. The goal of the adversary is to either identify the targeted records in the table or know the sensitive attributes of the targets, or improve its knowledge regarding the sensitive attributes of the targets. The privacy metrics are usually defined over these two definitions and privacy violation is due to implicit dependencies between sensitive and non-sensitive attributes of T and T'. This attack model assumes a weak adversary that uses some auxiliary information (also referred to as background knowledge of the adversary) to do linking or inference attacks in order to get information about some individuals. In our attack model, however, the adversary's goal is to unsanitized the published table, given the characteristics of the sanitized table and the privacy of the sanitization mechanism is defined against such a strong adversary. The effects of an adversary knowledge about the sanitization mechanism on the privacy definition has been studied before [31], but this is the first time that the privacy definition is directly defined considering this attack model. It is important to mention that using our framework it is possible to model the weak adversaries, when we only include one column of the channel's matrix and by changing the probabilities on input datasets to remove the unrelated inputs.

3.2.1 Modeling Adversarial's Knowledge

Measuring the privacy in the presence of additional adversarial knowledge allows the data holders to give higher protection to the individuals in the dataset when they are releasing the data to the public.

Recent studies consider many cases in which the adversary may possess different information about the data; known as adversarial's knowledge. Martin *et al.*[21] modeled background knowledge in the form of conjunctions of k basic implications. Each basic implication is a rule specifying the implication relationship between two predicate about a person and his sensitive values. This work was extended by Chen *et al.*[3] in a scheme called privacy skyline that uses a triple (ℓ, k, m) to quantify the three types of knowledge:(1) ℓ sensitive values that target individual t does not have, (2) the sensitive values of k other individuals, and (3) m people who tend to have the same sensitive values. The type of background knowledge in these models are the knowledge about the sensitive attributes of specific individuals in the population and/or the table and/or partial knowledge about the distribution of some sensitive and non sensitive attributes in the population. The adversary can acquire this knowledge from either public datasets that considered to be safe for access (they only contain identifier attributes and no sensitive information) or from previously released anonymized data from the same organizations or other organizations. It can be demonstrated that giving the adversary more background knowledge will result in more disclosure.

In our framework we model the additional background knowledge of the adversary by a probability distribution over the inputs of the channel, *i.e.*, the probability distribution over the input set T. We postulate that adversary may possess different types of knowledge ranging from access to external datasets to some piece of information about the individuals' attributes in the original dataset and *etc.*, but the results of all can be modeled in a probability distribution over the possible original datasets. In subsection 4.1, to evaluate the privacy of the mechanism or the error probability of the adversary we first assume that the background knowledge of the adversary is zero. In other words, we assume that the probability distribution over all possible datasets is uniform. It means that the adversary has maximum uncertainty about the possible data inputs before observing the output. We will then extend our model to include the prior knowledge of the adversary in the form of a probability distribution on inputs. We will show how the privacy metric will change using this prior knowledge.

The other types of knowledge that usually assist the adversary to jeopardize the individual privacy are the knowledge about the mechanism used for data publication and the optimality goal of the mechanism [31][30]. Our model is in fact taking into account the initial background knowledge of adversary about sanitization mechanism that is modeled as the probability distribution $\mathbb{P}(T'|T)$ or channel's matrix.

3.2.2 Modeling User's Knowledge

In the proposed information theoretic utility for a dataset, we include the amount of information a data user already has about the dataset. The fact that the prior knowledge of adversary about a dataset can affect the level of privacy that a mechanism offers, has long been considered in different analysis. Similarly, we show that the utility that a mechanism offers, not only depends on the application of the released dataset, but also to the knowledge level of potential users of the released dataset. For example, the utility of a released dataset for two different users p in population Ω is different if one of the users has more information about the released dataset, *i.e.*, has the previous release of the dataset in form of joint probability distribution of some attributes. Measuring the utility in the presence of additional user knowledge allows the data holders to give a better utility to the data users when they are releasing the data to the public.

We model the background knowledge of the user as prior probability distribution on different attributes of the dataset and joint probability distribution of any subsets of attributes. Since we will use probability distribution of different attributes as well as the joint probability distribution of any subsets of them to define the utility of a dataset, we model the background knowledge of the data user by her prior knowledge about these distributions. In subsection 4.2, to evaluate the utility of a mechanism we first assume that the background knowledge of user is zero. This means that user's prior knowledge about these distributions are in form of uniform distribution. In subsection 4.2.4, we will extend our model to include the background knowledge of the data users in the utility.

Most of the time, the purpose of data release is not known at the time of publication. Although this model of user's background knowledge does not depend on any specific application for dataset, we can customize it for specific applications of dataset. For example, assume that the goal of releasing dataset is rule association data mining. For this specific application, the joint probability distribution between the targeted attributes in dataset is a good indication of user's background knowledge. If the data is published for modeling the classification of a target attribute in the table, then probability distribution of the attributes that are essential for discriminating the class labels in the target attribute form the background knowledge of the user for that specific purpose.

If the user's prior knowledge about these distributions are in the form of uniform distribution, then the user will get the maximum utility from the dataset. On the other hand, if the background knowledge of the user is close to the knowledge that exists in the dataset, the utility of the dataset for that user is negligible.

4. PRIVACY AND UTILITY

In this section we show how to use the channel's matrix model of the sanitization mechanism to compute its privacy and utility.

4.1 Measuring Privacy

We define the privacy of a sanitization mechanism as the error probability of a guess by an adversary. The attack model in this work is different from the model in which the goal of the adversary is to infer the sensitive information of some targeted individuals. Here, the adversary's goal is to find the whole table T_1 of size r that was released by observing the released table T_1'. For now, the success of adversary is defined as the probability of guessing the exact input. Later, we will extend this definition to decrease the error probability. That is, another table T_1'' is guessed by the adversary that is not the exact Table T_1, but is close to it by some definition.

To compute our privacy metric, we follow MAP (maximum *a posteriori* probability) method. Let T be a random variable that gets its value from the input set to sanitization mechanism containing all n possible tables of size r. The probability distribution $\mathbb{P}(T)$, is *a priori* probability for this random variable. Let T' be another random variable that gets its value from possible outputs of the sanitization mechanism containing m possible released tables of size r.

We assume that there is a conditional probability (channel's matrix) $\mathbb{P}(T'|T)$, that is derived based on the characteristics of the sanitization and represents the possibility of releasing a table $T_1' \in T'$ by sanitization if the input table is $T_1 \in T$. Having $\mathbb{P}(T)$ and $\mathbb{P}(T'|T)$, we derive a posteriori distribution $\mathbb{P}(T|T')$ over all possible values for random variables T and T'. We then apply the MAP to compute the probability of guessing the wrong hypothesis. That is:

$$\mathbb{P}(T'|T) = \begin{bmatrix} p(T_1'|T_1) & \cdots & p(T_{m-1}'|T_1) & p(T_m'|T_1) \\ p(T_1'|T_2) & \cdots & p(T_{m-1}'|T_2) & p(T_m'|T_2) \\ \vdots & \vdots & \vdots & \vdots \\ p(T_1'|T_{n-1}) & \cdots & p(T_{m-1}'|T_{n-1}) & p(T_m'|T_{n-1}) \\ p(T_1'|T_n) & \cdots & p(T_{m-1}'|T_n) & p(T_m'|T_n) \end{bmatrix},$$

Suppose that function $f : T' \to T$ is a guess function or decision function that by observing an output $T_1' \in T'$, gives the input $f(T_1') \in T$ to the adversary. Suppose that for each $T_1 \in T$, $E(T_1)$ is the set of outputs that observing them do not give us T_1 as the input by function f. That is,

$$E(T_1) = T' - f^{-1}(T_1). \tag{1}$$

Probability of error for function f when we have uniform distribution $\mathbb{P}(T) = \frac{1}{n}$ is defined:

$$
\begin{aligned}
Error_f &= \sum_T \frac{1}{n} \sum_{E(T)} \mathbb{P}(T'|T) \\
&= \sum_T \frac{1}{n} (1 - \sum_{f^{-1}(T)} \mathbb{P}(T'|T)) \\
&= \sum_T \frac{1}{n} - \sum_T \sum_{f^{-1}(T)} \frac{1}{n} \mathbb{P}(T'|T) \\
&= 1 - \sum_T \sum_{f^{-1}(T)} \mathbb{P}(T')\mathbb{P}(T|T')
\end{aligned}
\tag{2}
$$

Based on MAP, we assume that $f(T') = T_1$ iff $\max_T \mathbb{P}(T|T') = P(T_1|T')$. We then obtain that:

$$Error_f = 1 - \frac{1}{n} \sum_{T'} \max_T \mathbb{P}(T'|T) \tag{3}$$

Having computed the channel's matrix for the sanitization mechanism, it is easy to compute 3. The higher this error probability, the less successful is the adversary and the higher the privacy of the protocol. The advantage of this metric is that it gives a value between 0 and 1 that is comparable for all different sanitization mechanisms, no matter what operations have been performed on data to achieve that privacy.

The maximum value for $\sum_{T'} \max_T \mathbb{P}(T'|T)$ is m and it happens when there is a deterministic sanitization mechanism that any output T' is the sanitization of at least one input set T with probability of 1 and when there are $m \leq n$ possible outputs for this mechanism. The minimum value for $\sum_{T'} \max_T \mathbb{P}(T'|T)$ is 1 and it happens when the maximum probability of $\mathbb{P}(T'|T)$ is $1/m$ in all columns or all the rows are the same:

$$1 - \frac{m}{n} \leq Error_f = 1 - \frac{1}{n}\sum_{T'}\max_T \mathbb{P}(T'|T) \leq 1 - 1/n$$

When the number of inputs (n) increases or the number of possible outputs decreases, this error probability gets closer to 1. It is a correct conclusion as privacy increases in these cases.

4.1.1 Effect of Adversarial's Knowledge on the Privacy Metric

When we model the channel's matrix we consider the adversary's knowledge about the sanitization mechanism in use. We take into account the adversary's additional background knowledge using a probability distribution over the set of all possible database instances $\mathbb{P}(T)$. To include this probability distribution, we rewrite our privacy metric as follows.

$$
\begin{aligned}
Error_f &= \sum_T \mathbb{P}(T) \sum_{E(T)} \mathbb{P}(T'|T) \\
&= \sum_T \mathbb{P}(T)(1 - \sum_{f^{-1}(T)} \mathbb{P}(T'|T)) \\
&= \sum_T \mathbb{P}(T) - \sum_T \sum_{f^{-1}(T)} \mathbb{P}(T)\mathbb{P}(T'|T) \\
&= 1 - \sum_T \sum_{f^{-1}(T)} \mathbb{P}(T')\mathbb{P}(T|T')
\end{aligned}
\tag{4}
$$

Based on MAP, we assume that $f(T') = T_1$ iff $\max_T \mathbb{P}(T|T') = P(T_1|T')$. We then obtain that:

$$
\begin{aligned}
Error_f &= 1 - \sum_T \sum_{f^{-1}(T)} \mathbb{P}(T')\mathbb{P}(T|T') \\
&= 1 - \sum_{T'} \mathbb{P}(T')\max_T \mathbb{P}(T|T') \\
&= 1 - \sum_{T'} \max_T \mathbb{P}(T'|T)\mathbb{P}(T)
\end{aligned}
\tag{5}
$$

The defined $Error_f$ is related to $H(T|T')$ by the Santhi-Vardy bound [25] as follows:

$$Error_f(\mathbb{P}(T)) \leq 1 - 2^{-H(T|T')} \tag{6}$$

where the conditional entropy $H(T|T')$ is defined as

$$H(T|T') = \sum_{T'} \mathbb{P}(T')\sum_T \mathbb{P}(T|T') \log \mathbb{P}(T|T') \tag{7}$$

Since the defined privacy depends on probability distribution of the input set (adversarial's knowledge), the minimum

error (minimum privacy) that a mechanism offers over all possible distributions of input set happens when the adversary does the maximum knowledge. It is easy to show that for all sanitization mechanisms (no matter what the $\mathbb{P}(T'|T)$ is), when the $H(T)$ is zero the error probability of adversary and hence the privacy of the mechanism will become zero.

In summary, when adversary does not know the probability distribution of the inputs $\mathbb{P}(T)$ but knows the mechanism of release, then the error probability of the adversary will be computed as stated in equation 3. If the adversary has not have access to channel matrix ($\mathbb{P}(T'|T)$) and does not have the probability distribution over the input, then if there are n possible input tables, adversary will randomly pick one of these tables with probability $1/n$. In this case the error probability of the adversary or the success rate of picking the right table is $1 - 1/n$. Now assume that adversary has the probability distribution of the inputs $\mathbb{P}(T)$ but does not know the mechanism of release ($\mathbb{P}(T'|T)$) (uniformly distributed). In this case if adversary chooses the input with the highest probability, the error probability is $1 - \max_T \mathbb{P}(T)$. If we add the mechanism of release to the adversary's knowledge, such that it enables him to derive the conditional probability $\mathbb{P}(T'|T)$, then the error probability of the adversary will be computed as stated in equation 5.

4.2 Measuring Utility

The cost of performing the privacy operations on the original collected data in order to achieve privacy is the loss of some information that could have been useful for a third party.

In our work, we argue that data utility is a specific measure since it depends on the specific application and on a dataset. To show this, we will first define an application-independent utility metric for a dataset and then will explain how this utility measure can be customized to be specific to a dataset regarding an application. We also argue that data utility is a relative measure when we consider how much utility is preserved in the released data after sanitization with respect to the original data. To cover this relativity, we propose a distance metric to measure the utility remained in the dataset after sanitization in general and with respect to an application. We also argue that the utility of a sanitization mechanism not only depends on the utility difference between a pair of original and released dataset, but also on the average utility that will be kept for different possible datasets. We also include the user background knowledge in these definitions.

4.2.1 Utility of a dataset

To understand the utility of a dataset, it is important to highlight that the utility of a dataset is the direct result of the correlation between the attributes of the dataset. As the result, data distribution of a dataset is a good indicator of its usefulness. For example suppose that the probability distribution (i.e., frequency) of an attribute's values in a dataset is uniformly distributed. Then, the utility of that dataset is less than another dataset with non-uniform distribution for the same attribute, if the application of the dataset only considers this attribute. Higher entropy of the dataset indicates that the distribution contains more information, and lower entropy indicates that it has less [26]. However, when the application concerns the correlations between several attributes together, the probability distributions of all these

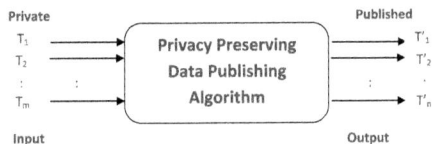

Figure 3: The Sanitization Mechanism as a Noisy Channel

attributes as well as their joint probability is important. The correlation between a subset of attributes may be independent of another subset of attributes and hence does not effect their utilities. For example, if the data is published for modeling the classification of a target attribute in the table, generalizing the values whose distributions are essential for discriminating the class labels in the target attribute will destroy the utility of it but generalizing other attributes may still keep the utility.

To define the utility of our dataset, we start with the utility of a single attribute $U(A_1)$ without considering the other attributes in the dataset and then extend it to the utility of multiple attributes:

$$U_1(A_1) = H_{max}(A_1) - H(A_1) \quad (8)$$

$H_{max}(A_1)$ or the maximum entropy of an attribute A_1 is $\log k$, where k is the number of values for attribute A_1 and it happens when A_1 has a uniform distribution. When there is a correlation between attribute A_1 with another attribute A_2, attribute A_2 can be use to reduce the uncertainty about it and to better predict the value of attribute A_1 . We use conditional entropy $H(A_1|A_2)$ (that can be computed using the joint entropy) to compute the utility of attribute A_1 as follows:

$$U_2(A_1) = H_{max}(A_1) - H(A_1|A_2) \quad (9)$$

Using this metric, we can justify why generalizing an attribute is considered a source of information loss. We can also relate the utility of a sensitive attribute to the metrics that in literature have been defined as privacy metric.

The increase of utility for attribute A_1 by using attribute A_2 or utility gain by using attribute A_2 is equal to

$$\begin{aligned} Utility_{gain} &= U_2(A_1) - U_1(A_1) \\ &= H(A_1) - H(A_1|A_2) = I(A_1; A_2) \end{aligned} \quad (10)$$

If we add another attribute A_3 in this utility measurement, the conditional entropy $H(A_1|A_2, A_3)$ can be used to compute the utility of attribute A_1:

$$U_3(A_1) = H_{max}(A_1) - H(A_1|A_2, A_3) \quad (11)$$

The increase of utility for attribute A_1 by using attributes A_2 and A_3 or utility gain by using attribute A_3 is equal to

$$\begin{aligned} Utility_{gain} &= U_3(A_1) - U_2(A_1) \\ &= H(A_1|A_2) - H(A_1|A_2, A_3) = I(A_1; A_3|A_2) \end{aligned}$$
$$(12)$$

We can similarly, compute the utility of a dataset, when the goal is to get knowledge about attribute A_1, considering the correlated attributes $A_2, A_3, \ldots, A_n$ as follows

$$U_{max}(A_1) = H_{max}(A_1) - H(A_1|A_2, A_3, \ldots, A_n) \quad (13)$$

Since the defined utility of an attribute is non-decreasing while considering all other attributes in the dataset, we call this the maximum utility of an attribute when all other attributes are used.

To compute the average utility of a dataset considering all possible usage of the dataset, we first compute the maximum utility for all attributes in the dataset, $U_{max}(A_1), U_{max}(A_2)$, ..., $U_{max}(A_n)$. We then assume that the data publisher has a priori distribution $\mathbb{P}(A)$ on the possibility of selection of attributes for an application and computes the average utility of a dataset over all possible applications. That is:

$$Utility_T = \Sigma_i \mathbb{P}(A_i) U_{max}(A_i) \quad (14)$$

4.2.2 Comparing the Utilities

In the previous section, we computed the utility of a dataset regardless of the fact that it is an original dataset or a sanitized one. Thus, the utility of a sanitized dataset can also be computed using the defined utility. For a dataset T and its sanitized version T', we define utility degradation as the reduction in quality of T when it is sanitized to T':

$$Utility_{Deg}(T, T') = Utility_T - Utility_{T'} \quad (15)$$

4.2.3 Utility Evaluation of a Sanitization Mechanism

Having the same data utility metric, we still have different utilities for different released tables by the same sanitization mechanism. To evaluate the utility performance of a mechanism regardless of its dataset inputs, we use the channel model as described before to compute the utility of a mechanism on average. This will allow us to compare the utility of different sanitization mechanisms. In the previous section, we quantified the average utility of a dataset and the average utility degradation of a dataset caused by applying a sanitization mechanism. We compute the utility degradation between all input and output datasets $Utility_{Deg}(T, T')$ and then obtain the expected value of the degradation to be used as a measure for utility comparison for the mechanism. The utility degradation is defined as:

$$Utility_G = \sum_T \mathbb{P}(T) \sum_{T'} Utility_{Deg}(T, T') \mathbb{P}(T'|T) \quad (16)$$

$Utility_{Deg}(T, T')$ is the utility degradation of an output table T', when the input table is T. $\mathbb{P}(T)$ is the probability distribution on the input table T and $\mathbb{P}(T'|T)$ is the probability of releasing T', when the input table is T.

The associated expected degradation provides a measure of utility loss of the perturbed datasets, in the intuitive sense that low degradation of a mechanism approximately preserves the values of the original data, and their joint statistical properties with respect to any other mechanism. This is the first time that the utility of a mechanism is defined over all possible usage of a mechanism.

We extend this metric in section 4.2.4 to include the previous knowledge of the user.

4.2.4 Effect of User Background Knowledge on the Utility Metric

To consider the user background knowledge in the utility metric, we assume that there is a population Ω of potential users of the released dataset. We model the background knowledge of the user as prior probability distribution on the different attributes of the dataset and joint probability distribution of any subsets of attributes. We then use the background knowledge of a user to define the background utility of that user for a dataset T with attributes $A_1, A_2, \ldots, A_n$ similar to what we did in equation 13. First the background utility of the user for an attribute A_1 is:

$$U_{Bg}^p(A_1) = H_{max}(A_1) - H'(A_1|A_2, A_3, \ldots, A_n) \quad (17)$$

The average background utility for a dataset considering background utility for all attributes in the dataset, $Umax_{A_1}$, $Umax_{A_2}, \ldots, Umax_{A_n}$ is computed as:

$$Utility_{Bg}^p(T) = \Sigma_i \mathbb{P}(A_i) U_{Bg}^p(A_i) \quad (18)$$

Where we assume that the same apriori distribution $\mathbb{P}(A)$ on the possibility of selection of attributes for an application.

When we consider the background utility, then the utility of a dataset T for a user p with background utility is given by:

$$Utility^p(T) = \Sigma_i \mathbb{P}(A_i)(U_{max}(A_i) - U_{Bg}^p(A_i)) \quad (19)$$

So far we have studied the influence of user's background knowledge on the utility of a dataset. Similarly, the effect of users background knowledge on the utility of a mechanism can be captured. Let $\mathbb{P}(p)$ be the probability of giving the released dataset to the user p in the population Ω, then

$$\begin{aligned}
Utiulity_G^\Omega &= \sum_{p \in \Omega} \mathbb{P}(p) Utility_G^p \\
&= \sum_{p \in \Omega} \mathbb{P}(p) \sum_T \mathbb{P}(T) \sum_{T'} Utility_{Deg}^p(T, T') \mathbb{P}(T'|T)
\end{aligned}$$
$$(20)$$

is the expected utility of a mechanism for population Ω. $Utility_{Deg}^p(T, T')$ is the utility degradation of an output table T', when the input table is T considering the background knowledge of user p for both datasets.

5. EVALUATION OF k-ANONYMITY

In this section we use our framework to represent a popular sanitization mechanism, i.e., k-anonymity [5][23] [29] as channel's matrix. This representation can be used in our defined framework to evaluate privacy and utility of this mechanism. To represent k-anonymity as a channel's matrix, we will first give the details of this mechanism that will lead us to define a representation for a dataset, a method to specify

the input set and output set of the mechanism and a way to compute the conditional probabilities. After computing these parameters, we are able to compute the privacy of the mechanism as described before.

5.1 Preliminaries and Assumptions

To enforce a specified privacy requirement on a dataset before being published based on a sanitization mechanism, a sequence of operations are applied on the dataset. Based on these operations the sanitization mechanism can be grouped in three general groups: (1) **generalization-based** methods that use generalization and suppression, (2) **anatomization** methods that use anatomization and permutation operations, and (3) **randomization** methods that use data perturbation operations such as adding noise, data swapping, and synthetic data generation. k-anonymity is an instance of a generalization method. To be able to represent a mechanism we need to know the details of it. Here we briefly review the basic definitions of a generalization-based sanitization mechanism in general and k-anonymity as a specific instance of these mechanisms.

A dataset to be released contains some **sensitive** attributes, **identifying** attributes, and *quasi-identifying* attributes. The values of quasi-identifying attributes can be used to uniquely identify at least a single individual in the dataset via linking attacks. In generalization-based mechanisms, the dataset is assumed to be in the form of a data table T and there is a domain associated with attributes of this table. Generalization and suppression are two operations that are used in these mechanisms that replace values of some attributes (usually are applied only to quasi identifiers, with sensitive attributes left intact), with less specific values. For example, ordered attributes such as "age" are partitioned into intervals, and categorical attributes are partitioned according to some domain or value generalization hierarchies (for example, cities are generalized to counties, counties to states, and states to regions). After theses operations, some subsets of tuples in dataset share the same values for quasi-identifiers. Every subset of tuples in dataset that share the same values for quasi-identifiers (and are indistinguishable from each other) is often referred to as an *equivalence class*. A released dataset is said to satisfy k-anonymity, if for each existing combination of quasi-identifier attribute values in the dataset, there are at least $k - 1$ other records in the database that contain such a combination.

The advantage of the generalization approach is that the released data is semantically consistent with the original data which means that it preserves the truthfulness of data. k-anonymity and most of its derivations follow this method for providing privacy. Because of its conceptual simplicity, k-anonymity has been widely discussed as a viable definition of privacy in data publishing. Also, due to algorithmic advances in creating k-anonymous versions of a dataset; k-anonymity has grown in popularity. For these reasons we also use it for evaluation using our framework.

There are different schemes in literature for generalizing one or several attributes such as **global recoding** in which if a value of an attribute is generalized, all its instances in the dataset are generalized to the same value or **local recoding** in which some instances of a value may remain ungeneralized while other instances may be generalized to different levels. For global recoding we have **full-domain** generalization[15][29] that generalizes all values in an attribute to the values of the same domain in domain generalization hierarchy and **subtree** generalization [16][13] generalizes all child values to the same value in a value generalization hierarchy. There are several methods to achieve k-anonymity. Among all possible ways of generalization, we will use the algorithm that uses global recoding, full-domain generalization in which a quasi-identifier is mapped to a generalized value at the same level of the hierarchy structure. We assume that there is no cell suppression and consider all possible generalizations by predefined generalization hierarchies.

5.2 Dataset Representation

We assume that the data table T follows the relational model. The relational model represents the dataset as a collection of relations, each one representing a collection of related data values. We consider a collected dataset as a single relational table T, containing non aggregate personal data. Based on this, we model the dataset of the data owner as a collection of n tuples $t_1, t_2, ..., t_n$ and m attributes $A = \{A_1, ..., A_m\}$. In a tuple $t = (a_1, ..., a_m) : D_1 \times ... \times D_m$, a_i represents the attribute value for A_i and D_i's denote the domain for attribute A_i.

If C is a subset of attributes: $C = \{C_1, C_2, \cdots, C_p\} \subseteq A$, for a tuple t, we use the notation $t[C]$ to denote the tuple $(t[C_1], ..., t[C_p])$, which is the projection of t onto the attributes in C.

5.3 Enumerating the Input Set (T)

To specify the input set T, we first assume that the number of tuples in each data table $T_1 \in T$ is r. For this, we assume that r also represents the number of tuples in the released table T' and can be specified by observing the output table T'. This is a valid assumption if we assume that the anonymization algorithm performs suppression by generalizing all the QI attributes to the last level.

To compute m, the size of input set T, assume that we have a table $T_1 \in T$ with r tuples and each tuple $t = (a_1, ..., a_p) \in T$ contains p attributes and a_i in tuple t presents the value for attribute A_i. Suppose that $|A_i|$ shows the size of the domain that the values of A_i are taken from.

Each row in this table can get $\prod_{i=1}^{p} |A_i|$ possible values. For r rows, there are

$$m = \binom{\prod_{i=1}^{p} |A_i| + r - 1}{r} = \frac{(\prod_{i=1}^{p} |A_i| + r - 1)!}{r!(\prod_{i=1}^{p} |A_i| - 1)!} \quad (21)$$

of ways of assigning values to the attributes. This number represents the size of input set T. It is easy to see that following this procedure, we can build the input set.

Example- Suppose that we have the released table which has 5 rows. From this we realize that $r = 5$. There are three attributes in the released table: Age, gender and disease. The disease attribute is a sensitive attribute and has not been generalized. It gets its value from domain $D = \{Cold, Heartattack, Diabetes\}$. Age and gender are QI attributes and have been generalized. The value and domain generalization hierarchy for these attributes are depicted in Fig 4 and 5:

For this example, where $p = 3$, so we will have $\prod_{i=1}^{3} |A_i| = 4 \times 2 \times 3 = 24$ possible values for each row. For 5 rows,

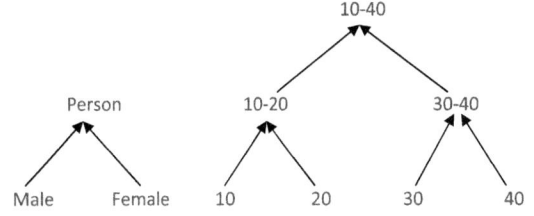

Figure 4: Value Generalization Hierarchy for Age and Gender Attributes

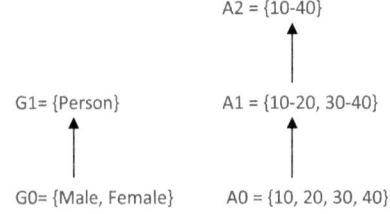

Figure 5: Domain Generalization Hierarchy for Age and Gender Attributes

there are $m = \binom{24+5-1}{5} = \frac{28!}{5!23!} = 98280$ of ways of assigning values to the attributes. This number represent $|T|$.

5.4 Enumerating the Output Set (T')

In generalization-based methods, the values in table T_1 are substituted with their generalized values according to a generalization hierarchy. The number of distinct values associated with each attribute is non-increasing in each level, so the substitution tends to map several values to the same result, thereby decreasing the number of distinct tuples in T. The number of possible outputs, *i.e.*, the size of T', depends on the generalization hierarchy that the anonymization algorithm is using and the generalization method. For example we consider full-domain generalization in our study. We assume that we have a table $T'_1 \in T'$ with r tuples and each tuple $t = (a_1, ..., a_p) \in T'$ contains p attributes and a_i in tuple t presents the value for attribute A_i. Suppose that $|A_i|$ shows the size of the domain that the values of A_i are taken from before generalization and $|DH_i|$ shows the height of generalization hierarchy for each attribute A_i.

The number of different generalizations of a table T, when generalization is enforced at the attribute level (full-domain generalization and single-domain), is equal to the number of different combinations of domains that the attributes in the table can assume. Given domain generalization hierarchies DH_i for attributes $A_i, i = 1, ..., p$; the number of generalizations, enforced at the attribute level, for table $T(A_1, ..., A_n)$ is computed as

$$N = \prod_{i=1}^{p} (|DH_i| + 1). \quad (22)$$

Given any of these generalizations such as $G_{l_1, l_2, ..., l_p}$ ($l_1 = 1 ... |DH_1| + 1, ... l_p = 1 ... |DH_p| + 1$) , we will now compute the possible ways of having a table with r rows and p attributes such that each attribute A_i gets its value from the level of l_i in the domain generalization hierarchy DH_i (suppose that $|l_i|$ shows the size of domain that the values of A_i are taken from in the level of l_i in the generalization).

Each row in this table can get $\prod_{i=1}^{p} |l_i|$ possible values. For r rows, there are

$$
n'_{l_1,l_2,\ldots,l_p} = \binom{\prod_{i=1}^{p} |l_i| + r - 1}{r}
$$
$$
= \frac{(\prod_{i=1}^{p} |l_i| + r - 1)!}{r!(\prod_{i=1}^{p} |l_i| - 1)!} \tag{23}
$$

of ways of assigning values to the attributes. Since we had $\prod_{i=1}^{p}(|DH_i| + 1)$ ways of generalization,

$$
n = \sum_{1,\ldots,1}^{|DH_1|+1,\ldots,|DH_p|+1} n'_{l_1,l_2,\ldots,l_p} \tag{24}
$$

will be the size of T'. It is easy to see that following this procedure, we can build the output set.

It is important to notice that not all of these computed output tables are k-anonymized. In fact we can reduce to the output tables that are k-anonymized:

First for any given generalization such as $G_{l_1,l_2,\ldots,l_p}$ ($l_1 = 1\ldots|DH_1| + 1, \ldots l_p = 1\ldots|DH_p| + 1$), we will compute all possible ways of having a table with r rows that are k-anonymized. Again we assume that each attribute A_i gets its value from the level of l_i in the domain generalization hierarchy DH_i and $|l_i|$ shows the size of domain that the values of A_i are taken from in the level of l_i in the generalization.

If we have r records, if the output satisfies k-anonymity, for any $k \leq r$, there would be $\lfloor \frac{r}{k} \rfloor \ldots 1$ quasi groups in the table. When we have $\lfloor \frac{r}{k} \rfloor$ quasi groups, then there will be $\binom{\prod_{i=1}^{p} |l_i|}{\lfloor \frac{r}{k} \rfloor}$ possible ways of having k-anonymized tables. Now assume that we have $\lfloor \frac{r}{k} \rfloor - 1$ quasi groups. In this case we will have $\lfloor \frac{r}{k} \rfloor - 1$ quasi groups with k records and we need to distribute additional k records in theses quasi groups, so we will have in total $\binom{\prod_{i=1}^{p} |l_i|}{\lfloor \frac{r}{k} \rfloor - 1}\binom{(\lfloor \frac{r}{k} \rfloor - 1)+k-1}{k}$ possible ways of having k-anonymized tables. Continuing this approach we will have $\binom{\prod_{i=1}^{p} |l_i|}{\lfloor \frac{r}{k} \rfloor - i}\binom{(\lfloor \frac{r}{k} \rfloor - i)+ik-1}{ik}$ k-anonymized tables with $\lfloor \frac{r}{k} \rfloor - i$ quasi groups.

The total k-anonymized tables that get their values from the generalization level $G_{l_1,l_2,\ldots,l_p}$ ($l_1 = 1\ldots|DH_1|+1, \ldots l_p = 1\ldots|DH_p| + 1$) is then computed as:

$$
n'_{l_1,l_2,\ldots,l_p} = \sum_{i=0}^{(\lfloor \frac{r}{k} \rfloor - 1)} \binom{\prod_{i=1}^{p} |l_i|}{\lfloor \frac{r}{k} \rfloor - i}\binom{(\lfloor \frac{r}{k} \rfloor - i)+ik-1}{ik} \tag{25}
$$

Since we had $\prod_{i=1}^{p}(|DH_i| + 1)$ ways of generalization, the

size of T' will be $n = \sum_{1,\ldots,1}^{|DH_1|+1,\ldots,|DH_p|+1} n'_{l_1,l_2,\ldots,l_p}$. It is easy to see that following this procedure, we can build the output set.

5.5 Computing the channel's matrix

After specifying the sets of input and output (T and T'), to compute the channel's matrix we first need to find the mapping between two sets and then compute the probability of this mapping.

To find the mapping between the input and output sets, we compute all possible inputs T that can be generalized to an output table T', for each generalized output T'. After determining the link between the input and output sets, for each (T, T') we will compute the probability of $\mathbb{P}(T'|T)$ in the following way:

We assume that for each input table T there are more than one possible outputs T', such that $\mathbb{P}(T'|T) > 0$. Suppose that for one row of the matrix, there are x possible outputs $T' \in DB'$, then $\mathbb{P}(T'|T) = \frac{1}{x}$. To see that the output table T' is the possible release of how many other input table T, any generalized value g_i of an attribute can be the generalization of ni values (all the leaf children of g_i in generalization hierarchy). For all the generalized values g_i in the table T', there are $\sum_{i=1}^{rp} n_i$ possible tables that will be the possible input.

6. CONCLUSIONS AND FUTURE WORK

We proposed the first general analytical framework for measuring both privacy and utility of sanitization mechanisms using information theory, which includes representation of the datasets and sanitization mechanisms and modeling the adversary and user's background knowledge. The proposed framework is general enough to formally express different sanitization mechanisms in the literature and specific enough to include the details of each mechanism to compute the privacy and utility of them. To use the proposed framework, we provided a formal representation of k-anonymity as a popular generalization-based sanitization mechanism as a channel's matrix.

We included two different types of background knowledge for our evaluation. The first type is the amount of information an adversary has about original dataset and about the privacy mechanism that will affect the privacy measure. We also included the amount of information the data user already has about the dataset that will affect the utility of the released dataset for that specific user.

The scope of our work is on non-interactive data publishing mechanisms, $i.e.$, the dataset is sanitized before publication and the whole sanitized dataset is published. For interactive data privacy mechanisms, either the dataset is sanitized and the queries are run on it, or the queries are run on the original database but query restriction-based methods are used to provide privacy. Our goal is to extend our proposed framework to be used for interactive sanitization mechanisms as well. In the future, we also plan to design an information theoretic-based sanitization mechanism that takes as the input a data user's current background knowledge about the data and its expected utility, the individuals expected privacy and the maximum level of adversary's current background knowledge about the data and generates a channel's matrix to be used to publish an input dataset.

7. REFERENCES

[1] D. Agrawal and C. C. Aggarwal. On the design and quantification of privacy preserving data mining algorithms. In *PODS*, 2001.

[2] K. Chatzikokolakis, C. Palamidessi, and P. Panangaden. On the bayes risk in information-hiding protocols. *J. Comput. Secur.*, 16(5):531–571, 2008.

[3] B.-C. Chen, K. LeFevre, and R. Ramakrishnan. Privacy skyline: privacy with multidimensional adversarial knowledge. In *VLDB '07: Proceedings of the 33rd international conference on Very large data bases*, pages 770–781. VLDB Endowment, 2007.

[4] T. Dalenius. Towards a methodology for statistical disclosure control. *Statistik Tidskrift*, 15:429–444, 1977.

[5] S. De Capitani di Vimercati and P. Samarati. k-Anonymity for protecting privacy. October 2006.

[6] J. Domingo-Ferrer, A. Oganian, and V. Torra. Information-theoretic disclosure risk measures in statistical disclosure control of tabular data. In *SSDBM*, pages 227–231, 2002.

[7] J. Domingo-Ferrer, F. Sebé, and J. Castellà-Roca. On the security of noise addition for privacy in statistical databases. In *Privacy in Statistical Databases*, pages 149–161, 2004.

[8] G. Duncan and D. Lambert. The risk of disclosure for microdata. *Journal of Business & Economic Statistics*, 7(2):207–17, April 1989.

[9] C. Dwork. Differential privacy. In *ICALP (2)*, pages 1–12, 2006.

[10] C. Dwork. Differential privacy: A survey of results. In *TAMC*, pages 1–19, 2008.

[11] A. V. Evfimievski, J. Gehrke, and R. Srikant. Limiting privacy breaches in privacy preserving data mining. In *PODS*, pages 211–222, 2003.

[12] B. C. M. Fung, K. Wang, and P. S. Yu. Top-down specialization for information and privacy preservation. In *ICDE*, pages 205–216, 2005.

[13] R. J. B. Jr. and R. Agrawal. Data privacy through optimal k-anonymization. In *ICDE*, pages 217–228, 2005.

[14] D. Lambert. Measures of disclosure risk and harm. *Journal of Official Statistics*, 9:313–331, 1993.

[15] K. LeFevre, R. Agrawal, V. Ercegovac, R. Ramakrishnan, Y. Xu, and D. J. DeWitt. Limiting disclosure in hippocratic databases. In *VLDB*, pages 108–119, 2004.

[16] K. LeFevre, D. J. DeWitt, and R. Ramakrishnan. Incognito: Efficient full-domain k-anonymity. In *SIGMOD Conference*, pages 49–60, 2005.

[17] K. LeFevre, D. J. DeWitt, and R. Ramakrishnan. Mondrian multidimensional k-anonymity. In *ICDE*, page 25, 2006.

[18] N. Li, T. Li, and S. Venkatasubramanian. t-closeness: Privacy beyond k-anonymity and l-diversity. *Data Engineering, 2007. ICDE 2007. IEEE 23rd International Conference on*, pages 106–115, April 2007.

[19] A. Machanavajjhala and J. Gehrke. On the efficiency of checking perfect privacy. In *PODS '06: Proceedings of the twenty-fifth ACM SIGMOD-SIGACT-SIGART symposium on Principles of database systems*, pages 163–172, New York, NY, USA, 2006. ACM.

[20] A. Machanavajjhala, D. Kifer, J. Gehrke, and M. Venkitasubramaniam. *l*-diversity: Privacy beyond *k*-anonymity. *TKDD*, 1(1), 2007.

[21] D. J. Martin, D. Kifer, A. Machanavajjhala, J. Gehrke, and J. Y. Halpern. Worst-case background knowledge for privacy-preserving data publishing. In *ICDE*, pages 126–135, 2007.

[22] D. Rebollo-Monedero, J. Forné, and J. Domingo-Ferrer. From t-closeness to pram and noise addition via information theory. In *Privacy in Statistical Databases*, pages 100–112, 2008.

[23] P. Samarati and L. Sweeney. Generalizing data to provide anonymity when disclosing information (abstract). In *PODS*, page 188, 1998.

[24] L. Sankar, S. R. Rajagopalan, and H. V. Poor. A theory of privacy and utility in databases. *CoRR*, abs/1102.3751, 2011.

[25] N. Santhi and A. Vardy. On an improvement over rényi's equivocation bound. *CoRR*, abs/cs/0608087, 2006.

[26] C. E. Shannon. A mathematical theory of communication. *The Bell System Technical Journal*, 27, 1948.

[27] A. Solanas, F. Sebé, and J. Domingo-Ferrer. Micro-aggregation-based heuristics for p-sensitive k-anonymity: one step beyond. In *PAIS*, pages 61–69, 2008.

[28] M. Sramka, R. Safavi-Naini, J. Denzinger, and M. Askari. A practice-oriented framework for measuring privacy and utility in data sanitization systems. In *EDBT/ICDT Workshops*, 2010.

[29] L. Sweeney. Achieving k-anonymity privacy protection using generalization and suppression. *International Journal on Uncertainty, Fuzziness and Knowledge-based Systems*, 10:2002, 2002.

[30] R. C.-W. Wong, A. W.-C. Fu, K. Wang, and J. Pei. Minimality attack in privacy preserving data publishing. In *VLDB*, pages 543–554, 2007.

[31] L. Zhang, S. Jajodia, and A. Brodsky. Information disclosure under realistic assumptions: privacy versus optimality. In *CCS '07: Proceedings of the 14th ACM conference on Computer and communications security*, pages 573–583, New York, NY, USA, 2007. ACM.

APPENDIX

A. EXAMPLE

Assume that we have computed the following channel's matrix for a given sanitization mechanism:

$p(T'\|T)$	T_1'	T_2'	T_3'	T_4'
T_1	5/17	2/17	0	10/17
T_2	0	20/35	5/35	10/35
T_3	15/28	5/28	3/28	5/28
T_4	5/20	8/20	0	7/20

Assume that the adversary's background knowledge is zero, *i.e.*, $P(T_1) = P(T_2) = P(T_3) = P(T_4) = 1/4$, then the privacy of this sanitization mechanism is computed as follows:

$$
\begin{aligned}
Error_f &= 1 - \sum_{T'} \max_T \mathbb{P}(T'|T)\mathbb{P}(T) \\
&= 1 - 1/4(15/28 + 20/35 + 5/35 + 10/17) \\
&= 1 - 0.46 = 0.54
\end{aligned}
\tag{26}
$$

However, if adversary has prior background knowledge of $P(T_1) = 1$ and $P(T_2) = P(T_3) = P(T_4) = 0$ about the input datasets the probability of error will become zero for the same sanitization mechanism. This example show the importance of adversary's background knowledge in privacy of a mechanism.

If the adversary did not know about the mechanism of release, he would randomly pick one of input tables with probability of 0.25 and error probability of 0.75. In fact this is similar to the case when the knowledge of adversary about the above mechanism can be modeled as:

$p(T'\|T)$	T_1'	T_2'	T_3'	T_4'
T_1	1/4	1/4	1/4	1/4
T_2	1/4	1/4	1/4	1/4
T_3	1/4	1/4	1/4	1/4
T_4	1/4	1/4	1/4	1/4

And the error probability is computed as:

$$
\begin{aligned}
Error_f &= 1 - \sum_{T'} \max_T \mathbb{P}(T'|T)\mathbb{P}(T) \\
&= 1 - 1/4(1/4 + 1/4 + 1/4 + 1/4) \\
&= 1 - 1/4 = 0.75
\end{aligned}
\tag{27}
$$

This means that for a non deterministic algorithm with the uniformly distributed channel's matrix the maximum privacy is achieved if the background knowledge of adversary is zero. For the same sanitization mechanism, if adversary has prior background knowledge of $P(T_1) = 1$ and $P(T_2) = P(T_3) = P(T_4) = 0$ about the input datasets, again the probability of error will become zero.

SWIPE: Eager Erasure of Sensitive Data in Large Scale Systems Software

Kalpana Gondi, Prithvi Bisht, Praveen Venkatachari[‡],
A. Prasad Sistla and V.N. Venkatakrishnan
Department of Computer Science, University of Illinois, Chicago, USA
{kgondi, pbisht, sistla, venkat}@cs.uic.edu, pvenka5@uic.edu[‡]

ABSTRACT

We describe SWIPE, an approach to reduce the life time of sensitive, memory resident data in large scale applications written in C. In contrast to prior approaches that used a delayed or lazy approach to the problem of erasing sensitive data, SWIPE uses a novel *eager erasure* approach that minimizes the risk of accidental sensitive data leakage. SWIPE achieves this by transforming a legacy C program to include additional instructions that erase sensitive data immediately after its intended use. SWIPE is guided by a highly-scalable static analysis technique that precisely identifies the locations to introduce erase instructions in the original program. The programs transformed using SWIPE enjoy several additional benefits: minimization of leaks that arise due to data dependencies; erasure of sensitive data with minimal developer guidance; and negligible performance overheads.

Categories and Subject Descriptors

D.4.6 [**Security and Protection**]: Verification; K.6.5 [**Security and Protection**]: Unauthorized access

General Terms

Languages, Security, Confidentiality, Verification

Keywords

Data Lifetime Minimization, Security, Static Analysis, Confidentiality

1. INTRODUCTION

The memory footprint of sensitive variables in software applications written in C is generally not ensured to be kept small. This state of practice results in the data being "left over" in memory long after its intended use in a program. The prolonged presence of sensitive data beyond its lifetime can lead to unauthorized disclosure.

Many security critical applications handle sensitive data such as passwords, credit-card numbers, social-security numbers, and various other forms of personally identifiable sensitive data. Most often the use of such sensitive data has a certain locality; its use is restricted to code that is confined to a certain small region of the program text. A typical example is an authentication routine in a trusted system program that handles sensitive data such as passwords. Sensitive data is typically not required beyond their intended use portion of the program (in this example, beyond the authentication step), and therefore can be erased to have a limited lifetime.

In developing system software, it is often the programmer's responsibility to ensure that sensitive data does not remain beyond its intended use. Unfortunately, only the most skilled application developers think about these issues, while many developers are simply unaware of these issues. This state of practice has led to prolonged sensitive data lifetimes opening the door to sensitive data disclosure attacks. As shown further (Section 2), there is a dire need to retrofit applications to minimize sensitive data lifetimes.

The problem is exacerbated in a type-unsafe language such as C. Due to the lack of memory safety, developers receive no assistance to protect data variables from exposures, resulting in leakage of sensitive data. An interesting SecurityFocus discussion [19] examined problems faced by developers in writing code that handles sensitive data in C programs. Chow et al., [13] performed a whole system simulation study with virtual machines to analyze the execution of several system applications such as browsers and authenticators that handle sensitive data. Using this study they demonstrated their claim that "*... applications take virtually no measure to limit the lifetime of sensitive data they handle... *".

The risks of sensitive data having an uncontrolled lifetime during the execution of a program are many fold. Such risks have implications not only during the lifetime of the program but even beyond that, sometimes even after an entire system shutdown. When resident in the memory space of the program long enough, sensitive information could leak through forensic examinations (or off-line attacks). For instance, offline examination of the swap space in disk can reveal passwords and other sensitive data, and it is not common for systems to have encrypted swap partitions. More recently, cold-boot attacks [21] have been demonstrated to be successful in recovering keys from memory long after a machine is powered down, by examining data resident in RAM even after a power recycle. Another source of offline leakage is from crash reports, as shown in [9] by demonstrating the presence of unmodified passphrases in the crash report (even when the cause of the crash itself was unrelated to sensitive data). In this case, sensitive information is available to a developer inspecting the crash report.

Prior Work Prior work in this area has been along several directions: residual data analysis in semiconductor devices [17, 18], use of memory management techniques such as garbage collection [8] and operating system / application-library level erasure methods [4, 26, 14]. The closest work is by Chow et al., [14], which augments the `free` library function with erase instructions. In general, pro-

```
 1    int  file_encrypt ( char *fname, char *userId ){        32        do {
 2       char key [255];                                       33            pass = getpasswd ();
 3       if ( getPrivateKey ( userId , key ) == 1 ){           34            char *epasswd = gethash( pass );
 4           int fd = open( fname, O_RDONLY );                 35            if ( strcmp( epasswd, shdwpwd ) != 0 ) {
 5           if ( fd == −1 ) exit ( 2 ); // error              36                attempts++;
 6           encrypt( fd, key );                               37            } else {
 7           // further processing 7−25 lines                 38                printf ( "Authentication  successful !" );
26       } else return −1;                                     39                getKeyfromDB( user, keyA );
27    } // end of file_encrypt                                 40                return 1;
28    int  getPrivateKey ( char *user, char *keyA ){           41            }
29       int attempts = 0; char *pass;                         42        } while( attempts < 3 );
30       char shdwpwd [255];                                   43        return 0; // end of getPrivateKey
31       readshdw( user , shdwpwd );                           44    }
```

Figure 1: Running example that illustrates the need for minimizing data lifetime. We are not showing `free` instructions for brevity.

grammers do not place `free` instructions to free the memory at the earliest possible program location i.e., they generally do not aim for minimizing the lifetime of unused data in the memory. As analyzed in Section 2, these approaches rely on a *deferred* or *pre-determined* location for erasing, introducing windows of instructions where sensitive data is present in the memory but no longer required by the program. Such exposures may lead to unauthorized data leakage.

Our Approach We propose a novel, *eager* strategy to aggressively reduce the lifetime of sensitive data items in legacy applications. More precisely, our technique aims to erase data in an eager fashion after completion of its intended use in the program. For the password example discussed earlier, once the password verification step is done, the use of our technique will result in immediate erasure of the user-supplied password, ideally as the very next instruction after the password checking step.

The underlying technique used in our approach is program transformation. Our approach transforms legacy applications by inserting erase (or scrub) instructions to clean-up sensitive data that is no longer required. This transformation is guided by a static analysis that precisely identifies the locations to which erase instructions are to be added. Our static-analysis approach includes a novel summary-based analysis technique that enables the approach to be highly scalable and efficient. Our approach has the benefit that it can handle a majority of information leaks due to data dependencies in the program. By statically introducing erases, our approach avoids high performance overheads typical of runtime techniques (such as taint tracking) that track and eliminate sensitive information at runtime.

We have implemented the approach in a tool called SWIPE, a source-to-source transformer that retrofits C programs to minimize the lifetime of data. Using SWIPE, we transform several commonly used open source desktop applications that handle sensitive data. Many of these programs do not attempt to minimize sensitive data lifetimes. We report our experiences in transforming these applications.

We finally note that our approach is conservative in its design. Specifically, if we are unable to correctly ascertain the "last use" points, we do not attempt to erase program data at these points, thus maintaining the original program semantics. Yet, our empirical results demonstrate that our approach is highly effective in erasing sensitive program data.

In summary, this paper makes the following contributions:

- A detailed security analysis of the threats due to *delayed* erasure of sensitive data.

- A novel, eager evaluation strategy for reducing data lifetime.

- A scalable static program analysis technique for identifying

erase points in a program, that includes a novel summary-based analysis.

- The implementation of a tool called SWIPE that implements the above approach and a discussion of implementation challenges.

- A comprehensive evaluation of some commonly used desktop applications along the dimensions of scalability, effectiveness of erasure and performance.

This paper is organized as follows: Section 2 presents a detailed analysis of the data lifetime reduction problem. Section 3 explains the approach used in the context of a simple imperative language that is modelled after the core constructs of the C language. Section 4 describes the key algorithms of our approach and key implementation challenges. We present an evaluation of SWIPE on many C programs that process sensitive data in Section 5. Section 6 presents related work and we conclude in Section 7.

2. PROBLEM ANALYSIS

In this section, we provide an analysis of the problem space by first highlighting some issues in minimizing sensitive data lifetime by the concept of exposure windows. We then use these concepts in an empirical analysis of a few applications that handle sensitive data. Our analysis highlights the prevalence of the problem.

Example We use a file encryption program shown in Figure 1 as a running example through out this paper. The `file_encrypt` function provides the functionality of encrypting the file (supplied as argument `fname`) with the private key of a user (identified by argument `userId`). The private key itself is obtained in the function `getPrivateKey` that first obtains and compares the user's password with the stored password. On successful authentication the function `getKeyfromDB` is invoked to retrieve the user's private key from a back-end database. The program makes three attempts to authenticate the user in a loop and aborts if the number of attempts exceed three. Lets consider a particular execution of this program in which the user supplies correct password in the second attempt and the program exits at line 5. In terms of the program's control flow, the loop at lines 32 - 42 executes twice, and the control exits on line 5. This control flow is shown as a linear trace in Figure 2, through which we will explain the concept of *exposure windows* in the program.

2.1 Exposure Windows

DEFINITION 1. *(Exposure Windows) In any given program P, for any object X, we coin the term exposure window as a sub-region of P that has access to X, when the value held in X is no longer required by P.*

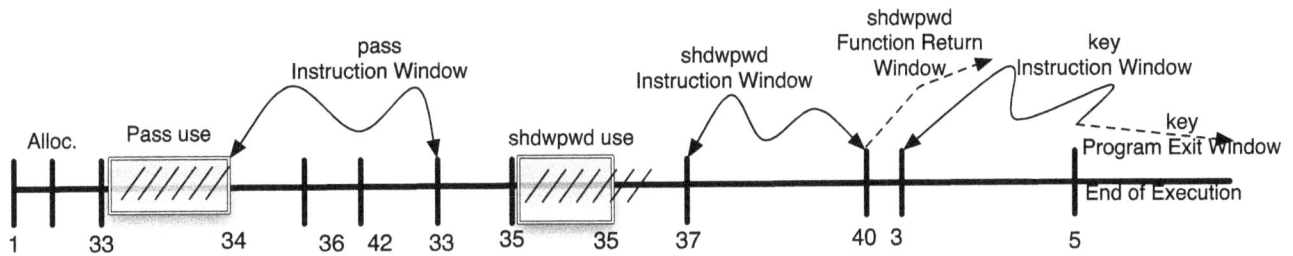

Figure 2: Windows of exposure for sensitive data

```
1    int  file_encrypt ( char *fname, char *userId ){
2       char key [255];
3       if ( getPrivateKey( userId , key ) == 1 ){
4           int fd = open( fname, O_RDONLY );
5           if ( fd == −1 ) {
5a              memset( key, 0, keySize );
5b              memset( userId, 0, userIdSize )
5c              memset( fname, 0, fnameSize );
5               exit ( 2 ); // error }
6           encrypt( fd, key );
7           // further processing 7−25 lines
18a         memset( fd, 0, intSize );
26      } else return −1;
27  } // end of file_encrypt
28  int getPrivateKey ( char *user, char *keyA ){
29      int attempts = 0; char *pass;
30      char shdwpwd [255];
31      readshdw( user, shdwpwd );
32      do {

33          pass = getpasswd ();
34          char *epasswd = gethash( pass );
34a         memset( pass, 0, passSize );
35          if ( strcmp( epasswd, shdwpwd ) != 0 ) {
35a             memset( epasswd, 0, epasswdSize );
36              attempts++;
37          } else {
37a             memset( shdwpwd, 0, 255 );
37b             memset( &attempts, 0, sizeOf( int ) );
37c             memset( epasswd, 0, epasswdSize );
38              printf ( " Authentication  successful !" );
39              getKeyfromDB( user, KeyA );
40              return 1;
41          }
42      } while( attempts < 3 );
42a     memset( shdwpwd, 0, 255 );
42b     memset( &attempts, 0, sizeOf( int ) );
43      return 0;
44  } // end of getPrivateKey
```

Figure 3: Transformed code of the running example from Figure 1. Newly added lines are highlighted with the gray color. The code for computing the size variables is not shown for brevity.

In the running example, consider the variable pass declared in line 29. This variable is initialized with the user supplied password in line 33 (through the method getpasswd) and subsequently used to compute the hash of the password in line 34. Subsequently, the data in pass is no longer required by the program but remains available in the rest of the function (lines 35 to 41 as shown in Figure 2).

We define three types of exposure windows as illustrated in Figure 2 and their implications for leakage of sensitive data.

1. Instruction Window This type of exposure window was explained above using the pass example. Basically, it arises from instructions in a program having access to data beyond its last use. A program crash in this window will yield a crash report containing sensitive data that if transmitted to a developer, will result in data leaks.

2. Function Return Window The local variables of a function that hold sensitive data, if not erased before returning from the function, create another type of exposure window that we term *function return window*. To illustrate this, consider the shdwpwd variable defined in line 31 of the function getPrivateKey. The sensitive data held in this variable is not erased at any of the two return statements (line 40 and line 43). Thus invocation of the function getPrivateKey leaves this sensitive data in the function stack. Since function returns do not by default clear the stack (As observed by us in several contemporary operating systems including Linux), subsequent function call records will have access to this data. Furthermore, if the program stack does not subsequently grow any larger after getPrivateKey was called, the sensitive data in shdwpwd will remain in the stack memory until the program exits.

3. Program Exit Window Similar to function return windows, another type of exposure window is created at program exit points that we call *program exit window*. Consider the exit instruction in line 5. As shown in Figure 2, content of the key variable remains in program memory even after the program exits. In contrast to function exit windows, this type of exposure window has implications *beyond* the program's execution lifetime. Sensitive data from programs, if not erased, remains in system memory pages and may become the target of forensic attacks (In Section 5.3.2 we demonstrate one such successful attack on OpenSSL).

An Empirical Analysis. We performed an empirical analysis to assess the prevalence of exposure windows in open source applications. For this purpose, we chose five widely used open source applications such as OpenSSL that handle sensitive data and analyzed their source code to measure exposure windows. We found a large number of instruction, function return and program exit exposure windows in all the five applications. As these popular applications fail to minimize the sensitive data lifetime, this analysis emphasized the clear need to reduce such exposure windows. Appendix B provides detailed results and methodology for this study.

3. OUR APPROACH

In this section we describe our high level approach for reducing extended data life time. A detailed treatment of algorithms developed to realize our approach is also provided (Section 3.3).

Transformed Running Example Our goal is to retrofit a given program's source code so that sensitive data lifetimes are minimized. Figure 3 illustrates the end result of transforming the running example (Figure 1) using our approach. Let us consider variables `key`, `userId`, `fname`, `fd`, `attempts`, `pass`, `shdwpwd` and `epasswd` as sensitive. The additional lines introduced (shown in gray) contain `memset` instructions to erase data objects.

We first note that the erase statement for `pass` is added at line 34a. Since `pass` is no longer required after the program computes the shadow password, the location at line 34a is the most precise location in source to erase this data item, addressing both the instruction window and the function return windows created by this piece of sensitive data. Another case is `epasswd`; the erase statements are introduced in a *path sensitive* manner, once at line 35a in the `then` branch of the conditional, and the other along the `else` branch at line 37c, closing both instruction windows. A third example is the erase of `fname` and `userId` introduced only before `exit(2)` at line 5, to address the program exit window. We do not erase them at other places in the example as the caller of the function `file_encrypt`, which is not shown in the running example, may continue to use those values.

3.1 Basic Idea

The transformation is performed based on the following idea.

> *In order to erase sensitive data precisely when they are no longer required by the program, our approach is to track and erase each sensitive data definition after its "last use".*

Notice that we make a distinction between the last use of a variable and the last use of a definition. A variable may be assigned many times in the program, and we do not attempt to find and erase the "last use" for the variable. Instead, we attempt to locate the "last use" for each definition of that variable, and erase after that use. Such a notion of "last use" is necessarily path sensitive, and there will be one such location along every control path of the program. (The notion of "last use" is formalized in Section 3.3.)

The intuition behind the approach can be explained as follows: typically, the use of definition is often restricted to a certain locality in the program. The lifetime of this definition is often much shorter and often can be estimated more precisely using static analysis. More importantly, analysis and erasure of definitions is better for security; a variable may have many uses in a program and may have large "idle times" between definitions. Any residual sensitive data that remains between definitions remains exposed, and our approach to erase definitions essentially closes this gap.

Our approach first identifies sensitive inputs to a program through a policy. By default this policy treats any data received through a standard C library input function as sensitive and can be overridden by the program developer to precisely identify sensitive inputs to the program. Our approach then employs standard information flow tracking techniques to track propagation of sensitive inputs in the program. Finally, it identifies last use points for each sensitive data definition and conservatively adds erase instructions. The following are two additional important benefits of our approach.

- *Secure factoring of data dependencies* Data dependencies in programs can often lead to sensitive residual data. For example, sensitive data may be propagated further in program's memory due to the effect of copying. Even if the original data is erased, this propagation will still leave residual data in memory. Since we capture all potentially sensitive definitions using information flow tracking, our approach offers the additional benefit of providing security factoring these data dependencies.

- *Usable without requiring specifications* In the absence of user annotations to identify sensitive inputs to a program, our system employs a default, conservative policy that still ensures the sound erasing of all sensitive data. Thus our approach can still be readily applied to the source code of any program by a user unfamiliar with the program's source code.

3.2 Overview

To realize the basic idea explained previously, we need to identify program locations where each definition of a sensitive input is *available but not required*. We employ the standard reachability analysis to identify program locations where a definition is available. We then partition the reachable program locations into two sets: `UsePoints` and `NoUse` (§3.3.2). All program locations that use a definition are in `UsePoints` set. Further, all program locations that have at least one successor in the `UsePoints` set are included in the `UsePoints` set. Intuitively, the `UsePoints` set contains all program locations that either use the definition or must retain the definition for subsequent use. Rest of the reachable program locations are in the `NoUse` set. Figure 4 depicts `UsePoints` and `NoUse` sets for the definition of `pass` at line 33 in running example given in Figure 1.

Interestingly, the identified `UsePoints` and `NoUse` sets provide us program locations, we call `ErasePoints`, where erase instructions must be added. Specifically, nodes in `NoUse` set that have predecessors in the `UsePoints` set are the `ErasePoints`. Intuitively, once control flows from `UsePoints` nodes to `NoUse` nodes for a definition, that definition will never be used again and essentially is available unnecessarily in each program location in the `NoUse` set. In Figure 4 for the definition of `pass` at line 33, the `ErasePoints` set includes line 35. As shown, an erase is introduced before line 35 (line 34a).

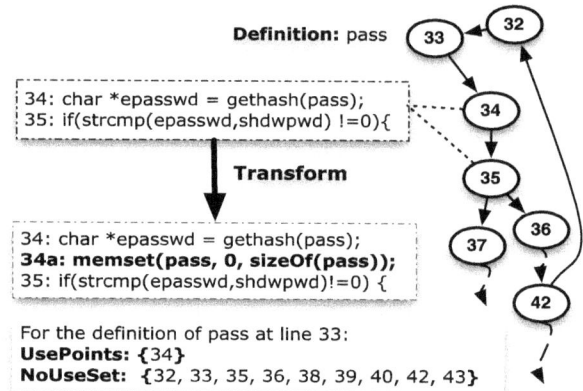

Figure 4: Illustration of `UsePoints` and `NoUse` sets and erase instruction for the definition of `pass` defined at line 33 (Erase is introduced after line 34).

Handling Aliasing The presence of aliases (pointers in C) require care in reachability computation described above. Specifically, aliases may extend or reduce the lifetime of certain definitions thus may impact correct computation of `UsePoints` sets and `ErasePoints`. Our approach incorporates an alias analysis to ensure correctness of reachability, `UsePoints` and `ErasePoints` computation. The results from our alias analysis are used conservatively: the *must aliases* (i.e., those that only point to one memory location) are used to identify definitions that can be erased, while the *may aliases* are used for computing the locations where data is used. Thus being conservative in computing both erase and use locations, we are able to achieve correctness of transformation. We provide more precise details of aliasing in Section 3.3.

Handling Procedure Calls The main challenge is to deal with the analysis of procedure calls to compute erase points. One straightforward way to deal with procedures is to inline procedure code and analyze the resulting program. However, this leads to a highly inefficient analysis that will not scale to large programs. We therefore develop a summary-based analysis (Section 3.3.3) that performs the analysis of a procedure *once* and reuses the results at every call site of the procedure.

3.3 Technical Description of the Approach

3.3.1 System Model and Terminology

Assumptions Similar to previous works on alias analysis [36, 7], we assume that the use of pointer arithmetic to shift through objects (array, scalar or structure types) is only within their allocated memory sizes. This assumption is needed by the alias analysis currently implemented in SWIPE [33, 5]. For those programs for which this assumption does not hold, bounds checking [22, 29] is needed to satisfy this assumption. We also assume that programs analyzed by SWIPE are single threaded, i.e., no concurrency.

$P ::= S$;	[PROGRAM]
$S ::= l$: *px := E	[ASSIGN1]
$\mid$ l: x := E	[ASSIGN2]
$\mid$ l: px := E	[ASSIGN3]
$\mid$ l: if E then S else S endif	[IF-ELSE]
$\mid$ l: while E do S done	[LOOP]
$\mid$ l: S ; S	[LIST]
$\mid$ l: exit	[EXIT]
$\mid$ l: return [x $\mid$ px]	[RETURN]
$E ::= c \mid x \mid \&x \mid *px \mid E$ bop E	
$\mid$ call f $(E, \dots, E)$	[EXPR]

Table 1: A small subset of C language

Terminology We consider programs in a subset of C whose grammar is given in Table 1. In this grammar, a statement is represented using S and each statement is prefixed with a label l that uniquely identifies its program location. We use the term base variable to denote a non-pointer variable that names a memory region. When memory allocation functions like `malloc` are invoked to assign memory to a pointer variable, SWIPE introduces a temporary variable as the base variable. SWIPE tracks only base variables and erases the data held by them. The variable x represents the base variable and px / py refer to pointer variables. The symbols & and * represent operators `address of` and `pointer dereference` in C language respectively.

A definition at a location l is an assignment statement consisting of base variable (or a dereference of its alias) on the left hand side of the assignment instruction. We also identify definitions generated by certain library function calls such as `strcpy` or through user annotations. We say that a definition at l is a *must definition* of a base variable x (i.e., *mustdefinition(x)*) if the left hand side of the assignment is either x or $*px$ where $*px$ aliases only x at location l. Each definition in the program is represented with a unique identifier id. Table 2 lists the set of notations used in the standard program analysis literature that we will use. These values are computed using slightly modified standard algorithms [5, 33].

3.3.2 Intra-Procedural Analysis

For each given function SWIPE computes a Control Flow Graph (CFG) that contains a node for each instruction in the function. For each *must definition* of some base variable x, denoted by id, SWIPE computes three sets of locations namely, UsePoints(id),

$A(v, l)$	Returns a set of variables aliased to variable v just before (in-aliases) and just after execution (out-
$A'(v, l)$	-aliases) of the statement at location l, respectively.
$preds(l)$	Returns a set of locations that represent immediate predecessors/successors of the program location l
$succs(l)$	in program's control flow graph.

Table 2: Standard terms used in SWIPE analysis

NoUse(id) and ErasePoints(id). UsePoints(id) denotes the set of locations where the definition denoted by id is used in statements at those locations. NoUse(id) is the set of locations where the definition denoted by id is available (or reachable) but not used. Effectively, NoUse(id) is the set of locations l such that, id is not used in l and is also not used on every control path from l until, and including the location l' such that $l' \in \{mustdefinition(x), exit, return\}$. Note that if $l \notin$ NoUse(id) then there is a location l', reachable from l, such that $l' \in$ UsePoints(id), i.e., the definition id is used at some location reachable from l.

ErasePoints(id) includes all those locations where the definition id can be erased immediately before those locations i.e., ErasePoints(id) is the set of locations l such that $l \in$ NoUse(id) and there exists an l' where $l' \in preds(l)$ and $l' \notin$ NoUse(id).

In the running example of Figure 1, variable pass receives a new definition *pass_d* at line 33 which is only used in line 34, so UsePoints(*pass_d*) = {34}, NoUse(*pass_d*) = {32, 33, 35, 36, 38, 39, 40, 42, 43} and ErasePoints(*pass_d*) = {35}, i.e., the transition point from UsePoints(*pass_d*) to NoUse(*pass_d*).

It is easy to see how ErasePoints(id) can be computed from UsePoints(id) and NoUse(id). Algorithms to compute NoUse(id) and UsePoints(id) are provided in Appendix A.

Alias Computation Exception We use the symbol $\perp$ to represent memory regions that cannot be named by a variable in the program. Such regions are generated when a `malloc` instruction at a given program location is executed more than once (in a `loop`). In such cases, the base variable corresponding to `malloc` denotes the latest memory allocation and all previously allocated memory is represented by the symbol $\perp$ (more discussion in Appendix A).

3.3.3 Inter-Procedural Analysis

Summary based approaches [3, 30] are used in the literature for inter-procedural pointer / alias analysis. Recent works such as [3, 30] generate summaries to capture the alias information purely for the purposes of analysis. In contrast, we employ the summary based approach for *transformation*. The main novelty of the technical approach developed here is to employ the summary-based approach to ensure that the instrumented code in a method is applicable for *all* calls to that method. To track and introduce erases for the data precisely, we build a summary-based approach with additional information that we describe in this section. Intuitively, the summary-based analysis computes the "net effect" of calling a function as a summary. In doing so, it factors in issues such as

1. new definitions introduced by the function,

2. changes to aliases in the calling function caused by updates to formal parameters in the called function,

3. whether it is safe to erase some formal parameters inside the function and

4. whether parameter values passed to the function are used inside it.

It is worth noting that traditional summary based analysis techniques usually consider only case 2 in the above list and not others. In the running example (Figure 1), after invoking the function

NewAllocVariables	Newly allocated memory variables inside called function which are accessible at call site.
NewDefinitions	New definitions that would propagate back to the caller. In Figure 1, after the call to `getpasswd` at line 33, `pass` points to a newly allocated variable. A new definition is also created (i.e., password).
AliasFunction	A function that captures changes to the alias relationship caused by the function. After the call to `gethash` at line 34 in Figure 1, `epasswd` becomes alias to newly allocated variable.
UsedIn	Denotes whether data passed to the function via the formal parameters is used inside. For `key` at line 6 in Figure 1, $\texttt{UsedIn}[2] = 1$, since `key` is used to encrypt the file.
UsedAfter	Denotes whether the definition held by a formal parameter is used after the function call in the caller. In Figure 1, if `key` is not used after the line 6, then $\texttt{UsedAfter}[2] = 0$.

Table 3: Summary captured by SWIPE

```
1   char * fun(int *f₁, int **f₂){        15   int *a₁, **a₂,*i₁;
2   int u = *f₁ + **f₂;                    16   a₁ = &x;
3   ...                                     17   ...
4   *f₂ = f₁;                               18   i₁ = &y;
5   char *l₃ = malloc(100);                 19   a₂ = &i₁;
6   if(u != 0) *f₁ = newData;               20   ...
7   ...                                     21   a₃ = fun(a₁,a₂);
8   return l₃; }                            22   int u = x;
```

Summary:
$$\texttt{NewAllocVariables} = \{malloc\_base_5\}$$
$$\texttt{AliasFunction}(*f_1) = \{**f_2', *f_1'\}$$
$$\texttt{AliasFunction}(**f_2) = \{\}$$
$$\texttt{AliasFunction}(malloc\_base_4) = \{*rp\}$$
$$\texttt{NewDefinitions} = \{Def\ for\ (*f_1')\}$$
$$\texttt{UsedIn} = [1,1], \texttt{UsedAfter} = [1,0]$$

Figure 5: (a) Function `fun()` (lines 1-8) (b) Calling context of `fun()` (lines 15-22) (c) Summary of `fun()`

`getPrivateKey` at line 3, the variable `key` would contain a new definition (case 1). Further, `key` passed to the function `encrypt` can be erased inside it provided that `key` is not used after the function call at line 6 (cases 3 and 4). Thus our detailed summary analysis readily facilitates eager erasure of sensitive data.

Once function summaries are available, our analysis computes the erase points and subsequently introduces erase instructions at these locations. For a given function f, SWIPE computes the summary of f into five components as shown in Table 3.

The component `AliasFunction` of the summary is obtained from aliases of variables at the return points inside the function. A Formal explanation of `AliasFunction` can be found in Appendix A. `UsedIn` ("used in") and `UsedAfter` ("used after") are m-bit vectors (where m is a natural number). $\texttt{UsedIn}[i] = 1$ if and only if i^{th} formal parameter is used inside the function, before being redefined. Similarly, $\texttt{UsedAfter}[i] = 1$ if and only if the ith actual parameter is used after some call site, before being redefined.

Note that the first four components of a function's summary are computed by analyzing the body of the function. The last component (`UsedAfter`) is contributed by call sites denoting whether an actual parameter is used after call sites. This "reverse feedback" from call sites is used to determine whether we could erase any formal parameters inside the functions. Use of an actual parameter after a call site would require that the corresponding formal parameter should not be erased inside the called function. If no such call site exists, we can erase the corresponding formal parameter inside the function.

Observe that in Figure 5(a), at the end of the execution of the function `fun`, $**f_2'$ [1] will be aliasing the same location as $*f_1$ at the beginning of the function. Similarly, memory location aliased by $**f_2$ before the execution of the function has no aliases at the end of function. This is reflected in the summary of the function $fun()$ given in 5(c). Also, observe that $malloc\_base_5$ is a newly allocated variable corresponding to $malloc()$ statement at line 5.

Applying Summaries At the call site l, the invocation of function f should capture all the changes to aliases and definitions. Using the `AliasFunction` component of the summary, the cor-

responding aliases are updated. Let $f_1, f_2, \ldots, f_m$ represent formal parameters of a function f and $a_1, a_2, \ldots, a_m$ represent actual parameters passed to function f from the call site at location l, i.e.,

$$l : p = f(a_1, a_2, \ldots, a_m);$$

At the call site, an actual parameter may alias other variables. For a variable y at the call site, let $act(y)$ denote the set of actual parameters, or their deferences that alias to y. Then the set $\texttt{AliasFunction}(f_i)$ represents new aliases for a formal parameter f_i after execution of the function call. Replacing a formal parameter by the corresponding actual parameter in this set provides new aliases of the actual parameter at the call site. For each variable y at the call site, updates to alias relations due to function execution are computed as below where m is the number of formal parameters.

$$A'(y,l) = \begin{Bmatrix} (A(y,l) - act(y)) \cup \\ \bigcup_{*^j a_i \in act(y)} \texttt{AliasFunction}(*^j f_i)[p/rp][a_k/f_k']_{k=1,\ldots,m} \end{Bmatrix}$$

Intuitively, the above expression replaces appearances of actual parameters in alias relations before the function call, with new values as returned by `AliasFunction`. The notations a_k/f_k and p/rp represent replacement of formal parameter f_k by actual parameter a_k and return pointer variable rp by the LHS pointer p at the call site.

In the example given in Figure 5, at the call site of function fun (line 21), the alias information changes as shown below.

Before call	$A(x,21) = \{*a_1\}, A(y,21) = \{*i_1, **a_2\},$ $A(i_1,21) = \{*a_2\}$
After fun call	$A(x,22) = \{*a_1, **a_2\},$ $A(y,22) = \{*i_1\}, A(a_1,22) = \{*a_2\}$ and $A(malloc\_base_4, 22) = \{*a_3\}$

Before calling the function, $act(x) = \{*a_1\}$, and $A(x,21) = \{*a_1\}$. After the call, aliases at the call site are computed as $A'(x,21) = \{\{*a_1\} - \{*a_1\}\} \cup \{*a_1, **a_2\}$ which is $A(x,22)$.

The value of `UsedAfter` is updated at each call site for each actual argument a_i. If $*^j a_i \in A(z,l)$ and the definition of z at program location l is used at some l' that is reachable from l, set $\texttt{UsedAfter}[i] = 1$. Essentially the above computation checks if definitions passed as parameters to invoked functions are being used after the call site. In Figure 5b, $*a_1$ is an alias to x and is not

---

[1] For each formal parameter we use f_i and f_i' to represent the value of parameter before and after the execution of the function respectively. Also, $*^j a_i$ means applying dereference operator $*$, j times.

redefined in all paths of the function `fun`. Thus the same definition may be available and is used at line 22, hence $\texttt{UsedAfter}[1] = 1$. However, the second argument a_2 is aliased to variable y. Also, y is not used at line 22 and later, hence $\texttt{UsedAfter}[2] = 0$. The `UsedAfter` values of $[1, 0]$ for function `fun` means that its first formal parameter cannot be erased within function `fun` but second can be erased as it is not used after the call site. Observe that for the function `fun` both parameters are used inside the function hence $\texttt{UsedIn} = [1, 1]$.

Soundness Soundness of our approach critically depends on the assumptions stated earlier and on the fact that we are erasing only *must definitions* and are using *may aliases* to compute `UsePoints`. Let P and P^T be original and transformed programs respectively. We say that, executions ρ of P and ρ' of P^T correspond to each other if ρ' executes the same sequence of statements as ρ executes (along with newly introduced erase instructions) and at every point l in ρ, the value of a variable, that is subsequently used in ρ, equals the value of the same variable at the corresponding point in ρ'. The soundness of our approach is stated by the following theorem.

THEOREM 1. *For every execution ρ of P there is a corresponding execution ρ' of P^T and vice versa.*[2]

4. IMPLEMENTATION

4.1 Implementation Overview & Algorithm

This section provides an overview of the implementation and presents the algorithm employed by SWIPE. The first and key requirement to generate all the required information described in Section 3 is to have the callgraph for an application to be transformed. SWIPE computes the callgraph of the application to process all the functions. The callgraph is traversed bottom-up to generate function summaries and use them at their invocation points. Also, bottom-up traversal of the callgraph is required to track the flow of sensitive data through formal parameters.

Once the call graph is generated, SWIPE uses a three step process as shown in Algorithm 1 to transform a given application. In the first step of the algorithm, SWIPE performs a bottom-up traversal of the callgraph to compute aliases, reaching definitions, reachability and other components of the summary of the function. SWIPE also sets `UsedAfter` values of invoked functions, using the information at the call sites in step one and two. The second step requires a top-down traversal of callgraph to track definitions that flow across functions through formal parameters. In the final step, SWIPE computes erase points for all the sensitive definitions in each function and introduces erases for the same.

4.2 Handling Special Cases

In this section, we discuss various challenges we have encountered while implementing SWIPE.

Dynamic Allocations: To erase dynamically allocated memory regions, their size information is required at erase points. SWIPE introduces unique temporary variables to hold the size information until erase points. (If a bounds checking approach is integrated with SWIPE, these variables will not be required.) To propagate the size information across function boundaries a size stack is used that mirrors function call stack i.e., for each entry in the function call stack it's size information is available in the size stack.

Global Variables: A global variable g which is an array is construed as an implicit parameter to every procedure. Otherwise, g is handled by introducing a temporary pointer variable pg (initialized

---

[2]Proof of the theorem is not provided due to space limitations.

Algorithm 1: SWIPE Implementation

Notation: f - Function
  n - Node in CFG of a function
  C - Called function
  id - unique identifier for a definition
  CG - callgraph

for *each f during bottom-up traversal of CG* **do**
  repeat
    update Aliases as in §3.3.2 and use `AliasFunction` of C to update Aliases in the presence of call to C;
  until *fixpoint*;
  repeat
    update Reaching Definitions as in §3.3.2 and in the presence of call to C use `NewDefinitions` of C to update them;
  until *fixpoint*;
  for *each definition id* **do**
    update reachability information;
    compute `UsePoints`(id);
    compute `NoUse`(id);
  update `UsedAfter` of each C called in f;
  compute `NewAllocVariables`, `NewDefinitions` `UsedIn` and `AliasFunction` of f as in §3.3.3;

for *each f during top-down traversal of CG* **do**
  update `UsedAfter` of each C called in f;

for *each f* **do**
  for *each definition id* **do**
    compute `ErasePoints`(id);
    introduce $Erase(id)$;

---

to point to g) which is considered as an implicit parameter to all functions. During the analysis, any references to g are considered as references to $*pg$. This way, we identify erase points for global variables in a manner similar to handling formal parameters to a function.

Arrays and Complex Data Structures: Standard alias analysis is not sufficient for arrays and complex data structures such as linked lists, to precisely erase data at its ideal lifetime. There are two techniques to tackle this problem:

1. A conservative approach where any reference to an element inside the data structure is considered as a reference to the entire data structure. Erases are introduced only after the use of all the elements. Thus this technique compromises precision to achieve soundness. This is employed by SWIPE.

2. Augment our approach with other sophisticated methods such as shape analysis [32] to reason about individual data items of complex data structures.

4.3 Policy Specification

In our approach, a policy dictates which data items are sensitive in a given program. This is desirable for cases where a developer who is familiar with the program can specify its sensitive variables. However, we do not expect all users of our tool to be developers, they could be system administrators who have a high-level knowledge of the tool but are not intimately familiar with the program source code. For this reason, we have also provided a default policy that is conservative. In our default policy, we treat all C library functions which take data from external sources such as user, network or file system as sensitive. This default policy may often be

Testsuite	# of files	# of tests taken	# of tests passed
gcc.c-torture	2076	20974	20974
compile	*811*	*5354*	*5354*
execute	*992*	*13912*	*13912*
unsorted	*273*	*1708*	*1708*
gcc.dg	2206	4068	4068
gcc.misc-tests	21	73	73
gcc.target	2	88	88
Total	4305	25203	25203

Table 4: GCC testsuite results for SWIPE

Application	C eLOC	CIL eLOC	Erase sens defs #eras	Erase sens defs %sz ovrhd
Bftpd	3348	62692	229	0.60
MySecureShell	4455	91817	109	0.36
SCP	18882	612672	196	0.28
SFTP	20835	632782	138	0.34
SSH	25619	722648	236	0.33
KeyRing	39230	1077533	59	0.40
GnuPg	68497	1006392	106	0.25
OpenSSL	137225	1085876	208	0.30

Table 5: Effect of SWIPE transformation on application sizes

used as a starting point for constructing actual policies by refinement.

Given the policy, we statically identify entry points for sensitive data in the program and then identify all definitions that may contain sensitive data because of propagation. This is done using a static dataflow analysis that merges results over paths, thus overapproximating the actual amount of sensitive data and thus is conservative. Being conservative here may add additional erase instructions for non-sensitive data but ensures that we do not miss erasing any sensitive data.

5. EVALUATION

Prototype Our tool SWIPE is implemented as a source-to-source transformer and uses the CIL framework [28] and consists of approximately 5K lines of OCaml code. The CIL framework has limitations in dealing with glibc, especially with code that is written using GNU C extensions. Our implementation therefore does not analyze library code. To ensure that our analysis is correct despite this limitation, SWIPE applies *over-approximated* summaries for functions whose sources are not being analyzed or available at the call site. The over-approximated summary makes all pointer variables used at the call site aliases to each other and assumes no new definitions because of invoked function. For a small number of cases (13), where this assumption did not hold, we used summaries generated through manual analysis.

5.1 Correctness

Our first experiment with SWIPE aims to ensure that the behavior of the transformed program is not altered through our transformation. For this purpose, we transformed the regression testsuite of GCC that is often used in testing of changes to the C code bases. This testsuite provides a large collection of tests that cover different aspects of the C language evaluating functionality and correctness of any program optimizations. Given the comprehensiveness of the GCC testsuite, it provided a rigorous empirical benchmark for testing the correctness of our approach.

The GCC testsuite is organized as directories. The GCC C-torture tests contain particular code fragments which have historically uncovered fragile program transformations. These tests are run with multiple optimization options. *gcc.c-torture/compile* directory contains test cases that should compile but do not need to link or run while the *gcc.c-torture/execute* directory contains test cases that should compile, link and run. The *gcc.dg* directory contains tests for specific features of the compiler while *gcc.misc-tests* contains tests that require special handling and the *gcc.target* contains architecture specific tests. For *gcc.target*, we chose only x86 specific tests.

Table 4 shows the split of the tests in the testsuite that were performed on CIL and SWIPE. From the collection of all GCC tests, we only chose those that passed successfully through CIL. It lists the number of files and the number of tests for each set of tests. The tests were run on a linux machine running Ubuntu 10.04 with GCC 4.3.3 and CIL 1.3.7. Out of 25203 tests performed on CIL across

4305 files, *programs transformed through* SWIPE *also passed all of them.* This experiment empirically demonstrates that our changes to the original program do not alter the original program semantics.

5.2 Scalability

Our next experiment is to check if SWIPE can scale to transform larger applications. We chose eight frequently used Linux applications of different sizes most of which handle sensitive information such as passwords, cryptographic keys, etc. We took three utilities from OpenSSH(5.6) - SFTP, SSH and SCP.

Size Overhead Table 5 presents the changes in size of applications because of our transformation. We used the RSM tool [1] to measure application codebase sizes in effective lines of code (eLOC). As shown in Table 5, CIL pre-processing of the original source code (column 2) led to significant increases in application source sizes (column 3). SWIPE transformation adds additional instructions as shown by erase instructions (column 4), and overall increase in the code size due to erase instructions (column 5). In all applications the size overhead due to SWIPE erase instructions was low (less than 1%).

5.3 Effectiveness in Erasing Data

5.3.1 Process Memory Snapshot Analysis

To assess effectiveness of SWIPE in erasing sensitive data, we analyzed runtime process memory of the original and the transformed applications. We used Gnu Debugger (GDB) to obtain backtraces and coredumps of running processes.

Our experiments were limited to single snapshots of the process memory. Some of the applications (SFTP, Bftpd) exited immediately after their execution and required artificial time delays to ensure that the program executed long enough to capture memory snapshots.

Other applications (OpenSSL, MySecureShell, GnuPg, SSH) were designed for manual termination through user interfaces and enabled us to attach to the running process after executing them with GDB. The processes were frozen at the point when the snapshot were taken. The backtraces provided valuable information on variable values whereas the coredumps gave us data not erased from the memory from the start of the program execution to that point.

We analyzed all backtraces and coredumps for the presence of known sensitive information and found that in many of the untransformed applications, sensitive data such as passwords, keys or file contents were present in the memory. Table 6 shows the occurrences of sensitive information found during analysis that was not being erased by original applications. The SWIPE transformed applications were then run through the same set of experiments and no traces of sensitive information were found in the memory.

An alternate technique called secure deallocation [14] which is close to our work, erases data at exit points, return instructions and augments free method calls with erase instructions. This tech-

Application	Sensitive Variable	In Original?	In Sec Dealloc?	In SWIPE?
Bftpd	password	Yes	Yes	No
MySecureShell	filename	Yes	Yes	No
	password	Yes	No	No
SFTP	hostname	Yes	Yes	No
	filename	Yes	Yes	No
SSH	hostname	Yes	Yes	No
	password	Yes	Yes	No
GnuPg	passphrase	Yes	Yes	No
OpenSSL	Key	Yes	No	No
	location	Yes	Yes	No

Table 6: Memory analysis for sensitive data

nique is simple to implement as there is no analysis required to retrofit the application. However, this technique will not be able to close instruction exposure windows. A program may spend more time in such instruction windows (because of loops or function calls) thus exposing the data for a longer duration. This is supported by our empirical analysis (Table 9 in Appendix B) which found significantly large instruction windows in the studied applications even without counting the effect of loops and any library calls. Closing such instruction windows will greatly mitigate the risks of sensitive data exposure. To perform a detailed comparison with the above method, we implemented the secure deallocation approach of [14], by transforming C applications using CIL for a comparison with our tool SWIPE. Table 6 also shows the occurrences of sensitive data in the memory snapshot of the applications transformed through secure deallocation approach. Note that in most applications, we noted presence of sensitive data in the secure deallocation approach that was absent in the SWIPE transformed application. For Bftpd and SFTP, there was no deallocation mechanism (such as free) for the data of interest. The program SSH still leaves a copy of user password in memory which is not being deallocated. In case of GnuPg, only one of the two occurrences of passphrase is erased by secure deallocation approach. Thus, the results from this experiment demonstrate that the secure deallocation is not completely effective in removing sensitive data from typical systems programs.

These experiments demonstrate that even popular applications fail to erase sensitive data from memory that, if leaked, can have serious implications. As observed earlier, SWIPE transformed applications did not leak any such information, thus demonstrating the security benefit provided by our transformation.

5.3.2 Cold Boot Attack

To underscore the importance of erasing data, we conducted an experiment to demonstrate how a malicious user can gain access to the sensitive data leaked in the memory. We used the approach devised by Halderman et. al [21] to perform the cold boot attack. In a cold boot attack, the attacker with physical access to a computer can retrieve encryption keys from a running operating system after using a cold reboot (typically by pressing and holding the power button until the machine switches off and then switching it back on) to restart the machine from an off-state. The attack exploits data remnant property of RAM, minutes after power is switched off. The application we chose for the demonstration was OpenSSL. The untransformed OpenSSL application was run on a Windows machine to generate a private-public key pair. Immediately after this, the machine was cold rebooted and the RAM snapshot was dumped into a USB memory stick using their tool [21]. This snapshot was then analyzed with Volatility (a memory forensic tool). We were able to confirm that the keys were indeed available. We performed the same experiment on the SWIPE transformed OpenSSL application by following the exact same steps. The subsequent RAM

Application	No. of C Files	No. of Funs	Call Depth	Call Sites	Xform Time (sec)
Bftpd	12	147	8	609	18
MySecureShell	26	189	9	1660	25
SCP	76	749	15	4775	120
SFTP	78	799	15	5577	133
SSH	84	906	24	7979	152
KeyRing	106	2589	15	12518	1544
GnuPg	140	1788	54	8224	498
OpenSSL	626	5669	33	53486	4109

Table 7: SWIPE transformation metrics

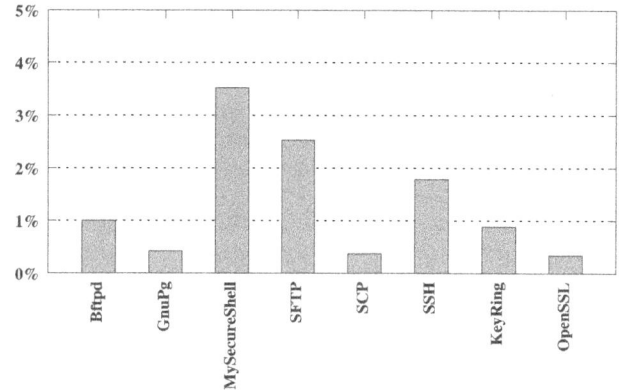

Figure 6: SWIPE performance overhead in percentage

snapshot obtained from the cold boot attack did not contain any keys. This demonstrates the effectiveness of our approach as a strong countermeasure against a very stealthy attack.

5.4 Performance

Transformation Time Table 7 depicts the time taken by SWIPE to transform applications. We also show the total number of files and functions SWIPE analyzed for each application. We can observe that the time taken for the analysis (transformation time) increases with the number of functions being analyzed.

We also compared the time taken to generate the compilation unit of an application with SWIPE and with an extended CFG that is described in Appendix B. As expected, the summarization based SWIPE implementation was able to handle larger programs in less time compared to the extended CFG (ECFG) implementation. One of the main reasons for this reduction is that performing fixed-point computation on large CFGs is costly. Further, in summarization based implementation each function body is analyzed only once (to generate summary), as opposed to the ECFG implementation where each function is analyzed once for each call site.

Runtime Overhead Figure 6 shows the runtime overhead of the transformed applications. Erasing sensitive data led to low overheads ranging from 0.34% to 3.5% and averaging 1.35%. We captured the overhead on a particular run for each application. Also, we disabled optimizations so that the optimizer does not remove instrumented instructions. In the presence of optimization flags, one could use compiler directives to retain erase instructions [2].

Improving Precision of Erases in Original Applications We further analyzed applications to assess SWIPE's precision in placing erase instructions. For this purpose, we identified applications that were already erasing some of their sensitive variables, and compared the placement of the programmer-introduced erase instruction and the SWIPE-introduced erase instruction. Table 8 lists application (column 1), analyzed variable (column 2) in the application, mechanism used to erase/free sensitive data (column 3) and SWIPE action (column 4).

Application - Variable	Original	SWIPE
SFTP- password	memset	memset (before 10 instr)
SSH- password	memset	memset (before 5 instr)
GnuPg- passphrase	free	memset (avg window 6)
OpenSSL- key	free	memset (avg window 10)
MySecureShell- password	free	memset (avg window > 10)
KeyRing-login_password	erases	No erase

Table 8: Erasing precision of SWIPE

This table shows that for five of the six analyzed applications, SWIPE was able to improve the precision by shortening the window of exposure. SWIPE identified locations before `free` calls to introduce erases (rows 4, 5 and 6). The KeyRing application (row 7) stored the identified sensitive data in a global variable, and could not be erased due to limitations in our current implementation.

For the programs that did erase sensitive information (rows 2 and 3), SWIPE improved precision by identifying an earlier point in the program to introduce erases, thus closing the exposure windows further. This is interesting because programmer introduced erase instructions are typically expected to be more precise than an automated tool such as ours. For example, the original SSH application erases sensitive password value. However, SWIPE identified erase point for `password` in a function (`ssh_put_password`) which is called prior to the original erase (`memset`) instruction. This experiment indicates that SWIPE can safeguard applications that fail to erase sensitive data as well as improve precision of the existing erases in applications.

6. RELATED WORK

Data Remanence The broad area of *data remanence* in systems development has been devoted to the problem of handling residual data in computer systems. This has been an important concern in secure operating system development and of MLS systems. Gutmann [17, 18] surveyed earlier work in this area, and specifically looked at the problem of secure deletion of information from magnetic disks [17] and semiconductor devices [18]. Our work of erasing data from legacy programs is complementary to these works which analyze issues related to erasing at the hardware level.

Memory Management It is possible to employ memory management methods such as garbage collection to address these issues. For instance, the Boer-Demers-Weiser [8] collector for C can be augmented with the task of erasing data i.e., erase data as and when the garbage collector is reclaiming the memory. This also requires no application instrumentation. However, the effectiveness of this approach is dependent on how frequently the garbage collector is scheduled to run. One can, in theory, invoke the garbage collector quite frequently to erase sensitive data but that would lead to very high performance overheads [20, 10].

Information Erasure Policies The property of secure data deletion has been studied formally by Chong and Myers [11]. In [12], the authors extend the Jif programming language with information erasure policies. In [11, 12], a developer explicitly specifies conditions under which data has to be erased whereas our approach automatically infers points of erasure through static analysis. The proposed framework in [11, 12] is suitable for developing new applications. In contrast, our approach can retrofit legacy applications with erase instructions.

Preventing Unauthorized Access There have been a number of works in operating systems to prevent unauthorized access or disclosure of sensitive data. Work related to DFIC operating systems [24, 35], Data Sandboxing [23], aim to minimize exposure of sensitive data by mitigating the effects of privilege escalation attacks on operating systems. TrustVisor [27] additionally provides data secrecy assurances for sensitive data by use of a micro-trusted platform module. Our work is focused on legacy operating systems implementation and the secure data erasure principles analyzed in this paper further minimize the risks in these systems.

Memory Safety of C Programs Another closely related line of work is memory safety of C programs. Most of these approaches have been based on program analysis and transformation. Approaches for memory safety for C programs [29] have contributed to research in the area but these approaches mostly rely on garbage collection for recollecting memory which is inherently unsuitable for our purpose. *Safe-C* [6] makes use of runtime checks to detect all memory errors. However, this approach introduces compatibility problems due to the use of fat pointers. Kelly [22] introduced techniques that stressed the importance of backwards compatibility in retrofitting programs.

Mapping Allocation Sites to Allocation Pools Work on managing memory to prevent security attacks is also related to our approach. Cling [4] is a memory allocator that aims to prevent use-after-free vulnerabilities by making use of address spaces. Automatic pool allocation [26] segregates heap memory into different pools for improving performance.

A number of approaches rely on static source code analysis to detect potential security-related memory errors prior to execution [15, 16, 34, 25, 31]. These are targeted towards many security problems with the C language but do not deal with the sensitive data residue issue.

7. CONCLUSION

The data lifetime reduction problem is a pressing issue for most security critical real world applications written in C. In this paper, we presented SWIPE, an automated approach and tool for reducing lifetime of sensitive variables. Our approach and tool employs static analysis for tracking information and automatically transforms the program with instructions that erase all the sensitive data after intended use. The effectiveness of SWIPE was demonstrated through a comprehensive evaluation over a set of real world C programs that handle sensitive information such as passwords and keys. SWIPE provides support for programmers and system administrators to retrofit software in order to minimize the memory footprint of sensitive information.

8. ACKNOWLEDGEMENTS

This work was partially supported by National Science Foundation grants CNS-0845894, DGE-1069311, CNS-1065537, CNS-1141863 CNS-1035914, CCF-0916438 and CNS-0917229. We thank anonymous referees for their feedback.

9. REFERENCES

[1] Resouce Standard Metrics. http://msquaredtechnologies.com.

[2] StackOverflow. http://stackoverflow.com/questions.

[3] AIKEN, A., BUGRARA, S., DILLIG, I., DILLIG, T., HACKETT, B., AND HAWKINS, P. An Overview of the Saturn Project. In *Program Analysis for Software Tools and Engineering* (San Diego, CA, 2007).

[4] AKRITIDIS, P. Cling: A Memory Allocator to Mitigate Dangling Pointers. In *USENIX Security Symposium* (Washington, DC, 2010).

[5] ANDERSENM, L. O. Program Analysis and Specialization for the C Programming Language. Tech. rep., 1994.

[6] AUSTIN, T. M., BREACH, S. E., AND SOHI, G. S. Efficient Detection of All Pointer and Array Access Errors. In

Programming Language Design and Implementation (Orlando, FL, 1994).

[7] AVOTS, D., DALTON, M., LIVSHITS, V. B., AND LAM, M. S. Improving Software Security with a C Pointer Analysis. In *International conference on Software engineering* (St. Louis, MO, 2005).

[8] BOEHM, H.-J. A Garbage Collector for C and C++. http://www.hpl.hp.com/personal/Hans_Boehm/gc, 2002.

[9] BROADWELL, P., HARREN, M., AND SASTRY, N. Scrash: A System for Generating Secure Crash Information. In *USENIX Security Symposium* (Washington, DC, 2003).

[10] CHEREM, S., AND RUGINA, R. Uniqueness Inference for Compile-time Object Deallocation. In *International Symposium on Memory Management* (Montreal, Quebec, Canada, 2007).

[11] CHONG, S., AND MYERS, A. C. Language-Based Information Erasure. In *Computer Security Foundations Workshop* (Aix-en-Provence, France, 2005).

[12] CHONG, S., AND MYERS, A. C. End-to-End Enforcement of Erasure and Declassification. In *Computer Security Foundations Symposium* (Pittsburgh, PA, 2008).

[13] CHOW, J., PFAFF, B., GARFINKEL, T., CHRISTOPHER, K., AND ROSENBLUM, M. Understanding Data Lifetime via Whole System Simulation. In *USENIX Security Symposium* (San Diego, CA, 2004).

[14] CHOW, J., PFAFF, B., GARFINKEL, T., AND ROSENBLUM, M. Shredding Your Garbage: Reducing Data Lifetime through Secure Deallocation. In *USENIX Security Symposium* (Baltimore, MD, 2005).

[15] DOR, N., RODEH, M., AND SAGIV, M. CSSV: Towards a Realistic Tool for Statically Detecting All Buffer Overflows in C. In *Programming Language Design and Implementation* (San Diego, CA, 2003).

[16] GANAPATHY, V., JHA, S., CHANDLER, D., MELSKI, D., AND VITEK, D. Buffer Overrun Detection using Linear Programming and Static Analysis. In *Computer and Communications Security* (Washington D.C., 2003).

[17] GUTMANN, P. Secure Deletion of Data from Magnetic and Solid-state Memory. In *USENIX Security Symposium* (San Jose, California, 1996).

[18] GUTMANN, P. Data Remanence in Semiconductor Devices. In *USENIX Security Symposium* (Washington, DC, 2001).

[19] GUTTMAN, P. Software Leaves Encryption Keys, Passwords Lying around in Memory. Security Focus Vuln Dev Mailing List, 2002.

[20] GUYER, S. Z., MCKINLEY, K. S., AND FRAMPTON, D. Free-Me: A Static Analysis for Automatic Individual Object Reclamation. In *Programming Language Design and Implementation* (Ottawa, Ontario, Canada, 2006).

[21] HALDERMAN, J. A., SCHOEN, S. D., HENINGER, N., CLARKSON, W., PAUL, W., CALANDRINO, J. A., FELDMAN, A. J., APPELBAUM, J., AND FELTEN, E. W. Lest We Remember: Cold Boot Attacks on Encryption Keys. In *Usenix Security Symposium* (San Jose, CA, 2008).

[22] JONES, R. W. M., H J KELLY, P., AND MOST C, AND UNCAUGHT ERRORS. Backwards-compatible Bounds Checking for Arrays and Pointers in C Programs. In *HP Labs Tech Report* (1997).

[23] KHATIWALA, T., SWAMINATHAN, R., AND VENKATAKRISHNAN, V. Data Sandboxing: A Technique for Enforcing Confidentiality Policies. In *Annual Computer Security Applications Conference* (Miami Beach, FL, 2006).

[24] KROHN, M., YIP, A., BRODSKY, M., CLIFFER, N., KAASHOEK, M. F., KOHLER, E., AND MORRIS, R. Information Flow Control for Standard OS Abstractions. In *Symposium on Operating Systems Principles* (Washington, WA, 2007).

[25] LAROCHELLE, D., AND EVANS, D. Statically Detecting Likely Buffer Overflow Vulnerabilities. In *USENIX Security Symposium* (Washington, D.C., 2001).

[26] LATTNER, C., AND ADVE, V. Automatic Pool Allocation: Improving Performance by Controlling Data Structure Layout in the Heap. In *Programming Language Design and Implementation* (Chicago, IL, 2005).

[27] MCCUNE, J. M., LI, Y., QU, N., ZHOU, Z., DATTA, A., GLIGOR, V., AND PERRIG, A. TrustVisor: Efficient TCB Reduction and Attestation. In *IEEE Symposium on Security and Privacy* (Oakland, CA, 2010).

[28] NECULA, G. C., MCPEAK, S., RAHUL, S. P., AND WEIMER, W. CIL: Intermediate Language and Tools for Analysis and Transformation of C Programs. In *Conference on Compiler Construction* (Grenoble, France, 2002).

[29] NECULA, G. C., MCPEAK, S., AND WEIMER, W. CCured: Type-safe Retrofitting of Legacy Code. In *Principles of Programming Languages* (Portland, OR, 2002).

[30] NYSTROM, E. M., KIM, H.-S., AND HWU, W.-M. W. Bottom-Up and Top-Down Context-Sensitive Summary-Based Pointer Analysis. In *Static Analysis Symposium* (Verona, Italy, 2004).

[31] RUGINA, R., AND RINARD, M. Symbolic Bounds Analysis of Pointers, Array Indices, and Accessed Memory Regions. In *Programming Language Design and Implementation* (Vancouver, British Columbia, Canada, 2000).

[32] SAGIV, M., REPS, T., AND WILHELM, R. Parametric Shape Analysis via 3-valued Logic. In *Principles of Programming Languages* (San Antonio, TX, 1999).

[33] STEENSGAARD, B. Points-to Analysis in Almost Linear Time. In *Principles of Programming Languages* (St. Petersburg Beach, FL, 1996).

[34] XIE, Y., CHOU, A., AND ENGLER, D. ARCHER: Using Symbolic, Path-sensitive Analysis to Detect Memory Access Errors. In *European Software Engineering Conference* (Helsinki, Finland, 2003).

[35] ZELDOVICH, N., BOYD-WICKIZER, S., KOHLER, E., AND MAZIÈRES, D. Making Information Flow Explicit in HiStar. In *Symposium on Operating Systems Design and Implementation* (Seattle, WA, 2006).

[36] ZHENG, X., AND RUGINA, R. Demand-driven Alias Analysis for C. In *Principles of Programming Languages* (San Francisco, CA, 2008).

APPENDIX

A. FORMAL EXPLANATION

Below we describe how $\texttt{UsePoints}(id)$ is computed. The set $\texttt{NoUse}(id)$ is computed from $\texttt{UsePoints}(id)$ using standard liveness analysis, which employs a simple fix point computation. We omit it's formal description due to space limitations.

Computing $\texttt{UsePoints}(id)$ In order to compute $\texttt{UsePoints}(id)$, we use the following functions ev and $DefsUsd$. Both of them take two arguments E, l where E is an expression and l is a program location. $ev(E, l)$ defines the set of base variables that are directly referenced in E and $DefsUsd(E, l)$ defines the set of definitions that are used in E. The function ev handles `address-of` and `dereference` operators specially as application of these operators may effectively reference aliased variables. ev finds all base variables that the resulting expression is aliased to by using the alias relations at the current program location. The function is defined inductively and is self explanatory. $DefsUsd$ is defined using the function ev.

$$ev(E, l) = \begin{cases} \phi & if E = c \\ x & if E = x \\ \&^{i+1}x & if E = \&y \ and \ \star^i y \in A(x, l) \\ \&^{i-1}x & if E = \star y \ and \ \&^i x \in A(y, l) \\ ev(E_1) \cup ev(E_2) \\ \quad if E = E_1 \ bop \ E_2 | call f(E_1, E_2) \end{cases}$$

$$DefsUsd(E, l) = \left\{ DefsHld(x, l) \ \middle| \ \begin{array}{l} x \in ev(E, l) \\ and \ x \ is \ a \\ base \ variable \end{array} \right\}$$

Where $DefsHld(x, l)$ is a set of identifiers representing definitions that the variable x may hold at the program location l. Now, `UsePoints(id)` is computed to be the set $\{l : id \in DefsUsd(E, l)\}$.

Alias computation exception In the presence of `malloc` instructions inside a loop, the alias computation needs to be appropriately changed as follows.

SWIPE adds the following rule to the standard alias computation where $malloc\_base_l$ is the temporary base variable introduced.

$l : p = malloc(...);$
$A'(x, l) = A(x, l) - \{*p\}, if * p \in A(x, l)$
$A'(\bot, l) = A(\bot, l) \cup A(malloc\_base_l, l)$
$A'(malloc\_base_l, l) = \{*p, malloc\_base_l\};$

This rule removes the LHS variable p from aliases of other variables. It updates alias information indicating $*p$ is an alias for $malloc\_base_l$.

We use the location specific $\bot$ i.e., $\bot_l$ to consider the definitions of $malloc\_base_l$ variables declared at each location l precisely. For malloc'd variables, the same algorithm to compute `NoUse` for non-malloc'd variables (described before) can be used with an exception to compute EP. The definition of $malloc\_base_l$ can not be erased at location l'' if -

- there exists a location l' where $\bot_l$ is referenced, i.e., there is a reference to $*p$ such that $*p \in A(\bot_l, l')$ and

- l appears in the path between l'' and l'.

This is to make sure that, we do not erase any previous definition of $malloc\_base_l$ inside a loop, before its use with the help of aliases of $\bot_l$. We can also erase data in memory locations allocated in earlier iterations (inside a *loop*) by tracking the references to $\bot_l$. This aids in erasing all the data without compromising the precision and soundness while applying rules to compute `ErasePoints`.

Computing `AliasFunction` Consider a function with formal parameters $f_1, f_2, ..., f_m$. Considering them as pointer variables, we let $level(f_i)$ denote the level of f_i. Thus, if f_i is a base variable then $level(f_i) = 0$. If it is a pointer to a base variable then $level(f_i) = 1$ and so on. Let rp be a special symbol that denotes a k-level pointer returned by the function. Let GPV denote the set of global variables. For each formal parameter we use f_i to denote the value of the formal before the execution and f_i' to represent the parameter after the execution of the function. Similarly, we use x' to represent the value of the global pointer variable x where $x \in GPV$, after the execution of the function.

`AliasFunction` is a function that denotes how the alias information of the formal parameters changes after execution of the function. Let D and R be sets as defined below.

Application	Size (eLoc)	# of Exit Wnd	# of Func Wnd	Instruction Windows	
				# of Wnd	Avg pth (Max)
SFTP	32970	60	238	804	79.73 (720)
OpenSSL	154056	70	265	1429	10.86 (80)
linux-utils	3862	2916	2652	12165	8.12 (102)
mpop	17995	11613	2153	24441	11.30 (104)
MySecureshell	10831	1583	169	10115	3.60 (42)

Table 9: Empirical analysis of data exposures in popular open source applications

- $D = NAV \cup \{*^i f_j | 1 \le i \le level(f_j), 1 \le j \le m\} \cup \{x | x \in GPV\} \cup \{\bot\}$.

- $R = \{*^i f_j' | 1 \le i \le level(f_j), 1 \le j \le m\} \cup \{x' | x \in GPV\} \cup \{*^k rp\}$.

Then, `AliasFunction` is a mapping from the domain D to the power set of R, i.e., $F : D \to 2^R$.

Significance of D and R If $*f_2' \in F(*f_1)$ then this denotes that after execution of the function, $*f_2$ aliases the same variable that $*f_1$ was aliasing before execution of the function. All references to formal parameters in `NewDefinitions`, refer to these values after the function has been executed. Observe that, for each x such that $x \in \{formals \ or \ GPV\}$, x' does not appear in D and x does not appear in R.

B. EMPIRICAL STUDY

Table 9 shows applications analyzed for the empirical study discussed in Section 2. We first inlined all function calls and using analysis tools built extended control flow graphs for these applications. For ease of analysis we made several approximations: each library function call was treated as a single instruction, loops were approximated by considering only zero or one iterations and effect of data flows (sensitive data being copied around in the program) was ignored. We note that all the above approximations are conservative, so the actual exposure windows are likely to be worse than what we report here.

Based on the definitions of Exit Window, Function Window and Instruction Window we measured various exposure windows in these applications. Since instruction window sizes are measured for each control path, we measured the average across all control paths.

Results We obtained the metrics measured across all program variables that appear in Table 9. We observe that the number of instances for Exit Window varies from 60 to 11613. The high number of instances of Exit Window (11613) for `mpop` is caused by a high number of exit instructions (144). The total number of Instruction Window ranged from 804 to 24,441 with average sizes from 3.60 to 79.73 instructions (maximum in paranthesis). This is larger than Exit Window or Function Window as programs often use a variable to hold multiple data items at different program points. We would like to note that for `SFTP`, `OpenSSL` and `linux-utils` this study could only analyze a subset of the source code because of scalability issues. The presence of numerous function and exit exposure windows and the average sizes of the instruction windows illustrate the prevalence of extedned data lifetime problem in popular open source applications.

Leakage-Free Redactable Signatures

Ashish Kundu[*]
IBM T J Watson Research Center
Hawthorne, New York, USA
akundu@us.ibm.com

Mikhail J. Atallah, Elisa Bertino
Department of Computer Science and CERIAS,
Purdue University.
West Lafayette, Indiana, USA
{mja,bertino}@cs.purdue.edu

ABSTRACT

Redactable signatures for linear-structured data such as strings have already been studied in the literature. In this paper, we propose a formal security model for leakage-free redactable signatures (LFRS) that is general enough to address authentication of not only trees but also graphs and forests. LFRS schemes have several applications, especially in enabling secure data management in the emerging cloud computing paradigm as well as in healthcare, finance and biological applications. We also formally define the notion of secure names. Such secure names facilitate leakage-free verification of ordering between siblings/nodes. The paper also proposes a construction for secure names, and a construction for leakage-free redactable signatures based on the secure naming scheme. The proposed construction computes a linear number of signatures with respect to the size of the data object, and outputs only one signature that is stored, transmitted and used for authentication of any tree, graph and forest.

Categories and Subject Descriptors

D.4.6 [**Security and Protection**]: Cryptographic controls

General Terms

Security

Keywords

Integrity, Authenticity, Cloud Computing, Trees, Graphs, Privacy, Leakages, Redactable Signatures

1. INTRODUCTION

In the emerging cloud computing paradigms, hosting and distribution of data is carried out by third party infrastructures and servers, which may not be trusted (e.g., Amazon EC2, Amazon Web Services AWS, "Database as a Service"). Public clouds as

---

[*]Part of this work was carried out by the author at the Department of Computer Science and CERIAS, Purdue University

well as hybrid clouds (an ecosystem of multiple clouds working together) not only host but also generate and distribute data that are sensitive with respect to confidentiality as well as privacy.

In such third-party data distribution settings, which are increasingly being employed in order to store and publish sensitive information belonging to individuals (such as healthcare and finance) and enterprises, protection of privacy and confidentiality is as important as verifying authenticity of data. A crucial requirement is therefore to ensure that the data authentication process does not lead to any leakages.

Some applications of leakage-free authentication of data in cloud computing are in database-as-a-service, in assuring healthcare (for HIPAA compliance), biological and financial data (such as credit card records and transactions in VISA databases), while protecting privacy and confidentiality. Data published through third-party architectures are very often organized as trees or graphs; for example, XML data or biological data.

Consider Figure 1(a). Assume that the tree T represents the XML-based heathcare record of an individual. Assume that element d represents a specific type of diseases such as "critical-diseases", and that elements a, b and c each refers to different diseases the patient has suffered from during his life. The order between these siblings refer to the temporal order in which the individual suffered from the diseases. Suppose a healthcare researcher queries the healthcare database on a specific set of diseases that an individual may have suffered from, and the query result is referred to by T_δ. Since c (e.g., "heart attack") is not part of T_δ due to privacy requirements, the lab should not be able to infer any information about c in the received information. At the same time, however, the researcher should be able to verify the authenticity of this query result – T_δ. Such requirements lead to the need of developing a security model for 'leakage-free authentication" of trees (as well as of graphs and forests, which have similar practical applications). We refer the reader to our earlier works [12][13] that describe information leakages and privacy issues due to authentication of healthcare data objects structured as trees and graphs.

The problem thus is how does *Alice* (the data owner) sign the data (a tree, a graph, or a forest (Figure 1)) *once*, so that the authenticity of a portion of the data (subtree(s)/subgraph(s)/sub-forest(s)) can be verified without leaking any information about the remaining part of the data. Integrity of the relationships represented by the edges and ordering among siblings is referred to as *structural integrity*, and the integrity of the contents of the nodes is referred to as *content integrity*. A leakage-free signature scheme must make it possible for the receiver of a subtree/subgraph/sub-forest (subtree T_δ, subgraph G_δ in Figure 1) to verify its integrity with the following additional requirement: the receiver should not be able to infer any extraneous information. Extraneous information in a

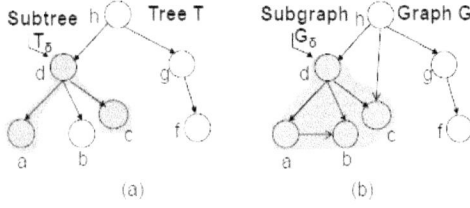

Figure 1: (a) Tree T and subtree T_δ. (b) Graph G and subgraph G_δ.

tree/graph $\Upsilon(V, E)$ with respect to its subtree $\Upsilon_\delta(V_\delta, E_\delta)$ comprises of $(\Upsilon \setminus \Upsilon_\delta)$ the nodes and edges that are in Υ but not in Υ_δ (such as b, f, g and h, edges: $e(d, b)$, $e(h, d)$, $e(h, g)$, and $e(g, f)$ w.r.t. T_δ in Figure 1).

Proving whether a sibling x is a left sibling of y without revealing any other information about other siblings of x and y, if any, can be achieved by assigning "secure names" to the nodes. Such names are secure, i.e., they are "leakage-free". By using secure names, we can construct leakage-free redactable signatures that are efficient. Leakage-free redactable signatures for trees exist in the literature [3], which require quadratic number of signatures to be computed per set of siblings. In this paper, we propose a solution that requires computation of only a linear number of signatures and that outputs only one signature, primarily by virtue of using the notion of secure names.

Contributions: In this paper, we propose (1) a formal model that supports query results to be not only connected subtrees as in [3] but also disconnected subtrees, and (disconnected) sub-graphs and sub-forests. Our formal model follows the definition of integrity of redactable signatures as defined by Johnson et al. [10]; (2) a formal model for secure naming schemes, and (3) a construction of leakage-free redactable signature for trees, graphs and forests.

2. PRELIMINARIES

Trees and Graphs: A directed graph $G(V, E)$ is a set of nodes (or vertices) V and a set of edges E between these nodes: $e(x, y)$ is an edge from x to y, $(x, y) \in V \times V$. A node x represents an atomic unit of data, which is always shared as a whole or is not shared at all. A node x is called the ancestor of a node y iff there exists a path consisting of one or more edges from x to y. Node x is an immediate ancestor of y in G iff there exists an edge $e(x, y)$ in E. Nodes having a common immediate ancestor are called siblings. If there is a specific order between siblings in G, then G is an ordered graph. The fact that x precedes one of its siblings y in an ordered graph is denoted by $x \prec y$; i.e., x is to the left of y. The contents, if any, of a node x is referred to as c_x. A *redacted subgraph* graph $G(V, E)$ is denoted by $G_\delta(V_\delta, E_\delta)$, and $G_\delta(V_\delta, E_\delta) \subseteq G(V, E)$. $G_\delta(V_\delta, E_\delta) \subseteq G(V, E)$ if and only if $V_\delta \subseteq V$ and $E_\delta \subseteq E$. $G_\delta(V_\delta, E_\delta) \subset G(V, E)$ if and only if $V_\delta \cup E_\delta \subset V \cup E$. Redacted subgraph $G_\delta(V_\delta, E_\delta)$ is derived from the graph $G(V, E)$ by redacting the set of nodes $V \setminus V_\delta$ and the set of edges $E \setminus E_\delta$ from G. A directed tree $T(V, E)$ is a directed graph with the following constraint: removal of any edge $e(x, y)$ from E leads to two disconnected trees with no edge or path between nodes x and y. Two nodes are siblings, if they have a common parent; x is a parent of node y iff there is an edge $e(x, y)$ in T; y is called the child of its parent x. In a tree, a parent node is nothing but the immediate ancestor of all its child nodes. An ordered tree is one where each pair of siblings have an order between them. A rooted tree has a special node called root, for which there is no parent node. As in the case of graphs,

a redacted subtree of tree $T(V, E)$ is denoted by $T_\delta(V_\delta, E_\delta)$ such that $T_\delta(V_\delta, E_\delta) \subseteq T(V, E)$. $T_\delta(V_\delta, E_\delta) \subseteq T(V, E)$ denotes that $V_\delta \subseteq V$ and $E_\delta \subseteq E$. Redacted subgraph $T_\delta(V_\delta, E_\delta)$ is derived from the tree $T(V, E)$ by redacting the set of nodes $V \setminus V_\delta$ and the set of edges $E \setminus E_\delta$ from T. Two trees/graphs/forests with the same nodes and edges, but *different ordering* between at least one pair of siblings are different trees/graphs/forests. In the rest of the paper, a tree refers to an ordered directed rooted tree, and a graph refers to an ordered directed graph, a subtree/subgraph refers to a redacted subtree/subgraph of a tree/graph unless otherwise stated. $\Upsilon(V, E)$ refers to either a tree $T(V, E)$ or a graph $G(V, E)$.

2.1 Signature Schemes

In this section, we review the standard definition of digital signatures (adopted from [11]).

DEFINITION 2.1 (STANDARD DIGITAL SIGNATURE SCHEME). *A digital signature scheme Π consists of two probabilistic polynomial-time algorithms and one deterministic polynomial-time algorithm $\Pi \equiv$ (Gen, Sign, Vrfy) satisfying the following requirements:*

KEY GENERATION: *The probabilistic key generation algorithm Gen takes as input a security parameter 1^n and outputs a pair of keys (pk, sk), where pk and sk are the public and private keys, respectively. We assume for convention that each of these keys has length n bits, and that n can be determined from (pk, sk).*

$$(\text{pk}, \text{sk}) \leftarrow \text{Gen}(1^n).$$

SIGNING: *The probabilistic signing algorithm Sign takes as input a private key sk and a message M, and outputs a signature σ.*

$$\sigma \leftarrow \text{Sign}_{\text{sk}}(M)$$

VERIFICATION: *The deterministic verification algorithm Vrfy takes as input a public key pk, a message M, and a signature σ, and outputs a bit b, with $b = 1$ meaning valid (i.e., σ is a valid signature of message M), and $b = 0$ meaning invalid (i.e., σ is not a valid signature of message M).*

$$b \leftarrow \text{Vrfy}_{\text{pk}}(\sigma, M)$$

2.2 Forgery

The strongest form of security for a digital signature scheme Π is to be *existentially unforgeable against chosen message attack* (EU-CMA). The following experiment $\text{Sig-Forge}_{\mathcal{A},\Pi}^{eu-cma}(\lambda)$ and definition review the unforgeability property of digital signatures (originally defined in [8]).

Unforgeability: Let us consider the following signature forging experiment. $\mathcal{A}$ is a probabilistic polynomial time (PPT) adversary with the knowledge of pk.

Signature Forging Experiment: $\text{Sig-Forge}_{\mathcal{A},\Pi}^{eu-cma}(\lambda)$

1. $(\text{pk}, \text{sk}) \leftarrow \text{Gen}(1^\lambda)$

2. $\mathcal{A}$ may know pk and has oracle accesses to $\text{Sign}_{\text{sk}}(\cdot)$ and $\text{Vrfy}_{\text{sk}}(\cdot)$. Let $\mathcal{Q}$ be the set of messages for which $\mathcal{A}$ queries $\text{Sign}_{\text{sk}}(\cdot)$.

3. $\mathcal{A}$ outputs (σ, M), where $M \notin \mathcal{Q}$.

4. The output of the experiment is 1 if and only if $\text{Vrfy}_{\text{pk}}(\sigma, M)$ outputs 1, else the experiment outputs 0.

DEFINITION 2.2. *The digital signature scheme* Π *is* $(t, q, \epsilon) -$ *secure if the experiment* $\text{Sig-Forge}_{\mathcal{A},\Pi}^{eu-cma}(\lambda)$ *outputs 1 with probability* $\epsilon(\lambda) = \frac{1}{2} + \text{negl}(\lambda)$, *where* $\text{negl}(\lambda)$ *is a negligible function in terms of* λ; *i.e.,*

$$\Pr(\text{Sig} - \text{Forge}_{\mathcal{A},\Pi}^{eu-cma}(\lambda) = 1) \leq \epsilon(\lambda) = \frac{1}{2} + \text{negl}(\lambda)$$

3. LEAKAGE-FREE REDACTABLE SIGNATURES

In this section, we present the formal model of the leakage-free redactable (LFR) signatures for trees, graphs and forests.

3.1 Why A New Model?

The standard notion of digital signatures (Section 2) has several shortcomings in our context. (1) It is not suitable for cases when a user has access only to a part of the message, and not the full message. (2) It is not suitable for messages that are trees, graphs or forests. Therefore, such notion does not define the notion of "leakage-free" signature. Redactable signatures have been proposed to address the first shortcoming. Such schemes allow signature of (a designated) part of a message to be computed from the signature of the complete message using the knowledge of the public key. Existing models for redactable and sanitizable signatures do not capture all our requirements in a holistic manner, and thus their security definitions are not directly applicable here as they are.

Brzuska et al. [3] are perhaps the first ones to have defined a formal security model for leakage-free redactable structural signatures for trees. Consider that a query on tree T evaluates to a subtree T_δ that is verified by the querier for its authenticity. The $sCut(\cdot)$ operation defined in [3], which "cuts" a leaf node from a tree, can be applied multiple times in order to compute the redacted subtree and its signature. However, by this cut operation, a tree can be reduced to only a connected subtree, not to a set of disconnected subtrees. The cases in which a receiver must receive multiple disconnected subtrees of a tree and verify their authenticity cannot be supported by such a definition. For example, consider Figure 1(a): the $sCut(\cdot)$ operation is applied on leaf b, and iteratively on leaf f. It then results on the subtree T_δ as shown shaded in the figure. The signature of T_δ is computed from the signature of the T without the knowledge of the secret key, with which T was signed. Now consider another scenario - a query on tree T evaluates to two disconnected subtrees: T_δ and the subtree consisting of g, f and the edge $g \rightarrow f$. Such a scenario *cannot* be modeled by the definition in [3]. However, such scenarios occur quite frequently in practical usages and databases, and cannot be ignored by a security model.

There is a need for a security model that would support graph-structured data (XML graphs, biological and genetic data, which have private and sensitive information encoded in them) as well as disconnected trees and graphs. Therefore, we have proposed a formal model for leakage-free redactable signatures for trees, graphs, and forests, which is the general model. Logically, our definitions resemble similarity to those in [3].

3.2 Definition of A General Scheme

In the following definition, $\Upsilon(V, E)$ refers to a tree, a graph, or a forest (a set of disconnected trees/graphs) with the set of vertices and edges being denoted by V and E, respectively.

DEFINITION 3.1 (LFRS $r\Pi$). *A leakage-free redactable signature scheme $r\Pi$ consists of four polynomial algorithms $r\Pi \equiv (\text{rGen}, \text{rSign}, \text{rRedact}, \text{rVrfy})$ satisfying the following requirements. Let $\Upsilon(V, E)$ refer to either a tree, graph, or a for-*est, *and let* $\Upsilon_\delta(V_\delta, E_\delta) \subseteq \Upsilon(V, E)$, *i.e.,* $\Upsilon_\delta(V_\delta, E_\delta)$ *be a redacted subtree/subgraph/sub-forest derived from* $\Upsilon(V, E)$.

KEY GENERATION: *A key generation algorithm* rGen *takes as input a security parameter* 1^λ *and outputs a pair of keys* (pk, sk), *where pk and sk are the public and private keys, respectively. We assume for convention that each of these keys has length* λ, *and that* λ *can be determined from* pk *and* sk.

$$(\text{pk}, \text{sk}) \leftarrow \text{rGen}(1^\lambda).$$

SIGNING: *The signing algorithm* rSign *takes as input a private key* sk *and a tree/graph/forest* $\Upsilon(V, E)$, *where the content* c_x *of each node* $x \in V$ *is such that* $c_x \in \{0, 1\}^*$. *It outputs a signature* σ_Υ.

$$(\sigma_\Upsilon, \Upsilon(V, E)) \leftarrow \text{rSign}_{\text{sk}}(\Upsilon(V, E)).$$

REDACTION: *The redaction algorithm* rRedact *takes as input* $\Upsilon(V, E)$, *its signature* σ_Υ, *and a set of nodes* V'_δ *and edges* E'_δ, *where* $V'_\delta \subset V$ *and* $E'_\delta \subseteq E$. rRedact *outputs a redacted signature* $\sigma_{\Upsilon_\delta(V_\delta, E_\delta)}$ *for* $\Upsilon_\delta(V_\delta, E_\delta)$, *where* $\Upsilon_\delta(V_\delta, E_\delta)$ *is a tree/graph/forest derived from* $\Upsilon(V, E)$ *consisting of vertices in* $V_\delta = V \setminus V'_\delta$, *and edges* $E_\delta = E \setminus E'_\delta$.

$$(\sigma_{\Upsilon_\delta}, \Upsilon_\delta(V_\delta, E_\delta)) \leftarrow \text{rRedact}_{\text{pk}}(\sigma_\Upsilon, \Upsilon(V, E), V'_\delta, E'_\delta)$$

VERIFICATION: *The verification algorithm* rVrfy *takes as input a public key* pk, *a tree/graph/forest* $\Upsilon(V, E)$, *whose authenticity needs to be verified, and a signature* σ. *It outputs a bit b, with b = 1 meaning* valid *(i.e.,* σ *is a valid signature of* $\Upsilon(V, E)$) *and b = 0 meaning* invalid *(i.e.,* σ *is not a valid signature of* $\Upsilon(V, E)$).

$$b \leftarrow \text{rVrfy}_{\text{pk}}(\sigma, \Upsilon(V, E))$$

An LFR signature scheme is correct if the following properties hold.

Signing Correctness: For any tree/graph/forest $\Upsilon(V, E)$, any positive integer value of λ, any key pair $(\text{pk}, \text{sk}) \leftarrow \text{rGen}(1^\lambda)$, and any $(\sigma_{\Upsilon(V,E)}, \Upsilon(V, E)) \leftarrow \text{rSign}_{\text{sk}}(\Upsilon(V, E))$, $\text{rVrfy}_{\text{pk}}(\sigma_{\Upsilon(V,E)}, \Upsilon(V, E))$ always outputs 1.

Redaction Correctness: For any tree/graph/forest $\Upsilon(V, E)$, any positive integer value of λ, any key pair $(\text{pk}, \text{sk}) \leftarrow \text{rGen}(1^\lambda)$, any $(\sigma_{\Upsilon(V,E)}, \Upsilon(V, E)) \leftarrow \text{rSign}_{\text{sk}}(\Upsilon(V, E))$, any subset of vertices $V'_\delta \subset V$, any subset of edges $E'_\delta \subseteq E$ such that $V_\delta = V \setminus V'_\delta$, and $E_\delta = E \setminus E'_\delta$, and any $(\sigma_{\Upsilon_\delta}, \Upsilon_\delta(V_\delta, E_\delta)) \leftarrow \text{rRedact}_{\text{pk}}(\sigma_\Upsilon, \Upsilon(V, E), V'_\delta, E'_\delta)$, $\text{rVrfy}_{\text{pk}}(\sigma_{\Upsilon_\delta}, \Upsilon_\delta(V_\delta, E_\delta))$ always outputs 1.

4. SECURITY OF LEAKAGE-FREE REDACTABLE SIGNATURES

In this section, we define the security requirements of the leakage-free redactable signature scheme $r\Pi$. Informally, these requirements are:

Unforgeability: Someone who does not know the secret key and does not know a valid signature for a tree/graph/forest Υ should not be able to compute a valid signature for Υ provided that (s)he does not know the valid signature for any tree/graph/forest Υ' such that $\Upsilon \subset \Upsilon'$. This is a bit different from the traditional notion of EU-CMA (More on this in Section 4.1).

309

Privacy: Someone who has access to $\Upsilon \subset \Upsilon'$ but not to Υ' should not be able to infer any information about the redacted nodes and edges (in Υ' but not in Υ) from the leakage-free redactable signature of Υ.

Transparency: Someone who has access to $\Upsilon \subset \Upsilon'$ but not to Υ' should not be able to infer whether the signature of Υ has been computed from scratch or through the process of redaction.

4.1 Unforgeability

In standard digital signature schemes, only the signer can compute the signature of a given message. However, a redactable signature scheme allows "anyone" with the public key pk to be able to compute the signature of a (designated) part of the data (In contrast, for sanitizable signatures, a designated sanitizer can only compute signatures on altered documents). The redactable signature scheme by Johnson et al. [10] computes the signature of a document M, which consists of n parts: $m_1, m_2, m_3, \ldots, m_n$. It allows anyone, who has a knowledge of the public key, to compute the signature of a redacted document M' that consists of a subset of m_i's. Due to such a property, redactable signature schemes cannot support the strongest notion of unforgeability, i.e., to be existentially unforgeable under adaptive chosen-message attack, as it is. It has to be adapted (in other words, weakened) in order incorporate the fact that the signatures of any redacted sub-document M' can be "legally forged" with respect to the operation that can be used to compute these sub-documents from the original document M (cf., [10]).

In what follows, we make use of the results of Johnson et al. [10] in defining the notion of unforgeability for the leakage-free redactable signature scheme $r\Pi$ defined in the previous section. The operation related to our notion of redaction is the subset $\subset$ operation: a redacted subtree T_δ is a tree with *subsets* of nodes and edges of the original tree T. Intuitively this notion means that if an adversary $\mathcal{A}$ has the knowledge of a subtree/subgraph/sub-forest Υ_δ, its valid signature σ_{Υ_δ}, and the public key, then $\mathcal{A}$ can in fact compute the valid signature of any subtree/subgraph/sub-forest of Υ_δ, and these are the *only* "messages" for which $\mathcal{A}$ can "forge" a signature without the knowledge of the secret key.

Existentially unforgeable under adaptive chosen-message attack with respect to the $\subset$ operation (EU-CMA-$\subset$): Let us consider the following signature forging experiment. As earlier, $\mathcal{A}$ is a PPT adversary has access to the signing oracle $\mathtt{rSign_{sk}}(\cdot)$ with the knowledge of pk. $\mathcal{A}$ should not be able to forge a valid signature σ for a "new" tree/graph/forest even after it has adaptively queried the signing oracle $\mathtt{rSign_{sk}}(\cdot)$. A "new" tree/graph/forest denotes a tree/graph/forest Υ', for which the $\mathcal{A}$ has not received a valid signature from the signing oracle and Υ' is not a redacted subtree/subgraph/sub-forest of another Υ for which $\mathcal{A}$ has received a valid signature from the signing oracle.

Signature Forging Experiment: $\mathtt{Sig\text{-}Forge}_{\mathcal{A},r\Pi}^{eu-cma-\subset}(\lambda)$

1. $(\mathtt{pk}, \mathtt{sk}) \leftarrow \mathtt{rGen}(1^\lambda)$

2. $\mathcal{A}$ is given the pk, and is allowed oracle accesses to $\mathtt{rSign_{sk}}(\cdot)$, $\mathtt{rRedact_{pk}}(\cdot, \cdot)$, and $\mathtt{rVrfy_{sk}}(\cdot)$. Let $\mathcal{Q}$ be the set of all trees/graphs/forests for which $\mathcal{A}$ queries $\mathtt{rSign_{sk}}(\cdot)$ for their signatures.

3. $\mathcal{A}$ outputs (σ, Υ'), such that

    (a) $\Upsilon' \notin \mathcal{Q}$: Υ' is a tree/graph/forest whose signature the $\mathcal{A}$ has not queried from the signing oracle, and

    (b) $\Upsilon' \notin \cup_{\Upsilon \in \mathcal{Q}} \Theta_\Upsilon$, where $\Theta_\Upsilon = \{\Upsilon'' | \Upsilon'' \subset \Upsilon\}$: Υ' is not a subtree/subgraph/sub-forest of any $\Upsilon(V, E)$, whose signature has been queried by $\mathcal{A}$ from $\mathtt{rSign_{sk}}(\cdot)$.

4. The output of the experiment is 1 if and only if $\mathtt{Vrfy_{pk}}(\sigma, \Upsilon')$ = 1, else the experiment outputs 0.

DEFINITION 4.1 (LFR SIGNATURE: INTEGRITY). *The leakage-free redactable signature scheme $r\Pi$ is existentially unforgeable under adaptive chosen-message attack over the $\subset$ operation, if the experiment* $\mathtt{Sig\text{-}Forge}_{\mathcal{A},r\Pi}^{eu-cma-\subset}(\lambda)$ *outputs 1 with probability* $\epsilon(\lambda) = \frac{1}{2} + \mathtt{negl}(\lambda)$:

$$\mathtt{Pr}(\mathtt{Sig} - \mathtt{Forge}_{\mathcal{A},r\Pi}^{eu-cma-\subset}(\lambda) = 1) \leq \epsilon(\lambda) = \frac{1}{2} + \mathtt{negl}(\lambda).$$

4.2 Leakage-Free Properties

There are two leakage-free properties: privacy and transparency. Transparency is the stronger property and subsumes privacy.

4.3 Privacy

An LFR signature scheme supporting privacy does not lead to leakage of the nodes and edges that have been redacted. Given a redacted subtree/subgraph/sub-forest and its LFR signature, one cannot infer any of the contents/existence/absence of the redacted nodes/edges. For example, given a subtree from a financial XML document that lists credit-card information, and given two such source XML documents, one cannot identify which source tree the subtree has been redacted from.

In the following adversarial experiment, a PPT adversary $\mathcal{A}$ outputs two trees/graphs/forests Υ_0 and Υ_1 such that (a) $\mathcal{A}$ has not queried the signatures for them nor has queried signatures for their super-trees/super-graphs/super-forests; (b) redacting a given set of vertices V_δ' and edges E_δ' from either of them lead to the same subtree/subgraph/sub-forest $\Upsilon_\delta'(V_\delta', E_\delta')$. The experiment randomly chooses either Υ_b (b = 0 or 1) to be signed, and then computes the signature for the redacted subtree Υ_δ'. A challenge consisting of the redacted subtree and its signature is given to the adversary. The experiment is successful, if the $\mathcal{A}$ can infer the Υ_b from which Υ_δ' has been redacted with a probability non-negligibly larger than $\frac{1}{2}$.

Privacy Experiment: $\mathtt{Sig\text{-}Priv}_{\mathcal{A},r\Pi}^{csa}(\lambda)$ Let us consider the following experiment on privacy of the LFR signature scheme $r\Pi$:

1. $\mathtt{rGen}(1^\lambda)$ is run to obtain keys $(\mathtt{pk}, \mathtt{sk})$.

2. Probabilistic polynomial-time adversary $\mathcal{A}$ is given pk and oracle access to $\mathtt{rSign_{sk}}(\cdot)$, $\mathtt{rRedact}(\cdot)$ and $\mathtt{rVrfy_{pk}}(\cdot)$. Let $\mathcal{Q}$ be the set of all trees/graphs/forests for which $\mathcal{A}$ queries $\mathtt{rSign_{sk}}(\cdot)$ for their signatures.

3. $\mathcal{A}$ outputs two trees/graphs/forests $\Upsilon_0(V_0, E_0)$, $\Upsilon_1(V_1, E_1)$, and another tree/graph/forest $\Upsilon_\delta(V_\delta, E_\delta)$, where $\Upsilon_\delta(V_\delta, E_\delta) \subset \Upsilon_0(V_0, E_0)$ and $\Upsilon_\delta(V_\delta, E_\delta) \subset \Upsilon_1(V_1, E_1)$.

4. A random b is drawn uniformly from $\{0,1\}$. $(\sigma_{\Upsilon_b}, \Upsilon_b(V_b, E_b))$ $\leftarrow \mathtt{rSign_{sk}}(\Upsilon_b(V_b, E_b))$. The signature for redacted subtree Υ_δ is computed from σ_{Υ_b}: $(\sigma_{\Upsilon_\delta}, \Upsilon_\delta) \leftarrow \mathtt{rRedact_{pk}}(\sigma_{\Upsilon_b}, \Upsilon_b(V_b, E_b), V_b \backslash V_\delta, E_b \backslash E_\delta)$. Then the *challenge* $(\sigma_{\Upsilon_\delta}, \Upsilon_\delta)$ is given to $\mathcal{A}$.

5. $\mathcal{A}$ continues to have oracle access to $\mathtt{rSign_{sk}}(\cdot)$, $\mathtt{rRedact_{pk}}(\cdot, \cdot)$, and $\mathtt{rVrfy_{pk}}(\cdot)$. Eventually, $\mathcal{A}$ outputs a bit b' (for the *challenge* $(\sigma_{\Upsilon_\delta}, \Upsilon_\delta)$).

6. The output of the experiment is 1 if $b' = b$, and 0 otherwise.

DEFINITION 4.2 (LFR SIGNATURE: PRIVACY). *The LFR signature scheme* $r\Pi$ *preserves privacy if* $\Pr(\texttt{Sig-Priv}_{\mathcal{A},r\Pi}^{csa}(\lambda)=1) \leq \frac{1}{2} + \texttt{negl}(\lambda)$.

4.4 Transparency

In this section, we formally define a transparent LFR scheme. In many applications, it is expected that the end-user should not be able to infer whether the received subtree/subgraph/sub-forest is a redacted one or not. If such information can be inferred, the adversary can learn that the source tree/graph/forest has a higher number of vertices/edges (which might represent the number of bank accounts, or number of critical diseases one has suffered from, or the number of surgeries one has gone through over a period of time). Therefore, the leakage-free redactable signature scheme should prevent inference of such information (prevention of leakage).

A similar notion exists in the literature for sanitizable signatures referred to as "signature transparency" [7], which however, is different from our notion of signature-indistinguishability in the sense that in our case, the adversary should not be able to infer any extraneous information (either contents or structural) in Υ with respect to Υ_δ (extraneous information is defined in Section 3). The existing notion transparency does not capture leakage of structural information.

In the following adversarial experiment, a PPT adversary $\mathcal{A}$ outputs two trees/graphs/forests Υ_0 and Υ_1 such that $\Upsilon_0 \subset \Upsilon_1$. The experiment randomly chooses either Υ_b ($b = 0$ or 1) to be signed; if Υ_1 is signed, then the signature for Υ_0 is computed by redaction from that of Υ_1. A challenge consisting of Υ_0 and its signature is given to the adversary. The experiment is successful (returns 1) if the adversary can infer whether the signature of Υ_b was computed by the signing oracle or by the redaction oracle, with a probability non-negligibly larger than $\frac{1}{2}$.

Transparency Experiment: $\texttt{Sig-Transp}_{\mathcal{A},r\Pi}^{csa}(\lambda)$ Let us consider the following experiment on transparency of the LFR signature scheme $r\Pi$:

1. $\texttt{rGen}(1^\lambda)$ is run to obtain keys $(\texttt{pk},\texttt{sk})$.

2. Probabilistic polynomial-time adversary $\mathcal{A}$ is given $\texttt{pk}$ and oracle access to $\texttt{rSign}_{\texttt{sk}}(\cdot)$, $\texttt{rRedact}(\cdot)$ and $\texttt{rVrfy}_{\texttt{pk}}(\cdot)$. Let $\mathcal{Q}$ be the set of all trees/graphs/forests for which $\mathcal{A}$ queries $\texttt{rSign}_{\texttt{sk}}(\cdot)$ for their signatures.

3. $\mathcal{A}$ outputs two trees/graphs/forests $\Upsilon_0(V_0, E_0)$, and $\Upsilon_1(V_1, E_1)$, such that $\Upsilon_0(V_0, E_0) \subset \Upsilon_1(V_1, E_1)$.

4. A random b is drawn uniformly from $\{0,1\}$. $(\sigma_{\Upsilon_b}, \Upsilon_b(V_b, E_b))$ $\leftarrow \texttt{rSign}_{\texttt{sk}}(\Upsilon_b(V_b, E_b))$. If b=1, then the signature for $\Upsilon_0(V_0, E_0)$ is computed from σ_{Υ_1}: $(\sigma_{\Upsilon_0(V_0,E_0)}, \Upsilon_0(V_0, E_0))$ $\leftarrow \texttt{rRedact}_{\texttt{pk}}(\sigma_{\Upsilon_1}, \Upsilon_1(V_1, E_1), V_1 \backslash V_0, E_1 \backslash E_0)$. Then the *challenge* $(\sigma_{\Upsilon_0(V_0,E_0)}, \Upsilon_0(V_0, E_0))$ is given to $\mathcal{A}$.

5. $\mathcal{A}$ continues to have oracle access to $\texttt{rSign}_{\texttt{sk}}(\cdot)$, $\texttt{rRedact}_{\texttt{pk}}(\cdot, \cdot)$, and $\texttt{rVrfy}_{\texttt{pk}}(\cdot)$. Eventually, $\mathcal{A}$ outputs a bit b' (for the *challenge* $(\sigma_{\Upsilon_\delta}, \Upsilon_\delta)$).

6. The output of the experiment is 1 if $b' = b$, and 0 otherwise.

DEFINITION 4.3 (LFR SIGNATURE: TRANSPARENCY). *The LFR signature scheme* $r\Pi$ *preserves transparency, if* $\Pr(\texttt{Sig-Priv}_{\mathcal{A},r\Pi}^{csa}(\lambda)=1) \leq \frac{1}{2} + \texttt{negl}(\lambda)$.

It should be noted that the definition of the general scheme (Definition 4.6) supports a form of "anonymization" related to

trees/graphs/forests (and is associated with privacy). Suppose that there are two structures Υ and Υ' such that $\Upsilon_\delta \subseteq \Upsilon$ and $\Upsilon_\delta \subseteq \Upsilon'$. Let σ_{Υ_δ} be a signature for Υ_δ and σ_{Υ_δ} be a redacted signature from the signature σ_Υ of Υ. However, given $(\sigma_{\Upsilon_\delta}, \Upsilon_\delta)$, the verification process does not leak whether Υ_δ is redacted from Υ or from Υ'. On the other hand, such a property of redactable signatures does not support the strongest form of non-repudiation notion supported by EU-CMA [10]. It is debatable whether such property should be supoorted by a leakage-free redactable signature scheme.

4.5 Relationships of Privacy and Transparency

In this section, we analyze the relationships between the two leakage-free properties of LFR signature schemes: privacy and transparency. In whatever follows, any mention of tree/subtree can be substituted by the term graph/subgraph or forest/sub-forest without any change to the semantics of the context.

PROPOSITION 4.4. *Privacy $\nRightarrow$ Transparency.*

Consider two trees: Υ_1: x is the parent of y and z, and $y \prec z$; Υ_2: x is the parent of y and w, and $y \prec w$. Consider the case in which a party receives subtrees x, y, and the edge from x and y, and its signature. If the signature scheme supports privacy, the signature does not leak contents of z or w, but may provide the fact that y has a right sibling. Such a scheme is privacy-preserving, but not transparent, because someone who knows Υ_1, and the subtree and its signature, can infer that the signature is a redacted signature from Υ_1.

PROPOSITION 4.5. *Transparency $\Rightarrow$ Privacy.*

Someone who cannot determine if a signature is a redacted signature, cannot in fact determine if the subtree is a redacted subtree or a source tree by itself. By taking negation of the implication, if an LFR scheme does not support privacy, then one can determine the source tree from whose signature, the signature of a subtree has been derived. Such inference in fact implies that the signature of the subtree has not been computed from scratch, but is a redacted signature, which is why transparency also does not hold for such a scheme. *The transparency property of a redactable signature scheme is indeed its leakage-free property.*

4.6 Formal Model for Secure Naming Schemes

We would now define a formal notion of secure names, and secure naming schemes. Secure names are assigned with nodes in order to prove/disprove the alleged order between a pair of nodes. Each secure (i.e., leakage-free) naming scheme $rN \equiv (\texttt{rNameGen}, \texttt{rNameVrfy})$ has two components: generation of secure names and verification of the order between secure names, and is defined as follows.

DEFINITION 4.6 (SECURE NAMING SCHEME rN). *A leakage-free naming scheme rN consists of two polynomial algorithms $rN \equiv (\texttt{rNameGen}, \texttt{rNameVrfy})$ satisfying the following requirements. Let V refer to a set of vertices such that $V = \{x_i | 1 \leq i \leq |V|\}$, and $x_i \prec x_j$, for all $1 \leq i < j \leq |\Theta|$. Let $V_\delta \subseteq V$, i.e., V_δ is a redacted set of vertices derived from V.*

NAME GENERATION: *A name generation algorithm $\texttt{rNameGen}$ takes as input two or less security parameters 1^{λ_1} and 1^{λ_2}, and V and outputs a set of $\Theta = \{\theta_i | 1 \leq i \leq |V|\}$ such that θ_i is a secure name for node x_i. We assume for convention that each of these secure names has length λ, and that λ can be determined from θ_i's. In case of one security parameter, 1^{λ_2} would just be replaced by 0.*

$$\Theta \leftarrow \texttt{rNameGen}(1^{\lambda_1}, 1^{\lambda_2}, V).$$

ORDER VERIFICATION: *The order verification algorithm* rNameVrfy *takes as input two or less security parameters* 1^{λ_1}, *and* 1^{λ_2} *and two pairs* (x_i, θ_i) *and* (x_j, θ_j), *where a pair is: (node x, secure name θ_x), and outputs a bit b, with* $b = 1$ *meaning* valid *(i.e., $x_i \prec x_j$) and $b = 0$ meaning* invalid *(i.e., $x_i \not\prec x_j$).*

$$b \leftarrow \texttt{rNameVrfy}(1^{\lambda_1}, 1^{\lambda_2}, (x_i, \theta_i), (x_j, \theta_j))$$

An LFR signature scheme is correct if the generated secure names are verified to be order-preserving.

Naming Correctness: For any set of vertices V such that between a pair of vertices $x, y \in V$, $x \prec y$, any positive integer values of λ_1, and λ_2, and any $\Theta \leftarrow \texttt{rNameGen}(1^{\lambda_1}, 1^{\lambda_2}, V)$, $\texttt{rNameVrfy}(1^{\lambda_1}, 1^{\lambda_2}, (x, \theta_x), (y, \theta_y))$ always outputs 1.

4.7 Security of Naming Schemes

In this section, we define the security requirement of the secure names. Informally, this requirement is as follows.

Name-Transparency: Someone who has access to an ordered set of secure names $\Theta_\delta \subset \Theta$ but not to Θ should not be able to infer whether $\Theta = \Theta_\delta$ or $\Theta \neq \Theta_\delta$.

Let us formally define a transparency notion for secure names. Such a notion is similar to that of transparency (Section 4.4).

In the following adversarial experiment, a PPT adversary $\mathcal{A}$ outputs two sets of vertices V_0 and V_1 such that $V_0 \subset V_1$, and $x_i \prec x_j$, where $1 \leq i < j \leq |V_1|$. The experiment randomly chooses either V_b (b = 0 or 1) for which secure names are to be generated; if V_1 is chosen, then the secure names for the vertices in V_0 are selected from V_1. A challenge consisting of V_0 and its set of secure names Θ_0 is given to the adversary. The experiment is successful (returns 1) if the adversary can infer whether the secure names in Θ_0 of Υ_b was computed from scratch or was selected from the Θ_1 after computing Θ_1, with a probability non-negligibly larger than $\frac{1}{2}$.

Name-Transparency Experiment: $\texttt{Name-Transp}_{\mathcal{A}, rN}^{transp}(\lambda)$ Let us consider the following experiment on name-transparency of the secure names $r\Pi$:

1. Probabilistic polynomial-time adversary $\mathcal{A}$ is given oracle access to
   rNameGen$(\lambda_1, \lambda_2, \cdot)$ and rNameVrfy$(\lambda_1, \lambda_2, \cdot)$.

2. $\mathcal{A}$ outputs two sets of vertices V_0, and V_1, such that $V_0 \subset V_1$.

3. A random b is drawn uniformly from $\{0, 1\}$.
   $\Theta_b \leftarrow$ rNameGen$(1^{\lambda_1}, 1^{\lambda_2}, V_b)$. If $b = 1$, then the set of secure names Θ_0 for the vertices in V_0 are selected from Θ_1. Then the *challenge* (Θ_0, V_0) is given to $\mathcal{A}$.

4. $\mathcal{A}$ continues to have oracle access to rNameGen$(\lambda_1, \lambda_2, \cdot)$ and rNameVrfy$(\lambda_1, \lambda_2, \cdot)$. Eventually, $\mathcal{A}$ outputs a bit b' (for the *challenge* (Θ_0, V_0)).

5. The output of the experiment is 1 if $b' = b$, and 0 otherwise.

DEFINITION 4.7 (NAME-TRANSPARENCY). *The secure naming scheme rN preserves transparency, if*
$Pr(\texttt{Name-Transp}_{\mathcal{A}, rN}^{transp}(\lambda)=1) \leq$
$\frac{1}{2} + max(\texttt{negl}(\lambda_1), \texttt{negl}(\lambda_2))$, *where* $max(i, j)$ *returns the larger of i and j.*

5. CONSTRUCTION

In this section, we propose a construction of leakage-free redactable signatures for trees that is transparent as well as efficient (it computes only one aggregate signature).

5.1 Secure Naming Scheme: rN

By definition, a secure naming scheme generates a set of names of a certain size. Such names can be assigned to an ordered set (of siblings, for example) that can be used for the purpose of verifying the order between any pair of elements in this set without revealing any information about the other elements or their relationships. In what follows we propose such a scheme.

In the computation of LR and RL below, the resulting values would be equal only with a negligible probability (in terms of the length of the parts). Note that each of these lengths are large enough to be a security parameter.

Name Generation:
rNameGen: Generate secure names for a set of nodes $x_1, x_2, ... x_k$.

1. Let N be the size of the secure names; let $\oplus$ denote the logical bit-wise XOR operation; let $\mathcal{H}$ be a collision-resistant hash function (which implies that it is an one-way function); let $m||n$ denote concatenation of m and n. Let the number of the siblings that need to be assigned secure names be k.

2. Without loss of generality, let $x_i \prec x_j$, where $i < j$, and $1 < i, j < k$.

3. Compute the secure names θ_{xi} and θ_{xj} for two siblings x_i and x_j, respectively, as follows. Let $i \leftarrow 1$ and $j \leftarrow 2$.

4. Assign θ_{xi} (i.e., the leftmost sibling for whom $i = 1$) a random.

5. All the bit positions of θ_{xi} are unmarked initially.

6. Compute the remaining secure names as follows.

   (a) Assign θ_{xj} a distinct random. All the bit positions of θ_{xj} are unmarked initially.

   (b) Divide θ_{xi} and θ_{xj} into three parts such as L_1, L_2, L_3, R_1, R_2, and R_3, respectively, such that lengths of the first and second parts are $\lceil \frac{N}{3} \rceil$, and the length of the third part is $N - 2\lceil \frac{N}{3} \rceil$.

   (c) Compute $LR \leftarrow L_1 \oplus R_3 || L_2 \oplus R_1 || L_3 \oplus R_2$.

   (d) $RL \leftarrow R_1 \oplus L_3 || R_2 \oplus L_1 || R_3 \oplus L_2$.

   (e) $r \leftarrow LR \mod N$, and $s \leftarrow RL \mod N$. r and s refer to the two indices in the bit-representation of the bit-strings θ_{xi} and θ_{xj}, respectively, with the left-most bit being the 0'th bit.

   (f) If the bit position r for θ_{xi} and/or s for θ_{xj} are not "unmarked", then repeat from step 7, else mark these positions in the respective secure names, i.e., they are used.

   (g) If $\theta_{xi}(r) \oplus \theta_{xj}(s) = 0$, then the random assigned to θ_{xj} can not be the secure name with respect to θ_{xi}, and vice versa. Repeat from step 7.

   (h) *Order-preserving property*: If $\theta_{xi}(r) \oplus \theta_{xj}(s) = 1$, then assign θ_{xi} and θ_{xj} as the secure names for x_i and x_j, respectively, and proceed as follows.

      i. $j \leftarrow j + 1$. Select a pair of siblings $x_{i'}$ and $x_{j'}$ such that the former is the left sibling of the latter.

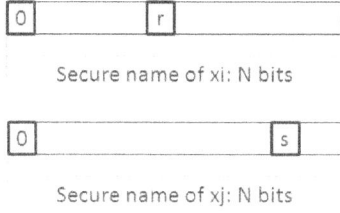

Figure 2: Secure names of two siblings.

ii. If the order-preserving property does not hold for the new pair, repeat from step 9. If there is no pair whose secure names do not satisfy the order-preserving property, then stop.

Order Verification:
`rNameVrfy`: Verify order between x and y: $x \prec y$, using secure names.

1. Let x and y be the two siblings such that $x \prec y$, and this order has to be verified.

2. Verify the order $x \prec y$ using the secure names L and R for the two siblings x and y, respectively, as follows.

   (a) Divide θ_{xi} and θ_{xj} into three parts such as L_1, L_2, L_3, R_1, R_2, and R_3, respectively, such that lengths of first and second parts are $\lceil \frac{N}{3} \rceil$, and the length of the third part is $N - 2\lceil \frac{N}{3} \rceil$. Note that each of these lengths are large enough to be a security parameter.

   (b) Compute $LR \leftarrow L_1 \oplus R_3 \parallel L_2 \oplus R_1 \parallel L_3 \oplus R_2$.

   (c) $RL \leftarrow R_1 \oplus L_3 \parallel R_2 \oplus L_1 \parallel R_3 \oplus L_2$.

   (d) $r \leftarrow LR \mod N$, and $s \leftarrow RL \mod N$. r and s refer to the two indices in the bit-representation of the bit-strings θ_{xi} and θ_{xj}, respectively, with the left-most bit being the 0'th bit.

   (e) Apply the *order-preserving property*: if and only if $\theta_{xi}(r) \oplus \theta_{xj}(s) = 1$, then the order $x_i \prec x_j$ is verified to be correct.

For the sake of generality, we should mention that the secure names L and R can be divided into $n' > 2$ parts. Moreover, LR, RL can be computed from these n' parts that leads to the non-commutative relationship between LR and RL. By the non-commutative property, we mean that $LR \neq RL$, which is the key for the order-verification process. The constraint is that each part of a name should have a size that is large enough to be a security parameter.

The above algorithm translates into a simple and constant-time test of which of two given siblings is to the left of the other. The above naming scheme computes secure names that are suitable for our notion of transparency (leakage-free property). If someone has access to one sibling node out of k siblings, then she cannot infer the existence of other siblings, because the attacker cannot compute the indices nor the bit value with a probability that is non-negligibly larger than $\frac{1}{2}$. This negligible probability is defined based on the size of the secure names. Given a subset of the k siblings, the attacker cannot learn existence of remaining other siblings. This is because of the properties of the random numbers assigned to the secure names, collision-resistant hash function, and the XOR operation.

5.2 LFR Signature for Trees

In this section, we describe the signature, distribution and verification protocols for trees. Prior to computing the signatures, a dummy node is inserted by splitting an edge: if $e(x, y)$ is an edge in the original tree, add a node w such that $e(x, w)$ and $e(w, y)$ are the new edges in the modified tree. Secure name θ_w of each inserted node w is a random. Such node w when given to a user only when the user has access to *both* x and y. The ordering between them is not needed to be verified by secure names.

The LFR signature scheme for trees is built using secure names, and Condensed-RSA scheme. The secure naming scheme has been described earlier in the paper. A brief summary of the Condensed-RSA (CRSA) scheme is given below.

5.2.1 Summary of CRSA

The public key and private keys of an RSA scheme are $(\bar{n}, \bar{e})$, and $\bar{d}$, respectively [16], where $\bar{n}$ is the product of two large random primes $\bar{p}$ and $\bar{q}$. $\bar{e}, \bar{d} \in Z_n^*$, such that $\bar{e}\bar{d} \equiv 1 \mod (\bar{p}-1)(\bar{q}-1)$. A message M is signed using RSA signature as follows: Signature of M $\sigma_M \leftarrow \mathcal{H}(M)^{\bar{d}} \mod \bar{n}$. A RSA signature σ_M is verified as follows: $\sigma_M^{\bar{e}} \stackrel{?}{=} \mathcal{H}(M) \mod \bar{n}$. Let $M_1, M_2, \ldots, M_m$ refer to m messages. The condensed signature of these m messages is computed as follows: first compute the RSA signature σ_i for each message i, $1 \leq i \leq m$; then compute the product of these signatures $\sigma_{1,m} \leftarrow \prod_{i=1}^{m} \sigma_i \mod \bar{n}$. The Condensed-RSA signature $\sigma_{1,m}$ is verified as follows: $(\sigma_{1,m})^{\bar{e}} \stackrel{?}{=} \prod_{i=1}^{m} \mathcal{H}(M_i) \pmod{\bar{n}}$. The definitions are simplified versions of RSA with no padding. Condensed-RSA is unforgeable against an adaptive chosen-message attack under the assumption that RSA is a one-way function [16][2].

5.2.2 Signing a Tree (rSign)

In order to sign a tree, we define a notion of an integrity verifier for each node. An integrity verifier (IV) of a node is the hash of the secure name of its parent, its secure name and its contents. In case of inserted nodes, no contents is used in IV. Using the IVs, we define a signature $\sigma_{T(V,E)}$ (also referred to as σ_T) for $T(V, E)$. In cases when "the received subtree (sent to the user) is the same as the original tree" is a sensitive information, the signature of a tree may be salted using a random value in order to protect this fact. The (salted) tree signature is publicly available or passed to the user alongwith the subtree that the user has access to. $\sigma_{T(V,E)}$ is an aggregate signature, computed over the IVs of its nodes. We define a signature for trees based on the condensed-RSA (CRSA) signatures [16].

DEFINITION 5.1 (INTEGRITY VERIFIER). *Let x be a node in tree $T(V, E)$, and c_x be the content of node x. Its integrity verifier (IV) denoted by ξ_x, is defined as: $\xi_x \leftarrow \mathcal{H}(\theta_{\hat{p}_x} \| \theta_x \| c_x)$.*

In this section, we define the signature of a tree based on Condensed-RSA signature scheme [16].

DEFINITION 5.2 (SIGNATURE OF TREES USING CRSA). *Let $T(V, E)$ be a tree, $\mathcal{H}$ denote a random oracle, the RSA signature σ_x of each node x be defined as follows $\sigma_x \leftarrow \xi_x^{\bar{d}} \mod \bar{n}$, where ξ_x is the IV of x. Let the salt be ω_T be a random, and let $\Omega_T \leftarrow \omega_T^{\bar{d}} \mod \bar{n}$. The signature of T, denoted by σ_T, is defined as*

$$\sigma_T = \Omega_T \prod_{x \in V} \sigma_x \mod \bar{n}. \tag{1}$$

rSign: Sign tree $T(V, E)$.

1. For each node $x \in V$, compute its secure name θ_x, and compute its IV: $\xi_x \leftarrow \mathcal{H}(\theta_{\hat{p}_x} \| \theta_x \| c_x)$.

2. Assign a salt ω_T to T.

3. Compute the "signature of the tree" $\sigma_{T(V,E)}$ using CRSA as follows:

   (a) For each $x \in V$, $\sigma_x \leftarrow (\xi_x)^{\bar{d}} \bmod \bar{n}$.

   (b) Compute the signature σ_T by evaluating Eq. 1, where $\Omega_T \leftarrow \omega_T{}^{\bar{d}} \bmod \bar{n}$.

Figure 3: Algorithm to sign a tree.

---

rRedact: Computed signature of the redacted subtree $T_\delta(V_\delta, E_\delta) \subseteq T(V, E)$.

1. $\sigma'_{T_\delta} \leftarrow \langle \sigma_{T_\delta}, \mathcal{VO}, \Theta_{T_\delta} \rangle$, computed as follows.

2. Θ_{T_δ} is the set of all secure names of the nodes and their respective parents in T_δ: $\Theta_{T_\delta} \leftarrow \{(\theta_x, \theta_{\hat{p}_x}) | x \in V_\delta\}$.

3. Compute the collective integrity verifier $\mathcal{VO}$ as follows.

4. CRSA: $\mathcal{VO} \leftarrow \omega_T \prod_{x \in (V - V_\delta)} \xi_x \bmod \bar{n}$;
   $\sigma_{T_\delta} \leftarrow \prod_{x \in V_\delta} \sigma_x \bmod \bar{n}$.

Figure 4: Algorithm to redact a subtree.

5.2.3 Distribution (rRedact)

The distributor $\mathcal{D}$ sends the following items to Bob, who has access to $T_\delta(V_\delta, E_\delta)$, a subtree of tree $T(V, E)$ $(T_\delta(V_\delta, E_\delta), \mathcal{VO}_{T_\delta}, \sigma_T)$, where $\mathcal{VO}_{T_\delta(V_\delta, E_\delta)}$ (also referred to as $\mathcal{VO}_{T_\delta}$) is the verification object of T_δ, and σ_T the signature of the $T(V, E)$. The following steps show how to compute $\mathcal{VO}_{T_\delta}$. $\mathcal{D}$ computes two collective IVs σ_{T_δ} and Δ_{T_δ} as part of $\mathcal{VO}_{T_\delta}$ over the IVs of all the nodes that are not in the subtree and also includes the salt.

$\mathcal{VO}$ is used to verify the signature of the tree and to detect if any node(s) has been dropped form T_δ in an unauthorized manner. σ_{T_δ} is used to verify the signature of all the nodes in the subtree in an aggregate manner, and is used to detect if any node(s) has been injected form T_δ in an unauthorized manner. θ_x is the secure name of x.

5.2.4 Authentication (rVrfy)

Bob receives the subtree $T_\delta(V_\delta, E_\delta)$, the signature of the tree σ_T, and the verification object $\mathcal{VO}$. As part of the content authentication process, Bob computes the IVs of the nodes in V_δ and combines them with the received collective IV $\mathcal{VO}$. If the contents of the nodes are valid, the structural integrity is verified with the help of secure names: the parent-child relationship, and the order among the siblings. Authentication of contents and structural positions of the subtree received includes (1) verification of integrity and, (2) verification of the source of the subtree. The integrity verification of structural relations in a tree involves traversing the tree and using the secure-name of two siblings of its parent or its sibling. The user can carry out verification of integrity of a n'-node subtree in $O(n')$-time. The verification procedure is given in Figure 5.

Two nodes are siblings in a graph if they have a common imme-

---

rVrfy: Verify authenticity of subtree $T_\delta(V_\delta, E_\delta)$.
Authentication of nodes:

1. For each node $y \in V_\delta$, compute $\xi_y \leftarrow \mathcal{H}(\theta_{\hat{p}_y} \| \theta_y \| c_y)$.

2. CRSA: Verify (a) and (b):
   (a) $(\sigma_{T_\delta})^{\bar{e}} \overset{?}{=} \prod_{y \in V_\delta} \xi_y \ (mod \ \bar{n})$, *and,*
   (b) $(\sigma_T)^{\bar{e}} \overset{?}{=} \mathcal{VO} \prod_{y \in V_\delta} \xi_y \ (mod \ \bar{n})$.

3. If (a) and (b) are valid, then the contents and secure names of T_δ are authenticated. Otherwise, if (b) is invalid and (a) is valid, then the received nodes are authenticated, but either some nodes have been dropped, or $\mathcal{VO}$ and/or σ_T have been tampered with.

Verification of edges and ordering among siblings:

1. Carry out a depth-first traversal on T_δ.

2. *Parent-child relationship:* Let x be the parent of y in T_δ; if $(\theta_x \neq \theta_{\hat{p}_y})$, then this relationship is incorrect.

3. *Order among siblings:* For ordered trees, in T_δ, let y and z are children of x, and let $y \prec z$.

4. Verify whether $y \prec z$ is true by carrying out the steps for "Order Verification" specified in Section 5.1.

Figure 5: Algorithm to verify a subtree.

diate ancestor. The number of signatures computed is 1, and the number of hashings carried out is $O(|V| + |E|)$.

Graphs and Forests: Ordered graphs and forests can be signed using the above scheme with a small modification: an edge verifier for each edge between x and y ($e(x, y)$) are computed as follows and is signed as part of the CRSA computation: $\mathcal{H}(\theta_x, \theta_y)$. Since the edge relationships are already accounted for, the secure name of a parent node is not included in the computation of the integrity verifier of a node any more.

5.3 Security

The following lemma states the security of the proposed construction rN.

LEMMA 5.3. *Under the standard model, rN preserves name-transparency.*

The following lemmas state the security of the proposed construction $r\Pi$.

LEMMA 5.4. *Under the random oracle hypothesis, and the assumption that the RSA problem is hard, $r\Pi$ is existentially unforgeable under chosen-message attack over subset operation over trees/graphs/forests.*

LEMMA 5.5. *Under the random oracle hypothesis, and the assumption that the RSA problem is hard, $r\Pi$ preserves transparency.*

6. RELATED WORK

Redactable signature [10] and sanitizable signature schemes [7] support computation of valid signatures for modified messages from the signatures of the source messages. However, such schemes leak structural information. Recently Kundu and Bertino proposed structural signatures for trees [12] and graphs [13] in order to compute signatures of redactable subtrees and subgraphs. They also show that leakages and privacy breaches occur due to the widely used "Merkle Hash Technique" [14]. However, (1) they have not provided a formal model of security, and (2) their approaches are quite expensive - the number of signatures computed is the linear in the size of the tree/graph. Brzuska et al [3] have proposed a formal model for the notion of structural signatures for trees and have proposed a construction for authentication of connected sub-trees, which is of quadratic complexity. Our proposed construction makes use of "secure names" and is of linear complexity.

Integrity assurance of tree-structured data is primarily carried by the Merkle hash technique [14]. This scheme requires information about other nodes and edges (extraneous information) in order to verify the integrity of a subtree, which is why it leaks. Merkle hash technique is integrity-preserving, but at the same time leaks [5, 12]. There are two types of sanitization of documents, where a document is a collection of several sub-documents: one that allows modification of sub-documents in a document, and another that allows only deletion of the sub-documents. Sanitizable signature schemes [7][4][15] focus on hiding only the sub-documents being sanitized, but not their structural position in the document and the structural relationships they have with other sub-documents. Homomorphic and redactable signatures [17] as well as content extraction signatures [6] (which are a form of redactable signatures [1]) leak information about the structural position. (Interested readers are referred to [1] for a conceptual analysis of sanitizable signatures, homomorphic, redactable, transitive and content extraction signatures.) Haber et al [9] proposed a signature scheme that prohibiting it. It however it leaks information about the existence of sub-documents and their structural positions.

7. CONCLUSION AND FUTURE WORKS

Redactable signatures are an important area of research especially for third-party data management and cloud computing models. Leakages of structural information due to (redactable) signatures lead to privacy and confidentiality breaches. In the literature, there has not been any formal model for leakage-free redactable signatures able to handle trees, graphs as well as forests.

In this paper, we propose a formal model that supports query results to be not only subtrees but also disconnected subtrees, and (disconnected) sub-graphs and sub-forests. Our formal model follows the definition of integrity of redactable signatures as defined by Johnson et al. [10]. We have also proposed a formal model for secure naming schemes, and a construction of leakage-free redactable signature for trees, graphs and forests based on secure names. In future, we plan to apply the scheme described here towards security of cloud-based data management especially of healthcare data.

8. ACKNOWLEDGEMENTS

Portions of this work were supported by National Science Foundation Grants CNS-0915436, CNS-0913875, Science and Technology Center CCF-0939370; by an NPRP grant from the Qatar National Research Fund; by Grant FA9550-09-1-0223 from the Air Force Office of Scientific Research; and by sponsors of the Center for Education and Research in Information Assurance and Security. The statements made herein are solely the responsibility of the authors.

9. REFERENCES

[1] G. Ateniese, D. H. Chou, B. de Medeiros, and G. Tsudik. Sanitizable signatures. In *ESORICS*, pages 159–177, 2005.

[2] Mihir Bellare, Juan A. Garay, and Tal Rabin. Fast batch verification for modular exponentiation and digital signatures. In *EUROCRYPT*, 1998.

[3] C. Brzuska, H. Busch, Ö. Dagdelen, M. Fischlin, M. Franz, S. Katzenbeisser, M. Manulis, C. Onete, A. Peter, B. Poettering, and D. Schröder. Redactable signatures for tree-structured data: Definitions and constructions. In *ACNS*, 2010.

[4] Christina Brzuska, Marc Fischlin, Anja Lehmann, and Dominique Schröder. Unlinkability of sanitizable signatures. In *Public Key Cryptography*, 2010.

[5] A. Buldas and S. Laur. Knowledge-binding commitments with applications in time-stamping. In *Public Key Cryptography*, pages 150–165, 2007.

[6] L. Bull, P. Stanski, and D. McG. Squire. Content extraction signatures using xml digital signatures and custom transforms on-demand. In *WWW*, 2003.

[7] Danielh. Chou, Breno De Medeiros, and Gene Tsudik. Sanitizable signatures. In *ESORICS*, 2005.

[8] S. Goldwasser, S. Micali, and R. L. Rivest. A digital signature scheme secure against adaptive chosen-message attacks. *SIAM J. Comput.*, 17(2), 1988.

[9] S. Haber, Y. Hatano, Y. Honda, W. Horne, K. Miyazaki, T. Sander, S. Tezoku, and D. Yao. Efficient signature schemes supporting redaction, pseudonymization, and data deidentification. In *ASIACCS*, 2008.

[10] R. Johnson, D. Molnar, D. Song, and D. Wagner. Homomorphic signature schemes. In *In CT-RSA*, 2002.

[11] J. Katz and Y. Lindell. *Introduction to Modern Cryptography: Principles and Protocols*. Chapman & Hall/CRC, 2007.

[12] A. Kundu and E. Bertino. Structural signatures for tree data structures. In *VLDB*, 2008.

[13] A. Kundu and E. Bertino. How to authenticate graphs without leaking. In *EDBT*, 2010.

[14] R. C. Merkle. A certified digital signature. In *CRYPTO*, 1989.

[15] K. Miyazaki, G. Hanaoka, and H. Imai. Digitally signed document sanitizing scheme based on bilinear maps. In *ASIACCS*, 2006.

[16] E. Mykletun, M. Narasimha, and G. Tsudik. Authentication and integrity in outsourced databases. *ACM Trans. of Storage*, 2(2):107–138, 2006.

[17] R. Rivest. "two new signature schemes", presented at cambridge seminar, 2001.

Detecting Repackaged Smartphone Applications in Third-Party Android Marketplaces

Wu Zhou, Yajin Zhou, Xuxian Jiang, Peng Ning

North Carolina State University
890 Oval Drive, Raleigh, NC 27695
{wzhou2, yajin_zhou xuxian_jiang, pning}@ncsu.edu

ABSTRACT

Recent years have witnessed incredible popularity and adoption of smartphones and mobile devices, which is accompanied by large amount and wide variety of feature-rich smartphone applications. These smartphone applications (or apps), typically organized in different application marketplaces, can be conveniently browsed by mobile users and then simply clicked to install on a variety of mobile devices. In practice, besides the official marketplaces from platform vendors (e.g., Google and Apple), a number of third-party alternative marketplaces have also been created to host thousands of apps (e.g., to meet regional or localization needs). To maintain and foster a hygienic smartphone app ecosystem, there is a need for each third-party marketplace to offer quality apps to mobile users.

In this paper, we perform a systematic study on six popular Android-based third-party marketplaces. Among them, we find a common "in-the-wild" practice of repackaging legitimate apps (from the official Android Market) and distributing repackaged ones via third-party marketplaces. To better understand the extent of such practice, we implement an app similarity measurement system called DroidMOSS that applies a fuzzy hashing technique to effectively localize and detect the changes from app-repackaging behavior. The experiments with DroidMOSS show a worrisome fact that 5% to 13% of apps hosted on these studied marketplaces are repackaged. Further manual investigation indicates that these repackaged apps are mainly used to replace existing in-app advertisements or embed new ones to "steal" or re-route ad revenues. We also identify a few cases with planted backdoors or malicious payloads among repackaged apps. The results call for the need of a rigorous vetting process for better regulation of third-party smartphone application marketplaces.

Categories and Subject Descriptors   C.4 [**Performance of Systems**]: Measurement techniques; K.6.5 [**Management of Computing and Information Systems**]: Security and protection – *Invasive software*

General Terms   Algorithms, Measurement, Security

Keywords   Smartphones, Privacy and Security, Repackaging

Permission to make digital or hard copies of all or part of this work for personal or classroom use is granted without fee provided that copies are not made or distributed for profit or commercial advantage and that copies bear this notice and the full citation on the first page. To copy otherwise, to republish, to post on servers or to redistribute to lists, requires prior specific permission and/or a fee.
CODASPY'12, February 7–9, 2012, San Antonio, Texas, USA.
Copyright 2012 ACM 978-1-4503-1091-8/12/02 ...$10.00.

1. INTRODUCTION

Smartphones have recently gained much popularity and demand. A recent report shows that in July of 2011, the number of Android smartphone activations reached $550,000$ each day [34]. Besides the portability and mobility, the popularity is also possibly due to the large amount and wide variety of feature-rich smartphone applications (or apps) mobile users can install and experience. As an example, there already have more than $200,000$ apps in the official Android Market [3] (starting May 2011). These feature-rich apps extend the capability of smartphones by empowering users to browse, socialize, entertain, and communicate on the go with unprecedented convenience and experiences, instead of limiting users for basic phone calls or simple text messages.

To allow for mobile users to conveniently browse and install these smartphone apps, platform vendors created centralized marketplaces, including Apple's App Store [23] and Google's Android Market [26]. Through the centralized marketplaces, developers can submit their apps to these marketplaces and make them available to thousands of users. Platform owners can also better control the quality of apps and block malicious ones to protect users. Meanwhile, a number of third-party marketplaces were also created for various purposes (e.g., to meet regional or localization needs). Cydia [10] and Amazon AppStore [22] are two such examples that host thousands of apps for iPhone and Android users, respectively.

To maintain and foster a hygienic smartphone app ecosystem, there is a need for third-party marketplaces to offer quality apps to mobile users. In this paper, we focus on six popular Android-based third-party marketplaces and perform a systematic study on the $22,906$ apps collected from them. Particularly, we observe that the apps hosted in these third-party marketplaces can be classified into three categories: The first category includes apps that are also available in the official Android Market. It is possible as app developers may choose to submit their apps to both official and alternative marketplaces to reach more users. The second category contains apps that are only available from the third-party marketplaces. The reason is that developers may create apps targeting specific customers (e.g., in their own regions, countries, or languages). The third category, which is the main focus of our study, consists of apps that are repackaged from the official Android Market and re-distributed to third-party marketplaces. Specifically, repackaged apps are based on legitimate ones, but for whatever reasons, include some "value-added" functionality or modification. Unfortunately, repackaged apps could lead to a number of problems. For example, if a legitimate app is repackaged with additional malicious payloads or exploits, users may find their phones compromised, phone bills increased or sensitive information (stored on the phones) stolen. App developers are also impacted as they find their intellectual properties violated, the in-app revenues stolen, and their reputation impaired. From the marketplace perspective, they are also seriously affected because mobile users and developers are their customers, who might turn away to other marketplaces for better-quality apps. As a result, the entire smartphone app ecosystem could seriously suffer from repackaged apps.

In this paper, we are motivated to systematically detect repackaged apps on third-party Android marketplaces. In particular, we aim to shed some light on questions such as: How serious is the overall app repackaging situation in our current marketplaces? What purposes are these repackaged apps used for? Can we systematically identify them? Note that the answers can be greatly helpful in assuring users that a downloaded app is legitimate and does not contain any malicious payload. Moreover, developers are also protected since their intellectual properties are not violated. For marketplace owners, they can also ensure that their marketplaces are not populated with repackaged or trojanized apps.

As our first step, we present a system called DroidMOSS[1] to measure the similarity between two different apps and use it as the basis to detect repackaged apps. Specifically, given each app from a third-party Android marketplace, we measure its similarity with those apps from the official Android Market. In order to handle a large number of apps in the official and alternative marketplaces, we choose to extract some distinguishing features from apps, and generate app-specific fingerprints. Our fingerprint generation is based on a fuzzy hashing technique to localize and detect the modifications repackagers apply over the original apps. After that, we calculate the edit distance to gauge how similar each app pair is. When the similarity exceeds certain threshold, we consider one app in the pair is repackaged.

We have implemented a DroidMOSS prototype and used it to study six third-party Android marketplaces worldwide, including two from United States (with $6,296$ apps), two from China (with $12,595$ apps), and two from East Europe (with $4,015$ apps). These apps were collected in the first week of March, 2011 and are measured against the $68,187$ apps collected from the official Android Market in the same time frame. To perform a concrete analysis, we randomly picked up 200 apps from each of these six marketplaces, and measured their similarity with the total $68,187$ apps in the official Android Market. From the resulting $81,824,400$ pair-wise similarity scores, DroidMOSS systematically reports the repackaged apps. For each reported one, we perform a manual analysis and then calculate the false positive rate. Our results show that 5% to 13% of apps hosted in these six marketplaces are re-packaged (with false positive rates ranging from 7.1% to 13.3%). Also, we found that 13.5% to 30% of apps in these alternative marketplaces are simply redistributed from the official Android Market. A further manual investigation indicates that these repackaged apps are mainly used to replace existing in-app advertisements or embed new ones to "steal" or re-route ad revenues. We also identified a few serious cases with planted backdoors or malicious payloads in repackaged apps. These worrisome facts call for the imperative need of a rigorous vetting process in third-party marketplaces.

The rest of this paper is organized as follows: We describe the DroidMOSS system design for app similarity measurement in Section 2, followed by its prototyping and evaluation results in Section 3. After that, we discuss the limitations of our system and suggest possible improvement in Section 4. Finally, we describe related work in Section 5 and conclude this paper in Section 6.

---

[1] The name comes from an earlier system called MOSS [39] that is designed to measure software similarity and has been primarily used in detecting plagiarism in programming classes (based on source code submissions).

2. DESIGN

To systematically detect repackaged apps in third-party marketplaces, we have three key design goals: *accuracy, scalability, and efficiency*. Accuracy is a natural requirement to effectively identify app-repackaging behavior in current marketplaces. However, challenges arise from the fact that the repackaging process might dramatically change the function naming or code layout in the repackaged app, which renders whole-app hashing schemes ineffective. Also, due to the large number of apps in various marketplaces, our approach needs to be scalable and efficient. As a matter of fact, our current data set for app similarity measurement has $81,824,400$ app pairs, which makes expensive semantics-aware full app analysis not feasible. Accordingly, in our design, we choose to collect syntactic instruction sequences from each app and then distill them for fingerprint generation. The generated fingerprints need to be robust in order to accommodate possible changes from app-repackaging behavior.

Assumption In this paper, we aim to uncover repackaged apps in current marketplaces and understand the overall situation. We focus on Java code inside Android apps without considering native code. One reason is that native code is harder for repackager to modify. Also our dataset shows that only a small number of (5%) apps contains native code. Moreover, the apps from the official Android Market are assumed to be trusted and not re-packaged. There may exist exceptions to this assumption, but DroidMOSS is still helpful in distinguishing app pairs with repackaging relationship (Section 4). Finally, we assume that the signing keys from app developers are not leaked. Therefore, it is not possible that a repackaged app will be signed by the same author as the original one.

2.1 Overview

Repackaged apps share two common characteristics: First, due to the repackaging nature, the code base is similar between the original app and the repackaged app. Second, since the developers' signing keys are not leaked, the original app and the repackaged app must be signed with different developer keys. DroidMOSS capitalizes on these two insights by extracting related features from apps and then discerning whether one app is repackaged from the other.

Figure 1 shows an overview of our approach. In essence, DroidMOSS has three key steps. The first step is to extract from each app two main features, i.e., instructions contained in the app and its author information. These two features are used to uniquely identify each app. After that, the second step is to generate a fingerprint for each app. The reason is that each app may contain hundreds of thousands of instructions. There is a need to significantly condense it into a much shorter sequence as its fingerprint (for similarity measurement). Finally, based on app fingerprints, the third step discerns the source of apps, i.e., either from the official Android Market or from the third-party marketplaces, and measures their pair-wise similarity scores (so that we can detect repackaged apps). In the following, we examine each step in more detail.

2.2 Feature Extraction

Each Android app is essentially a compressed archive file, which contains the *classes.dex* file and a *META-INF* subdirectory. The *classes.dex* file contains the actual Dalvik bytecode for execution while the *META-INF* subdirectory contains the author information.

To extract Dalvik bytecode from *classes.dex*, we leverage existing Dalvik disassemblers (i.e., *baksmali* [1]). Initially, we use the Dalvik bytecode (with opcodes and operands) as the code

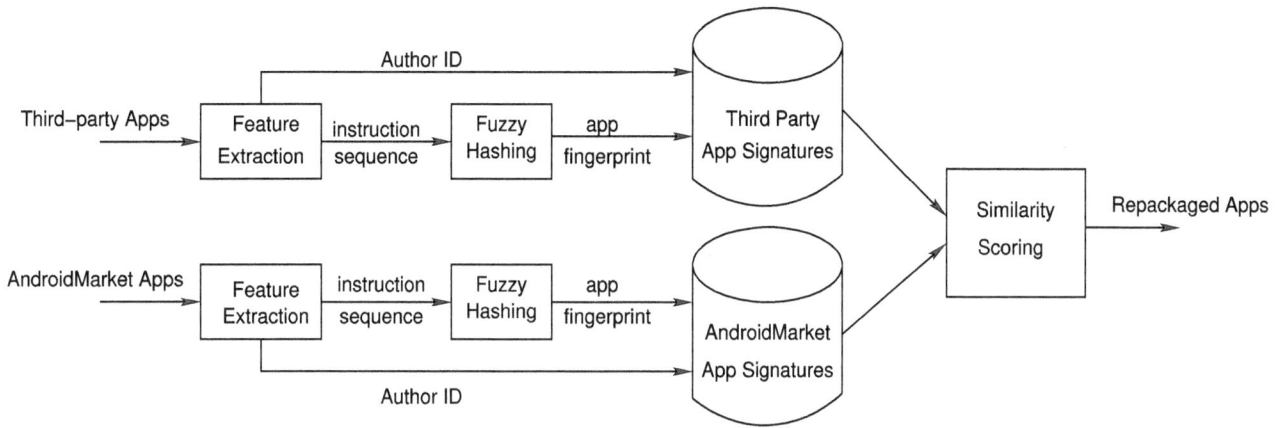

Figure 1: An Overview of DroidMOSS

feature directly. It turns out that it is not robust even for simple obfuscation that could just change some string operands (such as string names or hard-coded URLs). Because of that, we opt to make further abstraction by removing the operands and retaining only the opcode. The intuition is that it might be easy for repackagers to modify or rename the (non-critical) operands, but much harder to change the actual instructions. In the meantime, we also observe that apps intend to include various ad SDK libraries to fetch and display ads. After being disassembled, these shared ad libraries unnecessarily introduce noise to our feature extraction. Fortunately, there are a limited number of them and our current prototype builds a white-list to remove them from the extracted code.

For the author information, the *META-INF* subdirectory contains the full developer certificate, from which we can obtain the developer name, contact and organization information, as well as the public key fingerprints. For simplicity, we map each developer certificate into one unique 32-bit identifier (or authorID). This unique identifier is then integrated into the signature for comparison.

2.3 Fingerprint Generation

For each app, our second step generates a fingerprint from the extracted code. A common way of achieving that is through hashing. Although hashing the entire code sequence of an app can uniquely determine whether two apps are the same, they are not helpful to determine whether two files are similar. The reason is simply because one minor modification will dramatically change the hashing value. From another perspective, calculating the edit distance between two given sequences is a well-known technique to measure their similarity. Unfortunately, it cannot be directly applied either. Considering each instruction sequence (of an app) could have hundreds of thousands of instructions, it will be very expensive to calculate one single edit distance between two apps, not to mention the large number of apps each needs to be paired and compared with others.

In DroidMOSS, we adopt a specialized hashing technique called *fuzzy hashing* [21]. Instead of directly processing or comparing the entire (long) instruction sequences, it first condenses each sequence into one much shorter fingerprint. The similarity between two apps is then calculated based on the shorter fingerprints, not the original sequences. Therefore, a natural requirement for fuzzy hashing is that the reduction into shorter fingerprints should minimize the change, if any, to the similarity of two sequences.

To achieve that, we first divide the instruction sequence into smaller pieces. Each piece is considered as an independent unit

Algorithm 1 Generate the app fingerprint

Input: Instruction sequence *iseq* of the app
Output: Fingerprint *fp*
Description: wsize - sliding window size, rp - reset point value, sw - content in sliding window, ph - the piece hash

1: $set\_wsize(wsize)$
2: $set\_resetpoint(rp)$
3: $init\_sliding\_window(sw)$
4: $init\_piece\_hash(ph)$
5: **for all** byte d from $iseq$ **do**
6:    $update\_sliding\_window(sw, d)$
7:    $rh \leftarrow rolling\_hash(sw)$
8:    $update\_piece\_hash(ph, d)$
9:    **if** $rh = rp$ **then**
10:       $fp \leftarrow concatenate(fp, ph)$
11:       $init\_piece\_hash(ph)$
12:    **end if**
13: **end for**
14: **return** fp

to contribute to the final fingerprint. Therefore, if the repackaging process changes one piece, its impact on the final fingerprint is effectively localized and contained within this piece. For the rest pieces that are not changed, their contributions to the final fingerprint are still valid and persistent through the repackaging process, thus reflecting the similarity between the original app and the repackaged one. However, the challenge lies on the determination of the boundary of each piece. In DroidMOSS, we use a sliding window that starts from the very beginning of the instruction sequence and moves forward until its rolling hashing value equals a pre-selected *reset point*, which determines the boundary of the current piece. Specifically, if a reset point is reached, a new piece should be started. The concrete process is presented in Algorithm 1 and visually summarized in Figure 2.

For further elaboration, suppose a repackaged app has added a new instruction to invoke an external function. For simplicity, we assume the new instruction is inserted in the first piece of the instruction sequence (i.e., *piece 1* in Figure 2). Since our fuzzy hashing scheme uses a sliding window to calculate the rolling hash to determine the piece boundary, there are two possibilities about the placement of the new instruction in the first piece, either falling outside or inside the last sliding window. The former affects only

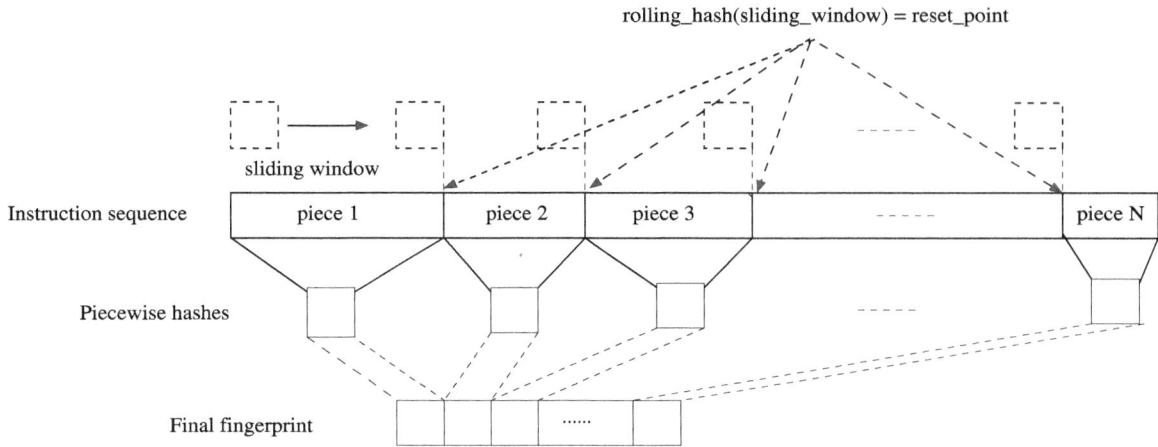

Figure 2: Fuzzy Hashing for Fingerprint Generation

the calculated hash value in the first piece while the rest pieces are intact. The latter changes the rolling hash value of the last sliding window (of the original *piece 1*). As a result, instead of stopping at the original boundary, we keep moving forward the sliding window until it hits the last sliding window in the second piece. In other words, it merges the first two pieces into one. Notice that it does not affect the determination of boundaries of the subsequent pieces. Therefore, for the final fingerprint generation, it only changes the hash values of the first two consecutive pieces. In either way, our scheme effectively localizes the changes.[2]

In our design, to derive the fingerprint, we need to apply traditional hash function twice. The first is to calculate the hash value of each piece (after its boundary is determined) and the calculated hash values of all pieces are combined into the final fingerprint. The second is to calculate a hash value on the content of the sliding window, which is matched against the reset point. In our prototype, we use a prime number as the reset point to enhance the randomization or robustness of our scheme against possible repackaging attacks.

2.4 Similarity Scoring

Our first two steps are applied for each app regardless of its source. In the third step, we divide the apps into two groups, one from the official Android Market and one from alternative marketplaces, and then calculate pair-wise similarity scores between the two. The similarity is based on the derived fingerprints, not the detailed (long) instruction sequence. Note that our fuzzy hashing scheme is deterministic in that if two apps from two groups are identical, the same fingerprints will be generated. In addition, it can also effectively localize the changes possibly made in repackaged apps.

Based on the above analysis, the similarity between the (shorter) fingerprints represents how similar their corresponding apps are. With that, our similarity scoring algorithm is to compute the edit distance between these two fingerprints, which is the number of minimum edit operations, including insertion, deletion and substitution of a single byte, needed to convert one fingerprint into another. The algorithm DroidMOSS adopts is a dynamic pro-

gramming algorithm as presented in Algorithm 2. In particular, for two fingerprints *fp1* and *fp2* (with lengths of *len1* and *len2*, respectively), we reserve a two-dimensional matrix (each value in the matrix is initialized to 0) to hold the edit distance between all prefixes of the first fingerprint and all prefixes of the second, and then compute the values in the matrix by flood filling the matrix. The distance between the two full strings will be the final value of the edit distance between the two fingerprints. The edit distance of any prefix subsequences of *fp1* and *fp2* can be derived from the minimum of three values: (1) $matrix(i-1,j)+1$, which means to add one insertion operation in *fp1*; (2) $matrix(i,j-1)+1$, which means to add one deletion operation in *fp2*; and (3) $matrix(i-1,j-1)+cost$, which means to add one substitution operation between *fp1* and *fp2*.

Algorithm 2 Calculate the edit distance between two apps

Input: Two fingerprints *fp1* and *fp2*
Output: Edit distance between *fp1* and *fp2*

1: $len1 \leftarrow strlen(fp1)$
2: $len2 \leftarrow strlen(fp2)$
3: $initialize\_two\_dimensional\_matrix(matrix, len1, len2)$
4: **for** $i = 0 \rightarrow len1$ **do**
5:     **for** $j = 0 \rightarrow len2$ **do**
6:         **if** $fp1[i] = fp[j]$ **then**
7:             $cost = 0$
8:         **else**
9:             $cost = 1$
10:         **end if**
11:         $matrix[i,j] = min(matrix[i-1,j]+1, matrix[i,j-1]+1, matrix[i-1,j-1]+cost)$
12:     **end for**
13: **end for**
14: **return** $matrix(len1, len2)$

Based on the calculated edit distance, we can derive a similarity score between two fingerprints. The formula we are using is as follows:

$$similarityScore = [1 - \frac{distance}{max(len1, len2)}] * 100 \quad (1)$$

If the calculated similarity score between two apps exceeds certain threshold and these two apps are signed with two different

---

Table 1: The Numbers of Collected Apps from Official or Alternative Android Marketplaces ([†]: the number in parenthesis shows the percentage of apps that are also hosted in the official Android Market.)

Marketplace	Total Number of Apps
US1 (slideme)	3108 (29.8%[†])
US2 (freewarelovers)	3188 (13.2%[†])
CN1 (eoemarket)	8261 (30%[†])
CN2 (goapk)	4334 (13.5%[†])
EE1 (softportal)	2305 (19.6%[†])
EE2 (proandroid)	1710 (20.2%[†])
Official Android Market	68187

Table 2: Repackaged App Detection from Six Studied Third-party Android Marketplaces (200 samples)

Third-party Marketplace	# Repackaged Apps from DroidMOSS	# Repackaged Apps from Manual Analysis	Percentage
US1	24	22	11%
US2	13	12	6%
EE1	11	10	5%
EE2	15	13	6.5%
CN1	27	25	12.5%
CN2	28	26	13%

developer keys, our system reports the one not from the official Android Market as repackaged. The threshold selection affects both false positives and false negatives of our system. Specifically, a high threshold likely leads to low false positives but also high false negatives while a low threshold introduces high false positives but with low false negatives. During our experiments, we empirically found the threshold 70 is a good balance between the two metrics (Section 3).

3. PROTOTYPING AND EVALUATION

We have implemented a prototype of DroidMOSS in Linux. In our prototype, the first step – feature extraction – is based on two open-source tools. Specifically, we use *baksmali* [1], a popular Dalvik disassembler to reverse *classes.dex* into an intermediate representation and then map it into Dalvik bytecode. A publicly available tool named *keytool* [25], which is already a part of Android SDK, is used to extract the author information. To glue them together, we created a number of *perl* scripts. For the next two steps, we implement our own C programs for fingerprint generation and similarity scoring. For efficiency reason, our rolling hash function is based on the spamsum algorithm proposed by Andrew [2] (originally for spam detection) and the sliding window size in our prototype is 7. The input to fingerprint generation is essentially those instruction sequences generated from the first step, while the output is used for similarity scoring. As mentioned earlier, the similarity scoring will also take into account the app author information: If two apps has the same authorID, we exclude them from repackaged app detection. If not, our prototype calculates the edit distance and derive the similarity score. The larger the score, the more similar the app pair.

To detect repackaged apps, we chose six popular third-party Android marketplaces worldwide: two in US, two in China, and two in Eastern Europe[3]. For each marketplace, we use a crawler to collect hosted apps. Our study is based on those apps collected in the first week of March, 2011. Meanwhile, we also collect more than sixty thousand apps from the official Android Market in the same time frame. The exact numbers of collected apps from official and alternative marketplaces are shown in Table 1. For each alternative marketplace, we also report the percentage of apps that are hosted in it but also have an identical copy in the official Android Market (i.e., the first category in Section 1). Table 1 shows our results.

---

[3]One domain is registered in Ukraine, but the resolved IP is actually located in US.

3.1 Repackaged Apps in Alternative Marketplaces

To perform a concrete study on the repackaged apps and measure the effectiveness of our approach, we randomly choose 200 samples from each third-party marketplace and detect whether they are repackaged from some official Android Market apps. Specifically, for each chosen app, we measure its similarity score with each of these $68,817$ ones inside the official Android Market. Among the calculated $68,817$ similarity scores, we choose the highest one for manual investigation. Among the total $1,200$ app pairs, we apply the threshold 70 to infer whether an app is repackaged or not.

Our results are shown in Table 2. The first column lists the name of these third-party marketplaces; the second column indicates the number of repackaged apps detected by DroidMOSS out of the 200 samples; the third column shows the manual analysis results; and the fourth one reports the corresponding repackaging rate. For each marketplace shown in the table, DroidMOSS reports that 5% to 13% of apps hosted on it are repackaged. Among the reported ones, we manually verify them and for each marketplace we only find one or two false positives, demonstrating the effectiveness of our approach. By further looking into the false positive cases, we notice that one main contributing factor is that our white-list of ad SDKs or shared libraries is incomplete. Note that by iterating the process to complete the white-list, there is a room for our system to be further improved.

Overall, our experiments show that the repackaging rates range from 5% to 13% among these third-party marketplaces. This is alarming as the repackaged apps seriously affect the entire smartphone app ecosystem. In the following paragraphs, we further look into individual repackaged apps and classify them into different categories for better understanding.

Injecting New In-App Advertisements In the first category, we observe new ad SDKs are added into the original app. Note that ad SDKs typically require adding a certain publisher identifier in the *AndroidManifest.xml* file, inserting layout description into the resource file, importing their own ad class files into the class directory, or even modifying the app bytecode. Recall that DroidMOSS considers ads as noise and thus filters them out for fingerprint generation and similarity scoring. With that, our system can easily spot them – as they share similar (or even identical) code sequences but are signed by different authors.

One example repackages a legitimate app *com.mmc.life49* by including the admob [24] SDK in the class hierarchy and adding a publisher identifier ADMOB_PUBLISHER_ID in *AndroidManifest.xml*. All the original bytecode remains intact. But some ad SDKs (e.g., wooboo [31] and youmi [42]) do require modifying existent class files in the original app to invoke ad-displaying code. Merely looking into the modified manifest file (or resource files)

Table 3: The Comparison of App Manifest Files from the Original App and the Repackaged App

Original *Angry Birds* (in the official Android Market)	Repackaged *Angry Birds* (in a US alternative marketplace)

<manifest android:versionCode="142"
   android:versionName="1.4.2"
   android:installLocation="preferExternal"
   package="com.rovio.angrybirds" xmlns:android="......">
 	
  <application android:label=......>
    ......
    <meta-data android:name="ADMOB_PUBLISHER_ID"
      android:value="**a14c9c5b4602e23**" />
    <meta-data android:name="ADMOB_INTERSTITIAL
      _PUBLISHER_ID" android:value="**a14ca2471ee0891**" />
    ......
  </application>
</manifest>
	<manifest android:versionCode="142"
	   android:versionName="1.4.2"
	   android:installLocation="preferExternal"
	   package="com.rovio.angrybirds" xmlns:android="......">
	
	  <application android:label=......>
	    ......
	    <meta-data android:name="ADMOB_PUBLISHER_ID"
	      android:value="**a14ce0cb83321d2**" />
	    <meta-data android:name="ADMOB_INTERSTITIAL
	      _PUBLISHER_ID" android:value="**a14ce0cbd3cc9a1**" />
	    ......
	  </application>
	</manifest>

and newly added class files is not enough to identify this kind of repackaging. In general, the modification is applied on small part of the original code. DroidMOSS can readily localize such kind of modification and detect the repackaging.

Usurping Existing In-App Advertisements In the second category, we also observe repackaged apps where existing ad SDKs still remain, but the corresponding publisher identifiers have been replaced likely with the repackagers' identifiers. Note that each developer can sign up various ad networks to get his own app publisher identifier. The publisher identifier is assigned and used by an ad network to correctly distinguish user clicks or ad traffics and then return the resulting ad revenues. For example, Admob, one of the most popular ad networks in Android, uses two identifiers *ADMOB_PUBLISHER_ID* and *ADMOB_INTERSTITIAL_PUBLISHER_ID*, whose values are assigned by Admob to the app developers during their enrollment. By repackaging apps with their own publisher identifiers, repackagers can collect ad revenues from ad networks, resulting in a financial loss for the original app developers.

In our experiments, we found that one popular repackaged target is the *Angry Birds* app (*com.rovio.angrybirds*) [40]. The vendor of this app (i.e., Rovio) does not charge for the download and installation. Instead it embeds certain ad SDKs (i.e., Admob) into this app to collect ad revenues. One repackaged *Angry Birds* DroidMOSS identified in a US marketplace did not modify any code in the original app. Instead, the only modification is on the Admob-specific identifiers. Table 3 shows the comparison of two corresponding manifest files.

During our evaluation, we initially thought that applying a common Unix utility program, i.e., *diff* [20], on these two manifest files and their corresponding class files can easily identify such repackaging behavior. However, our experience indicates that repackagers explored various unusual ways to substitute publisher identifiers (Table 3). For instance, besides modifying the app manifest file, they may modify the string resource file instead without changing the bytecode at all. Fortunately, with its capability of effectively localizing the changes from repackaging behaviors, DroidMOSS can help detect them.

Trojanizing Legitimate Apps with Malicious Payloads In the third category, we also observe trojanized apps with malicious payloads. Our findings are consistent with recent reports about discovered Android malware [7]. Specifically, the added payloads can be used to conduct a variety of malicious activities, such as

sending text messages to premium-rated numbers [35], downloading additional apps from the Internet [30], rooting the phone [32], and even registering the compromised phones as bots [28].

One example found by DroidMOSS is a repackaged app from *com.tencent.qq*, a popular instant messaging app. During our analysis, we found that the trojanized version requests more permissions as embodied in the first four lines of Figure 3. These permissions are requested to facilitate its wrongdoings. But having these added permissions is not sufficient to determine that one app is the repackaged version of another one. (Newer versions of an app may ask for more permissions than previous ones, and vice versa.) As a result, we need to further look into the code to collect additional evidences. In this particular case, the manifest file shows that a new receiver and a new service are added to the original app, and the receiver will be triggered when the system finished booting. Looking into the disassembled code, we know its purpose is to bootstrap a background service named *com.android.MainService*, whose code fetches and executes instructions from a remote server, effectively turning the compromised phones into bots. A further in-depth investigation of the code shows that the trojan app supports a number of commands, such as sending SMS messages to premium numbers, modifying the bookmarks of the built-in browsers, and downloading and installing additional apps onto the phones. All these actions are dispatched through a member function named *execTask* in *com.android.MainService*. The function is invoked to check a command and control (C&C) server using a hard-coded URL (*http://xml.XXX.com:8118/push/androidxml/?[parameters]*) to fetch and execute commands. In Figure 4, we show a code snippet from this function that demonstrates how different payloads are called according to the command it receives.

Another example found by DroidMOSS is a repackaged app based on *com.intsig.camscanner*. A similar background service is needed in this case, but it is triggered in a different way. Instead of using a new receiver to trigger the service, the repackager directly modifies the main activity of the original app to achieve the same purpose. Our analysis also indicates that some obfuscation techniques are being adopted by repackagers to evade analysis and detection. It seems that these malicious payloads are getting more powerful and harder to be analyzed.[4]

---

[4]Our study also shows that there is a fourth category of apps. In this category, repackagers essentially decompose original apps and re-package them by signing with their own developer keys. One possible reason is that repackagers want to build their own

```
. . . . .
<uses-permission android:name="android.permission.READ_SMS" />
<uses-permission android:name="android.permission.SEND_SMS" />
<uses-permission android:name="com.android.browser.permission.READ_HISTORY_BOOKMARKS" />
<uses-permission android:name="com.android.browser.permission.WRITE_HISTORY_BOOKMARKS" />
. . . . .
<receiver android:name="com.android.AndroidActionReceiver">
   <intent-filter>
      <action android:name="android.intent.action.SIG_STR" />
      <action android:name="android.intent.action.BOOT_COMPLETED" />
   </intent-filter>
</receiver>
. . . . .
<service android:name="com.android.MainService" android:process=":remote" />
```

Figure 3: The Manifest File of A Repackaged App *com.tencent.qq* (the listed receiver and service do not exist in the original app)

```
.method private execTask()V
   .registers 14
   ......
   const-string v10, "push"    ...
   invoke-direct p0, v0, v2, Lcom/android/MainService;->execPush(Ljava/lang/String;[Ljava/lang/String;)V
   ......
   const-string v10, "soft"    ...
   invoke-direct p0, v0, v2, Lcom/android/MainService;->execSoft(Ljava/lang/String;[Ljava/lang/String;)V
   ......
   const-string v10, "xbox"    ...
   invoke-direct p0, v0, v2, Lcom/android/MainService;->execXbox(Ljava/lang/String;[Ljava/lang/String;)V
   ......
   const-string v10, "mark"    ...
   invoke-direct p0, v0, v2, Lcom/android/MainService;->execMark(Ljava/lang/String;[Ljava/lang/String;)V
   ......
.end method
```

Figure 4: The Code Snippet of *execTask* (this function calls different malicious payloads – *execPush*, *execSoft* or *execMask* – based on the command it receives from the hard-coded C&C server – *push*, *soft*, or *mask*)

3.2 False Negative Measurement

While the above experiments focus on the understanding of overall repackaged apps in current third-party app marketplaces, they also show the effectiveness of our system in having a small low false positives. Next, we measure the false negative rates of our system. Because there are no public list of known repackaged apps available for us to use, we prepare such a set by ourselves. Specifically, we first collect those app pairs which have identical or similar package names, but are signed by different developer certificates. After that, we manually identify and confirm 150 repackaged apps as a test set to evaluate our system. As a result, DroidMOSS successfully reports 134 of them as repackaged, but misses 16 of them, implying a false negative rate of 10.7%. By examining those missed cases, we found two main reasons. (1) The first reason is that some repackager may add a large chunk of code into the original app. When the ratio between the added code and the original one is larger than certain threshold, the calculated fingerprints may differ a lot, leading to a small similarity score and causing a false negative. (2) The second reason is due to the fact our white-list is incomplete, which means some shared (ad) libraries are still contained in the sequence as noise. This added noise could result in considerable difference in the final fingerprints, thus leading to a miss in DroidMOSS.

To summarize, our experimental results show an alarming repackaging rate (ranging from 5% to 13%) among our current third-party marketplaces. The repackaged apps are mainly used to replace existing in-app advertisements or embed new ones to "steal" or re-route ad revenues. We also identified a few cases with planted backdoors or malicious payloads among repackaged apps. The results call for the need of a rigorous vetting process for better regulation of third-party smartphone app marketplaces.

4. DISCUSSION

Our evaluation results show that our prototype can effectively detect repackaged apps. In this section, we further examine possible limitations in our system and explore ways for future improvement.

First, our current prototype assumes that the official Android Market contains legitimate (and original) apps. However, this may not be the case in practice. For example, it has been reported that even in the official Android Market, there may exist malicious apps [29] repackaged from other legitimate apps. Also, it is possible that an app (from a third-party marketplace) might be an original one and the corresponding app from the official Android Market is actually repackaged. In either case, DroidMOSS is still helpful in distinguishing repackaged apps and answering the key questions that motivate this work.

reputation by providing benign, high-quality apps so that other users will trust them more when the time arrives for them to publish some bad or malicious apps.

Second, to discern any repackaged app, DroidMOSS depends on the existence of the corresponding original app in our data set. Due to various reasons, our current database is far from complete. For example, our current collection is comprised of those free apps and do not include paid apps in the official Android Market. As a result, we may miss some repackaged apps. Because of that, we have the reason to believe the overall repackaging rate is higher than we report in this paper. From another perspective, this also indicates the need of continuously expanding our current data set with more comprehensive samples.

Finally, our prototype still experiences difficulties due to the use of shared libraries or ad SDKs for repackaged app detection. Specifically, our current approach uses a white-list approach that may not detect possible malicious changes to the ad SDKs or shared libraries. A systematic method to automatically identify shared libraries and detect abnormal changes could greatly improve our prototype.

5. RELATED WORK

Software similarity measurement   The first category of related work includes prior efforts in measuring the similarity of software or documents in general. Among the most noted, MOSS [39] is designed to measure software similarity (at the source level) and has been widely used to detect plagiarism in college classes. Our system differs from it in two key aspects: First, DroidMOSS directly works at the Dalvik bytecode level without the source code access, which is required by MOSS. Second, both systems require the use of a sliding window to generate the fingerprint. However, MOSS uses it to generate a k-gram to directly compose the fingerprint, while DroidMOSS calculates the hash value to compare against a reset point to further localize repackaged changes. Our such design is needed and tailored to meet the scalability requirement (Section 2).

Our fuzzy hashing is due to Andrew Tridgell for the spamsum algorithm [2]. The original algorithm is proposed to detect spams and has been later extended by others for different purposes. For example, Payne *et al.* [21] applies it to expand the capability of his forensic tool. Kornblum *et al.* [33] materializes a similar concept for digital forensic analysis by identifying similar text documents. Our system instead applies it for repackaged app detection. To the best of our knowledge, we are the first to apply it for this purpose. Meanwhile, we notice an independent work from the App Genome project [27] that looks into the Android apps from two alternative China-based marketplaces and reports that nearly 11% of their apps also available on the Android Market were found to be repackaged. However, the study does not disclose any methodology as well as technical details behind their findings. Based on their summary-style description, we observe that the results are *only* applied to those apps also available on the official Android Market. Our work instead does not have this limitation by investigating apps we collected from six alternative geographically-scattered marketplaces. Moreover, our study further looks into possible motivations behind repackaged apps and leads to unique insights (e.g., stealing or re-routing ad revenues – Section 3), which have not been reported by others.

Instruction sequence-based security applications   As Droid-MOSS uses instruction sequences to generate a distinguishing feature to characterize Android apps, we also consider – as the second category of related work – recent security applications that are based on instruction sequences. For example, software birthmarks can be generated based on the k-gram of instructions (e.g., [36]). SigFree [41] applies the notion to network traffic stream by at-tempting to extract instruction sequence from incoming network requests or packets. By applying code abstraction analysis, SigFree can effectively test whether the packets contain executable instructions or not. Also closely related, recent work apply instruction instructions or even system call sequences in different ways to help detect known or unknown malware (e..g, [9]). DroidMOSS differs from them with a different focus on the app similarity measurement problem and applies instruction sequence in a different way. Specifically, based on the instruction sequence, DroidMOSS further applies fuzzy hashing to condense it to a shorter fingerprint for app similarity measurement.

Smartphone platform and app security   The third category include various systems [6,8,13–16,18,19,37,38,43,44] to improve the smartphone platform and app security. For example, TaintDroid [13] applies dynamic taint analysis to monitor apps and detect runtime privacy infringement behaviors in Android apps. PiOS [12] develops a static analysis tool to spot possible information leaks in iOS applications. ScanDroid [18] aims to automatically extract data flow policy from the app manifest, and then check whether data flows in the apps are consistent with the extracted specification. Kirin [15] proposes to enhance the install process in Android to block possibly unsafe apps that request dangerous permission combinations. A follow-up work of Kirin [14] reports a series of systematic findings in Android application security from the study of 1,100 popular free Android applications. Apex [37], MockDroid [6], and TISSA [44] enhance the Android infrastructure so that users can better control the access to specific resources or permission at runtime themselves. Stowaway [16] studies the over-privilege problem of a set of 940 apps and finds that about one-third are not following the least privilege principle. DroidRanger [43] leverages both static and dynamic analysis to detect malicious apps in existing Android marketplaces. Woodpecker [19] statically analyzes pre-loaded apps in smartphone firmware to uncover possible capability leaks. All these tools use either static or dynamic analysis techniques to infer relevant security properties from individual smartphone apps. In contrast, DroidMOSS measures the similarity of two apps (as a pair) by distilling their instruction sequences into corresponding fingerprints.

More recently, researchers also look into the interaction between different Android apps. For example, Saint [38] examines the interfaces one application exported to other and extends the Android framework to enforce inter-application security policy (at install and runtime). ComDroid [8] uncovers possible unintended consequences of exposing certain app components. A relevant work [17] goes further to study both unintentional and intentional exporting of internal components, which can cause apps with permissions to perform privileged task for apps without permissions. This paper also proposes IPC Inspection to address these vulnerabilities. Quire [11] similarly addresses the permission delegation problem by proposing an IPC call chain tracking mechanism to identify the provenance of these IPC requests and enforce certain policy. Stratus [4] explores the security of multi-market app ecosystem and proposes a new app installation model to retain the original single-market security semantics (e.g., kill switches or developer name consistency). Barrera *et al.* [5] uses a self-organization map to analyze 1,100 Android apps and identifies related usage patterns about android app permissions. DroidMOSS differs from them by systematically studying the app repackaging situation in our current third-party marketplaces by measuring the similarity of app pairs.

6. CONCLUSION

In this paper, we examine the problem of repackaged smartphone applications in current third-party marketplaces, and have accordingly developed a prototype system called DroidMOSS to detect them. Our system adopts a fuzzy hashing technique to effectively localize and detect possible changes from app repackaging. We have applied our system to detect repackaged apps in six third-party Android marketplaces and found that 5% to 13% of apps hosted in them are repackaged. Furthermore, we manually analyze those repackaged apps and our results show that apps are mainly repackaged to replace existing in-app advertisements (or embed new ones) to "steal" or re-route ad revenues, or even more seriously plant backdoors and malicious payloads. The results call for the need of a rigorous vetting process for better regulation of third-party smartphone app marketplaces.

Acknowledgements   The authors would like to thank the anonymous reviewers for their insightful comments that helped improve the presentation of this paper. Special thanks go to Shihong Zou, Qiang Zhang, and Yang Cao at NetQin for their constructive suggestions and feedbacks. This work was supported in part by the US National Science Foundation (NSF) under Grants 0855297, 0855036, 0910767, and 0952640. Any opinions, findings, and conclusions or recommendations expressed in this material are those of the authors and do not necessarily reflect the views of the NSF.

7. REFERENCES

[1] Smali - An Assembler/Disassembler for Android's dex Format. http://code.google.com/p/smali/. Online; accessed at May 17, 2011.

[2] Tridgell Andrew. Spamsum README. http://samba.org/ftp/unpacked/junkcode/spamsum/README. Online; accessed at May 17, 2011.

[3] AndroLib. Android Market Statistics from AndroLib. http://www.androlib.com/appstats.aspx. Online; accessed at June 1, 2011.

[4] David Barrera, William Enck, and Paul Oorschot. Seeding a Security-Enhancing Infrastructure for Multi-market Application Ecosystems. Technical report, School of Computer Science, Carleton University, http://www.scs.carleton.ca/shared/research/tech_reports/2010/TR-11-06%20Barrera.pdf. Online; accessed at May 17, 2011.

[5] David Barrera, H. Güneş Kayacik, Paul C. van Oorschot, and Anil Somayaji. A Methodology for Empirical Analysis of Permission-Based Security Models and Its Application to Android. In *Proceedings of the 17th ACM Conference on Computer and Communications Security*, CCS '10, 2010.

[6] Alastair Beresford, Andrew Rice, Nicholas Skehin, and Ripduman Sohan. MockDroid: Trading Privacy for Application Functionality on Smartphones. In *Proceedings of the 12th Workshop on Mobile Computing Systems and Applications*, HotMobile '11, 2011.

[7] Joany Boutet. Malicious Android Applications: Risks and Exploitation - A Spyware Story about Android Application and Reverse Engineering. http://www.sans.org/reading_room/whitepapers/malicious/malicious-android-applications_risks-exploitation_33578. Online; accessed at May 17, 2011.

[8] Erika Chin, Adrienne Felt, Kate Greenwood, and David Wagner. Analyzing Inter-Application Communication in Android. In *Proceedings of the 9th Annual International Conference on Mobile Systems, Applications, and Services*, MobiSys 2011, 2011.

[9] Mihai Christodorescu, Somesh Jha, and Christopher Kruegel. Mining Specifications of Malicious Behavior. In *Proceedings of the 6th Joint Meeting of the European Software Engineering Conference and the ACM SIGSOFT Symposium on the Foundations of Software Engineering*, ESEC-FSE '07, pages 5–14. ACM, 2007.

[10] Cydia. Cydia App Store. http://cydia.saurik.com/. Online; accessed at May 17, 2011.

[11] Michael Dietz, Shashi Shekhar, Yuliy Pisetsky, Anhei Shu, and Dan Wallach. QUIRE: Lightweight Provenance for Smart Phone Operating Systems. In *Proceedings of the 20th USENIX Security Symposium*, USENIX Security '11, San Francisco, CA, 2011.

[12] Manuel Egele, Christopher Kruegel, Engin Kirda, and Giovanni Vigna. PiOS: Detecting Privacy Leaks in iOS Applications. In *Proceedings of the 18th Annual Network and Distributed System Security Symposium*, NDSS '11, February 2011.

[13] William Enck, Peter Gilbert, Byung-gon Chun, Landon Cox, Jaeyeon Jung, Patrick McDaniel, and Anmol Sheth. TaintDroid: An Information-Flow Tracking System for Realtime Privacy Monitoring on Smartphones. In *Proceedings of the 9th USENIX Symposium on Operating Systems Design and Implementation*, USENIX OSDI '11, 2011.

[14] William Enck, Damien Octeau, Patrick McDaniel, and Swarat Chaudhuri. A Study of Android Application Security. In *Proceedings of the 20th USENIX Security Symposium*, USENIX Security '11, San Francisco, CA, 2011.

[15] William Enck, Machigar Ongtang, and Patrick McDaniel. On Lightweight Mobile Phone Application Certification. In *Proceedings of the 16th ACM Conference on Computer and Communications Security*, CCS '09, pages 235–245, New York, NY, USA, 2009. ACM.

[16] Adrienne Felt, Erika Chin, Steve Hanna, Dawn Song, and David Wagner. Android Permissions Demystified. In *Proceedings of the 18th ACM Conference on Computer and Communications Security*, CCS' 11, 2011.

[17] Adrienne Felt, Helen Wang, Alexander Moschhuk, Steve Hanna, and Erika Chin. Permission Re-Delegation: Attacks and Defense. In *Proceedings of the 20th USENIX Security Symposium*, USENIX Security '11, San Francisco, CA, 2011.

[18] Adam Fuchs, Avik Chaudhuri, and Jeffrey Foster. SCanDroid: Automated Security Certification of Android Applications. http://www.cs.umd.edu/~avik/projects/scandroidascaa/paper.pdf. Online; accessed at June 1, 2011.

[19] Michael Grace, Yajin Zhou, Zhi Wang, and Xuxian Jiang. Systematic Detection of Capability Leaks in Stock Android Smartphones. In *Proceedings of the 19th Annual Network and Distributed System Security Symposium*, NDSS '12, February 2012.

[20] James Hunt and McIlroy Douglas. An Algorithm for Differential File Comparison. Technical report, Computing Science Technical Report, Bell Laboratories, 1976.

[21] Dustin Hurlbut. Fuzzy Hashing for Digital Forensic Investigators. Technical report, Access Data Inc., http://accessdata.com/downloads/media/

Fuzzy_Hashing_for_Investigators.pdf. Online; accessed at May 17, 2011.

[22] Amazon.com Inc. Amazon AppStore for Android. http://www.amazon.com/mobile-apps/b?ie= UTF8&node=2350149011. Online; accessed at May 17, 2011.

[23] Apple Inc. Apple App Store for IPhone. http://www.apple.com/iphone/apps-for-iphone/. Online; accessed at May 17, 2011.

[24] Google Inc. Admob for Android Developers. http://developer.admob.com/wiki/Android. Online; accessed at May 17, 2011.

[25] Google Inc. Android Dvelopment Guide: Signing Your Applications. http://developer.android.com/guide/publishing/app-signing.html. Online; accessed at May 17, 2011.

[26] Google Inc. Android Market. https://market.android.com/. Online; accessed at May 17, 2011.

[27] Lookout Inc. App Genome Report: February 2011. https://www.mylookout.com/appgenome/. Online; accessed at May 17, 2011.

[28] Lookout Inc. Security Alert: Geinimi, Sophisticated New Android Trojan Found in Wild. http://blog.mylookout.com/2010/12/geinimi_trojan/. Online; accessed at May 17, 2011.

[29] Lookout Inc. Update: Security Alert: DroidDream Malware Found in Official Android Market. http://blog.mylookout.com/2011/03/security-alert-malware-found-in_official-android-market-droiddream/. Online; accessed at May 17, 2011.

[30] Symantec Inc. Android Threats Getting Steamy. http://www.symantec.com/connect/blogs/android-threats-getting-steamy. Online; accessed at May 17, 2011.

[31] Wooboo Inc. How to add Wooboo advertisement SDK into Android. http://admin.wooboo.com.cn:9001/cbFiles/down/1272545843644.swf. Online; accessed at May 17, 2011.

[32] Xuxian Jiang. Security Alert: New Sophisticated Android Malware DroidKungFu Found in Alternative Chinese App Markets. http://www.csc.ncsu.edu/faculty/jiang/DroidKungFu.html. Online; accessed at Sep 17, 2011.

[33] Jesse Kornblum. Identifying Almost Identical Files Using Context Triggered Piecewise Hashing. DFRWS '06, 2006.

[34] Greg Kumparak. TechCrunch: Android Now Seeing 550,000 Activations Per Day. http://techcrunch.com/2011/07/14/android-now-seeing-550000-activations-per-day/. Online; accessed at Sep 15, 2011.

[35] Kaspersky Lab. First SMS Trojan Detected for Smartphones Running Android. http://www.kaspersky.com/about/news/virus/2010/First_SMS_Trojan_detected_for_smartphones_running_Android. Online; Accessed at May 17, 2011.

[36] Ginger Myles and Christian Collberg. K-gram Based Software Birthmarks. In *Proceedings of the 2005 ACM Symposium on Applied Computing*, SAC '05, pages 314–318, New York, NY, USA, 2005. ACM.

[37] Mohammad Nauman, Sohail Khan, and Xinwen Zhang. Apex: Extending Android Permission Model and Enforcement with User-Defined Runtime Constraints. In *Proceedings of the 5th ACM Symposium on Information, Computer and Communications Security*, ASIACCS '10, 2010.

[38] Machigar Ongtang, Stephen McLaughlin, William Enck, and Patrick McDaniel. Semantically Rich Application-Centric Security in Android. In *Proceedings of the 2009 Annual Computer Security Applications Conference*, ACSAC '09, 2009.

[39] Saul Schleimer, Daniel S. Wilkerson, and Alex Aiken. Winnowing: Local Algorithms for Document Fingerprinting. In *Proceedings of the 2003 ACM SIGMOD International Conference on Management of Data*, SIGMOD '03, pages 76–85, New York, NY, USA, 2003. ACM.

[40] New York Times. Angry Birds, Flocking to Cellphones Everywhere. http://www.nytimes.com/2010/12/12/technology/12birds.htm. Online; accessed at May 17, 2011.

[41] Xinran Wang, Chi-Chun Pan, Peng Liu, and Sencun Zhu. SigFree: a Signature-Free Buffer Overflow Attack Blocker. In *Proceedings of the 15th Conference on USENIX Security Symposium - Volume 15*, Berkeley, CA, USA, 2006. USENIX Association.

[42] Youmi.net. Wiki - Youmi Android Banner Version 2.1. http://wiki.youmi.net/wiki/Youmi_Android_Banner_Version_2.1. Online; accessed at May 17, 2011.

[43] Yajin Zhou, Zhi Wang, Wu Zhou, and Xuxian Jiang. Hey, You, Get off of My Market: Detecting Malicious Apps in Official and Alternative Android Markets. In *Proceedings of the 19th Annual Network and Distributed System Security Symposium*, NDSS '12, February 2012.

[44] Yajin Zhou, Xinwen Zhang, Xuxian Jiang, and Vince Freeh. Taming Information-Stealing Smartphone Applications (on Android). In *Proceeding of the 4th International Conference on Trust and Trustworthy Computing*, TRUST '11, 2011.

Author Index

www.ingramcontent.com/pod-product-compliance
Lightning Source LLC
Chambersburg PA
CBHW080919220326
41598CB00034B/5624